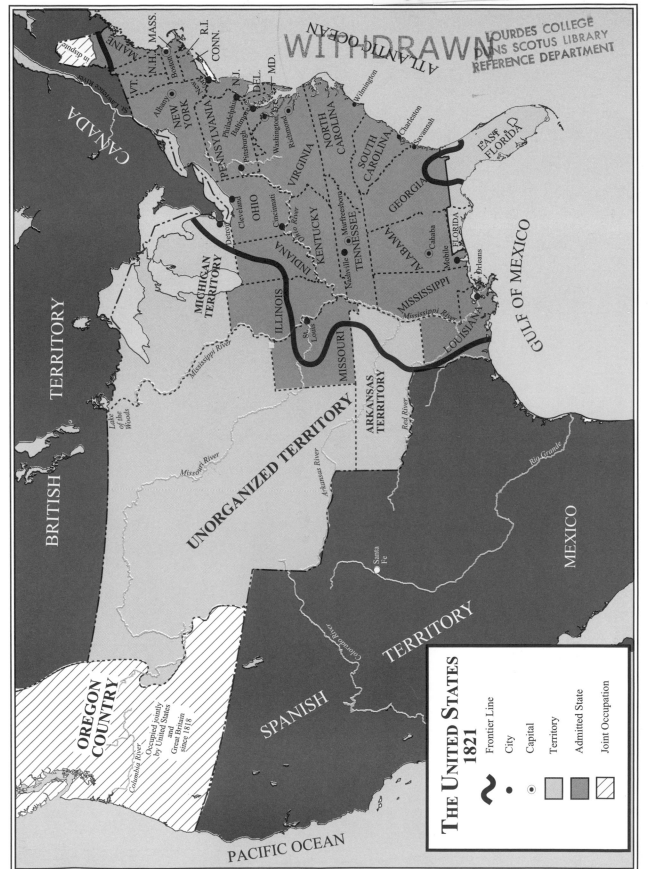

THE UNITED STATES
1821

Frontier Line
City
Capital
Territory
Admitted State
Joint Occupation

ENCYCLOPEDIA
OF THE
UNITED STATES
IN THE
NINETEENTH
CENTURY

Editorial Board

ENCYCLOPEDIA
OF THE
UNITED STATES
IN THE
NINETEENTH
CENTURY

Paul Finkelman

Editor in Chief

VOLUME 3

Printing Technology–Zoos

Systematic Outline
Directory of Contributors
Index

CHARLES SCRIBNER'S SONS

An Imprint of The Gale Group

NEW YORK   DETROIT   SAN FRANCISCO
LONDON   BOSTON   WOODBRIDGE, CT

02-202

Charles Scribner's Sons
1633 Broadway
New York, New York 10019

3 5 7 9 11 13 15 17 19   20 18 16 14 12 10 8 6 4 2

PRINTED IN THE UNITED STATES OF AMERICA

Library of Congress Cataloging-in-Publication Data

Encyclopedia of the United States in the nineteenth century / Paul Finkelman, editor in chief.
  p. cm.
  Includes bibliographical references and index.
  ISBN 0-684-80500-6 (set : hardcover : alk. paper)—ISBN 0-684-80497-2 (vol. 1 :
hardcover : alk. paper)—ISBN 0-684-80498-0 (vol. 2 : hardcover : alk. paper)—ISBN
0-684-80499-9 (vol. 3 : hardcover : alk. paper)
  1. United States—Civilization—19th century—Encyclopedias. I. Finkelman, Paul, 1949–

E169.1 .E626 2001
973.5—dc21
                       00-045811

Cover image credits *(clockwise, starting from the top left corner):* U.S. Capitol © Corbis; Native American group portrait © Planet Art; Andrew Jackson © Planet Art; Forty-niners © Planet Art; *Whistler's Mother* © EclectiCollections™; Frontier town © Planet Art; Frederick Douglass © Corbis; Drummer boy © Corbis; Abraham Lincoln © Corbis; Train © Planet Art.

CONTENTS OF OTHER VOLUMES

ENCYCLOPEDIA
OF THE
UNITED STATES
IN THE
NINETEENTH
CENTURY

P–Q

(continued)

PRINTING TECHNOLOGY Had Johannes Gutenberg, the man credited with inventing modern printing around 1450, entered an American printing shop at the beginning of the nineteenth century, he would have felt very much at home. Though many technological improvements had been made over the intervening 350 years, the fundamental processes of putting ink on paper remained essentially unchanged. But during the nineteenth century growing market demands for printed materials stimulated a search for increased speed and volume. By 1900 printing technology had undergone a revolution second only to that of Gutenberg's day—one that had a profound impact on commerce, culture, and information distribution.

Typesetting

In 1800 printing was done by a relief method called letterpress. In this painstaking process, printers arranged by hand individual pieces of type and blank spacing material into blocks of text. The text block was then locked into position in a press and inked by hand. The printer placed a sheet of paper over the type and engaged a lever, which pressed the paper onto the type. The type, made of a lead alloy or carved in wood, contained reversed images of the letters to be printed. When inked and pressed onto paper, the type left behind a right-reading impression.

The process was repeated for duplicate pages. Afterward the type block was broken up into individual letters, which were reset for the next printing job. Letterpress printing with handset type was slow, meticulous work.

This printing method was challenged first by the introduction of the stereotype in France during the last decades of the eighteenth century. The stereotype began with the same process of setting type by hand. With that type printers produced metal plates from which duplicate pages could be printed simultaneously on several presses. As the circulation of American newspapers, pamphlets, and books grew, the stereotype process allowed printers to increase their pressruns more efficiently.

Late into the nineteenth century, however, most printed text was still set by hand. This changed with the introduction of two typesetting machines, the Linotype and the Monotype. Ottmar Mergenthaler invented the Linotype in 1884. As the name implies, the Linotype produced a single line of type cast in metal for letterpress printing. The Linotype allowed a single keyboard operator to set a line of type much more quickly than a hand typesetter. These lines in turn were locked up in a press and printed traditionally. The Monotype, introduced in 1887 by Tolbert Lanston, was also operated by a keyboard, but it produced single type characters called sorts arranged in lines ready to be printed. The advantage of Monotype setting was that corrections or changes to the text could be done quickly and easily by replacing individual sorts. On the Linotype changing a word or a letter meant resetting the entire line.

Both typesetting inventions relied on traditional letterpress methods of presswork. By the end of the century innovations led to the invention of offset

1

A Print Shop. Compositors working in a print shop at the Hampton Institute, Hampton, Virginia. Photograph by Frances B. Johnston, c. 1899. LIBRARY OF CONGRESS: FRANCES BENJAMIN JOHNSTON COLLECTION

printing, which used an entirely different method— a chemical process—to put ink on paper. In offset, type and images were transferred by a photographic process to a flexible metal plate. The images on the plate attracted ink, and blank space on the plate repelled it, as in lithography. The positive image was transferred to a rubber blanket or roller and then to paper. The introduction of offset presses at the beginning of the twentieth century allowed significant increases in flexibility and speed.

The Press

The simple wood handpress of Gutenberg's time had been improved slightly by the early nineteenth century with the introduction of an iron frame and mechanism. To meet demands for more efficient newspaper printing, Frederick Koenig in 1810 developed a steam-powered press in England. By harnessing a power other than human and changing the configuration of the press to a revolving cylinder, Koenig's press dramatically increased output. Work done on a handpress, for example, could produce up to about two hundred sheets per hour. The first steam press increased that to eleven hundred. By the end of the Civil War a rotary steam-powered press fed from a continuous roll or "web" of paper raised the rate to twenty thousand sheets per hour. By the century's end American newspaper presses could print, cut, and fold twenty-four thousand copies of a complete newspaper in an hour.

While high-speed newspaper work was done on ro-

tary presses using flexible stereotype plates on cylinders, much book, stationery, and business form printing was done on new platen presses by the 1870s. These small, self-inking presses were operated by a single worker and were powered by a treadle and flywheel. Platen presses, ideal for smaller jobs and shorter runs, became extremely popular and were used well into the twentieth century.

Paper

The medium on which most printing appeared also changed as resources shifted and needs developed. From long before the advent of books until the middle of the nineteenth century, paper was produced by hand, made primarily of cotton fiber from recycled fabric or rags, and formed into individual sheets. The need for faster production and greater quantities of newspapers spurred the invention in 1799 of a mechanical process to produce paper on a continuous web that could be fed through new power presses.

New demands also spurred the manufacture of paper from wood pulp beginning in 1840. This opened the vast lumber resources of North America to paper production. Unfortunately wood-fiber paper was acidic, not very stable, and deteriorated much more quickly than cotton-fiber paper. Consequently, many mass-produced books, pamphlets, and newspapers from the later half of the nineteenth century have not survived as well as those printed before the advent of this low-quality wood-fiber paper.

By 1900 the mechanization of printing was almost

complete. From papermaking to type composition and image reproduction to printing itself, all processes could be accomplished by machines with greater speed and productivity than ever before. Typical of technological innovation, though, these developments occurred at varying rates. By the century's end many small print shops in the United States still set type by hand and individually printed small runs of newspapers and job work. Although complete mechanization was not accomplished until after World War I, the nineteenth-century revolution that swept other industries also transformed printing in substantial and abiding ways.

See also **Book Publishing; Communications; Inventors and Inventions; Literacy and Reading Habits; Lithography and Prints; Newspapers and the Press.**

Bibliography

Moran, James. *Printing Presses: History and Development from the Fifteenth Century to Modern Times.* Berkeley: University of California Press, 1973.

Silver, Rollo G. *The American Printer, 1787–1825.* Charlottesville: University Press of Virginia, 1967.

Steinberg, S. H. *Five Hundred Years of Printing.* New ed. Revised by John Trevitt. New Castle, Del.: Oak Knoll, 1996.

Twyman, Michael. *Printing 1770–1970: An Illustrated History of Its Development and Uses in England.* London: British Library, 1998.

GREGORY M. BRITTON

PRISONS AND PUNISHMENT   Since early colonial settlement, Americans have had a zeal for building prisons and incarcerating people. Yet while prisons had existed for centuries in both Europe and America, by the nineteenth century American reformers, politicians, and judges began using them intentionally as institutions to rehabilitate the nation's wayward, as a source of cheap labor, and as a means ostensibly to civilize the far reaches of the American frontier, among other things. By the 1820s and 1830s, as sweeping social and demographic changes began to transform the American economy, the fundamental ideology about the role of punishment in American society began to shift. Much of nineteenth-century American prison history is tied to various attempts and strategies directed toward detaining criminals for the express purpose of reforming their characters in institutions designed exclusively for that purpose, as opposed to merely exacting harsh punishment and retribution for their crimes.

This dramatic transformation in the function of American prisons in the early nineteenth century prompted various European politicians and observers, such as the famous French political philosopher Alexis de Tocqueville, to take notice as they traveled to the United States expressly to study the American penitentiary system in the early 1830s. Indeed, one of the most striking characteristics surrounding the development of prisons and penitentiaries over the course of the nineteenth century is the multiple functions and roles the increasingly large and complex institutions played in American society. The penal systems, prison architecture, and disciplinary procedures that developed in the nineteenth century became an integral part of the United States. As a result the history of nineteenth-century prisons and punishment patterns has attracted much attention from historians, sociologists, and cultural theorists.

From Retribution to Rehabilitation

In the seventeenth and early eighteenth centuries, communities along the eastern seaboard and in the South mostly punished criminals locally. Prior to the nineteenth century punishment was swift, retributive, violent, public, and inexpensive. Lynching and vigilante actions were common, especially in isolated rural areas. But the rapidly growing population and urbanization of the early nineteenth century, particularly in the Northeast, rendered the continued practices of such a tradition increasingly impractical.

By the late eighteenth century Quaker officials in Philadelphia advanced a series of humanitarian reforms that embodied a new philosophy of the role and purpose of punishment, namely that it provoke behavioral change in the criminal. In 1790 the Walnut Street Jail opened in Philadelphia to implement the ideals of the reformation philosophy. This institution served as a model for subsequent state penitentiaries along the eastern seaboard, including the large Newgate prison, which opened in New York State in 1797.

At Walnut Street, prison administrators significantly departed from past practices by segregating inmates by type of crime and gender. The facility also developed prison industries, provided some modest education and training for inmates, and subjected the inmate population to large doses of Christian suasion. Because Walnut Street and Newgate quickly became seriously overcrowded, a common occurrence, and because most of the prisoners were confined to large common rooms, where reforms found little fertile ground, these prototypical institutions failed. But the groundwork for reformist prisons had been laid.

Subsequent developments in punishment philosophy and penal architecture made further overtures toward reformation of the criminal. Yet complicating this new philosophical approach to criminality was

Andersonville Prison Camp. The Confederate prison camp at Andersonville, Georgia, originally designed for a population of 10,000 inmates, incarcerated more than 30,000 Union prisoners of war at its peak capacity. The conditions there led to the deaths of about 13,000 men in 1864 and 1865. © CORBIS

the stark fact that all nineteenth-century American prisons suffered to some extent from budgetary neglect, which resulted in appalling conditions, widespread corruption, and periodic abandonment of reform agendas in favor of mere warehousing, severe disciplining, and punishment. Over the course of the century American legislatures had difficulty reconciling the penal institution with its new role as an agent of humanitarian reform.

Rival Systems: Auburn versus Cherry Hill

By the 1820s New York legislators advocated adopting a new system of punishment that would be utilized in the new prison constructed at Auburn. The Auburn-style, or more formally "congregate system," prison relied almost exclusively on hard labor as a means to rehabilitation. Ideally, in an Auburn-style prison individual inmates occupied the cells only at night, leaving them to work in various prison-based industries during the day. They might have minimal interaction with other prisoners while they worked. During other activities—meals, bathing, and religious services—they were to maintain scrupulous silence in order to meditate upon their predicament and complete their penitence. They periodically received doses of moral, primarily Christian-oriented, instruction. Military discipline, including lockstep marching, characterized the Auburn-style prison experience.

The most important goal of the system was to inculcate habits of labor and self-discipline in the prisoners. During much of the remainder of the century new prisons built in the states and western territories more or less followed the Auburn pattern. In Pennsylvania, however, the Eastern State Penitentiary, also known as Cherry Hill, opened in 1829 and provided a variation on the Auburn system. The administrators at Cherry Hill implemented a system of punishment that was predicated on the solitary confinement of each individual and a rigid, almost monastic disciplinary routine. Prisoners were given minimal opportunity to speak with other inmates or staff during incarceration. The institution reflected Quaker notions that solitary reflection on one's sinful nature eventually cleansed the soul and produced a positive shift in behavior. Nevertheless, Cherry Hill abandoned the system within a few years due to the expense of the operation and serious overcrowding.

For good reason much scholarly attention has focused on the critical shift in penological practices after the turn of the nineteenth century and its acceleration during the Jacksonian era (1820–1840). Most American prison histories have examined in some detail this broad movement from public retribution to incarceration as a means to an end—to improve and redeem morally the individual with ultimate benefit to both the reformed criminal and society, which gained a productive member. The historian Christopher Lasch has argued that the entire enterprise of identifying and incarcerating societal miscreants and malcontents was one of the fundamental "preconditions of modern capitalism" and that it aided the United States in its massive efforts to organize individuals into productive cogs in the new freewheeling economic system (*The World of Nations,* p. 316). Historians and other scholars contend that the penitentiary as such must be viewed as a thoroughly social as well as socializing institution intended to serve as an agent of social control, particularly of the lower classes by those in power.

Moreover, even though long-term imprisonment was significantly more expensive than local, expedient punishment, most social reformers felt that it reflected the mark of a more civilized and advanced society. As the French prison theorist Michel Foucault notes in *Discipline and Punish,* a landmark 1975 study about prison evolution in Europe during this period, perhaps the most important aspect of the development was that those in power viewed imprisonment, no matter how atrocious the conditions, as "the most immediate and civilized form of all [societal] penalties" (p. 233). By the 1840s prisons (along with other Jacksonian-era humanitarian initiatives, including improved conditions in mental asylums, separate penal institutions for women and children, assistance to the homeless and indigent, and concern about alcoholism and prostitution), had become permanent fixtures in all states and were viewed as humane alternatives to earlier, near-barbaric practices.

Southern and Western Prisons

The U.S. government became involved in building and administering prisons in the 1820s with the creation of a national penitentiary outside of Washington, D.C. Later the federal government funded and administered territorial prisons in Iowa, Wisconsin, and Kansas, and by the 1850s it had constructed small facilities in New Mexico and Utah. Both the U.S. and Confederate governments constructed prisons and prisoner-of-war camps during the Civil War. The most infamous was the Confederate prisoner-of-war camp at Andersonville, Georgia, where some thirteen thousand Northern soldiers died from dysentery, malaria, and malnutrition. After the war the Union military commission tried and executed the camp's commander, Major Henry Wirz, for war crimes, the only individual charged with such abuses in the aftermath of the war. After the war, as the federal government faced the embarrassing problem of vigilante and extralegal criminal justice in the far-flung western mining districts, it financed construction of institutions in the new territories of Idaho,

Nebraska, Wyoming, Colorado, Dakota, and Montana. Despite skimpy budgets, all attempted to implement the Auburn-style system of architecture and punishment.

Though all nineteenth-century prisons were appalling by later standards, living and working conditions in western and southern prisons were particularly brutal. Running water was nonexistent in most institutions, disease was rampant and particularly devastating to Native Americans and immigrant prisoners—particularly Chinese and Hispanic prisoners who, like Native Americans, had no immunological experience with some communicable diseases—overcrowding was common and prison mismanagement and graft were prevalent. While in many local communities throughout the West the white majorities typically perpetrated the most vicious racism and violence against the most visible minorities, specifically Native Americans, Chinese, and Hispanics, surprisingly their overall rates of incarceration and sentence lengths in western prisons were not any higher or longer than those of their white counterparts. For most cash-strapped states and territories the cost of incarcerating inmates—of any race or color—based *solely* on racial fears or prejudices was simply too prohibitive during this formative period.

The pace of inmate labor was notoriously brutal, especially in the South, which utilized chain-gang la-

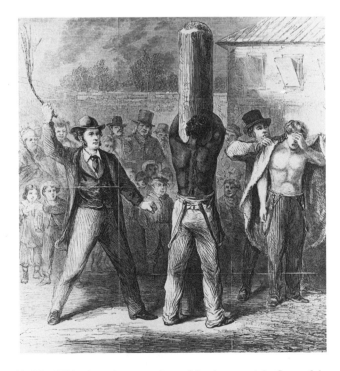

Public Whipping. A man at a whipping post is flogged in front of a crowd in New Castle, Delaware. LIBRARY OF CONGRESS

bor extensively in building and maintaining road systems. Black Americans, the primary targets of the racist Jim Crow legal system in the South after the Civil War, often constituted 75 percent or more of a given state's prison population.

Conditions in the South, particularly for black Americans, were abominable. After the Civil War many southern states practiced convict-leasing schemes, in which blacks were incarcerated on flimsy charges by racist courts and then leased out as laborers to plantation owners for indeterminate periods of time. In many cases the conditions were worse than blacks had faced during slavery.

Women and Children in Prisons

During much of the nineteenth century, few institutions existed primarily to house female adult offenders. Instead, if a woman committed an offense too egregious to be dealt with at the family level, local jails served as the principal institutions of confinement. Mount Pleasant Female Prison, which opened in New York in 1835, was the first exclusively women's prison in the United States. It initially operated under contemporary disciplinary regimes typical of the larger male prisons. At Mount Pleasant, and at other women's institutions that developed later in the century, monotonous and often petty labor was the chief rehabilitative means the institutions used.

In southern and western prisons women fared especially poorly. Until the 1890s few state institutions were built specifically to house female offenders. States and territories simply incarcerated women in separate quarters within male institutions. Violence, rape, and unwanted pregnancies were relatively commonplace. Few institutions—in any section of the nation—made any arrangements for prison nurseries. Western and southern state and territorial judicial systems often sentenced women of color to substantially longer prison terms than their white female counterparts.

The development of institutions primarily for the incarceration and rehabilitation of children followed roughly the same pattern as that for women. Early in the century families were primarily responsible for disciplining wayward children within local communities though teens and occasionally preteens convicted of particularly heinous crimes were often sentenced to adult institutions. By the 1820s reformers, in keeping with the general penological trends of the period, began developing ideas and practices that would lead ultimately to the first juvenile "reform school," the New York House of Refuge, which opened in 1825. Though the concept was slow to de-

velop (there were only three in the mid-1840s), by the 1870s there existed over fifty such schools scattered throughout every section of the nation except the South and the sparsely populated northern Great Plains. The goals of these institutions were similar to that of others of the century, namely to isolate deviant (and usually lower class) individuals from the rest of society and to reform their characters through a strict disciplinary regime and rigorous, though monotonous, labor. Unquestioned deference to authority, corporal punishment, and extended periods of isolation were often the norms at these institutions.

Nineteenth-Century Reform Efforts

Reformers argued periodically for changes in prison regimens and conditions. The feminist and humanitarian Dorothea Dix was the most indefatigable reformer of the Jacksonian era. She argued tirelessly for the improvement of prison and asylum conditions in Massachusetts specifically and New England generally. In the later half of the century two New York politicians, Enoch Wines and Theodore Dwight, urged rethinking of American penology. After studying eastern prisons for a number of years, the pair in 1867 issued a highly critical assessment entitled *Report on the Prisons and Reformatories of the United States and Canada*. They argued that the Auburn method of incarceration—shielding prisoners from the corrosive influences of other prisoners and of society through silence and solitary confinement—simply had not proven effective. Instead they argued for a gradual loosening of the system and for the integration of practical educational and behavioral incentives into penological practices. They criticized the widespread use of extended solitary confinement in dungeons, the floggings common in most prisons for relatively minor infractions, and the general dehumanizing effect of the prison experience.

Most prison administrators, however, were slow to accept suggestions for reform. A notable exception was Zebulon Brockway, who founded and ran the Elmira Reformatory in New York State. Wines and Dwight's report had heavily influenced Brockway's attempts to commit the institution to using education as its primary rehabilitative tool. Professors, principals, teachers, and lawyers participated in the program at Elmira during the latter part of the century, and it became a model for other reformatory institutions in northern and eastern states. Several of Brockway's pioneering behavioral incentives, such as the "good time" policy, also began to appear in other American prisons. Though the policy varied from region to region, it basically held that for every set period of time (a month, two months, six months) an inmate behaved, followed the rules, and worked diligently the prison administration would cut a proportionate amount of time from the inmate's sentence. For example, with good time an inmate could expect to serve eleven months of a one-year sentence.

Like earlier American penological innovations, Brockway's experiment at Elmira was compromised by severe overcrowding. It is a nearly universal rule that prisons in the nineteenth century were seriously overcrowded. In Montana, for instance, a small territorial penitentiary built by the United States to hold fourteen individuals in 1871 had five times that many on the prison grounds within just a few years of its opening. At its peak in the early 1890s, Elmira held twice as many prisoners as it had been designed for.

By the 1890s most states had taken measures to separate out the criminally insane from general inmate populations and to build separate facilities for juvenile and women offenders. By the turn of the century classification systems and parole were commonplace. Inmates in many institutions were segregated in various areas of the prison based on the nature of their crimes. State parole boards and commissions developed more rigorous oversight of released individuals in attempts to quell the chronically high percentages, often 33 percent, who returned to prison (recidivists).

Despite modest advances in some areas, official reports and firsthand accounts from prisoners indicate that penitentiaries at the close of the century remained overcrowded, idleness was common, administrative graft was normal, and brutality was the rule rather than the exception. Many states participated in lease arrangements with private contractors, who were paid a monthly flat rate based on inmate numbers. The lessees ran prisons in the cheapest way possible and leased inmate labor to supplement their administrative budgets and incomes. Abuse of the lease system was widespread, but vestiges of it remained in many regions well into the twentieth century.

Conclusion

At the turn of the twenty-first century, prison conditions demonstrated significant improvements. Despite these gains, however, prisons continue to grapple with issues such as finance, administration, and operations, which were shared by their nineteenth-century counterparts. The roots of penal practices, conflicts between punishment and rehabilitation, recidivism, chronic budgetary pressures, and debates over the role and scope of the penitentiary in society can be traced to the nineteenth century. The words of the nineteenth-century Russian writer and social critic Fyodor Dostoyevsky remain applicable: "The standards of a nation's civilization can be judged by opening the doors of its prisons" (Pisciotta, *Benevolent Repression,* p. 150).

See also **Chain Gangs; Convict Leasing.**

Bibliography

Ayers, Edward L. *Vengeance and Justice: Crime and Punishment in the Nineteenth Century American South.* New York: Oxford University Press, 1984.

Beaumont, Gustave de, and Alexis de Tocqueville. *On the Penitentiary System in the United States and Its Application in France.* Philadelphia: Carey, Lea, and Blanchard, 1833. Reprint, Carbondale: Southern Illinois University Press, 1964.

Butler, Anne M. *Gendered Justice in the American West: Women Prisoners in Men's Penitentiaries.* Urbana: University of Illinois Press, 1997.

Foucault, Michel. *Discipline and Punish: The Birth of the Prison,* translated by Alan Sheridan. New York: Vintage, 1979. The original French edition appeared in 1975.

Hirsch, Adam J. *The Rise of the Penitentiary: Prisons and Punishment in Early America.* New Haven, Conn.: Yale University Press, 1992.

Lasch, Christopher. *The World of Nations: Reflections on American History, Politics, and Culture.* New York: Knopf, 1973.

Mancini, Matthew J. *One Dies, Get Another: Convict Leasing in the American South, 1866–1928.* Columbia: University of South Carolina Press, 1996.

McKelvey, Blake. *American Prisons: A History of Good Intentions.* Montclair, N.J.: Patterson Smith, 1977.

Meranze, Michael. *Laboratories of Virtue: Punishment, Revolution, and Authority in Philadelphia, 1760–1835.* Chapel Hill: University of North Carolina Press, 1996.

Morris, Norval, and David J. Rothman, eds. *The Oxford History of the Prison: The Practice of Punishment in Western Society.* New York: Oxford University Press, 1995.

Pisciotta, Alexander W. *Benevolent Repression: Social Control and the American Reformatory-Prison Movement.* New York: New York University Press, 1994.

Rothman, David J. *The Discovery of the Asylum: Social Order and Disorder in the New Republic.* Rev. ed. Boston: Little Brown, 1990.

Sullivan, Larry E. *The Prison Reform Movement: Forlorn Hope.* Boston: Twayne, 1990.

Wines, E. C., and Theodore W. Dwight. *Report on the Prisons and Reformatories of the United States and Canada.* Albany, N.Y.: Van Benthuysen, 1867.

KEITH EDGERTON

PROFESSIONS

The Scope of Professionalism

The number of Americans identifying themselves as middle-class professionals and participating in the formation of professional associations expanded rapidly in the second half of the nineteenth century. In comparison to western European nations—England,

France, Germany—what differed in the United States was the breadth and inclusiveness of the movement. Occupations considered merely technical and trades in Europe raised themselves to professional status in the more permissive and less-structured environment of the United States. Novel types of occupational workers were required to build the rapidly developing nineteenth-century industrial and urban environment: engineers (civil, mechanical, electrical), research-oriented scientists and social scientists, white-collar managers, newspaper reporters, businessmen, real-estate and insurance agents. The "pro" baseball player and association appeared during this period. By the early twentieth century, "every man a professional" was a phrase being stretched to extend to "scientific" training for mothers, social reformers, and labor leaders as well as to calls for significant reforms of training and practices in the traditional professions of law and medicine.

The nineteenth-century movement toward a model of professionalization persisted relentlessly in the twentieth century. Its features included the opportunity for individual careers, boundary definitions of specialized work, schooling and certification, state licensing, self-regulating peer review and oversight, and codes of etiquette and ethics. As advocated by its turn-of-the-century, Progressive-era proponents, professionalization was an equal-opportunity initiative for middle-class (primarily white Protestant male) mobility, status, and independence. Historically, the model developed together with the expansion of the university system in America, which, unlike European systems, embraced professional schools, professional training, and large student enrollments within its expanding orbit.

Criticism of the U.S. professional model never was lacking, especially regarding gender, race, and religious discrimination and exclusionary practices. Often the ideals embraced by the model appeared hypocritical in the context of the historical realities of politics, partisanship, exclusionary practices, and the opportunities to profit from "expertise." Nevertheless, even with these criticisms, professions and professionals have proven to be remarkably adaptive and resilient. American higher education with its professional schools and the quality of U.S. professional work rank very high on any list of institutional success stories in modern world history.

What Professionals Do

What did professions and professionals do in the United States that put them in demand beginning in the middle of the nineteenth century? They convinced people that paying for professional services based on state-of-the-art, specialized knowledge was necessary to avoid a threat to existence or jeopardy to one's well-being in a sphere of vital concern. The legitimacy of the professional initiative was built on a credible threat (literal in physical health or engineering; metaphoric in social, psychological, and cultural specializations) to a client's interest.

As the nation became industrialized and urbanized, new technologies came on line, especially with revolutions in transportation and communications. Expectations for the personal quality of life, health, and activities rose with increased information and spendable income. The exposure to a variety of experiences and the speedup of life increased beyond what Americans had ever known. Under changed, even novel, circumstances, the application of empirical common sense to problems or threatening situations commonly was perceived to be seriously inadequate if not dangerous.

On matters great and small, where could ordinary, ambitious, literate persons turn for expert advice, judgment, and knowledge with some degree of confidence? The "con man" as a type first appeared in the 1840s. Clever quacks, frauds, humbugs, and the like easily exploited human needs for a broad variety of valued services. In a contemporaneous development, cheap and portable reference and information books—from housekeeping guides to detailed manuals for learning occupational skills—began appearing in the American marketplace in large numbers. Each sought to address an audience with a specific need for reliable information and tested procedures. In this context, the phrase "professional"—giving independent recognition to the individual practitioner in contrast to the gentleman, often nonpracticing, member of a corporate guild—emerged in popular vernacular. Additionally, "amateur"—one who pursued an activity for the love, delight, and charm of it—appeared. Every area from athletics to carpentry was crowded with amateurs, many of them knowing a great deal. However, when it came to the discipline of confronting a threat or sticking with a project through to resolution, amateurs lacked the commitment, systematic experience, and professional detachment necessary to encourage a client's trust.

The name of the professional game was winning, not loving it. For instance, when it came to the bloody business of winning a civil war that lasted longer than most everyone imagined, amateurs were no match against veteran professionals. Nor could amateurs build the railroad system. With the commercialization of the U.S. economy taking off in the post–Civil War decades, demands for competent and disinterested professional knowledge and services were widespread. These demands were accentuated by persistent public exposure to abuse, scandal, greed, politics, incompetence, and malpractice in the industrializing nation, and growing concerns about personal well-being and the effects of progress.

Professional Careers

Recruitment studies of young men entering professional work in the mid-period of the nineteenth century reveal a reasonably consistent pattern. They were the sons of clergymen, artisans, mechanics, local officials, and farmers, commonly referred to as the "middling" classes or sorts. In a republican context of producers where character counted, these young men were prepared by their fathers for a "fit calling" in the skills of a craft. As they matured after the 1840s, they found opportunities wanting in static or diminishing occupational fields. With an expanding youthful population of young men, including rising immigration from western Europe, it became increasingly harder to make a good living, open a shop, buy land, or afford to go to school. Farmers' sons, in particular, felt leaving the homestead offered a better quality of life—one without sweaty manual labor and concerns about the growing scarcity of good land. Gold in California, both in the hills and the rapidly growing cities, lured young men by the thousands beginning in 1849.

This middling class of young men began thinking in terms of professional "careers," a new, more positive meaning for what had formerly been a slur applied to criminals, itinerant evangelicals, shady politicians, drunks, and addicts. To career had meant to race precipitously and recklessly around a track, to cascade out of control down a race. Lacking integrity and stability of character, those who careered were headed for a deserved destruction. The older understanding of career was changing. A professional career, while neither as spiritually lofty as a learned profession nor as self-interested as mere trade or business, offered full-time work at a socially sanctioned activity in which one earned a permanent livelihood. In 1865 Samuel Clemens (Mark Twain, 1835–1910) wrote to his brother Orion from San Francisco, advising that the sermonic, noble Orion should hear his calling and enter the ministry so he could support his family. Clemens wrote he had no character or calling himself, but would pursue a career as a professional humorist and writer and succeed in making a very good living. Twain's lifelong career built around the written word—as a printer, river pilot, miner, reporter, humorist, author, and publisher—exhibited the new pattern of professional work among ambitious young men in the later nineteenth century.

Unlike the repetitive work of a job or the frugal self-sacrifice of a calling, work in a professional career moved along a track of specialization that made room for the challenges of change, variety, and development. Professions were not businesses in a conventional sense. Fiduciary trust, not commercial contract, became the basis of client relationships and independent judgment in performance, not outcome, became the basis of fee schedules. The practitioner whose responsibility was to diagnose and treat an illness was paid, whether the patient healed or not.

In the half century after the Civil War, self-regulating communities of peers or professional associations expanded rapidly. They served to raise the public credibility of professions by exercising oversight over standards for schooling, credentialing, licensing, practicing, and ethics. Theoretical papers, experimental findings, intellectual as well as practitioner concerns made up the typical program at annual conferences and retreats. Professions differed in emphasis: service-oriented teachers (the helping professions), research-oriented academics (knowledge-centered professions), performance-oriented actors (vocational professions). In differing degrees all professions shared the three spheres of helping, knowledge, and vocation. The object of professionalization was to establish independence and self-accountability in a field of necessary work, and the process of development was reasonably familiar across the spectrum. There was no lack of arrogance, snobbery, and backbiting among occupations as to which were real professions, and whether classes of people like women were capable of the concentrated study needed for a profession and disinterested practice. The infighting could be intense. Nevertheless, the basic values embodied in the professional model persisted over time and changed, albeit slowly.

Why Professional Authority Persists

In the nineteenth century, the emphasis on the expanding authority of independent professionalism was characteristically American. In part, it represented a response to the crisis of authority in the "public" sphere: Who spoke for the public in a marketplace, political as well as economic, of competing interests?

On the one hand, an administrative-centered government that could conduct itself objectively in a professional manner lacked plausibility. The American Revolution and the Constitution gave Americans a powerful legacy of skepticism toward the tyranny of the State, which might abuse individual rights, and the need for checks and balances. By the 1840s the newspaper-reading public commonly perceived that the spoils system dominated politics, government corruption was routine, and favoritism toward patrons ruled the public treasury. A design of extreme powers assumed by the federal government during the Civil War punctuated the point. On the other hand the capitalist marketplace in a laissez-faire economy made money and profit the measure of all worth. As marketplace entities, professions were no different than any other money-driven business. Between the government and the marketplace, promoting the independence of the professional—acting from the dual motives of personal career and public service in self-regulating associations—made good sense.

At the end of the twentieth century, there were few desirable alternatives regarding quality of life and opportunities to go to college and become a professional. Every one a professional, every one a career. Historically, radical Populists repudiated the professional model as elitist and authoritarian. Marxists rejected it as a false ideological cover for power, control, and money. Both movements stirred reflection and change within established professions, for instance on the limits of claims of expert objectivity, the exposure of bald commercial interest in public-service rhetoric, and the thorn of loyalty to a corporate body compromising the independent judgment at the core of professional credibility. But as movements neither the Populists nor the Marxists prevailed. In the twentieth century, professions became more regulated by an administrative government, but essentially they retained their original charter of independence either from the government or the marketplace. The fiduciary trust in the professional-client relationship remained intact.

See also **Academic and Professional Societies; Education,** *subentry on* **Graduate and Professional Education; Women,** *subentry on* **Women in the Professions; Work,** *subentry on* **Middle-Class Occupations.**

Bibliography

Bledstein, Burton J. *The Culture of Professionalism: The Middle Class and the Development of Higher Education in America.* New York: Norton, 1976.

Bloomfield, Maxwell. *American Lawyers in a Changing Society, 1776–1876.* Cambridge, Mass.: Harvard University Press, 1976.

Duffy, John. *From Humors to Medical Science: A History of American Medicine.* 2d ed. Urbana: University of Illinois Press, 1993.

Gawalt, Gerald W., ed. *The New High Priest: Lawyers in Post–Civil War America.* Wesport, Conn.: Greenwood, 1984.

Hatch, Nathan O., ed. *The Professions in American History.* Notre Dame, Ind.: University of Notre Dame Press, 1988.

Kimball, Bruce A. *The "True Professional Ideal" in America: A History.* Cambridge, Mass.: Blackwell, 1992.

BURTON J. BLEDSTEIN

PROGRESS, IDEA OF   Few themes echoed more resoundingly through American culture in the nineteenth century than the idea of progress. Americans were scarcely alone in believing in progress. Blossoming during the eighteenth century and enduring as an influential idea until World War I, progress "dominated the European mind to such an extent," observed the historian Christopher Dawson, "that any attempt to question it was regarded as a paradox or a heresy" (*Progress and Religion*, 1970, p. 7). But nowhere was public opinion so nearly unanimous on the certainty of progress as in the young United States. At the altar of progress, nineteenth-century Americans were often zealots and evangelists. "Old Europe will have to lean on our shoulders, and to hobble along by our side. . . . What a colossus shall we be, when the southern continent comes up to our mark!" exulted the elderly Thomas Jefferson in 1816 (Ekirch, *The Idea of Progress in America*, p. 32). The editor and reformer Orestes Brownson expressed the conviction of countless countrymen when he exclaimed in 1842, "We are THE PEOPLE OF THE FUTURE" (Ekirch, *The Idea of Progress in America*, p. 52).

What Americans had in mind when they contemplated the coming glories was subject to little exactness and less agreement. The "progress" they confidently expected referred to social improvement surely, but how was it to be measured? Probably a large majority of Americans anticipated gains in territory, population, wealth, productivity, and standard of living generated by westward expansion, advancing science, and industrialization. Less consensus existed about the likelihood of such material growth yielding the moral, educational, and aesthetic gains that, in the view of religious and intellectual leaders, constituted the truest kind of progress.

During the first decades of the new Republic, progress was sponsored chiefly by the Enlightenment, the movement of secular ideas that championed liberty and reason in support of empirical science and political revolution. Enlightened rationalists like Jefferson, Benjamin Franklin, and Benjamin Rush pointed to a multitude of historical circumstances favoring progress in the United States, including the bountiful natural resources and protected geographic position of the continent, the spirit of enterprise stimulated by political and economic freedom, the genius of republican governments, and the absence of burdensome feudal customs and undemocratic establishments. American thinking about progress was also colored by the evangelical religion that spread through the culture after 1800. Enlightened rationalists envisioned progress as a smooth ascent toward a more civilized way of life, with material gains predictably yielding moral ones. Protestant millennialists, believers in the imminent return of Christ, which would herald the establishment of God's kingdom on earth, typically envisioned progress as the product of hard struggle with Satan and sin, emphasized the need for divine grace, and held doubts about the moral outcome of worldly advances. Nonetheless, in the period before the Civil War, aspirations for spiritual perfection tended to merge with pride in material improvements. Later, when Darwin's theory of natural selection challenged traditional Christian doctrines, liberal clergymen joined with scientists in defending evolution as God's chosen method for redeeming humankind.

Thus God, nature, and reason came together in a master myth of progress that endured through the middle third of the nineteenth century. The Almighty endowed Americans with a bountiful continent and with the acumen they needed to build on it a just and prosperous and expansive society. Although European prophets of progress could lay equal claim to the benefits of reason and science, Americans were uniquely blessed with America, and often they spoke as though God the Creator were uniquely on their side, too.

Nineteenth-century Americans loved to contemplate the prospects of their youthful society, blessed with empty land and innocent of the historical burdens borne by older societies. Notwithstanding the awful fact of slavery, the idea of progress suffused Americans' sense of their national identity. The idea was invoked in speeches at every civic celebration. It was pictured in popular lithographs showing wagon trains and railroads rumbling steadily westward, conquering wilderness and barbarism as they went. It helped make Manifest Destiny a potent theme of both domestic and foreign policy. And it shaped the ideals of hundreds of thousands of earnest reformers and utopian communitarians. "Since the progress of the race appears to be the great purpose of Providence," wrote the historian George Bancroft, "it becomes us all to venerate the future. We must be ready to sacrifice ourselves for our successors, as they in turn must live for their posterity" (Marcell, *Progress and Pragmatism*, p. 75). Of all the societies caught up in the accelerating changes of the nineteenth century, no other was so inclined to look forward, no other was so prone to prefer its children to its ancestors.

The foremost prophet of this creed was the transcendentalist philosopher Ralph Waldo Emerson. Calling himself "a seeker with no Past at his back," Emerson expounded a vision of boundless potential

"**The Progress of the Century.**" Lithograph by Currier and Ives, 1876, depicting symbols of nineteenth-century progress, including the lightning steam press, the locomotive, the steamboat, and the electric telegraph. The words of Daniel Webster's famous 1830 denunciation of nullification in the Senate appear on the telegraph. LIBRARY OF CONGRESS

in a series of seminal essays. "Gentlemen, there is a sublime and friendly Destiny by which the human race is guided," Emerson wrote in "The Young American" in 1844. This destiny achieved its apogee in the United States. Emerson continued, "After all the deduction is made for our frivolities and insanities, there still remains [in America] an organic simplicity and liberty . . . which offers opportunity to the human mind not known to any other region" (Spiller, ed., *The Collected Works of Ralph Waldo Emerson,* pp. 230, 241–242).

But even at its zenith the American faith in progress was crossed by doubts that cast longer shadows as the century wore on. In "The American Scholar" (1837), Emerson exhorted Americans to fulfill the new nation's cultural promise. He complained, "We have listened too long to the courtly muses of Europe. The spirit of the American freeman is already suspected to be timid, imitative, tame." Meanwhile other writers, such as Nathaniel Hawthorne in the satirical story "The Celestial Railroad" (1843), mocked the optimism of the transcendentalists and all the airier dreamers of the time. By the 1830s the cancer of slavery and its associated festering sectional conflicts began to feed anxieties about the nation's future. Emerson's address to "gentlemen" in "The Young American" reminds us that progress had always been a thoroughly racialized and patriarchal doctrine, the preserve of educated white males who presumed that they alone had the capacity to move history forward. The idea had much less resonance among women, people of color, and other groups excluded from full citizenship and usually judged incapable of progress. It had no resonance at all among the Native Americans who were forcibly cast aside to make way for white enterprise. Moreover, what Emerson called the "insanities" of American life intruded ever more insistently on the consciousness even of progress-minded males. The slavery plague and sectional conflicts were finally eliminated, but only by the terrible bloodletting of the Civil War. After the war the contradictions and corruptions bred by industrialization and urbanization grew hard to reconcile with a simple faith in progress.

The prophets of material improvement found plenty to celebrate in the post–Civil War United States. The man who replaced Emerson as America's favorite philosopher, the agnostic Englishman Herbert Spencer, declared in one of his most popular books that "progress . . . is not an accident, but a necessity. . . . As surely as there is any efficacy in educational culture, or any meaning in such terms as habit, custom, practice, . . . so surely must the things we call evil and immorality disappear; so surely must man become perfect" (Buckley, *The Triumph of Time,* p. 48). World's fairs held in Philadelphia (1876), Chicago (1893), Atlanta (1887 and 1895), and other cities overflowed with displays of American technical and industrial genius. In *Triumphant Democracy* (1886) the steelmaker Andrew Carnegie bragged in characteristic railroad imagery, "The old nations of the earth creep on at a snail's pace; the Republic thunders past with the rush of the express. The United States in the growth of a single century, has already reached the foremost rank among nations, and is destined soon to out-distance all others in the race" (Wall, ed., *The Andrew Carnegie Reader,* p. 208).

These tributes to economic and technical wonders reflected a materialization of the meaning of progress that made the idea less universal and more controversial. Assumptions that abundance would bring social justice or improve manners and morals, always shaky, tended to break down. So did the alliance between science and religion in support of progress. The doctrine came to be associated increasingly with the mechanistic version of evolutionism taught by Spencer, which offended believers in biblical Christianity. Clergymen were joined by artists and intellectuals in criticizing it. William Dean Howells complained that America defined itself too much by its machines and expressed his growing disaffection with progressive dogmas in works such as *A Hazard of New Fortunes* (1890). Mark Twain's attitudes rapidly darkened on the way toward the apocalyptic vision of an industrial civilization destroying itself that concluded *A Connecticut Yankee in King Arthur's Court* (1889). At the turn of the century opponents of imperialism and historical pessimists like Van Wyck Brooks and Henry Adams warned of a gathering American decadence. Once a stimulus to reformers, the idea of progress tended to decay into a slogan that substituted for rather than invigorated reform commitments.

Even on its home ground of economic growth, the idea of progress encountered mounting skepticism. Industrial capitalism multiplied the nation's wealth but did a poor job of distributing it. The result was deepening class conflict and recurrent depressions. Less than a year after the 1876 Centennial Exposition a wave of railroad strikes stunned the nation. Less than a year after the 1893 Chicago World's Fair that city became the epicenter of the Pullman strike, the climax of many decades of struggle between capital and labor. Millions of southern and western farmers protested their exclusion from economic progress through the Farmers Alliances and the People's Party movement of the 1880s and 1890s. The reformer Henry George pondered the paradoxical combination in *Progress and Poverty,* a best-selling economic critique published in 1879. He wrote, "The enormous increase in productive power which has marked the present century and is still going on . . . simply widens the gulf between Dives and Lazarus. . . . This association of poverty with progress is the great enigma of our times" (pp. 8, 10).

Paradoxically, some of the groups that benefited least from the material bonanza of the Gilded Age found grounds for continuing to affirm progress for themselves if not for the whole society. Even though their expectations for emancipation were frustrated, even though Jim Crow laws, economic oppression, and lynching blighted their lives, most African Americans had to feel that for them the nineteenth century had been a century of progress. Women, too, could celebrate great strides in educational and economic opportunities despite lagging hopes in the 1890s for securing the vote. Spokesmen for the New South, prominent among them the black leader Booker T. Washington, never tried of projecting great things for their zone despite its persisting backwardness. But the dominant trend lay in the opposite direction. As the historian David Marcell has observed, "A vast and pervasive ambivalence toward the idea of progress marked American thought at the turn of the century" (*Progress and Pragmatism*, p. 36).

See also **Civil Rights; Communitarian Movements and Groups; Economic Theory; Labor Movement; Millennialism and Adventism; Nationalism; Panics and Depressions; Philosophy; Population; Poverty; Reform, Idea of; Transcendentalism; World's Fairs.**

Bibliography

Buckley, Jerome Hamilton. *The Triumph of Time: A Study of the Victorian Concepts of Time, History, Progress, and Decadence.* Cambridge: Mass.: Belknap Press of Harvard University, 1966.

Dawson, Christopher. *Progress and Religion: An Historical Inquiry.* 1929. Reprint, Westport, Conn.: Greenwood, 1970.

Ekirch, Arthur Alphonse, Jr. *The Idea of Progress in America, 1815–1860.* New York: Columbia University Press, 1944.

Emerson, Ralph Waldo. *The Selected Writings of Ralph Waldo Emerson.* Edited by Brooks Atkinson. New York: Modern Library, 1950.

George, Henry. *Progress and Poverty.* New York: Robert Schalkenback Foundation, 1979.

Marcell, David W. *Progress and Pragmatism: James, Dewey, Beard, and the American Idea of Progress.* Westport, Conn.: Greenwood, 1974.

Spadafora, David. *The Idea of Progress in Eighteenth-Century Britain.* New Haven, Conn.: Yale University Press, 1990.

Spiller, Robert E., ed. *The Collected Works of Ralph Waldo Emerson.* Volume 1. Cambridge, Mass.: Belknap Press of Harvard University Press, 1971.

Thomas, John L. *Alternative America: Henry George, Edward Bellamy, Henry Demarest Lloyd, and the Adversary Tradition.* Cambridge, Mass.: Belknap Press of Harvard University, 1983.

Tuveson, Ernest Lee. *Redeemer Nation: The Idea of America's Millennial Role.* Chicago: University of Chicago Press, 1968.

Wagar, W. Warren. *Good Tidings: The Belief in Progress from Darwin to Marcuse.* Bloomington: Indiana University Press, 1972.

Wall, Joseph Frazier, ed. *The Andrew Carnegie Reader.* Pittsburgh: University of Pittsburgh Press, 1992.

EUGENE E. LEACH

PROGRESSIVISM   Progressivism was a diverse, dynamic effort to assess and control the shattering changes that accompanied the growth of America from the end of the nineteenth century until the aftermath of World War I. Progressive activists in politics, social reform, education, and the arts recognized the transformation of the United States into an urban, heavily industrialized, multiethnic society. They were concerned about the damaging consequences of that rapid, largely unregulated expansion, which included overcrowding, poor city services, unsafe living and working conditions, alarming disparities in wealth and condition, unprecedented corporate power, and a corrupt, inefficient political system unsuited to the demands of modernity.

Although the motivations, methods, and issues of interest to particular progressive reformers varied considerably, certain key common features characterized their outlook. Progressives used the tools of bureaucracy, expertise, and efficiency—many of them forged in the corporate revolution of the late nineteenth century—to impose rationality and humane order on the complexities and disorganization of modern life. Economists, social workers, city planners, and other university-trained representatives of the young, professional middle class were central figures in progressive reform.

Progressive intellectuals and activists were willing to experiment in pursuit of truth or justice, placing great emphasis on environment, experience, and action. In academic fields such as philosophy and education, the progressive approach contributed to the development of pragmatism, which stressed the experiential or provisional nature of truth. In politics and social activism, the progressive commitment to action spurred a willingness to use government or expert authority to intervene in society to protect the public interest, thus producing laws regulating housing, factory safety, child labor and schooling, political campaigns, food, drugs, and liquor sales.

Progressives were notable also for their optimistic faith that social division would give way to harmony, that efficiency would advance democracy, and that social scientific methods would further the moral im-

Jane Addams, Social Reformer. With Ellen Gates Strarr, Jane Addams (1860–1935) was a founder in 1889 of Hull-House in Chicago. Photoprint c. 1914 by the Gerhard sisters, St. Louis. LIBRARY OF CONGRESS

peratives of Christianity. The moral fervor of the progressives, and their search for harmony as well as order in the new industrial metropolis, reveal the deep roots that bound progressivism to the nineteenth century, even as its topmost branches stretched into the twentieth century.

The depth and energy of the progressives' commitment flowed from their conviction that fundamental changes threatened to alter the basic character of American society at the end of the nineteenth century. The second phase of the industrial revolution, marked by heavy industry, the creation of the modern, centralized corporation, and a wave of business consolidations known as the Great Merger Movement, increased the prominence of business in the United States and sparked fears of predatory monopoly. In the late 1880s workers challenged the new order in a series of uprisings historians call the Great Upheaval. The sense of disorder was furthered by a new swell of immigration after 1880 that drew Slavs, Italians, and Greeks, Catholics, Orthodox Chris-

tians, and Jews from southern and eastern Europe to labor in American mines, fields, factories, and tenements. Between 1880 and 1919 over twenty-three million newcomers arrived in the United States. Several million "birds of passage" returned home after stints of labor, but even these temporary participants in the new immigration helped reconfigure American society and culture into more complex ethnic patterns.

By the 1890s the sense of pervasive change deepened into a crisis that directly influenced the development of progressivism. At the center of the crisis of the 1890s was the devastating depression of 1893. It not only created hard times for Americans but also caused many people to denounce corporations and seek greater protection through their government. In cities and towns in Wisconsin, among other states, citizens demanded strict regulation of corporations and political parties in the wake of the depression and endorsed expanded municipal services. By the end of the century mayors in Detroit, Toledo, and Cleveland championed publicly controlled utilities and dynamic reform action by municipal government. Embittered farmers in the South and West also called for government action against monopoly power in the 1890s. The Populist movement insisted that the national government intervene on behalf of its citizens against railroads, warehouses, and banks. The People's Party, founded by Populists in 1892, demanded postal savings banks, government-funded warehouses to store crops, an inflated currency, tight government supervision of railroads and telegraph companies, and the direct election of U.S. senators. Populism's challenge to the Gilded Age principle of party loyalty spread to the political system as a whole after 1896, as independent voting grew and party identification declined from its zenith in the 1880s. In the South the Populist revolt and an upsurge in violent racial antagonism in the 1890s sparked the more repressive features of southern progressivism, which attempted to tame corporations and politicians but also segregated and disfranchised blacks in the name of social peace, progress, and white supremacy.

The intersection of women's activism, social science, religious commitment, and urban problems in the late nineteenth century produced the settlement house movement, the most celebrated progressive reform innovation. Women in the late nineteenth century had become increasingly active in temperance work, social reform, and informal political action. A new generation of college-educated women, represented by Jane Addams and Ellen Gates Starr, yearned to apply their learning to the practical betterment of society, the Americanization of immigrants, and reconciliation between social groups. In 1889 Addams and Starr founded at Hull House in Chicago what they considered to be a social laboratory in a working-class, immigrant district. The community of women and several men who staffed Hull House completed a sociological survey of the neighborhood around them and published it as *Hull-House Maps and Papers* (1895). Settlement investigations generated the statistics upon which public policy reform was based. Florence Kelley, a Hull House resident, used the social survey method to expose the conditions of women and children laboring in sweatshops. Her study led to the creation of the Office of Factory Inspector in Illinois in 1893, with Kelley serving as the first chief inspector. By 1900 over one hundred settlements, many of them affiliated with universities, operated in American cities. Progressivism developed from this legacy.

See also **City and Regional Planning; Populism; Settlement Houses.**

Bibliography

Davis, Allen F. *Spearheads for Reform: The Social Settlements and the Progressive Movement, 1890–1914.* 1967. Reprint, New Brunswick, N.J.: Rutgers University Press, 1984.

Diner, Steven J. *A Very Different Age: Americans of the Progressive Era.* New York: Hill and Wang, 1998.

Sklar, Kathryn Kish. *Florence Kelley and the Nation's Work: The Rise of Women's Political Culture, 1830–1900.* New Haven, Conn.: Yale University Press, 1995.

Thelen, David P. *The New Citizenship: Origins of Progressivism in Wisconsin, 1885–1900.* Columbia: University of Missouri Press, 1972.

THOMAS R. PEGRAM

PROHIBITION.   See **Temperance Movement.**

PROPERTY   Americans in the nineteenth century inherited a constitutional system that placed a high value on the rights of property owners. Property ownership had long been associated with individual liberty in Anglo-American constitutional thought, and respect for property-holding delineated the legitimate powers of government. Moreover, it was widely believed that private ownership promoted the productive use of assets and maximization of societal wealth. Throughout the nineteenth century constitutional jurisprudence was markedly shaped by these considerations. From Chief Justice John Marshall to Chief Justice Melville W. Fuller, the Supreme Court devoted much of its energy to defending property

rights against legislative abridgment. Many state courts were even more active in championing property rights.

Yet, notwithstanding their devotion to private property, nineteenth-century Americans readily altered the legal rules governing property. Some changes were dictated by conflicting visions of property ownership. Policies designed to encourage economic development or to make room for new technologies often upset existing property relationships. Lawmakers had to balance security in property with the desire for economic growth. Judges, for example, modified the strict common law doctrine of nuisance to facilitate fledgling enterprise. Legislatures broadly delegated the power of eminent domain to acquire property for private businesses, such as railroads. Americans generally preferred property put to an entrepreneurial use rather than property dedicated to the status quo. Certain reform movements also affected property rights. Thus prohibitionists both before and after the Civil War sought to eradicate drunkenness by eliminating legal recognition of liquor as a type of property.

Another important set of legal changes reflected the view that land was a dynamic commodity similar to other types of property. Consequently, the law of conveyancing was simplified with the aim of making land readily alienable. In the same vein, by the mid–nineteenth century state legislatures began to enact married women's property laws. The effect of such statutes was to destroy the common law disability of coverture and thus to allow a married woman to use and dispose of her own property free of her husband's control and claims of the husband's creditors.

Although protected by several clauses in the Constitution, slavery became an increasingly controversial type of property by the mid–nineteenth century. Northern states gradually eliminated slavery, while southern lawmakers enacted comprehensive codes regulating slave property. Eventually the intense sectional conflict over slavery led to the Civil War, and the abolition of slave property by the Thirteenth Amendment in 1865.

During the nineteenth century both state and local governments relied heavily on a property tax on land and tangible personal property to meet revenue needs. By mid-century state constitutions were amended to embrace the Jacksonian principle that all property should be uniformly taxed, but this ideal proved difficult to achieve in practice. Criticism of the property tax mounted as the nineteenth century drew to a close.

Thinking about property evolved further toward the end of the nineteenth century. The emergence of large-scale corporate enterprise concentrated economic power and exacerbated disparities of wealth. This gave rise to demands for some form of public supervision of privately owned business. The disputes over property rights had a marked sectional dimension. By the 1890s agrarian discontent in the West and South coalesced into the Populist movement, which sought to curb private economic power. Although the federal and state courts upheld most regulations, judges clung to the view that they should safeguard traditional economic rights. Accordingly, they took a hard look at laws that limited contractual freedom, attempted to redistribute wealth, or benefited special groups. The continuing judicial solicitude for property rights was manifest when the Supreme Court, in *Pollock v. Farmers' Loan and Trust Company* (1895), struck down the first peacetime income tax.

See also Law, *subentry on* Common Law; Taxation and Public Finance.

Bibliography

Ely, James W., Jr. *The Guardian of Every Other Right: A Constitutional History of Property Rights.* 2d ed. New York: Oxford University Press, 1998.

Hall, Kermit L. *The Magic Mirror: Law in American History.* New York: Oxford University Press, 1989.

JAMES W. ELY JR.

PROSTITUTION Prostitution commonly refers to the performance of sex acts for hire. The single term covers a range of activities, including work as a paid mistress, a brothel inmate, a streetwalker, and various forms of casual prostitution.

At the opening of the nineteenth century, most prostitutes worked in port cities, serving sailors. Authorities rarely identified their presence as an important social problem. But westward expansion, urbanization, and industrialization all contributed to the increase of prostitution. Large populations of young men far from family and community supervision composed a clientele. Large numbers of young women trying to support themselves in an economy offering limited work options for women provided the workforce. By the end of the century, prostitution was part of life even in small towns, and it had become the object of national reform movements and international treaties.

Most prostitutes were between the ages of sixteen and thirty and tended to come from the poorest and most vulnerable populations of any region. The prostitutes in New York City in the 1830s were mostly American-born white women, often from rural areas. Around military posts in New Mexico in the 1870s,

they were Native American or Mexican women. A "fancy trade" in light-skinned slaves staffed brothels in New Orleans and other southern cities before the Civil War. Racist beliefs about black women's sexuality made them especially vulnerable to exploitation. Although most prostitutes were single, perhaps a third were married, widowed, or divorced. According to William Sanger, a physician who surveyed New York prostitutes in the 1850s, nearly half had at least one child. Birth rates among working prostitutes seem to have been low. Abortion and contraception account for some of this; infertility from venereal disease played an equally large role.

Types of Prostitution

Work in a parlor house or as a paid mistress were the elite prostitution trades. Before the 1850s, New York brothels were generally managed by women, and inmates, or resident prostitutes, of the more select houses exercised some autonomy in choosing clients and controlling their work. "Landladies" made money from room and board paid by inmates, and by selling liquor to callers. Men used brothels as social centers, not just for sexual recreation. In the last third of the century, New York brothels increasingly came under the control of male pimps, who offered "protection" and took profits. In other regions, pimps arrived much later or not at all. Even so, inmates everywhere in the last half of the century lacked the autonomy of earlier brothel prostitutes. They often paid a percentage of their earnings to the house, and some brothel keepers used coercion to keep women in the business.

The streetwalker's experience is less easy to document. She recruited her clients in public places, taking them to a rented room or even a dark alley. She earned less and frequently experienced a violent, unstable life. William Sanger believed that streetwalking was the last stage of a prostitute's downward career, but historians now challenge this view. Many prostitutes began as impoverished child streetwalkers, discovering at nine or ten that sex brought treats or contributed to the family purse. Streetwalking was also an option for casual prostitutes, women who occasionally turned to the sex trade to meet emergencies, then returned to other work. Prostitution was not merely a downward path; it could also be a revolving door.

In the West, conditions were especially harsh. Prostitutes often worked in tents, shacks, or even wagons. Among the most visible western prostitutes were indentured Chinese women brought to serve Chinese miners and railroad workers.

Male prostitution is far less well documented, but

evidence suggests that young men who sought sexual contact with other men were also part of the urban brothel culture of the late nineteenth century. "Gay" began as an expression for this underworld culture before becoming a term for sexual orientation.

Law and Reform

In states following Anglo-American legal tradition, both streetwalking and brothel keeping were common-law offenses—though by custom, a woman who worked alone and in private was not subject to prosecution. Over the course of the century, the body of law governing prostitution expanded in response to reform movements.

The earliest national movement emphasized not legal reform, but moral suasion. The American Moral Reform Association and the American Female Moral Reform Society were both organized in the early 1830s, when the growing population of young clerks in the cities raised fears about their association with prostitutes. Moral reformers sought to evangelize prostitutes and to urge a single standard of chastity for both men and women.

After the Civil War, physicians and police began to advocate not suppression, but regulation, of prostitution. They argued that medical examinations for prostitutes would control the spread of syphilis. A Missouri law of 1870 permitted St. Louis to legalize and license its brothels, but a national outcry led the legislature to reverse the law by 1874. After that, no state or city dared legalize prostitution, but many pursued extralegal regulation. In St. Paul, Minnesota, a system of regulation maintained public order and protected neighborhoods. In Davenport, Iowa, such regulation included medical examinations. Regulation in the South insured segregation. In New Orleans's Storyville district, established in 1896, prostitutes were white, black, and mixed-race, but they served only white clients. Where communities tolerated and regulated prostitution, stable conditions sometimes allowed women to save money and leave the business.

Two new anti-prostitution movements emerged in the 1870s, each with different goals and tactics. Anthony Comstock's New York Society for the Suppression of Vice investigated brothels and enforced censorship. The Woman's Christian Temperance Union blamed prostitution on predatory men. In 1885 the WCTU began lobbying states to raise the "age of consent," the age at which a girl's consent to sexual intercourse protected a man from prosecution for rape. In most states the age of consent was ten. Responding to pressure, many states raised it, usually to fifteen or sixteen.

By the 1890s, international anxiety focused on the "white slave" traffic. Historians disagree on the extent of any organized trade in women kidnapped and forced into prostitution, but fear led to an international convention in 1902 and, in the United States, to the White Slave Traffic Act of 1910.

See also **Cities and Urbanization; Health and Disease; Poverty; Recreation; Sexual Morality; Women,** *subentry on* **Women in the Professions.**

Bibliography

Best, Joel. *Controlling Vice: Regulating Brothel Prostitution in St. Paul, 1865–1883*. Columbus: Ohio State University Press, 1998.

Butler, Anne M. *Daughters of Joy, Sisters of Misery: Prostitutes in the American West, 1865–1890*. Urbana: University of Illinois Press, 1985.

Cohen, Patricia Cline. *The Murder of Helen Jewett: The Life and Death of a Prostitute in Nineteenth-Century New York*. New York: Knopf, 1998.

Gilfoyle, Timothy J. *City of Eros: New York City, Prostitution, and the Commercialization of Sex, 1790–1920*. New York: Norton, 1992.

Sanger, William. *The History of Prostitution*. New York: Harper, 1859.

Washburn, Josie. *The Underworld Sewer: A Prostitute Reflects on Life in the Trade, 1871–1909*. Lincoln: University of Nebraska Press, 1997.

SHARON E. WOOD

PROTESTANTISM

[This entry includes an overview and subentries on **Episcopalians, Congregationalists, Presbyterians, Methodists, Baptists, Lutherans, Mennonites,** and **Liberal Protestantism.**]

OVERVIEW

When the nineteenth century began, Protestantism was the dominant religious presence in the United States. Protestantism is a broad term denoting the diverse body of churches that stood in the tradition of the sixteenth-century Reformation. In one sense they were united only in their opposition to some of the doctrines of the Roman Catholic Church, especially its claim of the supremacy of the pope. Reflecting its commitment to the right of the laity to determine matters of polity for itself or the priesthood of all believers, Protestantism had proliferated into multiple denominations. While all Protestants accepted the authority of Scripture, they quarreled with each other and with Roman Catholicism over such issues as infant baptism, the use of a set liturgy, the nature of the sacraments, the nature of the ministry, the place of tradition, and other matters of faith and practice. The denominations that arose from these debates differed widely. For instance, the high church Episcopalians and the Disciples of Christ agreed only that they were not the Roman Catholic Church. Protestant hostility to Roman Catholicism continued throughout the century as Catholic immigrants arrived in larger numbers, though the virulent anti-Catholic crusade that began in earnest in 1830 diminished after the Civil War.

Despite their united front against Catholics, Protestants were divided among themselves over how to understand their relationship to American culture. Some adopted a paradoxical stance toward the culture, never fully embracing it but unable, like their Anabaptist cousins, to completely reject it, since to do so would be to fall into the sin of self-righteousness in a futile quest for moral purity. Other Protestant churches verged on an uncritical acceptance of the culture, in which they believed that they were the dominant actors because God's purpose was to make America Protestant. Despite those differences, Protestants profoundly shaped nineteenth-century American culture. Protestantism's influence was exerted through a number of specific themes and motifs, among them a belief in the freedom and responsibility of individual Christians to form their conscience solely by the word of God. Since Scripture, the supreme authority for Christian belief and practice, required literate readers, Protestantism put a strong emphasis on education. This gave rise to numerous colleges, seminaries, Bible societies, and the Sunday school movement. Toward the end of the century this commitment to education led many Protestants to embrace modern science and a liberal theology that in turn provoked a counterreaction known as fundamentalism.

For Protestants the freedom to be God's disciples in the world meant that they should be free from oversight by the state in the realm of religious thought and polity. They determined their moral responsibilities for themselves from within their gathered communities of faith. At the same time they accepted the legitimacy of the state as a divinely mandated institution that dealt with sinful human behavior in the world. The state was entitled to use means, such as coercion and legal repression, that were not appropriate for the internal life of the church. However, the state had to respect the right of individuals to form religious communities according to their rights. Thus Protestants made a major contribution to the political principles of constitutional government, especially the right of the people to free assembly and to control of their own political

destinies. After the demise of Puritanism and the disestablishment of most state churches at the beginning of the century, Protestants also committed themselves to the legal separation of church and state and to religious toleration, though most continued to believe that people who were not converted to Christ were damned.

Perhaps Protestantism's greatest contribution to nineteenth-century American culture was its program of evangelism and moral reform. Religious conversion was understood as carrying an obligation to spread the good news of Christ by evangelizing others. As a direct outgrowth of the revivalism of the Second Great Awakening, many Protestants saw both an evangelical opportunity and a divine imperative to carry the gospel and its call to conversion to non-Christians in America as well as abroad. The foreign missionary impulse brought the Protestant version of Christianity to more people in more places around the world than at any previous time in history. Domestically, missionary activity was most often directed toward the American Indians (and for a time to African slaves), as well as to white, unchurched settlers on the western frontier and later to immigrant populations in urban areas.

In turn, converted persons had a responsibility to reform the nation. All mainline Protestant churches shared, to various degrees, a dedication to transforming American morality. In what some have called "public Protestantism," this transformational intent sometimes focused on the spiritual renewal of individuals, who were then expected to change the culture. In other cases, especially under the Social Gospel movement of the late nineteenth century, the emphasis fell directly upon eliminating institutions considered structurally sinful, such as slavery or the industrial order.

Because the vast majority of Americans were affiliated with one denomination of Protestantism or another, a general Protestant morality easily dominated the moral agenda of the nation as a whole. The nineteenth was the century of revivalism, evangelicalism, and even millennialism, and many of these movements were inspired by a belief that they would help usher in the Kingdom of God. Protestants were, as a result, profoundly optimistic about social change. Some called for the evangelization of the world in their generation and espoused various degrees of spiritual and moral perfectionism. These movements rolled across the United States in waves, beginning with the Second Great Awakening in the first years of the century and continuing through the Third Awakening in the period after the Civil War, as Americans faced the challenges of industrialization, urbanization, and poverty. As a diverse group of religious communities, however, Protestants were often divided over moral issues. These divisions were most evident in the debates on slavery and wealth.

Protestantism was deeply divided over the issue of slavery in particular. Its divisions were within as well as between the various denominations. Some (e.g., the Episcopalians) dealt with the issue essentially by ignoring it in the belief that if it did not come up for discussion, it could not produce a divided church (for some a worse sin than slavery itself). Other denominations were not able to foreclose discussion of the issue and, as a result, some split into northern and southern factions, especially the Methodists, Presbyterians, and Baptists.

Many Protestants throughout the nation took either a proslavery position or advocated only a gradual elimination of slavery. The proslavery view was based on the claims that the Bible did not explicitly condemn slavery, and that slaves had every opportunity to do their moral duty even in a condition of bondage, since freedom was only a "contingent" right, not an "essential" right. The alternatives to slavery that were embraced by most northern Protestants ranged from colonization (a return of the slaves to Africa), a gradual ending to slavery, and immediate abolition.

Over the course of the century Protestantism underwent gradual secularization of many of its ideas and practices. It slowly gave up its suspicion of reason, its denial of free will, its emphasis on the depravity of the human soul, and the necessity for a conversion experience. Protestantism continued to dominate the institutional and cultural life of the nation, even though its denominational diversions dissipated its singular influence and reduced the differences between its ideas and those emerging from American culture itself.

See also **African Americans,** *subentry on* **African American Religions; Evangelicalism; Millennialism and Adventism; Missions; Religion,** *subentry on* **Religion in Nineteenth-Century America; Revivalism.**

Bibliography

Ahlstrom, Sydney E. *A Religious History of the American People.* New Haven, Conn.: Yale University Press, 1972.

Albanese, Catherine L. *America: Religions and Religion.* 2d ed. Belmont, Calif.: Wadsworth, 1992.

Hudson, Winthrop S. *The Great Tradition of the American Churches.* New York: Harper and Row, 1963.

Hudson, Winthrop S., and John Corrigan. *Religion in America.* 6th ed. Upper Saddle River, N.J.: Prentice-Hall, 1999.

Niebuhr, H. Richard. *Christ and Culture.* New York: Harper, 1951.

———. *The Social Sources of Denominationalism.* New York: Meridian, 1957.

FRANK G. KIRKPATRICK

EPISCOPALIANS

A Reorganized Church

Episcopalians in colonial America belonged to the Church of England, or Anglican Church. Such belonging became problematic during and after the time the colonies fought a War of Independence (1775–1783) against England. The ties to the Church of England were strained during the war, and it became difficult to sustain them or to use the name "England" in a church body's name after the war. Hence in 1789, during a postwar reorganization of their denomination, Episcopalians chose to name their body the Protestant Episcopal Church, after their polity. Distinctive among Protestants, Episcopalians organized around bishops in apostolic succession; that is, they intended to be in spiritual continuity with bishops from the early decades of the Christian church.

The War of Independence had been devastating for the fortunes of the Anglican church. When the war began, the church had been well-positioned to dominate in several colonies, due to the fact that it had been established by law in the southern colonies and was growing in numbers and influence in middle colonies, such as New York, and also in New England. But Anglican clergy had taken an oath of allegiance to the king against whom the colonies were fighting. Many clergy would not violate their oath, and they had instinctive loyalties to England and its established church.

For that reason many Anglican clergy, especially in the North, fled to Ontario and Nova Scotia in Canada or to England itself. In the South, more remained on the scene, and some adopted the patriots' cause. Many of the nation's founders, from General, later President, George Washington on down, were members of this church. Two-thirds of those who signed the Declaration of Independence were Anglicans, a fact that helped the postwar Episcopal Church gain and hold status in the nineteenth century.

Episcopal leaders met for their first general convention in Philadelphia on 27 September 1785 to organize a new kind of disestablished but national body. Organization meant agreeing on a version of *The Book of Common Prayer,* a constitution, and a mode of consecrating bishops. The laity also gained more voice and authority than it had had in England through the establishment of a house of bishops and a house of deputies at general conventions.

This process of formal organization occurred chiefly under the leadership of such bishops as Samuel Seabury (1729–1796) of Connecticut, William White (1748–1836) of Pennsylvania, and Samuel

Provoost (1742–1815) of New York. Seabury had to go to Scotland in 1784 to receive orders, which meant being consecrated in the apostolic succession. White and Provoost went to England for consecration three years later, by which time bishops no longer had to swear loyalty to the crown. Despite tensions between the various elements, the Protestant Episcopal Church was poised to serve and prosper in the new nation by the turn of the century.

The First Amendment to the U.S. Constitution in 1789 forbade the Congress from making laws affecting the establishment of religion in the nation. By 1800 all but three states, Connecticut, Massachusetts, and New Hampshire, had disestablished their churches. (Congregationalists were established in northern colonies, now states.) Disestablishment meant that churches could not rely on tax support and had to support their ventures and win converts and allegiance on their own.

A Century of Activity

For this work, such groups as the Baptists and the Methodist Episcopal Church—formally split from Episcopalianism in 1784—were more ambitious and better equipped to appeal to democracy-minded frontier people. Therefore, as the western areas were settled, especially in the South, the Episcopal Church did not increase as the populist Baptist and Methodist churches did. Never strong in their ministry among blacks, the Episcopalians also lost freemen and slave loyalty to Baptists and Methodists.

For many African Americans, memories of Episcopalians as slaveholders were vivid and off-putting. But it was the energies of Baptists and Methodists that did most to win blacks to their denominations. The Episcopal Church did found several colleges for African Americans after its pioneering effort in 1867, such as St. Augustine's College in Raleigh, North Carolina.

Episcopalians tended to be well educated, and they made efforts to carry their tradition of learning with them as their church moved west. To that end they developed a system of seminaries, beginning with the General Theological Seminary in New York in 1817 and the Protestant Episcopal Theological Seminary of Virginia in 1823. They also started academies, typified by Trinity College, founded in Connecticut in 1823, and Kenyon College, founded in Ohio in 1824. Through these educational outposts and a variety of other endeavors to gain strength, the Episcopalians experienced growth, but never enough to match that of Baptists, Methodists, and others. In 1829 there were about 30,000 Episcopalians, a number that grew to 150,000 by 1860.

The Protestant Episcopal Church was organized more around worship and governance than it was defined by dogma. It did not generate any theological movements to match those in Congregationalism, Presbyterianism, or Lutheranism. At the turn of the nineteenth century Episcopalian theological spirit had been influenced by the rationalism of the day, a pattern that was appearing in the church in England and among elites in the new United States. While this spirit meant a downplaying of the supernatural and the emotional elements in religion, it helped breed an interest in the church as a moral agent.

The Episcopal Church participated in several missionary movements as the century progressed. Bishops like Jackson Kemper (1789–1870) pioneered in work among western Native Americans. Another leader in this effort was Bishop Henry Whipple (1822–1901) of Minnesota. After the Civil War, President Ulysses S. Grant's administration collaborated with churches in striving to improve white relations with western Indians, and Episcopalians were assigned roles on Great Plains reservations.

When Americans began endeavors to convert people overseas, Episcopalians were not leaders, but they

Episcopal Churches of New York City. Lithographic views of some of the Episcopal churches in New York City. Lithograph published by Fersenheim and Witschief, 1867. LIBRARY OF CONGRESS

did participate. These endeavors began in 1828 when the Domestic and Foreign Missionary Society began work in Greece. In the period between 1835 and 1907, 50 percent of the listed missionaries of this church were women, ninety-five in all. Many were wives of missionaries, who were charged to engage in ministries closed to women domestically.

To serve missions and domestic social needs, the Episcopal Church devised any number of instruments. Prominent among these was the female diaconate, one of the ways of recognizing the talents of women and of seeing them put to work in varieties of charitable and educational causes. In a male-dominated church, Episcopalian women showed enterprise by organizing various auxiliaries, which became integral to the church's mission. Thus in 1871 the General Convention authorized Mary Abbot Emery to serve as executive secretary of a woman's auxiliary that became the first nationwide element in the Episcopal Church. To gain more power over funding, the auxiliary also began a United Thank Offering in 1889.

Conflicting Emphases

The Protestant Episcopal Church turned out to be anything but a unified body through the century. First there were tensions between leaders who had been loyalists and those who had been patriots during the Revolution. Also prominent and problematic were divisions that had to do with defining the very life of the church. One party, often dubbed "high church," and led by Bishop John Henry Hobart (1775–1830), favored clear, leading roles for bishops, formal liturgies, and sacramental life, including frequent communion. The high church party experienced some losses as about thirty priests left to join the Roman Catholic Church. As in England, this "Anglo-Catholic" movement was countered by "low church" and evangelical parties, which set out to accommodate themselves to informal and more democratic American values in culture and religion.

Two movements originating in England had proponents in the United States, and these served further to divide American Episcopalians. One was the Oxford Movement, a high church impulse in England, promoting "Anglo-Catholic" tendencies that looked to their critics too Roman Catholic. The other was the Cambridge Movement, which emphasized ritual and led to aesthetic, liturgical, and architectural changes in the United States. The architectural arrangements and decor favored by the Cambridge Movement, for example, exaggerated the differences between clergy and laity and accented the sacraments in a period of Gothic revival. While the Episcopal Church was far from being the largest church body in America, it had the wealthiest members, many of whom endowed churches that evoked medieval excesses, prominently displaying the wealth of the donors.

To these conflicts among Anglicans, one must note the conflict between the church in the North and that in the South. While the Episcopalians did not formally divide—as Methodists, Baptists, and Presbyterians did in the 1840s—almost all the leadership in the South supported the Confederacy, just as northerners virtually unanimously favored and aided the Union. Southern Episcopal bishop Leonidas K. Polk (1806–1864) became a Confederate general and lost his life in battle. For all their conflicts, the northern and southern Anglican churches came back together in 1865, and the church virtually doubled in size during the war decade.

After the Civil War, American churches turned increasingly to face social issues brought on by industrialization and immigration. Episcopalians worked to address many of these, particularly through movements that espoused the modernist Social Gospel that found favor among other American Protestants and related to a British movement of Christian Socialism. Such clerics as William D. P. Bliss (1856–1926) led such efforts to respond to new industrial conditions, and lay Episcopalians, such as Vida Scudder (1861–1954), promoted it through writings and organization. Wealthy laypeople, such as the banker J. P. Morgan (1837–1913) in New York, worked with Episcopal parishes and larger organizations to invent new forms of ministry that would serve new immigrants and citizens who would never become members of the church itself.

Thanks to these charitable endeavors, and to the popular preaching and hymn-writing of Phillips Brooks (1835–1893) and other prominent Anglican spokespersons, late-nineteenth-century Episcopalians established for themselves a respected place among the Protestant denominations in America.

See also **Catholicism; Social Gospel.**

Bibliography

Addison, James T. *The Episcopal Church in the United States, 1789–1931.* New York: Scribners, 1951.
Albright, Raymond W. *A History of the Protestant Episcopal Church.* New York: Macmillan, 1964.
Holmes, David L. *A Brief History of the Episcopal Church.* Valley Forge, Pa.: Trinity, 1993.
Prichard, Robert, *A History of the Episcopal Church.* Harrisburg, Pa.: Morehouse, 1991.
Sachs, William L. *The Transformation of Anglicanism: From State Church to Global Communion.* New York: Cambridge University Press, 1993.

MARTIN E. MARTY

CONGREGATIONALISTS

Congregationalism, the religion rooted in seventeenth-century New England, entered the nineteenth century in a state of turmoil and disarray, and left it completely transfigured. The general decline and pluralization of religion in New England in the post-revolutionary period, the theological and cultural fragmentation of Congregationalism, and the problems of geographical expansion prompted a thorough remaking of the denomination in the first third of the nineteenth century.

Turmoil and Disarray

Congregationalism languished during and after the American Revolution. The established religion of Massachusetts and Connecticut, Congregationalism was entitled to taxpayer support, except at times when citizens were formally given permission to designate their tax monies for the support of a minister of another authorized denomination. Yet during the Revolution ministers were in short supply, and their salaries were often unpaid or unadjusted for inflation. A number of churches by the 1790s possessed only a handful of members, many of them aged. Baptists and Anglicans, influential in New England since the Great Awakening of the 1740s, became alternative, if lesser, cultural authorities. Newer denominations, such as Methodism and Universalism, threatened to displace the elite prestige of Congregationalism with more populist theological and moral teachings. Newer nonreligious or antireligious philosophies such as deism captured the imaginations of enough of the younger generation, in the eyes of some Congregational ministers, to augur the destruction of all religion and morality.

Congregationalism's problems were not only external, however. Within the denomination adherents had drifted into distinct camps. The Old Lights, or moderate Calvinists, favored an inclusive church, in which children of church members were baptized, were subject to church discipline, and through gradualist and scriptural means were prepared for conversion. Arminian, or liberal Congregationalists, in contrast, were theologically vague. They focused on rational religion to promote morality and feelings for fellow humans, and they did not exclude or demarcate church members from the rest of the world. Liberal Congregationalists increasingly influenced curriculum and ministerial education through their cultural center, Harvard.

A third group, the Hopkinsians, provided the major impetus for both Congregationalist reorganization and schism during this period. The Hopkinsians,

New Light heirs who were firmly Calvinist, rooted their understanding of religious experience in the work and writings of Jonathan Edwards. Taking their name from Samuel Hopkins (1721–1803), a minister who provided them a systematic theology, they differed from Old Light Calvinists in their emphasis on experiential conversion, their insistence on the importance of benevolence, and their strict policy regarding church membership and church discipline. Conversion entailed a palpable reorientation of self, emotional as well as cognitive, in which one's will became conformed to God's. Individuals were expected to engage in pious practices to prepare themselves for God's grace, but true conversion was accomplished only through his sovereign intervention. Benevolence meant love of being in general rather than selfish self-love. With regard to church membership, Hopkinsians rejected the Half-Way Covenant—the practice of extending a kind of second-class church membership to children of baptized parents who had not themselves been admitted to church membership. By the end of the eighteenth century, a large number of the country ministers of Massachusetts and Connecticut were Hopkinsians, determined to purify the church. Their zeal sometimes led to contention with parishioners who were more latitudinarian in their religious values.

Congregationalism's nineteenth-century transformation was also generated by the stresses of an expanding population and communicants' need for religious instruction and leadership. The last part of the eighteenth century and the early part of the nineteenth saw a tremendous outmigration from Massachusetts and Connecticut to Vermont, New York, Pennsylvania, the eastern counties of Massachusetts (later Maine), as well as Ohio and westward. In search of land and opportunity, these migrating Congregationalists seldom included ministers who would establish churches, and church elders in New England worried that a lack of education in religion and literacy might lead them into barbarism or infidelity. Congregationalism faced the challenge of expanding over vast spaces into new communities that lacked capital and cultural resources.

Remaking Congregationalism

Beginning in the 1790s in Connecticut, Hopkinsian ministers centralized their evangelical efforts to maintain theological purity among the churches and to preserve church discipline. The General Association of Connecticut tightened ministerial control over individual parishes and churches and established communication both within Connecticut Congregationalism and with other Congregational and

Presbyterian bodies to ensure a coordination of effort. Recognizing kinship in theology with the Presbyterian General Assembly, for example, the General Association exchanged delegates with them at annual meetings. In 1801 they developed the Plan of Union for the evangelization of the West, whereby the two denominations agreed to work in harmony rather than in competition with each other. Their joint work endured until 1852.

As the nineteenth century began Jedidiah Morse (1761–1826), a moderate Calvinist from Connecticut, attempted to unite Massachusetts clergy in a similar consociational system. Although this plan was resisted at first by both the liberal Arminians, who perceived that they would be outnumbered in such a system, and the Hopkinsian core, who staunchly maintained the right to local autonomy in fear of a clerical dictatorship, Morse eventually succeeded in putting together a coalition of moderate Calvinists and Hopkinsians, who formed a General Association for Massachusetts. This union for the promotion of explicitly Calvinist interests marked a decisive break from the liberals, whom the General Association labeled a separate party with separate interests. A dispute with liberals in 1805 over the theological orientation of Henry Ware (1764–1845), a liberal candidate for the Hollis Professorship of Divinity at Harvard, was the first public evidence of the break. In 1808 Morse and his supporters established a seminary at Andover for the theological education of ministerial students in an evangelical, Calvinist mold.

Endorsing the revival impulse, the General Association of Connecticut in 1795 recommended a concert of prayer for the revival of religion among all Christian denominations. In 1800 the *Connecticut Evangelical Magazine* began publishing reports on the current state of piety, including detailed descriptions of revival activity. These descriptions became templates on which ministers and congregations who awaited the refreshing spirit of God might model their preparationist efforts. In 1803 a group of Massachusetts Hopkinsians began publishing the *Massachusetts Missionary Magazine* to generate revenue to support missionary efforts and to disseminate religious orthodoxy among far-flung populations without access to a regular minister. Its merger in 1809 with the *Panoplist*, edited by Morse, combined the Calvinist opposition to liberal Congregationalism and the promotion of revival activities. In 1815 a group of orthodox Massachusetts Congregational churches established a consociational system on the Connecticut model in an effort to ensure religious purity. Also that year Morse instigated a pamphlet war against the most liberal wing of the church, charging

it with infidelity and hypocrisy in refusing to divulge its true theological sentiments to the public.

The ideological split in Massachusetts extended to the grassroots level, as in town after town parishioners contended with church members over the settlement of ministers. From the first decade of the nineteenth century through the fourth, liberal parishes frequently clashed with conservative church members over calling or keeping a minister. The conservatives insisted on the right of the church to call ministers, and orthodox or Hopkinsian ministers, insisting on stringent requirements for church membership and baptism, ran afoul of congregations who differed. These disagreements sometimes resulted in splits, and both the minister's party and the congregation claimed the right to church property. In the Dedham Decision of 1820, a liberal-dominated court ruled that, in cases of splits, church property belonged to the members of the parish—nearly always the liberal side in the dispute. From that time on, the orthodox promoted disestablishment, which was finally accomplished in Massachusetts in 1833. By that time the liberals had labeled themselves Unitarians. Connecticut had disestablished in 1818 in response to Anglican and Baptist efforts. No liberal-conservative split occurred within Connecticut Congregationalism, perhaps because liberals had found other denominational homes earlier and the stronger consociational system there prevented the growth of Arminian Congregationalism.

Hallmarks of Congregationalism

The newly forming denomination of Congregationalism possessed several hallmarks. At its core were a common Calvinist theology and reliance on revivalism and strong church discipline. Emphasizing the proper education of children, evangelical Congregationalists in the first third of the nineteenth century saw themselves as the embodiment of Zion, opposed to an increasingly corrupt ethos in the surrounding culture. Willing to enter into benevolent coalitions with fellow evangelicals, Congregationalists were prominent in the formation of the American Board of Commissioners for Foreign Missions (1810), the American Education Society (1815), the American Bible Society (1816), and the American Tract Society (1825). These organizations along with a variety of local missionary and tract societies performed multiple functions. They gave adherents a common cause and occasions for interaction in the name of benevolence. Publishing materials that promoted the spread of true religion and piety, they disseminated the publications to areas where ministers were in undersupply, providing readers with a common vocabulary and a shared catalog of experiences. They pioneered sophisticated organizational methods, raising capital on a large scale, and they promoted their efforts at evangelization through specialized bureaucracies. Though Presbyterians and Baptists were prominent in these efforts, which later involved other denominations as well, Congregationalists provided much of the initial leadership.

Congregationalist women became involved in a variety of benevolent causes. In the majority among church members and among converts, women played a significant role in capitalizing and publicizing benevolent efforts. Forming auxiliaries to education or missionary societies, for example, church women produced constitutions, elected officers, and collected monies. Pastors sustained cordial relations with their women parishioners, who often provided the funding for ministerial life memberships in benevolent organizations. A good deal of the voluminous pious periodical and tract literature published during this period was written with female readership in mind.

Benevolence led some early-nineteenth-century Congregationalists into the antislavery cause. Hopkins voiced opposition to slavery and the slave trade, and many members of the New England and American Anti-Slavery Societies cut their organizational eyeteeth in the benevolent pursuits of the first third of the century. The presence of women in benevolent activities and in an ideology that emphasized the moral responsibilities of wives and mothers led many Congregationalist women to join antislavery societies and inspired some to speak publicly against slavery. The breach of established gender roles disturbed the Congregational ministerial establishment in Massachusetts, which in 1837 issued a pastoral letter condemning women who accepted such a public role. Clergy insisted on gendered lines of authority, in which women's power was covert rather than overt. Women were allowed to serve as missionaries or teachers, but they were always subject to the control of men.

By the middle third of the century, a variety of evangelical colleges and seminaries were training leaders for a denomination characterized by an emphasis on experiential religion and some degree of exclusivity in membership; social-reform efforts conducted in the name of benevolence; a membership that included a large female majority subject to male leadership; a commitment to mission work; and an inclination to spread the faith through publications and the work of an educated ministry.

Once Congregationalism had established an identity as a separate denomination rather than as a state-sponsored church, it accommodated itself both theologically and ecclesiastically to liberal American culture, which it had not done during the period of revival purification. The theology of Nathaniel William Taylor (1786–1858) in the 1830s and that of Horace Bushnell (1802–1876) in the 1840s emphasized the human capacity to actively seek grace. A righteous spirit could be attained through the efforts of the believer and with appropriate nurture. Congregationalism attenuated its Calvinist heritage but retained an interest in benevolent reform, encouraging active involvement in education and efforts on behalf of the racially disadvantaged, the deaf, the insane, and the poor. During the last third of the century Congregationalists such as Washington Gladden (1836–1918) became prominent in the Social Gospel movement, which stressed the importance of efforts to save society rather than individuals.

By the time of the Civil War, this denomination that had begun the century socially and theologically conservative had become markedly liberal and latitudinarian. National in scope, Congregationalism remained concentrated in New England and in areas populated by the descendants of New Englanders. Ecumenical in orientation and heavily attuned to education, Congregationalism declined in relative numbers but maintained a cultural importance disproportionate to its size through the end of the nineteenth century.

See also **Evangelicalism; Missions,** *subentries on* **Foreign Missions, North American Indians; New England; Religion,** *subentry on* **Religion in Nineteenth-Century America; Revivalism; Social Gospel; Unitarianism and Universalism.**

Bibliography

Abzug, Robert H. *Cosmos Crumbling: American Reform and the Religious Imagination.* New York: Oxford University Press, 1994.

Cayton, Mary K. "Congregationalism from Independence to the Present." In *Encyclopedia of the American Religious Experience.* Edited by Charles H. Lippy and Peter W. Williams. Volume 1. New York: Charles Scribner's Sons, 1988.

Mead, Sidney Earl. *Nathaniel William Taylor, 1786–1858: A Connecticut Liberal.* 1942. Reprint, Hamden, Conn.: Archon, 1967.

Moss, Richard J. *The Life of Jedidiah Morse: A Station of Peculiar Exposure.* Knoxville: University of Tennessee Press, 1995.

Rohrer, James R. *Keepers of the Covenant: Frontier Missions and the Decline of Congregationalism, 1774–1818.* New York: Oxford University Press, 1995.

Von Rohr, John. *The Shaping of American Congregationalism, 1620–1957.* Cleveland, Ohio: Pilgrim, 1992.

Walker, Williston. *The Creeds and Platforms of Congregationalism.* 1893. Reprint, Boston: Pilgrim, 1960.

Youngs, J. William T. *The Congregationalists.* New York: Greenwood, 1990.

MARY KUPIEC CAYTON

PRESBYTERIANS

As the United States of America formed in the late eighteenth century, a major Presbyterian denomination did as well, distinguishing itself from the less collegial Congregational wing of Reformed Christianity. The Reformed Protestants, who followed a middle road between Luther and the Anabaptists, listened especially to the teachings of John Calvin, a sixteenth-century humanist Bible scholar. Most connectional congregations from colonial synods joined to form the Presbyterian Church in the U.S.A. (PCUSA), and a 1788 general synod meeting led to the organization of a general assembly for the PCUSA. The PCUSA united Reformed Christians who had come from England, Wales, Scotland, northern Ireland (called Scots-Irish), and France. Some Dutch and German Calvinists also belonged to the PCUSA, as did a number of slaves and free African Americans. This denomination remained the major Presbyterian presence throughout the century, growing from about 20,000 members in 1800 to about 220,000 in 1837.

Numerous Scots-Irish families and congregations, however, still resisted the support of the PCUSA for a federal government, and they kept closed communions to form an Associate Reformed Church (ARC) in 1782 and several autonomous synods. In 1858 many of these Presbyterians gathered in the United Presbyterian Church in North America (UPCNA). Some Presbyterians retained identity in the ARC, and still others in the South formed an Associate Reformed Presbyterian Church (ARP).

Presbyterian Practice

Throughout the nineteenth century Presbyterians generally agreed among themselves on the nature of Christian practice, focusing on honesty in business, responsible participation in politics, and regular family devotional life. With a coalition of Protestant reformers and others, they extended the codes for Sabbath observance and accomplished related reforms. Presbyterians believed, as did other Reformed Christians, that universal literacy was necessary for the reading and comprehension of scripture. With varying coalitions, they founded common schools, private schools, colleges, and seminaries by the score as they settled across the country during the century. They also agreed that the Westminster Confession of Faith, a 1648 statement of belief commissioned by the English Parliament, and its catechisms bore authority in interpreting scripture. The strong affirmation of Providence and predestination in these standards distinguished Presbyterians from most Baptists and almost all Methodists, who increasingly emphasized human agency and free will, or God's goodness over God's godness.

Denominational Division

Four major issues in the nineteenth century divided and helped define the Presbyterians: the revival movement, the nature of mission, opposition to and defense of slavery, and the relationship between theology and science.

Evangelicalism

At the very beginning of the nineteenth century, a second Great Awakening took place. The Presbyterian James McGready led the first frontier revivals during the summers of 1799 and 1800. In 1801 the Cane Ridge revival in Bourbon County, Kentucky, featured thousands of participants and scores of ministers. The falling, "melting," boisterous verbal responses to preaching and other religious exercises were seen as the obvious work of the Holy Spirit by most there, but these actions were viewed with alarm by more staid Presbyterians from towns and cities. When many frontier Presbyterians sought to refashion the denominational requirements and theology to accommodate the perceived need for revivals and evangelists, a split occurred, resulting in the formation by 1810 of the Cumberland Presbyterian Church (CPC). Dissident Presbyterians also became members in the newly emergent Christian movement that yielded the Disciples of Christ and the communitarian Shaker movement.

The CPC-ordained ministers, who could engage in ministry while they gained a theological education, embraced revival techniques and amended the Westminster standards to provide a theological stance more open to human free will. The CPC thrived throughout the century, avoided a split during the Civil War, and subsequently formed the Second Cumberland Presbyterian Church (often referred to as the Negro Cumberland Presbyterian Church) among its black members in 1871. The Nolin Presbytery of the CPC in 1889 ordained Louisa Woosley, the first female Presbyterian minister in the United States. Her formal ministry stood out in a denomination in which women exercised informal leadership, holding office chiefly in women's organizations and Sunday schools. Presbyterians collaborated with other Protestants to promote temperance—moderation in or abstinence from alcohol.

By the 1830s these new measures for evangelism and worship also characterized the lives of many congregations in the PCUSA. Revivalists such as Charles G. Finney led the formation in 1837 and 1838 of a New School equal in size to the Old School. Each body consisted of more than 100,000 members. Important in this division were differences in methods of mission, attitudes toward slavery, and the authority of the Westminster standards as interpreter of scripture. Both divisions claimed to be the PCUSA.

Mission

In the 1810s and 1820s Presbyterians helped form Protestant societies to accomplish reform and mission. The American Bible Society (1816) sought to put Protestant versions of the scriptures in every pair of human hands. The American Tract Society (1823) sought to provide inexpensive expositions of the faith for Reformed Christians and those who might become such. The American Sunday School Union (1824) developed resources and programs for evangelism and instruction of children and adults. But the voluntary associations that spread the Gospel, the mission societies of various cities, the American Board of Commissioners for Foreign Missions (1810), the American Home Missionary Society (1826), and several groups that organized to evangelize particular regions and countries in Africa and Asia drew enormous Presbyterian energy. The growing Old School of the PCUSA sought to accomplish mission primarily through denominational efforts. In the words of Charles Hodge, a leader of Old School Presbyterians, "The Presbyterian church is a mission society."

Slavery and the Civil War

New School Presbyterians especially supported the voluntary mission and reform societies, and many in the North called for the immediate, uncompensated emancipation of slaves in the 1830s. In the division of 1837–1838 more New School churches were in the free states, while more than three-quarters of the Southern Presbyterians sided with the Old School. With the schism growing between free and slave states in the 1850s, the New School PCUSA divided between the North and the South in 1856 and 1857. The Old School remained united until 1861, when Federal loyalists demanded that commissioners from the South support the Union. Southern Old School Presbyterians in December 1861 formed the Presbyterian Church in the Confederate States of America (PCCSA).

After the Civil War the two PCUSAs in the North united in 1869, and their mission efforts among African Americans in the South soon yielded a truly national denomination, of more than a million members by 1900. Some Old Schoolers from border states and former New Schoolers from the South joined with the PCCSA to form the Presbyterian Church in the United States (PCUS), or Southern Presbyterian

Church, which by 1900 consisted of about 250,000 members.

Theology and Science

In the late nineteenth century Presbyterians struggled with the relationship of Darwinism to the Christian faith in general and the seventeenth-century Westminster Confession in particular, with critical historical study of scripture, and with an increasingly rigid fundamentalism that arose to combat modern interpretations of the Bible and the Gospel that accommodated the new science of the day. Heresy trials of Presbyterian leaders in South Carolina, Illinois, New York, and elsewhere made confrontations inevitable. On the other hand, mission efforts in the United States and abroad drew most Presbyterians into active, constructive Christian witness. The major foreign mission efforts of the Presbyterians extended to more than one hundred countries and colonial lands, especially after 1870. UPCNA special missions concentrated in the Middle East, and the missions of the PCUSA and PCUS were centered in Central Africa and China.

See also **Abolition and Antislavery; African Americans,** subentry on **African American Religions; Bible and Bible Reading, The; Evangelicalism; Literacy and Reading Habits; Missions,** subentry on **Foreign Missions; Religion,** subentry on **Religion in Nineteenth-Century America; Revivalism.**

Bibliography

Coalter, Milton J., John M. Mulder, and Louis B. Weeks, eds. *The Presbyterian Presence.* 7 vols. Louisville, Ky.: Westminster/John Knox, 1990–1992.

Lingle, Walter, and John Kuykendall. *Presbyterians: Their History and Beliefs.* Atlanta, Ga.: John Knox, 1978.

McNeill, John T. *The History and Character of Calvinism.* New York: Oxford University Press, 1960.

Smylie, James H. *A Brief History of the Presbyterians.* Louisville, Ky.: Geneva, 1996.

Weeks, Louis B. "Presbyterianism." In *Encyclopedia of the American Religious Experience.* Edited by Charles H. Lippy and Peter W. Williams. New York: Scribners, 1988.

Louis Weeks

METHODISTS

Methodism, part of the Evangelical Revival of the eighteenth century, was founded in England by John Wesley (1703–1791), a clergyman in the Church of England. Wesley's religious experience led him to preach an evangelical message that attracted a large number of people in the 1740s and later. He organized them into Methodist societies, with the purpose of bringing reform and renewal to the Church of England. Wesley did not originally intend that his movement lead to the formation of a new church, yet Methodism grew steadily in England, Scotland, and Ireland through the eighteenth century.

The Origins of Methodism in America

The earliest Methodist societies in America were organized about 1766 by Irish Methodist immigrants in Maryland and New York City. When Wesley learned that Methodist work in America was growing, he sent lay-preacher missionaries to assist its progress. Among them was Francis Asbury (1745–1816), the most celebrated leader in early American Methodism, who arrived in 1771.

By 1784 American Methodists numbered 15,000 and were served by eighty-four lay preachers. Wesley became convinced that these Methodists needed to be organized formally into a church led by ordained preachers who could administer the sacraments of baptism and the Lord's Supper. In a bold move he ordained two of his lay preachers and dispatched them to the United States with Thomas Coke (1747–1814), an Anglican clergyman sympathetic to Methodism, to organize a new church. About sixty American Methodist preachers gathered in Baltimore, Maryland, in December 1784 at what is called the Christmas Conference to form the Methodist Episcopal Church in America. The church ordained Asbury and twelve others and adopted a form of church government in which Asbury and Coke were named superintendents (later their title became bishop). Wesley sent a prayer book that included doctrinal articles. The American Methodist Church took a stand against slavery and formulated a mission statement: "To reform the continent, and to spread scriptural holiness over these lands."

American Methodism expanded rapidly in the early nineteenth century, becoming the largest Protestant denomination in the United States. In 1800 its membership was 65,000. By mid-century, despite divisions described below, membership was more than 1,482,000, and by 1900 the total membership in Methodist churches was more than 5,696,000. Although its earliest strength was south of the Mason-Dixon Line, Methodism grew quickly in the Middle Atlantic states, New England, the Midwest, and the West.

Several reasons explain Methodism's robust growth. First, it held that God's offer of forgiveness and salvation was freely available to everyone who would receive it by faith. Rich and poor, male and female, slave and free, all were invited to accept the Christian faith and live the Christian life. Second, Methodists were committed to a disciplined moral life, which included doing good to others and avoiding evil. In addition to worshiping with the congregation, usually on Sundays, each church member was expected to belong to a small group, called a class, that gathered weekly for prayer, study, admonition, and encouragement. Third, Methodism's leaders and preachers were convinced that they were divinely called to the urgent work of proclaiming and enacting the Christian message and thereby to reform the continent. They participated actively in revivals and camp meetings throughout the century. Fourth, Methodism was organized in an itinerant system, in which ordained and lay preachers were appointed by bishops to their preaching places, called circuits in the early days. Circuit-riding preachers braved weather and wilderness to reach even the most remote settlements of prospective Methodists with the gospel message. Between 1773 and 1792 all the itinerating American preachers met annually at one location to conduct their business. Geographical extension of the church made it increasingly difficult to gather all the preachers even once a year, so in 1792 they agreed to assemble every four years in a General Conference. Soon after, the preachers met annually in geographical units called annual conferences, presided over by bishops, to conduct business, experience spiritual renewal, and receive their preaching locations (appointments) from the bishops for the next year.

At the 1808 General Conference, the Methodist Episcopal Church adopted its first constitution, which shaped its life for the rest of the century. The document provided that future General Conferences consist of clergy delegates elected by their annual conferences and granted the General Conference unlimited powers except those prohibited by a series of "Restrictive Rules." Among other provisions, these rules protected the church's episcopal form of government and its doctrinal standards.

Schisms and Slavery

Several painful schisms split the Methodist Episcopal Church during the first half of the nineteenth century, two of which concerned the issue of race. In 1787 Richard Allen (1760–1831), an African American Methodist preacher, led a group of African Americans that walked out of St. George's Methodist Episcopal Church in Philadelphia when they were mistreated by white members of the congregation. Allen and his companions in 1816 formed a new denomination, the African Methodist Episcopal Church, devoted to Wesleyan theology and a Methodist form of organization. Allen was its first bishop.

The Power of the Pulpit. The original caption to this drawing reads, "A Methodist Preacher Drives the Devil from the John Street Church." Methodism originated in America during the colonial period. LIBRARY OF CONGRESS

The second schism caused by racial division occurred in 1796 in New York City under the leadership of James Varick (c. 1750–1827), Christopher Rush (1777–1873), and Peter Williams (c. 1750–1823). African American members of the John Street Methodist Episcopal Church, reacting to the discrimination of the white congregants, left the church and in 1821 formed the African Methodist Episcopal Zion Church with Varick as their first bishop. Their organization was also Methodist and their theology Wesleyan.

The democratic spirit that led to Andrew Jackson's election to the U.S. presidency in 1828 was a potent force in the Methodist Episcopal Church. Some laypeople wanted an official (voting) voice in the church's life. Local preachers, who were not full-time itinerant clergy members of an annual conference, desired equal voting rights with their itinerant brothers. Many preachers desperately wished to choose the presiding elders (superintendents) who directed their work rather than having them appointed by the bishop. When these reforms were not adopted, the advocates in 1830 founded a new denomination, the Methodist Protestant Church. Although committed to Wesleyan theological principles, the new body eliminated the office of bishop and presiding elder and granted equal voting representation to laypeople at its annual conferences and General Conferences. Local preachers, however, were not granted full clergy rights. At the time of organization, the Methodist Protestant Church had about five thousand members.

American Methodists argued for many years over slavery. Wesley condemned the slave trade as the "execrable sum of all villainies" in his journal on 12 February 1772. "Away with all whips, all chains, all compulsion! Be gentle toward all," he wrote in the tract *Thoughts upon Slavery* (1774), "and see that you invariably do unto every one as you would he should do unto you" (p. 27). At the Christmas Conference the American preachers wrote a strong rule against slavery. However, when it became clear that the rule was unpopular, especially with those whose livelihood depended on slavery, the rule was laid aside.

As slavery generated a bitter national debate, the Methodist Episcopal Church attempted to avoid discussion, but some Methodists were unwilling to accept sidestepping the question. In disgust Orange Scott (1800–1847), Luther Lee (1800–1889), and Lucius Matlack (1816–1883), New England Methodist leaders and abolitionists, left the Methodist Episcopal Church and in 1843 formed the Wesleyan Methodist Connection, which took a strong antislavery position. The 1844 Methodist Episcopal General Conference could not evade the matter of slavery any longer. The spotlight focused on a church bishop, James Osgood Andrew (1796–1871), who had acquired slaves through marriage. When Andrew was suspended from exercising his episcopal office by the antislavery majority, Southern Methodists drafted a Plan of Separation and formed the Methodist Episcopal Church, South, in Louisville, Kentucky, in May 1845. Considerable animosity developed between northern and southern Methodists in the years following, especially during the Civil War and Reconstruction. At the time of separation the Methodist Episcopal Church had about 800,000 members, and the Methodist Episcopal Church, South, had about 600,000. In 1870 about 65,000 African American members of the southern church formed the Colored Methodist Episcopal Church, also based on Wesleyan theology and Methodist organization.

Organization and Ministries

Missionary work in the United States and overseas was a major concern of nineteenth-century Methodism. One of the earliest missionaries was John Stewart (?–1823), who ministered among the Wyandot Indians of Ohio in 1816. Interest in missions moved the Methodist Episcopal Church to create the Methodist Missionary Society at its 1820 General Conference. The church's initial overseas missions were begun in Liberia in 1833 under the leadership of Melville Cox (1799–1833) and in South America in 1835. Women became increasingly active in promoting and supporting mission work and serving on mission fields, especially after the Civil War. In 1869 Methodist Episcopal women formed the Woman's Foreign Missionary Society and eleven years later the Woman's Home Missionary Society, both of which were at the forefront of the denomination's efforts. Similar groups were founded by women in the other Methodist denominations, and almost every local church had an active unit.

Methodists followed the example of their founder Wesley in promoting education. The Christmas Conference approved the creation in Abingdon, Maryland, of Cokesbury College, which was destroyed by fire in 1796. During the nineteenth century Methodists founded a number of preparatory schools, colleges, and universities, including McKendree College in Illinois (1828), Randolph-Macon College in Virginia (1830), and Wesleyan University in Connecticut (1831).

Acting on their widespread educational interests, American Methodists joined other Protestants in encouraging every local congregation to have a Sunday School. In 1827 the Methodist Sunday School Union was formed to foster the expansion of Sunday Schools in the Methodist Episcopal Church, and denominational printing presses produced literature for children and adults to use in their Sunday sessions. The Sunday Schools also prepared young people to become members of the church.

The role of laypeople in the government of the church was an important issue after the Civil War. Should laypeople be given an official voice and vote in the life of the church? Although the Methodist Protestants dealt with this question when they organized in 1830, the other Methodist churches debated it for several decades. The Methodist Episcopal Church, South, finally granted equal representation to laypeople and clergy at its 1870 General Conference but not at its annual conferences until 1930. The Methodist Episcopal Church equalized lay and clergy delegates at its 1900 General Conference but not at its annual conferences until 1932.

The role of women in the church was another critical topic with which the churches wrestled. By the end of the nineteenth century women were at the forefront of the churches' missionary work, they were celebrated teachers in Sunday Schools, and they were active in other areas of church life. Should they be given the same lay representational rights enjoyed by men, and should they be ordained and granted full clergy rights in the church? These questions were debated in the General Conferences of the churches. Frances E. Willard (1839–1898), a temperance leader and women's rights advocate, argued for women's equality in the Methodist Episcopal Church, but women were not admitted as delegates to the General Conference until 1904. At its 1880 General Conference the Methodist Episcopal Church denied ordination and full clergy rights to Anna Oliver (1840–1892). Women were not granted these opportunities until 1956.

From its origin Methodism emphasized holiness, that is, living a life of high moral standards devoted to complete love for God and neighbor and supported by God's presence and grace. Holiness included abstinence from alcoholic beverages. Most Methodists believed that the holy life was a gradual process of spiritual and moral growth. Others believed it was an instantaneous gift of God, a "second work" of God's grace, the "first work" being divine forgiveness. The quarrel between these two groups resulted in thousands of Methodists leaving the church and eventually forming new denominations called holiness churches, such as the Church of the Nazarene (1908) and the Pilgrim Holiness Church (1913).

By the end of the nineteenth century, despite the

divisions described above, Methodists comprised the largest and liveliest Protestant group in the United States. They claimed to be the "most American" of the churches because they had grown up with the nation. Methodist membership spread across the country, and Methodists were a highly influential force in the nation's life.

See also **Abolition and Antislavery; African Americans,** *subentry on* **African American Religions; Missions,** *subentries on* **Foreign Missions, North American Indians; Religion,** *subentry on* **Religion in Nineteenth-Century America.**

Bibliography

Heitzenrater, Richard P. *Wesley and the People Called Methodists.* Nashville, Tenn.: Abingdon, 1995.

McEllhenney, John G., ed. *United Methodism in America: A Compact History.* Nashville, Tenn.: Abingdon, 1992.

Norwood, Frederick A. *The Story of American Methodism.* Nashville, Tenn.: Abingdon, 1974.

Richey, Russell E., Kenneth E. Rowe, and Jean Miller Schmidt, eds. *Perspectives on American Methodism: Interpretive Essays.* Nashville, Tenn.: Kingswood, 1993.

CHARLES YRIGOYEN JR.

BAPTISTS

Baptists trace their origins to seventeenth-century Amsterdam, Holland, and the decision of a group of English Puritan Separatists to accept believer's baptism (baptism administered only to those who testified to a personal experience of faith and salvation) as a means of constituting the church. Led by John Smyth (c. 1570–1612) and Thomas Helwys (c. 1550–c. 1615), the little company formed in 1609 what is considered the first Baptist church, with each congregant receiving baptism by affusion (pouring) after making a profession of faith. The congregation soon divided when Smyth and others sought membership among the Mennonites. Helwys led the remaining faithful back to England and established the first Baptist church in London in 1612. Its congregants were General Baptists, so called because they adhered to the views of the Dutch theologian Jacob Arminius on free will, Christ's general atonement, and the possibility of falling from grace.

During the 1630s another Baptist group emerged in London after other Puritans accepted believer's baptism. These Particular or Calvinist Baptists stressed doctrines of election and predestination (God had chosen some for salvation before the foundation of the world), limited atonement (Christ's death was only for the sins of the elect), and perse-

verance of the saints (the elect could not resist God's grace and would persevere in Christian living until the end). The early Baptists thus began at either end of the Protestant theological spectrum, divided between Arminian and Calvinist dogmas while affirming certain common distinctive doctrines, among them the affirmation of biblical authority, liberty of conscience, local church autonomy, cooperation with like-minded congregations, the priesthood of the laity, an ordained clergy, and religious liberty.

The same doctrinal diversity is evident in the beginnings of the Baptist movement in America. Roger Williams (1603–1683), the quintessential colonial dissenter, founded the Rhode Island Colony in 1636 and, at Providence in 1639, the first Baptist church in the New World. Shortly thereafter he departed the Baptist ranks in search of newer revelations. A second church was established in Newport, Rhode Island, by the Baptist physician John Clarke (1609–1676). These two congregations had members of General and Particular Baptist sentiments as well as Seventh-Day Baptists, who observed Saturday as the Sabbath day, and Six Principle Baptists, whose beliefs were based on Hebrews 6:1–2. The Baptist family tree had many branches.

Baptist Beliefs

Like their colonial counterparts, nineteenth-century Baptists drew on a variety of theological traditions. While often hesitant to affirm "man-made" creeds that might undermine the authority of scripture, Baptists willingly composed confessions of faith that set forth basic dogmas. General and Particular Baptists wrote confessions that influenced Baptists in America. For example, the Philadelphia Confession of Faith, approved by Pennsylvania Baptists in 1742, was taken almost entirely from the Calvinistic Second London Confession of 1677.

Core beliefs, whether couched in Calvinism or Arminianism, received varying emphases and applications from Baptist denominations, churches, and individuals and included several facets. First was acceptance of the authority of scripture and the competency of the believer to interpret scripture. Baptists insisted that scripture was the primary authority for life and faith, yet they also insisted that the individual believer could interpret scripture according to the dictates of conscience. Baptists declared that the people of God could be trusted to interpret scripture for themselves in the context of Christian community under the guidance of the Holy Spirit.

Second was the notion of a believer's church as both individual and corporate. Baptists insisted that all who claimed membership in the church affirm personal faith in Christ as Savior. This individual experience led believers to seek the community of faith for worship and service.

Third was the pursuit of congregational autonomy and associational cooperation. While each congregation was autonomous in making decisions and pursuing ministries, Baptists did not hesitate to join in collective associations—locally, regionally, and nationally—linking churches in fellowship and common concern.

Fourth, the priesthood of the laity and the ordination of ministers were emphasized. Like other Protestants, Baptists held strongly that each Christian had direct access to God through Christ without the need for other mediators. Some early Baptists sometimes offered the laying on of hands to the newly baptized as a sign that each Christian was to serve as a minister. Yet they also set aside specific persons for direct ministerial functions, such as preaching and pastoral ministry, in the community of faith. Most Baptist churches recognized two church officers, pastors and deacons, the latter an office of the laity.

Fifth, observance of ordinances and the sacraments, particularly baptism by immersion and the Lord's Supper, was important. Baptismal immersion, begun by the 1640s, became the most identifiable ritual of the Baptist tradition. This act mirrored Jesus's own baptism in the river Jordan and symbolized the death and resurrection of the new believer with Christ. The Lord's Supper was administered to those who had received baptism as a sign of Christ's continuing presence with his church. Debates over admitting nonimmersed Christians to communion divided Baptists throughout their history. Some Baptists also observed foot washing as an ordinance of the church.

Sixth, religious liberty was balanced with loyalty to the state. Baptists were the first in Britain and America to call for complete religious liberty and full separation of church and state, insisting that the state could not judge the heretic or the atheist in matters of religious faith. God alone was judge of a person's conscience. This concern for religious liberty and freedom of conscience meant that Baptists were a dissenting people, challenging efforts to establish religion in any form. At the same time, they affirmed their loyalty to the state and their willingness to support the government as long as conscience was not undermined. The diversity of interpretations meant that the many Baptist "ways" often led to divisions and schisms among Baptist subgroups.

Colonial Baptists

During the colonial period Baptists experienced significant persecution from the religious establishments in New England and Virginia, often suffering imprisonment, fines, and even beatings for challenging those establishments. They were avid proponents of religious liberty, insisting, from the days of Roger Williams, that God alone is judge of conscience and that the state could not judge the heretic or the atheist. Strong supporters of the American Revolution, Baptists were among the first to lobby the First Continental Congress on behalf of religious freedom when the Warren Association of New England Baptists sent the pastor Isaac Backus (1724–1806) to represent their cause. Although his challenge to the idea of religious establishment in New England was not successful, it sowed the seeds of later religious liberty.

Baptists flourished during the religious enthusiasm associated with the eighteenth-century Great Awakening, yet not without divisions. Regular or Old Baptists were traditional Calvinists who affirmed the need for conversion while questioning certain revivalistic methods fostered by the Awakening. They favored orderly worship, educated ministers, scholarly sermons, and the singing of the Psalms in traditional Calvinist fashion.

A group of Separate Baptists developed out of the Great Awakening when certain prorevival New Light Separatists left Congregational churches to receive believer's baptism. Separate Baptists supported the theology and methodology evident in the Awakening. Their preachers offered colorful, spontaneous sermons, issued dramatic calls for personal conversion, and utilized hymns of "human composition." Many were suspicious of formal ministerial education, fearing it detrimental to genuine faith. Many Separates rejected the use of confessions of faith, believing that they were injurious to the centrality of scripture in the church. Shubael Stearns (1706–1771) and Daniel Marshall (1706–1784) were among those Separate Baptists who formed new congregations, such as the Sandy Creek Baptist Church in North Carolina. That congregation became the mother church of some forty new churches throughout the South. Although divisions were significant, by 1800 Regular and Separate Baptists were generally unified around the dogmas set forth in the Philadelphia Confession of Faith of 1742.

Confronting New Frontiers

The Baptist Church was well suited to the westward movement on the American frontier. Its autonomous local churches could be formed around a group of local believers without permission from any other ecclesiastical bodies. Many of its ministers were self-supporting farmer-preachers, who worked the land while exercising their ministerial gifts in frontier congrega-

Baptist Tent Meeting. Possibly a revival meeting following the second Great Awakening. Emanuel Baptist Church, Hattiesburg, Mississippi. LIBRARY OF CONGRESS

tions. Success in the camp meetings and protracted revivals made Baptists and Methodists the largest denominations in the United States by the 1840s.

As the Great Awakening of the 1730s and 1740s and Second Great Awakening from the 1790s to the 1830s sparked increased concern for evangelism and world mission, Baptists formed the General Missionary Convention of the Baptist Denomination in the United States for Foreign Missions, commonly known as the Triennial Convention because it convened every three years. This body provided funds for the work of Adoniram Judson (1788–1850) and his wife Ann Hasseltine Judson (1789–1826), Congregational missionaries sent to Burma who had accepted Baptist views while on their ship. The American Baptist Home Mission Society, with headquarters in Philadelphia, was founded in 1832 by churches in the North and in the South, due in part to the work of John Mason Peck (1789–1858), an itinerant preacher in the "western territories" of Missouri, Indiana, and Illinois.

Such Baptist societies were autonomous bodies funded by subscription from Baptist individuals, associations, and churches. Their independence was im-

portant to many Baptists, who feared that denominational hierarchies might undermine the authority of local congregations. The "society method" was an important means of organization for people who were suspicious of elaborate ecclesiastical structures.

Concern for education led Baptists to found numerous educational institutions, beginning with the College of Rhode Island (now Brown University) in 1764. Columbian College was established in Washington, D.C., in 1821 and later became part of George Washington University. During the nineteenth century Baptists formed numerous colleges, academies, and seminaries in the North and the South, including Hamilton Literary and Theological Institution (now Colgate University) in 1819, Newton Theological Institution in 1826, Richmond College in 1830, and Wake Forest College in 1834. These institutions provided basic education, particularly for ministers, while also helping to raise the social and economic status of new generations of Baptists.

Debates and Divisions

All these activities created significant controversy throughout Baptist history. Questions of mission methodology were particularly volatile. Daniel Parker (1781–1844), a strong Calvinist and one of the leaders of an antimission movement, believed that mission societies, revivals, and theological institutions were human efforts at creating salvation. He insisted that the New Testament gave no support for mission agencies outside the local church. Parker's doctrine of election involved concepts of "two seeds in the Spirit," whereby each person received at birth the seed of salvation or damnation as decreed by the sovereign God. These ideas influenced numerous "hyper-Calvinist" Baptist groups, including the Primitive Baptists and the Old Regular Baptists.

Arminianism also flourished. Benjamin Randall (1749–1808) led the Free Will Baptists in defining doctrine in terms of concern for free will, human choice, and Christ's death for all persons. Indeed, as Baptists participated in revivals, missions, and other evangelical endeavors, many moved toward Arminianism or at least a modified Calvinism that emphasized preaching for conversion and the possibility of conversion for all. Likewise democratic idealism and revivalistic evangelicalism significantly impacted Baptist understanding of free will and missionary outreach.

Throughout much of the nineteenth and twentieth centuries the Landmark movement further divided Baptists over the nature of the church. Taking their name from Proverbs 22:28, "Remove not the ancient landmark which thy fathers have set," Landmarkists declared that Baptists represented the true New Testament church, whose orthodoxy was kept intact through an unbroken succession of congregations stretching to Jesus's baptism in the Jordan. They required reimmersion of all not baptized in Baptist churches and promoted "close communion," which permitted only members of each specific church to receive the elements at the Lord's Supper. Landmarkist controversies led to the formation of new Baptist denominations, the Baptist Missionary Association in 1899 in Arkansas (renamed the American Baptist Association in 1924).

The great schism of the nineteenth century involved the question of slavery and southern secession. After years of compromise, the Triennial Convention was faced with the question of appointing a known slaveholder, James Reeves (1784–1858), as a missionary. When the mission board rejected his appointment, southerners gathered in Augusta, Georgia, in May 1845 to found the Southern Baptist Convention. Its "convention system" emphasized connections—linking agencies for missions, publications, and education—more than had the old society method. While southerners claimed the missionary impetus as their primary reason for beginning a new

denomination, slavery and its many complicating influences were at the heart of the schism.

After the Civil War Baptists in the North and the South remained divided, each group continuing to send its own missionaries, fund its own schools, and publish its own educational materials. A conference at Fortress Monroe, Virginia, in 1894 brought together representatives from the Southern Baptist Convention and the American Baptist Home Mission Society to discuss ministry to African Americans in the South and to establish certain territorial boundaries for the work of each group. These agreements lasted until 1909.

Baptist Women

Women were important contributors to the Baptist movement, though their stories have sometimes been overlooked. Married and single women were among the earliest Baptist missionaries, and many died from the harsh conditions (among them fever, cholera, plagues, and other diseases) experienced in every country to which they were assigned. Women such as Mary Webb (1779–1861) raised funds for overseas mission programs, while others like Joanna Moore (1832–1916) worked as home missionaries with southern freedmen and freedwomen.

The earliest Baptist ordinations of women occurred in the nineteenth century among the Free Will Baptists. Many Baptist groups did not ordain women until the mid–twentieth century. Some rejected such actions all together, as divisions over the ordination and the general role of women at home and in the church continued to characterize segments of the Baptist Church.

African American Baptists

During the early nineteenth century, white Baptists like other Christians, North and South, attempted to evangelize segments of the slave communities. Slaves accompanied their masters to camp meetings and often experienced Christian conversion. In the South, slaves shared membership with whites in Baptist churches. Southern Baptists sought the conversion of slaves in order to get them on the road to heaven and as a means of making them more docile. Their presence in white churches was also a way of monitoring their behavior. Southerners also made extensive use of "biblical arguments" for slavery, as found in Ephesians 6. Slaves nonetheless clung to the liberating elements of the Christian gospel as evidenced in the songs of slavery: "And before I'd be a slave, I'd be carried to my grave, and go home to my Lord and be free."

In the antebellum North, blacks and whites also shared membership in many Baptist churches. Before and after the Civil War, Baptists in the North sent missionaries to the South to work among the African Americans, helping to found schools and other training programs. Many Baptists outside the South were active in the abolitionist movement. The Baptized Licking Locust Association, Friends of Humanity, founded in 1807, was one of the earliest Baptist antislavery societies. After the Civil War, African Americans, sensitive to their second-class status, left white Baptist churches to found their own congregations and denominations.

African American Baptists also began mission boards and denominational organizations after the Civil War. The National Baptist Convention in the U.S.A., Inc., arose in 1895, the product of several earlier missionary conventions. The *National Baptist Magazine* was established in 1894. These and other programs helped shape Baptist identity in African American churches.

Baptists in the United States gave significant energy to evangelical, political, theological, and social concerns expressed through a wide spectrum of ideas and practices. From 1800 to 1830 Baptists increased from 100,000 to 313,138. In 1850 they claimed 815,212 members, making them second only to the Methodists, who claimed more than a million members. By 1890 Baptist membership was approaching two million. By the end of the nineteenth century, Baptists had become the largest Protestant denomination in the United States.

See also **Bible and Bible Reading, The; Education,** *subentry on* **Colleges and Universities; Evangelicalism; Missions,** *subentry on* **Foreign Missions; Protestantism; Religion,** *subentry on* **Religion in Nineteenth-Century America; Revivalism.**

Bibliography

Leonard, Bill J., ed. *Dictionary of Baptists in America.* Downers Grove, Ill.: InterVarsity, 1994.

Lumpkin, William. *Baptist Confessions of Faith.* Chicago: Judson, 1959.

McBeth, H. Leon. *The Baptist Heritage.* Nashville, Tenn.: Broadman, 1987.

Sweet, William W. *Religion on the American Frontier: The Baptists, 1783–1830.* Chicago: University of Chicago Press, 1931.

Torbet, Robert. *A History of the Baptists.* Philadelphia: Judson, 1963.

BILL J. LEONARD

LUTHERANS

The history of Lutheranism in the United States during the nineteenth century is closely linked to the history of American immigration. At the beginning of the 1830s less than a quarter of a million Lutherans lived in the United States; by 1900 the number had risen to more than a million and a half. New waves of immigration beginning in the 1830s contributed much of the increase.

Before the new immigration most Lutheran congregations in the United States were organized into larger cooperative bodies, usually called synods. Geographically based synods in the Atlantic and Appalachian states provided pastoral care to congregations founded by German-speaking Lutheran settlers and their descendants during the colonial and early national periods. Some of the synods participated in an intersynodical body known as the General Synod, which was organized in 1820. The General Synod, led by Samuel Simon Schmucker (1799–1873), professor at the Lutheran Theological Seminary in Gettysburg, Pennsylvania, promoted an alignment of Lutheranism with the broad consensus of American evangelical Protantism.

From the 1830s through the end of the century and beyond, Lutheran immigrants from the German territories, as well as Norway, Sweden, Denmark, and Finland, organized new congregations and synods throughout the United States but principally in the Midwest. Slovak Lutheran immigrants organized congregations in the late nineteenth century but did not succeed at synodical organization until the early twentieth century. Icelandic immigrants, who organized congregations in the United States and Canada, based their synodical organization in Winnipeg, Canada. Unlike the older American synods, the new synods founded by immigrants ran along ethnic rather than geographic lines, although Germans tended to name their synods geographically according to the states in which they were primarily based. The ethnically based congregations and synods founded by German and Scandinavian immigrants provided a cultural buffer that preserved some of the cherished traditions of the Old World and mitigated some of the traumas of Americanization.

Ethnic ties, however, did not ensure church unity. American religious freedom allowed immigrant Lutherans to organize church bodies according to differences of practice and belief. Thus by the end of the century, even after several synodical mergers, the United States counted five German synods that had organized after 1840; six Norwegian synods, counting the Lutheran Brethren and Lutheran Free Church; two Danish synods; and three Finnish synods, counting the Apostolic Lutheran Congregation, which organized formally as a synod in the twentieth century. Among the immigrant groups only the Swedes managed to avoid such division. The organization commonly known as the Augustana Synod represented the only Swedish Lutheran body in the United States. Swedish immigrants who desired an ecclesiastical alternative to the Augustana Synod affiliated with either non-Lutheran Swedes or non-Swedish Lutherans.

The proliferation of synodical bodies arose out of disagreements over church organization, theological doctrines, and American circumstances. Some of the disagreements originated in the Old World. Within the state churches of Scandinavia, for example, conflict had erupted over religious renewal movements that sought to elevate the authority of the laity in the life of the church. Norwegian, Danish, and Finnish Lutheran synods in the United States tended to organize along the lines of that conflict. The German synods in the United States were divided over doctrinal issues, such as the authority of the ordained ministry, the requirements of church fellowship, and, most notoriously, predestination, which concerns God's election of sinners to eternal salvation. Other theological controversies between divergent synods centered on the authority and interpretation of scripture and the Lutheran confessional documents collected in the Book of Concord, first published in 1580. The synods also diverged in their attitudes toward the circumstances of American life. For example, some synods supported the temperance movement while others did not, and some synods established parochial schools while others favored public schools.

As such divisions occurred among the synods founded by immigrant Lutherans in the Midwest, the older synods of the eastern states also experienced conflict and division. The Civil War ruptured the General Synod along the line between North and South. A further rupture occurred in 1867, when long-standing disagreements over the direction of the General Synod led to the formation of a rival intersynodical body known as the General Council. The General Council, based in Philadelphia and led by Charles Porterfield Krauth (1823–1883), promoted a recovery of historic Lutheranism in self-conscious distinction to other denominations.

The proliferation of Lutheran church bodies in the United States produced mixed results. Conflict between the synods often grew intense and acrimonious. Competition undermined limited resources as each synod endeavored to found and sustain its own supporting institutions, including publications, colleges, seminaries, and charities. If Lutheran unity generally suffered, however, Lutheran vitality generally increased. Synodical loyalties often promoted Lutheran identity and produced vibrant institutions. The history of the Missouri Synod, founded in 1847 by Carl Ferdinand Wilhelm Walther (1811–1887), provides a good example of both the impairment of Lutheran unity and the enhancement of Lutheran vitality. While the Missouri Synod was a protagonist of doctrinal controversy, it also established a strong network of congregations, schools, and missionary enterprises.

The basis of Lutheran church life throughout the nineteenth century was the local congregation. The religious commitments of Lutheran laity formed the bedrock upon which synodical bodies and their supporting institutions were established. Lutheran households throughout the United States normally contained Bibles, hymnals, prayer books, copies of Martin Luther's sermons and catechisms, and the works of Lutheran Pietists such as Johann Arndt (1555–1621). Family devotions nurtured the spiritual life. Lutheran laity frequently took the initiative in organizing congregations and religious schools, often before pastors were available.

Lutheran women contributed enormously to the establishment and support of churches. While congregations and synods precluded women from voting and exercising public leadership until the turn of the century, women nevertheless contributed money for church expenses, property for church buildings, and the labors of cleaning, cooking, and handiwork. As the institutional life of the churches developed, women organized aid societies and entered expanded roles as teachers, missionaries, and deaconesses. The American career of the Norwegian deaconess Elizabeth Fedde (1850–1921) illumines the expanded role of women by the end of the nineteenth century.

See also **Immigration and Immigrants,** *subentries on* **Germany, Scandinavia and Finland; Midwest, The; Religion,** *subentry on* **Religion in Nineteenth-Century America.**

Bibliography

Anderson, H. George. *Lutheranism in the Southeastern States, 1860–1886: A Social History.* The Hague, Netherlands: Mouton, 1969.

Forster, Walter O. *Zion on the Mississippi: The Settlement of the Saxon Lutherans in Missouri, 1839–1841.* St. Louis, Mo.: Concordia, 1953.

Gustafson, David A. *Lutherans in Crisis: The Question of Identity in the American Republic.* Minneapolis, Minn.: Fortress, 1993.

Lagerquist, L. DeAne. *In America the Men Milk the Cows: Factors of Gender, Ethnicity, and Religion in the Americanization of Norwegian-American Women.* Brooklyn, N.Y.: Carlson, 1991.

Nelson, E. Clifford, ed. *The Lutherans in North America.* 1975. Reprint with supplemental material, Philadelphia: Fortress, 1980.

PAUL A. BAGLYOS

MENNONITES

Mennonites are the spiritual descendants of the Anabaptists, the radical wing of the Protestant Reformation. Though their name derives from Menno Simons (1496–1561), an influential Dutch Anabaptist leader, most nineteenth-century Mennonites in America traced their spiritual roots to the Anabaptist movement in Switzerland and southern Germany, with a significant group of immigrants arriving in the second half of the century from Prussia and the Russian empire. The history of Mennonite settlement in North America is tied closely to that of the Amish, a conservative reform group that broke off from the Mennonites in the last decade of the seventeenth century in Switzerland and the Rhineland.

In 1683 Mennonite refugees from Krefeld, Germany, established the first permanent Mennonite congregation in North America, located at Germantown, Pennsylvania, just north of Philadelphia. During the following century, some seven thousand additional Mennonites and Amish immigrated to North America, settling first in a region northwest of Germantown known as Skippack, then about fifty miles west in Lancaster, before moving farther westward into the Cumberland Valley of Pennsylvania and the Shenandoah Valley of Maryland and Virginia. Although Mennonites in the colonial period initially shared much in common with other immigrant religious groups, especially those from German-speaking lands, the Revolutionary War brought a new sense of religious and political isolation that was to characterize Mennonite identity throughout much of the nineteenth century. The Mennonites' commitment to biblical pacifism and their hesitancy to swear oaths of allegiance or to pay war taxes tended to alienate them from all sides of the Revolution and prompted one group in Pennsylvania to immigrate to southern Ontario in search of greater religious toleration.

During the early nineteenth century Mennonites followed the general pattern of westward migration across the Allegheny Mountains into the central plains of western Pennsylvania, Ohio, Indiana, Illinois, and Iowa. Along the way, they established flourishing agrarian communities where religious identity was reinforced by strong endogamous marriage patterns, close kinship ties, congregationally based patterns of mutual aid, and a strong sense of cultural and ecclesiological separatism. Generally suspicious of higher education, Mennonite congregations throughout most of the nineteenth century were served by lay ministers—largely untrained and unsalaried—selected by lot. Memories of persecution and suffering in Europe persisted in Mennonite hymnody, devotional literature, sermon themes, and martyrologies well into the nineteenth century. Some scholars, however, have noted that by mid-century the religious language of suffering—increasingly anachronistic in the more tolerant climate of North America—gradually was being supplanted by the theological motif of humility.

Despite steady numerical growth, the Mennonite Church in North America experienced several significant strains throughout the course of the nineteenth century. Some of these resulted from tension between the more conservative forms of church life and thought inherited from established communities in the East and the frontier context of newer congregations, where stable leadership, economic resources, and traditional community patterns could not be assumed. A strong emphasis on moral probity, group conformity, and church discipline made Mennonites susceptible to the individualizing and spiritualist tendencies of Pietism and the emotional expressiveness of various revivalist movements. New forms of religious organization, such as Sunday schools and centralized boards, and more systematic approaches to theology challenged older patterns of group life and thought. Moreover, the linguistic transition from German to English—a symbol for many conservatives in the church of acculturation to "the world"—proved to be divisive in many Mennonite communities.

In 1847 a group of Mennonites in eastern Pennsylvania led by John H. Oberholtzer (1809–1895) established a more progressive Mennonite conference that called for greater individual freedom in matters of dress and expression, and the establishment of new institutions to promote education, missions, and church publications. In 1860 Oberholtzer's initiative found broader affirmation in the formation of the General Conference of the Mennonite Church of North America at West Point, Iowa. Bolstered by a recent influx of progressive-minded Mennonite immigrants from southwest Germany, the newly formed General Conference quickly established an orphanage, an educational program (the Wadsworth Institute in Wadsworth, Ohio), and a mission outreach to Native Americans in the western plains states. In the 1870s the character of the General Conference was transformed yet again by the arrival of some ten thousand Mennonite immigrants from the Russian empire and Prussia.

For the so-called Old Mennonites in the East, the Civil War posed another significant challenge to Mennonite identity, forcing them again to balance the pressures of acculturation against their traditional commitment to pacifism. Though some Mennonites eventually joined the Union and Confederate troops, many more bought substitutes or engaged in passive resistance to conscription.

The last decades of the nineteenth century were characterized by a concerted effort to renew the vitality of the Mennonite Church through the establishment of numerous new institutions. One key figure in these efforts was John F. Funk (1835–1930), a Mennonite from Bucks County, Pennsylvania, who left a flourishing lumber business in Chicago in 1867 to move to Elkhart, Indiana, where he established a church-related printing and publishing business. Converted to Christianity by D. L. Moody (1837–1899), Funk joined a progressivist spirit with a commitment to unifying the increasingly disparate congregations of the Mennonite Church. At Elkhart, Funk attracted future Mennonite leaders such as the noted evangelist John S. Coffman (1848–1899), the writer and historian John Horsch (1867–1941), the mission advocate George Bender (1867–1921), and Henry A. Mumaw (1850–1908), the founder of the Elkhart Institute (later Goshen College). Funk's press published not only the leading Mennonite Church paper of the day, *Herald of Truth* (German edition, *Herold der Wahrheit*, 1864–1902), but also a host of theological, historical, doctrinal, and devotional books that solidified a sense of Mennonite identity amid the rapid economic and cultural changes at the turn of the century.

Mennonites at the end of the nineteenth century were still a largely agrarian people and the church was not wholly unified. But the flurry of institutions established in the latter decades of the century—such as Sunday schools (1880s), the Mennonite Aid Plan (1882), Young Peoples' Meetings (1890s), the Chicago Home Mission (1893), a relief agency (1897), a foreign missionary outpost in India (1898), and Goshen College in Indiana (1903)—all pointed toward a Mennonite Church that was more confident and aggressive at the century's end than it was at the beginning. As the experiences of the twentieth century would bear out, many of these institutions would serve both as a means of sheltering Mennonite identity from corrosive outside influences and, paradoxically, as the structures through which American values would be mediated to the broader church.

In the late 1990s, there were slightly more than 1,000,000 Mennonites worldwide, with some 425,000 living in North America.

See also **Communitarian Movements and Groups; Immigration and Immigrants,** *subentries on* **Central and Eastern Europe, Germany; Midwest, The; Pennsylvania.**

Bibliography

Dyck, Cornelius J., ed. *An Introduction to Mennonite History: A Popular History of the Anabaptists and the Mennonites.* 3d ed. Scottdale, Pa.: Herald, 1993.
Horst, Samuel. *Mennonites in the Confederacy: A Study in Civil War Pacifism.* Scottdale, Pa.: Herald, 1967.
Nolt, Steven M. *A History of the Amish.* Intercourse, Pa.: Good Books, 1992.
Pannabecker, Samuel Floyd. *Open Doors: The History of the General Conference Mennonite Church.* Newton, Kans.: Faith and Life, 1975.
Schlabach, Theron F. *Peace, Faith, Nation: Mennonites and Amish in Nineteenth-Century America.* Volume 2: *The Mennonite Experience in America.* Scottdale, Pa: Herald, 1988.
Smith, C. Henry. *Story of the Mennonites.* 5th ed., rev. and enl. by Cornelius Krahn. Newton, Kans.: Faith and Life, 1981.

JOHN D. ROTH

LIBERAL PROTESTANTISM

Although dissent of various kinds—as practiced by such Christian nonconformists as Antinomians and Quakers—was a characteristic of colonial American religious life almost from its beginnings, dissent that might be termed theologically liberal did not appear until the era following the Great Awakening revivals of the 1740s. Response to these revivals created a number of camps among the Congregationalist clergy of New England; those who opposed both revivalistic religion and old-line Calvinism began to coalesce into a loosely organized but intellectually coherent party in subsequent decades. Among them were Charles Chauncy and Jonathan Mayhew of Boston and Ebenezer Gay of Hingham, Massachusetts.

By the beginning of the nineteenth century, these liberals, who had come to repudiate the traditional doctrines both of original sin and the Trinity, had acquired enough influence in the vicinity of Boston to take control of Harvard's Hollis Professorship of Divinity by 1805. Pamphlet warfare provoked by conservatives such as Jedidiah Morse ensued. The articulation of liberal principles in the public forum was exemplified in William Ellery Channing's sermon "Unitarian Christianity," preached at the ordination of Jared Sparks in Boston in 1819. In 1825 the founding of the American Unitarian Association (AUA) in Boston gave the movement its first institutional expression as something other than the left wing of the Congregational churches.

Unitarianism, said to trust in "the fatherhood of God, the brotherhood of Man, and the neighborhood of Boston," had seemingly no sooner emerged as an independent denomination than it began to experience severe internal stress as a result of challenges from within. This Second Unitarian Controversy was precipitated in part by an address delivered by the essayist Ralph Waldo Emerson to the graduating class of the Harvard Divinity School in 1838. Emerson, who had some years earlier renounced the Unitarian ministry, crossed the line of liberal acceptability by rejecting a Christianity based on belief in a Jesus who had demonstrated divinity by working miracles. Harvard's Andrews Norton attacked Emerson in his pamphlet *A Discourse on the Latest Form of Infidelity* in 1839, arguing for the necessity of the miraculous.

Emersonian dissent never achieved lasting institutional form; the spiritual impulse he represented was too individualistic. Rather, he was identified with a small group of like-minded Romantic thinkers loosely associated as transcendentalists, who expressed their thoughts through vehicles such as the *Dial*, edited by Emerson and Margaret Fuller, and experiments in living as varied as the Brook Farm community in Roxbury, Massachusetts, and Henry Thoreau's three-year solitary sojourn at Walden Pond in nearby Concord.

Two other institutionalized versions of Protestant liberalism did arise during the early and middle nineteenth century, however. Universalism had its origins in a variety of sources that coalesced in New England in the Revolutionary era and took confessional form in the so-called Winchester (New Hampshire) Profession of 1803. Universalism was theologically similar to Unitarianism but flourished more among the middling classes in the smaller towns than did its more cosmopolitan counterpart, which was favored by the Boston elite. The two groups ultimately merged in 1961 to form today's Unitarian-Universalist Association. In addition, the Free Religious Association, founded in 1867 by Francis Ellingwood Abbot and other Unitarians who rejected the AUA's continued avowal of an explicitly Christian identity, foreshadowed the humanistic thought that would characterize much of twentieth-century Unitarian opinion.

During the decades that followed the Civil War, the liberal impulse rapidly grew as a force within the larger Protestant denominations: Northern Baptists, Congregationalists, Episcopalians, Methodists, and Presbyterians. The related issues of Darwinian evolution and the historical criticism of the Bible were particular touchstones of a growing division within northern Protestantism that culminated in the Fundamentalist controversies and schisms of the 1920s. The great urban churches of the Victorian era and their "princes of the pulpit"—Phillips Brooks of Boston's Trinity Episcopal and Henry Ward Beecher of Brooklyn's Plymouth Congregational, among others—proclaimed a message of divine friendship rather than judgment and of nearly infinite human potential for material success as well as for spiritual growth.

The interdenominational divinity schools in Cambridge, Massachusetts; New Haven, Connecticut; and Chicago also became seedbeds for more sophisticated versions of the liberal themes initiated in pulpit oratory. The Social Gospel, promulgated by Rochester Theological Seminary's Walter Rauschenbusch and the Congregationalist parish minister Washington Gladden, turned liberal themes away from individualistic moral evolution to the redemption of the social order by the application of the Gospel to the economic and social ills of the day. Less rooted in traditional vocabulary were William James's ventures into psychology and comparative religion as he and others sought a scientific justification for religious belief.

Many themes of nineteenth-century liberalism, such as the historicist approach to revelation and the emphasis on social ethics, remained strong within mainline Protestantism. But the disasters of the subsequent era, beginning with World War I, cast doubt on the unqualified optimism of earlier liberalism, and the more pessimistic neoorthodoxy that began in the 1920s and lasted throughout the first half of the twentieth century—which was based on reappropriation of traditional Christian doctrines such as original sin and divine sovereignty—became the heir to the liberal legacy.

See also **Protestantism,** *subentries on* **Baptists, Congregationalists, Episcopalians, Methodists, Presbyterians; Social Gospel; Transcendentalism; Unitarianism and Universalism.**

Bibliography

Handy, Robert T., ed. *The Social Gospel in America, 1870–1920.* New York: Oxford University Press, 1966.

Hutchison, William R. *The Modernist Impulse in American Protestantism.* Cambridge, Mass.: Harvard University Press, 1976.

Lippy, Charles H., and Peter W. Williams, eds. *Encyclopedia of the American Religious Experience.* New York: Scribners, 1988. See especially chapters by Catherine L. Albanese, "Transcendentalism"; John Corrigan, "The Enlightenment"; William McGuire King, "Liberalism"; Charles H. Lippy, "Social Christianity"; George H. Shriver, "Romantic Religion"; and Peter W. Williams, "Unitarianism and Universalism."

Wright, Conrad. *The Beginnings of Unitarianism in America.* Boston: Starr King, 1955.

PETER W. WILLIAMS

PSYCHOLOGY   At the start of the nineteenth century the term "psychology" was not in general use, and no disciplinary specialty for the study of mental events existed. By the century's end American psychology was an established intellectual discipline with a distinct mission. Psychology had matured into a scientific movement that soon became an international force. Nineteenth-century psychological thought had diverse origins, and while those origins included links to intellectual work in Britain and Europe, it contained distinct indigenous characteristics. This diversity of ideas did not go uncontested. By mid-century many of the eclectic and popular features of American psychology were challenged by the rise of a scientific spirit committed to using experimental techniques to acquire knowledge and to investigate the observable (material) bases of mental phenomena. By the end of the century the United States boasted a "new psychology" that promised to produce predictive and useful knowledge about psychological events.

As Roger Smith demonstrated in *The Norton History of the Human Sciences* (1997), knowledge about human nature, even scientific knowledge, has definite foundations in public life, notably in views created through material and cultural practices. Early nineteenth-century American culture avowed its independence from European intellectual traditions, held deep commitments to religion, mainly Protestant, and fervently desired practical knowledge. Early nineteenth-century ideas about psychological phenomena were developed and transmitted in liberal arts colleges, most of which were affiliated with Protestant denominations. Teachers were attracted to the philosophers of the Scottish Enlightenment and adopted in particular their emphasis on common sense experiences over formal and abstract philosophical systems, the principle that humans have direct perceptions of the world, and the elaboration of God-given human faculties for perceiving and acting in the world. Called "common sense" or "faculty" philosophy, these ideas were taught under the rubric of "moral science" and became a regular feature in the college curriculum. American professors developed and refined Scottish thinking about human mental faculties. As early as 1831 Bowdoin College professor Thomas C. Upham published a moral science textbook, *Elements of Mental Philosophy*, that analyzed the basic psychological faculties and the foundations of moral character. In the 1880s Princeton University president James McCosh dedicated separate volumes of his textbook to the three basic faculties, respectively titled *The Emotions* (1880), *Psychology: The Cognitive Powers* (1886), and *Psychology: The Motive Powers, Emotions, Conscience, Will* (1887).

Outside college campuses Americans were exposed to popular versions of mental science, such as phre-

nology. For a fee individuals could attend lectures on the relation between physical characteristics of the head and individual psychology or have their characters deciphered.

By the middle of the century a number of intellectuals engaged in the scientific studies of human nature taking place in Europe. Physiology, neurology, biology, chemistry, and physics were demonstrating the importance of scientific method to produce valid knowledge and the idea that psychological phenomena had physical correlates. American scholars interested in the new scientific studies of mental life traveled to Europe to train in experimental laboratory techniques. William James, G. Stanley Hall, James McKeen Cattell, Joseph Jastrow, E. W. Scripture, and many others studied in Germany, often with the experimentalist Wilhelm Wundt, before establishing psychology laboratories at American universities. In these new laboratories researchers labored to observe, calibrate, and assess mental events and ultimately to demonstrate that psychology was a natural science distinct from philosophy and moral science. The vibrant work undertaken in other sciences fueled researchers' interest in applying rigorous scientific methods to psychological phenomena and influenced their choices of models and theories. Physics provided conceptions of energy, its transmission, and its conservation, which shaped theories of the nervous system. Chemistry inspired reductive theories of the structure and basic elements of consciousness, a mental chemistry.

In the last quarter of the century American psychology was shaped by the techniques and attitudes of experimental science and by the revised conceptions of human nature that derived from Charles Darwin's theory of evolution. Evolutionary theory provided further support for the belief that mental events had material bases and opened the way for comparative studies of mental processes in different species. In addition the Darwinian doctrine of natural variation intensified American psychologists' long-standing interest in individual differences and lent a framework for the assessment of difference. Stress on how organisms adapt to their environments fostered an interest in mental functions over structures and in psychological conduct over content. In addition it clearly differentiated the emerging scientific paradigm from the German models borrowed to establish the first laboratories.

The imported laboratory practices and scientific theories about psychological phenomena provided a defined and public foundation for the discipline's development. This discipline became a unique and culturally important enterprise through its continuation and maturation of the distinctly American interest in making psychology a moral and useful science. The development of research on the brain and other physical bases of psychological events indicated that religious doctrines were no longer relevant to mental science, but it did not mean that morality was irrelevant. Precise measurements of psychological processes found no evidence to sustain belief in the existence of the soul or even of the will, but they did not cancel deeply held cultural beliefs in human improvement or self-motivation. The vast majority of the psychological researchers who founded the laboratories, courses, and umbrella scientific organization, the American Psychological Association (1892), were committed to constructing a science that served society and improved the human condition. Thus American researchers expanded the subject matter of psychology. They investigated general mental processes, such as problem solving, habit formation, learning, and memory, but they also addressed clinical and practical topics, such as mental dysfunction, social problems, work performance, personality characteristics, and child development. By the turn of the century American psychologists pursued precise observation and measurement of differences related to race, ethnicity, gender, and age. From these interests evolved the specialties of developmental psychology, social psychology, clinical psychology, and industrial psychology. The objective of these plural enterprises was the production of scientific knowledge that could improve the functioning of individuals and society. At the end of the century several psychologists even created utopias based on scientific psychology. In the twentieth century psychology prospered by pursuing utilitarian and therapeutic aims marked out for the discipline by its pioneers in the late nineteenth century.

See also **Education,** *subentry on* **Colleges and Universities; Evolution; Mental Illness; Philosophy; Religion,** *subentry on* **Religion in Nineteenth-Century America.**

Bibliography

Leahey, Thomas Hardy. *A History of Psychology: Main Currents in Psychological Thought.* 4th ed. Upper Saddle River, N.J.: Prentice Hall, 1997.

Richards, Graham. *Mental Machinery: The Origins and Consequences of Psychological Ideas.* London: Athlone Press, 1992.

———. " 'To Know Our Fellow Men To Do Them Good': American Psychology's Enduring Moral Project." *History of the Human Sciences* 8 (1995): 1–24.

Smith, Roger. *The Norton History of the Human Sciences.* New York: Norton, 1997.

JILL G. MORAWSKI

PUERTO RICO   With just under a million people in 1898, many of whom were only one generation from slavery, the island of Puerto Rico had been a Spanish possession since the early 1500s. The main crop was sugarcane, and slavery had only been abolished in 1873. The Spanish had granted Puerto Rico autonomy in early 1898. Puerto Rico became a U.S. possession as a result of the Spanish-American War of 1898. During the fighting in July 1898, U.S. troops under General Nelson A. Miles landed in Puerto Rico and overwhelmed the small Spanish garrison in less than two weeks. Spain relinquished its sovereignty over Puerto Rico and its inhabitants to the United States in the Treaty of Paris, signed in December 1898.

Puerto Rico was placed under U.S. military rule on 18 October 1898 and remained so for the next year and a half. As the island moved toward territorial status, it faced a number of vexing economic and political issues. In September 1899 a devastating hurricane ruined the coffee crop, which accounted for the bulk of the island's revenue. To rebuild the shattered Puerto Rican economy, the administration of President William McKinley advocated that all tariff barriers between Puerto Rico and the United States be removed. In his annual message of 1899 President McKinley called for the abolition of all tariffs on Puerto Rican goods as the "plain duty" of the United States toward its new colonial possession.

Because the proposal called into question the protective tariff policy of the Republicans, Congress rebelled against the idea that it could not set rules for the newly acquired possessions. A controversy erupted that threatened for a time to imperil McKinley's relations with Capitol Hill. The result was legislation in April 1900 that imposed a 15 percent tariff on Puerto Rican products only until a civilian government could begin functioning.

Also in 1900 Congress passed the Foraker Act, named after its sponsor, Republican Senator Joseph B. Foraker of Ohio, which set up a civilian government for the island. Puerto Rico became an unincorporated territory that was not part of the United States. To represent the people of Puerto Rico in Congress, a resident commissioner would be elected to a two-year term but would not be able to vote, speak in congressional deliberations, or lobby on the floor.

The status of Puerto Rico became an issue in the Insular Cases that came before the Supreme Court between 1901 and 1922. On 27 May 1901, in the case of *Downes v. Bidwell,* the Court ruled that Puerto Rico and the Philippine Islands were possessions of the United States and thus were under the authority of Congress and the laws that it made. The key part of the decision, however, was that the inhabitants of Puerto Rico were not in fact citizens of the United States. The decision upheld the position that the McKinley administration had taken toward the status of the Philippines and Puerto Rico. In 1917 Congress made the people of Puerto Rico citizens of the United States.

Puerto Rico was not a major element in the deliberations that ended the war with Spain in 1898. Nevertheless acquisition of the territory necessitated important political, economic, and constitutional decisions, during the transition from the nineteenth to the twentieth century, decisions that shaped future U.S. foreign policy.

See also **Central America and the Caribbean; Foreign Trade and Tariffs; Spanish-American War.**

Bibliography

Campbell, Charles S. *The Transformation of American Foreign Relations, 1865–1900*. New York: Harper and Row, 1976.
Gould, Lewis L. *The Presidency of William McKinley.* Lawrence: University Press of Kansas, 1980.

LEWIS L. GOULD

QUAKERS The year 1800 found the Society of Friends in North America a united body, its membership scattered among the thirteen original states and just beginning to cross the Appalachians into the Ohio Valley. By 1900 American Friends had followed the general migration of Americans westward, but they were divided into three distinct strands.

Before 1830 the dominant outlook among American Friends was quietistic. Friends saw humans as incapable of any good action without a clear divine leading. Thus, to speak in a meeting for worship or even to pray or read the Bible required divine guidance. Growth was the dominant metaphor. Through obedience to the leadings of the Holy Spirit, observance of the Discipline that separated Friends from the rest of the world, and passive experiences of suffering, what Friends called "baptisms," Friends would ultimately be sanctified and fitted for heaven.

Quaker unity was first fractured in the Hicksite separation of 1827–1828. This division pitted Orthodox Friends, those whose views of the divinity of Christ and the authority of Scripture were similar to those of non-Quaker evangelicals, against a diverse group of opponents who rallied behind the leadership of Elias Hicks (1748–1830), a Long Island minister. Hicksite Friends perceived the Orthodox Friends as overly influenced by the larger religious culture while they themselves ranged from unbending conservatives skeptical of all non-Quaker influences to incip-

ient religious liberals. The separation began in the Philadelphia Yearly Meeting and spread from there to New York, Maryland, Virginia, Ohio, and Indiana. Precise statistics are not available, but the ultimate breakdown was probably about 60 percent Orthodox and 40 percent Hicksite.

The Hicksite separation did not end Quaker fractiousness. New splits appeared among Hicksite Friends in the 1830s. Some, most notably Lucretia Coffin Mott (1793–1880), were drawn into radical reform movements, especially abolition, nonresistance, and women's rights. A disproportionate number of the founders of the American Anti-Slavery Society were Hicksite Friends, who also dominated the Seneca Falls Women's Rights Convention of 1848. More conservative Hicksites feared ties with non-Quakers and denounced reformers. The result was a new round of separations in which many radicals left to form groups called Progressive or Congregational Friends.

Orthodox Friends also experienced splits. By the 1840s many were drawing closer to the larger evangelical religious culture, joining reform groups like Sunday school and Bible societies and emphasizing an instantaneous conversion experience. They found their inspiration in Joseph John Gurney (1788–1847), an English Friend who traveled in the United States from 1837 to 1840. A minority of Orthodox Friends viewed such innovations with dismay, particularly the Rhode Island minister John Wilbur (1773–1855). Between 1845 and 1855 Gurneyites and Wilburites separated in most of the Orthodox yearly meetings.

The Civil War presented all Friends with challenges, pitting their antislavery convictions against their pacifism. Hundreds, perhaps thousands, of male Friends joined the Union army, and for the first time some meetings tolerated such departures from tradition. Others went south as teachers and workers among the freedpeople.

Only the relatively small group of Wilburite Friends maintained traditional ways without compromise after 1870, and they depended almost entirely on keeping their children in their faith to survive. Hicksite Friends, while still holding to traditional ways of worship, gave up Quaker peculiarities of dress and speech. They softened enforcement of the Discipline and ended the practice of disowning Friends who married nonmembers. Many avowed a common identity with religious liberals.

Gurneyites saw the greatest change. Beginning about 1870 most Gurneyite meetings were swept by a wave of revivalism closely linked to the interdenominational second-experience holiness movement. Music, mourner's benches, and premillennialism be-

Quaker Meetinghouse. Immigrant Norwegian Quakers attending a Friends' meetinghouse in Newport, Rhode Island. Drawing by John Collins, 1857. LIBRARY OF CONGRESS

came articles of faith for many Friends. By the 1880s many Gurneyite meetings were calling themselves the Friends Church and hiring pastors. The traditional plain life was swept away as unnecessary. Quaker women followed the lead of other evangelical women and formed foreign and home missionary societies; many of the early Quaker pastors were women. Evangelism brought thousands of new members, but many received little instruction in Quaker beliefs. Some Gurneyites resisted these innovations, and in the 1870s a new round of separations took place.

A few blacks became Quakers during the nineteenth century. The best known was probably Paul Cuffe (1759–1817), a sea captain from New Bedford, Massachusetts. At least one black monthly meeting, Southland in Arkansas (associated with the black Southland College), was founded as a result of Quaker work among the freedpeople there in the 1860s. Friends made no concerted efforts to attract African American members, however, and blacks who did join the society sometimes encountered racial prejudice.

In the 1790s Friends began work to "civilize" Na-

tive Americans, focusing on education of children and teaching farming and housekeeping skills to adults. The first such efforts were among the Six Nations in New York. In 1804 Friends opened a farm and school among the Miamis on the Wabash River in Indiana, establishing a similar mission among the Shawnees at Wapakoneta, Ohio, in 1811. When the Shawnees were removed west of the Mississippi in the 1830s, Friends accompanied them. After the Civil War, both Gurneyite and Hicksite Friends were active participants in the Grant administration's "peace policy" of Indian civilization. Gurneyite Friends devoted considerable effort to winning converts among Native Americans in Kansas and Oklahoma.

By 1900 American Quakers included almost the full spectrum of American Protestantism. The financial status of Friends ranged from the great wealth of some Philadelphia families to relative poverty; virtually all Friends were native-born. Wilburite Friends maintained the old ways unbendingly. Hicksite Friends, while holding to traditional silent worship, increasingly saw themselves as tied to other liberal Protestants. Gurneyites, self-avowedly evangelical, were beginning to experience the tensions between incipient fundamentalists and modernists that would rend other Protestant denominations in the twentieth century.

See also **Protestantism; Reform, Social; Religion,** *subentry on* **Religion in Nineteenth-Century America.**

Bibliography

Barbour, Hugh, and J. William Frost. *The Quakers.* New York: Greenwood, 1988.

Doherty, Robert W. *The Hicksite Separation: A Sociological Analysis of Religious Schism in Early Nineteenth Century America.* New Brunswick, N.J.: Rutgers University Press, 1967.

Hamm, Thomas D. *The Transformation of American Quakerism: Orthodox Friends, 1800–1907.* Bloomington: Indiana University Press, 1988.

Ingle, H. Larry. *Quakers in Conflict: The Hicksite Reformation.* Knoxville: University of Tennessee Press, 1986.

Jones, Rufus M. *The Later Periods of Quakerism.* London: Macmillan, 1921.

THOMAS D. HAMM

R

RACE AND RACIAL THINKING The effort to identify scientific principles of race was perhaps the most insidious intellectual dead end of the nineteenth century. By claiming to use scientific methods to explain the differences between humans, the proponents of racial science encouraged white American leaders to institutionalize racist and repressive policies against nonwhites.

Ancient Greek and European Enlightenment students of human behavior argued that environmental factors produced the physical and cultural differences between people. John Locke (1632–1704), the English political theorist, wrote that an individual's mind was a tabula rasa (blank slate) at birth and that education and environmental surroundings formed character, personality, and intelligence. Enlightenment philosophers like Voltaire (1694–1778) held that favorable environmental conditions had allowed western Europeans to achieve a level of civilization superior to all others.

This environmental determinism implied that education could raise those of non-European ancestry to the level of Western civilization. This faith in the improvability of humans influenced the attitudes of early American leaders toward Native Americans. For example, in the 1790s the United States developed a comprehensive education and mission program to prepare Native Americans for assimilation. However, assimilation was not simply driven by benevolent motives. Instead U.S. officials used the "civilization program" to acquire native land. Ideally, U.S. policymakers hoped to instruct Indians in the principles of private property ownership, acquire

their tribal lands, allot small tracts to individual Indians, and sell the surplus land to white Americans.

American leaders of the early Republic were not as confident about the improvability of people of African descent. In his *Notes on the State of Virginia* (1785), Thomas Jefferson argued that blacks were so intellectually inferior to whites that they could never assimilate into American society. Jefferson even suggested that blacks represented a distinct genus or species, a suspicion that presaged the popularity of racial theory in the United States.

Racial Science

Beginning in the late eighteenth century, some European scholars contended that immutable biological distinctions between racial groups were transmissible by descent. Race determined not only physical appearance, they argued, but intelligence, character, and behavior as well. Students of race were not interested in the common characteristics that defined humans as a group but rather attempted to discern traits that particularized people into distinct ethnic and racial categories. Racial theorists debated the number of races, the characteristics of each race, and the relative position of each race on a putative hierarchy of human development. Carolus Linnaeus (1707–1778), a Swedish botanist, held that humans were a single species made up of four racial types, *Homo asiaticus, Homo afer, Homo americanus,* and *Homo europaeus*. Johann Friedrich Blumenbach (1752–1840), a German physician and zoologist, used skin color to divide humans into five races, Caucasian (white), Mongolian (yellow), Ethiopian (black), American (red), and Malay (brown). More extreme was Paul Broca (1824–1880), a French anthropologist, who broke down the human family into thirty-four distinct races.

The interest in racial traits produced new research in specialized areas of physiological study in Europe and the United States. Blumenbach and Pieter Camper (1722–1789) were forerunners in the science of anthropometry, the comparative study of human body measurements. Camper, a Dutch anatomist, attempted to determine the degree of intelligence of each race and constructed a hierarchy of the races based on the angles of the human face. Blumenbach and Georges-Louis Leclerc de Buffon (1707–1788) became known as the fathers of craniology, the study of the relationship between intelligence and the size, shape, and proportion of the skull. Blumenbach examined a single skull from the Caucasus Mountains, recognized a resemblance to the crania of his German specimens, and wrongly concluded that the original Europeans migrated from the Russian region into western Europe. Blumenbach's minimal evidence resulted in the common practice of identifying white people as Caucasians.

Samuel George Morton (1799–1851), a Philadelphia physician, was the most prominent American craniologist. Morton measured the size, structure, and capacity of more than eight hundred crania and categorized them by race and nationality. He concluded that the Caucasian race possessed larger average skulls than those of Africans and American Indians and were therefore generally more intelligent than the latter races. Morton's disciple, a southerner named Josiah Clark Nott (1804–1873), performed craniological studies of his own, including a survey of American hat sizes. Nott agreed with Morton's conclusions, used the evidence to justify southern slavery, and warned that Caucasians courted debilitation or annihilation by mixing with the "lower" races.

Johann Kaspar Lavater (1741–1801), a Swiss minister, reignited interest in the ancient theory of physiognomy, which contends that character can be discerned from physical appearance. Franz Joseph Gall (1758–1828), a German physician, founded the similar science of phrenology, which presumes that scientists can ascertain character traits and mental faculties by examining particular areas of the skull or brain. John Fiske (1842–1901), an American historian, exemplified phrenological study when he suggested that intelligence was determined by the number and depth of the convolutions of the brain. The more intelligent white race, Fiske held, possessed more deeply furrowed brains than those of nonwhites. The French physician Pierre Gratiolet (1815–1865) offered a similarly inventive theory when he proposed that the coronal sutures of blacks closed at an earlier age than those of whites. Black children were as intelligent as white children, Gratiolet argued, but the premature closing of the coronal suture inhibited the development of the brain and doomed blacks to an adulthood of intellectual inferiority.

Racial scientists were also particularly curious about racial distinctions in skin color and hair texture. Blumenbach, reflecting the continuing influence of the environmental approach, argued that the black skin of African peoples resulted from their absorption of carbon from the tropical atmosphere. Samuel Stanhope Smith (1750–1819), an American clergyman, believed that the African pigmentation was symptomatic of a noncontagious form of leprosy and held that an afflicted black would return to a natural white color if cured of the disease. James Cowles Prichard (1786–1848), an English physician, theorized that the original humans were black and that the lighter races emerged as an improved variation over time. Peter A. Browne, a lawyer from Philadelphia, argued in the 1840s that the differences in the hair textures of whites and blacks proved that they represented separate species.

Separate Species and Separate Creations

The separate species question infatuated students of race. According to Linnaeus, the test of species was whether two distinct organisms could propagate fertile offspring. Without any substantive evidence supporting his assertion, Morton argued that women of mixed racial ancestry had more difficulty in childbirth than women of "pure" racial backgrounds, that whites and blacks were separate species, and that the two races were naturally averse to social and sexual mixing. Subsequent scientists proved Morton wrong on all three counts.

The racialists who believed that all races were of the same species faced a difficult theological dilemma. Genesis, the first book of the Bible, held that humans originated when God created Adam and Eve in his own image. Considerable argument raged over how the various races could have been produced from the original couple. Blumenbach suggested that the nonwhite races had degenerated over time to their contemporary colors and levels of inferiority. On the other hand, Robert Chambers (1802–1871), an amateur scientist from Scotland, opined that the white race had passed through a series of stages, from black to Malay to Indian to Mongolian, until it reached its transcendent status of Caucasian. The implication was, of course, that the other races were still at lower stages of development.

Scholars as far back as the sixteenth century had proposed that God had intentionally separated the races geographically in a series of distinct creations, and scientists debated this proposition with fervor in the first half of the nineteenth century. The theory of polygenesis, or separate creations, adequately explained a particularistic world comprised of distinct peoples with unique racial characteristics. Many Christian Americans, however, including those who despised Indians and defended slavery, were unwilling to accept a theory that contradicted the orthodox view of human origins, even if it gave scientific credence to claims of white racial distinctiveness.

Social Darwinism

Charles Darwin's theory of evolution effectively ended the argument over polygenesis, because it provided scientists with a persuasive explanation for the physiological distinctions among the same species. Darwin (1809–1882) believed that the human races were of the same species and that racial distinctions were only minor variations. In some of his writings, however, Darwin extended the concept of evolution to the social realm and suggested in one passage that the people and progress of the United States were the products of natural selection. Social Darwinists, as

OUR GODDESS OF LIBERTY.
WHAT IS SHE TO BE? TO WHAT COMPLEXION ARE WE TO COME AT LAST?

The Many Faces of Liberty. A comment on the changing ethnicity of America, playing on fears in some quarters that the Anglo-Saxon race would be diminished. *Frank Leslie's Illustrated Newspaper,* 16 July 1870. LIBRARY OF CONGRESS

they came to be called, seized upon this aspect of Darwinian theory and maintained that the races had evolved slowly over time and that the white race was naturally selected for racial superiority.

Herbert Spencer (1820–1903), an English philosopher, was the foremost proponent of social Darwinism. Spencer described the evolutionary process as the "survival of the fittest" and argued that competition among humans improved society as a whole by eliminating weak and unintelligent individuals and races. Character traits were racially determined, Spencer believed, and therefore a race could not be improved except by the gradual process of social evolution. However, he added, the races were engaged in a fierce struggle for survival. The nonwhite races, he predicted, would not be able to compete with whites and were likely doomed to extinction. He warned that whites should refrain from polluting their race by mixing with people of other races.

Spencer also applied the idea of the survival of the fittest to economics and became a leading proponent of laissez-faire capitalism. Spencer and other social Darwinists argued that governments should allow individuals the absolute freedom to compete for survival and success, and they opposed progressive legislation that attempted to level the economic playing field between rich and poor and between owner and laborer.

Social Darwinism did not go unchallenged. Members of the Social Gospel movement, led by clergymen like Josiah Strong (1847–1916), accepted Darwin's theory of evolution but condemned the willingness of social Darwinists to allow the rich and powerful to exploit the poor and the weak. Despite their support for progressive ideas on class, the Social Gospel ministers, like the laissez-faire capitalists they criticized, believed the evolutionary process promoted the ultimate hegemony of whites. While they preached against the predatory nature of capitalism, the Social Gospel preachers generally avoided condemnation of the racial injustices of the times.

Eugenics

In the late nineteenth century the confidence in racial science and the belief in the improvability of humans combined to produce the eugenics movement. Francis Galton (1822–1911), perhaps the leading theorist of eugenics, proposed that humans could be improved through selective reproduction. Around the same time proponents of the germ plasm theory suggested that character traits and other adaptations that humans made to their environmental circumstances could become embedded into their hereditary pattern or "germ plasm." Accepting these ideas, eugenics proponents contended that criminal tendencies were inheritable, that certain races were biologically predisposed to antisocial behavior, and that society as a whole would benefit from the sterilization of certain groups. Thus, while social Darwinists wanted to limit governmental intrusion into the evolutionary struggle, eugenicists wanted governments to actively discourage or even prohibit reproduction by individuals or groups they deemed lacking in mental, moral, or physical faculties. The eugenics movement gained a considerable following after the turn of the century. Between 1911 and 1930 over two dozen states passed laws allowing for the sterilization of criminals and mental hospital patients.

Race and the Anglo-Saxons

Joseph-Arthur de Gobineau (1816–1882), a French diplomat, argued that the white peoples of northern Europe were the descendants of the Aryans, a mythically pure race of intelligent fair-haired and fair-skinned people who supposedly migrated from Persia into Europe in ancient times. The Nordic Europeans had generally retained their racial purity, Gobineau argued, and were the most advanced and intelligent race. While Gobineau's writings would have tremendous influence on German racial philosophers in the twentieth century, they were virtually ignored by nineteenth-century American scholars. Instead, an overwhelming number of American racial theorists focused their attention and praise on the Anglo-Saxons, a Germanic tribe in Saxony that invaded England in the fifth century. These scholars based their admiration of the Anglo-Saxons on the writings of the Roman historian Tacitus, who in *Germania* (98 C.E.) praised the Roman foes' virility, simplicity, and love of freedom. American admirers of the Anglo-Saxons also credited them with being the progenitors of the concepts of liberty and representative government and claimed that it was essential for the United States to recognize and preserve its Anglo-Saxon heritage. These arguments gained widespread acceptance among American expansionists, who declared that the United States had succeeded Great Britain as the guardian of Anglo-Saxon civilization. The new racial evidence, they claimed, proved that the Anglo-Saxon United States possessed a manifest destiny to expand across the Western Hemisphere. Exponents of the Anglo-Saxon mythology used it to justify the nineteenth-century wars against Mexico, Spain, and the western Indian tribes.

Interest in the Anglo-Saxons permeated American intellectual circles through the end of the nineteenth century. Many historians, for example, enthusiastically embraced the idea that the Anglo-Saxons were the force behind American success and progress. Herbert Baxter Adams (1850–1901) suggested that the environment that early settlers faced in America was similar to the one encountered by the Germanic tribes and that the colonial New England systems of land allotment, communal pastureland, and government by town meeting were similar to those found in Tacitus's descriptions of the ancient Germans. In other words, Adams held that the Anglo-Saxon strain motivated societies centuries apart to respond in a similar fashion to similar environments. Henry Adams (1838–1918) argued that the Anglo-American legal traditions of private property, the jury, and the rule of law could be traced back to Germanic roots. Other renowned historians like George Bancroft (1800–1891), John Lothrop Motley (1814–1877), Francis Parkman (1823–1893), and Albert Bushnell Hart (1854–1943) accepted in varying degrees the theory of Anglo-Saxon exceptionalism. The historical interest in the Anglo-Saxons also had a dramatic influence on college curricula. By 1875 twenty-three American colleges offered a course in the Anglo-Saxon language.

Anglo-Saxon themes and racial characterizations infected American literature as well. Ralph Waldo Emerson (1803–1882) wrote on how race determined character and appearance, and he described connections that he saw between the ancient Germans and American midwesterners. Barrett Wendell (1855–1921) attributed the achievements of New England writers to the racial homogeneity of the Anglo-Saxon peoples of the region. James Fenimore Cooper (1789–1851), Owen Wister (1860–1938), Jack London (1876–1916), and many others often used stereotypes of Anglo-Saxons and other races as a shortcut to characterization.

Consequences of Racial Science

While Enlightenment philosophy held that all humans could be improved to the same level of civilization, nineteenth-century racial theorists taught that the nonwhite races were biologically doomed to an inferior status. Because of their race nonwhites were intellectually incapable of rising to the level of the Anglo-Saxon American and could never be successfully assimilated into white America. Many writers depicted blacks and American Indians as dying races. According to the racial determinists, no amount of education or acculturation could remedy the fatal biological weaknesses imposed by their racial heritage.

These themes were particularly attractive to slaveholding American southerners, who were intent on preserving the institution of slavery. Southern racial ideologues, such as Thomas R. Dew (1802–1846), declared that the new scientific evidence demonstrated that blacks were naturally inferior and racially unfit for any occupation but bonded labor. George Fitzhugh (1806–1881), another prominent proslavery advocate, argued that slavery actually benefited laborers by providing protection, structure, and subsistence. He maintained that white laborers would be better off as slaves, or "warranties," as he called them, than as workers exploited by capitalists in the industrial system. After the emancipation of slaves at the end of the Civil War, southern politicians used the new racial theories to justify their disenfranchisement of blacks. As a whole, the United States after the war became a culture that adhered to a legal policy of racial segregation. In 1896 the U.S. Supreme Court issued its decision in *Plessy v. Ferguson*, which provided that separate public facilities for the white and black races were constitutional as long as they were equal in quality.

White Americans were just as accepting of the idea of Native American racial inferiority. Motivated in part by the findings of the racial scientists, U.S. leaders turned to a policy of racial separation in the nineteenth century. In the 1830s the United States removed the eastern tribes beyond the Mississippi River, and in the 1850s the federal government began consigning Native Americans to reservations.

For the first half of the nineteenth century racial thinkers in the United States were primarily concerned with distinguishing Anglo-Americans from Indians and blacks. After the Civil War, however, an influx of immigrants from Ireland, Italy, China, Japan, and eastern Europe captured the attention of racial determinists. Scientists and politicians began to focus on the perceived distinctions between the revered Anglo-Saxons and the newly arrived ethnic immigrants. A great upwelling of animosity developed among Anglo-American laborers, who feared that the recent immigrants would work for lower wages and take their jobs. A legacy of this xenophobia was the development and widespread acceptance of ethnic stereotypes among the Anglo-American public. In many cases the racial scientists purported theories and evidence that supported the ethnic stereotypes. In the 1880s and 1890s anti-immigrant groups, particularly in the industrial North, lobbied Congress for immigration quotas against specific races.

By the end of the nineteenth century the belief in Anglo-American racial superiority had infected almost every field of American academic study and had become part of the parlance of political rhetoric and social conversation. Many among the Anglo-American public felt that their race possessed a biological superiority over all other peoples that entitled their nation to expand its domain over the nonwhite races within and beyond U.S. borders. Through the twentieth century segments of the U.S. population continued to harbor racist sentiments espoused by the racial scientists of the nineteenth century.

Strong opposition to racial theory emerged late in the nineteenth century. Franz Boas (1858–1942) and other anthropologists moved away from the focus on racial categorization and toward the study of non-Western societies in culturally relativistic terms. Moreover, upon closer examination the idea of the pure Anglo-Saxon race proved to be a myth. While Germans from the area of Saxony had migrated to the British Isles before the Norman Conquest, they were certainly not a homogeneous group, and once there they had also integrated with a variety of ethnic groups already living on the island. The Anglo-Saxons who were wrongfully credited with producing the ideas of liberty and representative government were by no means the blue bloods that nineteenth-century racial theorists made them out to be. Slowly a new generation of social scientists dispatched the eccentric theories concocted by the racial scientists of the nineteenth century. By the second half of the twentieth century scientists had all but rejected the significance of race as a determinant of character and behavior.

For over a century the students of human behavior followed the siren song of race, a detour that left terrible consequences of death, discrimination, and displacement for millions. The atrocities of Nazi Germany in the name of race in the twentieth century demonstrated the disastrous road of racial theory and led scientists back to the study of the real and complicated factors that influence human behavior.

See also **Anthropology; Civilization; Evolution; Manifest Destiny; Miscegenation; Race Laws; Segregation,** *subentry on* **Segregation and Civil Rights; Slavery,** *subentry on* **Defense of Slavery; Social Gospel.**

Bibliography

Berkhofer, Robert F., Jr. *The White Man's Indian: Images of the American Indian from Columbus to the Present.* New York: Knopf, 1978.

Fredrickson, George M. *The Black Image in the White Mind.* New York: Harper and Row, 1971.

Gossett, Thomas F. *Race: The History of an Idea in America.* Oxford: Oxford University Press, 1997. The original edition was published in 1963.

Gould, Stephen Jay. *The Mismeasure of Man.* New York: Norton, 1996.

Haller, John S., Jr. *Outcasts from Evolution: Scientific Attitudes of Racial Inferiority, 1859–1900.* Urbana: University of Illinois Press, 1971.

Horsman, Reginald. *Race and Manifest Destiny: The Origins of*

American Racial Anglo-Saxonism. Cambridge, Mass.: Harvard University Press, 1981.

Jordan, Winthrop D. *White over Black: American Attitudes toward the Negro, 1550–1812.* Chapel Hill: University of North Carolina Press, 1968.

Mosse, George L. *The Crisis of German Ideology: Intellectual Origins of the Third Reich.* New York: Grosset and Dunlap, 1964.

Stanton, William Ragan. *The Leopard's Spots: Scientific Attitudes toward Race in America, 1815–1859.* Chicago: University of Chicago Press, 1960.

TIM ALAN GARRISON

RACE LAWS   Race laws, as distinct from those regulating slavery, were found in every state at the beginning of the nineteenth century. Racial discrimination varied, with the harshest laws generally in the South and the mildest in New England. By 1860 most of the South had restricted the rights, opportunities, and liberties of free blacks so severely that some twentieth-century scholars have called southern free blacks "slaves without masters." Nowhere in the South could blacks vote, serve on juries, or practice the learned professions, such as law, medicine, dentistry, and pharmacy. With few exceptions, they could never testify against whites. In parts of the South it was illegal to teach free blacks to read, and it was against the law for blacks to own weapons or to practice such skilled crafts as typesetting or gunsmithing. Every slave state required free blacks to carry papers to prove their nonslave status. Some states required that their real estate and other forms of property be controlled by white guardians.

In the North, conditions for free blacks were mixed. By 1860 most of New England gave blacks full civil and political rights, and in some instances these states prohibited discrimination by public facilities and certain other businesses. The middle states were more restrictive, allowing segregation at the option of local school boards. In New York, for example, Buffalo and Albany had segregated schools, but Syracuse and Rochester did not. In the early part of the nineteenth century, Ohio, Indiana, and Illinois placed severe restrictions on free blacks and actively discouraged them from moving to those states. These laws failed to stem the flow of free blacks and fugitive slaves out of the South to the North and West, and by 1860 antiblack immigration laws existed only in Indiana, Illinois, and Oregon. Most of the North outside of New England allowed private discrimination, had segregated schools and other facilities, and denied blacks some civil and most political rights. But these states also provided limited public education for blacks, and most passed personal-liberty laws to prevent southerners from kidnapping them into slavery.

During and after the Civil War most of the northern states did away with their race laws. In 1866 and 1875 the U.S. Congress passed two civil rights laws, designed to provide fundamental rights to blacks and to guarantee them equal access to public facilities. In the *Civil Rights Cases* (1883), the Supreme Court gutted the 1875 act, essentially leaving the regulation of race to the states. By the 1880s the New England and Middle Atlantic states had passed civil rights acts similar to the one passed by Congress in 1875.

Immediately after the Civil War the southern states adopted harsh black codes designed to replicate the oppression of slavery. The 1866 Civil Rights Act, the Reconstruction Act of 1867, and the Fourteenth Amendment (1868) led to the repeal of these laws. During Reconstruction (1866–1877) southern law became the most egalitarian in the nation, as integrated legislatures repealed the black codes and rewrote southern law to provide for substantial equality for former slaves. Following Reconstruction, however, the South gradually implemented de jure segregation across all phases of life. In a number of cases, culminating with *Plessy v. Ferguson* (1896), the U.S. Supreme Court gave its blessing to racial segregation and the concept of "separate but equal."

While mostly involving African Americans, discriminatory laws in some states were directed at people of Chinese and Japanese ancestry, Latinos, and Native Americans living away from their tribes. For example, California applied its race laws to the Chinese and Native Americans, as well as to blacks. When the state repealed its antiblack laws during the Civil War, its anti-Asian statutes were left in place. At the federal level, naturalization and immigration laws discriminated against blacks before the Civil War, and Asians, especially Chinese, after Reconstruction. Most importantly, neither the U.S. Congress nor the Supreme Court used the constitutional tools at hand, especially the Fourteenth and Fifteenth Amendments (1870), to protect racial minorities from discriminatory state action.

See also **African Americans,** *subentry on* **Free Blacks before the Civil War; Emancipation; Miscegenation; Reconstruction; Segregation,** *subentry on* **Segregation and Civil Rights; Slavery,** *subentry on* **Law of Slavery.**

Bibliography
Anderson, Eric, and Alfred A. Moss Jr., eds. *The Facts of Reconstruction: Essays in Honor of John Hope Franklin.* Baton Rouge: Louisiana State University Press, 1991.

Berlin, Ira. *Slaves without Masters: The Free Negro in the Antebellum South.* New York: New Press, 1992.

Litwack, Leon F. *North of Slavery: The Negro in the Free States, 1790–1860*. Chicago: University of Chicago Press, 1961.
Lofgren, Charles A. *The Plessy Case: A Legal-Historical Interpretation*. New York: Oxford University Press, 1987.

PAUL FINKELMAN

RADICALISM   Radicalism, both as a threat to the stability of governing groups and as a promise of expanded democracy, took on many forms in the course of national development. Both religious and secular utopian colonies were founded during the first half of the nineteenth century. Assorted groups of German pietists (many of them settling in Pennsylvania) and English Shakers were followed by artisans and intellectuals establishing such colonies as Brook Farm (in Massachusetts), Oneida (in New York), and New Harmony (in Indiana). Their peaceful quest for a cooperative order failed economically, although spiritually based colonies continued for generations, and the memory of utopian feminist Frances ("Fanny") Wright remained as dear to radicals as it was notorious to social conservatives.

The descendants of such efforts, political movements of socialists and anarchists sought to rally working people against the ascendant industrial capitalism. At the margins of organized movements but next to the infamous "color line," radical elements of African American, Asian American, Mexican American, and American Indian communities pressed their cases to advance their causes and often to recover stolen resources.

An unprecedented immigration of working-class German Americans from the late 1860s through the early 1870s gave shape and purpose to the radical movement. The International Workingmen's Association (IWA), guided by devotees of the German political philosopher Karl Marx, who espoused socialism, established branches in a scattering of cities, where they created unions, socialist newspapers, and educational-recreational facilities that served as sustaining centers of ethnic sensibilities.

The volatility of post–Civil War society and the influence of the radicals encouraged the affiliation of the National Labor Union with the IWA, the sudden rise of local labor federations, the Manhattan parade for the martyrs of the Paris Commune of 1871—the first time citizens had taken government directly into their own hands. The Tompkins Square police riot in New York City, two years later, quashed a mass movement of the unemployed guided by the Irish American socialist J. P. McDonnell. Still more dramatic from another standpoint, Victoria Woodhull, a suffragette, radical newspaper publisher, and free love advocate, emerged as an outstanding American socialist personality. Although she and her followers were scorned and expelled by the Marxists, Woodhull's prominence demonstrated that movements in the United States were likely to take even the organized radicals by surprise.

In 1877 socialists were unprepared for a violent railroad workers strike. Inspired by the public hatred of railroad barons and ignited by a walkout in West Virginia against deteriorating wages, the strike quickly spread to urban and industrial zones across the nation. Socialists provided guidance or at least propaganda and speakers for mass rallies, but they took no part in the widespread looting of railroad cars and rioting against brutal police responses. Socialists formed the core of the executive leadership for the general strike that held St. Louis in thrall for nearly a week. Within a year a dozen or so socialists won elected offices, but as was frequently the case, political insurgency was undercut by Democratic patronage, ethnocultural divisions, internal disorganization, and ballot stuffing.

Revolutionary Socialism

Disappointment led many radicals, especially in Chicago, to more violent actions. Quasi-military societies sprang up to defend workers against the law of the bayonet. Chicago socialists transferred their enthusiasm, their social and cultural institutions, and their influence with unionists to anarchism, known then as "revolutionary socialism." In scattered other sites, mainly the Rocky Mountain region and San Francisco, like-minded labor activists sought to form a "Black International" of anarchists and to prepare secretly for all-out class warfare if necessary.

Events seemed to point, though contradictorily, in their direction. The Knights of Labor, a new labor federation that urged cooperation between labor and capital, gained momentum after railroad workers successfully struck western lines. Enthusiasm for an eight-hour workday brought in a half million members nationwide by early 1886, including the largest number of African Americans in any labor movement until the 1930s. In the Southwest, Mexican American activists known as *las Gorras Blancas* affiliated with the Knights while taking direct action to end land enclosures and to reclaim land taken by Anglo settlers. Asian American laborers staged isolated protests at that time, and the Ghost Dance movement among Indians began in 1889 and ended in the massacre at Wounded Knee, South Dakota. The American Federation of Labor (AFL), established in the early 1880s by Samuel Gompers and others, rigidly excluded Asian Americans, and several of its key af-

The Five Anarchists.

Nineteenth-Century "Red Scare." The Haymarket anarchists were accused of instigating the May Day, 1886, riot in Chicago and were executed. Photograph, 1887. LIBRARY OF CONGRESS

genteel radicals embraced Edward Bellamy's novel *Looking Backward* (1888), which spurred a brief surge of utopian thought and peaceful plans for cooperative colonies. The severe depression of the 1890s provoked renewed violence but not on the part of radicals. Marches of the unemployed, led in some places by socialists, and insurgent agrarian politics spawned threats of violence against monopolists and machine politicians. In 1892 a strike in Homestead, Pennsylvania, became a pitched battle between displaced craft workers and steelmakers. In 1894 a peaceful strike of railroad workers boycotting the Pullman Company ended with the incarceration of the leader, Eugene V. Debs, and the suppression of the strikers. For almost a generation thereafter socialists generally held the high moral ground with their adamant resistance to violence.

Continuing gunplay, arrests, and sabotage in the battle between western hard-rock miners and private militias reminded radicals that the threat of armed retaliation held employers' worst impulses in check, at least in some extreme circumstances. Near the close of the century socialist propagandists urged soldiers to refuse military orders directed at slaughtering Filipino civilians during the Spanish-American War. One young anarchist made up his mind to go further against the architect of the war. Leon Czolgosz, the son of a prominent Polish American socialist, shot President William McKinley at the Pan American Exposition in Buffalo on 6 September 1901. Rather than bringing down the social system, this act brought about a new round of anti-immigrant hysteria and an unconstitutional roundup of known anarchists.

See also **Class, Social; Communitarian Movements and Groups; Immigration and Immigrants; Labor Movement,** *subentry on* **Unions and Strikes; Reform, Social; Third Parties; Violence.**

Bibliography

Buhle, Mari Jo, Paul Buhle, and Dan Georgakas, eds. *Encyclopedia of the American Left.* 2d ed. New York: Oxford University Press, 1998.

Buhle, Paul. *Marxism in the United States.* 2d ed. London: Verso, 1991.

Buhle, Paul, and Dan Georgakas, ed. *The Immigrant Left in the United States.* Albany: State University of New York, 1996.

Buhle, Paul, and Edmund B. Sullivan. *Images of American Radicalism.* Hanover, Mass.: Christopher Publishing House, 1998.

Foster, Lawrence. *Women, Family, and Utopia: Communal Experiments of the Shakers, the Oneida Community, and the Mormons.* Syracuse, N.Y.: Syracuse University Press, 1991.

Guarneri, Carl J. *The Utopian Alternative: Fourierism in Nine-*

filiated unions barred racial minorities. It enrolled many immigrant skilled workers, including German socialists, and used its strength to crush the rival Knights of Labor. The AFL gained better conditions for white male craft workers only.

Chicago, known by radicals as "Little Paris," experienced disaster on 4 May 1886. Police attacked a peaceful political rally in Haymarket Square, and an unknown assailant threw a bomb that killed eight policemen and sparked wild gunfire. In the "red scare" that followed immediately, radical newspapers, meeting halls, and unions were destroyed, known radical unionists were "blacklisted," and the press waged a campaign of sensational antiradicalism.

Anarchism or revolutionary socialism was effectively wiped out as a social movement, though circles of propagandists remained. Once again labor candidates, this time quietly supported by socialists, ran strong electoral races but faded quickly. As the distance between rich and poor continued to expand,

teenth-Century America. Ithaca, N.Y.: Cornell University Press, 1991.

PAUL BUHLE

RAILROADS

Building an Industry

Forerunners of the modern American railroad appeared in the 1830s, when pioneer companies such as the Baltimore & Ohio Rail Road, Mohawk & Hudson Rail Road, and South Carolina Canal & Rail Road opened for freight and passenger service. These early carriers typically used steam locomotives rather than horses or mules to pull a variety of largely wooden pieces of rolling stock, including boxcars, flatcars, baggage and package cars, and passenger coaches. The trains traveled over either wooden rails with iron-capped tops, known as strap rails, or solid iron rails bolted to stone blocks or spiked to wooden crossties. Early lines usually covered only a short distance, and often only one train travelled back and forth on a particular track. The first trains moved at speeds of ten to twenty-five miles per hour.

As business increased, the industry's physical plant underwent dramatic changes. After the Civil War, substantial iron and then steel "T" rails replaced the original ones, permitting ever-mightier steam locomotives pulling heavier equipment to travel at faster speeds. Engines with additional driving and auxiliary wheels and with larger fireboxes replaced less technologically advanced ones. Metal was used to build larger cars, especially passenger cars. By the outbreak of the Civil War, the newly perfected magnetic telegraph also helped railroad companies to increase speeds and enhance safety. Telegraphers reported the passage of trains to a dispatcher who then sent messages to personnel at trackside about where trains were and when they would arrive at a particular location.

As the century passed, freight and passenger trains moved with greater frequency. Between 1861 and 1890 the tons of freight carried by train skyrocketed from 55,073,000 to 691,344,000. This vastly increased activity went on between ever-expanding terminals, often the locations of maintenance and repair facilities and the places where train crews began and ended their work assignments. By the end of the century hundreds of communities owed their existence to the iron horse: Hornell, New York; Bradford, Ohio; Creston, Iowa; Huron, South Dakota; and Ogden, Utah, were all railroad towns. Terminals commonly were spaced about one hundred miles apart—the distance it would take a freight crew to travel in a normal work day.

Following the early gestation period, railroad leaders employed imaginative business techniques to foster and manage growth. Faced with expanding mileage, greater traffic, and a growing workforce, carriers adopted improved accounting methods, debt-financing schemes, and quasi-military organizational structures. By the 1880s railroad executives understood how to sell money-generating securities effectively and to manage the division or departmental system of operations, using their ubiquitous "book of rules." They also used innovative accounting methods that ended the chaos of individual, undefined criteria for decision making. Accountants could describe and analyze costs according to distinct types of expenditures, thus monitoring internal corporate spending by making the vital distinction between fixed expenses and those that varied with the volume and type of traffic transported. As America's first "big business," the railroads set an example for other industries, including iron, steel, and machine tool production, whose companies emulated these managerial practices.

Railroads also served as a revolutionary force in nineteenth-century America through their use in war. Although they contributed only modestly to victory in the Mexican War, their role in the Civil War was enormous. Armies of both the North and South used the rails to transport supplies, troops, the wounded, and other impedimenta of warfare. Rail lines became prime military targets, and the tide of battles often turned on the ability of military railroad personnel to provide reinforcements and to maintain a dependable flow of ammunition, forage, and rations. The War between the States could appropriately be called the first great "railroad war."

Managing Postwar Growth

The spectacular growth of railroads in the nineteenth century provided jobs for tens of thousands of Americans, whether farm boys or newly arrived immigrants. Early carriers hired personnel from the ranks of local clerks and stagecoach employees, along with skilled artisans and mechanics. Once a workforce was assembled, the railroad's employees were largely or wholly dependent upon the wage system.

Most railroad companies showed a paternalistic, anti-union spirit. Officials often expressed compassion toward workers, even though they generally preached a laissez-faire ideology. Nevertheless, railroad labor unions soon appeared. These organizations, the first of which was the Brotherhood of Locomotive Engineers, formed in 1863, usually rejected militancy,

A Meeting of Giants. The joining of Central Pacific and Union Pacific lines on 10 May 1869. LIBRARY OF CONGRESS

seeking instead to shelter members and their families from economic distress through mutual-aid programs. After the Civil War, however, the various craft unions more willingly took direct action and occasionally bitter strikes erupted. The most violent involved a walkout in 1877 of Baltimore and Ohio Railroad employees over pay and working conditions. The amount of property damage, particularly in Pittsburgh, was considerable. In 1888, locomotive engineers of the Chicago, Burlington & Quincy Railroad "hit the bricks" over low pay. In the ensuing months these men and their supporters caused considerable property damage and greatly disrupted operations before surrendering to the management, a common fate of the era's strikers.

Not all railroaders joined brotherhoods or operating unions. Some, especially craft workers in the South, found it difficult to form labor organizations.

For a few years there existed another alternative—an industrial union, which consisted of both skilled and unskilled workers. During the depression years of the 1890s the American Railway Union (ARU) made an impressive splash. Launched in 1893, the ARU was led by the charismatic Eugene Victor Debs (1855–1926), the general secretary and treasurer of the Brotherhood of Locomotive Firemen and Enginemen. After surviving an initial skirmish with James J. Hill's (1838–1916) Great Northern Railway, the ARU soon became involved in one of the greatest labor confrontations of the century—the Pullman strike (1894). The dispute erupted over treatment by the Pullman Palace Car Company of its workers in the company town of Pullman, Illinois. But the combination of the Chicago-based General Managers' Association and federal troops supplied by Grover Cleveland's (1837–1908) administration led to the walkout's failure, and conspiracy charges were filed against Debs and other ARU leaders. Soon this industrial union dissolved.

As post–Civil War America became more industrialized and urbanized, and commercial or market agriculture replaced subsistence farming, railroads became absolutely vital to the nation's transportation needs and their expansion accelerated. The landscape, especially in the East, became crisscrossed with trackage, aided by massive bridges, cuts, and tunnels. In 1830 the scope of the American rail net totalled a mere twenty-three miles. By 1850 it had reached 9,021 miles; in 1880, 93,262 miles; and a decade later, a staggering 166,703 miles. In 1916, mileage peaked at 254,037. Some overbuilding occurred, especially in the Midwest. But rail transport vastly surpassed anything else, particularly in an age of animal power and primitive roads. Trains were faster, cost effective for many cargoes, and dependable even during most winter weather.

One of the major developments in late-nineteenth-century railroading was system building. Railroad leaders, bankers, and prominent investors combined scores of short lines and small trunk roads under single corporate banners. Some of these lines had been constructed by states such as Illinois and Michigan in the 1830s and 1840s. At that time, private investors, both domestic and foreign, hesitated to finance construction through frontier country, sensing profitable opportunities in more developed locales. But the laissez-faire spirit of mid-century led to the privatization of virtually every publicly owned carrier. Yet early on, and for decades, local units of government, usually counties, provided subsidies, including purchase of stocks and bonds. By the 1890s most large railroads possessed a complex corporate genealogy—the legacy of purchases, leases, and construction.

The Erie is illustrative of the system-building process. The Erie Railway was the successor to the original New York & Erie Rail Road. In 1878 it became the New York, Lake Erie & Western Railroad and seventeen years later the Erie Railroad. During the 1860s, the Erie moved beyond its core New York route between New York City and Buffalo. In its quest to tap the potentially rich traffic of the Old Northwest, the company struggled to control the well-positioned Atlantic & Great Western Railway (A&GW). In 1865 the A&GW, itself an amalgamation of various lines, opened for through traffic between Salamanca, New York, and Dayton, Ohio. Two years later the A&GW fell into bankruptcy, and in 1868 it was leased by its receiver to the Erie. Then in 1869 another receiver took charge of the A&GW and again leased it to the Erie. The A&GW briefly

regained its independence in 1874, but in that same year the property returned to Erie domination through another lease agreement. In 1880 legal action led to a reorganization of the A&GW as the New York, Pennsylvania & Ohio Railroad (NYPANO). But the New York, Lake Erie & Western (Erie) ran NYPANO and in 1895, with reorganization of the Erie, the A&GW finally entered the Erie corporate structure. The Erie built on this acquisition to reach Chicago, already the nation's railroad center, by obtaining the assets of a faltering narrow-gauge road, the Chicago & Atlantic Railway (C&A), and a combination of new construction and trackage rights gave it entry into Chicago.

The fact that a narrow-gauge railroad allowed the Erie to become truly interregional was related to the debate over track width that had not been fully resolved by the 1870s and 1880s. Shortly after the Civil War a cadre of promoters considered standard-gauge lines (four feet eight and one-half inches) to be impractical for certain transportation needs. Instead, they argued for slimmer pikes (usually three feet in width) because they were easier and cheaper to build, maintain, and operate. Between 1871 and 1883 a national building boom produced approximately twelve thousand miles of narrow-gauge lines. But by the 1890s the narrow-gauge phenomenon largely had fizzled. The inherent inability to compete with standard-gauge roads, along with financial and managerial problems, halted construction. By 1900 most of the weaker companies had failed, although their lines were usually widened to become branches of larger carriers. The strongest narrow-gauge roads also converted gauge and joined established roads. A major exception was in the Rocky Mountains, where "slim princes" lasted well into the twentieth century.

The leaders of the nineteenth-century railroads, whether they were constructing conventional roads or not, hardly fit the category of robber barons. The vast majority were builders, not wreckers, and could arguably be called industrial statesmen. There were a few "bad apples," most notably Daniel Drew (1797–1879), John Eldridge (1811–1876), James Fisk (1834–1872), and "Commodore" Cornelius Vanderbilt (1794–1877). But even the Erie's free-booting organizer Jay Gould (1836–1892), "the most hated man in America," rehabilitated and expanded several key rail properties, including the Missouri Pacific and Wabash. Gould understood the importance of regional and interregional system building.

A typical railroad executive of the nineteenth century was Marvin Hughitt (1837–1928), the architect of the sprawling Chicago & North Western Railway. Hughitt, who joined the company in 1872 and rose to become its head in 1887, quickly sensed that the prosperity of this Chicago-based carrier depended on the overall economic health of its service area. Efficient and modern facilities would allow the company to flourish, and at the same time would produce lower rates and a safer environment.

Surviving Government and Popular Scrutiny

Benevolent and consumer-sensitive railroad officials such as Hughitt could not stem the nearly universal public desire to regulate America's first big business. Although some government oversight appeared prior to the Civil War, largely in New England, the first major movement for regulation erupted in the early 1870s. The Grangers (a coalition of farmers, merchants, and commercial groups), concentrated in the states of the upper Mississippi River valley, demanded rate relief, particularly an end to long-and-short-haul discrimination. In 1874, Iowa passed regulatory measures and launched a state railroad commission to ensure compliance. Similar measures were passed by Minnesota, Wisconsin, and Illinois. In 1877 the U.S. Supreme Court upheld the Granger

laws in *Munn v. Illinois*, but nine years later reversed itself in the case of *Wabash, Saint Louis, and Pacific Railroad Company v. Illinois*. Concern about rate-making abuses (antipooling sentiment that led to higher, non-competitive tariffs) prompted Congress in 1887 to pass the Interstate Commerce Act, creating the Interstate Commerce Commission, a federal agency that for decades set the tone for the interstate supervision of railroad corporations.

Despite these concerns, Americans found the iron horse exciting—it had a tenacious hold on the public imagination. The rapid construction of a transcontinental railroad across nearly two thousand miles of largely unsettled territory was completed in 1869; the golden spike ceremony at Promontory, Utah Territory, on 10 May 1869, thrilled the populace. Most citizens had an intimate knowledge of the railroad corridors in their home localities. The depot became a community focal point. It was the avenue through which people, freight, and mail flowed. Travelers planned itineraries, purchased tickets, and awaited their trains. Onlookers greeted and bid farewell to passengers or watched who was coming and going.

The Erie War. Competition over ownership of the Erie Railway between Cornelius Vanderbilt *(left)* and James Fisk *(right)* led to bitter machinations on the Stock Exchange. Lithograph by Currier & Ives, 1870. LIBRARY OF CONGRESS

Newspaper editors reported depot happenings and other rail-related events in popular railroad columns.

These strategically placed depots sported a rich variety of architectural styles, ranging from small, wooden, and standardized structures to massive brick and highly individualized monuments to the railway age. Although railroad officials initially utilized available buildings, they soon developed specialized ones. By the 1870s in nonurban locations the combination depot became popular, with a central office, a freight-express-baggage section, and a public waiting room.

Not everyone in nineteenth-century America welcomed the railroad. Those associated with competing forms of transportation, including steamboat captains and stagecoach drivers, felt the sting of competition. And some Americans did not want their isolation shattered. When in the 1870s the Norfolk & Western Railway arrived in the Tug Fork region of Kentucky and West Virginia, some residents found their previously placid lives disrupted, in part because rail service brought the rapid development of coal and timber resources. Thousands of Indians, especially those who inhabited the Great Plains, encountered a Euro-American civilization propelled by flanged wheels and soon found themselves on reservations, at times brought there by the iron horse itself.

Regardless of public attitudes, railroads became the dominant form of transportation and a major business enterprise. By 1900 five major systems, offering more dependable and cheaper service than had been known previously, served the nation. These were the Vanderbilt roads, the New York Central and Chicago & North Western; the Morgan properties, including the Erie, New Haven, and Southern railroads; the Pennsylvania system (the "Standard Railroad of the World"); the Harriman lines, principally the Union Pacific and Southern Pacific; and the Hill lines, consisting of the Great Northern, Northern Pacific, and Chicago, Burlington & Quincy. Railroad stocks made up the lion's share of securities traded on the New York Stock Exchange. When a major carrier faltered, the impact could be severe. The 1873 failure of the Northern Pacific triggered a national depression, just as the bankruptcy of the Philadelphia & Reading twenty years later contributed to the panic of 1893.

As Americans anticipated the twentieth century, they realized they were already living in the railway age. The public expected that railroads would continue to provide enhanced service. This meant more powerful steam and electric locomotives, and more luxurious and safer rolling stock that would speed along an increasingly dense network of steel rails.

See also **Corporations and Big Business; Interstate Commerce; Labor Movement,** *subentry on* **Unions and Strikes; Transportation,** *subentry on* **Railroads; Travel, Technology of.**

Bibliography

Chandler, Alfred D., Jr. *The Visible Hand: The Managerial Revolution in American Business.* Cambridge, Mass.: Belknap Press of Harvard University Press, 1977.

Cochran, Thomas C. *Railroad Leaders, 1845–1890: The Business Mind in Action.* 1953. Reprint, New York: Russell and Russell, 1966.

Fogel, Robert W. *Railroads and American Economic Growth: Essays in Econometric History.* Baltimore: Johns Hopkins University Press, 1964.

Gates, Paul W. *The Illinois Central Railroad and Its Colonization Work.* 1934. Reprint, New York: Johnson Reprint Corporation, 1968.

Goodrich, Carter. *Government Promotion of American Canals and Railroads, 1800–1890.* 1960. Reprint, Westport, Conn.: Greenwood, 1974.

Grodinsky, Julius. *Transcontinental Railway Strategy, 1869–1893: A Study of Businessmen.* Philadelphia: University of Pennsylvania Press, 1962.

Miller, George H. *Railroads and the Granger Laws.* Madison: University of Wisconsin Press, 1971.

Riegel, Robert Edgar. *The Story of the Western Railroads.* New York: Macmillan, 1926.

Stover, John F. *American Railroads.* 2d ed. Chicago: University of Chicago Press, 1997.

———. *Iron Road to the West: American Railroads in the 1850s.* New York: Columbia University Press, 1978.

Winther, Oscar O. *The Transportation Frontier: Trans-Mississippi West, 1865–1890.* New York: Holt, Rinehart, and Winston, 1964.

H. ROGER GRANT

RANCHING AND LIVESTOCK RAISING

Families with small herds of cattle, hogs, or sheep were the livestock raisers of the early nineteenth century. They butchered these animals for their own use or sold them in nearby towns. As states built a network of roads, canals, and railroads, some producers increased the size of their herds and shipped or drove their live animals greater distances to wholesale butchers near major cities.

As Americans began settling the Midwest after 1800, the livestock and meatpacking industries moved with them. In the early nineteenth century the Ohio River valley became the center of cattle and hog production, using corn as the primary feed. Through the 1820s farmers sold their excess cows and sheep, totaling a few thousand each year, to be driven east to urban centers for slaughter. The first commercial meatpacking plant opened in Cincinnati in

1818. Over the next decade that city was the leader in livestock sales and meatpacking in the country.

In the antebellum period packers and producers preferred pork over beef. Hogs were more easily maintained by farmers, who let swine run loose in the wild, then rounded them up and fattened them for six months on cheap midwestern corn. Packers butchered and packed pickled pork along with some beef for shipment to New Orleans, where they were exported to the East and the rest of the world. Packed meat could only be shipped in winter months because without refrigeration the meat spoiled. Local butchers obtained fresh meat by importing live cattle or hogs for slaughter.

The Civil War sharply altered livestock raising in the United States. Wartime needs, the devastation of farms and ranches in the South and East, the industrialization of the United States, and sharply increased immigration during and after the war raised the demand for meat. Chicago, St. Louis, and Kansas City were the new centers for meatpacking as the industry shifted westward to where cattle were becoming plentiful. Western cattlemen drove their cattle to railheads along the eastern edges of the Great Plains, where Abilene, Kansas, was one of the first cow towns at the end of the trails (see sidebar, "The Cattle Drive Era"). Cattle fattened by several months on range grass brought $40 to $50 profit per animal, making cattle drives very lucrative and worth the risks involved.

These prices, however, would not have been possible without the introduction of the refrigerated railroad car in 1867. Meatpackers could now ship partially or completely butchered carcasses from slaughterhouses in the central United States with little concern about meat spoilage. They avoided shipping the 60 percent of a steer considered either waste or inedible by-product and earned $60 to $70 more profit per steer. By the 1880s several cow towns had their own meatpacking plants.

The expansion of livestock raising during the cattle drive era came to a quick end in the mid-1880s as producers realized the industry had overexpanded. New settlers fenced off land on the formerly open range and fought with cattlemen over ownership and grazing rights. In addition, railroads extended their lines into the central cattle production regions of Texas, Wyoming, and Montana. Cattlemen responded in the 1880s and 1890s by establishing large ranches like the King Ranch, the XIT, and the Matador Land and Cattle Company in Texas and the Swan Land and Cattle Company of Wyoming. Many, like the Matador and the Swan, were ventures owned by easterners or European investors.

The large, corporate ranches emphasized scientific

The Cattle Drive Era

In the 1860s a longhorn steer sold in Texas for only $4 but brought $40 to $60 in major northern markets such as Chicago and Kansas City. In 1867 an Illinois merchant, Joseph McCoy, convinced railroad companies, town promoters, and Texas cattlemen that a new railhead should be built in central Kansas. This "cow town," Abilene, and others like it became the loading stations for Texas beef cattle destined for Midwest packing plants. Thus began the quarter-century era of the great cattle drives.

Cowboys drove over 3.5 million cattle north in herds of between fifteen hundred and five thousand animals from 1865 to 1880. The drives followed one of several trails (see map) to cow towns built along the railroads across Kansas and Nebraska. The Shawnee Trail, first opened in the 1840s but used only periodically before the Civil War, ran from South Texas to Baxter Springs, Kansas, and Sedalia, Missouri. In the 1850s and 1860s the state of Missouri and communities in Kansas posted quarantines against all Texas cattle because they carried the "Texas fever," which infected and killed local livestock.

After the Civil War the Chisholm Trail, running north from San Antonio to Abilene, Kansas, became the main cattle highway. Branches of the Chisholm and the Western Trail went to other new cow towns, including Wichita, Ellsworth, and Dodge City, Kansas. A western route, the Goodnight-Loving Trail, crossed out of West Texas through central New Mexico Territory to Denver and Cheyenne.

The cow towns became boomtowns, where cattle fresh from the trail were bought, sold, and shipped to Kansas City or Chicago and tired, overworked cowboys took advantage of the amenities. Cowboys used their pay, received when the cattle were sold, to buy new clothes or horse equipment, get a bath and a shave, and cut loose on cheap whiskey, gambling, and prostitutes. Their revelry earned cowboys a particularly bad reputation among the local citizenry, although usually they caused more mischief than actual harm. Cow towns also were centers of trade for buffalo hunters and railroad construction crews.

By the late 1880s the expansion of railroads farther into Texas, the introduction of barbed-wire fencing, and an overextended cattle industry in the midst of drought and depression brought the cattle drive era to a swift end. Many of the cow towns went into decline, and some disappeared altogether except for their "boot hill" graveyards.

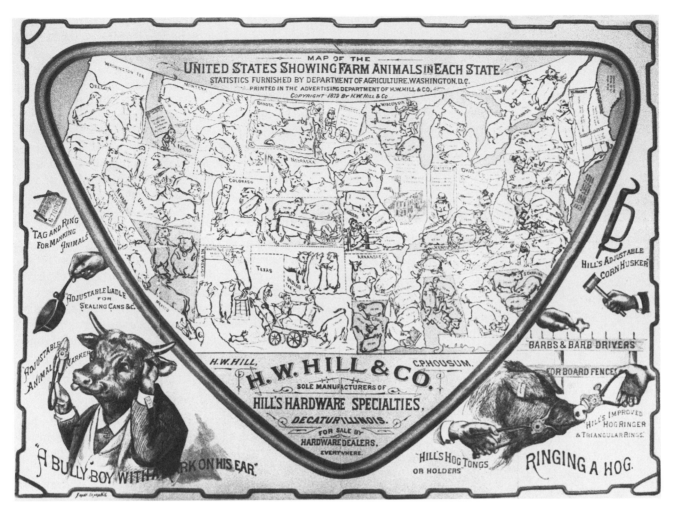

The Rise of Range Cattle. The range cattle industry, which began in California and Texas, spread during the late nineteenth century. Map, H. W. Hill Company, 1878. LIBRARY OF CONGRESS

range-management practices and careful breeding programs to restore purebred livestock, producing higher quality and more consistent beef. Many ranchers chose the hardy Hereford breed to improve their stock. To ensure sufficient water and grass for their herds, they had to be wary of overstocking their ranges, particularly in dry areas or during drought years. These large ranches and the corn feedlots in the Midwest produced most of the nation's cattle until the early twentieth century.

Sheep and Goats

Sheep and goats constituted a small portion of U.S. livestock production in the nineteenth century. Sheep, valuable as a source of wool and meat, generated more profit than cattle. Goats provided mohair, milk, and meat. In the early part of the century sheep and goats were largely concentrated in Ohio,

but by mid-century producers were raising and driving sheep and goats across the West, particularly in California, Montana, and the Southwest. Small sheep farms and ranches, similar to the cattle ranches of the late nineteenth century, were common. Sheep drives crossed the West to other ranges, to avoid overgrazing, and to feedlots and slaughterhouses in Kansas and the Midwest.

See also **Agriculture; Boomtowns; Cowboys and Cowgirls; Meatpacking; Transportation,** *subentry on* **Railroads; West, The.**

Bibliography

Dale, Edward Everett. *The Range Cattle Industry: Ranching on the Great Plains from 1865 to 1925.* Norman: University of Oklahoma Press, 1960.

Jordan, Terry G. *North American Cattle-Ranching Frontiers: Origins, Diffusion, and Differentiation.* Albuquerque: University of New Mexico Press, 1993.

Skaggs, Jimmy M. *Prime Cut: Livestock Raising and Meat-packing in the United States, 1607–1983.* College Station: Texas A&M University Press, 1986.

Wentworth, Edward Norris. *America's Sheep Trails: History, Personalities.* Ames: Iowa State College Press, 1948.

CAMERON L. SAFFELL

READING.   See **Literacy and Reading Habits.**

REALISM AND NATURALISM   The Chicago World's Fair of 1893 provided the setting for the convergence of two literary events that contributed to the dominance of naturalism and realism in fin-de-siècle American literary culture. As a consequence of the momentous transformations that took place within the temporal borderlands represented within its exhibits, the Chicago World's Fair of 1893 has been described as an encounter with change itself. It was there that the historian Frederick Jackson Turner first delivered the famous lecture "The Significance of the Frontier in American History," which explained the epochal transition from the original historical dynamic, that of eastern settlers encountering the ever-receding western frontier, to an unspecified new dynamic that would take hold in a now-crowded and mature society. In "The Dynamo and the Virgin," writer Henry Adams recounted his experience of having been brought face-to-face at the fair with industrial forces that he believed had utterly changed both historical reality as well as the methods needed to represent and analyze it.

A Convergence of Concepts

Turner's frontier thesis depended on the acceptance of particular themes—the errand into the wilderness, the westering of civilization—and mythological places—the Virgin Land, the Frontier. These concepts were the product of the romantic imagination that, in "The Dynamo and the Virgin" Adams repudiated as inadequate to an understanding of the dynamisms he had observed at the Chicago Fair. The international literary movements called realism and naturalism drew on this historical conjuncture—where Turner's romantic account of the end of the American frontier intersected with Henry Adams's discovery of the limits of the romantic imagination—for their cultural authority.

The fair's organizers had deployed these emergent literary formations, realism and naturalism, to produce the common sense that rendered comprehensible the disparate fields of endeavor on display. The Chicago World's Fair was a vast cultural bazaar wherein the expositions of historians like Turner took their place alongside the displays of anthropologists, scientists, geographers, imperial adventurers, and industrial capitalists. Realism and naturalism supplied the reflective media in which these displays were cognitively reproduced, classified, distributed and thereafter regulated as more or less agreed-upon worldly knowledges. These literary discourses jointly proposed that the fair's disparate exhibits all belonged to a collectively shared epistemological enterprise.

Realism and naturalism drew on mimetic and expressive conventions that extended across the entire history of the novel. But American literary historians have located the emergence of these new literary movements in the period after the Civil War, when a new generation of writers, including Mark Twain, Stephen Crane, and Frank Norris, brought a spirit of skepticism to the narrative form that up to that time had been dominated by romance. These novelists turned away from idealized representations of nature and the wilderness to face the hard facts of the new urban-industrial society.

New Structures and Genres

Conflicting accounts of the place of realism and naturalism in American literary history arise from different evaluations of their relation to the genre of literary romanticism. But no matter whether their writings are understood as outgrowths of romanticism or as alternatives to it, realist and naturalist writers reshaped the forms of literary discourse as well as the subjectivities that discourse effected. The shift from romanticism to realism and naturalism resulted in the promotion of the novel and the short story at the expense of the literary forms—the poem, the exploratory essay, and the autobiography—that the American romantics considered central to the literary imagination. The transition also involved a democratization of the subject, plot, and mode of narration. William Dean Howells provided this shift in literary sensibility with a kind of manifesto when he declared in the essay "Criticism and Fiction" (1891) that "I do not care to judge any work of the imagination without first applying this test to it. We must ask before anything else is it true—true to the motives, the impulses, the principles that shape the life of actual men and women."

As structures of fiction with demythologizing purposes, realism and naturalism became media for analysis and criticism of the social order. Realists and naturalists refused to idealize the world as had the American romantics. Both new genres took the commonplace seriously but without considering it a source of transcendental value. After removing literary discourse from the ambit of symbolic truth, realist and naturalist writers aspired to resituate it within the textures of a shared world. Realism and naturalism emerged as interdependent semantic practices, which played a part in the emergence of a broad new structure of feeling.

William Dean Howells, Mark Twain, Kate Chopin, Charles Chesnutt, Stephen Crane, Frank Norris, and Jack London freely borrowed from documentary history and urban sociology, from the industrial logic and technology of scientific engineering, as well as from cultural anthropology and the *faits divers* of the daily newspaper, to endow their literary constructions with the authority of literal reality. Seven years after the closing of the Chicago Fair, Theodore Dreiser published *Sister Carrie* (1900), a novel that reconnected this immense spectacle with the dynamics of everyday life.

The changing fortunes of literary realism and naturalism derived from pervasive social transformations. Industrialization converted what had once been rural and wilderness into functions of the dominant commercial system. These literary formations subsequently competed with science, economics, and history for the authority to analyze and make pronouncements about the decisive social issues of the day. They produced narrative frameworks supple enough to subsume the sometimes antagonistic interests of regionalism, racial uplift ideology, social Darwinism, women's causes, nationalism, and magazine culture.

In setting representations before the public that exposed the inhumanity of the factory and the prison systems, the realistic novels of Rebecca Harding Davis, Jack London, and Stephen Crane served as secularized sermons. They portrayed the ways in which individuals constructed, explored, responded to, fulfilled, or frustrated their social aspirations. In their efforts to transcribe the social evils besetting the everyday lives of actual men and women, these novelists afforded characters like Frank Norris's *McTeague* (1899) and Stephen Crane's *Maggie: A Girl of the Streets* (1893), who either did not or could not read literature, a literary franchise. Despite the numerous similarities in the historical conditions of their emergence and in their modes of narrative representation, however, realists and naturalists also disagreed in ways that recalled Turner's and Adams's different attitudes toward volatile social change.

Whereas the realists William Dean Howells and Henry James resembled Turner in their residual allegiance to the romantic imagination, the naturalists Frank Norris and Theodore Dreiser depicted characters moved by wholly impersonal forces on the order of Adams's laws of thermodynamics. Unlike the literary realists who were guided by the injunction that the writer should simply "portray things as they are," without artifice, naturalist writers openly acknowledged the part that literary conventions played in producing the illusion of reality. In place of claiming to free them from romantic dependencies, as had Howells in particular, the naturalists Jack London and Stephen Crane submitted their protagonists to a new complex of confinements and determinations posed by market and biological forces as well as by the mechanisms of a disciplinary society.

While American realists continued to respect the canons of bourgeois aesthetic ideology, the literary naturalists subverted the "universal" standards—disinterest, impartiality, purposiveness without a purpose—of aesthetic judgment by revealing them as socially constructed norms. Norris and London subordinated the aesthetic sphere to the laws of the market, and they recast that sphere's "subject without properties" into a subject that had to take into account the logics of economic scarcity and social injustice. Naturalists represented art's appeals to a transcendental standpoint and its enforcement of a universal standard of taste as having turned the aesthetic order against the experience and interests of the lower classes. Art's power as the legislator of taste—its ability to regulate the community that appreciated or comprehended the artwork—was as a consequence understood to be open to renegotiation.

Apropos of the differences between the two genres, scholar Leo Bersani has argued that the literary realists' overvaluation of the coherence of their plots and of the "truth" of their representation of social arrangements derived in part from their fear of the excessive desires released within commercial capitalism. But literary naturalists have grappled with the excessive and contradictory desires that the realists disavowed. The resolutely contradictory attitudes Norris and Dreiser adopted in their novels were designed to represent social conflicts, but neither believed himself obligated to resolve them. The naturalists' sprawling narratives were as a consequence reducible neither to the dimensions of a unified narrative plot nor to the gratifications of a coherent identity. In place of any confirmation of the order of things, the literary naturalists critically interrogated the rationalizing modes of thought through which their readers experienced the world.

See also **Civilization; Industrialization and the Market; Literature,** *subentries on* **Fiction, The Essay, Poetry; World's Fairs.**

Bibliography
Bersani, Leo. "Realism and the Fear of Desire." In *A Future for Astyanax*. New York: Columbia University Press, 1984.
Brodhead, Richard. *Cultures of Letters: Scenes of Reading and Writing in Nineteenth-Century America*. Chicago: University of Chicago, 1993.

Howard, June. *Form and History in American Literary Naturalism.* Chapel Hill: University of North Carolina Press, 1985.

Kaplan, Amy. *The Social Construction of American Realism.* Chicago: University of Chicago Press, 1988.

Levine, Lawrence. *Highbrow/Lowbrow: The Emergence of Cultural Hierarchy in America.* Cambridge, Mass.: Harvard University Press, 1988.

Michaels, Walter Benn. *The Gold Standard and the Logic of Naturalism.* Berkeley: University of California Press, 1987.

Mitchell, Lee Clark. *Determined Fictions: American Literary Naturalism.* New York: Columbia University Press, 1989.

Pizer, Donald. *Realism and Naturalism in Nineteenth-Century American Literature.* Carbondale: University of Southern Illinois Press, 1966.

Seltzer, Mark. *Bodies and Machines.* New York: Routledge, 1992.

Sundquist, Eric, ed. *American Realism: New Essays.* Baltimore: Johns Hopkins University Press, 1982.

Wilson, Christopher. *The Labor of Words: Literary Professionalism in the Progressive Era.* Athens: University of Georgia Press, 1985.

DONALD E. PEASE

RECESSIONS.   See **Panics and Depressions.**

RECONSTRUCTION

[This entry includes four subentries:
The Politics of Reconstruction and regional subentries on the South, North, and West.]

THE POLITICS OF RECONSTRUCTION

Reconstruction posed a profound challenge to the political system of the United States. Americans had to determine how to restore the Confederate States to normal relations in the Union, how far to go to make certain that loyal elements controlled the restored states while maintaining a democratic system, and how to define and protect the rights of former slaves. In the process they had to decide whether and how to expand the power of the federal government to protect Americans' rights. All this had to occur through the democratic process.

The test pushed the American political system to its limits. It led to the impeachment of a president, widespread violence in the former Confederate states, and a contested presidential election that raised the specter of violence for the whole country.

The Civil War and the Political Parties

The Civil War disrupted alliances among politicians. Many former Democrats had joined Republicans in a new Union Party called by various names, including Union Party, National Union Party, and Union Republican Party, at different times and in different states. Among these former Democrats was the former Tennessee governor and U.S. senator Andrew Johnson, who was elected Abraham Lincoln's vice president on the Union Party ticket. However, most Democratic politicians remained loyal to their political organization and criticized Union Party policies. Although these former Democrats disagreed over whether to keep fighting or to restore the Union through negotiations, they all opposed making emancipation a war aim and recognizing African Americans as citizens. At the grassroots, the Union Party appealed mainly to Republicans, the party of moral reform, especially among New Englanders, western settlers of New England origin, evangelical Protestants, and Scots-Irish immigrants. Democrats were strong in regions of the Old Northwest and West settled by southerners, who disliked the New England triumphalism that characterized antislavery Republicanism, and in cities with heavy concentrations of German, Irish, and French Catholics, who were attracted by the Democrats' tolerance of cultural and religious differences. For mediating between the party leaders and the rank and file, party activists were rewarded with "patronage," appointments to positions in the government civil service. Controlling the federal government, Republicans strengthened their party organization with federal patronage.

The Politics of Wartime Reconstruction

Reconstruction of the Union began almost as soon as the Civil War itself, as western Virginia remained loyal and Union forces occupied the northern tip of Virginia, the Sea Islands off the coast of South Carolina and Georgia, and New Orleans. The first question was the status of the states that were trying to secede. Democrats denied that secession was legal, arguing that the states remained part of the Union, entitled to all their privileges whenever their people resumed their allegiance. Democrats expected returning southerners to support their party because of its proslavery stance and its call for the immediate restoration of all states' rights.

Union Party leaders agreed that secession was a nullity, but they argued that the southern states were no longer in normal relations with the Union. Steps would have to be taken to reestablish such relations. However, they divided over how to proceed. The pragmatic President Lincoln wanted a quick restoration of southern states, hoping to provide rallying points for disaffected Confederates. Appointing provisional governors to administer occupied southern territory, in December 1863, to speed the Reconstruction process, he issued the Amnesty Proclamation, offering amnesty to all who took oaths of future loyalty and inviting them to reconstruct state governments based on freedom. Lincoln expected those who cooperated in this process to ally with the Union Party against those who remained loyal to the rebellion or who opposed the abolition of slavery. He hoped that his policy would give the Union Party a solid base in the South.

However, Lincoln's program promised too quick and unstable a restoration for most Union Party leaders in Congress. They wanted to delay Reconstruction until after the war ended and to abolish slavery through national legislation and a constitutional amendment. They feared that the leaders of Lincoln's restoration movement were too conservative and ultimately would ally with Democrats to preserve vestiges of slavery. The disagreement came to a head when in 1864 Congress passed the Wade-Davis Reconstruction Bill, which effectively delayed Reconstruction and required returning southern states to abolish slavery. Lincoln refused to sign it after Congress adjourned, killing it with a pocket veto.

Behind this disagreement lay the second key issue of Reconstruction—the place of African Americans in American society. As antislavery feeling grew in the North, Democrats appealed to racism to counteract it. They opposed any national measure to abolish slavery. Only a handful supported the Thirteenth Amendment, sent to the states for ratification in January 1865, and only a scattering of Democrats voted to ratify it in the state legislatures. As it became clear that slavery would be abolished, Democrats opposed granting African Americans more than the most basic rights of free people. Adhering to the position the Supreme Court had taken in *Dred Scott v. Sandford* (1857), Democrats insisted the United States was a white man's country. African Americans were entitled to none of the rights of national citizenship, and returning southern states could make any provision they wished for governing them.

Most Unionists, especially former Republicans, vigorously disagreed. Many favored making African Americans voters. This radical Unionist policy was consistent with the American principle of equal rights for all men, and it seemed attractive to Republicans' core New England and evangelical Protestant voters. In the South black voters could be expected to support truly loyal southern Unionists, giving the party a firmer base than that promised by Lincoln's conservative Reconstruction policy. But more conservative Unionists, including President Lincoln, feared that most white Americans, even in the North, would repudiate so radical a change. Lincoln hoped that white southern Unionists would provide reasonable protections for black southerners' basic rights, but he

Thaddeus Stevens (1792–1868). The House cochairman of a joint congressional committee on Reconstruction in 1865, Stevens of Pennsylvania pushed the Civil Rights Bill and the Freedman's Bureau Bill through Congress, overcoming President Andrew Johnson's veto. LIBRARY OF CONGRESS

and his allies in the party would not risk everything in a politically hopeless quest for racial justice.

Thus, when the war ended and Lincoln was assassinated in April 1865, the Union Party had not yet established a Reconstruction policy. Congress was adjourned, and the new president, Andrew Johnson, decided not to call a special session, fearing a disruptive fight over the issue. Instead he attempted to establish a policy through executive action, building upon the programs articulated both by Lincoln and Congress.

Radical Reconstruction

President Johnson combined the Reconstruction policies of Lincoln and Congress. He appointed provisional governors to supervise the reestablishment of loyal state governments, requiring southern states to ratify the Thirteenth Amendment and abolish slavery in their own constitutions. Intimately familiar with southern politics, he hoped to create a southern Unionist Party based on a reaction against secessionist leaders, support for emancipation among ordinary white southerners resentful of the old slave-owning aristocracy, and willingness to cooperate in Reconstruction. Having earlier faced strong resistance to his efforts to restore loyal government as provisional governor of Tennessee, Johnson was amazed and delighted to find ex-Confederates everywhere flocking to take the amnesty oath, cooperating in the restoration of state governments, and with only slight hesitation accepting the terms he had promulgated. By the time Congress met, most of the southern state governments had been reorganized under the control of leaders who clearly considered themselves Johnson's political allies.

Johnson's policy divided Unionists. It was clear that he was little concerned with securing the rights of the newly freed slaves. Unionists feared that the new governments he had fostered were coming under the control of ex-Confederates who would minimize changes in the South. The most radical wanted to treat the conquered southern states as territories subject to long-term federal supervision, and all Unionists wanted evidence that former Confederates fully accepted the results of the war. Radicals and many moderate Unionists favored giving black southerners the right to vote so they could defend their own interests under restored state governments.

Unionists' fears were confirmed as southerners elected former Confederates to political office and passed black codes that in many states severely limited African Americans' civil rights. But while sharing the concerns of their radical colleagues, many Unionists warned against alienating a president elected on their own ticket. Dividing the party could only lead to Democratic victory and the loss of much they had fought for.

As Unionists quarreled, Democrats hoped for a revival of their party's fortunes. They endorsed Johnson's policy, courted southern leaders, and invited former Democrats in the Union Party, including Johnson, to rejoin their old allies. In turn Unionists more and more turned to calling themselves Union Republicans or just Republicans. Johnson, ambitious to be elected president in his own right in 1868, flirted with the Democrats but also worked with ex-Whigs like Secretary of State William H. Seward to build up the conservative wing of the Union Party. Ideally he hoped to lead a broad, centrist Union Party against radical Republicans on the left and proslavery Democrats on the right. He was buoyed when voters in several northern states rejected proposals to enfranchise African Americans there. The results reaffirmed conservative Unionists' conviction that the voters would not support efforts to secure civil and political equality for African Americans.

Desperate to avoid a break with Johnson, Union Republican leaders in Congress framed a moderate Reconstruction program. They postponed seating congressmen from the southern states and created a Joint Committee on Reconstruction to study the issue. Moving cautiously, in April 1866 Congress overwhelmingly passed a Civil Rights Act that overturned the Supreme Court's *Dred Scott* decision by declaring that all persons born in the United States, except untaxed Native Americans, were citizens. To counteract the black codes, the bill specified that all citizens would have the same basic civil rights and be subject to the same criminal laws and procedures. But Johnson, unhappy at the delay, became progressively more critical of the Republicans, convinced that radicals had gained control of Congress. Although many of his closest Unionist allies in Congress had voted for the Civil Rights Act, Johnson vetoed it. The bill favored blacks over whites, he complained, and it invaded the rights of the states to define citizenship and govern their own people.

Johnson's course alienated nearly all Unionists, and they passed the Civil Rights Act over his veto. Johnson angrily completed the break in June by opposing ratification of the Fourteenth Amendment, which wrote the principles of the Civil Rights Act into the Constitution. Any southern state that ratified the amendment would be restored to normal relations in the Union, congressional leaders promised.

In the congressional elections of 1866, Unionists generally called themselves Republicans, and many former Democrats accepted that party allegiance. Johnson's cabinet broke apart, with three members resigning rather than break with the Republican Party. Another, Secretary of War Edwin M. Stanton, remained to insulate the army from the fight, even though he sympathized more with the congressional leaders than with Johnson.

Democrats urged Johnson to resume his Democratic allegiance, oust Republicans from federal offices, and replace them with Democrats, but he rejected their pleas. Instead, he tried to foster an alliance between Democrats and conservative Unionists. He sponsored a National Union Party convention, at which former Confederates and Unionists entered the hall arm-in-arm in a symbolic show of reconciliation. Democrats backed the movement, denouncing Republicans for trampling on states' rights and supporting racial equality. Johnson took the unusual step of campaigning in the North, blasting away at Republicans for delaying restoration. The result was an overwhelming Republican victory in the northern states.

With their victory, Republicans nervously awaited southern action on the Fourteenth Amendment, but Johnson intervened to nip any budding southern support for compromise. If the southern states simply refused to ratify, what many called "masterly inactivity" would either force Republicans to take unpopular, radical steps or look ineffectual. In two years impatient northern voters would throw them out and, Johnson expected, elect him president.

Republicans were unwilling to take the gamble. Fearing that inaction would lead to disaster, they passed new Reconstruction laws. The Reconstruction Acts of 1867 declared the existing southern state governments provisional and put them under the control of military commanders. Although leading radicals hoped the measures would be a stepping-stone to establishing territorial governments, most Republicans were anxious to restore the secessionist states to the Union, and they added provisions clearly setting the terms for restoration. To provide a political base for southerners who cooperated, a bill enfranchised African Americans. Southern states would be restored to normal relations in the Union when they ratified the Fourteenth Amendment and modified their state constitutions to eliminate racial discrimination in civil and political rights. Supplemental laws instructed the commanders to hold elections for constitutional conventions to set the process in motion. As Republicans hoped, northern immigrants to the South, joined by southern loyalists and some repentant Confederates, organized a Republican Party in the South to support the congressional Reconstruction program.

As Republicans fashioned a radical Reconstruction program, they debated about how to deal with President Johnson. Republicans passed the Tenure of Office Act over the president's veto, which limited Johnson's control of the patronage by continuing federal officials in office until the Senate agreed to a replacement. During a congressional recess Johnson could suspend an officeholder, but on reconvening, Congress could reinstate him. But Republicans disagreed about whether to include the cabinet in the act's provisions and thus protect Secretary of War Stanton from removal. A murky compromise left the law's application to Johnson's cabinet in doubt.

Radicals wanted to go further. As commander in chief of the armed forces, the belligerent Johnson would certainly interfere with the military supervision of the South, they warned, pointing out that he had already done so on several occasions, some of which had led to bloodshed. Radical Republicans warned that the only way to curb the president was to impeach and remove him. More conservative Republicans recoiled from so extreme a move.

These disagreements were echoed in local politics. Throughout the North aspiring Republican politicians endorsed or opposed radical policies as they sought influence in the party. Radical Republicanism seemed to gain ground. The Ohio radical Republicans Benjamin F. Wade and Salmon P. Chase emerged as the leading contenders for the 1868 Republican presidential nomination. More conservative Republicans worried that such a nominee would go down to defeat.

Yet Johnson's growing belligerence put them to the test. His attorney general, Henry Stanbery, inter-

Ulysses S. Grant and his Union Troops Confront the Confederate Army. One legacy of the Civil War was disagreement between North and South on the rights of newly freed slaves and the extent of federal control over the Southern states. Wood engraving from a drawing by Thomas Nast in *Harper's Weekly*, 1868. LIBRARY OF CONGRESS

preted the Reconstruction Act in a way that severely circumscribed the power of the military commanders. Congress had to come back into session and pass a new law to set matters straight. After Congress adjourned, Johnson suspended Stanton under the terms of the Tenure of Office Act and named the popular commander of the army, General Ulysses S. Grant, as Stanton's temporary replacement. Then Johnson ordered Grant to replace several commanders who were carrying out the Reconstruction Acts vigorously. Southern Republicans warned their northern allies that Congress's Reconstruction program was coming to a standstill.

Radical Republicans again urged Johnson's impeachment, but more conservative Republicans stoutly resisted. Radicals were running far ahead of popular opinion, they worried. Concerned that a radical, Chase or Wade, would win the Republican presidential nomination, they turned to Grant as a conservative alternative. State elections in 1867 justified their fears, as Republicans lost ground almost everywhere. Sobered party activists shifted toward conservatism. Grant's support boomed, while backing for impeachment and further radical reform in the South faded. When Congress reconvened in December 1867, the House overwhelmingly voted down an impeachment resolution. Emboldened, Johnson replaced yet more military commanders in the South with southern sympathizers. Southern Republicans despaired of meeting the Reconstruction Act's conditions for restoration.

Matters came to a head over the control of the War Department. In accordance with the Tenure of Office Act, Johnson notified the Senate of his reasons for suspending Stanton. The Senate rejected them, reinstating him. However, Johnson did not intend to obey the law, which he believed unconstitutional. On 21 February 1868 Johnson removed Stanton in defiance of the law. Republicans, both radical and conservative, voted to impeach him, but he was acquitted when seven conservative Republican senators broke ranks in the Senate trial.

To win acquittal, however, Johnson ceased interfering with Reconstruction. This enabled southern Republicans to succeed in reorganizing new southern governments that met the terms of the Reconstruction Act. Grant was elected president, and Republicans capped off Reconstruction by passing the Fifteenth Amendment, securing political rights regardless of race throughout the nation.

The Politics of Reconstruction after 1869

Republicans thought the election of Grant and the passage of the Fifteenth Amendment would take the Reconstruction issue out of politics. Under the moderate and respected Grant, they planned to concen-

The Politics of the Black Vote. The 1868 Democratic platform, which denied blacks a voice in government, made unlikely allies—the Irish, the former Confederates, and big businessmen. Woodcut after Thomas Nast in *Harper's Weekly*, 1868. LIBRARY OF CONGRESS

trate on rebuilding prosperity, paying off the national debt, and returning to a specie (gold and silver) currency in place of the paper money system the Union had adopted during the war. Southern Republicans expected emancipation to bring prosperity to the South and broaden the party's support there beyond southern loyalists and former slaves. Their opponents in the South were an amalgamation of former Democrats and Whigs who called themselves Conservatives. Republicans especially hoped that the former Whigs, who had generally opposed secession and favored government promotion of economic development, would come over to their support.

But the slavery issue had been the glue that held the Republicans together, and President Grant did not act energetically to create new ones to replace it. Republicans disagreed over financial issues and reducing the tariff. Efforts to impose such moral re-

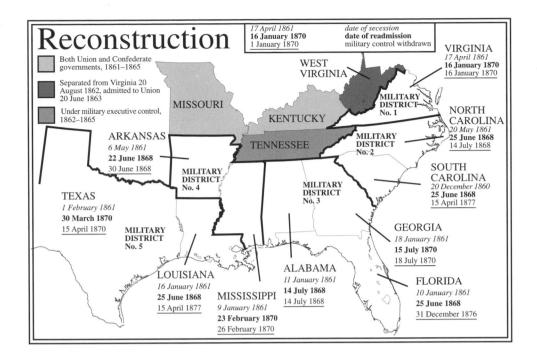

forms as prohibition of alcoholic beverages alienated many voters outside the party's core constituencies while they energized Democratic voters who had been dissatisfied with their party's prosouthern position. At the same time the growing influence of machine politicians in the Republican Party disturbed its intellectual leaders, including journalists, professional people, businesspeople, and academics, who called for a "reform" program of free trade, speedy resumption of specie currency, and the depoliticization of the civil service.

In the South, Republicans' need to serve their black constituents made it difficult to attract white voters. Most southern whites saw the promotion of economic development and the extension of public services to African Americans as a form of corruption because black southerners' poverty meant they paid a relatively small share of the taxes needed to support the programs. Those Republicans who tried to attract white support by minimizing their party's commitment to black rights lost power to those who worked with black leaders. The dissidents complained that unscrupulous party hacks were securing power by appealing to ignorant black voters and began to negotiate alliances with moderate Conservatives.

While reform Republicans sympathized with dissident Republicans in the South, the Grant administration and most northern Republican leaders urged party discipline and backed regular Republican organizations in the South. Although coalitions of Conservatives and dissident, "liberal" Republicans defeated regular Republicans in several border

states in 1869 and 1870, Republicans retained control of southern states with substantial black populations. Unable to oust Republicans by peaceful means, Conservatives turned to violence. Night riders like the Ku Klux Klan spread terror in Tennessee, Georgia, and the Carolinas. Afraid to admit that Reconstruction issues still festered, Republicans in Washington resisted southern Republican pleas for help. In 1871 Grant finally called for special legislation to put down the violence, and Republicans passed the Enforcement Act of 1871, often called the Force Act or Ku Klux Klan Act. Making it a crime for individuals to deprive people of the rights protected by the Fourteenth and Fifteenth Amendments, the law authorized President Grant to suspend the privilege of the writ of habeas corpus, that is, to jail offenders temporarily without trial, in counties beset by violence. The measure seemed to work, the Klan broke apart, and violence subsided.

Republican reformers denounced the Ku Klux Klan Act not only as a violation of constitutional rights but because it meant regular Republicans were seeking popular support by appealing to the old Civil War issues rather than by adopting reform programs. Hoping the Republicans would divide, Democrats announced a "new departure." They would accept the Civil War amendments and concede black rights. In 1872, supported by the Democrats, the reformers ran a Liberal Republican candidate, Horace Greeley, for president against Grant. But the war issues excited the voters, who swept President Grant and the Republicans back into office.

Despite their success in 1872, however, Republicans were on the defensive. Reformers and Democrats brought forward increasing evidence of corruption in the civil service and in the Republican governments of the South. In 1873 the economy soured, sending the country into an economic depression that lasted through the late 1870s. In 1874 angry voters gave the Democrats a huge majority in the House of Representatives and dramatically cut the Republican majority in the Senate. Support grew for issuing more paper money, a proposal that divided both parties and alienated reformers. At the same time, white southerners renewed violent attacks on Republicans, precipitating racial massacres that demoralized Republicans throughout the region.

In the 1875 lame-duck session of Congress, outgoing Republicans passed a new Civil Rights Act to secure African Americans equal access to public facilities, but they failed to pass a new force bill to protect southern Republicans against renewed violence. The southern Republicans' situation became critical when the Supreme Court decisions in the Slaughterhouse Cases (1873) and *U.S. v. Cruikshank* (1876) brought into question the constitutionality of important provisions of the laws enforcing the Fourteenth and Fifteenth Amendments. With popular support for federal action in the South waning, President Grant was reluctant to interfere, even in the most egregious cases.

Republicans passed the Resumption Act in 1875, which required a return to specie currency by 1879. Republicans became the party of "hard money," while Democrats were completely fractured on the issue. Republicans reinforced their position by running successfully on the financial issue in the state and local elections of 1875. Alienated on the one hand by Republican southern policy and on the other by the support of so many Democrats for "soft money," reformers did not know whom to support. Many backed the Republicans in 1875, encouraging Republican hopes of retaining the presidency the following year.

The Election of 1876

In 1876 Democrats papered over their differences about finances and nominated Samuel J. Tilden, a hard-money reformer, for the presidency with a soft-money vice presidential candidate. Republicans named Rutherford B. Hayes, who had run a hard-money campaign to win the Ohio governorship in 1875 and who indicated he supported civil service reform. With reformers dividing, the two candidates ran almost evenly. Violence in three southern states cast the returns in doubt both in the presidential election and in the elections for governors and state legislatures. If Hayes received all of the disputed elec-

toral votes, he would become president; Tilden would be inaugurated if he received even one.

Republicans claimed that the Republican president pro tempore of the Senate, who presided over the formal counting of the electoral vote in a joint session of Congress, had the right to decide which electoral votes to count. Democrats insisted that none of the disputed votes should be counted. In that case neither candidate would receive a majority of the electoral votes, and the Constitution delegated the decision to the House of Representatives, which the Democrats controlled.

Southern violence now threatened to spread to the nation as a whole. Each side threatened violence if the other did not give way, but the Republican president Grant commanded the army. He would tolerate no violent resistance to a decision, he warned. Democrats feared Republicans would count Hayes in and that they would be reduced to a legal challenge, which courts would be loathe to decide. Although some Democrats urged a belligerent stance, most leaders concluded that violent resistance would lead to political disaster. But many Republicans also worried about the political consequences of counting in a president. To the disgust of many of Hayes's advisers, both sides finally agreed to name an electoral commission, made up of five senators, five representatives, and five Supreme Court justices, to decide which set of disputed returns to count. After one independent justice was replaced by a Republican, Republicans outnumbered Democrats eight to seven.

Although more Democrats than Republicans had supported the compromise, the commission endorsed the Republican returns on a strictly party-line vote, giving Hayes the majority of the electoral votes. A Democratic threat to prevent the counting of the vote fizzled, but Hayes nonetheless promised southern Democrats he would not intervene to protect Republican claimants in the disputed state elections. With that the Republican party lost control of the last of the reconstructed southern states. Democrats quickly took action to suppress Republican voting through obstructive voting regulations, gerrymandered redistricting, and fraud.

With Democrats suppressing the Republican vote in the South and once more competitive in much of the North, the nation entered a new era of balanced politics. Each party predominated in different regions of the country but was competitive in the nation as a whole.

See also **African Americans; Civil War,** *subentry on* **Consequences of the Civil War; Constitutional Amendments,** *subentry on* **Thirteenth, Fourteenth, and Fifteenth Amendments; Democratic Party; Elections; Emancipation; Federal-State Relations,** *subentry on* **1861–1900; Ku Klux Klan; Law,** *subentries on* **Federal**

Law, State Law; Presidency, *subentry on* 1861–1877; Race Laws; Radicalism; Republican Party; Sectionalism; Segregation, *subentry on* Segregation and Civil Rights; States' Rights; Whig Party.

Bibliography

Benedict, Michael Les. *A Compromise of Principle: Congressional Republicans and Reconstruction, 1863–1869*. New York: Norton, 1974.

————. "The Politics of Reconstruction." In *American Political History: Essays on the State of the Discipline*. Edited by John F. Marszalek and Wilson D. Miscamble. Notre Dame, Ind.: University of Notre Dame Press, 1997.

Cox, LaWanda, and John H. Cox. *Politics, Principle, and Prejudice, 1865–1866*. New York: Free Press of Glencoe, 1963.

Donald, David Herbert. "The Republican Party, 1864–1876." In *History of U.S. Political Parties*. Edited by Arthur M. Schlesinger Jr. Volume 2. New York: Chelsea House, 1973.

Foner, Eric. *Reconstruction: America's Unfinished Revolution, 1863–1877*. New York: Harper and Row, 1988.

Gillette, William. *Retreat from Reconstruction, 1869–1879*. Baton Rouge: Louisiana State University Press, 1979.

Grossman, Lawrence. *The Democratic Party and the Negro: Northern and National Politics, 1868–92*. Urbana: University of Illinois Press, 1976.

Kleppner, Paul. *The Third Electoral System, 1853–1892: Parties, Voters, and Political Cultures*. Chapel Hill: University of North Carolina Press, 1979.

Perman, Michael. *The Road to Redemption: Southern Politics, 1869–1879*. Chapel Hill: University of North Carolina Press, 1984.

Polakoff, Keith I. *The Politics of Inertia: The Election of 1876 and the End of Reconstruction*. Baton Rouge: Louisiana State University Press, 1973.

Rable, George C. *But There Was No Peace: The Role of Violence in the Politics of Reconstruction*. Athens: University of Georgia Press, 1984.

Silbey, Joel H. *A Respectable Minority: The Democratic Party in the Civil War Era*. New York: W. W. Norton, 1979.

Sproat, John G. *"The Best Men": Liberal Reformers in the Gilded Age*. New York: Oxford University Press, 1968.

MICHAEL LES BENEDICT

THE SOUTH

At the end of the Civil War, Southerners faced an uncertain future. The region's material and financial losses were massive. Burned bridges and factories, wrecked rail lines, and ruined farms and plantations marked the paths of the armies. Away from areas visited by battle, neglect left farmlands in weeds and businesses languishing. Approximately one-third of the region's livestock was lost. Capital tied up in worthless Confederate money and bonds or invested in slaves disappeared. An estimated 260,000 Confederate soldiers had died. Thousands more returned physically and psychologically maimed to families that had endured their own hardships and disruptions. In addition to all of these problems the war had freed the South's nearly 4 million slaves but had not determined their place in the postwar society. Further, while the war had ensured the perpetuity of the Union, it had not settled how the seceding states would return to normal political relationships within the nation.

"Reconstruction" is the term applied to the era in which Southerners and the nation attempted to solve these problems. The traditional historical chronology of the period usually is tied to the course of the national government's efforts between 1862 and 1877 to restore the Southern states politically to the Union, even though many aspects of postwar life in the South do not fit conveniently within this political chronology. It provides, nonetheless, a useful framework within which to consider postwar history.

Presidential Reconstruction, 1862–1867

For some Southerners, political Reconstruction began before the war ended. In March 1862 President Abraham Lincoln named Andrew Johnson military governor of Tennessee, and Johnson attempted to organize a government using loyalists within that state. Military conditions delayed the completion of that task until March 1865. In Louisiana and Arkansas, local citizens attempted to organize under Lincoln's Proclamation of Amnesty and Reconstruction issued on 8 December 1863. This plan pardoned all Southerners, except for high Confederate political and military officers, who would take an oath of allegiance to the Constitution of the United States and agree to support any measures concerning the slaves taken by the federal government. When 10 percent of the legal voters within a state in 1860 took the oath, they could establish a loyal government.

Varied interests supported wartime Reconstruction in the states that attempted it. In Louisiana, a combination of planters and wealthy merchants, many of whom had been Whigs before the war, and a new radical element that emerged in New Orleans under Federal occupation organized a state government. In Arkansas, old Whigs were prominent in Reconstruction efforts, although the attempt to create a loyal government was dominated by men from the state's upland regions. These loyalists held constitutional conventions, in which Arkansas abolished slavery and Louisiana left that action to the state legislature. Subsequent elections selected state officials and congressional delegations. In part because of differences between the president and Congress over Reconstruction, Congress never recognized either state government.

While political Reconstruction proceeded, wartime conditions began to clarify the place of the freedpeople. As thousands of slaves came behind the lines of invading Union armies, many of them asserted their freedom by engaging in subsistence farming. Squatting on whatever land they could find, they withdrew from commercial agriculture and went to work supporting themselves. Federal officials believed the freedpeople's future was elsewhere, however, and across the South they experimented with means to put the freedpeople back to work in commercial agriculture. On the Sea Islands off of the coast of South Carolina and Georgia and in the Mississippi River valley, officers from the Treasury Department and the army developed a system of assigning freedpeople to leased plantations to work for wages as free laborers. The freedpeople had no choice in this matter, but they resisted working under this system. Federal officials observed that they worked better when farming a small plot of land on their own.

When the war ended, none of the states that had attempted wartime Reconstruction had been restored to the Union. The process continued under Lincoln's successor, Andrew Johnson, and now embraced the other eight Confederate states. Johnson's policy toward the South was similar to that of Lincoln. In his 29 May 1865 Proclamation of Amnesty he promised pardon, including the restoration of property rights, to those who would swear the oath of allegiance prescribed by Lincoln. Like Lincoln, he excluded high officials. Johnson also excluded individuals who possessed $20,000 or more in property, although he provided for their special pardon if they applied to him personally. The restoration of property rights was particularly important, for it ensured that the war-damaged antebellum landowning elites were not destroyed and that they would play a major role in reconstructing their states. It also prevented a redistribution of land to the former slaves. The "forty acres and a mule" many ex-slaves believed they would get proved a false hope.

On the same day as his amnesty proclamation, Johnson established the model for political restoration of the states with his North Carolina declaration. In this and subsequent proclamations for other Southern states he named provisional governors to supervise the election of delegates to constitutional conventions by voters who had taken the amnesty oath. Neither the governors nor the conventions received much advice on how to proceed, although Johnson did suggest they disavow secession, repudiate Confederate state debts, recognize the end of slavery, and ratify the Thirteenth Amendment. Possibly to allay growing concern in Congress, he also advised Governor William Sharkey that the Mississippi convention, the first to meet, should consider enfranchising a few qualified blacks.

For white Southerners the critical consideration of the president's policy was that he placed Reconstruction in their hands, and they quickly divided into parties to contest the election of delegates. Many in the South who had resisted secession and remained loyal to the Union throughout the war supported a total repudiation of the old Confederate leadership, full acceptance of the war's results regarding the freedpeople, and constitutions that gave the loyalists political power. This party was called the Union Party in most states. The Unionists' opponents, usually called Conservatives, included some die-hard states' rights advocates and secessionists but for the most part were men who had supported the Confederacy, accepted its loss, and now wanted a quick restoration of the Union. They differed with the Unionists mainly on the implications of the war for the freedpeople, supporting minimal changes, and on restructuring local political power, which they opposed.

The election of convention delegates began in the summer of 1865 with Mississippi and continued through the Texas election in the spring of 1866. In all states, Conservative candidates, including some who had failed to take the amnesty oath and were not qualified to participate in the election, won enough seats to control the conventions. Most of the conventions implemented the measures Johnson asked for, though they also showed limits as to how far they would go. Most nullified secession by conceding that it had been tried and failed, but they refused to deny the right of secession. All except South Carolina repudiated their Confederate debt, but North Carolina did so only under pressure from Johnson. None made provisions for black suffrage.

The same parties that vied for convention seats struggled for power in the elections that followed. Conservatives overwhelmed Unionists in most congressional, gubernatorial, legislative, and local elections. Typical of these Conservatives was Benjamin G. Humphreys, governor of Mississippi. Humphreys was a Whig who opposed secession in 1861 but served as a general in the Confederate army. He and others like him probably were loyal at this time, but such choices raised concerns in the North about Southern intentions. By December 1865 all of the Confederate states except Texas had held elections, and in his State of the Union message of December 1865 President Johnson declared that the Union had been restored.

Johnson's declaration was premature. The new state governments did much that reflected the interests of the victors and raised no criticism. Legislatures provided some relief for their citizens, particularly with stay laws to relieve debtors. They also moved to rebuild and expand their transportation systems, with most governments providing support for railroads. They rebuilt public facilities, and most created immigration bureaus to attract new residents. All demonstrated a new commitment to public education.

Other actions, however, raised concerns in the North. Frequently state legislative action suggested defiance, as in the case of Mississippi, which refused to ratify the Thirteenth Amendment and provided pensions to Confederate veterans. Georgia's legislature elected Alexander Stephens, former vice president of the Confederacy, to the U.S. Senate. The new governments also limited Unionist political power, especially through gerrymandering to destroy safe Unionist districts.

Actions toward the freedpeople produced the greatest apprehension in the North. The behavior of the freedpeople created great concern among most Southern whites. As a way of defining their independence, many of the freedpeople left their former masters at the war's end to find work elsewhere. The freedpeople also sought to gain control over their lives by establishing their own institutions (such as churches), strengthening family life, and pursuing education. They found support in achieving the last from the Bureau of Refugees, Freedmen, and Abandoned Lands, which was established in early 1865 to oversee the transition of the former slaves to freedom. In addition to supervising the adjustment to free labor, bureau agents helped organize schools for freedpeople.

Many Southern whites concluded that this behavior evidenced the irresponsibility of blacks and proved the need to restore control over them. Such fears were more illusory than real. Given their abject lack of resources, most freedpeople quickly went back to work on Southern farms, and the bureau agents actually encouraged this movement. They made many different types of labor contracts, but most involved some form of the share tenant system that had evolved during the war and accommodated the interests of the laborers and landowners. In sharecropping arrangements, the landowner provided the land and the materials necessary to farm it in return for a share of the crop, thus avoiding cash outlays. The freedpeople worked the crops individually for their shares, securing a degree of control over their work. Whatever form of contract was made, African Americans returned to the production of the region's crops, and thus helped move the South toward economic recovery.

Most white Southerners, however, had little faith in free labor or in the the new government's imposed legislative controls over African Americans, known as "black codes." These laws defined race and established African Americans as a separate people. Some of the laws were unexceptionable, legalizing slave marriages and the children of such unions, recognizing the right to own property, and allowing the freedpeople to sue and be sued. Other laws imposed serious restrictions. Most states passed vagrancy laws that required lawful employment at the beginning of each year, thus encouraging freedpeople to enter into annual contracts. Labor laws required strict obedience to contracts by laborers, restricted their movement, and subjected any who might leave an employer to arrest. Apprentice laws allowed minors not supported by their parents to be apprenticed as laborers to former masters. In contract disputes, laws that limited black testimony in cases involving whites and excluded them from juries biased the court system in favor of the landlords.

Concern for these measures played a role in Congress's passage in the spring of 1866 of a new Freedmen's Bureau Bill, which extended the life of the bureau and allowed it to establish courts to hear cases concerning the freedpeople. In addition, Congress passed a Civil Rights Bill, ultimately incorporated into the Fourteenth Amendment, declaring that all persons born in the United States, except American Indians, were citizens and giving federal courts power to intervene against any state that deprived a citizen of his or her rights. President Johnson vetoed both bills, but Congress passed them over the veto. Most importantly, Congress passed the Fourteenth Amendment and sent it to the states for ratification.

Of the two laws, the continuation of the bureau and the expansion of its powers had the most immediate effect in the South. In the autumn of 1866, bureau agents intervened in contract disputes between landlords and laborers. The freedpeople and bureau agents became convinced that landlords would cheat their workers whenever possible. Southern whites in turn resented what they considered an unconstitutional intervention of the federal government in their business affairs. Expansion of bureau power led to an increase in violence against both the agents of the bureau and the freedpeople who sought its help against white employers.

Congressional Reconstruction, 1867–1869

In 1866, Tennessee ratified the Fourteenth Amendment and was readmitted to the Union. In contrast, hostility to the president in Congress and concern with the actions of the Southern governments left all of the other states out of the Union and led to the inauguration of congressional Reconstruction in the spring of 1867. The Military Reconstruction Act of 2 March 1867 set new guidelines for the readmission of the ten unreconstructed states. It abolished the existing civil provisional governments and divided them into five districts under military commanders.

The commanders were to supervise the election of delegates to new constitutional conventions. Critical provisions were the act's enfranchisement of blacks in the elections and its exclusion of anyone who had sworn an oath to support the Constitution of the United States and then supported the Confederacy. Congress also required ratification of new constitutions and legislative ratification of the Fourteenth Amendment as prerequisites for readmission to the Union. When several states refused to call elections, Congress passed the Second Reconstruction Act of 23 March 1867, which authorized the military commanders to begin registering voters. A third act, passed on 19 July 1867, allowed registrars to determine whether or not registrants qualified and empowered military commanders to remove existing state officers who hindered the Reconstruction process. Despite this intervention, Reconstruction still was left in Southern hands.

The beginning of congressional Reconstruction saw the local emergence of the Republican Party across the South. This new party approved congressional intervention and accepted its demands for protection of blacks. Many Unionist politicians who had vied unsuccessfully for power in 1865 and 1866 joined the new party and backed black enfranchisement in particular as an essential condition for reforming the South. The Republican electorate varied in each state because of differences in the character of the population, but in every state blacks, Southern whites (called "scalawags" by their opponents), and Northern newcomers ("carpetbaggers") became part of the new party.

African Americans constituted the largest group within the Southern Republican Party, making up as much as 80 percent of the party's voting strength. Many freedmen came into the party through the Union League, a secret political organization. Condemned by Conservatives as ignorant and easily manipulated, African American voters actually had clear ideas about their interests and saw the Republican organizations as the best way to secure them. They often used their voting strength to force concessions on party policy from white Republicans.

Most white Republicans were natives of the South. Many had been opponents of the antebellum Democratic Party and had opposed secession. Quite a few served in the Union army during the war. Nu-

Alabamians Receiving Rations. The defeat of the Confederate army left the southern population in desperate straits. Sketch by A. R. Waud. *Harper's Weekly*, 1866. LIBRARY OF CONGRESS

merically, white Republicans were strongest in the mountainous areas of the South and in the German counties of Texas, but they appeared in every state. James Alcorn of Mississippi, an antebellum Whig, believed that aligning with national Republicans promised a speedier Reconstruction and more economic help for the South. One of the best-known of the Southern scalawags was the Confederate general James Longstreet.

Northern immigrants to the South constituted the third group associated with the party. The charge that they were carpetbaggers was based on the claim that most had come south to exploit its people politically, bringing all of their belongings in a carpetbag. While some fit this portrait, most, including many Union army veterans, were Northerners who came South seeking business and farming opportunities or who simply remained in the South when they were discharged from the army. Others were teachers and ministers who came to the region to help the freedpeople. Most came to the Republican Party because they believed it would further their social and economic goals.

Although election restrictions cut into its voting strength, the Conservative Party continued to develop under congressional Reconstruction, drawing on the combination of antebellum Democrats and Whigs developed after the war. They usually kept the name Conservative to reflect the multiparty origin of their leadership, but their connections with the national Democratic Party became stronger during this period. Opposition to congressional Reconstruction and the new Southern Republican party, considered by the Conservatives to be the creatures of Congress, became the focal points around which the Conservatives organized.

Convention elections began in 1867 and continued into 1868. Aided by the disfranchisement of approximately 10 percent of whites under the congressional provisions, Republicans dominated the conventions everywhere in the South. This success was achieved even though Conservatives often used violence to terrorize Republican candidates and voters. The constitutions that were written were revolutionary in their recognition of the rights of blacks. They also were generally more democratic and egalitarian than their predecessors. All of the constitutions made a commitment to the creation of public schools for both races.

When the conventions completed their work, each state elected state and local officials. North Carolina began the process in November 1867. Republicans gained control over state and local governments everywhere but in Virginia, where Conservatives won. The new legislatures ratified the Fourteenth Amend-

Political Poster Decrying the African American Vote. Tensions ran high in the South as whites contemplated the participation of African Americans in the federal government. Woodcut, c. 1867. LIBRARY OF CONGRESS: BROADSIDE COLLECTION

ment. When Texas, Mississippi, and Virginia did not hold their elections until 1869, they were forced to ratify the Fifteenth Amendment as well. As each state completed its requirements, Congress recognized the new governments and brought an end to the period of congressional Reconstruction.

Radical Reconstruction, 1868–1876

Following the return of the Southern states to normal relations in the Union, all except Tennessee and Virginia entered a period of Republican rule known as Radical Reconstruction. Their opponents criticized this period as one of "black rule" and unbridled corruption, although neither was the case. Overall, Republican governments often made great strides in improving local social and economic conditions.

The keystone of Republican policy was the improvement of local conditions through economic development, which officials promoted through state action. Legislatures supported railroad construction through state grants, underwriting railroad bonds, and tax breaks. New industries likewise were encouraged to move south with favorable tax policies. Immigration commissions were created to promote the movement of skilled laborers and entrepreneurs into the South. Most states created geological surveys to inform others of their natural resources.

In addition to these measures most states created public school systems. Public education appealed to Republicans because it promised to encourage economic development by creating a better-educated labor force. It also appealed to African American voters, who saw education as the means of breaking out of their situation. In Arkansas and Alabama, Republicans also created state universities. Republicans proved willing to accept the racial mores of the South, however, and virtually all of these schools were segregated.

For practical political reasons, Republican governments also attempted to suppress the endemic local violence, much of which was aimed at the freedpeople. It reflected the hostility of whites toward African Americans immediately after the war and was an effort to immobilize them so they would remain in the South as agricultural laborers. After 1867, violence was used to intimidate blacks as voters. An estimated 10 percent of black public officials were victims. Controlling these attacks on blacks was critical for Republicans to maintain voting strength. Most states were content with the passage of civil rights legislation and antiterrorism laws to accomplish this end, but the governors of Arkansas and North Carolina used the state militias on occasion, and Texas fielded a state police force. None of these measures eliminated violence completely. As a result, the assaults on Republicans continued and played a role in the overthrow of most Republican regimes.

In many states, Republican programs produced noteworthy successes. Efforts at spurring railroad construction doubled the miles of road in the South between 1860 and 1880. Public education reached nearly 50 percent of white children and 40 percent of blacks by the mid-1870s. South Carolina created a land commission in 1869 that made it possible for approximately five thousand African American families to gain their own land. Even though no other state directly assisted African Americans in achieving economic independence, the Republican regimes did provide a favorable legal and economic climate within which blacks improved their conditions. One mark of success in this area was the 1880 census report indicating that 20 percent of black farmers owned or were buying their own land.

The major drawback to Republican policies was

that they increased the cost of government and required a rapid increase in taxation. Party leaders hoped their programs would produce economic growth and an increase in the tax base that would relieve the burden on individuals, but none of their efforts produced an economic turnaround fast enough to head off increasing criticism. Worse, the tax base actually shrunk as declining cotton prices undercut land values. Even for voters who initially agreed with Republican policies, several years of increasing taxes created discontent.

Despite their efforts and accomplishments, the Southern Republican regimes faced strident opposition from the beginning. Conservatives effectively used increases in state and local taxes as a campaign issue in these struggles. When they connected the tax issue with charges of corruption among government officials, they further delegitimized the taxes. Yet the corruption issue was clearly a political ploy. While some Republican officials were guilty of extravagant use of public funds, graft, or outright embezzlement, most were not. In the context of contemporary governments, including those of the antebellum and the post-Reconstruction South, Republican fraud was relatively mild.

In addition to fiscal issues, Conservatives astutely used race in their attacks on Republican regimes. Taking their cue from national Democrats in the presidential election of 1868, local Conservatives turned their opposition to local Republicans into a crusade for white supremacy. Extreme measures were necessary, they claimed, to prevent blacks from taking over local government.

As in the case of charges of corruption, the assertion of a threat to white supremacy was a political tactic divorced from reality. In fact, African Americans never controlled any Southern government. Even though blacks constituted the majority of Republican voters, party leaders usually were white and most of the elected officials down to the county level were white. That is not to say that African Americans did not hold public office. Across the South about two thousand African Americans served as elected officials, and many played important and responsible roles in their governments. Mississippi even elected two blacks, Hiram R. Revels and Blanche K. Bruce, to the U.S. Senate. Still, this presence hardly indicated "black rule."

Conservative willingness to use the racial fear, however, helped unleash and justify a reign of terror against blacks and Republican officials after 1867. This violence first appeared in the 1867–1868 convention elections with the emergence of the Ku Klux Klan, whose members beat and murdered prominent Republican and African American leaders in an attempt to break up the Republican Party in the South. In subsequent elections the Klan, or similar groups such as the Knights of the White Camelia, the White Brotherhood, and the White League, assailed Republican officials and voters. While Conservative leaders did not publicly endorse what took place, the connection between waves of violence and political events disclosed its political purpose.

Violence was successful in most cases and demonstrated that without federal help Southern Republican regimes were doomed. Election violence that state officials were unable to control in Alabama, Georgia, and North Carolina in 1870 played a part in successful efforts to end Republican rule in those states. Conservative success led to a final effort by the federal government to bolster the remaining Republican governments. Congress responded with the Enforcement Act of May 1870, a second Enforcement Act in February 1871, and the Ku Klux Act of April 1871—all of which gave the federal government power to intervene in Southern elections. President Ulysses S. Grant used the Ku Klux Act to place troops in South Carolina in 1871 and in Louisiana in 1873 to protect black voters. Changing Northern opinion on Reconstruction, however, made Grant increasingly reluctant to intervene in Southern affairs. He refused to send troops into Texas in 1873, where victorious Conservatives removed the Republican governor before the expiration of his term; into Arkansas in 1873, where a virtual civil war had broken out between rival claimants to the governorship; or into Mississippi in 1875, where a particularly violent election led to Conservative victory.

By 1876, only Florida, Louisiana, and South Carolina remained under Republican control, and following the general elections of that year these last three state governments collapsed. In Florida, Conservatives regained control of the state following a court decision that ruled their candidate the winner in a disputed election. Republican governments in South Carolina and Louisiana collapsed as a result of the compromise of 1877, struck between Democrats and supporters of Republican presidential candidate Rutherford B. Hayes. In that agreement, Hayes promised to withdraw federal troops from the South. In return, Southern Democrats promised to refrain from blocking his inauguration and to respect the rights of both black and white Republicans in the South. As soon as he took office Hayes pulled the troops out of Louisiana and South Carolina, and in both states Conservatives quickly took power. Conservative redemption in these three states marked the end of national efforts at Reconstruction.

The end of national involvement in the South and the collapse of Republican state governments did not mean the end of Reconstruction at the local level, however. Blacks maintained their voting rights into the 1890s, and in many black majority counties Republican governments continued into the last part of the century. In addition, the process of social and economic Reconstruction continued through the legacy of public education and economic development initiated by the Republican governments. In many respects Reconstruction was a failure in its inability to establish Republican regimes in the South or to protect African Americans from subsequent legal discrimination. Yet it set in motion a process that continued into the twentieth century.

See also **Constitutional Amendments,** *subentry on* **Thirteenth, Fourteenth, and Fifteenth Amendments; Democratic Party; Ku Klux Klan; Republican Party; South,** *subentry on* **The New South after Reconstruction; Voters and Voting,** *subentry on* **Black Voters after the Civil War.**

Bibliography

Anderson, Eric, and Alfred A. Moss Jr., eds. *The Facts of Reconstruction: Essays in Honor of John Hope Franklin.* Baton Rouge: Louisiana State University Press, 1991.

Carter, Dan T. *When the War Was Over: The Failure of Self-Reconstruction in the South, 1865–1867.* Baton Rouge: Louisiana State University Press, 1985.

Foner, Eric. *Reconstruction: America's Unfinished Revolution, 1863–1877.* New York: Harper and Row, 1989.

Franklin, John Hope. *Reconstruction: After the Civil War.* Chicago: University of Chicago Press, 1961.

Litwack, Leon F. *Been in the Storm So Long: The Aftermath of Slavery.* New York: Knopf, 1979.

Moneyhon, Carl H. *Republicanism in Reconstruction Texas.* Austin and London: University of Texas Press, 1980.

———. *The Impact of the Civil War and Reconstruction of Arkansas: Persistence in the Midst of Ruin.* Baton Rouge and London: Louisiana State University Press, 1994.

Novack, Daniel A. *The Wheel of Servitude: Black Forced Labor after Slavery.* Lexington: University Press of Kentucky, 1978.

Perman, Michael. *Reunion without Compromise: The South and Reconstruction: 1865–1868.* Cambridge, U.K.: Cambridge University Press, 1973.

———. *The Road to Redemption: Southern Politics, 1869–1879.* Chapel Hill: University of North Carolina Press, 1984.

Rable, George C. *But There Was No Peace: The Role of Violence in the Politics of Reconstruction.* Athens: University of Georgia Press, 1984.

Roark, James L. *Masters without Slaves: Southern Planters in the Civil War and Reconstruction.* New York: Norton, 1977.

Summers, Mark W. *Railroads, Reconstruction, and the Gospel of Prosperity: Aid under the Radical Republicans, 1865–1877.* Princeton, N.J.: Princeton University Press, 1984.

Wayne, Michael. *The Reshaping of Plantation Society: The Natchez District, 1860–1880.* Baton Rouge: Louisiana State University Press, 1983.

Williamson, Joel. *The Crucible of Race: Black-White Relations in the American South since Emancipation.* New York: Oxford University Press, 1984.

CARL H. MONEYHON

THE NORTH

Surrender of the principal Confederate armies in the spring of 1865 touched off a period of celebration and relief across the North. As American armed forces raced through one of the fastest postwar demobilizations in modern history, northern communities hailed the triumph of the Union and congratulated themselves for ending slavery in the United States. A million men, nearly a third of the male population of the North between the ages of twenty and forty, returned to their families and to civilian life. But the end of the Civil War did not usher in a period of static relaxation or comfortable drift in the victorious Union states. While Reconstruction in the South, with its overt racial struggles and terrorist political violence, has long been recognized as a tumultuous era, Reconstruction in the North was just as dramatic in its way. Scholars now locate in the years between 1865 and 1877 many of the roots of modern America, as citizens in the northern states accommodated their own residual racism, wrestled with tremendous economic transitions, faced issues related to gender and diversity, and grappled with the appropriate applications of political power.

Racial Politics

President Abraham Lincoln's emancipation policy effectively ended slavery in the Confederate states by April 1865, but nationwide abolition was achieved only after ratification of the Thirteenth Amendment in December 1865. Even then the eradication of slavery as an institution did not settle the related but quite different question of what role black people would play in the postwar Union. Later generations of Americans have tended to assume that full civil and political rights for the freed slaves were implicit in emancipation, but that assumption was far from obvious to nineteenth-century Americans. The latter had plenty of experience in their own states with forms of citizenship that fell short of full civil and political rights: women could not vote, for example, and in some circumstances they could not hold property; unnaturalized immigrants had a special status; and restrictive forms of apprenticeship still existed in many states.

When the war ended, the only northern state constitutions that unambiguously permitted black males to vote were those of Maine, New Hampshire, Vermont, Massachusetts, and Rhode Island. In New York black males could vote if they met a property qualification not imposed upon white males. Elsewhere in the North blacks generally could not vote at all. A number of state-level Republican Party organizations promptly engineered ballot proposals to enable impartial male suffrage in their states, thereby giving Union voters a chance to address directly the issue of full political participation for black citizens. To the dismay of many Republicans, the first such proposals were roundly defeated in the autumn elections of 1865 in Minnesota, Wisconsin, and Connecticut. In subsequent referenda in 1866 and 1867, similar proposals were crushed in Nebraska Territory, Kansas, and Ohio. New York Republicans withdrew their impartial suffrage proposal in 1867 rather than risk certain defeat. In 1868 voters in Iowa and Minnesota approved black suffrage at the state level, while voters in Michigan and Missouri defeated black suffrage. Voters in New York rejected impartial suffrage in 1869. Black males were finally given the vote in all northern states in 1870, after the Republican Party successfully managed passage and ratification (by state legislatures rather than popular referenda) of the Fifteenth Amendment.

Most of the suffrage defeats took place in overwhelmingly Republican states, where the number of potential black voters in most areas was minuscule (blacks typically comprised fewer than 1 percent of the population in these northern states and nowhere more than 2 percent). It is therefore impossible not to conclude that the Union states harbored considerable residual racism after the Civil War. That racism was overcome occasionally by resolute political leadership, as in Iowa and Minnesota, but it proved a chilling political factor elsewhere and a serious threat to Republican office seekers. The Democratic Party recognized that residual racism and fanned it shamelessly in state and local campaigns, which helps to account for the relative quiescence of racial reform efforts at the state and local levels across the Reconstruction North after 1870.

Economic Tumult

The northern economy, by contrast, was anything but quiescent. Following a brief recession associated with rapid demobilization, it roared into an unprecedented industrial boom, underwritten by previously unimaginable concentrations of capital. More miles of railroad track were laid between 1865 and 1873 than existed in the entire national system at the outset of the war. Inspired by the scope of Union Army operations, corporate executives throughout the industrial sector expanded their postwar scales of operation. Perhaps most telling, the census of 1870 was the first in U.S. history to reveal that more laborers worked for someone else than for themselves. By 1873 only Great Britain had a larger manufacturing production than the United States, and virtually all American production came from the northern states. Citizens celebrated this great burst of national industrial energy and the rising standard of living that came with it (for most northern people), but they worried about abuses of corporate power, organized labor unions, formed farm cooperatives, and revived labor parties.

The panic of 1873 brought an abrupt halt to the postwar boom and plunged the United States into a depressive cycle that relentlessly contracted the economy month after month for more than five consecutive years, the longest stretch of uninterrupted depression in the nation's history. Half of the country's railroads were in receivership by 1876, and northern working people, who had organized during the late 1860s and early 1870s around the issue of an eight-hour day, now struggled to retain employment on any terms. Midwestern farmers, using their new Grange associations, experimented with legislative intervention at the state level in an effort to alleviate the crisis. As bewildered citizens groped for explanations and solutions, conspiracy theories abounded, especially around the issues of corporate capital and gold coinage. The frustrations and tensions of the period burst forth most dramatically in the Great Strike of 1877, which has been regarded as the most violent and extensive labor action in U.S. history. Begun against the Baltimore and Ohio Railroad, which lost most of its rolling stock to fire during the pitched battles that ensued, the strike spread quickly to most major northern cities and closed down northern mining operations. President Rutherford B. Hayes deployed federal troops against the strikers to restore order. Taken altogether, the years from 1865 to 1877 gave northern citizens a crash course on the pluses and minuses of the industrialized future that lay ahead.

Gender and Diversity

Northern women had played a major role in the Union victory. They ran farms and businesses while men were away fighting; they organized and ran massive civilian support systems, such as the Sanitary Commission; and they comprised roughly a third of the manufacturing workforce. Partly as a result, many northern women hoped that postwar political adjustments would improve their legal status in the Union. In particular they focused on the right to vote. Pressed by such leaders as Susan B. Anthony

Fears of Miscegenation. Northern Republicans regarded "Butternuts," from the border states and the Ohio River Valley, as ignorant as they did southern whites. Woodcut by Kilburn after Thomas Nast. From David R. Locke's *Ekkoes from Kentucky*, 1868. LIBRARY OF CONGRESS

and Elizabeth Cady Stanton, several northern state-level Republican organizations considered the issue of woman suffrage but failed to follow through. Northern feminists felt betrayed by the ultimate decision at the national level to promote racially impartial voting for men only, rather than universal suffrage for all citizens. In protest Anthony and Stanton opposed the Fifteenth Amendment, thereby signaling a symbolic end to the historic alliance between female reformers and racial reformers that had existed before the war.

Notwithstanding the suffrage setback, many northern women pushed forward after the war along paths not previously mapped in the sentimental domestic literature of the prewar period. They went south to teach in the new Freedmen's Bureau schools;

they began to enter the professions; they engaged policy issues, particularly temperance and education; and they found new jobs in the growing urban centers of the North. By 1880 the percentage of women in the nonfarm workforce in the North was nearly back to wartime levels. The demographic catastrophe of the war also helped ensure that women who reached adulthood during Reconstruction would be the first generation of women in U.S. history not to marry in near record percentages.

Immigration, which had almost stopped during the war, resumed quickly after 1865. In the first eight years after Appomattox, nearly three million people entered the country, a number equal to about 15 percent of the total northern population at the beginning of the war. Most of the newcomers were from northern Europe, and the vast majority of them settled in the northern states. Asian immigrants entered the far western states, principally as railroad construction workers. The presence of so many immigrants in the North rekindled ethnic tensions and nativist hostilities that had been suppressed during the war effort. Ethnic rioting, notably in New York City in 1871, and labor violence, perpetrated by native-born workers fearful of job loss, punctuated the entire Reconstruction era in the North. The political system eventually helped dampen such confrontations by subsuming these tensions into the structures of power. By the end of Reconstruction, both major parties across the North rested upon a bedrock of ethnocultural coalitions, in contrast to the race-dominated coalitions of the South.

Applications of Political Power

In an effort to solve residual problems and anticipate the needs of their industrial future, many northern states launched experiments during the early Reconstruction years that involved new applications of governmental power. Between 1867 and 1871, for example, New York, Connecticut, Rhode Island, Michigan, and New Jersey passed legislation that essentially established the state as guarantor of basic education. Between 1865 and 1870 Indiana, Vermont, New York, Wisconsin, Pennsylvania, Maine, Illinois, Kansas, and New Hampshire invested in teacher-training colleges. Boards of health were established across the North, pure food and drug laws were enacted at the state level, ad hoc systems of charity were reorganized and given governmental authority, and modern police and fire systems were put into place in major northern cities. The Union states also pioneered in areas that later would be called social welfare as they built asylums for the mentally impaired and special schools for the blind and the

deaf. They began to gather labor statistics, pass tenement safety codes, and experiment with industrial regulations. Most prominently in New York, where citizens overthrew William Marcy Tweed's notoriously corrupt New York City regime in 1871, but also in several other states, efforts were made to restructure antiquated city charters that no longer met real needs. Many of these governmental experiments eventually fell victim to the depression of the late Reconstruction period and were not revived until the end of the century, while others were elbowed outside the political arena into the hands of pressure groups and neutral commissions. But taken altogether, they represented the first large-scale manifestations and the crucial early building blocks of the modern activist state.

See also **Panics and Depressions; Progressivism; Voters and Voting.**

Bibliography

Adams, Charles Francis, Jr., and Henry Adams. *Chapters of Erie.* Ithaca, N.Y.: Great Seal, 1956. Reprint of lively and insightful essays about corporate power and political corruption.
DuBois, Ellen C. *Feminism and Suffrage: The Emergence of an Independent Women's Movement in America, 1848–1869.* Ithaca, N.Y.: Cornell University Press, 1978.
Dykstra, Robert R. "The Issue Squarely Met: Toward an Explanation of Iowans' Racial Attitudes, 1865–1868." *Annals of Iowa* 3d ser., 47 (1984): 430–450.
Foner, Eric. *Reconstruction: America's Unfinished Revolution, 1863–1877.* New York: Harper and Row, 1988.
Gillette, William. *The Right to Vote: Politics and the Passage of the Fifteenth Amendment.* Baltimore: Johns Hopkins University Press, 1965.
Mohr, James C. *The Radical Republicans and Reform in New York During Reconstruction.* Ithaca, N.Y.: Cornell University Press, 1973.
———, ed. *Radical Republicans in the North: State Politics during Reconstruction.* Baltimore: Johns Hopkins University Press, 1976.
Montgomery, David. *Beyond Equality: Labor and the Radical Republicans, 1862–1872.* New York: Knopf, 1967.

JAMES C. MOHR

THE WEST

The Reconstruction years from 1865 to 1877 brought increased migration into the region between the one hundredth meridian and the Sierra Nevada. Although California and Oregon were admitted to the Union before the Civil War and Salt Lake City, Utah, and Denver, Colorado, were established before the war, the greater part of the high plains and intermontane West lacked towns or settlements. The building of the Union Pacific Railroad resulted in the establishment of towns across Nebraska and Wyoming, while spur tracks connected outlying towns to the main route. By 1869 the Union Pacific linked up with the Central Pacific at Promontory Point, Utah, completing the first transcontinental railroad. The Southern Pacific Railroad served towns and villages along the Pacific Coast southward from San Francisco, California, but the railroad did not reach Los Angeles until 1876. The other major transcontinentals were built in the post-Reconstruction era.

The economy of the post–Civil War West varied from region to region. While agriculture served as the dominant means of livelihood for most people, mining was most important in Nevada, Montana, Idaho, and Colorado. In northern California, fishing, whaling, and shipping replaced mining when the gold fields had been exhausted. The most significant economic advance of the era was the development of the range cattle industry along the front range of the Rocky Mountains. Ranchers became powerful enough to dominate the legislatures of Colorado and Wyoming.

Before 1876 westerners seemed largely unperturbed by the social problems that concerned the Midwest and the East. They exhibited little interest in building hospitals and institutions for the physically and mentally handicapped or in attempting to curb prostitution, but great strides were made in education, especially in higher education. The Land Grant College Act, passed in 1862, gave the impetus for chartering public state universities. California established its state university in 1869, followed by Colorado in 1870, Nevada in 1874, and Oregon in 1876. During their earlier years many of the universities also served as preparatory schools due to the lack of public high schools throughout the region.

Elementary schools could be found in almost every town and village throughout the region. Many were privately or locally supported, but in California and Oregon elementary education was supervised by state superintendents of public education. The historian Ralph Roske estimated that 76 percent of the children in California between the ages of five and fourteen attended public schools in 1870, and in 1874 California made attendance compulsory until the age of fourteen.

During the Reconstruction period the Republican Party became politically dominant in the West. Pockets of Democratic strength existed, but the influx of Union veterans and the power of Republicans nationally, through their control of political patronage, led to the party's growth.

Support in the West for Radical Reconstruction and other policies affecting the defeated Confederacy

Satire on the 1867 California Gubernatorial Race. The Republican candidate George C. Gorham's view of Reconstruction supported the franchise for all races. Lithograph, 1867. LIBRARY OF CONGRESS: PRINTS AND PHOTOGRAPHS DIVISION

followed national patterns. Republicans, whose party continued to dominate the legislatures, supported congressional policies, while Democrats opposed those policies. The most contentious issue was black suffrage, which came to the West through the Territorial Suffrage Act of 1867 and the Fifteenth Amendment in 1870. The Territorial Suffrage Act was one of a series of laws, along with the District of Columbia Act and the First Reconstruction Act, that gave black men the right to vote. In the first elections held after the act became law, some whites in Colorado and Montana threatened violence to prevent blacks from voting, but the elections passed without incident. Resistance faded quickly because the number of black voters was too small to be meaningful, and Democratic politicians, although opposed to equal suffrage, disparaged violence.

For blacks the Reconstruction West offered an escape from the discrimination they encountered in the

South. Those who came to the West during and shortly after the Civil War settled mainly in cities, but in 1877 Benjamin "Pap" Singleton established Nicodemus in western Kansas. The idea of separate black communities appealed to many with the result that shortly after 1900 a number "black towns" were established in Oklahoma and eastern Colorado.

The Fifteenth Amendment, extending black suffrage into all states where it as yet had been denied, faced stiff opposition in the West. When Congress passed the amendment in 1869, the Wyoming territorial legislature, even though it was not affected by the measure, gave women the right to vote. The bill was passed in part to encourage women to settle in the territory but also to let national leaders know that Wyoming legislators regarded women as capable of casting a ballot as black men. Nevada was the first state in the nation to ratify the Fifteenth Amendment, but Oregon and California rejected it and did not ratify it until 1959 and 1962 respectively. Strong prejudices against blacks had existed in Oregon since the earliest settlement, and it was the only state admitted to the Union (in 1859) with a clause in its constitution prohibiting black immigration. California's rejection of the Fifteenth Amendment was prompted by the increasing Asian population rather than opposition to black voting. Asians, mainly Chinese, remained a separate caste in the state, and politicians, assuming that Asians would never assimilate into the general population, feared that their votes could be purchased by unscrupulous politicians in order to gain control.

Near the end of the Reconstruction era, in 1876, Colorado was admitted into the Union. Most western states remained sparsely populated well into the next century.

Bibliography

Berwanger, Eugene H. "The Absurd and the Spectacular: The Historiography of the Plains-Mountains States—Colorado, Montana, Wyoming." *Pacific Historical Review* 50 (1981): 445–474.

———. *The West and Reconstruction.* Urbana: University of Illinois Press, 1981.

Johansen, Dorothy O., and Charles M. Gates. *Empire of the Columbia: A History of the Pacific Northwest.* 2d ed. New York: Harper and Row, 1967.

Mohr, James C., ed. *Radical Republicans in the North: State Politics during Reconstruction.* Baltimore: Johns Hopkins University Press, 1976.

Riegel, Robert, and Robert G. Athearn. *America Moves West.* 4th ed. New York: Holt, Rinehart and Winston, 1964.

Roske, Ralph J. *Everyman's Eden: A History of California.* New York: Macmillan, 1968.

 EUGENE H. BERWANGER

RECREATION   America's agrarian and frontier character had a major impact on early-nineteenth-century leisure, which may be defined as activities freely chosen during nonobligated time. As late as 1820, 95 percent of Americans lived in rural areas and worked long, backbreaking hours, largely determined by the seasons and hours of available sunlight. Free time was especially limited during the seasons from spring planting to fall harvesting. Farmers' pastimes were not highly differentiated from their work, and they often incorporated amusement into their labor at husking bees and barn raisings. Births and weddings were occasions for parties, and religious revivals provided entertainment as well as spiritual fulfillment. Holidays like New Year's, May Day, the Fourth of July, and Thanksgiving, along with militia training days, fairs, and elections were times for socializing, marksmanship contests, wrestling, foot and horse races, orations, and musical entertainment.

Southern plantation owners employed their wealth to enjoy a robust social life that emulated the English gentry. They sponsored lavish balls and mock tournaments and were entertained by slaves who played banjos or fiddles, sang spirituals, recounted folktales, or trained fighting cocks. Planters also visited cities to attend the theater or Thoroughbred horse races. Their bondmen were given time off from labor only on Sundays and during Christmas week. When free of the master's supervision, slaves socialized, enjoyed their own music, performed line dances, and engaged in rural sports.

A Bachelor Subculture

The male bachelor subculture played a major role in early-nineteenth-century leisure. This subculture included frontiersmen, adventurous elites, and a large segment of the urban working class unaccustomed to timework discipline, especially apprentices, butchers, and unskilled Irishmen, who took off from work for birthdays or St. Monday (from the English tradition of inebriated workers taking off from work on Monday). They spent their free time mostly with other men who enjoyed drinking, chasing women, gambling, and watching blood sports like boxing and animal baiting. Participation in these pastimes was thought to demonstrate one's manliness, prowess, and, at times, even one's honor.

The bachelor subculture thrived in the era of rapid urbanization from 1830 to 1860. There was a large migration of rural youth into cities, where about 30 percent of male workers were single. They usually lived in anonymity in boardinghouses, free from social pressure to conform to accepted norms. They came together at volunteer firehouses (virtual social and athletic clubs) and other male bastions and provided a large market for leisure entrepreneurs in locales like New York's Bowery, which became an entertainment district in the 1840s. Entrepreneurs operated legal saloons, billiard parlors, theaters (melodrama and burlesque), and music halls, as well as commercialized vice. New York City alone had two hundred brothels by 1820 and six hundred by 1865. Better theaters seated poorer folk (and prostitutes) in the gallery, separated from the middle class in the pit and the upper class in boxes.

Reforming Recreation

Problems created by rapid urbanization in the Jacksonian era—overcrowding, crime, immigration, poverty, poor public health, and conflicts over values—encouraged numerous reform initiatives by journalists, scientists, and health activists, as well as by evangelists who wanted to eradicate sin and prepare the world for the Second Coming of Christ. Most reformers were middle-class Victorians who believed in hard work and domesticity and felt threatened by the bachelor subculture's anti-Victorian lifestyle. They gained their sense of manliness through work, not leisure, and made family the centerpiece of life. They believed, like the Puritans, that free time was for re-creation, that is, for the improvement of the individual and society.

In this context there developed a rational recreation movement that advocated uplifting and moral pleasures to replace vile amusements. Churches contributed space for fairs, bazaars, suppers, and religious festivals. In 1851 the Young Men's Christian Association (YMCA), founded in England in 1844, was established in Boston to help rural young men adjust to urban life by becoming muscular Christians, pure in body, soul, and spirit. In the name of national recreation, new sports emerged, especially baseball, which promised to promote morality, manliness, and good health. The temperance movement strove to deter drunkenness, and the park movement sought municipal space for active and receptive (passive) recreation. Boosters of New York's Central Park, initiated in 1858 and the model for future parks, anticipated that everyone would benefit from fresh air and beautiful grounds. However, most new parks were located at the outskirts of cities that were originally inaccessible to the urban poor. Furthermore, the park designer Frederick Law Olmsted opposed active forms of recreation in his parks to preserve decorum and protect the grass. Baseball diamonds and tennis courts were not laid out in city parks until the 1880s.

Immigrants and Workers

Ethnicity had a major influence on American leisure patterns. European immigrants brought with them traditional pastimes that helped them cope with culture shock and they followed the customs of the continental Sabbath that sanctioned entertainment after worship. Irish immigrants imported a male bachelor subculture with a strong sporting tradition and the stand-up pub, where heavy drinking was customary and inebriation not uncommon. Germans brought a proud cultural heritage and the family-oriented *bier garten*. They organized choral societies to sing German lieder, theater companies to perform German-language plays, and turnverein for gymnastics. New immigrants from Poland, Russia, and Italy who followed in the late nineteenth century similarly relaxed at ethnic theaters, saloons, and social clubs, but family get-togethers and religious festivals provided their social axes.

The flourishing of industrial capitalism in the late nineteenth century had a dramatic impact on leisure patterns by improving transportation to amusements by rail or streetcar, by producing new apparatus like bicycles, and by mass-producing equipment like sporting goods. More important, though, by reshaping the workplace and further skewing the distribution of wealth, industrial capitalism shrank the time and resources for leisure available to the working class. The factory displaced the small, traditional workshops where workers once had a large measure of control over a more casual pace of work. Factory workers were now governed by the factory whistle. They worked exhausting ten- or twelve-hour shifts six days a week for poor wages, giving them less leisure time and fewer recreational opportunities than in the past. Nonetheless, workers continued to rely on their amusements to gain a sense of self-worth that their jobs did not provide. Lower-class men mainly patronized cheap, gender-based sites of local entertainment, especially saloons, the "poor man's club," where they met friends, played billiards and other games, gambled, and drank. Opportunities to attend sporting events were limited by accessibility and the cost of tickets and often by Sunday blue laws. Wives and daughters in patriarchal working-class households had little independence, and their leisure was still primarily limited to socializing at home with friends and family or to church outings and festivals.

The Middle and Upper Classes

A new middle class emerged after the Civil War that was increasingly bureaucratized and less independent than in the past. But these white-collar employees typically worked only about forty-four hours a week,

Bathers at Play. Bathing was enjoyed by women along with other sports such as golf and tennis, which required less-restrictive clothing. Photograph by W. G. Davidson, 1897. LIBRARY OF CONGRESS

including a half-holiday on Saturdays. They used their leisure time to reinvigorate themselves for work, to improve themselves, to gain a sense of accomplishment not always achieved at the office, and to have fun. They attended the theater, light opera, lectures, and museums, joined sports clubs that sponsored clean games like baseball, cycling, and track, and attended professional baseball games. In addition, they spent considerable time with their families, playing music and singing at home, or on outings to picnic groves or vaudeville shows. Many middle-class wives had considerable leisure time because servants did their housework. Much of their entertainment was solitary, reading novels or magazines, playing the piano, or embroidering. They also entertained a great deal, visited and gossiped with other women, and shopped at expensive downtown department stores. In the 1860s younger middle-class women participated in nondebilitating sports, such as coed ice-skating and croquet, and in the 1890s many of them became avid riders of the new safety bicycle.

The old upper class continued to employ leisure to advertise their superior social status by sponsoring and participating in expensive and exclusive entertainment, while new-monied industrial capitalists used leisure to try to gain acceptance into the social elite. Wealthy men formed exclusive clubs to separate themselves from lesser folk, basing admission on wealth and family background. These prestigious organizations included downtown clubs focused on politics, culture, genteel sports such as racquets and track and field, as well as suburban country clubs that were modeled on the lifestyles of the English gentry. The elite were conspicuous consumers who made lavish expenditures on events like extravagant balls and parties attended by New York's "400," built luxurious summer homes like that of the Vanderbilts at Asheville, North Carolina, and vacationed at exclusive resorts like Newport, Rhode Island. The elite sponsored institutions of high culture like the New York Metropolitan Opera (1883), where they could be seen in their elegant box seats, and endowed zoos, libraries, and art and natural history museums to provide uplifting entertainment for the masses. Their wives enjoyed many of the same pastimes as middle-class women, only in more exclusive settings, socializing at elegant homes, the finest hotels, or at country clubs. Their daughters participated in country club sports like golf and tennis and rowed for varsity crews at elite women's colleges.

See also **Cities and Urbanization; Clubs,** *subentry on* **Fraternal Societies and Clubs; Holidays; Manliness; Saloons and the Drinking Life; Social Life; Sports; Vacations and Resorts.**

Bibliography

Duis, Perry. *The Saloon: Public Drinking in Chicago and Boston, 1880–1920.* Urbana: University of Illinois Press, 1983.

Dulles, Foster Rhea. *A History of Recreation: America Learns to Play.* 2d ed. New York: Appleton-Century-Crofts, 1965.

Gilfoyle, Timothy J. *City of Eros: New York City, Prostitution, and the Commercialization of Sex, 1790–1920.* New York: Norton, 1992.

Gorn, Elliott J., and Warren Goldstein. *A Brief History of American Sports.* New York: Hill and Wang, 1993.

Levine, Lawrence W. *Highbrow/Lowbrow: The Emergence of Cultural Hierarchy in America.* Cambridge, Mass.: Harvard University Press, 1988.

Riess, Steven A. *City Games: The Evolution of American Urban Society and the Rise of Sports.* Urbana: University of Illinois Press, 1989.

Rodgers, Daniel T. *The Work Ethic in Industrial America, 1850–1920.* Chicago: University of Chicago Press, 1978.

Rosenzweig, Roy. *Eight Hours for What We Will: Workers and Leisure in an Industrial City, 1870–1920.* Cambridge, U.K.: Cambridge University Press, 1983.

Rosenzweig, Roy, and Elizabeth Blackmar. *The Park and the People: A History of Central Park.* Ithaca, N.Y.: Cornell University Press, 1992.

STEVEN A. RIESS

REFORM, IDEA OF   Americans of the nineteenth century were famously patriotic, restless, sanctimonious, practical, and idealistic—all qualities that made them avid for reform. There was scarcely a dogma they did not attack, scarcely an institution they did not scrutinize for improvement. The nation held no patent on the idea of reform, but no other nation had so much of its history made by reformers.

The activity and influence of reformers peaked during the first decades of the nineteenth century. Surveying the missionary and charitable societies that abounded in 1817, an assembly of Presbyterian leaders exulted: "Such mighty plans of benevolence; such wonderful combinations; such a general movement of mankind, in promoting the great cause of human happiness was, surely, never before witnessed!" (Handy, *A Christian America*, pp. 45–46). In contrast to the politician who was bound always to public opinion, said the abolitionist Wendell Phillips, "The reformer is careless of numbers, disregards popularity, and deals only with ideas, conscience, and common sense" (Hofstadter, *The American Political Tradition*, p. 138).

By 1840 there were so many movements seeking to change American habits and institutions that a Convention of Friends of Universal Reform was held in Boston at which abolitionists, temperance crusaders, communitarians, water curers, and advocates of pantaloons for women all rubbed elbows. A significant fraction of these earnest improvers were women, their presence in itself a sign of the reforming temper of the time. The poet and essayist Ralph Waldo Emerson applauded the "keener scrutiny of institutions and domestic life" carried out by this motley "soldiery of dissent," but he also satirized the eccentricity that might make them decide that the insect world "had been too long neglected, and a society for the protection of ground-worms, slugs and mosquitos was to be incorporated without delay."

Reform flourished because the United States was a society undergoing several kinds of revolutionary transformations that legitimized both social change and public action to achieve it. Much reform activity in America represented the revolutionary impulse moderated and controlled—revolution by other means. One revolution that prepared the ground for reform was material: the application of capitalist market relations and mechanized production to all sectors of the economy. Rapid economic change demanded or facilitated social change. The ambitious farmers, mechanics, merchants, and industrialists who were transforming the economy frequently doubled as reformers of social institutions.

Even more fertile for reform was the religious revolution that swept through the country from the 1790s through the 1830s. The revivals of the Second Great Awakening taught Americans that Christians could voluntarily renounce their sins and achieve salvation. Belief in personal salvation fed belief in social reform. A utopian fervor spread through large sectors of the society. Evangelists like Charles Grandison Finney pronounced good works a Christian duty and spiritual perfection a possibility for people of strong faith. Finney assured a congregation in Rochester, New York, that "if Christians united and dedicated their lives to the task, they could convert the world and bring on the millennium in three months" (Johnson, *A Shopkeeper's Millennium*, p. 3).

Most important to promoting the idea of reform was the exhilarating stimulus of the American Revolution. The republican rebellion of 1776 created something new under the sun. It broke the age-old monopoly by elites of freedom and social power. By conferring liberty and citizenship on the majority of white adult males, the Revolution immensely widened the circle of people who had the standing and the means to change society. Under the terms of republican political philosophy, which tied liberty to civic virtue, reform became virtually an obligation of citizenship; the price of liberty was not just eternal vigilance but also an unceasing quest for social improvement. Reformers throughout the nineteenth century wrapped their causes in the principles and the rhetoric of the Revolution.

The advent of the new, the legitimation of change, the expectation of progress, the expansion of citizenship, the hope of salvation: the idea of reform took into itself and expressed each of these prominent themes of American culture in the early nineteenth century. But the Revolution that set reform in motion also set boundaries to that motion. First, just as the Revolution established a state that restricted sovereignty to white men, so it initially made reform the special prerogative of white men. Women and African Americans had to challenge this restriction in order to claim roles in movements for temperance and abolition of slavery. Ultimately they had to make movements of their own to pursue legal and political equality with white men. Second, living in the shadow of the Revolution, nineteenth-century Americans often felt they had only to safeguard its heritage. The mythicized achievements of the founders inspired but also limited the missions of reformers who came after them.

To believe social change was constant was not always to think it good. The idea of reform in nineteenth-century America was never uniformly democratic, optimistic, or progressive. For some reformers the purpose of directing social change was to discipline or moralize or simply to stop it. Many sought to curtail the egalitarian aspirations or correct the disorderly behavior they believed the Revolution had let loose. Alongside Christian perfectionists who regarded selfless benevolence as the test of true piety, there were conservative Christians who practiced benevolence as a means of gaining control over their sinful fellows.

Abraham Lincoln spoke in the idiom of antebellum reform when, addressing Congress in 1862, he called emancipation of the slaves the "last best hope of earth": America the champion of liberty and human rights, the redeemer nation, itself in need of redemption. But by then his majestic phrases invoked a waning spirit. The legacy of the Civil War proved less conducive to reform endeavors than the legacy of the Revolution had been. Costing more than 600,000 lives, the war exhausted the public's capacity for civic sacrifice. By vindicating the Union and ending slavery, the war seemed to complete the founders' business. Beyond abolition, the most crucial consequence of the Northern victory was to open the way for accelerating industrialization, urbanization, and immigration, which in turn deepened divisions along lines of class, religion, race, and ethnicity. The legions of reform, too, grew more divided.

The broad millennialist and utopian currents of antebellum reform lived on in Henry George, with his single tax panacea for the ills of modern America; in Edward Bellamy, with his semisocialist visions of the economy run by an industrial army; and in proponents of the Social Gospel, dedicated to Christian service to the disadvantaged. But goals of material abundance sponsored by an ascendant industrial capitalism largely superseded aims of national salvation, and the idea of reform registered this change. During the Gilded Age suffragists, agrarian radicals, labor reformers, temperance crusaders, and civil service advocates aspired not to save souls but to advance class interests. Reform in this period was predominantly secular, it focused on issues of economic and political justice, and it strove to guard the commonwealth against parasites and predators: corrupt politicians, plutocrats, and monopolists. Some reformers sought to protect America from aliens, socialists, and minorities seeking equality, but other reformers sought to improve the lives of aliens, achieve social justice, and even apply socialist ideas to the new industrial economy. But, for many Gilded Age reformers, the key aim was to forestall any future revolution rather than to sustain the revolutionary heritage of 1776.

Yet the reforming impulse also found new channels and new champions. Most northern white voters soon repudiated the great experiment of Reconstruction, but not before abolitionist ideals sent thousands of educators south to teach the former slaves. Many of these missionary-teachers were women who soon found other ways both to express their ideals and to pursue their rights. To the extent that humanitarian reform thrived in the materialistic Gilded Age, it lived largely in female, and eventually in feminist, endeavors. The preeminent reform leaders of the century's last decades included Frances Willard of the National Woman's Christian Temperance Union, Jane Addams of the settlement house movement, the antilynching crusader Ida B. Wells, and the many dauntless leaders of the suffrage movement. Women played large roles, too, in labor organizations, agrarian radicalism (the Farmers' Alliances and the People's Party), and the genteel socialism inspired by Edward Bellamy's 1888 utopian novel *Looking Backward*.

Feminized reform often represented domesticated reform, promoting the values and the interests of the idealized middle-class home. Beyond the home, some historians have argued, female reformers functioned as "municipal housekeepers," charitable ladies applying their supposed domestic talents to immigrants' slums. Yet leaders like Willard and Addams labored to win the dignity of full citizenship for women, a goal as momentous as any envisioned by male reformers. Moreover, women's reform endeavors of the 1880s and 1890s broke ground for the social justice wing of the Progressive movement, the principal reform initiative of the next decades.

If women's activism pointed toward the future of American reform, so did the defeat of labor and agrarian radicals during the depression-plagued 1890s. The movements of this decade represented the century's high-water mark of protest and organization by farmers and workers. These were far from revolutionary. Even the most militant Knights of Labor, Populists, Single Taxers, and Social Gospelers owed more to the earnest Evangelicals of antebellum America than to European theorists of class warfare. The heroes of Eugene V. Debs, the railway labor leader who converted to socialism after the Pullman Strike of 1894, were William Lloyd Garrison and Abraham Lincoln, not Karl Marx and Mikhail Bakunin. The Left in America barely clung to the fringes of the political system. To the defenders of property, law, and order, however, angry movements of debtor farmers and distressed workers looked profoundly subversive. The defeat and suppression of these movements decisively narrowed the province of American reform.

In this straitened province the Progressive movement grew. On the eve of the new century, reformers in industrial cities developed respectable alternatives to the ideas of insurgent workers and agrarians. Sometimes going by the name of "progressivism," this new model of reform practice would sponsor notable victories for social justice, economic fairness, and political openness in the early years of the twentieth century. Progressive reform was staunchly antiradical, predominantly white and middle-class, and sometimes rooted in religious values, as the principal movements of the nineteenth century had been. At the 1912 convention of the Progressive Party, the fullest gathering of progressive reformers, Theodore Roosevelt sounded like an old-fashioned moral crusader when he exhorted his followers to "stand at Armageddon and battle for the Lord!" But the Progressive model was more managerial than millennialist, more devoted to studies and regulation than to speeches and salvation, and more respectful of public opinion, in the way of politicians, than Wendell Phillips would have thought proper. Scientific, pragmatic, and interest group–based, it was committed to hard-headed lobbying, legislation, and government activism. In the twentieth century the Progressive style of reform would become virtually institutionalized in the politics and culture of a highly industrialized United States.

See also **Civil Service Reform; Muckrakers; Reform, Political; Reform, Social; Settlement Houses; Temperance Movement; Welfare and Charity; Work,** *subentry* on **Child Labor.**

Bibliography

Abzug, Robert H. *Cosmos Crumbling: American Reform and the Religious Imagination.* New York: Oxford University Press, 1994.
Boyer, Paul. *Urban Masses and Moral Order in America, 1820–1920.* Cambridge, Mass.: Harvard University Press, 1978.
Emerson, Ralph Waldo. *The Portable Emerson.* Edited by Mark Van Doren. New York: Viking Press, 1946.
Goodwyn, Lawrence. *The Populist Moment: A Short History of the Agrarian Revolt in America.* New York: Oxford University Press, 1978.
Handy, Robert T. *A Christian America: Protestant Hopes and Historical Realities.* New York: Oxford University Press, 1984.
Hewitt, Nancy A. *Women's Activism and Social Change: Rochester, New York, 1822–1872.* Ithaca, N.Y.: Cornell University Press, 1984.
Hofstadter, Richard. *The American Political Tradition and the Men Who Made It.* New York: Random House, 1948.
Johnson, Paul E. *A Shopkeeper's Millennium: Society and Revivals in Rochester, New York, 1815–1837.* New York: Hill and Wang, 1978.
McLoughlin, William G. *Revivals, Awakenings, and Reform: An Essay on Religion and Social Change in America, 1607–1977.* Chicago: University of Chicago Press, 1978.
Mintz, Steven. *Moralists and Modernizers: America's Pre-Civil War Reformers.* Baltimore: Johns Hopkins University Press, 1995.
Sproat, John G. *"The Best Men": Liberal Reformers in the Gilded Age.* New York: Oxford University Press, 1968.
Thomas, John L. *Alternative America: Henry George, Edward Bellamy, Henry Demarest Lloyd, and the Adversary Tradition.* Cambridge, Mass.: Harvard University Press, 1983.
Walters, Ronald G. *The Antislavery Appeal: American Abolitionism after 1830.* Baltimore: Johns Hopkins University Press, 1978.
Wood, Gordon S. *The Radicalism of the American Revolution.* New York: Random House, 1993.

EUGENE E. LEACH

REFORM, POLITICAL The moral reform of American politics was a cause that spanned the decades between the Civil War and World War I. It became a particularly urgent priority among college-educated gentlemen, a small fraction of the whole population. Many of these men practiced trained professions, including law and education, in the urban Northeast during the Gilded Age. Prominent among their spokesmen were Edwin L. Godkin, editor of the *Nation,* George William Curtis, and Dorman Eaton of New York; the peripatetic Carl Schurz, a German American; Edward Atkinson, Moorfield

Storey, and George Fred Williams of Massachusetts; and William Dudley Foulke of Indiana. As they led a sustained outcry of dismay over post–Civil War political conditions, they came to be called "mugwumps" because of their mistrust of conventional party discipline. Originally an Algonquian word meaning "chieftain," the name was used by scornful critics to describe a political fence-sitter with his "mug" on one side of the fence and his "wump" on the other.

Mugwumps reacted with indignant anxiety to the transforming triple impact on post–Civil War political behavior of rapid urbanization, industrialization, and mass immigration, a combination unprecedented in the histories of other nations. The mugwumps' response was to mount a concerted but often beleaguered effort to reassert the influence of their class-bound moralism on American governance—federal, state, and local—for the first time since the beginning of the age of Jackson. They offered themselves as a reformist elite to a political populace that no longer thought it needed one.

During the 1850s and 1860s control of the country's party system, from the municipal to the national level, shifted decisively to career politicians who scorned the rival pretensions of the genteel, educated amateurs they muscled aside. In reformist eyes the perceived decline in the quality of governance—quite aside from contested issues of policy—in Washington under Andrew Johnson and Ulysses Grant, in state houses from Pennsylvania west to the Pacific, and most spectacularly in the nation's largest city, the New York of "Boss" Tweed and Tammany Hall, made the arrival of the full-time professional politico seem like a triumph of corruption over republican virtue.

Municipal Reform

In fact it was the new power of industrial entrepreneurs, the surge of fresh city growth making American cities the fastest-growing urban places on Earth by the 1880s, and the need to assimilate waves of temporarily dependent European newcomers to the ways of American democratic politics that fostered maladjusted urban governance. Many twentieth-century historians and political sociologists defined mugwump reform in retrospect as an overly righteous condemnation of this maladjustment. The historians argued that the quality of American city government compared reasonably well with that of other countries, and they offered a sophisticated explanation of the corrupt practices of urban political machines by stressing the functional utility of this corruption. Corruption was the lubricant, they argued, that

made the boss-run machine work. Coercion at the ballot box; the award of monopoly franchises in coal, gas, and rapid transit to capitalists with open pocketbooks; the distribution of pick-and-shovel jobs on city building projects among loyal ward heelers; and the maintenance of rudimentary law and order, at a price, to the retail merchants who needed it, all served to hold the city together politically. Most graft was "honest" graft in this interpretation. Bribery became a "reward system," and the machine serviced the needs of the city in the teeth of galloping growth that overwhelmed formal structures of divided authority dating from the eighteenth century.

Reformers at the time saw it differently. In their minds corruption at any level of governance was arbitrary, manipulative, illicit, and unfair. In the city it seemed to subsidize an illegitimate "shadow" government of inner-city ward bosses, padrones, and wire-pullers who were beyond the reach of white-collar voters spread out along the city's residential rim and of the respectable officials they tried to elect.

Characteristic good-government (goo-goo) remedies sought to elevate and centralize the city's formal political power structure by endowing mayors with greater executive powers than ward-based common councils and boards of alderman, by seeking citywide at-large elections, and by creating boards of appointed experts with authority to regulate metropolitan police, utilities, parks, schools, and public finance. In some cases reformers used the charter authority of the state to promote these arrangements in the name of home rule. But in other cases rural-dominated state legislatures denied the cities greater authority to borrow, tax, and regulate because they mistrusted urban empowerment and the swelling growth of the cities' foreign-born masses.

Owing to their scattered suburban locations, their status as part-time, silk-stocking political amateurs, and their rather hygienic approach to urban reform, mugwumps and goo-goos struggled, with limited success, during the 1870s and 1880s to impose their political values on the cities. But by the 1890s reform-minded mayors in major cities—such as Hazen Pingree in Detroit, Tom Johnson in Cleveland, and Josiah Quincy (1859–1919) in Boston—provided successful models to follow. Meanwhile goo-goo reformers' accumulating political savvy, fortified by growing support from downtown businessmen and journalists, and the technology of the telephone and mimeograph, crucial for galvanizing shared purposes among reform clubs and citywide committees of one hundred, improved their chances for positive impact. In many cities they put into place the structural arrangements that urban Progressives of the post-1900

Seth Low (1860–1916). Although a Republican, as the reform mayor of Brooklyn in the early 1880s Low would not endorse his party's candidate for president, maintaining that local and national politics should not mix. LIBRARY OF CONGRESS

generation would use to pursue somewhat more generous and social-minded definitions of reform.

State Reform

In state governments, as in the cities, weak executive power, a long-term legacy of the American Revolution, remained a problem to overcome. For most governors influence over legislative behavior was largely confined to their authority to recommend, to appoint, and to veto. Their power to name new members to the state administrative commissions that proliferated after the Civil War rarely included the power of removal. Reform-minded governors often led demands for change in legislative behavior by curbing the influence of lobbyists, who in many states made up a virtual "third house" of the legislature, and by limiting in other ways the sway of corporate money over legislative outcomes. In the 1880s several farm states, led by Illinois, tried hard to impose rate regulation on rail corporations. Industrialized states, led by Massachusetts, began to invoke their constitutional police power to regulate factory hours and

work conditions more forcefully than ever before. Mugwump reformers supported these policy initiatives with varying degrees of enthusiasm.

A major new reform at the state level was the Australian (secret) ballot, designed to break the grip of political parties on the voting process. Introduced in Massachusetts in 1888, ballot reform spread swiftly to other states. Together with new voter registration laws, state-supervised voting helped to curb party discipline dramatized by torchlit mass political campaigning and partisan coercion at the ballot box on Election Day. These reforms probably reduced the high voter turnout rates characteristic of the Gilded Age. In addition, naturalization laws were codified to delay the right to vote among immigrants. The goal of most mugwump reformers was to purge the political system of its perceived flaws rather than to further its democratization.

Civil Service Reform

Central to the mugwump goal was the most important political reform achievement of the era, civil service reform. Partly inspired by British precedents, its aim was to dismantle the spoils system that had long tainted the distribution of public jobs. That system, called by its friends "rotation in office," used payroll patronage at all levels of government to reward loyal followers of the party in power. These patronage appointees were expected to give part of their salary to the party's campaign needs. The spoils system may well have been the most enervating sickness in American public life. It decentralized power by forcing executive deference to politicians with local clout. Patronage negotiation devoured the time and energy of these politicians and limited chances for technical competence and longevity among patronage winners. The radical expansion of federal and state bureaucracies during and after the Civil War exposed these drawbacks in the system. Its reform was an essential precondition for developing a modern, effective bureaucracy and strengthening executive efforts to solve public problems.

Civil service reform came on very slowly. Professional party politicians, eyeing its mugwump supporters, called it "snivel service reform" and resisted its threat to their entrenched patronage power. Despite Carl Schurz's efforts to install civil service reform while he was secretary of the Interior under Rutherford B. Hayes, most presidents wobbled on the issue. Finally the murder of President James Garfield by a frustrated office seeker in 1881 mobilized national support for the Pendleton Act, a reform measure largely written by Dorman Eaton, a New York lawyer-reformer, and passed by a skeptical Congress in 1883. Eaton designed the law to be incremental in its impact. At a pace to be determined by the president, it replaced party loyalty with merit determined by competitive exams as the key to access to positions in the federal civil service. The law's effect was to launch a gradual shift of control over the federal bureaucracy from congressmen to the executive branch.

Grover Cleveland's presidencies were crucial to this shift. During his quick rise from obscurity to the White House, first as "veto mayor" of Buffalo in 1882 and then as reform governor of New York in Albany, where he implemented the first state civil service reform law in 1883, Cleveland attracted enough mugwump supporters to ensure his election to the presidency in 1884. Only 11 percent of the federal workforce was covered by the merit system when he took office. A majority was covered when he completed his second term in 1897. The twentieth-century consequences of the Pendleton Act were more impressive than many historians have acknowledged. A dissenter among them, Paul Van Riper, put it this way:

The economic reforms considered so essential by others would not have been possible except for civil service reform. A relatively stable and effective civil service [was] indispensable for the functioning of the modern state. The civil service reformers diagnosed better than they knew or than others have usually given them credit. They did put first things first (*History of the United States Civil Service*, pp. 83–84).

Conclusion

The mugwump generation of political reformers receded from prominence in the 1890s, when a searing national depression and then the agrarian free-silver cause led by William Jennings Bryan riveted public concern. The anti-imperialist movement following the Spanish-American War of 1898 was for many mugwump reformers a final unsuccessful quest for national political influence. But they left their country with a better-functioning political structure than the one that provoked their anger in the 1870s. In their righteous indignation they had dreamed of operating as a vital third force within the American party system. This hope eluded them, perhaps because their reservations about the habits of a mass democracy prevented them from attracting much durable public support. Their legacy was a cleansing and aerating of party politics. Moreover, they opened political space where the collective professional intelligence of educated men and women could and did assert itself repeatedly in the country's public life during the decades ahead.

See also Civil Service Reform; Muckrakers; State Government.

Bibliography

Blodgett, Geoffrey. *The Gentle Reformers: Massachusetts Democrats in the Cleveland Era*. Cambridge, Mass.: Harvard University Press, 1966.
Hoogenboom, Ari A. *Outlawing the Spoils: A History of the Civil Service Reform Movement, 1865–1883*. Urbana: University of Illinois Press, 1961.
Lotchin, Roger W. "Machine Politics." In *Encyclopedia of American Political History*, edited by Jack P. Greene. Volume 2. New York: Scribners, 1984.
Mandelbaum, Seymour J. *Boss Tweed's New York*. New York: Wiley, 1965.
McGerr, Michael. *The Decline of Popular Politics: The American North, 1865–1928*. New York: Oxford University Press, 1986.
Sproat, John G. *"The Best Men": Liberal Reformers in the Gilded Age*. 1968. Reprint, Chicago: University of Chicago Press, 1982.
Van Riper, Paul P. *History of the United States Civil Service*. Evanston, Ill.: Row, Peterson, 1958.
Welch, Richard E. *The Presidencies of Grover Cleveland*. Lawrence: University Press of Kansas, 1988.

GEOFFREY BLODGETT

REFORM, SOCIAL   During the nineteenth century the United States changed from a rural, agricultural nation to an urban, industrial one with a diverse population. The resulting tensions focused attention on social issues, prompting a variety of reform efforts that occurred primarily during two thirty-year periods. The first period, from the 1820s through the 1850s, is often called the "Age of Reform" because of its many simultaneous efforts. The second period lasted from the 1870s to the end of the century. Each wave of reform contained a religious element and support for temperance. Some individuals were involved in more than one reform effort, and some attempts at social reform were tied to political or economic movements. Although few social reform efforts could claim complete success in the nineteenth century, most had some impact on American society, and scholars continue to debate their meaning and importance.

The Antebellum Age of Reform

One group of pre–Civil War reforms was moral, religious, and philosophical in nature. The Second Great Awakening, which reached full flower in the 1820s and 1830s, encouraged people to reform themselves and create a righteous society on earth in preparation for the Second Coming. An apparent increase in crime, vice, and general licentiousness associated with the growing cities disturbed leaders of the Second Great Awakening. Others equally disturbed by modern society chose to set an example for it rather than preach against it, and they formed small utopian or communal societies. Most, like Brook Farm, New Harmony, or the several Shaker settlements, were based on a philosophical or religious belief. Moral concerns also underlay the temperance movement of the late 1820s and the 1830s. Temperance leaders were concerned about the impure souls of those who drank too much as well as about the vice and crime they associated with drunkenness. The "common school" movement, largely inspired by Horace Mann, can also be considered moral or philosophical in nature, since its proponents believed that only a free public education for all would produce the virtuous and educated citizens needed to maintain a democracy. Of these morally based reform efforts, only the common school movement was really successful in the early nineteenth century.

A second group of pre–Civil War reform efforts focused attention on dependent individuals. These included those unable to care for themselves for any reason and sometimes criminals and paupers, who some reformers believed were morally disabled. Traditionally, dependent individuals had been cared for at home or in the community. Those viewed as a threat to society—criminals, the mentally retarded, and the mentally ill—were often housed together in a single facility. In the 1820s and 1830s churches, charities, and some governments began to create special institutions for different individuals. Reformatories or penitentiaries separated criminals from society so they could become penitent and reform themselves. Orphanages sheltered and taught proper values to parentless children. Asylums and hospitals provided care to those with physical or mental disabilities and tried to train some to be useful members of society.

In the 1840s and 1850s reformer and philanthropist Dorothea Dix, who had been a teacher, visited almshouses, jails, and other institutions. Outraged by what she saw, which included residents being treated cruelly or confined with chains or in cages, she began advocating separate institutions that could provide humane treatment and appropriate care for different types of individuals. Her 1843 petition to the Massachusetts legislature documented conditions in that state and led to some improvements. More than a dozen other states also responded to her first-hand reports and tireless calls for change. Her commitment, energy, knowledge, and skill led to her appointment during the Civil War as superintendent of women nurses for the North.

Slaves and women were also dependent individuals, and their conditions likewise sparked reform. By 1800, some northern states had dismantled slavery through constitutional provisions or emancipation statutes. Northern opponents of slavery then focused most of their attention on improving the conditions of former slaves and ensuring proper enforcement of emancipation statutes. In the South some early antislavery societies formed, but most people opposed to slavery there simply freed their slaves or took their slaves to the North and emancipated them there.

By the 1830s, some Northerners saw slavery as the most potent force for evil in the United States. In 1831, abolitionists in Boston began publishing an antislavery newspaper, *The Liberator*. In 1833 abolitionists founded the American Anti-Slavery Society. By the 1840s the antislavery movement in the North included black leaders, such as Frederick Douglass, William Wells Brown, Sojourner Truth, and Harriett Tubman; white abolitionists, such as William Lloyd Garrison and Wendell Phillips; and even young politicians, such as Salmon P. Chase of Ohio.

Northern abolitionists held public meetings and rallies to garner support for their cause, organized mass petition campaigns, and called upon officeholders and politicians to account for their views on slavery. Disagreements over tactics and what would happen to the freed slaves complicated the movement. From 1830 until the Civil War, however, the antislavery movement, which encompassed a variety of views, was a major engine for social reform. Many reformers involved in the abolition cause later supported women's rights, public education, and world peace.

Many women were active abolitionists and advocated for the disadvantaged or the disabled, and inevitably they recognized their own inequitable position with respect to men. In 1838 Sarah Grimké and Angelina Grimké published tracts on the rights denied to women. Ten years later Elizabeth Cady Stanton and Lucretia Mott organized a women's rights convention in Seneca Falls, New York. Some husbands of the women activists supported the call for women's rights, as did some leading abolitionists, in-

"Bar of Destruction." Temperance propaganda, including antidrinking cartoons and literature, was a leading form of social reform efforts. *Harper's Weekly*, 1874. LIBRARY OF CONGRESS

cluding Douglass and Garrison. Although the Civil War eventually rid the nation of slavery, neither blacks nor women gained real equality in the nineteenth century.

Social Reform in the Late Nineteenth Century

Industrialization played a key role during the Civil War and Reconstruction, which occupied much of the nation's attention during the 1860s. Industrialization was also a factor in late-nineteenth-century social reform. Beginning in the 1870s large groups of Europeans immigrated to the United States, where growing industries offered employment. Immigrants and industries spurred the exponential growth of cities. Three phenomena—industrialization, immigration, and urbanization—changed the American landscape at a rapid pace, producing great social tension.

Disparity of wealth was one source of tension. Industrialists' lives contrasted sharply with those of their employees. Although it was not a social reform in the narrowest sense, the labor movement attempted to improve workers' lives. Laborers worked long hours in hazardous conditions. Pay for men was so low that, to make a living, their wives and children worked alongside them for still lower wages. Injury or illness generally meant the loss of both job and income. In the 1870s the Knights of Labor tried to broaden the base for labor activism by including all types of workers, and in the next decade the craft unions combined to form the American Federation of Labor. However, major strikes, often quite violent, cost labor the public's support, as did the widely held belief that foreigners and Socialists were behind the labor movement. Major improvements in workers' conditions and the terms of employment did not occur until the twentieth century.

Laborers were not the only poor people in the country, of course. They joined a class of poverty-stricken citizens unable to provide for themselves. The traditional remedies for poverty were work relief for those who could work and almshouses for those who could not. Late nineteenth-century poverty, however, proved too weighty for these remedies. Moreover poor living conditions endangered others besides poor residents. Rapid population growth and inadequate incomes combined to produce tremendous overcrowding in industrial cities. Basement flats subject to flooding; sleeping rooms with no access to light or air; overflowing privies, fouled wells, and inadequate plumbing; and houses and flats subdivided to produce more dwellings of smaller size were common living conditions. Epidemics were frequent, crime rates were high, and fire was always a threat.

The problems associated with poverty and living conditions prompted a variety of reform efforts. The Salvation Army tried to uplift the poor, and the YMCA attempted to engage the youth so they could help themselves. "Friendly visitors," who were often associated with model tenements and were in essence the predecessors of social workers, made home visits to teach the poor and immigrants good domestic habits and to exhort them to overcome whatever weaknesses had produced their poverty. The temperance movement resurfaced with the Woman's Christian Temperance Union in 1874 and the Anti-Saloon League in 1893. Both viewed alcohol as the root of poverty and crime. Modeling their work on Toynbee Hall in England, in the 1880s and 1890s settlement workers like Jane Addams and Florence Kelley at Chicago's Hull House, and New York's Lillian Wald at the Henry Street Settlement and Mary Simkhovitch at Greenwich House, lived in the immigrant communities. There they worked to get parks and playgrounds in the cities and recreation programs for children and adults. Settlement houses were social and community centers for the immigrants, but they also taught them English and helped the immigrants deal with employers, landlords, and government officials. In many cities charity organization societies formed during the late 1870s and 1880s to coordinate the various efforts.

The publication of Jacob Riis's *How the Other Half Lives* in 1890 stimulated more calls for reform. Riis's vivid photographs of the living and working conditions of the poor illustrated his harsh statistics. The perception of the poor began to change. Traditionally individual poverty had been blamed on some weakness of character. By the 1890s, however, environmental determinism seemed another explanation as more people became aware of dismal and dangerous living conditions. The poor had been shaped by their miserable surroundings, reformers reasoned. If the poor could live in bright, airy, healthy homes, they would become strong and healthy people, able to work, improve their conditions, and contribute to society. This belief combined with a genuine concern about health and safety factors to produce advocates for housing regulations. New York State passed laws in 1867 and 1879 to increase the light, ventilation, and safety of newly constructed tenements, and other states followed suit. But that did not prevent the occupation of previously built, unsafe tenements. Increasing immigration and population growth in industrial cities meant that every available dwelling was occupied, sometimes by more than one household. As the nineteenth century neared its end, cities responded with building, housing, and sanitation

Dorothea Dix (1802–1887). The reformer and philanthropist Dorothea Dix was instrumental in promoting reform for the mentally ill in prisons and other institutions in Massachusetts and other states. LIBRARY OF CONGRESS

codes, and some reformers even called for zoning codes patterned after those in Germany.

A similar regulatory approach attempted to improve conditions for workers, particularly women and children. It had only marginal success, however, for such an approach required sympathetic legislators and judges. In this respect social reform merged with political reform, and the Social Gospel came into play. Such Social Gospel ministers as Walter Rauschenbusch of New York City and Washington Gladden of Columbus, Ohio, preached salvation through social responsibility. Responsibility to and for society was not limited to individuals, however. Government also should serve society. In agitating for city councils and state legislatures to pass reform legislation, Social Gospel pastors sought to address the root causes rather than just the symptoms of social problems. Social Gospel practitioners actively supported reform candidates for office, worked for political reforms that would make government more responsive to the people and their needs, and even ran for office. Social Gospel goals were often as radical as those of the labor movement. But the Social Gospel was led by mainline Protestant churches rather than the foreigners, Catholics, and Jews accused of labor agitation, so it was much less disturbing to many Americans. Social and political reforms merged and often included economic concerns in the Populist Party, which twice ran candidates for the presidency, and in some elements of Progressivism, which had a greater impact in the twentieth century. Some progress in addressing social issues was apparent by 1900, especially at the local and state levels, but not enough to conquer the underlying problems.

Historians have debated the meaning of nineteenth-century social reforms. Liberal progressive historians have taken the reformers at face value. Others have seen reform as social control. The pace of social, demographic, and economic change was rapid during both reform periods, and many people could well have believed that chaos threatened stable society. Faced with the impossibility of turning back the clock to a simpler time, when a more homogeneous population shared common views and values, they hoped to ingrain those views and values in the poor, the alcoholic, and the foreigner and thus to lessen social disorder and tension. According to this interpretation, self-preservation, not humanitarianism, motivated the reformers. Neither view can be proved conclusively, and the reality probably contained elements of each. Reform movements and individual reformers varied widely.

Still they shared some common elements. Reformers had strong beliefs about the causes of social problems and were optimistic, even idealistic, in believing their efforts could solve them. The multiplicity of efforts indicates that the reality was more complex than many early nineteenth-century reformers realized, although later reformers more often saw connections among different problems. This was not enough, however. In spite of individual and incremental successes, many of the same social problems continued well into the twentieth century.

See also **Abolition and Antislavery; Asylums; Cities and Urbanization; Progressivism; Reform, Idea of; Reform, Political; Settlement Houses; Social Gospel; Temperance Movement; Women,** *subentries on* **Woman's Rights** *and* **Women's Labor; Work.**

Bibliography

Boyer, Paul. *Urban Masses and Moral Order in America, 1820–1920.* Cambridge, Mass.: Harvard University Press, 1978.

Bremner, Robert H. *The Discovery of Poverty in the United States.* New Brunswick, N.J.: Transaction Publishers, 1992. Reprint, *From the Depths.* New York: New York University Press, 1956.

Cross, Whitney R. *The Burned-over District: The Social and Intellectual History of Enthusiastic Religion in Western New York, 1800–1850.* New York: Octagon Books, 1981.

Gladden, Washington. *Applied Christianity: Moral Aspects of Social Questions.* Boston and New York: Houghton, Mifflin, 1886.

Johnson, Paul E. *A Shopkeeper's Millennium: Society and Revivals in Rochester, New York, 1815–1837.* New York: Hill and Wang, 1978.

Kolko, Gabriel. *The Triumph of Conservatism: A Re-interpretation of American History.* Chicago: Quadrangle Books, 1963.

Rothman, David J. *The Discovery of the Asylum: Social Order and Disorder in the New Republic.* Rev. ed. Boston: Little, Brown, 1990.

Tyler, Alice Felt. *Freedom's Ferment: Phases of American Social History to 1860.* Freeport, N.Y.: Books for Libraries Press, 1970.

Walters, Ronald G. *The Antislavery Appeal: American Abolitionism after 1830.* Baltimore: Johns Hopkins University Press, 1976.

PATRICIA BURGESS

REGULATION OF BUSINESS

During the nineteenth century, business and government interacted at the local, state, and federal levels. Prior to 1830, when most commercial operations were managed by one individual and staffed largely by that individual's relatives, local governments kept business enterprises from becoming public nuisances, while state governments ensured that businesses contributed to the public good. Between 1830 and 1870, when small-scale mercantile enterprises gave way to large-scale transportation and manufacturing concerns as the nation's most prominent mode of business organization, state and local governments became increasingly less able to control business activity, and at times were themselves controlled by powerful business interests within their boundaries.

After 1870, when the rise of large corporations and monopolistic combinations threatened the economic independence of average citizens, states generally took a more confrontational stance with big business. Meanwhile, because the activities of such enterprises transcended state borders, the federal government was called on to play a more active role in business regulation. The government, however, generally failed to achieve much in the way of curtailing monopolistic behavior, in large part because its trust-busting powers were severely proscribed by the U.S. Supreme Court. Throughout the century, the Court generally followed a probusiness course, which stimulated the rise and growth of giant corporations.

Local Governments and Business

Prior to 1830 local governments regulated business in accordance with the time-honored provisions of English common law, which prevailed during the colonial period. These provisions were generally intended to make commercial activity as unobtrusive as possible with respect to daily life. To this end, local business regulations mostly addressed such things as the price and quality of goods and the frequency and place at which they could be sold. Licenses were required of some businesspeople, such as artisans, tavern keepers, and draymen, in order to both lessen the possibility of adverse competition and ensure the quality of goods and services. Many cities and towns erected market halls, with the intention of enclosing, both physically and legally, the oftentimes offensive sights, smells, and sounds of commercial activity. Blue laws, so called because they were often printed on blue paper, prohibited the sale of most goods and services on Sunday as a means of preserving community morals.

After 1830, as factories replaced artisans and railroads replaced carters, large business enterprises began to dominate the economies of many smaller communities. Consequently, many businesses gained local political clout and played an active role in their own regulation. By contributing land for a much-needed park, lining the pockets of corruptible council members, or threatening to ruin a community's economy by locating their thriving enterprise in or moving to a neighboring town, principals of big businesses usually managed to avoid substantive regulation of their companies by local authorities.

State Governments and Business

During the early half of the century, state governments regulated business in much the same way that local governments did. State laws stipulated the quality of goods to be exported as well as of those produced for home consumption. Business licenses provided a significant portion of a state's operating budget. Entrepreneurs who wished to incorporate could only do so through a special act of their state legislature.

After 1810 a number of states began encouraging the growth of business by "regulating" it in two important ways. Between 1815 and 1860 state governments used land grants and special bond issues to provide private companies with over two-thirds of the capital required to build the canals and railroads that came into existence during that period. These methods greatly encouraged the growth of commerce within a state's borders; however, they also served effectively as a means of preventing latecomers from participating in certain avenues of economic endeavor. Between 1811—when New York became the first state to do so—and 1880, most states encouraged business by passing general incorporation laws

enabling a business to obtain a charter simply by filling out a few forms and paying a fee. Moreover, these laws permitted an entrepreneur to determine the specific form and structure of a corporation, rather than leaving such details to legislators.

Following the emergence of regional railroads and large manufacturing enterprises during the middle part of the century, state governments sought ways to retain control of business activity. Massachusetts pioneered the public service commission, a "weak" regulatory agency composed of knowledgeable professionals who made suggestions about operating procedures rather than issuing decrees to the banks, railroads, or manufacturers that they oversaw. However, by the 1870s such commissions could no longer command the respect—and thus the compliance—of giant corporations whose operating units sprawled across the nation, and so state legislatures felt compelled to take a more antibusiness stance. This development led to the passage by four midwestern states of the Granger laws, which were intended to put an end to the monopolistic practices of railroads operating within their borders. Ohio and Pennsylvania, among others, began considering taxing the profits and assets of "foreign" corporations (those chartered in other states) at a higher rate than "home" corporations.

Unfortunately for the states, none of these measures succeeded completely or for long. In fact, several large business organizations actually turned the tables on regulators by gaining control of a state legislature. It was said, only half jokingly, that Standard Oil Company did everything to the Ohio legislature but refine it, and that a Pennsylvania legislator once moved to adjourn unless the Pennsylvania Railroad had more bills for the legislature to pass. In 1867 a particularly vicious takeover struggle involving the Erie Railroad was fought on the floor of the New York state assembly, where the rival parties were able to purchase votes at the going rate of $15,000 apiece. Matters were made worse for state regulators after 1889, when New Jersey became the first state to enact general incorporation laws that permitted a company to conduct all of its business affairs outside the state and to own stock in its competitors. This development facilitated the creation of holding companies, large corporations that produced no goods and provided no services but which served as a legal means to monopolize a particular industry. By the end of the century the size and scope of holding companies permitted them to replace factories and railroads as the largest form of business organization and made them virtually impossible for the states to regulate.

The Federal Government and Business

Prior to 1870 the federal government only sporadically involved itself with business regulation. In 1807, after Great Britain and France both interfered with American shipping, President Thomas Jefferson declared an embargo on U.S. trade that had near-ruinous effects on New England merchants. That same year Congress abolished the African slave trade, a move that had little effect on U.S. commercial interests. In 1816 Congress passed the first tariff bill designed to protect American manufacturers from competition with cheap British imports, a move that stimulated those business endeavors that were protected while doing nothing for those that were not. The National Banking Acts of 1863 and 1864 attempted to regulate the banking industry by creating nationally chartered banks and allowing them, and not state-chartered banks, to circulate national banknotes without paying a prohibitive tax. However, the acts failed to create a central bank to oversee the activities of the new national banks, and therefore they had little effect on the way banks behaved.

After 1870 the difficulty that the states encountered in trying to regulate the railroads and large manufacturing corporations led many people to call on the federal government for help. In 1887 Congress finally responded by creating the Interstate Commerce Commission (ICC) as a means of prohibiting monopolistic practices in the railroad industry. The ICC consisted of five disinterested individuals, each of whom was knowledgeable about railroading, who investigated complaints concerning unfair rates, rebates, and pooling arrangements, the practice whereby several competing railroads allocated among themselves a region's traffic or the profits from such traffic. The commission could subpoena witnesses, examine the records of railroad corporations, and pass binding judgments regarding the legality of whatever practices it uncovered. In 1890 Congress passed the Sherman Antitrust Act, which was intended to protect trade and commerce from unlawful restraint and the creation of monopolies by large manufacturers. Although English common law had long held that practices such as charging more than what was fair and creating a shortage via hoarding were illegal, this act was the first to make restraint of trade a crime against the government rather than against an individual. It also spelled out the penalties for monopolistic activity and permitted injured private parties to sue for damages.

Neither congressional initiative produced the desired result. The ICC was hamstrung by Supreme Court rulings that, by 1900, had reduced it to little more than a public information agency. Between 1890 and 1900 only seventeen antitrust cases were prosecuted by the U.S. Justice Department, and the bulk of these cases involved companies of intermediate size, not the giant corporations whose monopolistic behavior had inspired passage of the Sherman Act.

The Supreme Court and Business

During the century the Supreme Court made a number of decisions affecting state and federal efforts to regulate business. Although these decisions sometimes supported government's right to restrict business activity, for the most part they did more to dilute the effects of government regulation.

Prior to 1840 the Court made three important rulings limiting a state's right to regulate corporate behavior. In *Dartmouth College v. Woodward* (1819) the Court rejected the New Hampshire legislature's attempt to alter Dartmouth's corporate charter, which had been granted during the reign of King George III, on the grounds that it was a legal contract. Since most corporations received their charters via a special act of a state legislature, this ruling protected them from losing their legal status in a future legislative session. In *Gibbons v. Ogden* (1824) the Court rejected New York's granting of a monopoly to operate a steamboat within state waters, thus establishing the federal government, and not the states, as the arbiter of interstate commerce. This decision was invoked throughout the rest of the century by corporations that operated in more than one state, thus severely impeding state regulation of big business. In *Bank of Augusta v. Earle* (1839) the Court invoked the constitutional clause of interstate comity to establish a corporation's right to operate outside of the state that incorporated it. This decision had powerful implications fifty years later when New Jersey legalized the incorporation of holding companies at a time when most other states were attempting to abolish such monopolistic combinations.

After 1870 the Court made four rulings limiting the ability of state and federal governments to regulate big business. In *Munn v. Illinois* (1877) the Court found in favor of a state's right to regulate commerce that directly involved the public interest. However, it also left open to question a state's right to regulate a purely private business, a loophole that was used to great advantage by manufacturers seeking to overturn regulatory legislation. In *Santa Clara County v. Southern Pacific Railroad* (1886) the Court ruled that under the Fourteenth Amendment corporations enjoyed the same rights as persons. In *Wabash, St. Louis and Pacific Railway Company v. Illinois* (1886) the Court ruled that states had absolutely no right to regulate interstate commerce, even in the absence of federal regulation. In reaction to this decision, Congress established the Interstate Commerce Commission the following year. In *United States v. E. C. Knight Co.* (1895) the Court severely limited the federal government's ability to regulate giant manufacturing corporations via the Sherman Antitrust Act when it ruled that manufacturing and commerce had nothing to do with each other. Not until *Addystone Pipe and Steel Company v. United States* (1899), when the Court ruled that a price-fixing cartel of iron pipe manufacturers had violated the antimonopoly provisions of the Sherman Act, did the Court finally begin to cooperate with the executive branch in the regulation of monopolistic behavior.

Conclusion

As business enterprises increased in size and scope, local and state governments found it increasingly difficult to regulate corporate activity. The executive branch of the federal government offered these governments little substantive help, and the Supreme Court worked against them by ruling consistently in favor of corporations rather than governments. Although the situation changed in the early twentieth century, between 1830 and 1900 regional railroads and giant manufacturers generally were able to operate without much interference from government.

See also **Blue Laws; Corporations and Big Business; Foreign Trade and Tariffs,** *subentry on* **Trade and Tariffs; Interstate Commerce; Railroads; Supreme Court,** *subentry on* **The Economy; Trusts.**

Bibliography

Hall, Kermit L., William M. Wiecek, and Paul Finkelman. *American Legal History: Cases and Materials.* 2d ed. New York: Oxford University Press, 1996.

Hughes, Jonathan R. T. *The Governmental Habit Redux: Economic Controls from Colonial Times to the Present.* Princeton, N.J.: Princeton University Press, 1991.

McCraw, Thomas K. *Prophets of Regulation: Charles Francis Adams, Louis D. Brandeis, James M. Landis, Alfred E. Kahn.* Cambridge, Mass.: Belknap Press of Harvard University Press, 1984.

Pusateri, C. Joseph. *A History of American Business.* Arlington Heights, Ill.: Harlan Davidson, 1984.

Roy, William G. *Socializing Capital: The Rise of the Large Industrial Corporation in America.* Princeton, N.J.: Princeton University Press, 1996.

CHARLES W. CAREY JR.

RELIGION

[This entry includes two subentries:
Religion in Nineteenth-Century America
Religion as a Political Issue.]

RELIGION IN NINETEENTH-CENTURY AMERICA

Throughout the nineteenth century, religious participation in the United States steadily increased. Late in the eighteenth century the spirit of the Enlightenment, which motivated the most prominent of the nation's founders, appeared ready to prevail. Not without religious accents itself, this philosophy competed with the religion of most churches, downplayed divine revelation, and devoted itself not to a God revealed in scripture but a God of reason or a God of nature.

The Revivalist Pattern

While the Enlightenment ethos and ideals provided the foundation for most public institutions, they failed to touch the hearts of the masses. Challenging this philosophy at the turn of the century were the forces and fires of revivalism. While there had been what many called a Great Awakening of faith in the 1740s, religious fervor had waned during the Revolutionary War and nation-building era. But almost precisely with the coming of a new century, revivalism was manifest across the eastern seaboard, and when migrants crossed the Appalachians to encounter the vast western environments, it spread across the continent to the Pacific coast.

Revivalism, an emotional approach to practical Christianity, often appeared to rise by spontaneous combustion. Sometimes it was nurtured by already established local churches and spread to newly founded congregations in the South, Midwest, and eventually the West. Most often the revivalist tendencies were roused by skilled, if often rustic and untrained, preachers who gathered crowds, denounced sin, called for repentance, and welcomed converts into the community. The Methodists, a well-organized import from Great Britain, sent out circuit riders to advance their cause. The Baptists were another highly successful group. Organized democratically and empowered by and in local congregations, the Baptists won much of the South. Methodists and Baptists were successful at preaching revivalism to African American slaves, who, especially when they won or bought freedom or were emancipated en masse, went on to develop churches of their own. The Congregationalists and Presbyterians worked the North with evangelistic intent, but were eventually eclipsed.

The revivalist pattern had counterparts in Great Britain and in the Protestant areas of northern Europe, but nowhere were its exponents so successful as in the United States. In Europe most religion was sponsored by and tied to the state, a factor that led adherents to disregard freedom of choice in spiritual matters. In Europe apathy was widespread, causing a gradual drift from the churches, especially in the rapidly industrializing and urbanizing areas. In the United States, however, disestablishment—which was prefigured in the First Amendment to the United States Constitution and had been effected in all states by 1833—left the churches on their own. Those organizations that best understood the readiness of frontier people and new urbanites to choose their version of faith prospered at the expense of those that failed to employ a zealous, competitive spirit.

Revivalism moved with people from country to city. The best-known evangelizer in the first half of the century, Charles Grandison Finney, moved from the upstate New York frontier to metropolitan locales such as New York City and Boston, setting out to convert or create enthusiasm among newcomers to the city. His counterpart in the second half of the century, Dwight L. Moody, used Chicago as his base and constructed tabernacles and held huge rallies in cities more than in small towns. Revivalism had looked like a backwoods phenomenon, but at least among Protestants it was also becoming a main street and metropolitan affair.

Varieties of Millennialism

As the century moved on, one turn that developed in Protestant thought patterns had to do with millennial thinking. Early in the century, trends of thought that came to be called "postmillennial" dominated. In such evocations, history was moving under the hand of God to a destiny symbolized by the return of Christ to earth for a thousand-year reign. Many biblically prophesied traumas, it was said, had already occurred as signs of the end. These included the Protestant Reformation and the French Revolution. Now it was the task of reformers and missionaries to improve and convert the world in preparation for Christ's return.

Such thinking hardly touched Catholicism, but it was transformed in the second half of the century by spokespersons such as Moody, who was a kind of revivalist commuter between England and America. In the British Isles, Moody picked up new currents of thought that came to be called "premillennial." In this case, the traumas—wars and rumors of war, faithlessness, turmoil—were perceived as lying ahead. In the heart of an era that was turning progressive, here was a pessimistic philosophy of history for all but the properly converted, who looked beyond the bloodshed and earthquakes and apostasy to

Christ's thousand-year rule on earth. While premillennialism was initially a doctrine of only a few small denominations such as the Plymouth Brethren, a British import, it came to be a transdenominational movement of great power and was an antecedent to twentieth-century Protestant fundamentalism.

Postmillennialism tended to fade among liberal Protestants, who devoted themselves more to the doctrine of progress than to what came to be seen increasingly as mythical or mystical teachings about a millennium. No literal return of Christ was needed to bring about God's purposes in the world. The traditionalists and conservatives, protofundamentalists who objected to the modernists treating their Bible and its distinctive doctrines symbolically or spiritually, were quick to attack this view. Few of the antiliteralists formed new denominations, though Unitarians by 1825 had split off from Congregationalism. Most liberals, such as the Hartford, Connecticut, pastor Horace Bushnell, stayed in Congregationalism or other congenial denominations to propound nonrevivalist views of Christian nurture and progress. These modernist moves contributed to an increasing tension and schism.

The Protestant Empire

The disestablished churches, all on the same legal footing, came to be called "denominations," a word whose usage erased the line between the privileged "church" and the upstart "sects." Some called them "the voluntary churches," since they depended upon the will of the converts and propagators and were supported voluntarily. Whereas in Europe the established or legally privileged church was to take on many of the burdens of charitable work, in the United States efforts at reform, education, improvement, and care were undertaken on the initiative of lay people and clergy alike, many of them working across denominational boundaries.

What resulted was an endeavor sometimes called "an errand of mercy," which resulted in the formation of major groups like the American Bible Society, the American Temperance Union, and the American Tract Society. But imagination was evident in associations titled, for instance, the Association for the Relief of Respectable, Aged, Indigent Females or the Connecticut Society for the Suppression of Vice and the Promotion of Good Morals. As denominations grew in power and developed organizations, many of them developed their own errands of mercy and voluntary associations. Alexis de Tocqueville, the most perceptive European observer of American religion in the 1830s, saw these associations as great energizers of national life, movements with few counterparts in Europe.

In the course of the century, the energies of the voluntary churches and associations were channeled into the great moral issues of the times, notably slavery. One of the most traumatic events in nineteenth-century American religion was the division of what was still, by 1861, a Protestant empire, into separate northern and southern wings. Before the Civil War, the Baptists, Presbyterians, and Methodists went separate regional ways. In the North, the reactions to slavery ranged from quiet acquiescence to abolitionism, while in the South antislavery impulses, notable before 1830, all but disappeared when the Cotton Kingdom developed and the South moved toward secession. By century's end, these divided churches had taken few steps to reunite, and some never have.

The term "Protestant empire" might suggest that the United States included only Protestants—and to those who look at how denominational power was asserted, only English-speaking Protestants. But during the nineteenth century, great numbers of continental European Protestants, some of them Reformed but most of them Lutheran, migrated, especially to the Midwest, where they became a strong presence.

Non-Protestants

It is estimated that there may have been only about thirty thousand Roman Catholics and three thousand Jews in America at the end of colonial times. Catholics began to come to eastern seaboard cities from the European continent in the 1830s. Many emigrated from Ireland in the late 1840s due to potato famines and starvation. They quickly moved west

Catholic Mass Celebrated during the Atlanta Campaign. The many facets of Catholicism during the Civil War: in battle, in the hospital, and in the field. Published by American Oleograph Co., c. 1877. LIBRARY OF CONGRESS

Juliann Jane Tillman. Tillman was a preacher in the African American Episcopal Church, organized in 1816. The church numbered twenty thousand members by the Civil War. Lithograph by A. Hoffy, 1844. LIBRARY OF CONGRESS

and were joined by later immigrants who peopled midwestern cities such as Cincinnati, Milwaukee, St. Louis, and Chicago. Through missionary bishops and religious orders and even a kind of Catholic revivalism, they won the loyalty of millions of immigrants whose practice of the faith when in Europe may have been more relaxed. Catholicism did not become an empire, but it was an assertive power, a rival to Protestants who wanted to continue to dominate church and culture alike.

The Protestant population was easily stirred into anti-Catholicism, given its sense that American liberties and institutions depended upon Protestant teaching and practice and that as Catholics gained in numbers and power the United States would fall into papist thralldom. When Pope Pius IX issued the *Syllabus of Errors* in 1864, he denounced modernity, republicanism, and other "heresies" that Protestant America was manifesting, and this roused Protestants into a reactive state that has been called "The Protestant Crusade."

Alongside the largely white, evangelical Protestant churches, the African American denominations, and prospering Catholicism, other faiths established

themselves. While immigration from China and Japan (at first chiefly of men, often induced to come to build the railroads and work the mines in the West) brought Buddhists and other kinds of Asian religionists, their numbers did not challenge the Christian majority and they did not constitute a felt presence except in the West. Some Eastern Orthodox Christians also began to arrive in West Coast cities and in some midwestern industrial centers, but few churches of this sort developed by century's end.

The most visible new element in the religious mix was Judaism. All through the century, German Jewish immigrants to the United States brought a cultural consciousness to match that of European Christians. But after pogroms began in Europe in the early 1880s, thousands of poorer, often less educated, more "foreign" Jews began to arrive in New York and elsewhere. They began long processes of adaptation and sometimes assimilation and started to denominationalize into what became Reform, Conservative, and Orthodox Jewish branches. They experienced considerable anti-Semitism, especially among American literary and cultural elites, but most Christian Americans did not live near Jews or have week-to-week contact with synagogue goers.

Divergent Trends

Numerous new movements that represented religious innovation were more potent presences in Protestant and Catholic America than were Asians, Orthodox Christians, and Jews. It seemed as if wherever an ecological niche for spiritual development existed, someone would come along with what looked like, to the more conventional, irritating inventions. Prime among them grew from the visions and preachments of Joseph Smith, an upstate New Yorker who founded the Church of Jesus Christ of Latter-day Saints, or the Mormons, a much despised and persecuted people who made their way to Utah and came to dominate in that Great Basin region. William Miller, who in the 1840s foresaw the end of the world, founded the Seventh-Day Adventist sect, also in New York State. Many of them dispersed, but the movement was regathered and refashioned as a vegetarian communion by Ellen Gould White. And in 1870, under the ministrations of a Bible teacher named Charles Taze Russell, a movement formed in Pittsburgh to preach the imminent end of the world and to denounce church and state as they were constituted in the United States. Russell's organization became the Zion's Watch Tower Society in 1884, which adopted the name Jehovah's Witnesses in 1931. Another challenge to mainstream religion came in the form of the Church of Christ, Scientist,

who founded short-lived communities that challenged Christian majorities. But statistically, and for cultural power, none was a threat to the white Protestant denominations or the growing Catholic minority.

As the names Ellen Gould White, Mary Baker Eddy, and Ann Lee suggest, women took significant leadership roles in these marginal communities. Within the more mainstream groups were offshoots of revivalism and holiness movements, some of which came to be called Pentecostal in the twentieth century. Among them, revivalist leaders such as Phoebe Palmer advanced pioneer feminist causes in religion. So did Catherine Booth in the young and vigorous Salvation Army, and Frances Willard, founder of the Women's Christian Temperance Union.

The more staid and prestigious denominations did not ordain women to ministry, though many of them allowed for, often grudgingly, women preachers and teachers. Women outnumbered men in these denominations, where they put many of their energies into auxiliary organizations and served as educators or, most of all, as nourishers of faith in their homes. Some Catholic women excelled as leaders in religious orders, and two of them, Frances Cabrini and Elizabeth Ann Seton, were eventually canonized as saints.

The Social Question

After the Civil War, church leadership began to assess the new kinds of power produced in industrial and, eventually, corporate America. While the voluntary reform agencies continued their work with respect to individual needs, and while the Salvation Army and some counterparts addressed the problems of new immigrants, the poor, and victims of the new industrial order, some Protestants and Catholics thought it necessary to deal not only with individual but with corporate needs, to confront not only personal vices but structural and social "sin." The most prominent of these movements was the Social Gospel, which developed at century's end among mainstream Protestants. Just as the earlier movements eventually achieved transformation in American life—through temperance appeals and abolition—the Social Gospellers also worked for fundamental reform and change.

They were outnumbered, however, by middle-class Americans, who were partly isolated from the vision of poverty and need, and by followers of those whom the historian Winthrop Hudson called "Princes of the Pulpit." Preachers like Henry Ward Beecher attracted huge constituencies by offering messages that induced complacency or motivated personal ambition toward success. Beecher's bourgeois proclamations symbolized another growing division in the

THE AIM OF POPE PIUS IX.
"BEWARE! THERE IS DANGER IN THE DARK!"

Anti-Catholicism. Religious attitudes in nineteenth-century America were often marked by opposition to "immigrant" religions, such as Catholicism. Wood engraving from *Ballou's Pictorial Drawing-Room Companion*, 1855. LIBRARY OF CONGRESS

founded by Mary Baker Eddy in 1879. Christian Science was and is largely known as a healing movement in religion.

Many lesser movements, some of which barely survived or eventually disappeared, took advantage of spiritual hunger on the frontier. Among these were the Shakers, founded by Mother Ann Lee, an immigrant from England. This community shunned marriage and propagation. The Oneida Community was despised for propounding "free love" practices. The "infidel" Robert Owen was among other utopians

Protestant churches, as the respectable middle class came to look down on and fear the constant flow of non-Protestant immigrants from Catholic Europe. Under the leadership of James Cardinal Gibbons, Catholics alienated workers less than did Protestants or European Catholics, and many early labor movement leaders stayed with the Catholic Church.

New Patterns of Thought

New modes of thinking challenged the precepts of conventional and largely Christian America, first in the forms of "infidelity," or free thought, left over from Enlightenment days but rarely successful on the frontier. After mid-century, Darwinian theories of evolution came to prominence. Moderate and liberal church leaders initially adapted to the idea of evolutionism, while conservatives withdrew. But when natural selection came to dominate the scientific discussion, it was harder for many to coordinate evolutionary theory with belief in divine purpose, and only liberals voiced acceptance of Darwinism. Protestants in particular began to develop into a kind of "two-party" system of liberals and conservatives, who were to divide as modernists and fundamentalists well into the twentieth century.

Liberal theology was an internal challenge to revivalist, evangelical orthodoxies. Its advocates stressed an immanent God who induced progress in human affairs and downplayed sin and human limits in the interest of encouraging human aspiration toward progress or, in terms they found congenial, the Kingdom of God.

Often overlooked in accounts of American religion are the noninstitutional forms that never denominationalized. One could speak of this as the rise of what the sociologist Robert N. Bellah called "expressive individualism." At the opening of the century, churched America could still hear echoes of Enlightenment-era individualists such as Thomas Paine and President Thomas Jefferson, who averred that their own minds were their temples. They did not need organized religion and were highly critical of "priestcraft and superstition."

The frontier was characterized by both the formation of communities and by individualism, an inevitable by-product of population dispersal. Zealous though they might be, the revivalists, circuit riders, and chapel builders could never keep up with lonely adventurers in the wilderness and on the prairie. Yet when revivalists did come on the scene, they found that many of these entrepreneurs and homesteaders had developed some forms of piety on their own.

A more sophisticated conception of the frontier spirit came from modern philosophers such as William James, who at the turn of the twentieth century spoke for many when he defined religion as "the feelings, acts, and experiences of individual men in their solitude." While anticlericalism never developed on the American scene on a scale that matched European versions—perhaps largely because clericalism was easier to attack where a religious establishment prevailed—church and synagogue leaders found the rise of the modern forms of individualist, noninstitutional religion more puzzling and provoking than they found free thought or atheism. The latter was voiced by a few enterprising and courageous mavericks such as Robert G. Ingersoll, who in the 1880s charmed and shocked audiences with his clever attacks on Christian doctrine. But Ingersoll turned out to have more entertainment value than intellectual influence, and no native-born "God killers" rose on the American scene to rival the likes of Karl Marx, Friedrich Nietzsche, Charles Darwin, and Sigmund Freud across the Atlantic. Religion was very much a taken-for-granted force in respectable America.

See also **African Americans,** *subentry on* **African American Religions; Catholicism; Christian Science; Communitarian Movements and Groups; Evangelicalism; Judaism; Millennialism and Adventism; Mormonism; Protestantism; Social Gospel.**

Bibliography

Ahlstrom, Sydney E. *A Religious History of the American People.* New Haven, Conn.: Yale University Press, 1972.

Albanese, Catherine L. *America: Religions and Religion.* Belmont, Calif.: Wadsworth, 1981.

Butler, Jon. *Awash in a Sea of Faith: Christianizing the American People.* Cambridge, Mass.: Harvard University Press, 1990.

Dolan, Jay P. *The American Catholic Experience: A History from Colonial Times to the Present.* Garden City, N.Y.: Doubleday, 1985.

Glazer, Nathan. *American Judaism.* 2d ed. Chicago: University of Chicago Press, 1972.

Hansen, Klaus J. *Mormonism and the American Experience.* Chicago: University of Chicago Press, 1981.

Hatch, Nathan O. *The Democratization of American Christianity.* New Haven, Conn.: Yale University Press, 1989.

Marty, Martin E. *Righteous Empire: The Protestant Experience in America.* New York: Dial, 1970.

Moore, R. Laurence. *Religious Outsiders and the Making of America.* New York: Oxford University Press, 1986.

Raboteau, Albert J. *Slave Religion: The "Invisible Institution" in the Antebellum South.* New York: Oxford University Press, 1978.

Ruether, Rosemary Radford, and Rosemary Skinner Keller, eds. *Women and Religion in America.* Volume 1: *The Nineteenth Century.* San Francisco: Harper and Row, 1981.

Shipps, Jan. *Mormonism: The Story of a New Religious Tradition.* Urbana: University of Illinois Press, 1981.

MARTIN E. MARTY

RELIGION AS A POLITICAL ISSUE

The Constitution of the United States does not mention God. Its one reference to religion is a ban on religious qualifications for officeholders, and the First Amendment denies Congress the authority to establish a national faith or to abridge freedom of religion. When the First Amendment went into effect in 1791, however, five states provided tax support for ministers, and twelve maintained religious qualifications for office. The states dropped most of these practices early in the nineteenth century, and by mid-century most state constitutions mirrored the national compact in decreeing that government can neither support nor govern religion.

Even so, a few religiously identified organizations experienced direct political and governmental attacks. Among these were the Masonic Lodge and the Church of Jesus Christ of Latter-day Saints (Mormons). In the late 1820s an anti-Masonic movement, centered in the northeastern evangelical churches, attacked the Masonic Lodge as a secret society and an infidel substitute for a church. For a time anti-Masons were a political force in the rural Northeast, where they forced most Masonic Lodges to disband. In the 1830s and 1840s Mormon settlements in Missouri and Illinois were subject to government harassment that included invasions by state militias. The Mormons retreated to Utah in 1847, and in 1857 they engaged in armed conflict with the U.S. Army. Congress refused Utah's admission to the Union until 1896 and granted statehood then only after the Mormons agreed to abandon theocratic government and polygamous marriage.

While the amended Constitution separated church and state, it did not separate religion and politics. Indeed from the 1820s through the end of the nineteenth century and beyond questions grounded ultimately in religion, such as Sabbath keeping, antislavery, anti-Catholicism, prohibition, and Bible reading in schools, helped create and maintain the two-party system. In the North and West the National Republican (1820s–1830s), Whig (1830s–1850s), and Republican (1850s onward) Parties drew their core support from native-born evangelical Protestants, politicized moralizers who saw themselves as the keepers of America's historic national faith. Their Democratic opposition centered among sectarian Protestants, nonchurchgoers, evangelicals who refused to mix religion and politics, and, increasingly, immigrant Catholics. In the South, on the other hand, Baptist and Methodist cultural dominance was pervasive and seldom contested. While evangelicalism, white and black, was crucial to the making of southern society and culture, it was seldom a political issue in that section.

Northern evangelicals entered politics in the late 1820s with anti-Masonry and with calls for laws against Sabbath breaking. The Sabbatarians enjoyed some local success but failed in their petition campaign to make the federal government end the transportation of mail and the opening of post offices on Sunday. The Senate rejected their petitions, and Senator Richard M. Johnson of Kentucky, a devout Baptist who became vice president under President Martin Van Buren, answered them with a ringing defense of the constitutional wall between church and state. Even though they lost, the Sabbatarians in the process identified Senator Johnson's Democratic Party as the opponent of Protestant moral legislation. The contest between libertarian Democrats and the Whigs and Republicans who proposed Protestant moral laws persisted throughout the century.

In the 1830s, radical northern evangelicals launched an organized, sustained attack upon slavery in the southern states. The American Antislavery Society established branches in hundreds of northern and western communities, filled the mails with antislavery literature, and showered Congress with antislavery petitions. White southerners, recognizing that the activist, individualist implications of northern evangelicalism were at the base of the attack on slavery, responded with religious arguments of their own—arguments from the Old Testament that buttressed fixed social relationships and the patriarchal family. The controversy over slavery that began in the 1830s quickly expanded into questions of federalism, territorial expansion, and sectional political power, but it remained grounded in the moral and religious differences between the North and the South.

Another long-term battleground was public education. The schools mandated by state governments in the 1820s and 1830s included religious instruction and readings from the King James (English Protestant) Bible in particular. This was acceptable to Protestant churchgoers and to nonchurchgoers who were culturally Protestant. Religion in the schools became a political question when thousands of Irish and German Catholics entered the country in the 1840s and 1850s. Catholic parents and priests objected to the Protestant tenor of the schools. Many Catholics refused to send their children to the public schools, sometimes demanding tax support for Catholic education. Others simply called for the elimination of Protestant or anti-Catholic texts. Controversies over religion and the schools persisted throughout the nineteenth century and beyond, usually pitting middle-class Protestant Republicans, who wished to use the schools to "Americanize" immigrants, against immigrant Catholic Democrats, who refused to acknowledge that "American" meant "Protestant."

The most sustained moral issue in American politics was prohibition, beginning with the founding of the American Temperance Society in 1826. Rooted in middle-class evangelical churches, the early temperance movement tried to persuade Americans to give up alcohol. It soon switched to local campaigns for stricter liquor licensing laws, then to state-level prohibition. The first temperance success was the Massachusetts "Fifteen Gallon Law" of 1838, which forbade the sale of liquor by the drink. That law was repealed the following year, however. In the 1840s the Washingtonian Temperance Society and a number of temperance lodges brought new nondrinkers, many of them working-class Methodists and Baptists, into the fold. This enlarged constituency called for legal prohibition in the 1840s and 1850s, primarily as a nativist response to the mass immigration of Irish and German Catholics. An energized Protestant-nativist majority passed prohibition laws in seventeen northern states in the 1850s. The immigrants interpreted prohibition as Protestant coercion, and they turned consistently to the Democratic Party for help.

Following the Civil War, Republicans branded the Democrats as the party of "Rum, Romanism, and Rebellion," that is, of drunkenness, Catholicism, and southern secession. The antiliquor forces formed the Prohibition Party, which ran its first candidate for president in 1872. Under the leadership of the Methodist reformer Frances Willard, the Women's Christian Temperance Union campaigned for prohibition largely as a Protestant family issue. In 1895 the Anti-Saloon League began the systematic single-issue campaign centered among Protestant, overwhelmingly Republican households that resulted in national Prohibition in 1919. Democrats courted immigrant and southern votes, promising protection from intrusive moral legislation. But late in the century many southern evangelicals abandoned their old doubts about political activism and joined with the Prohibitionists. This added southern support made national Prohibition possible. It also created a powerful conservative coalition of northern Republicans and southern Democrats that could legislate on other issues. That coalition remained central to the organization of politics through changes in party names and partisan issues in the twentieth century.

See also **Abolition and Antislavery; Anti-Mormonism; Bill of Rights; Blue Laws; Clubs,** *subentry on* **Religious Clubs and Associations; Democratic Party; Immigra-** **tion and Immigrants: An Overview; Republican Party; Temperance Movement; Whig Party.**

Bibliography

Kramnick, Isaac, and R. Laurence Moore. *The Godless Constitution: The Case against Religious Correctness*. New York: Norton, 1996.

Noll, Mark A., *A History of Christianity in the United States and Canada*. Grand Rapids, Mich.: W. B. Eerdmans, 1992.

——, ed. *Religion and American Politics: From the Colonial Period to the 1980s*. New York: Oxford University Press, 1990.

PAUL E. JOHNSON

REPUBLICANISM

American historians once taught that the revolutionaries of 1776 created a republic without being republicans. The revolutionaries withdrew their allegiance from the English monarchy in 1776 because they cherished liberty, not because they aspired to set up a republic. For their ideas about government, patriot leaders relied principally on the Englishman John Locke (1632–1704), who had a great deal to say about natural rights and the consent of the governed, but little to say about republics. According to this historical interpretation, the political philosophy of eighteenth- and nineteenth-century America was the Lockean creed of natural rights and curbs on government that scholars would label "liberalism."

Defining Republicanism and Its Revolutionary Influence

The traditional account of early American political thought began to be questioned by Caroline Robbins as early as the 1940s; in the 1960s it was challenged aggressively by Bernard Bailyn and Gordon Wood. These revisionist historians argued that the men who made the Revolution had thought long and hard about the implications of erecting an American republic. In this thinking they were guided by the writings of English political dissenters—the radical Whigs or "Commonwealthmen" (heirs to the promise of the short-lived English republic, 1649 to 1653), who denounced corruption and various policies of the crown through much of the eighteenth century. Believing that all rulers craved power at the expense of their subjects, the radical Whigs looked back to the republics of ancient Greece and Rome (and to ancient writers like Cicero [106–43 B.C.] and Tacitus [c. A.D. 56–120]) for models of just governance. They did not call for an English republic—that would have been treason—but they did call on the king and Parliament to honor English constitutional principles which operated, in the spirit of the ancient republics, to safeguard liberty and check arbitrary power. Bailyn and Wood contended that the oppositionist "republicanism" developed by the radical Whigs structured the thinking of Americans who opposed the new imperial policies of George III (1738–1820).

Bailyn and Wood proceeded to remap the patriots' whole political universe. At its center was the conviction that men (and only men) were political beings who achieved their greatest fulfillment by participating in the affairs of the state. Monarchies and aristocracies accorded political rights to only a few, ruling the many by force and fear; republics conferred liberty and shares of sovereignty on common men, in the faith that they possessed the "civic virtue" required for participation in government. Yet American republicans were not democrats. They believed in property qualifications for full citizenship, on the grounds that only propertied men were sufficiently independent to be "disinterested"—to subordinate their private interests to the needs of the Commonwealth. Moreover, republicans believed that power tended to corrupt those who exercised it. Thus, depending on fragile virtue, republics themselves were fragile. "Liberty is never sure, 'till Virtue reigns triumphant," proclaimed a college commencement orator in 1795 (Kerber, *Women of the Republic*, p. 230). The American revolutionaries feared their countrymen also might eventually succumb to the civic degeneracy that had brought down the ancient republics and brought low the British. Nonetheless, they were encouraged by the extraordinary socioeconomic conditions (particularly the wide distribution of landed property) that seemed to promise health to an American republic.

What the Revolution achieved, then, was more than a separation from Great Britain. It forged a new republican worldview—a regenerative vision of a just and virtuous society. The pamphleteer Thomas Paine (1737–1809) told a French correspondent in 1782, "Our style and manner of thinking have undergone a revolution more extraordinary than the political revolution of the country. We see with other eyes; we hear with other ears; and think with other thoughts, than those we formerly used" (Wood, *The Creation of the American Republic, 1776–1787*, p. 48).

The "republican synthesis" crafted by Bailyn and Wood has altered permanently our understanding of the Revolution, its origins, and its legacy. Few historians now doubt the revolutionary leaders' debts to the radical Whigs, or their admiration for the political culture that once flourished, they believed, in ancient Rome. But questions persist about the nature and limits of American republicanism. Was it an aristocratic ideology, sponsoring an ideal of citizenship accessible only to propertied gentlemen? Was it nostalgic and defensive, or optimistic, even utopian?

Perhaps the most disputed question has to do with the longevity of republicanism in America. Some historians assert that it continued to exert influence on public affairs through much of the nineteenth century. Others contend that republican ideas receded from the center of the political culture soon after the Revolution. Republicanism helped make the Revolution, these doubters acknowledge, but in the nineteenth century the philosophy of liberalism, descended from the writings of Locke and Adam Smith (1723–1790), molded the way most Americans thought about liberty, government, and citizenship.

Understanding the Relationship between Republicanism and Liberalism

In debating the relative strengths of republicanism and liberalism, historians have tended to contrast them. Republicans sought to optimize conditions for good government; liberals sought to optimize conditions for economic growth. Republicans honored civic virtue; liberals prized enlightened self-interest. Republicans fretted about the degrading effects of commerce; liberals extolled the moral discipline of trading in free markets. Republicans had no objection to active government (provided it was virtuous); liberals distrusted state power.

However, in recent years, scholars on all sides have rejected the practice of reifying "republican" and "liberal." These are abstractions used by historians to interpret the behavior of people who did not think of themselves as republicans or liberals. Thus republicanism and liberalism should be understood as loose tendencies that intertwined, and not as systematic philosophies that clashed. In the career of a man like Benjamin Franklin (1706–1790) the two tendencies fused. The liberal Franklin made a small fortune as a printer and, as the canny "Poor Richard," told his countrymen how to succeed in business. The republican Franklin retired from the printing trade at age forty-two to become a gentleman, a paragon of civic virtue, and a hero of the Revolution. The historian Robert Shalhope suggests that while republican images shaped Americans' consciousness and identity during the revolutionary period, liberal values were already guiding their day-to-day conduct.

Rather than conflicting systems, republicanism and liberalism may be viewed as different dimensions of an elastic and diffuse ideology that revolved around the core value of liberty. Republicanism was liberty militant, the facet of American political culture that mobilized men to fight for their rights. The Revolutionary crisis summoned republican ideas to the forefront of Americans' political consciousness. The defensive imperative accounts for the martial and communitarian strains that many scholars have detected in republicanism. Knowing that power was predatory and liberty perpetually at risk, the good republican, like the good soldier, had to be perpetually vigilant and prepared for battle. The model republican was George Washington (1732–1799), the American reincarnation of the Roman hero Cincinnatus (b.c. 519 B.C.): a peace-loving man who was prepared to bear arms in defense of the Commonwealth.

If republicanism was liberty militant, liberalism was liberty triumphant: the dimension of Americans' political thinking that reflected their capitalist ambitions and their individualist proclivities. If Americans' republican values armed them intellectually to secure liberty, their liberal values moved them to exploit the opportunities opened up by a secured liberty.

Recruited to the revolutionary cause in the 1760s and victorious in the 1780s, republican ideas were gradually mustered out of service during the following decades. The classical republicanism of the founders died out with the Federalists, the party of Washington and Alexander Hamilton (1757–1804), in the 1810s. The farmers and artisans who revered Thomas Jefferson (1743–1826) and Andrew Jackson (1767–1845) were more intent on minimizing government than on making it virtuous. Liberal ideas better complemented Americans' drive to develop the continent. For many white men especially, the great imperative of the nineteenth century no longer was to defend liberty, but to use it and capitalize on it. Alexis de Tocqueville (1805–1859) remarked on the shift in emphasis from republican to liberal values in *Democracy in America* (1840): "Hardly anybody talks of the beauty of virtue." Instead "the Americans . . . are fond of explaining almost all the actions of their lives by the principle of self-interest rightly understood; they show with complacency how an enlightened regard for themselves constantly prompts them to assist one another and inclines them willingly to sacrifice a portion of their time and property to the welfare of the state" (vol. 2, pp. 129–130). Soon after the Revolution, Joyce Appleby notes, the word "virtue" began losing its reference to public service and was used more frequently to denote "a private quality, a man's capacity to look out for himself and his dependents" (Appleby, *Capitalism and a New Social Order*, pp. 14–15).

Following the Legacy of Republicanism

Despite these philosophical shifts, elements of the republican tradition endured into the nineteenth century, as alternatives to the dominant language of liberalism. Dissenters used republican standards of virtue and harmony for judging a society given over to capitalism and individualism; republicanism furnished moral and rhetorical resources to groups striving for citizenship. Whenever Americans sought to expand the boundaries of liberty, republicanism was called back into service. In this function the residual American republicanism of the nineteenth century resembled the English republicanism of the radical Whigs: it organized the perceptions and sustained the spirits of reformers and outsiders. Thus, for example, utopian experimenters commonly adopted ideals of commonwealth and civic virtue. Abolitionists identified slavery as the antithesis of republican values, the epitome of the arbitrary power which the Revolution had been fought to expunge. (Meanwhile, slaveholders devised a republican defense of slavery as a system that freed citizen-masters to perfect themselves as citizens.)

The republican legacy of the Revolution had ambiguous implications for women aspiring to equality with men. With its emphasis on independence, property, and worldly wisdom, the republican model of citizenship excluded women. So did the masculine ethos of "liberty militant." Yet in their role as "republican mothers," American women could claim a vital political function: nurturing the righteous citizen-sons who would sustain the Republic in the future. Before and after the Seneca Falls, New York, woman's rights convention of 1848, suffragists argued that if civic virtue began at home, the mothers who bred that virtue could themselves be virtuous citizens. Radical suffragists like Elizabeth Cady Stanton (1815–1902) and Susan B. Anthony (1820–1906) decided doctrines like republican motherhood were too timid. They contended that women had every right to political equality with men, not as mothers but as Americans.

Republican principles also animated movements to protest political corruption and the abuses of unregulated capitalism. Sean Wilentz contends that American artisans "elaborated their own democratic variant of American republican ideology," basing their claim to citizenship on the economic independence and moral virtue they derived from practicing their trades (Wilentz, *Chants Democratic*, p. 15). In republican fashion, the leaders of unions and workers' parties in the 1820s contrasted their devotion to the community with their employers' avarice and lust for power. This "artisan republicanism" died with the skilled crafts that supported it, but republican values of commonwealth, citizenly disinterestedness, and positive government appeared in the thoughts of Henry George (1839–1897), Edward Bellamy (1850–1898), labor and Populist leaders, and other critics of industrial capitalism in the 1880s and 1890s. All of these groups proposed to restore the true legacy of the Revolution, which they accused venal politicians and plutocrats of having stolen.

Liberal and republican principles mingled in the motives of the genteel reformers who founded the Liberal Republican Party in 1872. As liberals they opposed government meddling with currency values, market laws, and white supremacy in the South. They loathed the venality and vulgarity of the administration of Ulysses S. Grant (1822–1885). But they dreamed of purifying, not dismantling, the government, by creating a professional civil service that would put power in the hands of disinterested gentlemen like themselves.

The Liberal Republicans' thinking was laden with nostalgia for a never-never commonwealth of virtue. Yet for more creative and determined reformers, too, republican ideals retained a certain resonance a century after the Revolution. The Progressives who began their careers in the 1890s spoke a new language of pragmatic reform; but virtuous service to the commonwealth was central to the way Jane Addams (1860–1935), Frederic C. Howe (1868–1940), Robert LaFollette (1855–1925), and Theodore Roosevelt (1858–1919) conceived of their missions.

See also **Liberalism; Liberty; Politics,** *subentry on* **Political Thought; Revolutionary War Remembered.**

Bibliography

Appleby, Joyce. *Liberalism and Republicanism in the Historical Imagination.* Cambridge, Mass.: Harvard University Press, 1992.

Bailyn, Bernard. *The Ideological Origins of the American Revolution.* 1967. Enl. ed., Cambridge, Mass.: Belknap Press of Harvard University Press, 1992.

Kerber, Linda K. *Women of the Republic: Intellect and Ideology in Revolutionary America.* 1980. Reprint, New York: Norton, 1986.

Klein, Milton M., Richard D. Brown, and John B. Hench, eds. *The Republican Synthesis Revisited: Essays in Honor of George Athan Billias.* Worcester, Mass.: American Antiquarian Society, 1992.

McInerney, Daniel J. *The Fortunate Heirs of Freedom: Abolition and Republican Thought.* Lincoln: University of Nebraska Press, 1994.

Shalhope, Robert E. "Toward a Republican Synthesis: The Emergence of an Understanding of Republican in American Historiography." *William and Mary Quarterly* 3d ser., 29 (1972): 49–80.

Wilentz, Sean. *Chants Democratic: New York City and the Rise of the American Working Class, 1788–1850.* New York: Oxford University Press, 1984.

Wood, Gordon S. *The Creation of the American Republic, 1776–1787.* Chapel Hill: University of North Carolina Press, 1969.

———. *The Radicalism of the American Revolution.* New York: Vintage, 1993.

EUGENE E. LEACH

REPUBLICAN MOTHERHOOD

The term "republican mother" describes the model revolutionary republican woman of the late eighteenth and early nineteenth centuries. Such political philosophers as John Locke, the Baron de Montesquieu, and Jean-Jacques Rousseau proposed the creation of direct relationships between sovereign citizens and the state but excluded women from full membership in the constituent power. Republican theorists disagreed as to why the polity ought to be masculine. While Locke advocated male-female equality on such questions as child custody and divorce, for instance, he posited a sharp division between "conjugal society" and political governments. Rousseau, by contrast, refused to expand woman's sphere to include either domestic or political governance. But most European philosophes agreed that women had to be excluded from public life.

Such exclusion, however, presented problems, if only because it assumed a gender-based inequality at odds both with women's experience in the New World and with elements of radical republicanism. American and European thinkers, such as Judith Sargent Murray, Susanna Rowson, Benjamin Rush, Theodor Gottlieb von Hippel, and Mary Wollstonecraft, therefore promoted a remodeled republican mother entrusted with civic-minded work originating primarily in the maternal function. This construct affirmed women's worth while preserving traditional conceptions of the "good" wife and the male monopoly of public life. Even Locke, notwithstanding his insistence on the sex's equal claims to a direct relationship with nature's God, argued in the end that, in cases of disagreement between men and women, a male head of household ought to "lay down the law" to ensure efficient management of family and polity.

Into the 1770s, then, republican motherhood—a phrase coined in 1976 by the historian Linda Kerber—offered a way for upper- and middle-class white women to do patriotic work without direct participation in public affairs. Advocates of republican motherhood tried to combine domesticity and politics in a way that advanced revolutionary objectives without upsetting patriarchal applecarts. The ideal republican woman could not be idle, uneducated, or frivolous, nor could she be a wage laborer, an African American, or an American Indian, for whom republican motherhood was off-limits and whose very existence underscored the special properties and status of white women. Instead, she would be a well-educated, virtuous mother-citizen fluent in such disciplines as theology, literature, moral and political philosophy, and writing. She also would be a productive home worker although not a coarse laborer, the special custodian of republican idealism, and a worthy companion for virtuous Sons of Liberty.

These cultural changes were both limiting and emancipating. Before the mid–eighteenth century serious education had been largely a male undertaking. Now white middle- and upper-class women could hope to educate children in the fine points of republican political theory. They also could expect to be treated not as inferior helpmeets but as coequals who "governed" a separate, private, and tranquil domestic sphere while men did battle in public locations, such as the marketplace, jury boxes, the polls, and the militia. The republican mother would be the moral and cultural anchor of the revolutionary experiment but not a voter or a legislator. She also might carry her domestic concerns into the community as a reformer or educator. But, as Mercy Otis Warren learned the hard way, she could not cross the line between male and female realms. When Warren published a well-regarded history of the American Revolution, John Adams sharply castigated her for abandoning her patriotic post and poaching on masculine "science."

Historians have long debated the concept of republican womanhood and the related concept of separate spheres. Some emphasized the confining, unreconstructed character of these concepts, arguing that republican motherhood and separate spheres ensured the ongoing patriarchal control of women and the relative unimportance of eighteenth-century women's "revolutionary" innovations. Another group of scholars detected important shifts in the balance of power between men and women, related in part to women's augmented power within their families. In this view women in varying degrees made use of revolutionary ideas and indeed the revolutionary crisis itself to expand dramatically their sex's ambit. Still other historians emphasized the mixed character of revolutionary conceptions of the "ideal" republican woman-citizen in France and America. On the one hand, her power as a domestic rule-giver and educator had been augmented, but, on the other hand, the gendered line between public and private life had hardened. Thus, "republican motherhood" and "woman's sphere" had ideological rather than social significance, operating less as descriptors of social reality than as tools capable of warning off or punishing transgressive women.

Even farsighted egalitarian thinkers like Rush and Wollstonecraft were not ready to eliminate the separate spheres in which women and men functioned. Some scholars attributed this feature of eighteenth-century radicalism to the seeming claims of nature. Motherhood, a biologically determined female role, suggested the "naturalness" of republican motherhood and the "unnaturalness" of radical alternatives, such as male-female political equality. Moreover contemporaries described the role of the male citizen in opposition to the passive female role. The dependence of women and children thus helped to validate both the independence of male citizens and the otherwise traitorous rebellion of colonial "sons" against a tyrannical British "father." The revolutionaries thus undertook a rebellion in part for the benefit of classes deemed incapable of engaging in self-protection.

In the late eighteenth century republicans typically were not ready to revolutionize gender relations. Instead they fastened on the republican mother to ennoble women without fundamentally altering the terms of the social compact struck between male citizens. Women sometimes rebelled against the confines of woman's sphere and patriotic motherhood, but most did not. Indeed, as the nineteenth century advanced, both republican motherhood and the nation of separate spheres crystallized and exercised hegemonic authority within white society. It was precisely this sense of a republican revolution that inspired women's rights activists to foment another rebellion after 1848. In turn, these attempts by nineteenth-century women to abandon their patriotic stations and participate in politics elicited charges not merely of mannishness but of treachery against the Republic. Buttressed by the law of coverture, through which Anglo-Americans described and enforced married women's social and political disabilities, the concept of republican motherhood conditioned women's liberty prospects well into the late twentieth century.

See also **Character; Domestic Life; Education,** *subentry on* **Education of Girls and Women; Gender; Labor Movement,** *subentry on* **Women; Literature,** *subentry on* **Women's Literature; Magazines, Women's; Marriage; Women,** *subentries on* **Woman as Image and Icon** *and* **Women's Rights.**

Bibliography

Applewhite, Harriet B., and Darline G. Levy, eds. *Women and Politics in the Age of the Democratic Revolution.* Ann Arbor: University of Michigan Press, 1990.

Bloch, Ruth H. "The Gendered Meanings of Virtue in Revolutionary America." *Signs* 13 (1987): 37–58.

Gundersen, Joan R. *To Be Useful to the World: Women in Revolutionary America, 1740–1770.* New York: Twayne, 1996.

Hoffman, Ronald, and Peter J. Albert, eds. *Women in the Age of the American Revolution.* Charlottesville: University Press of Virginia, 1989.

Jones, Jacqueline. "Race, Sex, and Self-Evident Truths: The Status of Slave Women during the Era of the American Revolution." In *Half Sisters of History.* Edited by Catherine Clinton. Durham, N.C.: Duke University Press, 1994.

———. *Women of the Republic: Intellect and Ideology in Revolutionary America.* Chapel Hill: University of North Carolina Press, 1980.

Landes, Joan B. *Women and the Public Sphere in the Age of the French Revolution.* Ithaca, N.Y.: Cornell University Press, 1988.

Norton, Mary Beth. "The Evolution of White Women's Experience in Early America." *American Historical Review* 89, no. 3 (1984): 593–619.

———. *Liberty's Daughters: The Revolutionary Experience of American Women, 1750–1800.* Boston: Little, Brown, 1980.

Pateman, Carole. *The Sexual Contract.* Cambridge, U.K.: Polity, 1988.

SANDRA F. VANBURKLEO
ERIKA HANSINGER

REPUBLICAN PARTY   During the second half of the nineteenth century, the Republican Party established itself as one of the nation's two major political organizations. Advocating a strong national government as the means to promote economic growth, the Republicans became the driving force in American politics and set the agenda for several generations. By 1900 they had achieved a clear electoral supremacy over their Democratic rivals and were the majority party of the United States.

Although the Republican Party grew out of the agitation against slavery during the 1850s, its founders were not exclusively northern enemies of human bondage. The main component of the new Republican coalition consisted of former members of the Whig Party, who wanted to meld the economic doctrines of that organization with antislavery sentiment. Other elements included disaffected Democrats put off by the power of southerners in their party and exponents of moral reforms such as the prohibition of liquor.

The precipitating cause of the formation of the Republican Party was the debate over the Kansas-Nebraska Act in 1854. By reviving the slavery question, this act galvanized northerners to look for a party that could express their outrage and offer a means to pursue their antislavery agenda. Meetings were held to create a new political organization that embodied northern unhappiness. The first gathering of this kind took place in March 1854 at Ripon, Wisconsin; subsequent meetings led to the Republican Party's official formation.

Early Years of Republican Development

The Republican Party grew rapidly. In 1856 the Republicans fielded a presidential candidate, John C. Frémont, on an antislavery platform. Although Frémont lost, he ran well in the North, where he carried a majority of the region's electoral votes. During the remainder of the decade, the Republicans eclipsed the Know-Nothing Party and its nativist support. By 1860 Republicans offered the most effective means for northerners to express their opposition to the expansion of slavery.

In that year Abraham Lincoln campaigned for the presidency on the theme that the nation should be placed on a course leading to the extinction of slavery. He won the election even though he received no electoral votes from the South. His substantial electoral majorities in the North enabled him to outdistance his three rivals. The Civil War that followed stamped the Republicans as the party that preserved the Union against treason and rebellion. In the aftermath of the war, Republicans regarded Democrats as a party that had flirted with secession and lost its political legitimacy.

In the course of the Civil War, the Republican Party became identified as well with the causes of emancipation and of giving former slaves a chance to participate in the political and economic life of the nation. The Emancipation Proclamation was the most notable example of this wartime policy.

In the economic sphere, the Republicans used their majorities in Congress to enact the Morrill Tariff (1861), federal assistance to state colleges through the Morrill Act (1862), and the National Banking Act of 1863. These accomplishments further strengthened the image of the Republicans as the party of energy and change.

The Challenge of Reconstruction

Following the war and the assassination of Abraham Lincoln, the Republican Party sought to implement a Reconstruction policy for the defeated South that would assist the newly freed slaves and establish a Republican political base in the region. The major achievements of the Republicans in this regard were the three postwar amendments to the Constitution: the Thirteenth, which abolished slavery; the Fourteenth, which guaranteed blacks federal and state citizenship and equal protection under the law; and the Fifteenth, which ruled out race or color as a barrier to voting.

While successful in enacting these broad, general concepts into fundamental law, the Republicans encountered difficulty in transforming the South as they had envisioned. White resistance in the region seriously obstructed the Republican effort. In a blatantly partisan attempt to remove an obstacle to Re-

The 1856 Presidential Campaign. The Republican candidate John Charles Frémont (1813–1890) was not a natural politician; he was best known as an explorer of the western territories. LIBRARY OF CONGRESS

construction, the Republicans in Congress even went so far as to impeach President Andrew Johnson in 1868, but that effort proved unsuccessful. By the time Ulysses S. Grant was elected president in 1868, the momentum for Reconstruction had slowed.

The Grant presidency was a difficult time for the Republicans. Grant was not an effective executive, and the charges of corruption that swirled around his administration eroded the Party's moral standing. The president sought to maintain Republican regimes in southern states favorable to Reconstruction, but that proved increasingly difficult to do. By the mid-1870s the white South had returned to the Democratic fold. The Republicans had pockets of electoral strength in the region, but southern electoral votes were once again in the Democratic column.

Party divisions and economic problems plagued the Republicans in the 1870s. Grant faced a revolt from a dissident branch of the party, the Liberal Republicans, in 1872. This faction wanted easier treatment of the South, a lower tariff, and civil service reform. It joined the Democrats in support of the presidential candidate Horace Greeley in the 1872 election. Grant easily defeated Greeley in what would be the last decisive presidential election for a generation.

During Grant's second term, the Republican electoral position deteriorated. The economic depression that ensued from the panic of 1873 gave the Democrats a campaign issue that they used effectively in retaking the House of Representatives in 1874. Although the Republicans fought to repress the Ku Klux Klan in the South and achieved passage of the Civil Rights Act of 1875, the party's commitment to justice in the South was waning. More and more Republicans urged the party to concentrate on economic issues as a way of becoming a majority party once again. The growing influence of business interests in Republican affairs accelerated this trend.

The presidential election of 1876 proved to be a turning point in Republican history. The leading candidate for the nomination was James G. Blaine of Maine, a former Speaker of the House. Charismatic and eloquent, Blaine had legions of admirers across the country. Ethical problems involving assistance he had rendered an Arkansas railroad, however, cast a shadow over his candidacy, and the party turned to a safer choice, Rutherford B. Hayes of Ohio. The Democrats nominated Samuel J. Tilden of New York.

The disputed election resulted in a settlement bro-

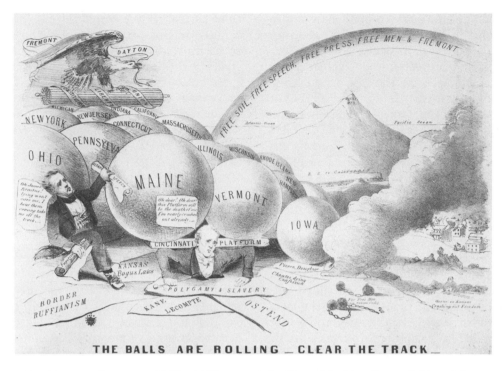

A Pro-Frémont Statement. Millard Fillmore of the Know-Nothing Party *(left)* and James Buchanan of the Democratic Party *(center)* are overcome by states that supported Republican candidate John Charles Frémont in the 1856 presidential election. Cartoon by Nathaniel Currier. LIBRARY OF CONGRESS: PRINTS AND PHOTOGRAPHS DIVISION

kered by the Electoral Commission, in which a sectional compromise was achieved. Hayes was elected in return for a tacit promise by the Republicans to end Reconstruction in the South. Although many elements in the party remained loyal to the ideals of the Civil War, the focus of Republicanism was shifting to the promotion of economic growth through a sound currency and, most notably, the protective tariff. As a result, party leaders made rhetorical bows toward the issue of black rights, but their hearts were in the economic issues that attracted larger numbers of voters in the North.

Republicans in the Gilded Age

The two decades that followed the election of Hayes were difficult for the Republican Party. Factionalism, the legacy of corruption under Grant, and a revived Democratic Party meant that the Republicans had to fight hard to maintain their electoral place. The resulting struggle proved to be an unexpected asset as Republicans strove to maintain internal cohesion. A tradition emerged within the party that no individual was more important than the larger institution.

The Republicans also had the benefit of strong national leadership in these years. In addition to Blaine, the Republicans counted among them James A. Garfield, Benjamin Harrison, Thomas B. Reed, and William McKinley. Such men found the positive pro-

grams of the Republicans attractive and profitable. They saw Republicanism as a springboard to national office. As a result, the party enabled younger politicians to build a following across the country.

The process of building a new national majority for the Republicans started slowly in the Hayes administration. The president maintained the prerogatives of his office against more patronage-minded party members such as Roscoe Conkling of New York. Hayes had less success strengthening the party in the South, where Democratic resistance to Republican inroads persisted. Democrats made gains in the congressional elections of 1878, as Republican infighting lingered and the effects of the depression of the 1870s continued. While Hayes was not a great president, he did recapture the moral authority that had been lost during the Grant years.

In the 1880 election the Republicans played down the southern question and turned their emphasis to the protective tariff under the leadership of Blaine and presidential candidate James A. Garfield. Garfield won the presidency by a close margin, and protectionism became a central tenet of Republican ideology for the next two decades.

The protective tariff enabled the Republicans to blend economic and emotional issues into an ideology that appealed to many in the North during the Gilded Age. Business leaders who faced competition from foreign economic interests responded to the protection that the tariff offered. The Republicans championed the tariff as beneficial to American workers, associating protectionism with prosperity and nationalism and accusing the Democrats of selling out to foreign interests. All Republicans, whatever their position on other issues, could rally behind the tariff as the embodiment of the Grand Old Party.

Garfield's assassination in 1881 once again disrupted the party's electoral momentum. The interim presidency of Chester Alan Arthur saw the unity of 1880 ebb away as the Republicans debated the civil service issue and tariff rates. The party suffered losses in the congressional elections of 1882, and economic conditions indicated that a Democratic victory was likely in the next presidential race.

The 1884 nomination went to Blaine, who campaigned against Democrat Grover Cleveland with energy and determination. In a year when the Democrats had the advantage, Blaine proved to be a formidable contender. A celebrated reference to the Democrats as the party of "Rum, Romanism, and Rebellion" made by the Reverend S. D. Burchard supposedly cost him the crucial state of New York. The presidency went to Cleveland in a close race, but Blaine was recognized as having retarded the electoral slide of the Republicans and helping put the party in a position to regain the White House in 1888.

During the first Cleveland administration, the Republicans worked on their party organization and waited for their adversaries to falter. Their chance came when Cleveland made lowering the protective tariff the sole theme of his annual message in 1887, in effect challenging the Republicans to base their presidential campaign on that issue. It was an opportunity that Blaine and others were glad to exploit. The Republicans happily rallied to the cause of the tariff.

To lead their campaign, the party selected Benjamin Harrison, an Indiana protectionist. Harrison was an adroit campaigner who captivated crowds with his speeches endorsing the tariff. The Republicans were well funded, purposeful, and organized. The Democrats were divided about the tariff and poorly managed. Although Cleveland won the popular vote, thanks to Democratic dominance of the South, Harrison had a clear majority in the electorate vote. The Republicans also won control of both houses of Congress.

The Limits of Republican Activism

In the Fifty-first Congress, the Republicans endeavored to enact their program of economic nationalism behind the leadership of Speaker Thomas B. Reed of Maine. The record of the Republicans was impressive. In 1890 they passed the Sherman Antitrust Act, the Sherman Silver Purchase Act, and the protectionist McKinley Tariff. Only in the case of the unsuccessful federal elections bill to preserve voting rights in the South did the Republicans falter.

To their dismay, the Republicans found that the voters were not pleased with this record of legislative productivity. In the fall election of 1890 the party suffered serious reverses, and the Democrats took control of the House. Republican losses in the Midwest stemmed from opposition at the state and local levels to party activism on ethnocultural issues such as prohibition and Sunday closing laws. Republicans also experienced losses in usually friendly states in the Great Plains, where the new People's Party made inroads.

The party faced a difficult task in the 1892 presidential race. Harrison had not proved to be a popular president. He alienated various segments of the party and inspired little loyalty. But despite a brief boomlet for Blaine, Harrison was nominated once again. He lost decisively to Grover Cleveland in the fall, and the Democrats took control of both houses of Congress. Some commentators suggested that the Republican Party was coming apart.

The onset of the panic of 1893 changed the political landscape. President Cleveland became identified with the economic hard times that characterized his four years in office. The Republicans' insistence on a protective tariff as the key to restoring prosperity resonated with northern and midwestern voters. In the congressional elections of 1894, the Republicans were on the offensive. Led by the governor of Ohio, William McKinley, they assailed the faltering Democrats and presented themselves as a more viable agent of change than the Populists.

Republicanism Triumphant

The outcome of the election was a decisive triumph for the Republicans. They gained 117 House seats and established a dominance in that body that lasted for sixteen years. The Republican platform of protectionism and cultural pluralism impressed the voters outside the South and Far West. The significance of the election went beyond its immediate results. The political balance that had existed since the 1870s gave way to a generation of Republican dominance. For the next thirty years, with the exception of Woodrow Wilson's two terms, the Republicans were the nation's majority party.

The presidential election of 1896 confirmed the results of the midterm election two years earlier. The contest brought to national prominence a political leader who would take the Republican Party into the twentieth century. William McKinley won the nomination on the first ballot. As the governor of Ohio, he had shown that he could carry a key midwestern

FOR PRESIDENT

ANY GOVERNMENT

FOR VICE PRESIDENT

IS SAFEST IN THE

HANDS OF ITS

PRESERVERS.

BENJAMIN HARRISON

LEVI P. MORTON.

PROTECTIVE TARIFF FOR ALL.

REPUBLICAN NOMINEES.

Presidential Campaign, 1888. Running against the incumbent Grover Cleveland, Benjamin Harrison and his running mate Levi P. Morton campaigned vigorously for high tariffs and promoted nationalism. LIBRARY OF CONGRESS

state during economic hard times. His years in the House of Representatives gave him a strong base within the party. Known as the champion of the protective tariff, he was an inclusive figure who had the diplomatic abilities necessary to maintain party harmony. While McKinley gained from the financial and organizational skills of his friend Mark Hanna, an industrialist from Cleveland, the Republican success in 1896 can largely be attributed to his own political acumen.

In the general election, McKinley faced William Jennings Bryan, the candidate of the Democrats and the Populists. Bryan ran on a program of inflation to bolster the flagging economy. Although Bryan started strongly, the Republicans used their abundant campaign funds, drawn from corporate contributions, to distribute several hundred million pamphlets outlining McKinley's message of tariff protection and sound money. McKinley delivered

speeches from his front porch in Canton to lead the Republican campaign. The result was the most decisive victory for a presidential candidate since 1872. McKinley won soundly in the electoral vote and had a 600,000-vote popular margin.

During his first administration, McKinley revived the authority and influence of the presidential office through adroit management of the press, frequent trips around the country, and effective courting of Congress. During the Spanish-American War of 1898, McKinley wielded the war power to govern the colonial empire acquired from Spain. He used the techniques of a strong presidency to secure ratification of the treaty with Spain and to fight the Philippine insurrection that followed American acquisition of those islands.

In 1900 McKinley ran against Bryan once again, with similar results. The president was reelected with wide margins in both the popular and electoral votes. With prosperity returned and an empire gained, the Republicans seemed to have their ascendancy in American politics well in hand. In the five decades of their existence they had achieved dominance in national affairs and had set the agenda for several generations of politicians.

Yet beneath the surface there were signs of trouble. At the end of the nineteenth century, the party's links to big business made it vulnerable as Americans debated the extent to which government should regulate an industrial society. Could a party that depended on corporate donors identify with the needs of ordinary Americans? The main ideological principle of the party, the protective tariff, came under fire from an increasingly consumer-conscious nation worried about inflation. In many midwestern states, factionalism stirred as talk of political and economic reform spread. An assassination attempt on 6 September 1901 led to the death of McKinley a week later and brought Theodore Roosevelt to the presidency. The transition from a Civil War veteran and traditional politician to the younger, charismatic, and more dynamic Roosevelt symbolized an important shift in focus for the Republicans. As they looked back on the nineteenth century, however, they had ample reason for pride in what they had accomplished in reshaping American politics and creating one of the two organizations that have defined the nation's politics since 1900.

See also **Abolition and Antislavery; Foreign Trade and Tariffs,** *subentry on* **The Politics of Tariffs; Politics; Presidency; Whig Party.**

Bibliography

De Santis, Vincent P. *Republicans Face the Southern Question: The New Departure Years, 1877–1897.* Baltimore: Johns Hopkins University Press, 1959.

Foner, Eric. *Free Soil, Free Labor, Free Men: The Ideology of the Republican Party before the Civil War.* New York: Oxford University Press, 1971.

Gienapp, William E. *The Origins of the Republican Party, 1852–1856.* New York: Oxford University Press, 1987.

Gould, Lewis L. *The Presidency of William McKinley.* Lawrence: Regents Press of Kansas, 1980.

Hoogenboom, Ari. *The Presidency of Rutherford B. Hayes.* Lawrence: University Press of Kansas, 1988.

Jensen, Richard J. *The Winning of the Midwest: Social and Political Conflict, 1888–1896.* Chicago: University of Chicago Press, 1971.

Marcus, Robert D. *Grand Old Party: Political Structure in the Gilded Age, 1880–1896.* New York: Oxford University Press, 1971.

Morgan, H. Wayne. *From Hayes to McKinley: National Party Politics, 1877–1896.* Syracuse, N.Y.: Syracuse University Press, 1969.

Paludan, Phillip Shaw. *The Presidency of Abraham Lincoln.* Lawrence: University Press of Kansas, 1994.

Peskin, Allan. *Garfield: A Biography.* Kent, Ohio: Kent State University Press, 1978.

Reitano, Joanne. *The Tariff Question in the Gilded Age: The Great Debate of 1888.* University Park: Pennsylvania State University Press, 1994.

Williams, R. Hal. *Years of Decision: American Politics in the 1890s.* New York: Wiley, 1978.

LEWIS L. GOULD

RESORTS.   See **Vacations and Resorts.**

REVIVALISM   Nineteenth-century America was framed by revival movements, with the Second Great Awakening occurring at the beginning of the century and a widespread premillennialism (the expectation of the second coming of Christ) at the end. Revivalism was a Protestant movement concerned with personal and public conversion and ultimate salvation. First practiced in the 1730s in the Middle Atlantic and New England colonies, revivalism was relatively constant in its existence throughout the century, though the underlying premises, visions, and emphases varied in both frequency and intensity.

The revivalist movement began with the Second Great Awakening. This event spanned the first four decades of the century, from the Cane Ridge Revival in Kentucky in 1801 all the way through to the 1840s, sweeping across portions of the frontier, the wilderness, and urban areas. The underlying theological premise of the Second Great Awakening was laden with longstanding Calvinistic ideas concerning the presence of God and his willful punishments inflicted upon a sinful world. According to this view, only a chosen few would be selected by God for salvation. The belief that any revelation and resurgence of faith was brought forth by God and not by man's design or effort was a tenet of the First Great Awakening of the eighteenth century. As the nation slowly shifted and matured, however, so too did revivalism.

By the 1830s, Charles Grandison Finney (1792–1875) had brought a new theological purpose to revivalism, one that reflected the social and physical changes underway in the nation at the time. These influences included a growing democratic movement, the slow yet steady growth of class distinctions, and the expansion of the nation to the west. Finney's worldview rejected the Calvinist idea of salvation of the select, and instead adopted the Arminian doctrine that all men could be saved through their own active acceptance of God's grace. Thus his conception of a revival meeting, the first of which was conducted in 1832, was one in which the event turned men and women, singly and collectively, toward God, and called for them to recognize their own role in preparing for salvation.

Finney's "new methods," and the writings through which they were espoused, were instrumental in determining the course of revivalism throughout the better part of the century. Revivalism as a method of inspiration and evocation of faith was parallel to the spiritualist and communitarian movements of the early national period, and it flourished among the antebellum humanitarian reforms of women's rights and abolition. Elements of revivalism could likewise be found among many of the utopian movements' worship services. These movements were precursors to the Social Gospel movement of the latter part of the century, which held that to serve humanity was to serve God and that individuals could create a society that was good and decent and adhered to the values of God without having to rely upon God to effect such changes.

Revivalism led directly to the success of the Baptists, Methodists, and Congregationalists, among many other churches, at winning converts and establishing congregations throughout the western frontier. These same missionary efforts were applied in America's urban centers, often through the construction of missions for the indigent and homeless, as well as in the creation of foreign mission societies, such as the Society for the Propagation of the Gospel, which reached out to people in the Pacific, Africa, and Asia. Missionaries, both at home and abroad, were charged with the responsibility to explain the teachings of their faith and try to inspire devotion to Jesus. They led services, preached, taught the Bible, wrote religious tracts, organized churches, and generally ministered to the physical and spiritual health of the intended converts. Revivals, which demonstrated the excitement and power of the faith that the missionaries hoped to bestow, were often an effective first step in gaining the attention, demonstrating the zeal, and keeping the interest among the people.

Both women and blacks played an important role in revivalism throughout the century. While they were rarely the central figures or initiators of revival movements, they were, in fact, the largest groups of participants. As such, they had a marked influence on the movements. Women, who were the social conscience of the nation, were the ones whose concerns and fears often underlaid the calling of revivals as they called for spiritual renewal of the nation's religious and social values from their separate sphere of society. They also kept the revival tents filled. Blacks, often excluded from white society in all matters except religion, took up revivals as a way to call for justice and equality in the safe confines of religion. Black revivals allowed them to be leaders, to channel their frustrations, and to implore whites to see their common needs. Revivalism was identified more closely with these two groups than with any other, and many aspects of revivalism found their way into the worship services of predominantly black churches.

Revivalism waxed and waned with the events of the century. Social conflicts and calls for social reform led to the belief that solutions could be provided by bringing people to God through a public forum. Revivalism was directly linked to the two major social reforms of the century, antislavery and temperance. Both were influenced by revivalism's calls for greater adherence to the teachings of Jesus and a desire to see an end to the violence and inhumanity brought on by slavery and alcohol. Revivalism also influenced other movements such as those focused on education, prison reform, and issues of mental and physical health. In all these movements women occupied a central role, often as the caregivers of society and the ones to whom these tasks fell as the result of the increasing separation between gender roles in American society.

Native Americans were also influenced by the revivalist impulse. The government programs to settle and Christianize the Indians brought them under direct influence of a host of revivalist ministers. As their discontent with the reservation policies grew, Indians heeded a call for the resurgence of their traditional ways. The Ghost Dance, first adopted by Indians in what is now Nevada in the late 1860s, became a movement that combined the elements of a Christian revival with Indian spiritual beliefs. Like earlier Christian revivals, the Ghost Dance went through its own spiritual decline and revival, coming to life again, though much stronger and more menacing, in 1889. Within a year the Ghost Dance, which used sacred objects and traditional songs and dance steps to evoke both human and animal ancestors, was rapidly spreading among the Great Plains Indians.

William A. (Billy) Sunday (1863–1935) and Dwight L. Moody (1837–1899) were leading figures of the postwar revivalist movement. Of the two, Moody was clearly the more dominant, and it was his views that defined the new avenue of revivalism. He merged the pre–Civil War era conceptions of religiosity with the immense industrial and social changes taking place. His approach was relatively unemotional, unlike earlier practices, and held that salvation was available to the individual "for the taking."

Moody went a step further than his predecessors, and under him revivals took on an organized and structured existence and became a regular attraction to combat what many felt was the moral and spiritual decline of American society. His ideas carried over into the emerging Progressive movement, which was optimistic in its own belief that the salvation of

Tent Meeting. Note that the meeting is segregated by sex: women on the left-hand side, men on the right. LIBRARY OF CONGRESS

the nation would come through solutions to social problems effected by individual citizens.

Revivalism throughout the century dictated much of America's religious, political, and social directions. Revivalism was at the core of evangelicalism—a movement among American Protestants toward increased scriptural authority, social reform, and religious conversion—and thus often had a profound influence on the nation's affairs. Both of these movements, however, often found themselves in tension with emerging scientific and intellectual trends.

By the end of the century, revivalism had accomplished many of its goals. It joined together many different Protestant traditions, brought about an increase in the presence of faith in the lives of many Americans, and accommodated the changing ideas of man's relationship to God and the need to evoke religion in everyday life. However, the growth in evolutionary science, an increasing ecumenical movement, and a growing acceptance in disbelief were increasingly challenging the tenets of revivalism.

See also **Evangelicalism; Millenialism and Adventism; Progressivism; Protestantism; Religion,** *subentry on* **Religion in Nineteenth-Century America; Social Gospel.**

Bibliography

Ahlstrom, Sydney E. *A Religious History of the American People.* New Haven, Conn.: Yale University Press, 1972.

Hardman, Keith. *Charles Grandison Finney, 1792–1875: Revivalist and Reformer.* Syracuse, N.Y.: Syracuse University Press, 1987.

Johnson, Paul E. *A Shopkeeper's Millennium: Society and Revivals in Rochester, NY, 1815–1837.* New York: Hill and Wang, 1978.

McLoughlin, William G. *Modern Revivalism: Charles Grandison Finney to Billy Graham.* New York: Ronald, 1959.

McLoughlin, William G. *Revivals, Awakenings, and Reform: An Essay on Religion and Social Change in America, 1607–1977.* Chicago: University of Chicago Press, 1978.

J. D. BOWERS

REVOLUTIONARY WAR REMEMBERED

Memories of the Revolutionary War changed with the century. During the first two decades of the 1800s, Americans sought a sense of identity, and the Revolutionary War represented a starting place. Aging revolutionaries published memoirs and made appearances at solemn Fourth of July celebrations.

George Washington quickly became an icon with the 1800 publication of Mason Weem's *The Life and Memorable Actions of George Washington.*

Yet a sense of ambivalence about the new nation's past persisted. The Revolution represented not only freedom from Britain but freedom from the Old World and all its trappings. Americans hesitated to build monuments to revolutionary era heroes for fear that such adulation had no place in a republic. The Society of Cincinnati, a veteran's organization restricted to officers from the war, met with public disdain for its exclusivity. Even the meaning of "revolution" itself was contested. Federalists and Democratic-Republicans squabbled over who were the true heirs to the war's legacy.

As the Revolutionary War generation died, memory of the war changed. Independence Day commemorations, once somber, almost religious occasions, became festive celebrations. Earlier reluctance to build monuments dissipated, and an increasing number of paintings, statues, and other types of monumental art appeared. Funding for such memorials, however, was limited, and the federal government played almost no role in supporting these efforts.

Although much of the public commemoration was local, memory of the Revolution began to pass into national mythology and legend, and it became more malleable and open to interpretation. Groups as diverse as temperance advocates, artisans, and abolitionists marched in parades and sprinkled their rhetoric with words of the founders. Each disparate group claimed to be the true keeper of the American Revolution's sacred legacy. At the same time, as the nation underwent increasing industrial change, growth, and expansion, many Americans turned away from history. To outsiders Americans appeared strikingly present-minded and little concerned with the past.

Entering the contentious 1850s the nation experienced a resurgence of interest in the Revolution and its main actors. New political coalitions, like the Republican Party and the Know-Nothing Party, claimed that the nation had changed beyond recognition from its exalted roots and must return to an earlier age of purity and self-sacrifice.

When the nation descended into civil war, each side drew on the Revolution both for inspiration and to justify its cause. U.S. president Abraham Lincoln used the emotional power of the public's memory of the Revolutionary War in his first inaugural address, calling on the "mystic chords of memory" to stir and reunite the divided nation. Confederate president Jefferson Davis similarly asked Southerners to recall the founding fathers. But while Northerners emphasized the creation of the Union and the Constitution, Southerners stressed the action of self-determination and rebellion. Confederates chose George Washington's image for their national emblem, and Union troops found inspiration in the memory of Valley Forge.

In the aftermath of the Civil War, memory of the Revolution changed yet again. In the South, whites stopped celebrating the Fourth of July, and black southerners made the holiday exclusively their own.

The one-hundredth anniversary of the Declaration of Independence revived the Spirit of '76 across the nation. The year 1876 marked the official end of Reconstruction, and celebrations highlighted reconciliation and the future. The shared exalted memory of the Revolution became a way to reunite North and South, even though the deep wounds of the Civil War still festered. Millions attended the Centennial Exhibition in Philadelphia. Congress showed new interest in completing the Washington Monument and began to appropriate money to help groups seeking to erect monuments on Revolutionary War battlefields. Hereditary societies like the Sons and Daughters of the American Revolution appeared, intent on acknowledging its members' connections to a glorified past and on claiming a privileged position in interpreting that past. These groups led efforts to preserve material remains of the Revolution, including homes, battlefields, and other important sites. They democratized memory of the Revolution by opening their membership to descendents of common soldiers, but at the same time these groups reflected the nativism of the era in their exclusion of Americans with recent immigrant roots.

As the century neared its end, popular memory of the Revolution enjoyed yet another revival. The 1890s witnessed renewed nationalism and patriotism. The influx of immigrants, continued industrialism, growing divisions between rich and poor, and racial strife all fueled Americans' anxieties about the present and the future. The Revolutionary War, stripped of its radicalism and complexity, became an outlet for nostalgia and ancestor worship.

See also **Holidays; Monuments and Memorials; Nationalism; Patriotic and Genealogical Societies.**

Bibliography

Forgie, George B. *Patricide in the House Divided: A Psychological Interpretation of Lincoln and His Age.* New York: Norton, 1979.

Kammen, Michael. *Mystic Chords of Memory: The Transformation of Tradition in American Culture.* New York: Knopf, 1991.

———. *A Season of Youth: The American Revolution and the Historical Imagination.* New York: Knopf, 1978.

Piehler, G. Kurt. *Remembering War the American Way.* Washington, D.C.: Smithsonian Institution Press, 1995.

LESLEY J. GORDON

RHODE ISLAND   The state of Rhode Island and Providence Plantations, dominated by Narragansett Bay, enjoys mild winters and temperate summers. Rhode Island began the nineteenth century in conflict. Merchants struggled with markets convulsed by the Napoleonic Wars, and farmers labored with dwindling acres and diminishing yields. Groups dissatisfied with political inequality pressed for franchise reform. Samuel Slater's pioneering textile mill created new opportunities in cotton and woolen manufacturing, but the paternalistic social structure and the growth of popular political parties promoted turmoil that led to a constitutional crisis in 1842. The resultant civil disorder, The Dorr Rebellion, forced the state government to ease voting rights and institute popular representation. Successive waves of turnpike, canal, and railroad construction provided access to the new industrial sites.

Increased transportation mobility fostered emigration of the state's residents and the arrival of newcomers. Rhode Island's population grew from 69,122 in 1800 to 428,556 at the end of the century. Among the residents in 1900, 64 percent had one or even two foreign-born parents. The flood of new workers into Rhode Island in the late nineteenth century transformed the towns and cities and fueled the continued growth of industry. At the same time a strong alliance between industrial owners and Republican leaders restricted trade union development. The "other Rhode Island," Newport and its summer "cottages," contrasted starkly with common workers. Providence, the capital city, was crowned with a new state house in 1900.

See also **New England; Textiles.**

Bibliography

Coleman, Peter J. *The Transformation of Rhode Island, 1790–1860.* Providence, R.I.: Brown University Press, 1963.

Conley, Patrick T. *Democracy in Decline: Rhode Island's Constitutional Development, 1776–1841.* Providence: Rhode Island Historical Society, 1977.

McLoughlin, William G. *Rhode Island: A Bicentennial History.* New York: Norton, 1978.

NORMAN W. SMITH

RICHMOND   The Virginia legislature established Richmond as a town in 1742 and as the state capital in 1779. Situated at the fall line on the James River in eastern Virginia, Richmond was always an important trading center, at first by river and later by canal and then railroad. Through much of the nineteenth century, Richmond's industrial workers, black and white, processed wheat and tobacco or labored in the Tredegar Iron Works. As the state capital, Richmond was the focus of political events in Virginia, and it also served as the capital of the Confederacy from 1861 to 1865.

Richmond's population grew from less than 6,000 in the 1790s to 37,910 in 1860 and 85,050 in 1900. The black population was always substantial, and in one census year, 1830, blacks outnumbered whites 8,305 to 7,755. In subsequent years, black and white figures both grew, but the white population usually grew more rapidly. Foreign-born residents, mostly from Ireland or Germany, numbered 4,956 of the city's 23,635 white residents in 1860. That year, Richmond's slave population peaked at 11,699, and the number of free black residents reached its pre–Civil War high of 2,576.

Significant tensions in nineteenth-century Richmond were revealed in the aborted conspiracy of a slave named Gabriel, a literate blacksmith who planned a slave uprising to be launched 30 August 1800, and in the wartime Bread Rebellion by white women on 2 April 1863. Disasters included the great fire of 26 December 1811 at the Richmond Theater and the collapse of the state government building on 27 April 1870. After the Civil War, white Richmonders memorialized the Lost Cause with statues along Monument Avenue of such Confederate heroes as Stonewall Jackson (1824–1863), unveiled in 1875, and Robert E. Lee (1807–1870), in 1890. Reflecting the development of urban services and amenities, Richmond inaugurated the first electric railway system in the United States, in 1888. Public entertainments ranged from horse racing and theater in the early 1800s to baseball and tennis in the late 1800s.

Richmonders clashed through the end of the century over who should run the city, and how. Black Richmonders gained the vote in 1867 and elected African American members of the city council as late as the 1890s. White Richmonders demonstrated their priorities through such organizations as the Southern Historical Association, founded to commemorate the Confederacy; black citizens read the *Planet*, an African American newspaper that put a different spin on public affairs and state history. Each group attended a different set of public schools, after which white men might attend Richmond College or the Medical College of Virginia, and their black counterparts might attend Virginia Union University. For a time, white workers and black workers together contested for political and economic power through their joint membership in the Knights of Labor. At the end of the century, Monument Avenue represented Richmond's dominant political and cultural realities.

See also **Civil War,** *subentry on* **Remembering the Civil War; Emancipation; Slavery; Virginia.**

Bibliography

Chesson, Michael B. *Richmond after the War, 1865–1890*. Richmond: Virginia State Library, 1981.

Click, Patricia C. *The Spirit of the Times: Amusements in Nineteenth-Century Baltimore, Norfolk, and Richmond*. Charlottesville: University Press of Virginia, 1989.

Dabney, Virginius. *Richmond: The Story of a City*. 1976. Revised and expanded ed., Charlottesville: University Press of Virginia, 1990.

Rachleff, Peter J. *Black Labor in the South: Richmond, Virginia, 1865–1890*. Philadelphia: Temple University Press, 1984.

Tyler-McGraw, Marie. *At the Falls: Richmond, Virginia, and Its People*. Chapel Hill: University of North Carolina Press, 1994.

PETER WALLENSTEIN

ROMAN CATHOLICISM.   See **Catholicism.**

ROMANTICISM   Romanticism refers to a worldwide movement that emerged in late-eighteenth-century Europe within the realms of literature, law, philosophy, religion, art, and politics as a collective reaction to perceived excesses of the Enlightenment ideal of reason. Spontaneous emotion and the free imagination were of greater importance to the romantic sensibility than analytic or calculative rationality. Refusing everything that had been imposed on the mind rather than spontaneously created, exponents of the romantic movement elevated dynamic organicism above the mind's rote formalizations. Romantic theory represented the poetic imagination as agent, as well as product of nature.

Romantic writers made claims for the capacity of single human beings to define themselves according to their own resources and to create their own vision of existence without the help of tradition. Romanticists valued the creative imagination as the motive for inspired literature and as the potential means for completely reorienting human culture. The reorientation that romanticism in fact effected involved the espousal of social progress and individual freedom, by way of feelings and sentiments that Enlightenment ideals were made to evoke.

Origins of American Romanticism

The specific forms that romanticism would assume differed from nation to nation. It emerged within the United States after the Revolutionary War when it was connected with the aspiration to forge a distinctive cultural identity correlative with the revolution's unprecedented political and social achievements. The first generation of American Romantics included the poets William Cullen Bryant and Henry Wadsworth Longfellow, the novelists James Fenimore Cooper and Catharine Sedgwick, and the landscape painters Thomas Cole and Asher Durand. Individually and as a group they ratified the conjoined beliefs that Americans were to proclaim liberty throughout the land and to serve as an example to the rest of the world.

In explaining what the Revolution meant, these artists turned to indigenous materials rather than replicating themes inherited from the parent culture. In their representation of the new nation as basically innocent and purged of Old World vices, however, these American romantics also correlated indigenous materials with images and figures of speech that were grounded in biblical typology. They cast the prototypical American hero as an Adamic figure chosen by Providence for a divine mission in the American wilderness, and they represented the United States as a redeemer nation with the manifest destiny to propagate the principles and the ideals of their democratic culture throughout the continent. The texts that formulated this secular scripture were understood to supplement the nation's foundational political compacts—the Declaration of Independence and the Constitution—by inventing a historical tradition for the principles recorded within them. Historian Eric Hobsbawm has observed, apropos of such romantic inventions, that a national tradition has reference to a set of practices that are normally governed by overtly or tacitly accepted rules and that are of a ritual or symbolic nature (Hobsbawm and Ranger, p. 1). Through the invention of a national tradition for the rights and liberties enshrined in the nation's foundational texts, the American romantics sought retroactively to inculcate them as values and norms of behavior indigenous to the nation. The romantics' creation of a national tradition constituted a struggle to turn the past into a myth for the present.

Invention of a Tradition

With the publication of *The Last of the Mohicans* in 1826, James Fenimore Cooper demonstrated how such an invented past might be made to accommodate a citizenry's contemporary imaginative needs. The state's execution of policies of Indian removal two years earlier had posed an insuperable contradiction to the citizenry's democratic ideals. Cooper's historical romance replaced the controversy surrounding the Indian Removal Act (1830) with representations of events that had taken place in the French and Indian Wars almost a half century earlier. The novelist made the last survivors of a noble tribe that was disappearing within a sublime national landscape the subject matter for a uniquely American romance, capable of arousing the most ennobling romantic sentiments.

In this historical romance, Cooper portrayed the imaginary Mohicans as the last Indian tribe who possessed legal title to the Northeastern territories from which the U.S. government had recently forcibly displaced all other native peoples. Both the fictional Mohican warrior Uncas and his father, the sagamore Chingachgook, would die before the Indian Removal bills had been passed into law. But before the last of the Mohicans died, he conveyed spiritual ownership of the landscape of his white blood brother, Hawkeye. Hawkeye in turn willed this visionary possession to the reading public in the form of the national epic that Cooper would call *The Leatherstocking Tales* (1823–1841).

In *The Marble Faun* (1860), Nathaniel Hawthorne distinguished the historical romance from the novel and shed light on American romantics' efforts to invent a national tradition: "No Author, without a trial can conceive of the difficulty of writing a romance about a country where there is no shadow, no antiquity, no mystery, no picturesque and gloomy wrong, nor anything but a commonplace prosperity, in broad and simple daylight, as is happily the case with my native land" (1888 ed., p. 15). The authors of historical romances were not alone in striving to invent a tradition for a nation that lacked a past. In his seven-volume *France and England in North America* (1851–1892), the romantic historian Francis Parkman produced a national mythology that rivaled Cooper's in its subordination of historical facts to the themes of manifest destiny and Indian savagery. And Washington Irving's mastery of both romantic history and historical romance disclosed the common allegiance of these different forms of literary production to the task of inventing America.

The primary foil for the natural democracy invented by the first generation of American romantics was the figure of the capitalist entrepreneur who had found in the industrial economy a frontier more suitable to his needs than Leatherstocking's forest. At a time when the economy provided citizens with unequalled opportunity to acquire personal wealth, the national culture came to be dominated by those with the capacity to capitalize on personal gains and losses. A second generation of American romantics emerged to repudiate the belief that public recognition could be obtained only by amassing money and power.

A Second Phase of Romanticism

The enthusiasms of this second generation were responsible for the founding of utopian communities like Brook Farm, established in 1841 at West Roxbury, Massachusetts, and the socialist community that the Scottish philanthropist Robert Owen created in 1825 in New Harmony, Indiana. The inhabitants of Brook Farm were unlike the Owenite community in that the members disallowed the rule of any authority or the formation of any bond that derived from any source other than the sincerity of one's heartfelt feeling. Nathaniel Hawthorne satirized his experiences as a recovering former member of the Brook Farm community in *The Blithedale Romance* (1852). In that narrative, Hawthorne critically interrogates the motives of those Brook Farm residents who had formerly dedicated their lives solely to radically individualistic pursuits.

The radical individualism that Nathaniel Hawthorne had discerned as the impediment to forming a Brook Farm community had earlier been the rallying cry for the transcendentalist movement, which originated outside of Boston in the 1830s. The transcendentalist movement was largely responsible for the swelling popularity of romanticism in the United States. American transcendentalists were like the members of the Brook Farm community in that they posed the personality of the individual against the impersonality of the commercial transaction. But they were unlike the Brook Farmers in their resistance to almost every form of cultural association.

The transcendentalists refused to define themselves after the norms that the culture prescribed, and instead endowed the individual identity with the principle of universality that they believed to ground the order of things in the natural as well as the cultural worlds. Their conviction that each individual was capable of encompassing the entirety of human nature also permitted them to believe in the individual's capacity to stand outside of culture and to refuse to submit to the laws of the marketplace. In pronouncing the imagination able to extract from the material world the spirit that had given rise to it, and to defeat thereby the acquisitive drives that might have otherwise predominated, these expressive individualists claimed an even greater domain of influence for the inner self than the industrialist's commercial empire.

The literature of these transcendentalists naturalized the transcendental self as timeless and immortal, as well as an organizing impulse for political reform. Through the essays, poetry, and public lectures of such writers as Ralph Waldo Emerson, Henry David Thoreau, Walt Whitman, and Margaret Fuller, literary romanticism conspired with the social ideals of the women's rights and the abolitionist movements. Fuller's essay "The Great Lawsuit: Man vs. Men, Woman vs. Women," which she first published in the transcendentalist periodical *The Dial* and subsequently expanded into book form as *Woman in the Nineteenth Century* (1845), remains an important document in the history of American feminism. And

Publ. & Print.by Th.Kelly.   17 Barclay St.N.Y.

THE OLD FARM HOUSE

Idyllic Winter Scene. Images of family life. Published by Thomas Kelly, 1874. LIBRARY OF CONGRESS

Thoreau's essays "Resistance to Civil Government" (better known as "Civil Disobedience" [1849], the title it was given after Thoreau's death) and "Slavery in Massachusetts" (1854) would become instrumental to the formation of civil rights movements in the antebellum period and again in late-twentieth-century America.

The sphere of transcendental freedom to which both Fuller and Thoreau claimed to have privileged access was in part the inverted reflection of slavery, which totalized the condition of unfreedom. Resolutely opposed to this institution, the transcendentalists denounced the government, which compromised with the slave power, as in contravention of the laws of nature. Remarking in his journal "I have other slaves to free than those negroes, to wit, imprisoned spirits, imprisoned minds," Emerson proposed the "Anti-Slave" as the figure of thought that consolidated the contradictory standpoints that American romanticism had inherited from the Enlightenment.

Emerson's attempt in the essay *Nature* (1836) to discover a deeper truth than that of the founding fathers led him to the belief that the natural world was an expression of the transcendental self. Whereas the nation's founders had transmitted to their descendants the conviction that the U.S. citizen-subject was the bearer of the universal rights to liberty, equality, and social justice, Emerson added the virtue of self-reliance to this disembodied remnant of Enlightenment thought. Describing enmeshment within everyday circumstances as a form of secular slavery, Emerson recommended that each individual become representative of the whole self. In their confident assertion of individuals' ability to transcend the contingency of ordinary circumstance, Emerson's essays purported to offer an imaginative technology through which transcendence might be achieved. Predicated on an aversion to associative life in all of its forms—the family, the community, the nation—Emerson's program for releasing the transcendental individual from cultural enslavement also rehabilitated the slave's condition of nonbelonging.

Thoreau explored the ironic potential of isolation as a principle of community when, in his account of the year he spent in a shack beside Walden Pond, he deployed terms that contrasted the socialist ideals of the Brook Farm community with his ability to survive the hardships of a subsistence economy on his own. In "Song of Myself" (1855), Walt Whitman attempted to produce an ironic community out of a nation of isolatoes, each of whom tried to define themselves without help from human others. Whitman saw every other individual as a partial version of his whole self whose separateness from these part selves constituted the precondition for their complete development.

If Walt Whitman constructed a poetic rationale for the nation of radical individualists, however, Herman Melville explored in *Moby-Dick* (1851) the susceptibility of such isolatoes to the imperial ambitions of ruthless men. Instead of distinguishing the transcendentalist's imagination from the industrialist's, whose enterprise involved taking possession of the continent, Melville imagined a convergence of their will to power in the figure of Captain Ahab. Melville's grim meditation on the ideological usages to which the radical individualism of the American romantics could be put was given material expression in the Civil War. But when exponents of the conflicting ideological standpoints of the North and of the South conscripted American romanticism's utopian aspirations into the business of mobilizing their respective armies, American romanticism lost its imaginative hold on its readers.

See also **American Indians,** *subentry on* **Indian Removal; Communitarian Movements and Groups; Frontier; Literature,** *subentries on* **Fiction, The Essay, Poetry, Women's Literature, The Influence of Foreign Literature; Manifest Destiny; Nature.**

Bibliography

Abrams, M. H. *Natural Supernaturalism.* New York: Norton, 1971.

Bloom, Harold. *The Anxiety of Influence.* New York: Oxford University Press, 1973.

Hobsbawm, Eric, and Terence Ranger, eds. *The Invention of Tradition.* Cambridge, U.K.: Cambridge University Press, 1983.

Kateb, George. *The Inner Ocean: Individualism and Democratic Culture.* Ithaca, N.Y.: Cornell University Press, 1992.

Matthiessen, F. O. *American Renaissance.* Oxford: Oxford University Press, 1941.

Pease, Donald E. *Visionary Compacts: American Renaissance Writings in Cultural Context.* Madison: University of Wisconsin Press, 1987.

DONALD E. PEASE

RUBBER   Household and industrial rubber products were largely unknown until the second half of the nineteenth century. As they gradually won popular acceptance, rubber manufacturing companies proliferated, overcame numerous technological obstacles, and introduced innovations in the composition, design, and fabrication of rubber goods. By the end of the century, they also played major roles in the organizational revolution that transformed American business.

Rubber is a natural polymer obtained by collecting and processing the sap of *Hevea brasiliensis,* a tree common to the tropics. South American natives had long used it to make simple objects, including footwear. Their activities gradually attracted the interest of British and American merchants, who exported crude rubber and boots to western Europe and the United States, where their elastic and water-repellent qualities attracted wide interest. The export trade between South America (particularly Brazil) and the United States grew rapidly, as demand increased; yet only at the end of the century, as the popularity of rubber products required larger and larger supplies of crude rubber, did producers shift to tree farming, notably in the British, Dutch, and French colonies of Southeast Asia.

In the meantime major innovations had occurred in the factory, as inventors and manufacturers devised better ways of processing rubber. The most critical of these breakthroughs occurred between 1839 and 1845, when Charles Goodyear, a New Haven, Connecticut, merchant and amateur scientist, discovered the process of vulcanization, patented it, and produced the first vulcanized tire. By heating natural rubber with sulfur and white lead, Goodyear was able to give rubber objects permanent form, greater elasticity, and other desirable qualities. Vulcanization was a major breakthrough; it made rubber a versatile material, opened new markets, and signaled the advent of the modern rubber industry. Goodyear personally derived little satisfaction from his seminal invention. His efforts to manufacture rubber products were only partially successful, and he died in 1860, just as the potential of his work was becoming apparent.

The combination of calendering (reinforcing rubber with a textile product, developed by the 1820s and 1830s) and vulcanization led to the development of improved boots and rainwear, and the appearance of new industrial products such as hoses, belts, and insulation, as well as balloons and surgical and dental products. The making of footwear, the leading rubber product until the 1890s, was concentrated in New England shoe centers. Most rainwear and industrial products were made near major markets, especially New York City. By 1889 there were 167 plants devoted to rubber production, including eleven large footwear factories averaging nearly a thousand employees; eleven substantial hose and belt plants; and more than a hundred smaller factories devoted to other products.

Between the 1860s and 1880s rubber boot and shoe manufacturers attempted repeatedly to stabilize prices and limit competition. After numerous failures, Charles R. Flint, a New York merchant, merged the largest companies in 1892. The resulting United States Rubber Company paid dividends during the severe depression of the mid-1890s, and gradually absorbed most of the leading makers of industrial products, creating a near monopoly. Its apparent success helped inspire the great industrial merger movement at the turn of the century. Yet many problems remained. Flint ran U.S. Rubber as a holding company, making no effort to consolidate operations or achieve the internal economies that were the hallmarks of successful combinations.

Regardless of Flint's policies, technological change soon made his goals of monopoly power and industry stability unattainable. The introduction of the safety bicycle (that featured two identical wheels) in the 1880s opened a vast new market, especially for pneumatic tires, which had a separate, inflatable inner tube inside the tire. The appearance of the clincher rim and tire in the early 1890s simplified tire repairs and removed the last major obstacle to their acceptance of pneumatic tires. By the time the first automobiles appeared, rubber manufacturers had mastered the essentials of the new technology.

Many industrial rubber goods producers, including U.S. Rubber, added tires to their product lines in the 1890s, but no firm made this transition more successfully than B. F. Goodrich, of Akron, Ohio. Benjamin Franklin Goodrich had moved his struggling industrial products firm to Akron in 1870; with the assistance of local capitalists, the Goodrich company became the largest maker of hoses and industrial products by the 1890s. With the addition of a tire department, it became almost as large and diversified as U.S. Rubber. Goodrich's success created a large group of individuals with technical skills in the Akron area. As automobile tire production grew, many of these technicians created or joined new firms, such as Goodyear Tire & Rubber, formed in Akron in 1898. By 1900 they had collectively made Akron the center of tire and industrial rubber products manufacture.

By the turn of the century, rubber boots, raincoats, hoses, balloons, and even tires had become familiar features of American life. The rubber industry, virtually nonexistent in 1850, had become known for rapid technological change and corporate power. A growing link to transportation promised additional dramatic changes in the future.

See also **Bicycling; Industrialization and the Market; Inventors and Inventions.**

Bibliography
Babcock, Glenn D. *History of the United States Rubber Company.* Bloomington: Bureau of Business Research, Indiana University, 1966.

Blackford, Mansel G., and K. Austin Kerr. *B. F. Goodrich: Tradition and Transformation, 1870–1995.* Columbus: Ohio State University Press, 1996.

French, M. J. *The U.S. Tire Industry: A History.* Boston: Twayne, 1990.

DANIEL NELSON

RUNAWAY SLAVES. See **Slavery,** subentry on **Runaway Slaves.**

RUSSIAN IMMIGRANTS. See **Immigration and Immigrants,** subentry on **Central and Eastern Europe.**

S

ST. LOUIS St. Louis, Missouri, is situated on the west bank of the Mississippi River, a few miles below the Mississippi's juncture with the Missouri River. At the time of the Louisiana Purchase in 1803, it was a small village. The Mississippi and Missouri River systems, according to promoters, gave St. Louis access to over fifty thousand miles of navigable water. The Missouri ran west as far as the Rocky Mountains. The Mississippi flowed to New Orleans and the sea. A Mississippi and Ohio River link provided a water route to eastern centers.

Settlers from other parts of the country boosted the St. Louis population to 4,593 in 1820, a year prior to Missouri statehood. The rise of agriculture diversified an economy based originally on furs from the West and lead from nearby fields. The city boomed as a steamboat center. Thousands of steamboats graced the waterfront annually, five thousand alone in 1859. St. Louis survived destructive floods, fires, epidemics, and depressions. The number of inhabitants swelled from 16,469 in 1840 to 77,850 in 1850, then more than doubled to 160,773 in 1860. There were significant numbers of German and Irish immigrants, as well as fifteen hundred slaves and over seventeen hundred free blacks.

During the Civil War, Union forces secured St. Louis, imposed martial law, restricted trade, and turned the city into a stronghold. The closing of the Mississippi, coupled with civil and military strife in Missouri, caused a severe business downturn. After the hostilities ended, postwar demand allowed trade to recover quickly, thereby spawning rapid growth.

St. Louisans numbered 310,864 in 1870 and 350,528 ten years later.

Logan U. Reavis, a local prophet of urban destiny, claimed in 1879 that St. Louis was destined to be a city of ten million, and even the site of the nation's capital. In reality, fundamental changes in transportation soon dashed such high hopes. The development of a nationwide railroad net led to a marked decline in river traffic. Although the magnificent Eads Bridge, completed over the Mississippi in 1874, gave the city direct rail connections to the East, the newer rival city of Chicago, fewer than three hundred miles away on Lake Michigan, almost overnight emerged as the number-one railroad hub in North America. Chicago gained a large percentage of the old upper Mississippi River steamboat trade at the expense of St. Louis, and secured direct trunk lines all the way to the Pacific coast. By 1880 Chicago, in existence fewer than fifty years, had surpassed St. Louis in wealth and population.

Despite inroads by Chicago, St. Louis continued to advance. It had 451,770 people in 1890. Gains in commerce, manufacturing, and finance helped to foster a civic renaissance in what had been a rather drab river city. Washington and St. Louis universities emerged as important institutions of higher learning. Imposing new buildings and large parks changed the cityscape. The construction of a costly, comprehensive waterworks was representative of new public projects. Sensational exposures of public corruption had little impact.

In 1900 St. Louis was the fourth largest city in the

United States, with a population of 575,238. The city had well over 100,000 immigrants and close to 36,000 African Americans. A successful and memorable world's fair, the Louisiana Purchase Exposition of 1904, signaled St. Louis's rise to metropolitan status.

See also **Missouri**.

Bibliography

Adler, Jeffrey S. *Yankee Merchants and the Making of the Urban West: The Rise and Fall of Antebellum St. Louis.* Cambridge, U.K.: Cambridge University Press, 1991.

Primm, James Neal. *Lion of the Valley: St. Louis, Missouri.* Boulder, Colo.: Pruett, 1981.

LAWRENCE H. LARSEN

SALOONS AND THE DRINKING LIFE

Throughout the nineteenth century most alcohol used in the United States was bought and consumed in public drinking houses. During the first third of the century a typical American annually drank as much as five gallons of distilled spirits, a rate three times that of Americans in the twentieth century. The country was dotted with taverns that lodged travelers and served both food and strong drink, mostly whiskey, to strangers as well as local residents. Often the largest building in a community, the tavern was a gathering place for political debates, social events, and even court sessions. In the 1830s temperance crusaders attacked these multipurpose establishments, and their numbers began to dwindle. By 1840 about half of all Americans, heavily influenced by Protestant revivals, had quit drinking, while the shift from stagecoaches to faster steamboats and trains reduced travelers' needs and thus also spurred the decline of taverns.

During the middle of the century taverns gradually gave way to saloons. The word "saloon," which originally meant any large room used for public gatherings, came from the French "salon" and suggested elegance. Around 1850 lavish drinking palaces opened in New York City. These early saloons featured marble floors, brass spittoons, mahogany bars, large mirrors, and cut-glass decanters. Well-dressed gentlemen ordered high-priced, specialty mixed drinks, such as manhattans. Beverages appeared with the luxurious novelty of crushed ice. In an attempt to be fashionable, rougher establishments, including both seedy city bars run by and for poor immigrants and crude watering holes in the West, adopted the term "saloon." While frontier saloons lacked marble floors and the wind often whistled through cracks in their wooden walls, they sometimes displayed mahogany bars and mirrors. By the late

1860s Americans used the word "saloon" in a general way to signify any place where alcohol was sold and consumed. Although most drinking was done on the premises, saloons commonly purveyed beer and liquor for off-site consumption.

Before the Civil War saloongoers primarily consumed whiskey. It was taken straight, except in the fancier establishments that specialized in mixed drinks. As large numbers of German immigrants arrived after 1840, saloons introduced lager beer, a trend that accelerated following the Civil War, when the federal government imposed high taxes on hard liquor. By the 1880s, when beer overtook whiskey as the dominant beverage, breweries owned or controlled many saloons, which were called tied houses because of their limited selections. Competition was cutthroat, and saloonkeepers at times turned to gambling or prostitution or sold doctored or stale beer to avoid financial ruin. By contrast, the new, highly capitalized, large-scale commercial brewers, such as Anheuser-Busch, Schlitz, and Pabst, flourished.

Workingmen's Clubs

In the late nineteenth century saloons became common in major cities. They were enormously popular, especially in largely immigrant, working-class neighborhoods of the burgeoning industrial areas. In such urban settings half a dozen or more saloons might operate on a block. In any given establishment most of the customers were regular patrons who combined alcohol with camaraderie. The desire for bonding led saloongoers to seek out like-minded companions, which explains why so many different drinking houses were located in such close proximity. Each saloon catered to a particular occupation, ethnic group, or political faction. Sailors congregated near the waterfront and swapped seafaring tales. German immigrants shared beer and their native tongue, the Irish mixed whiskey and folk songs, and Italians chose wine. Sometimes poker, slot machines, bowling, or pool also drew a particular clientele.

Like other nineteenth-century institutions, saloons reflected the popular view that life should be divided into separate male and female spheres. Saloons were for men. While respectable women avoided the main front bar, many saloons maintained a separate ladies' door at the side so women could unobtrusively enter the back room to join family gatherings or to participate in other special events. Housewives also used the side entrance to fill beer pails for home consumption. Even prostitutes seldom dared advance into the front bar, although they might lurk just beyond in a shadowy doorway. Some saloons rented upstairs rooms by the night or by the

"**Bachelors Carouse.**" Part of a series of temperance photographs demonstrating "The Drinkers' Progress." Created and published by G. W. Edmonson, c. 1874. LIBRARY OF CONGRESS

hour. In the front room, male saloongoers expressed working-class conviviality and fraternity at a time when middle-class advocates of domesticity, both female and male, argued that crude, violence-prone men could only be tamed in wholesome homes provided by morally pure wives and mothers. Some men went to saloons just to escape these civilizing influences. Many working-class men spent half their leisure time in drinking houses. For male drinkers the saloon provided a place to show manly courage, solidarity, and skill at repartee.

During the 1880s saloons began to offer a free lunch to anyone who bought a five-cent glass of beer. Originally a competitive lure, this buffet became a staple in many drinking houses for the rest of the century. Proprietors purchased food from wholesalers in such large quantities that they got heavily discounted prices. Although quality varied, lunches usually featured salty or spicy foods, such as potato salad, pickles, pretzels, or sausage, which encouraged

the purchase of a second beer. Some establishments served roast beef, but it was always sliced thin. The free lunch lured workingmen into taking midday meals in saloons. Unfortunately for the tranquility of drinking parlors, the free lunch also attracted derelicts and children, some of whom delighted in grabbing food from the buffet table and darting out the door. Workingwomen sometimes ate the free meal in the back room. Nothing angered reformers more than the free lunch, which they correctly considered to be a device to entice customers into drinking.

Saloon Practices and Politics

Saloons provided a place to drink, eat, and talk, but companionship within drinking houses had other dimensions, too. As a drug, alcohol reduced inhibitions and thereby encouraged social interaction. Saloons broke down psychological barriers and brought people together at an elemental level. At a time when

Extravagant Saloon Interior. The Grand Saloon in the Hoffman House, New York City, promoted as the "finest saloon in the world." Photograph c. 1888. LIBRARY OF CONGRESS

Americans ideologically embraced individualism and generally found few organized groups from which to draw support, men who lived and worked in a highly competitive and rapidly industrializing society could share feelings and bond into a group in their local saloons. Regular patrons expressed collective identity either by treating with rounds bought by each member for all who were part of the group or by a joint purchase of pails or kegs of beer that were then shared. These actions confirmed democratic equality even as they provided conviviality. Thus, imbibing together in a saloon both created community and fostered commerce in the beginning of industrial capitalism's consumer culture.

America's growing European immigrant population used saloons to maintain old-country traditions and to assimilate into new norms. Although some saloons were based on ethnicity, many welcomed persons of varying backgrounds. Even the free lunch encouraged takers to sample different ethnic foods. Few

establishments, however, were interracial. Back rooms sometimes offered boxing matches, card games, and dances, or they served as meeting places for neighborhood groups, various lodges, and social organizations. Drinking houses often provided the space free, so long as users purchased sufficient amounts of beer. Labor unionists also frequently met in saloons, where they could be confident that industrialists or middle-class managers would not bother them. Some saloons became bastions of radicalism. More commonly, bar owners were community leaders who kept track of job openings, cashed paychecks, loaned modest sums to regular patrons, organized entertainment, helped set and enforce community standards, and acted as arbitrators in disputes.

Saloonkeepers, many of whom were Irish Americans, learned to negotiate among different groups and thereby played an important role in politics. A large number, including President John Kennedy's two grandfathers, were elected to local offices. Bar ownering was often the occupation most represented on city councils, and saloon-based political machines came to dominate the country's cities. Because only men could vote, saloonkeepers had a good understanding of the electorate's desires. It was easy to coax patrons to the polls, especially if voting took place in the back room, where voters sometimes got chits for free drinks. Saloon-based gangs engaged in petty crime, including extortion, and intimidated political rivals. Because saloon-based political machines opposed almost all political change, reformers concluded that saloons had to be abolished for any reform program to succeed.

As cities grew, factories burgeoned, and Catholic and Jewish immigration increased, rural and small-town Protestants reacted negatively by lashing out at the resultant social changes. Often led by the Woman's Christian Temperance Union, they especially blamed saloons for all of society's ills, including poverty, crime, and family breakdown. Many Americans hated and feared drinking houses because they were the bastions of urban, immigrant, working-class men. Saloon connections to alcoholism, prostitution, liquor-related crimes, wife beating, and corrupt political machines led reformers to argue that only prohibition could end saloons and purify society. The dry campaign, largely an antisaloon movement, made little headway until after 1900. In 1917 Congress enacted wartime Prohibition to end saloons. Two years later, the Eighteenth Amendment made Prohibition permanent. When it was repealed in 1933, alcohol was regulated so that saloons did not reappear.

See also **Food; Immigration and Immigrants,** *subentry on* **The Immigrant Experience; Manliness; Popular Culture; Recreation; Working-Class Culture.**

Bibliography

Duis, Perry R. *The Saloon: Public Drinking in Chicago and Boston, 1880–1920.* Urbana: University of Illinois Press, 1983.

Noel, Thomas J. *The City and the Saloon, Denver, 1858–1916.* Lincoln: University of Nebraska Press, 1982.

Powers, Madelon. *Faces along the Bar: Lore and Order in the Workingman's Saloon, 1870–1920.* Chicago: University of Chicago Press, 1998.

Rorabaugh, W. J. *The Alcoholic Republic: An American Tradition.* New York: Oxford University Press, 1979.

Rosenzweig, Roy. *Eight Hours for What We Will: Workers and Leisure in an Industrial City, 1870–1920.* Cambridge, U.K. and New York: Cambridge University Press, 1983.

West, Elliott. *The Saloon on the Rocky Mountain Mining Frontier.* Lincoln: University of Nebraska Press, 1979.

W. J. RORABAUGH

SAN FRANCISCO   A dilapidated collection of military, religious, and commercial buildings housed several dozen residents on the windswept peninsular site at the entrance to the San Francisco Bay when the nineteenth century began. By the Mexican War (1846–1848) the settlement housed a motley collection of adventurers and entrepreneurs lured by profits from trade and commerce. The California gold rush brought the world's fortune seekers to the trading village, and during the thirty years between 1849 and 1879 the city played emporium and factory town to the gold and silver miners, railroaders, real estate developers, and farmers of the Pacific Coast region. People and profits poured into the city during those years, providing San Francisco the talent and the capital that allowed it to blossom into a cosmopolitan metropolis during the 1880s. By 1900 San Francisco dominated the Pacific Coast as the region's chief economic and cultural metropolis.

War and Gold

The gold rush transformed what had been a tiny trading village into a major city. While the influx of gold seekers provided the crucial spark for this transformation, nature contributed the necessary ingredients by creating the bay and a protected port. Military necessity and religion also contributed, for when the Spanish first arrived in the 1770s, soldiers fortified the entrance to the bay with a presidio, and Franciscan priests built Mission Dolores (1776).

By the 1830s Mexicans had replaced the Spanish as rulers, and the bay had become an important stopping point for ships plying the Pacific. Yerba Buena cove, which eventually was filled in, became the favored anchorage, and a small village grew up, named for the cove and dominated by English and American merchants. During the Mexican War, U.S. naval forces occupied Yerba Buena, and in 1847 local merchants persuaded the naval officer in charge of the port to change the name of the village to San Francisco. A year later James Marshall discovered gold at Sutter's Mill near Sacramento, and thousands thronged to California to make their fortunes. Given the rudimentary state of land transportation, most of the hopeful miners and nearly all of their supplies came by sea and disembarked in San Francisco.

By the summer of 1849 Yerba Buena cove was clogged with ships, some deserted by their gold-seeking crews. Within a year the village of 800 became a city of 8,000. In 1852 the first census counted 35,000 people, and by 1860 San Francisco ranked fifteenth among U.S. cities with 56,802 residents. In 1900 the city ranked number nine among the nation's cities with a population of 342,782 people.

San Francisco, 1895. View to the east from Hopkins' Art Association, showing Goat Island in the background. Very few structures from this period survived the 1906 earthquake. LIBRARY OF CONGRESS: PRINTS AND PHOTOGRAPHS DIVISION

Society and Economy

Besides its large number of residents, the city's economic power contributed to its development into a commercial metropolis on the Pacific Coast during the late nineteenth century. More than 20 percent of the total population of California, Oregon, and Washington lived in San Francisco during the last forty years of the century. The city controlled local trade with Bay Area counties, as well as coastal trade from Panama to Alaska. San Francisco manufacturers produced two-thirds of the region's goods, five railroad lines radiated from the city to its hinterland, and five ferry lines connected the city to other Bay Area communities. The city had more factories and workers, capital and value of products than all of the other twenty-four cities west of the Mississippi River combined. In 1875 the Palace Hotel, then the largest and most luxurious hotel in the nation, opened on Market Street, a short walk from the bustling waterfront, the commercial heart of the city. Ninety-nine percent of all imports to the Pacific Coast states and 83 percent of all exports passed over the city docks. By the beginning of the twentieth century San Francisco's corporate boardrooms held sway over the economy of the West, from salmon canneries in Alaska, to sugar plantations in Hawaii, logging in Washington State, the Coronado Hotel in San Diego, and mines throughout the western part of the nation.

San Francisco's diverse population and its cultural amenities earned the city a reputation for cosmopolitanism. With an opera house and numerous legitimate theaters, French restaurants, world-class hotels, and a Barbary Coast entertainment district, where anything and everything could be purchased, San Francisco ranked among the most famous international seaports of the second half of the nineteenth century. Chinatown became a tourist destination by the 1880s. Residents of foreign birth made up well over half of the population and at times more than 70 percent. The Irish arrived during the gold rush and remained numerically dominant throughout the century. Germans, including Protestants, Catholics, and Jews, made up the next largest group. Scandinavians and Italians were comparative latecomers, arriving in significant numbers only toward the end of the century. Most San Franciscans were white, especially after the 1890s, when the Chinese population declined from 8 percent of the total to just above 4 percent. Only a minuscule number of African Americans lived in the city.

Politics

San Francisco's politics reflected national trends with a few exceptions related to its gold rush experience, location, and population. Vigilantism erupted in 1851 and 1856, and former vigilantes dominated city government through the Civil War years. In the late 1870s the Workingmen's Party clamored for government controls on railroad monopolists and for exclusion of the Chinese workers first employed by the Central Pacific Railway and later by the city's factory owners. In 1869 San Francisco women organized the nation's first statewide organization dedicated to the cause of woman suffrage. Radical trade unionists established a branch of Karl Marx's First International, the International Workingmen's Association, in 1882. Ten years later John Muir and a handful of outdoor enthusiasts organized the Sierra Club, devoted to the preservation of the natural environment. By 1898, as the United States assembled its new overseas empire, San Francisco's leaders declared their metropolis to be America's Imperial City, the Paris of the Pacific.

See also **California; Chinese Exclusion Act; Gold Rushes and Silver Strikes; Immigration and Immigrants.**

Bibliography

Barth, Gunther. *Instant Cities: Urbanization and the Rise of San Francisco and Denver.* New York: Oxford University Press, 1975.

Ethington, Philip J. *The Public City: The Political Construction of Urban Life in San Francisco, 1850–1900.* New York: Cambridge University Press, 1994.

Issel, William, and Robert W. Cherny. *San Francisco, 1865–1932: Politics, Power, and Urban Development.* Berkeley: University of California Press, 1986.

Lotchin, Roger W. *San Francisco, 1846–1856: From Hamlet to City.* New York: Oxford University Press, 1974.

Shumsky, Neil Larry. *The Evolution of Political Protest and the Workingmen's Party of California.* Columbus: Ohio State University Press, 1991.

WILLIAM ISSEL

SCOTTISH IMMIGRANTS.   See **Immigration and Immigrants,** subentry on **Great Britain.**

SCULPTURE   The development of American sculpture during the nineteenth century paralleled that of painting in three main artistic periods: the Federal period, 1780–1828; the Jacksonian period, 1828–1865; and the Gilded Age, 1865–1900. Sculptors and painters experienced the same cultural revolution after the political liberation of the United States from England, except that sculptors were influenced more directly by neoclassicism than were painters. Neoclassical composition dominated sculpture, lending itself to standing and bust portraits of revolutionary leaders, as it similarly affected architecture.

The Federal Period: 1780–1828

Before 1800 the United States had no professional sculptors who could work in marble or metal, so the new nation met the demand for monumental official sculpture by placing orders with European sculptors. Not until the 1830s did local sculptors begin to replace foreigners in making important heroic images for the country. The foreigners, however, provided models for the native-born school, and most of the work was executed in the neoclassical tradition.

The earliest sculptor commissioned to execute a public work in marble was the French neoclassicist Jean-Antoine Houdon (1741–1828). Houdon came to the United States with Benjamin Franklin in 1785 to personally observe President George Washington and make studies of him. Houdon made a life mask and a terra-cotta bust before returning to Paris, where he finished his full-height, marble, standing portrait, *George Washington* (1791), dressed in contemporary clothing rather than in classical garments. A heroic, classical, *contrapposto* pose provides idealism to the otherwise realistic representation of Washington and the clothing he wore for his portrait, down to a button missing from his coat. The work was finished in 1791 and was installed in the Virginia Capitol (designed by Thomas Jefferson) in 1796. Houdon depicted other heroes of the American Revolution in terra-cotta during his stay in the United States. After returning to Europe he completed representations of Benjamin Franklin, Thomas Jefferson, and John Paul Jones. The bust *Benjamin Franklin* (c. 1790) is typical of the works that served as models for later, native-born sculptors. It has a realistic, aging face but with idealized classical drapery, calling attention to the prevailing characteristic of early and mid-nineteenth-century sculpture portraits, that is, a tension between the realistic details and idealism. Several Italian sculptors traveled to the United States during the Federal period to carve architectural decorations, such as the corncob capitals on the U.S. Capitol by Guiseppe Franzoni. Allegorical figures, such as *Car of History* (marble, 1819) by Carlo Franzoni, were commissioned by the U.S. Government.

From 1780 to 1828 most American-born sculptors were anonymous wood-carvers who produced store signs, ship figureheads, and the like. By 1800 most works exhibited a neoclassical influence, even ship figureheads. Samuel McIntire (1757–1811), an architect and architectural carver, also sculpted wood portraits and painted them white to resemble stone, such as his relief medallion *Portrait of George Washington* (1805). John Frazee (1790–1852), the son of a stonemason, learned to carve stone architectural decorations and created the earliest known American marble portrait, *John Wells* (1824). In addition Hezekial Augur (1791–1858) carved neoclassical works. Only one American sculptor, John Browere (1792–1834), worked in cast bronze. Browere learned how to make life masks from the French master Houdon while studying in Paris. He made life masks of several famous American leaders and cast the sculptures, including *James Madison* (1825), in Europe. The works exhibit the typical tension between realistic facial details and neoclassical drapery. By the end of the Federal period American sculpture had advanced in composition, but the technique of carving in stone and casting in metal still lagged behind work produced in Europe.

The Jacksonian Period: 1828–1865

The mid–nineteenth century was a favorable period for sculpture. Legislators on the national and state levels commissioned stone portraits of revolutionary heroes, local heroes, and allegorical figures. Many sculptors went abroad not only to apprentice in stone but also to set up studios where quality marble was available. Among those expatriates were Horatio Greenough (1805–1852), Hiram Powers (1805–1873), Thomas Crawford (1813–1857), and William Wetmore Story (1819–1895), the son of the Supreme Court justice Joseph Story. Neoclassicism was the dominant aesthetic, and works still exhibited tension between realism and idealism. Powers achieved international fame. His *Greek Slave* (marble, 1843) is an allegorical figure inspired by an episode of the Greek War for Independence in the 1820s that depicts, in the classical tradition of a nude Aphrodite, a woman in chains, representing captured Greek women being sold into slavery. This work, which was displayed at the first World's Exposition in London in 1851, inspired Powers to create several other Greek slaves in various scales into the 1860s. He also carved patriotic portraits of American heroes and allegorical figures for state governments.

A second generation of neoclassicists emerged during the Jacksonian period. Erastus Dow Palmer (1817–1904), influenced by Powers, continued the theme of a woman in trouble with *White Captive* (marble, 1858). Based on a human model rather than a Greek statue, Palmer's work is more realistic, reflecting the tastes of the 1850s. Henry Kirke Brown (1814–1886) executed one of the earliest public bronze monuments, *George Washington* (1856). In this equestrian statue the horse and rider have realistic detailing, but the neoclassical composition is based on Donatello's fifteenth century work and the Roman equestrian sculpture *Marcus Aurelius* (A.D. 180).

The Gilded Age: 1865–1900

American women struggled to receive an education in sculpting and to win commissions from male patrons. Harriet Hosmer (1830–1908) initially produced small, neoclassical marble pieces, but in 1868 she executed a sixteen-foot-tall portrait of Thomas Hart Benton. Elisabet Ney (1833–1907) was born and trained in Germany. Experiencing difficulty getting commissions of men, she pleaded with some older, notable German men to be her first subjects and thereby built up her clientele. Ney immigrated to the United States in 1870 and postponed her career while she raised a son. She built a sculpture studio in Austin, Texas, in 1890 with the expectation that she could get many commissions in a state that had no other professional sculptor. While the male-dominated legislature often overlooked her reasonable rates and local availability in favor of male artists, she did receive some important commissions. Her best-known works are the life-size, realistic, standing portraits *Samuel Houston* (plaster, 1892) and *Stephen Austin* (plaster, 1890s). The Houston piece, completed for the 1893 World's Columbian Exposition in Chicago, was paid for by the Texas Women's Auxiliary. After years of effort the Daughters of the Republic of Texas, aided by the state legislature, raised funding to commission Ney to complete marble statues of the Texas heroes for the state capitol and a set for the U.S. Capitol.

As in painting, genre subjects were popular during the mid– and late nineteenth century. John Rogers (1829–1904) made small, sentimental works, such as *Checkers at the Farm* (1859), with realistic details in the textures of actual objects. In the 1890s Frederic Remington (1861–1909) made realistic western-genre bronzes, such as *The Bronco Buster* (1895), which shows attention to detail on both horse and rider. The move toward realism began with a native-born generation influenced by neoclassicists that also wanted detail, as in the monumental bronze monument by Thomas Ball (1819–1911), *Emancipation* (1875). This sculpture of Abraham Lincoln and a slave, commissioned by freed slaves, captured the imagination of the public with its mix of naturalism and sentimentality. John Quincy Adams Ward (1830–1910) was successful with public sculptures of heroic monumentality or rugged masculine characterization, such as the *Monument to Henry Ward Beecher* (bronze, 1891). Mary Edmonia Lewis (1845–1911), the first African American woman in the country to gain international recognition as a sculptor, carved small allegorical pieces or naturalistic works, including *Old Indian Arrowmaker and Daughter* (marble, 1872). She was among the exhibitors at the Centennial Exposition in Philadelphia in 1876.

Much of her work, such as *Forever Free* (marble, 1867), has neoclassical and sentimental overtones due to a trip to Rome, where she was influenced by Greco-Roman sculpture.

During the post–Civil War years younger sculptors trained under neoclassicists in the United States as well as at the École des Beaux-Arts in Paris, which strongly influenced them in two phases. Augustus Saint-Gaudens (1848–1907) spent time in Paris and Rome between 1867 and 1877. His *Robert Gould Shaw Memorial* (1897) in Boston, a bronze relief on stone, is a group of realistic portraits of an army troop and their leader, Colonel Robert Gould Shaw. An idealized, allegorical Nike flies above the troops in the Renaissance-based Beaux-Arts style. The monument is dedicated to the famous "Glory Brigade," the Fifty-fourth Massachusetts, which was a black regiment organized in the North during the Civil War. Daniel Chester French (1850–1931) began his career with first-phase Beaux-Arts projects. *The Minute Man* (bronze, 1875), is of a patriotic, heroic scale and is realistic, possibly influenced by Ward, yet the figure is considered a naturalistic transformation of a cast of the *Apollo Belvedere* of antiquity. Later works by French, such as *Death Staying the Hand of the Young Sculptor* (marble, 1892), express naturalistic detail mixed with allegorical generality and volumes of classical drapery. Most second-phase Beaux-Arts sculptors exhibited the neorococo influence of the Beaux-Arts, including Frederick MacMonnies (1863–1937), who created the elegant, sensuous *Bacchante and Infant Faun* (bronze, 1893). Other sculptors, such as George Grey Barnard (1863–1938), were influenced by the impressionism of Auguste Rodin (1840–1917). Barnard's *Abraham Lincoln* (bronze, 1917) in Cincinnati, Ohio, depicts a lanky, roughly modeled figure that Barnard claimed was based naturalistically on a live model with lanky and awkward proportions.

Nineteenth-century American sculptors tended to mix realistic detailing with the prevailing style of the day—neoclassicism, genre, or Beaux-Arts. Sculptors of all periods experimented with allegorical or mythological subjects as well as with their main subject, portraiture. During the mid- and late century American sculptors divided into two groups, those who preferred a native realism and those who either moved to Europe or were strongly influenced by the Beaux-Arts movement. Unlike painters, who trained at a number of art centers throughout Europe, American sculptors working in marble preferred Italy, and those sculptors working in bronze preferred Paris. Like American impressionist painters, sculptors of the second-phase Beaux-Arts influence brought impressionism to American sculpture and extended its style into the early twentieth century.

See also **Folk Arts; Monuments and Memorials; Museums,** *subentry on* **Art Museums; Painting; Realism and Naturalism.**

Bibliography

Brown, Milton W., et al. *American Art.* New York: Abrams, 1979.

Craven, Wayne. *American Art: History and Culture.* Madison, Wis.: Brown and Benchmark Publishers, 1994.

———. *Sculpture in America.* Rev. ed. Newark, Del.: University of Delaware Press, 1984.

Green, Samuel M. *American Art: A Historical Survey.* New York: Ronald Press, 1966.

Lewis, Samella. *African American Art and Artists.* Berkeley: University of California Press, 1990.

Mendelowitz, David Marcus. *A History of American Art.* New York: Holt, Rinehart and Winston, 1970.

Pierson, William H., Jr., and Martha Davidson, eds. *Arts of the United States: A Pictorial Survey.* Athens: University of Georgia Press, 1960.

PHILIPPE OSZUSCIK

SEATTLE   A party of twenty-five settlers from Illinois arrived in the area near Puget Sound in November 1851, and three months later they staked claims on the eastern shore of Elliott Bay. In May 1853 the Washington territorial government received a plan of the new town, which the settlers called Seattle, a variation on the name of a local Suquamish Indian leader. Relations with nearby Indian communities soon deteriorated. On 26 January 1856 rumors of an imminent uprising prompted a contingent of U.S. Marines to attack a group of Indians. The ensuing battle, which lasted throughout the day, marked the last major conflict between whites and Indians in Seattle.

The construction of a steam sawmill in 1853 furthered the city's primary industry, supplying lumber to communities along the Pacific coast. The University of the Territory of Washington was established in 1861 (renamed the University of Washington in 1889). Its founder, Asa Mercer, gained fame for importing single women, the so-called "Mercer girls," into the male-dominated city for the purpose of matrimony during the 1860s.

After the Civil War, Seattle experienced rapid growth, increasing from 1,107 residents in 1870 to 80,671 in 1900, when the largest foreign-born groups were 3,786 from Canada and 3,091 from Japan. Racial discord recurred in the 1880s in the form of violence against Chinese immigrants, most of whom were forcibly expelled from the city in 1886.

A fire destroyed thirty blocks in downtown Seattle in 1889, but residents quickly rebuilt, replacing wooden structures with stone and brick. As its economy diversified, the city became the economic center of the Pacific Northwest, especially after it became the terminus for the Great Northern Railroad in 1893.

See also **American Indians,** *subentry on* **Wars and Warfare; Cities and Urbanization; City and Regional Planning; Immigration and Immigrants,** *subentry* on **Antiimmigrant Sentiment; Washington State.**

Bibliography

Jones, Nard. *Seattle.* Garden City, N.Y.: Doubleday, 1972.
Sale, Roger. *Seattle: Past to Present.* Seattle: University of Washington Press, 1976.

THOMAS CLARKIN

SECTIONALISM   From the Constitutional Convention until the Civil War, sectionalism was a constant of political life. Yet, paradoxically, it was also a constantly changing concept. During the Constitutional Convention delegates spoke of three major sections or regions: the South, the middle states, and the eastern states (New England). Before the War of 1812 the middle states had divided over slavery, with Delaware being seen as distinctly "southern" and Pennsylvania, New Jersey, and New York being seen as "northern." New England remained a distinct section until after the War of 1812, when it, too, was subsumed into "the North." The South retained its identity from the Constitutional Convention until the Civil War, growing ultimately to include the fifteen slave states in 1860. By 1812 "the West" had emerged. It initially consisted of the territories and states of the Old Northwest, plus Tennessee and Kentucky. By the 1850s the states of the original "West" had become politically aligned with the North and the South. Thus, Tennessee, which was "western" in 1800, had become distinctly southern by 1850. The West, by 1850, consisted mostly of the territories west of the Mississippi. Yet by this time the struggle over slavery had so consumed the politics of the nation that "the West" had ceased to have a political identity separate from the North-South conflict. Culturally, however, the West remained significant throughout the century, even as its definition changed.

The sections had distinct political needs throughout the period. The West needed access to the port of New Orleans before 1803, and to roads and canals later on. Westerners were aggressive in seeking new lands and confronting foreign powers. Thus, the West—Kentucky, Tennessee, and the Ohio valley—provided the greatest support for the War of 1812,

and the Northwest (Illinois, Indiana, and Ohio) was second only to the Southwest (Mississippi, Alabama, Louisiana, Arkansas, and Texas) in support of the war against Mexico in 1846. As it industrialized, the North—and especially the Northeast—sought protective tariffs, regulation of immigration, and a stable system of banking and currency. The North was generally less aggressive in foreign policy and western expansion, seeing economic development as more important than territorial growth.

The South demanded constant protection for slavery and the opportunity to find new lands to settle. Lacking an industrial base, it opposed tariffs, which raised the cost of manufactured goods. With four major exceptions the South preferred an inactive national government. The South wanted the national government to acquire new territory for slavery, and thus backed the Louisiana Purchase, Texas annexation, a war of territorial conquest against Mexico in 1846, and filibustering attempts to acquire Cuba and territory in Central America; similarly, the South wanted the national state to protect slavery through a strong fugitive slave law and the adoption of a federal slave code for the western territories; the South also favored an aggressive foreign policy that would force Great Britain to ignore American violations of the ban on the international slave trade and to return slaves who escaped to the protective umbrella of the Union Jack; finally, the South backed national policies that led to the removal of Indians from the region in the 1820s and 1830s.

New England and the North

From their dissenting Protestant heritage, as Puritans who evolved into Congregationalists or Unitarians, New Englanders developed a distinct culture by 1787. Although most were farmers, the economy depended heavily on the ocean. Shipbuilding, fishing, and whaling were major industries, and international and interstate commerce brought the most wealth to the region. New England merchants and sailors traveled the world in search of markets in which to buy and sell goods. In 1800 the region had the most homogeneous population in the nation. State-supported churches were maintained until the 1830s, and religious restrictions on officeholding existed long after the rest of the country had abandoned them. On the other hand, its sailors and merchants traveled far more than other Americans did, and its ports were filled with people from every place that salt water could be found. New Englanders sent missionaries to China and the Sandwich Islands (present-day Hawaii [Hawai'i]) well before the Civil War.

New England was the bastion of the Federalist

"**The Massachusetts Hoar.**" A political cartoon satirizing regional disagreements over the slavery issue. The man draped in codfish (a symbol of Massachusetts) holds the hand of a black man and defends slaves' right to freedom under the Constitution. In the center, a rich southerner dressed for a hunt disagrees vehemently, as his cohort calls the northerner's claims "nonsensical Codfish and Onion Notions." Meanwhile, the agitated crowd offer dissents in various ethnic dialects. Lithograph with watercolor, 1845. LIBRARY OF CONGRESS: PRINTS AND PHOTOGRAPHS DIVISION

Party, and when that party was long dead in the rest of the nation, it was still breathing, if not thriving, in Massachusetts and Connecticut. Suffering from Jefferson's embargo, and fed up with a nation seemingly dominated by slave owners, some New Englanders threatened to secede from the nation during the War of 1812. From 15 December, 1814, to 5 January, 1815, delegates from Connecticut, Rhode Island, and Massachusetts met at the Hartford Convention to discuss secession. In the end the convention urged the adoption of a series of constitutional amendments, including a prohibition on counting slaves for purposes of congressional representation. These amendments went nowhere, and the convention itself was the subject of ridicule and condemnation both within and outside New England. Indeed, its general opposition to the War of 1812, combined with the Hartford Convention, led to the final demise of the Federalist Party, after a strong showing in the 1812 presidential election.

The Hartford Convention also led to the end of New England as a "section" within the United States. By 1820 New England was part of "the North." From the 1820s until the Civil War, New England, in some ways, led the North. It became the intellectual center of the abolitionist movement, and the most important stronghold of the Republican Party in the 1850s. It would lead the North in the attack on slavery before the war, and Massachusetts would become the first northern state to enlist blacks during the Civil War. New England also led the northern economy; the American industrial revolution began in its mill towns. New England became the center of manufacturing for textiles, small machinery, firearms (at the Springfield armory), railroad cars, and shoes in the three decades before the Civil War. Laws and legal precedents coming out of New England were copied by the rest of the North. The treatises of Justice Joseph Story, a native of Massachusetts, helped nationalize law and constitutional

"The Hurly-Burly Pot." A political cartoon that casts sectionalist political figures as the witches of Shakespeare's *Macbeth*, plotting to instigate war and destroy the Union. Represented are, from left to right, Pennsylvania Free-Soil advocate David Wilmot, abolitionist William Lloyd Garrison, southern states' rights defender and Senator John C. Calhoun, and journalist Horace Greeley. Benedict Arnold, rising from the flames, is invoked as "our great patron saint." Published by James Bailley, 1850. LIBRARY OF CONGRESS

theories in the antebellum period, at least for the North.

Story's writing reflected a larger New England influence on the North in culture. Men and women of letters—such as Ralph Waldo Emerson, Henry David Thoreau, Herman Melville, Henry Wadsworth Longfellow, Nathaniel Hawthorne, Louisa May Alcott, and Lydia Maria Child—created much of American literary culture in the period. The most important novel of the century, *Uncle Tom's Cabin,* was the product of a Connecticut woman, Harriet Beecher Stowe. Stowe's father, Lyman Beecher; her sister, Catharine; and her brothers Henry Ward, Edward, Thomas, and Charles Beecher, were all significant figures in American religious and domestic culture during the century. Samuel Clemens, though raised in Missouri, wrote most of his important novels in Connecticut, after the Civil War. Meanwhile, New England colleges and law schools—Harvard, Yale, Williams, Litchfield College of Law, and later Harvard Law School—trained countless ministers, teachers, inventors, engineers, lawyers, business lead-

ers, and politicians who would lead their section and the nation in this period.

The most significant aspect of New England, and northern, culture in the antebellum period was the abolitionist movement, which began with the publication of William Lloyd Garrison's paper *The Liberator* at Boston in 1831. New England women and men lectured throughout the nation, spreading the antislavery gospel as well as arguments for women's rights. By 1860 the South would see the North as its enemy, but New England, and particularly Massachusetts, as the heart of opposition to slavery.

As New England merged with "the North" after the War of 1812, the North itself grew into an industrial center. Throughout this period a majority of Americans were involved in agricultural pursuits, but in the North a far greater percentage of the population was urban and employed in industrial work. The Northern population grew dramatically from the 1820s through 1861 as European immigrants, especially from Ireland and Germany, poured into the ports of Boston, New York, and Philadelphia.

"**Congressional Scales, a True Balance.**" Straddling the scale of justice, President Zachary Taylor is depicted as balancing and resolving northern and southern steadfastness on the issue of slavery. Henry Clay appears on the left, or northern, tray, while Lewis Cass and John Calhoun appear on the right, or southern, tray. Currier and Ives, 1850. LIBRARY OF CONGRESS: PRINTS AND PHOTOGRAPHS DIVISION

The West

The "West" was an ever-changing section during this period. In 1800 Ohio, Kentucky, and Tennessee were "the west." By 1850 Ohio, as well as Illinois, Indiana, Michigan, and Wisconsin, were as much "northern" as western, and during the Civil War they were solidly in the North, despite some Confederate sympathy in the Butternut (Copperhead) sections of southern Illinois and southern Indiana. By 1850 the "west" lay beyond the Mississippi, stretching from Kansas to California. Meanwhile, Kentucky, Tennessee, Arkansas, Missouri, and Texas, which were once part of the West, had become solidly southern as slavery came to define the great sectional divide in the nation.

Economically the West was dominated by small farmers in the first part of this period, and by ranchers and miners at the end of the period. In the Southwest, plantation-based agriculture—especially cotton in Texas, Arkansas, Missouri, and western Tennessee—led to a thriving plantation culture that quickly defined these places as more southern than western. Part of the definition of the West was the status of Native Americans. From the mid-1820s to the mid-1840s, the national government succeeded in removing most Native Americans in the East to "Indian Territory" (present-day Oklahoma). Remaining Indians, especially in upstate New York, Wisconsin, North Carolina, and Florida, were pushed onto reservations or marginal remote lands such as the Everglades in Florida and the mountains of western North Carolina. Thus, one definition of the West was where Indians could be found.

The West provided important cultural images for easterners: endless herds of buffalo, "wild" Indians, and abundant vacant land. It also produced powerful symbols of rugged independence, true "manhood," and the democratic spirit. The political power of the "West" emerged with the election of Andrew Jackson as president in 1828. From that year until 1852, with the exception of Jackson's protégé, Martin Van Buren, every elected president was, like Jackson, a native of the East who had moved West (often as a child) and was seen as a westerner. In 1840 William Henry Harrison, who was in fact born into a wealthy slave-owning planter family in Virginia, was successfully sold to the American voters as a man who grew up in a log cabin and drank hard cider, the beverage of the West. Even the losing candidates were "western" in this period. Henry Clay, running in 1844, campaigned under the slogan "Justice to Harry of the West." As late as 1856 John C. Frémont, the first candidate of the Republican Party, traded on his fame as a western explorer, as "The Pathfinder." As the first bearded presidential candidate, he personified the westerner under the slogan "Free Soil, Free Speech, Free Men and Frémont." Similarly, Lincoln, the first president actually born in the West, personified his section as "The Rail-splitter," in 1860.

By the 1850s, however, the political divide in the nation was over slavery. Kansas, which represented the West, literally became the battleground as proslavery settlers and border ruffians from Missouri fought against free state settlers. Only after the Civil War had ended the debate over slavery did the West reemerge as a section fighting for economic and political advantage against both the East and the South.

The South

The South is the easiest section of the nation to define: it consists of those states that maintained slavery until 1861: the eleven states of the Confederacy, plus Delaware, Maryland, Kentucky, and Missouri. Some of these states were "western," particularly before 1846, and presidential candidates from these states—Andrew Jackson, Henry Clay, James Polk, and Zachary Taylor—were usually portrayed as westerners, to make them more appealing to the North.

Slavery was the overwhelming factor in the definition of the South and dwarfed all other cultural factors. Indeed, without slavery the South looked much like the North. In the 1830s Evangelical Protestants were as common in Ohio or New York as in Georgia or Alabama. Temperance movements spread nationally. Whigs and Democrats competed for offices in both sections. But slavery made everything different. Slavery and plantation agriculture in much of the South made the region different from much of the North. But staple crop agriculture was not the cause of sectional difference. Slave-owning wheat farmers in Virginia were as committed to slavery as cotton planters in Alabama; urban masters in New Orleans were as devoted to slavery as their sugar-planting "country cousins"; and congressmen and senators from Delaware, with few slaves and virtually no plantations, voted with the deep South on issues involving slavery and race.

The South gradually became a closed society where free speech was proscribed and intellectual curiosity was suppressed by the need to protect slavery. Professors or ministers who expressed doubts about slavery were forced from their classrooms and pulpits. Science was corrupted by the need to find scientific and medical evidence of black suitability for slavery and of white superiority. Economic development was stifled by the needs of slavery. Immigrants avoided the South because they could not compete with slave labor; industrial development was hampered by a labor shortage. Masters were reluctant to allow their slaves to work in mines or factories, or on steamships and railroad crews. Thus the construction of roads, canals, and railroads was hampered by labor shortages as well.

The Sectional Crisis

Sectionalism first arose at the Constitutional Convention as delegates argued over the place of slavery in the constitutional structure and the relative power of Congress over commercial development. At one point in the convention, James Madison argued

> that the States were divided into different interests not by their difference of size, but by other circumstances; the most material of which resulted partly from climate, but principally from their having or not having slaves.

These two causes concurred in forming the great division of interests in the U. States. It did not lie between the large and small States: it lay between the Northern and Southern, and if any defensive power were necessary, it ought to be mutually given to these two interests. (Max Farrand, ed. *Records of the Federal Convention of 1787.* Rev. ed. 4 vols. [New Haven: Yale University Press, 1966] vol. 1, pp. 486–487.)

Madison proposed two branches of Congress, one in which slaves would be counted equally with free people to determine how many representatives each state would have, and one in which slaves would not be counted. Under this arrangement, "the Southern Scale would have the advantage in one House, and the Northern in the other." Madison made this proposal despite his reluctance to "urge any diversity of interests on an occasion when it is but too apt to arise of itself."

During a debate over commercial regulation, Pierce Butler of South Carolina declared that the interests of the southern and New England states were "as different as the interests of Russia and Turkey." Nevertheless, he was "desirous of conciliating the affections of the East," and in this debate supported a simple majority for commercial regulations. In a different context Gouverneur Morris, a delegate from Pennsylvania, complained that "when fairly explained," the system of representation "comes to this: that the inhabitant of Georgia and South Carolina who goes to the Coast of Africa, and in defiance of the most sacred laws of humanity tears away his fellow creatures from their dearest connections and damns them to the most cruel bondages, shall have more votes in a Government instituted for protection of the rights of mankind, than the Citizen of Pennsylvania or New Jersey who views with a laudable horror, so nefarious a practice."

The delegates managed to overcome these conflicts in 1787, but the sectionalism Madison and others observed could not disappear until its root cause—slavery—also disappeared.

In 1819 sectionalism led to divisive debates over the admission of Missouri as a state. Voting almost entirely on sectional lines, the northern congressmen (who included those from the states of the Old Northwest) voted to ban slavery in Missouri while southerners voted to allow slavery. The Missouri Compromise (1820) temporarily settled the issue of slavery in the West. The territories south of Missouri would be open to slavery; slavery would be banned from those north and west of Missouri. Texas independence in 1836, and annexation in 1845, did not violate the Missouri Compromise, but it exacerbated sectional tensions. In the 1830s a new abolitionist movement in the North petitioned Congress to attack slavery where it had the power to do so, and flooded the South with letters and pamphlets urging southerners, in the name of Christian morality, to end slavery.

Sectionalism soon came to national institutions as slavery led the Baptists, Methodists, and Presbyterians to divide into northern and southern branches. In the 1840s and 1850s southerners continued to send their sons to northern colleges, universities, law schools, and medical schools, but in declining numbers. Shared culture began to diminish. In the 1850s *Uncle Tom's Cabin* was read everywhere in the North but banned in the South.

Throughout the period southerners argued for various theories—nullification, state sovereignty, the concurrent majority, and the right to secede—that would allow them to prevent the enforcement of national laws they found objectionable, or even to leave the Union if they felt slavery was threatened by the national government. Meanwhile, in the 1840s and 1850s northerners made states' rights arguments to prevent fugitive slaves from being returned and to protect free blacks from being kidnapped. Open hostility to the enforcement of the 1850 Fugitive Slave Law led to the stationing of federal troops in some northern cities and federal prosecutions of abolitionists, free blacks, and even previously uncommitted bystanders who refused to cooperate in the return of fugitive slaves. Southerners interpreted this lawlessness as an indication that the North would never support its most important, and peculiar, institution.

In 1848 the sectional stress reached the political parties as antislavery Democrats, known as Barnburners, supported the candidacy of Martin Van Buren, running on the Free Soil ticket, support that led in part to the defeat of the Democratic Party's candidate, Lewis Cass. The Democrats had reunited by 1852, winning the White House by rallying around the Compromise of 1850, which briefly lowered sectional tensions. Trying to use this victory to end the debate over slavery, Senator Stephen A. Douglas of Illinois pushed through the Kansas-Nebraska Act (1854), which repealed the 1820 ban on slavery in territories west of Missouri and allowed settlers to decide the issue for themselves, under a concept known as popular sovereignty.

Douglas and the Democrats, blinded by their close ties to the slave South, misread the mood of their northern neighbors. A new political organization, the Republican Party, quickly emerged, pledged to stopping the spread of slavery into the territories. Meanwhile, a civil war in Kansas broke out as popular sovereignty degenerated into popular warfare. By 1856 the Whig Party was dead as a national institution.

Most northern Whigs became Republicans, as did many northern Democrats, disgusted by the party's continuing subservience to the slave South. In the South, Whigs backed the Know-Nothing candidacy of former President Millard Fillmore, a classic doughface (a northern man with southern principles) who had almost no support in his own region. James Buchanan, a Pennsylvania doughface, won the election, but was a truly sectional candidate, carrying every slave state except Maryland and losing eleven of sixteen free states to the Republican candidate, John C. Frémont.

In 1857–1858 Buchanan made Kansas admission as a slave state a test of party loyalty, splitting the Democratic Party in the North and setting the stage for a national division in 1860. The overwhelming majority of the settlers favored a free state, and the proposed Kansas constitution—the Lecompton Constitution—had been written by a convention that was fraudulently elected, and adopted in a referendum that prevented opponents of slavery from voting against either statehood or slavery. In order to protect his own career, Douglas, the most popular Democrat in the nation, successfully opposed Buchanan on the Lecompton Constitution and Kansas statehood. The president in turn tried to engineer Douglas's defeat in the 1858 senatorial election. This failed; Douglas narrowly beat the Republican challenger, Abraham Lincoln, a small-town lawyer with relatively little political experience.

The 1850s culminated with John Brown's raid on Harpers Ferry, Virginia (now West Virginia). Brown hoped to start a slave rebellion and lead a guerrilla war against slavery. He was easily captured, and quickly tried and executed. But southerners could not forgive the North for a public outpouring of support for Brown. With rhetorical flourish, northern poets and clergymen declared Brown a hero, a martyr, a new Christ. Ralph Waldo Emerson spoke of "the new saint awaiting his martyrdom, and who, if he shall suffer, will make the gallows glorious like the cross." And Henry Ward Beecher, whose sister Harriet had infuriated the South with her novel depicting the horrors of slavery, gloried in the prospect of Brown on the gallows. "Let Virginia make him a martyr!" Beecher thundered: "Now, he has only blundered. . . . But a cord and gibbet would redeem all that, and round up Brown's failure with a heroic success." John A. Andrew, a rising star in the Republican Party and future governor of Massachusetts, refused to commit himself on the wisdom of Brown's raid, but declared that "John Brown himself is right." For southerners, this was proof enough that the North, and its new political party, meant to make war on the South.

By 1860 the Democrats had completely unraveled.

The party convention was suspended when delegates from the deep South walked out rather than support the nomination of Douglas. In the election Douglas ran in the North and the South, but won only twelve electoral votes. John C. Breckinridge, running as southern Democrat, won eleven states and seventy-two electoral votes. Breckinridge argued that only he could save the Union, because if he were elected, the South would remain in the nation. John Bell of Tennessee, running under the banner of the newly created Constitutional Union Party, carried three states. Lincoln, on the ballot only in the North and a few border slave states, won all eighteen free states (although New Jersey divided its electoral vote between Lincoln and Douglas) and 59 percent of the electoral vote, but only 40 percent of the popular vote.

Sectionalism had triumphed in 1856 to elect a president, James Buchanan, whose appeal was almost entirely in the South; it triumphed again in 1860 to elect a northern candidate. What followed was the logical end point of sectionalism: secession and civil war. Following Lincoln's election, South Carolina declared it was no longer part of the United States. By the time of Lincoln's inauguration, six states had followed South Carolina out of the Union. Meeting in Montgomery, Alabama, delegates wrote a constitution for the Confederate States of America, elected Jefferson Davis their president, and prepared to make a new, southern nation. When Lincoln tried to send food and other supplies to Fort Sumter, in Charleston harbor, Confederate troops opened fire. The four years of war that followed destroyed slavery and the possibility of secession. Sectional disagreements would reemerge after the war. The West, the South, the Midwest, and the Northeast would disagree over programs and policies, but their disagreements would be settled by legislation, litigation, elections, and political compromises and trade-offs. The occasional use of federal troops or marshals in response to violent opposition to national policies would never again escalate to war.

See also **Abolition and Antislavery; Civil War,** *subentry* **on Causes of the Civil War; Democratic Party; Federal-State Relations,** *subentry on* **1831–1865; Federalist Party; Fugitive Slave Laws; Kansas-Nebraska Act; Missouri Compromise; Republican Party.**

Bibliography

Fehrenbacher, Don E. *The South and the Three Sectional Crises.* Baton Rouge: Louisiana State University Press, 1980.
Finkelman, Paul, ed. *His Soul Goes Marching On: Responses to John Brown and the Harpers Ferry Raid.* Charlottesville: University Press of Virginia, 1995.
Foner, Eric. *Free Soil, Free Labor, Free Men: The Ideology of the Republican Party Before the Civil War.* New York: Oxford University Press, 1970.
Freehling, William H. *Prelude to Civil War: The Nullification Controversy in South Carolina, 1816–1836.* New York: Harper and Row, 1966.
Freehling, William W. *The Road to Disunion: Secessionists at Bay, 1776–1854.* New York: Oxford University Press, 1990.
Holman, Hamilton. *Prologue to Conflict: The Crisis and Compromise of 1850.* Lexington: University of Kentucky Press, 1964.
Potter, David M. *The Impending Crisis, 1848–1861.* New York: Harper and Row, 1976.
Rawley, James A. *Secession: The Disruption of the American Republic, 1844–1861.* Malabar, Fla.: Krieger, 1990.
Sewell, Richard H. *Ballots for Freedom: Antislavery Politics in the United States, 1837–1860.* New York: Norton, 1976.

PAUL FINKELMAN

SEGREGATION

[This entry includes two subentries, **Segregation and Civil Rights** and **Urban Segregation.** See also **Education,** subentry on **School Segregation.**]

SEGREGATION AND CIVIL RIGHTS

In the U.S. South in 1900, racial considerations governed all human relations. Jim Crow had many faces: poverty, disfranchisement, exclusion, segregation, inequality. Violence and the threat of violence underlay the entire complex of social, economic, and political proscription based on race. In many respects, the broad contours of the racial landscape in 1900 resembled those of 1800, with systematic de jure segregation the most novel approach to organizing race relations in the region.

After 1865 slavery could no longer structure relations between the races. The Black Codes, enacted in 1865 and 1866 in every southern state to update or replace the Slave Codes, recognized certain civil rights: the right to make contracts, including marriages, though not interracial marriages; the right to own property, though not land in some states; and the right to testify in court proceedings, if blacks were involved. Rebutting the Black Codes, the Civil Rights Act of 1866 sought to expand the definition of such rights as property holding. Moreover, in a de facto kind of way, the right to attend school had already emerged in summer 1865 as schools for freed people began operations. In 1867 and 1868, political rights also became a reality for a time, as black men voted in all the former Confederate states. Meantime, segregation of a voluntary sort appeared, as freed people organized their own churches.

Segregation made no sense in some areas of public life (except perhaps in all-black jurisdictions like Mound Bayou, Mississippi). When black southerners were excluded from jury service, black plaintiffs or defendants had no alternative black system of justice to which they could turn. When black southerners were excluded from voting in elections, they could not maintain a "separate but equal" political system. In such instances, exclusion was exclusion, pure and simple.

Segregation had roots in the North, after slavery receded there, as well as in the antebellum South. Yet a regime of spatial separation in public facilities became a mainstay of southern custom and law only after 1865, and it reached full development only after 1890. Whether de facto or de jure, segregation in schools generally preceded segregation in transportation.

Segregation in Higher Education

Before 1865, black exclusion from higher education was universal in the South, and in fact the criminalization of black education—at any level—had been widespread. Nowhere in the South, therefore, was there an institution of higher education that black men or black women, no matter how well qualified, might attend. Several such schools opened within a few years of 1865, among them Fisk University, Atlanta University, Hampton Institute, and Howard University. Though these schools were designed primarily for black students, white students attended Howard in small numbers, and white children of white faculty members took classes at Atlanta University, for example. The University of South Carolina admitted black students during Reconstruction and became a predominantly black institution as whites withdrew.

The new rule, in public and private institutions alike, was that black students attended one set of schools and whites attended another. Exceptions to the new rule were unusual. The greatest change was the emergence of institutions that black southerners might attend at all, a marked change from the pre-Reconstruction era.

Segregation was soon codified. When the Virginia legislature inaugurated land-grant schooling in 1872 under the Morrill Act (1862), it divided the funds, with one-third of the money going to a black school, Hampton Normal and Agricultural Institute (later Hampton University), and two-thirds going to a white school, Virginia Agricultural and Mechanical College (later Virginia Polytechnic Institute and State University). Georgia applied the entire proceeds of its land-grant fund to a white school, the University of Georgia, but beginning in 1870 appropriated an equivalent amount of money to Atlanta University. In 1887 the Georgia legislature withdrew the funds from Atlanta University on the grounds that white students attended the school in violation of state policy against biracial education.

Congress passed a Second Morrill Act in 1890. Whereas the 1862 act had been silent on race, and states had varied in the ways they had chosen, if at all, to divide the benefits along racial lines, the 1890 act required them to supply benefits to black as well as white residents. The 1890 act offered more money than the 1862 act had, but made its availability contingent on its being shared. Yet it expressly permitted an "equitable" allocation to "separate" schools. Thus the "separate but equal" formula, generally ascribed to the Supreme Court in its 1896 decision in *Plessy v. Ferguson*, was already federal law (permitting segregation, not mandating it), so far as land-grant institutions were concerned, when that case was heard. Georgia proved typical when it satisfied the provisions of the new act by creating a new school in Savannah where only black faculty could teach and only black students could attend. Black access to segregated schools increasingly accompanied black exclusion from white schools.

Segregation in Elementary and Secondary Schools

Like higher education, elementary and secondary education was segregated. The freedpeople's schools that sprouted across the South's educational landscape in 1865 and 1866—sponsored by the Freedmen's Bureau, northern missionary societies, or the freedpeople themselves—revealed a transformation from the exclusionary practice of the past. By the early 1870s, every southern state had enacted a system of public schools that, on a segregated basis, admitted children of both races. New Orleans, which maintained a system of integrated schools for a time in the 1870s, was virtually unique in the region, and it soon fell into line with the prevailing practice and policy.

Segregated public elementary schools became less equal over time. In Alabama, for example, public money was divided far more equally on a per-student basis through the 1880s than was the case thereafter. Early in the twentieth century, every southern state greatly increased its financial support of public schools, but larger and larger shares went to schools in white communities. Segregated schools were surely better than no schools at all—segregation was an improvement over exclusion—but segregation also facilitated a growing inequality in funds and therefore in teachers' salaries, curricular offerings, and physical facilities. Many jurisdictions refused to support public education for blacks beyond elementary school, so exclusion continued to exist at the high school level.

Segregation in Other State Institutions

The shift from exclusion to segregation could be seen in other kinds of public institutions. South Carolina and Virginia had each admitted occasional black inmates into its insane asylum in the 1850s, but Georgia had followed an exclusionary model, based on the premise that slavery supplied a means of handling whatever problems might arise. After emancipation no such argument could be maintained. Every southern state adopted a policy of segregated access to mental hospitals, either in separate wings of the same institution or in separate institutions.

A similar development characterized state policy regarding special schools for people with impaired vision or hearing. By the 1850s Georgia was sponsoring schools to train handicapped whites. Emancipation did not bring an immediate change in the policy of exclusion, nor did the advent of Republican power during Reconstruction, but by the 1880s Georgia had more or less taken the "separate but equal" path and was doing much the same for handicapped blacks.

Segregated Inns and Theaters

Eating and sleeping establishments in the South remained generally segregated throughout the late nineteenth century. One way to implement segregation in restaurants was to have some establishments for black patrons and others for whites; another way was to separate patrons by race within one establishment.

Places of amusement such as parks and theaters also shifted from a policy of black exclusion to a policy of racial segregation. Savannah, addressing the postemancipation world by anticipating that freedpeople might wish to use the city park, simply closed the park for a time, but that expedient could hardly prevail. Theaters often practiced segregation by setting aside the balcony for black patrons. Sometimes segregation was achieved by separating the races in time rather than space, as when blacks might use a facility only at certain times.

The *Civil Rights Cases* (1883) overturned the public accommodations sections of the Civil Rights Act of 1875. The Supreme Court ruled that Congress could not act under the Fourteenth Amendment against private acts of discrimination, for that amendment authorized intervention only against state actions. Congress could act against individuals under the Thirteenth Amendment, but, according to

the Court, private acts of racial discrimination did not constitute marks of slavery. Therefore black plaintiffs had no constitutional ground to call on federal courts to curtail private actions of racial exclusion, segregation, or unequal treatment.

Segregation in Transportation

Public conveyances were far more segregated after 1900 than they had been in the 1870s, although segregation was at all times widespread in the post–Civil War South. Custom, state law, city ordinance, and company policy each played a role in establishing segregation as the norm on steamboats, railways, and streetcars. By petition, sit-in, boycott, and court challenge, black southerners often opposed the imposition of the rule of race in regulating travel. At the very least, they sought to seize the "equal" in "separate but equal."

A series of decisions by the U.S. Supreme Court opened the doors to a spate of segregation statutes and practices. *Hall v. DeCuir* (1877) overturned a Louisiana civil rights statute as a burden on interstate commerce. *Louisville, New Orleans & Texas Railway v. Mississippi* (1890) upheld a Mississippi law requiring the segregation of intrastate passengers, even on interstate railways, and *Plessy v. Ferguson* (1896) upheld a Louisiana statute requiring segregated intrastate railway accommodations. *Chiles v. Chesapeake & Ohio Railway* (1910) upheld company rules requiring segregation even in interstate travel. In these cases the Supreme Court neutralized every kind of legal effort to curtail segregation and upheld every kind of policy designed to achieve segregation.

Segregation in Marriage and Residence

Every southern state applied the ground rules of segregation to marriage and the family. The states varied in the approach taken before 1865, but soon after emancipation every one of them enacted a law to ban interracial marriage. Black southerners and white southerners alike, in the new postemancipation world of "separate but equal," had the right to marry, but only on their own side of the racial divide.

Soon after the dawn of the twentieth century, some southern cities—among them Baltimore, Maryland, and Louisville, Kentucky—mandated residential segregation. They enacted ordinances designed to achieve all-black and all-white neighborhoods. Only whites could move into majority-white districts, and only blacks could move into majority-black neighborhoods.

When challenges to these ordinances reached the U.S. Supreme Court, both sides agreed that state laws could employ racial categories to sort out who could ride in which railway car, attend which public school, or marry people of any particular racial identity. The two sides conceded that the Supreme Court had already validated such laws, but they differed as to whether the law could also designate residential zones according to racial identity. In *Buchanan v. Warley* (1917), the Supreme Court sided with the challengers and held that property rights could not be curtailed by such zoning ordinances. Restrictive covenants—private arrangements with similar objectives—became the preferred way to achieve residential segregation.

Leaders and Programs

African Americans espoused a wide range of programs and approaches to the proscriptions black southerners faced. One was situational withdrawal, or avoidance of the dangers and humiliations that confronting Jim Crow could evoke, whether within the South or outside it, such as choosing to walk rather than ride a Jim Crow streetcar in a southern city. That withdrawal could take the form of a quest for an all-black environment, whether that meant an all-black community within the South, the Exoduster migration to Kansas, or a "back to Africa" movement of the sort that Bishop Henry M. Turner (1834–1915) eventually adopted. It could also take the form of mass migration to the North, a phenomenon that brought large numbers north from Virginia by the 1880s and from the rest of the South by World War I.

For the first half century after emancipation, the vast majority of African Americans continued to live in the rural South. Most would have to make their lives there, but not all would, and African American leaders varied in their origins, their constituencies, and their programs for improving the situations of black southerners.

Frederick Douglass (1818?–1895), a Maryland slave turned prewar abolitionist, continued to fight for equality until his death in 1895, long after the Thirteenth, Fourteenth, and Fifteenth Amendments that he championed brought blacks freedom, citizenship, and political rights. Soon after the Civil War, he pushed for favorable federal policies on land distribution and freedpeople's schools. Late in his life, disheartened by the emerging constellation of oppression—disfranchisement, sharecropping, segregation, inequality, and violence—Douglass came especially to decry lynching.

Ida B. Wells (1862–1931), born a slave in Mississippi during the Civil War, became a teacher, a journalist, and an avowed opponent of transportation segregation. Beginning in Memphis in 1892, she launched her own crusade against lynching, an emerging phenomenon that she saw as a new weapon of terror promiscuously used to impose economic and political control on an entire race.

Booker T. Washington (1856–1915), a Virginia slave turned postwar educator, focused on the masses of rural black southerners and on training black teachers for black schools. His famous speech in Atlanta in 1895, the year Douglass died, urged black economic self-help and publicly acquiesced in segregation and disfranchisement. Yet Washington also surreptitiously promoted test cases in the courts to challenge the spreading blight of "separate but equal," especially as the "equal" in the formula receded.

W. E. B. Du Bois (1868–1963), born free in Massachusetts during the Reconstruction era, insisted on civil rights and on the role and the rights of what he called the "talented tenth," and he did historical and sociological research on African Americans and published widely. Early in the twentieth century, Du Bois helped found the National Association for the Advancement of Colored People (NAACP), a group that strived, mostly through test cases in federal courts, to break down segregation and enhance civil rights.

Civil Rights in the North

At the same time that African American civil rights were receding in the South and under federal law, they were expanding in the North under state law. Though critics decried the *Civil Rights Cases* and *Plessy* as echoing the 1857 *Dred Scott* decision (which had denied that African Americans could be citizens at all), one major difference was that the Court was not acting in a way that portended the nationalization of Jim Crow. During the very years that segregation emerged as a dominant characteristic of life in the South, it was receding still farther in the North.

Particularly in the 1880s, in the aftermath of the *Civil Rights Cases,* many northern and western states enacted state laws modeled on the Civil Rights Act of 1875. Moreover, some states repealed statutes that had long outlawed interracial marriage. In addition, court cases led to the desegregation of public schools in some jurisdictions. State legislatures and state courts, acting under the authority of state constitutions, could and did act to expand the definition of black freedom in the late-nineteenth-century North.

Northern state civil rights laws typically enumerated the kinds of places—restaurants, inns, and railroads, for example—where it was illegitimate to exercise racial discrimination. African American plaintiffs sometimes lost in court on the basis that they had suffered discrimination at a place that was not enumerated. On other occasions, they won the court decision, yet when the statute specified a maximum penalty but no minimum, they were awarded only a penny or some other minuscule figure. Nonetheless, these state civil rights laws reflected the small but emerging political power of black northerners, and they pointed toward a future in which de jure segregation might be far less widespread.

The Nineteenth Century's Legacy

The twentieth century inherited segregation. Yet segregation was not the central issue in the nineteenth century that it became in the twentieth. In the twentieth century, "civil rights" came to emphasize desegregation and reenfranchisement, rather than the matters addressed by the Black Codes or the Civil Rights Act of 1866. After the end of slavery, African Americans' first objective regarding public facilities was to achieve access at all, notably to schools. The next objective was to gain access to equal facilities, if not the same ones.

The various facets of segregation revealed multiple meanings. Black institutions of higher education, though poorly funded when compared to their white counterparts, provided invaluable training for black southerners who went on to become teachers, lawyers, doctors, and dentists in their communities. Over time, those institutions measured the advantages that "separate and unequal" brought when replacing a policy of exclusion. Black freedom long continued to carry a more restricted definition than did white freedom, but it was a far cry from black slavery. Moreover, black students at segregated colleges spearheaded much of the Civil Rights movement, as when four freshmen at North Carolina's black land-grant school began their sit-in at a Woolworth's lunch counter in downtown Greensboro in February 1960.

Black schools, elementary or secondary, might be poorly funded compared with white schools, but for generations they also provided employment opportunities for black teachers, opportunities that swiftly declined when desegregation took place in the 1960s. Desegregation brought real losses in black communities, just as it brought real gains, and the summing up is still in process.

For years, when historians argued about the timing of racial segregation—before the Civil War or after, directly after emancipation or not until the 1890s—they often focused on railroads and streetcars, not schools and colleges, let alone matters of marriage or residence. Yet segregation governed a wide range of activities, at many times and in many places, in the nineteenth-century United States.

See also **African Americans,** *subentries on* **Overview, Free Blacks before the Civil War; Civil Rights; Civil War,** *subentry on* **Consequences of the Civil War; Constitutional Amendments,** *subentry on* **Thirteenth, Fourteenth, and Fifteenth Amendments; Education,** *subentries on* **School Segregation, Education of African Americans, Education of the Blind and Deaf; Emancipation; Miscegenation; Race Laws; Reconstruction; Segregation, Urban; South,** *subentry on* **The New South after Reconstruction; Supreme Court,** *subentry on* **The Court during the Civil War and Reconstruction; Voters and Voting,** *subentry on* **Black Voters after the Civil War.**

Bibliography

Anderson, Eric, and Alfred A. Moss Jr., eds. *The Facts of Reconstruction: Essays in Honor of John Hope Franklin.* Baton Rouge: Louisiana State University Press, 1991.

Cell, John W. *The Highest Stage of White Supremacy: The Origins of Segregation in South Africa and the American South.* Cambridge, U.K.: Cambridge University Press, 1982.

Fredrickson, George M. *White Supremacy: A Comparative Study in American and South African History.* New York: Oxford University Press, 1981.

Harlan, Louis R. *Booker T. Washington: The Making of a Black Leader, 1856–1901.* New York: Oxford University Press, 1972.

Lewis, David Levering. *W. E. B. Du Bois: Biography of a Race, 1868–1919.* New York: Henry Holt, 1993.

Litwack, Leon F. *North of Slavery: The Negro in the Free States, 1790–1860.* Chicago: University of Chicago Press, 1961.

———. *Trouble in Mind: Black Southerners in the Age of Jim Crow.* New York: Knopf, 1998.

Lofgren, Charles A. *The Plessy Case: A Legal-Historical Interpretation.* New York: Oxford University Press, 1987.

McMurry, Linda O. *To Keep the Waters Troubled: The Life of Ida B. Wells.* New York: Oxford University Press, 1998.

Nieman, Donald G. *Promises to Keep: African-Americans and the Constitutional Order, 1776 to the Present.* New York: Oxford University Press, 1991.

Rabinowitz, Howard N. *Race Relations in the Urban South, 1865–1890.* New York: Oxford University Press, 1978.

Wallenstein, Peter. *From Slave South to New South: Public Policy in Nineteenth-Century Georgia.* Chapel Hill: University of North Carolina Press, 1987.

Williamson, Joel. *After Slavery: The Negro in South Carolina during Reconstruction, 1861–1877.* Chapel Hill: University of North Carolina Press, 1965.

Woodward, C. Vann. *The Strange Career of Jim Crow.* 1955. 3d ed., New York: Oxford University Press, 1974.

PETER WALLENSTEIN

SEGREGATION, URBAN

As American cities grew in the nineteenth century, they exhibited increasingly higher levels of segregation by class, ethnicity, and race. This trend, however, was hardly uniform across all regions or all social groups. The growth of segregation was uneven and unpredictable, strongly influenced by the spatial dynamics of the urban economy as well as the ethnic and racial demography of specific cities. Most urban groups experienced increased residential concentration to some extent, but by the beginning of the twentieth century the richest and poorest city dwellers, and those groups the larger society defined as racially inferior or suspect, tended to be the most highly segregated.

Between 1830 and the 1850s the expansion of urban economic activity, the influx of immigrants from Germany and Ireland, and the development of rudimentary mass transit systems, such as the omnibus, the horse-drawn railway, and the first commuter rail lines, all contributed to increased ethnic and class segregation in the nation's burgeoning cities, especially the large metropolises in the Northeast. The growth of central business districts, dock areas, and small factory districts promoted the expansion of inner-city working-class neighborhoods and also induced some of the upper middle class and elite to move to outlying suburbs.

This early differentiation by class within the urban context, however, was incomplete. Most urban dwellers in the mid-nineteenth century, regardless of their incomes, still walked to work and to local shops. Consequently, although middle-class and elite areas emerged, within the city proper they were of necessity not far removed from working-class neighborhoods. Many sections of the city remained mixed in both their class and land-use compositions.

The same was true of ethnic segregation. German and especially Irish immigrants clustered in the poorer, older parts of the cities. Middle-class members of these groups also lived in these sections, helping to create cohesive, cross-class communities whose residents shopped on the same streets and worshipped together in the local parish church. Despite clustering, however, these ethnic groups seldom comprised more than half of the total population of specific neighborhoods, even in a heavily Irish city like Boston. Even the small black population of antebellum northern cities remained relatively dispersed compared to conditions that would prevail in twentieth-century cities. At the time of the Civil War, African Americans were usually more segregated than any other group. Yet they almost always lived on streets interspersed to some degree with poor, often foreign-born, whites.

This moderate trend toward ethnic and racial segregation at mid-century was less evident in southern cities. With a few exceptions, like Louisville and New Orleans, southern urban centers did not attract immigrants, and the foreign-born seldom dominated particular neighborhoods. In contrast, African Americans, whether slaves or free, made up a substantial portion of the urban population in the South. They were more dispersed than blacks in northern cities, primarily because they often lived in shacks near the homes where they worked as servants. This pattern began to break down after emancipation, when the black populations of southern cities rapidly increased due to immigration and predominantly black districts of moderate size emerged. As late as the 1920s, however, older southern cities like Charleston, New Orleans, and Savannah did not have cohesive black ghettos, even though the races, by law, were then separated in most other aspects of life in these communities.

Urban segregation intensified in the post–Civil War decades, especially after 1880. Changes in business and transportation again played roles, as heavy industry, particularly in the Midwest, replaced small factory production, department stores and tall office buildings dominated downtown areas, and after 1887 the electric streetcar and elevated lines allowed the middle class to move to new housing developments in the outlying sections of cities. At the turn of the century the impoverished "new immigrants" from southern and eastern Europe crowded into the older sections, close to the growing industrial districts. There, to a much greater degree than had been true of their predecessors from northern Europe, they were segregated by both ethnicity and class. The new immigrants were usually separated from the increasingly middle-class Anglo-Saxon population, as well as from the Irish and Germans, some of whom were now upwardly mobile enough to join the exodus to the suburbs.

The maturing of the industrial city during the 1880–1915 period sharpened divisions along lines of class, ethnicity, and race. The upper class was perhaps the most segregated residentially, either in new elite suburbs, like parts of Long Island or Chestnut Hill in Philadelphia, or in smaller "gold coast" neighborhoods abutting the central business districts. A growing white-collar class was separated from largely working-class areas of Russian Jews, Italians, and other immigrant groups. African Americans also became more segregated, and by 1900 blacks in most large cities resided within a few well-defined areas. Except in Chicago and New York, however, prior to 1915 blacks did not live in ghettos but were still to some degree intermixed with poor immigrants, with whom they shared the most dilapidated sections of cities. As late as 1910 the segregation levels of Italians, Jews, and Poles were often little different from that of blacks. Only after World War I would this change, as the black population became ghettoized.

Immigrant areas began to shrink after immigration was virtually cut off in 1924.

At the end of the nineteenth century the Chinese were the most thoroughly segregated group in urban America. They were forced into densely populated Chinatowns, excluded from many occupations, and barred from political participation because they could not become naturalized citizens. Chinese immigrants, therefore, existed largely within self-contained communities. This was also increasingly true of the Mexican populations of California and Texas. In San Diego, Santa Barbara, and elsewhere, as the rapidly expanding Anglo population overwhelmed the older Mexican population, the Mexicans were confined to the historic pueblo districts of cities.

The growing segmentation of elements of the population within well-defined areas nurtured cultural differences and, at the same time, promoted stereotypes. Except in the workplace, and even then only among a defined social class, people from different ethnic, racial, and class groups had little direct contact with each other. Relatively few Americans at the time appreciated the marvelous diversity of their new urban scene. More typical was Jacob Riis's highly ambiguous description of New York's immigrant and black neighborhoods in *How the Other Half Lives* (1890), which moralistically judged various ethnic minorities according to how well they assimilated the mythical norms of Protestant, middle-class America.

See also **African Americans; Barrios; Chinatowns; Cities and Urbanization; Class, Social; Immigration and Immigrants; Industrialization and the Market; Population; Race and Racial Thinking; Segregation,** *subentry on* **Segregation and Civil Rights; Transportation,** *subentry on* **Urban and Interurban Transportation.**

Bibliography

Camarillo, Albert. *Chicanos in a Changing Society: From Mexican Pueblos to American Barrios in Santa Barbara and Southern California, 1848–1930.* Cambridge, Mass.: Harvard University Press, 1979.

Hershberg, Theodore, et al. "A Tale of Three Cities: Blacks, Immigrants, and Opportunity in Philadelphia, 1850–1880, 1930, 1970." In *Philadelphia: Work, Space, Family, and Group Experience in the Nineteenth Century.* Edited by Theodore Hershberg. New York: Oxford University Press, 1981.

Lieberson, Stanley. "Residential Segregation." In *A Piece of the Pie: Blacks and White Immigrants since 1880.* Berkeley: University of California Press, 1980.

Light, Ivan. "From Vice District to Tourist Attraction: The Evolution of America's Chinatowns." *Pacific Historical Review* 43 (1974): 367–394.

Riis, Jacob A. *How the Other Half Lives: Studies among the Ten-*

ements of New York. New York: Dover, 1971. Originally published in 1890.

Trotter, Joe William, Jr. *River Jordan: African American Urban Life in the Ohio Valley.* Lexington: University of Kentucky Press, 1998.

Warner, Sam Bass, and Colin Burke. "Cultural Change and the Ghetto." *Journal of Contemporary History* 4 (1969): 173–187.

Zunz, Olivier. *The Changing Face of Inequality: Urbanization, Industrial Development, and Immigrants in Detroit, 1880–1920.* Chicago: University of Chicago Press, 1982.

KENNETH L. KUSMER

SEMINOLE WARS   The three Seminole Wars were induced by white lust for land, irreconcilable cultural differences, and slavery. In the early nineteenth century the Florida borders were in constant turmoil as slaves escaped from Georgia and Alabama and parties of slave catchers roved through Spanish North Florida. The Spanish colonial government was unable to maintain order.

In 1818, to appease slaveholders in Georgia and Alabama, President James Monroe sent Major General Andrew Jackson to punish the Indians for harboring slaves, knowing that the general would seize Florida if given the chance. With 3,500 men, half of whom were Creek warriors, Jackson invaded West Florida. In eleven weeks, from 9 March to 24 May 1818, Jackson and his army destroyed Seminole settlements and fighting power west of the Suwannee River and captured the only two Spanish settlements in West Florida, Saint Marks and Pensacola. Jackson's conquests convinced Spain to relinquish Florida to the United States in 1819.

After this transfer of power, Seminole well-being deteriorated. The Seminoles, a loose aggregation of bands of Hitchiti, Coweta, Miccosukee, Hilibi, Eufaula, Uchi, and others, had migrated from the river valleys of Georgia and Alabama. In addition, numerous runaway slaves from the United States lived among them. The Southeastern borderland was in a constant state of agitation. Slaves from Georgia and Alabama and Creek Indians marauded continually, fighting that involved the Seminoles. White encroachment again drove the Seminoles to military action late in 1835, beginning the undeclared Second Seminole War. They ravaged the plantations along the Saint Johns River and on 28 December killed the U.S. Indian agent and his associates outside of Fort King. They then wiped out a column of U.S. soldiers marching to the relief of Fort King.

Osceola, who was half-white and was not a hereditary leader, provided generalship for the Seminoles until he fell ill late in 1836. Leadership passed vari-

Massacre of the Whites in Florida. Though outnumbered by whites forty to one, Indians engaged black allies during the Second Seminole War (1835), killing nearly four hundred whites. Woodcut. LIBRARY OF CONGRESS

ously to Wildcat, Alligator, Jumper, Halleck, Billy Bowlegs, and Sam Jones. The United States successively placed six generals in command. The fourth, Major General Thomas S. Jesup, frustrated by the perceived treachery of the Indians, began to capture Seminole leaders any way he could. Most notorious was his seizure of Osceola under a flag of truce on 27 October 1837. Jesup also succeeded in splitting the black warriors away from the Seminoles. Colonel Zachary Taylor commanded at the principal pitched battle, close to Lake Okeechobee on Christmas Day 1837. His casualties were high, 12 percent of 1,032 men, but he emerged a national hero and a brigadier general.

The last two commanders, Walker K. Armistead and William Jenkins Worth, relied on small detachments led by company officers. They hired blacks and Indian prisoners to guide them to the remaining Seminole hideaways, where they destroyed what was left of Seminole resistance. Band after band of Seminoles, ragged, hungry, and short of ammunition, surrendered, and in August 1842 the United States declared the action at an end. Over seven years the U.S. Army had committed every regiment to Florida, with a loss of about 1,500 men, most of them to disease. Thirty thousand citizen soldiers also were involved, and many of them perished. The financial costs were equally high. Of the Seminoles, 3,423 were forcibly emigrated, an unknown number were killed, and 350 remained in Florida in the Everglades south of Lake Okeechobee and Pease Creek.

White settlement during the next thirteen years pushed the Seminoles toward war once more. Led by Billy Bowlegs, they attacked a U.S. military camp on 20 December 1855, followed by fifteen months of guerrilla warfare. The last skirmish took place on 5 March 1857. Certain that the cause was lost, Billy Bowlegs accepted the U.S. offer of $8,000 and migrated with 165 followers. About 120 Seminoles remained behind. The United States officially affirmed the end of the Third Seminole War on 8 May 1858.

See also **American Indians; Florida.**

Bibliography

Covington, James W. *The Billy Bowlegs War, 1855–1858: The Final Stand of the Seminoles against the Whites.* Cluluota, Fla.: Mickler House, 1982.

Mahon, John K. *History of the Second Seminole War, 1835–1842.* Gainesville: University of Florida Press, 1967

Peters, Virginia Bergman. *The Florida Wars.* Hamden, Conn.: Archon, 1979.

JOHN K. MAHON

SERVANTS.   See **Work,** subentry on **Domestic Labor.**

SETTLEMENT.   See **Expansion; Homesteading.**

SETTLEMENT HOUSES   Settlement houses were residential community centers located in urban industrial districts. Middle-class young people came to live in these settlements to work with the poor residents in the house's neighborhood. The settlement-house movement in the United States was inspired by the founding of Toynbee Hall in London's East End in 1884. Using recent graduates of Oxford and Cambridge as the resident staff, Toynbee Hall tried to raise the status of the poor by providing tutoring and other services.

Development of U.S. Settlement Model

Americans such as Jane Addams (1860–1935) and Lillian Wald (1867–1940) brought the settlement movement across the ocean by the early 1890s. Addams founded Hull-House in Chicago in 1889, and Wald opened the Henry Street Settlement in New York in 1895. But the American movement differed significantly from the English model. First, a large number of the U.S. settlement founders and residents were women, while in Great Britain the residents were mostly men. Given the greater opportunities for women in higher education in the United States, many of the settlement women had college degrees.

TWENTY YEARS
AT HULL-HOUSE

JANE ADDAMS

In the Words of a Reformer. The cover of Addams's book about Hull-House, the Chicago settlement she founded in 1889; published in 1910, the book described her tireless defense of the nation's poor and marginalized, and would be followed by *The Second Twenty Years at Hull-House (1930)*. LIBRARY OF CONGRESS

Second, American settlement houses were much more willing to engage in policy advocacy, and residents played pioneering roles in the founding and administration of a variety of public and private social welfare, educational, correctional, and health movements and institutions. Third, beyond taking university students as residents, the U.S. settlement houses helped in the development of new academic disciplines. Finally, while the English settlements worked largely with poor British citizens from a common religious tradition, the American settlements mostly served immigrant families or ethnic minorities. These families were frequently Catholic or Jewish, with fundamental cultural differences from the overwhelmingly Protestant settlement leadership.

The ethnic and religious mix in American cities increased significantly in the last decade of the nineteenth century, and most settlements tried to address the problems growing from immigrant acculturation. Working on the *Hull-House Maps and Papers* in 1895, Agnes Holbrook (b. 1867) found, "Eighteen nations are thus represented in this small section of Chicago. They are more or less intermingled, but a decided tendency to drift into little colonies is apparent." There was a Jewish "ghetto" and nonimmigrant African Americans were "wedged" into another neighborhood. Facing such urban diversity, U.S. settlement-house residents, as well as American social policymakers, had the challenge of determining which neighborhood problems resulted from cultural factors and which were from political and economic causes. In contrast, the English settlement leaders could not blame the problems of their neighborhoods on ethnic weaknesses or different religious beliefs. Consequently, the English leaders more often saw poverty as the main problem, while the Americans were tempted to address customs, beliefs, and behavior in dealing with problems, rather than economic opportunity. Despite this temptation, many U.S. settlements promoted pride in the holidays, food, languages, and literature of their neighbors as a check on the social disintegration threatening immigrant families. Ellen Gates Starr (1859–1940), Jane Addams's major assistant, converted to Catholicism. Addams played a pioneering role in the battle against racism, especially after the arrival of large numbers of blacks in the North in the early twentieth century.

Emergence of Female Reform Leaders

The residents of settlement houses included many of the greatest leaders of North American social reform at the end of the nineteenth century. At Hull-House alone there were Florence Kelley (1859–1932), Julia Lathrop (1858–1932), Grace Abbott (1878–1939),

Edith Abbott (1876–1957), and Alice Hamilton (1869–1970). In 1893, Kelley became the first factory inspector in Illinois, and in 1899 she moved to the Henry Street Settlement, when she was invited to head the National Consumers' League. The league pioneered the development of labor standards, using consumer pressure to force firms to improve working conditions. Lathrop, who with Kelley refined the empirical study of social conditions, played a key role in organizing state care for the mentally ill. In 1912 she became the first woman to head a federal agency, the Children's Bureau. Hamilton, who came to Hull-House after receiving her medical degree from the University of Michigan, was a pioneer in the field of occupational health. These women were joined by some remarkable male reformers and political leaders. Even the future Canadian prime minister Mackenzie King (1874–1950) lived at Hull-House.

As reflected by the work of these women, settlement-house residents lobbied for new social policies and programs (often called maternalist) that protected families, women, and children. Their legacy included the development of a distinct juvenile justice system and of factory inspection laws. Much of the impetus for child-labor protections, limitations on work hours (especially for women), school-attendance requirements, and the struggle for pure milk found backing in the settlements. Settlement residents also became active in urban political reform movements.

For the female leaders, crossing the line from settlement work to politics meant departing the maternalist world. It was easiest to do so in coalition with mugwumps, Republicans willing to support reformers regardless of party; philanthropists; and especially professional males. In Chicago, Addams expressed frustration with the difficulty of opposing entrenched elected officials, who used patronage and favoritism to maintain support among the settlement's neighbors. Such officials appeared benevolent to the urban poor, while the settlement's call for fairness and equality seemed mean-spirited. Yet Addams, Lathrop, and Kelley joined several successful reform coalitions, such as the one led by Governor John Peter Altgeld (1847–1902). In Detroit, Hazen Pingree (1840–1901) included settlements in his coalition as did other municipal reformers. After the turn of the century, as more ethnic politicians rose to high office, with memories of places like Henry Street and Hull-House, settlement reformers became full coalition partners with leaders such as Al Smith (1873–1944) and Robert Wagner (1877–1953). Likewise, the settlements had much more influence in the professions after their early collaborators rose to leadership in fields such as medicine, law, and the so-

cial sciences. Abraham Jacobi (1830–1919), the head of the American Medical Association, worked closely with the Henry Street Settlement. Julian Mack (1866–1943), a law partner of Julius Rosenthal (1828–1905) and a juvenile justice pioneer, collaborated with Addams to bridge the gap between political regulars, ethnic leaders, and the middle-class Hull-House residents.

The settlements worked closely with key social and biological scientists, developing new information on conditions in urban America and making important methodological contributions. Hamilton turned industrial hygiene into a discipline, while Lathrop and Kelley worked with sociologists at the University of Chicago to produce the *Hull-House Maps and Papers*, which refined the methodology of the new discipline. Robert Woods (1865–1925), the founder of Andover House in Boston, spoke at Chicago's World's Columbian Exposition in 1893 and called settlements "laboratories in social science." Many settlements were linked directly to major universities, giving students experience with the urban working class and in applying the methods of the new social sciences. Addams served on the University of Chicago extension faculty, and regular faculty from the university came to Hull-House to give community lectures. The settlements also provided experiences that allowed women residents to overcome the barriers to entering academic positions; Sophonisba Breckinridge (1866–1948), the Abbott sisters, and Hamilton are notable examples of this process.

Historical Evaluation of Settlements

Some late-twentieth-century critics of the settlements believe the residents promoted policies that imposed social controls on the poor rather than liberating them or assuring social justice. Many contemporaries, in contrast, believed the settlements trained immigrants to be radicals or turned them away from ancestral faiths. Yet most historians have viewed the settlements as having left a remarkable and enduring legacy of social concern and reform, one especially distinctive in the United States because of the leadership by women. However, even those who have generally praised the settlements note that their leaders directed American social policy on an exceptional course, quite different from that in other industrial nations. Less often than in Europe, U.S. solutions to social problems ignored the need for income or economic equality, focusing instead on educational opportunity and social regulation. They often did not endorse public aid and lagged behind European counterparts in promoting social insurance. With the exception of a few notable political forays, such as Addams's involvement with the Pullman strikers in 1894, U.S. settlement leaders generally put their energies behind movements for practical social policy reform rather than partisan battles for economic change.

See also **Reform, Social; Sociology.**

Bibliography

Addams, Jane. *Jane Addams: A Centennial Reader.* Edited by Emily Cooper Johnson. New York: Macmillan, 1960.

Davis, Allen F. *Spearheads for Reform: The Social Settlements and the Progressive Movement, 1890–1914.* New Brunswick, N.J.: Rutgers University Press, 1984.

Meacham, Standish. *Toynbee Hall and Social Reform, 1880–1914: The Search for Community.* New Haven, Conn.: Yale University Press, 1987.

Residents of Hull-House. *Hull-House Maps and Papers: A Presentation of Nationalities and Wages in a Congested District of Chicago, Together with Comments and Essays on Problems Growing Out of the Social Conditions.* 1895. Reprint, New York: Arno, 1970.

Rousmaniere, John P. "Cultural Hybrid in the Slums: The College Women and the Settlement House, 1889–1894." *American Quarterly* 22 (1970): 45–66.

Sklar, Kathryn Kish. "The Historical Foundations of Women's Power in the Creation of the American Welfare State, 1830–1930." In *Mothers of a New World: Maternalist Politics and the Origins of Welfare States,* edited by Seth Koven and Sonya Michel. New York: Routledge, 1993.

Trolander, Judith Ann. *Professionalism and Social Change: From the Settlement House Movement to Neighborhood Centers, 1886 to the Present.* New York: Columbia University Press, 1987.

EDWARD C. LORENZ

SEXUAL MORALITY

SEXUAL MORALITY   A new system of sexual morality was one of the key social innovations in the United States during the early nineteenth century. The men and women of the new business classes that led commercial and economic development needed values appropriate to the industrial, urban society that they were building. The patriarchal values and gender roles that had seemed appropriate to a society of largely self-sufficient farmers, whose wives and children were necessary labor in a system of household production, were revised to reflect the aspirations of town dwellers, who were increasingly immersed in an interdependent market economy.

Under the influence of evangelical Protestants, social leaders redefined the roles of women and devised codes of Christian nurture for children. New values linked sexual expression to moral idealism, emphasized the innocence of children and the purity of "true women," and encouraged men to cultivate self-control. In the domestic advice manuals that became a staple of American culture in the 1830s, the family was presented as a private enclave rather than a part of a larger community. Virtuous women were exhorted to accept their place in the home, separated from the male world of market competition. If the wife was no longer her husband's partner in work, she was his moral superior within the domestic sphere, where her feelings were expected to regulate sexual conduct. This new code of "civilized morality" served as a marker of respectability that separated the successful and socially ambitious from the working classes and racial minorities, whose social inferiority was attributed to their deviation from the standards of "civilized," that is, middle-class Christian, morality.

Erotic expression had a prominent place in civilized morality but only when it was legitimated by romantic love, expressed in marriage. The new emphasis on idealized erotic expression as the justification for marriage could be problematic because middle-class Americans seldom felt that they could afford the large numbers of children that had been a necessity when the household was a unit of production. The rising standards of living of an industrial society implied smaller families and a greater emotional and financial investment in the nurture of each child. Civilized morality helped young adults cope with the sexual tensions they experienced by providing a powerful ethic of self-restraint that was reflected in declining rates of premarital pregnancy and declining fertility among the socially ambitious. Many married couples apparently heeded the advice of moralists and made the demographic transition to smaller families by limiting coitus. Others found advice in popular marriage manuals on how to practice contraception or learned from advertisements in cheap newspapers that unwanted pregnancies could be terminated by abortion.

Discontent with civilized morality was reflected in the burgeoning urban commercial vice districts, where large numbers of men pursued a double standard of morality that tolerated nonmarital and nonprocreative sex for men while defining unchaste women as "fallen creatures." In fact, prostitutes were usually working-class women for whom the wages gained by providing sexual services were far superior to work in sweatshops or as domestics. Rather than a fallen innocent, a prostitute was likely to be a woman of color or a member of an ethnic minority, whose community did not embrace the new sexual codes of middle-class Protestants.

Another counterculture emerged in the hundreds of utopian socialist communes that were established throughout the Northeast and Midwest before the Civil War. Based upon both secular and religious critiques of acquisitive individualism, these communes usually offered radical alternatives to middle-class sexual standards. For example, the Shakers embraced celibacy, the Oneida Perfectionists practiced sexual communism, and the Mormons practiced polygamy. Among the middle-class idealists who chose not to withdraw from society, a "free love" movement flourished, pushing republican ideals of individual free expression to the point of denying the right of the state to regulate sexual matters at all.

During the middle decades of the nineteenth century several "purity" movements led by middle-class reformers sought to make Americans live up to the values of civilized morality. While in the South a new emphasis on preserving the chastity of white women was part of the building of Jim Crow (the racial caste system that replaced slavery), purity crusaders in the North had often been moral reformers in the antebellum period and included many abolitionists. Beginning in the 1840s physicians led successful campaigns in state legislatures to criminalize abortion, apparently in response to the increasing demand by married women for pregnancy termination. In the 1870s some medical leaders, in response to the harm venereal diseases caused to mothers and children, attempted to regulate prostitution through medical inspections of prostitutes. These efforts evoked strong opposition from feminists and evangelical Christians, who defeated prostitution regulation but led major crusades to suppress commercial vice and the double standard of sexual morality. In 1873 the U.S. Congress passed the Comstock Act, a strong antiobscenity bill whose sweeping provisions banned not only smut but any information on abortion or contraception. This statute, used to prosecute free lovers, free thinkers, and artists well into the twentieth century, symbolizes the heroic but contradictory Victorian American endeavor to manage human sexuality.

See also **Contraception and Abortion; Communitarian Movements and Groups; Evangelicalism; Gender,** *subentry on* **Interpretations of Gender; Marriage; Prostitution; Victorianism; Women,** *subentries on* **Women's Rights, Woman as Image and Icon.**

Bibliography

Battan, Jesse F. "The 'Rights' of Husbands and the 'Duties' of Wives: Power and Desire in the American Bedroom, 1850–1910." *Journal of Family History* 24, no. 2 (1999): 165–186.

D'Emilio, John, and Estelle B. Freedman. *Intimate Matters: A History of Sexuality in America.* New York: Harper and Row, 1988.

Seidman, Steven. *Romantic Longings: Love in America, 1830–1980.* New York: Routledge, 1991.

JAMES W. REED

SHAKERS. See **Communitarian Movements and Groups.**

SHIPBUILDING.   See **Naval Technology.**

SHOPPING.   See **Consumerism and Consumption; Merchandising.**

SLAVERY

[This entry includes an overview and eight subentries:
Indian Slaveholding
Domestic Slave Trade and Migration
African Slave Trade
Slave Life
Slave Insurrections
Runaway Slaves
Law of Slavery
Defense of Slavery.]

OVERVIEW

By the dawn of the nineteenth century, slavery had been emerging for at least four generations in the Chesapeake region and for a shorter time elsewhere in the United States. In 1790 the nation's first census found nearly one in five Americans enslaved. As the nineteenth century unfolded, slavery receded as an institution in the North. Yet it spread across the South, propelled American economic and territorial growth, and became the central issue in the political life of the nation until a climactic war in the 1860s led to a national policy to extirpate it. From the beginning to the end of the nineteenth century, moreover, slavery supplied a marker for measuring independence for blacks and for whites.

Slavery and Freedom

For Abraham Lincoln the American ideal was best understood as the opportunity to achieve economic independence. The counterimage of the slave South gave Lincoln occasion to voice his image of the North with its free-labor basis, where young farmers did not all start out in possession of land, nor did young artisans begin work owning the tools they would need. But they need not labor for others all their lives, Lincoln argued in 1856, for they had the opportunity to obtain land or tools of their own: "The man who la-

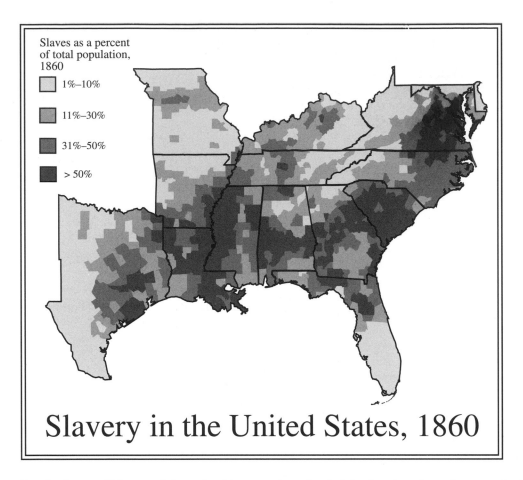

Slavery in the United States, 1860

bored for another last year, this year labors for himself, and next year he will hire others to labor for him" (Basler et al., eds., *The Collected Works of Abraham Lincoln*, vol. 2, p. 364).

Slavery was a system of unfree labor that ensnared most African Americans into the 1860s. It was also a measure by which free Americans gauged their liberty. In the eighteenth century, on the road to the American Revolution, colonists voiced their fears that powerlessness in the grip of the British Empire would render them slaves. The presence of slavery in every British colony in 1776 supplied a graphic representation of the fate that awaited them. To many antebellum northerners, southern slavery threatened free people's civil liberties, economic opportunities, and policymaking powers. Many Southerners fought the Civil War in an effort to fight off what they saw as their own enslavement. By the dawn of the twentieth century, many industrial workers came to view themselves as industrial slaves, that is, they came to recognize that Lincoln's ideal regarding the path to upward mobility no longer applied to their situations.

North of the Mason-Dixon line, between 1776 and 1830, slavery rapidly receded through freedom suits by slaves, individual acts of manumission by owners, and political action by legislators. Acts of manumis-

sion also led to freedom for a large majority of African Americans in Delaware and for significant black minorities in Maryland and Virginia. Especially after 1830, however, the Upper South also proved a bountiful source for slaves shipped south and west to satisfy the needs of cotton planters as new territory opened to staple cultivation by slave labor.

Despite slavery's near disappearance from the North, the total slave population in the United States grew from 697,624 in 1790 to 3,953,760 in 1860. Yet the free population grew as fast as the slave population did through natural increase, and immigration, mostly to the North, greatly augmented the free population. So the slave percentage of all Americans dropped by nearly half during those years.

The Politics and Economics of Slavery

Slaves constituted population majorities in South Carolina, Mississippi, and large areas of many other southern states. They made up the bulk of the wealth of countless owners and large fractions of the tax base in numerous jurisdictions. They produced the tobacco, sugar, rice, and cotton that comprised much of the value of exports from the United States. The cotton they grew spurred the growth of manufacturing in New England, but slaves' exclusion from the market economy in the South retarded the growth of cities and factories there.

Though caught in the toils of an enormous system of unfreedom, slaves worked with the materials at hand to forge lives and form families and communities. Neither statutory law nor public religion offered slaves much protection for their persons or their families. Slaves pursued recreation and held religious services with family, friends, and neighbors. They gardened and fished to supplement their rations. Yearning for freedom, slaves sometimes stole themselves, whether for a few days or for a lifetime, or even conspired to rebel.

Slavery was an important issue in the Constitutional Convention in 1787, and it became the central question of American politics in the nineteenth century. Delegates to the Hartford Convention in 1814–1815 sought to exclude slaves from calculations that determined a state's membership in the U.S. House of Representatives and the electoral college. After Missouri applied for statehood in 1819, the controversy that erupted over slavery led Thomas Jefferson to moan about the dim prospects for the nation's survival. A series of events in the 1850s—the Kansas-Nebraska Act, the *Dred Scott* decision, John Brown's raid on Harpers Ferry—presaged Lincoln's election on an antislavery platform.

When majorities of delegates to conventions in eleven southern states determined that slavery could not be secure under a Republican administration, they voted to take their states out of the Union and create the Confederate States of America. The Confederacy's vice president, Alexander H. Stephens, spoke of slavery as the new nation's "cornerstone."

As the Civil War ground on, President Lincoln came to see the institution in the same light. His Emancipation Proclamation put slavery in the South, too, on the road to extinction, and the Thirteenth Amendment, approved by Congress in January 1865 and ratified in December that year, completed the first stage of the process of terminating slavery. Looking for the end of slavery to lead directly to equality of opportunity, however, black and white advocates of emancipation were disappointed by early indications that fell far short of Lincoln's ideal.

Slavery's Long Aftermath

The death of slavery raised two crucial questions that demanded answers during Reconstruction. What would be the postemancipation place of African Americans, and who would hold political power in the South and in the nation? A century after 1865 those questions, basic to American society, politics, culture,

law, and economics, were still being asked, and they still demanded answers.

See also **Emancipation; Louisiana Purchase; Sectionalism; South, The.**

Bibliography

Basler, Roy F., et al., eds. *The Collected Works of Abraham Lincoln.* 9 vols. New Brunswick, N.J.: Rutgers University Press, 1953–1955.

Berlin, Ira. *Many Thousands Gone: The First Two Centuries of Slavery in North America.* Cambridge, Mass.: Belknap Press of Harvard University Press, 1998.

Campbell, Edward D. C., Jr., with Kym S. Rice, eds. *Before Freedom Came: African-American Life in the Antebellum South.* Charlottesville and Richmond: University Press of Virginia and the Museum of the Confederacy, 1991.

Freehling, William W. *The Road to Disunion,* Volume 1: *Secessionists at Bay, 1776–1854.* New York: Oxford University Press, 1990.

Malone, Ann Patton. *Sweet Chariot: Slave Family and Household Structure in Nineteenth-Century Louisiana.* Chapel Hill: University of North Carolina Press, 1992.

Oakes, James. *Slavery and Freedom: An Interpretation of the Old South.* New York: Knopf, 1990.

Stampp, Kenneth M. *The Peculiar Institution: Slavery in the Ante-Bellum South.* New York: Knopf, 1956.

Wallenstein, Peter. *From Slave South to New South: Public Policy in Nineteenth-Century Georgia.* Chapel Hill: University of North Carolina Press, 1987.

PETER WALLENSTEIN

INDIAN SLAVEHOLDING

The history of slavery and the history of Native Americans are closely intertwined in a complex web of multiple meanings and historically shifting conceptions and practices of slavery. In the period before contact with European civilization, Native Americans practiced various forms of slavery. In the post-contact period, many Native Americans were enslaved by white colonizers, and others actively participated as slaveholders in the African slave trade.

Indigenous Concepts of Slavery

The indigenous concept of slavery was based on the war-captive system. With the exception of the Northwest Coast tribes, this system was not commercially oriented, because war captives served social rather than economic purposes. Still, the war-captive system resembled slavery in a number of aspects: the captives endured often permanent and violent domination, were removed from their societies of birth, and often were allocated peripheral social positions, which involved performing menial tasks and strenuous work, in the capturing society.

Some warriors captured in conflict suffered torture and death in order to comfort those in the victorious tribe who had lost relatives in the conflict. Noncombatant captives usually were spared and performed menial tasks for their captors. Some were even adopted into new families to replace family members who had died in conflict. In the Pacific Northwest, hierarchical village peoples like the Tlingits, Haislas, Haidas, and Tsimshians presented an exceptional case. For them, slaves fulfilled a clearly defined economic function and symbolized wealth and prestige. Slaves were seen as property to be bought, sold, or given away.

Although the war-captive system carried multiple connotations of slavery and certainly contributed to the overall productivity of the capturing tribe, it differed markedly from the Euro-American concept of slavery in that it did not represent a major capital investment. Because most Native American economies existed at the subsistence level, they placed no premium on the accumulation of wealth. Consequently, their economic well-being did not depend on slaves.

Euro-American Conceptions of Slavery and Native American Culture

With the advent of white explorers and settlers, Native American concepts of slavery changed radically. The social function of the war-captive system was replaced as native leaders accepted the diplomatic and commercial value of slavery.

Beginning in the seventeenth century, a number of tribes captured slaves for economic gain. In the Plains and the Southwest, the Kiowas and Comanches often sold captive Apaches and Pawnees to Spanish authorities in New Mexico. The Kiowas, Comanches, and Navajos also captured Spanish subjects in slave raids and incorporated them into their own societies. The Treaty of Guadalupe Hidalgo, which ended the Mexican-American War in 1848, recognized this problem. The Americans agreed to interdict this practice and ransom Mexican citizens from the Plains tribes. The practice ended, however, only with the military subjugation of the Plains tribes in the 1870s.

Native Americans and African Slaves

Initially, southern planters enslaved Native Americans and attempted to integrate them into their agricultural enterprises. By 1800 this practice had proved impractical, both because Indian slaves could escape with relative ease and European diseases played havoc with their health. As the practice of enslaving Native Americans declined, the role of Native Americans shifted. The most severe change came with the U.S. government's "civilization programs," which since the 1790s had encouraged Indians to use African slaves to work in their fields. Many Native Americans adopted white notions of racial hierarchy and Euro-American conceptions of slavery, becoming owners of African slaves on a grand scale.

In the nineteenth century, Indians in the Southeast tried to enhance their economic standing through extensive participation in the slave economy. They bought slaves to work in their fields and ultimately enacted slave codes to protect their rights as property owners. They not only enhanced their economic standing but also radically altered their cultural traditions of matrilineal landownership and/or inheritance to emulate whites. With the cotton boom some Indian plantation owners became wealthy.

The Cherokees present the most dramatic example of the incorporation of Euro-American concepts of slavery into native culture. Their slave numbers increased from 583 in 1809 to almost sixteen hundred in 1835. These slaves were owned by a small Cherokee elite, who viewed complete adaptation to white ways as the only means to protect the Cherokee nation. These men replaced the traditional notion of communal landownership with privately owned plantations. They centralized the Cherokee government under a written constitution and enacted laws to protect their rights as owners of land and slaves. They established patrilineal inheritance and dominated the discourses on questions of national importance, such as land cessions. At the time of the Indian removal, many slaveowners took their human property with them on the "Trail of Tears." By 1860 the members of the Five Civilized Tribes in Indian Territory owned about four thousand slaves.

Native American attitudes on slavery varied sharply, however—even within the same tribe, particularly in the Cherokee and Creek nations. Other groups chose a different path. The Seminoles had resisted the "civilization program" and its inherent notions of race hierarchy. They counted hundreds of runaway slaves among their tribal members, and those former slaves enjoyed a semiautonomous existence with their own settlements and leaders. The circumstances of runaway slaves living a sheltered life were perceived by government authorities as a grave challenge to the institution of slavery. Combined with white land hunger, they provided the impetus for the Seminole Wars (1818; 1835–1842; 1855–1858) and the ultimate removal of the tribe westward.

Even after the removal of southeastern Indians

west of the Mississippi River in the 1830s, some tribes continued to use African slaves. During the Civil War, Indian slaveholders sided with the Confederacy. After the Union victory in 1865, the government and the Five Civilized Tribes of the Indian territory (Oklahoma) agreed by treaty that the freed slaves of the Five Civilized Tribes be adopted into the tribes as members with full rights of citizenship. Nevertheless, social and racial prejudice blocked many Indian freedpeople, including many black Cherokees, from gaining tribal citizenship.

As the nineteenth century ended, so did the involvement of Native Americans with slavery. Ironically, a people trying to escape subjugation and extermination not only turned on each other but also participated in the enslavement of another ethnic group. Native Americans played a double role in two of the darkest chapters of nineteenth-century American history, removal and slavery, as victims and perpetrators.

Bibliography

Littlefield, Daniel F., Jr., *Africans and Creeks: From the Colonial Period to the Civil War*. Westport, Conn.: Greenwood Press, 1979.

———. *Africans and Seminoles: From Removal to Emancipation*. Westport, Conn.: Greenwood Press, 1977.

May, Katja. *African Americans and Native Americans in the Creek and Cherokee Nations, 1830s to 1920s: Collision and Collusion*. New York: Garland, 1996.

McLoughlin, William G. "Indian Slaveholders and Presbyterian Missionaries 1837–1861." *Church History* 42 (December 1973): 535–551.

McLoughlin, William G. "Red, White, and Black in the Antebellum South." *American Quarterly* 26 (1974): 367–385.

Perdue, Theda. *Slavery and the Evolution of Cherokee Society, 1540–1866*. Knoxville: University of Tennessee Press, 1979.

FRANK SCHUMACHER

DOMESTIC SLAVE TRADE AND MIGRATION

The American plantation system began in the Chesapeake region late in the seventeenth century, and by the end of the eighteenth century plantation agriculture, and the slavery that supported it, had spread to the eastern seaboard of the Deep South and to the lower Mississippi valley. In the Chesapeake, this migration began in the late eighteenth century with small planters and the younger sons of the great planters moving west in search of new lands upon which to grow tobacco. During this early period, these new up-country planters relied on African imports as well as American-born slaves, but as the western and southern expansion continued (virtually nonstop from this time onward), more slaves were

moved off the older plantations, thus beginning one of the largest forced domestic migrations in American history. This migration, however, accounted for the smaller portion of the total numbers of slaves moved. It was instead the domestic slave trade that accounted for the larger numbers of slaves moved from the early nineteenth century (especially after 1820) until the Civil War.

During this period, states (and regions within states) imported slaves as new lands were opened and exported slaves as these lands became more agriculturally developed. Virginia, Maryland, and Delaware were already net exporters of slaves when the century opened, with North Carolina and the Dis-

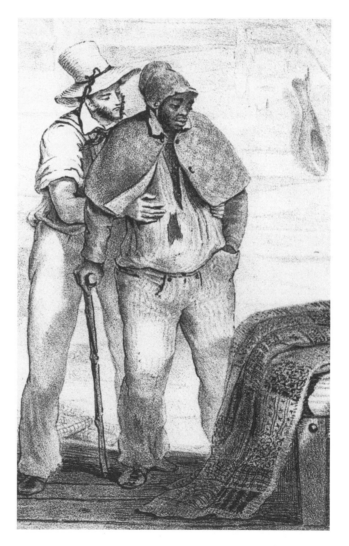

Slaveholder and Slave, Virginia, 1830s. A weary slave would not have been handled as compassionately as this 1832 illustration might convey—with plantations expanding into the South, slaveholders desired younger, more profitable slaves. Illustration from Frances Trollope's *Domestic Manners of the Americans*, 1832. LIBRARY OF CONGRESS

trict of Columbia following suit shortly thereafter. South Carolina and Kentucky became net exporting states by 1820, with Georgia and Tennessee joining the list by 1850. The rest of the southern states remained net importers until 1860, though Alabama and Missouri did have some exporting regions. Slaves bought by slave traders were moved to the markets of the Lower South by three methods. Some were transported by sea to New Orleans or down the Ohio, Missouri, and Mississippi Rivers on flatboats and steamers. The majority of these slaves, however, were driven overland, chained or roped together, and on foot in "coffles," that is, groups of thirty or more slaves. The number of slaves on these overland treks exceeded one hundred.

Planters preferred young men for field hands, and early plantation owners relied heavily on African imports to fulfill their labor needs. The influx of (primarily male) African imports, however, disrupted the nascent black community by creating problems such as low fertility, high mortality, and gender disparity. As the eighteenth century progressed, gender parity among blacks stabilized, and the slave population increased by natural means. This allowed for greater geographic expansion as non-slaveholders acquired slaves for working new land and the established planters added to their holdings. This natural increase also created a glut in the bound labor force, leading the Chesapeake planters to oppose the African slave trade and allowing them to criticize both the planters of the Lower South and northern merchants who supported the international trade.

The planters of the Upper South may have denounced the horrors of the international trade, but it is difficult to see their motives in an altruistic light, since the international trade also constituted competition. For the planters of the Upper South, "excess" slaves were a source of ready cash and great profit. To keep the labor force at what the planters considered to be optimum capacity, slaveholders regularly sold away their unneeded slaves, particularly the teenagers. Indeed, as lands on the oldest plantations became depleted, selling slaves became the best, and in some cases the only, source of profits.

The expansion of cotton production accelerated the expansion of slavery, and extended the migration of slaves in two ways. The first was due to migrating planters who moved from their spent plantations along the eastern seaboard to new cotton lands in the Lower South and the West. The second, more predominant means came by way of slave trading, as the plantations of the Upper South supplied slaves to the new cotton lands. The slave trading that supported the expansion of cotton was by necessity extremely age-specific (mainly young adults and teenagers),

while planter migrations tended to be less so (the migrating planters brought with them most of the slaves they then owned).

Conditions engendered by the domestic slave trade were at the heart of the debates over slavery that raged during the years preceding the Civil War. The abolitionists argued that slave trading compounded the miseries of slavery by breaking up slave families. According to the abolitionists, slave trading was central and necessary to the continuance of slavery as an institution, especially in the Upper South, where slave-driven monocrop agriculture had become unprofitable, and, for many planters, the only way to remain economically viable was to export their excess bondspeople to those states where cotton production was expanding.

The proslavery side countered that far from destroying the families of slaves, slaveholders encouraged and supported the institution of slave families. Delaware and Maryland attempted to regulate the interstate trade in slaves, but these efforts failed because such laws would interfere with the property rights of slaveholders. In fact, records belie claims of planter paternalism, indicating that market forces and economic self-interest were the driving forces behind the decision to separate slave families. In the case of local sales, as opposed to interstate or interregional sales, a planter might prefer to sell in lots, which were of mixed ages, and tended to keep families together. But even here, the motives were economic—mixed lots were perhaps the only way to sell slaves who were "unattractive" to traders. The interstate trade was much more selective. The desired groups included teenagers and children as young as eight (there was no practical reason for separating from their mothers children younger than this), females of childbearing age and young mothers with (typically) one child, and males in their prime (midteens to mid-twenties). Such selectivity thus necessitated the destruction of slave families. Because life for the enslaved Africans centered on family and community, the trade struck the point that was most disruptive, thus preventing blacks from establishing stable families and communities.

See also **Plantation, The; Slavery,** *subentry on* **Overview.**

Bibliography

Bancroft, Frederic. With a new introduction by Michael Tadman. *Slave Trading in the Old South.* Columbia: University of South Carolina Press, 1996.

Berlin, Ira. *Many Thousands Gone: The First Two Centuries of Slavery in North America.* Cambridge, Mass.: Belknap Press, 1998.

Tadman, Michael. *Speculators and Slaves: Masters, Traders, and Slaves in the Old South.* Madison: University of Wisconsin Press, 1996.

ALLEN L. MCDERMID

AFRICAN SLAVE TRADE

An extensive slave trade existed between the British colonies in America and the west coast of Africa, but during the American Revolution that trade effectively ended. In the Constitutional Convention of 1787 the states divided over the slave trade but not in a North-South dichotomy. The Middle Atlantic and Upper South regions opposed the trade, South Carolina and Georgia wished to import more slaves, and some New England states carried on the trade. The commerce clause (Article I, section 8, subsection 3) was limited by Article I, section 9, subsection 1: "The Migration or Importation of such Persons as any of the States now existing shall think proper to admit, shall not be prohibited by the Congress prior to the Year one thousand eight hundred and eight, but a Tax or duty may be imposed on such Importation, not exceeding ten dollars for each Person." Article V forbade amending this section before 1808.

In 1807 Congress enacted the Prohibition of the Slave Trade Act, to take effect in 1808, and in 1818 amended it, providing a sentence of three to seven years in addition to fines for engaging in the slave trade. Congress in 1819 authorized the use of warships in American waters and off Africa to intercept slave ships. In 1820 Congress defined slaving as piracy, punishable by death.

From 1807 onward Britain used the Royal Navy and its substantial diplomatic service to suppress the trade while convincing other nations to outlaw the trade and to enter into diplomatic conventions permitting the Royal Navy to search their ships. The United States refused to permit such searches. As a result, many foreign and American slavers displayed the U.S. flag to avoid visitation by the Royal Navy. Not until the Webster-Ashburton Treaty (1842) did the United States agree to station a naval force off Africa to suppress the trade.

An illegal slave trade continued in the United States virtually unabated prior to the Civil War, with fifty thousand slaves imported illegally. The usual federal penalty against slavers was the confiscation of ship and cargo. Many cases, such as *United States v. La Costa* (1820), were uncomplicated seizures. The Supreme Court justice Joseph Story heard *United States v. the La Jeune Eugenie* (1822), involving the prize claim by Robert Stockton, a naval officer, for award of a slaver flying the French flag that Stockton had captured off Africa. French ownership seemed to be a fiction to shield U.S. owners. With true ownership unverifiable, Story ordered the ship forfeited to France, because Stockton's prize claim required demonstrable U.S. ownership.

The 1858 *Echo* cases concerned the capture of the slave ship *Echo* in waters near the Florida Keys by a U.S. patrol ship. A habeas corpus hearing was followed by the trial of the crew members for slaving, but they gained acquittal through apparent jury nullification.

The cases of the *Wanderer* and *United States v. Corrie* (1860) involved confusion over the ownership of the slave vessel *Wanderer*. District judge Peleg Sprague heard the original owner of the vessel, Charles A. L. Lamar, claim the *Wanderer* on the grounds that no proof existed that it was a slaver and that the ship had been stolen from him. The crew aboard at the interception claimed the vessel in payment of accrued wages, while the United States claimed forfeiture for slaving. Judge Sprague found for the government, declaring that the odiousness of the trade and the prevalence of deceptions required that forfeiture be rigorously enforced.

Two of the most complex cases related to the slavers involved the ships *Antelope* and *Amistad*. In 1820 the *Antelope*, flying the revolutionary flag of José Artigas, the founder of the Uruguayan republic, was captured off northeastern Florida with 280 slaves aboard. The disposition of the case took eight years and ultimately involved the Supreme Court, both houses of Congress, two U.S. presidents—James Monroe and John Quincy Adams—and several of the presidents' respective cabinet ministers.

The *Antelope*, having engaged in African slaving, also seized slaves in piratical raids against Spanish and Portuguese vessels. Slaves taken directly from Africa would be freed by the court, but it seemed impossible to determine to which of those on board this applied. The courts had to determine the legality of the slave trade in international law to ascertain the status of the pirated Iberian slaves. If the slave trade was not contrary to international law, then the owners of the pirated slaves had a right to reclaim their property, in that they had not willfully violated the U.S. ban on that trade within U.S. jurisdiction. Did diplomats have the right to reclaim lost slaves? Did the U.S. marshal into whose custody the slaves had been placed have a lien against all the Africans until his expenses were reimbursed, or was a lien against the Africans directly enslaved by the *Antelope* repugnant to their free status? The Supreme Court upheld the legality of the slave trade in international law except as prohibited by domestic law, but it held that actual owners must apply for recaptured slaves to avoid frauds. Many blacks were repatriated to Liberia, while the remainder were awarded to their Spanish owners and sold to a U.S. citizen to pay costs. A lottery to assign slaves to be returned to the Spanish was avoided.

The *Antelope* case presented legal complexities, but the *Amistad* case raised ferocious sectional passions. In 1839 a U.S. revenue cutter intercepted the *Amistad*, crewed by Africans who had overthrown their captors. This Spanish schooner had left Havana with fifty-three slaves. The slaves rebelled, killing all but two of the crew. Captured off Long Island, New York, by a U.S. warship, the *Amistad* and cargo were claimed as salvage.

For proslavery people the slaves were mutineers and murderers who should be hanged, returned to the Spanish, or sold to reward the recoverer. For abolitionists the issue was the natural right of men to be free and to defend that freedom if unjustly threatened. The defense held that strong evidence proved that all or most of the blacks had been enslaved in Africa, contrary to the laws of most nations, including Spain. Therefore, their captivity was illegal. Justice Story wrote the decision for the Africans, denying that U.S. courts had to accept the position of Spanish authorities on the status of the Africans. The blacks were repatriated to Africa.

See also **Africa, Foreign Relations with; Supreme Court,** *subentry on* **Slavery.**

Bibliography

Finkelman, Paul. *The Law of Freedom and Bondage: A Casebook*. New York: Oceana, 1986.
———. *Slavery in the Courtroom: An Annotated Bibliography of American Cases*. Washington, D.C.: Library of Congress, 1985.
Franklin, John Hope. "Slavery and the Constitution." In *Encyclopedia of the American Constitution*. Edited by Leonard W. Levy, Kenneth L. Karst, and Dennis J. Mahoney. Volume 4. New York: Macmillan, 1986.
Jones, Howard. *Mutiny on the* Amistad: *The Saga of a Slave Revolt and Its Impact on American Abolition, Law, and Diplomacy*. New York: Oxford University Press, 1987.
Noonan, John T., Jr. *The* Antelope: *The Ordeal of the Recaptured Africans in the Administrations of James Monroe and John Quincy Adams*. Berkeley: University of California Press, 1977.
Rawley, James A. "Slave Trade, Atlantic." In *Dictionary of Afro-American Slavery*. Edited by Randall M. Miller and John David Smith. New York: Greenwood, 1988.
Thomas, Hugh. *The Slave Trade: The Story of the Atlantic Slave Trade, 1440–1870*. New York: Simon and Schuster, 1997.

PATRICK M. O'NEIL

SLAVE LIFE

Events of great magnitude changed the shape and appearance of American slavery during the first half of the nineteenth century. First, in 1808, the U.S. Congress banned the importation of new slaves from Africa or the Caribbean islands. The result was the "creolization" of the U.S. slave population, as the Africans enslaved before the ban gradually were replaced by slaves who had been born in the United States, spoke English, and were more removed from their African heritage. Second, following the Louisiana Purchase and the War of 1812, white Americans—and their slaves—went west. Together they filled the lower Mississippi River valley and began producing unprecedented amounts of cotton. As Americans from New Orleans to Boston got rich from this increased agricultural productivity, many became convinced of the value and indispensability of slave labor. Because of the profits generated in Northern seaports from the export of domestic staple products such as cotton, tobacco, and rice, which were the direct result of southern slave labor, even northerners with antislavery sentiments tolerated the existence of the peculiar institution. Third and last, with the gradual disappearance of slavery in the northern states, the institution became largely sectional. Conflicts intensified between northern abolitionists, those who wanted to arrest slavery's expansion as well as those who sought its abolition, and proslavery southerners, making a fiery clash appear imminent. Amid these changes, slaves continued their daily struggle to give meaning to their lives in a world that treated them not as people, but as property.

Resistance

Slaves proved remarkably resilient at securing a level of social and economic independence from their masters. As a result, white southerners enacted a series of strict statutes and regulations reinforcing masters' authority over their human property. These slave codes instituted curfews for slaves, required them to carry passes, and revoked their right to carry weapons. For committing petty offenses, slaves were whipped, beaten, or branded. Those guilty of more serious crimes were subject to physical mutilation, torture, or death. Southerners' belief in the necessity of slave codes was a testament to slaves' refusal to accept lives of bondage controlled by white masters.

Slaves resisted in a number of ways, from revolting and running away to committing individual acts of defiance. The decision to revolt was the most obvious, but it was also the most deadly. In Latin America and the Caribbean islands, slaves recently removed from Africa worked on plantations where they greatly outnumbered whites. These slaves rebelled quickly and often. In antebellum America, however, slaves usually were born into the institution, and

A Family's Flight. Poster dated 1 October 1847 from St. Louis. Suspected to have been aided by a white man, a slave family escaped its owner, Thomas Allen, Esq., and sought freedom in Chicago. LIBRARY OF CONGRESS: BROADSIDE COLLECTION

they lived in areas where the ratio between slaves and whites was more equal. Consequently, slave revolts occurred less often in the U.S. South than in Latin America and the West Indies.

Most U.S. slave revolts were put down quickly. In 1800 a slave named Gabriel Prosser (c. 1775–1800) led more than one thousand armed slaves toward Richmond, Virginia, to ignite a war of slave liberation. A storm halted the slaves' advance and, before they could regroup, whites learned of their intentions. Most of the slaves were arrested and more than thirty, including Prosser, were executed. That same year, Denmark Vesey (1767–1822) won $1,500 in a lottery and purchased his own freedom for $600. In 1822 he organized a revolt of several thousand slaves in Charleston, South Carolina. A house slave notified his master of the plan, and Vesey and more than thirty co-conspirators were executed.

In 1811 more than four hundred slaves armed with knives, axes, and clubs, marching to the beat of drums, killed several whites on the outskirts of New Orleans. A group of planters armed with guns met the insurgents, killing sixty-six. Charles Deslondes,

one slave leader who died during the insurrection, was an emigrant from Saint Domingue, once France's most profitable colony in the West Indies. Inspired by the French Revolution, 100,000 of the island's 500,000 slaves rose in rebellion in 1791. Led by the indomitable former slave Toussaint L'Ouverture (c. 1743–1803), Saint Domingue's slaves executed the first successful slave revolt in world history, creating the second independent nation in the Western Hemisphere—the future republic of Haiti. Prosser, Vesey, and Deslondes all were inspired by L'Ouverture and the slaves of Saint Domingue, who proved that black men and women could rise up and break the chains that bound them.

There is no evidence that Nat Turner (1800–1831) looked to the Caribbean for inspiration to rebel. Only Scripture and the memory of years in bondage were necessary to propel him to direct the bloodiest slave insurrection in U.S. history. Turner was an intensely religious man, well versed in the Bible. When not laboring under the hot Virginia sun, he preached the Word of God to fellow bondspeople. On 21 August 1831 Turner led more than sixty slaves on a night-

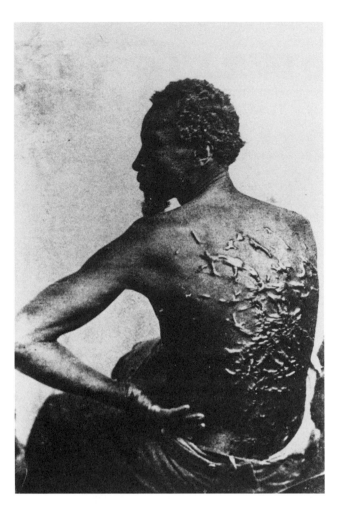

Slave's Back, 1863. The scars are from whippings, to which most slaves were subjected. NATIONAL ARCHIVES: RECORDS OF THE WAR DEPARTMENT GENERAL AND STAFFS

time trek across the plantations of Southampton County, Virginia, killing more than fifty whites. Approximately one hundred slaves, many of them innocent, died at the hands of the local militias and federal forces that arrived to quell the rebellion. Turner eventually was captured and executed.

While some slaves dared to revolt against insurmountable odds, others chose to run away. Many runaways, unwilling to leave family and friends behind, sought only a short respite from the life of slavery or a master's harsh treatment. Others ran away for good. Using a freed slave's manumission papers, Frederick Douglass (1817–1895) was able to board a ship traveling from Baltimore to New York. Henry "Box" Brown (1816–c. 1860) had himself nailed shut in a wooden crate and mailed from Richmond to Philadelphia to become free. Thousands of runaway slaves traveled the Underground Railroad, a clandestine, interracial network of men and women opposed to slavery that aided runaway slaves en route to free states north of the Mason-Dixon Line and the Ohio River and to Canada. In the three decades before the Civil War, as many as one thousand slaves per year followed the Underground Railroad and successfully reached the North. The most notorious conductor on the Underground Railroad, the escaped slave woman Harriet Tubman (c. 1821–1913), guided more than three hundred runaway slaves to freedom. While most slaves heading north traveled alone or in small groups, in Washington, D.C., in 1848, seventy-seven slaves fled at night aboard the schooner *Pearl*, which was docked in the Potomac River. White pilots steered the vessel south toward the Chesapeake Bay until bad weather forced them ashore. All were captured. The escaped slaves were returned to Washington and sold; some were taken as far as New Orleans.

In the Lower South, runaways absconded to hard-to-reach forests, mountains, and swamps. Known as maroons, fugitive slaves stole food and livestock from local plantations; harassed, and in some instances killed, slave owners; and encouraged other slaves to join them. In 1816 one maroon community living in an abandoned English fort in Florida had a population of nearly three hundred, until armed federal troops arrived, leaving but forty survivors among the inhabitants. Thousands of maroons fought with the Seminoles in a series of wars against the U.S. government. Many others ran away to cities, where their chances of avoiding recapture were enhanced greatly. The decision to run away never was easy, and the risk of being captured and severely punished was great. Still, many slaves took a chance at freedom.

The most widespread forms of resistance among antebellum slaves were sabotage and other personal acts of defiance. Slaves broke tools, feigned sickness, and pretended not to understand directions in order to avoid work. They poisoned masters and burned buildings to the ground. Forced to endure years of degradation, slaves used individual acts of resistance to provide a necessary psychological release.

Slaves' Work

While slaves yearned for freedom, they had to come to grips with the world in which they lived—one that revolved around labor. Every morning slaves awoke knowing they would spend the day working for the benefit of others. Late-twentieth-century historians rejected the idea that the typical antebellum slave worked on a cotton plantation surrounded by large numbers of fellow slaves and a white overseer. In fact, there was no typical American slave. Slavery was a diverse, amorphous institution that changed and took on various forms at different times and in different places. It flourished in the tropical climates of the Lower South and in the more temperate regions of the Upper South. Slaves labored on plantations, as well as on the plains and prairies. They worked at the docks, on ships, in factories, and in shops, performing myriad tasks. The forces of nature and those of the market determined what tasks slaves were required to perform.

Large plantations did exist throughout the South, especially along the fertile coastal regions, known as the low country, from northern Florida to Maryland. Labor was divided among three groups of plantation slaves. House servants lived in or near the "big house" with the master and performed the cooking, cleaning, and most other household chores, including nursery duties. Women and children dominated this group. Although they were decently clothed and fed, house servants had little privacy and often were isolated from other slaves. Field slaves were given less food, typically cornmeal and salt pork, and lower-quality clothing and were forced to perform the most physically challenging labor. Large numbers picked and planted cotton, while many others cultivated tobacco, rice, indigo, wheat, corn, and hemp. The third group of slaves, consisting of artisans, drivers, and black overseers, held an ambiguous position in the slave hierarchy. Because they were entrusted with high levels of responsibility, these slaves sometimes received better treatment. But when that trust was broken, masters dealt with these slaves unmercifully. In either case, this group played an important role on the plantation. Many gained the respect of their masters, who in turn granted them a level of independence never experienced by members of the other two slave groups.

Slaves on plantations usually faced one of two types of labor: the task or gang system. With the task system, slaves were assigned a specific task to complete each day. Following the completion of that task, they were allowed to pursue any useful activities for the remainder of the daylight hours, such as tending privately owned garden plots or livestock. The task system flourished, especially in the rice-growing regions of South Carolina and Georgia. The gang system of labor was harder on slaves. They were divided into two or more groups and, accompanied by one or more overseers, left their dwellings at dawn. Slave gangs labored in the fields until sundown. Throughout this long day, their thoughts, conversations, and songs were interrupted by the crack of the overseer's whip. Any slave who failed to move a tool rapidly enough, or was caught resting at an unauthorized time, might face the full wrath of the overseer. Sunday usually was reserved as a day for rest for slaves as well as for masters, but during harvest time this

day also was spent at work. Even in times of inclement weather, slaves were kept busy. Whether fixing a wagon, chopping wood, or repairing a fence, they were rarely without work.

Many slaves did not live on plantations, and many who did stayed only for a time. Masters and their slaves frequently moved from one location to another. Some moved from plantation to plantation, while others moved to the South's burgeoning small towns and cities. Work in Charleston, Baltimore, New Orleans, and Richmond rarely imitated that performed on plantations. In cities and towns, instead of producing cash crops, slaves were responsible for their finishing, transportation, and distribution. Urban slaves were not agricultural laborers; they were ironworkers, cigar makers, stevedores, and sailors. Some earned wages. Between harvests and in periods of economic decline, some masters rented their slaves out to work for other white men. These slaves forfeited all or a significant percentage of their earnings to their masters, yet the life led by an urban, wage-earning slave often was better than that of a field hand. Slaves who were allowed, or by some other means were able, to keep a percentage of their earnings supplemented their diet and wardrobe, entertained themselves, or even saved enough to purchase their freedom or that of others.

Female Slaves' Work

Women were not immune to the harshness of slave life. Visitors to southern plantations routinely commented on the backbreaking labor they witnessed slave women performing in cotton fields and rice paddies. Throughout the antebellum period, economic cycles of boom and bust, along with a paucity of white laborers, forced more male slaves to learn at least one skilled occupation. A number gained renown as blacksmiths, carpenters, and bricklayers. With fewer male slaves in the fields, masters increasingly relied upon female slaves to cultivate acres of staple crops. In addition to farming, cooking the master's food, washing the clothes, and taking care of the children, slave women also raised their own children. Collectively, these occupations kept slave women attached to their master's property.

As children, slave boys and girls were treated similarly. They played together, dressed alike, and worked alongside one another, often in the trash gang—a small group of slave women and children that worked in the fields pulling weeds, raking stubble, and cleaning up after field hands. In the teenage years, however, slave girls and boys were separated. Boys joined men in the fields, while girls joined women either in the fields or in the house. For the first time, these young women spent much of their time with women who were pregnant and married. It wasn't long before they too would be with child.

The child-bearing years often were the most difficult for slave women. Pregnant women were not excused from performing field labor and regular chores. Some were relegated to completing less strenuous tasks in the days just before and after the birth, but rarely was adequate time allotted for rest. Some masters hired doctors to assist in the delivery of slaves' children, but typically slave women were given little aid. More often slave women experienced in childbirth came to the aid of expectant mothers. By offering advice and medicine or conducting healing rituals, these women did their best to lessen the emotional and physical stresses on pregnant women. The medical care these women received was, nevertheless, inadequate.

After giving birth, mothers tried to provide their infants with care and attention. But masters had little sympathy for women who chose nursing over work. Consequently, infants and toddlers regularly accompanied their mothers to the field tied to their backs or were kept in a day nursery, where their mothers visited them periodically for nursing. Most slave women gave birth for the first time late in their teenage years: the average woman gave birth to approximately seven children throughout the course of

her adulthood. While premarital sex was not uncommon among slaves, most slave women gave birth to their husband's children.

Slave Family and Community

Despite the constant threat that they or one of their family members would be sold away, slaves tried to construct "normal" lives centered around family and community. Like their masters and white neighbors, slave men and women married and had children. Although southern laws did not recognize slave vows, slave owners often encouraged familial relations in order to promote reproduction and discourage running away. Typically, slave families lived in their own cabin and spent their spare time in the evenings and on Sundays together. They ate, prayed, and sang together. Parents told their children stories of the Bible, Africa, and slavery. One of the proudest moments slaves experienced was naming their children. It was customary to name children after relatives who had died or been sold away. Masters frequently ignored these names, giving slave children classical and biblical names, in addition to the master's surname.

Slaves spent most free time in the quarters, the groups of cabins where slaves lived. The quarters usually were at a distance from the master's house, thereby allowing the residents a level of privacy and

"The Sabbath Among Slaves." An illustration from Henry Bibb's *Narrative of the Life and Adventures of Henry Bibb, an American Slave,* 1849. LIBRARY OF CONGRESS: RARE BOOK AND SPECIAL COLLECTIONS DIVISION

intimacy not available to house servants. In this semi-private space, slaves were left to each other's company. They rested, exchanged stories, sang spirituals and played with their children. They tended their own gardens and traded goods and services with one another as well as with slaves from other locations. Some crossed plantation lines to spend time with loved ones on other properties, often without the master's knowledge. Despite the intrusion of masters and overseers, slave communities evolved within and beyond plantation boundaries.

Miscegenation

In the 1830s, the French historian Alexis de Tocqueville (1805–1859) commented in his *Democracy in America* on the lack of racial prejudice he found in the southern states where slavery existed, compared with the northern states, where slavery did not exist but racism flourished. On a Virginia train, the northerner Frederick Law Olmsted (1822–1903) was struck by "the close cohabitation and association of black and white. . . . Negro women are carrying black and white babies together in their arms; black and white children are playing together; . . . black and white faces are constantly thrust together out of doors, to see the train go by" (*A Journey in the Seaboard Slave States*, p. 17). In the slave states, whites and blacks lived and worked together. They sometimes even prayed together. The large African American population encouraged a degree of intimacy between the two races. The ubiquitous presence of mulattoes, or persons of biracial parentage, best illustrates the extent of this intimacy.

Sexual relations between slaves and whites rarely were voluntary. Masters took slave mistresses and, less often, the master's wife took male slave companions. Slaves and nonslaveholding whites also forged sexual bonds. In most cases white men forced sexual relationships upon slave women. Rapes were common although consensual relationships have been documented by historians. Attractive slave women especially found themselves the prey of licentious white masters. On the auction block, moreover, they sometimes sold for more than double the price for a skilled male slave. Some slaves considered female beauty a curse.

Mulattoes held an ambiguous position in slave society, since their fathers often were also their masters. Some mulattoes were relegated to the status of slaves. They worked in the fields and slept in the quarters. Others were treated better than the average slave, and many were set free. The manumission of large numbers of light-skinned slaves led to the development of a southern racial caste system: whites were free; blacks were slaves; and mulattoes were nominally free, yet relegated to a socially inferior status.

Every day slaves coped with the obstacles and conditions presented by bondage. Their reactions varied. Some lost hope; countless slaves committed suicide. But those who kept the dream of freedom alive survived. They laughed, cried, fell in love, married, and had children. They taught themselves to read and sang spirituals. They prayed for a brighter day. A new culture emerged that combined aspects of the black experience in both Africa and the United States. The unique evolution of African American language, religion, food, dress, music, and dance provides an enduring legacy of slaves' lives.

See also **Miscegenation; Music,** *subentry on* **Spirituals and African American Music; Plantation, The; Slavery; South,** *subentry on* **The South before the Civil War; Underground Railroad.**

Bibliography

Abrahams, Roger D. *Singing the Master: The Emergence of African American Culture in the Plantation South.* New York: Pantheon Books, 1992.

Aptheker, Herbert. *American Negro Slave Revolts.* New York: Columbia University Press, 1943.

Blassingane, John W. *The Slave Community: Plantation Life in the Antebellum South.* Rev. ed. New York: Oxford University Press, 1979.

Berlin, Ira, and Philip D. Morgan, eds. *Cultivation and Culture: Labor and the Shaping of Slave Life in the Americas.* Charlottesville: University Press of Virginia, 1993.

Dew, Charles B. *Bond of Iron: Master and Slave at Buffalo Forge.* New York: Norton, 1994.

Epstein, Dena J. *Sinful Tunes and Spirituals: Black Folk Music to the Civil War.* Urbana: University of Illinois Press, 1977.

Franklin, John Hope. *From Slavery to Freedom: A History of American Negroes.* 2d ed., rev. and enl. New York: Knopf, 1956.

Genovese, Eugene D. *Roll, Jordan, Roll: The World the Slaves Made.* New York: Vintage, 1976.

Gomez, Michael A. *Exchanging Our Country Marks: The Transformation of African Identities in the Colonial and Antebellum South.* Chapel Hill: University of North Carolina Press, 1998.

Gutman, Herbert G. *The Black Family in Slavery and Freedom, 1750–1925.* New York: Vintage, 1977.

Jones, Norrece T., Jr. *Born a Child of Freedom, Yet a Slave: Mechanisms of Control and Strategies of Resistance in Antebellum South Carolina.* Hanover, N.H.: University Press of New England, 1990.

Joyner, Charles. *Down by the Riverside: A South Carolina Slave Community.* Urbana: University of Illinois Press, 1984.

Kolchin, Peter. *American Slavery, 1619–1877.* New York: Hill and Wang, 1993.

———. *Unfree Labor: American Slavery and Russian Serfdom.* Cambridge, Mass.: Belknap Press of Harvard University Press, 1987.

Litwack, Leon F. *Been in the Storm So Long: The Aftermath of Slavery*. New York: Vintage, 1980.

Malone, Ann Patton. *Sweet Chariot: Slave Family and Household Structure in Nineteenth-Century Louisiana*. Chapel Hill: University of North Carolina Press, 1992.

Mullin, Michael. *Africa in America: Slave Acculturation and Resistance in the American South and the British Caribbean, 1736–1831*. Urbana: University of Illinois Press, 1992.

Olmsted, Frederick Law. *A Journey in the Seaboard Slave States, with Remarks on Their Economy*. 1856. Reprint, New York: Negro Universities Press, 1968.

Owens, Leslie Howard. *This Species of Property: Slave Life and Culture in the Old South*. New York: Oxford University Press, 1977.

Raboteau, Albert J. *Slave Religion: The "Invisible Institution" in the Antebellum South*. New York: Oxford University Press, 1978.

Rawick, George P. *From Sundown to Sunup: The Making of the Black Community*. Westport, Conn.: Greenwood Press, 1972.

Ricks, Mary Kay. "Escape on the Pearl." *Washington Post*, 12 August 1998.

Stevenson, Brenda E. *Life in Black and White: Family and Community in the Slave South*. New York: Oxford University Press, 1996.

Stuckey, Sterling. *Slave Culture: Nationalist Theory and the Foundations of Black America*. New York: Oxford University Press, 1987.

Vlach, John Michael. *By the Work of Their Hands: Studies in Afro-American Folklife*. Athens: University of Georgia Press, 1999.

Webber, Thomas L. *Deep like the Rivers: Education in the Slave Quarter Community, 1831–1865*. New York: Norton, 1978.

White, Deborah Gray. *Ar'n't I a Woman?: Female Slaves in the Plantation South*. Rev. ed. New York: Norton, 1999.

MATT CLAVIN

SLAVE INSURRECTIONS

America's bloodiest insurrections occurred between 1800 and 1859. A Mississippi farmer told the northern tourist Frederick Law Olmsted, "When I was a boy . . . folks was dreadful frightened. . . . [T]hey built pens in the woods where they could hide and Christmas time they went and got into the pens, 'fraid the niggers was risin'" (quoted in Wish, "American Slave Insurrections," p. 307). In the wake of abortive revolts and the growing influence and militancy of the North's abolitionist movement, the South's increasingly repressive slave codes seemed unable to prevent or to curb slave defiance. The Constitution required the federal government to protect slavery; Article IV, Section 4, guaranteed the states protection "against domestic violence." The South demanded and expected that federal troops help put down slave rebellions.

Collective and individual resistance included sabotage of tools, harming of livestock, or feigning illness; verbal or physical confrontations, such as arson, poisonings, or assaults; and escapes. Insurrections threatened plantations, towns, counties, and occasionally states. To most whites two or more discontented slaves constituted an insurrection waiting to explode. However, most conspiracies were detected or exposed by whites before any violence began, or the conspiracies represented escape or revenge plots that rarely got beyond the talking stage. Scaremongers blamed insurrections on everyone except the slaves: abolitionists, the British, free blacks, the French, Haitians, American Indians, northerners, Quakers, and nonslaveholders.

Rebellion and Revolution, 1800–1831

Gabriel Prosser (1776–1800) viewed himself as a revolutionary liberator who hoped to duplicate the success of Toussaint L'Ouverture's revolt in Haiti by reading military manuals and studying Toussaint's campaigns. By August 1800 he had a network of nearly two thousand slaves in ten Virginia counties, planned to seize the state capital at Richmond, and expected to become king. Fellow slaves betrayed his plot before it began, and a violent rainstorm disrupted mobilization of his forces. Twenty-seven blacks, including Prosser, were hanged. Sancho Booker, one of his former lieutenants, organized sixty slaves in four counties in 1802. He, too, was betrayed, and he and twenty-five slaves in Virginia and North Carolina were hanged.

A conspiracy by a free mulatto, Charles Deslondes, to capture New Orleans was betrayed by a slave recently sold from Virginia and was crushed by state and federal troops in January 1811. Vengeful Louisianans executed nearly a hundred blacks, including Deslondes, and displayed their severed heads on roads outside the city. Denmark Vesey (1767–1822) headed a politicized slave conspiracy. He won a lottery, purchased his freedom in 1800, and established himself as a prosperous Charleston, South Carolina, carpenter worth eight thousand dollars in 1822. Vesey cited the American, French, and Haitian revolutions as examples of justifiable and successful rebellions. He also claimed whites were illegally holding blacks in bondage because the Missouri Compromise (1820) banned slavery in the former Louisiana Purchase. His conspiracy, which included nine thousand slaves and free blacks, was set for July 1822, but a slave informed his master of the plot. Vesey and thirty-four other blacks were hanged.

Nat Turner's revolt is considered the largest American slave revolt because it killed more whites than any other. Turner (1800–1831), a slave in Southampton County, Virginia, plotted to kill as many

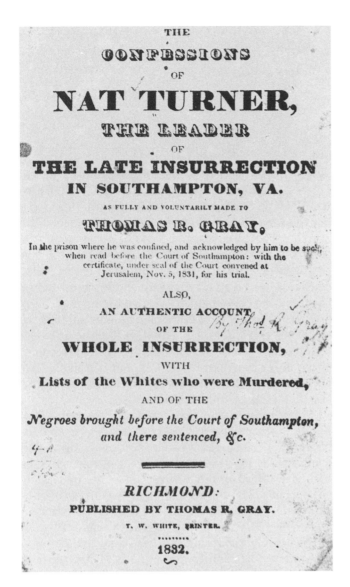

Proclamation of Capture. A poster dated 1832 announces the publication of Nat Turner's confessions. After Turner's bloody 1831 insurrection, southern slaveholders became increasingly anxious about controlling their slaves. LIBRARY OF CONGRESS: RARE BOOK AND SPECIAL COLLECTIONS DIVISION

whites as necessary, provoke terror while marching to the county seat at Jerusalem, seize its armory, then escape to the Dismal Swamp. On 21 August 1831 he and six followers (the group eventually grew to seventy-five) launched an attack that killed fifty-five whites during thirty-six hours. His divided troops spent most of their time looting instead of proceeding to Jerusalem. They were routed at plantations defended by loyal slaves and subjugated by militia and federal troops. Turner hid alone for two months, but he and most of his men were captured and hanged. The South enacted draconian laws against abolition-

ist societies, free blacks, and slaves. Nevertheless, slave unrest continued in urban and rural areas and often involved slaves allied with free blacks and sympathetic whites.

Revolts occurred on slave ships. In 1820 thirty slaves on a ship bound from Norfolk to New Orleans plotted to kill the white passengers and crew and sail to Haiti, but a female slave informed her mistress of the conspiracy. Thirty slaves took over the slaver *Decatur* and escaped to New York in 1827. Fifty-three Africans led by Joseph Cinque seized control of the Spanish slaver *Amistad* in 1839 and tried to return to Africa. The U.S. Navy seized the *Amistad* off Long Island, and the government put the Africans on trial for murder and piracy. In 1841 the Supreme Court ruled they were entitled to their freedom, and thirty-five survivors were returned to Africa. That same year Madison Washington, a slave from Virginia, led a rebellion of 134 slaves on the *Creole*, which was bound for New Orleans. The ship arrived in Nassau, the Bahamas, where British officials declared the slaves free despite American extradition demands and threats of war.

White Leaders of Black Revolts, 1816–1859

Among the South's greatest slave insurrection nightmares were those led by whites. George Boxley, who had been a soldier in the War of 1812, organized slaves in several Virginia counties and towns. He was betrayed by a slave woman and arrested in 1816 with thirty slaves. Six were hanged, but Boxley escaped from jail and disappeared. The militant abolitionist John Brown (1800–1859) led a band of twenty-one black and white men that captured the federal arsenal at Harpers Ferry, Virginia (now West Virginia), on 16 October 1859. Marines under the command of Colonel Robert E. Lee stormed the building, and most of Brown's raiders were killed or captured. Brown underestimated the determination of slaveholders and the government to put down slave rebellions and overestimated the enthusiasm of slaves to fight under the leadership of outsiders. Convicted of treason, murder, and slave insurrection, he was hanged in December at Charlestown. Afterward hundreds of blacks were arrested, tortured, killed, or driven from their homes. The South viewed Harpers Ferry as evidence of an abolitionist conspiracy; the national stage was set for civil war.

The Civil War

Limited outbreaks of insurrections continued during the Civil War as many emboldened slaves assumed Abraham Lincoln's inauguration and Emancipation Proclamation meant they were entitled to freedom.

Military and vigilante patrols sought to prevent uprisings, yet serious outbreaks occurred across the Confederate South: Alabama (December 1864), Florida (April 1863), Georgia (October 1863 and August 1864), Louisiana (May 1861), Mississippi (July 1862), South Carolina (April 1861), and Virginia (May 1861 and October 1862). Most either were insurrection panics or were foiled during the planning stage. The historian Winthrop Jordan has uncovered an 1861 conspiracy in Adams County, Mississippi, that resulted in the execution of forty slaves; authorities suppressed details of the plot and punishments.

Many slaves took up arms for personal revenge rather than as liberators. Although the federal government did not officially enlist black soldiers until 1863, from the war's beginning slaves forged military alliances with it. A South Carolina slave was caught stockpiling ammunition for Union troops on his master's rice plantation in May 1861. Union military authorities tentatively approved a plan for slaves to make a simultaneous uprising during August 1863, but Confederate agents thwarted it. Black guerrillas and maroons (fugitive slaves) launched hit-and-run raids on the outskirts of towns or isolated areas of the Confederate South. Some were so recurrent and prolonged that the Confederacy was forced to divert troops to maintain its internal security.

Slaves posed the greatest challenge to slavery. Their resistance, despite always being outnumbered and outgunned, was a bloody reminder of their willingness to kill and die for freedom. Ironically, slaves who expected their freedom or other rewards betrayed most insurrections. These racial renegades partly account for the overall failure of slave revolts. A leading scholar, Herbert Aptheker, suggested that at least 250 organized slave insurrections occurred (150 between 1800 and 1864), but the complete number can never be known.

See also **Abolition and Antislavery; Emancipation; Slavery,** subentry on **Slave Life.**

Bibliography

Aptheker, Herbert, *Negro Slave Revolts in the United States, 1526–1860.* New York: International, 1939.

Egerton, Douglas R. *Gabriel's Rebellion: The Virginia Slave Conspiracies of 1800 and 1802.* Chapel Hill and London: University of North Carolina Press, 1993.

Franklin, John Hope. *The Militant South, 1800–1861.* Cambridge, Mass.: Belknap Press of Harvard University Press, 1956.

Genovese, Eugene. *From Rebellion to Revolution: Afro-American Slave Revolts in the Making of the New World.* Baton Rouge: Louisiana State University Press, 1979.

Jordan, Winthrop. *Tumult and Silence at Second Creek: An Inquiry into a Civil War Slave Conspiracy.* Baton Rouge: Louisiana State University Press, 1993.

Slave Insurrections: Selected Documents. Westport, Conn.: Negro Universities Press, 1970.

Wish, Harvey. "American Slave Insurrections before 1861." *Journal of Negro History* 28 (July 1937): 299–320.

ERVIN L. JORDAN JR.

RUNAWAY SLAVES

Between 1800 and 1861 tens of thousands of slaves escaped, often making their way to the North, where they held on to a precarious freedom, or living in the South as free people. Legally, those who reached the North were still slaves, and could be seized under the fugitive slave clause of the Constitution and the federal laws of 1793 and 1850 adopted to enforce that clause. Relatively few runaway slaves who reached the free states were in fact returned to bondage. Nevertheless, the fear of capture made life for all fugitive slaves uncertain and dangerous. It is difficult to determine how many slaves actually reached freedom, either in the North or in Canada, but it is likely that the total was at least twenty-five thousand in the first six decades of the nineteenth century.

Many more slaves than that left their masters, hiding out in the woods, seeking freedom in the anonymity of the nearest town or city, or trying to find a relative or loved one who had been sold away or had been forced to move when his or her owner left the vicinity. The most comprehensive study of runaways, by John Hope Franklin and Loren Schweninger, concludes that most runaways remained close to the home of their master, where they could remain in contact with family and friends. These authors found that advertisements for runaways in Tennessee newspapers showed that masters rarely thought their slaves were headed north. Four times as many masters thought their slaves were still in the South than thought they had headed to Ohio, Indiana, or some free state. Most believed their slaves wanted to remain in Tennessee, with Nashville as the most likely destination. Reuniting with family seemed to be the most common motivation for slaves leaving their masters, especially if they were not heading north to freedom. Some slaves, particularly those who were literate, remained in the South, passing as free people. Some skilled and literate slaves from the upper South confused their masters by running south, not north, correctly assuming that their masters would never suspect that they had headed deeper into the world of slavery. In New Orleans, Mobile, or Natchez they were often able to pass themselves off as free people of color, find work, and live as they wished.

Escape to the North or Canada was more complicated. Most slaves who reached the North came from the upper South—Virginia, Maryland, Kentucky, Missouri, and Delaware—or from port cities, where they could use water transportation to make their escape. The majority traveled alone or in very small groups; if they were aided, it was by other slaves, free blacks, and the occasional white. Once they reached the North, many fugitive slaves were helped by members of "the underground railroad," like William Still in Philadelphia and Levi Coffin first in Newport, Indiana, and later in Cincinnati, who between them probably aided more than six thousand fugitives. Thomas Garrett, a Quaker in Delaware, took even greater risks in aiding hundreds of runaways. A few slaveowners successfully sued Garrett, who ultimately settled these cases for about $2,000, a huge sum at that time. Garrett did not seek fugitive slaves, aiding only those who passed by or were sent to him by knowledgeable blacks and white sympathizers.

A few fortunate slaves were aided by blacks and whites operating in the South. Harriet Tubman, the most famous "conductor" on the Underground Railroad, guided about three hundred slaves to freedom. Along the Ohio River and the Mason-Dixon Line, a few black and white opponents of slavery made forays into Kentucky and Virginia, helping slaves escape. Our knowledge of such adventures comes from memoirs written long after the events took place and from legal cases that resulted when these abolitionists were caught. Black and white sailors from northern ports occasionally helped slaves stow away on ships heading to free states. A few white ship captains helped slaves escape; some, like Jonathan Walker and Daniel Drayton, were severely punished when caught. In Richmond a white man named Smith packed Henry "Box" Brown in a wooden crate and shipped him by rail to the antislavery office. Smith was later sentenced to four and a half years in the penitentiary for facilitating two other escapes in this manner. John Brown, who would later be hanged for his raid on Harpers Ferry, helped nearly a score of slaves escape from Missouri, leading them to Canada.

Most runaways who made it to the North were not helped so directly. Frederick Douglass borrowed papers from a free northern black sailor, and then made his way to New York. Others, like Anthony Burns, simply hid on a ship, reached a free state port, and secretly disembarked. Some runaways were ingenious. Ellen Craft, a light-skinned, slim slave, wrapped her face in a bandage and placed her arm in a sling, so she would not be expected to write, and headed north, passing herself off as a young man traveling to Philadelphia to have surgery on her jaw. Her husband, William Craft, accompanied her as a "faithful" male slave. William did all the talking for

his poor, suffering "master." They reached Boston, wrote a narrative about their experiences, and then went to England.

Most runaways who reached the North sought anonymity. They simply wanted their freedom, and the best way to achieve it was to disappear into the larger cities or to go to small towns and farms in areas hostile to slavery. Upstate New York, northern Ohio, and parts of western Michigan provided safe havens for runaways. Some runaways became active in the antislavery movement. They often wrote, alone or with others, a narrative of their life that would be sold to raise money to support them and the cause of antislavery, as well as to help spread the word of the evils of slavery. Henry "Box" Brown, the Crafts, Rev. James Pennington (who called himself "The Fugitive Blacksmith"), Rev. Jermain Loguen, and scores of other fugitives wrote and sold their narratives. So, too, did some of the whites captured while attempting to help slaves, like Captain Drayton. Jonathan Walker, who was branded with the letters "s.s."—for slave stealer—published a particularly successful narrative, *The Man with the Branded Hand*.

The most important fugitive autobiography was *Narrative of the Life of Frederick Douglass*, which, along with his brilliant speaking abilities, made Douglass the most famous black in antebellum and Civil War America. He became so famous, in fact, that British abolitionists insisted on formally purchasing his freedom, so he could not be seized from a podium and returned to bondage. By the eve of the Civil War, Douglass had come to personify the fugitive slave while providing living proof, for whites willing to listen, of the equality of the races and the fundamental horror of slavery. During the war he would help recruit northern blacks—both free and fugitive—to enlist in a war that finally put an end to human bondage in the United States.

See also **Fugitive Slave Laws; Underground Railroad.**

Bibliography

Buckmaster, Henrietta. *Let My People Go: The Story of the Underground Railroad and the Growth of the Abolition Movement.* New York: Harper and Bros., 1941.
Campbell, Stanley. *The Slave Catchers: Enforcement of the Fugitive Slave Law, 1850–1860.* Chapel Hill: University of North Carolina Press, 1968.
Finkelman, Paul. *Slavery in the Courtroom: An Annotated Bibliography of American Cases.* Union, N.J.: Lawbook Exchange, 1985.
Franklin, John Hope, and Loren Schweninger. *Runaway Slaves: Rebels on the Plantation.* New York: Oxford University Press, 1999.
Gara, Larry. *The Liberty Line: The Legend of the Underground Railroad.* Lexington: University of Kentucky Press, 1961.
Horton, James Oliver, and Lois E. Horton. *In Hope of Liberty:*

Culture, Community, and Protest Among Northern Free Blacks, 1700–1860. New York: Oxford University Press, 1997.

PAUL FINKELMAN

LAW OF SLAVERY

From the early colonial period until the ratification of the Thirteenth Amendment (1865), the law shaped the development and eventual abolition of American slavery. Before the Revolutionary War four major principles of slave law emerged through statutes and court decisions. First, under colonial law, blacks were presumed to be slaves unless they could prove otherwise. Second, the law recognized that slaves held dual status as property and persons. As property they could be bought, sold, or given to other people and were subject to the authority of their owners, who could treat them as they wished. Most jurisdictions did not consider it a crime if a master killed a slave during punishment. At the same time, slaves were liable for their own actions and could be punished, after a proper trial, if they broke the law. Third, slaves had no fundamental rights, and could not testify against whites or claim any legal protections. Finally, in direct contradiction of English common law, the colonies, through statutes and common law, decided that the children of black women would follow the slave or free status of their mother, thus exempting white men from any legal consequences for having illicit sexual relations with slave women.

During the American Revolution the northern states began to dismantle slavery, through both direct abolition in Vermont, Massachusetts, and New Hampshire and gradual emancipation in the rest of the North. By 1804 every northern state had taken steps to abolish slavery. The Revolutionary War had less of an effect on southern law, although some states, like Virginia, adopted new laws allowing masters to voluntarily free their slaves. Similarly, North Carolina passed legislation criminalizing the intentional killing of a slave.

Southern Law

At the beginning of the nineteenth century, slave law was very much what it had been a century earlier. Southern law presumed that all blacks were slaves, to be treated as property with no basic rights. Slaves could not make contracts, own property, testify in court against whites, defend themselves against physical attacks by their masters, legally marry, or have any legal control over their children. These laws were mediated by the reality of human life, and thus

slaves did marry, raise their children, and sometimes grew their own crops, raised animals, and earned a little money on the side. But masters could, and did, sell children, separate spouses, and take property their slaves had acquired. Some slaves resisted the brutality of their masters, with mixed results. In his autobiography, Frederick Douglass (1817–1895) told of fighting back against a man he was hired out to, thereby gaining some respect and avoiding future beatings. Other slaves faced savage treatment, and even death, when they resisted their masters.

After 1800, southern courts and legislatures worked to strengthen the institution of slavery wherever possible. In 1806, for example, Virginia passed a law requiring that manumitted slaves leave the state within one year of being freed. By 1860 most southern states had enacted similar restrictions, and some refused to allow a master to free his slaves within the state, requiring the benevolent master to transport slaves elsewhere before manumitting them. By 1860 most slave states had made it a crime to teach a slave to read. It was a crime in most of the South to circulate antislavery literature, and in the 1850s most slave states banned the national bestseller *Uncle Tom's Cabin* (1852). Slaves could not even hold their own worship services without whites being present. Many of these restrictive laws also were applied to the more than 250,000 free blacks who lived in the South by 1860. Free blacks from the North or other countries who entered southern states as merchant seamen were routinely incarcerated while their ships were docked. Starting in the 1830s southern states began to reject claims to freedom by blacks who had lived in the North or Europe, where slavery was not allowed. In *Mitchell v. Wells* (1859) Mississippi even rejected the freedom of a slave whose owner had brought her to Ohio and voluntarily manumitted her there. By 1860 most of the South was a closed society, where neither whites nor blacks were allowed to question the value of slavery.

While fastening the bonds of servitude more firmly, southern law also made the system less harsh. Such changes made slave rebellions less likely while undercutting northern criticism of slavery. In the 1820s, for example, South Carolina prohibited castration, branding, dismembering, and other barbaric punishments of slaves. By 1860 all of the southern states had legislated that no one, not even a master, could murder a slave in cold blood. In *State v. Hoover* (1839), the North Carolina Supreme Court upheld the death sentence for a master who tortured his slave to death. Virginia's highest court upheld a five-year sentence of a master who tortured his slave to death, in *Souther v. Commonwealth* (1851). Shortly before the Civil War, a few southern states made it a crime for a male slave to rape a female slave. In *An Inquiry into the Law of Negro Slavery* (1858), the proslavery legal theorist Thomas R. R. Cobb (1823–1862) stated that the law should also punish whites who raped slaves, for "the honor of the statute-book."

Along the same lines, southern states provided due-process protections for slaves accused of crimes. Courts throughout the South overturned convictions of slaves who were denied a lawyer, coerced into confessing to a crime, improperly prohibited from calling witnesses, and incorrectly charged. In 1864 the Georgia Supreme Court reversed a slave's conviction based on his wife's testimony, because such testimony violated the ancient common-law right of spousal immunity. This was an extraordinary move, since southern law did not recognize the legality of slave marriages.

Such procedural victories were of little use to most slaves charged with crimes, since they usually faced quick trials and harsh punishments. The southern legislatures and courts readily accepted and supported the idea that slaves were at all times subordinate to whites. A few southern courts held that a slave could resist a white in order to save his or her life, and in *State v. Will* (1834) the North Carolina Supreme Court reduced to manslaughter the murder conviction of a slave who had killed his overseer after the overseer had wounded him with a shotgun. However, in *State v. Mann* (1829), the North Carolina justice Thomas Ruffin (1787–1870) reversed the conviction of a man who had shot and wounded a rented slave. Ruffin declared, "The slave, to remain a slave, must be made sensible, that there is no appeal from his master; that his power is in no instance usurped, but is conferred by the laws of man at least, if not by the law of God."

Northern Law

By 1830 only a few thousand aging slaves could be found in Pennsylvania, New Jersey, Connecticut, and Illinois; slavery had disappeared completely elsewhere in the North. In the four decades before the Civil War, northerners passed personal-liberty laws to protect their free black neighbors from being kidnapped, and sometimes to frustrate attempts by southerners to reclaim fugitive slaves. Before 1842 these laws gave jury trials to alleged fugitives. After 1842 northern states prohibited state officials from helping to return fugitive slaves to their owners—state magistrates could not issue warrants, state and local authorities were forbidden from making arrests, and no state jail could be used to hold fugitive slaves.

Before the 1830s most northern states allowed vis-iting masters to keep slaves in their jurisdictions for a short period of time. For example, a Pennsylvania law provided that masters could bring slaves into that state for up to six months, and only after six months had passed would the slave be free. New York gave masters a nine-month grace period. However, starting with *Commonwealth v. Aves* (1836) in Massachusetts, the free states began to emancipate slaves the moment they were brought into the North. While free blacks faced discrimination in most of the North, that area was nevertheless committed to freedom and opposed to slavery. Its legislation and jurisprudence reflected this.

Slavery and National Law

After the adoption of the Constitution (1788), the U.S. Congress and the Supreme Court generally supported slavery. In 1793 Congress passed the first fugitive slave act to help masters recover runaway slaves. An amendment to that law, known as the Fugitive Slave Law of 1850, provided federal help to masters and harsh penalties for anyone interfering with the return of runaway slaves. In *Prigg v. Pennsylvania* (1842), *Jones v. Van Zandt* (1847), and *Ableman v. Booth* (1859), the Supreme Court interpreted the fugitive slave laws to the benefit of masters and to the detriment of white abolitionists and blacks, including those who might have been legally free.

In 1808 Congress banned the importation of new slaves into the United States. Many slave owners in Virginia and Maryland favored this law because it increased the value of their slaves. However, no president before Abraham Lincoln tried to enforce the ban effectively. Meanwhile, in *The Antelope* (1825) and other cases, the Supreme Court upheld the legality of the international slave trade. In *United States v. Amistad* (1841) the Court ordered black men kidnapped from Africa to be set free, but only because they had been imported illegally to Cuba before entering U.S. waters. Had they been held legally as slaves in Cuba, the Court was prepared to return them to their owners.

In the Missouri Compromise (1820) the U.S. Congress banned slavery in all of the western territories north and west of Missouri's southern boundary. In the Compromise of 1850, Congress modified this ban to allow slavery in several of the territories ceded to the United States after the Mexican-American War (1846–1848). In the Kansas-Nebraska Act (1854) Congress repealed the ban on slavery in these territories, allowing popular sovereignty to determine whether these areas would restrict slavery. This led to a small civil war in Kansas, in which Congress and the administrations of Presidents Franklin Pierce and James Buchanan consistently sided with Kansas's slave owners.

In *Dred Scott v. Sandford* (1857) the Supreme Court ruled that all bans on slavery in the territories were unconstitutional, because southerners had a constitutional right to take their slaves into any federal territories. The Court also ruled that blacks had no legal rights under the Constitution and that they were not citizens of the United States. The *Dred Scott* decision led to an extraordinary backlash in the North. Lincoln's sharp critique of the decision helped to propel him to the Republican nomination for president in 1860.

During and after the Civil War the nation effectively overruled *Dred Scott*. During the war, Congress banned slavery in the territories, abolished slavery in the District of Columbia, and, with the enlistment of black troops starting in 1862, acknowledged that African Americans could be U.S. citizens. The Emancipation Proclamation (1863) had the force of law in ending slavery everywhere in the Confederacy. The Thirteenth Amendment (1865) ended slavery everywhere in the United States, and the Fourteenth Amendment (1868) declared that all people born in the United States were citizens of the nation and of the state in which they lived.

See also **Constitutional Amendments,** *subentry on* **Thirteenth, Fourteenth, and Fifteenth Amendments; Emancipation; Fugitive Slave Laws; Race Laws.**

Bibliography

Fehrenbacher, Don E. *The Dred Scott Case: Its Significance in American Law and Politics.* New York: Oxford University Press, 1978.

Finkelman, Paul. *Dred Scott v. Sandford: A Brief History with Documents.* Boston: Bedford, 1997.

———, ed. *Slavery and the Law.* Madison, Wis.: Madison House, 1996.

Morris, Thomas D. *Free Men All: The Personal Liberty Laws of the North, 1780–1861.* Baltimore: Johns Hopkins University Press, 1974.

Robinson, Donald L. *Southern Slavery and the Law, 1619–1860.* Chapel Hill: University of North Carolina Press, 1996.

Schafer, Judith Kelleher. *Slavery, the Civil Law, and the Supreme Court of Louisiana.* Baton Rouge: Louisiana State University Press, 1994.

Schwarz, Philip J. *Twice Condemned: Slaves and the Criminal Laws of Virginia, 1705–1865.* Union, N.J.: Lawbook Exchange, 1998.

Wiecek, William M. *The Sources of Antislavery Constitutionalism in America, 1760–1848.* Ithaca, N.Y.: Cornell University Press, 1977.

PAUL FINKELMAN

DEFENSE OF SLAVERY

Until the adoption of the Thirteenth Amendment (1865) many southerners, and occasionally some northerners, defended American slavery. Even after the demise of slavery, the arguments in favor of the institution remained alive, bolstering segregation, racism, and the "lost cause" of the Confederacy.

Before the American Revolution there were few significant defenses of slavery, in part because there were few sustained attacks on the institution. Slavery had existed in almost every human society and could be found everywhere in the Americas, as well as in Africa, Asia, and a good deal of Europe. It was seen as part of the natural order of the world. In 1688, Quakers in Germantown, Pennsylvania, challenged slavery on moral grounds, arguing that the institution was contrary to the Word of God and the Christian injunction to "do unto others as you would have others do unto you" (Matt. 7:12). By the 1770s such arguments were common among Quakers, Methodists, and some Baptists, but they had little effect on other faiths or most politicians.

The American Revolution had the potential to undermine slavery. The natural rights doctrine expressed in the Declaration of Independence—"that all men are created equal" and entitled to "life, liberty, and the pursuit of happiness"—was a powerful argument against slavery. How could one endorse such a concept and continue to own slaves? Critics of the American cause were quick to point out that many of the leaders of the Revolution, including Thomas Jefferson, the author of these words, were slaveholders.

In the North the Revolutionary War did, in fact, lead to universal male emancipation. Southerners, however, were unwilling to give up their slaves, as they represented a valuable form of property. With this decision, southerners had to explain to their fellow countrymen, and to the world, why they continued to own slaves while simultaneously proclaiming their allegiance to the natural rights of life and liberty. By the 1820s the southern defense of slavery had been recast into what is known as the "proslavery argument," which asserted that slavery was a "positive good" that benefited both the slave and the master, rather than a "necessary evil" that needed to be defended. Proslavery theorists supported slavery using a series of interrelated arguments based on race, economic necessity, history, and religion.

Racial Arguments

The proslavery argument was predicated on the notion that African Americans were inherently inferior to whites, and as such could *never* be equal. Thus their status was not only justifiable, but actually a blessing. Under this theory, white masters had a duty to take care of their racially inferior slaves. The seeds of this argument were planted by Jefferson in his

Proslavery Riot, November 1837. The murder in Alton, Illinois, of the abolitionist-printer Elijah P. Lovejoy by a proslavery mob from St. Louis led to northern fears of what was eventually called the "slavocracy." LIBRARY OF CONGRESS

book *Notes on the State of Virginia* (1787, first English edition). Jefferson argued against political equality for blacks because "the real distinctions which nature has made" between the races went beyond color and other physical attributes. In his *Notes* Jefferson asserted that a harsh bondage did not prevent Roman slaves from achieving distinction in art or science because "they were of the race of whites." American slaves could never achieve such distinction because they were not white.

Scientists and physicians of the mid–nineteenth century expanded on Jefferson's theories, arguing that blacks were in fact a separate species. Josiah C. Nott (1804–1873), a Mobile physician, published "scientific" research in which he claimed that mulattoes were a genuine hybrid of two separate races, and were weaker and less fertile than either. Nott argued that blacks had major anatomical differences from whites, including a larger head, smaller brain, defective mental powers, and larger nerves. He wrote that blacks reached their highest attainable goals when "tamed" and "educated to capacity" as slaves. Samuel Cartwright (1793–1863), a physician in New Orleans who specialized in "Negro diseases," believed that blacks' internal organs, flesh, and even brains were darker than whites'. He wrote that blacks "un-

der the compulsive power of the white man . . . are made to labor or exercise, which makes the lungs perform the duty of vitalizing the blood more perfectly than is done when they are left free to indulge in idleness. It is the red, vital blood sent to the brain that liberates their mind when under the white man's control, and it is the want of a sufficiency of red, vital blood that chains their mind to ignorance and barbarism when in freedom." Cartwright identified a disease called "drapetomania," which caused slaves to run away. The cure for the "running-away disease" was to whip slaves who showed symptoms, such as sullenness or discontent.

The scientific argument was crucial in the propaganda war against the North, but it was also weakened by the insistence by most scientists that blacks were a separate species from whites, and thus derived from a "separate creation." These pre-Darwinian scientists offered a theory that, in conflict with the biblical story of creation, put them at odds with the nation's Protestant majority.

Economic Necessity

Economic arguments rested on the importance of slave labor in developing the South and on the importance of cotton to the American economy. A subset of the economic argument was the claim that only blacks could survive and work hard in the heat of the Deep South. Thus, economics and geography fit neatly with racial theories to support not merely slavery, but black slavery. These arguments were grounded solidly in self-interest and directed at the northern business community. However, they also underscored the putative positive aspects of slavery. The system brought wealth and prosperity to whites, while at the same time providing sustenance to blacks, who, proslavery theorists argued, could not survive in freedom.

The high point of the economic argument came in an 1858 speech, known as the "mud-sill speech," by Senator James Henry Hammond (1807–1864) of South Carolina. Extolling the virtues of slavery, Hammond declared, "You dare not make war on cotton. No power on earth dares make war upon it. Cotton is king." Hammond rested this argument on the fact that much of the nation's economy was driven by cotton, cloth manufacturing, and cotton product exports. Textile mills in New England, and their tens of thousands of workers, all depended on cotton. So too did tens of thousands of workers in British mills. American shippers, shipbuilders, and sailors were equally tied to the plant. Cotton and cotton products made up half of all U.S. exports in 1850.

Hammond's economic arguments were not entirely wrong, but he and the South gravely overestimated the importance of southern cotton to the world economy. When the Civil War began, the Confederacy took its cotton off the world market, hoping to force Great Britain to recognize the new government. Instead, England turned to India and Egypt for cotton, and the South lost the opportunity to sell its product in Europe before U.S. naval ships made that impossible.

History

Since the earliest proslavery arguments, southerners had pointed out that all great societies had held slaves. In 1787, South Carolina's Charles Pinckney (1757–1824) told the Constitutional Convention, "If slavery be wrong, it is justified by the example of all the world." He offered the examples of "Greece Rome & other antient [sic] States; the sanction given by France England, Holland & other modern States." Pinckney asserted, "In all ages one half of mankind have been slaves."

The historical argument attempted to equate the South with ancient Greece and Rome. Plato, Aristotle, and most other classical writers accepted slavery and considered it vital to their societies. The Athenian democracy and the Roman Republic were slave-based societies. As Aristotle wrote, "It is clear then that by nature some are free, others slaves, and that for these it is both just and expedient that they should serve as slaves." In 1831, Alexander Knox, a Virginia politician, argued there was not "one solitary instance of a Government, since the institution of civil society, in which the principle of slavery was not tolerated in some form or other . . . in the republics of Greece and Rome, the cradles of liberty—slavery was tolerated in the severest form."

In *An Inquiry into the Law of Negro Slavery* (1858), Thomas R. R. Cobb (1823–1862), a cofounder of the first law school in Georgia, quoted Plato, Euripides, Juvenal, and other classical writers to teach his readers that slavery, especially black slavery, was accepted by the greatest minds of Western culture. Tying race to European history, Cobb insisted that at an "early day" the "negro was commonly used as a slave at Rome." Implicitly comparing the South to the Roman Republic, he noted, "For her footmen and couriers" the Roman "wife preferred always the negroes" and that "Negroes, being generally slaves of luxury, commanded a very high price." Cobb also asserted that in ancient Israel "many" of the slaves "were Africans of negro extraction" and that "among the Egyptians . . . there were numbers of negro slaves." Making similar claims for Assyria and Alexander the Great's empire, he concluded, "The negro was a favorite among slaves" in the ancient world. While there is no historical support for these ideas, Cobb's assertions went unchallenged by most readers, who had no access to any serious works of history.

The historical argument asserted that slavery was necessary for a great society. In addition, southerners argued that slavery allowed the leaders of the South—such as Jefferson, James Madison, and James Monroe—to devote their time to science, philosophy, and public service. Indeed, arguing from history, the proslavery theorists asserted that democracy itself was only possible in a slave society. In his "mud-sill" speech Senator Hammond tied this theory to his racial and economic theories, arguing that every society needs a bottom layer—a mud-sill—as a foundation for the rest of society. Hammond argued that, in the South, slaves provided this layer, thus elevating all whites to a state of political equality; in the free North, whites were in constant competition with each other, because whites occupied the lowest level of society. This meant that even the lowest class in the North, which owned no property and had little stake in society, could vote. In the South, he argued, democracy flourished precisely because the lowest social class was racially different and could not participate in the political process.

Religion

The most common defense of slavery was based on biblical scripture. This was in part because of the ubiquity of well-educated ministers in the antebellum South. In addition, the strongest attacks on slavery came from northern ministers and abolitionists whose opposition to slavery was religiously based.

Both the Old and New Testaments were cited in defense of slavery. Ancient Israel was a slave-owning society, and the Pentateuch (first five books of the Old Testament) is replete with rules for governing slavery, though many of Israel's rules were far kinder to slaves than the laws of the American South, and nowhere in the Bible was slavery predicated on race. Southern ministers, however, easily ignored any inconsistencies with their own practices and instead focused on the ways the Old Testament supported slavery.

The Israelite patriarchs—Abraham, Isaac, Jacob—had "slaves." Southerners found the story of Abraham useful. When Hagar runs away from Abraham, the angel of the Lord finds her in the wilderness and demands of her, "Hagar, Sarai's maid . . . whither wilt thou go?" Hagar answers, "I flee from the face of my mistress Sarai." The angel tells her, "Return to thy mistress, and submit thyself under her hands" (Gen. 16:8–9 AV). What better source could southerners ask for when defending their right to capture runaway slaves?

The story of Job was also used to illustrate the importance of slavery in a just society. Job was a slaveholder, and his good character, which God tested, was based in part on how he discharged his duty to his slaves. One of his trials was the loss of his slaves. Once returned to God's grace, Job obtained even more slaves. Leviticus offered ministers ironclad proof that their system was not only just, but blessed by God. For example, "Both thy bondmen, and thy bondmaids, which thou shalt have . . . ye shall take them as an inheritance for your children after you . . . for ever" (Lev. 25:44–46). According to the Pentateuch, there is no death penalty for killing a slave during punishment, because the law presumes that no one would intentionally kill his own slave, "for he is his money" (Exod. 21:21).

The New Testament was equally helpful. Even Jesus did not condemn slavery. Instead, the Gospels are full of statements about humble servants and good slaves, such as the injunction, "Servants, be obedient to them that are your masters" (Eph. 6:5). In other letters, Paul declares, "Let every man abide in the same calling wherein he was called. Art thou called being a servant? Care not for it" (1 Cor. 7:20–21). Paul's letter to Philemon sanctions the return of a fugitive slave. Similarly, the same letters tell readers, "Submit yourselves to every ordinance of man for the Lord's work. Servants, be subject to your masters with all fear."

Proslavery clergymen even found a biblical defense for the racially based slavery of the South in the story of Noah. After the ark came to rest, Noah planted grapes "and he drank of the wine, and was drunken; and he was uncovered within his tent. And Ham, the father of Canaan, saw the nakedness of his father, and told his two brethren without" (Gen. 9:21–22). For Ham's indiscretion, Noah cursed Ham's son, Canaan, declaring, "Cursed be Canaan; a servant of servants shall he be unto his brethren" (Gen. 9:25). Southern ministers interpreted the "curse" of Canaan to mean that he became black, and thus they argued that the Bible justified not merely slavery, but the enslavement of Africans, the descendants of Canaan.

Throughout the South, clergymen gave sermons on the duties of a Christian master, which included baptizing one's slaves and treating them humanely. But such duties never included emancipation.

Bibliography

Ambrose, Douglas. *Henry Hughes and Proslavery Thought in the Old South.* Baton Rouge: Louisiana State University Press, 1996.

Cobb, Thomas R. R. *An Inquiry into the Law of Negro Slavery in the United States of America.* 1858. Reprint, with an introduction by Paul Finkelman, Athens, Ga.: University of Georgia Press, 1999.

Davis, David Brion. *Slavery and Human Progress.* New York: Oxford University Press, 1984.

Genovese, Eugene D. *The World the Slaveholders Made: Two Essays in Interpretation.* New York: Pantheon, 1969.

Horsman, Reginald. *Josiah Nott of Mobile: Southerner, Physician, and Racial Theorist.* Baton Rouge: Louisiana State University Press, 1987.

Snay, Mitchell. *Gospel of Disunion: Religion and Separatism in the Antebllum South.* Chapel Hill: University of North Carolina Press, 1997.

Stanton, William. *The Leopard's Spots: Scientific Attitudes toward Race in America, 1815–1859.* Chicago: University of Chicago Press, 1960.

Tise, Larry E. *Proslavery: A History of the Defense of Slavery in America, 1701–1840.* Athens, Ga.: University of Georgia Press, 1987.

PAUL FINKELMAN

SLOGANS, SONGS, AND NICKNAMES, POLITICAL

America went through a largely peaceful political revolution—the expansion of voting rights—during the first half of the nineteenth century. By 1850 almost all white male adults were able to vote. These newly enfranchised voters were fiercely independent and quick to assert their equality. They embraced the promise of the Declaration of Independence—life, liberty, and the pursuit of happiness—and scorned aristocratic pretensions, real or imagined. The birth of mass political parties was an outgrowth of this trend. Politicians realized the power of the new voters to win elections and solicited their support by means that would have alarmed the founders, who hoped that elections would be characterized by measured debate and calm deliberation.

The use of political songs, slogans, and nicknames was an important part of the robust politics of American democracy in the nineteenth century. Designed to attract the attention, capture the imagination, and stir the emotions of the public, they were used by political parties to win the loyalty and the ballots of voters. Almost unknown at the century's beginning, by 1900 they were a universal and popular part of electioneering.

During the nineteenth century, the use of songs, slogans, and nicknames took place in the context of a wide range of campaign events and practices. For instance, most newspapers were affiliated with political parties and used their columns and editorial pages to boost the candidates of their choice. Moreover, during national elections, party organizers established hundreds of ad hoc periodicals to promote their campaigns. Flattering campaign biographies extolling candidates' virtues were standard features of electioneering. One of the most famous, of Abraham Lincoln, was written in 1860 by William Dean Howells (1837–1920), who later became a distinguished editor and novelist. Torchlight parades, tent meetings, and party rallies featuring bands, floats, fireworks, and patriotic images aroused the party faithful. Rallies and meetings were often held in conjunction with outdoor barbecues at which thousands were fed while listening to the party pitch. Candidate debates—the Lincoln-Douglas debates of the 1858 Illinois senate race were the most famous—drew enormous crowds.

The presidential candidates were not expected to campaign, on the theory that the office sought the man. Instead, they traditionally remained at home, issuing occasional statements and receiving delegations of supporters. Democratic candidate Stephen A. Douglas (1813–1861) was an early exception to this practice, traveling extensively from New England and the Midwest to the Deep South in the months leading up to the election of 1860. The custom was not seriously challenged again until 1896, when Democratic nominee William Jennings Bryan (1860–1925) campaigned across the country by train, covering eighteen thousand miles and delivering 569 speeches in the first of his three bids for the presidency.

Antebellum Politics

The new mass politics collided most dramatically with the established political culture when Andrew Jackson lost the presidency to John Adams in 1824. Jackson's supporters denounced the result, in a memorable and popular phrase, as a "corrupt bargain" between Speaker of the House Henry Clay (1777–1852) and Adams. Jackson's partisans, adopting the name the Democratic Party, plotted revenge in the election of 1828. They extolled the frontier roots of the candidate. His nickname, Old Hickory, in tribute to his physical toughness, contrasted his origins with those of the educated and reserved Adams. One of the first popular election songs of the century, "*The Jackson Toast,*" sung to the tune of "*Auld Lang Syne,*" dated from the 1828 election struggle:

> Though Adams now misrules the land,
> And strives t' oppress the free
> He must soon yield his high command
> Unto "Old Hickory"

The Democratic Party acquired its first symbol during Jackson's administration: a hickory pole and a broom, signifying a clean sweep against Adams and his National Republicans. Party symbols were useful at a time when many voters were illiterate. Ballots were customarily distributed at the polls by party officials, were often printed in distinctive colors, and featured the party emblem prominently; voters needed to know only the symbol to make their choice. In the 1840s, the broom and hickory pole gave way to the Democratic rooster, a symbol whose origins are uncertain. One legend attributes it to James Chapman, an Indiana Democratic leader whose "crowing" roused the party faithful.

By the mid-1830s, opposition to Jackson coalesced into the Whig Party. In 1840 the Whigs nominated William Henry Harrison (1773–1841) of Ohio for the presidency. Harrison, who had won the battle of Tippecanoe against a confederacy of Indian tribes in 1811, was lionized as the Log Cabin Candidate who enjoyed hard cider, though in reality he came from a distinguished Virginia family and, like Jackson, was a wealthy farmer. His running mate, John Tyler (1790–1862), contributed his name to one of the most famous campaign slogans of American history: Tippecanoe and Tyler Too. The Whigs portrayed their candidate as a humble workingman, contrasting him with the aristocratic President Martin Van Buren. Whig Party headquarters throughout the country featured log cabins, and hard cider was served at cam-

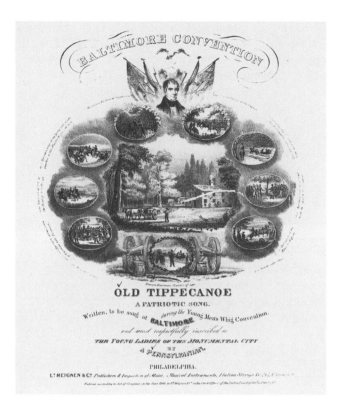

Campaign Sheet Music. A song and an illustration celebrating the military exploits of William Henry Harrison, Whig presidential candidate, 1840. LIBRARY OF CONGRESS: MUSIC DIVISION

paign rallies. Harrison triumphed, and his successful election effort became a model for future campaigns.

In 1844, the Democrats' nominee for president was the former Speaker of the House James Polk (1795–1849), dubbed Young Hickory for his Tennessee origins. Polk campaigned for American occupation of Oregon, parts of which were claimed by Britain, and the annexation of Texas. In a time of nationalist expansionism, termed "Manifest Destiny" by a journalist of the day, his popular proposals became enduring election slogans as Fifty-four Forty or Fight, a reference to the line of latitude defining the American claim in Oregon, and the immortal Remember the Alamo. Polk won the election, achieved his goals, and retired in 1848.

The unsuccessful Whig standard-bearer in 1844 was Henry Clay, making his third and last unsuccessful run for the presidency. He stirred strong emotions among the voters, earning the nicknames Prince Hal and the Star of the West from his admirers and the Old Coon (racoon) from friend and foe alike, in sometimes grudging tribute to his durability and political skill.

One of the many popular Clay campaign songs was set to the chorus of "Yankee Doodle":

For farmer Clay, then boys, hurrah
And proudly here proclaim him,
The great, the good, the valiant Hal
And shout whene'er you name him.

Campaign songs were usually set to popular melodies that were familiar to most people. "Yankee Doodle" was widely used, as were "Auld Lang Syne," "Wait for the Wagon," and "The Star-spangled Banner."

During the 1850s, the Whigs fractured, largely due to disagreements over slavery. Although the Democrats temporarily avoided this fate, they later broke into southern and northern factions. By the middle of the decade, a new party opposed to the expansion of slavery emerged—the Republicans, a name that recalled the Jeffersonian Republicans of early in the century. The party's original emblem, adopted in pointed contrast to the Democratic rooster, was the majestic American eagle.

The crucial presidential election of the century came in 1860. Four candidates—representing the two Democratic factions, a group favoring compromise, and the Republicans, who nominated the Illinois lawyer Abraham Lincoln—contested the election. With his rough-hewn features, Lincoln fit almost perfectly the model of the frontier statesman of humble origins. He was hailed as Honest Abe and the Rail-splitter, and his image was featured on countless posters and broadsides. Once again, campaign literature downplayed the fact that he was a prosperous attorney.

Two years earlier, a series of electrifying events led to the creation of perhaps the greatest political anthem in American history. In 1859, the abolitionist John Brown (1800–1859) seized the federal arsenal at Harpers Ferry, Virginia (now West Virginia), and proclaimed a slave uprising. He and his companions were quickly overpowered, and Brown was convicted of treason and hanged. In death, he became a martyr to the antislavery cause, and abolitionists soon put the words "John Brown's body lies a mouldering in the grave, but his truth goes marching on" to an earlier melody. Retitled and given new lyrics by Julia Ward Howe (1819–1910), "The Battle-Hymn of the Republic" became the most popular Union marching song of the war. Other songs of the war years were "We're Coming Father Abraham, Six Hundred Thousand More" and "Rally 'Round the Flag." For their part, southerners quickly adopted "Dixie," a popular minstrel song, as the unofficial anthem of the Confederacy.

Another political song popularized during the Civil War was "Hail to the Chief," with lyrics from Sir Walter Scott's poem "The Lady of the Lake" set to music attributed [sic] to James Sanderson. Played to announce presidents as early as 1845, the words became quickly forgotten, but the tune itself became so closely associated with the chief executive during Lincoln's administration that it was later reserved for the president's exclusive use.

As Lincoln guided the Union to victory, he implemented the emancipation of black slaves, first as a wartime expedient in rebellious states through the Emancipation Proclamation of 1863 and later throughout the nation by the Thirteenth Amendment to the Constitution, ratified in 1865. Assassinated on 14 April 1865, Lincoln gained the posthumous title the Great Emancipator. As President Lincoln died, Secretary of War Edwin Stanton (1814–1869) made the memorable remark "Now he belongs to the ages."

The Civil War continued to influence national politics throughout the balance of the century. Southerners referred to the Confederacy as the "lost cause," while northern Republicans repeatedly called attention to their party's wartime role by "waving the bloody shirt," accusing the Democrats of supporting secession and abetting the South.

After the War

The great political cartoonist Thomas Nast (1840–1902) bestowed new and enduring emblems on both the Democratic and Republican parties in the 1870s. He depicted the Democrats as a donkey in a cartoon that appeared in *Harper's Weekly* magazine in 1870, while the Republican elephant made its first appearance in the same publication in 1874. Although neither original caricature was flattering, the party faithful invested them with noble characteristics and adopted them as revered symbols. During the same period, the Republicans were known in the press as the "Grand Old Party"; in 1884, the *New York Tribune* abbreviated the sobriquet as "GOP" to save space in a headline, inventing a durable political acronym.

The GOP dominated the presidency in the last decades of the century in a series of closely contested elections. There were Democratic victories, however, such as the election of 1884, in which Republican candidate, James G. Blaine (1830–1893), known as the Plumed Knight for his dignified bearing and noble presence, faced a Democrat of decidedly less distinguished appearance, Grover Cleveland (1837–1908), who was accused of having fathered a child out of wedlock in his youth. This charge led to perhaps the most famous doggerel of the century, as Republicans chanted, "Ma, ma, where's my pa?" Democrats countered the attack when it was learned that a prominent Blaine supporter had called them the party

of "rum, Romanism [Catholicism], and rebellion." These slurs were widely publicized in Irish Catholic communities and the South and contributed materially to Cleveland's razor-thin margin of victory. Moreover, Blaine compounded the damage by failing to rupudiate the remark until three days before the election. Democrats then had the last laugh, completing the Republican doggerel with a final line, "Ma, ma, where's my pa? Gone to the White House, ha, ha, ha."

As the century drew to a close, the United States was mired in a deep economic depression, attributed by many to the nation's strict adherence to the gold standard. In 1896, the Democratic National Convention was stampeded by a thirty-six-year-old Nebraskan, William Jennings Bryan (1860–1925), who demanded coinage of silver money to revive the economy. Bryan's speech ("You shall not crucify mankind upon a cross of gold") electrified the convention and led to his nomination for president. Known as the Great Commoner and the Boy Orator of the Platte, Bryan campaigned across the nation, and the Democrats adopted Free Silver at Sixteen to One as their slogan. The GOP chose William McKinley (1843–1901) as its nominee, on a platform promising workers to restore the "full dinner pail" and prosperity by raising tariffs on imports. In contrast to Bryan, McKinley conducted a "front porch" campaign from his home in Canton, Ohio, speaking to delegations of voters brought in by special trains. His well-financed organization gained victory over Bryan, inaugurating a period of Republican political dominance that lasted well into the twentieth century.

The relative peace and prosperity of McKinley's first administration was shattered on 15 February, 1898, when the U.S. battleship *Maine* suddenly exploded while at anchor in the harbor of Havana, Cuba. Although no cause for the explosion was ever established, a number of American newspapers blamed Spain and called for war. Initially reluctant, McKinley was subjected to increasing pressure as the "yellow press" popularized the memorable rallying cry Remember the *Maine*! When Spain refused U.S. demands to end the insurrection, Congress declared war. American forces triumphed, and the United States entered the twentieth century as a newly recognized power. The force of a political slogan had transformed the nation's role in the world.

See also **Cartoons, Political; Elections,** *subentries on* **Campaigns and Elections, Presidential Elections; Politics,** *subentry on* **Parties and the Press.**

Bibliography

Dinkin, Robert J. *Campaigning in America: A History of Election Practices*. New York: Greenwood Press, 1989.

Kelly, Kate. *Election Day: An American Holiday, An American History.* New York: Facts on File, 1991.

Nevins, Allan, and Frank Weitenkampf. *A Century of Political Cartoons: Caricature in the United States from 1800 to 1900.* New York: Scribners, 1944.

Nichols, Roy F. "It Happens Every Four Years." *American Heritage* 7, no. 4 (June 1956): 20–33. Includes illustrations of election paraphernalia.

Safire, William. *Safire's New Political Dictionary: The Definitive Guide to the New Language of Politics.* New York: Random House, 1993. A comprehensive contemporary and historical collection of political slogans, phrases, and practices.

Shankle, George Earlie. *American Mottoes and Slogans.* New York: Wilson, 1941.

Silber, Erwin. *Songs America Voted By.* Harrisburg, Pa.: Stackpole Books, 1971.

Weisberger, Bernard. "How to Get Elected." *American Heritage* 15, no. 5 (August 1964): 62–77. Includes illustrations of election paraphernalia.

THOMAS H. NEALE

SMALL BUSINESSES   Prior to the Civil War the term "small business" was a redundancy. Nearly all businesses employed only a few people and served a limited number of customers. The vast majority were organized not as corporations but as sole proprietorships and partnerships with owners acting as hands-on managers.

By the 1880s technical and organizational breakthroughs had allowed large corporations to emerge in a number of industries, including railroads, textiles, flour, meatpacking, rubber, iron, and steel. Small businesses did not disappear, of course, not even in manufacturing. In fact small establishments increased in absolute numbers in all sectors of the economy, and in 1900 they employed nearly two-thirds of working Americans. The economy remained hospitable to new business formations, as demonstrated by the fact that in the last three decades of the century the country's population doubled while the number of businesses tripled. Still, the rise of big business undeniably changed the status and prospects of small enterprises as well as the public's ideas about their cultural significance.

Characteristics of Small Businesses

Painting a detailed picture of small businesses in the nineteenth century is difficult because the national census data is incomplete, especially for the first seven decades. The existing information concerns specific firms and industries, types of business owners (such as immigrants and women), or communities. Definitional problems also hinder attempts at synthesis. Historians have used a functionalist definition, in which "small" means that a business was simply structured and personally managed by its owner. But can a manufacturing plant employing more than one hundred workers really be considered small? On the other end of the scale, should the definition include barbers, peddlers, craftspeople, boardinghouse keepers, and other self-employed individuals?

A few generalizations are possible, however. Agriculture was the largest sector of the economy for most of the century, and small family farms produced the bulk of foodstuffs. Historians have disagreed about whether or not farmers should be classed as small businesspeople, particularly during the earlier decades. Even in the colonial era many American farmers displayed businesslike traits, including avidly speculating on land. When domestic and foreign demand for American meat and grain exploded during the antebellum period, farmers participated in the market and tried to run their farms more efficiently and profitably. By mid-century family farms in the Midwest and the Northeast produced substantial surpluses—two to three times subsistence level—and earned an estimated 12 percent return on investment. In the last three decades of the century all but one-quarter of American exports consisted of farm goods, and large corporate farms of one thousand or more acres had emerged in the West and the Great Plains. Yet even in 1900 the average farm was small, consisting of 146 acres of which only 72 were cultivated.

Small firms thrived in the service sector. By the 1830s banking and insurance, functions previously performed by merchants, had become businesses in their own right. Most operated as single-unit establishments. By 1861 more than half the states had passed free banking laws, making it easier for entrepreneurs to start banks. As a result and in contrast to most other countries at the time, the number of small independent banks soared. In 1866 the United States had two thousand banks, and in 1900 the country had more than twelve thousand, most of them small local enterprises. The distribution function, too, split into its component functions: retail, wholesale, export, and import. Small establishments were especially numerous in retail, which required relatively low capital investment for entry and which remained open to different individuals, including women, recent immigrants, ethnic minorities, and blacks. In 1839 the United States had more than fifty-seven thousand retail stores with an average capital investment per store of $4,350. This figure included goods bought on credit from larger suppliers, who in effect provided a large portion of the start-up and working capital for storekeepers. Even though large department and chain stores appeared after the Civil War, the small general store remained a fixture of American life until well into the twentieth century.

No sector was more profoundly affected by the rise of big business than manufacturing. By 1904 a mere handful of large corporations accounted for half of the output in seventy-eight industries. Even so, such industries as furniture, apparel, leather, lumber, and the construction trades never developed adequate economies of scale during the nineteenth century and therefore remained the domain of small firms. In the clothing and shoe industries, many firms remained technically small because they outsourced ("put out") much of the actual sewing and assembly to households, who were paid by the piece. Sometimes companies in the same industry but in different locations exhibited divergent patterns. For example, by mid-century textile mills had become large in New England but remained small in the Philadelphia area. As large firms became more powerful, small manufacturers employed new strategies to survive, including serving as suppliers and subcontractors to their larger brethren. Successful small manufacturers in textiles and steel employed advanced or specialized technology to exploit niches that larger firms could not efficiently serve.

Cultural Significance

Because most small businesses were single-unit operations, they were strongly identified with their particular communities. Local business owners were among their towns' most prominent boosters and were active in civic and cultural affairs. Small businesses also allowed marginalized groups to participate in the economy. At a time when women were shut out of most areas of the public sphere and some ethnic groups and all blacks faced substantial discrimination, small business ownership provided a means of survival and the basis for a sense of personal accomplishment or failure.

In the last two decades of the century Americans developed a nostalgic regard for small businesses, seeing them as the last bastions of personal and financial independence as well as important transmitters of family, community, and artisanal values. At the same time, however, Americans welcomed the many new products and opportunities that big business made possible. An uneasy, although often mutually beneficial, relationship developed between large and small enterprises. The tensions continued into the twentieth century, which saw increased political activity on behalf of small business owners.

See also **Agriculture; Banking and Finance,** *subentry on* **The Banking Industry; Boosterism; Corporations and Big Business; Entrepreneurs; Entrepreneurs, Women.**

Bibliography

Atherton, Lewis E. *The Frontier Merchant in Mid-America.* Columbia: University of Missouri Press, 1971.
Blackford, Mansel G. *A History of Small Business in America.* New York: Twayne Publishers, 1991.
Bruchey, Stuart, ed. *Small Business in American Life.* New York: Columbia University Press, 1980.
Gamber, Wendy. *The Female Economy: The Millinery and Dressmaking Trades, 1860–1930.* Urbana: University of Illinois Press, 1997.

ROWENA OLEGARIO

SOCIAL CLASS.   See **Class, Social.**

SOCIAL DARWINISM.   See **Biology; Race and Racial Thinking; Sociology.**

SOCIAL GOSPEL   The Social Gospel was a religiously based movement for social change that began around 1865 and lasted roughly until the outbreak of World War II. While owing most of its initial impulse and original theology to Protestantism, the movement included initiatives for social change within Judaism and Roman Catholicism as well. For Christians the Social Gospel expressed the social side of a perennial tension in their religion between seeking the salvation of the individual soul and seeking the redemption of the human community. Premillennialists, Adventists, and millennialists had stressed the rescue of individuals from personal sin. Postmillennialists, who comprised most of the Social Gospelists, were often evangelically inspired and stressed the importance of establishing the kingdom of God on Earth in the form of a whole society built on principles of economic and social justice. As Shailer Mathers put it (in his article "Social Gospel" in *A Dictionary of Religion and Ethics* in 1921), the gospel was intended to be applied to "society, the economic life, and social institutions . . . as well as to individuals."

The earliest Protestant Social Gospelists, the clergymen Washington Gladden (1836–1918), called the "father of the Social Gospel," and Walter Rauschenbusch (1861–1918), reacted against what they took to be the rampant social injustices caused by an unregulated capitalism and the individualistic philosophy that undergirded it. The unprecedented wealth accumulated by industrial entrepreneurs in the years after the Civil War left grinding poverty for the workers whose labor made that wealth possible. The effects of this unjust distribution of economic and po-

Walter Rauschenbusch

Rauschenbusch was the most important articulator of the theology of the Social Gospel during its mature period at the turn of the century. His exposure to the poverty surrounding his first parish in Hell's Kitchen, New York City, stimulated him to address the problems of the working class. He helped publish a workingman's newspaper, *For the Right,* and later brought the Brotherhood of the Kingdom group into existence. When deafness caused him to step back from direct involvement in the movement, he drew upon the emerging biblical scholarship in Europe to support his conviction that the primary message of Scripture was one of prophecy against unjust social exploitation. He argued that Jesus must be seen as a revolutionary prophet who put love and social justice higher than property and self. Jesus proclaimed not just an individual salvation but the establishment of a "kingdom" of God in the world to be led into existence by the forces of labor.

The publication in 1907 of Rauschenbusch's book *Christianity and the Social Crisis* began a process of applying gospel principles to social causes that was continued in his *Christianizing the Social Order* (1912). Both books subjected capitalism to detailed criticism. Capitalism, according to Rauschenbusch, was based on the individualistic notion of competition instead of the biblical notions of love and justice in community. He called for the creation of a Christian economic order that would be marked by collective property rights, industrial democracy, approximate economic equality, cooperation between capital and labor, and governmental regulation of the workplace. An optimist, he concluded *Christianity and the Social Crisis* with these words:

> Perhaps these nineteen centuries of Christian influence have been a long preliminary stage of growth, and now the flower and fruit are almost here. If at this juncture we can rally sufficient religious faith and moral strength to snap the bonds of evil and turn the present unparalleled economic and intellectual resources of humanity to the harmonious development of a true social life, the generations yet unborn will mark this as that great day of the Lord for which the ages waited, and count us blessed for sharing in the apostolate that proclaimed it.

In one of his final books, *A Theology for the Social Gospel* (1917), he tried to wed the movement's social message with an evangelical foundation for each individual who would embrace it. He argued that sin is selfishness and that the institutions of society, not just individuals, can embody this selfishness, for example in slavery and capitalism, and become sinful. Many nonreligious activists agreed with the social critique but not the evangelical notion of sin, while more traditional religious persons accepted the evangelical foundation without the commitment to social justice. Rauschenbusch's latent perfectionism was ultimately rejected by "Christian realist" critics, such as Reinhold Niebuhr. Not until the mid–twentieth century did Rauschenbusch's optimistic call for social change become once again a rallying point for many Christian activists, such as Martin Luther King Jr.

litical power were seen most often in the burgeoning cities that were attracting millions of immigrants as well as migrants from the American countryside. As long as religious teaching focused on the salvation of individual souls, no sustained criticism of the dominant economic and social policies was possible. The theology that justified concentration of wealth in the hands of a few while urging the poor to work their own way out of poverty had come to be known as the "Gospel of Wealth." The Social Gospel sought to shift the emphasis of moral accountability to the social order as a whole and away from exclusive reliance on the individual.

A cause that initially attracted the Social Gospelists was the right of workingmen to organize into unions, then implacably resisted by corporate employers. Worker protests, beginning with the railroad strikes of 1877, forced many church people to question the oppressive working conditions that led the strikers to such desperate actions.

The Social Gospel was never a single, unified movement. It spawned a number of different groups, some of which overlapped with secular progressive groups in the American political arena. Because most of the Social Gospelists took politics seriously as an avenue for reform, they were not averse to joining political parties, but few embraced the parties uncritically or abandoned their primary religious allegiances. Some Social Gospelists created action groups to put their principles into practice. One of the most influential of these was the Church Association for the Advancement of the Interests of Labor, founded in 1887. The association defined labor as the sole standard of social worth and called upon its members to use the press to advance its point of view, to vote on labor issues, and to require churches to do business only with companies that met its criteria for just relations with laborers. Another group, the Brotherhood of the Kingdom, lasted for twenty years as a study and fellowship community for Protestant clergy struggling to address the social issues of the time. Arguably its most important member was Rauschenbusch, whose writings, especially *Christianity and the Social Crisis* (1907) and *A Theology for the Social Gospel* (1917), summarized and gave theological depth to the movement.

Drawing upon precedents in Great Britain, such as the Christian Socialist movement in the 1840s and 1850s, American Social Gospelists made much use of emerging scientific, especially sociological, data to buttress their religious arguments against the injustices of the industrial order. The economist Richard T. Ely (1854–1943) was one of the leading Social Gospel writers whose analyses proved useful to the movement. Two Protestant ministers, W. D. P. Bliss (1856–1926) and George Davis Herron (1862–1925), combined hard data with organizing skill to put the themes of the Social Gospel into action. Bliss called his views "Christian socialism" and founded the Society of Christian Socialists in 1889. Herron called for a "Christian state" based on the principle of social sacrifice, which meant a public ownership of the means of production. But even the Social Gospelists most committed to the welfare of the working class never embraced doctrinaire Marxism because of its perceived hostility to religion.

The involvement of the Roman Catholic Church in the Social Gospel debate resulted largely from Pope Leo XIII's encyclical "Rerum novarum" (1891), in which he argued for a middle road between socialism and unregulated free enterprise in which government would make the promotion of human welfare its highest priority.

The Jewish community, especially under the leadership of Rabbi Stephen S. Wise (1874–1949), also made contributions to the Social Gospel movement. Wise attacked an economic system that permitted some to gather up great wealth while others were denied the opportunity to obtain even basic necessities for themselves and their families.

In the decades after World War I the legacy of the Social Gospel was carried into a number of church agencies, among them the Federal Council of Churches, which adopted a social creed in 1908. However, the movement never made strong inroads into the working class whose interests it claimed to champion, in large part because it never fully accepted the necessity of permanent countervailing power within the political process. Its proponents never gave up hope that love would eventually melt the hearts of the antagonistic classes. Also, because it was often allied with liberalism in theology, the movement failed to address the growing desire of evangelicals for a more personal, individual gospel of salvation squarely rooted in a conservative or fundamentalist reading of the Bible.

See also **Millennialism and Adventism; Reform, Social; Religion;** *subentry on* **Religion in Nineteenth-Century America.**

Bibliography

Abell, Aaron I. *American Catholicism and Social Action.* Notre Dame, Ind.: University of Notre Dame Press, 1963.

Handy, Robert T., ed. *The Social Gospel in America, 1870–1920.* New York: Oxford University Press, 1966.

Hopkins, C. Howard. *The Rise of the Social Gospel in American Protestantism, 1865–1915.* New Haven, Conn.: Yale University Press, 1940.

May, Henry F. *Protestant Churches and Industrial America.* New York: Harper and Row, 1949.

Phillips, Paul T. *A Kingdom on Earth: Anglo-American Social Christianity, 1880–1940.* University Park: Pennsylvania State University Press, 1996.

Rauschenbusch, Walter. *Christianity and the Social Crisis.* Edited by Robert D. Cross. 1907. Reprint, New York: Harper and Row, 1964.

White, Ronald C., and C. Howard Hopkins, eds. *The Social Gospel: Religion and Reform in Changing America.* Philadelphia: Temple University Press, 1976.

FRANK G. KIRKPATRICK

SOCIALIST MOVEMENTS.   See **Radicalism.**

SOCIAL LIFE

[This entry includes subentries on **Rural Social Life** and **Urban Social Life.**]

RURAL SOCIAL LIFE

All celebrated the Fourth. Picnic at Allentown. Stopt for Matthew Allen's folks but found Aunt Lucy unwell so made a visit instead. Ice cream 15 cents, just for

Juddie and Lucy Ann, but I suppose for a good cause too. Ida off somewheres with Bert. Mostly long, dull speeches, tho Marshall Delano talked about the Grange depot where farmers can get the worth of their money. Good Templars sang, Maine band played marches. Married men beat young men at baseball for once. Home at chore time. In eve, went to Union with Bert's folks to see the fireworks, a poor display. Must be up early next morning for haying. (Diary of George Riley, 4 July 1876, Nanticoke Valley Historical Society, Maine, New York)

Went down to Maine, got a little fireworks for the children, Lucy made ice cream and we had a fine time with our neighbors in the evening. (Diary of George Riley, 4 July 1887)

George Riley's celebrations of the Fourth of July in 1876 and 1887 typify the range of social activities that flourished in rural communities. On the nation's centennial (though he did not remark the year) George, his wife Lucy Ann, their young son Judson, their newlywed daughter Ida, and her husband Bert all attended a community-wide picnic at Allentown, near their farm in Maine, New York. The Rileys first visited his elderly relatives and then participated in events organized by local groups. The Women's Benevolent Society of the Methodist Church made the ice cream, and the proceeds funded improvements to the church building and the parsonage. While the partisan political speeches passed George by, the speech by the storekeeper who represented the Patrons of Husbandry aroused his interest. Lucy Ann and George were active Grange members and had attended its educational programs since 1874, but this was the local farmers' first venture into cooperative purchasing. Soon Grange members set up a cooperative creamery as well. Temperance songs and a band formed by Civil War veterans provided entertainment. The annual baseball game pitted fathers and uncles against sons and nephews. Riley's rheumatism kept him on the sidelines, but he rejoiced in the married men's rare triumph over the single men. In the evening the family traveled down Nanticoke Creek to the village of Union for a disappointing fireworks display. Finally, George's day was punctuated by barn chores and framed by thoughts of work. July Fourth signified the beginning of haying season as much as it did the anniversary of American independence. Like many farmers, the Rileys celebrated before rather than after a bout of intense work because, when the job was finished, all hands would be much too tired for merrymaking.

The Riley's celebration of the Fourth in 1887 was less formal and more local. Ida and Bert Davey had young children on the farm next door. If the Rileys and Daveys had gone to the celebration in Maine or Binghamton, a longer journey "over the hill," Ida or Lucy Ann would have had to stay home to care for the baby, violating the first, unwritten rule of rural social life: no one was to be left out. So the Rileys, the Daveys, and their stay-at-home neighbors, including their friends from Mount Ettrick, the settlement at the top of the hill, made their own celebration, with ice cream and firecrackers. The Hoags, from a family of famous Scottish poets, recited some verses made up for the occasion. One set of verses humorously described the dozens of cousins who shared first names because "their fathers were brothers, their mothers sisters, and their grandparents all the same." Another sentimentally retold the story of emigration, as the children sadly bade good-bye to their "aulde house" in Scotland. The spontaneity and inclusiveness of this gathering and the participants' ability to improvise entertainment typify the sociability of open-country neighborhoods during the nineteenth century.

Both the communitywide observance of 1876 and the neighborhood celebration in 1887 brought together men and women, parents and children, old and young, and "folks and friends"—that is, relatives and neighbors. Farm labor was customarily divided by gender, business and politics were usually the provinces of men, and caregiving and charity were primarily the responsibilities of women, but social life united rural residents across all these lines of division. Farmers with rich valley land dressed as modestly as the hardscrabble hill dwellers, and storekeepers acted as if they were unaware of the balance between credits and debits in their account books. Even neighbors who deliberately avoided working together sat next to each other at dish-to-pass suppers. Protestant churches held fund-raising socials that members of other Protestant denominations and even Catholics were welcome—indeed, expected—to attend. Opposing political parties debated controversial questions, such as "female influence" and the money supply, in a spirit of good fellowship.

Only whites' racist exclusion of blacks withstood the power of sociability. Since most rural communities in the North and Midwest were segregated by race, this exclusion was seldom visible to white people. African Americans in the North recorded making long journeys to other communities to see their scattered kin and kind. Those living in the South enjoyed the benefits of proximity—at least after emancipation gave them a greater measure of control over their own lives. During slavery days African Americans were permitted to congregate only between sundown and sunup, and often did so in secret, to call on the

Quilting Party. Leisurely community gatherings included people of both sexes, and of varying age, faith, and economic status, despite their segregation in the working world. 1854. LIBRARY OF CONGRESS

spirit with song and dance, bury their dead, and seek hope and consolation. In freedom black churches were centers of social as well as religious life, and mutual aid encompassed both work and worship. Those who gathered on Sundays to praise God also shared their burdens and their joys throughout the week.

The social rituals of rural communities varied with their cultural inheritances, settlement patterns, and work rhythms. The occasions that people who moved from the country to the city remembered most fondly—barn raisings, quilting bees, and harvest dances—had already shifted from labor to leisure. Rural residents followed the fads and fashions of popular culture not only as spectators but also as participants. Traveling theater companies staged "home talent" plays, for example, and handbooks for ladies' aid societies introduced new themes for church socials. The "play-party songs" recommended for those forbidden to dance resembled the ring shout. White Oklahomans had no idea that their circular, hand-clapping shuffle originated in Africa. The "shivaree," a raucous ritual that interrupted couples on their wedding nights, originated in the charivari, a community sanction against unacceptable couplings in early modern Europe. In nineteenth-century America the practice celebrated legitimate marital pleasure with a round of treats. A masculine culture of drinking, gambling, and commercial sex flourished in lumber and mining camps, but those were isolated subcultures. Flirting and courting, games of chance and skill, and sharing of food and drink were integrated into the family-based, gender-mixed, intergenerational, and cross-class forms of social life that characterized rural America.

See also **African Americans; Class, Social; Clubs; Country Fairs; Holidays; Music; Popular Culture; Recreation; Revolutionary War Remembered; Slavery,** *subentry on* **Slave Life; Social Life,** *subentry on* **Urban Social Life; Theater.**

Bibliography

Bethel, Elizabeth Rauh. *Promiseland: A Century of Life in a Negro Community.* Philadelphia: Temple University Press, 1981.

Hansen, Karen V. *A Very Social Time: Crafting Community in Antebellum New England.* Berkeley: University of California Press, 1994.

Joyner, Charles. *Down by the Riverside: A South Carolina Slave Community.* Urbana: University of Illinois Press, 1984.

Matsumoto, Valerie J. *Farming the Home Place: A Japanese American Community in California, 1919–1982.* Ithaca, N.Y.: Cornell University Press, 1993.

Neth, Mary. *Preserving the Family Farm: Women, Community, and the Foundations of Agribusiness in the Midwest, 1900–1940.* Baltimore: Johns Hopkins University Press, 1995.

Osterud, Nancy Grey. *Bonds of Community: The Lives of Farm Women in Nineteenth-Century New York.* Ithaca, N.Y.: Cornell University Press, 1991.

GREY OSTERUD

URBAN SOCIAL LIFE

At the beginning of the nineteenth century the social life of most Americans was rooted in the economic dynamics and social structures of rural communities or small villages or market towns of fewer than a thousand people. The only cities in the United States were the old colonial port towns that developed through trade with Britain over the course of the eighteenth century. Among them, only New York City had begun to grow rapidly as a commercial center. While its increasingly diversified economy accelerated differentiation by wealth and social status, however, most New Yorkers lived, worked, and socialized in densely occupied neighborhoods, where face-to-face social interaction predominated. In New York and other cities, towns, and even rural villages a small elite, usually descendants of the early founders of the place, maintained social leadership by holding public office; supporting and managing churches, associations, and institutions; and living genteel material lives. Beneath them in status, a mixed group of larger farmers, professionals, entrepreneurs, and clergy referred to as the "middling sort" were paragons of "good society" who lived stoic, frugal, and simple material lives. In some towns and larger cities "good society" also included master craftspeople, journeymen, and apprentices. Bound to each other within the craft shop by a web of reciprocal social obligations, they produced bespoken goods by hand for a limited market to achieve a certain level of "competency." Those unable to achieve artisan status belonged to a broader, lower social group that included laborers, farm workers, tenant farmers, free blacks, widows, slaves, and the poor.

Though some towns and cities were growing well beyond the ability of every resident to know or to know about every other, most people acquired identity and meaning by living within corporate occupational, family, kin, and community networks. At the beginning of the nineteenth century "society" was an organic framework handed down by tradition that most individuals accepted and within which they lived their lives. Identity came from playing a part and fulfilling certain duties and obligations. Though some people became more individualistic and sought social mobility by pursuing self-interests, most accepted their positions, deferred to the elites, and lived according to traditions. Within such a relatively stable society, most events, occasions, and rituals confirmed order rather than defined boundaries. Hence urban social life tended to be more inclusive, varied, and relaxed than later in the century.

The market revolution and industrialization triggered increasing urban growth throughout the nineteenth century. Driven by competition, craftspeople, merchants, professionals, and capitalists, indeed all people, were compelled to use ideas, technological innovations, financial capital, and ultimately intensified personal effort to keep up in the broadening marketplace. On farms as well as in towns and cities market-oriented behavior caused individuals to focus more on their own particular activities and to differentiate them from those of other people. People who succeeded and prevailed over others experienced increased status and wealth. As social differentiation increased, the lines between social groups became more porous, compelling people to draw markers of social identity and boundaries more sharply. Individuals intensified their efforts to socially define and distinguish themselves from "others." Behavior, speech, clothes, education, comportment, housing, and material style became signs of social and cultural identity. In an impersonal society composed mostly of strangers, social status depended largely on an individual's ability to externally or materially demonstrate class through work, consumption, behavior, and institutional affiliation.

During the 1820s and 1830s distinctive upper, middle, and working classes emerged in American towns and cities. The old colonial elite transformed into a patrician capitalist elite or upper class, whose great wealth placed them above an increasingly self-conscious middle class. Middle-class people pursued social mobility and control by living moral, disciplined lives. While middle-class women maintained households in which they focused on raising fewer children, middle-class men worked hard to be breadwinners, fathers, and gentlemen. In their focus on morality, work, and family, middle-class people differed from the rich, whose genteel material culture they admired but whose values they disdained, as well as the working class, whose values and lives they sought to reform and elevate. As middle-class ideology began to shape the center ground of urban society in the 1830s, a working class articulated oppositional values more self-consciously. Working people valued physical labor, unrestrained physical and verbal expression, and patriarchal authority. Lack of domestic privacy, poor housing and material resources, and high birthrates prevented working-class women from creating a separate sphere and establishing a social presence. Working-class men exhibited mastery of themselves and others through aggressive self-expression, sexual prowess, and physical force. Single men in particular manifested these values to flout middle-class ideology. Over time immigrants from across Europe, Latin America, and Asia infiltrated

and transformed this native-born working class. On the bottom edge of the working class were laborers, free blacks, widows, the indigent, and in southern cities slaves. Though their struggle to find jobs and find housing precluded the formation of a self-conscious social identity, free blacks established churches, social networks, associations, and schools that laid the foundations of an African American working-class identity.

For most early nineteenth-century Americans, whether on the farm or in a town or city, social life focused on participation in weekly and monthly rounds of festivities. Families defined culture through constant gatherings, visits, and dinners as well as occasional weddings, christenings, and funerals that

Great Russian Ball, New York City Academy of Music. Grand balls, attended by only the social elite, were characterized by ornate halls and fancy dress. LIBRARY OF CONGRESS

demarcated the cycles of family life. They connected to neighbors and the larger community within the social contexts of religious activities and work. Among both rural and urban people, Sunday services followed by a family or congregation dinner in mid-afternoon was the central social event of most weeks. Before church, town and village residents, dressed in their best clothes, gathered outside the sanctuary to visit and to transact business. The church service was preceded by a procession of members to their respective pews, the proximity to the pulpit and cost of which were directly proportional to social status. Afterward family and friends gathered at the household for a large dinner. Often set on plank tables and in summer out of doors, this ritual meal was usually followed by conversation, singing, and games.

Similar socializing occurred at harvest festivals, barn raisings, quilting bees, and public events, such as Election Days, court days, or county fairs. Racing, hunting, swimming, hiking, riding in hay wagons, and even billiards sometimes accompanied these occasions. If drinking was involved, a "dancing party" or ball with music, dancing, and singing might escalate into a "frolic"—a general merrymaking involving running about or parading through fields or streets accompanied by roughhousing, cheering, and sometimes a good-natured brawl. From such collective frolicking evolved customs of staging parades on regional holidays, such as Evacuation Day or among the black community Emancipation Day in New York City, Pope's Day or Thanksgiving in Massachusetts, Mardi Gras in southern cities like Mobile and New Orleans, or Admission Day in San Francisco; on national holidays, like George Washington's birthday and the Fourth of July; and on religious holidays, such as Christmas. These events were held in the public spaces of the town—the village square, the common fields, the public highways, or main street—and constituted public life in the community. Smaller events were held in the town taverns or coffeehouses, many of which in the early nineteenth century added a "hall" or a "ballroom" to facilitate such occasions and which often served as local social and business centers. Within these venues men formed private social clubs to facilitate learning, promote the town, or plan the development of a public institution. Benjamin Franklin's Friday evening Junto Club or the Wednesday Club in Annapolis were two examples of such clubs that, meeting both in taverns and in private homes, cultivated a public institutional life.

In the larger, more impersonal towns and cities of early-nineteenth-century America the elements of social life distilled into formal events designed for defining social identity and for gate keeping. By the 1820s the urban upper class embraced the court cul-

Coney Island Summer. In this section of Brooklyn, New York, amusements were geared toward classes other than the elite. Cover illustration for *Frank Leslie's Illustrated Newspaper*, July 1886. LIBRARY OF CONGRESS

ture of gentility or "elegant civility" even more than their colonial predecessors. They separated themselves from the lower orders by establishing churches, associations, clubs, theaters, operas, restaurants, and hotels that controlled entrance with high membership dues, tithes, fees, or prices. Each city established a Union Club, the first founded in New York in the 1830s, with strictly limited memberships. Grace, Trinity, and St. Paul's Churches in New York reserved pews for the old elite. Certain hotels, such as the Astor, the St. Nicholas, the Gisley House, or the Waldorf, and restaurants, such as Delmonico's, all in New York, became social institutions where the elegant civility of the upper class reigned.

Members of this old elite further separated themselves from other classes through intermarriage customs, a narrow range of institutional associations, and a precisely orchestrated social season involving an incessant round of parties, balls, charity events, and performances to which only the select few in "society" were invited. Guided by increasingly elaborate rules of etiquette and decorum after the Civil War, those events assured that members of the elite society only met, socialized, and married each other. Minor hierarchies within the narrow social circle determined who was invited to which events, who sat where, who led the cotillion, or who debuted when.

By the 1880s increased numbers of participants made society more impersonal and eroded the ability of even Mrs. John Jacob Astor of New York, who coined the notion of an elite "400," to rule "society." "Blue books," which stated a person's name, residence, calling hours, club memberships, and philanthropic activities, clarified nuances of status. Moreover, society pages tracked elite social events in newspapers from New York to Seattle, providing voyeuristic enjoyment for middle-class readers. Sequestered in exclusive neighborhoods, the elite built increasingly elaborate "art" houses decorated in aristocratic styles. Houses on Fifth Avenue in New York, Du Pont Circle in Washington, D.C., Prairie Avenue in Chicago, and Nob Hill in San Francisco became showpieces of society. Though members of the elite lost political power in most cities by the 1870s and 1880s and their values, tastes, and attitudes drifted away from mainstream American culture, they continued to set the behavioral standards that other classes emulated through the 1890s. The aristocratic beaux-arts style they patronized was for a decade or more the style of public buildings that transformed the appearance of the American metropolis.

Beneath the elite the middle class began to imprint its values and ideals on urban social life. As people in middling occupations achieved economic mobility, they sought ways to secure and display that achievement socially. Borrowing from the elite, they adopted modest versions of the culture of gentility to differentiate their family and group social occasions from those of the working class. As urban society became more impersonal and individuals knew fewer people, social occasions in general became more exclusive and private. The construction of more formal housing in the federal and Italianate styles, with differentiated parlors, dining rooms, and sometimes a ballroom, enabled middle-class and upper-middle-class people to emulate the elite with soirees, parties, and balls.

Where appropriate houses had not yet been built, such as in western towns, balls or parties were held at the best hotel in town. Sometimes called "bachelor assembly balls" because men often outnumbered women five to one, these affairs became more formal and charged admission to maintain some control over the door. Though usually held on holidays, for instance, the Washington's birthday ball was a commonplace social occasion in mid-century, they were not held as frequently and were not guided by as rigid rules as elite balls. Most middle-class people socialized with each other in an increasingly structured private social realm.

To increase the frequency of socializing and to define social sets more securely, middle-class Americans adopted the English tactic of forming clubs. In the diverse and crowded cities, circles of middle-class men could no longer count on privacy in taverns and coffeehouses. For a while many men retreated to their private homes and held meetings of reading and philanthropic clubs in family parlors. This practice continued for smaller clubs in most cities throughout the century. In small towns and cities men's discussion groups, given a wide variety of locally meaningful names like Kent, Lotus, and Round Table, met in the private homes of members. Clubs that grew too large or had a more public purpose sought more public venues. Sometimes clubs, like the ubiquitous Commercial Club, met in the public rooms of hotels or rented rooms or halls in commercial buildings downtown. As the next step they established these rooms as permanent clubhouses. By the 1850s richer clubs in the cities occupied or built clubhouses downtown.

This proliferation of club culture among middle-class men included the establishment or reinvigoration of fraternal associations. The Masons, the International Order of Odd Fellows, the Red Men, the Knights of Pythias, the Knights Templars, and the Elks were founded or revived during the 1860s through the 1890s. By the 1890s, when as many as one in five middle-class men were members, mutual benefit and service associations, such as the Rotary Foundation, the Lions, the Ancient Order of Workmen, or the Modern Woodmen of America, and ethnic associations, such as the Knights of Columbus and B'nai Brith, filled out their ranks. Each of these clubs added rituals, costumes, secret meetings, and nicknames to their activities to enhance the meaning of membership. Likewise from the 1830s on urban men founded athletic clubs and specialized horse racing, sailing, tennis, hunting, or golf clubs, providing private spaces within which members pursued their social and recreational goals.

Some of these clubs, taking the lead from elite clubs, provided food, mostly lunch, as middle-class men working downtown demanded better eating establishments. The traditional gentleman's restaurant, a more comfortable alternative to the dark and smoky tavern, improved eating out somewhat, but few women ever went to such establishments. For most of the century the primary place to dine in public was in a hotel, usually at a banquet for a specific occasion, or for the elite in a private club. The banquet emerged as a key part of public celebrations by the 1820s. Larger hotels, with larger public rooms and kitchens, made such events more feasible. With the formation of professional associations after the Civil War, banquets in large urban hotels became ubiquitous events. Elections, holidays, openings of canals, visits of dignitaries to a city, railroad excursions, and annual or monthly meetings of clubs, professional associations, or the chamber of commerce all warranted a banquet. By the 1870s, following the elite style, printed invitations were sent to hundreds of guests for a several course meal, and the table was elaborately set with printed menus and badges or name tags in a decorated room. Until late in the century banquets were predominantly all-male events. Since much drinking and cigar smoking accompanied speeches and toasts, banquets often grew loud and raucous. This was especially true of "roasts," all-male banquets at which a series of speakers sarcastically mocked a person or event before some bawdy entertainment came on. As the occasions for banquets broadened to include more decorous meetings of reform associations, philanthropic societies, churches, and charity events, both men and women attended, and some banquets were held exclusively for women.

In general the banquet remained the primary site of public dining. Not until the 1870s and 1880s did a real choice among genteel restaurants appear in American cities. In most cities the dining room of the newest or largest hotel replaced the tavern as the place to buy the best food in town. But as restaurants opened, following the lead of Delmonico's in New York, middle-class married couples increasingly ventured out to eat together, even though many eateries still maintained separate men's and women's cafés and a separate women's entrance into the 1890s. More couples dined out, and going out transformed from a public obligation into a middle-class social diversion, which it had already become for the elite. As the system of chaperoning single men and women relaxed by the end of the century, single couples also dined out as a form of socializing.

Urban middle-class women constructed their own parallel social world. Men and women met, of course, at balls, soirees, and dinner parties, and later in the century they went to shows and to dinner together. But as with the upper class, most middle-class socializing was carried on by and for women. Within smaller social circles, middle-class women increasingly attended tea parties in late afternoons. Introduced in the 1810s in the East, tea parties took place even on the urban frontier by the 1830s. Such occasions allowed women to screen newcomers or to see occasional acquaintances without making a significant social commitment or imposing a social burden on guests. Less socially demanding was the practice of "calling." On a certain day each week the middle-class or upper-middle-class woman of the house, emulating elite practices, was available at home to greet "callers." Early on callers included anyone who wanted to say hello, but over time they were only people who had specific reasons to call or who had been asked by the hostess to pay a call. Establishing a certain day as her calling day enabled a woman to handle unwanted strangers. A stranger who did not know a family's calling time or who had not looked at the social register if the family was on the edge of the elite usually found the woman of the house "not at home." Following proper etiquette, the stranger was asked to leave a card, possession of which indicated a certain social station, and the visitor turned up one of the corners to indicate the purpose of the call. If a call was desired, a note invited the caller to come on the family's appointed day. This system of calls thus gave families a chance to meet new people, old friends, acquaintances, and visitors and to exchange pleasantries without placing social pressure on either party. It provided the middle class with a way to regulate associations through aggressive gate keeping.

The inadequacies of weekly calling led to the revival in the early 1800s of the old practice of calling on New Year's Day. By the 1830s middle-class men called at the houses of their friends and acquaintances on New Year's Day, and middle-class women served cakes, sweets, coffee, and tea. Some men made as many as fifty calls in the course of a long day, while hostesses often received hundreds of people going to and fro on foot, by carriage, or in sleighs. In Washington, D.C., New Year's Day calling merged into the old practice of public officials having open houses or soirees and became a great day for calling on the president, members of the cabinet, senators, and military officials. Later, officials who spent the morning calling opened their houses to greet callers until late in the day. A similar ritual of calling developed in state capitals. With these formal events the urban middle class drew lines of demarcation around themselves while allowing newcomers and upwardly mobile individuals access through sponsorship.

Within their private social realm of friends and associates, genteel middle-class people socialized in a steady round of private dinners, a midday meal usually on Sunday, or dinner parties on weekend evenings. Those affairs were for groups of a dozen or fewer guests. Less frequently the middle class hosted soirees or parties, often after a dinner party, to which they invited a larger number of people. The formality of these social occasions varied with the gentility of the household. Gentility demanded elevated standards in household decoration, bodily hygiene, dignified personal comportment, and proper etiquette. Having a tea, paying or receiving a call, or giving or attending a dinner party or soiree obligated a display of manners, which were judged by the guests accordingly. Likewise hosts assumed the hygiene, dress, and behavior of the guests would be appropriate to the genteel occasion. Increasingly elaborate guidebooks provided middle-class people with rules and advice on what was or was not proper. Within some leeway, a knowledge of etiquette and the material ability to participate in social rituals were accepted markers of class boundaries.

Responding to the impulse to circumscribe and demarcate their social realm, many middle-class women in the 1860s and 1870s formed private clubs and public service associations that paralleled recently founded men's clubs. The first woman's club, Sorosis, was founded in New York before the Civil War. By the 1880s genteel women in nearly every town and city had formed a Sorosis club. Women also formed Female Moral Reform Associations, formed Ladies Protective Relief Associations, and joined the Women's Christian Temperance Union. By the 1880s a national Federation of Women's Clubs helped coordinate the activities of a variety of women's clubs and associations.

Club culture emerged as one aspect of a broadening public role for middle-class women. Genteel department stores, ice cream parlors, tea saloons, and theaters clustered around a shopping district, usually called the "Ladies Mile" after Broadway in New York City, in most towns and cities after the Civil War. Meanwhile women altered the manner in which the middle class celebrated public events and holidays. Valentine's Day, a genteel exercise in celebrating love, and Easter and May Day, spring holidays celebrating rebirth and fertility, were commemorated more formally with dinners, parties, and the exchange of gifts. Parades, sporting events, barbecues, and picnics, large outside gatherings that became popular as political gatherings and social events by the 1850s, gradually replaced the great Fourth of July dinners or feasts of the early part of the century. By mid-century middle-class women elevated Thanksgiving, a New England holiday celebrated with an autumnal harvest feast, into a major holiday across the urban North. It officially became a national holiday in 1863. But the greatest transformation occurred in the celebration of Christmas. The traditional boisterous Christmas festivities, two- or three-day frolics of drinking, dancing, and carousing, were decried as pagan by the Puritans and Congregationalists in New England, who thus did not celebrate at all. Christians across the United States sought more genteel ways of celebrating Christmas in the 1830s, and Americans adopted the Christmas customs of England in the early 1840s. Within a decade Americans appropriated Santa Claus as patron of the holiday, decorated a Christmas tree indoors, decorated the house and public venues with greens, nuts, cones, and fruits, exchanged gifts and cards, and sang Christmas carols. By the 1860s these traditions transformed Christmas into a fantasy world for adults and children alike and imposed gentility and order on what had been for many workers a day of revelry.

In response to middle-class efforts at moral reform and social control, many workers, immigrants, and blacks self-consciously asserted their own distinctive identities. Forced to live in crowded housing, urban workers developed a social life within the public realm of the street and its adjacent venue, the public tavern, saloon, or "groggery." Working-class taverns often served as the workingmen's clubs, where men could eat, drink, talk sports, cavort, and fight. As the cities became more diverse, certain taverns specialized in the food part of their businesses. Nearby saloons, where only liquor was available, became clubhouses associated with certain street groups, gangs, fire company volunteers, or ethnic groups. Friends and associates met at all hours and in the course of talk and drink forged male bonds among a few dozen regulars. Sometimes groups of men formed more formal drinking clubs with specific attire, special toasts, and a leadership structure. Some saloons, later called "concert saloons," began to offer music, singing, dancing, and comedy variety shows as well as boxing matches. Other saloons became gambling dens, where patrons played faro, poker, dice games, and roulette. Since no respectable woman entered such places, the women present were mostly prostitutes. Most were amateurs who worked in nearby hotels or upstairs in the concert saloon. Some saloons catered to this trade, offering lewd dance shows and sexual exhibitions that encouraged patrons to become paying customers. More deeply submerged were private meeting places for gay men. Throughout the "sporting male" urban subculture, working and transient men, whether immigrants, native born, or African American, asserted their manhood through heavy drinking, exaggerated bravado and street language, florid attire, and aggressive sexuality in sharp contrast to the prevalent middle-class ethos of gentlemanliness rooted in self-discipline and control.

Many workers joined volunteer fire companies and competed in boisterous competitions with other companies to provide fire service. Militia companies organized, drilled, and marched in parades on public occasions. Workingmen and immigrants alike joined fraternal organizations that cultivated fraternity through rituals, secrecy, and public activities. Less formal organizations such as gangs provided more rudimentary male bonding in initiation rituals, distinctive clothing, and nicknames. Bonding was reinforced by rough group activities like drinking bouts, sometimes called "jollifications," that often spilled over into traditional frolics, called "skimmington" music. Usually this violence involved turf wars with other gangs, resulting in general melees and drinking "benders" that continued after the fighting ended. Gang members also attacked brothels, not to hurt the male customers but to intimidate the women who would not provide their services to workingmen by destroying their property or by committing a gang sexual assault. Ethnic and racial tensions often simmered over into vigilante actions or general street riots. The worst in the nineteenth century included the riots in Philadelphia in the 1830s and 1840s, the draft riots in New York in 1863, and the riots in New Orleans and Memphis just after the Civil War ended.

Though workers created a separate social realm, the clubs, taverns, and houses of prostitution in working-class areas were not patronized solely by working-class men. These districts and the nearby areas where houses of prostitution catered to a middle-class clientele gradually developed into a broader entertainment district. There middle-class men and workingmen rubbed shoulders and created a vibrant urban male subculture. Whites, blacks, Asian immigrants, and European immigrants mingled in a diversity and excitement that foreshadowed twentieth-century urban society. In these districts concert saloons, variety clubs, and dance halls evolved into vaudeville and burlesque theaters, dinner clubs, and nightclubs, the mixed-gender nightlife of the modern American metropolis.

Ethnic communities and neighborhoods developed from the foundations of the social order of the streets. Specific taverns became social clubs. Local stores catering to the local clientele opened up and down the streets. Beyond saloons and their male subculture, the ethnic groceries, newspaper stands, shops, and restaurants became the building blocks of working-class neighborhoods. Residents formed congregations, built churches and temples, established benevolent associations, founded schools, and started newspapers. On religious holidays neighborhoods and parishes held festivals that included parades around the edges of the neighborhoods. In larger cities parades to mark Steuben Day, Santa Lucia Day, or Chinese New Year later moved to nearby major avenues and became multineighborhood or even citywide ethnic events. This was especially true of the Saint Patrick's Day parades that ran through the centers of most cities by mid-century. But it did not take parades to impel the social life of working-class neighborhoods into the streets. Mothers sat on stoops and visited, children played games, gangs patrolled their turf, police walked the beat, and the sounds of parties in clubs and taverns mingled on the streets. In these activities immigrant and black residents of cities created their own social space. For some it was the equivalent of the village in the Old World or the South, in which they pursued the universal goals of social life, that is, social maintenance, procreation, and the construction of identity.

See also **Class, Social; Clubs; Gender,** *subentry on* **Interpretations of Gender; Holidays; Manliness; Manners; Personal Appearance; Prostitution; Recreation; Saloons and the Drinking Life; Segregation,** *subentry on* **Urban Segregation; Vaudeville and Burlesque; Wealth; Working-class Culture.**

Bibliography

Blumin, Stuart M. *The Emergence of the Middle Class.* New York: Cambridge University Press, 1989.

Carnes, Mark C. *Secret Ritual and Manhood in Victorian America.* New Haven, Conn.: Yale University Press, 1989.

Cohen, Patricia Cline. *The Murder of Helen Jewett: The Life and Death of a Prostitute in Nineteenth-Century New York.* New York: Knopf, 1998.

Duis, Perry R. *Challenging Chicago: Coping with Everyday Life, 1837–1920.* Urbana: University of Illinois Press, 1998.

Erenberg, Lewis A. *Steppin' Out: New York Nightlife and the Transformation of American Culture, 1890–1930.* Westport, Conn.: Greenwood Press, 1981.

Gilfoyle, Timothy J. *City of Eros: New York City, Prostitution, and the Commercialization of Sex, 1820–1920.* New York: Norton, 1992.

Kaplan, Michael. "New York City Tavern Violence and the Creation of Working-Class Identity." *Journal of the Early Republic* 15 (winter 1995): 591–617.

Kasson, John F. *Rudeness and Civility: Manners in Nineteenth-Century Urban America.* New York: Hill and Wang, 1990.

Mahoney, Timothy R. *Provincial Lives: Middle-Class Experience in the Antebellum Middle West.* New York: Cambridge University Press, 1999.

McNamara, Brooks. *Day of Jubilee: The Great Age of Public Celebrations in New York, 1788–1909.* New Brunswick, N.J.: Rutgers University Press, 1997.

Ryan, Mary P. *Civic Wars: Democracy and Public Life in the American City during the Nineteenth Century.* Berkeley: University of California Press, 1997.

Wilentz, Sean. *Chants Democratic: New York City and the Rise of the American Working Class, 1788–1850.* New York: Oxford University Press, 1984.

TIMOTHY R. MAHONEY

SOCIOLOGY   In the United States sociology did not begin until the 1880s, when a scattering of universities first offered a course or a series of lectures in this new field. In 1883 Lester Ward published *Dynamic Sociology,* and in another decade sufficient academic growth in sociology warranted the publication of two textbooks, by Albion Small and George Vincent (1894) and Franklin H. Giddings (1896). Sociology gained further impetus in 1892, when the newly founded University of Chicago included a Department of Sociology. The department's first chair, Small, founded the *American Journal of Sociology* in 1895.

The onset of American sociology was influenced by the changing American university and by the rapidly developing industrialization and urbanization of American society. The first American sociologists believed beyond any doubt that natural laws governed the behavior of human beings while insisting that intellect and rationality enabled humans to rise above biological determinism. Regarding social change as progress, they thought progress would be accomplished by a rational intervention into social relations, that is, by social reform. Furthermore they possessed an individualistic conception of social life, viewing social groups as arrangements of interacting individuals. They held that the psychological makeup of those individuals was the source of social change.

The development of sociology in the 1880s and 1890s was not strictly an academic process carried on by gentrified scholars interested only in theory. To the contrary, pioneering American sociologists were deeply concerned with the social conflict and disorganization that accompanied urbanization and industrialization. Beginning in the 1870s a continuous stream of social protest by farmers, workers, and even middle-class citizens told sociologists that the United States was not "exceptional" but was subject to the same class struggles and other serious disruptions of social life characteristic of Europe. Another European import, socialism, appeared on the American scene, but in the American university it was less likely to be Marxian. Rather, it was likely to be a Christian socialism of voluntary cooperatives and other forms of an idealized cooperative commonwealth.

Sociology began with two divergent emphases: first, an interest in social problems and, second, a desire to provide a rational and scientific foundation for the discipline. An interest in social problems came easily to the first generation of sociologists, who were native-born sons of the economically prosperous. Many of them also were Protestant clergy or the sons of clergy, and some aspired to produce a specifically Christian sociology. Most of this first generation of sociologists shared white Americans' common assumption of biological inferiority among people of color and immigrants from southern and eastern Europe. They applied this assumption to interpretations of the behavior and social characteristics of the urban poor and the immigrant working class, who were labeled "dependents, defectives, and delinquents" in courses on "social pathology."

Herbert Spencer (1820–1903). The sociologist Herbert Spencer believed in the theory of Social Darwinism, which posed competition as the root of social progress. Steel engraving. LIBRARY OF CONGRESS: PRINTS AND PHOTOGRAPHS DIVISION

Other sociologists, however, had more sympathy for immigrants and the urban poor, and they joined with the emerging profession of social work and its settlement houses, the reforming Protestant clergy, the muckrakers from urban journalism, and other social reformers to advocate for progressive legislation and a more just and efficient government in an industrialized society. These social reformers instituted the first efforts at empirical social research. The impetus came from British reformers, particularly Charles Booth, whose study of the London poor was a model for the American researchers. The staff of the pioneering settlement house Hull-House, founded by Jane Addams in Chicago in 1889, carried out a great deal of similar research. The black sociologist W. E. B. Du Bois knew of Hull-House and of Booth's work, and in 1896 he undertook an impressive empirical study of the black population of Philadelphia, the best social research undertaken before 1900. In his systematic fieldwork, Du Bois attended meetings, churches, and social and political gatherings, and he visited house-to-house with the black families of Philadelphia's Seventh Ward. He presented his data in tables, charts, and graphs supported by comparisons of black and white families. In 1897 Du Bois moved to Atlanta University to begin a series of empirical studies of the "Negro American." However, white sociologists simply ignored his work.

Sociologists' association with social reformers

SOUTH, THE 189

helped sociology gain acceptance and a foothold at a time when American universities were expanding, but the association also had a downside. Their work with reformers and focus on social problems detracted from the idea that sociology was a sober, scientific discipline and sometimes linked sociologists with controversial political positions. For instance, Edward A. Ross lost his job at Stanford University because of his populist opinions. As a consequence, some sociologists focused on legitimate sociology as a true science, deserving of a place in the university. Some, however, held interests in both scientific sociology and reforming sociology. Lester Ward, for example, believed that rational scientific knowledge was the key to social progress because such knowledge allowed intelligent human intervention, that is, intelligent social reform. He became the chief opponent of William Graham Sumner, a Yale sociologist who combined Herbert Spencer's theory of social evolution and the ideology of social Darwinism with an advocacy of laissez-faire economics. Like Ward, many American sociologists accepted Spencer's concept of social evolution, which they viewed as social progress, but few were social Darwinists like Sumner. The sociologists who worked to legitimize sociology wrote divergent and even conflicting theses on what sociology was or should be and made programmatic statements to justify their new discipline. They relied on Europeans, such as Ludwig Gumplowicz, Gustav Ratzenhofer, and Albert Schäffle, long-forgotten theorists, for intellectual guidance. But in the late 1890s the work of Charles Horton Cooley and Ross produced fruitful scholarship. Cooley constructed a sociological social psychology with a central concept of socialization, which in time became incorporated into the vocabulary of most middle-class Americans. Ross developed the key concept of social control.

Sociology remained an unorganized and diffuse entity to the end of the 1890s. The American Sociological Society was finally established in 1905. During the last two decades of the nineteenth century sociology suffered from all the travails of a beginning science seeking to academically and intellectually legitimate itself. The mature development that gave it a distinct disciplinary shape came in the early decades of the twentieth century.

Another scholar whose early work before 1900 was further developed in the next decade was the unconventional economist Thorstein Veblen. He influenced reform-minded sociologists through his savage critiques of "higher learning" in the United States, of an emerging capitalism, and of class privilege, from which came his famous concept of "conspicuous consumption."

See also **Education,** *subentry on* **Colleges and Univer-**

sities; **Philosophy; Populism; Progress, Idea of; Progressivism; Psychology; Reform, Idea of; Reform, Social; Settlement Houses; Social Gospel.**

Bibliography

Barnes, Harry Elmer. *An Introduction to the History of Sociology.* Chicago: University of Chicago Press, 1948.
Hinkle, Roscoe C., Jr., and Gisela J. Hinkle. *The Development of Modern Sociology.* New York: Random House, 1954.
House, Floyd Nelson. *The Development of Sociology.* New York: McGraw-Hill, 1936.
Oberschall, Anthony. "The Institutionalization of American Sociology." In *The Establishment of Empirical Sociology: Studies in Continuity, Discontinuity, and Institutionalization.* Edited by Anthony Oberschall. New York: Harper and Row, 1972.
Ross, Dorothy. *The Origins of American Social Science.* Cambridge, U.K.: Cambridge University Press, 1991.

JAMES B. MCKEE

SONGS. See **Music,** subentry on **Folk Songs, Parlor Music, and Popular Music.**

SOUTH, THE

[This entry includes subentries on **The South before the Civil War** and **The New South after Reconstruction.** See also **Reconstruction,** subentry on **The South.**]

THE SOUTH BEFORE THE CIVIL WAR

Migration westward and the rise in cotton production defined the political, social, and economic spheres of southern life from 1790 to 1860. During the colonial period the South's economy was as diverse as the North's, but the two regions' economic systems diverged in the early nineteenth century, when many plantation owners in the Deep South began to rely heavily upon a single cash crop, cotton. The dependency upon cotton, hastened by ideal climatic conditions for cotton growing in many areas of the South, also produced a dependency upon northern textile manufacturers. Moreover, the rapid industrialization of the northern, free states from 1820 to 1860 sharpened the division between the regions. The Mason-Dixon line—simply a surveying boundary established in 1763 between Maryland and Pennsylvania—became by 1850 an intangible but real demarcation between two socially, economically, and politically distinct areas of the country. During the 1850s Southerners increased their manufactures, even eclipsing the rate of industrial expansion in the

North, but the manufacturing deficit of the 1830s and 1840s outweighed the impressive gains of the 1850s. By 1860, on the eve of the Civil War, the South had invested so much financial and political capital into becoming a Cotton Kingdom that the defense of that system and its associated institution of slavery was tantamount to the union of the states.

Development of "King Cotton"

In 1790 southern states in the United States were not unlike their northern counterparts. The southern coastal cities of Baltimore, Charleston, and Savannah surpassed northern urban areas in cultural life and rivaled New York City as major ports. While it was more agrarian than the North, the South did not rely solely upon the production of its major cash crops of tobacco, rice, sugar, and hemp: in the 1810 census, the South's economy was economically more diverse than that of the North, in large part because of its thriving urban areas.

By the early nineteenth century, however, three events dovetailed to change forever the trajectory of North and South. The end of the War of 1812 and the beginning of Indian removal from the southeast freed resources and opened new land, which was crucial, because of population growth and overused soil in the Upper South. Coinciding with these two developments was Eli Whitney's invention of the cotton gin in 1793, which streamlined the most labor-intensive phase of growing cotton. Consequently, by 1815, with a stable national economy, growing worldwide demand, available fertile land, and a crucial technological advance, cotton surpassed tobacco as the primary staple crop of the southern states.

After 1815 southern cotton growers found little reason to produce different crops. World demand for cotton increased 5 percent each year from 1820 to 1860. The 8 percent return on cotton harvesting easily surpassed planters' return on tobacco, and middling farmers became small producers of cotton because little capital was required to begin growing the crop. Moreover, southern port cities continued to specialize in exporting cotton, and the construction of rail lines beginning in the 1830s increased efficiency and profitability. The result of these developments was astounding. In 1812 southern growers produced 150,000 bales of cotton; by 1860 they produced more than 3.8 million bales, 75 percent of worldwide production of cotton. Clearly, the Deep South between 1815 and 1860 became the Cotton Kingdom.

Importance of Slavery

Escalating cotton production was made possible by the availability of unfree labor. While every northern state had taken steps to end slavery by 1804, the institution had become the foundation upon which the South's agrarian economy rested. The emergence of cotton as the primary cash crop in the South further entrenched enslavement as the center of southern economic livelihood.

From 1790 to 1860, the slave population in the South skyrocketed. Although the importation of slaves was outlawed in 1808, natural increase among enslaved African Americans accounted almost exclusively for the population explosion. In 1790, 690,000 African Americans were enslaved in the South. The number grew to two million by 1830 and doubled yet again by 1860, when four million blacks lived in bondage within the southern slave states. This enormous increase in population over seventy years ensured the continuation of unfree labor as the chief factor in the increase in cotton growers' profits. Additionally, with their chattel property reproducing itself every three decades, slave owners had yet another dimension of profiteering that was built upon black slavery.

Cotton and slavery were so inextricably linked that the Cotton Belt, the major cotton-producing region of the South, held the largest concentrations of African Americans in the nation. Although cotton growers were successful from Virginia to Texas and as far north as southern Illinois, they found the soils of central Georgia through eastern Texas to be the best for their crop. The interrelatedness of cotton and slavery meant economic prosperity in the short term but ruin in the long term for the economically one-dimensional South.

Rural Southern Society

Although planters propelled the southern economy, they represented a minuscule portion of the region's population. Overall, only one-fourth of white southerners lived in slave-owning families. In 1860 only forty-six thousand individuals, or 12 percent of the slaveholding population, owned twenty or more slaves, the level at which a slave owner was considered to be a "planter." Less than 1 percent of slave owners, or 2,300 individuals, owned a hundred or more bondspeople. Primarily concentrated in the Plantation Belt, or the section of the South that encompassed the lowlands of the Carolinas and Georgia, the rich delta acreage of Mississippi and Louisiana, and the fertile valleys that extended from central Virginia to northern Alabama, planters were not numerous enough to overwhelm the other classes with sheer numbers. In spite of being numerically inferior, southern planters wielded influence in every facet of southern society because by 1860 they owned about 60 percent of the South's four million slaves. Planters held sway over much of the southern "plain folk," or middle-class, rural people whose ties to the Cotton Kingdom and slavery were less direct than those of the planters.

One segment of these middle-class (or yeomen) farmers comprised the Plantation Belt yeomen. Although these farmers owned few slaves, they shared important business and community relationships with their more affluent neighbors. Reliance upon planters' cotton gins and mills often meant the difference between profit and loss, and planters themselves were sometimes important consumers of the subsistence crops that yeomen produced. In addition, family ties bound planter and yeoman and created pockets of overlapping economic, kinship, and social webs. In communities where plantations existed, they were the hubs of economics, politics, and social life for all classes of people who lived nearby. Finally, the goal of many (perhaps most) of these small farmers was to become planters.

Yeomen farmers who lived in other parts of the South, however, shared few ties to the planter class. Geographically isolated, middle-class farmers in the southern backcountry, a swath of hills and mountains that encircles the western portions of Virginia and the Carolinas, the northern portions of Georgia and Alabama, and eastern Tennessee and Kentucky, developed an individual economy and social life that did not depend upon planter class influence. These non-slaveholding farmers of Appalachia were primarily subsistence farmers, agricultural producers who farmed mostly for their families' daily needs. The backcountry yeomanry, who were for the most part evangelical Christians, centered their lives around the Baptist, Methodist, or Presbyterian churches in their community.

Although they did not have a direct connection to plantation owners, backcountry yeomen did not necessarily oppose the political hegemony of the planters. The wealthy slave owners of the South succeeded in equating the livelihood of all whites with the perpetuation of slavery, so that even the non-slaveholding, backcountry yeomen could exist peripherally but not in opposition to the southern plantation economy. Racial and not class or regional differences were the most distinguishing in southern society. Race was the only connecting factor between planters and poor whites. Mostly tenant farmers and rural day laborers, poor whites lived a marginal existence. Although poverty was temporary for some whites, by the 1850s land prices had soared beyond the level of affordability for many farmers who aspired to join the ranks of the yeomanry. By 1860, one-fourth of southern white farmers were landless.

Another marginal group that ranked economically and socially below poor whites was the small but significant free black population. In 1860, more than 260,000 free blacks, or 6 percent of the population, lived in the South. While a few free African Americans were slave owners themselves, the vast majority of free blacks in the South were unskilled laborers living in rural areas. Their barely adequate economic status was further cemented by the passage of restrictive legislation during the 1820s and 1830s. In addition to proscribing the behavior of enslaved and free African Americans, black codes enacted by each southern legislature, prevented the free black population from growing by severely limiting the circumstances in which a slave could be granted freedom.

Southern Women

White southern women, like their northern counterparts, were seen as guardians of the domestic sphere. Responsible for raising children and providing a stable family life for their working husbands, these women found that the ideal of women's roles often conflicted with reality. Instead of living in luxury, planters' wives found that they shared in significant responsibilities in the management of their families' enslaved workforce. Wives of yeomen frequently aided their husbands in the fields in addition to raising their children, and poor white women had little choice but to endure by any means necessary, which commonly entailed holding degrading jobs away from home. The gap between reality and myth became so stark that Sarah and Angelina Grimké, daughters of a prominent South Carolina plantation owner, moved north in the 1820s and spoke out against slavery and the position of women in southern society. In addition to the declining birth rates and rising divorce rates at mid-century, Sarah Grimké's book *Letters on the Equality of the Sexes* is evidence that southern women did not accept unquestioningly the positive image of the South propagated by white male slave owners.

Southerners in the Cities

In part because of the small population, urban groups in the South rarely challenged the political influence of the planters. Moreover, merchants, bankers, and manufacturers relied upon the capital produced by the planter class for their own livelihoods. Nonetheless, following the panic of 1837, in which cotton prices dropped dramatically, southern industrialists began meeting annually in Augusta, Georgia. Headed by James D. B. DeBow, these businessmen warned southern political leaders that the region could not subsist forever with an agrarian economy and called for economic diversification that would make the South less dependent upon northern industry.

These meetings sparked impressive gains in southern industrialization. The Tredegar Iron Works opened in Richmond in 1838 and quickly became the most important industrial source in the South. Increased production of coal, iron, and salt bolstered the South's economy, and during the 1850s the region's total railroad mileage quadrupled from 2,340 miles in 1850 to 10,500 miles in 1860. In 1860, however, even the strides of the previous decade did not close the industrial gap between North and South: with 30 percent of the country's population, the South accounted for only 20 percent of the nation's industrial capital.

Lack of urbanization and an industrial economy prohibited immigrants from moving to the South at the same rate that they migrated to the North. Rejecting the competition of slave labor and seeking opportunities in urban areas, most European immigrants avoided the South. In 1860, only 550,000 foreign-born whites, or 13 percent of the total foreign-born population in the nation, lived in southern

states, and they were concentrated largely in Baltimore, Richmond, Charleston, Mobile, and New Orleans. The absence of a growing immigrant population that viewed slavery as a threat to obtaining employment contributed to the stale political position of the South.

Southern Politics

By 1860, with differences between North and South becoming more pronounced, southern political leaders viewed the situation as urgent. The abolitionist movement, spurred by the publication of Harriet Beecher Stowe's *Uncle Tom's Cabin* in 1852, galvanized proslavery advocates in the South. Describing enslaved African Americans as a depraved people, defenders of slavery rejected the moral justification for abolition, arguing that enslavement imbued bondspeople with the teachings of Christianity. Moreover, these apologists argued that the southern system of slavery prevented the region from being plagued by a white, laboring "underclass" that the free labor ideology of the North had produced. Their successful defense of the South's Cotton Kingdom and slavery

"The 'Secession Movement'." A political cartoon depicting the imminent danger in southern states' quest for secession from the union. Lithograph by Currier & Ives, 1861. LIBRARY OF CONGRESS: PRINTS AND PHOTOGRAPHS DIVISION

empire against northern threats of abolition made all southerners, including nonslaveholders, dependent upon the prosperity of the system. By 1860, the division between northern and southern political leaders over the issue of slavery rendered the Republican Party powerless in the South, which had become during the emergence of the "kingdom" a single-party, Democratic stronghold. When the planter and South Carolina senator James Henry Hammond remarked to the Senate in 1858 that "cotton is king," he unknowingly described the teetering balance the region had achieved between prosperity and decline.

See also **American Indians,** *subentry on* **Indian Removal; Appalachia; Civil War,** *subentry on* **Causes of the Civil War; Cotton; Market Revolution; Slavery,** *subentry on* **Overview; Women; Work,** *subentries on* **Agricultural Labor, Domestic Labor.**

Bibliography

Boles, John B. *The South through Time: A History of an American Region.* 2d ed. Englewood Cliffs, N.J.: Prentice Hall, 1999.

Cash, W. J. *The Mind of the South.* New York: Knopf, 1941.

Cooper, William J., and Thomas E. Terrill. *The American South: A History.* 2d ed. New York: McGraw-Hill, 1996.

Oakes, James. *Slavery and Freedom: An Interpretation of the Old South.* New York: Knopf, 1990.

Stampp, Kenneth M. *The Peculiar Institution: Slavery in the Ante-bellum South.* New York: Random House, 1956.

Stevenson, Brenda E. *Life in Black and White: Family and Community in the Slave South.* New York: Oxford University Press, 1996.

Woodman, Harold D. *King Cotton and His Retainers: Financing and Marketing the Cotton Crop of the South, 1800–1925.* Columbia: University of South Carolina Press, 1990.

Woodward, C. Vann. *The Burden of Southern History.* Baton Rouge: Louisiana State University Press, 1968.

KEVIN D. ROBERTS

THE NEW SOUTH AFTER RECONSTRUCTION

The term "New South" first surfaced during the Civil War, as events portended an end to the older South, but the Atlanta journalist Henry Grady, a New South booster in the 1880s, is most closely associated with the phrase, which had to do with a prospective transformation of the economy—a rise in industry and a general prosperity. In the mythical New South, the economy would be more industrial, society more urban, and agriculture less dependent on cotton. Although race relations would be less turbulent than during Reconstruction as well as less benighted than under slavery, whites would rule. Slavery, the Civil War, and Reconstruction would all belong to the past.

Historians later adopted the phrase, but they continued to seek evidence of a New South's existence, not just its assertion. Applying their own wishes to the phenomenon, they also tended to look for a New South that was less ridden by the twin oppressions of class and race—less poor, more just. Three books in a multivolume history of the South illustrate this view. C. Vann Woodward sought the *Origins of the New South* during the years 1877–1913, and, in the next volume in the same series, George B. Tindall explored *The Emergence of the New South* between 1913 and 1945. If Woodward was wistful and ironic and Tindall optimistic, Numan V. Bartley was bold in concluding the series with *The New South, 1945–1980.*

The Former Confederacy after Reconstruction

Despite the elusive nature of a New South, the term has been employed largely as a tag to identify the South of the late nineteenth century, the time when Grady flourished and the place where Woodward first looked. Contrasted with the Old South, where slavery was the dominant institution within the South itself and generally the dominant issue in regional and national politics, the New South is taken as an era, also comprising approximately a generation, that followed the Civil War and Reconstruction. Such a division in time to work, presupposes that Reconstruction ended in 1877, and historians have in fact displayed a near consensus on this subject.

The dominant facts of the New South were the twin legacies of racial slavery and Civil War. The war brought massive destruction, human and physical. It also brought an end to slavery, though abolition raised a host of issues regarding the future status of black southerners and relations between blacks and whites. Segregation—separate facilities for the races, or at least black exclusion from facilities open to whites—became the rule. From the first postwar years, schools at every level were rigidly segregated almost everywhere. The exceptions soon vanished, and by the early twentieth century, segregation spread in just as systematic a fashion to other venues, like transportation.

Throughout the New South years, more than four of every five African Americans lived in the eleven former states of the Confederacy (see the accompanying table). Whites constituted a majority in most states; blacks were a majority in South Carolina and Mississippi into the twentieth century. But whites were not a very large majority; in every one of the eleven states, blacks constituted at least one in four residents as late as 1880. Black southerners proved to be major players in the New South, whether as

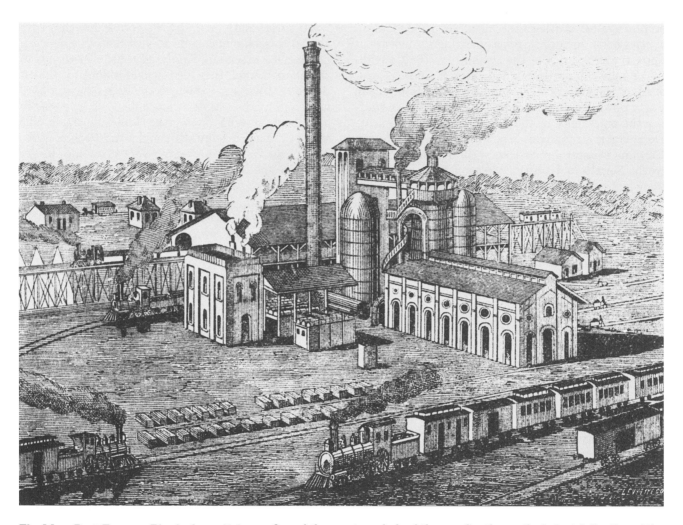

The Mary Pratt Furnace, Birmingham, Alabama. One of the great symbols of the new South was the industrialization of the region, especially the steel industry in Birmingham. Engraving in Dubose's *Alabama and Birmingham Illustrated*, 1886. LIBRARY OF CONGRESS

agents, with votes of their own, or as the central issue among white southerners.

The New South had need of reconciliation in any number of ways. Black southerners had to do what they could to match their aspirations to a changing structure of opportunity, as slavery turned to freedom and then the promise of freedom faded. White southerners had to bring their values and behavior of the past to terms with their own aspirations for the future. How might they, in particular, reconcile with the New South the sacrifice of the Civil War, suffered in a sustained effort to maintain the Old South? There was scant evidence of rapprochement between the races in the late nineteenth century.

Transportation and Urbanization

Rapid development of a rail grid, particularly in the 1880s, brought markets within reach of more and more southern areas and southern people. Thousands of upland farmers responded by producing much more cotton for market. In the mountain regions of the South, railroads made possible the extraction of massive quantities of coal and timber. On 30 May 1886 the nation adopted a standard railroad gauge, and thousands of miles of track in the South had to be adjusted to meet the new standard.

In degree, as regards urbanization, a New South was emerging. Standing as he did in Atlanta in the 1880s, Henry Grady understandably could hope that what he saw in that burgeoning city might be happening elsewhere, soon if not already. Unlike cities that originated as ports or on the fall lines of rivers, Atlanta emerged before the Civil War at a point where several railroads intersected. In 1900 New Orleans, though it was declining in the ranks of major U.S. cities, remained the largest city in the South, but by then Atlanta had vaulted past such traditional

Cotton States Exposition in Atlanta, 1895. At this exposition Booker T. Washington became a national figure for his speech urging greater cooperation between blacks and whites in the South. © CORBIS

southern cities as Mobile, Savannah, Charleston, Norfolk, and Richmond.

Yet all the world was not Atlanta, and not until later would such metropolitan Sun Belt centers as Houston and Miami emerge. Meanwhile, the New South remained the Old South in that most people lived on the land or, if not on farms, in small towns. Substantial migration of whites and blacks within the region took many people west to farms in Arkansas or Texas and from farms to mills or mines. Rapid growth among black and white residents alike also took place in Florida and Georgia. By contrast, the black population figures were more stagnant, and the black percentage was in decline, in the eastern Upper South, particularly in Virginia, where migration to the District of Columbia, Baltimore, Philadelphia, and New York was already well under way before World War I. The New South was a place that people moved from, not to. Foreign immigration played a far smaller role in the South's urban growth in the late nineteenth century than it had before the Civil War.

Economics: Tenancy and Textile Mills

The South did not become less dependent on cotton during the late nineteenth century. To the contrary, cotton production continued to climb, as did the numbers of southern farm families dependent on cotton crops and cotton prices. In the cotton states of Alabama, Arkansas, Georgia, Louisiana, Mississippi, South Carolina, and Texas, at least half of all farm families worked on land that someone else owned. Even higher percentages of black families than white families were caught in this trap, but in a region in which a majority of families were white, there were more white than black sharecroppers. Grinding poverty in the rural South was something of an equal opportunity employer, though far more whites than blacks escaped.

Cotton proved as much the base of southern industrial growth as of agriculture. By 1900 the South had surpassed New England in textile manufacturing, and South Carolina was the capital of the textile empire of the South. Textile jobs were reserved for whites. Whites therefore also monopolized brown lung disease (byssinosis, the counterpart of coal miners' black lung), which came with sustained work in damp surroundings and exposure to airborne cotton fibers.

Other industries also grew increasingly important in the New South's economy. Tobacco processing, an outgrowth of tobacco cultivation, employed ever more hands, particularly in North Carolina. In Alabama, the city of Birmingham grew up in the center

Black Southerners in Each State of the Former Confederacy (1880 and 1910): Total Number (Rounded to the Nearest Thousand), Percentage of Each State's Population, and Percentage of All African Americans.

	1880			1910		
	Total	State (%)	United States (%)	Total	State (%)	United States (%)
Alabama	600	48	9	908	42	9
Arkansas	211	26	3	443	28	5
Florida	127	47	2	309	41	3
Georgia	725	47	11	1,177	45	12
Louisiana	484	51	7	714	43	7
Mississippi	650	57	10	1,009	56	10
North Carolina	531	38	8	698	32	7
South Carolina	604	61	9	836	55	9
Tennessee	403	26	6	473	22	5
Texas	393	25	6	690	18	7
Virginia	632	42	10	671	33	7

of a new iron and steel industry. Railroad construction was a growth industry in much of the South through much of the era. Coal mining and timber extraction also became major industries, particularly in the Appalachian parts of several states.

Politics: Power and Policy

The leading feature of political history in the generation beginning in the 1870s was the rise of a one-party political system in which the Democratic Party could be counted on to win almost every election. The New South followed Reconstruction, according to most measures, when the Democrats "redeemed" the states, one by one, and the Republican Party fell from power. The change did not take place everywhere in 1877. When the final four Republican regimes fell—in South Carolina and Mississippi in 1876 and in Louisiana and Florida in 1877—they completed a pattern that had been occurring ever since Virginia, Tennessee, North Carolina, and Georgia had gone that way at about the beginning of the decade.

Redemption carried no guarantees. Into the 1880s and 1890s, the possibility of electoral victory continued to animate opponents of the Redeemer regimes. This real possibility reflected two facts of political life during the era of the New South. Redeemer policies were anathema to many whites, and many blacks continued to vote. The Readjuster movement in Virginia can stand as a proxy for developments elsewhere. The Virginia Redeemers were committed to full payment of an enormous public debt that originated before the Civil War, even if that meant high taxes yet few funds for public schools. Black and

white voters combined to take the legislature in 1879 and the governorship in 1881. The Readjusters' dominance lasted only a few years, but when they relinquished power, most of their policy innovations persisted. To retrieve and retain power, the Democrats had to accept the new terms of public finance that the Readjusters had forced. The 1890s supplied renewed evidence of restiveness among southern electorates, as a coalition of black and white voters, calling themselves Populists, or the People's Party, sought to obtain power and to promote policies more friendly to small farmers.

Class and race combined, however, to make these efforts as short-lived as the Readjuster episode, and it seemed that each state had only one opportunity to make a bid for an alternative power arrangement before the Democrats took control for the duration. In state after state, Democrats did what they could to escape contingency. First, they disfranchised as many black voters as possible. Second, they lived comfortably with the fact that since race itself could not be used as the basis for restricting the franchise, some of the many poverty-struck white voters would also leave the electorate when faced with such impediments as high poll taxes. Third, they rallied whites through race-baiting campaigns that made it virtually impossible for white voters to permit themselves to be seen as sympathetic to black political aspirations.

The Redeemer regimes—or Bourbon or Conservative regimes—took pleasure and political advantage in campaigning against alleged fiscal excesses of their Republican predecessors during Reconstruction. Sometimes retrenchment was genuine but distinctly temporary, as when Georgia Democrats slashed social spending for a year or two and then found that schools and other institutions did, after all, need to be funded. Sometimes it was an illusion, as when the Redeemer regimes held back in some areas but promoted increasingly vast new expenditures on their favorite object of treasury largess, pensions for Confederate veterans, itself designed to shore up electoral support among constituents.

The New South of the 1880s and 1890s remained a time of turbulence in state politics. The one-party South had not yet taken on the permanence that it soon would, but New South politicians took care to end the time of transition. Markers are many. Mississippi accomplished its coup in 1890, and black Mississippians would struggle mightily in the 1960s to retrieve the political rights that had once been theirs. Voters in North Carolina sent George H. White, a black lawyer and former slave, to the U.S. House of Representatives in 1896 and 1898, but after he left office at the end of his second term he had no black successor there for many years. In 1902, Virginia established obstacles to voting, such as a poll tax and thus merrily disfranchised many of the voters, black and white, who had supported the old Readjuster coalition. Black political power remained scant in Georgia from the 1870s through the end of the century, but coastal McIntosh County continued to send a black representative to Atlanta until almost total disfranchisement ended that possibility throughout the state in 1908.

For the next half-century, a minority of whites in black-majority areas—the "black belt" areas of each state—dominated the political scene in each state. Elected by small numbers of white voters from the black belt, the leading politicians faced little organized resistance. Their white constituents, the only ones with political voices, saw themselves as having the most to lose if they lost control, and they were prepared to put up great resistance to change.

The time of transition came to an end with emphatic punctuation in such dramatic white-on-black violence on a large scale as at Wilmington (North Carolina) in 1898 and in Atlanta in 1906. Violence at retail was no less horrific, as lynchings, whether by rope or by fire, grew ever more frequent at the turn of the century. The New South bequeathed to the twentieth century the trappings of political democracy, together with an illusion of consensus, constructed upon twin foundations of exclusion and terror.

A New Century

By the dawn of the twentieth century, the New South had ossified in patterns that were to endure far longer than had the transitional decades of the 1880s and 1890s. In politics, the one-party system incorporated relatively few people who were not white and did not live in the rotten boroughs of the black belt. In social relations, a system of racial segregation had emerged that included schooling from elementary education to higher education and travel on all such transportation facilities as streetcars and railroads. A universe of segregation laws was enacted that rendered it a serious crime, for example, to marry across racial lines between black and white. In the world of making a living, across the Deep South in particular, a majority of farm families engaged in sharecropping or some other form of tenancy, and the major alternatives for work were in the hard and dangerous industries of coal mining, timbering, or textile manufacture.

See also **Agriculture; Cities and Urbanization; Civil War,** *subentry on* **Consequences of the Civil War; Education,** *subentry on* **Public Policy toward Education; Emancipation; Miscegenation; Railroads; Reconstruction,** *subentry on* **The South; Segregation,** *subentry on* **Segregation and Civil Rights; Textiles; Virginia; Voters and Voting,** *subentry on* **Black Voters after the Civil War.**

Bibliography

Ayers, Edward L. *The Promise of the New South: Life after Reconstruction.* New York: Oxford University Press, 1992.

Carlton, David L. *Mill and Town in South Carolina, 1880–1920.* Baton Rouge: Louisiana State University Press, 1982.

Doyle, Don H. *New Men, New Cities, New South: Atlanta, Nashville, Charleston, Mobile, 1860–1910.* Chapel Hill: University of North Carolina Press, 1990.

Foster, Gaines M. *Ghosts of the Confederacy: Defeat, the Lost Cause, and the Emergence of the New South, 1865–1913.* New York: Oxford University Press, 1987.

Gaston, Paul M. *The New South Creed: A Study in Southern Mythmaking.* New York: Knopf, 1970.

Kousser, J. Morgan. *The Shaping of Southern Politics: Suffrage Restriction and the Establishment of the One-Party South, 1880–1910.* New Haven, Conn.: Yale University Press, 1974.

Litwack, Leon F. *Trouble in Mind: Black Southerners in the Age of Jim Crow.* New York: Knopf, 1998.

Newby, I. A. *Plain Folk in the New South: Social Change and Cultural Persistence, 1880–1915.* Baton Rouge: Louisiana State University Press, 1989.

Rabinowitz, Howard N. *The First New South, 1865–1920.* Arlington Heights, Ill.: Harlan Davidson, 1992.

Wallenstein, Peter. *From Slave South to New South: Public Policy in Nineteenth-Century Georgia.* Chapel Hill: University of North Carolina Press, 1987.

Wilson, Charles Reagan. *Baptized in Blood: The Religion of the Lost Cause, 1865–1920.* Athens: University of Georgia Press, 1980.

Woodman, Harold D. *New South, New Law: The Legal Foundations of Credit and Labor Relations in the Postbellum Ag-*

ricultural South. Baton Rouge: Louisiana State University Press, 1995.

Woodward, C. Vann. *Origins of the New South, 1877–1913*. With a critical essay on recent works by Charles B. Dew. Baton Rouge: Louisiana State University Press, 1971.

PETER WALLENSTEIN

SOUTH AMERICA, FOREIGN RELATIONS WITH

For most of the nineteenth century, U.S. relations with South America were relatively distant, lacking the significance U.S. policymakers placed on relations with Mexico and Central America. This circumstance stemmed in part from the fact that for the first half of the 1800s, the United States was primarily concerned with continental expansion; Mexico, Central America, and the Caribbean were the areas arousing the most interest. In addition, until the last half of the nineteenth century, U.S. trade with regions such as South America—while never insignificant—was considered less important than building the nation's internal commercial infrastructure. Finally, it was obvious to any observer than the United States had been outmaneuvered by the British, who had been assiduously establishing economic and political footholds in South America following the revolts that broke out there at the start of the nineteenth century. By the latter decades of the 1800s, however, all of this began to change, and U.S. relations with South America gained new prominence.

The Era of Independence

When the Spanish and Portuguese colonies in South America began to assert their independence in the early 1800s, most people in the United States were uninformed about the region. Although trading contacts had existed between the colonies and the United States, these had been inconsistent (as a result of the vagaries of the colonial regimes that ruled the area) and often illegal. Nevertheless, the response of the American public to the revolts was generally enthusiastic. While the U.S. government remained officially neutral, private Americans made sure that arms, supplies, money, and even a few volunteers made their way to South America. The idea of New World "brothers" taking up arms against Old World monarchies appealed to many in the United States. Economic self-interest also played a role in this enthusiasm, as U.S. traders and merchants eagerly anticipated the opening of previously unavailable markets.

The U.S. government was cautious in dealing with the situation. While some statesmen, such as Henry Clay, became ardent supporters of the Latin American independence movements, many others, such as James Madison, James Monroe, and John Quincy Adams, were more circumspect. They did not want to take rash actions that might endanger America's thriving trade with European nations such as Spain or even France. The United States was in negotiations with Spain for control of the Florida territory; recognition of the revolutionary governments in South America would surely end the talks. As the negotiations became more intense, the United States went so far as to ban arms shipments to South America and forbade U.S. citizens to take commissions in the rebels' armed forces. Furthermore, war with Great Britain was an ever-present fear, and the United States did not want to stretch its limited resources too thinly.

Finally, despite the initial enthusiasm shown by some in the United States, most Americans could not completely shake their negative impressions of the Spanish and Portuguese people. The Black Legend, which arose from the writings of European travelers to the New World who argued that Spanish colonial rule in Latin America was venal, violent, and backward, was widely accepted among the English and Americans. The fear that the rebels would not be able to divorce themselves from that past haunted many in the United States. Racism was also a factor. The majority of Americans were appalled at the mixing of races that had taken place in the Spanish and Portuguese empires. The resultant "mongrel" populations did not strike most people in the United States as a solid foundation on which to build republican governments. And the fact that those leading the South American revolutions (like their enemies) were Catholic also troubled Americans, who felt that people who gave their allegiance to the "decadent" precepts of "popism" were unlikely to be solid adherents to the ideas of democracy and freedom.

By the late 1810s and early 1820s, however, a confluence of events pushed the United States toward recognition of the revolutionary governments in South America. War with Great Britain had come and gone, and the negotiations with Spain over Florida finally came to fruition, removing important stumbling blocks. In South America the revolutions, which had struggled for years, seemed to be on the road to success. The tremendous success of the British in snapping up the new markets, and the fear that Spain (or perhaps France) might launch serious and disruptive campaigns to recapture the colonies in South America, forced the United States to the conclusion that if it did not act now, there would be nothing to act upon. Accordingly, in 1822 the United States became the first nation to grant recognition to the newly proclaimed republics in South America when it established diplomatic relations with Colombia and Mexico. In 1823 U.S. recognition was granted to the United Provinces of Río de la Plata (Argentina) and Chile, and in 1824 to Brazil and Central America. Peru was officially recognized in 1826.

The Monroe Doctrine and the Panama Congress

In 1823 the British had made a surprising offer: the United States and Great Britain should produce a joint declaration disavowing any territorial goals in Latin America, recognizing the de facto independence of the Spanish and Portuguese colonies, and calling on those colonial powers to refrain from any attempts at reconquest. Secretary of State John Quincy Adams demurred. He preferred a purely U.S. statement of policy in regard to the situation in Latin America. Such a statement was found in President James Monroe's message to Congress in December 1823. What came to be known as the Monroe Doctrine laid out the basics of U.S. policy toward Latin America: no European interference with the independent Latin American republics and no further European colonization in the region.

The response to the Monroe Doctrine in Latin America was measured. Most of the governments of the area were delighted with the basic sentiments but could not fail to notice that the declaration contained nothing about U.S. interference or colonization. Furthermore, Latin American officials were well aware that the British navy, not statements from the young and relatively powerless United States, would protect them from any future recolonization schemes by the Europeans.

The Panama Congress of 1826, called by Colombia's president, Simón Bolívar, might have provided an opportunity for the airing of some of these concerns. Bolívar originally saw the meeting as one for former Spanish colonies only; eventually, however, both Brazil and the United States were invited to attend. He desired some sort of confederation among the new Latin American republics and wished to discuss protection of the hemisphere from outside forces. Although the United States was invited, its two representatives—Richard C. Anderson, ambassador to Colombia, and John Sergeant, a lawyer from Pennsylvania—never reached the meeting. Anderson died en route; Sergeant arrived after the main meetings were over. Given the nature of their instructions, it is unlikely that their presence would have made much difference. The U.S. goals for the meeting were generally negative: to refuse any multilateral defense

James Monroe (1758–1831). The Monroe Doctrine of 1823 restricted European interference with Latin America. Painting by C. B. King, published in 1817. LIBRARY OF CONGRESS: PRINTS AND PHOTOGRAPHS DIVISION

plans and to dissuade the Latin American republics from any attempts to free Cuba. Only in terms of seeking trade advantages for the United States were they to involve themselves in any positive discussions.

Early Contacts

Despite the failure at Panama, many in South America looked to the example of the United States. Its tremendous economic growth and stable national government were considered models. Both the United States and South America desired closer economic relations, but the British dominated trade and commerce in the southern hemisphere. Contributing to the lack of closeness were the U.S. diplomatic representatives sent to the South American republics. They were a motley crew, chosen not for abilities but for their political allegiances. Some expressed great fondness for South America and its people, but many were clumsy, arrogant, and outwardly racist. As was the case with American representation in Central America, it was often difficult to sustain a U.S. diplomatic presence. The first two U.S. representatives to Argentina died at the post; the third left after less than six months. From 1832 to 1844 there was no U.S. representative to Argentina. Even when U.S. diplomats did reach their posts and stayed long enough to function, they often felt deserted by their own government. Instructions were few and far between. One of the U.S. representatives in Chile in the 1820s heard nothing from the Department of State for over two years.

United States economic interests in Latin America grew from the 1820s to the 1860s. Total U.S. trade with Latin America in 1821 had been $28 million; in 1861, that figure had increased to nearly $110 million, or about 25 percent of total U.S. foreign trade. In addition to trade, there were other contacts between the United States and Latin America. As U.S. economic interests in South America grew during the 1830s and 1840s, there were increasing contacts between the two areas. These were not always friendly. In 1832 President Andrew Jackson ordered a raid on Las Malvinas (also known as the Falkland Islands), which had been claimed by Argentina. An American trading vessel had been seized by Argentine officials there, and the ensuing raid by an American warship led to the capture of half a dozen Argentine government officials. By the late 1840s and 1850s the United States—now a nation stretching from the Atlantic to the Pacific—became even more interested in expanding its South American trade. In the 1850s Congress authorized the U.S. Navy to undertake extensive mapping expeditions. Some of these ventured up the Amazon River in Brazil; others mapped the region of the River Plate; and some groups managed overland treks from Argentina to Chile. What they saw was a vast continent awaiting economic development and the construction of adequate transportation and communication lines. At the same time a scientific interest in South America developed as naturalists and others investigated the continent.

Reports of many of these investigations, while breathlessly describing the possibilities in South America, also revealed disappointment with the direction of economic and political development there. There was a sense that the South Americans had been unable to overcome their colonial heritage: the corruption and inefficiency of their Spanish forebears, the decadent lassitude of the Catholic Church, and the wasteful and dangerous militarism that had emerged from their revolutions. More and more, U.S. observers were prone to make comparisons between the republics of South America and their own nation. While, in their view, the former sank farther and farther into economic underdevelopment and political instability, the latter went on to greatness. Searching for reasons why led many of those observers to go

beyond the colonial legacy, and focus on racial and climatic factors. According to many observers' accounts, the people in Latin America were, quite simply, racially inferior; years of mixing Spanish, black, and Native American populations had resulted in a distinctively degraded populace, and the tropical climate of much of Latin America had sapped the willpower and initiative of the people who lived there. No wonder American visitors to South America were generally more impressed with Argentina and Chile (more "Europeanized" and in a temperate climate zone) than with Brazil ("mongrelized" and tropical). Since the British and other European nations had established their hegemony in trade and investment in South America from the early 1800s, there was little for the United States to do but despair of the future of the region.

The post–Civil War economic expansion of the United States refocused American interest on South America. Determined to push its way into foreign markets around the globe, the United States became equally determined to push the Europeans out of the Western Hemisphere. James G. Blaine, who served as secretary of state in 1881 and again from 1889 to 1892, was one of the most consistent advocates of U.S. economic penetration of Latin America. Under the banner of "Pan-Americanism," Blaine sought to bring uniformity to the Western Hemisphere's economic connections, arguing for uniform customs, duties, and trade regulations, and to develop some system whereby national differences could be arbitrated. Few concrete results flowed from the 1889–1890 conference of Western Hemisphere nations called by Blaine and held in Washington. A weak treaty for arbitration of hemispheric disputes was passed. The Commercial Bureau of the American Republics was also created, designed to facilitate commercial intercourse among the assembled nations; it had little immediate impact. Latin American suspicions concerning U.S. intentions and a lack of follow-up by American diplomats rendered the Pan-American idea relatively devoid of substance.

A More Aggressive U.S. Stance

Yet, as other events in the late 1800s showed, the United States was determined to take a more aggressive stance in South America. In 1893 a revolt broke out in Brazil. The government threatened by the uprising had, in 1890, signed a reciprocal trade agreement with the United States; trade between the two nations flourished. The United States was concerned, not simply because of the threat to the friendly Brazilian government but also because, according to rumor, Britain supported the rebels. President Grover

Cleveland responded by ordering the U.S. Navy to protect American shippers loading and unloading at Brazilian ports. Since the Brazilian government received most of its revenue from imports and exports, the U.S. action was a decided benefit. The revolt ended shortly thereafter, and U.S. relations with Brazil were cemented.

The Venezuelan crisis of 1895–1896 brought about the new and forceful diplomacy used by the United States in dealing with South America. The crisis arose, as so many had in South America, over a border dispute. Venezuela and British Guiana had for years claimed the same piece of territory. Perhaps in response to the growing U.S. presence in South America, or perhaps because stories of large deposits of gold in the disputed land began to surface, Britain in the early 1890s began to more aggressively push its case. Officials in the United States were concerned, first and foremost, that the British would gain an even larger foothold in South America. Second, the area under dispute contained the mouth of the Orinoco River, which had long been hailed by American mapping expeditions as the route into the inland markets of northern South America. President Cleveland sent a sharp note to the British, demanding that the case be arbitrated. This note was ignored. Secretary of State Richard Olney thereupon put the matter far less diplomatically than his president had. In a note that became known as the Olney Corollary, the secretary astounded the British by arguing that the United States was "practically sovereign in this continent, and its fiat is law upon the subjects to which it confines its interposition." The British, facing even larger problems with Germany in Europe, finally gave in to the demand for arbitration. Most of the territory, including the mouth of the Orinoco, was deemed to be Venezuela's. Interestingly, while the United States and Great Britain were represented on the arbitration board, Venezuela was not.

While the United States was not exactly "sovereign" in South America by 1900, it was well on the way to becoming the dominant foreign power in the region. By 1901, total U.S. trade with Latin America was $348 million (total U.S. world trade was about $2.3 billion). The Spanish-American War and the growing impulse for a Central American canal pushed the United States to more keenly consider the nations to the south. By the end of the nineteenth century, the United States had made its position in South America clear: it would act to support friendly governments against insurrection; it desired an expansion of U.S. trade and investment in the region; and it had in no uncertain terms indicated its desire for European powers to cease their interference in the South American republics. Nearly ignored by U.S. policymakers in the early nineteenth century, South America had become a testing ground for America's new economic, military, and political power.

See also **Monroe Doctrine.**

Bibliography

Fifer, J. Valerie. *United States Perceptions of Latin America, 1850–1930: A "New West" South of Capricorn?* Manchester, U.K.: Manchester University Press, 1991.

Johnson, John J. *A Hemisphere Apart: The Foundations of United States Policy toward Latin America.* Baltimore: Johns Hopkins University Press, 1990.

Langley, Lester D. *America and the Americas: The United States in the Western Hemisphere.* Athens, Ga.: University of Georgia Press, 1989.

Park, James William. *Latin American Underdevelopment: A History of Perspectives in the United States, 1870–1965.* Baton Rouge: Louisiana State University Press, 1995.

Shurbutt, T. Ray, ed. *United States–Latin American Relations, 1800–1850: The Formative Generations.* Tuscaloosa: University of Alabama Press, 1991.

Whitaker, Arthur P. *The Western Hemisphere Idea: Its Rise and Decline.* Ithaca, N.Y.: Cornell University Press, 1954.

MICHAEL L. KRENN

SOUTH CAROLINA The heat of the "Palmetto State," its plentiful rain, and its vast pool of slave labor allowed it to grow rich rice crops in the eighteenth century, but from about 1810 cotton began to dominate the lowland. With the collapse of cotton prices in the 1820s and 1830s, the state's economic well-being worsened dramatically.

South Carolina inherited from colonial days a political division between the great planters of the lowlands, especially around Charleston, and the smaller farmers of the uplands. Quiet was maintained by compromises. In 1786 the state legislature, the General Assembly, moved the state capital from Charleston to Columbia. The constitution of 1808 expanded the suffrage, but representation was still deliberately unequal, the uplands being represented by counties and the lowlands by the much smaller unit of the parish; this imbalance lasted until after the Civil War. For most of the nineteenth century blacks made up more than half the total population and formed a huge majority in the lowlands. The conspiracy in 1822 of Denmark Vesey, a free black who planned a large slave rebellion in Charleston, terrified whites and hardened their already extreme proslavery views.

Charleston became the great southern city; South Carolina (only the seventh most populous state at the century's start) gradually replaced Virginia as the leader of the South and became the most strenuous and extreme of the southern states in its articulation

The Seceding South Carolina Delegation. When South Carolina left the Union, most of the other Southern states followed suit. Photography by Mathew Brady. *Harper's Weekly,* 22 December 1860. LIBRARY OF CONGRESS

of proslavery thought and southern nationalist ideology. Antebellum South Carolina was the most "southern" of the states, the most out of sympathy with the democratic, egalitarian, and progressive spirit of the age. It was, for instance, the only state in which presidential electors were chosen by the legislature and not by popular vote. And South Carolina took the lead in Southern political advocacy, vigorously asserting the rightness of her "peculiar institution" of slavery, the rights of states against federal authority, and antiprotectionism.

All these arguments were pressed fiercely by John C. Calhoun, the state's greatest son, secretary of state and vice president, and the South's most famous theoretician, rhetorician, and evil genius. In 1832, inspired by Calhoun, a state convention nullified the federal tariff and threatened secession. Congress responded with a Force Act, while President Andrew Jackson warned that he would use the military to crush the state; although both sides backed off, the tone of South Carolina politics had been set. The nullification crisis reduced state politics to two groups, quite different from the national parties: nullifiers, or "states-righters," for whom secession from the Union remained an attractive possibility, and unionists.

The events of the final crisis of union all centered on South Carolina's metropolis, Charleston. It was in Charleston that the old Democratic Party died, for at the 1860 party convention southern firebrands insisted that a Calhounite slavery plank be written into the platform. "Gentlemen of the South, you mistake us; we shall not do it!" exclaimed the Northern Democracy, which broke away. This split guaranteed Democratic defeat in 1860. With the election of Abraham Lincoln, a convention was called at once in Charleston and voted almost unanimously for immediate secession (20 December 1860), the moderates having at last agreed with the radicals that the Union was now intolerable. The Lower South followed the Palmetto State out of the United States and organized themselves as the Confederate States of America. Meanwhile, federal troops still held a federal fortress in the mouth of Charleston harbor, Fort Sumter, and when Lincoln cautiously tried to reprovision the beleaguered garrison, the batteries of Charleston opened fire (12 April 1861): the Civil War had begun.

Although Beaufort and Port Royal fell to the North in November 1861, large Union armies only arrived in the state with William Tecumseh Sherman's invasion early in 1865. When the war ended, the state had suffered monstrously: the cotton crop for four years was an almost total loss, the slaves (the bulk of the state's property in dollar terms) were now free, and one-fourth of the sixty-three thousand South Carolinians who served in the Confederate armies were dead, a fair proportion of the entire white male population.

During Reconstruction, affairs were in the hands of the Republicans, made up of a small number of white unionists (northen whites who had moved to the state) and blacks, most of whom were former slaves. Most native whites remained loyal to the Democrats, did not accept the legitimacy of black suffrage, and resisted Reconstruction—often with violence through such terrorist organizations as the Ku Klux Klan and the Knights of the White Camelia. In the disputed election of 1876, both Republicans and Democrats (the "Redeemers") claimed victory: in South Carolina there were two rival governors and legislatures, and a civil war within the state seemed likely. But in return for the presidency, the federal Republicans abandoned the last southern Republicans; Wade Hampton, who had been a Confederate colonel, was allowed to seize power as governor, and Reconstruction was over. Thereafter, until the 1960s, South Carolina was effectively a one-party state, wholly in the hands of conservative Democrats who implicitly, and then, with the new state constitution of 1895, explicitly disenfranchised the state's blacks.

Recovered self-government did little to reverse South Carolina's severe economic decline, as cotton

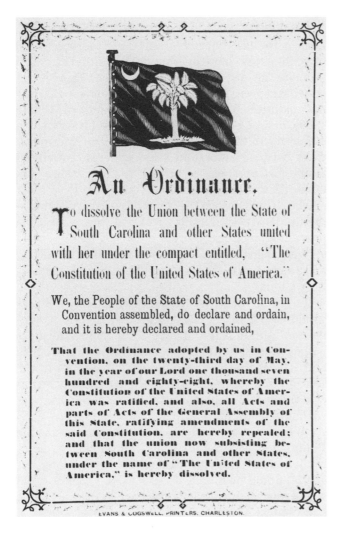

An Ordinance.

To dissolve the Union between the State of South Carolina and other States united with her under the compact entitled, "The Constitution of the United States of America."

We, the People of the State of South Carolina, in Convention assembled, do declare and ordain, and it is hereby declared and ordained,

That the Ordinance adopted by us in Convention, on the twenty-third day of May, in the year of our Lord one thousand seven hundred and eighty-eight, whereby the Constitution of the United States of America was ratified, and also, all Acts and parts of Acts of the General Assembly of this State, ratifying amendments of the said Constitution, are hereby repealed; and that the union now subsisting between South Carolina and other States, under the name of "The United States of America," is hereby dissolved.

EVANS & COGSWELL, PRINTERS, CHARLESTON.

"We, the People of the State of South Carolina." South Carolina's 1860 ordinance repealed its ratification of the U.S. Constitution and declared its union with other states "hereby dissolved." LIBRARY OF CONGRESS: RARE BOOK COLLECTION

prices continued to fall and soil erosion worsened. Emigration of blacks lessened their presence in the population; urban centers like Spartanburg and Greenville began to grow in the Piedmont, rice almost vanished as a crop, and tenant farmers became the norm. Intimidation, violence, and lynching kept the state's large black population subordinate and segregated. In reaction to the patrician arrangements before the war, the state's politics became noticeably populist; agrarian radicalism allowed the long dominance of Benjamin Ryan ("Pitchfork Ben") Tillman, governor (1890–1894) and senator (1895–1918).

See also Cotton; Reconstruction, *subentry on* The South; Slavery, *subentry on* Slave Insurrections; South, The, *subentries on* The South before the Civil War, The New South after Reconstruction.

Bibliography

Carleton, David L. *Mill and Town in South Carolina, 1880–1920.* Baton Rouge: Louisiana State University Press, 1982.

Chesnutt, David R., and Clyde N. Wilson. *The Meaning of South Carolina History: Essays in Honor of George C. Rogers, Jr.* Columbia: University of South Carolina Press, 1991.

Freehling, William W. *Prelude to Civil War: The Nullification Controversy in South Carolina, 1816–1836.* New York: Harper and Row, 1966.

Lander, Ernest McPherson. *South Carolina: An Illustrated History of the Palmetto State.* Edited by Amy Adelstein. Columbia: University of South Carolina Press, 1988.

Williamson, Joel. *After Slavery: The Negro in South Carolina during Reconstruction, 1861–1877.* Chapel Hill: University of North Carolina Press, 1965.

RICHARD MAJOR

SOUTH DAKOTA   The area of the Dakotas, in the northern Great Plains, came into U.S. possession through the Louisiana Purchase in 1803. In 1861 Congress created the Territory of Dakota, the southern half of which was inhabited by perhaps 28,000 Sioux and no more than 1,000 non-Indians. The 1868 the Fort Laramie Treaty recognized the Great Sioux Reservation, comprising more than sixty million acres, but the Sioux Agreement of 1889 dissolved that reservation. In the 1870s, the discovery of gold in the Black Hills had led to the Great Sioux War, as Indians—under such leaders as Crazy Horse and Sitting Bull—tried to defend their land. By 1889, Indians were largely confined to six reservations in central and western South Dakota—Crow Creek, Pine Ridge, Rosebud, Lower Brule, Cheyenne River, and Standing Rock—plus the Yankton and Lake Traverse reservations in the southeast and northeast, all together covering little more than fourteen million acres. In 1889 Congress created the new states of South Dakota, North Dakota, Montana, and Washington by passing the Omnibus Statehood Act. The massacre at Wounded Knee the next year marked the effective end of Sioux resistance.

Non-Indian ethnic diversity fast became a hallmark of South Dakota. In 1890 the census counted 328,808 inhabitants, a number that rose to 629,849 by 1930. The largest ethnic groups were Norwegians; Germans from Germany, Switzerland, and Russia; Czechs; Irish; Austrians; Finns; Scotts; and Poles. These groups established a broad range of churches and a great number of schools for settlers. Parishes and educational facilities on Indian reservations came to be controlled by Episcopalians, Presbyterians, Catholics, and Congregationalists.

What motivated immigrants to an environment marked by such inhospitable natural conditions? Incentives included the lure of economic opportunity in the fur trade and the gold rush; the employment opportunities in Indian agencies, missions, and schools; and the availability of land for settlement, especially as it became increasingly scarce elsewhere in the West. The area also benefited from the publicity of famous travelers, artists, and businessmen, including the writings of the explorers Meriwether Lewis and William Clark and the travel writer Maximilian of Wied, the paintings of Karl Bodmer and George Catlin, and the adventures of the fur trader Pierre Chouteau Jr. (whose first name was given to the state capital, established in the vicinity of Fort Pierre).

A century after statehood, South Dakota's nearly fifty million acres had yet to gain a population much higher than 700,000. A sparse population still endeavored to sustain itself mainly by means established during the nineteenth century—farming, ranching, tourist economies, and military installations—together with generous help from Congress in support of grassland, forest, river valley, and recreational area management.

See also **American Indian Societies**, *subentry on* **The Plains; Great Plains; Louisiana Purchase.**

Bibliography

Hoover, Herbert T. *The Yankton Sioux*. New York: Chelsea House, 1988.

Hoover, Herbert T., and Karen P. Zimmerman, comps. *The Sioux and Other Native American Cultures of the Dakotas: An Annotated Bibliography*. Westport, Conn.: Greenwood, 1993.

———. *South Dakota History: An Annotated Bibliography*. Westport, Conn.: Greenwood, 1993.

Milton, John R. *South Dakota: A Bicentennial History*. New York: Norton, 1977.

Schell, Herbert S. *History of South Dakota*. 3d ed. Lincoln: University of Nebraska Press, 1975.

HERBERT T. HOOVER

SPANISH-AMERICAN WAR The Spanish-American War, waged in Cuba, the Philippines, and Puerto Rico from April to August 1898, was the result of a combination of a severe and prolonged political crisis in Cuba and the increased desire of late-nineteenth-century America for overseas expansion. By the time the conflict was over, the United States had acquired a small empire and the status of a world power.

Background

During the last quarter of the nineteenth century, several factors came together in the United States to promote the idea of overseas expansion. There was a growing concern for new markets and new sources for raw materials. The up-and-down economy of the late 1800s, during which major depressions hit with some regularity (often accompanied by violent confrontations between labor and management), convinced many that perhaps the answer to the nation's economic ills was the expansion of foreign trade. Foreign markets could absorb the country's industrial and agricultural overproduction, while at the same time providing much-needed raw materials for America's growing industrial base. Two of the most promising areas were Latin America and the Far East, particularly China.

To penetrate those markets the United States would need a strong navy to protect American commerce. Captain Alfred Thayer Mahan was the most noted publicist for this point of view, arguing in books and articles that a strong navy was essential to the security and future growth of the nation. In the Pacific this would mean the establishment of a series of coaling and supply stations across the ocean. Such stations were eventually established in Hawaii, the Philippines, Guam, and American Samoa. In addition, a canal through Central America—long desired—would now be a necessity. And such a canal would mean a greater U.S. presence in the Caribbean and Central America.

There were other factors at work as well. The late nineteenth century marked the height of the missionary movement among America's Protestant churches. The desire to spread the gospel to the "heathens" around the globe was powerful, and the missionaries sent far and wide often served as unofficial agents for American business and political penetration. At the same time the idea of social Darwinism was in vogue, which argued that the "fittest" among the human race would emerge to lead and to perpetuate it. It became, in the words of Rudyard Kipling, the British poet for imperialism, the "white man's burden" to uplift their "little brown brothers." By implication social Darwinists believed it was also necessary to bring a new vigor and aggressiveness to the Anglo-Saxon race, in order to meet the challenge of racially inferior, but more numerous, peoples. Among some American males, caught in the throes of the new industrial America, there grew a belief that masculinity was becoming a thing of the past. With no wildernesses to be conquered or wars to be fought, the martial spirit that had defined American manhood for so many years was fading away. Perhaps foreign adventure would reinvigorate America's diminishing manliness.

Crisis in Cuba

While these developments were unfolding in the United States, a crisis had evolved in Cuba. The United States, which had long coveted the island, had tried earlier in the century, just after the Mexican-American War, to buy Cuba or coerce Spain into giving it up. In 1868 rebellion broke out on Spain's "ever-faithful isle." The Ten Years' War that followed devastated the colony. U.S. investors quickly filled the economic vacuum, and Cuba proved to be an economic bonanza. By the 1890s the United States had over $50 million invested in Cuba, and annual trade with the island—mostly in sugar—was over $100 million. Best of all the United States had no overhead associated with its involvement in Cuba. Spain handled administration and policing, but was so weak and inefficient that U.S. businessmen and traders did not feel unduly constrained. In 1895 revolt broke out anew; this time it was more powerful and more destructive. Spanish troops, led by General Valeriano Weyler y Nícolau, established concentration camps into which they herded Cuban civilians to deprive the rebels of recruits and supplies. The rebels responded with a scorched earth policy. Inevitably American properties were damaged in the growing conflict.

President Grover Cleveland and his successor, William McKinley, watched with concern but declared the United States neutral in the war. Many Americans disagreed with the policy. As they had with other wars for independence in Latin America, many U.S. citizens expressed initial enthusiasm for the rebels. Cuban lobbyists in the United States worked tirelessly to whip up support and to gain recognition for the rebellion. American newspapers, particularly those of Joseph Pulitzer (*New York World*) and William Randolph Hearst (*New York Journal*), were quick to sense a dramatic story. The "yellow journalism" of late-nineteenth-century America sensationalized the events in Cuba, treating the rebellion against Spain as a David-versus-Goliath battle. The Spanish were portrayed as venal, licentious cowards and weaklings who were nevertheless capable of tremendous cruelty. Stories of rape, mutilation, and torture abounded. The Cuban revolutionaries were pictured as heroic freedom fighters and as "bronzed Europeans" not much different from their North American neighbors. Editorial cartoons were fond of portraying the struggle as one in which villainous, immoral Spaniards tried to take advantage of virtuous and defenseless damsels. The Spanish commander quickly became "Butcher" Weyler.

Presidents Cleveland and McKinley and most of their advisers took a more cautious stance. The situation in Cuba was becoming intolerable, but U.S. policy was conflicted. Few doubted that Spain was primarily responsible for the war; its weak and corrupt administration of the island was notorious. Yet there were few willing to side with the rebels—an unknown group of nationalists (and possibly radicals) of uncertain racial cast. The United States had, it appeared, four options. First, it could intervene militarily and annex the island. The uncertainties of war (especially the reactions from other European nations) just as the nation was climbing out of a depression, and the antipathy toward assimilating the Cuban population into Anglo-Saxon America, made this a dubious choice. Second, the United States could side with the Spanish in putting down the revolt. This solution was unlikely to have any long-lasting impact. Spain was weak and growing weaker; the rebels were obviously not going to give up the struggle. Endless warfare and instability would be the results. Third, the United States could side with the rebels. But while rebel success was more likely, there were problems. American officials distrusted the rebel leadership—would it protect American investments and trade? In addition Spain, realizing the hopelessness of its situation, might, rather than fight, sell the island to a more powerful European nation, such as Germany or England. Finally, the United States could do what it eventually did—remain neutral; press the Spanish to grant reforms to quiet the revolt; and warn the rebels that American property and lives must be respected.

The Course of the War

The American position held out the slim hope that perhaps the status quo ante might obtain in Cuba. Spain's inability (or unwillingness) to grant real reforms or deal effectively with the deteriorating situation, and the rebels' dismissal of the limited reforms Spain did grant, soon led to a crisis for American diplomacy. In February 1898 a letter written by the Spanish minister to the United States, Enrique Dupuy de Lôme, was leaked to the American press. In it he declared that McKinley was "weak and a bidder for the admiration of the crowd." Americans seethed at the insult. A few days later an even more dramatic event occurred. In January 1898 President McKinley had ordered the battleship USS *Maine* to Havana Harbor, perhaps to protect American lives but more likely to send a message to both the Spanish government and the rebels about U.S. concerns. On 15 February 1898 the ship exploded, killing more than 250 servicemen. Although the explosion was likely the re-

Wreckage of the *Maine*. The 1898 explosion of the U.S. battleship in Havana Harbor heightened anti-Spanish sentiments and precipitated President McKinley's declaration of war. LIBRARY OF CONGRESS

sult of an onboard accident, many Americans (and U.S. newspapers) quickly jumped to the conclusion that Spain was behind the incident.

McKinley prepared the country for war. In the Far East, U.S. naval vessels were ordered to prepare for attacks on the Spanish colony of the Philippines if war broke out. The president sought and received funds to buttress the nation's weak military forces. American business interests pushed McKinley for a decision, arguing that the uncertainty was bad for the economy. McKinley made several more efforts to push the Spanish into changing their policies in Cuba, but it was too late. On 11 April 1898, McKinley asked Congress for a declaration of war. The war resolution passed, but not without debate. Several congressmen urged that a declaration of Cuba's independence be attached, but McKinley rejected this. The war would not be fought to "free" Cuba. In place of the defeated amendment, the Teller Amendment (introduced by Senator Henry M. Teller), which stated that the United States had no territorial designs on Cuba, was passed.

The war was quick and decisive. On 1 May, Commodore George Dewey's forces soundly defeated the Spanish fleet at Manila Bay in the Philippines. In July the Spanish fleet in Cuba was destroyed, with the loss of one American sailor. The refurbishment of the U.S. Navy, which had begun during the administration of Chester A. Arthur, had paid off.

The U.S. ground war was run somewhat less efficiently. The first difficulty was in forming a reasonable American fighting force out of a fairly dilapidated institution. In the thirty years since the end of the Civil War, the army had been used mostly in combating Native Americans on the frontier, but even those battles had basically ended nearly a decade before. There was no shortage of recruits; more than a quarter-million American men would join the armed forces before the brief war ended. These recruits, however, were outfitted with heavy winter uniforms, and forced to use outdated weapons and consume awful rations. American military leadership also was suspect. The commander of U.S. ground forces in Cuba, Major General William R. Shafter, was out of shape and lacked much martial spirit. He became the butt of numerous jokes and sarcastic songs among his troops. Training the new men and finding adequate transport for them (this was to be America's first overseas war) went on for weeks, with little discernible progress.

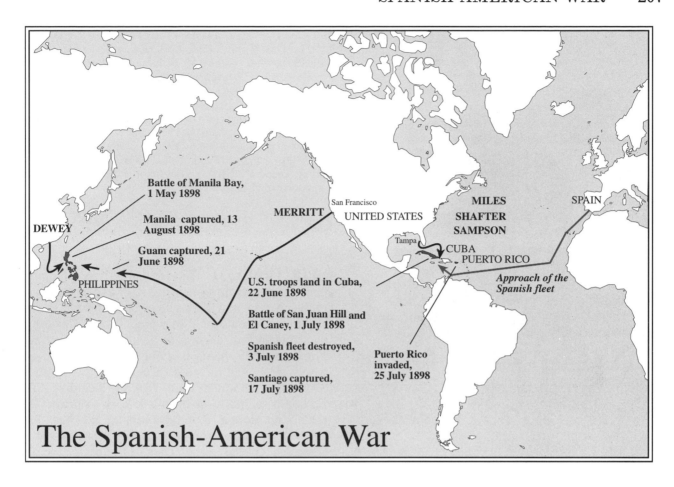

Battle of Manila Bay, 1 May 1898

Manila captured, 13 August 1898

Guam captured, 21 June 1898

DEWEY

PHILIPPINES

MERRITT

San Francisco
UNITED STATES

MILES
SHAFTER
SAMPSON

SPAIN

Tampa
CUBA
PUERTO RICO

Approach of the Spanish fleet

U.S. troops land in Cuba, 22 June 1898

Battle of San Juan Hill and El Caney, 1 July 1898

Spanish fleet destroyed, 3 July 1898

Santiago captured, 17 July 1898

Puerto Rico invaded, 25 July 1898

The Spanish-American War

Fortunately the Spanish were at least as poorly supplied, and lacked much spirit to fight and die so far from home. There were, nevertheless, several sharp battles in Cuba, especially around Santiago following the landing of U.S. troops in late June. The most famous battle was the attack by Lieutenant Colonel Theodore Roosevelt and his Rough Riders on San Juan Heights, in June 1898. By the middle of July, the fighting in Cuba was basically over. More devastating than warfare to the U.S. troops was disease, particularly yellow fever. In July, McKinley ordered the seizure of the Spanish colony of Puerto Rico. By August the war was over. The United States had lost nearly three thousand men, more than twenty-five hundred of them dying from disease and accidents. For a relatively small price the United States had acquired Cuba, Puerto Rico, and the Philippines. America had cleared a European power out of the Caribbean (and away from the route of the contemplated canal) and had obtained a base of operations near the valued China market.

Results

Exactly what territory the United States had acquired was somewhat unclear. There was little dis-

cussion of actually annexing the areas as parts of the United States. The initial enthusiasm for the Cuban rebels in American newspapers had changed. Reports from U.S. servicemen and officials in Cuba indicated that large numbers of the rebels were black or of mixed racial heritage. Almost overnight the "bronzed Europeans" began to be portrayed in editorial cartoons with the same "Sambo" stereotypical qualities the media used to portray African Americans. Accounts of the Philippines and Puerto Rico elicited the same reactions. Indeed, many of the so-called anti-imperialists in the United States used the racial issue as the basis for their stance: the peoples of those areas were unassimilable. These same perceptions, however, also argued against granting Cubans, Filipinos, and Puerto Ricans independence. These peoples were seen, at best, as mischievous children; at worst, as racial inferiors incapable of self-government. Americans worried that independence would mean anarchy, which in turn would invite foreign intervention. For the time being, at least, the three areas would exist in a constitutional limbo—not exactly colonies, not exactly territories, and not independent nations by any stretch of the imagination.

In the Philippines the American presence led to violence. Rebels, who had been fighting the Spanish

Rough Riders. Colonel Theodore Roosevelt and his men at the site they captured in the Battle of San Juan Heights; though not shown in the photograph, African American soldiers did most of the fighting. Photo by William Dinwiddie, 1898. LIBRARY OF CONGRESS: PRINTS AND PHOTOGRAPHS DIVISION

for some time before the arrival of the United States, turned their wrath on the new occupiers. In three years of brutal warfare beginning in February 1899, more than four thousand Americans were lost, and fifteen thousand rebels died in the fighting. By the time the insurrection ended in 1902, thousands of other Filipino civilians had died of hunger and war.

The ratification of a peace treaty in early 1899 brought to a close the "splendid little war," as the U.S. ambassador in London, John Hay, described the Spanish-American War. Almost instantly the United States had entered the circle of imperial powers, with an empire that stretched from the Caribbean to the shores of Asia. As the United States soon discovered, especially in the Philippines, the price of empire could be high.

See also **Cuba; Overseas Possessions; Puerto Rico.**

Bibliography

LaFeber, Walter. *The New Empire: An Interpretation of American Expansion, 1860–1898*. Ithaca, N.Y.: Cornell University Press, 1963.

Morgan, H. Wayne. *America's Road to Empire: The War with Spain and Overseas Expansion*. New York: Knopf, 1965.

Musicant, Ivan. *Empire by Default: The Spanish-American War and the Dawn of the American Century*. New York: Henry Holt, 1998.

Offner, John L. *An Unwanted War: The Diplomacy of the United States and Spain over Cuba, 1895–1898*. Chapel Hill: University of North Carolina Press, 1992.

Paterson, Thomas G., and Stephen G. Rabe, eds. *Imperial Surge*. Lexington, Mass.: D.C. Heath, 1992.

Trask, David F. *The War with Spain in 1898*. Lincoln: University of Nebraska Press, 1997.

MICHAEL L. KRENN

SPIRITUALISM In 1848 Spiritualism burst upon the American scene when a series of occurrences in the upstate New York village of Hydesville caused a national sensation. Two young sisters, Katie Fox and Maggie Fox, claimed to be able to elicit strange rapping sounds produced by the "spirits" of the dead, who were communicating through the two women. Soon some prominent New Yorkers, including John Edmunds, a judge on the New York Court of Appeals, and Horace Greeley, editor of the *New York Tribune*, expressed the opinion that the Fox sisters possessed special gifts. They did not. Later the women confessed that they had participated in a great fraud, prompted by family tensions. They had made the rapping noises by cracking the joints of their toes.

The Fox sisters' confession did not spell the death of Spiritualism. The belief persisted that through mediums humans could commune with those who "had passed over." In fact, Spiritualist belief spread and intensified. Before the revelations at Hydesville, Spiritualism had only scattered adherents, most prominently Shakers and Swedenborgians. After Hydesville, Spiritualism attracted a large, increasingly diverse following, especially among women. The movement did not denigrate or oppress women, and it also lacked an orientation toward male authority. Spiritualism therefore offered women new roles, such as that of medium. Additionally, the trauma caused by the bloodbath of the Civil War created a milieu conducive to further growth. Moreover, the supposedly scientific dimensions of Spiritualism helped to attract followers. Spiritualist interest in atomic theory and the wonders of mesmerism and psychic powers gave the movement a pseudorationalistic flavor. Just as Edmunds and Greeley had become fascinated, so did Hamlin Garland, Lester Ward, and other well-known personalities of the late nineteenth century. These supporters gave the faith credibility, and indeed, it became fashionable. In

1893 thousands of Spiritualists from throughout the nation joined the newly launched National Spiritualist Association (NSA), which remained the main body of Spiritualism in the United States for over a century. NSA churches conducted Protestant-like services, usually with some aspect of spiritual healing involved in their weekly worship and always with the message that Spiritualism is the key to all religion and the life of all reform.

In the post–Civil War years Spiritualists created dozens of encampments or assemblies for séances, healings, and related activities, including "spiritual writings" from the beyond. Two of the principal Spiritualist Meccas were Liberal in Barton County, Missouri, and Lily Dale in Chautauqua County, New York, both of which had been centers of the earlier free thought or "infidel" phenomenon. A link between freethinkers and Spiritualists is understandable because followers of both embraced the spirit of scientific inquiry and challenged religious orthodoxy. Some advocates of Spiritualism preached social reconstruction as a handmaiden to spiritual regeneration, and they created several utopian communal colonies during the Gilded Age and after. Fountain Grove, California, the creation of Thomas Lake Harris; Spirit Fruit Society, which began in Ohio and relocated to Illinois and then California, founded by Jacob Beilhart; and Shalam, New Mexico, led by Elizabeth Rowell Thompson, are examples.

Just as some freethinkers and communitarians moved into Spiritualism, Spiritualists drifted into other contemporary metaphysical faiths, most notably theosophy. During the nineteenth century Spiritualism was vibrantly alive, expanding rather than contracting as it would throughout most of the next century.

See also **Religion,** *subentry on* **Religion in Nineteenth-Century America.**

Bibliography

Kerr, Howard, and Charles L. Crow, eds. *The Occult in America: New Historical Perspectives.* Urbana: University of Illinois Press, 1983.

Moore, R. Laurence. *In Search of White Crows: Spiritualism, Parapsychology, and American Culture.* New York: Oxford University Press, 1977.

Taylor, William George Langworthy. *Katie Fox, Epochmaking Medium and the Making of the Fox-Taylor Record.* New York and London: Putnam, 1933.

H. ROGER GRANT

SPORTS

[This entry includes subentries on **Sports and the Sporting Life** and **Baseball.**]

SPORTS AND THE SPORTING LIFE

Sport before the Civil War

Antebellum sport was dominated by elite and working-class members of the male bachelor subculture, who believed in immediate gratification and who challenged Victorian morality and capitalist values of hard work, sexual continence, avoidence of idleness, moderation, self-control, and frugality. They constituted a sporting fraternity whose contests embodied such masculine traits as aggression, courage, honor, and vigor. Their pastimes were castigated as immoral and socially debilitating wastes of time by members of the respectable middle class, who believed in hard work, domesticity, sobriety, and piety.

Sporting activities in the early Republic were primarily participatory and rural. They included horse racing, gouging (a no-holds-barred combat between frontiersmen), boxing, fishing, hunting, billiards, cockfighting, and animal baiting. These premodern pastimes were characterized by local competition, simple rules, gambling, limited organization, and little role differentiation, publicity, or record keeping and provided opportunities to demonstrate prowess and honor. Tavern owners were the first sports promoters, attracting thirsty customers with billiard tables, outdoor bowling lanes, marksmanship contests, cockfights, and illegal backroom boxing matches. Most pugilists were Irish immigrants, such as John Morrissey, a street brawler who grew up in Troy, New York. Morrissey won the American championship in 1853 against John L. "Yankee" Sullivan in the thirty-seventh round and later became an important gambler and Tammany Hall politician.

Because of the notable persons involved, the amount of money wagered, the number of spectators, and the attention of the press, horse racing was the most important spectator sport. It was barred, however, in the northeast after the Revolution for its aristocratic associations, considered inappropriate to the lives of hardworking, moral citizens. In 1821 New York State legalized racing, and two years later John Cox Stevens, son of a wealthy inventor-merchant, organized the Eclipse–Sir Henry race, the first of five great North-South matches between contestants that symbolized each region's social and economic systems. Horse racing languished in the North in the 1840s because of the impact of the Depression of 1837 and growing moral opposition to gambling. In 1835 Stevens organized the first major professional pedestrian (running) race, won by a competitor who ran ten miles in under an hour. He also founded the prestigious New York Yacht Club (NYYC) in 1844 and in 1851 sponsored the boat *America,* which defeated seventeen of the finest British vessels in the Royal Yacht Squadron's regatta, demonstrating the excellence of American seamanship and naval architecture.

A New Ideology of Sport

At mid-century the sporting culture underwent important changes that enabled sport to become respectable, helping set the stage for a postwar sporting boom. The key was the creation of a positive sport ideology in the 1840s and 1850s by social reformers and evangelists. Reformers, including physicians, journalists, scientists, and health faddists, were concerned about the declining quality of city life owing to immigration, poverty, disease, and crime. Evangelists were inspired by the Second Great Awakening to prepare a more perfect society for the Second Coming of Christ. Public health, municipal park, and fitness movements emerged to ameliorate living conditions for slum dwellers and sedentary white-collar workers by getting them involved in outdoor "rational recreation," that is, uplifting leisure that would improve the participants. These crusades were justified by a new sports creed, based on Ancient Greek athletics, Enlightenment thought, and European educational reform, which argued that participation in uplifting sports would improve morality, build character, promote public health, and produce muscular Christians. Americans were urged to emulate the sporting cultures of English, Scottish, and German immigrants, who brought their athletic traditions with them and organized athletic clubs to promote their ethnic heritages. By the 1830s Englishmen were renowned for cricket, rowing, and long-distance running. Scotsmen in the 1850s formed Caledonian societies to sponsor professional track and field meets that included traditional events like throwing a tall, heavy pole called the caber. By the 1870s the Caledonian games drew up to twenty thousand paying spectators. In the late 1840s, Germans introduced turnvereins, athletic clubs that promoted exercise, gymnastics, liberal politics, German culture, and unions.

Americans were also encouraged to eschew evil gambling sports in favor of uplifting ones, especially baseball. Baseball fulfilled the requirements of the new sports creed as a manly game that improved character and fitness. It evolved from British boys' games, with rules drawn up in 1845 by a New Yorker, Alexander Cartwright, for his Knickerbocker Club. Three years later the first recorded game was played by the New York and Brooklyn clubs. Baseball quickly surpassed the more difficult, less exciting, and seemingly interminable game of cricket as the leading team sport and by the 1850s was known as "the national pastime." Most notable teams were in metropolitan New York, where clubs in 1857 organized the National Association of Base Ball Players. Within a few years the best teams were recruiting players with cash or government sinecures.

Post–Civil War Sport

Sport took off after the Civil War because of the new sport ideology, the modernization of particular sports, and the impact of urbanization and industrialization. Sport became highly organized into institutions that arranged national championships and standardized rules. Roles became specialized, events were well publicized, and statistics and records were carefully maintained. Athletes were drawn from the newly enlarged industrial radial cities, where sports were becoming organized, commercialized, and professionalized. A variety of external factors, such as evolutions in urban physical structures, social organizations, and values (group attitudes, behavior, and ideologies) shaped the rise of sport.

The sports world was profoundly influenced by technological innovations in communication and transportation. Railroads dramatically shortened travel time, facilitating access to sites of competition. Major-league baseball teams traveled by rail, and race horses were shipped cross-country by train. Commuter lines brought spectators to suburban racecourses and the elite to their country clubs. Railroads transported fighters and fans to secret locations beyond the arm of the law, such as Richburg, Mississippi, site of the John L. Sullivan–Jake Kilrain heavyweight championship fight in 1889. In addition, mass transit enabled fans to travel to ballparks and the middle class to visit distant city parks.

Communications innovations like the telegraph and telephone made possible instantaneous transmission of sporting news to newspapers and gambling halls. The antebellum press, particularly the *New York Herald*, began to cover sport in some detail by the 1840s. Joseph Pulitzer's *New York World* established the first sports department and took advantage of inventions like the rotary press and the linotype machine (1886) to mass-produce newspapers, increasing its circulation from 15,000 in 1883 to 250,000 in 1887. Sport later became a staple of the penny press and was also widely covered in mainstream magazines and specialized weeklies, like the *Spirit of the Times* (1831–1902), the *Police Gazette* (1845–1916), and the *Sporting News* (1886–).

Technological innovations aided record keeping, helped preserve great moments in sports, and improved the ambience of indoor sport. Stopwatches re-

Poster for *Bearings* Magazine, 1896. *Bearings* was a magazine for bicycle enthusiasts. LIBRARY OF CONGRESS

corded times in fifths of seconds, and photographs helped determine close horse races. Thomas A. Edison's kinetoscope (1894) was soon used to film boxing matches. Indoor sports were lit first by dangerous gas lamps in the 1880s and then by electric arc lights. These were in turn superseded by Edison's incandescent lightbulb, which required simpler wiring and emitted consistent candle power. By 1890 electric lighting was common at major indoor sporting sites.

The factory system made possible the manufacture of cheap and improved sporting goods. Spalding baseballs cost just five cents in 1892 and were available from specialized retail shops, department stores, and mail-order catalogs. The 1895 Sears, Roebuck catalog advertised over eighty pages of sporting goods. New products, like sliding seats (1870) and lightweight racing shells for crew, enhanced athletic performance, and streamlined sulkies with pneumatic tires (1888) sped up harness racing. Catchers' masks, chest protectors, shin guards, and gloves improved baseball safety.

The bicycle was the most important new manufactured sporting product, enabling millions of middle-class men and women to escape crowded industrial cities. Pierre Lallement's velocipede or "boneshaker," introduced in 1866, caused a brief riding fad in 1868 and 1869. It was supplanted in 1876 by the English "ordinary," with a front wheel sixty inches in diameter and a tiny rear wheel to lighten its weight. The ordinary was expensive, hard to master, uncomfortable, and dangerous. By 1878 local cycling clubs were organized to sponsor long-distance road races and to promote riders' interests with the assistance of the League of American Wheelmen, founded in 1880. The English safety bicycle, invented in the late 1880s, had equal-sized pneumatic tires and coaster brakes and was easy to ride. A huge cycling fad recruited four million riders by 1896. Cycling became women's most popular physical activity, offering exercise and independence. Women's sports clothes, bloomers and split skirts, replaced floor-length dresses. Cycling was also a popular spectator sport, featuring events like indoor six-day races at New York's Madison Square Garden beginning in 1895.

Middle-Class Sport

The direction of late-nineteenth-century sport was heavily influenced by social structure. Upper-class men with ample wealth and leisure time demonstrated their manliness and certified or achieved high social status by playing expensive sports and joining elite sports clubs. These sportsmen were epitomized by the *New York Herald* publisher James G. Bennett Jr. Bennett was a member of the NYYC and the American Jockey Club; an organizer in 1876 of the Westchester (New York) Polo Club, the first in the United States; and the builder of the Newport (Rhode Island) Casino Club, site of the U.S. men's tennis championships (1881–1914). Upper-class clubs limited membership by strict admission policies and fees. The least prestigious were downtown athletic clubs that emphasized track and field. The first such club, the New York Athletic Club (NYAC), was founded in 1866, and by the mid-1880s nearly every major city had one. The NYAC supported strict amateurism and in 1888 helped found the Amateur Athletic Union. Amateur athletes were defined as those who had never competed for money, vied with professionals for a prize, or taught athletics to earn a living. Elite amateurs dominated the first U.S. Olympic squad in 1896.

Suburban country clubs also became focal points of elite sportsmen, following the example of the Brookline (Massachusetts) County Club, established in 1882. Country clubs provided an escape from ur-

Lawn-Tennis Tournament, New Brighton, Staten Island. Sporting competitions were new arenas for men to showcase their dominance, leadership, and wit. Engraving from sketch by H. A. Ogden, 1880. LIBRARY OF CONGRESS

ban life, helped integrate families into an elite subculture, and promoted a sense of community and stability. They quickly became known for golf and tennis. St. Andrews, a nine-hole course built in Yonkers in 1888, was the first U.S. golf course, but William K. Vanderbilt's eighteen-hole Shinnecock Hills Golf Club (1891) in Southhampton, Long Island, became the American prototype. Thirteen years later about one thousand American golf clubs were in operation. Tennis was less popular among men until the international Davis Cup competition in 1900.

Upper-class young women were among the first sportswomen. Their social prestige protected them against having their femininity questioned and made their breaking of social conventions more possible. Enjoying the facilities at private athletic and country clubs as both spectators and competitors, they became models for the independent, attractive, corsetfree "Gibson girl" of the 1890s magazines who participated in coed cycling, golf, tennis, and horseback riding. Women responded to both the physical and social dimensions of golf, and a women's national championship was started in 1895, one year after the

men's. Lawn tennis, an English game developed in 1873, was introduced in the United States one year later by Mary Outerbridge. Tennis was also popular among women, who played in full-length skirts. A women's national tennis championship was established in 1887.

Sports flourished in the late nineteenth century among middle-class men because of the increase in their leisure time and discretionary income, the influence of the sports creed, newly invented "clean" sports (i.e., those that did not involve gambling or abuse of animals and were not connected to corrupting institutions like saloons) like croquet and volleyball, and the need they shared with the elite to demonstrate manliness to counter the perceived feminization of American culture. The new professionals and bureaucrats, who had less control over their work than independent antebellum shopkeepers, turned to their pastimes to demonstrate their manliness, creativity, and self-worth. They joined athletic clubs, cycled, played tennis and baseball, and attended baseball games.

Middle-class women's participation was controversial. Physicians, writers, and female physical educators recommended moderate exercise to improve health, although many critics felt women were too frail or that competitive sport would render them aggressive and unfeminine. Exercise and sports like horseback riding, ice skating, croquet, cycling, and tennis that promoted grace and beauty were encouraged. Fitness proponents emphasized calisthenics, Swedish drilling (a complicated system of calisthenics that used no apparatus, designed to develop every part of the body), Dr. Dio Lewis's system of gymnastics that relied on apparatus, and Dr. Dudley Sargent's "corrective gymnastics" program of individualized exercises, which developed in the 1880s.

Working-Class Sport

Working-class sport was a male sphere, influenced by limited leisure time, low incomes, declining access to traditional playing areas, and amateurism. Semiskilled and unskilled men worked about sixty hours a week, skilled men about fifty-four hours. Workers had few holidays and only Sundays off, but most states had blue laws that limited Sabbath-day pastimes. Working-class athletes were mainly Irishmen or German-American members of the labor aristocracy. The new immigrants from eastern and southern Europe who were at the bottom of the social ladder arrived without a sporting tradition and disdained American sport as time-wasting.

Lower-class athletes participated in activities that fit their socioeconomic circumstances and were especially drawn to sports that offered professional opportunities, such as pedestrianism, pugilism, and baseball. Long-distance racing was lucrative for several years, especially in 1878 and 1879, when the international Astley Belt races paid up to $20,000 to the winner, who covered over 500 miles in six days. Boxers typically came from urban slums. Prominent among them were Irish Americans, who produced nine of nineteen American world champions in the 1890s. Opportunities in amateur sport were limited, but in the 1880s welfare capitalists, most notably the railroad car manufacturer George Pullman, organized athletic programs to attract and keep workers, provide a moral alternative to vile amusements, and advertise their companies.

The African American athletic experience differed from that of immigrants because former slaves had grown up with American sports. Slaves had trained fighting birds, raced in boats, ridden thoroughbreds at southern tracks, and boxed in matches arranged by their owners. The former slave Tom Molineaux, the first prominent American pugilist, fought the English boxing champion Tom Cribb in 1810. After the

Civil War outstanding black athletes had some success in professional sports. The premier jockeys until the 1890s were mainly black, including Isaac Murphy, winner of three Kentucky Derbies (1884, 1890, 1891). Successful black pugilists included the Canadian-born George Dixon, a bantamweight (1888) and featherweight champion (1891–1897). About seventy-five African Americans played professional baseball from 1872 to 1898, including the brothers Moses Fleetwood Walker and Weldon W. Walker in the major league American Association in 1884. However, prejudice forced African Americans out of baseball and horse racing at the end of the century. Black fighters had a hard time getting matches, and the color line was drawn against the black heavyweight contender Peter Jackson.

Intercollegiate Sport

Intercollegiate sport began in 1852 with the Harvard-Yale boat race. Within two decades colleges also competed in baseball, football, and track and field. Initially competition was limited to the elite eastern institutions, where it was sponsored by student associations. By 1900 college sports were played throughout the country and had become rationalized, commercialized, and professionalized. Female students also participated and, like men, used sports to display prowess, organize extracurricular activities, and promote school spirit. College men played sports to demonstrate their manliness, while women played sports to shape their self-images, fitness, and public attitudes toward femininity.

Baseball was the second college sport. In the inaugural game in 1859, Amherst College defeated Williams College 73 to 32. By the 1870s baseball was the principal game on American campuses.

Football competition began in 1869, when Rutgers beat Princeton six goals to four using soccer-like rules. Modern football actually began in 1874, when Harvard used rugby rules that permitted physical contact and ball carrying in a game with McGill University. Winning became very important. Yale dominated football under the volunteer coach Walter Camp, who employed repetitive drills and rough scrimmages to develop efficient and precise play, communicated plays by signals, and introduced strategy. Yale outscored the opposition by 4,600 to 92 between 1883 and 1891. Camp introduced major rule changes to make the game more entertaining. In 1880 he cut the number of players from fifteen to eleven and introduced the scrimmage system to put the ball in play and the downs system to maintain possession. Remaining a rough game, football was considered a "moral equivalent of war" that tested the manliness of upper-middle and upper-class young men.

College sports soon developed problems, such as weak eligibility rules. Colleges recruited players with jobs, scholarships, and easy course loads, with little regard to academic standards. In response, faculties formed organizations, such as the Intercollegiate Conference of Faculty Representatives (1895), to set and enforce rules for eligibility and fair play. These efforts were followed by the creation of the National Collegiate Athletic Association in 1905.

Elite eastern women's colleges introduced physical education shortly after the Civil War, teaching calisthenics with dumbbells, Indian clubs, and wands. Although most physical educators of women discouraged competition and preferred intramural participation, many student athletes preferred team sports, and by 1866 women at Vassar College were playing baseball. In 1892, one year after James Naismith invented basketball, the Smith College gymnasium director, Senda Berenson, modified the rules and the court size of the game to make it more appropriate for women athletes. Stanford defeated the University of California 2 to 1 in the first intercollegiate women's basketball match in 1896. Women also competed in crew, field hockey, and track and field.

Professional Sport

The major innovation in post–Civil War sport was the growth of commercialized spectator sports. The product of the new sporting ideology, urbanization, and the modernization of sport, professionalized sport received the backing of politically connected entrepreneurs. Events were staged in enclosed arenas, racetracks, and fields, where fees were charged to see professional athletes perform. Although prizefighting remained widely barred because of its brutality, its corruption, and the gambling nexus, heavyweight champion John L. Sullivan (1882–1892) nevertheless became the most famous sportsman of the century. Pugilism was increasingly regulated in the 1880s by the Marquis of Queensberry rules, which required three-minute rounds, ten-second knockouts, and gloved competition. Prizefighting was legalized in New Orleans in 1890 and in New York City, the national sporting capital, from 1896 to 1900.

Horse racing revived after the war at prestigious elite tracks, starting with New York's Jerome Park (1866) and including Baltimore's Pimlico (1870), Brooklyn's Sheepshead Bay (1880), and Chicago's Washington Park (1884). By 1900 major races were contested by thoroughbreds costing up to $40,000

Yale Football Team. After the Civil War, sport came to be viewed as a means of moral, as well as physical, vitality. Photograph, 1878. LIBRARY OF CONGRESS: PRINTS AND PHOTOGRAPHS DIVISION

and were attended by more than 30,000 spectators. Their success encouraged the establishment of proprietary tracks, like Brooklyn's Brighton Beach (1870), that attracted a plebeian audience. By the 1890s major tracks in such racing centers as Illinois and New Jersey were closed because of opposition to gambling.

In the latter half of the century, baseball was the preeminent professional sport. In 1869 the Cincinnati Reds, the first all-salaried team, was organized and won fifty-seven games and tied one. Two years later the National Association of Professional Base Ball Players was established, superseded in 1876 by the more rationalized and profit-oriented National League. The National League instituted important reforms, like the reserve clause in 1879 (a clause in a player's contract that gives the team an option to renew the player's contract, trade the player, or release him without any reciprocity on the team's part), to put the sport on a more businesslike basis. National League clubs also waged a moral crusade against playing ball on Sundays, gambling, and rowdyism to attract middle-class audiences and charged fifty cents to keep out the rabble. The league became profitable and attracted competition, particularly the American Association (1882–1891), whose franchises, located in the largest cities, sought working-class fans by charging twenty-five cents, selling liquor, and playing on Sundays. The game on the field in the 1880s had modernized its rules, equipment, and tactics, including place hitting, sacrifices, and hit and run, which emphasized scientific but rough play. By 1900 only the eight-team National League operated, setting the stage for the rise of the American League.

See also **Bicycling; Health Consciousness and Fitness; Inventors and Inventions; Recreation; Saloons and the Drinking Life; Sports,** *subentry on* **Baseball; Victorianism; Working-class Culture.**

Bibliography

Adelman, Melvin L. *A Sporting Time: New York City and the Rise of Modern Athletics, 1820–1870.* Urbana: University of Illinois Press, 1986.

Betts, John R. "Mind and Body in Early American Thought." *Journal of American History* 54 (1968): 787–805.

———. "The Technological Revolution and the Rise of Sports, 1850–1900." *Mississippi Valley Historical Review* 40 (1953): 231–256.

Gorn, Elliott. *The Manly Art: Bare-Knuckle Prize Fighting in America.* Ithaca, N.Y.: Cornell University Press, 1986.

Hardy, Stephen. *How Boston Played: Sport, Recreation, and Community, 1865–1915.* Boston: Northeastern University Press, 1982.

Himes, Cindy L. "The Female Athlete in American Society, 1860–1940." Ph.D. diss., University of Pennsylvania, 1986.

Kirsch, George. *The Creation of American Team Sports: Baseball and Cricket, 1838–1872.* Urbana: University of Illinois Press, 1989.

Rader, Benjamin G. *American Sports: From the Age of Folk Games to the Age of Televised Sports.* 4th ed. Englewood Cliffs, N.J.: Prentice Hall, 1998.

Riess, Steven A. *City Games: The Evolution of American Urban Society and the Rise of Sports.* Urbana: University of Illinois Press, 1989.

Seymour, Harold. *Baseball.* New York: Oxford University Press, 1960.

Smith, Ronald A. *Sports and Freedom: The Rise of Big Time College Athletics.* New York: Oxford University Press, 1988.

Somers, Dale A. *The Rise of Sports in New Orleans, 1850–1900.* Baton Rouge: Louisiana State University Press, 1972.

STEVEN A. RIESS

BASEBALL

By the end of the nineteenth century, baseball had become America's sport, the national pastime. Its lineage is not without controversy, but most contemporary scholars trace the game directly to the English countryside and games like cricket, rounders, and one old cat. There are references to "base ball," two words then, in eighteenth-century children's books and in Jane Austen's novel, *Northanger Abbey* (1818).

A Gentleman's Game

Before the Civil War there were early versions of baseball, variously called soak ball, town ball, the Massachusetts game, and the New York game, played mostly in northeastern cities. The playing fields were square, with posts or stones for bases. Baseball evolved most quickly in and around New York City, where Alexander Cartwright (1820–1892), the guiding hand behind the Knickerbocker Base Ball Club and the "father of modern baseball," mapped out playing field dimensions and rules. The first game under Cartwright's rules was played on 19 June 1846 at the Elysian Fields in Hoboken, New Jersey, as even then recreational space in Manhattan was scarce. Played mostly by middle-class gentlemen, the games were models of propriety, often followed by friendly dinners. Baseball was then as social as it was athletic. The New York game's popularity increased, but for the most part excluded working-class men, whose manners were disparaged, and whose long workdays did not leave time to play games.

A loose and largely ineffective organization of amateurs, the National Association of Base Ball Play-

Morris Brown College Baseball Team. The coach *(center)* and his team in Atlanta, Georgia. Though excluded from playing white college baseball teams, African American colleges formed their own teams and participated in what was becoming an American institution. LIBRARY OF CONGRESS: PRINTS AND PHOTOGRAPHS DIVISION

ers, was formed in 1858. This league, primarily comprised of "gentlemen," opposed paying players as unsporting, although in 1860 a pitcher, James Creighton, was paid to play for the Brooklyn Excelsiors. Two years later, Brooklyn businessman William Cammeyer converted his skating rink into a baseball field and charged admission. Spectators paid ten cents, though the players were not remunerated. In those years few sporting events charged admission and few athletes were paid for playing. During the Civil War the game was spread to the South by Union troops in Confederate prison camps. After the war, fan interest, promoted by an enthusiastic sports press, created profitable opportunities for both entrepreneurs and players. Spectators, sometimes in the thousands, went "out to the ballgame." Commercial interests were beginning to reshape the "gentleman's" game, and professional baseball was on the horizon.

Professional Baseball

Although most teams were located in the East, in 1869 Harry Wright (1835–1895) founded the first all-professional team, the Red Stockings, in Cincinnati. That team, with most of its players from the New York City area, won fifty-seven games, lost none, and tied one in its first season. A few annual salaries reached two thousand dollars. To organize competition, players in 1871 formed the National Association of Professional Base Ball Players (NAPBBP). The league, poorly managed and overwhelmed by the superlative Boston Red Stockings, was a commercial failure. Unable to keep out unprofitable small-town teams—franchises cost only ten dollars—and failing to control owners or players, gambling, drunkenness, or corruption, the league lasted only five years.

In 1876, William A. Hulbert (1832–1882), a Chicago businessman and owner of the Chicago White Stockings, raided other leagues for star players, including future Hall of Famer Albert G. Spalding (1850–1915). Hulbert and Spalding planned the National League of Professional Base Ball Clubs. They enticed four eastern teams from the NAPBBP to join four western teams to create the new league, setting the pattern for the future American League. In an effort to improve the league's image, boisterous spec-

A Day at the Ballpark. The professional Boston team gathers for a photograph while gentleman fans pack the stadium. Photograph, F. L. Howe, 1886. LIBRARY OF CONGRESS

tators were ejected and Sunday games, as well as the sale of liquor and gambling on club grounds, were prohibited.

The National League, unlike the player-controlled Association, had a strong, owner-dominated administration. When they did not meet their schedules, the New York and Philadelphia clubs were expelled from the league. Players who threw games were permanently barred. Umpires were paid; previously they had been volunteers. Spalding, captain of the White Stockings, played for a year and then retired to build a sporting goods empire. Later, in an effort to portray baseball as a uniquely American sport by denying its English antecedents, Spalding promoted the myth that in 1839 Abner Doubleday (1819–1893) had invented baseball in Cooperstown, New York. There is little evidence to support, and much to deny, the claim that Doubleday, a Civil War general, had anything to do with baseball.

In the prosperous 1880s, ticket prices rose to fifty cents, baseball stars were glorified, umpires were vilified, and hot dogs became a baseball institution. The game turned scientific, stressing strategy and finesse. New equipment was introduced: gloves for fielders (earlier they had fielded barehanded), masks and shin guards for catchers. The distance between pitcher and batter increased gradually from forty-five feet, reaching the present sixty feet, six inches, in 1893, and rules were changed to allow pitchers to throw overhand. The National League inserted the reserve clause in contracts to prevent players from jumping from one club or league to another. During the depression of the 1890s, baseball profits declined, but the National League survived and in 1903 was joined by the American League, creating the foundation for the major league structure in the twentieth century. This, then, was the dawn of modern professional baseball.

A National Game

New Americans took to the diamond sport. By the end of the nineteenth century Irish-American players made up as much as one third of the National League. Popular players like Mike "King" Kelly (1857–1894), regaled in the hit song "Slide Kelly Slide," were celebrated. German-Americans were also well represented in professional ranks. It was not until the twentieth century, however, that significant numbers of sons of poor southern and eastern European immigrants, groups without a strong sports heritage, were commonly found on professional rosters.

Despite a strong black sports tradition—and although there were significant exceptions like Moses Walker (1857–1924)—professional baseball allowed few opportunities for African Americans. Jim Crow laws also restricted black participation at school and amateur levels, so African Americans formed sports clubs of their own and outstanding professional teams like the Cuban Giants. Complete segregation in organized baseball came in 1898, to be broken only in 1946, when Jackie Robinson (1919–1972) joined the Montreal farm team of the Brooklyn Dodgers.

In *God's Country and Mine* (1954), Jacques Barzun writes that "whoever wants to know the heart and mind of America had better learn baseball, the rules and realities of the game—and do it by watching first some high school or small town teams." As American industry flourished and cities grew during the Gilded Age, the work ethic gave ground to the idea of leisure time. In the second half of the century, baseball became a truly national game. Across the country youngsters played with five-cent baseballs in public parks, open fields, and vacant lots. Companies sponsored teams to advertise their products; politicians supported teams to win elections, and ethnic organizations backed teams to boost pride. In communities across the nation, baseball provided a common experience. Reformers such as the Progressives believed that baseball could transform and Americanize immigrants. Baseball was played in every corner of America: indoors in armories, unsuccessfully at night under artificial light in Fort Wayne, Indiana, and on ice skates in Brooklyn. At the end of the nineteenth century, baseball—a city game resonating with agrarian values—mirrored the face of America.

See also **Recreation**.

Bibliography

Barzun, Jacques. *God's Country and Mine: A Declaration of Love with a Few Harsh Words*. Boston: Little, Brown, 1954.
Goldstein, Warren. *Playing for Keeps: A History of Early Baseball*. Ithaca, N.Y.: Cornell University Press, 1989.
Rader, Benjamin. *American Sports: From the Age of Folk Games to the Age of Spectators*. Englewood Cliffs, N.J.: Prentice-Hall, 1983.
Reiss, Steven A. *Sport in Industrial America, 1850–1920*. Wheeling, Ill.: Harlan Davidson, 1995.
Seymour, Harold. *Baseball*. Vol. 1. *The Early Years*. New York: Oxford University Press, 1960.
Voight, David Quentin. *American Baseball*. Vol. 1. *From Gentleman's Sport to the Commissioner System*. Norman: University of Oklahoma Press, 1966.

ARNOLD MARKOE

STAGECOACHES.   See **Transportation**, subentry on **Animal Power**.

STATE GOVERNMENT   The states are fundamental parts of American government. This relationship was established during the American Revolution and was reaffirmed by the Constitution of the United States, which acknowledged the existing states and authorized the creation of new ones. The nation contained sixteen states in 1800 and added twenty-nine over the next one hundred years. Most new states were admitted by the process outlined in the Northwest Ordinance (1787), which authorized Congress to organize territorial governments and allowed territorial officials to petition for statehood. Ohio (admitted in 1803) was the first of five states carved out of the original Northwest Territory, which also contained Indiana (1816), Illinois (1818), Michigan (1837), and Wisconsin (1848). Congress created a succession of territories as the U.S. population spread across North America during the nineteenth century. Louisiana (1812) was the first state created from the Louisiana Purchase tract.

Sectional conflict between northern and southern citizens ruffled the politics of statehood before 1861. The Missouri Compromise resulted in the admission of Maine (1820), formerly part of Massachusetts, as a nonslave state and Missouri (1821) as a slave state. In 1845 Congress annexed Texas, which had broken from Mexico and declared itself independent. Congress balanced the number of slave and nonslave states until after 1848, the year that Wisconsin entered as the thirtieth state. California, which split from Mexico during the Mexican War, formed its own government prior to admission as a free state (1850). The conflict between slave and antislave factions took a bloody turn in Kansas, which achieved statehood (1861) on the eve of the Civil War. West Virginia seceded from Virginia during the war (1863), and Nevada joined the Union a year later. The postwar admissions were concentrated in the western region of the country. The Omnibus Bill added four states in 1889 (North Dakota, South Dakota, Montana, and Washington), with Wyoming and Idaho following the next year. Congress delayed the admission of Utah (1896) until the Mormon Church disavowed polygamy.

Each state possessed its own constitution, which created a government and detailed operational procedures. Most of these documents contained a bill of rights that guaranteed liberties to citizens of the state. Fifteen southern states permitted slavery prior to the Thirteenth Amendment (1865) to the U.S. Constitution. The Fourteenth (1868) and Fifteenth (1870) Amendments placed additional restrictions on state governments, as did internal provisions in the Constitution. State constitutions underwent numerous changes by means of amendment; and the original charters of new states reflected current political trends. Early constitutions lodged most power in state legislatures and limited the authority of governors and judges, some of whom were selected by legislators. Reforms in the course of the nineteenth century established universal suffrage for white males, directly elected governors and most judges, and limited legislative prerogatives. Governors were permitted to veto legislation in New York in 1821, in Illinois in 1848, and in Virginia in 1870. The latter two states followed the majority of states in converting their legislatures from annual to biennial meetings. Reformers restricted the ability of states to incur debt and prohibited investments in private companies. State judiciaries in many states struck down an increasing number of statutes after 1850.

Constitutional and judicial restrictions impeded but did not stop the passage of legislation that covered a widening assortment of subjects during the 1800s. This outpouring of law rested on two fundamental legal principles. First, the Constitution of the United States reserved numerous policy subjects to the states, which coexisted with the national government within a federal system. Second, a legal doctrine called the police power emerged by the 1830s that justified state regulations intended to protect the health, safety, welfare, and morals of their citizens. The police power was an elastic concept that evolved over the century in legislative actions, judicial review, and constitutional revision. State lawmakers assigned the enforcement of most regulations to city and county governments, which states created and empowered.

This reliance on local officials was a major reason why state governments were slow to develop an extensive administrative capacity before 1900. Most taxation and expenditure occurred at the local level. State lawmakers tended to concentrate on formulating general policies that guided their lower-level and local officials. State legislation fell into three distinct public policy eras over the course of the century. The first, the 1780s to the 1830s, was characterized by political deference to elites, "mercantilist" promotion of commercial development such as canals and railroads, legislative supremacy, and a bare-bones administrative structure. Suffrage during this stage was confined to property owners, and legislatures tended to enact particularistic laws that chartered companies and cities individually. Many states, mainly in the north, sponsored ambitious transportation improvements, such as New York's Erie Canal, which opened in 1825. This stage gave way to the egalitarian era, 1830–1870, when a movement toward universal white male suffrage and wider applications of democracy appeared. Legislatures adopted general laws to incorporate businesses and cities; social regulations appeared in the form of municipal police, free schools, attacks on slavery in the North, and attacks on liquor everywhere; and urban services such as fresh water were provided. Constitutional revisions imposed limitations on legislatures, especially concerning loans and debt, which reduced, but did not eliminate, state-sponsored transportation projects. During the Civil War state and local governments played a major role in raising troops for the Union Army, spending half a billion dollars on enlistment bounties. The Civil War increased indebtedness and led to new taxes but did not produce fundamental alterations in northern governance, unlike the constitutional and other changes that occurred in southern state governments during the war and Reconstruction. The Civil War expanded state tax bases but had minimal impact on other areas of statecraft.

The states gravitated toward a regulatory policy regime (1870–1900) after the depression of the 1870s. During this stage, which blossomed into progressive reform after 1900, legislators expanded the range of regulation over commercial activities, social behavior, and local finances. The imposition of railroad rate regulations, some authorized by commissions, and the adoption of controls over alcoholic beverages constitute prime examples. The era also witnessed the beginning of laws governing the conditions of work, especially for women and children, and political parties. Services such as free high schools and textbooks, public health activities, and road building began, some of them administered by semiautonomous bureaus and commissions. Despite weak executives, fragmented administrative structures, and political corruption, state governments spearheaded a major expansion of civic activity during the last quarter of the century.

See also **Courts, State and Federal; Federal-State Relations; Internal Improvements; Law,** subentry on **State Law; Local Government; Reform, Political; Statehood and Admission; States' Rights; Territorial Government.**

Bibliography

Campbell, Ballard C. "Public Policy and State Government." In *The Gilded Age: Essays on the Origins of Modern America.* Edited by Charles W. Calhoun. Wilmington, Del.: Scholarly Resources, 1996.

Hall, Kermit L. "Mostly Anchor and Little Sail: The Evolution of American State Constitutions." In *Toward a Usable Past: Liberty under State Constitutions.* Edited by Paul Finkelman and Stephen E. Gottlieb. Athens, Ga.: University of Georgia Press, 1991.

Scheiber, Harry N. "Government and the Economy: Studies of the 'Commonwealth' Policy in Nineteenth Century America." *Journal of Interdisciplinary History* 3 (1972): 135–151.

Shade, William G. "State Legislatures in the Nineteenth Century." In *Encyclopedia of the America Legislative System.* Edited by Joel H. Silbey. Volume 1. New York: Scribners, 1994.

BALLARD C. CAMPBELL

STATEHOOD AND ADMISSION

The notion of the expansion of the United States by the accession of additional states was present from the birth of the Republic. In the Articles of Confederation, Article 11 provided, "Canada, acceding to the Confederation, and joining in the measures of the United States, shall be admitted into and entitled to all the advantages of this Union; but no other colony shall be admitted into the same, unless such admission be agreed to by nine States."

The cession of the Northwest Territory to the United States by the peace treaty with Britain (1783), and the abandonment of Western land claims by the seaboard states, raised the question of how this new territory was to be governed. Although some proposed that the western territories be kept perpetually as federal colonies for the benefit of the original states, the Northwest Ordinance of 1787—enacted by the Congress of the Articles and reenacted in 1789 by Congress under the Constitution—established the principle that new states would be created on an equal footing with the original states.

Although not legally binding, the ordinance became a kind of covenant between the national government and the people of the territories. Article 4, Section 3 of the federal Constitution provided that "New states may be admitted by the Congress into this Union; but no new state shall be formed or erected within the jurisdiction of any other state; nor any state be formed by the junction of two or more states, or parts of states, without the consent of the legislatures of the states concerned as well as of the Congress."

Although Congress is under no legal obligation to grant statehood to any territory, it has considered three conditions to be the criteria determining suitability for statehood: The majority of eligible voters within a territory should support statehood; the people should have an ingrained devotion to democracy and the principles of the U.S. Constitution; and the territory should have sufficient population and resources to support a state government.

Vermont became the fourteenth state in 1791, after New York and New Hampshire agreed to give up their claims to that region. Kentucky followed in 1792, but again, this was possible only when Virginia had ceded its claim to that area. That pattern continued with Tennessee in 1796 after the cession of North Carolina's claims.

The first statehood application to raise serious problems was that of Missouri in 1818, which, although part of the Louisiana Purchase, was located northwest of the Ohio River and should, in theory, have been free of all slavery. The balance of slave and free states had become an issue because the South with its largely rural economy and its intemperate climate began to fall behind the other regions of the country in population growth by the 1820s, with no prospect of a reversal of that tendency. It therefore became vital for the effective defense of slavery that at least one major organ of the federal government maintain securely a balance of regional influence. The U.S. Senate was the logical choice, given its equality of suffrage for each state, and it could serve as a block to any legislation hostile to slaveholding interests. Congress solved the difficulty with the Compromise of 1820, or the Missouri Compromise, whereby Missouri was admitted as a slave state and Maine (which had been part of Massachusetts) was admitted as a free state. Finally, a line was drawn at the southern boundary of Missouri (36 degrees, 30 minutes) as the boundary between free and slave territory.

The admission of Texas also provoked political controversy. As soon as Texas achieved de facto independence from Mexico, it applied for admission to the Union. Fear of war with Mexico and Northern opposition to the admission of another slave state combined to block this. President Tyler's Secretary of State John C. Calhoun submitted a treaty of annexation to the Senate in 1844, but it failed to be ratified. In 1845 Tyler got around the two-thirds requirement for the ratification of treaties by proposing that Texas be admitted to statehood by an act of Congress, requiring only a majority of both houses.

Texas passed its own appropriate legislation to give effect to the federal statute.

When the Mexican War ended during the administration of President James K. Polk, the United States found itself in possession of an enormous tract of land composed of the northern provinces of Mexico. As had been the case with the Louisiana Purchase, disputes arose as to whether this newly acquired land would ultimately enter the Union as free states or as slave states. Once again, a great political compromise had to be worked out in the Congress.

At first the House of Representatives passed the Wilmot Proviso, which provided that no land ceded by Mexico would be open to slavery, but the proviso failed to pass in the Senate. Two years after the Treaty of Guadalupe Hidalgo transferred it to U.S. ownership, California applied for statehood as a free state. The Compromise of 1850 admitted California as a free state while extending the Missouri Compromise line through the rest of the Mexican Cession, demarcating the boundary between slave and free territory.

The next bone of contention over statehood between North and South was the Kansas-Nebraska Act. In 1854 Senator Stephen A. Douglas attempted to remove the nettlesome issue of the admission of particular territories as slave or free states from Congress and leave it up to "popular sovereignty." Territorial legislatures and then state constitutional conventions would decide the status of slavery in newly admitted states. But the resort to popular sovereignty did not solve the problem, because the South maintained that neither the territorial legislatures (nor Congress) had the right to ban slavery. The Republicans, on the other hand, held that neither Congress nor a territorial legislature had the constitutional authority to permit slavery within a territory. When this practical experiment in popular sovereignty was actually undertaken in Kansas, the result was near civil war. In 1861 Kansas was admitted as a free state.

The story of the development of statehood for West Virginia is full of constitutional controversy. On 11 June 1861 delegates from the western region of Virginia met at Wheeling and established a "restored government" of Virginia, rejecting the ordinance of secession that had been enacted by the Old Dominion. But the admission of West Virginia as a separate state provoked furious debate. One of the most serious objections was that it created a new state within the jurisdiction of another state, without that state's consent, a seeming violation of the restrictions of Article 4, Section 3 of the U.S. Constitution.

Representative Thaddeus Stevens argued for the right to admit West Virginia out of the "absolute power which the laws of war give us." The argument that seemed to prevail, however, was the legalistic one, which would regard West Virginia both as the state of Virginia for the purpose of approving the division of its jurisdiction and as the new state for the purposes of applying for and accepting the elevation to statehood. On 20 June 1863, West Virginia became a state.

Statehood for Utah was complicated by popular hostility to the Mormon Church's practice of polygamy. Utah had sought admission to statehood under the name of the State of Deseret as early as 1849, but its settlers achieved only territorial status. In the meantime Congress passed the Anti-Polygamy Act (1862), the Poland Act (1874), the Edmunds Anti-Polygamy Act (1882), and the Edmunds-Tucker Act (1887), all designed to outlaw plural marriages and to diminish the political power of the Mormon Church. In the 1890s the Church repudiated the practice of polygamy, greatly reducing opposition to Utah statehood. In 1896 Utah became a state, with minimal congressional dissent.

Spurts of congressional admissions of territories to statehood have been typical. From 1803 to 1821, many states were formed from the territory ceded by Britain—the eastern side of the Mississippi (Alabama, Mississippi, and Missouri) and the lower tier of the Northwest Territory (Ohio, Indiana, and Illinois). Louisiana and Maine were also admitted. Four of these were slave states and four were free, but the particular patterns of admissions seemed to flow more from internal migration patterns than from congressional politics.

From 1845 to 1861, two slave states (Florida and Texas) were admitted, as were six free states (Iowa, Wisconsin, California, Oregon, Minnesota, and Kansas). The South seemed to abandon as futile and counterproductive any attempt to maintain a balance by blocking the admission of more free states. The South needed allies in the West in disputes such as those over tariffs, and a growing abolitionist challenge meant that the South had to seek new legislation, such as the Fugitive Slave Act of 1850, to protect its interests. A simple veto of unfavorable legislation was no longer adequate.

Between 1889 and 1890, six other states were admitted—North and South Dakota, Montana, Washington, Idaho, and Wyoming. These reflected not only internal settlement patterns, but political balances between the Republican and Democratic parties and certain economic interests, especially the railroads.

Barring statehood for the District of Columbia or the subdivision of an existing state, such as California, the admission of more states to the Union seems unlikely. Puerto Rico, Guam, and the Virgin Islands have geographical distances and cultural and linguistic differences that make it unlikely that they will receive statehood. Nonetheless, it has been fairly remarkable how various political compromises and acts of statesmanship have permitted the United States to keep its pledge, made more than two centuries ago in the Northwest Ordinance, that when territories were capable of fulfilling the obligations of statehood, they would be admitted to the Union with full political equality.

See also **Bleeding Kansas; Compromise of 1850; Expansion; Mexican Cession; Mexican War; Missouri Compromise; Northwest Territory; States' Rights.**

Bibliography
Brinkley, Alan. *American History: A Survey.* 10th ed. Boston: McGraw-Hill College, 1999.

Dávila-Colón, Luis R. "Statehood." In *The Encyclopedia of the United States Congress.* Edited by Donald C. Bacon, Roger H. Davidson, and Morton Keller. New York: Simon and Schuster, 1995.

Randall, J. G. *Constitutional Problems under Lincoln.* 2d ed. Urbana: University of Illinois Press, 1951.

Woodward, Isaiah A. *West Virginia and Its Struggle for Statehood, 1861–1863.* Baltimore: Wolk, 1954.

PATRICK M. O'NEIL

STATES' RIGHTS States' rights was the political rallying cry of those who believed that under the federal system of government created by the U.S. Constitution, the balance of power remained in the hands of the states. The roots of this belief were cultural, historical, political, and theoretical. Many of the colonists had brought to the New World a fear of the centralizing tendency of the English monarchy. Because the colonies were settled separately and developed independently of each other, attempts to unite them before 1776 proved ineffectual and short-lived. The American Revolution in many ways reinforced these tendencies, because it was fought to deny the authority of Great Britain, the only central government that the colonists had ever known. Beyond this there was a pervasive belief that only through the decentralization of authority could the republican governments created after independence survive and the democratic potential of the Revolution be fulfilled.

During the 1790s opposition to Federalist attempts to expand the authority of the central government, in particular, to the Alien and Sedition Acts (1798), gave birth to the Kentucky and Virginia Resolutions (1798 and 1799). These were an important

Jeffersonian-Republican statement regarding the origin and nature of the federal union. The resolutions raised the states' rights argument to the level of legal procedure. They argued that the Union was a compact between the different states, granting limited and specific powers to the federal government. Should the federal government overstep its bounds, the states had a right to "interpose" by declaring an act of Congress unconstitutional. The resolutions were designed to help overthrow the Federalists in the election of 1800. This accomplished, many Republicans, including Thomas Jefferson and James Madison, abandoned states' rights principles. But a substantial number of other supporters of the party, known as Old Republicans (John Taylor, Spencer Roane, John Randolph, and Nathaniel Macon), remained committed to what they called the "spirit of '98."

After 1800 the Federalists, becoming an ineffective minority, rallied behind states' rights to obstruct the Louisiana Purchase, Jefferson's embargo, and the policies of the federal government during and after the War of 1812. Much more significant were the Old Republicans, who, in the name of the states' rights, denounced the creation of the second Bank of the United States, a federal program of internal improvements, and the jurisdiction and decisions of the Supreme Court in cases involving federal-state relations. It was these Old Republicans who provided the ideological basis for the movement that brought the Jacksonians to power in 1828 and who then proceeded, in the name of majoritarianism and states' rights, to dismantle the highly nationalistic Jeffersonian economic program known as the American System.

At about the same time there developed a new strain of states' rights thought in South Carolina, under the leadership of John C. Calhoun. Denouncing the protective tariffs of 1828 and 1832, Calhoun argued that a single state, by calling a special constitutional convention, could declare such laws unconstitutional and unenforceable within its boundaries. States' rights were not linked to the protection of minority rights. Calhoun held as well that should the federal government try to enforce an unwanted law or legitimize it through a constitutional amendment, a state had the right to withdraw peacefully from the Union. Although a compromise was reached in 1833, during the second third of the nineteenth century the matter became the dominant form of states' rights, inextricably linked with the defense of slavery and providing a rationale for the South's secession in the crisis of 1860–1861.

In the 1840s and 1850s most northern states adopted states' rights arguments and passed personal liberty laws to withdraw state support for the enforcement of the federal fugitive slave laws. In *In re Sherman Booth* (1854) and *In re Booth and Rycraft* (1854), the Wisconsin Supreme Court declared that the federal Fugitive Slave Law of 1850 was unconstitutional and then, using states' rights theory, defied attempts by the U.S. Supreme Court to review its decisions. This ultimately led to a forceful denunciation of states' rights by the U.S. Supreme Court in *Ableman v. Booth* (1859). From the 1830s to the eve of the Civil War, governors in Maine, New York, Ohio, and elsewhere refused to extradite free blacks, fugitive slaves, and white abolitionists accused of crimes in the South, including "larceny" for "stealing" slave property. In *Kentucky v. Dennison* (1861) the U.S. Supreme Court affirmed the power of the state to act in this manner. Chief Justice Roger Taney's goal in this case was to immunize state governors from the federal government on the eve of the Civil War.

The North's victory in the Civil War discredited much of the states' rights argument, especially its view of the right to secede. And there was a definite (if slow) drift in the last third of the nineteenth century toward the expansion of the federal government's power. But the belief persisted that it was safer, more efficient, and more democratic to leave control of many aspects of daily life—education, criminal justice, family relations, property and labor law, and much business regulation—to state control. That view would continue through the twentieth century.

See also **Nullification.**

Bibliography

Bestor, Arthur. "State Sovereignty and Slavery: A Reinterpretation of Proslavery Constitutional Doctrine, 1846–1860." *Journal of the Illinois State Historical Society* 54 (summer 1961).

Ellis, Richard E. *The Union at Risk: Jacksonian Democracy, States' Rights and the Nullification Crisis.* New York: Oxford University Press, 1987.

Finkelman, Paul. "States Rights North and South in Antebellum America." In *An Uncertain Tradition: Constitutionalism and the History of the South.* Edited by Kermit Hall and James W. Ely, Jr. Athens: University of Georgia Press, 1989.

Morris, Thomas D. *Free Men All: The Personal Liberty Laws of the North, 1780–1861.* Baltimore: Johns Hopkins University Press, 1974.

RICHARD E. ELLIS

STEAM POWER   Steam power was essential in transforming the nineteenth-century United States from an agrarian society into an industrial economy.

Industrialization required vast amounts of energy that traditional sources, such as water, wind, and animal or human muscle, simply could not provide. The dramatic expansion of steam power was a prerequisite for the entry of the United States into the wealthy industrial world. Those countries that failed to shift their economy to steam power remained poor agrarian societies and could not escape their poverty even in the twentieth century.

The Origins of Steam Engines

Distinct models for use on ships, railroads, and factories had emerged out of the basic steam engine by the early 1820s. This entry focuses mainly on the stationary or standing engine, originally called the mill engine. During the nineteenth century almost all steam engines in the United States were of the reciprocating type. In the simplest description, steam came from a boiler to push a piston back and forth inside a cylinder. A factory owner used the resulting motion in the rod of the piston to operate machinery. Thomas Newcomen in 1712 had invented the atmospheric steam engine to pump water out of coal mines

Steam-Powered Printing. An advertisement for Jacob Haehnlen's press, located at Goldsmith's Hall in New York City, decorated with illustrations of his craft. Created by Jacob Haehnlen, c. 1867. LIBRARY OF CONGRESS

in England. Steam pushed the piston in only one direction, but when cold water cooled the steam in the cylinder, the resulting vacuum allowed the pressure of the atmosphere to push the piston back in the other direction. A major improvement came in 1776, when James Watt designed a new engine that exhausted the steam for cooling into a separate condenser, where the vacuum now formed. Not having to cool and heat the cylinder saved fuel but required a bulkier, heavier machine. All the early models had the cylinder in an upright position, and the piston rod moved an overhead beam, similar to those used for pumping in oil wells. The back-and-forth motion of the beam was well suited to pumping the water out of the mine shafts.

When this eighteenth-century engine crossed the Atlantic, very few found any use for the unwieldy contraption. Fuel consumption, even under the Watt model, was outrageous but had not been a concern inside British coal mines. In 1803 only five steam engines were in use in the United States, and three of these powered pumps for urban water supply. The limited manufacturing that existed in New England relied on abundant waterpower, and the Watt model was expensive to buy and costly to operate in a region without abundant coal supplies. Until new uses for steam power materialized, few needed the Watt model, and not until a better engine appeared would the demand for steam power increase.

To escape this circle, in 1803 the American inventor and manufacturer Oliver Evans decided to make a different steam engine, whose characteristics he expounded in easy-to-read manuals that inspired fruitful tinkering among mechanics, soon to be called by the newly coined word "engineers." The key to the Evans engine was high pressure, a term then used to designate steam exceeding the 15 pounds per square inch (psi) of the atmosphere. Pressures over 30 psi had not been possible before because of weak boilers, but the new Evans design provided ample steam safely. Evans used steam to drive the piston first in one direction and then in the opposite direction to complete each "stroke" of the piston. He had in effect created a workable double-acting engine. The condensers and air pumps were now unnecessary, making the engine lighter, more compact, and less expensive than the Watt model. He also eliminated the bulky beam and connected the piston rod to a flywheel, thus obtaining more than 25 revolutions per minute (rpm).

Riverboat Steam Engines

The market for the Evans engine eventually came not from manufacturing but from transportation. In 1803 the Louisiana Purchase doubled the size of the country, and the previous demand for fast and reliable transportation became even more urgent. Robert Fulton, who was born in 1755, the same year as Evans, concluded that steam transportation by inland waters was the best way to connect the vast country. He adapted a Watt engine to navigation and established the first regular steamboat service in the world in 1807. Although the pioneering *Clermont* operated in the Hudson River, Fulton's real goal was the vast rivers of the West. Experience soon showed that, while the Watt engine was tolerable in the rivers of the East Coast, in the West only the Evans engine met the requirements of navigation in vastly changing river currents. In 1816, riverboats in the West took the revolutionary measure of placing the cylinder of the Evans engine horizontal to the boat rather than vertical as had been the rule since Newcomen's days. The horizontal engine allowed engineers to eliminate the cumbersome overhead beam and to connect the piston rod to a flywheel, which turned the paddle wheels. Just a few years later innovators dropped the flywheel altogether and connected the piston rod directly to the paddle wheels. The low cost of the new engine made it affordable to a capital-scarce region.

Steam pressures reached 80 psi in 1830, and since higher pressure was the easiest way to obtain more horsepower (hp) and rpms from the engine, the normal operating pressure reached 100 psi in 1840 and 150 psi in 1850. Although fuel consumption was high, firewood was cheap and abundant at the frequent stops for cargo and passengers. The excavation of waterways, in particular the Erie Canal linking the eastern seaboard to the Great Lakes, enlarged the demand for river transportation, and inland waters accounted for the most widespread use of steam engines. Indeed in 1838 steamboats produced 57 percent of the steam power in the United States. Besides their many direct contributions to transportation, riverboats were responsible for the successful introduction of the steam engine into the United States.

Steam Power and the National Market

Once the steamboats demonstrated the benefits of the Evans engine, the way was clear for the introduction of steam power on land. While the atmospheric engines needed a huge water supply to cool the cylinders, the Evans engine needed only a small amount of water for the steam. New England manufacturers, rather than install the expensive Watt model in the cities, preferred to rely on the traditional waterpower in the countryside. With the Evans engine, steam power came into the eastern cities and spread to the flat western territories lacking falling water. The five stationary steam engines of 1803 multiplied to about 2,000 with a total horsepower of 40,000 in 1838. The average stationary engine was of 20 hp, and 50 percent had less than 11 hp; no more than 20 engines exceeded 100 hp in the whole country. Industry now became possible where waterpower was unavailable; equally significant, many shops and early factories in the United States now replaced the often unreliable waterpower with the Evans engine. In addition, the replacement of the muscle power of men and animals with the Evans engine brought large savings to owners. Thanks to the stationary steam engine, shops could produce more goods at lower prices than before, while the riverboats carried the merchandise to markets throughout most of the country.

By the early 1840s the economic expansion of the United States faced a transportation bottleneck. To reach all the potential consumers with the products from the factories, the country needed a transportation network more extensive than the waterways. The railroad, perhaps the most famous application of steam power, launched the United States into the next stage of industrialization. The railroad had been developed in England, but because of the cheapness and apparent abundance of water transportation, it initially played only a secondary role in the United States. The tracks in existence in 1850 were a modest nine thousand miles, and more significantly, most railroads were either feeders to or links for waterways. By the 1840s the demand was mounting for more transportation, but before the railroads could meet the demand, they first had to improve their performance.

Many innovations ranging from brakes to lights gradually appeared, but the most significant development concerned steam power for the locomotive. The earliest railroads had captured the popular imagination because for the first time humans experienced speeds faster than those possible by either wind or muscle power. The engineers in the locomotive were no less caught up in the enthusiasm, and they experimented with new ways to increase the speed of the steam engine. The upright engine with overhead beam soon gave way to the horizontal cylinder, whose piston rod acted directly on the wheels of the locomotive. A new multitubular boiler drove the exhaust steam up the smokestack and made possible higher steam pressures. Some locomotives had already reached 90 psi by 1850 and long before then had put into practice what Evans had urged in 1803, the expansive use of steam.

Letting the inflow of steam continue until the piston reached the end of the cylinder produced the maximum power, which was suitable for starts and heavy loads. Riverboats by 1840 provided the choice of either this maximum power or two other options to cut off the inflow of steam before the piston reached the end of the cylinder; the steam continued to expand and completed the piston movement. For the locomotives, however, the engineers needed many settings to adjust the amount of steam let into the cylinder to compensate for the turns and inclines on the railroad track. Also, without cutoff all the steam in the other end of the piston did not have time to escape, and the trapped steam slowed down or "cushioned" the stroke and kept the locomotive from reaching high speeds. In 1842 the Stephenson valve gear at last gave the engineer the freedom to adjust the steam intake in the cylinder as needed. Full steam pulled the locomotive for heavy loads and starting, but once speed increased the engineer set the Stephenson valve gear to cut off the steam at the level appropriate for the track and the desired speed. As steam pressures continued to rise, the locomotive became more efficient. After 1850 the railroad spread across the United States but at a faster pace in the North, which by the start of the Civil War had twice as much track as the South. Railroads contributed to the North's victory, and after the war the North completed the first transcontinental railroad in 1869. The improved locomotive made possible economical long-distance travel and created a national market of a size that at last forced industrialists to adopt steam power on a wide scale as their main source of energy.

Steam Power and Manufacturing

The Stephenson valve gear, however, was not practical for factories. Every locomotive needed an engineer, who by playing with the steam valves and other instruments did his best to enhance the mystery of the operation of trains. The appeal of locomotives enchanted many, but industrialists on land had no time or patience for a machine with a personality or for cranky engineers. For factory and shop owners power production was an input and not their main business, so simple operation, easy maintenance, and small investment remained the principal concerns. As late as 1899, 77 percent of factory owners continued to rely on the Evans engine with a fixed cutoff valve. But from the 1850s on, as the spreading railroad network created a national market, the largest industrialists needed more power to increase their output. To compete against local producers, these large industrialists also required a smooth-running engine capable of producing high-quality goods. The solution came in 1849, when the American inventor George H. Corliss patented his automatic valve cutoff, which self-adjusted the amount of steam going into the cylinder. If an increased load slowed down the wheel, the automatic valve lengthened the time period of the cutoff a corresponding amount to increase the quantity of steam going into the cylinder. Likewise, if the load decreased and the wheel speeded up, the automatic valve shortened the time period of the cutoff to decrease the quantity of steam going into the cylinder. The Corliss engine became the standard for large factories and adequately satisfied the requirements for both more power and smooth, carefree operation.

The one major disadvantage of the Corliss engine was the overhead beam, which wasted power. As late as the Philadelphia Centennial Exhibition in 1876, the Corliss engine with its massive beam remained the center of public attention. The rocking motion of the beam seemed to satisfy some inner human need, while the vast size of the engine, over two stories high, impressed citizens just emerging from an agrarian society. Yet at that same exhibition Charles T. Porter and John F. Allen presented the fast-speed Porter-Allen engine as a substitute for the Corliss engine. The American inventors had devised an engine that at less than half the size easily produced an incredible 200 rpm. Among their innovations the two most important were a short stroke from smaller components (for example, the flywheel was less than half the normal size) and direct action without any beam. Nevertheless the higher operating costs because of wasted steam cooled the enthusiasm for the engine. In 1899 less than 20 percent of the horsepower in manufacturing came from the Porter-Allen engine. Ironically, its most important contribution was to kill off the beam once and for all. Any owner of a steam engine who substituted direct action for the beam could reduce costs and increase rpms. When interplanetary voyages are the concern of a later age, it may be hard to imagine that the decisive improvement in steam power in the last quarter of the nineteenth century came from the seemingly obvious decision to drop the overhead beam.

Only establishments needing the high speed of 200 rpm and unconcerned with fuel costs adopted the Porter-Allen engines. Factories that needed more horsepower but not high speed found the answer in marine engines. Aboard oceangoing ships more space devoted to coal meant less cargo-carrying capacity. Any reduction in coal consumption increased the income-earning potential of a steamship. In the late 1850s, English engineers revived their earlier discovery of the compound engine. In the compound engine the exhaust steam from a first cylinder flows to a second cylinder of more than twice the diameter of the first. The two pistons connected to the crankshaft

also give a greater uniformity to the rotating motion. The compound engine cut fuel costs almost by half, and by the late 1860s it had become universal in ocean shipping. However, the compound engine was slow to spread on land in the United States, and even railroads did not adopt it until the 1900s. As in the early nineteenth century, urban water systems took the technological lead and were the first to use compound engines to power pumps. Slowly the engine spread to the largest establishments, particularly ironworks and steelworks. Attractive as the savings in coal were to the factory owner, the larger initial investment did not seem justified if the compound engine—no matter of what size horsepower—was to function only sporadically. Manufacturers continued to acquire the simpler and cheaper engines until steam provided more than 80 percent of the power for U.S. manufacturing in 1899, the highest percentage steam power ever attained.

Steam Power and Electricity

The reliance on steam power in manufacturing began to decline after 1900 because of the appearance of electric utilities, which paradoxically eventually became the principal users of steam power. In 1897 an engineer claimed that the impact of electricity had transformed the steam engine more drastically in the previous ten years than in the preceding fifty years. To produce electricity a steam engine had to turn a generator at 1200 rpm, a speed not even the Porter-Allen engine could reach. In addition, the Porter-Allen engine's high fuel costs made it unacceptable to a utility, whose main business was the production of electricity. The rising demand for cheap electricity forced utilities to adopt the compound engine during the 1890s. Gearing up and pulleys in some cases helped the steam engine reach higher rpms, but a better solution soon emerged. After connecting the compound engines by direct drive to the generators, engineers increased the size of the generators several times to produce the same amount of electricity at the low engine speed as would have been produced had the engine been able to turn a small-sized generator at 1200 rpm. Besides the huge expense of massive engines and generators four stories high, the machinery also required vast space inside enormous buildings. The climax of development came with the Manhattan power station for the New York Elevated Railway in 1901. There the largest stationary engines ever built turned the massive generators at 75 rpm.

By then the reciprocating steam engine was obsolete because of the appearance of the turbine, in which steam hits the blades of a rotor to produce motion. Although the history of the steam turbine belongs mainly to the twentieth century, in 1884 the first model made by the British inventor Sir Charles A. Parsons had reached an unbelievable speed of 18,000 rpm. Whereas before engineers had to slow down the generator to match the low engine speed, they now had to speed up the generator and slow down the turbine. The turbine was so revolutionary that it did not begin to displace the reciprocating engine in the utilities until 1900. But once the turbine made possible abundant and cheap electricity, steam engines gave way to electric motors in manufacturing. In the last quarter of the nineteenth century the growing floor area of factories created the problem of how to transmit power from the central steam engine to the outlying shops. Once electric motors became readily available, the steam engine began its decades-long disappearance from the factories it had once helped to create. Steam powered most trains and ships until the 1950s, and at the end of the twentieth century it remained the source of 80 percent of the electricity in the United States. Whether directly through motion or indirectly through electricity, steam power transformed the agrarian society into an industrial power and made possible the material abundance of the wealthiest country in the world.

See also **Industrialization and the Market; Travel, Technology of; Waterpower.**

Bibliography

Briggs, Asa. *The Power of Steam: An Illustrated History of the World's Steam Age.* Chicago: University of Chicago Press, 1982. An appealing and reliable visual introduction to the impact of steam power on the industrialized world.

Comstock, Henry B. *The Iron Horse: An Illustrated History of Steam Locomotives.* 2d ed. Waukesha, Wis.: Greenberg, 1993. Superb drawings and photographs help make understandable the evolution of locomotives in the United States.

De La Pedraja, René. *A Historical Dictionary of the U.S. Merchant Marine and Shipping Industry: Since the Introduction of Steam.* Westport, Conn.: Greenwood, 1994. See especially "Marine Propulsion" and entries for individual engines.

Dickinson, H. W. *A Short History of the Steam Engine.* New York: Macmillan, 1939. A minor classic with very helpful diagrams and many delightful passages.

Evans, Oliver. *The Young Steam Engineer's Guide.* Philadelphia: H. C. Carey and I. Lea, 1805. An easy-to-read primary account by one of the great American inventors; available on microform.

Fenichel, Allen H. "Growth and Diffusion of Power in Manufacturing, 1838–1919." In *Output, Employment, and Productivity in the United States after 1800.* Studies in Income and Wealth. Volume 30. New York: National Bureau of Economic Research, 1966.

Hunter, Louis C. *A History of Industrial Power in the United States, 1780–1930.* Volume 1: *Waterpower in the Century of the Steam Engine.* Charlottesville: University Press of Virginia, 1979. Volume 2: *Steam Power.* Charlottesville: University Press of Virginia, 1985. Volume 3: *The Transmission of Power,* coauthored with Lynwood Bryant. Cambridge, Mass.: MIT Press, 1991. These three volumes comprise the single most important source on the history of steam power in the United States. This is a monumental reference source that provides encyclopedic coverage and is also well illustrated.

———. *Steamboats on the Western Rivers: An Economic and Technological History.* New York: Octagon, 1969. The definitive work on the topic.

Stewart, James. *Steam Engineering on Sugar Plantations, Steamships, and Locomotive Engines.* New York: Russell's American Steam Printing House, 1867. One of the many nineteenth-century manuals for engineers; exceptionally clear and also available on microform.

Taylor, George R. *The Transportation Revolution, 1815–1860.* New York: Rinehart, 1951.

Temin, Peter. "Steam and Waterpower in the Early Nineteenth Century." *Journal of Economic History* 26 (1966): 187–205.

RENÉ DE LA PEDRAJA

STEEL AND THE STEEL INDUSTRY

The steel industry was fundamental to the economic and social development of the United States in the nineteenth century. Steel was a major force in the country's transition from a mercantile to an industrial economy. Iron and steel manufacturers, responding to demands created by the westward migration of European Americans, aggressively competed for diverse markets. As late as 1900 small merchant iron mills shared the stage with newly formed steel conglomerates.

Mass production of steel was an outgrowth of the nineteenth-century "transportation revolution." Beginning in 1815 the development of extensive canal systems, steamboats and especially railroads accelerated westward migration. By 1860 railroads were the major form of inland transportation in the United States, and they voraciously consumed iron, especially iron rails. Seeking to cut costs, railroads were a ready market for rails made of more durable steel if they were mass-produced affordably.

Roots of Iron

New technologies and an expanding transportation system increased the demand for iron and changed the structure of the American iron industry. At the beginning of the nineteenth century the country's iron manufactories reflected the American agricultural-mercantile economy. Wood, a plentiful and easily exploited natural resource, was the most widely used material. Iron was a relatively expensive commodity produced in scattered locations, although migration down the Ohio Valley was an incentive for

Cambria Steel Company, Johnstown, Pennsylvania. The steel industry originated in the Mid-Atlantic states, with Pennsylvania dominating for decades. Postcard, between 1880 and 1920. LIBRARY OF CONGRESS

entrepreneurs to concentrate iron manufactories in the river port of Pittsburgh.

Early-nineteenth-century iron production was centered in Pennsylvania. Iron "plantations" included mines, limestone quarries, thousands of acres of woodland that produced charcoal for smelting and forging iron, and the workforce. Self-sufficiency was dictated by the isolation of charcoal ironworks, which were remote from existing towns and villages because iron production required large tracts of undeveloped land.

These iron plantations typically were owned by small partnerships of two or three merchants with close personal, often familial, ties. They produced commercial castings and wrought bar iron for sale on the open market. The heart of an iron plantation was its charcoal-fueled blast furnace. Limited to about thirty feet in height because of the weight of its fuel, it typically produced a maximum of fifteen tons of pig iron a week. At the base of the furnace workers poured molten pig iron directly into molds for commercial castings or into ingots called pigs. Most iron plantations included waterpowered finery forges, where iron pigs were reheated and hammered into wrought iron bars for sale to local blacksmiths, farmers, or independent forges. By the 1830s Pennsylvania's rural iron masters found markets for raw iron pigs in the foundries and rolling mills around Pittsburgh and in southeastern Pennsylvania.

In the 1830s the expanding national transportation network and important technological developments in the manufacture of iron combined to make charcoal blast furnaces and finery forges obsolete. The coal-fueled puddling furnace and the rolling mill, invented in England, far surpassed the capacity of the finery forge in both quantity and quality of finished product. In 1816 Isaac Meason hired Welsh ironworkers to build America's first ironworks with a puddling furnace and a rolling mill in Connellsville, southwest of Pittsburgh. By 1850 such plants were common throughout the state. But perhaps no other technology played as significant a role in the antebellum iron industry as the steam engine, the catalyst for the industrialization of American iron manufacture.

The Steam Engine, Railroads, and Industrialization

Steam-engine manufacturers required varieties and quantities of iron plate that exceeded the production capabilities of finery forges. Steamboats proliferated in the Ohio and Mississippi Valleys after 1815, and Pittsburgh developed a thriving steam-engine and boat-building industry. More than one thousand steam engines were in operation in the Mid-Atlantic states by 1830, and Pittsburgh alone produced one hundred steam engines that year.

Steam engines also stimulated technological advances in the American iron industry. Steam power led to a shift from charcoal to mineral fuels in blast furnaces. Anthracite coal and bituminous coke were more resistant than charcoal to crushing under the weight of ore and limestone in a blast furnace. Furthermore coal and coke could be transported in bulk and stockpiled for use year-round. These characteristics and the increased power and geographical freedom of steam engines allowed iron manufacturers to erect larger, more productive blast furnaces closer to the puddling furnaces and rolling mills in the emerging urban industrial centers.

Locomotive steam engines ensured the economic viability of railroads. Rail mileage in the United States grew from less than three thousand in 1840 to more than thirty thousand in 1861. This tenfold increase created a huge demand for cheap iron rails, and the iron industry responded accordingly. After years of experimentation, the English rolled-iron "T" rail became the accepted standard in the 1840s. The first iron "T" rails made in the United States were rolled in 1845 at the Mount Savage Iron Works near Cumberland, Maryland, using pig iron smelted with locally mined bituminous coal and iron ore. At about that time several rolling mills in eastern Pennsylvania and New Jersey began to manufacture "T" rails from iron made in anthracite furnaces.

The completion of the Pennsylvania Railroad (PRR) between Philadelphia and Pittsburgh in 1854 coincided with the expansion of iron rail production west of the Allegheny Mountains. Fifteen firms constructed new rail mills with puddling furnaces in western Pennsylvania during the mid-1850s, and chief among them were the Cambria Iron Works at Johnstown and the Jones and Laughlins Company of Pittsburgh. The PRR's continuous rail link between western Pennsylvania and the anthracite region ended Pittsburgh's dependence on charcoal pig iron. Even with the cost of cross-state rail shipment, anthracite pig iron had a clear advantage in the western market because it cost half as much to produce as charcoal pig iron.

Anthracite iron's advantage was short-lived, however. Railroads soon built branch lines to tap Pennsylvania's rich deposits of bituminous coal. Coal from the Connellsville region proved especially suitable for making coke, a nearly pure carbon residue left after baking coal in the absence of oxygen. Coke was an even cheaper fuel than anthracite. After the Civil War, Connellsville coke became the dominant fuel in the mass production of iron centered in Pittsburgh.

Steel and Railroads

The accelerated expansion of railroads after the Civil War required even greater rates of rail production. Faster and heavier locomotives along with greater traffic density reduced the effective lives of iron rails to cost-prohibitive levels. Before the Civil War iron replaced wood as the bridge-building material of choice for railroads; and expansion, increasing train weights, and higher speeds placed further demands on iron manufacturers. The chief problem was not increasing wrought iron output but reducing costs.

In the mid-nineteenth century manufacturing technologies for wrought iron reached the pinnacle of their development. The superior durability of steel was well known, and some iron rail manufacturers, among them Andrew Carnegie, a relative newcomer to the industry, experimented unsuccessfully with a technique for fusing steel tops to wrought iron rails. The railroad industry continued to demand solid steel rails, which required a mechanized mass-production technology.

At the time of the Civil War the most common form of steel made in the United States was blister steel. Skilled artisans immersed malleable wrought iron bars into a bed of charcoal, and under the high heat of the forge, carbon from the charcoal combined with the iron to form a hard surface. Making blister steel required many hours of hard labor and was an expensive process that yielded small quantities. Used primarily in the manufacture of edged tools, such as axes and plowshares, blister steel was also melted in small clay pots called crucibles for casting critical parts of machine tools. As did wrought iron puddling, the manufacture of blister and crucible steel defied mechanization, the key to cheap mass production.

The breakthrough that gave steel dominance over iron in the United States ironically stemmed from attempts to make wrought iron without the laborious puddling process. Two men working independently, the Englishman Henry Bessemer and the American William Kelly, simultaneously invented the pneumatic process for blowing air into vessels called converters that were filled with molten pig iron. Oxygen in the airstream combined with carbon in the molten iron to produce a violent chemical reaction, during which the impurities in the pig iron were eliminated in a matter of minutes. The same process in a puddling furnace required several hours. Although Bessemer and Kelly filed American patents in 1856 and 1857 respectively, Bessemer's converter apparatus was the key to commercial viability, and steel made by the pneumatic process in the United States bore his name.

The importance of Bessemer's invention was clear to American manufacturers of iron rails. In a fraction of the time required for a skilled puddler and his assistants to make three hundred pounds of wrought iron, a Bessemer converter operated by a small crew of semiskilled attendants could produce several tons of more durable steel. In 1865 Alexander Holley, a self-taught mechanical engineer, built the first commercially successful Bessemer steelworks in the United States at the Rensselaer Iron Works in Troy, New York. Holley became the most important engineer in the nineteenth-century U.S. steel industry. His next project was the Bessemer plant of the Pennsylvania Steel Company at Steelton, Pennsylvania.

In 1867 steel ingots from the Steelton plant were used in the Cambria Iron Works rolling mill at Johnstown, Pennsylvania, for the first American-made steel rails. Cambria Iron erected its own Bessemer plant in 1871. By 1875 two firms, the Jones and Laughlins Company and Andrew Carnegie's Edgar Thompson Steel Company had established Bessemer plants near Pittsburgh. Although wrought iron production continued to grow, Bessemer steel production exploded from 2,000 tons in 1867 to 470,000 tons in 1876 and more than 2 million tons in 1886, nearly all of which went to roll steel rails.

Steel Diversifies

The production of Bessemer steel rails dominated the steel industry into the mid-1880s and was responsible for making the United States the world's leading producer of steel by 1886. But American railroad expansion slowed in the mid-1880s, forcing steel manufacturers to seek other markets. In this quest Bessemer steel was at a double disadvantage. Outside of the very rich deposits in the Great Lakes region, most available iron ore in the United States contained relatively high amounts of phosphorous, which weakened steel, that the Bessemer process could not remove. In addition the speed of the chemical reaction in a Bessemer converter limited manufacturers' ability to control the quality and composition of steel for customers outside the rail market.

These problems were solved by the open-hearth method developed in Europe by William Siemens, Friederich Siemens, and Pierre-Émile Martin at about the time that Bessemer invented the pneumatic process. The Trenton Iron Works installed America's first Siemens-Martin open-hearth furnace in 1868, and other steel manufacturers followed. Open-hearth steel grew from less than a tenth of all steel manufactured in the United States in 1886 to more than a third of the market in 1900.

The open-hearth process was based on advanced puddling technology that increased the heat in the furnace to the level needed to make steel. In contrast to Bessemer technology, open-hearth furnaces could process pig iron of varying compositions. The greater length of time required to convert iron to steel was offset by a greater capacity and allowed manufactur-

ers to blend carefully measured additives, including recycled scrap iron and steel, for custom orders.

The flexibility and easy quality control of the open-hearth method opened new markets for mass-produced steel and encouraged many small iron firms to enter the specialty steel business, an important development. Even as large, integrated iron and steel corporations attracted national attention in the 1880s and 1890s, small, independent iron and steel manufacturers continued to be an important segment of the national economy well into the twentieth century.

Between 1880 and 1900 American iron and steel production more than tripled, and the industry diversified as steel replaced iron in the manufacture of finished products. Overall rail production nearly doubled, but it dropped from 45 percent to 25 percent of all rolled products during those twenty years. During that period production of plates and sheets increased by nearly 600 percent to equal rail production in market share, while wire rods, structural shapes, and other products accounted for approximately 55 percent of the total. The proportion of steel in finished products rose dramatically.

Geographical Expansion and Corporate Consolidation

The iron and steel industry expanded geographically as its output and diversity grew. During the first half of the century iron and steel production was concentrated in the Mid-Atlantic states. After the Civil War iron and steel manufacture expanded westward, first taking root in the Ohio Valley, near Wheeling, West Virginia, and Cincinnati, Ohio, and in the vicinity of Youngstown and Cleveland, Ohio. Wheeling ironworks specialized in nail production to satisfy the post–Civil War trans-Appalachian housing boom, while Cincinnati became known for its machine tool industry. Ironworks and steelworks located on Ohio's Lake Erie shore took advantage of the proximity of rich ore deposits that were only beginning to be exploited in the Lake Superior region. In the Deep South, Birmingham, Alabama, developed as an important source of pig iron when northern capitalists explored nearby deposits of iron ore in the 1870s. Chicago's emergence as a western metropolis attracted ironworks and steelworks during the late nineteenth century.

At the beginning of its post–Civil War expansion, the iron and steel industry was heavily decentralized. Few producers controlled the costs of their raw materials or the markets for their output, which made them particularly vulnerable to sudden changes, such as the financial panics of 1873 and 1893.

Consolidation initially took the form of rearward integration. The Carnegie Steel Company, already one of the largest American iron and steel producers, acquired an interest in the H. C. Frick Coke Company in 1882, which guaranteed Carnegie favored access to the best fuel available. Carnegie Steel then embarked on an expansion program, buying out competitors at Homestead and Duquesne near the company's own Edgar Thompson Works. In the 1890s Carnegie Steel built its own railroad to serve its ironworks and steelworks, secured ownership or leases to large supplies of Great Lakes iron ore, and built the Pittsburgh, Bessemer & Lake Erie Railroad to haul the ore between the Lake Erie docks and the company's blast furnaces.

By the end of the nineteenth century Carnegie Steel was a holding company, wherein a single entity held controlling interest in several lesser firms. While typically holding companies were publicly traded stock, Carnegie Steel's securities were privately held. Andrew Carnegie owned an absolute majority of shares. Carnegie and his fellow shareholders were, in fact, partners in the tradition of merchant capitalism and were directly involved in the management of day-to-day operations. Carnegie financed the expansion and consolidation of his company internally, while other holding companies secured their transactions with the help of investment banks.

The iron and steel empire formed by the Wall Street financier J. P. Morgan was more typical of holding companies. Morgan played a major role in rationalizing the railroad network in the industrial Northeast during the 1880s, and in the following decade he turned to the iron and steel industry. Between 1898 and 1900 he established control, through interconnected banking arrangements, over the Federal Steel Company, the American Bridge Company, and the National Tube Company, an integrated iron and steel empire that included all facets of production, from raw materials to finished products.

The formation of fully integrated holding companies by Morgan and others in the 1890s posed a major threat to Carnegie Steel, since a large amount of that company's product was semifinished steel for sale to independent finishing mills. Faced with the loss of his traditional markets as the century came to a close, Carnegie announced plans to construct his own steel tube works. Carnegie's challenge to Morgan's carefully crafted "community of interest" in iron and steel production led to negotiations between the two in 1901. Carnegie agreed to sell Carnegie Steel, and Morgan merged it with his other companies to form the United States Steel Corporation, the first billion-dollar corporation in American history.

Workers and the Workplace

The formation of U.S. Steel was the culmination of half a century of change in the American iron and steel industry. The advent of mass-produced steel transformed both the industry and the national economy. Industrialization also brought significant change to the communities where iron and steel were made.

Industrialization altered the composition of the workforce and the nature of the workplace. Manufacturers' efforts to increase efficiency and productivity in their mills challenged the traditional control of skilled puddlers and rollers over the rates and costs of production. The resulting conflicts between labor organizations and iron and steel manufacturers throughout the post–Civil War period culminated in a bloody conflict at Carnegie's Homestead Works in 1892.

Workers were hampered by their inability to present a united front due to the structure of their union, the Amalgamated Association of Iron and Steel Workers, formed in 1876. The Amalgamated Association was a craft union that admitted only skilled workers directly engaged in the puddling and rolling processes. They were mostly of English or German descent, while common laborers, who were excluded from the union, were primarily unskilled immigrants from southern and eastern Europe who streamed into the United States after the Civil War. The skilled workers exercised wide freedom in hiring their assistants and preferred men of their own ethnic backgrounds.

Mechanization of the steelmaking process replaced skilled workers with machines run by easily trained operators and increased the number of manual laborers in the mills. While the Amalgamated Association remained predominantly Anglo-Saxon through the 1880s and 1890s, the mass of laborers changed from English-speaking Irish to a heterogeneous group of eastern Europeans with different cultures and languages. Large iron and steel manufacturers quickly exploited the ethnic divisions in their workforces, and none more so than Carnegie and Henry Clay Frick, Carnegie's principal associate after 1882. By 1889 they had effectively eliminated the Amalgamated Association from all of their mills except Homestead.

Carnegie and Frick decided to break the Homestead union when the existing agreement expired in 1892. But the Amalgamated Association convinced Homestead's common laborers that worker solidarity was in their best interest. Carnegie and Frick closed the plant rather than meet the union's demands, and when they attempted to occupy the works with armed guards, a violent confrontation ensued. Pennsylvania's governor sent the state militia to the town,

Homestead Steel Mill Lockout. After a lockout at Andrew Carnegie's mill, unionized workers continued to protest wage cuts; their violent reaction to armed Pinkerton guards became the Battle of Homestead, 1892. LIBRARY OF CONGRESS

and within a few months the strike ended in total defeat for the Amalgamated Association.

Labor historians generally equate Homestead with the beginning of the nonunion period in American history. Unionism certainly was dealt a crushing blow there. But the many independent iron and steel manufacturers making wrought iron or crucible steel still depended on skilled puddlers and heaters. The Amalgamated Association retained influence in wrought iron and specialty steel manufacture for many years after Homestead.

Conclusion

America's emergence as the world's greatest industrial power at the end of the nineteenth century was based on the mass production of steel. In the process of contributing to the transformation of the country's economy, the steel industry itself was transformed. The technological and organizational changes in the American steel industry during the nineteenth century were both causes and effects of an increasingly diverse, rapidly urbanizing industrial society.

See also **Coal; Corporations and Big Business; Industrialization and the Market; Inventors and Inventions; Iron; Labor Force; Labor Movement,** *subentry on*
Unions and Strikes; Mining and Extraction; Natural Resources; Pennsylvania; Railroads; Regulation of Business; Steam Power; Work, *subentries on* **Artisans and Craftsworkers, Factory Labor.**

Bibliography

Eggert, Gerald G. *The Iron Industry in Pennsylvania.* Middletown, Pa.: Pennsylvania Historical Association, 1994.

Gordon, Robert B. *American Iron, 1607–1900.* Baltimore: Johns Hopkins University Press, 1996.

Hogan, William T. *Economic History of the Iron and Steel Industry in the United States.* Lexington, Mass.: Heath, 1971.

Ingham, John N. *Making Iron and Steel: Independent Mills in Pittsburgh, 1820–1920.* Columbus: Ohio State University Press, 1991.

Lewis, W. David. *Iron and Steel in America.* Greenville, Del.: Hagley Museum, 1976.

McHugh, Jeanne. *Alexander Holley and the Makers of Steel.* Baltimore: Johns Hopkins University Press, 1980.

Misa, Thomas J. *A Nation of Steel: The Making of Modern America, 1865–1925.* Baltimore: Johns Hopkins University Press, 1995.

Montgomery, David. *The Fall of the House of Labor: The Workplace, the State, and American Labor Activism, 1865–1925.* Cambridge, U.K.: Cambridge University Press, 1987.

Paskoff, Paul E. *Industrial Evolution: Organization, Structure, and Growth of the Pennsylvania Iron Industry, 1750–1860.* Baltimore: Johns Hopkins University Press, 1983.

Taylor, George Rogers. *The Transportation Revolution, 1815–1860.* New York: Rinehart, 1951.

Temin, Peter. *Iron and Steel in Nineteenth-Century America: An Economic Inquiry.* Cambridge, Mass.: MIT Press, 1964.

Wall, Joseph Frazier. *Andrew Carnegie.* New York: Oxford University Press, 1970.

Warren, Kenneth. *The American Steel Industry, 1850–1970: A Geographical Interpretation.* Oxford: Clarendon, 1973.

VAGEL C. KELLER JR.

STOCK MARKETS The predecessors of American stock markets were the seventeenth-century European bourses, which enabled governments and mercantile companies to raise money. Although Philadelphia established the first stock exchange, and Boston also ran a thriving bourse, New York City has been the heart of U.S. investment banking for two centuries.

During the Republic's infancy, lower Manhattan hosted curbside markets comprising of auctioneers and dealers in securities. But when the bankruptcy of speculator William Duer disrupted the system, traders decided to establish a formal exchange, with membership fees and standard commissions. In May 1792 they signed the Buttonwood Agreement under a buttonwood tree located at present-day 68 Wall Street.

Trade initially consisted primarily of bonds, especially government bonds. Most sales were in cash,

Stockbrokers, New York City. No industry was immune to the erratic spikes and plummets of the stock market. LIBRARY OF CONGRESS

because forward contracts were not legally enforceable at the time. Then as later, banks forged links to securities markets via loans to investors and speculators.

Birth of the Exchange

The War of 1812 generated a flurry of activity. The federal government attempted to raise money to finance the war, but was left with $10 million of bonds on its hands. Financiers John Jacob Astor, Stephen Girard, and David Parish bought the bonds at forty cents on the dollar and resold them for eighty-two cents. After a public outcry, the traders decided to organize themselves at a central location and establish more formal membership criteria. The New York Stock and Exchange Board (renamed the New York Stock Exchange in 1863) was born in 1817. Objecting to the $25 membership fee, rogue traders formed the New York Club Market, which later became the American Stock Exchange and moved indoors only in the 1920s.

Sharp practices, such as stock cornering, characterized trading at the unregulated exchange. And, despite centralization, the public still found obtaining information about prices difficult. Still, the exchange flourished initially as New York City, bank, and canal stocks began to appear. But volume declined 75 percent when the Franklin Bank failed in 1825, and the exchange did not recover for six years.

The period from 1830 to the Civil War was a turbulent one for the exchange. In 1839 it listed 144 stocks, almost half from banks. Two decades later, fraud and panics had caused the number of companies to shrink to 114. Foreign investors, who bulked large in the securities market, suffered substantial losses from municipal bond defaults when Congress failed to renew the charter of the second Bank of the United States, thus spurring the financial panic of 1837. One consequence was the creation of the business credit rating, established in 1841 by Lewis Tappan through a company later known as Dun and Bradstreet.

Investors and Speculators

The antebellum years also heralded the rise of investment houses, designed to help people raise large amounts of capital and trade shares and foreign exchange. Among the more famous was the Peabody (later Morgan) firm, founded in 1851. Jay Cooke began his career in 1839 as a clerk at E. W. Clark's Philadelphia house, which went under in the panic of 1857. Cooke started his own establishment in 1861, and made a name for himself when he persuaded Pennsylvania officials to sell bonds at par rather than at the typical discount. Because the bonds were intended to raise money to defend the state against Confederate invasion, Cooke successfully tied their sale to people's patriotic impulses. As a result, Secretary of the Treasury Salmon Chase later chose Cooke to help raise massive amounts of capital for the U.S. government during and just after the Civil War.

Cooke was overshadowed by the grand speculations of Jay Gould, who made his first killing by cornering the gold market in 1869. On 24 September—known as Black Friday—Gould's actions caused the stock market to collapse. Four years later, Gould and other speculators helped bring on another financial panic, which put Cooke, among others, out of business. The panic of 1873 did much to enhance the attractiveness of stock companies, which offered limited liability to their owners. It led also to the emergence of large conglomerate companies, as robber barons like Gould, Jim Fisk, Cornelius Vanderbilt, Russell Sage, and Daniel Drew bought up firms in distress.

Technological Developments

Railroad securities proved especially popular during the postbellum period, in part because railroads provided collateral through their rolling stock. But railroads were also associated with the biggest scandal in American history to date. To facilitate construction of the transcontinental railroad just after the Civil War, Oakes Ames set up a construction company, the Crédit Mobilier. Using a scheme of bribes and graft, Ames charged the government twice what the project cost and pocketed the profit.

The perennial paroxysms on Wall Street led to a demand for more market information. The invention of the telegraph in 1844 made the stock ticker possible by 1867. Seats on the exchange became transferable after 1868, costing about $7,000 to $8,000 each. Dow Jones founded the *Wall Street Journal* in 1889 and began reporting a daily index in 1896. Statistical evidence suggests that the securities markets of the late nineteenth century seem to have operated with reasonable efficiency despite the lack of regulation. In part, this occurred because Wall Street consisted of a fairly narrow set of investors who estab-

lished good private information networks. Still, sharp practices continued. Among the more famous victims was Ulysses S. Grant, who lost most of his wealth in 1884. (As a happy consequence of his misfortune, however, Grant produced a highly regarded autobiography [1885], which he wrote so that his family would not fall destitute after his death from throat cancer.)

The consolidation of companies that began in the 1870s continued through the rest of the century, despite the passage of the Sherman Antitrust Act in 1890. The number and value of shares exchanged doubled between 1875 and 1885, and stocks began to outnumber bonds in the market. The first million-share day occurred in 1885. Until the 1900s, railroad bonds and commercial paper typically did better than stocks.

J. P. Morgan

The burgeoning need for new capital in the last quarter of the century led to large profits for investment bankers, whose fees averaged about 10 percent of the proceeds. They padded their pocketbooks further by taking large stakes in companies and gaining inside information about the firm's commercial prospects. Leading the pack for fifty years after 1880 was the house run by John Pierpont Morgan, who was instrumental in the formation of U.S. Steel and General Electric.

Morgan played an important role in the panics of 1893 and 1907. President Grover Cleveland turned to him to stanch the outward flow of gold in 1894. Although Morgan succeeded, his syndicate was the target of much ire for making $6 million on the deal. His role in bailing out the banks and the stock exchange in 1907 won both plaudits and criticism. Ultimately, people decided that the public sector rather than private individuals should act as the lender of last resort. This led to the creation of the Federal Reserve system in 1913—in the same year that J. P. Morgan died.

See also **Banking and Finance,** *subentry on* **The Banking Industry; Entrepreneurs; Investment and Capital Formation; Wealth.**

Bibliography

Carosso, Vincent. *Investment Banking in America: A History.* Cambridge, Mass.: Harvard University Press, 1970.

Friedman, Milton, and Anna Schwartz. *A Monetary History of the United States.* Princeton, N.J.: Princeton University Press, 1963.

Geisst, Charles. *Wall Street: A History.* New York: Oxford University Press, 1997.

Lamoreaux, Naomi. *The Great Merger Movement in American*

Business, 1895–1904. Cambridge, U.K., and New York: Cambridge University Press, 1985.

JENNY WAHL

STRIKES.   See **Labor Movement,** subentry on **Unions and Strikes.**

SUBURBS   During the nineteenth century suburban communities developed at the edges of city borders. Several factors stimulated this phenomenon. As cities industrialized, upper-class residents could not avoid the negative physical and social impacts of urban life. A steep increase in immigration from eastern and southern Europe caused crowding and congestion. Air and water pollution were prevalent. Social problems, such as crime and disease, affected many neighborhoods. Thus wealthier people were drawn from the cities to more comfortable, bucolic environments along new commuter rail lines in the country. Many urban residents theorized that living in the country was not only healthier and more peaceful but also morally prudent. Living in the country put distance between its residents and all the vices of the city.

Transportation

New transportation technologies, including the steam railroad and the electric rail trolley car, made suburban development possible. Prior to rail transportation, intraurban transit was based on the horse-drawn omnibus, which operated at slow speeds and traveled short distances. Steam railroads provided commuters with the opportunity to live farther distances from their jobs in the central city. However, commuting on the steam railroad was costly. As a result, suburban communities along steam rail lines, such as the towns in Westchester County, New York, or the town of Riverside, Illinois, were primarily composed of wealthy professionals.

The first electric trolley car was tested in 1888.

Scramble at a Typical Suburban Station. Professionals who could afford to board the commuter rail each day escaped city life for the quieter suburbs. Created and published by Currier and Ives, c. 1884. LIBRARY OF CONGRESS: PRINTS AND PHOTOGRAPHS DIVISION

The trolley was faster and quieter, and it traveled longer distances. Because it was cheaper to maintain, the fare was less expensive than railroad fares. This opened up the suburbs to the middle classes. Soon after the first test, the trolley car was put to use in the Boston suburb of Brookline. Following Boston's lead, most major cities in the United States built electric trolley lines to serve suburban communities.

Development Followed Transportation

As rail lines extended, suburban communities developed at rapid rates. In 1830 Brooklyn was a suburban community of Manhattan, but growing at a faster rate than Manhattan. Many of the wealthier, established communities located farther from central cities, such as Montclair, New Jersey, and Chicago's Northshore, blocked rail line development in fear of being inundated with immigrants and the lower classes.

Many suburban communities closer to central cities, including Chicago's Hyde Park and the Bronx in New York City, were annexed, a common practice during the nineteenth century. Residents of the suburban communities preferred to give up their autonomy because cities had more capital and provided better services during the late nineteenth century. In 1850 a single annexation by the city of Philadelphia increased its land area from 2 square miles to 129 square miles. In 1889 Chicago, then 43 square miles, annexed an additional 133 square miles. In 1898 New York City consolidated with the suburban boroughs of Brooklyn, Queens, the Bronx, and Staten Island to create the nation's largest city. However, not all suburban communities agreed to annexation. Evanston to the north of Chicago and Oak Park to the west and the suburban Boston communities of Brookline, Cambridge, and Somerville all rejected annexation attempts.

See also **Cities and Urbanization; City and Regional Planning; Class, Social; Population; Transportation,** *subentries on* **Animal Power, Railroads, Urban and Interurban Transportation; Travel, Technology of.**

Bibliography

Foner, Eric, and John A. Garraty, eds. *The Reader's Companion to American History.* Boston: Houghton Mifflin, 1991.

Jackson, Kenneth T. *Crabgrass Frontier: The Suburbanization of the United States.* New York: Oxford University Press, 1985.

McKelvey, Blake. *The City in American History.* London: Allen and Unwin, 1969.

Stilgoe, John R. *Borderland: Origins of the American Suburb, 1820–1939.* New Haven, Conn.: Yale University Press, 1988.

BARRY BAIN

SUFFRAGE.   See **Voters and Voting.**

SUNDAY-CLOSING LAWS.   See **Blue Laws.**

SUPREME COURT

[This entry includes seven subentries:
The Marshall Court
The Antebellum Court
The Court during the Civil War and Reconstruction
The Gilded Age
Slavery
The Economy
Supreme Court Justices.]

THE MARSHALL COURT

The institutional framework for the nineteenth-century Supreme Court and the outline of U.S. constitutional law before 1865 were established during the chief justiceship (1801–1835) of John Marshall. A Virginia lawyer, Marshall served as President John Adams's secretary of state from 1800 to 1801, immediately prior to his appointment to the Court.

The Court's first decade was occupied with establishing its jurisdiction, formalizing its procedures, and dealing with international affairs and national security issues. Many associate justices resigned after short periods of service, and both Chief Justices John Jay and Oliver Ellsworth accepted diplomatic appointments that resulted in long absences from the Court. Marshall's long tenure provided continuity, as did the dedicated service of many associate justices. No members of Marshall's Court took leave to perform other governmental duties.

The Marshall Court differed from its predecessors in a political way. It found itself in conflict with state power when its decisions invalidated state statutes contrary to the U.S. Constitution's contract clause, when state action encroached on the regulation of interstate commerce, or when states chose to challenge the supremacy of the U.S. Constitution. Composed largely of property-oriented justices, the Marshall Court found itself in persistent conflict with legislative programs espoused by the presidential administrations of Thomas Jefferson and Andrew Jackson and their congressional majorities. The Jay and Ells-

John Marshall (1755–1835). Marshall, chief justice of the Supreme Court from 1801 to 1835, established the foundation of constitutional law, unified the majority as one voice, and strengthened the judicial branch of government. LIBRARY OF CONGRESS: PRINTS AND PHOTOGRAPHS DIVISION

worth Courts were of the same Federalist orientation as the presidents and Congresses of their day and were not challenged politically and ideologically as was the Supreme Court under Marshall.

Supremacy and Judicial Review

The Marshall Court's first significant case, *Marbury v. Madison* (1803), also known as the Mandamus Case, involved a request that the Supreme Court order Secretary of State James Madison to deliver a commission to a justice of the peace. The writ of mandamus, derived from English practice, commanded an official to perform a routine duty established by law. Because the Court's original jurisdiction was established by the Constitution and did not include issuance of mandamus writs, Marshall held that the congressional statute authorizing the procedure was void. The *Marbury* case represented the first time the

Supreme Court applied judicial review, a doctrine earlier developed by state courts and some lower federal courts. Judicial review occurs when a court concludes that a statute or administrative regulation conflicts with a higher legal authority. In these situations the court must declare the provision invalid or inoperative in the case being considered.

The Court's power of judicial review also existed in regard to state legislation or court decisions that clashed with the U.S. Constitution. In *Martin v. Hunter's Lessee* (1816) Justice Joseph Story held that Virginia legislative acts that attempted to escheat land were contrary to the provisions of the 1783 peace treaty with Britain. When a question of federal authority was involved, whether resulting from a constitutional provision, a congressional statute, or a treaty negotiated by the United States, uniformity of law throughout the nation could only be obtained through Supreme Court decisions.

In *McCullough v. Maryland* (1819) the Marshall Court delineated the supremacy of the federal government in activities committed to its authority by the Constitution. This included the implied power to establish a national bank that would be exempt from state taxation. Looking to the "necessary and proper" clause of the Constitution, Marshall held that it authorized all federal activities appropriate or useful in implementing powers enumerated in the Constitution.

In *Cohens v. Virginia* (1821) the Court affirmed its authority to exercise judicial review in cases that raised federal questions—that is, cases that brought into issue rights claimed under the Constitution, federal statutes, or treaties negotiated under the authority of the United States. *Cohens* rejected the claim that the Eleventh Amendment precluded the Court from deciding federal question cases when a state was a party to the action.

Property Rights and Economic Regulation

Because the Constitution was designed to establish a common market throughout the United States, the Marshall Court was called upon to delineate the economic consequences of political union. This was accomplished through a broad reading of the contract clause in *Fletcher v. Peck* (1810), involving cancellation of state land grants, and in *Dartmouth College v. Woodward* (1819), which prohibited legislative cancellation of a royal grant to the college. In *Ogden v. Saunders* (1827), over Marshall's dissent, the Court held that since Congress had not enacted a uniform bankruptcy statute as authorized by the Constitution, the states might provide debtor relief through insolvency laws.

Viewing the free flow of goods and passengers in interstate commerce as central to the economic integration of the Union, the Court, in *Gibbons v. Ogden* (1824), invalidated a New York State steamboat navigation monopoly, holding that congressional enactment of a federal licensing statute precluded state restrictions on the licensee. Subsequent cases, such as *Willson v. Black-Bird Creek Marsh Company* (1829), recognized that congressional control of interstate commerce would be implemented in balance with the police powers traditionally vested in the states.

Human Rights: Slavery, the Slave Trade, and the Indian Removals

As sectional controversy over slavery intensified during Marshall's chief justiceship, the justices took a moderate and restrictive approach in construing the scope of the statutes prohibiting the slave trade and in evaluating petitions for freedom from individuals held in slavery. In the *Antelope* case (1825) the court refused to consider the slave trade to be a form of piracy and limited the federal prohibition of the slave trade to penalize only attempts to import slaves into the United States. The Court pointed out that slavery was an established part of the laws of nations in Europe and the Americas. The same narrow approach is found in the Court's attitude toward petitions for freedom. In *Mima Queen v. Hepburn* (1813) Marshall, on behalf of the Court, refused to allow the introduction of hearsay evidence to prove the petitioner's status. Justice Gabriel Duvall took strong exception to this, pointing out that hearsay evidence was common, that hearsay was the only available evidence, and that in Maryland—whose law governed the case—hearsay had been traditionally accepted in support of freedom petition cases.

Natural law played a more significant role in the Marshall Court's discussion of the status of Indian tribes and the nature of their rights. Compromising the justices' variant views on the legal status of Indian tribes, Marshall held in *Cherokee Nation v. Georgia* (1831) that Indian tribes were "domestic dependent nations." As such, they did not have standing to invoke the original jurisdiction of the Supreme Court, because they were neither a foreign power nor a state. Subsequently, when the appellate case of *Worcester v. Georgia* (1832) collaterally raised the issue of tribal status, the Court held that Georgia's attempt to exert criminal jurisdiction within Cherokee territory was null and void. The decision upheld tribal treaty rights and based Cherokee authority on paramount federal law. President Jackson's preoccupation with the 1833 nullification crisis, an early step in the secession movement, prevented a direct clash between the Supreme Court and President Jackson. However, Jackson eventually prevailed, and most of the Cherokee tribe was forced to migrate to Indian Territory, now Oklahoma.

Institutional Development

Under Chief Justice Marshall's leadership the Supreme Court developed into a powerful branch of the federal government. This was in part because of the personality and political acumen of Marshall himself. However, several other justices, including Joseph Story, Bushrod Washington, William Johnson, and Brockholst Livingston, made substantial contributions to the growth of the Court. Story's erudition strengthened the Court's opinions in all fields. His contributions in admiralty, commercial, and international law were noteworthy. As the first Jeffersonian appointee, Johnson tempered the Court's opinions by arguing for the primacy of legislative power and asserting a broad federal authority in interstate commerce. Marshall's habit of taking advice from his colleagues capitalized on their wisdom and recruited them into the fraternal atmosphere of the Court.

Like their predecessors, Marshall Court justices rode the circuit to try civil and criminal cases in the circuit courts, including the treason trial of Aaron Burr (1805). The former vice president was charged with an alleged treasonable conspiracy to raise a rebellion in the western territories of the United States or, in the alternative, of raising an armed force to invade the territory of a friendly power contrary to a federal statute. Burr was acquitted of treason in a high-profile trial, during which Marshall sharply restricted a hitherto broad construction of the constitutional clause concerning treason. The indictments based on federal criminal statutes were never brought to trial. Presiding in circuit courts gave the justices contact with all geographical areas of the nation, and it also brought federal judicial authority to each state. In addition the justices gained firsthand knowledge of the abilities of district court judges and the administration of their courts.

Virtually all of the cases appealed to the Marshall Court were from lower federal courts, the largest number being from the District of Columbia Circuit Court. This limited the likelihood of direct clashes with state authority, and it permitted the Supreme Court to develop both public and private law precedents. Implementation in 1802 of a system of certifying questions from the circuit courts to the Supreme Court permitted the justices to initiate Supreme Court consideration of matters that otherwise might not have been reviewed.

Unlike the earlier Jay and Ellsworth Courts, the

Marshall Court adopted the practice of delivering majority opinions in all significant cases, also known as "Opinions of the Court." This development was supplemented by the practice of having the senior justice present deliver the Court's opinion. Before 1812 Chief Justice Marshall predominated in opinion delivery, and thereafter he shared in a substantial but declining percentage of opinions delivered. The strong likelihood is that Marshall wrote all of the 443 reported opinions he delivered on behalf of the Court. The use of Court opinions provided anonymity to the views adopted by various justices, and it provided greater certainty to the points of law expounded. Solidarity within the Marshall Court was based on the personality and persuasiveness of the chief justice. Collegiality was enhanced by justices rooming together during their Washington sittings. When they were ostracized from governmental social affairs during the administration of Thomas Jefferson, members of the Marshall Court found comradeship within their own ranks.

Dissent from Court opinions or the expression of concurring opinions were rare events. *Ogden v. Saunders* was Marshall's dissent in a constitutional case. While other justices were more frequently in dissent, particularly in the last years of Marshall's tenure, the chief justice was successful in minimizing the incidence of discontent and in maintaining ostensible unanimity. That unanimity was based in part on the threatened situation of the Court in a hostile political environment. It also was produced by changed procedures within the Court, including the adoption of the majority opinion, the rooming house arrangements, and the justices' shared experience of law practice and judicial service. However, the most cohesive element was the personality of Chief Justice Marshall, which facilitated compromise of conflicting opinions, shared and consultative decision-making, and supportive relationships among all the justices.

See also **American Indians,** *subentry on* **Indian Removal; Constitutional Law,** *subentry on* **Before the Civil War; Courts, State and Federal; Federal-State Relations,** *subentries on* **1800–1833, 1831–1865; Interstate Commerce; Judicial Review.**

Bibliography

Frankfurter, Felix, and James M. Landis. *The Business of the Supreme Court: A Study in the Federal Judicial System.* New York: Macmillan, 1928.

Haskins, George L., and Herbert A. Johnson. *Foundations of Power: John Marshall, 1801–1815.* Volume 2 of *History of the Supreme Court of the United States.* New York: Macmillan, 1981.

Johnson, Herbert A. *The Chief Justiceship of John Marshall.* Columbia: University of South Carolina Press, 1997.

Seddig, Robert G. "John Marshall and the Origins of Supreme Court Leadership." *University of Pittsburgh Law Review* 36 (1975): 785–833.

White, G. Edward. *The Marshall Court and Cultural Change, 1815–1835.* Volumes 3 and 4 of *History of the Supreme Court of the United States.* New York: Macmillan, 1988.

HERBERT A. JOHNSON

THE ANTEBELLUM COURT

The U.S. Supreme Court came to life with the rest of the new federal government in 1789. In its first decade the Court inspired neither awe nor acclaim. John Jay, the first chief justice, considered the judiciary the feeblest arm of the federal government and resigned his seat due to the Court's mediocre reputation and estate. The stature of the judiciary rose immensely, however, after John Marshall became chief justice in 1801. During Marshall's thirty-four-year tenure, the Court waxed in dignity and prestige, becoming a truly august institution that commanded both authority and reverence.

The defining principle of Marshall's jurisprudence was judicial nationalism, expanding the scope of national power at the expense of the states. At the same time Marshall established the Supreme Court as the final arbiter in all matters of constitutional interpretation. In *Marbury v. Madison* (1803), the Court claimed the power of judicial review, that is, the authority to judge the constitutionality of congressional and presidential actions. This step catapulted the formerly weak Court into a position of full equality with the other branches of the federal government. In *Martin v. Hunter's Lessee* (1816) the Court firmly established its appellate jurisdiction over state courts. In *Cohens v. Virginia* (1821) Marshall reasserted this prerogative as part of a sweeping ruling in favor of federal judicial primacy. Marshall's most forceful national-supremacy decree came in *McCulloch v. Maryland* (1819). Grafting the concept of implied powers into constitutional law, he greatly enhanced the sphere of congressional authority. He also pronounced a nationalist solution to questions of federalism, boldly asserting that whenever federal and state powers collided, the latter must yield to the paramount sovereignty of the former.

The Marshall Court also exerted a shaping influence on American economic development through a broad construction of the contract clause of the Constitution. In *Fletcher v. Peck* (1810) Marshall ruled that, because the original conveyance formed a contract, a state legislature could not rescind a land grant that was subsequently proved fraudulent. The Constitution prohibited states from impairing the obligations of contracts. In *Dartmouth College v. Woodward* (1819) he extended this principle to protect corporate charters from alteration or annulment by the states. By enshrining the inviolability of contractual property rights in this way, the Marshall Court became a powerful instrument for the promotion of corporate enterprise and capitalist development.

Marshall died in 1835 and was succeeded as chief justice by Roger B. Taney, who led the Court until 1864. The Taney period coincided with an explosion of interstate trade and market growth, so much of its jurisprudence involved commercial suits. In this respect the Taney Court diverged somewhat from the nationalistic tone of its predecessor. In *Gibbons v. Ogden* (1824) Marshall curtailed the states' role in economic development by declaring that Congress possessed exclusive authority to regulate interstate commerce. Contrarily, in a series of cases—*Charles River Bridge v. Warren Bridge* (1837), *New York v. Miln* (1837), and the *License Cases* (1847)—Taney and his associates accorded the states a measure of regulatory initiative as part of their general police power to provide for the public welfare. In particular the Court adhered to the doctrine of concurrent powers, which allowed the states to regulate commerce in the absence of federal legislation. The Court refined its position in *Cooley v. Board of Wardens* (1852) by articulating the doctrine of "selective exclusiveness." This formula recognized dual aspects of interstate commerce, some purely local that permitted state action and others fundamentally national that fell solely within congressional purview.

In other commerce-related cases, the Taney Court sought to accommodate market development and economic progress. In *Bank of Augusta v. Earle* (1839) the Court ruled that corporations could conduct business freely across state lines except where states excluded foreign companies as a matter of positive law. *West River Bridge v. Dix* (1848) sanctioned the doctrine of eminent domain, which served as a catalyst for the proliferation of railroads.

Slavery was an important issue for the Taney Court, whose jurisprudence on the subject gave the tribunal a proslavery cast. In *Prigg v. Pennsylvania* (1842) the Court struck down a state personal liberty law, designed to prevent the kidnapping and arbitrary reenslavement of alleged escaped slaves, as repugnant to the fugitive slave provisions of the Constitution. The Court proscribed all state legislation that interfered with the return of fugitive slaves, even state acts designed to prevent the mistaken or intentional removal of free blacks. Rather, the Court held that only the federal government possessed authority over the rendition of fugitive slaves. The Court

handed down a similar ruling in *Jones v. Van Zandt* (1847), in which antislavery interests challenged the constitutionality of the Fugitive Slave Act and insisted that a "higher law" than the Constitution repudiated slavery and all ordinances recognizing property rights in man. Rejecting this higher-law moralism, the Court sustained the Fugitive Slave Law, affirmed the right of property in man, and acknowledged slavery as one of the "sacred compromises" upon which the Constitution and the Union were founded (Hyman and Wiecek, *Equal Justice under Law*, p. 111).

The Court maintained its proslavery posture in *Dred Scott v. Sandford* (1857), the most notorious slave case in American history. Led by Taney, the Court majority sanctified the racial and constitutional doctrines of the Old South. Taney decreed that no black person, slave or free, could sue in federal court because blacks were not citizens under the Constitution and, furthermore, were "regarded as beings of an inferior order" with "no rights which the white man was bound to respect" (Fehrenbacher, *The Dred Scott Case*, p. 347). He also ruled that Congress had no constitutional authority to retard the territorial expansion of slavery. Overall the *Dred Scott* decision raised a political furor and exacerbated the sectional tensions that produced the Civil War.

Despite the ignominy that temporarily attached to the Court in the wake of *Dred Scott*, the tribunal suffered no lasting damage. On the whole, in fact, the antebellum Court compiled an impressive record. By the time of the Civil War, the Court had successfully established its own constitutional authority, expounded the scope of national power, and defined relations between the central and state governments.

See also **Constitutional Law,** *subentry on* **Before the Civil War; Economic Regulation; Federal-State Relations,** *subentries on* **1800–1833, 1831–1865; Fugitive Slave Laws; Interstate Commerce; Judicial Review; Law; Race Laws; Slavery,** *subentry on* **Law of Slavery; States' Rights.**

Bibliography

Fehrenbacher, Don E. *The Dred Scott Case: Its Significance in American Law and Politics.* New York: Oxford University Press, 1978.

Hobson, Charles F. *The Great Chief Justice: John Marshall and the Rule of Law.* Lawrence: University Press of Kansas, 1996.

Hyman, Harold M., and William M. Wiecek. *Equal Justice under Law: Constitutional Development, 1835–1875.* New York: Harper and Row, 1982.

Johnson, Herbert A. *The Chief Justiceship of John Marshall, 1801–1835.* Columbia: University of South Carolina Press, 1997.

Newmyer, R. Kent. *The Supreme Court under Marshall and Taney.* Arlington Heights, Ill.: Harlan Davidson, 1986.

Swisher, Carl Brent. *Roger B. Taney.* New York: Macmillan, 1935.

——. *The Taney Period, 1836–1864.* Volume 5 of *History of the Supreme Court of the United States.* New York: Macmillan, 1974.

White, G. Edward. *The Marshall Court and Cultural Change, 1815–1835.* Abridged ed. New York: Oxford University Press, 1991.

ERIC TSCHESCHLOK

THE COURT DURING THE CIVIL WAR AND RECONSTRUCTION

Scholars often view the Supreme Court from 1861 through the early 1870s as relatively ineffectual. Radical Republican congressmen cowed the justices by juggling their numbers, altering jurisdictions, and threatening impeachments. Made timid, jurists failed to condemn constitutionally questionable policies. An alternative perspective is that by 1860 or 1861 all governing branches were floundering, and the unexpectedly aggressive Supreme Court affected both war and nonwar policies.

The Civil War

The Court's docket in early 1861 reflected the effects of its Dred Scott (1857) decision that the government could not exclude slavery from U.S. territories. In *Lemmon v. New York* (1861), Virginians sojourning in New York with their slaves insisted that the Fifth Amendment to the Constitution protected their property (i.e., civil) rights, traditionally state-defined, from New York's antislavery constitution. The right to acquire and protect private property was sanctified in legal doctrines, constitutional decisions, and political rhetoric as the source of all other rights. The outbreak of the Civil War made the *Lemmon* case moot as wartime civil liberties issues upstaged concerns that transitory voting majorities could erode civil rights.

Reluctantly, most justices sustained emergency infringements on the traditional civil liberties of speech, press, and association. Chief Justice Roger B. Taney was an exception. In his circuit opinion in *Ex parte Merryman* (1861), he condemned President Abraham Lincoln for suspending the habeas corpus writ and authorizing military arrests of civilian disloyalists in Maryland, which had almost seceded. Taney asserted that the habeas writ had always shielded all Americans' civil liberties, and he contradicted his own principle, established in *Luther v. Borden* (1849),

that in undeclarable civil wars only popularly elected officials, not judges, could legitimize a winner.

Comparatively few civil liberties issues reached the Court during the war. In the *Prize Cases* (1863) a majority sustained Lincoln's imposition of a naval blockade of rebel ports. Despite Taney's claims in *Merryman*, the justices, in *Ex parte Vallandigham* (1864), rejected jurisdiction in an appeal of an army court's verdict by an antiwar civilian. In short, when balancing the nation's security needs against individual civil liberties, the wartime Court was cautious but not supine.

In rebuttal to Taney's *Merryman* views, several law writers, including Timothy Farrar, Sidney George Fisher, Francis Lieber, and William Whiting, concluded that the framers had built crisis powers into the Constitution and that congressmen and presidents, not judges, must determine when the nation's survival requires their exercise. Such arguments undergirded the laws passed in 1861 and 1862 confiscating rebels' private property and resparked civil rights concerns. Since 1789 even antislavery activists had acknowledged that constitutionally the nation could not inhibit slave owners' property rights in slave states, and reverence for state-defined property rights still dominated. As a result, confiscation required a federal trial to prove an owner disloyal before a slave gained freedom, so few slaves benefited.

By mid-1862 Union troops policed several states. In 1863 Lincoln ordered slaves in still-defiant rebel areas freed without confiscation trials, recruited blacks for the Union Army, and initiated state reconstructions requiring whites to accept emancipation unless the Supreme Court ruled otherwise. Through 1864 and early 1865 Lincoln encouraged the nationwide eradication of private property rights in slaves, a step heatedly opposed as a violation of civil rights. In December 1865, almost nine months after General Robert E. Lee's surrender and Lincoln's murder, voters took this daring step by ratifying the Thirteenth Amendment.

In 1863, more nervous about civil rights than civil liberties, the justices, in *Gelpcke v. Dubuque*, had invalidated attempts to repudiate Dubuque's bonded debts. While monitoring the money morality of Northern cities and states, the justices respected the nation's wartime fiscal needs. Denying itself jurisdiction in *Roosevelt v. Meyer* (1863), the Court implicitly sustained the Union's authority to make paper money legal tender for private debts. The issue would reappear on the Court's docket.

Reconstruction

Taney's death in late 1864 and Lee's surrender at Appomattox in April 1865 altered the Court's composition and the nation's priorities. Chief Justice Salmon P. Chase faced tensions that alienated Congress from President Andrew Johnson. Alleging violations of their civil liberties, whites initiated numerous famous lawsuits, in sharp contrast with the small number and deep obscurity of blacks' litigations to secure equal civil rights.

In *Ex parte Milligan* (1866) the Court questioned the use of military courts where civil tribunals operated. The next year, in *Mississippi v. Johnson* and *Georgia v. Stanton*, the justices refused to enjoin presidential implementation of the Military Reconstruction Act (1867). But voting 5 to 4 in *Ex parte Garland* (1867) and *Cummings v. Missouri* (1867), the "test oath" cases, the justices voided federal laws and state constitution clauses requiring the past loyalty of all public officials, as well as licensed professionals and tradesmen, as violating both civil liberties and civil rights. By redefining public office and licensed professions and trades as federally protected property rights, the justices expanded the interpretation of *Roosevelt* and *Gelpcke*, and opened most leadership positions in the South to former rebels.

Some implications in those cases initially benefited blacks. Inequities in contract and criminal provisions in the former slave states' revised constitutions and laws prompted Congress to craft the first Civil Rights Act in 1866. Implementing the Thirteenth Amendment and anticipating the Fourteenth, the act defined federal citizenship to include blacks; stipulated that states must equalize the rights to contract, marry, sue, be sued, and testify; and widened access to federal courts if state officials denied individuals equal justice because of race.

On his Maryland circuit in 1867, Chief Justice Chase decided in favor of the plaintiff of *In re Elizabeth Turner*. A former slave, Turner wanted release from her apprentice contract made under Maryland's labor law, which disfavored blacks in violation of the Thirteenth Amendment and the Civil Rights Act. Ruling that all residents of every state were owed equal state justice, Chase hoped to settle the issue of blacks' civil equality. His other circuit opinions legitimizing southerners' nonwar civil obligations incurred in marriages, bequests, wills, and business deals were attempts to stabilize social and market relationships. In *Texas v. White* (1869) Chase extended his position. Envisaging a federally reconstructed and improved union of indestructible and equal states, he concluded that in each state all residents, white and black, male and female, should be equally empowered by and accountable to state justice.

Most of the other justices did not share Chase's priority to racially equalize civil rights, and they re-

duced aspirations like his to legalistic rhetoric. In 1873, Chase was deeply troubled by the Court's decision in the *Slaughterhouse* cases. Louisiana's legislators had granted a meatpacking monopoly to a favored corporation, ostensibly to protect public health, and the ousted competitors sued. All parties were white. Lauding the fact that the amended Constitution had nominally equalized all persons' legal rights in their states of residence, the majority asserted nevertheless that the federal system was fundamentally unaltered by the Civil War and Reconstruction. Therefore federal civil rights protections did not embrace ordinary trades and livelihoods like butchering, precisely those to which blacks needed access.

The *Slaughterhouse* majority represented the prevailing doctrines about the sanctity of contracts and the justices' particular mission to determine which implementations of the states' police powers or federal commerce or tax powers were acceptable. In *Hepburn v. Griswold* (1870) a majority of the Court voided the wartime Legal Tender Act (1862) with respect to contracts that called specifically for specie payments. Also in 1870, in *United States v. DeWitt*, the Court unanimously voided a federal tax on highly volatile naphtha, as a disguised federal police regulation. Meanwhile, indications multiplied that most of the justices were disinclined to pursue Chase's pioneering assertions in *Turner* that the Thirteenth Amendment and the Civil Rights Act protected even black women and that the actual fairness of written and unwritten contracts governing life and labor should guide judges' decisions.

In 1873, with Chase dissenting, the Court in *Bradwell v. Illinois* denied a white woman's appeal of Illinois's refusal to license her as a lawyer because of her sex, despite her obvious professional competence. Like Turner and the Louisiana butchers, this female complainant claimed the protection of the Thirteenth Amendment and the Civil Rights Act, asserting that the denial of her license reduced her to involuntary servitude. In rejecting her plea the majority held that while women were persons, they did not enjoy a full range of federally protected civil rights. In *White v. Hart* (1873), Chase again dissenting, the majority of the Court held that prewar contracts for the sale of slaves still were enforceable.

The Civil War and Reconstruction loosed the potential for race and gender equality in civil rights and civil liberties, as well as in political and social rights. Nevertheless, only twenty-three years after the *Slaughterhouse* cases, the Supreme Court, in *Plessy v. Ferguson* (1896), accepted separate-but-equal arguments. The Supreme Court would not reflect the meanings of the Civil War and Reconstruction until the "second Reconstruction" of the 1950s.

See also **Bill of Rights; Civil Rights; Constitutional Amendments,** *subentry on* **Thirteenth, Fourteenth, and Fifteenth Amendments; Law,** *subentry on* **Women and the Law.**

Bibliography

Foner, Eric. *Reconstruction: America's Unfinished Revolution, 1863–1877.* New York: Harper and Row, 1988.

Hyman, Harold M. *The Reconstruction Justice of Salmon P. Chase:* In re Turner *and* Texas v. White. Lawrence: University of Kansas Press, 1997.

Hyman, Harold M., and William M. Wiecek. *Equal Justice under Law: Constitutional Development, 1835–1875.* New York: Harper and Row, 1982.

HAROLD HYMAN

THE GILDED AGE

The Gilded Age ran through the tenure of Chief Justice Morrison R. Waite (1874–1888) and into the early chief justiceship of Melville Weston Fuller (1888–1910). Both presided over a Supreme Court dominated by the forceful and often conflicting personalities of Stephen J. Field, Samuel F. Miller, Joseph P. Bradley, and John Marshall Harlan. These justices played a premier role in determining how the nation would deal with the aftermath of civil war and its development into an industrialized society.

Amendments to the Constitution provided new principles with which to work. The Thirteenth Amendment abolished slavery, and the Fifteenth Amendment gave former slaves the right to vote. But parts of the Fourteenth Amendment that prohibited states from denying any person equal protection of the laws or depriving any person of life, liberty, or property without due process of law were even more important in terms of the development of constitutional doctrine. The Court used this broad language, along with other provisions of the Constitution, to mold the law to fit what was, in its view, the needs of a changing society. Its most important decisions involved business regulation, civil rights, and individual liberties.

Business Regulation

Many landmark cases of the Gilded Age involved the relationship between government and business. In the *Slaughterhouse Cases* (1873) New Orleans butchers complained that a state law requiring them to use a central slaughterhouse deprived them of their rights under the Fourteenth Amendment. The majority of the Court disagreed, but dissents by Justices Stephen Field and Joseph Bradley maintained that the amendment guaranteed a right to pursue a lawful trade or calling. This idea provided the seed for two related theories that would eventually allow the Court to act as censor of state efforts to regulate business. One of these theories, "substantive due process," greatly expanded the meaning of due process by changing it from a guarantee of correct judicial procedure into a tool the Court could use to overrule state regulations that interfered with individual liberty. The other theory, "liberty of contract," suggested that among the liberties guaranteed by the Fourteenth Amendment was the right of individuals to enter into virtually any contract they might desire.

These new theories did not immediately take hold. Ruling in *Munn v. Illinois* (1877) that states had the power to regulate "business affected with a public interest," the Court seemed to allow states free play to regulate. But *Santa Clara County v. Southern Pacific Railroad Company* (1886) determined that corporations were "persons" entitled to the rights guaranteed by the Fourteenth Amendment. In *Allgeyer v. Louisiana* (1897) the majority agreed that the Fourteenth Amendment guaranteed liberty of contract, and in *Smyth v. Ames* (1898) it ruled that state regulations could not deny a business a fair rate of return on its investment. By the end of the century the Court had developed a doctrine that significantly limited state power to regulate business.

The Court also placed limits on the federal government's power. In *United States v. E. C. Knight Company* (1895) it ruled that the Sherman Antitrust Act (1890) could not stop a sale giving American Sugar Refining Company control of 98 percent of the U.S. sugar market. Adopting a narrow view of the commerce clause, Chief Justice Fuller ruled that the power to regulate interstate commerce meant only that Congress could regulate the transportation of goods across state lines; it did not permit Congress to regulate the manufacture of goods.

Two other cases that same year demonstrated that the Court of the Gilded Age had assumed the role of protector of property and bastion of conservatism. *In re Debs* (1895) sanctioned the concept of the federal labor injunction, a device employers could use to put an end to strikes. And in *Pollock v. Farmers' Loan and Trust Company* (1895) the Court overruled the progressive income tax.

Civil Rights

The Gilded Age Court was not as aggressive in using the new amendments to end discrimination. In its earliest cases involving civil rights, the Court ruled that although the Fourteenth Amendment's equal protection clause prohibited states from discriminating on the basis of race, it did not prohibit discrimination by private individuals. Applying this "state action doctrine" in the *Civil Rights Cases* (1883), the Court overruled provisions of the Civil Rights Act of 1875 that prohibited inns, theaters, and other businesses serving the public from denying the use of their facilities to any person on the basis of race. Thirteen years later, in *Plessy v. Ferguson* (1896), the Court established the "separate but equal doctrine" when it upheld a Louisiana law requiring blacks to ride in separate railroad cars. The *Plessy* case is also known for Justice John Harlan's dissent: "Our Constitution is color-blind," Harlan admonished. It "neither knows nor tolerates classes among citizens."

Chinese fared slightly better. *Yick Wo v. Hopkins* (1886), for example, overruled a state law discriminating against Chinese launderers. But Chinese cases were complicated because they involved state laws that interfered with the federal treaty-making power. When Congress passed the Chinese Exclusion Act of 1882, the Court joined the movement to end immigration and prohibit those Chinese who temporarily left the country from returning.

Women saw no better results in matters of equal rights. In *Bradwell v. Illinois* (1873), for example, the Court ruled that Illinois had the authority to exclude women from the legal profession.

Individual Liberties

In cases involving individual liberties, the Gilded Age Court followed prevailing political and social trends that emphasized Victorian morality. It regularly upheld Sunday closing laws and laws prohibiting the sale of liquor. *Reynolds v. United States* (1878) upheld a federal law prohibiting polygamy, despite Mormon objections that the prohibition violated their First Amendment right to free exercise of their religion. This pattern extended to free speech cases. *Ex Parte Jackson* (1878) upheld a federal law prohibiting transmission of gambling materials through the mail.

Following *Barron v. Baltimore* (1833), standard constitutional doctrine held that the Bill of Rights did not apply against the states. The Gilded Age Court continued to follow this rule in *Hurtado v. California* (1884), which held the Fifth Amendment right to a grand jury did not apply to the states. The lasting importance of *Hurtado*, however, lay in the defendant's theory and Harlan's dissent suggesting that the Fourteenth Amendment guarantee that no state shall deprive any person of life, liberty, or property without due process of law meant no state could de-

prive any person of the guarantees of the Bill of Rights. Inspired by this "incorporation doctrine," later Courts selectively applied most of the Bill of Rights to the states.

Conclusion

By adopting a philosophy that discouraged government interference with business, the Court helped release powerful forces of economic change in Gilded Age America. Its opinions had less favorable implications for political and social equality.

See also **Bill of Rights; Civil Rights; Economic Regulation.**

Bibliography

Benedict, Michael Les. *The Blessings of Liberty: A Concise History of the Constitution of the United States.* Lexington, Mass.: D. C. Heath, 1996.

Fairman, Charles. *Reconstruction and Reunion, 1864–1888,* part 2. Volume 7 of *Oliver Wendell Holmes Devise History of the Supreme Court of the United States.* New York: Macmillan, 1987.

Fiss, Owen M. *Troubled Beginnings of the Modern State, 1888–1910.* Volume 8 of *Oliver Wendell Holmes Devise History of the Supreme Court of the United States.* New York: Macmillan, 1993.

Kelly, Alfred H., Winfred A. Harbison, and Herman Belz. *The American Constitution: Its Origins and Development.* 7th ed. Volume 2. New York: Norton, 1991.

Kens, Paul. *Justice Stephen Field: Shaping Liberty from the Gold Rush to the Gilded Age.* Lawrence: University Press of Kansas, 1997.

PAUL KENS

SLAVERY

The words "slave" and "slavery" appear in about 280 U.S. Supreme Court cases before 1866. Usually the "peculiar institution" was incidental to the case, as in *Bank of Augusta v. Earle* (1839), where counsel used slaves as an example of goods that were sold in interstate commerce. Because slavery provided an important and valuable form of property, slaves were often involved or mentioned in litigation involving business, debts, banking, and accidents where a slave had been working on a railroad or steamboat.

The antebellum Court heard all appeals from the District of Columbia courts. In this capacity it heard numerous run-of-the-mill cases affecting such matters as the status of blacks, the criminal law of slavery, and economic disputes involving slaves. These set no new precedents and had little effect on the law of slavery at the local or national level.

In six areas of law, Supreme Court decisions involving slavery and free blacks significantly affected both national politics and legal development. Such cases involved (1) the African Slave Trade; (2) interstate business and commerce directly involving slaves; (3) fugitive slaves; (4) the status of slaves brought to free states; (5) federal regulation of slavery in the territories; (6) the rights of free blacks under the federal constitution. After 1839 the greatest volume of these cases involved fugitive slaves while one case, *Dred Scott v. Sandford* (1857), determined the constitutional standard on the last three issues listed above.

Court Makeup

From 1800 to 1861 (with the exception of a few years in the late 1820s and early 1830s), the majority of Supreme Court justices were southerners, almost all of whom were also slaveowners. In addition, most of the northerners on the Court were "doughface Democrats"—northern men with southern principles—including Justices Henry Baldwin (Pennsylvania), Robert Grier (Pennsylvania), Samuel Nelson (New York), and Levi Woodbury (New Hampshire). Until 1864 the Court was led by a southerner, either the moderate Virginian John Marshall (1801–1835) or Roger B. Taney (1836–1864), the latter consistently proslavery, always hostile to the rights of free blacks, and ultimately a supporter of southern nationalism. With the exception of a few slave trade cases, the most important slavery-related cases were decided after 1836, and reflected Taney's passionate support for slavery and the South.

The Slave Trade

After 1 January 1808, the United States prohibited the importation of slaves from Africa and barred Americans from participating in the trade to other countries. Congress strengthened this law with an 1819 act designed to stop Americans and American ships from participating in the trade by using foreign papers and committing other frauds.

Nevertheless, in *The Antelope* (1825) Chief Justice John Marshall refused to examine the true ownership of a ship that had been involved in the African trade, seized by pirates, and then taken by the U.S. Coast Guard near Florida. On board were nearly three hundred blacks, some captured in Africa and some removed from Spanish and Portuguese ships. Marshall ruled that the African slave trade did not violate international law, even though it was "contrary to the law of nature." Ultimately the Court ordered that the Africans on the ship be separated by lottery and 120 of them returned to Africa, as products of the illegal slave trade. Some forty others were determined to be

legally owned by Spanish claimants, and were subsequently sold in the United States to a Georgia congressman. About 125 of the blacks died while the case was in litigation.

In *United States v. Gooding* (1827) the Court actually examined ownership of a slaving vessel, and upheld the prosecution of Americans who were secretly, and illegally, participating in the trade. In *United States v. The Amistad* (1841) the Court refused to accept the fraudulent papers of slave owners and in the end held in favor of a shipload of Africans, known as the "Amistads," who had been illegally imported to Cuba. The Amistads were being transported to another part of that island when they seized the ship, killed the captain and crew, and forced their owners to sail toward Africa. The crew sailed east during the day, but at night headed northwest, hoping to reach the American South. The ship ended up in Long Island Sound, out of food and water, and was towed to Connecticut by a U.S. Coast Guard vessel. The owners claimed that the blacks were Cuban slaves, but their utter ignorance of Spanish and their obvious African origins led the U.S. courts to reject this idea. Speaking for the U.S. Supreme Court, Justice Joseph Story held that the "Amistads" had been imported illegally, and set them free. Eventually they were returned to Africa. Had the blacks been legally slaves in Cuba, however, the Court would have ordered their return to bondage. In *The Slavers* (1864) the Court sustained condemnation proceedings of vessels being prepared for the illegal trade.

The Business of Slavery

Most issues involving the business aspects of slavery, including buying, selling, and renting slaves, were governed by local or state law, and rarely raised federal questions. After 1808 Congress had the power to regulate the interstate slave trade, but no such regulation was ever considered since it would have immediately threatened the Union. Arguments of counsel and the opinions of the justices in Supreme Court commerce clause cases, such as *Gibbons v. Ogden* (1824), *New York v. Miln* (1837), *The License Cases* (1847), and the *Passenger Cases* (1849), recognized the special status of slaves in the general regulation of commerce, thereby implying that the Supreme Court would not interpret the commerce clause or other aspects of the Constitution in ways that would harm slavery.

Groves v. Slaughter (1841) forced the Court to rule on slavery and commerce. In an attempt to reduce the flow of capital out of the state, the Mississippi Constitution of 1832 prohibited the importation of slaves for sale. In violation of this provision, Robert

Slaughter, a slave trader, sold slaves in Mississippi and received notes signed by Moses Groves. Groves later defaulted on the notes, arguing that the sales were void under Mississippi's constitution. The Court concluded that Mississippi's constitutional prohibition on the importation of slaves was not self-executing, and absent legislation implementing the prohibition, the sale was valid and the notes had to be honored. In separate concurrences northern and southern justices agreed that a state might legally ban the importation of slaves. This principle supported northerners who wanted to keep slaves out of their states and southerners who wanted to make sure that the federal courts would not interfere with slavery at the local level.

Fugitive Slaves

The jurisprudence concerning fugitive slaves was the most divisive constitutional issue in antebellum America. The Supreme Court heard four major cases involving fugitive slaves: *Prigg v. Pennsylvania* (1842), *Jones v. Van Zandt* (1847), *Ableman v. Booth* (1859), and *Kentucky v. Dennison* (1861). These cases exacerbated the sectional crisis by failing to deal adequately with the moral and political questions raised when human beings escaped to freedom. Ultimately, these issues were decided not by constitutional arguments and ballots, but by war.

The cases were based on the fugitive slave clause of Article IV, Section 2, of the Constitution. The Framers had adopted this clause late in the Constitutional Convention, without any serious debate or discussion. Congress's Fugitive Slave Act of 1793 was the first of two statutes to enforce this clause. In *Prigg v. Pennsylvania* (1842) Justice Story falsely characterized the Constitution's provision as "a fundamental article without the adoption of which the Union could not have been formed." The Supreme Court maintained this view until the end of slavery, and thus virtually always ruled in favor of slaveowners and federal enforcement in fugitive slave cases.

Starting in the 1820s, some northern states passed personal liberty laws requiring higher standards of evidence for the removal of an alleged fugitive slave than the federal law required. These laws were a good faith effort to protect free blacks from enslavement through kidnapping or mistaken identity, as well as to provide procedures by which state officials could aid in the rendition of actual fugitives. Before the 1830s the northern states generally tried to balance their desire to protect the freedom of their free black population with their desire to comply with the obligations placed upon them by the Constitution to return runaway slaves.

The constitutionality of the federal law of 1793, as well as the state personal liberty laws, was not tested in the Supreme Court until *Prigg v. Pennsylvania* (1842). In *Prigg*, Justice Story held that the Fugitive Slave Law of 1793 was constitutional; that Pennsylvania's personal liberty law of 1826 (and by extension all similar laws) unconstitutionally added new requirements to the rendition process; that the Constitution's fugitive slave clause implied a common-law right of recapture, and so any slaveowner or his agent could remove a fugitive slave without complying with the federal law of 1793 if such a capture could be done without a breach of the peace; and that although all state judges and other officials should enforce the federal law, the national government could not require them to do so. Chief Justice Taney concurred, but objected to Story's assertion that state judges did not have to enforce the fugitive slave law, correctly predicting that the states would use Story's opinion to undermine the effectiveness of the 1793 statute. Indeed, after *Prigg* some states simply withdrew all support for the return of fugitives.

The Court's interpretation of the 1793 statute in *Jones v. Van Zandt* (1847) further stimulated northern opposition to fugitive slave rendition. Jones sued Van Zandt for the value of a slave who had escaped into Ohio, because Van Zandt had given the black a ride in his wagon. The Court, through Justice Levi Woodbury, essentially adopted the southern legal rule that all blacks should be presumed to be slaves, and thus held Van Zandt liable for the value of the slave. Representing Van Zandt was the abolitionist attorney Salmon P. Chase.

In response to growing northern hostility to returning runaway slaves, southerners in 1850 gained a new, stronger fugitive slave law with federal enforcement. The 1850 act, which was a key component of the compromise of 1850, authorized the appointment of federal commissioners in every county of the United States. The commissioners could issue certificates of removal for fugitive slaves and were empowered to call on federal marshals, the military, and "bystanders, or *posse comitatus*," to enforce the law. People interfering in the enforcement of the law could be jailed for up to six months and fined up to one thousand dollars.

The law seemed to mock due process and fairness. Alleged fugitives could be remanded on minimal evidence, or mere affidavit; seized blacks were not allowed to testify on their own behalf; and no jury trial was allowed to determine the status of the alleged fugitive. Worst of all, federal commissioners received a fee of ten dollars if they found on behalf of the claimant, but only five dollars if they decided the alleged fugitive was in fact a free person. To many northerners this seemed like a blatant attempt at bribery.

In *Ableman v. Booth* (1859) the Court rejected an attempt by the state of Wisconsin to declare the federal law unconstitutional. Speaking for a unanimous Court, Taney wrote a powerful opinion upholding federal judicial power at the expense of the states. He held that every state was pledged *"to support this Constitution,"* and that "no power is more clearly conferred than the power of this court to decide ultimately and finally, all cases arising under [the federal] Constitution and laws" (21 Howard [62 U.S.] 525 [1859]). *Ableman* is still cited for the proposition that the federal government "should be supreme, and strong enough to execute its laws by its own tribunals, without interruption from a State or from State authorities," and that "the supremacy thus conferred on this Government could not peacefully be maintained unless it was clothed with judicial power, equally paramount in authority to carry it into execution" (21 Howard [62 U.S.] 517 [1859]).

Kentucky v. Dennison (1861), decided after secession had begun, was the Court's last major decision on slavery. Willis Lago, a free black living in Ohio, had helped a Kentucky slave escape to Ohio. Governors Salmon P. Chase and William Dennison of Ohio refused to extradite Lago so that he could stand trial for helping a slave escape. Kentucky asked the Supreme Court to intervene. With the Confederacy already formed, and the Civil War on the horizon, Taney did not want to give authority to the federal government to compel the actions of a state governor. In an opinion reminiscent of Marshall's in *Marbury v. Madison* (1803), he castigated Dennison for his refusal to act, but ultimately refused to issue a mandamus against the governor. Taney ruled that interstate extradition was a matter of gubernatorial discretion, to be performed out of comity and good citizenship.

Slaves in the Territories and the Free States

In the Northwest Ordinance (1787) and the Missouri Compromise (1820), Congress prohibited slavery in most of the territories owned by the United States. The meaning of the slavery prohibition in the Northwest Ordinance came before the Supreme Court in *LaGrange v. Chouteau* (1830), *Menard v. Aspasia* (1831), and *Strader v. Graham* (1851). In each case the Court refused to support freedom claims of slaves who had lived or worked in the old Northwest. In *Strader* the Court held that the slavery prohibition ceased to be in force when the territories became states. Thus each state could determine for itself the

status of persons within its jurisdiction, and this was not subject to review by the Supreme Court.

The *Dred Scott* Case

Dred Scott v. Sandford (1857) and *Marbury v. Madison* (1803) are the only antebellum cases in which the Supreme Court held a federal law unconstitutional. The Missouri Compromise (1820) prohibited slavery in the territory north of Missouri, which became the Wisconsin Territory. Dr. John Emerson, an army surgeon, took his slave Dred Scott to Fort Armstrong in the free state of Illinois, and then to Fort Snelling in the Wisconsin Territory (in what later became Minnesota). After Dr. Emerson died, Scott sued for his freedom, and in 1850 a Missouri trial court declared him free, under the principle that he had become free by living in nonslave jurisdictions. Although this decision followed Missouri precedents dating from 1824, the Missouri Supreme Court, reflecting the growing proslavery ideology of the South, reversed it.

By this time Scott was owned by John F. A. Sanford, a New Yorker. (The Supreme Court reporter would misspell his name in the case as "Sandford.") Scott sued Sanford in federal court under diversity jurisdiction, which allowed citizens of one state to sue citizens of another state in federal court. By the time the case reached Chief Justice Taney's court, the question of slavery in the territories had become the central political issue of the decade.

Answering the prayers of proslavery politicians, especially president-elect James Buchanan, the strongly proslavery Taney used *Dred Scott* to decide this pressing political issue in favor of the South. His two most controversial points dealt with the constitutionality of the Missouri Compromise and the rights of free blacks under the federal Constitution.

With strained logic, Taney argued that the territories clause of Article IV of the Constitution applied only to the territories owned by the United States in 1787 and not to territories acquired after that date. This led him to conclude that the ban on slavery in the Missouri Compromise was unconstitutional. In addition, Taney argued that freeing slaves in the territories constituted a taking of property without due process, which violated the Fifth Amendment. This was the Supreme Court's first use of the concept of substantive due process. Thus, under Taney's theory of the Constitution, Dred Scott had not been entitled to freedom even while he lived at Fort Snelling. More important, Taney implied that all congressional limitations on slavery in the territories were unconstitutional. This was a direct assault on northerners who had been working to make the territories free, and a frontal assault on the new Republican Party,

Roger B. Taney (1777–1864). Taney's most significant decision as chief justice was in *Dred Scott v. Sandford* (1857). He declared that blacks, even if free, could never be citizens of the United States, and thus could not sue in federal court. Photograph taken between 1850 and 1864. LIBRARY OF CONGRESS: PRINTS AND PHOTOGRAPHS DIVISION

which was dedicated to ending the spread of slavery in the West.

Taney compounded this attack on northern attitudes with a gratuitous denial of any rights for free blacks, including the right to sue in federal court. Rigorously applying a jurisprudence of original intent, Taney concluded that even those free blacks living in the North with full state citizenship could never be citizens of the United States. He argued that blacks

> are not included, and were not intended to be included, under the word "citizens" in the Constitution, and can therefore claim none of the rights and privileges which that instrument provides and secures to citizens of the United States. On the contrary, they were at that time [1787] considered as a subordinate and inferior class of beings, who had been subjugated by the dominant race, and, whether emancipated or not, yet remained subject to their authority, and had no rights or privilege but such as those who held the power and the Government might choose to grant them (19 Howard 404–405 [1857]).

In an analysis that was historically incorrect and shocking to the North, Taney asserted that when the Constitution was adopted, blacks were universally considered "beings of an inferior order, and altogether unfit to associate with the white race, either in social or political relations; and so far inferior, that they had no rights which the white man was bound to respect; and that the negro might justly and lawfully be reduced to slavery for his [white people's] benefit" (19 Howard 407 [1857]). In dissent, Justices John McLean and Benjamin Curtis pointed out that Taney ignored the fact that at the time of the Revolution, free blacks in fact voted in a number of states, including Massachusetts, Pennsylvania, and North Carolina, and were clearly constituent members of the American society that adopted the Constitution.

All nine justices wrote opinions in *Dred Scott*. Six concurred with Taney, including two northerners, Robert Grier and Samuel Nelson. Justices John McLean of Ohio and Benjamin R. Curtis of Massachusetts wrote long and powerful dissents. Curtis noted that everyone, including Taney, admitted that "Congress has some power to institute temporary Governments over the territory" (19 Howard 609 [1857]). Curtis believed that this power came from the territories clause of Article IV. Curtis demonstrated that this power was a broad power, not the narrow and constricted one that Taney found. Curtis reasoned that the words "needful regulation" in the territories clause empowered Congress to regulate or ban slavery in the territories.

Curtis's dissent heartened Northerners like Horace Greeley, the editor of the *New York Tribune*, who wrote that Taney's decision was an "atrocious," "wicked," "abominable," "false" opinion. It was a "collection of false statements and shallow sophistries," a "detestable hypocrisy" and a "mean and skulking cowardice." The *Chicago Tribune* expressed the reaction of many Northerners: "We scarcely know how to express our detestation of its inhuman dicta, or to fathom the wicked consequences which may flow from it."

The *Dred Scott* case gave Taney an opportunity to try to settle the issue of slavery, once and for all, in favor of the South. He hoped that his magisterial decision would end the controversy over slavery in the territories, and in the process destroy the new Republican Party, which so threatened slavery. But his decision had just the opposite affect. In 1858 and 1860, Republicans successfully made Taney and the decision the focus of their campaigns. In his "House Divided" speech (1858), Abraham Lincoln argued that Taney's opinion was part of a proslavery conspiracy to nationalize slavery and a prelude to future proslavery jurisprudence. By 1860 a majority of northern voters accepted Lincoln's arguments and supported his presidential candidacy. In 1864 Lincoln, as president, replaced the deceased Taney with Salmon P. Chase, a lawyer called the "attorney general for fugitive slaves," who had spent much of his life fighting the proslavery jurisprudence of the Taney court.

See also **Constitutional Law,** *subentry on* **Before the Civil War; Law,** *subentry on* **State Law; Slavery,** *subentry on* **Law of Slavery; Supreme Court,** *subentry on* **The Antebellum Court.**

Bibliography

Fehrenbacher, Don E. *The Dred Scott Case: Its Significance in American Law and Politics.* New York: Oxford University Press, 1978.

Finkelman, Paul. *An Imperfect Union: Slavery, Federalism, and Comity.* Chapel Hill: University of North Carolina Press, 1981.

Finkelman, Paul. *Dred Scott v. Sandford: A Brief History with Documents.* Boston: Bedford Books, 1997.

Finkelman, Paul. " 'Hooted Down the Page of History': Reconsidering the Greatness of Chief Justice Taney." *Journal of Supreme Court History* 1994 (1995): 83–102.

Finkelman, Paul. "Story Telling on the Supreme Court: *Prigg v. Pennsylvania* and Justice Joseph Story's Judicial Nationalism." *Supreme Court Review* 1994 (1995): 247–294.

Hyman, Harold M., and William M. Wiecek. *Equal Justice under Law: Constitutional Development, 1835–1875.* New York: Harper and Row, 1982.

Morris, Thomas D. *Free Men All: The Personal Liberty Laws of the North, 1780–1861.* Baltimore: Johns Hopkins University Press, 1974.

Wiecek, William M. *The Sources of Antislavery Constitutionalism in America, 1760–1848.* Ithaca, N.Y.: Cornell University Press, 1977.

Wiecek, William M. "Slavery and Abolition Before the United States Supreme Court, 1820–1860." *Journal of American History* 65 (1978–1979): 34–59.

PAUL FINKELMAN

THE ECONOMY

The system of government established by the Constitution was instituted with a number of purposes in mind, as that document's preamble makes clear: "to form a more perfect union, establish justice, insure domestic tranquility, provide for the common defense, promote the general welfare, and secure the blessings of liberty." The vagueness of the references to social and economic policymaking—ensuring domestic tranquility, promoting the general welfare, securing the blessings of liberty—is revealing. It sug-

gests that the need to establish a more effective system of government rather than a particular policy agenda lay at the heart of the creation of the Constitution.

Within the document itself, economic policy is covered not by reference to specific purposes but by the limitation or delegation of powers: no abrogation of contract, specific federal authority over commerce and the tariff, and some power of taxation. Not until the addition of the Bill of Rights did the Constitution refer to such social matters as the government's relationship to freedom of speech and religion. The prevailing assumption, which James Madison expressed in *The Federalist* (1787), was that the states retained primary responsibility for most economic and social policymaking.

In practice economic policy in its largest sense quickly assumed a major place in the governance of the new nation. In the 1790s Congress enacted significant economic legislation affecting debt, currency, banking, tariff, finance, commerce, and land. The Supreme Court under Chief Justice John Marshall emerged during the early nineteenth century as a critical force in shaping economic policy in the young Republic.

For all the commitments to liberty that infused the Revolution and the Constitution, the prevailing mercantilist mind-set of the eighteenth century was not easily put aside. True, the founders were as one in their desire to get rid of the cankers of preference, monopoly, and corruption that disfigured the English-imposed economic policies of the colonial period. But they were by no means ready to enter into an economic state of nature, where an untrammeled market reigned supreme. While belief in the productive capacity of free men was widespread, so too was the belief that economic growth depended as well on confidence in the stability of existing arrangements and relationships. Property and contractual relationships needed to be freely entered into, but they also needed to be secured and guaranteed. All of this raises the general question of the nineteenth-century Supreme Court's influence on the course of American economic development.

Antebellum: The Marshall and Taney Courts

John Marshall and his Supreme Court reflected that predisposition to influence economic development in two important cases, *Fletcher v. Peck* (1810) and *Dartmouth College v. Woodward* (1819). *Fletcher* involved a spectacular land fraud. In 1795 an all but completely bribed Georgia legislature awarded a huge tract of territory, called the Yazoo, to a land company. A later legislature, chosen in good part because of public outrage over this jobbery, rescinded the original act. This of course cast a shadow over the title of the original Yazoo Company purchasers and over the titles of those who bought land from them. Marshall for the first time invoked the contract clause of the Constitution to sustain the original grant of land. Tolerated corruption, that major source of revolutionary indignation, is part of the price to be paid for firm contractual guarantees as a necessary condition of economic growth.

This protectionist mind-set is seen as well in the *Dartmouth College* case, where the issue was not an overtly economic one. In 1816 the New Hampshire Republican state legislature altered the colonial charter to change Dartmouth's name to the University of New Hampshire and to shift its control from private trustees to trustees appointed by the governor of the state. Marshall in response came to the profoundly important conclusion that a charter was in fact a contract and that Dartmouth College was a "private eleemosynary [charitable] institution." The state's action violated the Constitutional requirement that no state could pass a law "impairing the obligation of contracts" (Article 1, Section 10).

This decision cast a long shadow. State-chartered private corporations from the 1820s on became the chosen instrument for the large-scale accumulation of capital and organization of enterprise in the American economy. *Dartmouth College* implied that they could call on the Constitution's contract clause to protect them from state-imposed restrictions deemed by the courts to be a violation of existing contractual arrangements.

The flow of American economic development during the early and mid–nineteenth century was away from the cosseted early Republic environment in which the sanctity of contract seemed to be the most important prop to economic growth. It soon became apparent that the most useful spur to economic growth was not to protect existing enterprise but to ease the path for new enterprise. In this springtime of the American Industrial Revolution, the unleashing of individual energy and enterprise following the War of 1812 and the development of new technologies, such as the steamboat, the railroad, and the factory, created a fresh set of economic imperatives.

Marshall's Court duly responded in *Gibbons v. Ogden* (1824). In 1808 the New York legislature gave the steamboat inventor Robert Fulton and his partner and political financier Robert Livingston the exclusive right to run steamboats on the waters of the state. Fulton and Livingston licensed Aaron Ogden to exercise that privilege on the lucrative New York–New Jersey crossing. Meanwhile Thomas Gibbons,

another entrepreneur, secured a license under the federal Coasting Act to run steamboats in the same waters. Ogden challenged this threat to his monopoly grant from New York State.

In sharp contrast to his opinions in *Fletcher* and *Dartmouth College*, Marshall found not for the original grantee Ogden but for the challenger Gibbons. He argued that the commerce clause of the Constitution trumped state authority, particularly when the commerce under question was so clearly interstate. This is an instance of Marshall's nationalism, his gradual, subtle development of the authority of the central government, but it had equal economic importance. It helped make the federal power over interstate commerce an enormously influential force for the development of a national economy. More immediate, by subjecting preexisting, exclusive state grants to the modifying restraint of a larger national power, it opened the door to economic development untrammeled by prior monopoly rights.

The tendency not to let existing state charter monopoly grants block economic development reached its high-water mark in the decision of Marshall's successor, Roger B. Taney, in *Charles River Bridge v. Warren Bridge* (1837). The Charles River Bridge Company had a Massachusetts charter dating from 1785 that gave it the right to build a bridge over the Charles River and collect tolls for forty years. In 1792 the charter was extended to seventy years. Rapidly rising traffic between Boston and Charlestown led the legislature to charter another firm, the Warren Bridge Company, to build another bridge close by. After earning enough to pay off its bondholders, the company would turn the bridge over to the state to be run without tolls. The Charles River Bridge Company sought to block the new bridge as a violation of its vested rights as protected by the contract clause.

Given the *Fletcher* and *Dartmouth College* precedents, the company might well have seemed to be in the right. The Jacksonian Democrat Taney was not the early Republic Federalist Marshall, however, and the 1830s were not the 1810s. It no longer made economic sense to protect existing contractual arrangements at the cost of present and future economic needs. Taney argued for the states' fundamental "power over their own internal police and improvement, which is so necessary to their well-being and prosperity." Since the Massachusetts legislature had not specifically given indefinite exclusive rights to the Charles River Bridge Company, he saw no impairment of its charter by the new bridge charter. Rapid changes in internal improvements imposed on the state the obligation to make benefits available to its inhabitants as expeditiously as possible.

Over the course of the first half century of the Republic, the Supreme Court set down the lineaments of its economic policymaking. Marshall's concern for the sanctity of contractual arrangements, steeped in the protective mercantilism of the eighteenth century, later found new life with the rise of substantive due process. In *Cohen v. Virginia* (1821), Marshall affirmed the power of a state to ban the sale of lottery tickets, even though the lottery was authorized by Congress. His real purpose—typical of Marshall—was to establish the Court's power to review state court decisions. In the course of doing so, however, he set the stage for judicial acceptance of a wide range of state economic and social regulation, which came to be justified under the police power to protect the public health, safety, mores, and welfare.

During the second half of the century, the Court had to deal with a growing body of state regulation and taxation. It responded by using the test for the doctrines of due process and police power. Two questions were asked: does the statute at issue violate the substantive due process rights of the plaintiff, and is the statute a proper application of the police power?

The Supreme Court also of necessity had a hand in purely commercial decision making. The question of the respective obligations of debtors and the rights of creditors in bankruptcy was an early and recurring issue. The states sought to ease the plight of debtors, initially out of a revolutionary distaste for English-style imprisonment of bankrupts, rather than out of the belief that a second chance was both a part of the American ethos and wise economic policy. Marshall in *Sturges v. Crowninshield* (1819) struck down a New York law that retroactively relieved insolvent debtors as a violation of the contract clause. But in *Ogden v. Saunders* (1827) the Court accepted a state law easing the constraints on debtors. Marshall vigorously dissented, the only time he did so on a constitutional issue. The Taney Court in *Swift v. Tyson* (1842) sought to establish a national commercial law, but the dictates of states' rights and sectionalism meant that in decades to come federal and state commercial law coexisted as separate, at times conflicting, and often confusing entities.

The Taney Court's support of American development assumed its darkest character in its defense of slavery. In *Groves v. Slaughter* (1841), the Court held that although the Missouri constitution forbade the importation of slaves in order to sell them, the failure of the legislature to pass an enabling act allowed such sales to take place. In *Dred Scott v. Sandford* (1857) the Court disastrously sought to legitimate slavery as a national institution and reduce black Americans to a condition somewhere between property and personhood.

Postbellum: The Supreme Court and Industrial America

The Civil War remains the customary dividing line between the agrarian-commercial young Republic and corporate-industrial-urban America. In reality, of course, the transition was far less abrupt and dramatic. Certainly in terms of politics and government and especially in terms of constitutional law and ideology the war was a watershed. The Civil War's most significant constitutional legacy to the Court's economic decision making was the Fourteenth Amendment (1868), particularly its first section: "No State shall make or enforce any law which shall abridge the privileges or immunities of citizens of the United States; nor shall any State deprive any person of life, liberty, or property, without due process of law; nor deny to any person within its jurisdiction the equal protection of the laws."

No part of American constitutional history has been the subject of more debate than the intention that lay behind these words. One school holds that the amendment was drafted with the economic implications of the due process and other clauses very much in mind, that is, that they could be used to oppose state tax and regulatory laws. The other, more persuasive opinion holds that the primary purpose of the amendment was to afford newly freed slaves protection from vengeful former Confederate states seeking to return them to servile status. Certainly this was the context—the high noon of Radical Reconstruction after the Civil War—in which the Fourteenth Amendment was passed. It was, after all, sandwiched between the Thirteenth Amendment of 1865, which ended slavery, and the Fifteenth Amendment of 1870, which in principle enfranchised the black population.

Whatever the Fourteenth Amendment's original intent, the Supreme Court, in a stunning display of constitutional creativity during the late nineteenth and early twentieth centuries, turned the due process clause into a major instrument of economic policymaking. Simply put, the Court came to accept the idea that corporations were legal "persons" and thus entitled to the safeguards afforded by the Fourteenth Amendment.

This did not come with a rush. The Court was slow to use the amendment to protect any rights, civil or property. Between 1872 and 1886 forty-six Fourteenth Amendment cases came before the Court. Corporations were parties in only a dozen of them, blacks in only eight. The Court decided only six cases in favor of the plaintiff pleading the amendment. Justice Stephen J. Field warned in 1886, "This Court is not a harbor where refuge can be found from every act of ill-advised and oppressive State legislation." Then what has been called a judicial revolution occurred. Between 1887 and 1910 the Supreme Court handed down 558 decisions based primarily on the Fourteenth Amendment's due process, privileges and immunities, and equal protection clauses. The larger economic context for this explosion is clear: the rise of interstate corporations and the attempts of the states to regulate and tax them.

The traditional view is that procorporation judges turned the amendment into a bulwark against state regulation and taxation of big business. Statistically a more complex picture emerges. Of the 243 Fourteenth Amendment decisions before 1901, 93 percent upheld the state law at issue. In the early 1900s that portion went down to 76 percent. It seems clear that the Court more vigorously applied Fourteenth Amendment constraints when, in the Progressive Era, regulatory laws largely increased in volume. Most of that legislation was upheld, but a one-in-four rejection rate may well have had a depressing effect on regulatory efforts. It may be argued also that the shape of the turn-of-the-century American economy was determined by technology, markets, and capital far more than by the decisions of the Court.

Corporations and other business interests challenged state regulation in other ways. They often sought protection under Marshall's standby, the contract clause, or they argued, again in the Marshall tradition, that state regulation violated the federal government's right to control interstate commerce. But here, too, the victory of private interests over state regulation was limited. Between 1873 and 1912 the Court upheld the constitutionality of the state laws at issue in 83 percent of its contract clause cases and 75 percent of its commerce clause cases.

This is the quantitative picture, but what of the qualitative one? Just how significant a force was the Supreme Court in shaping the course and character of the American economy in the late nineteenth and early twentieth centuries?

Railroads made the most frequent and substantive calls on the Court for protection from state regulation and taxation. They were the first big business; and as they combined into interstate monoliths during the middle decades of the nineteenth century, state legislatures responded. The result was a growing body of state laws governing railroad rates, corporate organization, taxation, safety, and labor. States commonly created railroad commissions to oversee the lines. In 1887 Congress established the Interstate Commerce Commission, the first federal regulatory body, to pass on rates and other railroad regulatory matters.

Most of this regulatory structure grew with little

or no restraint from the Supreme Court—although in *Loan Association v. Topeka* (1875) the Court did put a damper on local government subsidies to business enterprises, which lasted for almost a century. In 1877 *Munn v. Illinois* upheld a state law setting maximum grain storage rates. Chief Justice Morrison Waite justified rate regulation, which implicitly included that of railroads, on the basis of a centuries-old English common-law doctrine regarding "business . . . affected with a public interest." *Munn* has been called "a brief in behalf of judicial deference to legislative decisions." The Supreme Court notably was not disposed to favor railroads as litigants. Of the railroad cases that came before the Court from 1884 to 1889, forty-nine decisions went against the lines and forty-eight for them. From 1892 to 1897 the Court decided ninety-six cases against railroads and forty-eight in favor.

From the mid-1880s on the Court responded to the belief that state regulation and taxation had an adverse effect on the national flow of commerce. In *Wabash, St. Louis and Pacific v. Illinois* (1886) the Court struck down a state law regulating freight rates on the grounds that this disrupted interstate commerce. That decision led directly to the creation of the Interstate Commerce Commission. In *Chicago, Milwaukee and St. Paul v. Minnesota* (1890) the Court went further. In effect it overturned *Munn*, holding that the reasonableness of rate regulation was a judicial and not a legislative matter. The implication is that rate making should rest in the hands of the managers of interstate rail lines, subject to review by nationally minded federal courts rather than locally minded state courts and legislatures. Starting in the 1870s federal district courts took over bankrupt railroads and appointed receivers, almost always the existing management. One contemporary thought that "long tables of railway statistics, with the accompanying analyses, look strangely out of place in a volume of United States Reports." In fact, the Court had assumed a quasi-administrative supervisory role.

The federal courts did not affect greatly the evolution of American railroads. The economic forces that led to growth and consolidation were far stronger than legal or constitutional considerations. The factors that made the railroads profitable Goliaths in the age before motor vehicles and then transformed them into money-losing mastodons after the coming of automobiles, trucks, and buses went far beyond the writ of any court.

Insurance, like railroads, was a pioneering interstate business in the nineteenth century. The Court's decision in *Paul v. Virginia* (1869) upheld a Virginia law that regulated salespeople for foreign, that is, chartered by another state, insurance companies.

"The corporation," said Justice Field, "being the mere creation of local law, can have no legal existence beyond the limits of the sovereignty where created." *Paul* implies that states have wide authority to regulate the activities of foreign corporations as well as their own. Indeed, the protective cloak of the charter as a contract that Marshall wove in *Dartmouth College* came in for much post–Civil War judicial criticism as an unwarranted limit on the regulatory power of the states.

The idea of a powerful and active government, state or national, failed to take hold in late-nineteenth-century America. As the experience of the Civil War faded into memory, the old American hostility to strong government reemerged. The view that state regulation impeded the growth of an increasingly national economy reinforced that inclination. The courts, including the Supreme Court, accepted the view that the states were free to impose a broad range of requirements and restraints in corporation charters and that the companies could be closely held to them. Once made, the charter had much of the sanctity of a contract, and with the legal concept that a corporation was a citizen under the Fourteenth Amendment, the protections of substantive due process, privileges and immunities, and equal protection came into play.

In its constant balancing act between the police power and substantive due process, the Supreme Court began to put greater weight on due process. In *Barron v. Burnside* (1887) the Court for the first time decided that state regulation of foreign corporations might be of doubtful constitutionality. In another insurance case, *Allgeyer v. Louisiana* (1897), the Court struck down a Louisiana law that forbade its citizens from doing business with a New York life insurance company. By the early twentieth century the prevailing "liberal theory" of foreign corporations held that, like any American citizen, they were immune to special obligations imposed on them by the states.

The courts also had to respond to rising concern over the capacity of large corporations to crush competition and fix prices. Monopolies and other restraints on the free market had long been objects of legal and legislative concern, and the rise of big business gave new force to old threats to a free market economy. In a stunning example of legal creativity, a Standard Oil attorney, Samuel C. T. Dodd, in the late 1870s created the first corporate trust agreement. Stock in Standard Oil and a number of its competitors was turned over to a Standard Oil–dominated board of trustees, who issued trust certificates in return. That arrangement allowed the company to circumvent its Ohio charter, which, as was common at the time, forbade it from holding the stock of other companies or having property outside the state.

A number of states passed laws aimed at trusts; as a result only about ten trusts were created in the 1880s. Meanwhile Delaware, New Jersey, and West Virginia amended their corporation laws to allow one company to hold the stock of another firm, opening the door to another legal invention, the holding company. Not a trust, a holding company is a corporation created solely to hold the stock of and thus control other companies. A great wave of corporate consolidation took this form around the turn of the century, and the modern American big business economy emerged.

The major political response to these developments was the Sherman Antitrust Act of 1890. Relying on the federal power over interstate commerce, the act outlawed "every contract, combination in the form of trust or otherwise, or conspiracy, in restraint of trade or commerce." The Sherman Act seemed constitutionally impregnable, but the Supreme Court dealt a heavy blow to antitrust enforcement in *United States v. E. C. Knight* (1895). The Court struck down a Justice Department suit against the American Sugar Refining Company, even though that firm controlled more than 90 percent of the nation's sugar refining capacity. The Court reasoned that sugar refining was manufacturing and hence was not interstate commerce.

Why did the Court do this? Certainly in part because some of the justices feared a radical assault on vested corporate interests and the developing national economy. The Sugar Trust decision also showed the Court's sensitivity to the principle of federalism, in which certain powers are delegated to the national government and the others, as the Tenth Amendment prescribes, are reserved to the states or to the people.

When private parties, injured competitors and the like, brought suit charging unfair practices, such as unfair trade practices and price-fixing cartels, the Supreme Court readily allowed Sherman Act suits to void them. In *Standard Oil Company v. United States* (1911) the Court put forward a "rule of reason," which in effect said that it would review antitrust cases in an administrative as much as a purely legal or constitutional context.

In the nineteenth century the modern American economy became national and corporate. Also during that period the courts set down the ground rules, including the police power of the state, the due process, and other protections of corporations as persons, that made up a distinctive American system of business regulation. The Supreme Court definition of the legal character of the corporation helped make it the preferred form of American business organization. The

Court's response to the rise of big business encouraged the growth of large, state-chartered firms that were free to tap national markets, vertically integrated from raw materials to marketing, and under constant legal pressure not to crush competition with price-fixing cartels or other forms of unfair competition. The Court promoted oligopoly, not monopoly.

One observer in 1899 noted that the problem of corporate regulation was "rapidly assuming phases which seem beyond the scope of courts of justice." The "state of warfare between producers and consumers" and capital and labor called for political rather than judicial solutions. The Court's impact on the American economy was greater in the nineteenth century than in the century that followed. Certainly the forces of technology and the business cycle have done more than courts and legislatures to create the American economy of the twentieth century.

See also **Banking and Finance; Constitutional Amendments,** *subentry on* **Thirteenth, Fourteenth, and Fifteenth Amendments; Constitutional Law; Corporations and Big Business; Courts, State and Federal; Economic Regulation; Insurance; Interstate Commerce; Judicial Review; Law,** *subentries on* **Federal Law, State Law; Property; Railroads; Regulation of Business; States' Rights; Trusts.**

Bibliography

Baxter, Maurice G. *The Steamboat Monopoly: "Gibbons v. Ogden," 1824.* New York: Knopf, 1992.

Commager, Henry Steele. "The Constitution: Was It an Economic Document?" *American Heritage* 10 (1958): 58–61, 100–103.

Hovenkamp, Herbert. *Enterprise and American Law, 1836–1937.* Cambridge, Mass.: Harvard University Press, 1991.

Hurst, James Willard. *Law and the Conditions of Freedom in the Nineteenth-century United States.* Madison: University of Wisconsin Press, 1956.

Keller, Morton. *Affairs of State: Public Life in Late Nineteenth Century America.* Cambridge, Mass.: Harvard University Press, 1977.

———. "The Making of the Modern Corporation." *Wilson Quarterly* (autumn 1997): 58–69.

Kutler, Stanley I. *Privilege and Creative Destruction: The "Charles River Bridge" Case.* Philadelphia: Lippincott, 1971.

Magrath, C. Peter. *Yazoo: Law and Politics in the New Republic.* Providence, R.I.: Brown University Press, 1966.

McCurdy, Charles W. "The Knight Sugar Decision of 1895 and the Modernization of American Corporation Law, 1869–1903." *Business History Review* 53 (autumn 1979): 304–342.

Newmyer, R. Kent. *The Supreme Court under Marshall and Taney.* Arlington Heights, Ill.: Harlan Davidson, 1986.

Stites, Francis N. *Private Interest and Public Gain: The "Dartmouth College" Case, 1819.* Amherst: University of Massachusetts Press, 1972.

MORTON KELLER

SUPREME COURT JUSTICES

The six chief justices and forty-four associate justices who served on the U.S. Supreme Court during the nineteenth century helped strengthen the Court's institutional power to offer binding interpretations of the U.S. Constitution. In interpreting the Constitution, the justices enhanced the federal government's power at the expense of the states while protecting private property interests in a manner that facilitated the economic expansion of the nation.

The Marshall Court (1801–1835)

The most towering figure on the Court during the nineteenth century was John Marshall, who served as chief justice from 1801 to 1835. Marshall was appointed during the final days of the administration of President John Adams, who hoped that the Court under Marshall's leadership would promote the ideals of the Federalist Party, which had lost control of the presidency and the Congress in the election of 1800. By strengthening the federal government's power, protecting private property interests, and fostering capitalistic economic development, the Marshall Court helped perpetuate Federalist policies throughout decades in which the presidency and Congress were controlled by Jeffersonian Republicans. Marshall's intellect and forceful personality enabled him to dominate the Court even after all the associate justices had been appointed by Republican presidents. William Johnson (1804–1834) was the only associate justice who frequently and forcefully dissented from the Marshall Court's nationalizing decisions.

Marshall is best remembered for his opinions in *Marbury v. Madison* (1803), which established the power of the Court to review the constitutionality of congressional legislation; *Fletcher v. Peck* (1810), establishing the Court's power to review the constitutionality of state legislation and limiting the power of the states to interfere with private contracts; *McCulloch v. Maryland* (1819), which espoused a broad view of Congress's power to legislate in the national interest; *Dartmouth College v. Woodward* (1819), providing constitutional protection for corporations; and *Gibbons v. Ogden* (1824), espousing a broad view of congressional power to regulate interstate commerce.

Marshall found a powerful ally in Joseph Story, who served as associate justice from 1811 to 1845. Story, one of the nation's most distinguished legal scholars, provided intellectual resonance and credibility to many of the Marshall Court's decisions. Story is perhaps best remembered for his opinion in *Martin v. Hunter's Lessee* (1816), which established

The Taney Court (1836–1864)

Marshall was succeeded as chief justice by Roger B. Taney, who served from 1836 to 1864 and was the dominant figure on the Court throughout his tenure. Although many of Taney's associates, particularly John McLean (1829–1861) and James M. Wayne (1835–1867), were able and influential, none are counted among the Court's greatest justices. In appointing Taney, Andrew Jackson hoped the Court would reduce the power of the federal government and provide less constitutional protection for nascent capitalism. Taney and his associates, however, did not significantly retreat from the decisions of the Marshall Court. Although the Court was less protective of vested economic interests, its decisions stimulated the continued growth of capitalism by encouraging economic competition. For example, Taney's opinion in *Charles River Bridge v. Warren Bridge* (1837) declared that owners of a bridge could not pre-vent a state from permitting the construction of a rival bridge. Taney and his associates also contravened the libertarian spirit of Jacksonianism by pioneering the doctrine that state governments have an inherent police power that permits them to act on behalf of the public health, safety, welfare, and morals. While Taney is widely hailed for his farsighted decisions on economic issues, his record is blotted by his decision in *Dred Scott v. Sandford* (1857), in which Taney argued that blacks, slave or free, were not American citizens and that Congress had no power to exclude slavery from the territories.

The Post–Civil War Court

During the last third of the nineteenth century the Court was shaped more by the work of powerful associate justices than by the three chief justices who served during that time, Salmon Portland Chase (1864–1873), Morrison R. Waite (1874–1888), and Melville W. Fuller (1888–1910). Justices during this period differed sharply on the constitutionality of social and economic regulatory legislation. Stephen J.

Robes of Justice. Chief Justice Morrison R. Waite *(center)* and the Associate Justices of the Supreme Court. From left to right: Joseph P. Bradley, Samuel Blatchford, Samuel F. Miller, Stanley Matthews, Waite, Horace Gray, Stephen J. Field, Lucius Q. C. Lamar, John Marshall Harlan, c. 1888. LIBRARY OF CONGRESS

Field (1863–1897) and David J. Brewer (1890–1910) were influential advocates of the theory that the Constitution's due-process clauses impose substantive limitations on the power of federal and state governments to regulate private businesses. Field, Brewer, and several other justices during this period also espoused a narrow view of the power of Congress to regulate business pursuant to the commerce clause. John Marshall Harlan (1877–1911) and Samuel F. Miller (1862–1890) were the only justices who consistently articulated a broad vision of governmental regulatory power. Several other justices, notably Joseph P. Bradley (1870–1892) and Horace Gray (1882–1902), generally accepted a broad view of federal power but sometimes voted to strike down state and federal regulatory legislation.

The justices of the late nineteenth century increasingly imposed restrictions on the power of the federal government to prevent racial inequality. The only justice who regularly and forcefully dissented from these decisions was Harlan, who is best remembered as the sole dissenter in *Plessy v. Ferguson* (1896), in which the Court upheld a state statute that mandated racial segregation in public transportation under a theory of "separate but equal."

The Appointment Process

Political ideology was the most important criterion for appointment during the nineteenth century, although its importance receded late in the century as conflicts over federalism and the Court's role became less pronounced. Throughout the nineteenth century and during the twentieth century presidents usually appointed justices who were members of the president's political party. Although the Senate generally did not probe deeply into the judicial philosophies of nominees or reject nominees on ideological grounds, it often rejected the nominees of lame-duck or politically vulnerable presidents.

In contrast to late-twentieth-century practice, geographical balance was a major factor in appointments throughout the nineteenth century. Presidents usually attempted to ensure that each of the federal judicial circuits was informally "represented" by a justice at all times. Accordingly a new justice frequently replaced a justice from the same judicial circuit and sometimes from the same state. The matching of justices with judicial districts was particularly important before 1891, when justices spent much of their time sitting as members of circuit courts, since justices were believed to serve most effectively in their home circuits.

Personal political loyalty to the president was an important factor in many nineteenth-century appointments. While few appointments were the result of sheer cronyism, many presidents preferred to appoint able lawyers with whom they were personally familiar, often as a reward for their political support. For example, President Abraham Lincoln appointed his personal friend and political adviser David Davis to the Court in 1862.

Professional and Social Backgrounds of Justices

Nineteenth-century justices had homogeneous personal and professional backgrounds. Before ascending the bench, virtually all had distinguished careers at the bar and were active in partisan politics in their communities. Approximately two-thirds had previous judicial experience, mostly in state courts. Although many had served as elected executive officials or legislators, few had held high political office. The only nineteenth-century justices who held a major national political office before joining the Court were Marshall, who had served as secretary of state, and Chase, who was secretary of the Treasury. The large majority came from affluent backgrounds, all of them were of northwestern European ethnicity, and except for the Roman Catholics Taney and Edward Douglass White (associate justice 1894–1910 and chief justice 1910–1921), all were Protestant. In an age in which few lawyers had formal legal educations, fewer than a dozen of the nineteenth-century justices attended law school and only five had law degrees. Most, however, had college degrees and were highly educated. A handful, particularly Story and Bradley, were distinguished legal scholars.

Length of Tenure and Disability

Most of the justices who served during the nineteenth century had long tenures. More than one-third of the justices who were appointed during the century served for more than twenty years. The growing power and prestige of the Court ensured that nearly all justices regarded service on the Court as the apex of their careers, although a few justices, especially Chase and McLean, harbored presidential ambitions. The only nineteenth-century justices who resigned to pursue other careers were Benjamin R. Curtis (1851–1857), who resumed a lucrative private law practice; Davis, who became a U.S. senator; and William Strong (1870–1880), who was active in Christian organizations after leaving the Court. John A. Campbell (1853–1861) resigned from the Court at the outbreak of the Civil War to return to his native Alabama to serve the Confederacy. The two other justices from Confederate states, John

Catron of Tennessee (1837–1865) and James M. Wayne of Georgia (1835–1867), remained on the Court.

Many of the justices served well into old age and suffered from physical or mental disabilities that impaired their performance and reduced their capacity to carry their full burden of work. No federal pension for justices existed before 1869, so some disabled justices remained on the bench for financial reasons. At a time when the Court received little scrutiny from the press, the public was generally unaware of this chronic problem. Healthy justices generally tolerated the infirmities of their brethren, although in some instances they gently urged their ailing colleagues, including Field and Robert C. Grier (1846–1870), to resign.

See also **Courts, State and Federal; Jacksonian Era; Jeffersonian Era; Judicial Review; Law; Legal Profession; Slavery,** *subentry on* **Law of Slavery.**

Bibliography

Abraham, Henry J. *Justices and Presidents: A Political History of Appointments to the Supreme Court.* 3d ed. New York: Oxford University Press, 1992.

Atkinson, David N. *Leaving the Bench: Supreme Court Justices at the End.* Lawrence: University Press of Kansas, 1999.

Biskupic, Joan, and Elder Witt, eds. *Guide to the U.S. Supreme Court.* 2 vols. Washington, D.C.: Congressional Quarterly, 1997.

Friedman, Leon, and Fred L. Israel, eds. *The Justices of the United States Supreme Court, 1789–1969: Their Lives and Major Opinions.* Vols. 1 and 2. New York: Chelsea House, 1969–1978.

Urofsky, Melvin I., ed. *The Supreme Court Justices: A Biographical Dictionary.* New York: Garland, 1994.

WILLIAM G. ROSS

SWEDISH IMMIGRANTS.   See **Immigration and Immigrants,** subentry on **Scandinavia and Finland.**

T

TARIFFS. See **Foreign Trade and Tariffs.**

TAXATION AND PUBLIC FINANCE American taxation began with the colonial settlements, which collected local property taxes or levied fees on sales or transactions. English colonists in particular, operating under mercantilist policies of duties and subsidies on enumerated goods, were comfortable with this system of "indirect" taxes—that is, taxes levied on products rather than on income—as long as those duties remained equitably applied throughout the British Empire and as long as they remained light. Indeed, on the eve of the Revolution, the American colonists were among the most lightly taxed people in the world. The problems arose within the imperial system when the British changed the nature of taxation from regulatory (ensuring that certain colonies specialized in certain products) to revenue-raising after the French and Indian War. That change was instituted with the Stamp Act of 1765, which was repealed in 1766 and then revived with the Tea Act of 1773. Opposition to these and other taxes elicited a heated response from the colonists that eventually triggered the Revolutionary War with its antitax slogan "taxation without representation is tyranny." Thus, it was not surprising that when the Articles of Confederation were drafted, Congress made provisions for levying taxes but did not allow for adequate collection mechanisms. Even with the hostility to taxes inherent in the new nation, in a brief time delegates gathered to address the weaknesses of the Ar-

ticles of Confederation, at which point taxation issues received more thorough consideration.

With the ratification of the Constitution in 1789, Congress received the power to impose indirect taxes on commerce, and provision was made for a collection mechanism through the Treasury Department. Export taxes were prohibited, but Congress expected import duties to circumvent the need for direct taxation. Americans were still wary of giving the government broader powers to level direct taxes on individuals, however, as seen in Article 1, section 9 of the Constitution. Leaders such as Secretary of the Treasury Alexander Hamilton viewed import duties as important both to protect infant industries and to raise revenue. A series of generally low-rate import duties applied to many items accounted for about 90 percent of the total federal tax revenues in the first twenty years of the Republic.

Occasionally, as in the case of the whiskey tax, imposed in 1793 on the production of spirits, the government attempted to enact excise taxes. The excise tax on whiskey struck at farmers who made extra money by running stills; the tax singled them out for special federal taxation, mainly to display the power and authority of the federal government. While the government managed to confirm that it had the authority to levy such taxes, the resulting Whiskey Rebellion (1794) in Pennsylvania reflected the dangers in testing those powers. The rebellion served as a reminder that most Americans were hostile to taxes from any source, not just England. Relying on Alexander Hamilton's advice, George Washington concluded that excise taxes and other taxing authority resided in the federal government and had to be employed once in a while, both to prepare for emergencies when foreign revenue would dry up (as occurred with the War of 1812) and to develop a spirit of civic duty among taxpayers. As a result, Washington used military force to put down the Whiskey Rebellion, more to establish the principle of federal authority than to set a precedent for tax policy.

Fortunately, during the first half of the nineteenth century the federal government usually did not require large amounts of money from taxation; land sales and customs receipts provided the bulk of its revenue. State governments, without land to sell, relied on property taxation, which addressed other concerns, most notably avoiding the public endorsement of European-style large landed estates. In America, the state did not care how much land anyone had as long as taxes were paid on it. This corresponded with a trend in early American courts that favored development rights over pristine property rights (i.e., rights that envisaged the use of land whereby all surrounding scenery is considered part of the property). In a series of cases known as the Mill Acts, courts ruled that individuals who sought to benefit the public through the construction of mills, dams, turnpikes, and other large-scale works were immune from damage suits for changing the nature of the property of others. Thus, the public received the benefits of large-scale, capital-intensive activities without taxation, which some critics of the courts' rulings complained was inequitable. In addition, large-scale projects such as roads, bridges, and harbor facilities often were constructed with private funds. Entrepreneurs built canals and early railroads with the assistance of states and localities, usually in the form of public guarantees of private bond issues. Thus, little demand existed for widespread public finance, nor was it accepted that government should engage in such activities. However, in the 1830s the Whig Party in particular started to advocate public financing of road construction, river improvements, and other large-scale projects.

Meanwhile, the purposes of the states' property taxes soon grew to include a host of measures best described as "social engineering." By the 1830s Jacksonian reformers taxed everything from stocks and bonds to tools, equipment, and furnishings as property. The expansion of taxes beyond real estate undercut the goal of encouraging property development by ensuring that no one could "sit" on land. By the 1840s just the contrary had occurred: people were penalized for seeking to improve the land. These excesses led several states to revise their property tax rates, beginning with Ohio in 1851.

The American South, in general, sought to avoid property taxes, sometimes exempting slaves from taxation and instead imposing levies on the profits of banks and railroads. Many of the southern states had exceptionally healthy banking systems, and thus they were able to avoid enacting large property taxes. The notion of financing public services from taxes on profits of specific activities reached into the northern states as well. Maryland used bank tax revenues for schools, and northern states such as Ohio, for example, used some specific bank taxes for public projects on a specific case basis.

The tariff remained a point of contention between the sections. Between 1810 and 1830 several disputes arose over tariff revisions. Southern leaders had become convinced that in the course of protecting northern manufacturers, high tariffs were harming southern consumers by creating higher prices for finished products. In 1828 southerners attempted to defeat the tariff movement by proposing even higher duties on a range of goods that included a number of raw materials needed in New England. The bill's sponsors intended it to force the New England delegations to vote against a tariff, and when they did so, the southerners then would vote against their own measure, effectively killing tariff increases for a time. But as the astonished southern delegations looked on, the northern representatives voted in favor of the bill. Suddenly saddled with extremely high tariff rates, the South—a victim of its own strategy—denounced it as an abomination, and South Carolina in particular threatened to prevent collection by nullifying the tariff. By imposing an exceptionally burdensome tariff on the South, the North had raised the issue of

Federal Revenues from Customs and Land Sales, 1800–1900

Year	Total $	Customs	Land Sales
1800	10,849	9,081	Not avail.
1810	9,384	8,583	697
1820	17,881	15,006	1,636
1830	24,844	21,922	2,329
1840	19,480	13,500	3,293
1850	43,603	39,669	1,860
1860	56,065	53,188	1,000
1870	411,255	194,538	1,414
1880	333,527	186,522	1,017
1890	403,081	229,669	6,358
1900	567,241	233,165	2,837

Source: *Historical Statistics of the United States, Colonial Times to 1970*, pt. 2 (Washington, D.C.: U.S. Bureau of the Census, 1975), Y 352–357, p. 1106.

whether any tariff was legitimate, a question that was resolved by the nullification crisis, wherein it was ruled that the federal government's laws could not be rendered null and void by individual states (a ruling that set a precedent for all sorts of federal taxes).

President Andrew Jackson stated that he would put down any attempt to interfere with the enforcement of federal law and would hang those responsible. This episode, heralded as a prelude to the Civil War by some historians, resulted in a compromise fashioned by Henry Clay of Kentucky in which most rates were lowered from their "abominable" levels, and while protection remained for nine years, it was to be phased out gradually. After 1842, according to the compromise, sharp tariff reductions were to occur. Clay had managed to avert a crisis, but the South still saw the tariff as a tool of "northern aggression." Many southern leaders took from their experience with the so-called Tariff of Abominations the view that the South more than ever had to specialize in cotton, which it could use as leverage in England and thus avoid being subject to future tariffs originating in or supported by the North.

After the 1842 tariff reductions, tariff rates fell even further prior to the Civil War. Whether or not protective tariffs actually encouraged the growth of the industries they sought to protect, the tariff issue could generate votes in the North. Thus both the Whig and Republican Parties adopted a protective tariff as a platform plank. The Republicans subordinated the tariff to slavery as the party's central platform plank. Tariffs also redistributed wealth from one section (the South, and later the West) to another (the North). Regardless, then, of the overall effectiveness in increasing economic growth, that growth imposed hardships on some to benefit others.

When the Civil War broke out, the U.S. government examined a number of options for raising revenue, including an income tax. Excise taxes included "sin" taxes on whiskey and tobacco, which were pared down but not eliminated after the war. The first American income tax, enacted in 1861, provided a personal exemption of $800 and imposed a rate of 3 percent on all incomes. In 1865 the rate on "the rich" (those with incomes above $600) was increased to 5 percent, and the rate on the "superrich" (above $5,000) was set at 10 percent. A critical element in obtaining support for the tax lay in the claim that it would raise necessary revenues. In the short run that appeared to be true, with the tax generating over 20 percent of the government's total income during the war. Only later would it emerge that higher rates could result in lower revenues. The short life of the tax and the patriotic nature of the war effort made resistance and avoidance infrequent. In addition to

the notion that it was needed to fund the war effort, another point in the tax's favor came from the unwarranted notion that any tax would be equitably shared among eligible taxpayers. Of course it was not: only 10 percent of the North's population, and perhaps 15 percent of northeastern households, paid income taxes.

In 1862 the U.S. government created the Office of the Commissioner of Internal Revenue, foreshadowing the twentieth-century creation of the Internal Revenue Service. The first commissioner, George S. Boutwell, calling his office the "largest Government department ever organized," recognized that even with his large administration, he would have to rely on the accounting systems of the state and local governments to assess property valuations. But the chief source of tax revenue remained import duties and excise taxes, which the primitive accounting methods of the day could deal with more easily.

Some have sought to portray the Republicans as particularly devious in devising a wartime tax structure that could be continued after the conflict. In reality they sought the most expedient system that could generate the revenue needed to win the war. They appealed to patriotic sentiments to enlist support for the tax structure, as they did with bond sales, national bank charters, press censorship, and all other wartime acts. Of course many resisted what they saw as an unconstitutional expansion of the powers of the federal government.

What often has gone unnoticed, however, is the expansion of tax policy in the hands of the Confederacy and the level of tax resistance that those policies generated in the other half of the nation during the Civil War. The Southern government had even greater difficulty than the U.S. government in raising revenues through taxation, partly because of the lower level of consumption for excise taxes and partly because of the rural character of the South and the problems that imposed on assessments and accounting. Eventually, tax resistance in the South led the Confederate government to resort to the confiscation of goods for the war effort, which hardly reflected an endorsement of its taxation policies. Historians have tended to downplay the Confederacy's internal policies as unimportant to its overall defeat. Richard Bensel's comparison of Union and Confederate "domestic" policies, however, reveals that the Southern expansion of government power at the expense of the private sector helped account for its defeat on the battlefield.

After the war the Republicans eliminated most of the wartime excise taxes and did away with the income tax as well. They continued to maintain the tariff, both as a source of revenue from consumption and for the protection of American industries. Tariffs in the late nineteenth century were mostly on manufactured items, such as steel, iron, metal products, and cotton textiles. Except for those tariffs on cotton goods the duties could be defended as being in the interest of national security; the U.S. Navy in particular had emerged as the largest customer of the American steel companies. The consumption elements of the tariffs also underscored the long-held bias in the American economic structure that encouraged capital investment and savings. Tariffs accounted for a larger share of federal revenues after the Civil War, when western land sales began to tail off (see table). From 1865 to 1900, with a few exceptions, tariff revenues constituted the most important part of federal income.

Some historians have attributed the widespread postwar public support for the Republicans' tax policies (as noted by the increased willingness of state legislatures to pass income taxes, by interest in books such as *Progress and Poverty* by Henry George, and by the popularity of the Progressives) to the effective role taxation played in Civil War finance. It is also suggested that the public endorsed the programs that the tax policies funded, such as naval construction, pacification of the West, and Reconstruction. But Reconstruction lasted only a few years, and the cost of the U.S. Army's operations in the West was small compared with the Civil War effort. The public in fact supported the consumption tax because it was familiar; because, despite sectional complaints, it was fair to all individuals in the nation; and because taxing consumption rather than savings and investment seemed the prudent thing to do for the economic health of the country. While it is true that various pork barrel projects were financed by tariff revenues, it is not at all clear that the citizenry of the day saw the direct connection between higher costs of, say, their iron skillets and the harbor that allowed ships to deliver those skillets.

A stronger argument can be made for the linkage between veterans' pensions and the tariff. It is likely that the veterans, as an early special interest group, had a much clearer notion of where the funding for their pensions came from. It is unlikely, though, that most Americans regarded the system as government interference either in the economy or in regulating consumer choice. It was the best system available, given that a national sales tax (which would have achieved most of the same results) would have been viewed as an intrusion of government power. Indeed, the tariff system, while viewed in purely free-market terms as a protectionist policy, appealed to many Americans as a small-government alternative to direct taxation and big government. Virtually all nations (except free-trade England) had tariffs, and

the Constitution had authorized the use of tariffs. Employing a power already granted in the Constitution seemed like a reasonable function of government compared with creating broad, new taxes not specifically enumerated by the founders.

Manufacturers liked tariffs, because heavy industries benefited from higher prices. Many, therefore, could and did pay higher wages made possible by protection. Labor, in that sense, was induced into supporting high tariffs, thus reflecting Adam Smith's observation that neither business nor labor really likes free and unfettered competition. Over time, however, tariffs came to be viewed in a negative light by an increasing number of people, most of whom thought that industry had used tariffs to protect itself against competition, which of course it had. Finally, tariffs provided a point of partisan difference for Democrats to adopt in the two-party system. If Republicans were going to be in favor of tariffs, Democrats would take the opposite position.

Thus, a crack appeared in the public support for tariffs that was exploited by the Democrats and some Republicans: farmers, large groups in the South and West, and small businesses that thought they could not compete with the protected manufacturers. By the late nineteenth century that dissatisfaction, coupled with the income disparities in the postbellum period, led to a movement to enact new taxes on income and corporate profits. The progressive tax—progressive both because it was eventually sponsored by the Republicans known as the Progressives and because the rates became higher as income levels increased—was from the outset an attempt to redistribute wealth and had virtually no connection with the need for government revenues. Indeed, during the late nineteenth century, when the progressive tax measures were debated, the government seldom ran a deficit, and tariffs and land sales provided more than enough money to fill federal coffers. Virtually none of the early proponents of the income tax advocated it on grounds of supplying revenue for the government, while almost all endorsed it as a "fairness" measure.

Much of the impetus for change in the tax system came from the writings of Henry George, who advocated a "single tax" in place of myriad import duties. In *Progress and Poverty* (1879) he endorsed a broad tax on the unimproved value of land, a stand that won him support in his race for mayor of New York City. George reflected the views of a new political movement that marched under the banner of the Populist Party, which advocated inflation and taxation to redistribute wealth.

Courts, however, consistently stood in the way of imposing such taxes, especially on income. In 1895

"Without a Friend." A dog representing income tax is pelted with bricks labeled "public disapproval" and "press." The 1895 Supreme Court case *Pollock v. Farmers' Loan and Trust Co.*, which stated that income tax was unconstitutional, is represented by the bucket. *Puck,* May 1895. LIBRARY OF CONGRESS: PRINTS AND PHOTOGRAPHS DIVISION

the Supreme Court, in *Pollock v. Farmers' Loan and Trust Co.*, declared the income tax component of the Wilson-Gorman tariff unconstitutional. If the government could not levy income taxes on corporations (as individuals), neither could it apply such taxes to private citizens. The only way around the Constitution, in this case, was to change it.

In 1896 the Democratic Party, which had reinvented itself as the party of income redistribution, formally endorsed the income tax. But it was not until a cadre within the Republican Party picked up on the political support that existed in some segments of society for redistributive taxation that the income tax finally gained a wider audience. The perception arose that property owners, especially farmers, paid more than their share of taxes and that a national corporate income tax was needed to reach "unearned" profits. Republicans, therefore, allowed themselves to be manipulated into endorsing this predominantly Marxist principle of division between labor and capital. This resulted in the inescapable position that risk, innovation, invention, and skill were without value and thus had to be taxed differently than labor. By the early 1900s such well-known Republicans as Robert M. La Follette of Wisconsin and President

Theodore Roosevelt endorsed an income tax, and in 1911 Wisconsin became the first state to adopt an income tax, which hit corporations especially hard.

Some historians have interpreted the shift in both parties toward an income tax as a means of preventing more significant social upheaval and thereby maintaining the power of elites. According to that interpretation the eventual adoption of the income tax represented a meaningless concession by the entrenched interests to the masses in which little real power changed hands. Such a view, however, mischaracterizes both the arguments used to sell the income tax amendment to the population as a whole and the public's response to income taxes when the true nature of the system became apparent after World War I. Indeed, one of the great Progressive myths was that there was widespread grassroots support for the income tax. Rather, the Sixteenth Amendment appeared to be a panacea: a way of taking from the rich and giving to the poor. When the income tax amendment was ratified in 1913, it marked the fruition of the redistributionist movement of the late nineteenth century. To ensure that the income tax appeared sufficiently targeted at the upper classes, the Underwood Tariff reduced tariff duties, reflecting a fundamental shift in American taxation away from consumption and toward income.

Achieving an amendment that instituted the income tax required broad support, which the income tax had for several reasons. First, the rates were extremely low, with the top bracket paying 7 percent, but most taxpayers paying the average rate of 1 percent. A high exemption of $3,000 allowed most Americans to escape paying any taxes under the new law. In that way the tax appeared to be an efficient way to "soak the rich" and excuse the middle class from paying taxes. Second, even for those who had to pay taxes, the form was simple, consisting of a single page. By combining simplicity with the appearance that most Americans would pay no tax at all, the Progressives of both parties succeeded in implementing a tax structure that seven years later would affect virtually everyone, with top rates reaching 77 percent (on incomes over $1 million) and the lowest rate increasing fourfold. World War I showed how quickly and drastically both the exemptions and the rates could change, exposing the majority of people to significant levels of taxation, under the guise of "soaking the rich." Only reforms enacted by Secretary of the Treasury Andrew Mellon, which dramatically lowered all rates, saved the system from a potentially fatal backlash.

See also **Foreign Trade and Tariffs; Nullification; Populism.**

Bibliography

Bensel, Richard F. *Yankee Leviathan: The Origins of Central State Authority in America, 1859–1877.* Cambridge, U.K.: Cambridge University Press, 1990.

Benson, George C. S., Sumner Benson, Harold McClelland, and Procter Thomson. *The American Property Tax: Its History, Administration, and Economic Impact.* Claremont, Calif.: Claremont Men's College, 1956.

Brownlee, W. Elliot. *Federal Taxation in America: A Short History.* Washington, D.C.: Woodrow Wilson Center Press, 1996.

Ellis, Elmer. "Public Opinion and the Income Tax, 1860–1900." *Mississippi Valley Historical Review* 27 (September 1940): 225–242.

Seligman, Edwin. *The Income Tax: A Study of the History, Theory and Practice of Income Taxation at Home and Abroad.* 2d ed., revised and enlarged. New York: Macmillan, 1914.

Stanley, Robert. *Dimensions of Law in the Service of Order: Origins of the Federal Income Tax, 1861–1913.* New York: Oxford University Press, 1993.

Sylla, Richard. "Long-Term Trends in State and Local Finance: Sources and Uses of Funds in North Carolina, 1800–1977." In *Long-term Factors in American Economic Growth.* Edited by Stanley L. Engerman and Robert E. Gallman. Chicago: University of Chicago Press, 1986.

Taussig, Frank W. *The Tariff History of the United States.* 8th rev. ed. New York: G. P. Putnam's Sons, 1931.

LARRY SCHWEIKART

TELEGRAPH   During the nineteenth century the American telegraph system grew from a single experimental line into a national network used for a variety of communications purposes. As the telegraph evolved into a national system, it helped engender changes in corporate organizations and in the forms of information, and it also encouraged inventive activity.

Development of the Telegraph

The electric telegraph was originally conceived in 1832 by the American artist Samuel F. B. Morse (1791–1872). Its potential was not realized, however, until congressional interest in establishing a national system of semaphore telegraphs enabled Morse, who proposed his electrical system as a superior alternative, to gain the assistance of the mechanic Alfred Vail (1807–1859). Vail made Morse's crude instruments into commercially practical devices. Morse had additional help regarding batteries and electric circuits from the chemist Leonard Gale and the physicist Joseph Henry. After obtaining a $30,000 grant from Congress in 1843, Morse and his associates built an experimental line between Washington and Baltimore, and on 24 May 1844 Morse transmitted the first message, "What hath God wrought."

The congressional appropriation provided substantial development capital, which was difficult for an untried system to obtain from private entrepreneurs in a still-emerging capitalist economy. But with American development policy turning away from direct public funding of internal improvement projects, Congress decided not to adopt the telegraph as a public enterprise. Instead, the federal patent system and state incorporation laws fostered the subsequent commercial development of the telegraph. Under the protection of his patent, Morse and his partners licensed the use of their invention to private entrepreneurs, who established companies under state laws and raised the necessary funds from local investors. Morse achieved both wealth and fame from his invention, and his success stimulated other pioneers in electric telegraphy, who patented their own systems. These new telegraph systems became the basis for competing companies, which spurred the extension of telegraph lines throughout the country.

Competition and Consolidation

While many small, regional companies helped establish a network of lines throughout the country by the mid-1850s, the problems of interconnection forced these small companies to consolidate into a few large firms, led by the Western Union and American Telegraph companies. In 1857 these two firms joined with

Telegraph Room. General operating department, Western Union Telegraph Building, 1875. Photographic print on stereocard. Photographer, C. K. Bill. LIBRARY OF CONGRESS

four other companies to sign a cartel agreement known as the "Treaty of Six Nations," which carved the market into clearly defined territories. The agreement was shortlived, however, as Western Union broke ranks in 1860 to win a government subsidy to construct the first transcontinental telegraph. The Civil War soon gave Western Union additional competitive advantages because the company controlled the principal east-west lines, while the system of its main rival, American Telegraph, was made up primarily of north-south lines, which were ruptured by the war. After the war Western Union was in a position to take over its rivals and achieve a near monopoly of the industry.

As Western Union developed the first truly national telecommunications network, the firm's president, William Orton, reorganized the company's bureaucracy. Historians generally have considered railroads the first modern corporations, but Western Union was the first company to operate on a nationwide scale and to draw criticism as a dangerous new form of monopoly. For the remainder of the century, Western Union faced challenges from rivals hoping to break into its profitable business and from antimonopoly reformers seeking a postal telegraph system to compete with or replace it.

The most serious challenge to Western Union came from the financier Jay Gould (1836–1892), who used his railroad connections and large financial resources to build a competing network. Western Union had created its national system in large part using railroad rights-of-way for its lines. Gould used his financial interests in railroads with telegraph lines not controlled by Western Union to mount two challenges to the railroad baron Cornelius Vanderbilt (1843–1899), who was Western Union's major stockholder. Although Gould failed in his first effort, his Atlantic and Pacific Telegraph Company merged into Western Union in 1877, giving him a significant block of Western Union stock and valuable experience in the telegraph industry. He used these advantages to gain control of Western Union through his new American Union Telegraph Company. A merger of the two companies in 1881 consolidated Western Union's place as the nation's dominant telegraph company. By the time of the Sherman Anti-Trust Act (1890), only the Postal Telegraph and Cable Company remained as a minor, though significant, competitor to Western Union.

Telegraph Use

Telegraph use grew slowly in the antebellum era; mail remained a more important method for transmitting most information. However, the speed and reliability of telegraph service improved with new technology that automatically relayed messages between stations and with the consolidation of many small lines into a national network, and the telegraph became an increasingly important communications system. It became particularly important for business, as the telegraph proved especially well suited for transmitting time-sensitive information such as market reports and shipping information. By the 1880s an estimated 80 percent of Western Union's messages were business-related. Commercial news and business messages also dominated cable telegraph lines to Europe, which were largely controlled by British firms.

The most significant nonbusiness users of the telegraph were newspapers, which by the 1850s published about two columns of Associated Press telegraph dispatches, primarily concerning market reports, shipping news, and legislative proceedings. Spurred in part by the success of Civil War dispatches, the factual and impartial Associated Press reports grew in importance after the war, and competing telegraph news agencies developed. By the end of the century Associated Press and other newsbrokers leased telegraph lines exclusively devoted to their press reports.

The telegraph also was employed for a host of other communications services during the late nineteenth century. Stock tickers, which were small printing telegraphs, provided market reports from central exchanges for stocks, gold, and commodities. Fire alarm telegraphs, developed before the war, came into extensive use afterward. Besides those employed by city fire departments, private fire and burglar alarm telegraphs operated through central district stations, enabling users to call for other services, such as taxis or doctors.

Another system of communication evolved from the telegraph in the 1870s. The telephone was developed by inventors working on telegraphy, and Western Union held important patent rights, including those of Elisha Gray and Thomas Edison, who developed his famous Menlo Park laboratory with Western Union support. Faced with challenges from Gould in its principal intercity market, Western Union in 1879 decided to sell its telephone interests to the National Bell Telephone Company in exchange for a percentage of profits, the transfer of all telegraph messages received by telephone, and Bell Telephone's promise to refrain from entering the long-distance market during the life of the patents. By the end of the century, however, Western Union faced a growing challenge from American Telephone and Telegraph, the long-distance arm of the Bell Telephone Company, which briefly took over Western Union in 1909.

See also **Communications; Electricity; Inventors and Inventions; Railroads; Stock Markets; Trusts.**

Bibliography

Du Boff, Richard B. "Business Demand and the Development of the Telegraph in the United States, 1844–1860." *Business History Review* 54 (1980): 459–479.

———. "The Telegraph and the Structure of Markets in the United States, 1845–1890." *Research in Economic History* 8 (1983): 253–277.

Israel, Paul. *From Machine Shop to Industrial Laboratory: Telegraphy and the Changing Context of American Invention, 1830–1920.* Baltimore: Johns Hopkins University Press, 1992.

Lindley, Lester G. *The Constitution Faces Technology: The Relationship of the National Government to the Telegraph, 1866–1884.* New York: Arno Press, 1975.

Thompson, Robert Luther. *Wiring a Continent: The History of the Telegraph Industry in the United States, 1832–1866.* Princeton, N.J.: Princeton University Press, 1947.

PAUL ISRAEL

TELEPHONE.   See **Communications.**

TEMPERANCE MOVEMENT   The temperance movement, an unprecedented reform agitation, began in the nineteenth century and reached its climax in the early twentieth century. Its attack on the previously accepted consumption of alcoholic beverages ignited popular enthusiasm in the United States, other parts of the English-speaking world, and Scandinavia. Before the 1800s a few people abstained from alcoholic drink, but almost nobody tried to convert the general public to do likewise. Only excessive drinking had been considered a social and moral problem.

In the United States the temperance movement seems to have been a product of a collision in the early 1800s involving the growing consumption of alcohol, mostly by men, that cheap whiskey encouraged and the growing sentiment in favor of moral reform. During the nineteenth century the Second Great Awakening optimistically aimed to reform the country on Christian principles through nondenominational voluntary societies. Temperance quickly became intertwined with evangelical Protestantism, the status of women, modernizing capitalism, and electoral politics. Temperance often meant the imposition of middle-class and middle-aged values on the poor, immigrants, African Americans, Native Americans, and more generally young men.

Although temperance societies had formed earlier, the first temperance organization to build a mass membership was the American Society for the Promotion of Temperance, better known as the American Temperance Society, founded in New England in 1826. Like previous evangelical religious societies, it energetically published and distributed tracts. Although its leaders were men of elite status, it welcomed women as members. By 1835 the society claimed more than 1.5 million members in eight thousand locations throughout the country. Committed to moderation in drinking, specifically by abstinence from spirits, its program was one of moral suasion, employing education and good example to encourage reform.

In a major shift in temperance objectives, the American Temperance Union, pledged to total abstinence, replaced the American Temperance Society in 1836. By thus radicalizing its objectives, the temperance movement lost some wealthy supporters everywhere and most of its southern sympathizers. The movement remained strongest in New England and New York State, which were, not coincidentally, bastions of abolitionism and other reform agitations that challenged deeply rooted social attitudes and practices.

In the early 1840s Washingtonianism, popular among the working and lower-middle classes, democratized the previously middle-class temperance movement. In contrast with earlier temperance societies, which scorned drunkards as beyond help, the Washingtonians featured testimony by repentant former drunkards to encourage pledges of total abstinence. In Martha Washington societies women worked to make husbands and sons sober. After a few years of notoriety, most Washingtonian societies disappeared. They were handicapped by the lack of a central organization and by strained relations with the ministers and business entrepreneurs who had dominated earlier temperance societies. Moreover most Washingtonians were out of step with the American temperance movement because they relied exclusively on persuasion to create a dry country, a strategy the temperance movement in general abandoned. As early as the 1830s the movement edged toward legal coercion by supporting no-license campaigns intended to prevent the sale of alcohol in localities. After the Washingtonians faded into obscurity, the largest temperance organizations were prohibition-minded fraternal ritual societies, such as the Sons of Temperance. In the 1840s the Sons of Temperance outnumbered older nontemperance fraternal societies, like the Freemasons and the Odd Fellows.

Voluntary commitment always remained at the core of the temperance movement. For teetotalers, "taking the pledge" was analogous to a religious con-

Woman's Holy War. Grand Charge on the Enemy's Works. The Temperance movement wages battle. Note the leg of a fleeing man *(lower right)*. Lithograph, Currier & Ives, 1874. LIBRARY OF CONGRESS

version experience. They often pledged during childhood before ever consuming a glass of alcohol. Yet coercion came to supplement personal acceptance of total abstinence and teetotal propaganda directed at others. Most temperance reformers were uncomfortable with community involvement in the drink trade through regulation and taxation, even when the goals were to restrict it and reduce it. But they were eager to use governmental power to make alcohol sales illegal. Although drinking was seen as a sinful, personal moral failing, it was also viewed as a social evil for which government bore responsibility. By making it more difficult to get drink, society could reduce the temptation that overwhelmed weak-willed drinkers.

In the 1850s many teetotalers turned unequivocally to prohibition. Maine pioneered statewide prohibition, enacting a statute to that effect in 1851. Other states imitated the Maine law, but enforcement difficulties made many people turn away from statewide prohibition as impracticable. Moreover the disruption of the sectional crisis and the Civil War eclipsed the temperance cause temporarily.

After the war the temperance movement re-

bounded. Its program henceforth focused on prohibition, whether by local option, by statewide statute, by amendment to the state constitution, or eventually by a national law. For instance, the most popular fraternal temperance society, the Good Templars, required its members to pledge themselves to support prohibition legislation. In the post-Reconstruction era the rural South joined the rural Midwest as prohibition strongholds, particularly after the disfranchisement of blacks made whites comfortable confronting controversial issues. In contrast, immigration from such countries as Ireland and Germany, where drinking was still accepted, diluted temperance sentiment in large cities. As a result temperance reformers in old prohibition strongholds, such as Massachusetts and New York State, could not expect statewide prohibition.

Frustrated with the major political parties, temperance reformers organized the National Prohibition Party in 1869. At first it proposed a broad reform program, but later the party narrowed its focus to eliminating the sale of alcohol. Regardless of the scope of its program, the National Prohibition Party got few votes in any elections, while the Republican and Democratic Parties remained politically dominant.

Despite lacking the vote, women, who were much less likely to drink than men, took a more prominent role in the political agitation against drink in the United States than in any other country. In such midwestern states as Ohio women closed many saloons in 1873 and 1874 by extralegal means, such as obstructing entrances with prayer meetings. Later in 1874 the Woman's Christian Temperance Union (WCTU) organized to fight for prohibition by the more conventional means of propaganda and lobbying. The WCTU leader Frances Willard became the best-known woman reformer in the country. Under her leadership the WCTU adopted a broad program of woman suffrage and social reform and cooperated with radical-minded third parties.

In the late nineteenth century the American temperance movement seemed stalled. A large minority of the country embraced its objectives, but except for local option, popular in rural districts, prohibition seemed unattainable. After the National Prohibition Party failed, prohibition supporters formed the Anti-Saloon League of America in 1895. The Anti-Saloon League worked pragmatically through the existing political parties, particularly the Republican Party in the midwestern states, to get whatever antidrink laws the circumstances in a particular state permitted.

Prohibition made temperance controversial and political. It raised questions about personal freedom and property rights and whether coercive legislation regulating private behavior could be enforced without empowering government to an unacceptable degree. Moreover prohibition was divisive for the major political parties, which struggled to accommodate both the prohibitionists and their drinking, drink-selling, and drink-making enemies.

Complex and ever changing, the temperance movement defies easy generalization. Like many other reform movements, it suffered from factionalism. In addition it interacted with changes in drinking practices. Over the course of the nineteenth century, per capita consumption declined. Alcohol disappeared from many social gatherings, such as Protestant funerals. After the Civil War lager beer, which is less intoxicating, replaced whiskey as the typical alcoholic drink. By the end of the century many temperance reformers were life abstainers. The intensity of their fear and hatred of intoxicating drink foreshadowed that of the enemies of illegal drugs a hundred years later.

See also **Alcoholic Beverages; Brewing and Distilling; Evangelicalism; Reform, Social; Saloons and the Drinking Life.**

Bibliography
Blocker, Jack S., Jr. *American Temperance Movements: Cycles of Reform.* Boston: Twayne, 1989. Standard survey.

Gusfield, Joseph R. *Symbolic Crusade: Status Politics and the American Temperance Movement.* 1963. 2d ed., Urbana: University of Illinois Press, 1986. Helped begin revival in temperance history studies.

Lender, Mark Edward. *Dictionary of American Temperance Biography.* Westport, Conn.: Greenwood, 1984. Contains 373 short biographical entries.

Pegram, Thomas R. *Battling Demon Rum: The Struggle for a Dry America, 1800–1933.* Chicago: Ivan R. Dee, 1998. New survey; strong on politics.

Tyrrell, Ian R. *Sobering Up: From Temperance to Prohibition in Antebellum America, 1800–1860.* Westport, Conn.: Greenwood, 1979. Groundbreaking scholarly monograph.

DAVID M. FAHEY

TENNESSEE   Tennessee has three major regions. East Tennessee contains Knoxville and borders the Appalachian Mountains on the east and the Cumberland Plateau on the west. West Tennessee is anchored by the city of Memphis on the Mississippi River. Middle Tennessee includes Nashville.

Tennessee became the sixteenth state on 1 June 1796. At the turn of the century it was a frontier state with 91,709 white residents, 13,584 slaves, and 309 free African Americans. The population concentrated mostly north and east of Knoxville and in the Cumberland River basin of north central Tennessee. John Sevier, the state's first governor, was still in office when the nineteenth century opened. Approximately thirty thousand Cherokees, Creeks, and Chickasaws controlled all of West Tennessee, the southern half of Middle Tennessee, the Cumberland Plateau, and the area south of the Little Tennessee River in East Tennessee.

Numerous conflicts between whites and Indians climaxed in the Red Stick Creek War, fought in Alabama in 1813–1814 during the War of 1812. Tennessee Cherokees and the Tennessee militia serving under Andrew Jackson crushed the Creeks at the Battle of Tohopetra (Horseshoe Bend) on 27 March 1814. When the British invaded the Gulf Coast, Jackson was called into national service. On 8 January 1815 his soldiers defeated the British at New Orleans, where Tennessee riflemen under John Coffee inflicted much of the damage. In 1818 Jackson and Isaac Shelby, a former Kentucky governor, purchased West Tennessee from the Chickasaws. Settlers poured into the area and created sixteen new counties in six years.

Tennessee supplied the United States with three presidents during the nineteenth century, although all three were born in the Carolinas. A fourth Tennessee politician, born in Virginia, became the first president of the independent Republic of Texas. Two of these men dominated politics in the state and the nation in the 1830s and the 1840s. Jackson, one of the strongest of all American presidents, served from 1829 to 1837. He broke the power of the second Bank of the United States, set up the system of "pet banks," defeated South Carolina's attempt to nullify a tariff act, vetoed numerous bills, and helped establish the Democratic Party. Jackson was also responsible for the federal removal of many American Indians from their native lands. The passage of the Indian Removal Act of 1830, followed by the fraudulent 1835 Treaty of New Echota, moved the Cherokees along the infamous Trail of Tears to Indian Territory during the winter of 1838–1839. Jackson retired to the "Hermitage," his home near Nashville.

While Jackson governed the nation, Davy Crockett, a former congressman from Tennessee, moved to the Mexican province of Tejas, where he helped foment a revolution and create the new country of Texas. The hero of this revolution, Sam Houston, a former governor of Tennessee, became the first president of the Republic of Texas.

James K. Polk from Columbia, Tennessee, served as Speaker of the U.S. House of Representatives, governor of Tennessee, and then U.S. president from 1845 to 1849. His administration acquired vast new territories for the United States through the annexation of Texas, the Oregon Treaty with Great Britain, and the seizure of California and the Southwest in a war with Mexico. Sarah Polk, who served as press secretary and political adviser to her husband, was the first important political first lady.

In 1860 Tennessee had 1,109,801 residents— 826,722 whites; 7,360 free people of color; and 275,719 slaves. Like other states of the Upper South, Tennessee did not rush to secede when Abraham Lincoln won the presidency in 1860. In February 1861 Tennessee voters rejected the call for a secession convention. After shooting began at Fort Sumter, South Carolina, however, Tennessee joined the Confederate States of America, although the state's citizens remained divided over the war. Some one hundred thousand men served in the Confederate military, yet some forty thousand white men and former slaves fought for the Union. Bordered by the Mississippi River, divided by the Tennessee and Cumberland Rivers, and crossed by several major railroads, Tennessee was the scene of more Civil War battles than any other state except Virginia. Among those battles were Fort Donelson, Shiloh, Stones River, Chattanooga, Fort Pillow, and Nashville.

The Civil War left Tennessee with physical, economic, and psychological devastation. Andrew Johnson from Greeneville, Tennessee, succeeded to the presidency after Lincoln's death in April 1865. Johnson's administration evicted the French from Mexico and purchased Alaska from Russia. However, Johnson had a difficult term, barely escaping removal after being impeached. Political reconstruction went more easily in Tennessee than in the rest of the former Confederacy after President Johnson's home state rebuffed him and ratified the Fourteenth Amendment in July 1866. Yet economic reconstruction was slow, and agriculture did not recover until the end of the century. Sharecropping replaced slavery, and farmers remained tied to tobacco and cotton as cash crops.

Tennessee typified the South in adopting racial segregation in schools and public accommodations, but it differed from other southern states in significant ways. Most states of the former Confederacy embraced the Democratic Party, but Tennesseans also gave strong support to the Republicans. The best example is the "War of the Roses" governor's race in 1886, in which the Democrat Robert Taylor (the white rose) defeated his brother, the Republican Alfred Taylor (the red rose). Continued close elections rendered white Tennesseans undecided about whether to disfranchise black men, so African Americans retained the vote.

By 1900 the population of Tennessee stood at 2,020,616—1,540,186 white and 480,430 black. Among the population 99 percent were U.S. natives. The state's largest cities were Memphis and Nashville. The Tennessee centennial celebration in 1896

and its participation in the Spanish-American War of 1898 helped bring the state back into the mainstream of national political culture. But at the beginning of the twentieth century Tennessee was still struggling to regain the position of national prominence it had held half a century earlier.

See also **American Indians,** *subentry on* **Indian Removal; Appalachia; Civil War,** *subentries on* **Causes of the Civil War, Battles and Combatants; Reconstruction,** *subentry on* **The South.**

Bibliography

Bergeron, Paul H., Stephen V. Ash, and Jeanette Keith. *Tennesseans and Their History.* Knoxville: University of Tennessee Press, 1999.

Lamon, Lester C. *Blacks in Tennessee, 1791–1790.* Knoxville: University of Tennessee Press, 1981.

Satz, Ronald N. *Tennessee's Indian Peoples.* Knoxville: University of Tennessee Press, 1979.

West, Carroll Van, ed. *Tennessee History: The Land, the People, and the Culture.* Knoxville: University of Tennessee Press, 1998.

FRED S. ROLATER

TERRITORIAL GOVERNMENT With independence, the governance of territories outside the effective jurisdiction of states became an issue for the United States. In 1780 the Continental Congress resolved that any western land ceded to the national government would be organized into states on an equal footing with the existing commonwealths. In the Treaty of Paris (1783), which ended the American Revolution, the crown ceded the lands northwest of the Ohio River, commonly known as the Northwest Territory, to the newly independent American Confederation. This territory was claimed, in whole or in part, by a number of states, but none effectively ruled the region. Virginia, New York, Massachusetts, and Connecticut ceded their land claims to the Confederation. In 1785 Congress passed a land ordinance providing for the division of the territory into townships, the sale of which was to benefit the Treasury of the new republic.

On 13 July 1787 Congress passed the Northwest Ordinance, setting up a form of government for the territory. At the Constitutional Convention meeting in Philadelphia that year, the delegates proposed, in Article IV, section 3, of the Constitution, to give Congress "Power to dispose of and make all needful Rules and Regulations respecting the Territory or other Property belonging to the United States," and in Article I, section 8, they gave Congress the power "to exercise exclusive Legislation in all Cases whatsoever, over such District (not exceeding ten Miles square) as may, by Cession of particular States, and the Acceptance of Congress, become the Seat of the Government of the United States." James Madison, in the *Federalist*, number 38, pointed out that the failure of the Articles of Confederation to provide a power for Congress to acquire, govern, and dispose of territory had forced Congress to establish the Northwest Ordinance without constitutional warrant.

Once the Constitution had been ratified, Congress passed a slightly modified version of the Northwest Ordinance on 7 August 1789, since all nontreaty statutory enactments under the Articles of Confederation lapsed with the adoption of the Constitution. The ordinance is listed with the Declaration of Independence and the Constitution of the United States as part of the Organic Law in the Statutes-at-Large of the United States, primarily because it contains the covenant (morally but not legally binding) by which the national government promised to admit to statehood territories with sufficient population and adequate political organization. Some U.S. statesmen had advocated holding the territories as colonies to be governed for the benefit of the existing states, but this view did not prevail.

The ordinance provided for a governor, a secretary (who would also act as a kind of lieutenant governor), and a three-judge panel with common-law jurisdiction. Until it was practical to create legislative assemblies, the governor and his judges could extend to the territory any criminal or civil law of the original thirteen states. Congress had the authority to overrule such enactments, and legislative assemblies subsequently created could alter or abolish them. The requirement that a new law be found on the books of an existing state limited the arbitrary exercise of power by the governor and his council.

From 1784 on, each territory could send a nonvoting delegate to the Confederation Congress and subsequently to the House of Representatives. After the Louisiana Purchase (1803) the House in 1805 established the Committee on Public Lands, which dealt with most territorial matters, although the House and Senate Committees on the Judiciary handled territorial judicial proceedings and the statutory law of the territories. In 1825 the House created the Committee on Territories, and in 1844 the Senate created a similar committee.

As new territories—the Louisiana Territory, Florida, the northern provinces of Mexico (Upper California and New Mexico), and the Oregon Territory—were annexed by the United States, the system first employed in the Northwest Territory was extended. While populations remained sparse, territorial governors with plenary powers ruled, to be supplemented when population allowed by popularly elected territorial legislatures.

The first major U.S. territorial dispute to enter the federal courts was *American Insurance Company v. Canter* (1828), which was appealed to the Supreme Court. Chief Justice John Marshall found that the territorial court was constitutional.

The single greatest issue in the governance of the territories in the first half of the nineteenth century was the status of slavery within the territories. There was no great controversy concerning the banning of slavery in the Northwest Territory, because southerners at the time had no interest in moving there. By 1820, however, contention had arisen over the application of Missouri to enter the Union as a slave state, despite its geographic location north of the Ohio River. In the Missouri Compromise of 1820 Congress admitted Missouri as a slave state, paired with the admission of Maine as a free state, and a line was drawn across the continent from the mouth of the Ohio River, dividing the remainder of the Louisiana Territory into slave and free territory.

Once slavery had become the focus of sectional controversy, the balancing of free with slave states became central to the strategy of the South in protecting its "peculiar institution." Equality in numbers of free and slave states would have preserved the Senate as an effective southern check on any antislavery legislation.

In the Compromise of 1850, which followed the Mexican War, California was admitted as a free state, the domestic slave trade was prohibited in the District of Columbia, a strong fugitive slave law was enacted, and the Missouri Compromise line was applied to the territory ceded by Mexico. Great concessions had to be made to the South in this compromise because, for the first time since the sectional tensions arose, a free state was not paired with a slave state for admission. The South, however, felt it essential to obtain an effective fugitive slave law. The geographic division could not quell sectional agitation, and both sides denounced the legislation. Free-Soilers and many Republicans held that Congress must prohibit slavery in any territory because of the Fifth Amendment's provision that no person shall "be deprived of life, liberty, or property, without due process of law." Southerners held that any act that proscribed slavery in the territories deprived the slaveholder of his property without due process of law.

In 1854 Congress attempted to solve the problem of slavery in the territories by making it an issue of popular sovereignty. Senator Stephen A. Douglas introduced the Kansas-Nebraska Act to allow the settlers of those territories to decide at the time of their application for statehood whether they would be

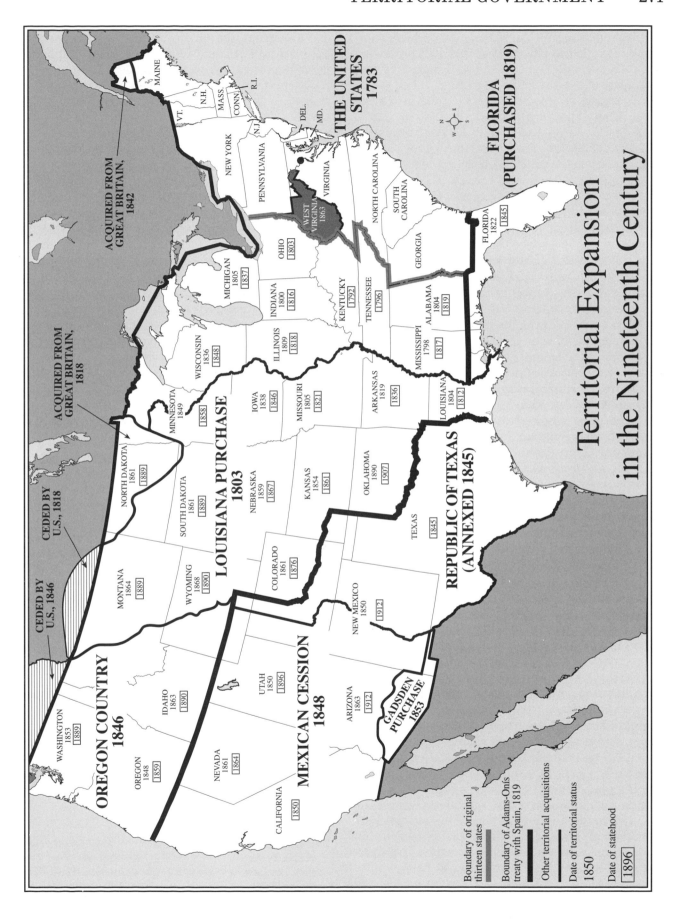

Territorial Expansion in the Nineteenth Century

slave or free. Rather than solving the problem, however, the law led to violent strife between proslavery and antislavery settlers. "Bleeding Kansas" became a foretaste of the Civil War to come.

The climax of this controversy came in the Supreme Court case of *Dred Scott v. Sanford* (1857). Chief Justice Roger Taney held the Compromises of 1820 and 1850 to be unconstitutional, ruling that the federal government could not deprive the slaveholder of his property without due process of law and that the federal government had no municipal authority over the territories and thus could pass no laws on their behalf, except to provide for the sale or other disposal of public lands within them. The First Congress was able to legislate for the Northwest Territory only with respect to Virginia's desire to enact certain measures as specified in its deed of cession. Each person who enters a territory (according to Taney) takes with him the body of laws of his state of origin, in a kind of municipal extraterritoriality. The sole power of the federal government was its duty to enforce these various state statutes.

Despite the obiter dicta of the *Dred Scott* decision, Congress never ceased to legislate for the territories, and subsequent administrations continued to apply federal statutory and administrative law. In a series of Supreme Court decisions between 1901 and 1922, the court set down what has become standard legal doctrine concerning territorial governance. Congress was recognized as having plenary power over the territories. In addition, the Court distinguished between incorporated and unincorporated territory. Incorporated territory, which at some future time Congress intended to admit to the Union, was defined as being covered by the Constitution; its inhabitants were understood to be U.S. citizens.

When particular territories were annexed to the United States, they were often temporarily placed under military authority. Many contiguous continental territories, including the Louisiana Territory, were under the authority of the War Department when first acquired. Overseas colonies, particularly small islands with strategic potential, were often administered by the Department of the Navy. For example, American Samoa was placed under the navy from 1900 to 1929, as were the U.S. Virgin Islands from 1917 to 1931. The uninhabited islands annexed over the years under the provisions of the U.S. Guano Islands Act (1856) were the special concern of the U.S. Navy and the Department of State. In 1907 the Office of Territorial Affairs was created within the Interior Department, and the various U.S. overseas territories were slowly reassigned to that office from the War Department, the Department of the Navy, the Department of State, and elsewhere.

Throughout the nineteenth century, the general approach to territorial governance was to emphasize flexibility, economy, and practicality. Large territories were divided and subdivided as populations increased, reflecting geographic, economic, and political considerations. Rigidity of forms was avoided, and in general territorial governments were allowed to reflect the preferences of those subject to them as well as peculiarities of circumstances. Before the final partition of the Oregon Territory, for example, British and American authority coexisted, operating with a minimum of friction. In the case of the guano islands, various guano extraction companies that were given exclusive mining rights to particular islands were allowed to operate virtually in the manner of the famous charter companies of the British Empire: in exchange for their privileges, they were expected to carry on quasi-governmental functions, including mail delivery and the maintenance of law and order.

Admissions to statehood have often come in spurts caused in large part by the contemporaneous settlement of contiguous territories. From 1803 to 1821 many states created from the Northwest Territories, the Georgia cessions, and the Louisiana Purchase were admitted. From 1845 to 1861 Florida, Arkansas, Texas, California, and Oregon—as well as the states of the upper Midwest, including Michigan, Wisconsin, Minnesota, and Iowa, joined the Union. Finally, in 1889–1890 the admissions of North and South Dakota, Montana, Washington, Wyoming, and Idaho completed the upper tier of western states.

With regard to populational requirements, the Northwest Ordinance set a minimum of sixty thousand free inhabitants as the standard for statehood, and this was generally followed. In the case of the admission of Nevada in 1864, however, that minimum was not required because in the crisis of the Civil War the silver from Nevada was important to the Union cause. Admission for Nevada helped to secure the loyalty of that region.

See also **Missouri Compromise; Northwest Territory; Oregon; Statehood and Admission.**

Bibliography

Becker, Carl. "Law and Practice of the United States in the Acquisition and Government of Dependent Territory." *Annals of the American Academy of Political and Social Science* 16 (1900): 60–76.

Bloom, John Porter, ed. *The American Territorial System*. Athens, Ohio: Ohio University Press, 1973.

Karst, Kenneth L. "Territorial Court." In *Encyclopedia of the American Constitution*. Edited by Leonard W. Levy, Kenneth L. Karst, and Dennis J. Mahoney. New York: Macmillan, 1986.

Laney, Garrine P. "Territories and Possessions." In *Encyclo-*

pedia of the United States Congress. Edited by Donald C. Bacon, Roger H. Davidson, and Morton Keller. New York: Simon and Schuster, 1995.

Mahoney, Dennis J. "Insular Cases" and "Territory." In *Encyclopedia of the American Constitution.* Edited by Leonard W. Levy, Kenneth L. Karst, and Dennis J. Mahoney. New York: Macmillan, 1986.

Thomas, David Yancy. *A History of Military Government in Newly Acquired Territory of the United States.* Studies in History, Economics, and Public Law. Volume 20, no. 2. New York: AMS, 1967.

Van Cleve, Ruth G. *The Office of Territorial Affairs.* New York: Praeger, 1974.

PATRICK M. O'NEIL

TEXAS

At the beginning of the nineteenth century, Texas was a sparsely settled frontier outpost in Spain's North American empire. A century later Texas was part of the United States, rich in agriculture and poised to become a major industrial and urban area.

Texas occupies a crossroads position in North America, between the English-speaking North and the Spanish-speaking South. Geographically it consists of four major regions: the forested plains of east Texas, the semiarid grasslands of north Texas and the Panhandle, the arid lands of south and southwest Texas, and the Llano basin and Edwards Plateau of central Texas. The climate in Texas ranges from the moderate, humid climate of east Texas to the semitropical Gulf Coast, the continental climate of the north Texas plains, and the desert climate of west and southwest Texas. Because of the state's climate and terrain, farming is confined mostly to the east and north and the Rio Grande valley of the south. Central, west, and southwest Texas are suitable primarily for grazing.

Texas in 1800

Prior to the arrival of the Europeans, Texas was home to many Native American cultures. The agricultural Caddos inhabited the woodlands of east Texas, while the hunter-gatherer Western Gulf Culture lived in the harsh, arid lands of south Texas. The Jumanos occupied the upper Rio Grande valley, while Plains Indians—first Apaches and then Comanches—began moving into this western region in the seventeenth century.

In 1800 approximately four thousand Spanish subjects of mixed racial and ethnic backgrounds resided in Texas. The center of Spanish activity was in San Antonio and the ranches and missions along the San Antonio River. The city was the administrative capital of Texas and its population center, with approx-

imately twenty-five hundred residents. The Nacogdoches area had another five hundred residents, while the mission and ranching settlements around La Bahía (or Goliad) had twelve hundred. The economy of Spanish Texas centered on farming, primarily for local consumption, and ranching.

As the nineteenth century opened, Spanish control of Texas was waning. Since first establishing settlements in Texas, the Spanish had failed to populate Texas or develop a prosperous colony there. The collapse of the Spanish colonial empire and the expansionist tendencies of the newly independent United States radically transformed Texas in the nineteenth century.

Anglo Texas

The first serious effort to plant a colony of U.S. settlers in Texas took place in 1820, when Moses Austin (1761–1821) arrived in San Antonio seeking permission to bring three hundred families to Texas. Neither Moses Austin nor the Spanish government in Mexico survived long enough to see the colony take root. Moses's son, Stephen F. Austin (1793–1836), actually directed the settlement of the colony, and the newly independent Mexican government authorized it.

The Austin colony transformed Texas. All in all Austin brought more than 4,000 colonists and initiated the Americanization of the province. The non-Indian population in 1834 was composed of approximately 15,000 Anglos, 2,000 African American slaves, and 4,000 Tejanos (Mexican Texans, a group that includes Creoles and mestizos). Anglos dominated Texas demographically and redefined the economic, social, and racial character of the province. The majority of Texan immigrants had come from the U.S. South and had brought with them that region's cotton, plantation, and slave cultures.

As the Anglo population of Texas increased, conflicts developed between the residents of Texas and the Mexican government. Political chaos following the Mexican war for independence from Spain undermined Anglo confidence in the Mexican government and reinforced their prejudice against the Mexican people. At the same time, the Anglos' demographic dominance fed Mexican fears that the settlers planned to overthrow Mexican rule and lead Texas into the United States. In the early 1830s squabbles over immigration, slavery, and efforts to collect customs duties resulted in sporadic outbreaks of violence. Efforts to resolve the conflicts through compromise unraveled when General Antonio López de Santa Anna (1794–1876) seized power in 1834, abolished the Mexican Constitution, and dissolved Mexico's state governments.

"**Texan Mounted Militia.**" A British perspective of the West. Wood engraving from *The Illustrated London News*, 18 June 1842. LIBRARY OF CONGRESS

Independence and the Republic

Armed conflict between Texas and Mexico began in the summer and fall of 1835, and war erupted in December when Texas militia units (made up of Anglos and Tejanos) drove the Mexican army from San Antonio and Texas. In response General Santa Anna began a march northward determined to crush the Texas uprising and to drive all Anglos from the territory. Santa Anna's forces defeated Texas militia units at the Alamo and at Goliad in March 1836. While Mexican forces dominated the battlefield, political leaders of Texas assembled at the hamlet of Washington on the Brazos River to organize a government. On 2 March 1836 they declared Texas's independence.

After his victory at the Alamo, Santa Anna divided his army and sent soldiers across the countryside to stamp out any vestiges of resistance. Cut off from reinforcements, Santa Anna and about half of the Mexican troops were defeated in April at the Battle of San Jacinto by the Texas army of Sam Houston (1793–1863). Santa Anna, captured following the battle, ordered the Mexican army's remaining units to withdraw from Texas, and, as a prisoner of the Texas government, he signed a treaty in which he agreed to use his influence to get the Mexican government to recognize Texas's independence.

Texas existed for nine difficult years as an independent republic. It faced constant danger of invasion from Mexico, which had disavowed Santa Anna's treaty and refused to recognize Texas's independence. Efforts to negotiate immediate annexation by the United States were frustrated by the growing U.S. debate over the expansion of slavery. President Sam Houston (1836–1838 and 1841–1844) pursued conservative fiscal policies and attempted to avoid armed conflict with Mexico or the Indians while trying to maneuver Texas into the United States. From 1838 to 1841, President Mirabeau B. Lamar (1798–1859) sought to expand Texas westward, drive out the Indians, and implement an ambitious program for public education. But the only results of Lamar's efforts were a soaring national debt and collapse of the Texan dollar.

Texas achieved one success during its independence: population growth. Both Houston and Lamar used cheap land to lure settlers to the Republic, and its population increased from an estimated 34,000 in 1836 to 142,000 in 1847. Just as the influx of Anglo immigrants overwhelmed the Hispanic population and paved the way for the Anglo takeover of Texas in the 1820s and 1830s, continued Anglo immigration in the 1830s and 1840s solidified their control of the region and made Mexican reconquest unlikely. The most dramatic aspect of the Republic's population growth was the increase in its slave population, from approximately 5,000 in 1836 to 38,753 in 1847. This influx strengthened the slave plantation economy in Texas. The 1840s also saw the beginning of German immigration to central Texas.

Annexation, the Mexican War, and the Civil War

In 1844 the issue of annexation surfaced again in Texas and the United States. Desires for American expansion and fears of British imperial ambitions in Texas undermined the anti-annexation arguments in the United States. When the pro-annexation candidate, James Polk (1795–1849), won the presidency in 1844, Congress approved a joint resolution annexing Texas into the United States. On 29 December 1845 President Polk signed the act making Texas the twenty-eighth state in the Union. On 19 February 1846 Anson Jones (1798–1858), the last president of Texas, formally relinquished power, announcing, "The Republic of Texas is no more."

The annexation of Texas provoked a U.S. war with Mexico and brought the slavery issue to the forefront of the American political debate. The underlying causes of the Mexican War (1846–1848) included the territorial ambitions of U.S. expansionists and the determination of Mexican nationalists to avenge their loss of Texas. Actual fighting erupted in April 1846 over a dispute about the Texas-Mexico boundary. While America's victory in the war set the Rio Grande as the southern boundary of Texas, it precipitated a conflict over the state's western boundary and provoked a new debate over slavery in the western territories. Both the slavery issue and the west Texas border dispute were addressed in the Compromise of 1850. Texans transferred their claims to New Mexican territory to the U.S. government for $10 million. Efforts to resolve the slavery issue failed.

In the 1850s Texas continued to experience rapid growth. By 1860 its population had soared to 604,000, including 183,000 African American slaves. The growth of slavery tightened the bonds between Texas and the other southern states. However, with its large German and Mexican American minorities, Texas enjoyed greater ethnic diversity than the other slave states. At mid-century almost all Texans lived in the eastern third of the state. West and southwest Texas were controlled by Native Americans. Most Texans were farmers who had migrated there from the southern states. Approximately one-third of the population consisted of slaves, most of whom worked the plantations that stretched along the Brazos and Colorado Rivers or were in northeast Texas. German immigrants were concentrated in the counties west and north of San Antonio, and Mexican Americans mostly lived in the San Antonio area and south Texas.

As the sectional conflict deepened in the late 1850s, Texas found itself drawn more closely into the South's orbit. When the 1860 election of Abraham Lincoln (1809–1865) sparked secession, Texans, over the objections of Governor Sam Houston, voted by a three-to-one margin to join the Confederacy. Approximately 68,500 Texans served in the Confederate Army, where they experienced their share of casualties. However, as the western frontier of the Confederacy, Texas did not suffer greatly from the devastation of war. No major battles were fought on Texan soil, and at the end of the war the state was relatively free of Federal troops.

The Civil War ended in Texas on 2 June 1865, over six weeks after Appomattox, when General Edmund Kirby Smith (1824–1893), commander of the Confederate forces in Texas, surrendered to the United States. On 19 June 1865 the first units of the U.S. Army arrived in Galveston to begin the federal occupation of Texas. The U.S. commander, General Gordon Granger (1822–1876), issued orders furloughing all Confederate troops in Texas and freeing all of Texas's slaves. Juneteenth (derived from "June nineteenth") is still celebrated by African American Texans as emancipation day.

Reconstruction in Texas was similar to that in other former Confederate states. Texas resisted granting civil and political rights to the freed slaves. Although some African Americans achieved political influence or economic prosperity, most former slaves remained mired in poverty, growing cotton as sharecroppers or tenant farmers for white landowners. By the mid-1870s conservative Democrats had regained political power in Texas, and the period of Reconstruction had come to an end.

From a Southern to a Western State

In the post–Civil War period, Texas's government was dominated by conservative Democrats. African Americans remained active in politics, especially in the Republican Party, but the Republicans no longer competed seriously with the Democrats for power. Texas became a one-party state. The relationship between whites and African Americans followed the pattern of that in other former Confederate states, with the gradual but steady erosion of African American rights.

Other aspects of race relations in Texas more closely resembled those of the western states. The 1870s brought Texas its most protracted Indian wars. Military campaigns against the Comanches and

Apaches ultimately drove those peoples out of the state. By the mid-1880s all of Texas was open for settlement. Force was also used to pacify the Mexican borderlands, where the Texas Rangers served as the instrument of white supremacy.

Politically and economically, Texas also shared much with the western states in the late nineteenth century. Although Texas continued as a major cotton producer and much of its cotton crop was produced by African American labor, cotton became a less dominant factor in the state's economy, and between 1870 and 1890 the percentage of African Americans in the population declined from 31 percent to 22 percent. Texas remained predominantly agricultural and rural, but the ranching industry that spread out of south Texas in the late 1860s became an important new source of wealth in the state, and the settlement of the plains of north Texas had more in common with the settlement of Nebraska than with that of Alabama. Texas also differed from other southern states in its continuing ability to attract significant numbers of immigrants. The state's population soared from 604,000 in 1860 to more than 3,000,000 in 1900.

The political issues of late-nineteenth-century Texas reflected the state's changing economic structure. Farmers and ranchers—not planters—set the political agenda, and issues such as land policy, fencing, and railroad regulation dominated the political debates. In the absence of a viable Republican Party, farmers' organizations provided the most serious challenge to the Democrats. The issue of the railroads was central to Texan politics in this period. Railroads had promoted the settlement of the frontier, shipped cattle to market, and provided the transportation system necessary for industrial development. But railroads also charged discriminatory freight rates and exerted political influence. Farmers saw unregulated railroad rates as the center of their economic problems. Railroad regulation was the issue that ultimately derailed the conservative Democrats. In the 1880s Texas Congressman John H. Reagan (1818–1905) spearheaded efforts to create the Interstate Commerce Commission (1887), and in 1890 Texas's reform-minded attorney general, James S. Hogg (1851–1906), used the issue of railroad regulation to win the governor's office and bring reform government to Texas.

Texas in 1900

As the nineteenth century came to a close, Texas was poised to become a major industrial, urban state. In 1900, however, it was still rural and agricultural. Its population had spread across the plains of north Texas, but only the city of San Antonio had over fifty thousand residents, and major industrial development was yet to come. But the infrastructure was in place—a transportation system that connected cities and markets and a government friendly to industrial development. The 1880s had witnessed the development of the state's first real industry, the lumber business. The event that would transform the Texas economy, however, occurred at the very beginning of the twentieth century: on 10 January 1901, Captain Anthony F. Lucas (1855–1921) struck oil at Spindletop. The magnitude of this discovery and of subsequent oil strikes made Texas a major industrial state.

See also **Mexican War; Mexico; Sectionalism; Statehood and Admission.**

Bibliography

Barr, Alwyn. *Reconstruction to Reform: Texas Politics, 1876–1906.* Austin: University of Texas Press, 1971.

Campbell, Randolph B. *An Empire for Slavery: The Peculiar Institution in Texas, 1821–1865.* Baton Rouge: Louisiana State University Press, 1989.

De Leon, Arnoldo. *The Tejano Community, 1836–1900.* Albuquerque: University of New Mexico Press, 1982.

Jordan, Terry G. "A Century and a Half of Ethnic Change in Texas, 1836–1986." *Southwestern Historical Quarterly* 73 (April 1986): 385–422.

Moneyhon, Carl H. *Republicanism in Reconstruction Texas.* Austin: University of Texas Press, 1980.

Newcomb, W. W. *The Indians of Texas, from Prehistoric to Modern Times.* Austin: University of Texas Press, 1974.

Richardson, Rupert N., Adrian Anderson, and Ernest Wallace. *Texas: The Lone Star State.* 7th ed. Upper Saddle River, N.J.: Prentice Hall, 1997.

Weber, David J. *The Mexican Frontier, 1821–1846: The American Southwest under Mexico.* Albuquerque: University of New Mexico Press, 1982.

CARY DECORDOVA WINTZ

TEXTILES   Before the American Revolution the barest beginnings of a textile industry existed in the United States, producing low volumes of coarse cloth that was sold locally to those who could not afford expensive imports. Household and putting-out systems dominated. Workers spun raw cotton and sold the thread, and others purchased the thread and produced goods for use or sale.

Machinery, such as looms, shuttles, jennies, and mules, was an essential ingredient in nineteenth-century textile development. Machines drew out cotton fibers and coordinated the size, placement, and speed of various rollers and bobbins to create thread with consistent strength and thickness. The flying shuttle, which was patented by John Kay in 1733, improved the process further. Before 1810 almost all weaving was done on hand looms. The power loom, which was patented in 1785 by Edmund Cartwright, became practical and was used widely in England by the 1810s. The English textile industry became mechanized with inventions such as the spinning jenny (patented by James Hargreaves in 1770) the water frame, which was patented in 1769 by Richard Arkwright, and the mule, which was invented by Samuel Crompton in 1779. The jenny had several spindles and a reciprocating action driven by a hand-powered spinning wheel, and the water frame used rollers to spin thread. The mule combined the reciprocating action of the jenny with the power drive of the water frame.

Americans had difficulty acquiring machines from Britain, however, because the British did not want competition from mechanized American mills. Some Americans advertised in Britain and sent agents to recruit mill workers to emigrate under assumed names or assumed occupations. As technological expertise slowly crossed the Atlantic the U.S. textile industry became a reality.

New England Textiles and the Rise of Corporations

In the 1790s Samuel Slater (1768–1835) built America's first textile factory for mechanized cotton yarn production in Pawtucket, Rhode Island. Slater, who had gained expertise working at a British mill, emigrated claiming he was a farmer. He brought the new machine designs to America, reproducing them from memory. He became a partner in the firm of Almy and Brown in Rhode Island, agreeing to build the equipment and a mill, supervise it on a day-to-day basis, and pay half the expenses. The firm agreed to purchase the raw material, lend Slater money, have the yarn from the mill woven into cloth, sell the cloth, and pay the other half of the expenses. Eventually Slater branched out and built mills of his own.

Domestic demand grew during the turmoil of the Napoleonic Wars and the War of 1812. In 1805, both Rhode Island and Massachusetts had at least twelve mills operating. The number of mills grew even more when President Thomas Jefferson placed an embargo on English goods in 1808. Over the next four years thirty-six cotton mills and forty-one woolen mills opened in the United States. After the War of 1812, however, English textile manufacturers dumped textiles on the U.S. market, and a number of overcapitalized U.S. mills went bankrupt.

Slater established the early practice of building mills in rural settings, where waterpower was readily available and idyllic landscapes contrasted with the dirty, dark cities British factories had created. These

Samuel Slater (1768–1835). Founder of the American cotton industry, Slater was an English textile worker who produced English-type machinery in America in 1790. By 1798 he had built his first manufacturing plant. LIBRARY OF CONGRESS

mills relied on child workers, who were poor or orphaned and whose ages ranged from seven to fourteen. The Slater system evolved into a family labor system, in which the mill built adjacent housing and rented it to families. Older children worked in the mills, and their younger siblings followed. Fathers worked in the mills or in other capacities, such as hand loom weavers. In this paternalistic system mill owners imposed requirements on families, including regular church attendance. Mills were sometimes owned by a family, with a family member living at the mill site and running the business.

Eventually the Slater system gave way to the Lowell, or Waltham, system. After visiting England's textile manufacturers in 1810, Francis Cabot Lowell (1775–1817), a Boston merchant, effected a revolution in the textile industry. He created a limited liability corporation, the Boston Manufacturing Company, with some family members and business associates, including Nathan Appleton (1779–1861). With large amounts of capital, they opened their first mill in Waltham, Massachusetts, in 1814. In 1822 they built a second mill upstream on the Merrimack

River at the site that became Lowell, Massachusetts, a major textile center of the nineteenth century. The essential components of this system were integrated production, heavy capital, labor recruitment, purchasing of supplies, marketing of finished goods, and waterpower. The Boston group undertook everything on an unprecedented scale. Historians generally have referred to this group, eventually composed of several different companies, as the "Boston Associates."

Lowell and his partners reduced cloth production to its simplest elements and minimized the amount of skill required, choosing machines that were easily operated. They also subscribed to the idea that U.S. industry was "good," as opposed to the "bad" industry that had dirtied up Britain and oppressed its people. The Boston group wanted to make money but in a better, kinder, and more profitable way than the English.

The money generated from these mills poured into railroads, banks, other financial investments, and philanthropic efforts. In England, Lowell had seen not only the power loom, but also the "dark satanic mills" (William Blake) that the Industrial Revolution had created. Money from the Lowell mills flowed to hospitals, universities, and other cultural institutions. But historians, who originally viewed the Lowell system as a forward-looking development devised by adventuresome entrepreneurs, began in the twentieth century to stress the owners' conservatism and taste for social control of their employees.

The new mills integrated all aspects of cloth production. Raw cotton entered the mill complex, and finished cloth exited. The cotton proceeded upward from the first floor through raw cotton preparation, spinning, weaving, dyeing and finishing, to the finished product. Power for the highly mechanized process came from a waterwheel in the basement and rose upward through as many as four stories in a system of shafts and belts.

Relationships at Lowell differed from those at earlier mills. The owners hired managers to run the mills, and mill hands, recruited from local farm families, were young, unmarried women who lived on the mill site and abided by a strict moral code. Management sometimes became bossy and interfering. The intent was to teach the workforce not only a new job but a new way of life. That way of life, of course, forbade disrupting millwork or protesting working conditions. Large, capital-intensive corporations rather than individuals or families owned the mills. By 1855 Lowell had fifty-two mills.

Power looms in the United States made rapid development possible. They changed the nature of work in the new Massachusetts mills, requiring that people work at a pace set by machines rather than allowing the workers to set the pace. The limited number of skilled positions were often held by men. Many women developed the dexterity, quickness, and keen eyesight required to work the machines, bringing into question whether or not mill jobs of this era were truly unskilled. As workers became more skilled, management raised the number of machines per employee, a practice known as stretch-out, or they increased the machines' operating speeds, which was called speedup. After the 1840s mill owners increased productivity by adding machinery rather than by increasing labor or wages.

By 1840 textiles had become a major U.S. industry, and the Lowell system had begun to change. Paternalism faded as mill housing was sold into private hands. Housing conditions soon became as deplorable as those in English mill cities. The composition of the workforce in New England mills changed as well. The young farm women left, replaced by Irish immigrants. In the 1870s French Canadians began to replace the Irish as the labor source. The percentage of male workers also increased over the decades.

The Lowell mill experienced little labor organization early on, but it increased in the latter half of the century. Strikes remained infrequent, brief, and unsuccessful through the 1880s. As the workforce diversified, efforts toward labor organization actually lost momentum because the workers' aims were divided. Owner responses to strikes, particularly in the second half of the century, proved swift and decisive. They dismissed strikers, closed mills, and refused reemployment to activists.

In the 1850s, several Lowell mills failed. Rapid expansion had saturated the market, and prices fell. During the Civil War the New England companies that had stockpiled raw cotton or that found supplies outside the U.S. South survived. In the 1860s the products being made began to vary, but the mills did not move all the way toward finer cotton goods. The emphasis remained on low-skill, mass-scale processes.

The Lowell system did not outlast the Civil War, but the war was not the main cause of its demise. While the war brought layoffs and shutdowns, the mills' efforts to compromise between modern industrialization and traditional values failed. Those that survived into the late nineteenth century copied other industries, which often meant bad working conditions and no concern for the quality of workers' lives. By 1870 the conservatism of the owners had left many mills with old buildings, antiquated machinery, and managements focused on short-term profits, often derived from squeezing labor costs. The inflexibility of large-scale operations, which often purchased large amounts of raw cotton a year in advance, also caused problems, making it difficult for a

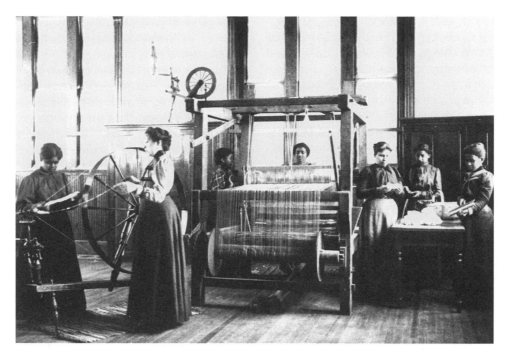

Textile Production. The manufacturing stages of cotton: combing, spinning, and weaving on a loom. LIBRARY OF CONGRESS

mill to reduce production during periods of uncertain markets.

The New England mills that survived after 1870 abandoned any effort at a new kind of industrialization and concentrated on rapid development and expansion. Some shifted from production of long runs of coarse cloth for inventory to production of a variety of finer goods made to order. By the mid-1880s Lowell was at the forefront of a gradual shift toward small, specialized textile firms.

Pennsylvania and Flexible Production

The textile industry developed differently in other areas of the country. Rockdale and Philadelphia, Pennsylvania, experienced smaller factories, modest capital investment, and gradual growth, and owners and workers came from the community and continued to live in the community. Mills in rural settings like Lowell ranged from Maine to Ohio. In the 1820s they started with small capital and were mainly proprietary firms or partnerships. Many began with a single portion of the process and produced staple goods with little variety. Staple production required less machinery, which was difficult to obtain and maintain in remote areas.

Relationships between management and workers varied. In some cases owners practiced Christian industrialism, converting their workers and teaching Christian obedience. In other cases management at-

tempted to deal straightforwardly with workers. They explained market declines to their employees, who took a wage cut and an increase when the market improved. Treatment with dignity often staved off strikes. The owners frequently had more experience as merchants and farmers than as millers and depended on outside managers. Early labor included women and children as well as male mechanics and loom bosses. By the 1850s many rural areas experienced influxes of immigrants, who went to work in the mills.

The noncorporate model, which historians have called "proprietary capitalism," was at least as prevalent in the textile industry as the Lowell-Waltham corporate model. By 1860, Philadelphia boasted a complex of specialized and flexible textile manufacturing enterprises that produced woolens, cottons, blends, hosiery, carpet, and silks rather than cotton goods alone. Owners often ran the businesses directly, and the firms merged new ideas of capitalism and profit with older, traditional values and culture from an artisanal and paternalist past. Immigrants played larger roles in these firms than in the early New England firms. Within these companies various combinations of old and new technologies, or artisanal and factory forms of production, coexisted.

In the 1880s, however, textile labor and textile capital clashed in Philadelphia. By that time the size and skill of the city's textile labor force was unequaled anywhere in the nation due to rapid development of small firms during the 1870s. Some local workers joined the national Knights of Labor, and labor unrest and activity occurred in periods of economic decline, and in faltering industry sectors. The more prosperous and flexible sectors, such as silk and woolens, saw few labor conflicts.

Some similarities existed between the Massachusetts and Pennsylvania textile mills. Pennsylvania mills appeared to be carefully structured compromises between modern industrial systems and traditional cultural and social values. The Boston Associates made similar compromises, using the advantages of the industrial revolution to place themselves higher within the traditional social and cultural hierarchy that they wanted preserved.

Two things set Philadelphia apart from Lowell: smaller firms and more skilled workers. Philadelphia's textile entrepreneurs, short of capital, shifted toward product flexibility, outwork, and interfirm linkages. The manufacturing group consisted mainly of non-elite immigrants, who infused their own cultures into businesses. During the Civil War, while the rigid Lowell mills stumbled, the flexible Philadelphia mills became an integral part of war production.

Textile manufacturing had shaped Lowell and Waltham, whereas Philadelphia shaped its textile manufacturing. Philadelphia and its industry developed together and provided other economic outlets beyond textile manufacture and trade. Technology also differed. The machinery developed and used at Lowell pushed speed and bulk. Machinery for Philadelphia mills tended toward flexibility and specialized functions.

The Rise of the South

New England's dominant position in the textile industry faded over the course of the century. During the 1870s and 1880s the bulk of coarse cotton production shifted to the South, which sought to establish a textile industry as a base for its general economic recovery. The effort to bring the cotton factories to the cotton fields accompanied the effort to promote the southern economy abroad. Textile mills offered the defeated southerners an avenue into industrial development that might branch out and save the South from its weak economy, which was dependent on one product, raw cotton. Some historians have called the southern cotton mill campaign a continuation of the battle that was lost militarily in 1865.

A few textile firms operated in the South before the Civil War. Southern states built mills between 1808 and 1812 in an attempt to achieve economic independence, particularly from England. After the War of 1812 ended, England dumped cheap fabrics on the American market, and most southern mills, not as heavily capitalized or as large as their northern counterparts, collapsed. Demand for English goods raised prices for raw cotton and shifted southern efforts back toward that production.

In the late 1820s the South again attempted to build mills, prompted by a desire to lessen the region's economic dependence on New England markets and manufacturers. As cotton prices rose again in the 1830s, investment in the mills again declined. Another cotton mill boom occurred in the South between 1845 and 1850, although the United States experienced agricultural depression at this time. But once again the shift toward manufacturing reduced the overproduction of cotton and raised raw cotton prices, ending the boom. Wealthy landowners and planters often added their voices to the call for mill building, which they envisioned being financed through foreign trade rather than raw cotton.

Among southern states, Virginia and Tennessee played large roles in the early nineteenth century textile industry, but by 1870, however, South Carolina had the most mills in the South, and by the 1890s Georgia and North Carolina also had substantial numbers of mills.

After the Civil War, southern factories began with a shortage of capital but with abundant sources of cheap labor. Due to the lack of milling and spinning skills, the region mostly produced coarse cloth, which was manufactured with machinery requiring minimal skill. However, the fall of cotton prices in the 1870s urged capital out of agriculture and into industry, and the early 1880s saw rapid development in the southern textile manufacturing industry. Business slumped in the mid-1880s, and southerners sought an expansion of markets abroad. By the end of the century the American South rivaled Great Britain on the world market for rough cotton fabrics.

Southern industrialization stimulated mill growth, but the substantial wage differential between North and South was the major impetus. The average southern wage could be as much as 25 percent below the average northern wage in the late nineteenth century. The South also had a large unskilled labor force, primarily women and children. Child labor and long hours prevailed in southern mills, which often hired family groups. The South's elastic labor supply adjusted to cotton market highs and lows. In lean times for the mills the workers flowed back to agricultural labor, yet they remained available when mills expanded. Consequently southern mills experienced few labor shortages, in contrast to the northern mills, which increased labor by hiring immigrants, a less-elastic labor supply.

Other economic factors aided southern mill expansion. Southern mill building coincided with a growth in the export market for coarse goods. Since northern mills decreased their coarse goods production in favor of finer goods, this growth aided the southern mills more than the northern ones. Lower taxes and the quick adoption of new technology also boosted southern enterprises.

While the number of spindles, generally accepted as a measure of the size of the industry, increased in the North during the last decades of the nineteenth century, expansion in the South far outpaced that in the North. At the end of the nineteenth century the southern states were producing more coarse goods than northern states, and there was also an increased production of finer fabrics in the South in the 1890s. The total number of spindles in the South did not overtake the North until the 1920s, when many New England firms closed their northern shops and moved to the South.

The century began with only limited American textile production. When it ended the United States was a major participant in the world textile market.

See also **Cotton; Industrialization and the Market; Labor Force; Labor Movement; New England; Philadelphia; South, The; Waterpower; Women,** *subentry on* **Women's Labor; Work,** *subentries on* **The Workshop, Factory Labor, Child Labor.**

Bibliography

Dalzell, Robert F., Jr. *Enterprising Elite: The Boston Associates and the World They Made.* Cambridge, Mass.: Harvard University Press, 1987.

Dublin, Thomas. *Women at Work: The Transformation of Work and Community in Lowell, Massachusetts, 1826–1860.* New York: Columbia University Press, 1979.

Galenson, Alice. *The Migration of the Cotton Textile Industry from New England to the South, 1880–1930.* New York: Garland Publishing, 1985.

Gross, Laurence F. *The Course of Industrial Decline: The Boott Cotton Mills of Lowell, Massachusetts, 1835–1955.* Baltimore: Johns Hopkins University Press, 1993.

Hearden, Patrick J. *Independence and Empire: The New South's Cotton Mill Campaign, 1865–1901.* Dekalb: Northern Illinois University Press, 1982.

Jeremy, David J. *Transatlantic Industrial Revolution: The Diffusion of Textile Technologies between Britain and America, 1790–1830s.* Cambridge, Mass.: MIT Press, 1981.

Kulik, Gary, Roger Parks, and Theodore Z. Penn, eds. *The New England Mill Village, 1790–1860.* Cambridge, Mass.: MIT Press, 1982.

Lander, Ernest McPherson. *The Textile Industry in Antebellum South Carolina.* Baton Rouge: Louisiana State University Press, 1969.

McLaurin, Melton Alonza. *Paternalism and Protest: Southern Cotton Mill Workers and Organized Labor, 1875–1905.* Westport, Conn.: Greenwood Publishing, 1971.

Scranton, Philip. *Proprietary Capitalism: The Textile Manufacture at Philadelphia, 1800–1885.* Cambridge, U.K.: Cambridge University Press, 1983.

Shelton, Cynthia J. *The Mills of Manayunk: Industrialization and Social Conflict in the Philadelphia Region, 1787–1837.* Baltimore: Johns Hopkins University Press, 1986.

Steinberg, Theodore. *Nature Incorporated: Industrialization and the Waters of New England.* Cambridge, U.K.: Cambridge University Press, 1991.

Tucker, Barbara M. *Samuel Slater and the Origins of the American Textile Industry, 1790–1860.* Ithaca, N.Y.: Cornell University Press, 1984.

Wallace, Anthony F. C. *Rockdale: The Growth of an American Village in the Early Industrial Revolution.* New York: Knopf, 1978.

LINDA EIKMEIER ENDERSBY

THEATER   During the nineteenth century, theater in the United States flourished as the most common type of public amusement and as a central social and aesthetic gathering place in communities of any size. Theaters' broad range of drama and entertainment catered to diverse patrons, and both variety and clientele steadily increased as the nation grew. While never lacking for moral and aesthetic detractors or for entertainment competitors, such as taverns, churches, politics, and lectures, theaters remained located near the center of the public square of American cities, towns, and hearts. That one of the nation's major riots, in New York City in 1849, developed from a feud between fans and the Astor Place Opera House, and that the tragic assassination of President Abraham Lincoln in 1865 took place in a playhouse, symbolized how theaters were knitted into the fabric of American life.

Expansion

In 1800 professional theater was limited to the larger eastern cities and was just beginning to expand beyond its origins in a single troupe that had emigrated from England in 1752. That English troupe built the earliest playhouses in several cities and patriotically renamed itself the American Company in 1766. During the American Revolution theatricals were banned by politicians as wasteful, joining the earlier religiously inspired bans in New England, but British soldiers kept the dramatic torch alive by presenting seasons of plays in the cities they occupied. At the war's end laws against the theater disappeared, and dramatic companies regrouped and expanded.

The range of the theater grew with the nation's wealth and transportation network. By 1830 most

American towns with a population of more than ten thousand, including those in the Mississippi Valley, had their own theaters and attracted visiting companies, with some "stars" lighting the place for a few nights. By 1850 major cities had a panoply of theaters for different sorts of entertainments and audiences. Actors followed miners to the Far West and played a central role in local lives and lore wherever sudden wealth appeared.

In the 1840s "gardens" and "museums" helped reduce remaining religious opposition to theater by offering moral dramas untainted by the liquor and prostitutes available in most earlier theaters. In 1843 the Boston Museum presented W. H. Smith's play *The Drunkard*, which ran for one hundred nights to launch what was through most of the century America's strongest resident company, centered around William Warren's comic genius. At the Boston Museum and theaters like P. T. Barnum's in New York and Louisa Lane Drew's in Philadelphia, good productions, high tone, and low prices expanded the audience, especially among middle-income and poorer people. Matinees also widened the attendance of women and children.

In the century's later decades the railroad and mass communication networks created a new dramatic system in which touring companies, featuring plays and players that had triumphed in big cities, especially New York, went from place to place for months and even years at a time. Smaller troupes went to less populous communities, sometimes on showboats or in tent shows, offering their versions of the publicized successes. Dramatic and musical entertainments were also increasingly packaged into Chautauqua and other lecture series, while amateur and school plays were common in those areas unpenetrated by even such mobile professionals.

Varied Attractions

Theatrical entertainment was broad-ranging. In 1800 long evenings might include William Shakespeare's *Hamlet* followed by a farce, with songs, dances, acrobatics, and juggling featured between the acts. Bills under this repertoire system changed frequently, sometimes every night, and the dramas ranged from the plays of Shakespeare to those of Richard Brinsley Sheridan to contemporary comedy, melodrama, or plays grounded in music, dance, or scenic effect. Genres did not so much disappear as become divided. By mid-century long runs of more elaborate productions had undercut the ever-changing repertoire and the need to attract with such a variety of offerings. Special theaters also formed around spin-offs from earlier playhouses. In the early 1840s the immensely

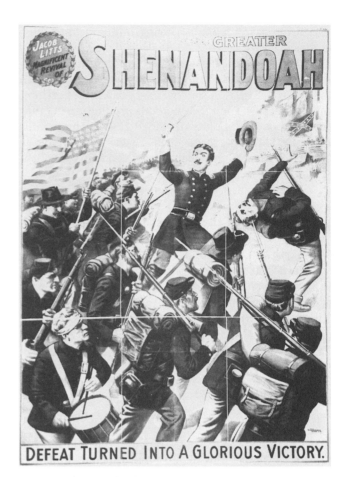

Poster for the Dramatization of a Civil War Battle. Bronson Howard (1842–1908), one of the first American Indian playwrights, drew from American subjects for his plays. Lithograph, Strobridge & Co., 1898. LIBRARY OF CONGRESS

popular minstrel shows, evolved from T. D. Rice's "Jim Crow" performances (1828), led the way to a separate existence. Vaudeville, opera, and burlesque theaters soon followed, the latter offering farcical takeoffs on dramas and current events.

During the early 1860s leg shows leavened a few plays, and in 1868 Lydia Thompson led her British Blondes in burlesques in which nimble legs and wits decorated and satirized literary and gender forms and formulas, the intellectual ancestor of what slowly devolved into the twentieth-century strip burlesque. Vaudeville, with its mélange of earlier entre-act entertainments, grew in popularity, especially after 1885, when B. F. Keith and E. F. Albee centralized the system and lowered prices to a dime. Increasingly large circuses housed the animals, acrobats, clowns, and "feats" that had once enlivened the playhouse. Like minstrelsy, ethnic theaters developed from the comic stereotypes of earlier plays, and immigrant audiences laughed at and with their farcical representatives. The theater of Edward Harrigan and Tony

Hart in New York City was perhaps the most beloved of these.

Stars

"Stars" of the stage drew large audiences to the theater. Most of the earliest sensations had established London reputations, as had George Frederick Cooke (whose U.S. debut was in 1810), Edmund Kean (1821, 1825), Charles Kemble and Fanny Kemble (1832), and William Macready (1827, 1849). Later imported talent was more international and included Jenny Lind (1850), Fanny Janauschek (1867), Helena Modjeska (1877), Sarah Bernhardt (1880), and Eleonora Duse (1893). In the 1830s the United States produced its own stars, beginning with Edwin Forrest, Charlotte Cushman, and Junius Brutus Booth, a permanently transplanted Englishman. The black tragedian Ira Aldridge, on the other hand, had to find stardom in England and on the Continent rather than on the stages of his racist native land. The foreign stars Maria Malibran (1825) and Fanny Ellsler (1840) and the American-raised Adelina Patti (1859) stimulated broad American enthusiasm for the opera and ballet.

The early stars worked in the repertoire system and specialized in Shakespeare, although all played modern roles as well. Cushman and especially Forrest actively encouraged American dramatists; Forrest found one of his most popular roles in John Augustus Stone's play *Metamora* (1829), a melodramatic tragedy centered on an American Indian hero. Later stars, including the comedian John Gilbert; Clara Morris, famed for her ability to pour forth tears; Lester Wallack; and Richard Mansfield, shifted the balance of their performances from Shakespeare toward the modern. The touring system encouraged some stars to play a single role for decades. Joseph Jefferson became permanently identified with Dion Boucicault's interpretation of *Rip Van Winkle* and James O'Neill with Charles Fechter's adaptation of Alexandre Dumas's *The Count of Monte Cristo*.

The Play's the Thing

Drama remained the core of American theater. Shakespeare was the most performed dramatist, but even early in the century melodrama was the dominant form. Named for plays that arose during the French Revolution, melodrama had roots in eighteenth-century sentimental drama and comedy, which assured audiences of a world of moral meaning where the good and usually long-suffering would triumph over the powerfully vile. The theater's desire for immediacy of audience response encouraged absolute distinctions between the selfless good characters and vicious villains at the center of these plays. Low comic characters—Irish, Yankees, servants, sailors, farmboys and farmgirls, fire boys and their girls, and frontiersmen—could show everyday interest in sex, money, liquor, and brawling, because these enthusiasms were bound within the parable of higher moral meaning. Melodramas were imported first from France and then from England and Germany, but Americans quickly began to produce native variants. For example, William Dunlap, who managed New York's John Street Theater (1796–1811) and later wrote the first and definitive account of the American stage, *History of the American Theater* (1832), adapted plays from French works and from the dramas of August von Kotzebue, but he also wrote many original dramas on American themes.

Melodrama's basic structure was easily adapted to comedy, tragedy, musical drama, and plays centered on spectacle, feats, animals, and prodigies. The first successful American play was Royall Tyler's melodramatic comedy *The Contrast* (1787), which introduced the stage Yankee (the comically naive but shrewd New Englander) as well as the theme of the follies of the pretentious rich. Both motifs threaded later American plays, such as Samuel Woodworth's comic musical melodrama *The Forest Rose; or, American Farmers* (1825), the first American play to win large British as well as American audiences, and the successful drama *Fashion* (1845) by the socialite-actress Anna Cora Mowatt.

The moralism of melodrama cushioned its handling of controversial political issues, usually with sympathy directed toward the victims of social power. Such was the orientation of the many historical plays related to the Salem witchcraft trials or dealing with incidents of Native American history. After 1840 melodramas increasingly attacked contemporary social evils such as alcoholism, corrupt and aggressive business greed, and urban poverty. The most controversial religious and political issues were handled in plays like Thomas Dunn English's *The Mormons* (1858) and Mrs. J. C. Swayze's *Ossawatomie Brown; or, the Insurrection at Harpers Ferry* (1859). No plays were more successful in the nineteenth century than the two that questioned slavery and racism when those issues were dividing the nation—Dion Boucicault's *The Octoroon* (1859) and the many versions of Harriet Beecher Stowe's *Uncle Tom's Cabin* (from 1852 on). So popular was the latter that the "Tom show" remained a distinctly successful theatrical genre throughout the century.

Toward Realism

Awareness of melodrama's aesthetic limitations was strong, but dramatists found its moralism hard to escape. Even the best attempts to rise higher, such as Robert Montgomery Bird's *The Broker of Bogota* (1834) and George Henry Boker's *Francesca da Rimini* (1855), occupied some uneasy middle ground between honesty, Shakespearean aspiration, and moralism that prohibited great power on either page or stage. In the century's second half theater moved toward greater realism within its melodramatic conventions. Acting styles became less dependent on emotive outbursts. Edwin Booth's brilliant portrayal of Hamlet in 1864 set the quieter standard in classic drama, while Matilda Heron and Minnie Maddern Fiske worked toward a realistic style in contemporary plays. Stage settings and productions as well as many surface aspects of plays became more realistic. Modern trends were clear in the dramas Boucicault wrote and produced, in Augustin Daly's highly controlled productions, and in David Belasco's super-realistic sets and props. James Herne's drama *Margaret Fleming* (1890), with its attack on the sexual double standard, best showed the desire for greater realism and the limitations of American efforts toward it compared to those in Scandinavia, Russia, Ireland, and England at the century's end.

American theater had difficulty escaping melodrama because it was grounded in the popular will rather than in the hands of cultural institutions and aesthetic arbiters. Ordinary folks were reluctant to give up what their theater had long offered, comfortable amusement amid the moral assurances and decencies of melodrama, even though the brutal waves of honest modernism were about to break over them.

See also **Circuses; Minstrel Shows; Vaudeville and Burlesque.**

Bibliography

Grimsted, David. *Melodrama Unveiled: American Theater and Culture, 1800–1850.* Chicago: University of Chicago Press, 1968.

McConachie, Bruce A. *Melodramatic Formations: American Theatre and Society, 1820–1870.* Iowa City: University of Iowa Press, 1992.

Meserve, Walter J. *Heralds of Promise: The Drama of the American People during the Age of Jackson, 1829–1840.* New York: Greenwood, 1986.

Odell, George C. D. *Annals of the New York Stage.* 15 vols. New York: Columbia University Press, 1927–1949.

Quinn, Arthur Hobson. *A History of the American Drama from the Beginning to the Civil War.* New York: Harper and Brothers, 1923.

———. *A History of the American Drama from the Civil War to the Present Day.* New York: Harper and Brothers, 1927.

Shattuck, Charles H. *The Hamlet of Edwin Booth.* Urbana: University of Illinois Press, 1969.

Wilson, Garff B. *History of American Acting.* Bloomington: University of Indiana Press, 1966.

DAVID GRIMSTED

THIRD PARTIES   Although the U.S. political process normally revolves around the two-party system, during the nineteenth century dozens of third parties came into existence. Several parties originated to influence politics in one particular state, such as the Equal Rights Party or Locofoco Party in New York and the Nullifiers in South Carolina during the 1830s, the Law and Order Party in Rhode Island during the 1840s, the Readjusters in Virginia during the 1880s, and the Silver Party in Nevada during the 1890s. However, most third parties intended to become a major party by displacing the Democrats or Whigs in the antebellum period or the Democrats or Republicans after the Civil War. After 1900 third parties became an increasingly rare phenomenon because the Democrats and Republicans dominated the political process almost completely in terms of issues. Consequently, twentieth-century third parties almost always appeared only as a vehicle for the presidential aspirations of a particular candidate. Once that candidate's popularity faded, so did the fortunes of the party. Some third parties played a major role for a few elections before disappearing, while others played a minor role for decades. Most focused attention on issues the major parties either skirted or ignored. No third party ever became a major party. Nevertheless, third parties influenced several important national elections and espoused innovations and ideas that were later co-opted by the major parties.

Major Third Parties before the Civil War

The first national third party was the Anti-Masonic Party. It was formed in 1826 in Batavia, New York, following the murder of William Morgan, a New York resident and a former Mason who wrote a book revealing the darkest secrets of Freemasonry, the world's largest secret fraternal society. New Yorkers, outraged by Morgan's information that the Masons were a secular, elitist institution and by the fact that his murderers were never brought to trial, made the Anti-Masons a major party in their state within two years. The party also became popular in Pennsylvania and Vermont, capturing both state houses. Abhorring secrecy and elitism, the Anti-Masons in 1831 became the first party to select their presidential candidate and write a platform at a national convention rather than in a closed congressional caucus, an innovation that was quickly adopted by the major parties. The party's fortunes peaked in 1832, when it elected twenty-five representatives from six states. That year its presidential candidate won 8 percent of the popular vote and seven electoral votes.

During the antebellum period a number of third parties arose over the question of slavery. The first was the Liberty Party, formed in 1839 in Warsaw, New York. The party preached abolition and nothing else, which cost it the support of nonabolitionists at a time when most northerners cared little about slavery. Moreover, many abolitionists avoided politics because they believed abolition was a moral cause, not a political one. The Libertymen twice ran James G. Birney, a minor politician, for president. After a miserable showing in 1840, he drew slightly over 2 percent of the popular vote in 1844 and may have affected the outcome of the election. Birney polled fifteen thousand votes in New York, which James K. Polk, the Democratic candidate, carried by only five thousand votes. Had Henry Clay, the Whig candidate, gotten just over a third of Birney's votes, then Clay rather than Polk would have won New York and the presidency. Many experts agree that Clay probably would have received Birney's votes. However, other scholars doubt that many of the Libertymen would have voted for Clay, a slaveholder, had Birney not been in the race.

In 1848 the Free-Soil Party picked up where the Liberty Party left off. Composed primarily of former Libertymen and disaffected antislavery factions from both major parties, the Free-Soil Party opposed the expansion of slavery into the territories acquired in the Mexican War. It also took a stand on most of the day's other issues. In 1848 the former president Martin Van Buren, the party's presidential nominee, captured more than 10 percent of the popular vote but carried no state. The party did win two seats in the U.S. Senate and nine in the House of Representatives. By 1852 the more pragmatic Free-Soilers had become Democrats, leaving the party in the hands of the former Libertymen. After winning less than 5 percent of the popular vote in 1852, the party collapsed. Despite its lack of success, the Free-Soil Party served as the foundation from which the Republican Party rose in 1854.

The third party that came closest to achieving major-party status was the American or Know-Nothing Party. Formed to restrict the immigration of Irish Catholics and Germans and to prohibit the foreign-born from voting and holding public office, the party elected ten representatives from New York and Pennsylvania in 1844. Unlike the Anti-Masons, the Know-Nothing Party went to great lengths to conceal its inner workings from the general public. Candidates often ran as independents, and members frequently claimed to know nothing about party ac-

tivities. By 1854 the party had taken on a more moderate look, permitting it to gain control of eight state legislatures and supplant the Whigs as the principal opposition in twelve others. In 1854 the party won five gubernatorial contests and elected five senators and forty-three representatives from seventeen states. One of them, Nathaniel Banks, became the first third-party member to be elected Speaker of the House in 1856. The Know-Nothing candidate for president in 1856, the former president Millard Fillmore, won 21 percent of the popular vote (over 40 percent in the South) and carried one state. Four years later the party was dead, because of its refusal to take a clear-cut stand on the expansion of slavery.

In 1850, as the slavery issue became increasingly important, the Constitutional Union Party was formed in Georgia. That same year the party captured Georgia's governorship and elected ten members from three states to the U.S. House of Representatives. Party members tended to be southern elitists who were overly sentimental for a bygone day, but as the debate over the Compromise of 1850 proved, eloquent appeals to nationalism were losing their ability to prevent antislavery and proslavery factions

Advertising and Politics. A Boston soap manufacturing firm took the name of the Know-Nothing Party, possibly to ally the product with the party's nativist beliefs. Lithograph by H. L. H. Bradford & Co., c. 1854. LIBRARY OF CONGRESS: PRINTS AND PHOTOGRAPHS DIVISION

from tearing apart the national fabric. The party went national in Baltimore in 1859. The former U.S. senator John Bell, the party's nominee for president in 1860, captured more than 12 percent of the popular vote (over 40 percent in the South) and thirty-nine electoral votes. Southern secession in 1860 and 1861 doomed the party to extinction.

The crisis over slavery also led to the formation of the only third party that openly supported slavery. In 1860, when the Democrats refused to put a pro-slavery plank in its platform at the national convention in Charleston, South Carolina, delegates from nine slave states walked out. At subsequent Democratic conclaves in Baltimore and in Richmond, these disaffected delegates joined with other proslavery elements to form the Southern Democratic Party. The party nominated Vice President John C. Breckinridge for president and pledged to remove all barriers to the expansion of slavery into the territories. Despite the total lack of a party organization outside the South, Breckinridge polled over 18 percent of the popular vote and captured seventy-two electoral votes. He ran surprisingly well in Pennsylvania, where more than a third of the voters cast their ballots for him, and in Oregon, where he missed carrying the state by 254 votes. As with the Constitutional Unionists, southern secession killed the party.

The Republican Party

The Republican Party is unique among nineteenth-century political parties in that it acquired major party status as soon as it was founded. When the Whigs faded from the political scene in 1854 most of their northern members became Republicans. These former Whigs were joined by a number of Democrats who were disgruntled over their party's stand on slavery and by the remnants of the Free-Soil Party. By taking a strong stand concerning slavery, the Republicans did what the Whigs had never done; because it was a stand against slavery, the burning issue of the 1850s, the party became immediately successful in the North. In 1856 the party's first presidential candidate carried eleven states, and in 1860 its second candidate, Abraham Lincoln, won the election. It has been one of the two major political parties ever since.

Third Parties after the Civil War

Economic issues replaced slavery as the principal spawner of third parties following the Civil War. The most important exception to this rule was the Prohibition Party, founded in 1869 in Chicago as the political arm of the temperance movement. For the next hundred years the party regularly fielded a presidential candidate, although only in 1888 and 1892 did that candidate poll over 2 percent of the popular vote. This party was the first to espouse woman suffrage in its platform and the first to give voting rights to women delegates at its conventions. The party's lack of success resulted from its "narrow gauge" focus on only one issue, prohibition. For this reason in 1896 the National Party broke off from the Prohibition Party to work for a number of other political initiatives in addition to prohibition. Known as the "broad gaugers" because their stance was more expansive than narrow-gauge prohibitionists, its members supported most of the issues advocated by the Populists in addition to prohibition.

In 1872 dissident Republicans broke away to form the Liberal Republican Party. These dissidents were upset that big business and commerce were taking over the Grand Old Party and that corruption seemed to pervade Ulysses S. Grant's presidential administration as a result. In addition to being the first party to espouse civil service reform, Liberal Republicans opposed the continuation of Reconstruction, a position that found ready allies among southern Democrats. In 1872 the party's nominee for president, Horace Greeley, and its entire national platform were adopted by the Democrats. The fusion ticket polled almost 44 percent of the popular vote and gained sixty-six electoral votes. The Liberal Republicans also elected seven senators and four representatives from eleven states. Despite the party's economic focus, its demise four years later resulted in part from the Republican decision to end Reconstruction.

In 1874 the National or Greenback Party was formed in Indianapolis, to enhance the political clout of midwestern farmers. The party sought to end the monopolistic practices of railroads and to increase the circulation of unbacked paper currency, or greenbacks. The greenback issue appealed to factory workers as well because it enabled them to pay their bills more easily, especially since the panic of 1873 had dried up credit and constricted the nation's supply of gold, which backed the currency then in circulation. Greenbackers fashioned the first U.S. alliance between agrarian and industrial workers. In 1878 the party elected fourteen representatives from ten states, and Greenback-Democratic fusion candidates won gubernatorial contests in three states. In 1880 the party's candidate for president polled over 3 percent of the popular vote but carried no state. Although Greenbackers were elected to Congress as late as 1886, the end of the recession in 1880 began the party's decline.

The demise of the Greenbackers led directly to the rise of the People's or Populist Party. In addition to espousing railroad regulation, Populists promoted

"**Candidate Billy's Busy Day.**" Political cartoon commemorating the day William Jennings Bryan received three nominations for the presidency. Drawing by George Yost Coffin, 1896. LIBRARY OF CONGRESS: PRINTS AND PHOTOGRAPHS DIVISION

civil service reforms, shorter work hours, a graduated income tax, equal rights for women, the secret ballot, initiative and referendum, and the direct election of the president, the vice president, and senators. The party's most important issue was the free coinage of silver, which gained the support of those yearning for an increase in the money supply and of western mining interests. In 1890 the party elected two senators and eight representatives from five states. Over the next several years Populist and Populist-Democratic fusion candidates won gubernatorial contests in eleven states. In 1892 the Populist candidate for president won 8 percent of the popular vote and carried four states. In 1896, the party's heyday, it elected five senators and twenty-two representatives from eight states, while its candidate for president, William Jennings Bryan, and its main issue, the free coinage of silver, were adopted by the Democrats. Although Populists continued to be elected to Congress until 1900, Bryan's heartbreaking defeat in 1896, when he polled 48 percent of the popular vote and carried twenty-two states, brought Populism to an end.

Dissident Republicans formed the Silver Republican Party in 1896, when the GOP refused to support the free coinage of silver. That year the party held a joint convention with the Populists, at which it endorsed Bryan's candidacy for president, and it elected five senators and three representatives from five states. In the election of 1898 those figures dropped to three and two, respectively. By 1900, the year the Currency or Gold Standard Act reaffirmed U.S. commitment to the gold standard, the party had reunited with the Republicans.

Minor Third Parties

Most third parties of the nineteenth century lasted only a few years, primarily because they arose in consequence of a short-lived political phenomenon. Once the causes that brought about their existence ceased to be matters of importance, which normally occurred by the time the next election rolled around, these parties faded away as rapidly as they had sprung to life. Those that espoused a more enduring platform persisted for decades, often well into the twentieth century. However, during the nineteenth century no minor third party ever elected a single congressman or gained more than 2 percent of the presidential vote.

Several third parties were born to champion the cause of working people, whose needs were largely ignored by the major parties. In 1828 the Workingmen's Party was formed in Philadelphia to involve the working class more fully in the political process. This party advocated doing away with militia service and imprisonment for debt, and it supported the establishment of free public education and maintenance of the ten-hour workday. In 1872 the National Labor Reform Party was formed in Columbus, Ohio, to elect prolabor candidates and to advance the objectives of labor unions in general. This party espoused an eight-hour workday, the abolition of convict labor, the exclusion of Chinese immigrants, and federal regulation of railroad and telegraph companies. In 1877 the United Labor Party was formed in Pittsburgh by trade unionists. Its platform advanced the single tax, whereby land would be taxed according to its value rather than its acreage, but otherwise its platform greatly resembled that of the National Labor Reform Party.

In 1877 the Socialist Democratic Workingman's Party, better known as the Socialist Labor Party, was formed in Newark, New Jersey. The first Marxist party to gain a national following in the United States, it advocated placing control of government and industry in the hands of the working class. To this end it espoused laws protecting the rights of the working people, nationalization of railroads and telegraphs, municipal control of utilities, and equal wages for women. Its most radical proposal called for replacing the president, vice president, and Senate with an executive board that served at the whim of the House of Representatives. While rarely successful in electing candidates, the Socialist Labor Party appeared on the ballot in elections throughout the rest of the nineteenth century and the entire twentieth century.

In 1884 the Antimonopoly Party was established in Chicago, in opposition to the economic hegemony of railroads, banks, and large corporations. Its platform supported government regulation of industry and commerce, specifically calling for the federal government to end monopolistic practices and its preference for the interests of industry and commerce over those of agriculture. It also called for a graduated income tax, direct election of senators, and restrictions on the immigration of Chinese laborers. In 1887 the Union Labor Party was formed in Cincinnati, Ohio, to promote the interests of farmers and trade unionists. Its platform proposed limitations on the amount of land an individual or corporation could own and public ownership of the railroads and telegraphs. In 1897 the Social Democratic Party was formed in Chicago, with a platform closely resembling that of the Socialist Labor Party.

Some minor third parties were formed by disgruntled major-party members to protest a major party's action. In 1864 the Independent Republican Party was formed in Cleveland, Ohio, to oppose the reelection of President Abraham Lincoln. In 1872 the Straight-Out Democratic Party was founded in Louisville, Kentucky, to oppose the Democratic nomination of Horace Greeley for president. In 1896 the National Democratic Party was formed in Indianapolis, in support of retaining the gold standard after the Democrats took a stand in favor of the free coinage of silver.

Other third parties were formed to address a single issue. In 1884 the Equal Rights Party was formed in San Francisco to advance the cause of woman suffrage. That year the party nominated the first woman presidential candidate, Belva Lockwood. At the time women could not vote, meaning that all of the 4,149 votes Lockwood received were cast by men.

Conclusion

Third parties arose in such great numbers during the nineteenth century for several reasons, but most importantly because the United States had not adopted a two-party system. Third parties adopted an agenda different from the two major parties of their day, but they also entertained hopes of displacing one of those parties. Although most third parties were short-lived,

they contributed significantly to the American political structure. National nominating conventions, greater involvement in the political process for the average citizen, and the first female candidate for president are only a few of the advancements put forth by third parties.

See also **Government; Politics,** *subentry on* **Political Thought; Voters and Voting.**

Bibliography

Gillespie, J. David. *Politics at the Periphery: Third Parties in Two-Party America.* Columbia: University of South Carolina Press, 1993.

Kruschke, Earl R. *Encyclopedia of Third Parties in the United States.* Santa Barbara, Calif.: ABC-CLIO, 1991.

Mazmanian, Daniel A. *Third Parties in Presidential Elections.* Washington, D.C.: Brookings Institution, 1974.

Rosenstone, Steven J., Roy L. Behr, and Edward H. Lazarus. *Third Parties in America: Citizen Response to Major Party Failure.* Princeton, N.J.: Princeton University Press, 1984.

Schapsmeier, Edward L., and Frederick H. Schapsmeier. *Political Parties and Civic Action Groups.* Westport, Conn.: Greenwood, 1981.

CHARLES W. CAREY JR.

THIRTEENTH AMENDMENT. See **Constitutional Amendments,** subentry on the **Thirteenth, Fourteenth, and Fifteenth Amendments.**

TOURISM. See **Foreign Observers; Grand Tour; Recreation; Vacations and Resorts.**

TOYS. See **Games and Toys, Children's.**

TRADE. See **Foreign Trade and Tariffs.**

TRAILS TO THE WEST   During the early nineteenth century, explorers, fur traders, and government agents mapped dozens of trails in the trans-Mississippi West. The years 1821 to 1869 marked the heyday of the western trails: Missouri traders and merchants crossed the southern Plains to New Mexico via the Santa Fe Trail; midwestern families arrived at the Willamette River valley and Sacramento River valley on the Oregon-California Trails; gold prospectors hurried along the Bozeman Trail to seek their riches in Montana; and Mormons arrived at their religious haven in Utah by way of the Mormon

Trail. These trails, and many others, served as major transportation routes before the construction of the western railroads.

Euro-American trailblazers certainly did not discover these routes. The well-traveled Oregon and Santa Fe Trails, for example, were part of extensive Native American trade networks that had existed for centuries. After Europeans began establishing settlements along the western coast in the seventeenth and eighteenth centuries, the native trails were used extensively by Indian trading groups, such as the Comanches and Shoshones, to move horses, guns, cloth, and other goods across the continent. However, it was the efforts of such mountain men as Jedediah Smith (1799–1831), who made the first effective discovery of South Pass, and Joseph Reddeford Walker (1798–1876), who pioneered the California Trail, that made it possible for eastern whites and commerce to come west via land.

The Santa Fe Trail, a twelve-hundred-mile commercial route that linked Independence, Missouri, and Santa Fe, New Mexico, was one of the earliest western trails. This route first was traveled in 1821 when, following Spain's withdrawal from Mexico, the Missouri trader William Becknell (c. 1796–1865) realized that huge profits could be made in New Mexico. Thereafter a brisk trade developed between the two regions, reaching $5 million annually by 1855. Although the Santa Fe Trail primarily was used for commerce, it was followed by the U.S. military during the Mexican War as well as many California-bound gold seekers in 1849 to 1850.

Several trails radiated out from Santa Fe. The Chihuahua Trail ran south to El Paso, while the Old Spanish Trail and the Gila River Trail connected New Mexico to southern California. The Gila River Trail, the southernmost route to California, was pioneered in 1828 by Sylvester and James Ohio Pattie (1804–c. 1850). Sections of the Old Spanish Trail were mapped as early as the 1770s, but a viable route to California was not established until the 1830s, when such traders as Antonio Armijo and William Wolfskill pushed through to Los Angeles.

The Oregon-California Trail was the most heavily traveled western route. The trail first was used by fur traders and missionaries, but during the 1840s it became the principal route for Oregon- and California-bound emigrants. Between 1840 and 1860 some 350,000 people traversed the two-thousand-mile trail. Wagon trains began their journey at various towns along the Missouri River, including Independence, Westport, and Council Bluffs. The trail followed the Platte and North Platte Rivers to Fort Laramie, then up the Sweetwater River and through the Rocky Mountains at South Pass. Once over the

Continental Divide, wagons proceeded to Fort Hall, where the trail split. Oregon-bound wagons arrived at the Willamette River valley by way of the Snake and Columbia Rivers, while wagons headed to California turned southwest to the Humboldt River, pushed across the Nevada desert, and then climbed over the Sierra Nevada through one of several passes.

The overland journey was long and difficult. Wagons traveled fifteen to twenty miles per day, and the journey took four to six months to complete. Approximately thirty thousand people died on the trails; the biggest killers were disease (specifically cholera), accidental gunshots, and drowning. In the best-known tragedy, forty-four members of the Donner party perished in 1846 to 1847 while trapped high in the snow-covered Sierra Nevada.

Led by Brigham Young (1801–1877) in 1847, the Mormons popularized another western route—the Mormon Trail—which followed the north bank of the Platte River to Fort Bridger, Wyoming. From there the trail veered southwest, following a branch of the California Trail through the Wasatch Range to Salt Lake City. Between 1846 and 1869, approximately thirty thousand to forty thousand Mormons traveled this route.

Not all overland trails ran east to west. The Bozeman Trail, for example, mapped in 1863 to 1865 by John Bozeman (1835–1867), followed a northwesterly path from southeastern Wyoming to Virginia City, Montana. This path provided a direct route to Montana's goldfields, but it also cut through the Powder River country, the prized hunting grounds of the northern Plains Indians. Lakotas, Cheyennes, and Arapahos resisted this incursion by attacking travelers and the army. On 21 December 1866, they annihilated eighty soldiers under the command of William J. Fetterman (c. 1833–1866) near Fort Phil Kearny in Wyoming. In signing the Second Treaty of Fort Laramie (1868), the federal government abandoned the Bozeman Trail.

Conflicts between emigrants and Native Americans actually were quite rare on the overland trails: Native American attacks accounted for less than four hundred of the approximately thirty thousand deaths. Heavy traffic on the trails, however, quickened Native American dispossession in other ways. Native Americans, for example, contracted European diseases from which they had no immunities. Overland travel also launched an assault on trans-Mississippi ecosystems. Heavy traffic destroyed native grasses, accelerated soil erosion, polluted waterways, and disrupted bison migration patterns.

Although the completion of the transcontinental railroad in 1869 ended most overland travel, these paths have not disappeared. Railroads and interstate highways largely follow defunct western trails. Interstate 80, for example, crosses the Great Plains over the same path traveled by Oregon- and California-bound wagon trains, and tourists still can view wagon ruts carved into the landscape from the thousands of wagons that passed over the trails during the nineteenth century.

See also **American Indian Societies,** *subentry on* **The Plains; Frontier; Mormonism.**

Bibliography

Faragher, John Mack. *Women and Men on the Overland Trail.* New Haven, Conn.: Yale University Press, 1979.

Hafen, LeRoy R., and Ann W. Hafen. *Old Spanish Trail: Santa Fé to Los Angeles.* Glendale, Calif.: Clark, 1954. Reprint, Lincoln: University of Nebraska Press, 1993.

Reid, John Phillip. *Law for the Elephant: Property and Social Behavior on the Overland Trail.* San Marino, Calif.: Huntington Library, 1997.

Stegner, Wallace. *The Gathering of Zion: The Story of the Mormon Trail.* New York: McGraw-Hill, 1964. Reprint, Lincoln: University of Nebraska Press, 1992.

Stewart, George R. *The California Trail: An Epic with Many Heroes.* New York: McGraw-Hill, 1962. Reprint, Lincoln: University of Nebraska Press, 1983.

———. *Ordeal by Hunger: The Story of the Donner Party.* 1960. Reprint, Boston: Houghton Mifflin, 1992.

Unruh, John D., Jr. *The Plains Across: The Overland Emigrants and the Trans-Mississippi West, 1840–1860.* Urbana: University of Illinois Press, 1979.

MARK R. ELLIS

TRANSCENDENTALISM   Arguably the single most important philosophical, literary, and religious movement in American history, "transcendentalism" took its name from the "Transcendental Club," which began to meet in 1836, the year in which its most famous member, Ralph Waldo Emerson (1803–1882), published his brief and anonymous first book, *Nature.* Among those in attendance at these conversations were George Ripley (1802–1880), Amos Bronson Alcott (1799–1888), James Freeman Clarke (1810–1888), and Elizabeth Palmer Peabody (1804–1894). The word "transcendentalism" refers to the individual's innate capacity to directly intuit truth without the mediation of institutions.

"Transcendentalism" was a name originally applied by others to Emerson, Alcott, and their circle of friends, who frequently wrote about the movement as if they were not part of it. These authors saw themselves as the literary and philosophical equals of European and English counterparts like Johann Goethe, Samuel Coleridge, and Thomas Carlyle. The transcendentalists were remarkable for the catholic-

ity and ambition of their thought. Emerson and his iconoclast friend Henry David Thoreau (1817–1862) wrote on a vast array of topics, and their works had bearings on fields ranging from economics and literature to philosophy and religion. Their daring universality, while by no means a purely American characteristic, was nonetheless in part a reflection of nineteenth-century America's commercial and political emergence onto the world stage. The transcendentalists in general rejected what they saw as the crass commercialism of American society, and looked instead to establish a new American literary, religious, and philosophic universalism based on the sovereignty of the individual's spiritual intuition.

Although transcendentalism is often associated with the German philosopher Immanuel Kant (1724–1804), who held that sense phenomena could be distinguished from the noumenal, that which can be intuited directly by the mind, Emerson himself wrote, in the essay "The Transcendentalist," that what was popularly called "Transcendentalism" was in fact "Idealism," and that it was a form of "the very oldest of thoughts . . . Buddhism is an expression of it." American transcendentalism in fact shares with Kant little more than the word "transcendental" and an emphasis on intuitive perception. It derives, more precisely, from a wide variety of sources: Platonism/Neoplatonism as filtered through the translations of the Englishman Thomas Taylor (1758–1835); English and German Romanticism as represented by Thomas Carlyle, William Wordsworth, and Novalis (Freidrich von Hardenberg); the Christian theosophy of Jakob Böhme (1575–1624) and James Pierrepont Greaves (1777–1842), with whom Alcott corresponded; and the sacred writings of Hinduism, and to a lesser degree, Buddhism.

As a specifically religious movement, American transcendentalism derived in part from Unitarianism. The majority of its early figures were Unitarian ministers, who had grown up in an atmosphere of mingled Unitarian liberalism and Calvinist conservatism and then rebelled against both. But the transcendentalists—whether like Emerson they resigned their ministry, or like Clarke, remained prominent ministers, or like Thoreau, had nothing to do with institutional religion—were almost all concerned with questions of comparative religion. They, for the most part, rejected what they saw as the shallowness of merely social religion that did not awaken the individual's realization of his own spiritual authority. Thus the transcendentalists drew on whatever religious and philosophical sources they saw as affirming the individual's spiritual awakening, be those sources Sufi, Buddhist, Hindu, Taoist, Confucian, Jewish, or Christian. Emerson and Thoreau were more literary than religious authors, but the influence of Hindu works runs through Emerson's essays and Thoreau's most important book, *Walden* (1854).

It is true that American transcendentalism—particularly in the first cycle of Emerson, Thoreau, and friends—represented in part a reaction against the prevailing Unitarian rationalism and against the materialism of its day, but at the same time the transcendentalists emerged out of and reflected their ambience. Like virtually all of the American writers of the period, the transcendentalists drew upon nonmaterialist Western esoteric traditions like Christian theosophy as well as upon Asian religious traditions, and one might well see these influences as representing alternatives to the growing New England commercialism with which these authors were surrounded. Yet Emerson in particular drew upon some of the spirit of that same commercialism in his essays when he wrote that the world would beat a path to the door of the one who invents a better mousetrap. In brief, the American transcendentalists reacted against the rationalism and materialism of their era, but for that very reason they could hardly be conceived of outside such a period, and in their sense of

Ralph Waldo Emerson (1803–1882). Emerson's book *Nature* (1836) was the first expression of transcendentalist thought. LIBRARY OF CONGRESS

American boundlessness they also to some degree reflected it.

Emerson remains the most important figure of this movement. His greatest influence derived from his earlier works, in particular *Nature*, published anonymously in 1836, and his first and second collection of essays. His "American Scholar" (1837) and "Divinity School Address" (1838) were startlingly bold declarations of independence from Old World cultural authority and historical Christianity, both delivered at his alma mater, Harvard University, the main citadel of intellectual propriety in his day. His aphoristic prose was, though often scattershot, brilliantly evocative and lucid. He celebrated individual spiritual intuition and independence from dogmatic structures and institutions. Lecturing and publishing widely, Emerson continued to be a major public figure until his death. He gave the inaugural address at the first meeting of the Boston Radical Club, also known as the Chestnut Street Club, which met in the 1870s. Accounts of its conversations, held among such figures as Bronson Alcott, Emerson, and Thomas Wentworth Higginson (1823–1911), were often published in the *New York Tribune* and other newspapers of the day.

Thoreau was, next to Emerson, the most important figure of this movement, even though he himself refused to subscribe to any movement and even went so far as to resign from any to which he might have been committed without his knowledge. Thoreau was a brilliant if irascible literary and philosophical author as well as naturalist. His greatest achievement unquestionably was his account of his 1845–1847 sojourn at Walden Pond, near Concord, Massachusetts, published in 1854, but he is also well known for his essays. His "Civil Disobedience" (1849) inspired practitioners of nonviolent protest, including Indian leader Mahatma Gandhi, in the twentieth century. In Thoreau's later years, he was occupied with naturalistic observations in his extensive journals. He died prematurely of tuberculosis in 1862.

Among the primary concerns of the early transcendentalists was social reform. Margaret Fuller (1810–1850), an editor of the transcendentalist periodical *The Dial*, in 1843 published a lengthy article that would become her most well-known book, *Woman in the Nineteenth Century* (1845), a protofeminist work mingled with literary criticism. Like Elizabeth Peabody, Fuller—who, as Emerson once commented, had a "mountainous ME" and who is quoted as saying that she had never met her intellectual equal—grew dedicated to both the abolitionist and women's rights causes.

Perhaps the most celebrated expression of first-cycle transcendentalism efforts at social reform was the emergence of the utopian communities Brook Farm (1841–1846) and Fruitlands (1842–1943). Brook Farm was inspired by the concepts of French socialist Charles Fourier and led by George Ripley. The community included not only a number of the original transcendentalists but also the writer Nathaniel Hawthorne, who was rather sardonic in his view of the group. Notably absent were Emerson and Thoreau, who were neither joiners by nature nor interested in socialist utopias. Bronson Alcott's Fruitlands, based at a ninety-acre Massachusetts farm, was home to just a handful of people, including Alcott's beleaguered family and the Englishman Charles Lane and his son. While Brook Farm ran out of steam after a promising beginning, Fruitlands failed promptly, not least because its members lacked practical experience in matters like farming.

One of the most interesting efforts at transcendentalist social reform was made by Alcott, who for some years taught children at his own school on principles formulated by the Swiss educational reformer Johann Heinrich Pestalozzi. In 1835 Alcott began a series of conversation on the New Testament with his students, which were recorded by Elizabeth Peabody and her sister Sophia. The basic premise of Alcott's work was that children have an intuitive spiritual understanding and that the task of the educator is to draw this out. In 1836–1837 Alcott published his two-volume *Conversations on the Gospel with Children*, causing a controversy that eventually forced him to close his school. The leading Unitarian, Andrews Norton, called the work one-third absurd, one-third blasphemous and one-third obscene.

In the second, mostly postbellum, cycle of American transcendentalism, the fascination with comparative religion and Asian traditions flourished. James Freeman Clarke, for instance, published *Ten Great Religions* (1871); the fiery John Weiss (1818–1870) wrote *American Religion* (1871) and translated the German philosopher Goethe's *West-östlicher Divan*; Samuel Johnson (1822–1882) wrote a series of books titled *Oriental Religions and Their Relation to Universal Religion* (1872, 1877, 1885) that surveyed world religions and argued for the emergence of a universal religion. Other second-cycle transcendentalist figures included William Rounseville Alger (1822–1905), whose *The Poetry of the East* (1856) was drawn from Buddhist, Hindu, and Persian Sufi sources, and Octavius Brooks Frothingham (1822–1895), who like Johnson envisaged an emerging universal religion in which humanity would recognize religion not as the revelation of God to man, but of one human being to another.

To a considerable extent, American transcendentalism was a New England movement (it was particularly strong in Massachusetts). Nearly all of its major figures lived relatively near one another in Concord or Boston. It is no accident that the transcendentalists came together in the 1830s for "Conversations," and thirty to forty years later were still engaged in public conversations. Emerson and Alcott traveled in the Midwest and other regions as lecturers, helping to make the Massachusetts movement a national one. Some of the transcendentalist Conversations were summarized and published in national newspapers toward the end of Emerson's life. Clarke and William Henry Channing (1810–1884) spent time in Louisville, Kentucky, and Cincinnati, Ohio, respectively, widening the movement's scope; and Moncure Conway (1832–1907) also represented a transcendentalist perspective in Ohio.

From its inception, transcendentalism was seen as a threat by evangelical Christians, and by Catholics led by erstwhile transcendentalist and Catholic convert Orestes Brownson (1803–1876), for its emphasis on immediate individual spiritual understanding over institutional and ritualized religious faith. From the literary side, too, transcendentalists were often attacked for refusing to acknowledge the reality of evil. The prominent English author Thomas Carlyle once took Emerson on a harrowing trip through a London slum and then exclaimed "Well, do you believe in a devil now?" Other American writers also expressed doubt about the transcendentalists' optimism: Nathaniel Hawthorne satirized transcendentalism in "The Celestial Railroad" (1843); Herman Melville sneered at the movement in such works as *The Confidence-Man* (1857), while his masterpiece, *Moby-Dick* (1851), could well be seen as a repudiation of transcendentalist affirmations about nature and the cosmos; and Edgar Allan Poe (1809–1844) said that he would like to see the editor of *The Dial* hanged.

Such criticism notwithstanding, transcendentalism remains the single most influential and characteristically American contribution to nineteenth-century Western philosophy, literature, social reform, and arguably, religion. As a philosophical and literary religious movement, transcendentalism was inspired not least by Asian religious traditions and a comparative religious or syncretic approach represented both by first-cycle transcendentalists like Emerson, and by second-cycle transcendentalists like Samuel Johnson. From a literary perspective, it demonstrated that Americans could stand with their British and European counterparts and predecessors. And in the realm of social reform, its adherents' efforts were ahead of their time, for the issues with which they struggled anticipated many of those with which Americans still struggle today.

See also **Communitarian Movements and Groups; Literature,** *subentries on* **Fiction, The Essay, Poetry; Massachusetts; Reform, Social; Religion,** *subentry on* **Religion in Nineteenth-Century America.**

Bibliography

Albanese, Catherine. *Corresponding Motion: Transcendental Religion and the New America.* Philadelphia: Temple University Press, 1977.

Allen, Gay Wilson. *Waldo Emerson.* New York: Viking Press, 1981.

Boller, Paul, Jr. *American Transcendentalism, 1830–1860.* New York: Putnam, 1974.

Caruthers, J. Wade. *Octavius Brooks Frothingham, Gentle Radical.* Birmingham, Ala.: University of Alabama Press, 1977.

Dahlstrand, Frederick. *Amos Bronson Alcott.* Rutherford, N.J.: Fairleigh Dickinson University Press, 1982.

Edelstein, Tilden. *Strange Enthusiasm: A Life of Thomas Wentworth Higginson.* New Haven, Conn.: Yale University Press, 1968.

Fuller, Margaret. *The Essential Margaret Fuller.* Edited by Jeffrey Steele. New Brunswick, N.J.: Rutgers University Press, 1992.

Miller, Perry. *The American Transcendentalists: Their Prose and Poetry.* New York: Doubleday, 1957.

Richardson, Robert, Jr. *Emerson: The Mind on Fire.* Berkeley: University of California Press, 1995.

Versluis, Arthur. *American Transcendentalism and Asian Religions.* New York: Oxford University Press, 1993.

———. *The Esoteric Origins of the American Renaissance.* New York: Oxford University Press, 2001.

———. *The Hermetic Book of Nature.* St. Paul, Minn.: Grail, 1997.

Weisbuch, Robert. *Atlantic Double-cross.* Chicago: University of Chicago Press, 1986.

ARTHUR VERSLUIS

TRANSPORTATION

[This entry includes six subentries:
Animal Power
Roads and Turnpikes
Canals and Waterways
Railroads
Urban and Interurban Transportation
Automobiles.]

ANIMAL POWER

For generations horses, mules, and oxen powered transport in the United States. By the mid–nineteenth century horses were ubiquitous, tens of thousands of them taking riders to their destinations. For example, the saddle horse allowed hardy Methodist circuit riders to spread the gospel and establish that Protestant denomination as one of the country's lead-ing faiths. The animal population soared from 5,950,000 in 1849 to 18,730,000 fifty years later. Animals pulled carriages, carts, hacks, omnibuses, and other types of wheeled vehicles. Mules, because of their better resistance to heat and humidity, were prevalent in the South; but horses, such as Clydesdales, Morgans, and Percherons, dominated elsewhere. In suitable conditions "Old Dobbin" might be hitched to a sleigh, bobsled, or similar contraption with runners, and a mule or ox might draw a "mudboat" or some other conveyance.

Before the advent of canals and railroads, long-distance interior movement depended heavily on freight wagons and stagecoaches. Often a team of plodding oxen propelled the former and a team of spirited horses the latter. The popular Conestoga wagon, with its trademark white canvas cover, generally carried commercial goods or the possessions of emigrants. The wagon's capacity was significant; the amount of cargo might exceed several tons. Less impressive, wagon speeds were slow at best, depending on the weather and the overall condition of roadways. In the 1820s it might take twenty days or longer for a loaded Conestoga wagon to travel between Philadelphia and Pittsburgh, a distance of approximately 350 miles.

Stagecoaches, which first appeared toward the end of the eighteenth century and operated in scattered parts of the nation until the early years of the twentieth century, differed dramatically from the lumbering Conestogas and other freight wagons. The most famous coaches, known as Concords, originated in the mid-1820s in Concord, New Hampshire. These coaches, patterned after ones used in Great Britain, were durable, relatively lightweight, and partially enclosed. The driver, however, rode outside the enclosure, and extra passengers took rooftop space. The style worked so well that it became the standard. Usually a team of four or occasionally six or eight horses, depending upon the terrain and the weight of the passengers, baggage, and mail, could manage an acceptable speed at a brisk trot or steady gallop. The peak period of stagecoach operations was usually immediately prior to the availability of steam railroad service. Therefore the "stagecoach era" ended in the 1830s along the Atlantic seaboard and fifty years later in the Far West.

Early in the nineteenth century, canals—the principal predecessors of railroads and at times competitors of roadways—depended on animals in both the construction and operational stages. Horses, mules, and oxen helped workers shape these artificial waterways, and when canals opened, teams of mules commonly pulled freight boats while horses handled passenger packets. Speeds were restricted, for the bow

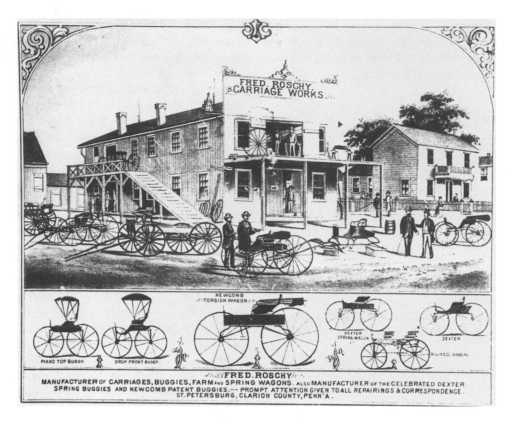

Advertisement for Carriage Works. Fred Roschy manufactured a variety of wheeled vehicles such as *(left to right)* the piano-top buggy, the drop-front buggy, the Newcomb torsion wagon, the Dexter Spring wagon, the business wagon, and the Dexter. LIBRARY OF CONGRESS

wave from a craft traveling more than about three miles an hour rapidly eroded the earthen banks.

As railroads superseded canals, they also relied upon animals, particularly during the demonstration phase. Mules, horses, and ponies pulled mine cars laden with coal or ore, and this primitive rail technology was applied to intercity railroad propulsion. Horses rather than steam engines propelled the nation's pioneer railways, including such early carriers as the Baltimore and Ohio, the Erie and Kalamazoo, and the South Carolina Canal and Railroad. But animals were better used with vehicles with flanged wheels.

Americans commonly encountered horses and mules on the streets of their cities, towns, and villages. Beginning in the 1830s these animals pulled small railroad-like cars that moved along lightweight rails. On a street railway a single horse could move a score or more of revenue-paying passengers at a rate of about three miles per hour, a pace somewhat slower than an individual could walk. But patrons preferred animal cars. They could sit, albeit in cars that frequently lacked heat or illumination, and they no longer had to slog through dust, mud, or snow. Service, too, was usually convenient, with only a few minutes of lapsed time between "cars" in major urban centers.

Horse cars or "equine traction" had limitations. Horses suitable for street railways were expensive, costing up to two hundred dollars each, and they were good for an average of only four years of active service. Moreover, they were susceptible to injury and death. In the 1870s a respiratory and lymphatic disease, epizootic apthnae or the "great epizootic," struck the eastern United States, killing thousands of animals and in the process either disrupting or stopping urban transport. Animals on public thoroughfares were a nuisance and a health risk. A horse dropped about ten pounds of manure daily and periodically discharged large quantities of urine, which slickened streets, produced offensive odors, and caused tetanus. A skin abrasion incurred on these roadways increased the chances of contracting a deadly illness, and disposing of manure from stables and other localities was an aggravation. Nevertheless, the age of real horsepower continued largely unchallenged until the 1890s, when the electric trolley rapidly eclipsed animal transport.

Stagecoach Outing. Sioux City passengers travel on a Tallyho Coaching conveyance at the Great Hot Springs of Dakota. Photograph by Crabill, 1889. LIBRARY OF CONGRESS

Before the railroad shattered the sectional isolation of the nation, travel was particularly difficult in the West, especially the mountainous and arid regions. The available solutions included pack animals, mule teams, and camels. Pack animals, horses or mules, could be strung together to haul supplies ranging from mining equipment to foodstuffs, and a single movement might employ as many as 100 animals, each carrying 250 to 500 pounds. These pack or saddle trains were well suited for the most rugged terrain. In more level areas powerful mules were hitched to freight wagons, such as the twenty-mule teams that transported borax in the California deserts. Camel caravans were much less numerous. As early as the 1840s the federal government discussed the possibility of importing these beasts of burden but did not embark upon the experiment, which was endorsed by two secretaries of war, Jefferson Davis and John Floyd, until 1855. In 1856 thirty-four camels arrived in Texas from the Middle East, and others subsequently came. A few army officials saw camels not so much as carriers of freight but rather as potential "gunships of the desert." They thought the animals might serve both as mobile bases for small howitzers and as rugged mounts for cavalry troops. But the trial fizzled, and by the late 1860s the War Department had sold its camel herds. A few of the animals were used into the 1870s by private freight operations. The reasons for failure were varied. Camels caused horses and mules to stampede, drivers bitterly disliked camels because they spit on them without provocation, and camels had strong, unpleasant odors. Finally technology caught up with them. The iron horse, which made its debut in the early 1830s, had by the immediate post–Civil War period revolutionized the nature of travel over long distances.

The memorable Pony Express experience lasted for an even shorter time. By the 1830s the all-weather National Road linked the Mid-Atlantic with the Midwest, prompting a creative response. Although stagecoaches carried the U.S. mail, in 1836 Postmaster General Amos Kendall endorsed an unusual experiment. The government hired boys, fifteen to seventeen years of age, to race their horses along the fifty-six miles of the National Road between Columbus and Zanesville, Ohio. These plucky young riders, who changed their mounts every six miles, dramatically reduced the time of the trip, covering the distance in five hours rather than the usual nine hours by stagecoach. By 1838 this expedited mail service was discontinued because of cost considerations, but the concept persisted. Between 1860 and 1861 young Pony Express horsemen rode their mounts at a full gallop for ten-mile segments between St. Joseph, Missouri, and San Francisco, California, the century's most spectacular experiment in lightning animal transportation. Their special equipment, close-fitting clothes for riders, light racing saddles, and mail pouches that could be tossed from horse to horse in a few seconds, caught the nation's imagination. With the introduction of the transcontinental telegraph in 1861, the Pony Express horses, which had been selected for speed and stamina, returned to more mundane lives. Once again animals served well, but technology replaced them.

Horses and mules contributed to the development of the nation during the nineteenth century, helping to bind neighborhoods, cities, and regions. Though lacking some of the excitement and glamor of steam locomotives or electric trolleys, horses particularly were much beloved. These animals were capable of affection and frequently endeared themselves to their owners or attendants, many of whom resented their animals' lost status in the evolving transport world. In the early twentieth century the internal combustion engine, which sparked the motorized era of the automobile and bus, brought permanent changes.

See also **Pony Express; Travel, Technology of.**

Bibliography

Ambler, Charles Henry. *A History of Transportation in the Ohio Valley.* Glendale, Calif.: Arthur H. Clark, 1932.
Rittenhouse, Jack D. *American Horse-Drawn Vehicles.* Los Angeles, Calif.: J. D. Rittenhouse, 1948.
Taylor, George Rogers. *The Transportation Revolution, 1815–1860.* New York: Rinehart, 1951.

H. ROGER GRANT

ROADS AND TURNPIKES

The nineteenth century witnessed a great expansion in the total mileage of American roads. As a result of the differing methods of financing and construction, however, the roads throughout the United States varied greatly in their quality, ranging from rutted dirt paths that lacked drainage to granite or brick roads that could handle large loads.

During the early years of the century, roads in urban and coastal regions were hard surfaced and wide enough for wagon traffic. Rural roads, however, were usually little more than pathways through woods and fields that became virtually impassable in wet weather. On occasion these roads were surfaced with logs, but local governments, which were responsible for road construction and maintenance, often lacked the capital and manpower to make such improvements.

Poor road quality inhibited economic growth and hampered westward expansion, but disputes over the constitutionality of funding internal improvements and conflicts between the states for access to any such funds limited federal involvement in road construction projects. The federal government financed the National Road, which by 1818 stretched from Cumberland, Maryland, to Wheeling, West Virginia. Congress, however, refused to appropriate the funds necessary for maintenance, and the road fell into disrepair. President Andrew Jackson then gave the National Road, which ultimately reached Vandalia, Illinois, to the several states through which it passed. For a brief period during the 1820s the federal government granted public lands to the states for use as roadways, or, in some cases, to sell in order to raise funds for road construction. This practice ended in 1830, when Jackson vetoed the proposed Maysville Turnpike in Kentucky on the grounds that the road lay entirely in one state and therefore did not merit assistance from the national government. Thus, federal aid for road construction ceased.

To facilitate road construction, many states permitted private companies to build roads and charge a fee for their use. These toll roads were commonly known as turnpikes because a pike blocked the way until the toll was paid. On average thirty feet wide, these roads consisted of heavy foundation stones topped with smaller rocks. Traffic included freight wagons loaded with agricultural merchandise and stagecoaches carrying passengers and mail. In 1820 builders stopped using foundation stones.

Turnpike construction boomed during the first three decades of the nineteenth century. By the 1830s there were twelve thousand miles of turnpikes, most of which were in the Northeast, since southerners rarely followed through on plans to build turnpikes. Many southerners felt that since cotton was nonperishable, the reduction in time that turnpikes provided in shipping cotton to market did not offset the increased cost of tolls. Turnpike construction slowed as competition from canals began to reduce turnpike traffic. The primary cause for the decline of turnpikes, however, was the inadequate return on investment: many companies failed to turn a profit.

In the late 1800s, local governments took over

most turnpike operations. Traffic flow determined the quality of road maintenance: routes with heavy traffic were usually well-maintained, while less-used routes deteriorated. To build and maintain new roads, governments levied taxes or required citizens to contribute labor to road construction projects. As a cost-cutting measure, some governments turned from stone to wooden planks to surface roads. The vogue for plank roads ended shortly before the Civil War, by which time it became apparent that such roads did not last long.

Road construction followed a slightly different path of development in western regions. Between 1807 and 1880, the U.S. Army built over one hundred roads for military purposes, a federal expenditure that the Constitution allowed. These routes, which included the Natchez Trace and the Santa Fe Trail, later become important routes for settlers moving onto the western frontier. The army played no role in the building of local roads, which were again the responsibility of local governments. In 1866 Congress granted a free right-of-way for public roads on unreserved public lands, a boon to central and western states, which no longer had to purchase land for road construction. Spending on maintenance was very low, however, and western roads quickly earned a reputation as the worst in the nation.

Between 1850 and 1900 more than 1.5 million miles of roads were constructed in rural areas. During the final decades of the century, public demand for road improvements grew, in part because after 1884, with the introduction of the "safety" bicycle design, an increasing number of Americans took to riding bicycles. Local and national good road associations organized during this period, and some states assumed responsibility for many road projects. In addition, the federal government showed a renewed interest in financing road construction. In 1893, Congress authorized the Agriculture Department to study road management. The department implemented a program of building small, quality roads to demonstrate the advantages that good roads brought to communities. Known as the object lesson road program, this project marked a turning point in the development of American roadways, resulting in increased interest in road construction by local officials.

See also **Travel, Technology of.**

Bibliography

Stover, John F. "Canals and Turnpikes: America's Early-Nineteenth-Century Transportation Network." In *An Emerging Independent American Economy, 1815–1875.* Edited by Joseph R. Frese, S. J. Judd, and Jacob Judd. Tarrytown, N.Y.: Sleepy Hollow, 1980.

Taylor, George Rogers. *The Transportation Revolution, 1815–1860.* New York: Rinehart, 1951.

U.S. Department of Transportation, Federal Highway Administration. *America's Highways, 1776–1976: A History of the Federal-Aid Program.* Washington, D.C.: U.S. Government Printing Office, 1976.

Winther, Oscar Osburn. *The Transportation Frontier: Trans-Mississippi West, 1865–1890.* New York: Holt, Rinehart, and Winston, 1964.

THOMAS CLARKIN

CANALS AND WATERWAYS

Nineteenth-century waterways were pathways for travel and development in the United States. They opened the land to exploration and helped determine patterns of settlement. Canals served as artificial rivers, supplying arteries for a water-connected society.

Waterways and Development

Rivers were central to American history. Explorers and fur traders followed them west in canoes and keelboats. Meriwether Lewis and William Clark moved upstream on the Missouri and the Yellowstone and downstream on the Clearwater and the Columbia, tracing their route to the Pacific. Wagon trains on the Oregon Trail set out along the Platte, and the Humboldt sustained the forty-niners in their trek across the high plains. Steamboats facilitated the westward movement of the Cotton Kingdom, and transportation on the Mississippi was decisive in the Civil War.

Eastern rivers flowed from the Appalachians and the mountains of New England toward the Atlantic Ocean. In New England steep river descents made travel difficult but supplied waterpower for factories, which helped make the region the most industrial section of the nation. Maine logging drives on the rivers supplied timber for coastal shipbuilding. At the mouth of the Hudson River, New York became the great Atlantic seaport. In Pennsylvania the Delaware, Schuylkill, and Susquehanna carried the products of forests, farms, and industries to Delaware Bay and Chesapeake Bay, contributing to the growth of Philadelphia and Baltimore.

Travel on the Potomac and James Rivers helped define a Tidewater society, and long rivers such as the Neuse, the Cape Fear, and the Savannah carried corn, cotton, tobacco, and rice to the coast. Southern rivers, lined with plantations, traversed the Piedmont and Tidewater, creating fall-line cities such as Alexandria and Richmond, Virginia, and Columbia, South Carolina, as well as coastal seaports.

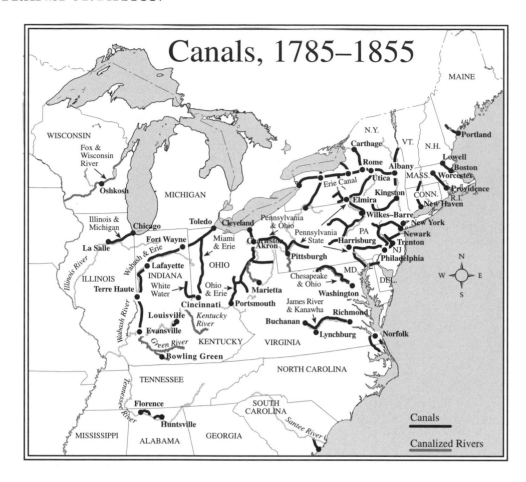

Canals, 1785–1855

Cities grew at the confluence of rivers, such as Pittsburgh, located where the Ohio River begins at the junction of the Allegheny and the Monongahela. The vast watershed of the Ohio includes the Kentucky, Cumberland, and Tennessee Rivers and from the north the Muskingum, Scioto, Little and Great Miami, and Wabash Rivers. Travelers from Kentucky and Tennessee reached the Ohio by riverboat, and southern influences penetrated the Old Northwest on Ohio tributaries. A canal bypassed the falls of the Ohio at Louisville in 1830, and in 1885 engineers introduced the Chanoine movable dam along with a lock 110 feet by 600 feet at Davis Island to enable boats and rafts to pass rapids below Pittsburgh. Other such dams were added downstream to the Beaver River and elsewhere on western waters.

The Mississippi drains the American heartland, fed by the Wisconsin, Illinois, Ohio, Sunflower, and Yazoo Rivers from the east and the Missouri, Platte, Arkansas, and Red Rivers from the west. Southern tributaries nourished the Cotton Kingdom, and western rivers opened the way to the Great Plains. After 1879 the Mississippi River Commission, created by Congress, began to improve river transportation by installing low-water dams, closing secondary channels, and creating reservoirs for times of low water.

River Vessels

Flatboats, keelboats, and steamboats were the primary agents of development on western rivers. The flatboat was shaped like a large box, had no keel, used long "sweeps" on either side, and was steered by a long oar astern. Flatboats floated with the current and sometimes carried a sail. Keelboats were forty to eighty feet long, had pointed ends and a shallow keel, and carried from fifteen to fifty tons. Moving upstream, crews pushed long poles into the mud, faced the stern, and put their shoulders to their poles as they walked the craft against the current. Where necessary, they pulled the keelboat by a cordelle or towline.

American steamboats reached their most phenomenal development on western rivers. A steamboat moved up the Ohio to Louisville in 1815 and up the Missouri in 1819. The steamboat captain Henry Shreve moved the steam boilers from the hold to the main deck, allowing a long hull with a shallow draft, and the addition of a second and a third deck placed the passengers on an upper deck. Giant sidewheels and tall smokestacks rose on the superstructure. Steamboats grew in size and luxury as the Mark Twain era developed. Flatboats continued to be used well into the nineteenth century, and steamboats in-

The Construction of the Erie Canal. Pulley cranes were used to dig the Erie Canal lock at Lockport, New York. Lithograph, 1825. © CORBIS

creased in the 1850s in spite of railroad competition. Steam snag boats invented by Shreve began to clear the Mississippi in 1829.

Canal Construction

The canal era emerging in the nineteenth-century United States responded to the need to improve navigation of rivers, which were often too low, too high, or obstructed. Two eighteenth-century canals, the Middlesex Canal linking the Merrimack and Charles Rivers in Massachusetts and the Santee and Cooper Canal in South Carolina, continued to be used into the nineteenth century. Short canals serving bateaux on the Mohawk River in New York germinated into the Erie Canal.

The Erie Canal was the great success of the canal era. It extended 363 miles from the Hudson River to Lake Erie, with eighty-seven locks and a succession of great aqueducts crossing streams and rivers. Its original dimensions of forty feet wide and four feet deep served New York for a decade. But in 1836 an enlargement program began to expand the canal in order to accommodate trade from around the Great Lakes. This trade in grain, lumber, and other products was stimulated by the thousands of emigrants traveling west on the canal and by the increase after the 1820s of steamboats on the lakes. The Erie Canal accommodated four thousand boats in the 1840s and carried 1.8 million tons to the tidewater in 1860. When the enlargement program was completed in 1862, the Erie Canal was seventy feet wide and seven feet deep. Its peak year of tonnage was 1872. The Erie Canal became a school for engineers, including Benjamin Wright, James Geddes, and John B. Jervis, many of whom later built canals in other states.

Other states sought to imitate or compete with the Erie Canal. Eastern states attempted to surmount the Appalachian barrier using canals to draw western trade to their river and ocean ports. In Pennsylvania the Union Canal, whose most dramatic feature was a 729-foot tunnel, connected the valleys of the Schuylkill and Susquehanna Rivers. The ambitious Pennsylvania Mainline Canal combined short segments of railroad with longer stretches of canal. First the Columbia and Philadelphia Railroad ran to the Susquehanna. Then the Mainline Canal followed the Susquehanna and the Juniata Rivers until it crossed the high mountains on the Allegheny Portage Railroad between Hollidaysburg and Johnstown. There stationary engines pulled cars carrying canal boats up a series of inclined planes on each slope. The western portion of the Mainline Canal followed the Conemaugh, Kiskiminetas, Allegheny, and Monongahela Rivers to Pittsburgh.

Along the upper Susquehanna the North Branch and the West Branch Canals entered the anthracite coalfields. Southeast of the coalfields a company dominated by Josiah White and Erskine Hazard built the Lehigh Valley Navigation, which extended from White Haven and Mauch Chunk to Easton on the Delaware River. Below Easton the Delaware Division Canal followed the Delaware to Bristol above Philadelphia.

Canals from the Pennsylvania coalfields made a

Cruising Through a Canal. The steamboat *Josie W.* with tow leaves Tuscaloosa for Mobile, Alabama. Photograph, c. 1870–1890. LIBRARY OF CONGRESS

network of interconnections with the canals of New York, New Jersey, and the Chesapeake Bay. The Delaware and Hudson Canal left Honesdale in Pennsylvania, followed the Delaware to Port Jervis, and turned northeast to Rondout on the lower Hudson River. Coal could also be carried from Easton across the Delaware to Phillipsburg to enter the Morris Canal, which crossed New Jersey to Newark opposite New York City. This high canal rose 760 feet to Lake Hopatcong, using lift locks and inclined planes powered by water turbines. A second New Jersey canal, the Delaware and Raritan Canal, carried Pennsylvania coal to New York. A long navigable feeder tapped the Delaware at Raven Rock near New Hope, reached Trenton where the Delaware and Raritan connected to Bordentown on the Delaware, and then turned north to New Brunswick on the Raritan River with access to New York.

The Chesapeake and Delaware Canal crossed the short fourteen miles through the Delmarva Peninsula between the Chesapeake and Delaware Bays. It was built between 1824 and 1828 by a company chartered in Pennsylvania, Maryland, and Delaware, aided by two congressional stock subscriptions. Its width of sixty-six feet accepted steam propeller vessels that carried coal, forest products, grain, and flour bound for Philadelphia. Some of this trade came down the shallow lower Susquehanna on arks and flatboats, and some came through the Susquehanna and Tidewater Canal, which was part of the rivalry between

Baltimore and Philadelphia for the Susquehanna trade.

Two Chesapeake canals attempted to cross the Appalachians to reach the Ohio River. The Chesapeake and Ohio Canal from Alexandria, Virginia, and Washington, D.C., to Cumberland, Maryland, began with the Potomac Company of the late eighteenth century and was aided in 1828 by a congressional stock subscription. Stymied by the Baltimore and Ohio Railroad and delayed by strikes by Irish laborers, it never reached its destination on the Ohio. The James River and Kanawha Canal, designed to link Richmond and the Ohio River, met a similar fate after it became a state work in 1823. It stopped at Balcony Falls, and the Kanawha Valley portion remained unfinished.

Two canals entered the Chesapeake Bay from the south, both joining the Elizabeth River a few miles from Norfolk. The first was the Dismal Swamp Canal, a low-level waterway with a southern terminus at Elizabeth City on the Pasquotauk River, which flows into Albemarle Sound. The second took a more easterly course through the Dismal Swamp to the Chesapeake. These canals, along with the Chesapeake and Delaware and the Delaware and Raritan Canals, gave a north-south direction to the canal network in the East.

Southern canals, built with the labor of slaves, included the short Roanoke Canal in North Carolina, the coastal Savannah, Ogeechee, and Altamaha Canal in Georgia, and the Barataria and Lafourche Canal in Louisiana. The latter was a partially successful route from New Orleans to the Attakapas country that became part of the Gulf Intracoastal Waterway.

Canals in western states reached from Lake Erie to the Ohio River and from Lake Michigan to the Illinois River, which flows to the Mississippi. Ohio began the Ohio and Erie Canal and the Miami Canal in 1825. The former joined Lake Erie at Cleveland, climbed southward along the Cuyahoga Valley to Akron, turned west to a feeder from Columbus, and then followed the Scioto Valley to Portsmouth on the Ohio. From this waterway the Pennsylvania and Ohio Canal was built eastward from Akron, intersecting the Erie Extension Canal across the Pennsylvania border and joining the Pennsylvania Mainline Canal. The Sandy and Beaver Canal ran eastward for the short distance from Bolivar to the Ohio. Farther south the Muskingum Improvement followed the Muskingum Valley to reach the Ohio at Marietta.

In southwestern Ohio the Miami Canal was built from Cincinnati to Dayton and then was extended to Toledo. The entire waterway was known as the Miami and Erie Canal. This canal joined the Wabash and Erie Canal, which followed the old Wabash route to the Ohio at Evansville. In southeastern Indiana the Whitewater Canal climbed the steep valley of the Whitewater River to Cambridge City. Farthest west the Illinois and Michigan Canal followed the paths of the Chicago and Illinois Rivers to the Mississippi.

On the Ohio River itself the Louisville and Portland Canal bypassed the falls of the Ohio and brought a rapid increase in steamboat traffic. A similar venture was the Saint Marys Falls canal at Sault Sainte Marie in Michigan, which passed the falls of the Saint Marys and allowed passage for lake boats from Lake Huron to Lake Superior in 1855.

The canals of the era were built primarily by states and private companies, and only a few received national aid. Most were begun in the 1820s, and a "canal mania" developed. The panic of 1837 led to stop laws that halted construction, and some states defaulted on their canal indebtedness. Most states followed the model of the Erie Canal, but dimensions varied widely, often within the same state. Larger boats on the Pennsylvania Mainline Canal could not travel the narrower Union Canal. The narrow Morris Canal in New Jersey drove coal traffic to the wider navigable feeder of the Delaware and Raritan Canal along the Delaware River. The eastern and western parts of the Erie Canal had different widths, as did the northern and southern parts of the Miami and Erie Canal in Ohio. Canals exhibited remarkable engineering triumphs, such as the Irondequoit embankment on the Erie Canal, the Paw Paw tunnel on the Chesapeake and Ohio, and the mountain sections of the Pennsylvania Mainline Canal. The canal era added locks, basins, aqueducts, and inland ports to the infrastructure of the United States.

Changes in elevation on canals were surmounted by locks, in which a boat entered a lock chamber, gates were closed, and the boat was raised or lowered as the lock was filled or emptied. Canal boat size was limited by lock size, 90 feet by 15 feet on the original Erie Canal and 110 feet by 18 feet after the canal was enlarged. Packets on the original Erie Canal were 80 feet long and 14 feet wide and 100 feet long on the enlarged canal. Interiors were divided into men's and women's sections, with long tables in the center for eating. Three tiers of folding bunks for sleeping lined the sides and were folded for sitting by day. Line boats carried both passengers and freight. Freighters hauled 70 to 90 tons, 1,000 barrels of flour, or 4,000 bushels of wheat. Like steamboats, canal boats added luxuries and refinements in their later years of development.

Like rivers, canals stimulated urban growth in cities, such as Rochester, Syracuse, and Buffalo in New York, Cleveland, Akron, Toledo, and Dayton in Ohio, and a long line of inland ports in Indiana. Some unprofitable canals have been judged successful for their developmental impact.

See also **Cities and Urbanization; Exploration and Explorers; Industrialization and the Market.**

Bibliography

Gray, Ralph D. *The National Waterway: A History of the Chesapeake and Delaware Canal, 1769–1985.* 2d ed. Urbana: University of Illinois Press, 1989. The original edition was published in 1967.

Haites, Erik F., James Mak, and Gary M. Walton. *Western River Transportation: The Era of Early Internal Development, 1810–1860.* Baltimore: Johns Hopkins University Press, 1975.

Hunter, Louis C. *Steamboats on the Western Rivers: An Economic and Technological History.* Cambridge, Mass.: Harvard University Press, 1949.

Johnson, Leland R. *The Davis Island Lock and Dam, 1870–1922.* Pittsburgh: U.S. Army Engineer District, 1985.

McCall, Edith. *Conquering the Rivers: Henry Miller Shreve and the Navigation of America's Inland Waterways.* Baton Rouge: Louisiana State University Press, 1984.

Scheiber, Harry N. *Ohio Canal Era: A Case Study of Government and the Economy, 1820–1861.* Athens, Ohio: Ohio University Press, 1969. Reprinted with a new preface in 1987.

Shaw, Ronald E. *Canals for a Nation: The Canal Era in the United States, 1790–1860.* Lexington: University Press of Kentucky, 1990.

———. *Erie Water West: A History of the Erie Canal, 1792–1854.* Lexington: University Press of Kentucky, 1966. Reprinted in 1990.

Way, Peter. *Common Labor: Workers and the Digging of North American Canals, 1780–1860.* Reprint. Baltimore: Johns

Hopkins University Press, 1997. Originally published in 1993.

RONALD E. SHAW

RAILROADS

The development of the railroad system in the nineteenth century was a major event that defined the course of the United States's history like no other. As a new technology in the 1830s, the railways spread the benefits and demands of the industrial era everywhere they went, pushing relentlessly against the boundaries of the western frontier. In speeding up the course of settlement, the railroad also paved the way for an increasingly diverse population of immigrants. After the first generation of pioneers who ventured out with handcarts and wagons, virtually everyone who settled west of the Mississippi traveled there by train. Of equal importance, the railroad enabled western products to reach eastern markets, and ultimately its greatest value was in the transportation of freight. Prior to the Civil War, the pattern of railway expansion reinforced the sectional split between the industrial North, with a rail corridor to the West, and the increasingly isolated South. After the war, however, the railroads helped weld the country back together and create a national economy.

The frenetic pace of railroad expansion in the decades following the Civil War also revealed the harmful aspects of unrestrained growth and the harsh methods of big business. Railway owners often engaged in a merciless competition that left their customers and their workers angry and disillusioned. By the turn of the century, however, the public's interest in railway transportation had been established through legislation, and the railroad had been tamed by the very conditions it created. Along the way, the story of American railway transportation combined machinery, industry, and society in a unique way.

The First Railways

From its beginning, railway steam locomotion was an amalgam of borrowed technologies. The basic form grew out of the tramway, a common feature at mines and quarries in Great Britain, where trains of ore cars ran along wooden beams. Initially, horses and mules provided the power to drive these primitive railways, but by the late 1700s many of them utilized stationary steam engines. At about the same time, cast iron strips were added to the rails to help smooth the track and reduce rolling resistance. Building on this experience, English and Scottish inventors such as James Watt, Richard Trevithick, and George Stephenson became the leading innovators of steam-powered transportation. Trevithick and Stephenson patented the first locomotive designs, and their engines were hauling goods and passengers along short rail lines by the early 1800s. Thereafter, the development of railroads in Britain and western Europe focused on refining a mass transit system that gave them an enviable lead over the United States in the development of passenger service.

Early American Railroads

The physical makeup of the American landscape made building a railway system considerably different than it was in England. The distances were daunting, and the climate was extreme. And in the rush to point the rails into open territory, expediency was often the primary construction requirement. At the turn of the nineteenth century, Americans were still a remarkably isolated and parochial people. Outside of the major seacoast cities, most communities were self-centered and proud of their independence. Travel was primarily performed on foot and on horseback, along wooded trails or rough country roads. The stagecoach was the standard method of long-distance overland travel, although the cramped quarters and punishing ride were universally reviled and avoided if at all possible.

All of this began to change in the first decades of the 1800s, when the deficiencies of the transportation and communication system of the nation became impossible to ignore. The situation was most acute during the economic embargoes and naval blockades associated with the War of 1812, when Great Britain tried to cut the United States off from overseas trade and brought coastal shipping between American cities to a standstill. With few interior routes to fall back on, the need for internal improvements became a major political topic of the period and set off a spate of turnpike and canal construction to make up the difference. Unfortunately, most of these projects involved privately funded corporations that failed to return a profit to their stockholders and were not the building blocks of a national transportation network. Although the Erie Canal, completed in 1825, was a magnificent accomplishment, its success was not easy to duplicate. Dozens of smaller operations throughout the northwestern states failed, despite massive public assistance, for every one that managed to turn a profit. Furthermore, even the viable canals had to shut down for months at a time because of winter ice and spring floods, leaving the local population as isolated as they had been in the past. Despite their limited success, the canals attracted thousands of people to new settlements along their routes and

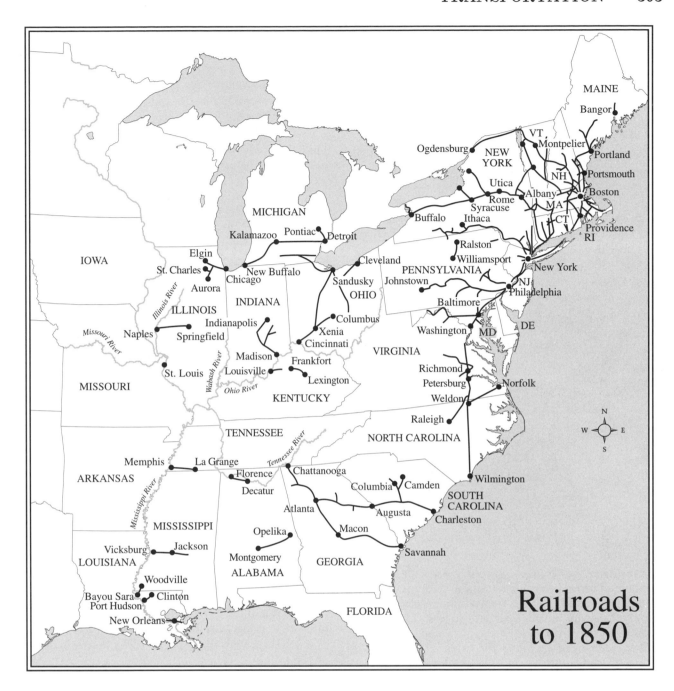

Railroads
to 1850

raised public expectations for something faster and more reliable.

During the debate over the construction of the Erie Canal in 1812, John Stevens, a Revolutionary War veteran from New Jersey, announced that he could build and operate a railroad over the same route for much less money. Stevens's claim that a steam locomotive pulling cars would be cheaper and faster than the boats on the canal was met with ridicule and with a tinge of sympathy for a man who had obviously lost his senses. Three years later, Stevens obtained a charter from the New Jersey legislature authorizing him to construct a rail line near

Trenton. Unable to find investors, Stevens retreated to his Hoboken estate, where in 1825 he built the first operating railroad in America, a toy-like locomotive that ran on a circular track.

The first railroad of effective size built in America was the Quincy Tramway of Massachusetts, completed in 1827. About three miles long, the Quincy road operated between a granite quarry and a shipping point along the Neponset River. It consisted of pine rails covered with an oak plate and topped with flat iron. The rails were five feet apart and were anchored to granite cross blocks set into the ground every eight feet. But even this effort must be quali-

Fine Dining on the Cincinnati, Hamilton & Dayton Railroad. This advertisement promotes various products, such as Peebles' Sons whisky. The railroad may have sought to suggest excellence by allying their service with luxury products, or the advertisement of products may have offset printing costs. Lithograph, Strobridge Lithographing Company, 1894. LIBRARY OF CONGRESS

fied, since horses were used to haul the cars along the way. The same was true of the second American railway, the Mauch Chunk Railroad of Pennsylvania, built in 1828, which ran nine miles from the Lehigh River to the local coal mines. The initial section of this line consisted of a gravity railroad from the top of Summit Hill to Mauch Chunk (now Jim Thorpe), where coal cars descended the track by their own weight. Empty cars were towed up the incline by teams of mules. Later, by the mid-1840s, the line relied on stationary steam engines to take the cars uphill.

It was in August 1829, on the newly formed Dela-

ware and Hudson Railroad, that the first true locomotive ran in America. Horatio Allen, an engineer for the Delaware and Hudson Canal, maneuvered the British-built *Stourbridge Lion* down the track. Thereafter, American inventors quickly put their own designs to work. Peter Cooper's diminutive *Tom Thumb*, built for the Baltimore and Ohio Railroad, hauled a passenger car and twenty-four people along a thirteen-mile line in August 1830. When other working engines ranged from five to ten tons in weight, the *Tom Thumb* weighed only one ton, making its performance remarkable. Cooper's real achievement, however, was in proving that a steam locomotive could negotiate a tightly curved track without incident, something that English experts and potential investors had seriously doubted. His speed, which reached fifteen miles per hour along certain sections of the road, was also promising.

The next two years marked a turning point in the push for railway transportation in the United States. In 1831 the South Carolina Railroad began the first regularly scheduled passenger service using an American-built engine, the *Best Friend of Charleston*. South Carolina also began carrying the U.S. mail by railroad later that year. In 1832 the Mohawk and Hudson Railroad in New York and the Camden and Amboy Railroad in New Jersey inaugurated passenger service on their lines. And Matthias Baldwin, the eventual founder of the Baldwin Locomotive Works, which built the bulk of the nation's engines, delivered his first locomotive *Old Iron Sides* for the Philadelphia, Germantown, and Norristown Railroad the same year.

Machinery and Operations

In building the Camden and Amboy line, the line's president, Robert Stevens, helped vindicate the ideas of his father, John Stevens, and was instrumental in altering track design and the configuration of the best British engines to fit the rough conditions found on American lines. His first innovation was the Stevens rail, a T-shaped design spiked to wooden cross beams with the lengths joined by iron plate fasteners. The earlier method of laying track on granite blocks did not stand up to the harsh American winters, during which frozen ground split and shattered the foundation stones. And the old iron-covered wooden rails often broke under the increasing weight of the trains, sometimes curling up through the floorboards of the cars, endangering the passengers sitting above. Although the Camden and Amboy still laid some sections of track in the old manner, Stevens's design was clearly superior and by the 1870s was adopted throughout the United States.

Stevens was also partially responsible for another major innovation when he ordered a British locomotive for the Camden line that arrived unassembled and without instructions in August 1831. Fortunately, Stevens turned to a young machinist named Isaac Dripps to put the engine together. Dripps knew something about steamboats and had the *John Bull*, as it was later named, ready for a trial run within a month. Over the next few years, as Stevens completed his railway, he and Dripps modified the *John Bull* to meet their needs. In its original form, the British locomotive ran on four equally sized driving wheels designed for the slightly curved, well-groomed rails in England. American tracks were just the opposite: cheaply made, uneven, and full of turns. To negotiate the sharp curves in the Camden line, Dripps and Stevens added a smaller set of wheels, attached by beams to the front drivers and suspension of the engine. These pilot wheels guided the locomotive over the undulating track without derailing. They later added a cowcatcher to complete the design, if not to actually clear the rails.

John Jervis, chief engineer on the Mohawk and Hudson railway, made a similar modification to an engine when he cut away the rigid front axle and wheels of an English locomotive and replaced them with a smaller four-wheel, two-axle truck that swiveled several degrees around a center pivot. This redistributed the weight of the engine and allowed it to negotiate the uneven rails. Bringing all these ideas together, Henry Campbell, a Philadelphia engineer, patented the "American Standard" engine in 1836. The 4-4-0 design incorporated four leading wheels on a truck, four driving wheels (unlike Jervis's 4-2-0 locomotive), and no trailing wheels. Although the Jervis-style engine dominated American production through the 1840s, the 4-4-0 soon became the U.S. standard, and some twenty-five thousand of them had been placed in service by 1900. At the same time, the ever increasing demands of freight service led to the development of much larger engines with six, eight, and even ten driving wheels. Depending on the location, steam engines burned either wood or coal. On the West Coast, where coal was expensive, oil burners were common by the turn of the century.

An 1837 survey of the first decade of railway transportation revealed that there were approximately 1,650 miles of operating track in the country, divided among fifty-six roads. The South Carolina Railroad had the longest line at 136 miles, but there were more than a dozen others with less than 10 miles apiece. In all, twelve states, from Maine to Georgia and as far west as Louisiana, had at least one road of their own. Within the next three years, total mileage would almost double, making the United States the world leader in railway lines by 1840, with nearly 3,000 miles compared to less than 2,000 in Great Britain. Mileage tripled again in each of the next two decades, leaving the nation with some 30,000 miles of track on the eve of the Civil War.

Despite this steady growth, the American railway system progressed in a peculiar manner that not only mirrored the impending sectional crisis but also reflected the nation's adherence to the philosophy of free enterprise. To begin with, the bulk of the rail system lay along the northeastern seaboard and stretched westward from Pennsylvania to Illinois. In 1860 the rail lines of four principal northern states, New York, Massachusetts, Pennsylvania, and Ohio, exceeded all the miles in the eleven states that joined the confederacy. But there was more at work than just political or cultural differences; within each section of the country, railroads competed across state lines and between communities.

Most of the nation's rail lines were still relatively short and disinclined to accommodate the services of another road. Through-schedules for passengers and freight were not available, and companies deliberately disrupted the flow of traffic to ensure that their line was included in the passage. The primary means for doing this was to alter the gauge of railway, the distance between the inside edges of the rails, so that passengers wanting to go on in a certain direction continually had to get off and reboard a succession of trains to reach their destination. Communities wanting a share of this transfer business joined in by offering or demanding a particular gauge track into their town. While a majority of railroads in America adopted the British standard of 4 feet, 8½ inches, the gauge in use on any particular line could vary by several inches or more, including some 6-foot-wide tracks.

Debate over the construction of the first transcontinental line in 1863 led Congress to pass a bill setting the gauge at the British standard to ensure that the western railways became part of a national system. The completion of the transcontinental railway, the Union Pacific Railroad, in May 1869 was justifiably celebrated as a turning point in the unification of the country.

Over the course of the Civil War, the need for uniformity between the lines became painfully obvious to both sides. One solution that had been used for years was to lay down a third rail to match the gauge of a connecting line. More ingenious alternatives included the use of five-inch-wide "compromise" wheels to ride along slightly varying widths of track and the use of a sliding wheel that could accommodate standard- and wide-gauge rails. But these were all temporary measures in the process of converting the roads to standard gauge. There was a brief push in the 1870s for a narrow, three-foot gauge as a cheaper alternative, but it never caught on and was mainly reserved for the mountainous sections of the western roads.

Other technological changes that added to the speed, comfort, and safety of rail travel dealt with the design of the cars themselves. Passenger coaches started out as nothing more than stagecoach bodies on rails. But major changes came quickly, and by 1831 passenger cars started riding on two independent four-wheel trucks placed under each end. As with engines, these swiveling trucks immediately improved the ride and allowed for larger cars. The length of passenger compartments evolved from less than twenty feet to more than sixty feet by the 1890s. And, unlike the British trains that segregated cars into different-class compartments, the longer American coaches adopted an open style of seating, with rows of seats lining both sides of a center isle. The early cars of the 1840s and 1850s still offered few amenities beyond a dry toilet, a potbellied stove, and a candle lantern at each end. The move toward more sumptuous accommodations started in the late 1860s, when George Pullman's palace car gained widespread acceptance. Thereafter, specialized cars for dining, smoking, and sleeping became a regular part of the service as the major lines competed for passenger traffic.

Several major safety innovations were also crucial to the development of the modern railroad. The first involved the method of coupling cars together. For thirty years, railways relied on a link-and-pin coupling system that required trainmen to stand between the cars and make the connection by hand. That single operation accounted for more serious injury and death to railway employees than any other. An automatic hook was invented in 1863 that saved thousands of lives and led to later innovations and a proliferation of designs. Unfortunately, most of them were not interchangeable. Ultimately, it took an act of Congress in 1893, the Railroad Safety Appliance Act, to force many railroads to adopt an automatic device of any type. And it was well after the turn of the century before a standard design for a railroad car coupler was chosen and universally applied.

Stopping trains was almost as dangerous as linking them together. In the early days, cars were equipped with wooden brake blocks that were not unlike the handbrake used on wagons and stagecoaches and that worked only at the slowest speed. Later, chain-operated brakes on individual cars allowed for more leverage against the blocks, but required the brakeman to climb on top of a fast-moving train to activate them. Then, in 1869, George Westinghouse patented

the compressed-air brake that truly revolutionized the process. An automatic braking system followed in 1873 that stopped the whole train if a car broke loose or was accidentally uncoupled. Taken together, these innovations—along with the use of steel for rails and car frames (in place of iron and wood) by the 1890s—allowed railroads to make tremendous gains in locomotive size and carrying capacity. By the end of the century, a fully loaded freight train could measure as much as a mile long and weigh as much as six thousand tons.

As impressive as the gains were in constructing a large-scale national rail system by the end of the nineteenth century, the railroad industry had left a legacy of public mistrust. This stemmed in part from the decades after the Civil War when railways fanned out across the nation in every direction and railway managers waged war on each other to dominate lines and territory. The rate wars, pooling agreements, and stock manipulations of the period invited government regulation. The Interstate Commerce Act of 1887 established a committee to investigate complaints against the railroads. That it failed to codify the behavior of the roads was no surprise, and the weeding out of weak competitors and unprofitable lines continued into the 1900s, along with the call for government intervention. Nevertheless, the railway system by this time was vastly more efficient and was unquestionably the engine of America's industrial growth.

See also **Interstate Commerce; Railroads; Travel, Technology of.**

Bibliography

Chandler, Alfred D., Jr. *The Railroads: The Nation's First Big Business, Sources and Readings.* New York: Harcourt, Brace, 1965.

Cochran, Thomas C. *Railroad Leaders, 1845–1890: The Business Mind in Action.* Cambridge, Mass.: Harvard University Press, 1953.

Dale, Rodney. *Early Railways.* New York: Oxford University Press, 1993.

Douglas, George H. *All Aboard! The Railroad in American Life.* New York: Paragon, 1992.

Gordon, Sarah H. *Passage to Union: How the Railroads Transformed American Life, 1829–1929.* Chicago: Ivan R. Dee, 1996.

Henry, Robert Selph. *This Fascinating Railroad Business.* Indianapolis and New York: Bobbs-Merrill, 1946.

Holbrook, Stewart H. *The Story of the American Railroads.* New York: Crown, 1947.

Johnson, Emory R. *American Railway Transportation.* New York: D. Appleton, 1904.

Riegel, Robert Edgar. *The Story of the Western Railroads: From 1852 through the Reign of the Giants.* New York: Macmillan, 1926.

Taylor, George Rogers, and Irene D. Neu. *The American Rail-*

road Network: 1861–1890. Cambridge, Mass.: Harvard University Press, 1956.

MARTIN R. ANSELL

URBAN AND INTERURBAN TRANSPORTATION

The invention and refinement of urban mass transit is among the most important developments of the nineteenth century. Urban mass transit did not exist in the United States or anywhere else until the 1820s. Before then most people traveled around cities on foot. Pedestrian traffic had an important effect on the urban environment, setting the radius of the preindustrial city at two or three miles, the distance a person can walk in about half an hour.

Omnibuses and Horse Railways

The world's first mass transit conveyance was the omnibus, which was inaugurated in Nantes, France, in 1826. The omnibus was a horse-drawn wagon that hauled up to twenty passengers and reached a speed of five miles per hour. Although its physical design and passenger accommodations were similar to those of the intercity stagecoach, the omnibus offered a particular kind of service that qualified it as a mass transit mode. The omnibus was an intra-urban conveyance that traveled over fixed routes, made regular stops, operated on a frequent schedule, and charged a set fare.

Although innovated in Europe, the omnibus was soon adopted in the United States, where it had its greatest impact. In the late 1820s Abram Brower, a New York City stable owner and stagecoach operator, introduced the omnibus in the United States, putting several vehicles in operation in Manhattan. By 1832 Boston, Philadelphia, Brooklyn, Washington, D.C., and New Orleans had omnibus lines. The early transit industry consisted of small businesses that were undercapitalized, financially unstable, and highly localized. Omnibus companies were generally confined to a particular city, where they were run by entrepreneurs who often had worked in related enterprises such as livery stables. Many operators were closely associated with local politicians. Most cities had a number of omnibus companies, which generally operated a few routes rather than serving entire urban areas. Private omnibus companies received franchises from local governments that gave them the right to use city streets. In exchange the companies had to pay licensing fees, pass vehicular safety inspections, and satisfy other elementary operating standards. As limited as they were, such early transit regulations were frequently neutralized by political corruption. The chief mechanism for controlling transit companies for much of the nineteenth century was not government regulation but rather the vicissitudes of a highly competitive and unstable marketplace that kept its operators localized and small in scale.

A second transit form, the horse railway, was introduced in New York City. On 26 November 1832 the New York and Harlem Railroad inaugurated the world's first horsecar in lower Manhattan. Although the horse railway and omnibus were both wooden boxes on wheels that were pulled by animals, the horse railway was superior. Its cars glided on iron rails that reduced friction to a minimum, while omnibuses ran on rough city streets. The use of iron rails permitted horsecars to reach speeds of up to eight miles per hour, a third faster than the omnibus; carry three times more passengers; and provide more comfortable rides. Boston, Brooklyn, Philadelphia, Pittsburgh, Cincinnati, Chicago, and New Orleans had horse railways by the 1850s. By then the horse railway had become the nation's primary form of mass transit. Like the omnibus firms, horse railway companies were small businesses that were financially unstable and geographically localized.

Horse railways transformed the urban spatial structure. Although the slow-moving omnibus had little effect on urban geography, the horsecar's faster speeds let people live farther from their jobs without having to spend more time commuting. Horse railways consequently triggered residential development on the outskirts of American cities, leading to the construction of a ring of suburbs three or four miles from the urban center. In New York City the edge of the built-up area on Manhattan Island reached Forty-second Street by 1860, having moved twice as far in thirty years as in the past two centuries. These new suburbs represented a departure from the earlier pattern of cities that covered small physical areas. Horse railways were a precursor of later transportation technologies, such as the electric street railway and the automobile, that would extend the urban landscape across much greater distances.

As the urban spatial structure changed and cities covered larger areas, residents became dependent on the horse railways as part of their everyday lives. One result of the indispensability of horse railways was that they were increasingly blamed for urban problems. People complained that the cars caused traffic jams and that the animals fouled the streets with their waste. Horse railways were also blamed for inflaming social tensions. By mixing together all sorts of people in a crowded public space, the cars led to class, racial, ethnic, and gender animosities. This social tension was partly a result of the popularity of horse railways. While the high price of an omnibus ride—ten cents usually—confined its ridership to middle-class residents, the average cost of a horse railway trip was only five cents, affordable for working-class as well as middle-class patrons.

Cable Railways and Electric Railways

By mid-century a search had begun for a mechanical form of propulsion that could replace the horse railway. In 1873 Andrew S. Hallidie, a wire rope manufacturer, opened the world's first cable railway on a San Francisco route that ran up the steep Nob Hill. The cable railway was adopted by more than twenty-five cities, yet it never challenged the dominant position of the horse railways and only became an important means of transportation in a few cities, such as San Francisco and Chicago. The total U.S. cable railway trackage peaked in 1893 at a mere 305 miles. The cable railway had financial and design flaws that reduced its influence. High capital costs confined the construction of cable lines to built-up areas that could generate heavy traffic loads, and frequent breakdowns disrupted cable operations and alienated riders. The proliferation of cable lines was due as much to the weaknesses of horse railways as to the strengths of cable railways. After a more advanced

form of mechanical power was introduced later in the nineteenth century, cable railways were abandoned almost everywhere, except in San Francisco.

The advent of electrical power revolutionized mass transit. The first completely successful electrification of a railway line took place in 1888, when a former U.S. Navy officer named Frank J. Sprague electrified the Union Passenger Railway of Richmond, Virginia. Sprague's electric railway provided a fast, cheap, lightweight, clean, and mechanically reliable propulsion system vastly superior to existing transit modes. It had lower capital costs than cable railways and lower operating costs than horse railways, and it was faster than either. Electric railway construction boomed during the 1890s. The trolley, as the electric streetcar was nicknamed, replaced the horse railway as the primary mass transit mode. By 1902 electric streetcars constituted 97 percent of the total U.S. railway trackage. Electrification also made mass transit a more important part of urban life. The new technology stimulated the construction of streetcar suburbs in outlying areas of American cities, and as travel became more convenient, residents rode more frequently. Per capita ridership doubled between 1890 and 1902, increasing from thirty-two to seventy-nine trips per year.

Streetcar in Washington, D.C. Streetcar designers experimented with a surface contact system, using a skate to supply power at the front of the car. Photograph, 1895. LIBRARY OF CONGRESS

A New Era in Rapid Transit. The elevated railroad—the world's first—commenced in New York City on 3 July 1868. LIBRARY OF CONGRESS

The adoption of electric power also enabled the transit industry to expand its service beyond urban borders. With the electric cars providing faster speeds and greater passenger comfort, interurban railways were built into the countryside. A pioneering interurban enterprise was Oregon's East Side Railway, which in 1893 began operating between Portland and Oregon City, a distance of more than fifteen miles. Chicago, Cincinnati, Los Angeles, Rochester (New York), and other cities developed extensive interurban systems.

Electrification brought about the restructuring of the mass transit industry. The small, independent businesses that had prevailed during the era of the omnibus and the horse railway were replaced by huge corporations that operated nearly all of a city's transit lines. New York City's Metropolitan Street Railway Company controlled most of the traction lines in Manhattan, for example, while the Union Traction Company monopolized Philadelphia's streetcars. These traction trusts became notorious for the poor quality of their service and for their unresponsiveness to public demands for transit improvements. The trusts were also infamous for cultivating alliances with local politicians and were accused of corrupting municipal governments. The career of Charles Tyson Yerkes Jr., a traction magnate who ran Chicago's street and elevated railways and who later consolidated London's underground railways, inspired Theodore Dreiser's scathing portrait of the robber baron Frank A. Cowperwood in the trilogy *The Financier* (1912), *The Titan* (1914), and *The Stoic* (1947). Reacting to the widespread disenchantment with mass transit, progressive reformers tried to reign in the traction trusts. Some supported public ownership of mass transit, but most reformers wanted government to regulate private industry rather than own and operate the streetcars. The chief progressive remedy was the creation of powerful state regulatory commissions that could hold hearings, investigate complaints, order service changes, and approve fare increases. Although the formation of these regulatory commissions was an improvement, the public disdain for mass transit became deeply embedded in the urban political culture. This popular distrust thwarted efforts to rescue street railway companies from a financial crisis that ravaged the industry following World War I and contributed to the decline of mass transit during the 1920s and the 1930s.

Elevated Railways and Subways

Another major transportation improvement was the development of rapid transit. Rapid transit consists of any mass transit mode that operates on its own right-of-way, running either above the street surface, as in the case of elevated railways, or wholly or partially below the surface, as in the case of subways. Rapid transit's advantage is speed. By operating on independent rights-of-way, elevateds and subways avoid the traffic congestion that slows surface vehicles.

The world's first elevated railway opened in New York City on 3 July 1868 in lower Manhattan. By 1880 New York City had an extensive elevated network, with three lines running the length of Manhattan. By providing access to areas that had previously been beyond the edge of the built-up sections, the elevated railways spurred real estate development in upper Manhattan. At first New York's elevated railways made use of steam propulsion. They began to switch to electrical power in 1901, following the development three years earlier of a multiple-unit control that enabled trains to be operated as an integrated system. Brooklyn, Chicago, Kansas City, Missouri, and Sioux City, Iowa, also built elevated railways.

Subways were a European, not an American, innovation. The first subway in the world was London's Metropolitan Railway, which entered service in 1863. Budapest inaugurated a subway in 1896, and Glasgow followed suit two years later. The first North American subway opened in Boston on 1 September 1897 and was designed to relieve traffic congestion in the central business district. It consisted of a tunnel below Washington and Tremont Streets that gave the West End Railway Company's trolleys easy access to downtown and permitted the removal of streetcar tracks from Boston's most crowded streets. Even though it was very short, the Boston subway was so expensive, costing $4.2 million, that it prompted a change in U.S. mass transit financing. Most earlier urban railways had been privately financed and owned, but subways cost so much more to build per mile of track than elevated or surface railways that the Boston project required a combination of private and public control. A public agency, the Boston Transit Commission, financed and built the subway, while a private corporation, the West End Railway Company, leased and operated it.

This formula of private-public cooperation was adopted by the two other American cities that built subways before World War I. New York City unveiled its first subway in 1904, the interborough subway line from lower Manhattan to the Bronx. Philadelphia opened a subway in 1907. Although Philadelphia's first subway, the Market Street route, was privately financed, subsequent lines used the Boston formula.

See also **Cities and Urbanization; Suburbs.**

Bibliography

Barrett, Paul. *The Automobile and Urban Transit: The Formation of Public Policy in Chicago, 1900–1930.* Philadelphia: Temple University Press, 1983.

Cudahy, Brian J. *Cash, Tokens, and Transfers: A History of Urban Mass Transit in North America.* New York: Fordham University Press, 1990.

Hilton, George W. *The Cable Car in America: A New Treatise upon Cable or Rope Traction as Applied to the Working of Street and Other Railways.* Rev. ed. San Diego, Calif.: Howell-North, 1982.

Hilton, George W., and John F. Due. *The Electric Interurban Railways in America.* Stanford, Calif.: Stanford University Press, 1960.

Holt, Glen E. "The Changing Perception of Urban Pathology: An Essay on the Development of Mass Transit in the United States." In *Cities in American History.* Edited by Kenneth T. Jackson and Stanley K. Schultz. New York: Knopf, 1972.

Hood, Clifton. *722 Miles: The Building of the Subways and How They Transformed New York.* New York: Simon and Schuster, 1993.

Middleton, William D. *The Time of the Trolley.* 2d ed. San Marino, Calif.: Golden West, 1987.

Taylor, George Rogers. "The Beginnings of Mass Transportation in Urban America," Parts 1 and 2. *The Smithsonian Journal of History* 1, no. 2 (summer 1966): 35–50, and no. 3 (fall 1966): 31–54.

Warner, Sam B. *Streetcar Suburbs: The Process of Growth in Boston, 1870–1900.* Cambridge, Mass.: Harvard University Press, 1962.

CLIFTON HOOD

AUTOMOBILES

Although few realized the significance of the automobile at the time, its mechanical configuration had already largely been delineated by the late nineteenth century. Historians generally agree that the first automobiles powered by internal combustion engines were created in Germany (1876) and reached their highest level of early development in France. The United States lagged behind these two countries through the remainder of the century, but some important steps were taken.

The precursors of the American automobile were steam-powered devices of the sort created by Sylvester Roper, who built at least ten road-going vehicles from 1859 onward. Electric vehicles also made an early appearance. One of the first electrics was a tricycle built in 1884 by Andrew Riker, who went on to manufacture electric cars from 1896 to 1901. As the century drew to a close it was not at all obvious that the gasoline-fueled internal combustion engine would become the nearly universal means to power the automobile. Production figures for 1900 showed that 1,681 cars were steamers; 1,575 were electrics; and only 936 had internal combustion engines.

With benefit of hindsight we can note that the basic pattern of the automobile was set by Charles E. Duryea and J. Frank Duryea, when in 1893 they fashioned the first American gasoline-powered automobile in Springfield, Massachusetts. Series production of a sort began in 1896, when the brothers and their associates assembled thirteen cars. In that same year Henry Ford took his "Quadricycle" for its first drive, and by 1899 he was superintendent of the Detroit Automobile Company.

After the founding of the Ford Motor Company in 1903, Ford challenged one unfortunate legacy of the nineteenth century, the Selden patent. Awarded to George B. Selden in 1895, the patent "for an improved road engine" was finally voided in 1911. The patent had been used to encourage oligopoly through the formation of the Association of Licensed Automobile Manufacturers, but the association was never able to bring the industry under its control. Spurred on by production improvements wrought by Ford and others, the automobile rapidly outstripped its nineteenth-century origins and became one of the key artifacts of the twentieth century.

See also **Detroit; Entrepreneurs.**

Bibliography

Automobile Quarterly, eds. *The American Car since 1775.* New York: L. S. Bailey, 1971.

Flink, James J. *America Adopts the Automobile, 1895–1910.* Cambridge, Mass., and London: MIT Press, 1970.

RUDI VOLTI

TRAVEL, TECHNOLOGY OF

As the nineteenth century dawned, a newborn republic of fifteen agricultural states and 5.3 million people clustered along the Atlantic seaboard. Early roads were abominable, and most Americans traveled by water. The federal government took the first steps to improve the worst form of transportation. In 1784, England had replaced post riders with its first coaches, and a year later, the U.S. Post Office subsidized the delivery of mail by wagon or coach. Yet, apart from the National Road, which the federal government began in 1815 at Cumberland, Maryland, and completed in 1818 at Wheeling, (West) Virginia, on the Ohio River, private enterprise—aided by army civil engineers—built the inland transportation network. In the early nineteenth century, turnpike or toll road joint-stock companies flourished and built roads to carry the nation's freight.

By 1820, when a postwar boom had collapsed, forty thousand miles of graded roads were in use. In 1800, Boston had 27 stage lines radiating outward; in 1820, 40; in 1825, 61; and in 1835, 110. In 1827, stage coach owner "Land Admiral" James Reeside cut the running time of his fleet of coaches from Philadelphia to New York from twenty-three hours to sixteen, and then to twelve. Passengers traveled throughout the year, at night, with less mud, and on lighter, higher, faster coaches after 1826, when J. Stephen Abbot and Lewis Downing of New Hampshire developed the classic Concord Coach supported with flexible leather thoroughbraces.

In the sparsely settled West, the federal government actively built wagon roads, subsidized freight contracts for scattered forts and mail contracts between distant cities, and encouraged railroads with land grants. Farmland in Oregon in the 1840s and gold in California in the 1850s brought an overland migration by plodding, ox-drawn, canvas-topped wagons that lasted into the 1880s.

The hurried population of 1850s California, however, demanded faster communication with the East, and in 1858, Overland Mail Company stages began running between San Francisco and St. Louis, Missouri, by way of El Paso, Texas. Rolling along at five miles per hour, twenty-four hours a day, these vehicles took a hot, dusty twenty-one days to traverse their route. The completion of the transcontinental railroad in 1869 made even western stagecoaches into feeder lines, for stage travel was not cheap. In California between the 1860s and 1890s, the cost of stage travel was ten to seventeen cents a mile, compared to three to five cents a mile by railroad. From 1880 onward, bicycle riders led the fight for improved roads, paving the way for the automobile.

At the start of the century, boats powered by wind and muscle traveled the nation's rivers, at very slow speeds. At first only flatboats and keelboats cruised the two thousand miles of the Ohio and Mississippi Rivers. Downriver flatboats, merely long boxes with a cabin for families, an open deck for livestock, and two long steering oars, took fifty days to reach New Orleans from Pittsburgh. Keelboats, up to eighty feet long and twelve feet wide, carried three hundred barrels of freight, and showed the shipbuilders' art through rounded bow and stern, cabin, mast, and sail. In 1815 the legendary Mike Fink and his friends used long poles to maneuver three hundred of these craft upriver to Pittsburgh and points in between.

Technology soon came to the aid of rivermen and Great Lakes sailors. In 1807, Robert Fulton launched the steamer *Clermont* on the Hudson River, and within two decades, its descendants churned the nation's waters at thirty miles per hour. Launched in

1811 on the Ohio River, the Pittsburgh-built steamer *New Orleans* reached its namesake city in January 1812. Five years later, the *Washington*, a two-decker with a high-pressure engine, made the upriver trip with a full load of cargo in twenty-five days and set the style for steamboats. In 1850, 740 steamers sped downriver at twenty-five miles per hour, and chugged upriver at sixteen.

Canals formed another segment of the inland network east of the Mississippi River. New York State built the greatest of all between 1817 and 1825. The Erie Canal, running between Albany on the Hudson River and Buffalo on Lake Erie, made New York City the financial center of the nation. Currents sent canal boats downstream at four miles an hour; mules plodding along towpaths returned them at half that speed.

Steam-powered railroads also appeared in the

Riding the Rails, 1841

The infant express business took off in the early 1840s. Pioneer expressmen, such as William Harnden, Alvin Adams, Henry Wells, and William Fargo, rapidly moved money and valuables over water, road, and rail. In 1864, the gregarious Henry Wells, then president of the American Express Company and a founder (1852) of Wells, Fargo, and Company, reminisced about his early years as an expressman delivering fresh oysters to Buffalo, New York. In 1841 as a messenger Wells had greeted the riverboats from New York City at Albany. From there, heading west to Buffalo, he would "travel by rail to Auburn, by stage to Geneva, by rail to Rochester, to Lockport by stage, and thence to Buffalo by private conveyance." He added, "The through trip occupied four nights and three days at the quickest attainable rate of traveling." He tersely dismissed stage-coaching: "The common road was, in summer, *endurable,* but for the greater part of the year, simply *horrible.*" However, memories of crude, early railroads still provoked him. "The line," Wells recalled painfully, "was laid with a 'strap-rail,' which, as you doubtless well know, was nothing more than a flat bar of iron spiked down to the sleepers and afforded no very great security against 'run-offs.' The spikes, too, were continually getting loose, and, under the pressure of the passing train, the rails curved upward and, in the form of 'snake-heads,' often tore through the bottom of the cars to the imminent peril and, sometimes, serious injury of the limbs and lives of the passengers."

Henry Wells, *Sketch of the Rise, Progress, and Present Condition of the Express System* (1864), pp. 12–13.

1820s. On 28 February 1827, the Baltimore and Ohio Railroad incorporated, changing the face of America. By 1840, the United States had 3,328 miles of railroads, compared to 1,818 in Europe. Dubbed the iron horse, the American train reached maturity in the 1850s, racing along at twenty-five miles per hour. In 1851 the Illinois Central received the first land grants; in 1853 the Baltimore and Ohio arrived at Wheeling, West Virginia, on the Ohio River; the Chicago and Rock Island reached the Mississippi in 1854 and crossed it in 1856. The Central Pacific and Union Pacific railroads connected to form the transcontinental railway on 10 May 1869, and rapid railroad expansion continued until the end of the century. Symbolic of their dominance in American life, railroads agreed, in 1883, on four standard time zones across the United States, one hour apart.

By the 1860s horse-drawn omnibus cars, often on rails, commonly whisked residents of the nation's larger cities from home to work and back again. In 1873 Andrew Hallidie, of San Francisco, California, gave a boost to hilly cities with the development of the cable car, while in 1888, electric street cars appeared in Richmond, Virginia, again on rails.

In 1818–1819 the sea-going ship *Savannah* reached Liverpool, England, partially under steam, but at the same time, "black ball" ships (named after the black ball on their top sails) became the first regularly scheduled transatlantic sailing packets, making the crossing in six weeks. Soon, hard-driven at twelve knots, some sped to England in sixteen days, and these vessels carried the high tide of German and Irish immigration that began in the late 1840s.

In 1845 the first of the fast three-masted clipper ships, the *Rainbow,* was built for the China and California markets, for which speed mattered more than size of cargo. In 1854 Captain Joseph Cressy rushed the *Flying Cloud* in eighty-nine days from New York around Cape Horn to San Francisco, a record for a wind-powered ship not broken until 1989. In contrast, the slower merchantmen vessels took up to six months to make the same trip. The Down-Easters (large, two-thousand-ton grain ships built in New England) followed after the Civil War, transporting California grain trade and eastern commerce.

Americans returned to steam on the seas in 1847. Two years later, the E. K. Collins line used four well-designed side-wheelers to rush across the Atlantic in nine days. Heading in the opposite direction, the Pacific Mail Steam Ship Company put gold seekers through to California, by way of the Panama Isthmus, in less than a month.

At the close of the nineteenth century, America had become a manufacturing nation of 76.1 million residents, stretching from sea to sea and beyond. Although steam power dominated, the development of gasoline-powered automobiles and airplanes loomed on the twentieth-century horizon.

See also **Maritime Technology.**

Bibliography

General

Hill, Forest G. *Roads, Rails, and Waterways: The Army Engineers and Early Transportation.* Norman: University of Oklahoma Press, 1957.

Lamar, Howard R., ed. *The New Encyclopedia of the American West.* New Haven, Conn.: Yale University Press, 1998.

Nevin, David. *The Expressmen.* New York: Time-Life, 1974.

Shipping

Lubbock, Basil. *The Down Easters: American Deep-Water Sailing Ships, 1869–1929.* Glasgow: Brown, Son, and Ferguson, 1929.

Mills, Randall V. *Stern-Wheelers up Columbia: A Century of Steamboating in the Oregon Country.* Palo Alto, Calif.: Pacific Books, 1947. Reprint, Lincoln: University of Nebraska Press, 1977.

Morrison, John H. *History of American Steam Navigation.* New York: Stephen Daye, 1958.

Shaw, Ronald E. *Canals for a Nation: The Canal Era in the United States, 1790–1860.* Lexington: University Press of Kentucky, 1990.

Worden, William L. *Cargoes: Matson's First Century in the Pacific.* Honolulu: University Press of Hawaii, 1981.

Horses, Wagons, and Stagecoaches

Berkebile, Don. *Carriage Terminology: An Historical Dictionary.* Washington, D.C.: Smithsonian Institution Press, 1978.

Boggs, Mae Hélène Bacon, comp. *My Playhouse Was a Concord Coach.* Berkeley, Calif.: Howell-North, 1942.

Clemens, Samuel [Mark Twain]. *Roughing It.* Hartford, Conn.: American Publishing, 1872. Reprint, Berkeley: University of California Press, 1972.

Fox, Charles Philip. *Horses in Harness.* Greendale, Wis.: Reiman, 1987.

Frederick, J. V. *Ben Holladay: The Stagecoach King.* Glendale, Calif.: Arthur H. Clark, 1940.

Fuller, Wayne E. *The American Mail: Enlarger of the Common Life.* Chicago: University of Chicago Press, 1972.

Hafen, Le Roy R. *The Overland Mail, 1849–1869.* Glendale, Calif.: Arthur H. Clark, 1926. Reprint, 1976.

Howard, Thomas F. *Sierra Crossing: First Roads to California.* Berkeley: University of California Press, 1998.

Jackson, W. Turrentine. *Wagon Roads West: A Study of Federal Road Surveys and Construction in the Trans-Mississippi West, 1846–1869.* New Haven, Conn.: Yale University Press, 1965.

———. *Wells Fargo in Colorado Territory.* Denver: Colorado Historical Society, 1982.

John, Richard R. *Spreading the News: The American Postal System from Franklin to Morse.* Cambridge, Mass.: Harvard University Press, 1995.

Madsen, Betty M., and Brigham D. Madsen. *North to Montana! Jehus, Bullwhackers, and Mule Skinners on the Montana Trail.* Salt Lake City: University of Utah Press, 1980.

Meier, Gary, and Gloria Meier. *Knights of the Whip: Stagecoach Days in Oregon.* Bellevue, Wash.: Timeline, 1987.

Outland, Charles F. *Stagecoaching on El Camino Real: Los Angeles to San Francisco, 1861–1901.* Glendale, Calif.: Arthur H. Clark, 1973.

Root, Frank A., and William Elsey Connelley. *The Overland Stage to California.* Topeka, Kans.: W. Y. Morgan, 1901. Reprint, Glorieta, N. Mex.: Rio Grande, 1970.

Settle, Raymond W., and Mary Lund-Settle. *War Drums and Wagon Wheels: The Story of Russell, Majors, and Waddell.* Lincoln: University of Nebraska Press, 1966.

Strahorn, Carrie Adell. *Fifteen Thousand Miles by Stage, 1877–1898.* New York: Putnam, 1911. Reprint, Lincoln: University of Nebraska Press, 1988.

Walker, Henry Pickering. *The Wagonmasters: High Plains Freighting from the Earliest Days of the Sante Fe Trail to 1880.* Norman: University of Oklahoma Press, 1966.

Railroads

Athearn, Robert G. *Union Pacific Country.* Chicago: Rand McNally, 1971.

Frey, Robert L, ed. *Railroads in the Nineteenth Century.* New York: Facts on File, 1988.

ROBERT J. CHANDLER

TRUSTS After the Civil War business competition in the United States became increasingly cutthroat. As industry's capacity to produce goods exceeded consumers' ability to buy them, many companies resorted to price slashing and sharp business practices that drove other companies from the field and reduced the profits of those that survived. Consequently entrepreneurs sought ways to reduce competition in their industries by forming various monopolistic combinations. Known collectively as trusts, a term that refers specifically to a short-lived form of combination, these entities dominated American business in the nineteenth century's last three decades. Because these combinations controlled the market and supplies and could raise prices at will, many Americans perceived trusts as working against the people's economic interests and threatening to undermine their individual liberties. Those fears resulted in federal and state attempts to regulate the formation and activities of trusts. However, prior to 1900 the attempts did more to encourage than to impede the formation of monopolistic combinations.

Generally speaking, such combinations took four forms. Pooling agreements, or pools, prevailed in the railroad industry. These arrangements allotted percentages of either the traffic controlled by or the profits accruing to the pool's member railroads. Cartels, also known as federations and trade associations, were gentlemen's agreements among competitors in the same industry to ensure that each member received an equitable amount of revenue by improving cooperation among pool members. Trusts were legal arrangements whereby stockholders in a number of competing companies surrendered their stock to a board of trustees, which generally consisted of the most important figures in the industry in question, in exchange for stock in the trust. The board then managed the various companies whose stock it held in monopolistic fashion and distributed the profits among the holders of the trust's stock. Holding companies produced neither goods nor services. Instead these corporations bought controlling interest in competing companies and administered them in the same way as did a board of trustees.

Pools

Railroads were particularly vulnerable to sharp competition for several reasons. Building a railroad entailed spending huge amounts of capital to obtain and prepare rights-of-way, lay hundreds of miles of iron rails, and purchase a fleet of locomotives and passenger and freight cars. Compared with other businesses, railroads were very immobile. Unlike a store or factory that could be dismantled and relocated to a more promising site, railroad tracks remained in place long after they ceased to be profitable. Most railroad entrepreneurs eagerly sought ways to create combinations that reduced what they considered to be ruinous competition.

To this end railroad entrepreneurs implemented pooling arrangements, a form of corporate profit sharing. The first such arrangement was the Iowa Pool, established in 1870 by the Burlington, the Rock Island, and the Chicago and Northwestern railroads to distribute equally among the three lines approximately 50 percent of their total traffic revenue. Other railroads quickly formed their own pools.

Almost as quickly pools demonstrated themselves to be unsatisfactory arrangements. The four-year recession resulting from the panic of 1873 reduced traffic levels, thus making it difficult for any railroad to surrender business voluntarily to a competitor. Negative public response to pools and other monopolistic practices by railroads led four midwestern states to place restrictions on pools. When the railroads appealed to the U.S. Supreme Court, that body rendered an ambivalent decision. The Court refused to endorse pools; *Munn v. Illinois* (1877) upheld the state's right to regulate an enterprise operating in the public interest, which railroads did. On the other hand it also implied that the states could not regulate a purely private enterprise, which railroads were. Almost immediately railroad entrepreneurs began using this loophole to create legal monopolistic combinations.

Cartels

Cartels were formal arrangements designed to improve cooperation among pool members. In addition to allocating available business to members on a percentage basis, cartels set rates by which all members must abide and established executive committees with the power to fire employees who disregarded cartel-established rates and allocations. In 1877 the Eastern Trunk Line Association allocated 33 percent of the cartel's traffic to the Pennsylvania Railroad, 33 percent to the Erie, 25 percent to the New York Central, and 9 percent to the Baltimore and Ohio. The Southern Railway and Steamship Association, the Southwestern Railway Rate Association, and the Western Traffic Association made similar arrangements for their regions.

Many manufacturing entrepreneurs, eager to reduce competition and increase profits, followed the railroads' lead and formed their own cartels. Known as trade associations, industrial cartels fixed prices, established production quotas, determined the market in which a firm could compete, and created revenue-sharing arrangements similar to railroad pools. They also possessed the theoretical power to fine companies that overproduced or made false reports concerning sales and production, or failed to report at all. By the mid-1880s most of the corporations that produced lumber, furniture, shoes, leather goods, petroleum, explosives, glass, paper, iron, steel, copper, brass, and lead belonged to a trade association. Among hardware manufacturers fifty different trade associations regulated the production of such things as sledgehammers, screws, shears, straps, shovels, saws, and kitchen sinks.

Although most cartels succeeded in stabilizing prices and production, they proved to be unsatisfactory by the mid-1880s. Cartels were federations, not conglomerates, and an association's executive committee could not examine a member company's books to determine whether or not it was abiding by the agreements. Therefore many firms got away with cutting prices by giving rebates and submitting false sales and production reports. Moreover, cartels were extralegal entities, and cartel agreements were not legal contracts. Even when a cartel member blatantly violated the agreement, it could not be sued. Consequently, after a cartel had reduced competition in a given industry, one of its members usually withdrew from the association and attempted to gain a commanding share of the market by cutting prices and increasing production.

In order for a cartel to work for an extended period of time, its executive committee had to gain legal control of the companies that composed it. Then the committee could dictate, rather than suggest, to a member company how it would behave in the marketplace. A simple merger of all of a cartel's companies into one giant corporation would have worked nicely, but several factors prevented entrepreneurs from moving in this direction. First, a corporate merger could be effected only by a special act of a state legislature, and gaining passage of a merger bill required the expenditure of much time, effort, and money. Second, any commercial organization or device that even appeared to restrain trade, as giant corporations most certainly did, was generally considered to be in violation of the common law. Unless a merger could be presented as benefiting the public, which made it more susceptible to state regulation, its chances of passage were nil. Third, in the early 1880s state legislatures began demonstrating considerable animosity toward "big business." The Pennsylvania legislature contemplated taxing the assets and revenues of out-of-state corporations at a higher rate than in-state corporations. Several other legislatures passed antimonopoly laws, although their wording was too vague to be of much threat. Thus entrepreneurs wishing to reduce competition effectively developed a new legal device, the trust.

Trusts

The first trust was established to consolidate the petroleum industry. When the National Refiners Association failed to control prices and production in the early 1870s, John D. Rockefeller, president of the Standard Oil Company, and his four associates set out to gain control of the industry. By exchanging Standard stock for stock in other member companies of the petroleum cartel, they created a tight-knit association of forty refiners. Although representatives met regularly to fix prices and establish production quotas, each company operated independently of the others. This situation became a problem for the association in 1879, when competition from nonmember refiners compelled the association to contemplate building new refineries and either modernizing or shutting down existing ones. To meet this challenge without going through a prolonged debate in a state legislature, the Standard Oil Trust was created. Stockholders in the forty companies exchanged their stock for shares in the trust, thus ceding control over day-to-day operations to a nine-man board of trustees headed by Rockefeller. By 1882, when the trust was revised, it had closed thirty-one refineries and built three huge, state-of-the-art refineries, thereby reducing the trust's cost of producing refined oil by two-thirds. The trust also integrated vertically by

John D. Rockefeller (1839–1937). Rockefeller's companies created the first modern trust in 1881 when his attorney Samuel Calvin Tate Dodd organized Standard Oil of Ohio and its subsidiary companies under a board of nine trustees. LIBRARY OF CONGRESS: PRINTS AND PHOTOGRAPHS DIVISION

obtaining control of its own pipelines, tankers, barrel factories, and crude oil wells and by establishing its own purchasing and marketing organizations. Standard Oil at that time controlled approximately 90 percent of all the oil refined in the United States.

Other successful trusts were established in the cotton oil and lead-processing industries. Formed in 1884, the American Cotton Oil Trust had closed all but seven older refineries and built seven new ones by the mid-1890s. It also integrated vertically by creating a central purchasing network for obtaining cottonseed directly from farmers; operating over one hundred cotton gins and extracting mills; acquiring a tank ship and a fleet of tank cars; developing its own brands of food oil, soap powder, lard, margarine, cattle feed, and fertilizer; and organizing an international marketing operation to sell these products. The National Lead Trust was formed in 1887 and soon controlled 60 percent or more of the white lead, red lead, and lead acetate processed in the United States. After consolidating production of these commodities and acquiring and expanding a mining and smelting operation, the trust became the nation's leading producer of paint and a significant producer of fabricated lead products.

The linseed oil, whiskey, and sugar trusts, also created during the 1880s, were not as successful as the petroleum, cotton oil, and lead-processing trusts. Formed in 1885, the National Linseed Oil Trust consolidated production and gained control of the transportation and marketing of its products, but it was never able to acquire an inexpensive and reliable source of flaxseed. The whiskey trust, created in 1887, closed over fifty small distilleries and consolidated production in twenty-one big ones. However, the overall management of individual operating units was more decentralized than in the petroleum, cotton oil, and lead-processing trusts, and it was not until 1895 that the Distillers Corporation, the trust's corporate successor, began to integrate vertically by acquiring liquor wholesalers. The American Sugar Trust, formed in 1887, was never able consistently to control more than 50 percent of the market and was continually beset by competition from large independent sugar producers, including a nationwide grocery wholesaler that tried to acquire control of its own source of sugar. Despite these shortcomings, the linseed oil, whiskey, and sugar trusts introduced significant cost-saving measures into their respective industries that resulted in substantial profits for manufacturers and cheaper prices for consumers.

Unlike these six successful trusts, the cattle and cordage trusts failed miserably. Formed in 1887, the American Cattle Trust was little more than a cooperative venture by western cattle ranchers to obtain better prices for their herds. It was never able to get a handle on distribution and ceased to exist in 1890. The National Cordage Trust established purchasing and marketing organizations but never succeeded in consolidating production. In 1893 its corporate successor, the National Cordage Company, failed so completely that it helped to bring on a financial panic that year.

American ambivalence about the rise of the trusts was most clearly demonstrated by the 1892 decision of the Ohio Supreme Court in an antitrust suit brought by that state against the Standard Oil Trust. The court applauded the trust for improving the quality of petroleum products and lowering consumer prices. However, the court also fretted that trusts consolidated too much economic power in the hands of too few entrepreneurs, who might be tempted to use that power to ruinous effect. Two other statutory developments reflected ambivalence toward monopolistic combinations. In 1889 the New Jersey legislature removed the legal obstacles that prevented cartels from converting into giant corporations by passing a new state corporation law and in the process earned the hatred of many antimonopolists. This law permitted the creation of holding companies, which could buy and hold stock in other companies, including their competitors. In 1890 Congress passed the Sherman Antitrust Act, the first law to make monopolistic practices a crime against the government rather than against a competitor. Although these two developments seem contradictory in their intent—one encouraged monopolies while the other threatened to discourage them—over the next ten years they worked together to bring about the creation of over two hundred holding companies.

Holding Companies

In 1889 the cotton oil and lead-processing trusts incorporated as holding companies. Both holding companies then reincorporated all of their business operations within a state into one corporation chartered in that state in order to avoid the kind of tax discrimination threatened by Pennsylvania. By 1893 over fifty holding companies had been created.

The panic of 1893 impeded the formation of holding companies. Only twenty-seven were formed between 1894 and 1896. However, in 1897 a wave of mergers began that lasted into the twentieth century. During that year thirty holding companies were established. They were joined by another 24 in 1898, 105 in 1899, and 34 more in 1900. Although many of the decade's mergers involved only two companies, approximately half involved five or more competitors. Altogether the creation of holding companies during the 1890s resulted in the disappearance of approximately two thousand firms.

The merger craze resulted from the growing attractiveness of corporate securities among financiers and investors and the ambivalence of the U.S. Supreme Court toward the legality of holding companies. By 1890 railroad stocks had lost much of their appeal, largely because many lines had declared bankruptcy. Manufacturing concerns were demonstrating a remarkable ability to generate profits, and in the 1890s industrial stocks became the darlings of the New York Stock Exchange. Several corporate mergers were prompted by investors' willingness to pay more for a newly created holding company's initial stock issue than the total value of its individual companies.

A more important factor was the limited way in which the executive and judicial branches of the federal government applied the provisions of the Sherman Act, which outlawed "every contract, combination in the form of trust or otherwise, or conspiracy, in restraint of trade or commerce among the several States." Only seventeen antitrust cases were begun during the 1890s, and the first was not heard by the Supreme Court until five years after the act's passage. *United States v. E. C. Knight Company* (1895) involved a federal antitrust suit against a holding company that, by purchasing the last of its major competitors, controlled over 90 percent of the sugar refined in the United States. The Court found in Knight's favor, ruling somewhat surprisingly that manufacturing and commerce had nothing to do with one another. Because holding companies seemed to be exempt from antitrust prosecution while trusts and other forms of monopolistic combinations clearly were not, after 1895 companies rushed to merge in order to avoid litigation.

The federal government moved more frequently against monopolistic activity after 1900, motivated in large part by the rise of Progressivism. In 1902 President Theodore Roosevelt initiated a suit against the Northern Securities Company, a $400 million enterprise that had gained control of the major railroads in the Northeast. In 1906 the federal government filed suit against Standard Oil of New Jersey, the largest of all holding companies. And under Presidents William Taft and Woodrow Wilson the federal government launched dozens of suits against monopolistic combinations.

Monopolistic combinations did not appear until the 1870s, but by 1900 they dominated the American economy. Many people felt ambivalent toward them, as reflected in the manner in which state and federal governments addressed them, and popular authors wrote about them. Frank Norris outlined the problems caused to farmers by monopolistic railroad practices in *Octopus* (1901), and Ida Tarbell wrote an exposé on the Standard Oil Trust in 1904. Combinations thrived well into the twentieth century.

See also **Corporations and Big Business; Entrepreneurs; Regulation of Business.**

Bibliography

Chandler, Alfred D., Jr. *The Visible Hand: The Managerial Revolution in American Business.* Cambridge, Mass.: Belknap Press of Harvard University Press, 1977.
Lamoreaux, Naomi R. *The Great Merger Movement in American Business, 1895–1904.* Cambridge, U.K., and New York: Cambridge University Press, 1985.
Pusateri, C. Joseph. *A History of American Business.* Arlington Heights, Ill.: Harlan Davidson, 1984.
Roy, William G. *Socializing Capital: The Rise of the Large Industrial Corporation in America.* Princeton, N.J.: Princeton University Press, 1997.

CHARLES W. CAREY JR.

TURKISH EMPIRE IMMIGRANTS. See **Immigration and Immigrants**, subentry on **The Ottoman Empire and the Middle East.**

TWELFTH AMENDMENT. See **Constitutional Amendments**, subentry on the **Twelfth Amendment.**

U–V

UNDERGROUND RAILROAD The Underground Railroad offered freedom-seeking African American slaves assistance in escaping their masters. Fugitives, called passengers, traveled along a loose network of safe houses, called stations, operated by agents or station masters. Engineers or conductors transported the runaways from one station to another. Stockholders contributed food, clothing, and money.

Origin and Operation

Though linked most strongly with abolitionism in the first half of the nineteenth century, the Underground Railroad predates the organization of the American Anti-Slavery Society in 1833. In the era of the American Revolution, Quakers and others opposed to slavery provided covert support for refugees from the South's "peculiar institution." The runaway problem was significant enough that politicians from the slaveholding states argued for and got in 1793 a Fugitive Slave Law, which demanded the recapture of runaways.

Historians are unsure of the origin of the metaphor "Underground Railroad." Some point to the year 1831 when Tice Davids ran away, crossed the Ohio River near Ripley, Ohio, and took refuge with a white abolitionist. Frustrated in his attempt to recapture Davids, his owner complained that the slave had "gone off on an underground road." The story was repeated and, in an age when steam locomotives captured the popular imagination, the "underground road" became the "underground railroad" with a vocabulary of railroad terms such as depots, lines, spurs, stations, and conductors.

Underground Railroad routes ran through the northern states, with stations between ten and thirty miles apart. Some forty thousand fugitives are said to have made their way to freedom in Canada, particularly to present-day Ontario, known until 1841 as Canada West. There they set up colonies, such as Buxton and Dawn. Others settled in the northern states, where slavery had been abolished. Additional destinations included Spanish Florida, where some runaways were taken in by Native Americans, secluded areas of the South, such as the swamps and bayous where there were colonies of "maroons," or fugitive black slaves, and the unorganized territory of the West. Most of the fugitives who escaped to the free states originated from the border states of the upper South. Underground operations relied on runaways' making the most difficult part of the road to freedom by themselves, though some agents operated below the Mason-Dixon line. Most runaways were men between the ages of sixteen and thirty-five.

Freedom Seekers

In the post–Civil War decades, Union veterans and supporters of abolition elaborated the legend of the Underground Railroad by making it appear to be more of an organized effort than it actually had been. The folklore about daring rescues, secret tunnels, hidey-holes, and runaways transported by dark of night or covered under a load of straw in a farmer's wagon also tended to minimize the importance of Af-

Harriet Tubman *(far left)* **with Former Slaves She Had Helped Free.** The most famous of all the "conductors" of the Underground Railroad was Harriet Tubman (c. 1820–1913), herself an escaped slave. She brought an estimated three hundred slaves from the South to freedom in the North. © BETTMANN/CORBIS

rican Americans themselves. One of the most important black agents was the Philadelphian William Still, who for eight years secretly kept a record of his Underground Railroad labors while secretary of the Philadelphia Vigilance Committee. Published in 1872, with a second edition in 1879 and a third in 1883, Still's book contained anecdotes, letters, and excerpts from newspaper articles, and ran to nearly eight hundred pages. Jermain Loguen of Syracuse and Frederick Douglass of Rochester, both of New York State, and the legendary Harriet Tubman, known as the "Moses of her people," also belong to the cohort of the most famous black conductors and station masters. Tubman ran away from the Eastern Shore of Maryland in 1849 and thereafter made as many as nineteen raids into the southern states, bringing out an estimated three hundred slaves.

Tubman and others seeking freedom followed the North Star, which they could find in the sky by locating the constellation called the Drinkin' Gourd, or Big Dipper. Old slave spirituals such as "Steal Away," "Sweet Canaan," and "Go Down, Moses" were encoded with messages about escaping slavery. A large oral tradition developed about hairbreadth escapes and ingenious devices, such as the box in which Henry "Box" Brown of Richmond had himself shipped by a white friend in Virginia to the Phila-

delphia Vigilance Committee. This friend later served time in prison after being discovered attempting to ship another slave north. William and Ellen Craft escaped in 1848 by disguising Ellen with bandages as an invalid planter and masquerading as master and slave.

Some of the most famous white agents and station masters included Harriet Tubman's collaborator Thomas Garrett of Wilmington, Delaware, a Quaker who aided more than twenty-seven hundred slaves to freedom; Levi Coffin, also a Quaker, of Newport, Indiana, credited with aiding two thousand runaways; and John Rankin, a Presbyterian minister whose farm on the Ohio River was a heavily frequented station. Gerrit Smith's mansion in upstate New York at Peterboro was a well-known stop. Scores of white abolitionists provided shelter to runaways out of humanitarian motives as well as political ones, especially after the passage of the Fugitive Slave Act of 1850.

The Fugitive Slave Act of 1850

This law was designed to counteract the Personal Liberty laws northern states had passed to thwart southern slave catchers and mollify proslavery forces angered by the failure of the Supreme Court in *Prigg v. Pennsylvania* (1842) to provide a clear mandate that northern state officials must assist in the recapture of runaways. The Fugitive Slave Act authorized federal "commissioners" to issue warrants for the arrest of fugitives and prohibited interference with the rendition process. It also required private citizens to assist slave catchers.

Challenges to the Fugitive Slave Act involved fugitive slave resistance and rescues. On 11 September 1851, William Parker and other blacks fired on Edward Gorsuch and a party of slave catchers who had surrounded Parker's home near the village of Christiana, in southeastern Pennsylvania. Called the "Christiana Riot," the encounter resulted in Gorsuch's death and the arrest of thirty-six blacks. Parker and five others escaped to Canada. Abolitionists, including Jermain Loguen and Gerrit Smith, aided in the rescue of Jerry Henry, formerly of Missouri, on 1 October 1851 in Syracuse, New York. Rescuers stormed the police building, freed Henry, and spirited him to Canada. The arrest of Anthony Burns in 1854 in Boston sparked another contest with the Fugitive Slave Act. Abolitionists tried and failed to free Burns from jail, and authorities, with the aid of U.S. soldiers, shipped him back to Virginia. Friends would later purchase his freedom. In 1858 abolitionists living in Oberlin, Ohio, used force to free John Price. Known as the Oberlin-Wellington rescue, their actions led to imprisonment and a controversial trial that revealed how deeply divided the nation was. Among the Oberlin-Wellington rescuers was John A. Copeland Jr., one of the five black participants in John Brown's Harpers Ferry raid. The Emancipation Proclamation and the defeat of the South in the Civil War put an end to Underground Railroad traffic.

See also **Abolition and Antislavery; African Americans; Slavery.**

Bibliography

Blockson, Charles L. "Escape from Slavery: The Underground Railroad." *National Geographic* (July 1984): 3–39.

Finkelman, Paul. *Slavery in the Courtroom: An Annotated Bibliography of American Cases.* Washington, D.C.: Library of Congress, 1985.

———. "Story Telling on the Supreme Court: *Prigg v. Pennsylvania* and Justice Joseph Story's Judicial Nationalism." *Supreme Court Review* (1994): 247–294.

Gara, Larry. *The Liberty Line: The Legend of the Underground Railroad.* Lexington: University of Kentucky Press, 1961.

Siebert, Wilbur H. *The Underground Railroad from Slavery to Freedom.* New York: Macmillan, 1898. Reprint, New York: zArno, 1968.

Still, William. *The Underground Rail Road: A Record of Facts, Authentic Narratives, Letters, Etc.* Philadelphia: Porter and Coates, 1872. Reprint, Chicago: Johnson, 1970.

MILTON C. SERNETT

UNIONS See **Labor Movement,** subentry on **Unions and Strikes.**

UNITARIANISM AND UNIVERSALISM

The most significant channels for liberal currents in antebellum American Christianity, Unitarianism and Universalism developed as distinct religious movements in the early decades of the nineteenth century. Although Unitarians and Universalists shared a strong respect for the role of reason in religious faith and an opposition to certain traditional Christian, particularly Calvinist, tenets of faith, they represented differing strains of religious thought. Initially the two movements posed separate challenges to Calvinist orthodoxy and evangelical religion. But by the 1870s, as American religious culture grew more engaged with social action than with matters of faith, the denominations had become closely associated forms of American religious liberalism.

Unitarianism

Unitarianism grew from deep roots in the theology of seventeenth- and eighteenth-century Puritan New England, but it also strongly reflected the Enlightenment emphasis on the benevolence of God and the essential goodness of humankind. Unitarians were critical of many traditional Calvinist notions, especially the idea that God elected or predestined only a limited portion of the human family for salvation. Strongly asserting the freedom of the will, Unitarians accentuated the responsibility of the individual for his or her moral development and ultimate salvation.

The Boston ministers Charles Chauncy (1705–1787) and Jonathan Mayhew (1720–1766) held views that were precursors of those later termed Unitarian. By the opening of the nineteenth century the spread of such liberal ideas had begun to divide the ecclesiastical establishment of eastern Massachusetts, known as the Standing Order, and they played a primary role in its abolition by 1833. The 1805 election of the liberal Henry Ware (1764–1845) as Harvard's Hollis Professor of Divinity inaugurated the "Unitarian controversy" or schism between Calvinist orthodoxy and liberal opponents.

William Ellery Channing (1780–1842), minister of Boston's Federal Street Church, became Unitarianism's most distinguished intellectual figure. His landmark 1819 sermon, "Unitarian Christianity," openly rejected orthodox Christian trinitarianism. The founding in 1825 of the American Unitarian Association, an educational and publishing society, helped establish Unitarianism's national identity.

The important American literary and religious movement known as transcendentalism sprouted from Unitarianism in the 1830s and 1840s. Disenchanted by the institutional church and the biblically based Unitarianism represented by the Harvard professor Andrews Norton (1786–1853), transcendentalists elevated individual spiritual intuition. Leading transcendentalists included the renowned lecturer and essayist Ralph Waldo Emerson (1803–1882) and the minister and reformer Theodore Parker (1810–1860).

Seeking to fortify Unitarianism's institutional foundations, the New York City minister Henry Bellows (1814–1882) initiated the National Conferenceof Unitarian Churches in 1865. Together with the Harvard professor Frederic Henry Hedge (1805–1890) and the theologian James Freeman Clarke (1810–1888), Bellows led the influential Broad Church movement seeking wide institutional inclusiveness. Independent Unitarians who shared more radical commitments to scientific or humanistic ideals gathered in the Free Religious Association in 1867. Leading proponents of Free Religion included the educator Francis Ellingwood Abbot (1836–1903) and the New York City minister John White Chadwick (1840–1904).

Universalism

While Unitarianism initially developed within New England's Standing Order, Universalism originated among Baptists and other independent dissenters from the Congregational establishment in the late eighteenth century. Early Universalists sought to reconcile the Calvinist doctrine of God's sovereignty with the Enlightenment assertion of God's benevolence through the single idea of the universal election or salvation of humanity. Unitarianism departed from Calvinism in its focus on human freedom and capacity for moral growth. But early Universalism, which asserted that divine will and power were irresistible, retained a sensibility in many ways closer to traditional Calvinism.

The New England ministers John Murray (1741–1815), who is often termed the "Father of Universalism," Caleb Rich (1750–1821), and Elhanan Winchester (1751–1797) of Philadelphia were key framers of the late-eighteenth-century faith. But Hosea Ballou (1771–1852), a Boston minister and editor, became Universalism's most outstanding theologian and revered figure. His *Treatise on Atonement* (1805) laid the intellectual cornerstone of the movement and established its antitrinitarian aspect.

The brief Winchester Profession of Faith (1803) served as a statement of faith for most Universalists

---

Key Unitarian and Universalist Figures

William Ellery Channing (1780–1842)

Channing was the pivotal figure in the history of American Unitarianism. A graduate of Harvard College, Channing was minister of the Federal Street Church in Boston from 1803 until his death in 1842. The intellectual father of Unitarianism, Channing gave theological definition to the liberal wing of the New England Congregational establishment, the Standing Order. His 1819 sermon "Unitarian Christianity" was a manifesto for an independent Unitarian denomination and the moral theology that undergirded it. In the second half of the century Unitarians venerated Channing for his strong opposition to slavery as well as for his theological contributions to the foundation of the Unitarian denomination.

Hosea Ballou (1771–1852)

Born in rural New Hampshire and largely self-educated, Hosea Ballou became the most important theologian and honored elder statesman of the Universalist denomination. His 1805 *Treatise on Atonement* charted the course for the movement in the nineteenth century. Pastor of Boston's Second Universalist Church from 1817 until his death in 1852, Ballou was also an editor and Universalism's most skilled polemicist. He acquired a reputation for his wit and for his reasoned criticism of aspects of orthodox Calvinism. In testament to Ballou's contributions to their movement, Universalists in 1859 erected a large statue over his grave in Mount Auburn Cemetery in Cambridge, Massachusetts.

Olympia Brown (1835–1926)

A graduate of Antioch College and Canton (New York) Theological Seminary, Brown became in 1863 the first woman in the United States to be ordained with full denominational authority. Brown later became involved in the woman suffrage movement as a cofounder of the New England Woman Suffrage Association and as vice president of the National Woman Suffrage Association organized by Elizabeth Cady Stanton and Susan B. Anthony in 1869. Brown lived to witness the passage of the Nineteenth Amendment in 1920 and to vote in a national election.

Thomas Whittemore (1800–1861)

Whittemore was one of Universalism's most ardent defenders and the editor of *Trumpet and Universalist* magazine, a major denominational journal. Like many other antebellum Universalists, he was convinced that revivalists who threatened the unregenerate with endless punishment in hell promoted a form of insanity. Indeed, he was known to comb the records of the Massachusetts state lunatic asylum in Worcester, seeking cases of insanity stemming from "religious fanaticism," "religious excitement," and "dread of future punishment" (Miller, *The Larger Hope,* p. 269).

throughout the nineteenth century. It avowed a belief in biblical revelation, the assurance of ultimate salvation, and the duty to obey the moral law. The movement's unity was threatened in the 1830s by controversy over the doctrine known as restorationism, which posited punishment after death but before ultimate salvation. By the 1850s restorationism had all but eclipsed ultra-Universalism, the position that denied any retribution after death.

Widely regarded as dangerous heretics, Universalists were active antagonists of revivalism and evangelical religion in the first half of the nineteenth century. Led by controversialists such as the Boston editor Thomas Whittemore (1800–1861), proponents of Universalism were far less occupied with denominational organization and institution building than with doctrinal debate and religious polemic. In 1862 the Boston editor Thomas B. Thayer (1812–1886) published his systematic *Theology of Universalism*, which emphasizes the movement's biblical foundations. The national Universalist General Convention, organized in 1833, finally passed a comprehensive constitution in 1865.

Social Reform

Many Unitarians and Universalists were prominent figures in nineteenth-century social reform. The Unitarian Joseph Tuckerman (1778–1840) ministered to Boston's urban poor, and the Universalist prison reformer Charles Spear (1801–1863) opposed capital punishment. The Unitarian writer Lydia Child (1802–1880) and the Universalist editor Sylvanus Cobb (1798–1866) condemned slavery. The Universalist Horace Greeley (1811–1872), editor of the *New York Tribune*, was an active social reformer. Both denominations pioneered in the ordination of women. The first denominationally ordained woman in the United States was the Universalist Olympia Brown (1835–1926) in 1863, and Unitarians ordained Celia Burleigh (1826–1875) in 1871. Similarly, Unitarians and Universalists, including Brown, the Universalist Mary Livermore (1820–1905), and the Unitarian Julia Ward Howe (1819–1910), were leading advocates of woman suffrage.

Liberal Unity

In the late nineteenth century both denominations remained heavily concentrated in the Northeast, but Universalism had also established a presence in the Midwest and the South. By 1900, Unitarians claimed about 50,000 members in 455 churches, and Universalists had some 50,000 members in 1,000 separate societies. By that time increasing cooperation between the two movements already hinted at their

eventual union in 1961. Indeed, as the pragmatism of the social gospel came to dominate American religion in the last quarter of the century, Unitarians and Universalists grew closer to liberal Protestantism generally. The Harvard theologian Francis Greenwood Peabody (1847–1936) was a major Unitarian voice on social ethics. The belief in the ultimate salvation of every soul—the central Universalist tenet that had made even earlier Unitarians uncomfortable—evoked only mild controversy as theological concerns waned. Unitarians and Universalists gradually lost much of their distinctiveness and became complementary liberal wings of American Protestantism.

See also **Protestantism,** *subentry on* **Liberal Protestantism; Reform, Social; Religion,** *subentry on* **Religion in Nineteenth-Century America.**

Bibliography

Ahlstrom, Sydney E., and Jonathan S. Carey, eds. *An American Reformation: A Documentary History of Unitarian Christianity.* Middletown, Conn.: Wesleyan University Press, 1985. Documents with good theological background.

Cassara, Ernest, comp. *Universalism in America: A Documentary History.* Boston: Beacon, 1971. Major documents with good interpretive introduction.

Miller, Russell E. *The Larger Hope.* Vol. 1. *The First Century of the Universalist Church in America 1770–1880.* Boston: Unitarian Universalist Association, 1979. Standard institutional history of American Universalism.

Robinson, David. *The Unitarians and the Universalists.* Westport, Conn.: Greenwood, 1985. Concise history of both movements with biographies of major figures.

ANN LEE BRESSLER

URBANIZATION   See Cities and Urbanization.

UTAH   Utah overlaps three geographic regions—the Great Basin, the Colorado Plateau, and the Rocky Mountains—and it contains high-alpine to upper-Sonoran biomes. It is an arid area, but the confluence of regions of the Green and Colorado Rivers and the Great Salt Lake along the north-south-running Wasatch Range produces localized "oasis" environments that have long invited human land use. Archaeological evidence indicates human habitation of the area from 10,000 B.C. by the Desert Culture, and then cliff-dwelling Fremont and Anasazi agriculturalists from 400 B.C. to A.D. 1300. American Indian inhabitants have included the Ute, Navajo, Paiute, Shoshone, and Gosiute peoples. By the mid-1600s, Utah Indians engaged in trade with Spanish

New Mexico. Spanish *entradas* into Utah did not occur until the 1770s, and their failure to establish settlements limited their influence.

In the 1810s and 1820s, fur traders from Taos, New Mexico, trappers from the Northwest and Hudson's Bay companies, and Ashley-Henry trappers from St. Louis, Missouri, converged on northern Utah. Utah was the site of three of the first four fur-trade rendezvous, held between 1825 and 1840. Etienne Provost, Peter Skene Ogden, Jedediah Smith, Jim Bridger, and other early trappers pioneered routes across Utah, followed in the early 1840s by government explorer John C. Frémont and several California-bound overland companies (including the ill-fated Donner Party) who established wagon roads.

In 1847 the first Mormon pioneers entered Utah, settling in the valley of the Great Salt Lake. Fleeing persecution in Illinois for their political theocracy, cooperative economics, millennialism, polygamy, and clannish self-righteousness, members of the Church of Jesus Christ of Latter-day Saints (Mormons) set out to build their Kingdom of God in isolation. But the territory they settled passed from Mexican to American control in 1848, and thousands of California gold seekers rushed through Utah over the next few years. Nevertheless, the Mormon church president Brigham Young maintained firm theocratic control of Utah's society and economy.

Mormon settlement was highly organized. Young scouted the region for suitable settlement sites, most located on the eastern benches of the Wasatch Range, where water, arable land, and timber were readily available. He then organized companies of settlers with a variety of skills to establish town sites, located roughly a day's ride apart and laid out according to the "plat of the City of Zion"—a grid system oriented to the compass, centered on the church, surrounded by blocks of town lots, encircled by individual fields and pastures, all irrigated from a canyon stream. While Mormon communities were agricultural in nature, Young did establish specialty colonies to provide iron, coal, and other necessities, but he eschewed precious metal mining as contrary to good order and doctrine. One year before the transcontinental railroad neared completion at Promontory Summit, Utah, in May 1869, Young organized the United Order, a communal economic experiment to ensure Mormon self-sufficiency and insularity. Unsuccessful in the long run, the United Order marked Utah's economic development and highlighted the theocratic nature of Utah society.

The nature and location of Mormon communities brought settlers into competition with Indians for subsistence resources. In the wake of several conflicts with the Indians between 1853 and 1868, settlers and the federal government forced Utes onto the Uintah Reservation, while Shoshones and Paiutes were removed to Fort Hall, Idaho, or remained on the margins of Mormon communities. In 1881 the government relocated Colorado Utes to the Uintah and Ouray Reservation and it gave Navajos reserved land in southeastern Utah in 1884.

Utah became a territory as part of the Compromise of 1850, but was refused statehood six times between 1849 and 1890. The stumbling block was polygamy and Mormon political domination. In Utah, territorial appointees and non-Mormons found they had little power against the entrenched theocracy, and President James Buchanan sent an army to Utah in 1857 and 1858 to bridle the Mormon patriarchs. In the 1860s, Colonel Patrick Connor, commander of Fort Douglas, challenged Young's political control of Utah by precipitating a mining boom. Metal mining and smelting became a significant element of Utah's economy, but Connor and the non-Mormon miners who organized the Liberal Party (siding nationally with the Republicans) could not break the voting bloc of the Mormon-dominated People's Party. Women, given the territorial vote in 1870, ensured Mormon control.

In Washington, D.C., Republican lawmakers set out to destroy polygamy and reconstruct Utah as they had destroyed slavery and reconstructed the South. The Morrill Anti-bigamy Act (1862), the Edmunds Act (1882), and the Edmunds-Tucker Act (1887) attempted to disincorporate the Mormon church, disenfranchise and imprison polygamists, and break their political domination. In 1890, facing the ultimate demise of his church, the Mormon president Wilford Woodruff issued a manifesto renouncing the practice of polygamy, and in the following years he supervised a division of Mormon voters between the Democratic and Republican parties. In the face of this more apparent than real victory, President Grover Cleveland signed Utah's statehood proclamation on 4 January 1896, making Utah the forty-fifth state. Census takers counted 276,749 residents of Utah in 1900, up from 11,380 in 1850.

See also **American Indians**, *subentry on* **Wars and Warfare; Anti-Mormonism; Mormonism; Polygamy, Mormon.**

Bibliography

Alexander, Thomas G. *Utah, The Right Place: The Official Centennial History.* Salt Lake City: Gibbs Smith, 1995.
Arrington, Leonard J. *Great Basin Kingdom: An Economic History of the Latter-day Saints, 1830–1900.* Cambridge, Mass.: Harvard University Press, 1958.
Bigler, David L. *Forgotten Kingdom: The Mormon Theocracy in*

the American West, 1847–1896. Logan: Utah State University Press, 1998.

Papanikolas, Helen Z., ed. The Peoples of Utah. Salt Lake City: Utah State Historical Society, 1976.

Poll, Richard D., ed. Utah's History. Provo, Utah: Brigham Young University Press, 1978. Reprint, Logan: Utah State University, 1989.

Powell, Allan Kent, ed. Utah History Encyclopedia. Salt Lake City: University of Utah Press, 1994.

DAVID RICH LEWIS

UTOPIAN COMMUNITIES. See **Communitarian Movements and Groups.**

VACATIONS AND RESORTS Vacationing caught on rapidly in the nineteenth-century United States. By the 1820s, spa vacations were popular from Virginia to upstate New York. The establishment of the Catskill Mountain House in 1824 presaged the popularity of landscape tourism, and the opening of the Erie Canal in 1825 brought Niagara Falls within reach of the eastern seaboard. Resorts like Newport, Rhode Island, and Long Branch, New Jersey, established themselves as breezy retreats for privileged city dwellers, and wealthy southerners summered on the cool New England coast. At the same time, intrepid citizens of the new republic were venturing to Europe, where by the early 1840s, the American version of the grand tour was being conducted. A path was beaten from Liverpool to London, England, via Warwick and Stratford-upon-Avon—or, less directly, via the Lake District, the "[Sir Walter] Scott country," and Edinburgh, Scotland—then on to Paris or the Rhine, Switzerland, and Italy.

As the century progressed and railroads were built, the possibilities for vacationing expanded. The writer Washington Irving toured the prairies in 1832, and the future historian Francis Parkman retraced the Oregon Trail in 1846. By 1868 the Springfield newspaperman Samuel Bowles could take a large company of men and women to Colorado for a summer vacation in what he called "the Switzerland of America." Harriet Beecher Stowe, meanwhile, was already wintering in Florida in 1867. By the end of the century, the Florida East Coast Railroad had reached Miami, and the Southern Pacific was touting the advantages of the American Riviera in southern California.

Beginning in mid-century some vacationers seeking more active forms of recreation went camping, hiking, and canoeing in the lakes and mountains and later built "camps" in remote and scenic settings. One famous example was the camping trip in the Adirondacks undertaken in 1858 by a group of Boston-area notables, including Ralph Waldo Emerson, the poet James Russell Lowell, and the Harvard naturalist Louis Agassiz. Henry David Thoreau, it is said, refused to go when he heard that Emerson would be carrying a gun. In 1869 the one-time Connecticut clergyman William H. H. "Adirondack" Murray started a craze for healthy camping for men and women alike with the glowing and somewhat unrealistic accounts of a summer in the Adirondacks that made up his book Adventures in the Wilderness. Also beginning in the 1860s, groups of outdoor-minded men and women began banding together for excursions and exploring expeditions. The predominantly female Alpine Club of Williamstown, Massachusetts, was founded in 1863; the Appalachian Mountain Club followed in 1876; and the Sierra Club formed in 1892.

Vacationing was not limited to the wealthy. Over the course of the nineteenth century, vacations became central features of the lives of many Americans and cherished goals for many more. By mid-century, as Dona Brown points out in Inventing New England (1995), office workers, teachers, and shopkeepers were regularly taking a week or two in the country. By 1890 many retail workers enjoyed regular paid vacations. Vacation facilities naturally kept pace with the growing trend. Families of modest means could board in farmhouses or, later, in seaside boardinghouses. Those of a religious persuasion could attend one of the annual camp meetings at Ocean Grove on the New Jersey Shore or Cottage City on Martha's Vineyard.

Vacationing was important for many African Americans. In the antebellum period, slaves sometimes traveled with their owners, making contact with free blacks and learning of the possibilities for freedom. After the Civil War, elite African Americans visited resorts like Saratoga, New York, and Newport, Rhode Island, and established summer colonies within reach of major cities from Washington to Boston.

Vacationing was also a popular subject for painters and writers in the period. Thomas Cole, the founder of the Hudson River School of landscape painters, painted many vacation spots, including the Catskill Mountain House. The artist Winslow Homer depicted tourists in the White Mountains and coastal resorts from Maine to New Jersey. Emerson, Stowe, Mark Twain, and others published travel accounts, and aspiring amateurs imitated them. The "international theme" was a great success in fiction, beginning with works like Irving's The Sketch Book (1819–

1820) and Nathaniel Hawthorne's *The Marble Faun* (1860) and reaching its height with Henry James's *The American* (1877) and *Daisy Miller* (1879) and William Dean's *The Lady of the Aroostook* (1879). Regional writers, notably Sarah Orne Jewett, the author of *Deephaven* (1877) and *The Country of the Pointed Firs* (1896), also contributed to vacation fiction, as did popular writers like Edward Bellamy, with *Six to One: A Nantucket Idyl* (1890); Charles Dudley Warner, with *Their Pilgrimage* (1886); and the African American writer Emma Dunham Kelley, with *Four Girls at Cottage City* (1895).

See also **Grand Tour; National Parks; Recreation; Social Life.**

Bibliography

Brodhead, Richard H. *Cultures of Letters: Scenes of Reading and Writing in Nineteenth-Century America.* Chicago: University of Chicago Press, 1993.

Brown, Dona. *Inventing New England: Regional Tourism in the Nineteenth Century.* Washington, D.C.: Smithsonian Institution Press, 1995.

Sears, John F. *Sacred Places: American Tourist Attractions in the Nineteenth Century.* New York and Oxford: Oxford University Press, 1989.

Stowe, William W. *Going Abroad: European Travel in Nineteenth-Century American Culture.* Princeton, N.J.: Princeton University Press, 1994.

WILLIAM W. STOWE

VAUDEVILLE AND BURLESQUE

Vaudeville and burlesque were quite different forms of entertainment during much of the nineteenth century. As the century came to a close, however, their formats and their acts were more similar.

Vaudeville

Variety acts such as rope dancing and songs were popular as diversions between the acts of legitimate drama in America in the 1700s. Variety became a part of other forms of entertainment, such as minstrel shows and circuses, in the nineteenth century. Niblo's Gardens was a popular spot in the 1830s for summer variety shows. Variety acts were featured in honky-tonks and museums and helped train performers for big-time vaudeville.

Concert saloons also helped in the growth of vaudeville. They charged little or no admission but profited from the sale of food, drink, and tobacco, and they offered a range of variety acts. Concert saloons were enormously popular during the 1850s in cities across the United States.

Variety shows came to be known for their lewdness

Vaudeville Promotional Poster. Daring physical acts were a standard component of family-trade vaudeville. Photograph c. 1899. LIBRARY OF CONGRESS: PRINTS AND PHOTOGRAPHS DIVISION (THEATRICAL POSTER COLLECTION)

and by the 1860s were considered entertainment for men only. Tony Pastor, sometimes called the "father of American vaudeville," had performed in minstrel shows and circuses and was concerned, as were a few other impresarios, with cleaning up vaudeville. In 1865 his first theater, in New York City, discouraged drinking and attempted to achieve a family trade. His methods proved successful, and he opened larger theaters in 1875 and 1881, the latter on Fourteenth

Street, where he was immensely successful. His usual format was typical of vaudeville: songs, dances, comedy, circus acts, and drama.

The next step in what was now called vaudeville was taken by B. F. Keith. His training, like Pastor's, had been with the circus before he went into theater management in Boston. His Gaiety Musee (1885) offered continuous entertainment (two or three shows daily), which became popular across the country. He and his associate, E. F. Albee, soon controlled more than one hundred theaters.

Vaudeville expanded greatly during the years from 1890 to 1910. In 1900 the Vaudeville Managers Protection Association was organized in an effort to achieve a monopoly on vaudeville talent.

Burlesque

The American stage featured burlesques, or parodies, throughout the nineteenth century. Any serious event, literary work, or opera was fair game for burlesques. No sooner did a play open than it was burlesqued in another theater. The leading actor in burlesque was George L. Fox, well known for his takeoff on *Hamlet*. John Brougham was the leading U.S. writer of burlesques, and his satire of *Metamora* (1847) was probably the best burlesque of the century.

The composition of the typical burlesque show had three sources. The first influence was Lydia Thompson and her British Blondes, who came to the United States in 1868 and burlesqued myths, opening with *Ixion, Ex-King of Thessaly*. Their principal contribution to the genre was having women in tights play male roles, thereby establishing one element of the burlesque show. The second source in the development of burlesque, the honky-tonk, was coarse, vulgar, enormously popular entertainment played before a rowdy audience in a setting part saloon and part brothel. The final element was derived from the minstrel show, which had begun with the Virginia Minstrels in 1843. Composed of three parts, minstrel shows provided the basis for the structure of the burlesque show, which consisted of comic questions and answers with musical interludes, specialty acts, and a burlesque of a popular show. The interplay between the end men, Tambo and Bones, became the model for the interplay of burlesque comedians.

The three strands were woven together into the burlesque show by A. J. Leavitt in 1870. His Rentz-Santley Novelty and Burlesque Company used a female minstrel company combined with vaudeville acts and travesties. Belly dancers, also called cooch dancers, were added in about 1890 and remained a permanent part of the burlesque show. During the 1890s at least fifteen to twenty cities featured bur-

lesque shows. Attempts were made in 1900 to organize the various burlesque houses to exchange bookings and to protect against contract jumping.

See also **Circuses; Minstrel Shows; Recreation; Theater.**

Bibliography

Allen, Robert C. *Horrible Prettiness: Burlesque and American Culture*. Chapel Hill: University of North Carolina Press, 1991.

DiMeglio, John E. *Vaudeville U.S.A.* Bowling Green, Ohio: Bowling Green University Popular Press, 1973.

Gilbert, Douglas. *American Vaudeville, Its Life and Times*. New York: McGraw-Hill, 1940.

Green, William. "Strippers and Coochers: The Quintessence of American Burlesque." In *Western Popular Theatre*, edited by David Mayer and Kenneth Richards. London: Methuen, 1977.

Laurie, Joe, Jr. *Vaudeville: From the Honky-Tonks to the Palace*. Port Washington, N.Y.: Kennikat, 1972.

Zeidman, Irving. *The American Burlesque Show*. New York: Hawthorn, 1967.

JULIAN MATES

VERMONT   Over the course of the nineteenth century, Vermont moved from the fringes of the American experience, to the vortex of the market revolution, and finally to the margins of the American economy.

By 1800, Vermont's aboriginal people, the western Abenakis, had been reduced to small clusters living in the state's northern reaches. Though essentially unsettled until after the French and Indian War, Vermont quickly passed through its frontier stage; in the decade following its entry into the Union as the fourteenth state in 1791, it had the fastest-growing population of any state. Residents previously had been concentrated almost exclusively in the fertile river valleys that lie on either side of the Green Mountains, which bisect the state. Turn-of-the-century land pressures drove them north onto the marginal land in the state's hill country. By 1820 the state was widely settled and radically deforested.

These late arrivals inherited not only Vermont's unique revolutionary legacy but also the divisions that increasingly characterized the state. In the early 1800s extreme cultural tensions emerged between those who idolized the older yeoman republic and those with a commercial vision for the state. In addition, Vermont was divided by geography, bisected not only into east and west by mountains but also north and south by rivers.

The completion of the Champlain Canal in 1823, which linked Lake Champlain with the Hudson

River, concentrated trade to the south and opened Vermont to a period of tumultuous change. Vermont farmers had previously exported limited amounts of such commodities as timber, potash, maple products, and wheat. The opening of the canal touched off what was known as the "sheep craze"; in large numbers farmers shifted to wool production. That transition initiated an era of intense political, religious, and reformist passion. The Anti-Mason Party experienced its greatest success in Vermont, which elected an Anti-Mason governor, William Palmer, four consecutive times and cast its 1832 electoral votes for that party's presidential candidate. Repeated bursts of revivalist fervor, which peaked in 1831, supplied the breeding ground for many prominent evangelists of the era. By 1854, the many areas of Vermont life toward which reformist fervor had been directed, such as temperance, education, and criminal incarceration, had been largely supplanted by abolitionism. Vermont immediately became a devoutly Republican state upon that party's formation in 1854 and remained so throughout the century. Vermonters served and died in the Civil War at rates among the highest of all Union states.

By the start of the Civil War, those farmers who remained in Vermont had almost wholly shifted from wool to dairy products. Many had not stayed behind, however; the single most important characteristic of the state from the 1830s on was a steady population shift. Over the rest of the century, Vermont's total population remained essentially static, but almost every small town dramatically lost population. Those losses were only counteracted by the growth of a few industrial centers—such as Burlington, Rutland, Barre, and Springfield—engaged notably in quarrying, textiles, and machine-tool production.

As the century ended, Vermont was characterized by a profound ambivalence. Prominent Vermonters, almost wholly drawn from the ranks of industry, fretted about a decline in the state's rural districts, yet Vermont emerged as a potent symbol to an industrializing nation of lost rural values and virtues. That idealized image attracted turn-of-the-century tourists, but hardly reflected the great changes the state had undergone in the previous century.

See also Masons; New England.

Bibliography

Barron, Hal. *Those Who Stayed Behind: Rural Society in Nineteenth-Century New England.* New York: Cambridge University Press, 1984.

Morrissey, Charles T. *Vermont: A Bicentennial History.* New York: Norton, 1981.

Roth, Randolph. *The Democratic Dilemma: Religion, Reform, and the Social Order in the Connecticut River Valley of Vermont, 1791–1850.* New York: Cambridge University Press, 1987.

PAUL M. SEARLS

VETERANS ORGANIZATIONS

American veterans of its wars did not seek comprehensive organization until the middle of the nineteenth century. The Revolutionary War had fostered the Society of Cincinnati (instigated in 1783 by General Henry Knox), an exclusive group restricted to officers and their heirs that proved unpopular with Americans concerned with a virtuous and democratic republic. The War of 1812 and the Mexican War produced veterans, but little serious organization. Aging veterans of the War of 1812 formed state societies and sponsored a national convention nearly forty years after the conflict. Opening their membership to all ranks, these associations promoted their members' service, and stirred renewed interest in both the War of 1812 and the War for Independence. They sought, with mixed success, land bounties, pensions, and federal funds to commemorate battlefields.

Mexican War officers modeled their Aztec Club of 1847 after the exclusive Society of Cincinnati, but the club did little beyond providing a social outlet for its members. After Reconstruction, Mexican War veteran organizations began appearing in various states, especially in the South, seeking pensions from the federal government. But they, like veterans of wars before them, failed to create any serious national affiliation.

The Civil War produced the most veterans in American history. Northerners and southerners who had fought sought ways to come together at local, state, and national levels. Advancements in communication and transportation enabled former Civil War soldiers to congregate with greater frequency and from greater distances than any previous generation of veterans. The largest and most successful of all the veteran organizations of the nineteenth century was the Grand Army of the Republic (GAR). There are at least two versions of its founding in 1866: One account attests that the GAR was the brainchild of two Illinois veterans, one a chaplain, the other a doctor, who simply missed the camaraderie of camp. The other account, which is apparently more accurate, maintains that the GAR was founded as a political club to mobilize Union veterans in support of the Radical Republicans and their agenda for Reconstruction. Either way, the GAR quickly became firmly associated with the Radical Republicans, playing a prominent role in supporting the party through the 1870s. There was even fear that armed members of the GAR would march on Washington, D.C., during the impeachment crisis and forcefully remove President Andrew Johnson from office.

The GAR had a pseudomilitary structure and secret ritual of initiation, but its first posts lacked unity and conformity. Membership fluctuated through the 1870s, and by the late 1870s numbers dropped as a result of a variety of factors, including the introduction of an unpopular grade system, distaste for the GAR's partisanship, bad economic times, and a general lack of interest in the war. Posts dissolved and numbers declined, but the GAR did not entirely vanish. In the 1880s it was revived, and by 1890 the GAR reached its highest numbers, about 400,000 members; still only a fraction of the entire number of Union veterans. Yet its national influence was dramatic, especially during the final two decades of the century. During the 1880s, the GAR shifted its focus to funding orphanages and soldiers' homes and to its successful campaign for federal pensions. By the 1890s the GAR actively advocated its own brand of patriotism that included promoting Memorial Day celebrations, military preparedness, and encouraging schools to use certain preapproved history textbooks and fly the American flag. The GAR became perhaps the most powerful political lobby of the late nineteenth century. In 1884, former GAR commander-in-chief John A. Logan ran as Republican James G. Blaine's running mate for president. Logan used his GAR connections to bring strong veteran support to Blaine, who did not serve in the army during the Civil War. However, Logan's addition to the ticket was not enough to beat the Democrat Grover Cleveland, the only elected president between 1868 and 1900 who was not a GAR member.

From its founding, the GAR opened its membership to all Union veterans of the war, including blacks, but talk constantly arose about segregation and complete racial exclusion, particularly among southern posts. Women and sons of veterans formed auxiliary groups—the Ladies of the Grand Army of the Republic (1886) and the Sons of the Union Veterans of the Civil War (1881)—although women's status was considered of secondary importance, and sons were viewed as not entirely worthy of full-fledged membership. In 1898 the GAR refused to admit Spanish-American War veterans into the fold, mainly because this would have included some former Confederates. The GAR also contested pensions for Mexican War veterans because of the large number of former Confederates who would be eligible.

Though none proved as successful as the GAR, other Union veteran organizations included the Military Order of the Loyal Legion, the Society of the Army of the James, the United States Soldiers and Sailors Protective Society, and the United Service Society. Many of these associations had both fraternal

Veterans Reunion. Members of the Grand Army of the Republic, the national organization of Union Civil War veterans, convened regularly after the end of the Civil War through 1949. Their 1892 encampment was held near the Washington Monument in the national capital. LIBRARY OF CONGRESS

and political purposes, seeking jobs and bounties for their members, sponsoring banquets and conventions, and providing help for the disabled and needy. Some restricted their eligibility for membership to officers or prisoners of war; others limited membership to men with active service records.

Confederate veterans too sought to organize, but not until several decades after the war ended. During Reconstruction, former Confederates refused to participate in Memorial Day and Fourth of July celebrations sponsored by the GAR, and many veterans joined the secretive Ku Klux Klan, disguising themselves as ghosts of the Confederacy and terrorizing southern blacks and southern Republicans. By the 1880s and 1890s, interest in Confederate organizations grew as the mythology of the "Lost Cause" evolved and spread. A coalition of state veteran groups from Louisiana, Tennessee, and Mississippi created the United Confederate Veterans in 1889 in New Orleans, and the UCV quickly spread throughout the South. By the early 1900s it is estimated that one-third of all living Confederate veterans belonged to the UCV. The United Daughters of the Confederacy was formed in 1894 and the Sons of Confederate Veterans in 1896, and along with the UCV they promoted the basic tenets of the "Lost Cause." They built monuments, orphanages, and soldiers' homes, celebrated Confederate Memorial Day, and petitioned southern legislatures and school officials to teach their version of the past, which acknowledged little about the evils of slavery or the humiliation of defeat.

By the 1890s, active veterans groups could be found throughout the country. Confederate and Union veterans sponsored shared reunions and encouraged reconciliation, and veterans played a prominent role in endorsing the prevalent nostalgia and nationalism that marked the decade.

The Spanish-American War produced a new wave of veterans. When the GAR resisted their admittance, men who had served in Cuba and the Philippines started their own groups, including the American Veterans of Foreign Service (1899) and the Army of the Philippines. These two bodies merged in 1913 to become the Veterans of Foreign Wars.

See also **Civil War,** *subentry on* **Remembering the Civil War; Clubs,** *subentry on* **Fraternal Societies and Clubs; Holidays; Military Service; Republican Party; South,** *subentry on* **The New South after Reconstruction.**

Bibliography

Davies, Wallace Evan. *Patriotism on Parade: The Story of the Veterans' and Hereditary Organizations in America, 1783–1900*. Cambridge, Mass.: Harvard University Press, 1955.

Dearing, Mary R. *Veterans in Politics: The Story of the GAR*. Baton Rouge: Louisiana State University Press, 1952.

Foster, Gaines M. *Ghosts of the Confederacy: Defeat, the Lost Cause, and the Emergence of the New South*. New York: Oxford University Press, 1987.

McConnell, Stuart. *Glorious Contentment: The Grand Army of the Republic, 1865–1900*. Chapel Hill: University of North Carolina Press, 1992.

Piehler, G. Kurt. *Remembering War the American Way*. Washington, D.C.: Smithsonian Institution Press, 1995.

LESLEY J. GORDON

VICTORIANISM The Victorian concept of character has exerted a powerful influence upon Americans for about three hundred years. Even the coolest late-twentieth-century gangsta rapper had internalized Victorian ideas, values, and behavior patterns to a large extent. Victorian values implicit in messages from parents, teachers, ministers, friends, relatives, and the media have permeated American society, demonstrating that the basic elements of a culture are transmitted early in an individual's development and change very slowly.

Victorian Character

The home was the vital institution of Victorian America. Loving, middle-class mothers and fathers sought to inculcate in their children a quality they called "character." Character connoted some different traits for males and females, but its attainment was crucial for middle-class respectability.

An analysis of hundreds of statements about character from a great variety of Victorian sources shows that a person of character was expected to be dependably self-controlled, punctual, orderly, hard working, conscientious, sober, respectful of other Victorians' property rights, and ready to postpone immediate gratification to achieve long-term goals. Most important, such a person prayed at least daily to a usually friendly God, believed that the Bible was literally true, and was oriented strongly toward home and family.

Victorianism in the United States was basically the culture of an ethnic and religious group. The largely British American ethnic group that dominated American society between 1830 and 1890 excluded members of certain other ethnic groups from acceptance as persons of character, even when members of those groups exhibited Victorian character traits. African Americans and Mexican Americans, most of whose ancestors had lived in America longer than the ancestors of the majority of British Americans, were among those regarded as "foreign." So were virtually all Asians, Jews, and Catholics.

The Victorian concept of character originated at least as far back as the sixteenth century. According to R. H. Tawney, by the seventeenth century a secularized Puritan creed had developed, and at its core lay an "ideal of personal character and conduct to be realized by the punctual discharge of public and private duties" (*Religion and the Rise of Capitalism*, p. 12).

William Dean Howells, a realist who understood his fellow Victorians as well as anyone, wrote *A Modern Instance* in 1882. In this novel, which Howells considered his best, the most perceptive character states: "Character is a superstition, a wretched fetish. Once a year wouldn't be too often to seize upon sinners whose blameless life has placed them above suspicion, and turn them upside down before a community, so as to show people how the smoke of the Pit had been quietly blackening their interior. That would destroy character as a cult" (p. 629). The most significant aspect of this statement lies not in Howell's cynical allegation of widespread hypocrisy, a common charge in any era. Rather its significance is in the confident assumption that readers would understand that a quality called character obliged Victorians to live an outwardly blameless life.

The Alcotts

The fashion in which parents inculcated Victorian values in their children was described best by Bronson Alcott, father of Louisa May Alcott, whose family members were the models for the main characters in her *Little Women* (1868). Bronson Alcott, whose chief object was to instill in his children all the virtues of Victorian character, tested his educational theories on his young daughters and recorded the results in great detail. In a typical exercise (recorded in his unpublished journal) he left an apple on the wardrobe in the room occupied by Louisa and her older sister Anna, who were about two and a half and four years of age respectively. As he left the room Bronson Alcott led this conversation:

> Anna, should little girls take things that do not belong to them without asking their fathers and mothers?
> No, they should not.
> Do you think that you shall ever do so—take an apple, or such thing if you should see one, without asking for it?
> No, father.
> And shall you, Louisa?
> No, father. ("Researches on Childhood," pp. 156–164)

After dinner, Alcott found the apple core on the nursery dining table. The two girls quickly confessed that, after a period of restraint, they had rushed for

A Rebel Against Victorianism. An unidentified woman defies Victorian convention by smoking, drinking beer, and revealing her petticoats. Self-portrait, c. 1896. LIBRARY OF CONGRESS

the apple and devoured it while telling each other that they must not. Alcott explained to the girls that he had left the apple as a trial and he would exact no punishment. He expressed his disappointment, which was the most severe penalty he could have inflicted on his adoring daughters.

The next day the same scene was reenacted. This time the girls withstood the intense temptation for an entire morning before ravishing the apple in the afternoon. Nevertheless, both father and mother were pleased. With aid from the most powerful tool available for the purpose—manipulation through affection by a close-knit team of parents—their daughters' characters were developing (Coben, *Rebellion against Victorianism*, pp. 11–12).

Experiences like these prepared Louisa May Alcott for a career as Victorian America's foremost chronicler of the lives of boys, girls, young men, and young women. Prior to the publication of *Little Women*, Louisa May Alcott confided in her diary that if the novel succeeded it would be because it was "simple and true, for we really lived most of it" (Cheney, *Louisa May Alcott*, p. 36). *Little Women* quickly became one of the Victorian era's best-sellers. All of Alcott's novels and stories dealt with the struggles of parents to create homes in which their children would develop Victorian character.

Victorians believed that what parents left undone or found impossible to accomplish, a good man or woman might still influence in the adult. In most cases women were the expected agents of cultural conformity. Victorians assumed that women were naturally more virtuous and could teach purity to men. Louisa May Alcott's nobler women sometimes carried out their obligations in a fashion that twentieth-century readers found objectionable. Meg, the first of the "little women" to marry, took advantage of her wedding day to extract from her friend Laurie, then a college student who as a boy had been raised to enjoy fine wine, a pledge of perpetual abstinence from alcoholic beverages. Similar incidents occurred in Alcott's other novels.

Women's Sphere

Alcott's novels show the author's sensitivity to the contradictions inherent in the roles assigned to women and girls during the Victorian era. Hers may be the clearest fictional depictions of the cooperative form of marriage urged by American marriage manuals after the mid–nineteenth century. Yet Alcott also described the thwarting of emotional and intellectual growth in young women expected to carry heavy responsibilities as partners in marriage and child rearing.

In *Little Women* Meg's mother gives Meg advice about her husband that mimics the advice offered in the most popular contemporary manuals: "Don't shut him out of the nursery, but teach him to help in it. . . . The children need him; let him feel that he has a part to do, and he will do it gladly and faithfully, and it will be better for you all" (Alcott, *Little Women*, p. 397). However, Alcott's ideal cooperative home did not leave every individual free to choose among all possible roles. When Meg counsels her own son indirectly by praising one of his schoolmates, she declares: "Now there's a girl after my own heart. Pretty, well-bred, educated and yet domestic, a real companion as well as a helpmate for some good and intelligent man" (Alcott, *Jo's Boys*, p. 28).

Catharine Beecher and her sister Harriet Beecher Stowe, in their volume of domestic advice, *The Amer-*

ican Woman's Home (1869), declared in a related spirit, "It is far more needful for children that a father should attend to the formation of their character and habits . . . than it is that he should earn money to furnish them with handsome clothes and a variety of tempting foods" (p. 299).

Unfortunately, in that harshly competitive age the overwhelming majority of fathers, even those of the middle class, worked extremely long hours to provide their families with food, clothing, and shelter. As always, a large gap divided the ideal and reality.

A Resilient Tradition

Henry Seidel Canby, the editor of the *Saturday Review of Literature* and a professor of literature at Yale University, attempted to recapture for readers in the 1930s his impressions of Wilmington, Delaware, during his adolescence in the late 1880s and early 1890s. He recalled:

> Our houses moved with felt rhythms, not set, not identical, yet so sensible that what one felt first in a strange home was the tempo of life there. We [children] were away for brief intervals only, at home long enough to be harmonized, and even the heads of families, whose working hours were incredible in their length, seemed never to lose their conditioning by the home. If business and the home lived by different ethical standards, as was commonly said, it may be because the worker was a different man outside the rhythm of the house. And women lived almost exclusively within. (*The Age of Confidence*, p. 54)

He believed that something valuable from his youth had been lost. "There has been no such certainty in American life since" (p. 79).

Unquestionably, American Victorianism became more flexible between the mid–nineteenth century and the end of the twentieth century. The extreme restraint and confidence of Alcott and Canby's world declined among most of the middle class. It is a tribute to the resiliency of Victorianism and to the satisfactions it provided that these shifts occurred without seriously threatening its essence or its predominance. The powerful assaults launched against Victorianism during the twentieth century, especially in the 1920s, the 1960s, and the early 1970s, failed to offer acceptable substitutes for the gratifications it provided. During the mid- and late-1990s, a survey of over five hundred conservative, largely fundamentalist Protestants, Catholics, and Orthodox Jews revealed a high correlation between fervent religious beliefs and adherence to Victorian character traits.

During the twentieth century, hard-working, religious, family-oriented Latin Americans and eastern Europeans immigrated to the United States. The majority of Americans also possessed these characteristics, guaranteeing that Victorian ideas, values, and behavior patterns would persist in the United States.

See also **Character; Civilization; Domestic Life; Home; Manners.**

Bibliography

Alcott, Louisa May. *Jo's Boys*. Boston: Little, Brown, 1914.
———. *Little Women*. Boston: Little, Brown, 1946.
Beecher, Catharine E., and Harriet Beecher Stowe. *The American Woman's Home; or, Principles of Domestic Science*. New York: J. B. Ford, 1869.
Canby, Henry Seidel. *The Age of Confidence*. New York: Farrar and Rinehart, 1934.
Cheney, Ednah D., ed. *Louisa May Alcott: Her Life, Letters, and Journals*. Boston: Little, Brown, 1928.
Coben, Stanley. *Rebellion against Victorianism: The Impetus for Cultural Change in 1920s America*. New York: Oxford University Press, 1991.
———. *Relationships between Strong Religious Beliefs and Political, Social, Economic, and Moral Beliefs and Behavior*. Forthcoming.
Howe, Daniel Walker, ed. *Victorian America*. Philadelphia: University of Pennsylvania Press, 1976.
Howells, William Dean. *A Modern Instance*. Boston: James R. Osgood, 1882.
Tawney, R. H. *Religion and the Rise of Capitalism*. New York: Harcourt, Brace, 1974.

STANLEY COBEN

VIGILANTES   Vigilantism, like lynching, is a label applied to situations where crowds outside the law punish a person accused of some deviant behavior. Lynchers and vigilantes both justify themselves as legitimate expressions of popular sovereignty, but vigilantism usually suggests a higher degree of organization than lynching. In some cases vigilantes organize extralegal "courts," complete with "jurors," a "judge," and "counsel," while lynching crowds are often thought to act more spontaneously, with little or no internal organization.

Nineteenth-century vigilantism began in the wake of the American Revolution. With the close of hostilities, veterans and their families flooded the Trans-Appalachian frontier. These settlers regularly resorted to extralegal means to punish persons they believed guilty of crimes, explaining that the absence of strong government forced them to act outside the law. Many Revolutionary War veterans had used extralegal means against Tories during the war, and some writers have reported that Trans-Appalachian vigilantes continued wartime practices.

The most famous vigilante episodes before the Civil War came in 1835. On 6 July, Vicksburg, Mississippi, residents hung five gamblers for threatening the public peace. At about the same time, in nearby Madison County, whites organized a vigilante court and hung whites and some blacks for plotting a slave insurrection. The slave panic behind both of these episodes can be traced to implausible rumors that John A. Murrell (c. 1804–c. 1850) had organized a vast slave conspiracy to rebel against whites. Whites organized vigilante patrols up and down the Mississippi River valley.

In the 1840s and 1850s vigilantism was rampant. Missouri "slickers" whipped or "slicked" outlaws. In Illinois, hundreds of Massac County residents acted as regulators, forming a ruling council to make important decisions. Nebraska settlers practiced "club law," meaning they formed clubs to combat claim jumpers and horse thieves. In 1851, San Francisco merchants and others operated as a "committee of vigilance" for one month, hanging four men and forcibly expelling twenty-eight more. In 1856, six to eight thousand San Franciscans joined a reorganized committee, this time claiming to fight political corruption. These vigilantes did not disband for three months, until they had put in place a political organization that controlled the city for a decade.

Vigilantism continued through the Civil War. In 1862 residents of northern Texas formed a "citizen's court" to try and hang persons charged with collaborating with the Yankees. In 1864, Montana vigilantes executed at least twenty-two men, including Sheriff Henry Plummer. The men were accused of being "road agents" or highway robbers, but the evidence against Plummer seems thin. Another of the hanged men, a Mexican named Joe Pizanthia, committed no crime other than to criticize the vigilantes, and the vigilantes exhibited gruesome bigotry when they used a cannon to go after Pizanthia, whom they called "the Greaser." After shelling Pizanthia's house with a howitzer, the vigilantes shot and then hanged his body.

During Reconstruction, conservative white southerners embraced vigilantism to resist federal power and Republican rule. First organized as a social club in Pulaski, Tennessee, probably in May or June 1866, the Ku Klux Klan turned violent with the advent of congressional Reconstruction. In March 1867 the U.S. Congress passed the first Reconstruction Act, dividing the South into military districts. The authors of this legislation meant to unseat state governments established by Presidents Abraham Lincoln (1809–1865) and Andrew Johnson (1808–1875), and to extend the right of suffrage to African Americans. This congressional plan to enfranchise blacks led enraged white southerners to make the Ku Klux Klan into a vigilante organization. The Klan probably did not appear in other southern states until the spring of 1868, after Republicans acted to rewrite state constitutions. Klan vigilantes only briefly acted under any kind of central direction, and for most of this period the Klan operated with little or no central direction. Local Klansmen decided for themselves whom to attack, taking votes at regular meetings. Congress passed tough laws to control Klan violence and President Ulysses S. Grant (1822–1885) dispatched troops to arrest Klansmen. Although the U.S. Supreme Court weakened these laws, the Klan subsided under pressure from Grant.

For many Americans, the idea that communities could, and should, organize themselves to punish "crime" outside the courts remained just as strong at the end of the nineteenth century as at the beginning. In the 1880s and 1890s, vigilantes often called themselves "white caps" and tried to regulate morality, including punishing abusive or immoral husbands. In 1892, Wyoming cattlemen hired regulators to attack settlers they accused of rustling. At the same time, the lynching of African Americans reached new levels of savagery and brutality. The novelist Owen Wister (1860–1938) and other western writers sought to distinguish "civilized" western vigilantism from "savage" southern lynching, but at the end of the nineteenth century, antilynching campaigns by Ida B. Wells (1862–1931) and others had done much to associate the vigilante impulse with racial violence.

See also **Ku Klux Klan; Lynching.**

Bibliography

Bancroft, Hubert Howe. *Popular Tribunals*. 2 vols. San Francisco: The History Company, 1887.

Dimsdale, Thomas J. *The Vigilantes of Montana*. Norman: University of Oklahoma Press, 1953. First published as a series of newspaper articles in 1865.

Mather, R. E., and F. E. Boswell. *Hanging the Sheriff: A Biography of Henry Plummer*. Salt Lake City: University of Utah Press, 1987.

Trelease, Allen W. *White Terror: The Ku Klux Klan Conspiracy and Southern Reconstruction*. Westport, Conn.: Greenwood, 1979.

CHRISTOPHER WALDREP

VIOLENCE The pattern of violence in nineteenth-century America was uneven. Some areas, such as rural New England, were quite peaceful. Others, such as the mining frontier, were unusually violent. Social and ethnic differences were also apparent. Young, unmarried, lower-class workers were at high risk, as were American Indians, Irish immigrants, and black and white southerners.

Patterns of Violence

During the antebellum years, acts of public and private violence—dueling, brawling, eye gouging, child beating—were most common in the slaveholding states and territories. It is no coincidence that the most memorable characters in Mark Twain's novel *The Adventures of Huckleberry Finn* (1884) are either violent, like the feuding Shepherdsons and Grangerfords; fantasists of violence, like Tom Sawyer; or victims of violence, like Huck Finn. Huck is nearly killed by his drunken "Pap," who is later shot dead.

The everyday cruelties of slavery contributed to the southern climate of violence, as did the weakness and unpredictability of legal sanctions, the habit of carrying knives and guns, and the popularity of corn liquor. The southern tradition of honor, of prompt physical response to any slight or challenge, was another important factor. The first European settlers of the southern and midlands frontiers—displaced Cavaliers, Scots, Scots-Irish, north Britons, and Savo-Karelian Finns—all came from cultures that stressed the imperatives of masculine honor and skill in using deadly weapons. Their nineteenth-century descendants continued the cultural imperatives, leaving a legacy of insult-triggered fights and killings that has not entirely disappeared.

The other primary zone of violence was the nonagricultural frontier. Frontier regions settled by farm families or religious colonists like the Mormons were peaceful, although raids by Indians (or outlaws dressed as Indians) did occur. But frontier regions populated by soldiers, cowboys, hunters, miners, lumberjacks, and other itinerant workers had very high levels of violence relative to both farming regions and eastern cities. From 1878 to 1882 the homicide rate of Bodie, California, a mining boom town, was more than thirty times that of Philadelphia.

Conflict between the encroaching Anglo-Americans and the indigenous Indian and Hispanic peoples was an obvious and recurring source of frontier violence. Yet even in the absence of such clashes, life on the nonagricultural frontier was relatively dangerous. Activities such as prospecting or cattle ranching attracted mostly young, single men, the most volatile group in any population. Young, single women were scarce in the early years. Miners and cowboys had to delay or forgo marriage, which ordinarily operates as a restraint on male behavior. What they had instead of wives and children were prostitutes and faro dealers. Vice institutions became flash points of violence.

Though the region's reputation for gaudy violence was preserved in such popular entertainments as "Buffalo Bill" Cody's Wild West, launched as a touring show in 1883, the era of saloon shootouts and Indian clashes was essentially over by 1890. The Battle of Wounded Knee fought that year was more fiasco than denouement, the fate of the Indians having already been settled.

If a common thread runs through violence in all regions and subcultures, it is alcohol. Nineteenth-century America was full of self-destructive drunks, from quarreling teamsters to reeling Indians cheated of their furs for a few gallons of adulterated whiskey. Drinking impaired judgment and gave rise to accidents and clumsy offenses, always dangerous when men carry weapons and are sensitive about reputation. Drunks blundered into fights. No homicide scenario was more common than two men in a crowded saloon who had been innocent of any intention of murder before they began drinking.

Drinking was an important source of domestic violence. Alcohol did not automatically turn men into brutes, as the prohibition stereotype had it. It was, however, a common source of marital discord. Wives, concerned for their children, resented the pay spent on drink and the time spent in saloons. Husbands resented the resentment, and retaliated against their wives' "nagging" or other interference with masculine prerogatives. "We had trouble," explained one battered Boston woman in 1880, "because I would not get him beer."

Chronological Trends in Violence

Statistics for homicide and other violent crimes are patchy for the first half of the century. Studies of northeastern cities show an increase during the 1840s and 1850s, a rise partly due to the influx of impoverished Irish immigrants. The reputation of the Irish for drinking and fighting was deserved. New York City coroners' records for 1865 and the period 1871–1873 show that an average of 42 percent of the slain were Irish-born, who made up just 21 percent of the city's population in 1870.

The absorption of millions of men into the Union and Confederate Armies temporarily reversed the mid-century urban crime wave. Men busy killing one another at Antietam and Gettysburg were constrained from mischief in the streets of Boston and Charleston. Out-of-uniform violence surged again after 1865, as hardened veterans returned home or headed west. (One observer likened former Confederates who took up ranching in Texas to "TNT dressed in buckskin.") A combination of factors made the 1860s and 1870s the most violent decades of the century: the war and its aftermath, depredations and racial terrorism against the freedmen, the rapid expansion of the frontier and ensuing conflicts with

Indians, the depression and labor turbulence of the mid-1870s, widespread attacks on Chinese immigrants, and the proliferation of handguns, including war-surplus revolvers.

Much of the violence in the 1860s and 1870s had a political—or, what amounts to the same thing, a racial—edge. Mostly Irish and Democratic, New York City draft protesters made known their displeasure at the prospect of fighting in a Yankee Protestant war for black freedom by staging the worst riot in American history in July 1863. At least 105 people were killed, including eleven blacks, eight soldiers, and two policemen. The harassment and murder of indentured Chinese laborers, culminating in a full-scale riot in San Francisco in 1877, was also fundamentally political in character. White, particularly Irish, workers viewed Chinese "coolies" as threats to their jobs. Their attacks persisted even after 1882 legislation excluded further legal Chinese immigration. Twenty-eight Chinese, fleeing for their lives, were gunned down like antelope in the Rock Springs Massacre in Wyoming Territory in 1885. Their deaths caused an international episode; ultimately the United States government had to pay more than $147,000 in damages. Though sixteen white men were arrested for the murders, none was ever convicted.

By the early 1880s, however, the overall level of violence in the nation was at last beginning to fall. The winding down of the Indian wars and the increase in the number of women, children, and older persons brought a measure of peace to the West. Southerners—impoverished, honor-conscious, and racially divided—still suffered from more than their share of murders, but the homicide rate was beginning to decline in northern and western industrial cities. In Boston it fell from about 4 per 100,000 in the late 1870s to just 2 per 100,000 at the turn of the century. The growing number and professionalism of uniformed police helped, as did the decelerating growth of education and industry. The historian Roger Lane has argued that the proliferation of schools and factories, with their bells and whistles, their knuckle-rapping teachers and gimlet-eyed foremen, instilled discipline in children and sobriety in workers. This sort of regimentation helps explain the general decline in violent crime in the late Victorian era, both in the United States and in other industrial nations. However, groups with fewer opportunities for education and steady work, most notably African Americans, were less socially disciplined and hence more prone to criminal violence. This essentially circular problem would become ever more apparent as the nineteenth century turned into the twentieth and millions of southern blacks poured into the ghettos of northern and western cities.

See also **American Indians,** *subentry on* **Wars and Warfare; Anti-Catholicism; Anti-Mormonism; Assassinations; Dueling; Lynching.**

Bibliography

Ayers, Edward L. *Vengeance and Justice: Crime and Punishment in the Nineteenth-Century American South.* New York: Oxford University Press, 1984.

Courtwright, David T. *Violent Land: Single Men and Social Disorder from the Frontier to the Inner City.* Cambridge, Mass.: Harvard University Press, 1996.

Ferdinand, Theodore. "The Criminal Patterns of Boston since 1849." *American Journal of Sociology* 73 (1967): 84–99.

Gurr, Ted Robert, ed. *Violence in America.* Volume 1: *The History of Crime.* Newbury Park, Calif.: Sage, 1989.

Lane, Roger. *Violent Death in the City: Suicide, Accident, and Murder in Nineteenth-Century Philadelphia.* Cambridge, Mass.: Harvard University Press, 1979.

McPherson, James M. *Battle Cry of Freedom: The Civil War Era.* New York: Oxford University Press, 1988.

DAVID COURTWRIGHT

VIRGINIA   England's first effort at transplanting British society to take root in North America was nearly two hundred years old by the dawn of the nineteenth century. By then, settlers from Europe and Africa and their descendants had largely supplanted the aboriginal residents. Only in the eighteenth century had settlements moved into the area west of the Blue Ridge Mountains. East of that barrier, the white and black populations grew to great numbers, nearly equal by the American Revolution. Virginia began the nineteenth century at the center of the American Republic, midway between New England and Georgia and preeminent by many measures.

In the nineteenth century a three-way struggle for political power, economic well-being, and social autonomy characterized Virginia. Race, class, and region divided blacks from whites, free people who owned slaves from those who did not, and people dwelling east of the Blue Ridge from those to the west. Commercial farmers—slave owners from the eastern region until the 1860s—dominated politics in Virginia at both ends of the century, but they had a preponderant say in national politics only in the early decades. Nondominant white households, especially in the western half of the state, contended for political power and economic advantage. Black Virginians, most of them slaves until the 1860s, carried out their own challenges to planter domination.

Challenges to Dominance, 1790–1860

Virginia entered the new United States as the most populous state, with the largest black population, the most total residents, and (if the Maine District is subtracted from Massachusetts) the largest white population. Virginians with American Indian ancestry, whether slave or free, were typically counted either black or white. In 1790 whites numbered 747,610, free blacks 12,866, and slaves 292,627.

Between 1790 and 1860 new states like Kentucky, Ohio, and Mississippi absorbed large numbers of Virginians, and the Virginia population grew slowly while other states surged ahead. Some slave owners moved with their slaves south and west to other slave states. Larger numbers converted excess slaves to cash by shipping them to the cotton South. Non-elite white Virginians moved in large numbers to the Ohio Valley and beyond. Smaller numbers of free blacks, like John Mercer Langston, and escaped slaves, like Henry "Box" Brown, made their way to the North. In 1860 white Virginians numbered 1,047,299, free blacks 58,154, and slaves 490,865. Only the number of whites in the western part of the state had grown appreciably in the preceding three decades. In seventy years Virginia's percentage of white Americans dropped from 14 to 4, and its percentage of U.S. slaves dropped from 42 to 12. Those various demographic developments were central to the social, economic, and political history of Virginia in the nineteenth century.

Political developments of the first quarter-century forecast a future different from the one that actually emerged, for the years of the Virginia dynasty had no sequel. Thomas Jefferson, a Virginian elected president in 1800, served two terms, as did the next two presidents, Virginians James Madison and James Monroe. Two other native Virginians, William Henry Harrison and John Tyler, served as president in the nineteenth century, but they shared a single term, and neither was elected to the presidency from Virginia.

During Madison's presidency and the War of 1812, southern New Englanders found themselves so disaffected by Virginia political leaders and Republican Party policies that delegates to the Hartford Convention in the winter of 1814–1815 demanded constitutional amendments to curtail Virginia's power in national politics. If those amendments failed, the New Englanders threatened secession. As it happened, the 1810s proved a high-water mark in the Old Dominion's power in national politics, and Virginia left the Union in 1861 to join the Confederacy. Much as the generation of 1776 broke away from the British Empire when outside power threatened local prerogatives, the generation of 1861 declared its political independence from the United States. Unlike the revolution of 1776, however, that of 1861 failed.

Black Virginians challenged planter domination from early to late in the century. Near Richmond in

The Confederate Capital Under Union Siege. The James River was a conduit for vessels such as the steamboat *Monohansett (center)*, used as a dispatch vessel by the Union general Ulysses S. Grant. Photograph c. 1864. © THE MARINERS' MUSEUM/CORBIS.

August 1800 Gabriel Prosser conspired to attack the city, seize arms, and ignite a larger slave uprising, though slave informants and torrential rains averted the rebellion. Nat Turner's bloody slave uprising in Southampton County in August 1831 led white Virginians in the 1832 legislature's lower house to a ferocious debate over slavery's future. When slaves escaped north, planters sought a stronger Fugitive Slave Act (1850) and then feared for its weak enforcement in hostile hands. During the Civil War black Virginians escaped behind Federal lines and even took up arms against the Confederacy. Black men secured political rights in the late 1860s and, during the Readjuster insurgency of the early 1880s, became a majority in a coalition that briefly dominated Virginia politics.

Middling and landless white farmers, mostly from west of the Blue Ridge, sought a greater say in state politics and policymaking. In a constitutional convention in 1829–1830, they demanded, but failed to obtain, universal white manhood suffrage and a legislative apportionment that would give them a louder voice. In 1832, in the wake of Nat Turner's rebellion, they led the charge against slavery but were narrowly turned back. In a second constitutional convention in 1850–1851 they obtained a wider suffrage and a reapportionment. But the new constitution also restricted their power to tax planters' slaves and thus obtain enhanced revenues with which to fund education and transportation for their part of the state.

Civil War and Emancipation

Revolution caught Virginia in the years between 1859 and 1870. John Brown's raid at Harpers Ferry, Virginia, in October 1859, and the support for Brown that his execution evoked in the North, led whites in the eastern half of the state to perceive an equation between the small abolitionist movement and mainstream public opinion in the North. Abraham Lincoln's election as president on the new Republican Party's antislavery platform did not itself drive Virginia out of the Union. But his refusal to agree to new safeguards for slavery, together with his response to the attack on Fort Sumter, led the state convention to adopt secession.

A history of political and cultural differences, heightened by western Virginians' frustration over their fiscal powerlessness, had enormous consequences during and after the secession crisis of 1860–1861. After the eastern counties took Virginia out of the Union in April 1861, the northwestern third of Virginia broke

The Readjusters

The Readjuster movement challenges conventional assumptions about late-nineteenth-century southern politics, as class trumped race for a time, and conventional periodization of southern history, as Reconstruction can be said to have continued in or come to Virginia after 1877. Republicans controlled the state constitutional convention of 1867–1868 and took the governorship in 1869, but they did not control the legislature. Through the 1870s the Democratic Party insisted on full payment of a huge public debt left over from the prewar period, even at the cost of seeing the public schools wither for lack of funding.

Challenging the ruling Democrats' power and policies, a biracial coalition—Republicans and disaffected Democrats; the majority black, a large minority white—took power, winning both houses of the legislature in 1879 and the governorship in 1881. Later than the 1877 cutoff traditionally taken by historians to mark the end of Reconstruction, black political power flourished for a time in a biracial coalition in Virginia.

The new regime "readjusted" the public debt, slashing payments on it, and expenditures for public schools surged. The legislature also eliminated the connection between a poll tax and voting rights, and it established Virginia Normal and Collegiate Institute (present-day Virginia State University) for black Virginians. The Readjuster legislature sent William Mahone to the U.S. Senate for the 1881–1887 term, and Mahone took his seat as a Republican. The Readjusters' policy initiatives persisted long after their loss at the polls in 1883 (when Democrats exploited a racial incident in Danville to stampede white voters). In 1888 the Petersburg area elected a black candidate for Congress, John Mercer Langston, a former president of Virginia Normal and Collegiate. Seated only after a long contest in the House, he was not present when Congress in 1890 passed what might well be considered the final Reconstruction measure, the Second Morrill Act.

away and formed West Virginia. The new state supplied tens of thousands of Federal soldiers, although it also provided Confederate troops.

Virginia brought the Confederacy manpower, materials, and military leadership, including Robert E. Lee. After four years of war, the great gamble ended in defeat. Dead were slavery, the Confederacy, and many thousands of Virginia soldiers. Much of the fighting had taken place on Virginia soil, and tens of thousands of encamped soldiers, no matter the color of their uniforms, had devastated the countryside, much as the burning of Richmond had ravaged the capital city.

The conflict did not end when the war did, but the western region proved far weaker in state politics than it would have had West Virginia not gone its separate way. Reconstruction brought the enfranchisement of black men, and former slaves served in the state legislature until late in the century. A new school system established in 1870 made space for black children and white children alike, though in separate schools. Implementing the new federal land-grant system of higher education, the legislature divided Virginia's Morrill Act funds, two-thirds to a new white school, Virginia Agricultural and Mechanical College (founded in 1872, present-day Virginia Polytechnic Institute and State University), and one-third to a black school, Hampton Normal and Agricultural Institute (founded in 1868, present-day Hampton University).

In the 1880s the Readjusters established a public college for black Virginians near Petersburg (Virginia Normal and Collegiate Institute, present-day Virginia State University), and their successors established a school in Farmville (present-day Longwood College), the first of four institutions designed to train white women to teach in the public schools. By World War I each of the four great divisions of the state had such a school—two east of the Blue Ridge (one north and one south of the James River) and two west of it.

A Whitening of Virginia Society and Politics

Meanwhile a collection of economic and demographic developments in the 1880s and 1890s, including a resumption of out-migration, altered east and west. As railroad construction and the burgeoning demand for coal and timber began their transformation of Appalachia, many black Virginians and western white Virginians moved into the emerging coalfields and timberlands of southwestern Virginia and West Virginia.

Even larger numbers of black Virginians—long before the "Great Migration" of the 1910s through the 1960s—moved north to Washington, Baltimore, Philadelphia, and New York. That migration was well under way in the 1880s. The 1900 census counted 1,192,855 whites in Virginia (the limited change since 1860 reflected the loss of West Virginia) and 661,329 blacks. Between 1900 and World War II the black population figure stagnated while the white figure doubled.

In a constitutional convention in 1901–1902 Virginia's traditional elite resumed control over state

Virginia After the Civil War. Industrialization in the New South did little to relieve the region's widespread rural povery, which affected both blacks and whites, as shown in a photograph taken in Stony Creek, Virginia, by George Baker in 1886. LIBRARY OF CONGRESS: PRINTS AND PHOTOGRAPHS DIVISION

politics. A poll tax and other measures achieved their purpose of circumscribing the political activities of both wings of the Readjuster coalition. The electorate of the early twentieth century looked remarkably similar to that of the late eighteenth. Though a system of public schools had taken root after the Civil War, far greater state and local funding went into schools for white easterners than for any other group. Slavery did not return under the new regime, but segregation, disfranchisement, and sharecropping left black Virginians with only a down payment toward social, economic, or political freedom. Into the 1960s eastern blacks and western whites would continue to have little say in, and to see little benefit from, state programs.

Virginia's journey through the nineteenth century revealed enormous conflict and great short-term change, but it also exhibited long-term continuity. Virginia remained largely rural, agricultural, and dependent on tobacco production. The cataclysm of the 1860s brought an end to the legal enslavement of some Virginians by others, and it broke the commonwealth into two states. Joining the Confederacy re-flected a perception by dominant Virginians that their place had become insufficiently secure in the United States. Yet in the postwar years Virginia's planter families of 1860 retrieved their dominance within the state, and their children and grandchildren entered the twentieth century still in the saddle.

See also **Appalachia; Civil Rights; Civil War,** *subentries on* **Battles and Combatants, The Home Front in the South, Consequences of the Civil War, Remembering the Civil War; Confederate States of America; Education,** *subentry on* **School Segregation; Fugitive Slave Laws; Harpers Ferry and John Brown; Reconstruction,** *subentry on* **The South; Sectionalism; Slavery; South, The; States' Rights; Voters and Voting;** *subentries on* **White Male Franchise, Black Voters before the Civil War, Black Voters after the Civil War; West Virginia.**

Bibliography

Crofts, Daniel W. *Old Southampton: Politics and Society in a Virginia County, 1834–1869.* Charlottesville: University Press of Virginia, 1992.

Dew, Charles B. *Bond of Iron: Master and Slave at Buffalo Forge.* New York: Norton, 1994.

Jordan, Ervin L., Jr. *Black Confederates and Afro-Yankees in Civil War Virginia*. Charlottesville: University Press of Virginia, 1995.

Lowe, Richard. *Republicans and Reconstruction in Virginia, 1856–70*. Charlottesville: University Press of Virginia, 1991.

Moger, Allen W. *Virginia: Bourbonism to Byrd, 1870–1925*. Charlottesville: University Press of Virginia, 1968.

Shade, William G. *Democratizing the Old Dominion: Virginia and the Second Party System, 1824–1861*. Charlottesville: University Press of Virginia, 1996.

Stevenson, Brenda E. *Life in Black and White: Family and Community in the Slave South*. New York: Oxford University Press, 1996. A study of antebellum Loudoun County, Virginia.

Varon, Elizabeth R. *We Mean To Be Counted: White Women and Politics in Antebellum Virginia*. Chapel Hill: University of North Carolina Press, 1998.

Wallenstein, Peter. *Virginia Tech, Land-Grant University, 1872–1997: History of a School, a State, a Nation*. Blacksburg, Va.: Pocahontas, 1997.

PETER WALLENSTEIN

VIRGIN ISLANDS Because of their strategic location at the eastern end of the Caribbean Sea and their relationship to the approaches of a possible canal across Central America, the three Virgin Islands, long possessions of Denmark, attracted the attention of various American presidential administrations during the second half of the nineteenth century. In October 1867 President Andrew Johnson and Secretary of State William H. Seward negotiated a treaty to purchase the islands for $7.5 million. After a devastating hurricane hit the islands, Congress refused to appropriate the money, and the treaty was never considered in the Senate. The United States tried twice more to acquire the islands. The first of these initiatives came in 1893, during the administration of Grover Cleveland. The second was in 1902, when Theodore Roosevelt, reflecting the growing apprehension about German military influence in the Western Hemisphere, again asked Denmark to cede the islands. On that occasion the Danes declined to approve the treaty.

In late 1916, with tensions between Washington and Berlin rising just before American entry into World War I, acquisition of the harbor at St. Thomas to block a possible German presence in the region took on a new urgency. On 4 August 1916 Secretary of State Robert Lansing signed a treaty, which the U.S. Senate and its legislative counterpart in Denmark approved. For the sum of $25 million, the Virgin Islands became an American possession on 31 March 1917. Their fate was a minor episode in the period of U.S. expansionism.

See also **Expansion.**

Bibliography

Campbell, Charles S. *The Transformation of American Foreign Relations, 1865–1900*. New York: Harper and Row, 1976.

Tansill, Charles Callan. *The Purchase of the Danish West Indies*. Baltimore: Johns Hopkins Press, 1932.

LEWIS L. GOULD

VOTERS AND VOTING

[This entry includes four subentries:
White Male Franchise
Black Voters before the Civil War
Black Voters after the Civil War
The Women's Vote]

WHITE MALE FRANCHISE

In 1800 the young American Republic had experienced one revolution and was entering the first stages of a second. The nation had gained independence, the states had adopted republican constitutions, and the new federal system established by the U.S. Constitution and implemented by the Federalist administrations of Presidents George Washington and John Adams was secure. Yet the election of 1800, in which Thomas Jefferson was elected president, heralded a second wave of change that was both social and political. Jefferson's followers, who characterized the Federalists as a coalition of aristocrats and moneyed interests, successfully mobilized the "common people" in jurisdictions where they could vote. Known as the Democratic-Republicans, they comprised the nation's first popular political party.

The "Revolution of 1800" produced its most pronounced change in voting and suffrage. Over the next half-century the right to vote was inexorably expanded in state after state until, by the outbreak of the Civil War in 1861, it included the vast majority of white male adults. This change occurred almost entirely on the state level.

Conversely, during the same period various groups were denied the franchise. Nascent efforts by women to attain voting rights were summarily rebuffed, many immigrant groups were denied the vote, and free African Americans throughout the nation were increasingly excluded from the voting rolls.

Voting Practices in the Nineteenth Century

Throughout much of the nineteenth century voting was a public act. At the century's start voting *viva voce*, by voice, was still widespread, and the secret ballot was largely unknown. Particularly in rural areas and on the frontier, a person's choice was known to his neighbors as a point of honor. Voters gathered at polling places on election day and called out their choices to election officials, who duly recorded the results. The use of paper ballots, introduced after the Revolution, increased throughout the century, until Kentucky became the last state to abandon voice voting for local and state elections in 1892. Differing state requirements led to a wide array of ballot practices. In some states the parties provided ballots, often printed in distinctive colors and emblazoned with the party symbol, such as the Democratic rooster, for the benefit of nonliterate voters. In others electors were required to sign their ballots, while in still other instances ballots were sealed in envelopes for secrecy.

Aside from early experiments, voter registration by the states was unknown until midway into the century. Election clerks usually knew would-be voters personally, especially in rural areas and the backcountry. Persons known to election officials as accepted members of the community were generally allowed to cast a ballot whether or not they met formal qualifications. Personal identification worked less well in the growing cities, however, where multiple voting at different polling places remained a regular phenomenon until registration was introduced in the 1850s. This kind of fraud even crossed state lines until 1845, when Congress established a national presidential election day. Later extended to elections for the U.S. House of Representatives, the federal election day was set for Tuesday after the first Monday of November in even-numbered years.

Elections were administered on the local level, in towns in New England and in counties throughout the rest of the nation, and each jurisdiction provided a single polling place, typically the county courthouse. Larger population centers were usually organized into precincts. Distance from the polls often influenced voter turnout, as voters who faced a long trip to the polls voted in fewer numbers. Weather also influenced participation, so state and local election days were scheduled for the autumn months, when travel was easy, the harvest had been gathered, and farmers had more free time, or in winter prior to the spring thaw and the arrival of "mud time," when primitive roads were impassable.

Early Expansion of the Franchise

The U.S. Constitution was largely silent on the question of voting qualifications. Under the Constitution the president was chosen by an electoral college, while senators were selected by state legislatures. This left the House of Representatives as a popularly elected chamber, chosen by "the people." As to voting qualifications, Article I, section 2 of the Constitution states that "the electors in each State shall have the qualifications requisite for electors of the most numerous branch of the State Legislature." While voting rights were thus left to the states, the framers clearly intended that the House electorate be as large as possible. As James Madison wrote in *The Federalist* (1788), number 57: "The electors are to be the great body of the people of the United States. They are to be the same who exercise the right in every State of electing the corresponding branch of the legislature of the State" (1961 ed., p. 384).

Estimates of the number of eligible voters in the early eighteenth century vary widely, ranging between 6 percent and 50 percent of free white adult males. This proportion had already undergone considerable expansion by the beginning of the nineteenth century. Religious restrictions aimed at Catholics, Jews, and members of dissident Protestant groups, such as Baptists, had been largely repealed following the Revolution.

Another prevalent restriction, the freehold requirement by which voters were required to own a piece of land, usually twenty-five or fifty acres, or other property of a certain value in order to vote, was also easing at the time. Between 1788 and 1805 six states either modified or abandoned the freehold requirement substituting proof of tax payment or a poll tax. Simultaneously new states had even more liberal voting requirements. Vermont extended voting rights to all "freemen" when it joined the Union in 1791, and Kentucky established a similar qualification upon admission in 1792. Tennessee (1796), Ohio (1803), and Louisiana (1812) were admitted with land ownership or tax qualifications, but no state that entered the Union after Mississippi (1817) imposed freehold requirements on its voters. Voters in every state were required to be free white males who had attained twenty-one years of age, a common feature that remained unchanged throughout the nineteenth century.

The Drive for Universal Suffrage

Pressures for an expanded franchise accelerated in the decades following the War of 1812, as the United States continued to evolve socially. Beyond the Appalachian Mountains a frontier society developed that emphasized independence, individualism, and the equality proclaimed in the Declaration of Independence. Colonial habits of social deference that lingered in the East were explicitly rejected. This new model also strongly influenced small landholders, tenant farmers, and city dwellers in more settled parts of the country, where many had only limited

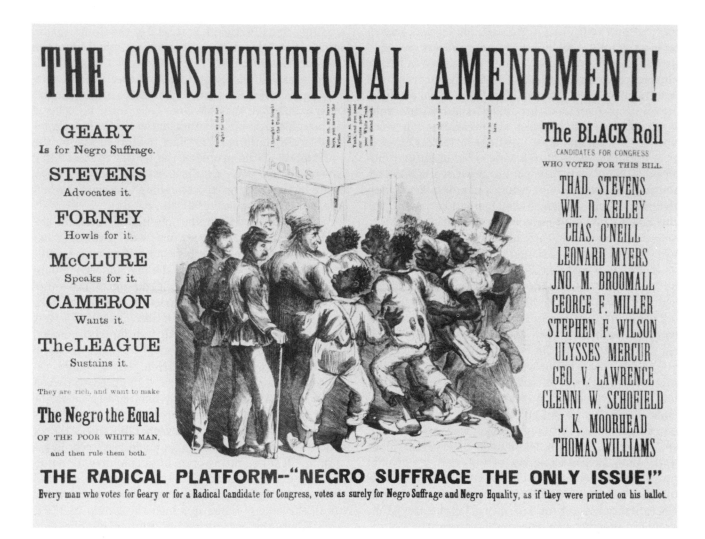

THE CONSTITUTIONAL AMENDMENT!

GEARY
Is for Negro Suffrage.

STEVENS
Advocates it.

FORNEY
Howls for it.

McCLURE
Speaks for it.

CAMERON
Wants it.

The LEAGUE
Sustains it.

They are rich, and want to make

The Negro the Equal
OF THE POOR WHITE MAN,
and then rule them both.

The BLACK Roll
CANDIDATES FOR CONGRESS
WHO VOTED FOR THIS BILL.

THAD. STEVENS
WM. D. KELLEY
CHAS. O'NEILL
LEONARD MYERS
JNO. M. BROOMALL
GEORGE F. MILLER
STEPHEN F. WILSON
ULYSSES MERCUR
GEO. V. LAWRENCE
GLENNI W. SCHOFIELD
J. K. MOORHEAD
THOMAS WILLIAMS

THE RADICAL PLATFORM--"NEGRO SUFFRAGE THE ONLY ISSUE!"

Every man who votes for Geary or for a Radical Candidate for Congress, votes as surely for Negro Suffrage and Negro Equality, as if they were printed on his ballot.

"The Constitutional Amendment!" A poster, created in 1866, opposing the Fourteenth Amendment. The text warns that whites who elect radical Republican candidates to Congress are, in so doing, voting for suffrage and equality for blacks. LIBRARY OF CONGRESS: BROADSIDE COLLECTION

voting rights or were unable to vote at all. Jefferson's mass political party, the Democratic-Republican Party, enshrined the frontier principles and crushed the less organized, more conservative Federalists in the decades following the election of 1800. The common people ultimately triumphed with the election of Andrew Jackson to the first of two terms as president in 1828. A military hero who rose from humble beginnings, Jackson championed the democratic ideal and gave his name to the age and the phenomenon of Jacksonian Democracy. The Whigs emerged as a new opposition party in the 1830s and, forced by necessity to compete for the votes of the common citizens, emulated Jackson's devotion to democratic ideology despite reservations.

Opponents of universal suffrage defended the established order on several grounds. They upheld revolutionary-era restrictions, calling voting a gift bequeathed by the founding fathers that contributed to "balanced" government, in which wealthy interests shared power with the less well-off. They also warned against the empowerment of "king numbers," claiming that the landless and the urban poor had a lesser "stake" in society, were ill-educated and prone to mob instinct, and were incapable of giving dispassionate consideration to public questions. They were fighting a rearguard action, however, as one state after another moved toward voting rights for all white adult males.

The decade of the 1820s was characterized by several dramatic developments in the movement to broaden the franchise. Three of the most important states in the Union, Massachusetts, New York, and Virginia, dealt with the question in constitutional conventions held during the decade. The results in each case were different and were incomplete successes for universal suffrage, but all three spurred the national trend. The 1820 Massachusetts convention—called to consider amendments to the Constitution of 1780—included John Adams, Supreme Court Justice Joseph Story, and Daniel Webster among its members, and all three defended the status quo. Although the Massachusetts convention concerned itself primarily with other issues, it did approve Amendment III, which expanded the franchise and established a revised voting formula that combined age, residence, citizenship, and payment of a token poll tax. The New York convention met a year later, in 1821, and reflected the shift of power from the Hudson River valley to newly settled western lands and New York City. The state's revolutionary-era constitution had long been criticized for its two-tier voting requirement. Renters and small freeholders were eligible to vote only for the lower house of the state legislature, while large landowners and the well-off constituted a separate electorate for the state senate and the governor. Once again reformers gained only a partial victory. The convention eliminated dual electorates but retained the requirements of a tax payment and militia service. Five years later a constitutional amendment finally implemented universal suffrage. Like the Massachusetts convention, Virginia's 1829–1830 convention numbered the commonwealth's most distinguished citizens among its members, including James Madison, James Monroe, John Randolph, and John Marshall. It pitted the small farmers of the western and mountain counties against the aristocratic Tidewater establishment that had dominated Virginia since before the Revolution and arrived at a compromise formula that extended voting rights to leaseholders and heads of households who paid taxes. A modified freehold requirement remained in force until 1851.

Perhaps the most dramatic incident of this era was Dorr's War in 1842, when disfranchised Rhode Islanders rebelled unsuccessfully against the state's restrictive colonial-era freehold clause. The governor called out the militia to restore order, but the state subsequently adopted a new constitution reducing the freehold requirement.

During the 1840s the steady stream of European immigration into the United States expanded, spurred by famine in Ireland and political upheavals in Germany. Several of the more severely affected eastern states sought to deter immigrant voting, particularly among Irish Catholics, by establishing more restrictive literacy and residency requirements. Western and southern states sought to attract settlers by offering noncitizens the right to vote once they pledged to become U.S. citizens. By 1875 twenty-two states and territories had adopted some form of noncitizen voting.

Women and Minorities

While voting rights were gradually secured by most white male adults, few members of ethnic minorities and almost no women were allowed to vote in the nineteenth century. In its 1776 constitution, New Jersey required that its electors be "inhabitants of this Colony, of full age" rather than the more common formulations of "men," "freemen," or "male inhabitants." Some women thus voted regularly in New Jersey until an 1807 constitutional amendment restricted suffrage to "male citizen[s]." During its first stirrings, the women's rights movement held a convention in Seneca Falls, New York, in 1848. The convention issued the first call for female suffrage when it resolved on 19 July that "it is the duty of the women of this country to secure to themselves their sacred right to the elective franchise." Vehemently opposed by many interests, the woman suffrage movement made little headway until late in the nineteenth century, although in 1869 the Wyoming Territory became the first major jurisdiction to extend voting rights to women.

Free African Americans, who constituted about 8 percent of the black population in the 1790 census, were at that time specifically denied the right to vote in Georgia, South Carolina, and Virginia. During the first half of the nineteenth century both free and slave states moved to prohibit blacks from voting. Among the original states, Connecticut, Delaware, Maryland, New Jersey, North Carolina, and Pennsylvania excluded free blacks between 1792 and 1835, while every new state that joined the Union prior to the Civil War, except Maine, Vermont, and Tennessee, specifically barred blacks from voting. In the 1830s Tennessee, following North Carolina's lead, also prohibited black suffrage. Rhode Island granted blacks equal suffrage after Dorr's War. The other New England states had no statutory prohibition, but New York maintained restrictive property ownership and tax requirements that applied exclusively to African Americans. Blacks voted in some parts of Ohio, Wisconsin, and Michigan during this period, notwithstanding state law. Participation in these instances depended on the level of support for emancipation and black equality in different communities.

Throughout the century most states excluded Native Americans on the grounds that they were neither citizens nor white. In some cases, however, Indians who had been assimilated into the local community, many of whom were of mixed ancestry, were allowed to vote if they met standard qualifications. Asians, few in number outside California, were denied citizenship and voting rights, but Latino residents of Texas and the areas ceded to the United States by Mexico in 1848 who adopted American citizenship were widely admitted to the franchise.

The Civil War and the Fifteenth Amendment

At the outbreak of the Civil War in 1861, most states retained a number of minor requirements, such as residency, literacy, citizenship, and a poll tax. Some restrictions were aimed at immigrants, but universal white male suffrage had been attained for all practical purposes.

As the war drew to a close in 1865 Congress proposed the first of three amendments that incorporated Union war aims into the Constitution. The Thirteenth Amendment, ratified in 1865, abolishes black slavery, and the Fourteenth, ratified in 1868, defines citizens as "all persons born or naturalized in the United States." The Fifteenth Amendment, ratified in 1870, states, "The right of citizens of the United States to vote shall not be denied or abridged by the United States or by any State on account of race, color, or previous condition of servitude."

For the first decade following the war the U.S. government enforced the provisions of the Fifteenth Amendment, defending black voting in the South through military occupation. Following the end of Reconstruction in 1876, however, conservative state governments established throughout the region gradually restricted African American suffrage and extinguished it by the 1890s.

As the century drew to a close women increasingly demanded the right to vote. While successfully rebuffed in the East, the suffrage movement enjoyed successes in the Rocky Mountain states, where Colorado, Utah, and Idaho joined pioneering Wyoming in enacting woman suffrage by 1900.

Other late-nineteenth-century innovations included widespread adoption of the secret or Australian ballot, establishment of voter registration systems, and strengthened residence requirements. Although these reforms helped reduce election fraud, they also had the effect of making it difficult if not impossible for recent arrivals, transients, and the poor to vote. At the end of the century the Populist and Progressive movements also began their campaigns for popular election of U.S. senators, a struggle that successfully culminated in the Seventeenth Amendment in 1913.

See also **Civil Rights; Constitutional Amendments,** *subentry on* **Thirteenth, Fourteenth, and Fifteenth Amendments; Elections,** *subentry on* **Campaigns and Elec-** tions; **Immigration and Immigrants,** *subentry on* **Anti-immigrant Sentiment; Jeffersonian Era; Politics,** *subentry on* **Party Organization and Operations; Race Laws; Reform, Political.**

Bibliography

Chute, Marchette Gaylord. *The First Liberty: A History of the Right to Vote in America, 1619–1850*. New York: Dutton, 1969.

De Grazia, Alfred. *Public and Republic: Political Representation in America*. New York: Knopf, 1951.

Madison, James. "The Popular Basis of the House." In *The Federalist*, Alexander Hamilton, James Madison, and John Jay. 1788. Reprint, Cambridge, Mass.: Belknap Press of Harvard University Press, 1961.

Mason, Alpheus Thomas. "Expanding the Base of Popular Power." In *Free Government in the Making: Readings in American Political Thought*. 3d ed. New York: Oxford University Press, 1965.

McGovney, Dudley Odell. *The American Suffrage Medley: The Need for a National Uniform Suffrage*. Chicago: University of Chicago Press, 1949.

Peirce, Neal R. "The Right to Vote in America." In *The People's President: The Electoral College in American History and the Direct Vote Alternative*. 1st ed. New York: Simon and Schuster, 1968. This chapter was eliminated from the 1981 revised edition.

Peterson, Merrill D., ed. *Democracy, Liberty, and Property: The State Constitutional Conventions of the 1820s*. Indianapolis, Ind.: Bobbs-Merrill, 1966.

Porter, Kirk Harold. *A History of Suffrage in the United States*. 1918. Reprint, New York: AMS, 1971.

Wilentz, Sean. "Property and Power: Suffrage Reform in the United States, 1787–1860." In *Voting and the Spirit of American Democracy*. Edited by Donald W. Rogers. Urbana: University of Illinois Press, 1992.

Williamson, Chilton. *American Suffrage: From Property to Democracy, 1760–1860*. Princeton, N.J.: Princeton University Press, 1960.

THOMAS H. NEALE

BLACK VOTERS BEFORE THE CIVIL WAR

At the time the United States was founded, free blacks could vote on the same basis as whites in a number of states. Between the turn of the century and the Civil War this situation changed. In 1800, free black men in Massachusetts, New Hampshire, Rhode Island, Vermont, New York, New Jersey, Pennsylvania, Maryland, North Carolina, and Tennessee were all entitled to vote. When Maine became a state in 1820 it also allowed black suffrage. In 1822, and again in 1836, the Rhode Island legislature explicitly banned black voters, but the state adopted equal suffrage under its 1842 constitution. Ohio prohibited nonwhites from voting, but in a decision unique to that state, the Ohio Supreme Court ruled in *Anderson v. Milliken* (1859) that people of mixed racial ancestry could vote if they were more than half white. Ohio blacks could vote in school board elections where the schools were segregated. In Michigan, blacks could also vote in school board elections, and there is strong evidence of blacks voting in some regular elections in Detroit.

In 1810, Maryland took the vote away from blacks. This decision may have been a result of the growing number of free blacks in the state. Ironically, freedom for many blacks may have led to the loss of political power for those already free. New York's constitution of 1777 had a property requirement of $250 for all voters. The constitution of 1821 removed this requirement for whites, but maintained it for blacks. This blatantly unfair system was the result of a compromise within the constitutional convention; the old Federalists, led by Judge James Kent (1763–1847), wanted equal suffrage for all men, while the Democrats wanted to expand white suffrage and eliminate black suffrage. In part, these positions were political, as black voters in New York had traditionally been Federalists, but they also reflected the racism of the Democrats.

In the 1830s the connection between Jacksonian democracy and racism became more clear. A new constitution in Tennessee (1834), as well as a constitutional amendment in North Carolina (1835), led to universal white male suffrage and a complete denial of black suffrage in those states. In *Hobbs v. Fogg* (1837) the Pennsylvania Supreme Court declared that blacks had never had the legal right to vote in the state, despite six decades of black voting. The court regretted that Pennsylvania's constitution lacked a provision similar to the 1835 North Carolina amendment. However, a year later the state enacted just such a provision, limiting suffrage to "every white freeman" in its 1838 constitution. Philadelphia's black community vigorously protested this change in Pennsylvania law, but the protests led nowhere.

During the first two decades of the century, blacks in Massachusetts, New York, Pennsylvania, and North Carolina generally supported the Federalists. This made sense, since the Democratic-Republican Party, led by Thomas Jefferson, James Madison, and James Monroe, was clearly dominated by slave owners. In the 1830s and 1840s, black voters in New York and New England supported opponents of slavery, who were more likely to be Whigs than Democrats. In 1860, black voters and political leaders, such as Frederick Douglass, supported Lincoln and the Republicans. The Republican Party, in turn, pushed for equal suffrage laws or state constitutional amendments in New York, Connecticut, Iowa, and Wisconsin.

Where they could vote, blacks did so. In 1845, black voters in Boston voted at almost twice the rate of white voters. Jeffersonians complained about black voters in New York, presumably because their votes were decisive in Federalist victories. The evidence for this decisive nature of black votes is slim, but the Jeffersonian racism against black voters is clear.

Despite the small number of eligible black voters and the racism of the antebellum period, at least a few blacks won elective office before the Civil War. In 1855 the Ohio attorney John Mercer Langston (1829–1897) was elected township clerk in Brownhelm, Ohio, even though as a black he could not vote for himself. In Providence, Rhode Island, a black was elected to a minor office in 1857.

See also **African Americans,** *subentry on* **Free Blacks before the Civil War; Race Laws.**

Bibliography

Curry, Leonard P. *The Free Black in Urban America, 1800–1850: The Shadow of the Dream.* Chicago: University of Chicago Press, 1981.

Finkelman, Paul. "Prelude to the Fourteenth Amendment: Black Legal Rights in the Antebellum North." *Rutgers Law Journal* 17 (1986): 415–482.

Horton, James Oliver. *Free People of Color: Inside the African American Community.* Washington, D.C.: Smithsonian Institution Press, 1993.

PAUL FINKELMAN

BLACK VOTERS AFTER THE CIVIL WAR

Black male enfranchisement was an unexpected and highly revolutionary outcome of the Civil War. On the eve of the Civil War, the Republican Party vowed to stop the expansion of slavery into free federal territories but was not prepared to emancipate slaves, much less enfranchise them. As soon as the war started, Southern slaves took the initiative of seeking freedom by running to the Union army lines. This act of self-emancipation compelled the Republican-controlled Congress and President Abraham Lincoln to move more rapidly and firmly to undertake emancipation. By the invitation of Lincoln's Emancipation Proclamation (1 January 1863), nearly 180,000 black men enlisted in the Union army and another 300,000 black men and women served as laborers for the Union cause. Blacks' participation in the Civil War not only helped the Union to defeat the Confederacy but also, and more important, laid the foundation for their demand for political rights in the Reconstruction era.

Black agitation for suffrage began before the Civil War ended. The National Convention of the Colored Men, held in Syracuse, New York, in 1864, urged the federal government to grant all blacks the right to vote. Such leading black abolitionists as Frederick Douglass warned that without enfranchisement, neither blacks' freedom nor the nation's freedom could be permanently guaranteed. Blacks in New Orleans sent two representatives—Jean-Baptiste Roudanez and Arnold Bertonneau—to Washington, D.C., to petition for suffrage. Black enfranchisement was enthusiastically supported by Radical Republicans in Congress, but it was not included in the early Reconstruction programs of Lincoln and the Congress. The Thirteenth Amendment, ratified in 1865, recognized black freedom nationwide without offering any specific civil or political rights substantiating this freedom. Contributing to the Republicans' refusal to grant blacks voting rights in the early stage of Reconstruction was the party's reluctance to break the conventional division of powers between the federal and state governments, as well as the practice of black disfranchisement prevailing in much of the North.

The enactment of "Black Codes" in 1865–1866 by the former Confederate states quickly changed the minds of many Republicans. Attempting to offer some federal protection for the freedmen's civil rights, which was missing from the presidential reconstruction plans, in early 1866 Congress passed a Civil Rights Act and a bill to extend the Freedmen's Bureau. President Andrew Johnson, who succeeded Lincoln in April 1865, vetoed both bills, insisting that the issue of freedmen's rights should be left with the states. Alienated by Johnson's unsympathetic attitude toward blacks, moderate Republicans joined the Radicals not only to override Johnson's vetoes but also to adopt the Fourteenth Amendment (ratified 1868), which granted blacks federal citizenship, along with its accompanying privileges and immunities. The amendment, in its second section, provided that a state's representation in the House would be reduced "in the proportion" to its disqualification of eligible males from voting, but it avoided an affirmative declaration of black suffrage.

The open defiance of the South, which Johnson supported, convinced the Republican majority in Congress that black suffrage was indispensable to the establishment of the "republican form of government" in the South, as well as to the maintenance of the party's control of the national government. Encouraged by their triumph in the congressional elections of 1866, in 1867–1868 the Republicans in Congress enacted a number of Reconstruction Acts that prescribed the process of the reorganization of the former Confederate states, including provisions for black participation in the process.

Enabled by the congressional Reconstruction policy, about 700,000 black males in the South registered and exercised voting rights in 1867 and 1868. Black votes were instrumental in the formation of new state governments, which complied with the conditions for readmission prescribed by Congress, including abolition of slavery, ratification of the Fourteenth Amendment, and repudiation of the Confederate debts. Southern black votes—at least half a million of them—also played a vital role in Ulysses S. Grant's victory in the presidential election of 1868; his majority of the popular vote was only 300,000 out of the 5.7 million total votes. The impact of black votes, as demonstrated in these contests, led the Republicans to enfranchise blacks living in the North and border states. The Fifteenth Amendment, adopted in February 1870, nationalized black suffrage by barring federal and state governments from depriving U.S. citizens of the right to vote on account of race, color, or previous condition of servitude.

Black participation in Reconstruction was further evidenced by the large number of black officeholders during this period. Even at the national level, from 1870 until 1901 blacks served in every session of Congress but one. Two sat in the U.S. Senate and fourteen in the House of Representatives. Hiram R. Revels, a former slave and a Methodist minister from Mississippi, was the nation's first African American to serve in the Senate; in 1870 he took the seat at one time occupied by Jefferson Davis (1847–1853). Blacks constituted a majority in South Carolina's House of Representatives up to 1876, but in most of the southern state legislatures they were not a majority. Meanwhile, more than fourteen hundred blacks were either elected or appointed to occupy positions of political importance at the state and local levels. These positions included governor (Pinckney B. S. Pinchback in Louisiana), lieutenant governors, state supreme court justices, state secretaries, mayors, aldermen, tax collectors, and sheriffs. Since their backgrounds varied, black politicians did not always display unanimity on issues. Lack of education and political inexperience sometimes hindered the effectiveness of black statesmen in political negotiations, but black officials generally supported such progressive legislation as state-supported public education, civil rights laws, prison reform, land distribution, and antisegregation laws.

From the very beginning blacks voting and holding office were confronted with political terrorism by such white supremacist organizations as the Ku Klux

Extending the Franchise. Columbia, the personification of the United States, advocates voting rights for a black soldier who had lost a leg in the Civil War. Wood engraving by Thomas Nast published in *Harper's Weekly*, 5 August 1865. LIBRARY OF CONGRESS

Klan. To protect the rights of the freedmen and to sustain black voters as a loyal constituency for the Republican-led Reconstruction in the South, Congress enacted three enforcement laws in 1870–1871. These acts established a uniform system of election supervision, prescribed the voting procedures, provided federal machinery, granted federal courts the exclusive power to hear cases arising under these laws, and empowered the president to use the army to keep peace at polling places and to suspend habeas corpus in the Klan-ridden areas. Aided by federal troops, the Department of Justice carried out an effective enforcement. In 1873 more than a thousand cases under the enforcement laws were brought to the federal courts in the South, and the conviction rate was as high as 40 percent.

The vigorous federal enforcement, however, did not extend beyond 1875. It declined as a result of the oscillations of the Grant administration, financial restraints, bureaucratic inefficiency, decline of northern popular support, and the split between the Liberal and regular Republicans. Institutionally, the recapture of the House of Representatives by the Democratic Party in 1875 blocked the passage of any new enforcement law. Meanwhile, the white South carried on an effective movement of "redeeming" the South—the "Mississippi Plan" of the mid-1870s—that employed an array of techniques to oust Radical Republican administrations and replace them with white supremacist Democratic regimes. The official ending of Reconstruction was marked by the Compromise of 1877, in which southern Democrats accepted Rutherford B. Hayes, the Republican candidate, as the victor in the presidential election of 1876 in return for his pledge to restore home rule in the South. Following the withdrawal of the federal troops from the statehouses of South Carolina and Louisiana by the end of April 1877, the Democrats recaptured full control of the South.

Federal enforcement of black voting rights received another major blow from the Republican-dominated Supreme Court, which in *United States v. Reese* (1876) and *United States v. Cruikshank* (1876) found two sections of the 1870 enforcement law inappropriate and ordered the revocation of the indictments based on the act. The court declared that in order to secure convictions under the enforcement acts, it must be proved that the accused had acted for racially motivated reasons. Later, in *Ex parte Siebold* (1880), *Ex parte Clarke* (1880), and *Ex parte Yarbrough* (1884), the Court confirmed that the Fifteenth Amendment had indeed established the principle of black male suffrage, but its earlier opinions on Reconstruction amendments and enforcement laws had nullified effective federal enforcement.

Despite the decline of federal enforcement, blacks in both the North and the South continued to vote whenever and wherever they could. In the 1880s, when northern Democrats pursued a new strategy to compete with the Republicans for black votes, black voters in some northern states were able to negotiate with the Democrats for positions at the local level and to demand the implementation of state civil rights laws in exchange for their support. In several places in the South, such as eastern Texas and North Carolina, blacks continued to vote as late as the early 1890s. The Republican Party, on the other hand, did not completely abandon black suffrage, as traditionally believed. In 1879–1880 President Hayes stood firmly for enforcement by vetoing all seven bills to repeal the enforcement acts that were presented to him by a Democrat-controlled Congress. In 1890–1891 the party used its control of the White House

"The First Vote." A southern polling place during state elections in 1867, as illustrated in *Harper's Weekly*. LIBRARY OF CONGRESS

and both houses of Congress to introduce the Lodge Federal Elections Bill. This initiative aimed at stopping the black disfranchisement under way in the South and preventing fraudulent elections nationwide. The bill passed the House but was defeated in the Senate by the defection of a small number of Republicans from the West.

Parallel to the Republican failure to reenforce black suffrage was the rapid development of black disfranchisement in the South. In 1890 the constitutional convention of Mississippi imposed a literacy test, which required a prospective voter to read any section of the state constitution or give a "reasonable" interpretation of any section read to him. State-appointed officials who administered the test were given the discretion to determine the "reasonableness" of the interpretation and, consequently, used the opportunity to reject most black voters and pass most whites. Between 1890 and 1910 other southern states followed suit by adding new voting qualifications to their state constitutions so as to exclude blacks from the electorate. In addition to the literacy test a number of other devices and techniques were adopted by the Redeemer governments, including the use of multiple ballot boxes (with the

intention of confusing illiterate black voters), advance payment of poll taxes (a financial burden on many poor black farmers), a complicated registration process and inconvenient timing (a constant frustration for rural blacks), the "good character" test, a long-residence requirement, and, later, a white primary (a device to permit only whites to have a voice in the nomination of the Democratic Party candidate). Most notorious of the disfranchisement plans was the "grandfather" plan, adopted by Louisiana in 1898, by which no male—or son or grandson of such male—who was entitled to vote on 1 January 1867 was to be denied the right to vote. Despite the protests of black voters, several other southern states— Alabama, Virginia, Georgia—adopted the same device in the next decade.

Consequently many former black voters in the South were deprived of the right to vote. In 1900, two years after the new suffrage qualifications went into effect in Louisiana, only about five thousand black voters were registered as qualified voters, a decline of 96 percent from 1896, when about 130,000 blacks registered to vote. The Georgia state constitution reduced black registration from 28 percent in 1904 to 4 percent in 1910. Black voters in Mississippi simply disappeared after 1890. Black disfranchisement in the South was accepted by the federal government. In 1894 the Democrat-controlled Congress repealed significant portions of the enforcement acts in spite of the opposition of the Republican minority. Four years later the Supreme Court, in *Williams v. Mississippi*, refused to recognize the states' disfranchising devices (literacy test, poll tax, lengthy residency requirements) as potential political discrimination against black voters. In *Giles v. Harris* (1903) and *Giles v. Teasley* (1904) the Court ignored a black voter's challenge to the "grandfather" clause and the "good character" clause of the 1901 Alabama constitution.

See also **Constitutional Amendments,** *subentry on* **Thirteenth, Fourteenth, and Fifteenth Amendments; Ku Klux Klan; Reconstruction,** *subentries on* **The Politics of Reconstruction, The South.**

Bibliography

Belz, Herman. "Origins of Negro Suffrage during the Civil War." *Southern Studies* 17 (summer 1978): 115–130.

Benedict, Michael Les. "Preserving Federalism: The Waite Court and Reconstruction." *Supreme Court Review* (1978): 39–79.

Foner, Eric. *Freedom's Lawmakers: A Directory of Black Office-holders during Reconstruction.* New York: Oxford University Press, 1993. See especially the introduction.

———. *Reconstruction: America's Unfinished Revolution, 1863–1877.* New York: Harper and Row, 1988.

Gillette, William. *Retreat from Reconstruction, 1869–1879*. Baton Rouge: Louisiana State University Press, 1979.

———. *The Right to Vote: Politics and the Passage of the Fifteenth Amendment*. Baltimore: Johns Hopkins University Press, 1965.

Goldman, Robert M. *"A Free Ballot and a Fair Count": The Department of Justice and the Enforcement of Voting Rights in the South, 1877–1893*. New York: Garland, 1990.

Goodwyn, Lawrence C. "Populist Dreams and Negro Rights: East Texas as a Case Study." *American Historical Review* 76 (December 1971): 1435–1456.

Grossman, Lawrence. *The Democratic Party and the Negro: Northern and National Politics, 1868–92*. Urbana: University of Illinois Press, 1976.

Holt, Thomas. *Black over White: Negro Political Leadership in South Carolina during Reconstruction*. Urbana: University of Illinois Press, 1977.

Kousser, J. Morgan. *The Shaping of Southern Politics: Suffrage Restriction and the Establishment of the One-Party South, 1880–1910*. New Haven, Conn.: Yale University Press, 1974.

Lewinson, Paul. *Race, Class, and Party: A History of Negro Suffrage and White Politics in the South*. New York: Russell and Russell, 1963.

Litwack, Leon F. *Trouble in Mind: Black Southerners in the Age of Jim Crow*. New York: Knopf, 1998. See chapter 5.

Nieman, Donald G. *Promises to Keep: African Americans and the Constitutional Order: 1776 to the Present*. New York: Oxford University Press, 1992. See chapters 3–5.

Swinney, Everette. *Suppressing the Ku Klux Klan: The Enforcement of the Reconstruction Amendments, 1870–1877*. New York: Garland, 1987.

Wang, Xi. *The Trial of Democracy: Black Suffrage and Northern Republicans, 1860–1910*. Athens, Ga.: University of Georgia Press, 1997.

Woodward, C. Vann. *The Strange Career of Jim Crow*. 3d rev. ed. New York: Oxford University Press, 1974.

XI WANG

THE WOMEN'S VOTE

"Suffrage," Susan B. Anthony maintained, "involves every basic principle of republican government, all of our social, civil, religious, educational, and political rights." Accordingly it is "the pivotal right, the one that underlies all other rights." Women's struggle to obtain the ballot in the United States began soon after the American Revolution and marched forward for more than a century as the nation, with an almost exclusively male electorate, contemplated the value of enfranchising women. With many trailblazers, the movement for women's political inclusion prevailed in 1919, when Congress passed the Nineteenth Amendment. Ensuring that a citizen's right to vote could not be denied "on account of sex," the amendment was ratified by the states in August 1920.

In the years before the English colonies gained independence, some colonies, most notably New York, allowed propertied women to "vote their estates." With independence, however, the new nation effectively eliminated women's participation at the polls. Voting was a privilege granted by the states, and women retained the franchise only in New Jersey in the wake of the American Revolution. With the adoption of a constitution in 1776 that enfranchised "all free inhabitants" worth fifty pounds and the use of the words "he or she" in a 1790 revision of the election codes, New Jersey confirmed women's inclusion in the state's electorate. By the turn of the century, however, even politicians in New Jersey retreated. Declaring it "highly necessary to the safety, quiet, good order, and dignity of the state," they limited the franchise to "white male citizens" in 1807.

Reform Movements

The early national extension of voting rights enfranchised most white men, including the nonpropertied, Catholics, Jews, and sometimes aliens. Although excluded, women nonetheless forged a public role for themselves. Led primarily by radical Protestants, women between 1810 and 1860 increasingly participated in a variety of reform movements to improve their status in the United States while remaking the Republic. Educators like Emma Willard, Mary Lyon, and Catharine Beecher successfully improved women's educational opportunities. Women joined moral reform societies and voluntary organizations, combating the growing evils in American society associated with poverty, crime, and licentiousness. Thousands actively participated in female temperance societies, seeking to deliver women and children from abuse by and dependence on drunken husbands and fathers. Others, such as Ernestine Rose and Jane Swisshelm, sought to expand the legal rights of women by campaigning for married women's property rights, as well as the full enfranchisement of women. Coinciding with these efforts, reformers actively defended the right of women to speak more freely, openly, and publicly. Early in her career Anthony asserted women's right to speak publicly at state conventions for teachers in New York; Paulina Wright Davis initiated a public speaking career as a lecturer on female physiology; and in her campaign to win humane treatment for the mentally ill, Dorothea Dix launched a fierce defense of women's participation in politics and public speaking.

Women's commitment to improving both their own conditions and the commonweal led to their involvement in the abolitionist movement established in the early 1830s. Intent on destroying the "sin of slavery," abolitionists welcomed women's involvement—though usually by organizing separate female abolitionist societies. By 1838 more than one hundred female antislavery societies had emerged. The movement's radical wing, the American Anti-Slavery Society led by William Lloyd Garrison, however, readily received women into its own ranks. Following the lead of such zealous campaigners as Lucretia Mott, Abbey Kelly Foster, Elizabeth Cady Stanton, Angelina Grimké, Sarah Grimké, and Lucy Stone, thousands of women joined the abolitionist movement during the 1840s and 1850s. The activism of such women did not go unnoticed. Indeed, it sparked bitter debate over the public role of women.

As abolitionists and temperance workers forced to defend their rights to participate equally and fully and to speak publicly before audiences of both sexes, women began to transform the understanding of their own oppression into the beginnings of a political movement to liberate women. "The investigation of the rights of the slave has led me to a better understanding of my own," Angelina Grimké wrote to Catharine Beecher in 1836. Drawing parallels between the positions of slaves and women, they began to justify their demands for equality. In her *Letters on the Equality of the Sexes and the Condition of Women* (1838), Sarah Grimké articulated the question of equality in political as well as moral and religious terms:

> I ask no favors for my sex. I surrender not our claim to equality. All I ask of our brethren is that they will take their feet from our necks, and permit us to stand upright on the ground which God has designed us to occupy. . . . God has made no distinction between men and women as moral beings. . . . To me it is perfectly clear *that whatsoever it is morally right for a man to do, it is morally right for a woman to do* (p. 10).

Abolitionism taught women, as the historian Ellen Carol DuBois has argued, "less that they were oppressed than what to do with that perception, how to turn it into a political movement" (1981, p. 57). By teaching women how to organize, build a constituency, conduct massive petition drives, and step out of the confines of the domestic sphere, abolitionism provided women with a political framework to transform an idea into a movement for political inclusion.

The Seneca Falls Convention

The first large-scale women's rights meeting in the United States was held in Seneca Falls, New York, in July 1848. Organized by Lucretia Mott and Elizabeth Cady Stanton, the meeting was first proposed in response to the exclusion of eight American women delegates, including Mott and Stanton, from the World's Anti-Slavery Convention in London in 1840. Denied a seat and a vote on account of their sex, the delegates left London agreeing that a women's protest meeting in the United States was needed. Announced on 14 July 1848 in the *Seneca County Courier* as a meeting "to discuss the social, civil, and religious condition and rights of women," the Seneca Falls convention attracted three hundred women and men. Identifying the moral, social, economic, legal, and political injustices facing American women, its proceedings marked the first formal assertion of the equal rights of women. Consciously intending to initiate a broader movement for the emancipation of women, the organizers' demand for equality was revolutionary. Denouncing the "absolute tyranny" of men, convention participants issued the Declaration of Sentiments. Modeled after the Declaration of Independence, the document proclaimed "that all men and women are created equal" and enumerated the "repeated injuries and usurpa-

Leading Advocates for Women's Suffrage. Elizabeth Cady Stanton (1815–1902), seated, and Susan B. Anthony (1820–1906). LIBRARY OF CONGRESS: PRINTS AND PHOTOGRAPHS DIVISION

tions on the part of man toward woman." Delegates charged men with denying women the full benefits of citizenship, including the ability "to exercise her inalienable right to the elective franchise." Supplementing the Declaration of Sentiments were resolutions calling for the freedom to address public audiences, expansion of educational opportunities, equal property rights, liberalization of divorce, and equal pay. The most controversial resolution claimed suffrage for women. Directly rejecting women's dependence on men, it was the only resolution not passed unanimously. Nonetheless, the demand for political inclusion at Seneca Falls launched a campaign for women suffrage that intensified in the late 1860s.

In the years following Seneca Falls, the woman's rights movement accelerated its efforts to gain the full benefits of citizenship for women. Holding annual conventions and promoting a broad agenda, the movement before 1860 experienced limited victories, including, most notably, increased access to higher education and passage of married women's property laws by several states. As the nation turned its at-

President and Suffragist. The suffragist leader Susan B. Anthony gives chase to former president Grover Cleveland, who carries a book entitled *What I Know About Women's Clubs.* An article by Cleveland in the *Ladies' Home Journal* decried suffragist women's clubs as a menace to home life. Drawing by Charles Lewis Bartholomew, 1905. LIBRARY OF CONGRESS: PRINTS AND PHOTOGRAPHS DIVISION (CARTOON DRAWINGS)

tention to the Civil War in 1861, so too did the woman's rights movement. During the war the movement supported the Union war effort and maintained its alliance with abolitionists, advocating emancipation and the Thirteenth Amendment. The war's end brought bitter disappointment to the woman's rights movement, however. Somewhat dismayed, its leaders found that abolitionists were much less concerned about women's rights than those of emancipated slaves. The contentious issue of black citizenship and political rights embodied in debates over the Fourteenth and Fifteenth Amendments forced the woman's rights movement to reconsider both its alliances and its objectives.

Divided Strategies: Persuasion and Rebellion

In the wake of emancipation, women's rights leaders were divided over how best to achieve the full benefits of citizenship. While support for the Thirteenth Amendment, which abolished slavery, had come easily, the same was not true for the Fourteenth and Fifteenth Amendments. The movement's leaders were alarmed by the Fourteenth Amendment's introduction of the word "male" into the Constitution and the Fifteenth Amendment's failure to prohibit the denial of voting rights on the basis of sex as well as race, and conflicts arose among them. Refusing to support a suffrage amendment that extended the right to vote to African American men but not to women, Stanton and Anthony in 1869 formed the National Woman Suffrage Association (NWSA), denounced the Fifteenth Amendment, and advocated woman suffrage through the Constitution. Later that year Stone and Julia Ward Howe organized the American Woman Suffrage Association (AWSA), which supported the Fifteenth Amendment as a step toward universal suffrage and worked to persuade states to extend the ballot to women.

Although the debate over the Fifteenth Amendment had divided and thus weakened the women's rights movement, from it emerged an independent movement focused on a single purpose. As women came to see political standing and participation as essential preconditions for the achievement of other reforms, the movement increasingly emphasized universal suffrage. Largely avoiding all other "side issues," as Stone put it in 1869, both the NWSA and the AWSA focused on securing women the vote. To be sure, women had voted in so-called "partial suffrage" states, among them, Kentucky, Arkansas, and Mississippi, since the late 1830s, but women, unlike all men, lacked constitutional authority for claiming the ballot as an incident of citizenship. While the AWSA pursued a state-by-state campaign for the ballot, the NWSA adopted a new strategy following ratification of the Fifteenth Amendment. A constitutional approach known at the time as the "New Departure" contended that women were already enfranchised. Relying on an egalitarian interpretation of the Constitution and a broad understanding of the Fourteenth Amendment, the NWSA contended that, as citizens exercising their "privileges and immunities," women need only go to the polls, assert their constitutional right, and vote. The Supreme Court disagreed in *Minor v. Happersett* (1875), however, and rejected the case for universal suffrage. By the end of the 1870s the NWSA abandoned the New Departure for a different strategy, a federal suffrage amendment.

State by State toward National Woman Suffrage

Whatever course was chosen, women found progress painstakingly slow. By 1890, when the movement finally reunited as the National American Woman Suffrage Association (NAWSA) under pressure from younger women convinced of the need to pool constituencies and resources, only the women in Wyoming possessed unlimited suffrage. In the ensuing years several western states followed the lead of Wyoming. Colorado granted women the ballot in 1893, Utah and Idaho in 1896, Washington in 1910, California in 1911, Arizona, Kansas, and Oregon in 1912, Alaska Territory in 1913, and Nevada and Montana in 1914. Women east of the Mississippi River gained access to the polls much more gradually, often securing the ballot first in local elections or elections involving educational and bond issues. Prior to 1917 Illinois was the only state east of the Mississippi to enfranchise women in presidential elections.

Under the leadership of Anna Howard Shaw and Carrie Chapman Catt, the NAWSA worked to broaden its influence and reinvigorate the call for woman suffrage. Introducing new arguments for woman suffrage, the movement claimed that it was not only "just" to enfranchise women, but also "expedient." Depicting suffrage as a natural extension of women's duty to protect the home, they argued that women's virtue would purify politics, curb corruption, and promote reform. Leaders insisted that allowing women to vote would lead to improvements

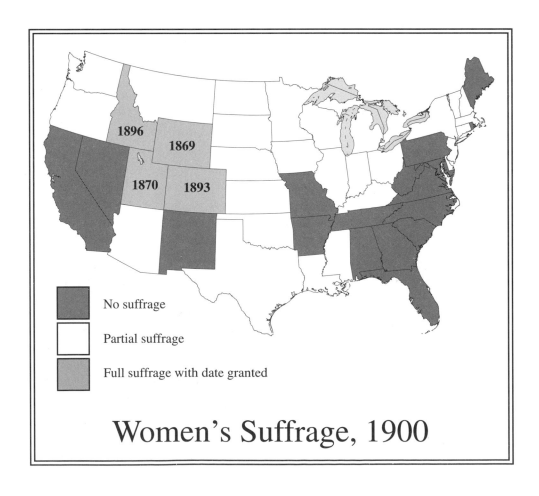

Women's Suffrage, 1900

in education, the workplace, and the family. This approach appealed more broadly to middle-class white women, resulting in an increase in NAWSA membership from 13,000 in 1893 to about 75,000 in 1910. By the second decade of the twentieth century two million women across the nation supported the push for woman suffrage. Employing tactics such as suffrage parades, silent picketing, leaflet and petition campaigns, open-air rallies, touring lectures, legislative lobbying, and testifying at congressional hearings, the NAWSA coordinated state campaigns with efforts in Washington, D.C., to obtain a federal suffrage amendment. At the same time the National Woman's Party, formed in 1916 by Alice Paul and other reformer-lobbyists, initiated more militant tactics to secure the ballot for women. Its efforts gained national headlines in 1917 as women were arrested and jailed for picketing the White House.

Victory ultimately came to the women's rights movement in January 1918, when President Woodrow Wilson announced his support for a federal suffrage amendment. In 1919 Congress passed the "Anthony Amendment," as it was known. Following Tennessee's tumultuous ratification, it became the Nineteenth Amendment in August 1920, just in time to enable women to vote in the 1920 presidential election. The Nineteenth Amendment did not revolutionize American politics or women's place in the polity, however. Contrary to the hopes of its supporters, women did not turn out to vote in large numbers, and those who did go to the polls tended to vote like their male relatives. Suffrage also failed to bring women of all classes and colors the full benefits of citizenship. Female jury service and to a lesser extent female officeholding, for example, continued to be rare until the 1960s. Nevertheless, the Nineteenth Amendment secured for women the crucial right of republican citizenship and an open door to the political process that would enable a future generation to move closer to the full equality their foremothers had envisioned.

See also **Abolition and Antislavery; Clubs,** *subentry on* **Women's Clubs and Associations; Constitutional Amendments,** *subentry on* **Thirteenth, Fourteenth, and Fifteenth Amendments; Education,** *subentry on* **Education of Girls and Women; Labor Movement,** *subentry on* **Women; Law,** *subentry on* **Women and the Law; Literature,** *subentry on* **Women's Literature; Marriage; Reform, Political; Reform, Social; Republican Motherhood; Temperance Movement; Women,** *subentries on* **Women's Rights, Woman as Image and Icon.**

Bibliography

Buechler, Steven M. *Women's Movements in the United States: Woman Suffrage, Equal Rights, and Beyond.* New Brunswick, N.J.: Rutgers University Press, 1990.

DuBois, Ellen Carol. *Feminism and Suffrage: The Emergence of an Independent Women's Movement in America, 1848–1869.* Ithaca, N.Y.: Cornell University Press, 1978.

———. *Woman Suffrage and Women's Rights.* New York: New York University Press, 1998.

Flexner, Eleanor. *Century of Struggle: The Woman's Rights Movement in the United States.* Cambridge, Mass.: Belknap Press of Harvard University Press, 1959.

Kerber, Linda K. *No Constitutional Right to Be Ladies: Women and the Obligations of Citizenship.* New York: Hill and Wang, 1998.

Kraditor, Aileen S. *The Ideas of the Woman Suffrage Movement, 1890–1920.* New York: Columbia University Press, 1965.

Scott, Anne Firor, and Andrew MacKay Scott. *One Half the People: The Fight for Woman Suffrage.* Urbana: University of Illinois Press, 1982.

Weatherford, Doris. *A History of the American Suffragist Movement.* Santa Barbara, Calif.: ABC–CLIO, 1998.

MARY J. FARMER

W–Z

WAR OF 1812 The War of 1812 is one of the least known and most inglorious wars in U.S. history. Sometimes described as the "forgotten conflict," the War of 1812 is unlikely to become the topic of a long-running popular documentary series, such as Ken Burns's *Civil War*. Indeed, sandwiched between the American Revolution and the Civil War, the War of 1812 is perennially overlooked. The war was so obscure in its roots and consequences as to be named for the year in which it broke out rather than for any cause or outcome. The conflict is best understood as a second war for American independence.

In the larger scheme of early-nineteenth-century world affairs, the War of 1812 was a sideshow in the titanic struggle between Napoleonic France and Great Britain. The United States, adhering to a diplomacy of neutrality as set down by President George Washington in his 1796 Farewell Address, sided with neither European power in their conflict. At the same time both France and Britain denied the United States the legitimacy it craved as a newly independent nation. The United States may have won its independence in fact in 1783, but British ministers, especially on matters of trade, continued to view the Americans as colonials. Nothing grated more on American sensibilities.

Issues of trade and honor lay at the heart of the conflict between the United States and Great Britain. Following the renewal of Anglo-French warfare in 1803, both European powers enforced embargoes, blockades, and other measures to cut off trade in an effort to cripple one another economically as well as on the battlefield. Great Britain dominated the seas, while French general Napoleon Bonaparte, envisioning the establishment of a new Rome, attempted to seal off and dominate the European continent. The United States and other weaker neutrals thus found themselves catapulted into the epic struggle between the greatest land and sea powers the world had ever witnessed.

Following the revolutionary era, American leaders had perceived free trade as the key to U.S. prosperity and republicanism. Dependent on American natural resources and agricultural commodities, Europeans would be compelled to trade on favorable terms with the United States. Such an idyllic world of international commerce could not prevail, however, in the midst of a life-and-death struggle for Europe. Neither Britain nor France, nor their allies, would adhere strictly to neutral rights in wartime.

In 1805 Great Britain began to clamp restraints on U.S. commerce with Europe, announcing a blockade of the entire northern coast of the Continent to enforce the measures. New duties on trade with the British West Indies and elsewhere amounted to nothing less than a reimposition of colonialism. France followed an essentially parallel course under Napoleon but lacked the sea power to enforce the controls as effectively. Americans viewed these wartime measures as assaults on their economic viability and ultimately as threats to independence itself. In reality, U.S. commerce could have survived under the trade restraints, although the economy might not have grown at the desired pace.

The War of 1812 was thus an affair of honor more than a conflict over a real challenge to economic vi-

The Battle of Lake Erie. Oliver Hazard Perry is shown during the engagement that forced the British out of Detroit on 9 September 1813. Copy of engraving by Phillibrown after W. H. Powell, 1858. NATIONAL ARCHIVES

ability or national security. While both Britain and France trampled on American neutral rights, London especially showed its contempt for U.S. nationalism through the practice of impressment of seamen into the Royal Navy. Thousands of British subjects had escaped or deserted from naval service, which was characterized by low pay; strict discipline, including frequent lashings; and horrid food, water, and living conditions, as well as the dangers of battle at sea. Desperate for manpower in its war with a more populous France, by 1812 Britain had impressed more than 10,000 American sailors into its fleet. British naval commanders showed no hesitancy about forcing weaker American vessels to heave to and have their crews mustered for inspection and ultimately impressed into British naval service. The American diplomat John Quincy Adams described the odious practice as tantamount to a state system of kidnapping on the high seas.

The most infamous case of impressment demonstrating London's contempt for U.S. neutral rights occurred in June 1807 off the Virginia coast. The American frigate *Chesapeake* had just left Norfolk when the British warship *Leopard,* hovering off the U.S. coast for such a purpose, demanded that the Americans consent to boarding and inspection. When the captain of the *Chesapeake* refused, the *Leopard* delivered a series of broadsides, causing twenty-one casualties and prompting the *Chesapeake*'s captain,

who was later court-martialed, to lower the flag. The British boarded the ship and impressed four seamen, one of whom they later hanged for desertion at Halifax. Conditioned since the Revolution to view Great Britain as the nation's chief enemy, the American press and public exploded in outrage at the assault on U.S. national dignity.

President Thomas Jefferson confronted pressure to take some action in the face of continual affronts to American honor. Jefferson knew that his nation lacked adequate preparation for war, and he and other classical republicans did not want to see the United States take up heavy armaments, increase taxes, and expand the federal bureaucracy as would be required to put the nation on a war footing. Although Jefferson strengthened coastal emplacements and outfitted new gunboats, he sought to respond to British provocations with measures short of war.

With an exaggerated perception of European dependence on American markets, Jefferson implemented a program of economic warfare. The Virginian believed, as did many early American idealists, that the nation's foodstuffs, cotton, and natural resources were so crucial to the British economy that London would be forced to remove its trade restrictions and respect U.S. neutral rights. The centerpiece of Jefferson's diplomacy was the Embargo Act, which he pushed through Congress in December 1807. Under this policy the United States ceased all exports

The Taking of the City of Washington . . . by the British Forces under Major Genl. Ross on Augt. 24, 1814. The burning of the capitol and the presidential mansion underscored American vulnerability. Copy of engraving, 1814. NA-TIONAL ARCHIVES

to Europe and closed American ports to the European powers.

Jefferson miscalculated. U.S. trade alone could not make or break the British economy. While failing as a method of diplomatic coercion, Jefferson's policy also undermined the American economy, which was dependent on British textiles, iron, and consumer goods. The embargo heightened dissent to a rebellious level in Federalist New England, already alienated by the Republican president's policies and his reputation from the revolutionary years as a Francophile. Smugglers daily violated the embargo, encouraging contempt for the authority of the national government. Under pressure from Congress, Jefferson lifted the embargo as he left office in 1809.

Jefferson's chosen successor, James Madison, persisted in the effort to apply various economic sanctions to garner respect for U.S. neutral rights and end impressment. The Non-Intercourse Act (1809) in theory opened commerce with nations other than the two European belligerents but proved no more successful than the embargo. In sum, the economic warfare initiatives of Jefferson and Madison failed to achieve their design. They instead spurred frustration at home while increasing momentum toward military conflict with the world's preeminent power.

Much of the domestic discontent centered on the frontier. Farmers in the West and South bitterly resented British violations of neutral rights, a menace to their export-based economies. Cotton exports from the South dropped sharply between 1809 and 1811. Discontent on the frontier produced a more belligerent "War Hawk" Congress, chosen in state elections in 1810 and 1811. Many of the War Hawk congressmen represented western states, whose settlers often came into conflict with American Indian tribes that

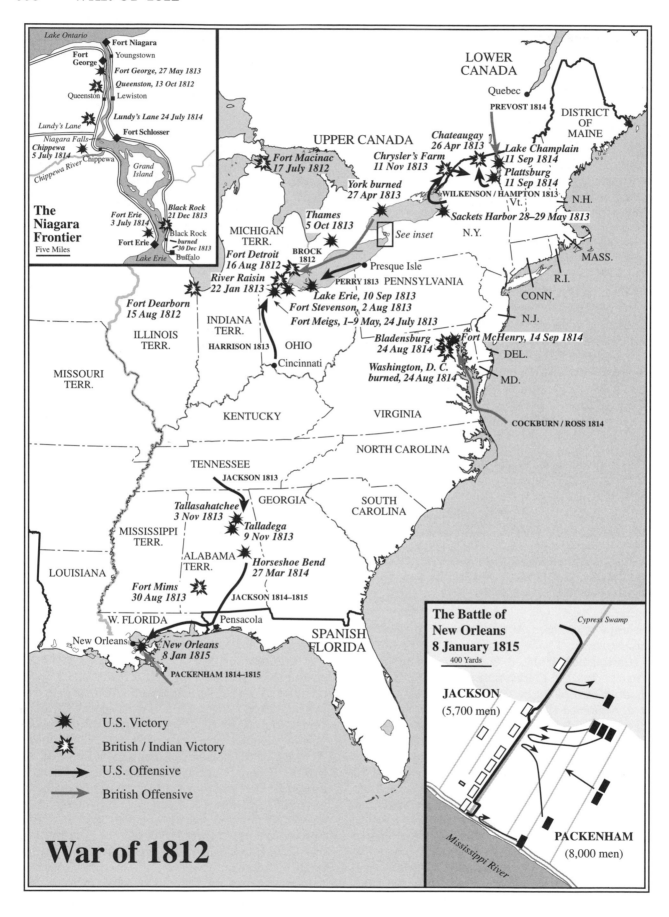

The Niagara Frontier
Five Miles

Lake Ontario
Fort Niagara
Youngstown
Fort George
Fort George, 27 May 1813
Queenston, 13 Oct 1812
Queenston   Lewiston
Lundy's Lane 24 July 1814
Lundy's Lane
Fort Schlosser
Niagara Falls
Chippewa 5 July 1814
Chippewa River   Chippewa
Grand Island
Fort Erie 3 July 1814
Black Rock 21 Dec 1813
Black Rock *burned 30 Dec 1813*
Fort Erie
Lake Erie   Buffalo

LOWER CANADA
Quebec
PREVOST 1814
DISTRICT OF MAINE

UPPER CANADA
Fort Macinac 17 July 1812
Chateaugay 26 Apr 1813
Chrysler's Farm 11 Nov 1813
Lake Champlain 11 Sep 1814
Plattsburg 11 Sep 1814
WILKENSON / HAMPTON 1813
Vt.
N.H.
York burned 27 Apr 1813
Thames 5 Oct 1813
See inset
Sackets Harbor 28–29 May 1813
N.Y.
MASS.
BROCK 1812
Presque Isle
R.I.
PERRY 1813
PENNSYLVANIA
CONN.
MICHIGAN TERR.
Fort Detroit 16 Aug 1812
River Raisin 22 Jan 1813
Lake Erie, 10 Sep 1813
Fort Stevenson, 2 Aug 1813
Fort Meigs, 1–9 May, 24 July 1813
N.J.
Fort Dearborn 15 Aug 1812
INDIANA TERR.
HARRISON 1813
OHIO
Cincinnati
Bladensburg 24 Aug 1814
Fort McHenry, 14 Sep 1814
DEL.
Washington, D. C. burned, 24 Aug 1814
MD.
ILLINOIS TERR.
MISSOURI TERR.
KENTUCKY
VIRGINIA
COCKBURN / ROSS 1814
NORTH CAROLINA
TENNESSEE
JACKSON 1813
Tallasahatchee 3 Nov 1813
GEORGIA
SOUTH CAROLINA
Talladega 9 Nov 1813
MISSISSIPPI TERR.
ALABAMA TERR.
Horseshoe Bend 27 Mar 1814
LOUISIANA
Fort Mims 30 Aug 1813
JACKSON 1814–1815
W. FLORIDA   Pensacola
New Orleans
SPANISH FLORIDA
New Orleans 8 Jan 1815
PACKENHAM 1814–1815

★ U.S. Victory
✸ British / Indian Victory
→ U.S. Offensive
→ British Offensive

War of 1812

The Battle of New Orleans 8 January 1815
400 Yards
Cypress Swamp
JACKSON (5,700 men)
PACKENHAM (8,000 men)
Mississippi River

had long-standing alliances with the British. Men such as John C. Calhoun of South Carolina and Speaker of the House Henry Clay of Kentucky declared that Britain's restrictions on trade and support of the Indian "savages" represented nothing less than an effort to deprive the United States of its liberty and independence.

Reaching the end of his own patience with the British, President Madison convened Congress a month early in November 1811 to assess the deteriorating international situation. Their influence often exaggerated, the so-called War Hawks were not in fact eager for war, yet they came to see no alternative except continued humiliation at the hands of Great Britain. Congress felt the need to do something other than continue to endure ignominious treatment, and war appeared to be the only option that remained.

Abetted by the War Hawks, the Madison administration stumbled into a potentially devastating conflict with Great Britain. The president drafted a war message, citing impressment, illegal blockades and trade restrictions, and incitement of Indians on the frontier. Considerable opposition remained, especially in New England, which had been hit hardest by the embargo and where some pro-British sentiment still prevailed. After seventeen days of sometimes vicious debate, Congress approved the president's call for a declaration of war against Great Britain in a vote along party lines, 79 to 49 in the House and 19 to 13 in the Senate. Madison signed the declaration of war on 18 June 1812.

The United States chose armed conflict as its ultimate response to British maritime restrictions, encouragement of Indian resistance, and the contempt that London continued to display for U.S. neutral rights. Many Americans remained convinced that Britain anchored a worldwide plot to destroy republicanism, which the United States was obliged to defend. At the time Congress declared war Britain was on the verge of lifting the most severe restraints on American trade. Yet Americans sensed that another defense of the Revolution was required for the country to go forward.

The new nation, however, was pathetically ill equipped for war. It possessed a deliberately weak central government, had no effective plan to finance the war, lacked strong military leadership, and was badly outclassed at sea by the Royal Navy. Moreover, at virtually the same time that the United States declared war, Napoleon launched his invasion of Russia, which would lead to his defeat and in turn would render the American war with Britain unnecessary. Other than emotional and psychological responses—anger, resentment, humiliation, and insecurity—the United States had no reason to go to war.

But in postrevolutionary America, where men still engaged in duels over individual affronts, an affair of honor with another nation was not easily overlooked.

The War of 1812 was ineffectively led and poorly fought on the American side. Madison, the "Father of the Constitution" and a brilliant intellectual, was indecisive, remote, and utterly unable to mobilize the nation for war. The U.S. strategy was to strike out at Great Britain in Canada, which the Americans viewed as vulnerable because British forces were concentrated against Napoleon's armies in Europe. By defeating the British in Canada, Madison reasoned, the United States could drive Britain from the continent and ensure U.S. security for years to come. Such an outcome would obviate the need for a large standing army and perpetual military conflict, both of which were anathema to the Republican ideologist.

Actions on the ground failed to conform to expectations. A smaller force not only repelled the U.S. invasion of Ontario in the summer of 1812 but drove the Americans in retreat into the Michigan Territory. A combined British and Indian force sacked Detroit and Fort Dearborn (now Chicago). U.S. forces rallied in 1813. Oliver Hazard Perry won control of Lake Erie and forced the British out of Detroit, which they had occupied since the failed U.S. thrust into Canada. A second attack on Canada, led by William Henry Harrison, enjoyed initial success, but U.S. forces, many of whom were farmers who needed to return home to their crops, eventually vacated the territory. As with much of the war, the fighting in Canada proved inconclusive.

While the Americans could not defeat British and Candian forces, Indian tribes ultimately suffered devastating losses in the War of 1812. Even before the conflict began, Harrison outlasted the Indians at Tippecanoe in the Indiana Territory, slaughtering noncombatants in the process. During the 1813 campaign, Kentucky volunteers killed Tecumseh, the charismatic leader of the pan-Indian movement in the Old Northwest, in the Battle of the Thames. In the Old Southwest, Tennessee border captain Andrew Jackson led a defeat of the Creeks in 1814, clearing the southern states and the Gulf Coast for U.S. dominance.

Sporadic battlefield victories notwithstanding, the United States was weak and increasingly vulnerable before an angry British Empire. Napoleon's total defeat and abdication in April 1814 gave London the option of focusing its war machine on the upstart Americans. The British talked of punishing the Americans, exacting trade and territorial concessions, returning Louisiana to the Spanish, and even dissolving the republican union of states. The British underscored American vulnerability by marching into Washington, D.C., and torching the city, including the Capitol and the presidential mansion, as James and Dolley Madison fled to the hills across the Potomac. The U.S. forces acquitted themselves well, however, against the British at Baltimore and Plattsburgh (New York), as the inconclusive war ground on.

Financial weakness and internal dissent wracked the United States in wartime. The country, indebted since the 1803 Louisiana Purchase, lacked the financial and bureaucratic structures necessary to prosecute a successful national war effort. State militias and the regular army were poorly outfitted and lacked coordination. Opposition to "Mr. Madison's War" heightened across the country, and by the late war years the New England states verged on open rebellion. At Hartford, Connecticut, in October 1814 Federalists decried the "rule of Virginia"—a reference to the three American presidents from a single slaveholding southern state—and called for fundamental revision of the Constitution. They did not, however, as some Republicans later charged, advocate secession.

British exhaustion from more than a decade of total war with Napoleon provided salvation for the United States. Neither crown officials nor the British public wanted to pay for and prosecute yet another war on far-off American shores. British diplomats focused their attention on the more immediate need to reshape the European continent at the Congress of Vienna. Despite the country's palpable weaknesses and sectional differences, American patriotism remained strong, and British officials judged correctly that the young nation was not on the verge of collapse.

Negotiations aimed at ending the War of 1812 began in August 1814 at Ghent. The diplomats Madison dispatched to Europe, including John Quincy Adams, Henry Clay, and Albert Gallatin, possessed far more talent than the generals who had been assembled on the various battlefields. Despite considerable tension within the U.S. delegation, the Americans conceded little and gained nothing other than an end to the war. After twenty weeks of fruitless negotiations, both sides settled for an armistice rather than a formal peace treaty. The British refused to renounce impressment, but with the peace in Europe it would no longer be an issue. U.S. and British diplomats signed the Treaty of Ghent, terminating the war at the status quo ante, in December 1814.

Before news of the accord reached American shores, Andrew Jackson won a spectacular U.S. victory, slaughtering a British invading force at New Orleans on 8 January 1815. The victory ignited an "Era of Good Feeling" and catapulted Jackson to national political prominence. Congress quickly ratified

the Treaty of Ghent, formally ending the war. Despite inept handling of war issues by Jefferson and Madison, the Republicans succeeded in equating Federalist dissent with treason. The "rule of Virginia" continued for two more terms under James Monroe, and the Federalists disappeared from the face of American politics.

The United States did little more than survive a potential threat to its national independence that it had brought on by declaring a war for which it was ill equipped. The ineffectiveness of the war effort attested to the limited progress in nation building on the part of the young Republic. The United States not only failed to sack Canada, its invasions spurred Britain's determination to secure the northern outpost as a permanent barrier to American "Manifest Destiny." U.S. expansionists delivered decisive blows to Indian tribes in the West and South, furthering the merciless momentum of removal and extermination.

The War of 1812 is most appropriately conceptualized as a Second War for Independence. The Americans did not win their independence over two years of inconsequential military campaigns, yet the signing of another treaty with Great Britain confirmed the reality of national existence. Americans had rallied around the flag, embraced "Uncle Sam" as a national symbol, and adopted "The Star Spangled Banner" as a national anthem. Inspired by the "rockets' red glare," Francis Scott Key wrote the words to the anthem after witnessing the successful American defense of Baltimore and Fort McHenry. In the end the United States had survived yet another clash with the world's most powerful empire, and never again would Americans feel as vulnerable to foreign powers. Such psychological reassurance was an appropriate outcome of a war that at its essence had been an affair of honor.

"Victory" in the War of 1812 provided the stability and reassurance Americans needed to embark on a new era of national expansion and internal development. Congress authorized a second National Bank to address the weaknesses, revealed under the stress of war, of the new nation's financial institutions. The first national tariff sought to protect nascent U.S. industry from the sort of vulnerability to foreign powers that had been demonstrated in the war. Stung by Jackson's victory in New Orleans, Great Britain accorded the United States the grudging respect of negotiating settlements to a variety of border and economic disputes in the postwar years. The Anglo-American rapprochement freed Washington to enter into a sweeping agreement with Spain, the 1819 Adams-Onís Treaty, that facilitated continental expansion and to flex its muscles in Latin

America through the Monroe Doctrine of 1823. While the fighting had been inconclusive and probably avoidable, the War of 1812 ultimately confirmed the emergence of a rising American empire.

See also **Baltimore; Canada; Era of Good Feeling; Federalist Party; Foreign Relations,** *subentry on 1789–1860;* **Foreign Trade and Tariffs; Great Britain, Foreign Relations with; Jeffersonian Era; Militia, State; Nationalism,** *subentry on 1800–1865;* **Navy.**

Bibliography

Cohen, Warren I., ed. *The Cambridge History of American Foreign Relations.* Vol. 1. *The Creation of a Republican Empire, 1776–1865,* by Bradford Perkins. New York: Cambridge University Press, 1993.

Hickey, Donald R. *The War of 1812: A Forgotten Conflict.* Urbana: University of Illinois Press, 1989.

Stagg, J. C. A. *Mr. Madison's War: Politics, Diplomacy, and Warfare in the Early American Republic, 1783–1830.* Princeton, N.J.: Princeton University Press, 1983.

Tucker, Robert W., and David C. Hendrickson. *Empire of Liberty: The Statecraft of Thomas Jefferson.* New York: Oxford University Press, 1990.

WALTER L. HIXSON

WASHINGTON, GEORGE The American public's fascination with the image of George Washington (1732–1799) in the nineteenth century was an outgrowth of an ambiguous but genuine cult of hero worship that began to emerge soon after his appointment as commander in chief of the Continental army in 1775. At that time America settled on Washington as a collective symbol around which it could rally in its struggle against Great Britain.

By the dawn of the nineteenth century physical images of Washington had become so commonplace across the country that visitors to America remarked that every home had a likeness of the former president. Indeed, it was not unusual to see Washington's visage on coins, banknotes, tavern signs, coach panels, ships' mastheads, coat buttons, and cotton prints and samplers. Such likenesses, which multiplied exponentially during the nineteenth century, became inseparably intertwined with the more abstract, evolving image of Washington as the hero of the American Revolution and of the republican experiment.

Creating a Demigod

The mythmaking and even transformation of Washington into a demigod began in earnest upon his death in mid-December 1799. A year-long outpouring of public grief was expressed in parades and mock funerals, militia reenactments, religious sermons and prayers, and hundreds of eulogies celebrating his military and political achievements. This early veneration of Washington, culminating in *The Columbiad* (1807), a book-length poem by Joel Barlow (1754–1812) that celebrated Washington as a god, became especially noted in the ensuing decades at Fourth of July celebrations, Tree of Liberty fireworks, birthday commemorations, and numerous anniversary balls and dinners. Indeed, the public's desire for immediacy to Washington enabled P. T. Barnum (1810–1891) to begin his illustrious career as a huckster in 1835 by exhibiting an old slave woman as Washington's nurse.

America's grieving citizens also demanded tangible representations of Washington, resulting in a wide variety of mass-produced images. Moreover, the reaction to Washington's death and the ensuing celebrations of his life set precedents for the wholesale manufacture of Washingtoniana at anniversaries throughout the nineteenth century: the 1832 anniversary of his birth; the semicentennial celebration of his presidential inauguration in 1839 (featuring a two-hour speech by John Quincy Adams [1767–1848] and a special ode composed by William Cullen Bryant [1794–1878]); the 1876 centennial of the Decla-

George Washington. Engraving after a painting by Gilbert Stuart (1755–1828), published between 1840 and 1860. LIBRARY OF CONGRESS

ration of Independence; the 1889 celebration of his inauguration; and the 1899 centennial of his death.

Larger public gestures to honor Washington in a more permanent way began shortly after his death, when Martha Washington (1732–1802) reluctantly acquiesced to Congress's request that her husband's remains be moved from Mount Vernon, Virginia, to rest in the new federal capital; the removal of the body failed to take place, although designs for a public tomb were submitted and debated in Congress. A petition to build a national memorial to Washington first circulated in 1810, but it was 1833 before the Washington Monument Society was organized. Finally, on Independence Day 1848, the foundations of the Washington Monument were laid in Washington, D.C. Designed by the architect Robert Mills (1781–1855), the hollow marble obelisk, measuring 555 feet high and 55 feet square at the base, finally was dedicated in 1885 and opened to the public in 1888.

Meanwhile, representations of Washington in painting and sculpture proliferated in postrevolutionary America. Constantino Brumidi (1805–1880) painted *The Apotheosis of George Washington* (1865) and John Trumbull (1756–1843) included Washington in several of the massive murals of the American Revolution in the Capitol (1817–1824). *Washington Crossing the Delaware* (1851), by Emanuel Leutze (1816–1868), is one of the century's most famous images. Classical likenesses of Washington appeared in Antonio Canova's (1757–1822) severely criticized 1821 statue in the North Carolina statehouse at Raleigh and in the 1843 statue by Horatio Greenough (1805–1852), which portrays Washington in a Roman toga. Later, large equestrian statues of Washington were erected in New York, Richmond, Washington, and Boston.

In 1847 Washington and Benjamin Franklin (1706–1790), the first postmaster general for the united thirteen colonies, appeared on the first U.S. postage stamps. Before the Civil War, Washington's image had appeared on the 3¢, 12¢, 24¢, and 90¢ stamps, while the Confederate government issued a 20¢ stamp with his portrait. Washington's image also was used on government bonds, securities, and notes. Gilbert Stuart's (1755–1828) famous portrait of Washington (1796) was chosen to adorn the dollar bill when the federal government began issuing paper currency in the 1860s.

State coins and anniversary medals honoring Washington slowly opened the way for the appearance of human likenesses on federal coins. Funeral medals of 1800 set the precedent for more than a dozen nineteenth-century medals that commemorated various aspects of Washington's life and career.

Mount Vernon

Probably the most lasting legacy of Washington's nineteenth-century image has been his Virginia home, Mount Vernon—the first permanent shrine in the nation to attract multitudes of visitors. In shambles on the eve of the Civil War, Mount Vernon's decline was mourned by those who made pilgrimages to Washington's tomb. Ann Pamela Cunningham (1816–1875) of South Carolina led a group of women dedicated to saving the estate, and it was restored between 1853 and 1890. As the century ended the mansion was packed with artifacts related to the period 1759 to 1799. Martha Washington teas were held in Richmond and Baltimore in the 1870s to raise an endowment for the preservation of Mount Vernon. This began the historic house movement in America, and soon other houses connected with Washington were slated for preservation, among them the Hasbrouck House in Newburgh, New York; the Longfellow House in Cambridge, Massachusetts; the Ford Mansion in Morristown, New Jersey; and Washington's headquarters in Valley Forge, Pennsylvania. Nineteenth-century tourists from far and wide were sure to take in Mount Vernon and the tomb in their travels. Even General William T. Sherman's victorious Union army passed through in 1865 on its way to a grand review in Washington, D.C. Before the end of the century, recognition of Mount Vernon as a major tribute to its owner was so widespread that the state of Virginia paid for a facsimile to be erected at the 1893 World's Columbian Exposition in Chicago.

Also, a flurry of medals appeared on the eve of the Civil War, almost all with Revolutionary War themes. While proposals to place images of the first president on U.S. coins in 1864, 1865, and 1876 all failed, Washington became the first American citizen to appear on a federal coin when he and the Marquis de Lafayette (1757–1834) appeared on the Lafayette dollar in 1900.

Defining the Man and His Ideas

Washington's legacy to the nineteenth century went beyond his physical image and hero status. After Washington's death, various political figures embraced his strong leanings toward federalism and union, which were apparent in his Farewell Address (1796). Washington enumerated several important themes in this document—sacred union, the Constitution and the rule of law, reservations about party and faction, civic responsibility and moral and religious obligations of the citizenry in a republic, education, and warnings about foreign entanglements.

Two of these themes informed American political character in significant ways in the nineteenth century. First, Washington's idea (as paraphrased in an 1830 speech by Daniel Webster) of "Liberty and Union, now and forever, one and inseparable" became especially important during the sectional crises from 1820 to 1860, as men like John C. Calhoun (1782–1850), Jefferson Davis (1808–1889), and Stephen A. Douglas (1813–1861), elevating liberty at the expense of union, lined up against men like Daniel Webster (1782–1852), Henry Clay (1777–1852), and Abraham Lincoln (1809–1865), who stressed the sanctity of union. The attempt to preserve Washington's link between liberty and union remained the central issue in American politics until Lincoln's Gettysburg Address (1863) settled the matter by placing the Declaration of Independence at the core of the Union. The second important theme, neutrality in foreign (especially European) affairs—codified by Thomas Jefferson's (1743–1826) phrase "entangling alliances with none" (1801)—became, with some modifications, the cornerstone of U.S. foreign policy well into the twentieth century.

Between 1800 and the eve of the Civil War, more than four hundred books, essays, and articles on Washington's life appeared in print. Following a pattern set by hundreds of eulogies lamenting Washington's death and celebrating his military and political achievements, these writings invariably emphasized Washington's reputation as the disinterested embodiment of republican virtues, and his character and conduct became the ideals not only desired but expected of all Americans.

The style of these writings varied considerably. Mason Locke Weems's (1759–1825) well-known *The Life and Memorable Actions of George Washington* deviated from the content of the eulogies by revealing a private side of Washington. Parson Weems's inclusion of anecdotes (many of obvious questionable authenticity) and his emphasis on the development of character as one of the book's central themes made it an interesting and meaningful source to most Americans, especially to children. Originally printed in 1800, but quickly reprinted and enlarged in subsequent new editions, Weems's book became the best-known and most influential of all Washington-related publications in the nineteenth century; fifty-nine editions had been printed by 1850. Other writers, perhaps more factual but just as reverent and romantic as Weems, began to fashion Washington in their own

image. In the 1830s Jared Sparks (1789–1866), touting the inability of getting to know Washington except through the president's own writings, published a twelve-volume edition (1834–1837) of Washington's letters. Others, such as John Marshall (1755–1835), Washington Irving (1783–1859), John Frederick Schroeder (1800–1857), and Washington's step-grandson, George Washington Parke Custis (1781–1857), variously focused on Washington as a federalist, soldier, and moral role model.

Washington's image was co-opted, adapted, and modified by a divergent variety of groups for a variety of reasons. Politicians and theorists appealed to Washington as the embodiment of personal sacrifice, private virtues, and self-governance on which the republican experiment rested. Presidential candidates freely appropriated Washington in their campaign rhetoric and election paraphernalia. A myriad of government and private organizations claimed Washington's legacy for their own. During the Civil War both the Union and the Confederacy appropriated Washington for their side.

After the Civil War and Lincoln's assassination, the nation had a new savior to vie with Washington for citizens' affections. Predictably, the number of publications on Lincoln dramatically multiplied after his death but did not surpass the number still being published on Washington. Even when the latter fell off, Lincoln's appeal could not cross sectional lines as easily as Washington's.

Finding the Real Washington

A resurgence of respect for Washington occurred in the three decades after the Civil War, as attempts to humanize Washington replaced the old tendency to deify him. Consequently, he became more accessible to average Americans; this accessibility ironically ensured his mythic endurance. The ideals of virtue and morality that characterized the older image were replaced by those of self-reliance and self-improvement—ideals aptly suited to America's rising middle class. The new image was enthusiastically and nearly universally appropriated, even as grand pageants like the centennial celebrations of the Declaration of Independence and of Washington's first inauguration and death perpetuated Washington's older, idealized image.

Serious scholars also began to focus on the real Washington. In 1896 Paul Leicester Ford (1865–1902), whose brother Worthington C. Ford (1858–1941) edited a new edition of Washington's letters, published *The True George Washington*, which for the first time openly called into question Washington's religious commitments, in contrast to the pious and religious Washington who had appeared in the 1830s. In 1897 the historian and future president Woodrow Wilson (1856–1924) published a biography of Washington that did not even mention religion, but which included a series of celebrated illustrations by Howard Pyle (1853–1911). Despite this resurgence of interest in Washington, however, by the end of the nineteenth century, Lincoln's image had emerged as superior to that of Washington, as the nation came to emphasize equality over liberty.

See also **Monuments and Memorials; Politics,** *subentry* *on* **Political Thought; Presidency,** *subentry on* **The Presidency as an Institution; Republicanism; Revolutionary War Remembered.**

Bibliography

Albanese, Catherine L. "Our Father, Our Washington." Chapter 5 in *Sons of the Fathers: The Civil Religion of the American Revolution.* Philadelphia: Temple University Press, 1976.

Klapthor, Margaret Brown, and Howard Alexander Morrison. *G. Washington, a Figure upon the Stage.* Catalog edited by Carole J. Jacobs. Washington, D.C.: Smithsonian Institution Press, 1982.

Longmore, Paul K. *The Invention of George Washington.* 2d ed. Charlottesville: University Press of Virginia, 1999.

Marling, Karal Ann. *George Washington Slept Here: Colonial Revivals and American Culture, 1876–1986.* Cambridge, Mass.: Harvard University Press, 1988.

Pessolano-Filos, Francis. *Selected Washington Medals and Tokens, 1792–1977.* Edited by Margaret M. Walsh. New York: Eros, 1984.

Schwartz, Barry. *George Washington: The Making of an American Symbol.* New York: Free Press, 1987.

Spalding, Matthew, and Patrick J. Garrity. *A Sacred Union of Citizens: George Washington's Farewell Address and the American Character.* Lanham, Md.: Rowman and Littlefield, 1996.

FRANK E. GRIZZARD JR.

WASHINGTON, D.C.

WASHINGTON, D.C.   In the spring of 1800, 131 federal bureaucrats set up shop in the new capital along the Potomac River, which despite a decade of effort had attracted only three thousand residents in hamlets scattered in the woods. Capitol Hill, around which clustered ramshackle boardinghouses where homesick members of Congress lived during sessions, and Lafayette Square, planned as the hub of the executive branch, functioned as distinct villages in the city's early decades, connected by an unpaved Pennsylvania Avenue that turned to a bog after storms. After the British raid in 1814, Congress debated giving up on the city until local bankers provided funds to rebuild the Capitol and White House.

City of Magnificent Intentions

The French engineer Pierre Charles L'Enfant had designed Washington on a scale far in excess of its early requirements and resources. Jeffersonian Congresses did little to implement L'Enfant's system of radiating avenues punctuated by circles and squares. George Washington had selected the confluence of the Potomac and Anacostia rivers in part because he envisioned a mercantile center able to fund its own embellishment. Erosion from land clearance upstream, however, turned the riverfront into a marsh. Both river ports included in the one hundred square miles of the original District of Columbia—Georgetown on the Maryland side of the Potomac and Alexandria on the Virginia side—languished. Alexandria voted to return to Virginia in 1846. Meanwhile, Washington City, incorporated in 1802 to govern the thirteen square miles encompassed in L'Enfant's plan, bankrupted itself through efforts to promote commerce, such as the Chesapeake and Ohio Canal. Congress bailed out its capital in 1836 and began to improve the Mall, Pennsylvania Avenue, and other major features of L'Enfant's plan. One innovative prewar project was the Washington Aqueduct, designed by Montgomery Meigs, an army engineer. It was completed in December 1863, the same month as the wings and dome of the Capitol, also supervised by Meigs.

By 1860 the District's population was 75,080. Of that number, 61,122 resided in Washington City, making it the country's fourteenth largest city. Still, the straggling capital justified Charles Dickens's epithet "City of Magnificent Intentions." The crowning indignity was the Washington Monument, abandoned half-finished for want of funds in 1854—"a factory chimney with the top broken off," in Mark Twain's words—until its completion in 1884. The lack of trade and industry explains Washington's having attracted the lowest proportion of immigrants among the country's twenty largest cities.

Heart of a Troubled Nation

Situated amid the Chesapeake plantation country, Washington quickly acquired a large African American community. Free blacks soon outnumbered slaves—9,209 to 1,774 in Washington City—in 1860. Most free blacks toiled in laboring or service jobs, but some gained success despite the constraints of local black codes. Hostility to the black presence manifested itself in the Snow Riot of 1835, when a mob vandalized a black school along with black churches and businesses, and the *Pearl* Riot of 1848, when a crowd, agitated over an attempt to sail a shipload of runaway slaves to freedom, attacked the office of the

Construction of the U.S. Capitol, East Front, 9 May 1861. The completion of the dome in 1863 was deemed a sign of national solidarity by President Lincoln. LIBRARY OF CONGRESS

antislavery publication *National Era*. The Compromise of 1850 eliminated Washington's slave trade, but slavery endured there until 1862.

The Civil War brought unprecedented activity and attention to the capital. The influx of war workers, along with forty thousand "contraband" slaves, doubled the population in four years. The city acquired expanded police and fire service, streetcars, and modern school buildings. Soldiers and horses trampled the Mall. Army wagons ground the cobblestones of Pennsylvania Avenue to rubble. Nurses tended the wounded in hotels, churches, and houses seized from Confederate sympathizers, hundreds of whom, including the city's mayor, were jailed.

In December 1866, over local opposition and a presidential veto, Congress mandated black suffrage in District of Columbia elections. Radical Republicans, winners in a disputed municipal election in June 1868, endeavored to extend civil rights and educational opportunities to local blacks, but their rule collapsed in 1870. By the 1880s segregation prevailed, with the black third of the city's population dispro-

portionately consigned to menial employment and alley housing. The presence of institutions such as Howard University, founded in 1867, along with limited minority access to jobs in the professions, business, and government, nevertheless enabled Washington to evolve into a black intellectual and political metropolis.

The New Washington

In 1871 a group of Republican businessmen persuaded Congress to consolidate Washington City and Georgetown and the unincorporated highlands known as Washington County into the Territory of the District of Columbia, with a mix of elected and appointed officials. Led by Alexander "Boss" Shepherd, this pro-growth regime undertook a massive public works program that in three years transformed Washington's appearance and reputation. The millions of dollars in unauthorized spending and rampant conflict of interest that accompanied creation of this "New Washington" compelled Congress in 1874 to place the city under a board of commissioners appointed by the president, an arrangement made permanent in 1878. White Washingtonians acquiesced in the loss of home rule in part because it eliminated black suffrage, but largely because Congress agreed to pay half the municipal budget, which at last ensured adequate funds to maintain a capital "worthy of the nation," as contemporaries termed the goal. With blacks largely excluded, white Washingtonians exerted influence over their appointed rulers through a network of civic organizations, at the center of which stood the Board of Trade, an organization of bankers, merchants, and property investors founded in 1889.

The Gilded Age expansion of institutions such as the Smithsonian, the Library of Congress, and the U.S. Geological Survey set the stage for the capital's emergence as a center of science and learning. Although ties to the South remained strong, a postwar generation of entrepreneurs with roots in the North and West poured capital into fashionable neighborhoods such as Dupont Circle, as well as into utilities, transit lines, and suburban subdivisions. The clash between Antiques and Parvenus, satirized in Mark Twain and Charles Dudley Warner's *The Gilded Age: A Tale of Today* (1873), formed a theme in Washington's high society.

Placed under the Army Corps of Engineers, the once-decrepit Washington street system gained an international reputation for solid construction. The Corps of Engineers also won acclaim for its fifteen-year effort to fill the riverfront marshes and create Potomac Park. Meanwhile, James McMillan, a Republican from Michigan who served as the longtime chair of the Senate's District of Columbia Committee, commissioned renowned urban affairs experts to redesign social services and infrastructure. These efforts culminated in the McMillan Plan of 1902, the nation's first "comprehensive" urban plan. By Washington's centennial celebration in 1900, civic leaders could point with pride to the attractions and amenities of their city of 278,781, including 28,044 federal workers. Yet through the acceptance of nonelected government and racial segregation, the capital had embraced maladies that would plague it through the next century.

Bibliography

Gillette, Howard, Jr. *Between Justice and Beauty: Race, Planning, and the Failure of Urban Policy in Washington, D.C.* Baltimore: Johns Hopkins University Press, 1995.

Green, Constance McLaughlin. *Washington.* 2 vols. Princeton, N.J.: Princeton University Press, 1962–1963.

Lessoff, Alan. *The Nation and Its City: Politics, "Corruption," and Progress in Washington, D.C., 1861–1902.* Baltimore: Johns Hopkins University Press, 1994.

Lewis, David L. *District of Columbia: A Bicentennial History.* New York: Norton, 1976.

Melder, Keith E., ed. *City of Magnificent Intentions: A History of Washington, D.C.* 2d ed. Washington, D.C.: Intac, 1997.

ALAN LESSOFF

WASHINGTON STATE

The future state of Washington became a part of the United States as a result of the Anglo-American treaty of 1846. Washington was created as a territory in 1853 and admitted as a state in 1889. American interest in the state during the nineteenth century was based principally upon its extractive industries: furs, timber, and agriculture.

The major geographical features of the state are the Cascade Mountains running north and south and the Columbia River, the seventh longest river in North America, on the south. To the west of the Cascades the soil is fertile, the waters abundant with fish, and the climate far more humid than to the east. American Indians who lived in the area originally included the Coast Salish in the west and the Interior Salish and Sahaptin speakers east of the Cascades.

The maritime fur trade first drew Europeans and Americans to Washington in the 1780s. By the early nineteenth century American and British land-based beaver trappers operated in the region, led by John Jacob Astor's Pacific Fur Company (1811–1813) and the British North West Company (1813–1821). They were following the path of Lewis and Clark, who traversed the north bank of the Columbia River in 1805 and 1806.

Astor's company and the North West Company sent parties along the Columbia and Snake Rivers deep into the interior. Astor sold out to the North West Company in 1813. The British Hudson's Bay Company absorbed the North West Company in 1821 and remained a force in the Washington fur trade until the treaty of 1846.

Knowledge of the Indians publicized by the fur traders led to the arrival of religious missionaries. The American Board of Commissioners for Foreign Missions sent a party led by Marcus Whitman to Waiilatpu in southern Washington in 1836, and Roman Catholic priests followed in 1838. The missionary endeavor suffered a setback in 1847, when the Cayuse Indians attacked the Waiilatpu Mission and killed Marcus Whitman, Narcissa Whitman, and twelve others. The advance of the whites, however, could not be checked.

In western Washington, settlers began arriving over the Oregon Trail in the 1840s. Towns were soon laid out along Puget Sound, and Seattle was founded in 1853. These communities served as transportation centers for the first export, lumber from around Puget Sound that was sent to California after the gold rush began in 1848. Settlers also began farming the valleys of the sound region at this time. The advance east of the Cascades began with a mining rush into northern Washington in 1855. The native inhabitants were forced to make treaties in 1854 and 1855. The treaties placed the Indians on reservations, of which the Yakima and Colville reservations still exist. After the Indian wars were over, more settlers filtered into eastern Washington.

Washington Territory was created in 1853 from Oregon Territory. The first governor was Isaac Ingalls Stevens. The population reached 11,594 in 1860. Washingtonians largely ignored the Civil War, although Stevens joined the Union Army and was killed at the Battle of Chantilly. Citizens held a constitutional convention in 1878, but Washington was not admitted to the Union as the forty-second state until 1889.

The major event in nineteenth-century Washington was the coming of the transcontinental railroad. The Northern Pacific reached Tacoma in 1883, and the Great Northern reached Seattle in 1893. The railroads led to greater exports of lumber, beef, and wheat; brought an increase in migration and imports of manufactured goods; and opened up much of the dry country of eastern Washington to settlement. The gold rush to Alaska in 1897 had an enormous effect upon Seattle and, along with the coming of the Great Northern, made it the metropolis of the Pacific Northwest.

Major political issues of the late nineteenth century included labor disputes, woman suffrage, the movement to halt the migration of Chinese, and struggles between the eastern and western parts of the state over regulation of railroad rates and the supply of money. Republicans were the majority party in these years, although the Democrats were formidable rivals. By 1900 the population was 518,103.

See also **American Indian Societies,** *subentry on* **The Northwest Plateau; Fur Trade; Oregon; Seattle.**

Bibliography

Clark, Norman H. *Washington: A Bicentennial History.* New York: Norton, 1976.

Ficken, Robert E., and Charles P. LeWarne. *Washington: A Centennial History.* Seattle: University of Washington Press, 1988.

Morgan, Murray. *Puget's Sound: A Narrative of Early Tacoma and the Southern Sound.* Seattle: University of Washington Press, 1979.

GORDON B. DODDS

WATERPOWER

For much of the nineteenth century, America led the world in the large-scale development and use of waterpower. From the earliest days of colonial settlement, water-driven mills, powered by streams, rivers, and tides, were among the first structures erected in new settlements; gristmills and sawmills often took precedence over schools, churches, stores, and wagon roads. The water-driven mills played a central role in pioneer and rural settlements by providing settlers with the two essential staples of frontier life: bread and lumber. The water mill, in its various early manifestations, ushered the machine age into American culture by demonstrating the laborsaving benefits of mechanical power.

The Water Mill

Most counties had scores of water mills. By the beginning of the nineteenth century, America had at least 10,000 mills. In 1840, according to that year's census, over 66,000 mills were in operation—31,650 sawmills, 23,700 gristmills, 8,200 tanneries, and 2,600 fulling mills (where cloth was cleansed and prepared for manufacture)—one mill for every 245 people. The typical mill of the early 1800s consisted of a waterwheel, placed beside or beneath the mill building; a dam, located upstream, that ponded water overnight for use the next day and controlled the volume of water flowing to the mill; a millrace, or headrace, a canal that carried water to the mill; a penstock, or sluice, that carried the water to the waterwheel; and a tailrace that carried the spent water away from the wheel.

Types of waterwheels

Various types of waterwheels were used for power. All were circular, though of varying diameters and widths, with paddles or buckets arranged around their circumference. These paddles or buckets came into contact with falling water and captured a portion of the energy produced by the water's fall. The least sophisticated was the wooden tub wheel, which rotated horizontally on a vertical axis; it was usually connected directly to a millstone, and primarily used in rural gristmills. Undershot wheels also provided an uncomplicated means of exploiting waterpower. Water flowed into buckets on the upstream side of this wheel, which, unlike the tub wheel, spun vertically on a horizontal axis. Overshot wheels used the same principle, but water was carried over the top of the wheel. A more sophisticated version of the undershot wheel was the breast wheel, which was fitted with deep buckets that enabled the wheel to be turned by the weight of the water as well as the force of the water striking the wheel. Water flowed onto the upstream side of the wheel at a point roughly halfway

Dam Construction on the Cumberland River above Nashville, Tennessee, 1891. LIBRARY OF CONGRESS: PRINTS AND PHOTOGRAPHS DIVISION

up the wheel. An apron, or breast, formed a tightly fitted enclosure around the back portion of the wheel, preventing water from flowing out of the buckets prematurely, thereby maximizing the rotation given by the weight of the water.

The Rise of Industry in America

As American technological skill grew, waterpower was given new applications and the age of water milling gave way to the age of waterpower. As industries increased in scale and sophistication, their resemblance to rural water mills vanished. In a factory setting, waterpower needed a system of shafting, pulleys, and belting to carry power from the "prime mover" (waterwheel) to locations throughout the site. Efficient power transmission had much greater importance, and thus higher demands were placed upon it.

Lowell, Massachusetts

The textile mills at Lowell, Massachusetts, broke new ground for American industrial development in the nineteenth century. The pioneering efforts in the design, construction, and operation of waterpower works in Lowell surpassed all previous accomplishments. It was likewise at Lowell that waterpower became a product that could be measured, managed, bought, and sold. Here, the rule-of-thumb methods

formerly used at creekside mills were replaced by the highest order of engineering competence; what had been a craft became a science. Although still based upon a system of dams, millraces, waterwheels, and other supporting structures, the massive scale, sophistication, and complexity of the new establishments at Lowell marked a new stage in waterpower application in which hydraulic science played an ever increasing role. The Merrimack River, which flooded on a seasonal basis, was controlled, to a degree, by a series of dams and guard gates, and its powerful waters were channeled through massive millraces to the penstocks and waterwheels of the mills being erected at Lowell. By the mid–nineteenth century, the extensive network of canals, whose combined length was more than five miles, powered ten major mill complexes employing more than 10,000 workers. Imposing five- and six-story brick mills lined the Merrimack River for nearly a mile. The canals fed the waterwheels of forty mill buildings, powering 320,000 spindles and nearly 10,000 looms. Water rights were purchased in nearby New Hampshire, where water was stored in lakes during the spring, and then released into the Merrimack during low water periods in the summer and autumn.

The development of Lowell, which gradually unfolded between the 1820s and 1850s, led to the creation of other industrial towns in New England—

Manchester and Nashua, New Hampshire, and Lawrence, Fall River, and Chicopee, Massachusetts—all dedicated to textile manufacturing and strongly influenced by the hydraulic and civil engineering principles that were developed at Lowell. Similarly inspired water-powered industries arose in Minneapolis, Minnesota; Troy and Cohoes, New York; Richmond and Manchester, Virginia; and Augusta and Columbus, Georgia.

The Development of the Turbine

The turbine came onto the American scene in the 1840s. Its design was significantly different from the waterwheel. Unlike the waterwheel, the turbine was not driven by water falling onto its blades or buckets; instead, the wheel was put into motion by reacting to the pressure of the water flowing into the turbine case. At locations like Lowell the demand for waterpower began to exceed its availability, and the conversion to turbines, which in Lowell increased the capacity of the power system by one-fourth, provided mills with badly needed additional power. By the end of the Civil War, the turbine had become the leading source of stationary power in New England's textile industry, displacing all previous forms of waterwheels, which were substantially more wasteful in their use of water. The turbine's efficiency was about one-third higher than that of a breast wheel, and twice that of overshot and undershot wheels.

During the rapid industrialization that took place after 1865, many American inventors and manufacturers applied themselves to the development of a better and cheaper turbine. Their innovations were not a result of engineering theory but of empiricism; their goal was a simple, durable turbine that could be used in a wide variety of applications. The end product of this movement was the American mixed-flow turbine, which, compared with the turbines of the 1840s, provided an equal amount of power in half the space, at one-fifth the cost, and with a much simpler design.

Waterpower in Mining

While the turbine was undergoing improvements in design, waterpower was finding new applications in the American West. For the burgeoning mining industry, the need for water was exceeded only by the need for labor, its power being used to remove minerals, waste, and water. Unique conditions were often encountered in the mountains of the West. Among the challenges was a way to use small volumes of water with "high head" (water that fell from great heights, often more than a thousand feet). This led to the development of the tangential waterwheel,

which was immune to the damage that sand and silt would cause to turbines used in mining applications. Its simple design, ease of installation and maintenance, and flexible operating characteristics made its use widespread. The kinetic energy of water was put into direct application with hydraulic mining, by which hills were leveled and mountainsides demolished in the relentless quest for gold.

Steam Power

In spite of the widespread interest in the development of turbines after the Civil War, the use of waterpower began to lag behind steam power. In 1860 the ratio of waterpower use to steam power was 56 to 44; by the following decade, steam had come to dominate waterpower by a ratio of 52 to 48. By 1889 nearly 80 percent of the power being used was steam, and by 1899 waterpower accounted for only 15 percent of the power being generated. This transition was largely due to three variables: the industrialization of the economy, the urbanization of manufacturing, and the proliferation of railroads. The most critical factor in industrial location became transportation facilities, which gave manufacturers access to markets, capital, labor, raw materials, and service facilities. This stands in marked contrast to the 1820s and 1830s, when the need for waterpower outweighed any other consideration. Only with the coming of hydroelectric power in the 1890s did waterpower regain its standing.

The Return of Waterpower: Hydroelectric Power at Niagara

Efforts to harness the waterpower of Niagara Falls for industrial purposes were well under way in the 1850s, but it was not until the 1880s that flour and paper mills began to utilize, albeit in a meager way, 7,000 horsepower, only a small fraction of the available power. In 1886 a proposal was made to construct a network of twelve supply canals on the Niagara River above the falls that would supply water to 238 mills, each with a 500-horsepower waterwheel placed in a wheel pit approximately 150 feet deep. The 2.5-mile-long tailrace tunnel for these wheel pits would empty into the river below the falls. Conceptually, the proposal had much in common with what had been done at Lowell over half a century earlier, but on a much vaster scale. This plan led to the formation of the Niagara River Hydraulic Tunnel, Power, and Sewer Company that same year.

It was not until 1889, however, that investors agreed to back the development. The investors, who renamed the company the Niagara Falls Power Company, were reluctant to proceed with the plan as it stood, and consulted with European and American scientists and engineers. In 1890 it was decided to do away with supplying water to individual mills; instead, one central power station would be built. In October of that year, construction began on the power development's tailrace tunnel, and excavation of the power station's inlet canal began shortly thereafter. It was not until 1892 that tentative designs for the 5,000-horsepower turbines, the largest yet to be constructed, were ready. Ten turbines would be placed at the bottom of one large wheel pit located beneath the power station, and would utilize a 150-foot head of water. In May 1893 the decision was made to use alternating current to generate and transmit the power created by the turbines. The first hydroelectric turbine-generator unit went into operation in April 1895. Three more went into operation during the following year, and by 1900 all ten units were running. The first long-distance transmission of power was in 1896, to Buffalo, New York, twenty-six miles away. In 1904, a second powerhouse went into operation, bringing the total capacity of the power station to 105,000 horsepower, one-fifth of the total electrical energy used in the United States.

The construction of the Niagara Falls Power Company's power station, at that time the largest power plant in the world, was a landmark in power engineering both in its magnitude and in the myriad difficulties that had to be surmounted. Its success assured the mass acceptance of the alternating-current system, and marked the beginning of the rush to develop hydroelectric power that took place in the twentieth century. It showed the world the possibilities of power generation on a gargantuan scale and of the long-distance transmission of power. It also marked the end of what had been the traditional American system of distributing power to industrial consumers as water in canals, such as at Lowell; power would now be generated at central power stations, from which it would be sent wherever it was needed.

See also **Electricity; Mining and Extraction; Steam Power; Textiles.**

Bibliography

Adams, Edward Dean. *Niagara Power: History of the Niagara Falls Power Company, 1886–1918.* Vol. 2, *Construction and Operation.* Niagara Falls, N.Y.: Niagara Falls Power Company, 1927.
Hindle, Brooke, and Steven Lubar. *Engines of Change: The American Industrial Revolution, 1790–1860.* Washington, D.C.: Smithsonian Institution Press, 1986.
Hughes, Thomas P. *Networks of Power: Electrification in Western Society, 1880–1930.* Baltimore: Johns Hopkins University Press, 1993.
Hunter, Louis C. *A History of Industrial Power in the United States, 1780–1930.* Vol. 1, *Waterpower in the Century of the Steam Engine.* Charlottesville: University Press of Virginia, 1979.
Hunter, Louis C., and Lynwood Bryant. *A History of Industrial Power in the United States, 1780–1930.* Vol. 3, *The Transmission of Power.* Cambridge, Mass.: MIT Press, 1991.
Layton, Edward T. *From Rule of Thumb to Scientific Engineering: James B. Francis and the Invention of the Francis Turbine.* Stony Brook, N.Y.: Research Foundation of the State University of New York, 1992.
National Park Service. *Lowell: The Story of an Industrial City.* Washington, D.C.: U.S. Department of the Interior, 1992.
Passer, Harold C. *The Electrical Manufacturers, 1875–1900: A Study in Competition, Entrepreneurship, Technical Change, and Economic Growth.* Cambridge, Mass.: Harvard University Press, 1953.
Rawson, Marion Nicholl. *Little Old Mills.* New York: E. P. Dutton, 1935.

DANIEL MARTIN DUMYCH

WEALTH   The wealth of a country and its citizens reveals much about the national and individual quality of life. To most people, the term "wealth" connotes physical wealth or financial assets, real estate, buildings, equipment, inventories, and the like. Yet the know-how and intelligence of citizens should also count. Both physical and "human" capital are needed to engage in productive activities, which in turn lead to greater wealth, higher purchasing power, and better living standards. Most wealth estimates include only physical assets, in part because human capital is hard to measure. Fortunately the rankings of physical capital for comparative purposes—across persons, places, and time periods—often parallel the rankings of total, physical plus human, capital. Despite measurement difficulties, however, at least the concept of wealth should include human capital, even if official measures do not.

Physical-capital measures are hard to come by for the nineteenth-century United States. Not until 1850 did the federal census begin to include measures of wealth. That year the census reported real estate values, and starting in 1860 both real estate and personal property values appeared. Probate records, newspaper accounts, and business documents constitute the primary sources of wealth information about the years before 1850. Researchers sometimes use income as an imperfect proxy for wealth, particularly when considering distributional issues.

For most of the century average Americans held much of their wealth in land. Perhaps the greatest bargain in U.S. history, the Louisiana Purchase added $12 million worth of land to the country in mid-1803. This and other public land made its way into private hands via auctions; land grants, particularly to railroads; and special laws such as the Homestead Acts. In antebellum days southerners also held large portions of their wealth in slaves. Roger Ransom and Richard Sutch estimated that slaves constituted 60 percent of agricultural wealth in the five cotton states and that slaves accounted for two-thirds of the average slaveholder's wealth. Total value of slaves across the entire South was about $3 billion on the eve of the Civil War. After the war the Gilded Age produced multimillionaires whose wealth was invested in industrial and transportation concerns, financial assets, and raw materials, such as copper, coal, and oil.

According to estimates made by Robert Gallman, the U.S. capital stock grew rapidly—faster than the gross national product (GNP)—from 1840 to 1900. Other research found average real household wealth doubled in Ohio between 1860 and 1900. Estimated national per capita income (1860 prices) was $95 in 1839, $109 in 1840, $130 in 1859, and $144 in 1860. Per capita GNP (1958 prices) averaged $531 in the decade 1869–1878 and $774 in the decade 1879–1888. Yearly averages from 1889 to 1899 were $795, $836, $856, $920, $859, $819, $900, $865, $930, $933, and $1,000, respectively.

Any average wealth measure cloaks large variations across regions, sectors, factors of production, and individuals. For example, the 1825 tariff on manufactured goods redistributed wealth from the South to protected industries located in the Northeast. Jeremy Atack and Fred Batemen estimate that as of 1860 wealth was more equally distributed in northern rural areas than in cities, which contained many poor immigrants, and in the rural South, where large plantations nestled next to small farms. Mid-century per capita income measures indicate that the richest areas of the country were the Northeast and the Southwest Central, whereas the North Central region was relatively poor. By 1880 the average wealth per person outside the South was nearly three times that of the average southerner. Agricultural wealth accounted for 40 percent of national wealth in 1860, but this figure dropped to 20 percent in 1890. The share of income earned by labor declined in the 1860s, then increased through the 1880s and 1890s.

The period from 1774 to 1860 was one of high and increasing inequality in wealth across individuals partly because immigrants and babies, both notorious for their poverty, swelled the population. Jeffrey Williamson and Peter Lindert estimate that in 1774 the top 1 percent of wealthholders possessed 12.6 percent of all assets and the top 10 percent held nearly half of the total assets. In 1860 the respective figures were 29 percent and 73 percent. Slaves, who were not counted as persons in the census, typically held no wealth. Consequently, the true proportion of families without wealth in 1860 exceeded 50 percent.

Inequality remained after 1860, but some movement toward parity occurred. For example, the country experienced a large redistribution of wealth at the end of the Civil War, when former slaves became entitled to the fruits of their own labor. The postbellum years also featured variability in wealth as a series of financial panics plagued the nation. The longest period of economic contraction of the nineteenth century began in fall 1873 and lasted five years and five months. The 1890s experienced another major financial crisis.

Still, standards of living improved over the century for most Americans, with the probable exception of indigenous people. Per capita consumption of butter in pounds went from 13.7 in 1849 and 14.8 in 1859 down to 10 or 11 in the early 1870s. The figure increased through the 1880s to peak at 22.2 in 1886, then fell slightly to 20 in 1900. Sugar consumption ranged from 40 pounds in the 1870s to 65 pounds by the century's end. Cheese consumption fluctuated, with a low of 2.2 pounds in 1879 increasing to 4.5 pounds by 1901.

For some Americans the nineteenth century brought huge wealth. In the 1870s lucrative products and techniques developed, and industries consolidated. Cornelius Vanderbilt (1794–1877) and Jay Gould (1836–1892) both accumulated fortunes of more than $100 million, and John D. Rockefeller (1839–1937) and Andrew Carnegie (1835–1919) made far more than that. Many people have criticized the way various captains of industry made and spent their money. Sharp business practices and conspicuous consumption of ostentatious mansions, luxurious yachts, and expensive food and clothing certainly characterized many Gilded Age grandees. Yet these wealthy individuals also bankrolled new products and services, bringing prices within the range of the average pocketbook. They sometimes stabilized markets and often returned considerable wealth to the community. J. Pierpont Morgan (1837–1913) played a key role in suppressing incipient financial panics in 1895 and 1907. Others, such as Carnegie, who helped establish community libraries, donated millions. In his life, Rockefeller gave away about $530 million, $450 directly or indirectly to medicine and much of the remainder to educational and research institutions. Rockefeller's son gave away $537 million directly and $540 million through philanthropic organizations. One notable exception to this philanthropic group was the wealthiest woman of her time, Henrietta "Hetty" Green (1834–1916). In 1865

Home of John Jacob Astor, New York City. Fifth Avenue became the street of millionaires' mansions after the Civil War. LIBRARY OF CONGRESS

Green inherited $10 million from her family's shipping, trading, and whaling interests, and she shrewdly increased her fortune tenfold over the next half-century. In addition to leaving nothing to charity, Green reputedly spent little on clothes or soap, and her son lost his leg because she refused to pay for his medical care.

See also **Banking and Finance,** *subentry on* **The Banking Industry; Consumerism and Consumption; Corporations and Big Business; Economic Regulation; Entrepreneurs; Entrepreneurs, Women; Federal Land Policy; Foreign Trade and Tariffs,** *subentry on* **Trade and Tariffs; Gilded Age; Investment and Capital Formation; Monetary Policy; Panics and Depressions; Property; Railroads; Trusts.**

Bibliography

Atack, Jeremy, and Fred Bateman. *To Their Own Soil: Agriculture in the Antebellum North.* Ames: Iowa State University Press, 1987.

Atack, Jeremy, and Peter Passell. *A New Economic View of American History.* New York: Norton, 1994.

Fogel, Robert William, and Stanley L. Engerman. "The Economics of Slavery." In *The Reinterpretation of American Economic History.* Edited by Robert William Fogel and Stanley L. Engerman. New York: Harper and Row, 1971.

Gallaway, Lowell E., and Richard K. Vedder. "Migration and the Old Northwest." In *Essays in Nineteenth Century Economic History.* Edited by David C. Klingaman and Richard K. Vedder. Athens, Ohio: Ohio University Press, 1975.

Gallman, Robert E. "The United States Capital Stock in the Nineteenth Century." In *Long-Term Factors in American Economic Growth.* Edited by Stanley L. Engerman and Robert E. Gallman. Chicago: University of Chicago Press, 1986.

Ransom, Roger L., and Richard Sutch. *One Kind of Freedom.* Cambridge, U.K., and New York: Cambridge University Press, 1977.

Ratner, Sidney, James H. Soltow, and Richard Sylla. *The Evolution of the American Economy.* New York: Macmillan, 1993.

Soltow, Lee. *Men and Wealth in the United States, 1850–1870.* New Haven, Conn.: Yale University Press, 1975.

United States Bureau of the Census. *Historical Statistics of the United States, Colonial Times to 1957.* Washington, D.C.: U.S. Government Printing Office, 1960.

Williamson, Jeffrey G., and Peter H. Lindert. *American Inequality: A Macroeconomic History.* New York: Academic Press, 1980.

JENNY BOURNE WAHL

WELFARE AND CHARITY The United States began the nineteenth century with a system of care for the indigent based on two centuries of English practice under the Elizabethan Poor Law. In 1800 the indigent were the responsibility of their local community, supported by local property taxes. However, with industrialization and urbanization, the demands of the poor overwhelmed many local governments. Pleas by local officials for aid from higher levels of government prompted a reevaluation of the roles of public and private charities in meeting the needs of the growing number of indigents. Throughout the century officials took numerous small steps to increase the state and federal roles in protecting the welfare of selected groups. By 1900 a comparatively large private and public welfare system had emerged. However, the system was distinctly American, causing historians to question what accounted for this American exceptionalism. Generally, changes in welfare during the century included intense study and a growing ideological debate concerning the relationship of the industrial economy to welfare needs; development of new public policies to deal with the poor, especially in assessing their worthiness to receive various forms of public assistance; and reform and expansion of private charities to meet the growing human needs. These innovations raised, and in turn helped answer, important questions about the nature of policymaking in the United States and the goals of public welfare and private charity.

Ideological Foundations

Several factors restrained changes in welfare and charity during the century. First, the country had inherited two centuries of experience with the Elizabethan Poor Law that fit well within a large federal union, where local governments and private charities could best identify those in need. Second, the American religious tradition, with its emphasis on personal moral responsibility and the separation of religious questions from state control, reinforced oversight of charity by local and private institutions. Finally, beginning with Adam Smith's theory of capitalist political economy, the English-speaking world became enamored of laissez-faire ideas of minimal government intervention in the economy. Reinforced first by the work of the Manchester school of economists in England, laissez-faire theory held that government could not make life better by interfering to protect people from market forces.

After mid-century new support appeared for Smith's ideas from Charles Darwin's cousin Herbert Spencer. His theory of social Darwinism held that government regulation of sanitary conditions, provision of public education, and other protection of the poor was not simply unwise, it contradicted the biological law of natural selection. Government should not interfere with the survival of the fittest. William Graham Sumner spread the message of social Darwinism in the United States through works such as *What Social Classes Owe to Each Other* (1883), which attacked vigorously any intervention by government in protecting the indigent. Richard Dugdale's *The Jukes* (1877), a study of a degenerate family, popularized the related eugenic theory that personal failure was based in heredity. Amos Warner's *American Charities* (1894), the standard text regarding work among the poor, reinforced these ideas. The popularity of laissez-faire economics and social Darwinism combined with political and religious traditions to limit innovations in welfare policies, yet by the end of the century major new theories redefined the proper responsibility of the state and society to the poor.

Several factors account for these new ideas. First, the abject poverty evident in cities, especially some of the new industrial centers, could not be ignored easily. In addition to the laissez-faire ideas coming to the United States from Europe, important counter arguments grew out of the responses to urbanization in Great Britain and to a lesser extent in France and Germany. Americans learned much from the reports of the English Poor Law Commission in the 1830s and 1840s. In the same era the early statistical movement produced better data on the conditions of the poor.

Among the non-English immigrants to the United States were various defenders of continental organic conceptions of society. Americans learned about both religious and secular utopian ideas and socialist alternatives to capitalism. From France came the ideas of Charles Fourier, who called for breaking down mass industrial society into small producing communities called phalanxes. Robert Owen, the Welsh reform industrialist from Scotland, received an official reception from President James Monroe and the U.S. Congress when he arrived to promote the establishment of model industrial communities in 1825. Later in the century, in 1872, the international Socialist headquarters moved to New York from London, and a small Socialist movement arose in the United States. Yet during the nineteenth century the Socialists had a limited following, and none of the utopian communities experienced overwhelming success.

The two most influential European critiques of capitalism that spawned significant American welfare reforms originated in the German universities and continental religious movements. Throughout the century a number of German economists developed a historical critique of English laissez-faire economics that called upon the government to develop new policies to ameliorate the worst consequences of industrialization. With the rising reputation of German higher education, many American academics

Dwight Moody *(center, with beard)* **and Chicago Street Urchins**. The evangelical minister and social reformer was active in the Young Men's Christian Association and other charitable organizations in Chicago. Photograph, 1877. LIBRARY OF CONGRESS

went to Germany for their graduate training or attended the new American institutions, such as Johns Hopkins University, that copied the German institutions. Richard Ely played a leading role in advocating welfare policy. After attending the University of Heidelberg, he returned to teach at Johns Hopkins and founded the American Economic Association to promote social reform. Ely also reported on another continental contribution to welfare policy, Christian social thought. Pope Leo XIII's *Rerum Novarum*, published in 1891, the most dramatic and influential example of Christian social thought, supported a variety of reforms.

Throughout the century, American churches repeatedly focused on questions related to the growing number of poor. Many of the new charitable and welfare programs originated in the century's periodic evangelical crusades, including movements to help the deaf, the mentally ill, orphans, freedmen, and Native Americans. Church links became a distinctive feature of many American reform movements, partially accounting for the exceptional American focus on voluntarism rather than public provision of charity. The work of Charles Loring Brace, a Congregational minister from Connecticut, is a good example

of the role of religion in reform. Beginning with a personal "mission to the children" in 1852, he helped found the Children's Aid Society of New York, and he and his son led the development of American policies regarding children into the early twentieth century. Later, ministers such as Washington Gladden and Josiah Strong formalized the links between Christian thought and welfare policy in the Social Gospel movement. While usually emphasizing private voluntary charity, their work added sophisticated services for the indigent to the programs of churches in urban America. Strong especially spread support for social reform and community responses to poverty through the nationwide Evangelical Alliance, which he headed for many years. Both Gladden and Ely built bridges between the Social Gospel movement and Christian social thought. Gladden joined Ely in founding the American Economic Association, and Ely wrote a number of scholarly accounts of Christian social theory. Although church leaders often minimized the role of public aid, Strong increasingly criticized the fixation on private charity among the churches and in 1898 created the League for Social Service to advocate expansion of both public and private welfare programs.

Salvation Army Sermon. The organization, founded in London by William Booth in 1865, used Gospel teachings to rehabilitate the poor. Wood engraving in *Harper's Weekly*, 3 April 1880. LIBRARY OF CONGRESS

Government and the Deserving Poor

During the nineteenth century, one of the exceptional features of American social policy was the effort to improve assessment of the worthiness of individuals for charity and public aid. Concern with identifying the deserving poor originated with the increase in the number of indigent that accompanied industrialization. Local control of, and responsibility for, welfare policy required some industrialized cities and towns to shoulder a disproportionate share of the welfare burden. When these cities pleaded for funding assistance, state governments demanded that they stop providing aid to people who continued to live in their own homes, a practice called "outdoor relief." Instead, states ordered local governments to force the indigent to move into almshouses, where they could be observed and made to work while receiving aid (indoor relief). These poorhouses were wretched places, and pressure mounted to determine who should be placed in them and who deserved aid outside. Each addition to the ranks of the deserving poor resulted in new institutions and forms of assistance, a recurring feature of American welfare policy.

Among the first to be defined as deserving were those with obvious physical handicaps. In 1817 Thomas Gallaudet, a Congregational minister inspired and assisted by French reformers, launched the Connecticut Asylum for Deaf and Dumb Persons with a grant from the state and support from private charity. Two years later the U.S. Congress contributed a land grant to support the school. Gallaudet's work became a model for converting a group of people needing control into a group deserving aid. He found that the state and national governments would contribute to ameliorating a group's condition once it proved worthy. In 1831, emulating Gallaudet, New York State incorporated a school for the blind and moved blind children there from the almshouses. Within a year other eastern states followed that example, and several states even established special asylums for juvenile delinquents. Before the Civil War, Dorothea Dix led an effort to remove the mentally ill from prisons and poorhouses and place them in special hospitals.

After mid-century, federal provisions for the deserving indigent increased remarkably, stimulated by several factors. First, experiences treating various Civil War injuries influenced the understanding and treatment of certain disabilities, including mental illness. Second, following the Civil War many deserving handicapped veterans and veterans seeking pensions returned to their communities. Consequently, the U.S. Pension Bureau became a major welfare agency for a generation of Northerners. Third, the Freedmen's Bureau gave the federal government its first major experience with providing social services. A decade after the war's end, the shock of the Battle of Little Bighorn, the embarrassment of the flight of the Nez Percé Indians, and Helen Hunt Jackson's *A Century of Dishonor* (1881) permanently changed the status of American Indians. The general public no longer saw Native Americans as hostile savages, and they, too, became deserving wards of the federal government, a change recognized by the Supreme Court in *United States v. Kagama* (1886). In reality, the *Kagama* decision only confirmed a trend begun much earlier with the removal of the Indians from the Southeast to Oklahoma. By mid-century the federal government transferred the Bureau of Indian Affairs (BIA) from the War Department to the Interior Department. Reflecting the new worthiness of Indians, the BIA established its first hospital in the 1850s on the Nez Percé reservation and opened its first Indian school in 1860 in Yakima, Washington.

Despite these impressive steps, the federal government provided comparatively few public welfare services. The new roles for the government in protecting public welfare emerged largely at the state and local levels. While almshouses were the most negative consequence of this trend, in fields such as health, sanitation, and housing, state and local governments brought significant improvements to the lives of the urban poor, especially through public health programs targeted at infants and children. New professional societies, such as the American Public Health Association, supported such initiatives. Governments created research institutions, such as the Lawrence Experimentation Station in Massachusetts, that brought marked improvement to urban sanitation and water supplies. Led by the work of Carroll Wright at the Massachusetts Bureau of Statistics of Labor, states collected data to better understand the needs of the industrial population. Consequently, by the 1890s bureaus of factory inspection studied factories further and enforced new regulations related to working conditions. Florence Kelley, the first state factory inspector in Illinois, and other female reformers played remarkable roles in launching those programs. Finally, big-city political machines provided many informal but vitally important protective services to the urban poor, such as aid to widows and help in securing jobs and burial funds. Unfortunately, the corruption associated with both urban bosses and various federal welfare programs, especially those for veterans, tainted the reputation of public welfare well into the next century.

Reforms of Private Charity

Despite the many public-policy initiatives of the nineteenth century, U.S. welfare policy continued to rely heavily on private initiative and institutions for most charity. The scope and methods of private charity changed in four major ways during the century. First, new private institutions developed for each new category of worthy poor. Often these private initiatives received government subsidies, as in the case of institutions for the deaf, mentally ill, freedmen, and Indians. Second, national and international conferences and other institutions shared information on charitable procedures. For example, Brace participated in international conferences on children's charities, and the infant mortality movement spawned a network of international meetings and publications. Also, American reformers went to Europe to learn comparative methods for working with the indigent.

A third major change came in the last quarter of the century with the development of new institutions to coordinate the varied charitable activities in each community. Copying efforts in London, most American cities, beginning with Buffalo in 1877, developed a Charity Organization Society (COS). The COS generally did not dispense payments to the poor; it centralized information on the indigent, gathered relevant statistics, and employed friendly visitors to check on the living conditions of the needy. Historians of social policy have criticized the COS movement as an effort to control the poor rather than solve their problems. While that often proved true in the early years, the COS movement was also a step on the path to remedial reforms. Before the end of the century Josephine Shaw Lowell joined other COS leaders in founding the National Consumers' League, which attacked the economic factors causing poverty.

Finally, a number of older institutions that worked with the poor changed fundamentally during the century, especially hospitals and health care, both of which evolved rapidly after 1850. With the professionalization of nursing, and improved treatment techniques such as antiseptic surgery that developed during the Civil War, hospitals abandoned their historic role of primarily caring for the dying indigent and provided better care for all. The rise of middle-class medical professionals converted hospitals from a tragic final step in the life of the poor into centers of expert medical cures. As with so much other American charity, religious groups played an important role in sponsoring hospitals, both to fulfill their charitable mission and to assure that their members received care in accordance with religious principles, whether it be providing kosher food or access to the last rites.

The change in hospital roles corresponded with the important general policy transition near the end of the century that converted the timeless condition of the poor into a solvable problem. That transition accelerated after the depression of 1893, which more than previous economic downturns influenced leaders of private charitable activities to see the limits of their efforts. Lowell, Strong, and other leaders whose earlier focus had been on improving private charitable efforts became supporters of public-welfare programs and general social reform movements.

American Exceptionalism

When compared with the policies of other industrial societies, American welfare policy had several exceptional characteristics, including a reliance on the private sector and the continual emphasis upon assessments of worthiness. When some New York matrons opened a hospital for former slaves, they named it the Home for Worthy, Aged, and Indigent Colored People. Clearly, the United States faced the confounding problem of sorting out the racial and ethnic causes of poverty from the economic ones. In contrast the poor of countries like England or Germany were usually of the same ethnicity as the affluent. Americans were tempted to blame poverty on ethnicity.

Historians have debated why the U.S. public social welfare process differed so greatly from that in other industrial nations. The numerous theories can be grouped into four broad categories that place the emphasis on either cultural, economic, political, or social factors.

The cultural argument, articulated by Louis Hartz and Daniel Levine, finds that America's liberal consensus limits the options Americans consider when making policy decisions. Americans grant to business a privileged position socioeconomically and culturally. As theorists like William Graham Sumner assumed, laissez-faire business practices and the resulting prosperity—not conscious public intervention—solve social problems.

Harold Wilensky and other historians, however, have emphasized that industrialization causes the development of social welfare policies and that America's exceptionalism arises from its unique industrialization. With its vast farmlands, not available in Europe and Japan, the United States became a leading industrial power while still being a leading agricultural nation. Except in a few industrial states in the American Northeast, officials did not face the need for ameliorative public policies that their counterparts in other industrializing nations faced.

A variety of political historians from Stephen Skowronek to Theda Skocpol have found the source of exceptionalism in the limited capacity or development of the American state. The constitutional limits on public power, such as federalism and the separation of powers, and the absence of a skilled civil service left the United States incapable of administering complex social welfare policy. The government's in-

capacity forced Americans to rely on private charity and voluntarism.

Finally, Walter Korpi and others have proposed that the lack of strong labor unions and strong leftist parties explains the level of social policy. A variation of this theory emphasizes the unique treatment of women in the United States. Women were empowered with control over social welfare policy, but they could not vote. Therefore welfare remained private, removed from the public sphere controlled by men. The contrasting roles of women in the settlement house movements of the United States and Britain supports this interpretation.

Another point of interpretative dispute is the intent of social policy. The most common perspective holds that the intent of social policies, whether schools for the blind or the Freedmen's Bureau, was to provide social opportunity or to bring social justice. However, Paul Boyer and Robert Wiebe have emphasized that social welfare reformers frequently wanted to bring order to a chaotic society, that is, to impose social control. The desire for social control may have reached its most sinister form among the supporters of Francis Galton's eugenics and other implicitly racist assessments of the causes for social problems. While some social Darwinists advocated minimal social welfare policy to avoid tinkering with the survival of the fittest, David Noble has maintained that some advocated quite intrusive social engineering, most often applied in a crude form by the friendly visitors from the COS.

Conclusion

While the nineteenth century left a mixed legacy in addressing the welfare needs of society, clearly the existence of women factory inspectors, the Consumers' League campaign for labor standards, government hospitals and schools for Indians and the disabled, and a substantial federal pension bureaucracy made welfare and charity in 1900 far more similar to that of 2000 than to that of 1800. By the close of the century the exceptional American approach to providing welfare protections had been defined, including minimal social insurance and maximum reliance on charity and voluntarism. Federalism continued to restrict the national government's role in public welfare. Americans remained interested in assessing the worthiness of the poor, and those efforts were complicated by the difficulty of sorting out economic and ethnic patterns in poverty.

See also **Asylums; Civil War,** *subentry on* **Consequences of the Civil War; Class, Social; Economic Theory; Hobos, Tramps, and the Homeless; Immigration and Immigrants,** *subentry on* **Anti-immigrant Sentiment; Local Government; Mental Illness; Orphans and Orphan-**

ages; **Panics and Depressions; Politics,** *subentry on* **Machines and Bosses; Population; Poverty; Race and Racial Thinking; Reform, Social; Settlement Houses.**

Bibliography

Bannister, Robert C. *Social Darwinism: Science and Myth in Anglo-American Social Thought.* Philadelphia: Temple University Press, 1979.

Boyer, Paul S. *Urban Masses and Moral Order in America, 1820–1920.* Cambridge, Mass.: Harvard University Press, 1978.

Bremner, Robert H. *From the Depths: The Discovery of Poverty in the United States.* New York: New York University Press, 1956.

Dowbiggin, Ian Robert. *Keeping America Sane: Psychiatry and Eugenics in the United States and Canada, 1880–1940.* Ithaca, N.Y.: Cornell University Press, 1997.

Flora, Peter, and Arnold Heidenheimer, eds. *The Development of Welfare States in Europe and America.* New Brunswick, N.J.: Transaction, 1981.

Gittens, Joan. *Poor Relations: The Children of the State in Illinois, 1818–1990.* Urbana: University of Illinois Press, 1994.

Hartz, Louis. *The Liberal Tradition in America: An Interpretation of American Political Thought since the Revolution.* New York: Harcourt, Brace, 1955.

Hofstadter, Richard. *Social Darwinism in American Thought.* Revised ed. Boston: Beacon, 1955.

Katz, Michael B. *Poverty and Policy in American History.* New York: Academic, 1983.

Korpi, Walter. *The Democratic Class Struggle.* Boston: Routledge and K. Paul, 1983.

Koven, Seth, and Sonya Michel, eds. *Mothers of a New World: Maternalist Politics and the Origins of Welfare States.* New York: Routledge, 1993.

Levine, Daniel. *Poverty and Society.* New Brunswick, N.J.: Rutgers University Press, 1988.

May, Henry Farnham. *Protestant Churches and Industrial America.* New York: Harper, 1949.

McLoughlin, William G. *Revivals, Awakenings, and Reform: An Essay on Religion and Social Change in America, 1607–1977.* Chicago: University of Chicago Press, 1978.

Meckel, Richard A. *"Save the Babies": American Public Health Reform and the Prevention of Infant Mortality, 1850–1929.* Baltimore: Johns Hopkins University Press, 1990.

Noble, David F. *America by Design: Science, Technology, and the Rise of Corporate Capitalism.* New York: Knopf, 1977.

Orloff, Ann Shola. *The Politics of Pensions: A Comparative Analysis of Britain, Canada, and the United States, 1880–1940.* Madison: University of Wisconsin Press, 1993.

Ross, Dorothy. *The Origins of American Social Science.* Cambridge, U.K., and New York: Cambridge University Press, 1991.

Rothman, David J. *The Discovery of the Asylum.* Boston: Little, Brown, 1971.

Skocpol, Theda. *Protecting Soldiers and Mothers: The Political Origins of Social Policy in the United States.* Cambridge, Mass.: Belknap Press of Harvard University, 1992.

Skowronek, Stephen. *Building a New American State: The Expansion of National Administrative Capacities, 1877–1920.* Cambridge, U.K., and New York: Cambridge University Press, 1982.

Starr, Paul. *The Social Transformation of American Medicine.* New York: Basic Books, 1982.

Trattner, Walter I. *From Poor Law to Welfare State: A History of Social Welfare in America.* New York: Free Press, 1974.

———, ed. *Social Welfare or Social Control? Some Historical Reflections on Regulating the Poor.* Knoxville: University of Tennessee Press, 1983.

Wiebe, Robert H. *The Search for Order, 1877–1920.* New York: Hill and Wang, 1967.

Wilensky, Harold L., and Charles N. Lebeaux. *Industrial Society and Social Welfare: The Impact of Industrialization on the Supply and Organization of Social Welfare Services in the United States.* New York: Russell Sage Foundation, 1958.

EDWARD C. LORENZ

WELLS FARGO   New York expressmen Henry Wells and William George Fargo formed Wells Fargo on 18 March 1852 to offer all residents of the Pacific Coast three interconnected services: expressing, banking, and letter delivery. It immediately inaugurated ocean service between New York and San Francisco via Panama and, within a decade, had come to dominate the market, establishing itself as the most powerful company in the Far West.

Wells Fargo handled the transport of money rapidly and guarded by messengers with shotguns. From miners, the company safely carried so much gold and silver as to compile statistics on precious metals production in the West. The company administered bank loans that developed the economy, while its reliable Letter Express carried 75 percent of the mail within California. Wells Fargo did virtually everything. "It is the Ready Companion of civilization, the Universal Friend and Agent of the miner, his errand man, his banker, his post-office," the eastern newspaper editor Samuel Bowles remarked in his book *Across the Continent* (1865).

It was the policy of Wells Fargo to serve all prospective customers. "Proper respect must be shown to all—let them be men, women or children, rich or poor, white or black," company regulations declared. "It must not be forgotten that the Company is dependent on these same people for its business." Among its employees, too, were African Americans, Chinese, Hispanics, Japanese, and Native Americans.

In 1858 Wells Fargo helped form the Overland Mail Company, instituting the first regular cross-country passenger service; in 1861 it ran the Pony Express; and in 1866 it inaugurated a vast overland stagecoaching network. By 1888 Wells Fargo's express lines extended over a multitude of railroads into Mexico and reached "ocean to ocean" across the continent to New York City. Wells Fargo's express business split off in 1905; in 1918, ten thousand offices

Wells Fargo Agent John Q. Jackson

Wells Fargo agent John Quincy Jackson summed up his experiences in letters home to Petersburg, Virginia. "My position," he told his parents in October 1852, "throws me in contact with the heaviest business men of the state—Bankers, Lawyers, Merchants & all do business through us." Only twenty years old, Jackson exulted that in Auburn, California, where he had "charge of a large Express Office and Banking house," he could "make as much here in one month as I can in Virginia in two years."

A younger brother received a detailed explanation later that month. "What I have to do is quite confining," Jackson wrote, "staying in my office all day till 10 at night buying dust, forwarding & receiving packages of every kind, from and to everywhere—filling out drafts for the Eastern Mails in all sorts of sums from $50 to $1,000, and drawing checks on the Offices below [Sacramento and San Francisco], when men wish to take money to the cities—as it is a great convenience to them to have a check instead [of gold coin at 3.5 pounds per $1,000]—and it saves us the trouble of shipping coin up from below for purchasing dust.

"I have just come from the Post Office, from which I have got 100 letters [from the Atlantic States] to be forwarded to the different parts of the country to which they are ordered by Express. On these I make $25, as my charge on each is 25 cents."

Jackson closed, "I am spinning out this letter when I have something else bearing down on my mind which has to be done to night—all my letters on business are to be written; always five or six each night, and the same number during the day. The Gold dust bought during the last two days is to be cleansed, weighed, sealed and packed, ready to be forwarded in the morning—my books balanced—letters to be sorted for the different offices to which they are to be forwarded—a list made of those received from Sacramento to day—and bundled for the river messenger who leaves at daylight. This done with half dozen other things, and I go to sleep after being kindly remembered to all."

nationwide became part of American Railway Express during World War I. Wells Fargo Bank remained in San Francisco, establishing itself, as Bowles concluded in 1865, as "the omnipresent, universal business agent" of the West.

See also **Banking and Finance,** *subentry on* **The Banking Industry; Pony Express; Post Office; Transportation,** *subentry on* **Railroads.**

Bibliography

Bartz, James Lynn. *Company Property of Wells, Fargo & Co.'s Express, 1852–1918*. Lake Forest, Calif.: Westbound Stage, 1993.

Coburn, Jesse. *Letters of Gold: California Postal History through 1869*. New York: Philatelic Foundation, 1984.

Loomis, Noel. *Wells Fargo*. New York: Clarkson N. Potter, 1968.

Nevin, David. *The Expressmen*. New York: Time-Life, 1974.

ROBERT J. CHANDLER

WEST, THE   In the broadest sense, the "West" in the nineteenth century referred to the western portion of the United States. Yet the boundaries of the region shifted throughout the century. By the close of the century the West meant the region west of the Mississippi River. Early in the century, however, Americans employed the term to describe areas as far east as trans-Appalachia. Indeed, before 1803 Wisconsin and Illinois were the "Far West."

One reason for the West's historical movability is the link between the region or place called the West and the Anglo-American "frontier." In this conception the West moved with the line of Anglo expansion. In fact, for some the two terms became interchangeable. Because it is often conflated with the frontier experience, the "West" is a value-laden and iconic term. For many Americans the West remains a land of cowboys and Indians caught in a timeless, epic conflict; of rugged frontiersmen braving the wilderness; and, of course, of sheriffs, gunfighters, and "soiled doves" (prostitutes). This vision of the West was mythologized in numerous nineteenth-century dime novels and Buffalo Bill's Wild West Shows and later in twentieth-century films and television programs.

For an early-nineteenth-century Anglo-American, the West usually referred to the Ohio River valley, the old Northwest Territory, and states like Tennessee and Kentucky or the trans-Appalachian West. By the mid–nineteenth century the United States had expanded from the Atlantic to the Pacific Coast. The West then stretched from the Mississippi River to the Pacific, north to the Canadian border, and south to

Black Hawk City, Colorado Territory, 1864. Photograph by George D. Wakely, a pioneer Rocky Mountain photographer. LIBRARY OF CONGRESS: PRINTS AND PHOTOGRAPHS DIVISION

the newly established, as a result of the Mexican War (1846–1848), Mexican border.

Eighteenth-century American colonists thought of the West in terms of frontier expansion into the interior. In 1763 the British Crown forbade further expansion across a Proclamation Line, which ran along the crest of the Appalachians, because Britain rightly felt that Anglo-Indian conflict inspired by expansion had been a primary cause of the costly French and Indian War. Many colonists decried this interference with expansion into the "West." After the Revolution, Americans resumed migration into the interior, and the West increasingly was identified with the area across the Appalachians. During this period of expansion the West as an idea began to take shape. Individuals like the explorer-entrepreneur Daniel Boone were deified by writers like James Fenimore Cooper, who modeled his character Leatherstocking after Boone.

After Thomas Jefferson purchased Louisiana from France in 1803, Americans began to identify the West as the area across the Mississippi or the so-called trans-Mississippi West. Thus, when Meriwether Lewis and William Clark set out from St. Louis in

1804 to explore the Louisiana Purchase territory with the Corps of Discovery, they were voyaging into the West.

The Politics of Expansion

By the early nineteenth century Anglo-American expansion into the interior touched off conflict in places like the Ohio River valley. In 1811 William Henry Harrison won fame battling the followers of the Shawnee leader Tecumseh at Tippecanoe Creek in Indiana Territory. Harrison did not defeat the Shawnees; Tecumseh later fell in battle during the War of 1812. Nevertheless, Harrison eventually rose to the presidency on his fame as an Indian fighter out West, the hero of Tippecanoe Creek.

Expansion west brought about sectional conflict as proslavery southerners vied with "free soil" northerners over the question of whether the region would allow ownership of slaves. The question of admittance of Missouri as a slave state, which threatened to upset the political balance between slave and free states, ended with the Missouri Compromise of 1820. In 1846 Congressman David Wilmot introduced his

Taos Pueblo, 1878. Note the beehive ovens in the foreground. LIBRARY OF CONGRESS: PRINTS AND PHOTOGRAPHS DIVISION

proviso declaring all territory taken from Mexico as a result of the Mexican War should be closed to slavery. The Wilmot Proviso failed to become law, but the contentious debate it engendered was a premonition of things to come. When Kansas-Nebraska was opened under the doctrine of popular sovereignty (the people of the territory would determine if it was to be slave or free) with the Kansas-Nebraska Act of 1854, Kansas erupted into an internal civil war between free soilers and proslavery forces.

The nineteenth-century West exhibited several defining characteristics. First, it was marked by significant ethnic and racial diversity. Some scholars have viewed the West less as a place defined by geographic or environmental factors and more as a region defined by the intensive interactions among peoples of European, American Indian, Asian, and African ancestry. Geography and climate, however, also defined the region. It is a dry place. Despite pockets of moisture and verdancy, in the Pacific Northwest, for instance, the West is arid. Some observers have pointed to this factor as the definition of where the West begins and where it ends. The West begins on or about the ninety-eighth meridian, which severs the western Plains from the greener eastern Plains. Thus Lawrence, Kansas, is not "western," whereas the dry Sand Hills of western Nebraska are. In general, however, this was a late-nineteenth-century perception that developed among individuals like the explorer-

scientist John Wesley Powell. By and large, for those Americans who thought about it, after 1803 the Mississippi and not some imaginary line on a map marked the eastern boundary of the West.

The West is a land of extremes in aridity, temperature, and geography. The West boasts high mountains in vast ranges like the Rockies, Cascades, and Sierra Nevada. Yet it is also flat, best exemplified by the Great Plains. Indeed many nineteenth-century Americans accepted the image, created by the explorer and army engineer Stephen Long, of a "Great American Desert" in the interior West until well into the last decades of the century.

The nineteenth-century West also was noted for a drastic boom-and-bust economy and its eventual domination by large economic interests. While settlers and homesteaders on the Plains remained an enduring image, the economy of the region rapidly was dominated by large-scale extractive industries like timber and mining. The mining frontier expanded into the Rocky Mountains and beyond, fueled by a series of gold discoveries and the subsequent rush of prospectors eager to stake their claims in Colorado and Nevada in the 1850s and 1860s, and in Alaska's Yukon in the 1890s. Big companies predominated in the cattle industry, rendering the mythic cowboy more like a migrant wageworker than a knight-errant. Even agriculture, which began in the region in the mode of Jefferson's yeoman farmers, ended with the increased agglomeration of holdings and extensive control exerted by the railroad companies.

Several Wests

For the peoples who lived in the region, many nineteenth-century "Wests" existed, with different meanings. To some groups the nineteenth-century West meant new hope and new beginnings. For immigrants from western and eastern Europe, who came to the Great Plains to take up federal lands opened by the 1862 Homestead Act, the West was a place to start anew, to build new towns and agricultural communities. By the century's end scores of immigrants had taken advantage of this major land reform policy.

For many Asian immigrants the West initially represented a "gold mountain," where fortunes could be realized so young men could return home rich. Unfortunately for most of the Chinese men who came to the goldfields as part of the gold rush of 1849, gold mountain proved to be always a little farther across the horizon. Dreams of riches transformed into back-breaking agricultural work, railroad building, and laboring in San Francisco laundries. Ultimately, a successful anti-Asian movement excluded the Chinese from the United States with the Chinese Exclusion

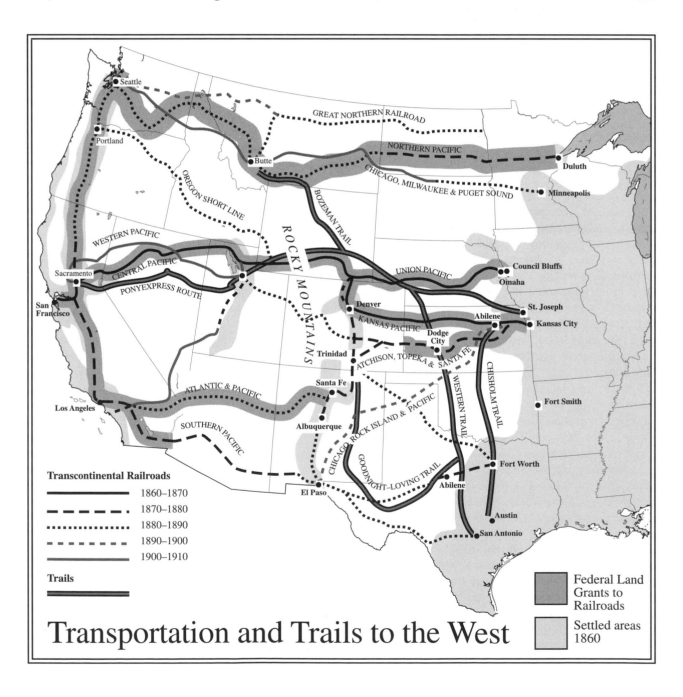

Transportation and Trails to the West

Transcontinental Railroads

——————— 1860–1870

— — — — 1870–1880

·············· 1880–1890

– – – – 1890–1900

——————— 1900–1910

Trails

═══════════

Federal Land Grants to Railroads

Settled areas 1860

Act of 1882. The Japanese immigrants who came in the late 1890s perhaps fared a little better, but all Asian immigrants to the American West faced economic exploitation, legalized discrimination, and sometimes murderous racial violence.

For Hispanics in northern Mexico or, after the Mexican War, the American Southwest, the early nineteenth century brought independence from Spain in 1821. But within a few decades the residents of such communities as San Antonio, Monterey, and Santa Fe were citizens of the United States. The terms of the Treaty of Guadalupe Hidalgo (1848), which ended the Mexican War and brought the Southwest under U.S. control, guaranteed protection of the rights and privileges that Mexicans had enjoyed first as Spanish subjects and then as Mexican citizens. Nonetheless, the Anglo and *Tejano* (Texans of Mexican descent) cooperation that had characterized the Texas revolt of 1836 quickly disappeared after Texas independence, and the remainder of the century was characterized by the circumscribing of Hispanic rights and their loss of their lands.

The West also meant a promised land, a new Zion. For Brigham Young and the members of the Church of Jesus Christ of Latter-day Saints (Mormons) it offered a refuge from religious persecution in the Midwest and a chance to establish a new godly community in the Great Basin in 1847. For Benjamin "Pap" Singleton, a former slave, and his followers, the West also promised new hope. A nineteenth-century Moses, Singleton launched an exodus of African American settlers from the Jim Crow South and sharecropping into the west of Kansas. The Exodusters, as they came to be known, established new towns at places like Nicodemus, Kansas. Nicodemus lasted, but the far-flung hope of a new promised land never materialized, and the exodus quickly dropped off. Not until the mid–twentieth century did another significant African American migration to the West occur.

Beginnings and Endings

The possibility of cooperation with Native Americans that first characterized westward expansion when Lewis and Clark and the Corps of Discovery first set foot in the new lands acquired by the United States under the Louisiana Purchase eventually gave way to resistance and violence with the Massacre at Wounded Knee in 1890. Lewis and Clark's latter-day *entrada* signaled a new beginning characterized by significant cross-cultural contact. As the century progressed the multiethnic, multiracial character of the West became even more prominent. The West be-

came an area of intensive interactions, both peaceful and contentious, between European, Native, Asian, and African Americans. Lewis and Clark's expedition also highlighted two different models of how the process of interaction might play out. It was a journey marked by cooperation, as seen with the bonds the members of that expedition formed with their Mandan hosts over the winter of 1804–1805. Yet the voyage was also marred by misunderstanding, cultural arrogance, and the potential for violence, as evidenced by the intense encounter between the intrepid explorers and the Teton Lakotas, an incident that barely avoided bloodshed.

By mid-century the United States had begun its ultimately successful drive for regional hegemony. Native Americans found themselves increasingly pressured to surrender their lands or face the consequences. In the 1830s, southeastern tribes like the Cherokees were forced to relocate to Indian Territory (Oklahoma) on a march aptly remembered as the Trail of Tears. In 1864, Christopher "Kit" Carson forced resistant Navajos on the Long Walk to Fort Sumner in eastern New Mexico, although Navajo leaders later negotiated a return to their homeland in 1868. By the century's end the region had been conquered, and railroads linked the eastern seaboard with the Pacific Coast. The region was incorporated into the United States, and it assumed a large role in defining who Americans were.

In 1893 Frederick Jackson Turner delivered an address to the American Historical Association at the Chicago World's Fair. In his address, a reading of his essay "The Significance of the Frontier in American History," Turner captured what many Americans felt instinctively about the role of the westward movement. He maintained that the frontier experience had made Americans what they were, individualistic, rugged, and democratic. Thus, according to Turner, the westward movement of the nineteenth century was not merely part of the American experience, it was in fact its central defining moment. Turner believed, based on his reading of the 1890 census, that the moment had passed, the frontier had ended, and that defining event had drifted into the annals of history.

If 1890 carried momentous meaning for Turner as the end of something special, for others it also meant a crucial turning point. In that same year U.S. Army troops opened fire on a group of Lakotas under the leadership of Big Foot, who had surrendered near Wounded Knee Creek. The massacre of Big Foot's people came amidst heightened tension as the Ghost Dance revitalization movement spread to the northern Plains. The movement, which had begun in Nevada and was led by a spiritual figure named Wovoka, spread to other native peoples assisted by the railroads. Its attraction was facilitated by the increasingly harsh conditions on reservations and the threat of loss of Indian lands posed by the General Allotment Act (Dawes Act) of 1887. The movement, which offered spiritual renewal, became increasingly militant as it was adopted and transformed among the Lakotas. White settlers and military officials interpreted the Ghost Dance as an ominous threat.

On a cold December day in 1890 the heightened tensions reached a tragic point. Big Foot and the men, women, and children of his band met their terrible fate at the hands of the U.S. Army. It was the final tragic incident in a century that for many Native Americans meant the end of one way of life and the beginning of a new one of reservations and boarding schools. After Wounded Knee, the West was characterized by the enforcement of one vision, a West of reservations, regiments, and railroads. By the century's end one peoples' western star had risen, while another's had eclipsed.

See also **Arizona; California; Colorado; Denver; Idaho; Indian Territory; Kansas; Montana; Nebraska; Nevada; New Mexico; North Dakota; Oregon; St. Louis; San Francisco; South Dakota; Texas; Utah; Washington State; Wyoming.**

Bibliography

Lamar, Howard R. *The New Encyclopedia of the American West.* New Haven, Conn.: Yale University Press, 1998.

Milner, Clyde A. II, Carol A. O'Connor, and Martha A. Sandweiss, eds. *The Oxford History of the American West.* New York: Oxford University Press, 1994.

Nash, Gerald D. *Creating the West: Historical Interpretations, 1890–1990.* Albuquerque: University of New Mexico Press, 1991.

Ronda, James P. *Lewis and Clark among the Indians.* Lincoln: University of Nebraska Press, 1984.

Slotkin, Richard. *The Fatal Environment: The Myth of the Frontier in the Age of Industrialization, 1800–1890.* New York: Atheneum, 1985.

White, Richard. *"It's Your Misfortune and None of My Own": A History of the American West.* Norman: University of Oklahoma Press, 1991.

SCOTT C. ZEMAN

WEST POINT.   See Military Academy, U.S.

WEST VIRGINIA   In the last third of the nineteenth century, war and politics created a new American commonwealth in the heart of the Appalachian highlands. West Virginia, embracing fifty counties or roughly one-third of Virginia, became the thirty-fifth state in the Union on 20 June 1863, in the midst of the Civil War. Its creation was controversial. Wartime circumstances complicated the democratic process and forced the Unionist founders into complex legalisms to avoid the appearance that West Virginia had illegally seceded from Virginia. They created a "restored" Virginia government, complete with a full set of officials. This government then gave the constitutionally-required permission for West Virginia to be formed from its territory. A great many Virginians were incorporated into the new state who opposed its existence. Combining with disaffected Unionists, the dissidents gained control of the state in 1870 and turned the statemakers out of office. The state itself endured, however. Though its politics retained a Virginian cast until nearly the end of the century, the creation of the state of West Virginia was one of the few unambiguous outcomes and the only permanent boundary change of the Civil War.

The new state's unusual borders were determined by the pattern of earlier settlements. Several districts planted during the mid– and late eighteenth century matured between 1800 and 1850. In the north these included a commercial farming and agricultural processing area in the lower Shenandoah Valley; a stock-raising area along the upper Potomac's South Branch; a region of small-scale farming and manufacturing in the upper Monongahela Valley; and the iron- and glass-making city of Wheeling and the river town of Parkersburg, where an oil boom mushroomed just before the war, both in the Ohio Valley. Connected first by trails, then by turnpikes, and eventually (1852–1857) by the Baltimore and Ohio Railroad, these areas were bracketed by two "panhandles," one extending northward along the Ohio, the other eastward along the Potomac. Although Confederates predominated in the South Branch and Shenandoah Valleys, the Monongahela and Ohio Valleys formed the Unionist heartland. Conquered swiftly by the Union army in the war's initial campaigns in 1861, this region provided the core public support for a new state.

In the south another transportation corridor connected the Kanawha–New River system with central Virginia. A well-traveled turnpike followed this corridor, but railroad promoters faced the formidable barrier of New River Gorge, an obstacle not surmounted until the completion of the Chesapeake and Ohio Railroad in 1873. The Kanawha Valley, which combined tobacco plantations with a large and innovative salt industry, became a Union military base in 1861. The Greenbrier Valley, a stock-raising area with a nascent resort industry, remained a rebel stronghold until nearly the end of the war.

Separating and surrounding these southern zones was a wildly beautiful "interior," rich in timber, coal, and other minerals. While fossil fuels had figured in the growth of the salt industry and the Kanawha and Monongahela districts undertook small-scale mining before the Civil War, the long-anticipated growth of extractive industry did not materialize on a large scale until the 1880s. Then southern, central, and eastern West Virginia underwent rapid economic and demographic changes. The interior counties, with roughly one-fifth of the state's population in 1870, had more than a third by 1900 and were dotted with dozens of new railroad towns (of which Huntington and Bluefield were the largest) and hundreds of lumber and coal "camps." Following the initial boom, the depression of the 1890s introduced the first of many "busts" along with an outbreak of labor conflict, another harbinger of the state's future. Meanwhile a corps of resident speculators and "distinguished land attorneys" worked at transferring ownership of mineral and timber resources from small landholders to absentee investors. Abundant supplies of natural gas fostered an expansion of the glass industry, while a new chemical process industry took shape amid the ruins of the Kanawha salt trade.

Not surprisingly, the rapid transformation of the interior led to political change. An influx of new voters usually tilted political balances against the party that held power before the newcomers arrived. Mining and railroad magnates used their personal fortunes to acquire U.S. Senate seats and control of political party organizations. Such competition and the economic rivalry that it foreshadowed were usually peaceful, but not always. One conflict involving locals and outsiders contending for control of resources along the West Virginia–Kentucky border became famous as the Hatfield-McCoy feud.

By 1900, the population totaled 568,000, of whom 98,500 (about 17 percent) were African American. For the first time, West Virginia began to attract significant numbers of immigrants; 22,500 persons were foreign-born in 1900. Coal, oil, and natural gas booms were again under way, and another round of railroad building and town founding had begun. Conventional economic dogma held that West Virginia's industrial expansion depended upon low wages and low taxation of extractive industries, most of which were now controlled by nonresident corporations. Challenges to these premises shaped much of West Virginia's history during the twentieth century.

See also **Appalachia; Civil War,** *subentry on* **Consequences of the Civil War; Mining and Extraction; Virginia.**

Bibliography

Ambler, Charles Henry. *Sectionalism in Virginia from 1776 to 1861*. Chicago: University of Chicago Press, 1910. The classic account that derives West Virginia separatism from environmental and institutional differences from Virginia.

Curry, Richard Orr. *A House Divided: A Study of Statehood Politics and the Copperhead Movement in West Virginia*. Pittsburgh, Pa.: University of Pittsburgh Press, 1964. A revisionist account that emphasizes internal divisions during the Civil War.

Rice, Otis K., and Stephen W. Brown. *West Virginia: A History*. Lexington: University Press of Kentucky, 1993. An updated restatement of the Ambler interpretation.

Williams, John Alexander. *West Virginia: A History*. New York: Norton, 1976. An interpretive account emphasizing social and economic history.

———. *West Virginia and the Captains of Industry*. Morgantown: West Virginia University Press, 1976; reissued 1999. A political and economic history of the period 1870–1910.

JOHN ALEXANDER WILLIAMS

WHALING   For most of the nineteenth century, the United States was the center of the world's whaling industry. From the eighth to the eighteenth centuries the industry had been dominated first by the Basques, then by the Dutch, and finally by the British. As the nineteenth century ebbed, leadership passed to the Norwegians; later they were joined by the Japanese and Russians. The tonnage of U.S. vessels engaged in whaling increased from an annual average of 18,000 between 1816 and 1820 to 196,000 in the years from 1851 to 1855, before falling to 10,000 in the first five years of the twentieth century. Over the same period, in constant 1880 dollars, the value of output rose from an annual average of $765,000 to $9,630,000 and then fell to $878,000. Although whaling was never as important in terms of value of output as brewing or cotton textiles, as late as 1860 it was on a par with calico printing, carpet weaving, and hosiery knitting. A decade later the industry had declined in both absolute and relative terms but still bulked large in the economic life of a number of New England ports.

American whalers systematically hunted only five species of whales: principally, sperm whales and two types of baleens—bowheads and rights—and secondarily, humpbacks and grays (also baleens). The Americans would have liked to catch the faster-swimming rorquals—blues, seis, minkes, and finners—but, given the existing technology, that goal proved almost impossible. Unlike the later entrants—the Norwegians, Russians, and Japanese—who caught whales because they could be used in the production of a number of products that continued to be demanded, such as meat, fertilizer, cooking oils, and margarine, American whalers sought sperm whales for their sperm oil and baleen whales for their whale oil and whalebone. Until the 1850s sperm oil was a highly valued illuminate (it produced a bright, clean light), and even well into the twentieth century it continued to be valued as a lubricant for high-speed and heavy machinery. Inferior to sperm oil but much cheaper, whale oil was the illuminate chosen by the average consumer and was also used to lubricate heavy machinery. Whalebone (baleen) is not bone, but plates of cartilage through which the whale screens seawater in order to remove food. Before the widespread innovation of spring steel, baleen was used when a strong but flexible material was needed, as in such products as corset stays, whips, and umbrellas.

Successful whaling involved the coordinated efforts of owners, agents, captains, and crew. A whaling vessel usually made a number of voyages, varying in length from a few to sixty-nine months and averaging just fewer than thirty-three. Because of the wear and tear that often resulted from a long voyage and the severe climatic conditions encountered on voyages directed toward hunting grounds in Hudson's Bay and Davis Straight and the South Atlantic, Pacific, Indian, and western Arctic Oceans, it was often necessary for a vessel to undergo major repairs and refitting at the end of a voyage. At this point it was usual for an owner to sell the vessel and for a whaling agent to purchase it, undertake the necessary repairs, sell shares, and organize the next voyage. Over the course of the nineteenth century more than half of American whaling tonnage (50.8 percent) sailed from New Bedford, Massachusetts.

Whaling excursions usually required a number of shareholders. While their ranks often included agents and captains, more than half were merchants. Manufacturers, artisans, financiers, and service workers made up an additional 30 percent. The agents and to a lesser extent the captains organized and directed the voyage. The agent, almost always a major shareholder, was the entrepreneur. His first major decision was the choice of vessel. In the early years the choice was most often a three-masted ship, square rigged on all three masts. Once the whaling grounds in the western Arctic were opened, however, the need for speed and maneuverability became more important. Thus, when technical improvements in sails and in steam-operated winches made such rigging changes economically feasible, the choice was increasingly a bark (three-masted, square rigged on the fore and main masts but fore-and-aft rigged on the mizzen).

The agent next chose the captain, and together they selected officers, boatsteerers, and skilled artisans. Agents usually chose the rest of the crew as well, but over time they began to contract out that function to specialized firms. The captain and agent together selected the equipment and the provisions to be carried. Finally, the agent, perhaps with the advice of the captain, decided on the length of time the vessel was to be at sea, the whaling grounds to be hunted, and the places and dates at which the vessel would put into a port to resupply, take on new crew members, and ship oil and bone home. Once the vessel had sailed the agent turned most day-to-day decisions over to the captain while retaining a surprising level of overall control. At sea the captain's management responsibilities included any refitting, reprovisioning, and recruiting that was required, but his chief task was to find whales and catch them. Given the importance of that latter task, the captain's management responsibilities were much greater than those of a typical merchant captain.

Depending on the size and rigging of the vessel, the whaler's crew typically consisted of three or four officers other than the captain, about the same number of boatsteerers, almost always a cook, a steward, a cooper, frequently a carpenter, often a blacksmith, usually four to six skilled and semiskilled seamen, and ten or eleven green hands (nonsailors recruited for unskilled tasks). While most labor contracts reward workers on the basis of time worked or individual output, each member of a whaler's crew, from captain to green hand, received an individually negotiated fraction of a vessel's net catch, termed the "lay." The method of payment provided two benefits. Individual voyages were very risky, and by making "wages" depend on the catch a part of that risk was transferred from the owners to the crew. Catching whales efficiently required close cooperation among the crew members, which this method of payment encouraged.

Technically, the lay was expressed as a fraction of the net catch (for example, 1/16), but often it was referred to by the denominator alone (a 16). At the peak of American whaling, in the 1840s, average lays ranged from 1/15 for captains to 1/186 for green hands. Although whalers' "wages" were much more variable in terms of comparative incomes, whaling captains earned about three times as much as merchant captains, and mates earned about twice as much as their peers in the merchant marine. The crew did less well: the earnings of cooks and skilled and semiskilled seaman were about three-quarters of the merchant marine standard. In comparison with wages ashore, officers earned about a quarter more than skilled artisans, while boatsteerers, coopers, cooks, and stewards earned slightly more than that benchmark. Skilled and semiskilled seamen and green hands earned approximately as much as unskilled factory workers and common laborers.

In the final analysis, while the agent and captain were responsible for finding whales, the vessel's entire crew was involved in catching them. Despite technical improvements (better harpoons, for example), there was little change in the method of capture over the course of nineteenth-century American whaling. Almost all American whalers were sailing vessels; and, given the speed at which the whales could swim (a sperm whale cruised at nine miles per hour and could reach speeds of twenty-seven miles per hour), capture could not be managed from the vessel itself. Search and capture thus were separate and distinct operations.

Once a whale had been sighted, the attack was launched from small whaleboats. Two or three men were left on the vessel to maintain steerage and to signal the whale's movements, but the rest of the crew were assigned to the boats. A whaleboat had a crew of six: a steersman (usually an officer) and five oarsmen—two on the port side and three, one the boat-steerer, on the starboard. The crew rowed or sailed close to the whale, and the boatsteerer attempted to harpoon it and attach it to the boat by a line connected to the harpoon. At this point the whale usually began to flee, towing the boat on what whalemen termed a "Nantucket sleigh ride." When the whale tired, the boat reapproached the animal, and the steersman (who had changed places with the boat-steerer) used a lance in an attempt to kill it. If successful, with the whale dead and floating, the whaling vessel hoved to. A work stage was rigged; the whale was winched toward the mast; baleen or spermaceti were removed; the crewmen sliced off the blubber and loaded it aboard the vessel. There, the blubber was "tried out"—boiled over a fire built in a brick "try" works—and barreled. Meanwhile the whaleboats had been reloaded, and the search for whales continued. In the early years, when the vessel was fully loaded, it returned to its home port. Later, the cargo was frequently unloaded at transshipment points, such as Lahaina, Hawaii, and San Francisco, California, and the vessel returned to the whaling grounds. Since the process was often repeated, over time voyage length increased.

The evidence indicates that the rise and decline of the American whale industry was driven by demand rather than supply. Although some local whalestocks may have been depleted, the opening of new grounds more than compensated for this. On the demand side, after 1815 in both America and northwestern Europe, the growth of population, particularly urban population, was rapid, per capita income rose, the share of industry and transportation in aggregate output increased, and machinery and equipment accounted for a rising fraction of the capital stock. All these factors led to a dramatic expansion in the demand for illuminants and lubricants. The American whaling industry responded. During the four decades from 1817 to 1856, with the New Bedford fleet taken as an overall indicator, the whaling industry performed very well indeed. Profits, including capital losses, averaged 16.1 percent. Thereafter, the industry fared less well. Average profits fell to 11.7 percent in the decade from 1857 to 1866, to 9.5 percent between 1867 and 1876, and, if the banner year 1877 is excluded, to 7.3 percent between 1877 and 1886.

Initially, whale oil had faced little competition as a commodity, but by mid-century, old products were improved and new products innovated. In the decade before the Civil War innovative activity was especially intense, and the importance of competing products, particularly of gas manufactured from coal, increased dramatically. By 1860 the whale fishery, which at mid-century had been the most important supplier of illuminants and lubricants, retained only a tiny fraction of those markets, both at home and abroad. The fishery was almost as large as it had ever been, but the overall market was very much larger. The first successful oil well in 1859 and the exploitation of petroleum, however, soon settled the future of both coal and whale oils. There were still markets for lubricants, but they were limited. Whalebone continued in high demand until the first decade of the twentieth century, but alone it was insufficient to support the industry. In the decades after 1890 others, not Americans, were to exploit an industry revitalized by new technologies and products.

See also **Maritime Technology; Petroleum.**

Bibliography

Bockstoce, John R. *Whales, Ice, and Men: The History of Whaling in the Western Arctic.* Seattle: University of Washington Press and New Bedford Whaling Museum, 1986.

Chatterton, E. Keble. *Whalers and Whaling: The Story of Whaling Ships up to the Present Day.* Philadelphia: Lippincott, 1926.

Davis, Lance E., Robert E. Gallman, and Karin Gleiter. *In Pursuit of Leviathan: Technology, Institutions, Productivity, and Profits in American Whaling, 1816–1906.* Chicago: University of Chicago Press, 1997.

Hegarty, Reginald B. *Returns of Whaling Vessels Sailing from American Ports: A Continuation of Alexander Starbuck's* History of the American Whale Fishery, *1876–1928.* With additions by Philip F. Purrington, New Bedford, Mass.: Old Dartmouth Historical Society and Whaling Museum, 1959.

Hohman, Elmo Paul. *The American Whaleman: A Study of Life and Labor in the Whaling Industry.* New York: Longmans, Green, 1928.

Scammon, Charles M. *The Marine Mammals of the Northwestern Coast of North America, Together with an Account of the American Whale-Fishery.* 1874. Reprint, New York: Dover, 1968.

Starbuck, Alexander. *History of the American Whale Fishery.* 1878. Reprint, Secaucus, N.J.: Castle, 1989.

LANCE E. DAVIS

WHIG PARTY

WHIG PARTY The Whigs and the Democrats were the two major political parties in the United States between 1834 and 1854. On the federal, state, and local levels, the two parties competed for elective office, articulated distinctive and often opposing ideologies, staked out positions on policy issues, fought against one another in legislative arenas, and claimed loyal partisans who intensely identified with them. Whig candidates were elected president in 1840 and 1848, and the party controlled both houses of Congress between 1841 and 1843, the Senate between 1843 and 1845, and the House of Representatives between 1847 and 1849. Together, Whigs and Democrats were the principal components of what is often called "the second party system" in American political history, as distinguished from the first party system of Jeffersonian Republicans and Federalists and subsequent party systems composed of Republicans and Democrats.

Roots of the Party

Although the Whig Party's birth can be traced to a caucus of politicians who assembled in December 1833, it had its roots in a series of political, social, and economic developments beginning in the late 1810s. In the first two decades of the nineteenth century, the Jeffersonian Republicans were the dominant political party in the federal government and in most of the country. Jeffersonians normally employed a congressional caucus to choose their presidential candidate, invariably a Virginian, and their vice presidential candidate, a weak politician and often a New Yorker. By the early 1820s this system was unraveling. The lack of credible opposition to the Jeffersonians weakened party discipline and harmony. Moreover, the absence of an obvious successor to President James Monroe, coupled with a growing wariness of the undemocratic nature of the caucus, led that method of selection to fall into disrepute. In the vacuum thus created, four aspirants, reflecting different regional and ideological reactions to the economic and social developments of the previous decade, arose to harness support in the 1824 presidential election.

Two of these candidates, John Quincy Adams of Massachusetts and Henry Clay of Kentucky, favored relatively coherent national policies geared toward economic development and integration. They came from different backgrounds: Clay was a native Vir-

ginian from the nationalist wing of the Jeffersonian party, and Adams was the son of a president and a former Federalist. But both favored high protective tariffs to enable American farmers and manufacturers to compete against more developed British producers, a privately and publicly funded national bank to provide a stable currency by facilitating commerce and serving as a check against the overextension of notes issued by state banks, and the distribution of the proceeds of federal land sales to the states to finance internal improvements and common schools. By the end of the decade these leaders and their followers would be known as National Republicans, and they would bring to the Whig Party a belief that governmental activism in the economy was desirable. National Republicans were strong in New England and the smaller Middle Atlantic states, but they had little support, outside of Kentucky and Louisiana, in the slave states or in most of the Northwest.

Those who deplored the increasing commercialization of the economy saw antirepublican forms of

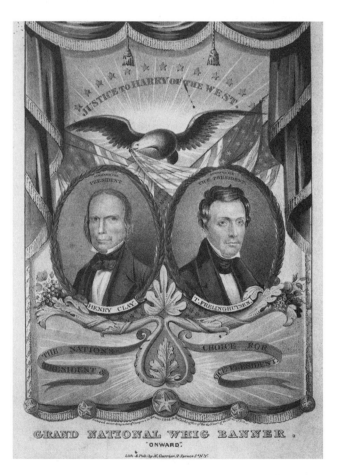

Whig Election Banner, 1844. Nathaniel Currier produced banners for both the Democrats and the Whigs. Lithograph, 1844. LIBRARY OF CONGRESS: PRINTS AND PHOTOGRAPHS DIVISION

privilege in corporate charters and banking institutions. They blamed paper money and speculators for economic hard times, and gravitated in 1824 toward former military hero Andrew Jackson of Tennessee and a group of politicians who by the early 1830s would become known as Democrats. Jackson's support billowed when a debilitating stroke ended the candidacy of Treasury Secretary William Crawford, a Georgian whose followers, like Jackson's, saw the debates over Missouri's admission into the Union as a slave state, high tariffs, and the very idea of an active federal government as portents of a Leviathan state and a possible menace to the institution of chattel slavery. Despite winning a plurality of the electoral and the popular votes cast, Jackson lost the presidency to Adams when the contest went into the House of Representatives. For the next four years, Jackson's allies pummeled Adams as an elitist who had been undemocratically elected and whose visionary proposals (such as a national university and observatory), coupled with his Federalist upbringing and distaste for slavery, made him unfit for the presidency. Jackson was triumphantly elected in 1828 and reelected in a campaign against Clay four years after that.

The Jacksonian Age

Part of Jackson's appeal lay in his humble origins and his exploitation of the egalitarian impulses of the electorate. The National Republicans at first eschewed such appeals as demagogic. But as they evolved into the Whig Party in the 1830s, they gained the adherents of another faction, the Anti-Masons. Originating in a local dispute over the disappearance of William Morgan, a member of a Masonic lodge in rural New York, the Anti-Masonic movement emerged first as an expression of outrage against the corrupt power of the Masons, but then expanded to include people worried about immorality and social instability. Drawing most of its supporters from middling farmers and artisans, and heavily influenced by the Second Great Awakening—a religious revival that blended an urgency for salvation with a postmillennial view toward perfecting society—the Anti-Masons emerged as the principal opponents of the Democrats in New York, Pennsylvania, and Vermont, and they were strong in many other northern states as well. Anti-Masons would bring to the Whig Party an evangelical zeal that found expression in social policies seeking to uplift even as they sought to control the lower classes.

Jackson's vetoes of bills funding internal improvements and rechartering the Second Bank of the United States angered National Republicans, and his harsh Indian removal policy and support of Sunday mail transportation galvanized opposition from Anti-Masons. But it was not just Jackson's policies that helped to unite his opponents in the form of the Whig Party. His liberal use of the veto, his personal confrontations with congressional and judicial leaders, his high-handed use of authority in removing the government's funds from the Second Bank, and his threats of force against South Carolina during the nullification crisis frightened many voters, north and south. The National Republicans and the Anti-Masons united gradually and unofficially (merging mostly in the congressional election of 1834) to form the Whig Party, using the name given to opponents of British colonial policies in the eighteenth century in an effort to liken "King Andrew I" to King George III. Throughout the life of their party, Whigs championed restraint on the part of presidents and state governors.

Jackson's "executive tyranny" diminished his popularity in the South, but at least equally important

Daniel Webster. Daguerreotype of the Whig senator from Massachusetts, from the studio of Matthew Brady between 1845 and 1849. LIBRARY OF CONGRESS: PRINTS AND PHOTOGRAPHS DIVISION

to the rise of the Whig Party was his retirement, because his Democratic successor from New York, Martin Van Buren, was more vulnerable to a southern Whig attack. In 1836 southern Whigs favored a former Jacksonian, Hugh L. White of Tennessee, for president, claiming that he was far more trustworthy on the slavery issue than Van Buren. Most northern Whigs championed William Henry Harrison, who had cultivated support among the Anti-Masons; those in Massachusetts favored Daniel Webster. The hydra-headed Whig campaign was not, as historians once thought, part of a scheme to throw the election into the House. Instead, it reflected the Whigs' lack of cohesion. Nonetheless, Van Buren won the election by a slim margin.

The Zenith of Party Conflict

Until 1837 the ideological contrast between Whigs and Democrats, though sharp in terms of rhetoric, did not lead to consistent policy differences. The economic boom of the early and mid-1830s led most Democrats on the state level to favor business expansion. Moreover, the southern Whig strategy of claiming that White was an ardent defender of states' rights did not harmonize well with the northern Whigs' support for higher tariffs and a rechartering of the national bank. But an economic depression that lasted almost without interruption from 1837 to 1843, and that many blamed on Jackson's hard money policies, catapulted the Whigs into the position of a formidable competitor. It led to sharp differences in congressional and state legislative voting behavior, especially on national and state economic policies. Democrats demanded an "independent treasury" system in which the government divorced itself from the business of banking—in some states they refused to incorporate banks or other companies—and they generally opposed any governmental involvement in the economy, claiming that any such involvement benefited some people at the expense of others. Whigs, by contrast, deplored such restrictive policies as the worst possible remedy to hard times and spoke of the harmony of the country's economic interests.

The depression also galvanized people who previously had been apathetic toward politics. Just over half of all eligible voters participated in the presidential elections of 1828 through 1836, while over 70 percent cast ballots in the congressional contests of 1838 and over 80 percent participated in the 1840 presidential election—possibly the highest level of voter turnout in any presidential election. Harrison easily won the election, taking all but seven of twenty-six states, and the Whigs won control of Congress and

most state governments as well. They not only capitalized on economic hard times; they also appropriated Democratic appeals to the common man by portraying Harrison—a wealthy Virginian by birth—as a humble frontiersmen who lived in a log cabin and drank hard cider (considered a morally acceptable alternative to rum and whiskey); Van Buren, by contrast, though in fact the son of a middling tavern keeper, was depicted as an aristocrat leading a royal lifestyle amid mass privation.

Once matured, Whigs and Democrats articulated differences not only on state and national economic policy, but on social issues as well. Whigs championed the right and duty of state and local governments to "improve" the morals of society. They advocated an increase in the funding of common schools, and even favored compulsory school attendance in some states. Whigs favored local restrictions on the sale of liquor, Sabbatarian legislation, the funding of asylums, and prison reform. Some even advocated the abolition of capital punishment in the name of human perfectibility. Whereas Democrats were proponents of negative liberty (freedom from government restrictions), Whigs championed a positive form of liberty whereby governmental intervention ensured a more prosperous, healthier, and progressive society. For that reason, the Whigs opposed unchecked territorial expansion, arguing that the nation should develop temporally rather than spatially—that it should improve the soil it had, and who and what inhabited it, before grasping for more.

To some extent, party differences emerged over race relations as well. Though both parties clung to the doctrine of white supremacy, Whigs championed a more paternalistic racism than did Democrats. They opposed harsh Indian removal policies, were more willing than Democrats to fund schools for black children, and in some northern states a sizable minority of Whigs favored extending the right of suffrage to African Americans—usually against vociferous Democratic opposition. Even in the South, where both parties defended the institution of slavery, Whigs were, after 1836, more moderate on racial issues. They were not as insistent as Democrats on expanding the institution of slavery or prohibiting the discussion of abolitionist petitions in Congress. Southern Whigs opposed state laws that made the manumission of slaves more difficult, and they were less disposed than Democrats to restrict the rights of free blacks. Perhaps because they held to notions of meritocracy, Whigs found it easier than Democrats to position minorities on a hierarchical scale and accord them some rights without contradicting the racism that both parties espoused. But whereas Democrats were willing to treat foreign-born whites as equals, Whigs believed that aliens, like other "inferior" groups, needed to be uplifted socially and "Americanized" before gaining full political equality. As a result, they vigorously defended stronger naturalization laws.

The 1840s constituted the heyday of the second party system. Each party was strong in every region of the country, though Democrats tended to be more powerful in the Deep South and the West, and the Whigs more powerful in the Northeast. Northern Whig strongholds included Massachusetts, Vermont, New Jersey, Rhode Island, and Ohio; in the South they were the majority party in Maryland, Delaware, Kentucky, North Carolina, Louisiana, and Florida. New York, Pennsylvania, Connecticut, Indiana, Tennessee, and Georgia were more equally divided between the two parties, and elections in these states were hotly contested. Each party commanded deep loyalties, and millions of voters identified with one or the other of them. During these years voter turnout remained at exceptionally high levels, and split-ticket voting was not common. In the North, Whigs were the party of the urban and rural middle classes, and they gained a good share of votes from native-born factory workers as well. In the Deep South, they fared well among wealthy planters and in the few urban pockets of the region. By contrast, in the Upper South, they often had the support of yeomen farmers from the Piedmont, who demanded transportation improvements. Whigs gained a great deal of support from evangelical and pietist religious groups such as Presbyterians and Congregationalists, as well as from well-to-do Unitarians and Episcopalians, though the demographics of party identity varied considerably because of local factors.

Collapse of the Party

The Whigs were the last major American political party to fade away, and historians have long debated why this happened. Given the lack of formal, government-supplied ballots in the nineteenth century (parties printed and distributed their own paper ballots), the same thing that made it easy to launch a new party made it easy to destroy an existing one. And so, the more specific question is, Why did the Whigs, and not the Democrats, die? There were several reasons, though it is difficult to determine their relative importance.

Both Whigs and Democrats were adept at fighting over sectionally neutral issues like banking, turning military figures into politicians, and conducting crowd-pleasing campaigns. But the volatile issue of the status of slavery in western territories ultimately destroyed both parties' national organizations. Be-

cause the Whigs were the more heterogeneous group and were more inclined toward an activist government, sectional differences sundered them first. After William Henry Harrison's untimely death in 1841, his successor, John Tyler of Virginia, defied his party's congressional leaders and vetoed Whig economic legislation, causing a party rupture. When Henry Clay ran as the Whig candidate in 1844, he was forced to waffle over the annexation of Texas, perhaps hurting him in the South while perhaps costing him the votes of some northern opponents of slavery. James Polk, the Democratic candidate, won the election. Weakened by differences arising out of the Compromise of 1850, especially the Fugitive Slave Act of 1850 (differences that made the administrations of Zachary Taylor, a Whig elected in 1848, and his successor, Millard Fillmore, also a Whig, as unsuccessful as Tyler's), the Whigs were routed in the 1852 presidential election. They carried only four of thirty-one states because their nominee, Winfield Scott, was perceived in the South as unsafe on slavery. Two years later the Kansas-Nebraska Act, which opened up those territories to slavery, irreparably divided the party into sectional factions. To be sure, the two parties had for years opposed each other, within each region, on the slavery issue. Northern Whigs and southern Democrats usually staked out more sectionally conscious positions than did northern Democrats and southern Whigs, who tended to champion sectional harmony and love of the Union. But the Whigs were clearly more capable of campaigning against incumbent Democratic presidents, as in the 1834, 1838, and 1846 congressional campaigns, and profiting from economic hard times, as in 1840 and 1848, than they were in governing once they obtained power.

The Democrats survived the realignment of the 1850s because their policy of popular sovereignty in the territories—by which settlers could themselves decide the status of slavery there—was sufficiently ambiguous to buy them enough time to become a different kind of party, though still under the same name. The question of whether the federal government should actively protect the institution of slavery in the territories divided the Democrats by 1860, but they had survived long enough, and had become the object of such scorn by their new opponents, that their most loyal voters, especially southerners and Catholic immigrants, were remobilized. The Civil War would produce new issues over which Democrats and Republicans could fight.

Although a sectional-conflict interpretation is most persuasive as an explanation of the Whigs' underlying weakness, and possibly the principal reason for their demise in the Deep South, it does not delineate very well the *proximate* cause of the party's death in the North and Upper South. Indeed, it was during a lull in the sectional conflict (1851–1853), when most voters accepted the finality of the Compromise of 1850, that the Whig Party collapsed. Local issues such as prohibition, Bible reading in the public schools, and general cultural animosities between zealous native-born Protestants, on the one hand, and Catholic immigrants and casual Protestants among the native-born, on the other, were the primary reasons why the Whigs fell apart in the North and Upper South. The push for statewide prohibition laws and opposition to the burgeoning population of Catholic immigrants, more than proslavery or antislavery sentiments, led to the creation of independent parties that eroded the second party system and especially the Whigs, who were divided over whether to soften or strengthen their nativist proclivities. The Whigs' failed effort to appeal to Catholic voters in the 1852 campaign produced a nativist and prohibitionist backlash against the party. In the following year, independent parties formed on the local and state level, paving the way for the rise of the anti-immigrant Know-Nothing Party, which replaced the Whigs in many states.

This culture-conflict interpretation, however, does little to account for political developments in the Deep South, where nativism and prohibitionism were not politically important. Nor does it explain why the Republican Party ultimately replaced the Know-Nothings. Even if Republicans were anti-Catholic, their fundamental thrust was opposition to slavery. Sectional- and cultural-conflict interpretations should be viewed as partial but mutually supportive reasons for the collapse of the Whigs.

One further cause of the Whigs' collapse was their inability to exploit economic issues in the early 1850s, something they desperately needed to do in light of sectional divisions and strategic problems they faced on ethnic and religious issues. The discovery of gold in California and heavy British investment in America after the revolutions of 1848 in France and Germany resulted in an economic boom that obviated the Whigs' national economic policies and blurred the differences between themselves and Democrats on state-level economic issues. As in earlier booms, both parties advocated the expansion of banks. Proposed railroad company charters pitted regions, rather than the parties, against each other. With no significant economic issues to exploit, Whigs were vulnerable to the national party divisions over slavery, and to local divisions over how to react to immigrants and the problems of urbanization.

Though short-lived, the Whigs had a lasting impact on American political life. Together with Dem-

ocrats they turned elections into populistic and emotionally powerful events. They preserved earlier notions of government playing a proactive role in the economy, and combined them with a belief in a particular type of progress that sought to bridge, even as it reflected and exacerbated, social divisions. Most Whigs, even northern antislavery Whigs who were often reacting to perceived southern aggressions, valued the Union above sectional animosity. Those antislavery Whigs would form an important component of the Republican Party, which eventually achieved by war the emancipation and concept of one nation that could not be attained by peace.

See also **Democratic Party; Elections; Jacksonian Era; Masons; Politics,** *subentry on* **The Second Party System; Presidency; Republican Party.**

Bibliography

Ashworth, John. *Slavery, Capitalism, and Politics in the Antebellum Republic.* Vol. 1, *Commerce and Compromise, 1820–1850.* New York: Cambridge University Press, 1995.

Brown, Thomas. *Politics and Statesmanship: Essays on the American Whig Party.* New York: Columbia University Press, 1985.

Cooper, William J., Jr. *The South and the Politics of Slavery, 1828–1856.* Baton Rouge: Louisiana State University Press, 1978.

Formisano, Ronald P. *The Birth of Mass Political Parties: Michigan, 1827–1861.* Princeton, N.J.: Princeton University Press, 1971.

Holt, Michael F. *The Political Crisis of the 1850s.* New York: John Wiley, 1978.

———. *The Rise and Fall of the American Whig Party: Jacksonian Politics and the Onset of the Civil War.* New York: Oxford University Press, 1999.

Howe, Daniel Walker. *The Political Culture of the American Whigs.* Chicago: University of Chicago Press, 1979.

McCormick, Richard P. *The Second American Party System: Party Formation in the Jacksonian Era.* Chapel Hill: University of North Carolina Press, 1966.

Watson, Harry L. *Liberty and Power: The Politics of Jacksonian America.* New York: Hill and Wang, 1990.

LEX RENDA

WILD WEST SHOWS   The romantic image of the American West as an untamed frontier was propagated by Wild West shows. Demonstrating facets of western life and Indian cultures, these gaudy displays were driven by U.S. and European curiosity about the trans-Mississippi West.

George Catlin (1796–1872), an artist of the American West, started the first Wild West show in 1833. Using his paintings of American Indians to elicit sympathy for their plight, Catlin perpetuated the image of Indians as "noble savages," or a benevolent

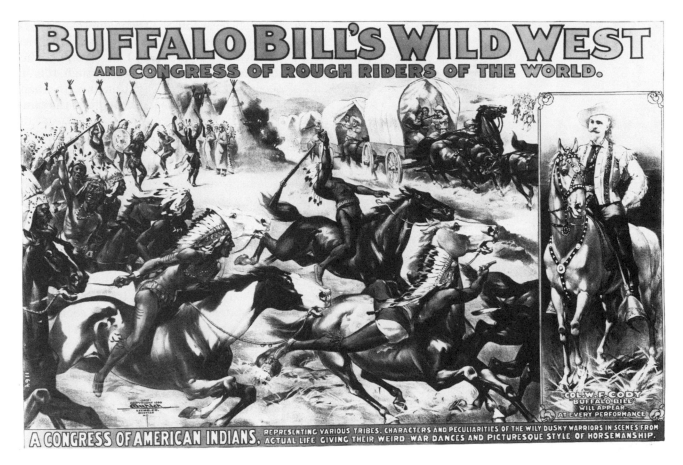

Poster for Buffalo Bill's Wild West Show, 1898. "Buffalo Bill" Cody continued to produce his famous shows until his death in 1917. LIBRARY OF CONGRESS

people unfit for white society. In 1840 Catlin moved his exhibit to Europe, where it garnered as much popularity as it had in the United States.

After the Civil War, William F. "Buffalo Bill" Cody (1846–1917), a former U.S. Army scout and cavalryman, rejuvenated the Wild West show idea by re-creating western imagery with "authentic" western personalities on a small stage. Annie Oakley, who represented frontier women, and the Sioux chief Sitting Bull, who represented "noble savages," became central attractions of his shows (see photograph overleaf). Cody orchestrated his first production in Omaha, Nebraska, on 17 May 1883 and toured the United States and Europe into the early twentieth century.

Themes of Cody's productions evolved from the first modern rodeo, which Cody organized in 1882, into re-creations of bank robberies, buffalo hunts, and fights with Indians. By 1900, competition with another major Wild West show produced by Gordon William "Pawnee Bill" Lillie prompted the decline of Cody's touring troupe. Lillie merged with Cody in 1909, but he retired in 1913, his shows having lost audiences to motion pictures and rodeos. Cody, however, continued to perform until shortly before his death in 1917.

See also **American Indians,** *subentry on* **The Image of the Indian; Interpretations of the Nineteenth Century,** *subentry on* **Popular Interpretations of the Frontier West; Theater.**

Bibliography

Brown, Dee. *The American West.* New York: Charles Scribner's Sons, 1994.

Reddin, Paul. *Wild West Shows.* Urbana: University of Illinois Press, 1999.

KEVIN D. ROBERTS

WISCONSIN   The region known today as Wisconsin lies in the northernmost tier of the United States, bounded on the east by Lake Michigan and on the west by the Mississippi River, and separated from Canada by Lake Superior. In 1800 its aboriginal forests and prairies were thinly populated by six autonomous native peoples, who migrated seasonally in

Wild West Show Performer (see previous page). Annie Oakley (1860–1926), photographed in 1899. LIBRARY OF CONGRESS: PRINTS AND PHOTOGRAPHICS DIVISION

pursuit of food, and a handful of whites who occupied four fur-trading posts on strategic waterways. By century's end, in contrast, its prairies had been plowed under and its forests leveled, most original inhabitants had been driven away or confined, and a population of two million, mostly white, grappled with problems caused by industrialization and urbanization.

This extraordinary transformation of land and peoples occurred in only three generations. Although French-speaking traders and missionaries had trickled across the region since the early seventeenth century, significant numbers of white settlers did not spread north into Wisconsin until two centuries later. In the 1820s, hundreds of white prospectors, miners, and entrepreneurs appropriated the southwestern corner of the state to extract lead used in bullets and paint, even though no treaty had been properly sanctioned by native landowners. Most Sauk inhabitants evacuated across the Mississippi, but in 1832 a community led by the chief Black Hawk resisted the white incursion with force. This calamitous "Black Hawk War" is remembered today for Black Hawk's tactical shrewdness in the face of the overpowering American forces that pursued him through Illinois and Wisconsin, and for briefly bringing Abraham Lincoln and Jefferson Davis together under the same command.

After the defeat of Black Hawk in 1832, new treaties with the Ho-Chunks (Winnebagos), Ojibwas, Menominees, and others threw the region open to white settlement, and the entire territory north to Lake Superior was in government hands within a few years. When the General Land Office began surveying the landscape in 1831, white Americans were flowing quickly north along streams and across prairies to turn Indian cornfields and hunting grounds into farms, mines, factories, and towns. English-speaking settlers from New York, New England, and the southern states came first, followed soon by organized immigrant societies from England, Wales, Switzerland, and elsewhere in Europe. Germans and Norwegians also began arriving in the 1830s, and by mid-century, some 300,000 white Americans, a third of them foreign-born, had overwhelmed the 6,500 Indian inhabitants.

Wisconsin was granted statehood in 1848, with its capital already established at Madison. The University of Wisconsin was founded at the capital the same year, intended by the legislature to be a public, secular, democratic, and utilitarian institution. Railroads reached the state in 1851, and an intricate latticework of lines soon extended to all but the smallest towns. These carried wheat grown by Scandinavian farmers, boards milled by Yankee lumberjacks, and beer made by German brewers to markets in Milwaukee, Chicago, and points east. Industries such as furniture-making and ship-building sprang up along Lake Michigan, while mining for iron developed near Lake Superior. During the middle third of the century, this capitalist transformation of the native arcadia, driven primarily by lumbering and agriculture, drew new settlers by the tens of thousands and provided them with a quality of life unobtainable at home.

By the time of the Civil War, Wisconsin residents belonged to several races and spoke a babel of languages from Dutch to Ojibwa. Many, such as the "Forty-eighters" (Germans who had emigrated after the failed uprisings in their homeland in 1848) in cities and Norwegian farmers on the prairies, had escaped Old World feudal institutions. Others, like the Ho-Chunks around Black River Falls and former slaves in the lakeshore towns, were refugees from America's own social institutions. Despite their very different origins, a critical mass of the state's residents were liberal democrats who believed passionately in ideals of freedom and justice: seven utopian communes were founded between 1840 and 1860, the Wisconsin Supreme Court repudiated the Fugitive Slave Law several times, and 80,595 Wisconsin soldiers flooded Union ranks in the 1860s. After the Civil War, thousands formed labor unions, created radical political parties, advocated women's rights, or helped create the Progressive movement. The University of Wisconsin, meanwhile, swelled from five hundred students in 1887 to nearly five thousand in the early twentieth century. It was a major force in the national movement for academic freedom, as expressed in its Regents' 1894 declaration that a university "should ever encourage that continual and fearless sifting and winnowing by which alone the truth can be found."

Ethnic variety, economic opportunity, democratic values, and rapid change were the chief features of Wisconsin society in the nineteenth century. This mix of cultural diversity, optimism, and idealism shaped the Wisconsin childhoods of the environmentalist John Muir, the suffragist Carrie Chapman Catt, the historian Frederick Jackson Turner, the temperance leader Frances Willard, the presidential candidate Robert M. La Follette, the architect Frank Lloyd Wright, and the painter Georgia O'Keeffe, each of whom had a profound influence on national life. Isolated and sparsely settled when the century began, Wisconsin in just three or four generations saw its population explode from 17,000 to 2,069,042 as it moved from the frontier fringe into the mainstream of American life.

See also **American Indians**, *subentry on* **Wars and Warfare; Immigration and Immigrants**, *subentries on* **Great Britain, Germany, Scandinavia and Finland; Midwest, The.**

Bibliography

Black Hawk. *Black Hawk: An Autobiography.* Edited by Donald Jackson. Urbana: University of Illinois Press, 1964.

Current, Richard Nelson. *Wisconsin: A Bicentennial History.* New York: Norton, 1977.

Kinzie, Juliette A. *Wau-Bun: The "Early Day" in the Northwest.* 1856. Reprint, Urbana: University of Illinois Press, 1992.

La Follette, Robert M. *La Follette's Autobiography: A Personal Narrative of Political Experiences.* Madison, Wis.: Robert M. La Follette Co., 1913.

Muir, John. *The Story of My Boyhood and Youth.* Boston: Houghton Mifflin, 1925.

Schurz, Carl. *Intimate Letters of Carl Schurz, 1841–1869.* Edited by Joseph Schafer. Madison: State Historical Society of Wisconsin, 1929.

Thompson, William Fletcher, ed. *The History of Wisconsin.* 6 vols. Madison: State Historical Society of Wisconsin, 1973–1998.

MICHAEL EDMONDS

WOMEN

[This entry includes an overview and subentries on **Women's Rights, Women's Labor, Women in the Professions,** and **Woman as Image and Icon.** See also **Clubs,** subentry on **Women's Clubs and Associations; Magazines, Women's; Voters and Voting,** subentry on **The Women's Vote.**]

OVERVIEW

The history of women in the nineteenth-century United States is complicated and difficult to narrate. The difficulty stems in part from the category "women," which encompasses women of all classes—working class, middle class, and elite—as well as a variety of ethnicities. Regardless of the differences and the unique life experiences of women living in the nineteenth-century United States, perhaps the American feminist Elizabeth Cady Stanton's (1815–1902) observation ties these women together across class, ethnic, and racial lines. In *Eighty Years and More,* Stanton recalled the birth of a sister: "I heard so many friends remark, 'What a pity it is she's a girl!' that I felt a kind of compassion for the little baby. True, our family consisted of five girls and only one boy, but I did not understand at that time that girls were considered an inferior order of beings" (p. 4). This notion of women as "inferior beings" may have resonated in individual women's lives and encouraged to some extent the ideology of woman's sphere or, as some historians have called it, the "cult of true womanhood."

The cult of true womanhood combined piety and domesticity with submissiveness and passivity; popular magazines and books of the day reinforced the ideology. In July 1832 Sarah Josepha Hale, editor of the women's magazine *Godey's Lady's Book,* described the "true woman" as one who was "delicate and timid," "required protection," and "possessed a sweet dependency." The cult of true womanhood developed as a distinctive middle-class ideology in the first half of the century. Concentrated in the Northeast, overwhelmingly Protestant and white, the new middle class had higher incomes, higher living standards, and greater literacy than their less fortunate neighbors. An additional characteristic was the distinctive gender roles: "competitive, aggressive, and materialistic" men belonged outside the home in the world of business; "gentle, spiritual, and nurturing" women belonged in the home.

Although the cult of true womanhood became the ideal against which all nineteenth-century women were measured, in order to attain the ideal a woman needed a husband who could support her financially. For the majority of women—immigrant women, poor women, black women, workingwomen, and others—this ideal remained beyond their reach. Nevertheless, the cult of true womanhood ideology extended middle-class ideals far beyond the middle class and affected marriage, female education, and employment choices, as well as strategies for obtaining women's rights, throughout the nineteenth century.

1800–1830

After the American Revolution, the process of redefining women's sphere had begun with the insistence of clergy and political leaders that women's special domestic skills could make an important contribution to society. They urged women to use their modesty and purity, believed to be inherent in their nature, to ensure the republican integrity of American men by educating children at home. By the 1820s the notion of women's higher moral status encouraged some women to educate children in school.

Marriage

Marriage offered white women the best route to fulfillment as true women. Therefore, it is not surprising that society expected women to marry, and the majority of them did so at some point in their lives. The trend to marriage based increasingly on love and affection, begun in the mid-eighteenth century, continued into the nineteenth century. These companionate unions, at least according to the ideal, romanticized women as nurturing mothers and sexually pure moral guardians. Middle-class marriages adhered to the strict gender-specific roles centered on family responsibilities. Among the southern planter class, marriage relations seemed an exaggerated version of the cult of true womanhood. In extolling and exaggerating the virtues of plantation women, southern planters were able to offset the inhumanity of slavery, in their own minds at least.

Nineteenth-century marriage was burdened with contradictions. For southern plantation women these contradictions were often glaring; wives might have to assume ignorance of their husbands' extramarital affairs with slave women. Thus they would have to ignore the violent rape their husbands were capable of committing. For women, north and south, marriage legally erased them throughout much of the nineteenth century.

State law governed marriage. In all states, married women were legal possessions rather than legal persons. Under coverture (the status a woman acquired upon marriage, under common law), married women had no control over their real or personal property, no right to their own earnings, no contract rights, and no guardianship rights over their children. Before 1800, a divorced woman rarely gained custody of her children, because most judges believed that fathers were the "natural custodians" of their offspring. Coverture assumed "spousal unity," which meant that legally, partners in marriage became united in the husband—in other words, a married woman's legal existence was extinguished by the status of marriage. In Louisiana, Texas, and California, the law nominally recognized a marital community of goods but vested in the husband control over all community property and similarly restricted the wife's legal capacity.

In contrast to the experience of most white women, married women on the Mexican frontier had certain legal advantages; they retained control of their land after marriage and held one-half interest in the community property they shared with their spouses. Many Native American women also retained some economic power in marriage. Traditionally, Indian women had been responsible for growing staple foods and often had controlled the inheritance of cultivation rights. Among the Cherokees, after marriage the husband lived with his wife's relations; if the marriage dissolved, the children remained with the mother. In addition to some rights in marriage, their importance in the economic sphere gave Indian women some political power as well. When missionaries and some Cherokee leaders introduced white middle-class domesticity, Cherokee women lost their economic and political power.

Slaves could not enter into any contracts, including the marriage contract. But most slaves did enter into formal unions solemnized either in church weddings before black or white preachers or through simple ceremonies, such as jumping over a broomstick. Because most slaves lived on small plantations, many sought partners elsewhere, in what were called "broad marriages." Slaves had to have their owners' permission to marry, and about one in six marriages was broken up by the sale of one of the partners.

Education

The idealized middle-class white marriage emphasized the valuable task that mothers performed in educating their children to be productive and moral citizens; therefore women's education became increasingly important. A marked improvement in the education of girls occurred around the end of the eighteenth century. In the early 1800s, as more white girls

A Milliner's Shop. Woodcut in Edward Hazen's *Panorama of Professions and Trades* (1836). LIBRARY OF CONGRESS

attended primary school, female literacy rose, but secondary education existed mostly for the daughters of affluent white men and reinforced upper-class women's domestic talents. Female academies featured subjects like French, English, and embroidery. By the 1810s, however, a new ideal of women's education began to take shape, an ideal still heavily influenced by accepted wisdom on what constituted "natural" and "appropriate" subjects for the female sex.

In 1819 Emma Willard, a teacher at a girls' academy, sought funding for an institution of higher learning for women. She argued that her curriculum would produce better homemakers and well-trained mothers—and, if necessary, self-supporting teachers. Eventually raising money from citizens in Troy, New York, Willard opened the Troy Female Seminary (1821), a model training school for teachers. Catharine Beecher opened the better-known Hartford Female Seminary in 1823. Over the next two decades, Beecher became an intellectual leader of women educators and inspired a multitude of women teachers. In a series of publications she argued that "moral and religious education must be the foundation of national instruction" and that "energetic and benevolent women" were the best qualified to impart moral and intellectual instruction to the young. At the same time that private schools became more readily available to girls, publicly supported education expanded

in the first decades of the nineteenth century and almost invariably included girls along with boys.

Inspired by their education and the evangelical fervor of the Second Great Awakening then sweeping the United States, some middle-class women took their moral mission outside the home. Prostitutes and their male customers became the focus of reformers' attention. Moral reform was among the first of women's efforts in the public arena. As the first quarter of the century gave way to the second, women expanded their reform efforts to include temperance, education reform, the abolition of slavery, and, finally, rights for themselves.

Work outside the home

Not only did educational and reform opportunities open up for women but wage-paying jobs did as well. In the 1820s, the development of water-powered mills in New England provided American women with their first chance at respectable, relatively safe work at reasonable wages. A method of factory management evolved in the textile mills of Lowell, Massachusetts. With the production process fully mechanized, the principal limitation on the firm's output was the availability of labor, and here the company made an innovation: it recruited young farm girls from the surrounding countryside. In order to attract these women and to reassure their families, the owners developed a paternalistic approach to management that became known as the Lowell system.

A Kitchen Interior. Frontispiece of Mrs. E. A. Howland's *The New England Economical Housekeeper* (1845). LIBRARY OF CONGRESS

The owners built boardinghouses to accommodate their labor force and enforced strict curfews, prohibited alcohol, and required church attendance. The twenty-five or so women residing in each house worked, ate, and spent leisure time together. Although Lowell provided cultural and economic advantages, it was not a "finishing school for young ladies." The mill workers had come to work, and they expected to be paid for their labor and treated with respect.

The farm girls became renowned as excellent employees. Studies have shown that the female mill employees worked to earn money primarily for themselves, often using it for a dowry. Most Lowell women worked only a few years. By the early 1830s more than forty thousand young women were working in the textile mills in New England. The Boston Manu-

facturing Company had managed to achieve competitive superiority over its British rivals by using new technology and cheap female labor.

By 1830 changes in women's roles were clearly in evidence, and they accelerated over the next few decades. Middle-class white women continued to use society's acceptance of their moral superiority to push for more educational opportunities, to expand their reform activities, and to campaign for women's rights. At the same time that white middle-class women's position appeared to be growing in influence, if not in power, women in other classes and of other ethnicities seemed to remain in the same position or actually lose some of their power.

1830–1848

In *The Bonds of Womanhood*, historian Nancy Cott argued that the 1830s became a turning point in women's history. Trends begun in the previous two decades bore fruit beginning in the 1830s. More young women worked at the new textile factories, and many of them became involved with industrial strikes. Women used petitions, a political tool, to demand legislation granting married women their property rights. Educational options continued to expand, and female literacy grew (by 1850, the census indicated that over 87 percent of all white women could read and write). Without directly challenging male domination of social and political institutions, women expanded the concept of domesticity and widened their role in the public sphere. However, the roles of wife and mother still provided women with their main purpose in life.

Marriage

Between 1840 and 1865, more than half a million people left the eastern United States and journeyed west. Great numbers of men went west, leaving their wives and children at home; women, in contrast, usually traveled with families. During the early years of settlement, men significantly outnumbered women in the West. These population imbalances on the frontier intensified the pressure upon women to marry, but anecdotal evidence suggests that not all women chose marriage. Women and men carried the "cult of true womanhood" ideal of domesticity westward, and the sexual division of labor remained basically intact. However, one aspect of women's lives did not remain the same. In the East most wives had drawn upon friends and family for help in their rounds of work and for physical and emotional support. The move west usually shattered that network and made women's work even more arduous.

Many nineteenth-century utopian and religious movements considered the transformation of marriage to be fundamental to their particular visions of

A New York Medical College for Women. From *Frank Leslie's Illustrated Newspaper*, 16 April 1870. LIBRARY OF CONGRESS

a reordered society. The Shakers eschewed marriage altogether and advocated celibacy for their members in their marriageless society. John Humphrey Noyes's Oneida Community, seeking to reform marriage with its problems of exclusiveness, jealousy, and quarreling, developed the doctrine of complex marriage. Complex marriage meant that all the members of the Oneida Community were married to one another. This complex doctrine attempted to achieve several social goals, including freeing women from being regarded as the property of their husbands. The Mormons, or the Church of Jesus Christ of Latter-day Saints, founded in 1830 by Joseph Smith, adopted polygamy—the practice of a man having multiple wives at the same time—in 1843.

Although for most white middle-class Americans the ideal of marriage remained the same, some women actively campaigned to change the laws governing married women's property, and some states responded. Mississippi was the first state to pass a married women's property law (1839). This law (most of which dealt specifically with slaveholdings) guaranteed the right of a married woman to receive income from her property and protected it against being seized for her husband's debts; however, the law left husbands in sole charge of buying, selling, or managing the property. In 1848, after a thirteen-year petition campaign, New York State lawmakers gave women control over their property and wages but refused to give them the right to sell or will property or money. By 1850 most states had passed laws giving married women some limited rights to own property. One motivation behind these laws was to protect large property owners who wanted to leave their holdings to their female children, who would pass these holdings on to their male descendants.

Education

The debate over married women's property rights was part of a larger contest over woman's proper "place" in society, and nowhere was this more evident than in the arena of education. Both as reformers and as teachers, women played a significant role in education. Women vigorously supported the movement led by the educator Horace Mann to expand public elementary schools. As secretary of the newly created Massachusetts Board of Education from 1837 to 1848, Mann lengthened the school year; established teaching standards in reading, writing, and arithmetic; and improved instruction by recruiting well-educated women as teachers.

Among some Hispanic residents of New Mexico traditions insisted that women be cloistered and protected, which led them to protest the establishment of coeducational public schools after 1850. Public education reform had little effect on slaves in the South, where it was illegal to teach slaves—and often free blacks—to read. In the North, free African American children were usually, but not always, relegated to segregated schools, and in some places they were denied access to education. By 1860 all northern states provided some public education for blacks, although some rural areas, especially in the southern portions of the Midwest, refused to fund schools for blacks and maintained segregated schools for whites. By the 1850s most teachers—especially in white schools—were women, in part because women could be paid less than men. And female education still emphasized moral and religious education, domestic science, and teacher training.

The total exclusion of women from colleges was broken in 1837, when Oberlin College in Ohio permitted women to enroll with men. However, most women at Oberlin enrolled in the "Ladies' Courses," which did not require Latin, Greek, or higher mathematics. The college required female students to wash male students' clothing, clean their rooms, and serve them at meals.

Mary Lyon, a teacher at a female academy, wanted to establish an endowed school of higher learning for women. In 1837, after four years of fundraising, she opened the Mount Holyoke Female Seminary in South Hadley, Massachusetts (now Mount Holyoke College). Its three-year curriculum covered many subjects studied by college men: grammar, ancient and modern geography, ancient and modern history, algebra, human physiology, botany, natural and intellectual philosophy, calisthenics, music, and French. Oberlin College and the Normal School for Colored Girls in Washington, D.C., founded in 1851, were among the few institutions where free black women could receive higher education.

In 1833, Prudence Crandall, a Quaker who conducted a successful school for "young ladies" in Canterbury, Connecticut, at the request of her free black servant accepted an African American girl, Sarah Harris, as a student. The admission caused a storm of protest, and rather than dismiss Harris, Crandall closed her school. Two months later she opened a new school with seventeen African American students. After community members threatened Crandall and the school to no avail, they employed other, more drastic tactics: Crandall was arrested for vagrancy, school windows were broken, pupils and teachers were stoned, and local merchants and doctors refused to serve the school. Nevertheless, for a year and a half Crandall and her students carried on, until one night men with battering rams demolished the school. The next day Crandall announced the closing of the school.

Antislavery activity

In the early nineteenth century, both white and African American women directly engaged in antislavery activity. Sarah and Angelina Grimké, two of the most active and best-known abolitionist speakers, grew up on a plantation in South Carolina and traveled north to speak to others about the horrors of slavery. Almost twenty years before Harriet Beecher Stowe's *Uncle Tom's Cabin* (1852) set publication records, Angelina Grimké published *An Appeal to the Christian Women of the South* (1836). Less-well-known women organized petition drives for abolition, campaigned for antislavery candidates, embarked on lecture tours, and formed abolitionist societies. African American women founded the nation's first women's antislavery society, in Salem, Massachusetts (1832). In 1833 Lucretia Mott, Charlotte Grimké Forten, and others formed the Philadelphia Female Anti-Slavery Society. The fugitive slave Harriet Tubman placed her life at risk helping others escape to freedom, and the former slave Sojourner Truth joined white women abolitionists in their effort to achieve the dual emancipation of slaves and women. In 1836 members of the Boston Female Anti-Slavery Society hired counsel who, in *Commonwealth v. Aves*, successfully secured the liberty of Med, a six-year-old slave whose owner had brought her to Massachusetts.

Surprisingly, all-female abolitionist meetings attracted male attendance, and before long women were speaking to mixed audiences, though they drew sharp criticism for doing so. Their actions provoked widespread outrage, and the female abolitionists were told that they were out of their "place" or "sphere" and behaving in an "unwomanly" manner. They continued their activities.

In 1840, the World Antislavery Convention refused to seat Lucretia Mott, one of six American women elected as delegates to the London convention. Mott and the other women had to sit upstairs in the balcony and watch; they could neither speak nor vote. In London, Mott met Elizabeth Cady Stanton, who was outraged at not being allowed to take part in the convention. They vowed to hold a women's rights meeting when they returned to the United States. Eight years later, in 1848, they placed a small ad in a newspaper announcing that a women's rights convention would be held in Seneca Falls, New York. More than three hundred women and a few dozen men attended the meeting. Three years earlier Margaret Fuller had published *Women in the Nineteenth Century*, an influential publication urging women's rights.

Women workers

As middle-class women participated in reform movements and began campaigning for women's rights, the Lowell mill workers agitated for better pay and working conditions. These workers had come to expect a certain level of respect from the mill owners. When the owners responded to increased competition and poor business conditions with sharp reductions in wages and increases in the rents they charged in their boardinghouses, many women workers were outraged. As conditions continued to decline during the 1840s, mill owners began to turn to newly arrived immigrant women, who would accept lower pay and more work.

When New England mill owners lowered their wages in 1834, women workers decided to walk out, leaving the mills short-staffed, to pressure owners into maintaining the wage rates. The *Boston Evening Transcript* reported that in Lowell, eight hundred strikers had formed a procession "and marched about town. We are told that one of the leaders mounted a pump and made a flaming . . . speech on the rights of women and the iniquities of the 'moneyed aristocracy,' which produced a powerful effect on her auditors, and they determined to 'have their own way if they died for it.' "

The women developed local organizations to sustain their protests; the Factory Girls' Association, formed in 1836, immediately signed up more than 2,500 members. Workers in other factory towns across New England followed Lowell's lead and developed local organizations to bring about strikes. With the onset of the 1837 depression, workers had little choice but to accept cuts in pay. But when the 1840s brought an upturn in both the national economy and the textile industry, a new generation of mill workers pressed their case again. Their activities expanded the idea of "woman's sphere."

1848–1865

In 1848 New York, following the lead of Texas and Mississippi, passed the Married Woman's Property Act, which gave married women ownership over property inherited or acquired. In July of that year, the first women's rights convention in the United States met at Seneca Falls, New York. A second women's rights convention met in Rochester, New York, in August. Black women made their first official bid for equality in meetings with black men in 1848. At the annual meeting of the National Convention of Colored Freedmen in Cleveland, Ohio, a black woman proposed that women delegates be allowed to speak and vote as equals. The former slave and now lecturer and writer Frederick Douglass supported her proposal. After much debate, convention delegates reclassified eligible voters as "persons" instead of men and allowed women to participate equally.

At the Seneca Falls woman's rights convention, Stanton read the "Declaration of Sentiments," which described many of the ways that men had power over women. It further stated that women were equal to men and should have all the same rights and responsibilities in society that men did. The statement also raised, for the first time, the idea that women should have the right to vote—the most radical idea presented at the convention. Although they hoped to enlarge women's opportunities beyond the home, most women's rights activists accepted traditional ideas about women's special maternal qualities and their moral and spiritual superiority. The Quaker reformer Susan B. Anthony had heard about the Seneca Falls Convention, but she deemed its goals of secondary importance to temperance and antislavery. All that changed in 1851 when she met Stanton, with whom she formed a lifelong political partnership.

In general, the period immediately preceding the Civil War showed evidence of women changing society. In 1849, Amelia Bloomer established the *Lily*, a temperance journal that shifted its focus to women's rights. That same year, Elizabeth Blackwell received her medical degree at Geneva, New York, and became the first "regular" woman doctor in the United States. In 1850, the Female Medical College of Pennsylvania, the first medical school for women, was established. And on 23 October of that year, at the women's rights convention in Worcester, Massachusetts, delegates decided to circulate petitions for woman suffrage. Paulina Wright Davis established the *Una*, one of the first women's rights journals, in 1853.

The inequality of married women before the law and the inequality within most marriages delayed abolitionist and women's rights activist Lucy Stone's decision to marry Henry Blackwell, an ardent abolitionist. They took the word "obey" out of their marriage vows and read a protest against the marriage laws at their 1855 wedding ceremony. The protest was later published and widely circulated. After marriage, Stone kept her surname. Other women's rights activists demonstrated that marriage did not equal the sum total of their lives; they retained their birth names, added on their husbands' last names, and preferred not to be called by their husband's first names. Elizabeth Cady Stanton, for instance, did not want to be called "Mrs. Henry Stanton" and identified herself as Elizabeth Cady Stanton or simply Mrs. Stanton.

By 1860, Indiana, Maine, Missouri, Ohio, and other states had passed laws to allow married women to keep their own earnings. At the Tenth National Woman's Rights Convention, Stanton introduced ten resolutions favoring more liberal divorce laws. At that time, women in New York State were entitled to sue for divorce only on the ground of adultery. A few other states allowed women to sue for divorce on the ground of the husband's desertion or failure to provide for his wife and children as well as of adultery. Stanton wanted marriages to be treated as simple contracts that could be dissolved quickly and quietly on the grounds of drunkenness, insanity, desertion, brutality, adultery, or incompatibility. Although her resolutions were tabled, they expanded the discussion of marriage rights to include divorce.

During the Civil War (1861–1865) white and free black women in the North established soldiers' aid societies, including the U.S. Sanitary Commission. In the South, white Confederate women organized hundreds of local soldiers' relief societies and volunteered to make weapons and other war supplies. Confederate and Union women served as nurses (several women acted as doctors and surgeons at the front) as well as spies, scouts, and smugglers. An estimated four hundred women disguised themselves as soldiers and fought during the war. Susan B. Anthony organized the National Women's Loyal League to collect signatures for passage of the Thirteenth Amendment, abolishing slavery. Northern women entered government offices to replace clerks who went to war. Like their northern counterparts, southern women took over the work of men who had gone off to fight and managed family farms and plantations. Additionally, women on the southern homefront bore the worst hardships because the war was largely fought on their soil. Busy with the war effort, the leaders of the women's rights movement decided to discontinue their conventions until the war's end and concentrate all their energies into relief societies, fund-raising, abolitionist activities, and nursing. Some considered the pause a strategic move: they reasoned that women would prove themselves worthy of the vote by their patriotic endeavors during the war. In 1865, the year the Civil War ended, Vassar College opened, offering the first college-level curriculum for women.

1865–1900

In the final third of the nineteenth century, American society as a whole embraced the theory of female moral superiority. Middle- and upper-class women continued to use this belief to extend their sphere beyond the home. Many women argued that the services of morally superior women were needed to help correct the "evils" of the world. Just as reform in the middle of the century permitted women to venture out of the home, so at the end of the century reform movements grew to encompass political and economic issues as well.

Between 1870 and 1900 the number of wage-earning women grew by almost two-thirds; their sex shaped their role as workers. Contemporary beliefs about womanhood determined which women entered the workforce and how they were treated once they became wage earners. Wives were not supposed to work outside the home. By 1890, only 4.5 percent of married white women, 30 percent of married African American women, and 40.5 percent of single women worked outside the home. At the turn of the century, women worked as domestic servants; held "female" white-collar jobs in teaching, nursing, sales, and office work; or worked in industry, especially the garment trades and textile mills.

By the mid-1870s almost all the states in the North had passed married women's property acts, and by the end of the century, the southern states had as well. Although the scope of these laws varied widely from state to state, taken together, they represented a sweeping transfer of property rights and a historic improvement in the status of American married women.

As part of Reconstruction, northern teachers were appointed to the Freedmen's Bureau to educate the former slaves. By 1869, nine thousand teachers had been recruited to instruct the former slaves, and 600,000 African Americans of all ages were enrolled in elementary schools. For most southern black girls, receiving an education had been impossible before the Civil War.

Secondary education for whites of either sex was not widespread until after 1870, when there were only 160 high schools in the whole country. Ten years later, the figure was almost eight hundred, and by the end of the century the number was six thousand. The continued refusal of men to grant women an opportunity for higher education provided the impetus for the establishment of separate female colleges; the number of women college students throughout the United

States increased from eleven thousand in 1879 to eighty-five thousand in 1900.

Chinese immigrants

The widespread belief that Chinese Americans were inferior to whites barred them from public education. In 1859, after years of petitioning by the Chinese to get their children into San Francisco's schools, the board of education reluctantly allowed the Chinese into evening classes for foreigners and opened a day school for Chinese children. But by the late 1860s anti-Chinese feeling closed the day school and banned the Chinese from evening classes. Chinese children went to church-sponsored day schools, and working adults attended evening classes in churches.

The number of Chinese women who traveled to the United States in the nineteenth century was so small that by 1882, in California, there were twenty-two Chinese men for every Chinese woman. This population imbalance created a demand for sexual services and sustained organized prostitution in Chinese immigrant communities. Only a few married Chinese women traveled to America; most of the female immigrants were young women who were placed into prostitution. They did not necessarily enter prostitution voluntarily. Many had been enticed into sham marriages in China, only to be sold into the trade on their arrival in America. Others had been purchased from their poverty-stricken parents; still others had been kidnapped by procurers and smuggled into American ports.

"Rescue homes" run by white Protestant women attempted to "redeem" Chinese women from prostitution, reform them, and help them marry. The homes emphasized the ideals of the cult of true womanhood—purity, piety, and domesticity—as they trained immigrant women for new roles as mothers in Christian homes. Apparently the rescue homes were so successful that they had a high marriage rate (but a lesser rate of conversion to Christianity). The Page Act, "An Act to Prevent the Kidnapping and Importation of Mongolian, Chinese and Japanese Females for Demoralizing Purposes," passed by Congress in 1875, assumed that all Asian women entering the United States were doing so for "criminal and demoralizing purposes" unless it was proved otherwise. It effectively ended the immigration of unmarried Asian women to the United States.

Women's suffrage

After passage of the Fourteenth Amendment, granting citizenship to all people born in the United States, and of the Fifteenth Amendment, prohibiting racial discrimination in voting, leaders of the women's rights movement determined to press their own claims more vigorously. The Supreme Court's refusal to extend most Fourteenth Amendment rights to women anchored the prevailing "separate spheres" gender ideology. In 1869, two suffrage organizations were formed: Elizabeth Cady Stanton and Susan B. Anthony founded the National Woman Suffrage Association (NWSA); Lucy Stone and Henry Blackwell organized the American Woman Suffrage Association (AWSA). The two groups worked independently for the next twenty years.

NWSA's primary goal was a woman suffrage amendment. Its members also wanted women to have the rights to inherit or own property, to attend college, to control the money they made if they held a paying job, and to obtain custody of their children in divorce cases. They also were concerned about the terrible working conditions for women in the factories and textile mills. AWSA leaders chose to work on smaller, separate referenda campaigns in each individual state to gain the right to vote, and they avoided involvement with other women's issues. Antisuffragists asserted that suffrage would divert women's attention toward politics and the public sphere and away from home and family.

In 1890 the two rival suffrage organizations merged to form the National American Woman Suffrage Association. By this time many states had passed married women's property rights laws, equalized guardianship of children, and granted women legal standing to make contracts and bring suit. Nearly one-third of college students were female, and nineteen states allowed women to vote in local school board elections. In two western territories—Wyoming and Utah—women voted on an equal basis with men.

The garment industry

The garment industry became a major employer of women, especially immigrant women, around 1882. Female workers could make a living only by working long hours or by taking work home with them. In sweatshops women routinely worked ten hours a day, six days a week. Supervisors locked doors to prevent workers from going to the bathroom without permission. A variety of schemes cheated women of some of their meager wages. Employers turned back clocks to add extra minutes to the day or distributed tiny ticket stubs, easily lost, as tokens for work completed. Whispers of easy tasks for sexual favors filtered through the industry. The term sweatshop, first used in the clothing industry, later became synonymous with low-wage, unsanitary work in many industries.

The investigators of sweatshops denounced them as a "system of making clothes under filthy and inhuman conditions" and as a "process of grinding the faces of the poor" (Louis Levine, *The Women's Garment Workers* [New York: Huebsh, 1924]). In explaining these conditions, investigators generally took the view that the sweatshop was the result of the inferior standards introduced by the immigrants. Some even declared the sweatshop a special Jewish institution explicable by the "racial" and "national" characteristics of the Jewish workers. The bias involved in such explanations is evident. Sweating in the United States existed in the clothing trades long before the coming of Jewish and Italian immigrants.

Women's organizations

The last decades of the nineteenth century were characterized by the founding of women's institutions and organizations. These separate institutions both reflected and intensified the assumptions that women had an identity so different from men that they needed a separate sphere to fulfill their womanly roles. Separate institutions also enabled women to forge positive identities, strengthen the bonds of sisterhood, and create supportive networks. White middle-class and upper-class clubwomen lobbied for uncontaminated food and milk, clean streets, and better "municipal housekeeping." In 1890, thousands of local clubs formed the General Federation of Women's Clubs, which helped secure the passage of the Pure Food and Drug Act and promoted protective legislation for women and children in the early twentieth century.

Denied access to white-only clubs, African American middle-class women launched their own club movement committed to community service and female sociability. They also sought to eradicate the racist stereotyping of black females as sexually promiscuous. The National Association of Colored Women, organized in 1896, was the first nationally organized civil rights association. Antilynching strategies accounted for a major part of its reform work. African American women's antilynching activity began with Ida Wells-Barnett, who conducted a systematic investigation of the real reasons blacks were lynched.

At the turn of the century, ideas about women and women's habits were changing: mothers had fewer children, more women demanded a voice in politics, and more worked outside the home. Urbanization and expansion of the female labor force offered unmarried women the chance to live apart from their families. The term New Woman, first coined in the 1890s, described confident and self-sufficient young women whose lifestyles differed radically from those of preceding generations. The New Woman, as portrayed in periodicals, was white, sophisticated and city-dwelling, usually college-educated, and interested in social issues. Just as the cult of true womanhood did not reflect adequately the realities of most nineteenth-century women's lives, neither did the New Woman.

See also **Beauty Contests; Birth and Childbearing; Civil War,** *subentry on* **Women on the Front; Clubs,** *subentry on* **Women's Clubs and Associations; Contraception and Abortion; Divorce and Desertion; Domestic Life; Education,** *subentry on* **Education of Girls and Women; Entrepreneurs, Women; First Ladies; Gender; Labor Movement,** *subentry on* **Women; Law,** *subentry on* **Women and the Law; Marriage; Midwives; Voters and Voting,** *subentry on* **The Women's Vote; Women,** *subentries on* **Women's Rights, Women in the Professions, Woman as Image and Icon; Work,** *subentry on* **Domestic Labor.**

Bibliography

Clinton, Catherine, and Nina Silber, eds. *Divided Houses: Gender and the Civil War.* New York: Oxford University Press, 1992.

Cott, Nancy F. *The Bonds of Womanhood: "Woman's Sphere" in New England, 1780–1835.* New Haven, Conn.: Yale University Press, 1977.

Degler, Carl. *At Odds: Women and the Family in America from the Revolution to the Present.* New York: Oxford University Press, 1980.

Dublin, Thomas. *Women at Work: The Transformation of Work and Community in Lowell, Massachusetts, 1826–1860.* New York: Columbia University Press, 1979.

DuBois, Ellen Carol. *Feminism and Suffrage: The Emergence of an Independent Women's Movement in America, 1848–1869.* Ithaca, N.Y.: Cornell University Press, 1978.

Faragher, John Mack. *Women and Men on the Overland Trail.* New Haven, Conn.: Yale University Press, 1979.

Flexner, Eleanor. *Century of Struggle: The Woman's Rights Movement in the United States.* Cambridge, Mass.: Belknap Press of Harvard University Press, 1975.

Ginzberg, Lori D. *Women and the Work of Benevolence: Morality, Politics, and Class in the Nineteenth-Century.* New Haven, Conn.: Yale University Press, 1990.

Hersh, Blanche Glassman. *The Slavery of Sex: Feminist-Abolitionists in America.* Urbana: University of Illinois Press, 1978.

Kessler-Harris, Alice. *Out to Work: A History of Wage-Earning Women in the United States.* New York: Oxford University Press, 1982.

Riley, Glenda. *Women and Indians on the Frontier, 1825–1915.* Albuquerque: University of New Mexico Press, 1984.

Scott, Anne Firor. *The Southern Lady: From Pedestal to Politics.* Chicago: University of Chicago Press, 1970.

Sklar, Kathryn Kish. *Catharine Beecher: A Study in American Domesticity.* New Haven, Conn.: Yale University Press, 1973.

Solomon, Barbara Miller. *In the Company of Educated Women: A History of Women and Higher Education in America.* New Haven, Conn.: Yale University Press, 1985.

Stanton, Elizabeth Cady. *Eighty Years and More, 1815–1897:*

Reminiscences of Elizabeth Cady Stanton. New York: Schocken Books, 1971.

Weatherford, Doris. *Foreign and Female: Immigrant Women in America 1840–1930.* New York: Schocken Books, 1986.

Welter, Barbara. "The Cult of True Womanhood, 1820–1860." *American Quarterly* 18 (Summer 1966): 151–175.

White, Deborah Gray. *Ar'n't I a Woman?: Female Slaves in the Plantation South.* New York: Norton, 1985.

GAYLE V. FISCHER

WOMEN'S RIGHTS

In the antebellum era demands for women's rights were articulated in the speeches and writings of such women as Frances Wright, Ernestine Rose, and Angelina Grimké. In this period of widespread reform endeavors, women's demands were a logical response to the discriminations against women in law, religion, education, the professions, and politics. Women who began their reform involvement in religious missionary societies often were drawn to the temperance movement, where they easily connected alcoholism with spousal abuse. At the same time abolitionist women began to see their own oppression reflected in that of the southern slaves, while women moral reformers attempted to end prostitution by publishing the names of male customers. In 1848 in Seneca Falls, New York, the first national women's rights convention ratified a Declaration of Sentiments, written mostly by Elizabeth Cady Stanton. Women's rights leaders organized similar conventions in various other cities until the onset of the Civil War.

During the war, women's rights reformers suspended their work on behalf of women to focus on the war effort. In the North the U.S. Sanitary Commission, largely a women's organization, raised funds, collected supplies, and oversaw nursing resources. After the war, women's rights reformers focused on attaining women's suffrage, which was overlooked by the Reconstruction amendments that enfranchised black males. Women's clubs, which first appeared in New York City in 1868, advocated social reform, and by the end of the century they had spread throughout the nation. Late in the century various women's rights groups, including the Women's Christian Temperance Union headed by Frances Willard, joined in a coalition, reflecting Willard's "do everything" policy of reform. In 1890 many white women's clubs formed the General Federation of Women's Clubs.

During the nineteenth century the U.S. culture's core belief in the moral superiority of women encouraged them to take up reform. In addition an increasing number of women attended college and entered the professions, encouraging women to agitate on the state level for elimination of laws that denied married women control over their property, earnings, and children. Women fought for admission to law and medical schools and persuaded state boards to certify them. Elizabeth Blackwell, the first woman doctor in the United States, graduated from Geneva Medical College in 1849, and Arabella Mansfield, the nation's first woman lawyer, was trained by her brother and licensed by the Iowa bar in 1869.

In cities women secured such reforms as improved sanitation and schools, which benefited their families. Individuals such as Jane Addams improved material conditions for working-class women at home and at work and established reform vocations. Addams sparked the nationwide settlement house movement in 1889, when she founded Hull-House in Chicago.

African-American women were for the most part denied membership in white women's organizations. Working for social reform and the elimination of the mainstream sexualization of black women, they formed separate clubs, which federated in the National Association of Colored Women in 1895.

See also **Abolition and Antislavery; Civil Rights; Clubs,** *subentry on* **Women's Clubs and Associations; Education,** *subentry on* **Education of Girls and Women; Law,** *subentry on* **Women and the Law; Literature,** *subentry on* **Women's Literature; Professions; Reform, Social; Settlement Houses; Temperance Movement; Voters and Voting,** *subentry on* **The Women's Vote; Women.**

Bibliography

Banner, Lois W. *Elizabeth Cady Stanton: A Radical for Woman's Rights.* Boston: Little, Brown, 1979.

DuBois, Ellen Carol, ed. *Elizabeth Cady Stanton, Susan B. Anthony: Correspondence, Writings, Speeches.* New York: Schocken, 1981.

Flexner, Eleanor, and Ellen Fitzpatrick, *Century of Struggle: The Woman's Rights Movement in the United States.* Cambridge, Mass.: Belknap Press of Harvard University Press, 1996.

Hoffert, Sylvia D. *When Hens Crow: The Woman's Rights Movements in Antebellum America.* Bloomington: Indiana University Press, 1995.

LOIS W. BANNER

WOMEN'S LABOR

Motivated by patriotism, survival, or service, nineteenth-century women entered the paid labor force in large numbers. Female workers experienced wage labor differently, depending on marital status, race, class, and citizenship.

Historical Context

U.S. ideology discouraged women from doing paid work. Under the cult of domesticity, developed from 1820 to 1860, women were viewed as naturally inferior, physically weaker, and more emotional than men. These arguments justified women's relegation to a separate sphere in the home. No longer viewed as a place for the production of goods, the family home was a domain for the nurturing of children and spiritual guidance. Women were also dissuaded from wage labor by the sharp dichotomy between the home and the marketplace. The participation of women in paid work was viewed as a temporary stage to be replaced by marriage and homemaking.

During 1820 to 1865, the industrial revolution forced women to seek paid work outside the home. Formerly, women had played an active role in the household production of goods controlled by the family. However, by utilizing traditional skills of sewing, stitching, and looming cotton in large-scale production, the manufacturing industry diminished the importance of the domestic sphere and stripped the family unit of a market for its goods. The shift away from household production and the depression of 1837–1839 forced women to seek income opportunities outside the home. During the Civil War there was a shortage of male laborers, and in response, increasing numbers of women aided soldiers on the battlefields as nurses, sewed soldiers' uniforms, produced war supplies in factories, and performed clerical duties in government offices.

Labor Occupations

By the mid-1800s women were employed in more than two hundred occupations. The leading jobs for women in 1850 were in domestic service (330,000), the clothing industry (62,000), cotton textiles (59,000), wool textiles (19,000), shoe manufacturing (33,000), hatmaking (8,000), and teaching (55,000). By 1890, women made up 17.1 percent of the labor force in the United States. The majority of these were employed in domestic service. In return for room, board, or wages, domestic servants assisted in household tasks such as cooking, cleaning, and caring for children. Immigrant women represented one-third of all domestic servants. By 1900 domestic servants were primarily Irish immigrants and black women. Domestic service also included female laundresses, dressmakers, and seamstresses. In these areas women worked in their own homes and sold their goods to other households.

The clothing industry underwent a transformation in the nineteenth century. In the 1820s, urbanization created a demand for ready-made clothing, and women worked as seamstresses, dressmakers, tailors, and shirt, cuff, and collar makers in their homes or in small garment shops. However, with the emergence of the sewing machine in the 1840s, the sewing trades expanded into a large-scale garment industry. In the 1840s and 1850s, immigrant women, who were more willing to work in harsh conditions for low wages, replaced native-born women. Women typically worked in these sweatshops for fourteen hours a day and earned from $3 to $6 a week.

The textile industry both exploited and liberated nineteenth-century women. Lowell, Massachusetts, was the largest textile center in the United States, and in the early 1800s single women from surrounding farm communities found work in the mills. In 1836, 85 percent of the mill workers in Lowell were women, of whom 96 percent were native-born. Often finding a sense of independence, these mill girls transformed Lowell into a cultural center that provided lectures, language classes, sewing groups, and other self-improvement activities. Women lived in boarding houses that created a sense of community, provided little privacy, and imposed strict curfews. Employment in the mills was considered temporary for native-born females, who were expected to marry. However, the textile industry began to lose profits in the 1830s due to competition and overproduction. As a result, conditions in the mills deteriorated, and wages were lowered.

In response, female millworkers formed labor unions and staged protests. Groups such as the Knights of Labor, the Factory Girls Association, and the Lowell Female Labor Reform Association unionized women laborers. The first recorded strike by female textile workers was in Dover, New Hampshire, in December 1828. Female millworkers in Lowell organized strikes in 1834 and 1836. The second strike proved more successful, rallying 1,500 workers and shutting the mills down for several months. In addition, labor groups lobbied for ten-hour workdays through rallies and petition drives. However, these efforts generally proved unsuccessful in changing working conditions. In the 1840s Italian, English, Welsh, Irish, French Canadian, and eastern European immigrant workers began to replace native-born female workers. By the late 1800s large numbers of immigrant women labored under poor conditions and lived in dilapidated houses on dirty streets.

Nineteenth-century women were also employed in the shoe-binding trades. Initially performed within households, shoe binding was relegated to small shops, and labor was divided along gender lines. Men constructed the leather materials, and women stitched the shoes together. Employers believed that, because women generally had smaller hands, they were more dexterous and better suited to stitching than men. In the 1840s the introduction of the sewing

Milking a Cow. LIBRARY OF CONGRESS

machine transformed the boot and shoe trades into a large-scale industry. By 1900 women comprised 33 percent of the shoe industry employees.

Clerical work was open only to middle-class, native-born women. The emergence of the typewriter created opportunities for women as stenographers and typists, and by the mid-1870s numerous women were employed in large office typing pools. Clerical work provided higher salaries and was cleaner and quieter than factory work. However, female office workers faced discrimination and were rarely promoted.

Nursing and teaching were also only available to middle-class, native-born women. Nursing attracted many women interested in service work. Women were considered well suited for the field of nursing because of the prevailing view that they were natural caregivers. Working under unsanitary conditions, female nurses received no professional training and were paid low wages. The profession of choice for many nineteenth-century middle-class women was teaching. Female teachers were largely concentrated at the elementary level and earned one-half to one-third of what males earned. Beginning in 1907 teachers were required to complete high school and earn a license.

Women in the Midwest and West primarily worked in domestic service and agriculture. White female homesteaders performed domestic duties, worked on family farms, and helped male family members run small businesses. Many Mexican women worked with their families under poor conditions in the sugar beet fields or performed domestic duties for male workers living in boarding houses. Similarly, after emancipation black women worked as domestic servants and as agricultural workers under harsh conditions. Immigrating to the West coast, Asian women were met with hostility and were ostracized to isolated Asian communities. Many Asian women in urban areas worked as domestic servants and prostitutes, or in family businesses. In the rural Midwest, Asian women worked as domestic servants, agricultural workers, or on family farms. In contrast, Native American women were thrust into the center of battle during a series of wars with whites that began in 1865. Native American women engaged in activities such as weaving, pottery, and farming while maintaining the survival of their tribal communities.

See also **Entrepreneurs, Women; Gender; Industrialization and the Market; Labor Movement; Textiles;**

Zuni Women Grinding Corn. Lithograph by Ackerman Lithographers after R. H. Kern. From *Report of an Expedition down the Zuni and Colorado Rivers, by Captain L. Sitgreaves* (1854). LIBRARY OF CONGRESS: PRINTS AND PHOTOGRAPHS DIVISION

Women, *subentries on* **Women's Rights, Women in the Professions; Work.**

Bibliography

Applebaum, Herbert. *The American Work Ethic and the Changing Work Force: An Historical Perspective.* Westport, Conn.: Greenwood Press, 1998.

Baxandall, Rosalyn, and Linda Gordon, eds. and comps. *America's Working Women: A Documentary History, 1600 to the Present.* New York: Norton, 1995.

Brownlee, W. Elliot, and Mary M. Brownlee. *Women in the American Economy: A Documentary History, 1675 to 1929.* New Haven, Conn.: Yale University Press, 1976.

Butler, Anne M., and Ona Siporin. *Uncommon Common Women: Ordinary Lives of the West.* Logan: Utah State University Press, 1996.

Cantor, Milton, and Bruce Laurie, eds. *Class, Sex, and the Woman Worker.* Westport, Conn.: Greenwood Press, 1977.

Kessler-Harris, Alice. *Out to Work: A History of Wage-Earning Women in the United States.* New York: Oxford University Press, 1982.

Matthaei, Julie. *An Economic History of Women in America: Women's Work, the Sexual Division of Labor, and the Development of Capitalism.* New York: Schocken Books, 1982.

LAURA ANN FOSTER

WOMEN IN THE PROFESSIONS

Women first demanded equal access to the professions of medicine, law, and university teaching in the late 1800s. Pioneering females entering male-dominated professions braved cultural bias and discrimination.

Historical Context

The public viewed women as intellectually inferior to men and believed that respectable middle- and upper-class women should not work outside the home. These beliefs became known as the cult of domesticity. The public believed in a sharp dichotomy between the home and the business world. The home, in contrast to the marketplace, was a domain for nurturing and spirituality and became a woman's proper sphere. Women, seen as morally superior to men, were restricted to the roles of wife and mother. The public believed that the female mind, in contrast to the male mind of reason and intellect, was innately connected with nature, emotions, spirituality, and biology. Darwinism and medical experiments revealing the smaller size of the female brain seemed to support these views.

Marginalized by the cult of domesticity, lower-class women were constructed as amoral and promiscuous, thus they were excluded from the professions and considered well suited for the agricultural and domestic labor in which they predominated. Thus nineteenth-century ideology discouraged women from entering the professions.

However, several historical events influenced women to enter the professions. The Industrial Revolution took production out of the home and into the marketplace. By diminishing the importance of the domestic sphere, the Industrial Revolution inspired white middle- and upper-class women to seek alternatives to being a homemaker. After caring for injured soldiers as nurses and aides during the Civil War, women were strongly influenced to become physicians. Women's rights advocates, encouraging women to enter professional careers, protested the ideals of domesticity and pushed for education reforms.

Influence of Higher Education

Women's opportunities for higher education dramatically increased with the founding of women's colleges, including Mount Holyoke (1837), Vassar

Kindergarten in the North-End Industrial Home, Boston. Wood engraving after sketch by Charles Upham, in *Frank Leslie's Illustrated Newspaper*, no. 52:229 (1881). LIBRARY OF CONGRESS

(1861), Wellesley (1870), Smith (1871), Radcliffe (1879), and Bryn Mawr (1880). These exclusive women's colleges created a supportive environment for the intellectual and professional growth of women. However, women's colleges debated on whether to educate women for the domestic sphere or the business world. This debate manifested itself in the curriculum of early coed schools such as Oberlin (founded in 1833), where women were encouraged to learn home economics and the humanities rather than attend math and science lectures with male classmates. Women's educational opportunities also expanded in the 1870s with the opening of state universities, such as California, Indiana, Iowa, Kansas, Michigan, Minnesota, Missouri, and Wisconsin, to females. In fact women made up 21 percent of the total college student population in 1870 and 32 percent in 1880. Although the educational opportunities for women dramatically expanded, universities often trained women for homemaking, thus dissuading them from higher intellectual pursuits.

Physicians, Lawyers, and University Teachers

Despite obstacles, women of the nineteenth century began entering professional fields of study. The majority of women who pursued professional careers were middle- or upper-class and white. Women first made progress in the field of medicine. Prior to the Civil War women received medical training from exclusive female medical colleges, such as Gregory's Medical School in Boston and Women's Medical College of Pennsylvania in Philadelphia. Elizabeth Blackwell became the first female to receive a medical degree when she graduated from Geneva Medical College in 1849.

Women's opportunities in the field of medicine expanded after the Civil War increased the need for hospitals and physicians. Marie Zahrzewska, a German immigrant, graduated from Cleveland Medical College in 1856 and established the New England Hospital for Women and Children in 1862 to train female physicians. Two years later Rebecca Lee Crumpler became the first African American female to receive a medical degree, graduating from New England Female Medical College. By the late nineteenth century, sixty-five black women physicians practiced medicine. Opportunities further expanded when public medical schools, such as those in Boston; Buffalo, New York; Ann Arbor, Michigan; and Syracuse, New York, became coeducational in 1880. A decade later training hospitals for women opened up in Boston, Chicago, New York, Philadelphia, Minneapolis, and San Francisco. Susan La Flesche Picotte became the first Native American to earn an M.D., graduating

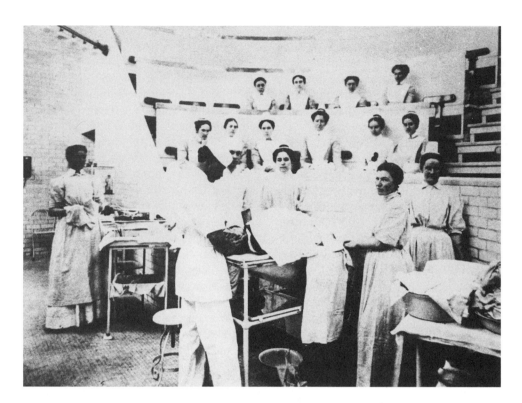

Operating Room Demonstration at St. Luke's Hospital, New York. Photograph by R. F. Turnbull. LIBRARY OF CONGRESS

from the Women's Medical College of Pennsylvania in 1889. Despite this progress women faced obstacles. Medical schools set higher admissions standards for women and demonstrated gender and racial discrimination. Professional associations prevented women from securing necessary internships and training.

Women faced greater opposition in the legal field. Associated with logic and reason rather than the nurturing element of medicine, the study of law was considered antithetical to a woman's capacity. In addition the legal profession was highly regulated, and the common law prohibited women from being lawyers. In 1869 Arabella Mansfield was the first American woman admitted to the bar. The Illinois State Supreme Court denied Myra Bradwell entrance to the bar in 1869, however, during the same year Washington University in St. Louis and the University of Iowa opened their doors to women. Ada Kepley, the first female law graduate, was awarded a degree from the present-day Northwestern University in 1870. At the same time the University of Michigan and Boston University began admitting women as well. Charlotte Ray became the first African American female to receive a law degree when she graduated from Howard University Law School in 1872. In 1879 Belva Lockwood became the first female admitted to practice law before the U.S. Supreme Court. The

number of female attorneys totaled 75 in 1881 and 208 in 1891. However, female law students, isolated from male students, were disadvantaged, and practicing female attorneys faced discrimination and doubt over their ability to argue legal principles in a public courtroom. In fact many female attorneys resorted to assisting their husbands' legal practices as office clerks. African American, Jewish, and immigrant women did not enter the legal profession in significant numbers until the twentieth century, when night law schools opened.

Women made pioneering strides as university professors beginning in the late 1800s. Women's colleges were the most receptive to hiring female faculty. Maria Mitchell became one of the first female faculty members of Vassar in 1865, and Katherine Lee Bates was hired in 1885 as an English instructor at Wellesley. Marie Louise Sanford entered the faculty of University of Minnesota, and Ellen Swallow Richards began teaching at MIT in 1884. However, female professors faced discrimination and limited opportunities to pursue high intellectual scholarship.

Females in the West and South were less represented in the professions than females in the East. In contrast to the industrial progress of the eastern United States, the southern and western regions of the country were primarily agrarian. Thus, women in the West and South were concentrated in professions like agriculture, domestic service, and teaching, and found limited opportunity to enter other professions.

Despite their triumphs, women represented a small percentage of the total number of professionals. From 1870 to 1920 females represented less than 8 percent of the college professors, 5 percent of the physicians, and 3 percent of the lawyers in the United States. These low numbers were due to the cult of domesticity, stricter admissions standards, and discrimination. Nineteenth-century women in the professions were underpaid and not respected. However, they paved the way for future generations of females in the professions.

Women were considered well suited for the professions of nursing and teaching. Middle- and upper-class white women interested in service work predominated in these fields. Immigrant and black women participated in these fields in very small numbers compared to whites. The first nursing school was established at New York's Bellevue Hospital, in 1873. However, nurses received little formal training. Living in crowded, ill-equipped hospital dormitories and receiving meager wages, nurses trained on the job by caring for patients. Teaching did not require formal education and became the primary career for middle- and upper-class white women. By the end of the nineteenth century, half a million women were teachers. Female teachers often worked in one-room schoolhouses at the elementary level and were paid substantially less than male teachers.

See also **Education,** *subentries on* **Colleges and Universities, Graduate and Professional Education, Education of Girls and Women; Gender; Law,** *subentry on* **Women and the Law; Legal Profession; Medicine; Professions; Women,** *subentry on* **Women's Rights.**

Bibliography

Drachman, Virginia G. *Women Lawyers and the Origins of Professional Identity in America: The Letters of the Equity Club, 1887 to 1890*. Ann Arbor: University of Michigan Press, 1993.

Falk, Gerhard. *Sex, Gender, and Social Change: The Great Revolution*. Lanham, Md.: University Press of America, 1998.

Glazer, Penina Migdal, and Miriam Slater. *Unequal Colleagues: The Entrance of Women into the Professions, 1890–1940*. New Brunswick, N.J.: Rutgers University Press, 1987.

Harris, Anita M. *Broken Patterns: Professional Women and the Quest for a New Feminine Identity*. Detroit: Wayne State University Press, 1995.

Harris, Barbara J. *Beyond Her Sphere: Women and the Professions in American History*. Westport, Conn.: Greenwood, 1978.

LAURA FOSTER

WOMAN AS IMAGE AND ICON

Nineteenth-century illustrations interpreted white women in a complex visual language of race and class. The century commenced with the Enlightenment challenge to define the meanings of citizenship. Mary Wollstonecraft Godwin's *A Vindication of the Rights of Woman* (1792) articulated women's political aspirations and stimulated debate over the symbolic terms for women's civic and legal rights throughout the nineteenth century. Opponents to women's public lives warned that women who left the home would become "unsexed" or masculine women. Popular media depicted the century's most controversial female political activists, including Fanny Wright in the 1830s and Victoria Woodhull in the 1870s, as at once unsexed and sexually dangerous. Within a visual culture of patriarchy, largely produced by male artists, women struggled to appropriate the political potential of the symbolic order.

The dominant gender ideology among middle-class and upper-class whites of the first half of the nineteenth century was the "cult of true womanhood," whose archetypal female was the mother. The symbolic language of Christian religious tradition pitted negative icons of womanhood, such as Eve the temptress or Mary Magdalen the harlot, against the purity of the Madonna, a figure adapted by American Protestantism into the ideal of "helpmeet," a frail, private, and virtuous woman, guardian of domesticity. The religious revivals of the Second Great Awakening (c. 1800–1830) led religious leaders to view women as inherently devout and thus possessing greater moral authority than men. Quaker women like Sarah Grimké and Angelina Grimké, for example, used such religious justifications in publishing their criticism of the oppression of slaves and the oppression of women. Evangelical Christianity, though steeped in the language of domesticity, thus allowed many women to challenge their relegation to the private sphere in defense of the family.

The white, bourgeois ideal of Christian domesticity stood in direct contrast to the alternative iconography of class and racial difference. Workingwomen, by virtue of economic necessity, were financially excluded from the domestic ideal. Popular images of such women, from laundresses to shop girls, rendered them as morally suspect and sexually dangerous. "Public women" or prostitutes were easy targets for such stereotyping, but most depictions of workingwomen through the century blurred distinctions between the selling of goods and the selling of sexual favors. The growth of theater opened a controversial public forum for women as performers. For example, the "Swedish Nightingale" Jenny Lind, skillfully

A Modern Odalisque. Photograph by E. Donald Roberts Jr., Detroit. LIBRARY OF CONGRESS

marketed by the showman P. T. Barnum, found enormous commercial success in the 1850s. After the Civil War, with the rise of burlesque and the concert saloon, women's bodies became a newly sexualized source of entertainment. Such reformers as Charles Loring Brace decried such developments. In *The Dangerous Classes of New York, and Twenty Years' Work among Them* (1872) he represented the public sphere as a slippery slope for women in which any kind of public work led inevitably to disrepute.

Race likewise offered a symbolic counterpoint to the "true woman." Representations of women in slavery, for example, oscillated between two primary stereotypes, the "temptress," whose sexual depravity justified her sexual abuse during and after slavery, and the "Mammy," a nonthreatening nurturer of white supremacy. To highlight the abuses of slavery, abolitionists, including Lydia Maria Child in *An Appeal in Favor of That Class of Americans Called Africans* (1833), represented an alternative image of the slave woman as the victim of slaveholders' sexual predation. Women's slave narratives, including Harriet Jacobs's *Incidents in the Life of a Slave Girl*

(1861), represented a more complex sexual landscape for slave women, in which resistance to owners had grave consequences and no clear distinctions existed between consent and abuse.

Representations of other women of color in popular culture were equally negative. As white Americans drove American Indians westward, depictions of Native American women were limited to either the highly sexualized image of the pagan "squaw" or the symbol of Pocahontas, the Indian princess who protected her European friend John Smith from death at the hands of her people. As the American empire expanded southward, sexualized or bestialized images of Mexicana and Mexican American women became a staple nineteenth-century representation. Similarly the equation of Chinese women with prostitution in popular media facilitated the passage of the Page Law (1875), which restricted their immigration on moral grounds.

The Civil War was an important point of transition in visual culture that elevated race distinctions over class and ethnic difference. Access to ready-made clothing by the end of the century made visible

Ophelia. Post–Civil War participation of women in saloon and stage entertainments coincided with an increase of sexualized images. LIBRARY OF CONGRESS

markers of class difference less salient in popular image. Physiognomic distinctions of German and Irish women, for example, gradually faded into a more generic European-type in illustrated media, though the "new immigrants" from southern and eastern Europe remained symbolically distinct through the early decades of the 1900s. By the end of the nineteenth century popular depictions of African Americans became increasingly racist, drawing upon scientific theories of immutable biological differences. As the ideal of white womanhood became more democratic in class terms, African American women and men paid the price. As Ida B. Wells noted in *The Red Record* (1895), the epidemic of lynching of African American men for alleged rapes of white women after the Civil War denied both the abuses of slavery and the complicity of whites in interracial sexual relations.

By the time the Statue of Liberty was placed in New York Harbor in 1886, the image of the woman on the statue no longer represented the sexually dangerous revolutionary at the barricades of the French Revolution. Both as "Miss Liberty" and as the "Mother of Exiles," the statue embodied a tamed republicanism and universal maternalism. With the birth of modernism at the fin de siècle and with the growing sophistication of reproductions, images of womanhood coalesced into increasingly rigid categories. Advertising capitalized on sexualized renderings of women's bodies to sell products. The "Gibson Girl," the "new woman" in a shirtwaist with an hourglass figure, finally entered the public sphere. The trade-off was the extreme degree of sexualization she encountered there. Such advertising trademarks as "Pocahontas" and "Aunt Jemima" paved the way for unflattering twentieth-century racial representations in photographs and the cinema. These stereotypes posed new challenges to twentieth-century women seeking alternative expressions of womanhood.

See also **African Americans; American Indians; Clothing; Domestic Life; Gender,** *subentry on* **Interpretations of Gender; Immigration and Immigrants; Literature,** *subentry on* **Women's Literature; Magazines, Women's; Marriage; Prostitution; Republican Motherhood; Women,** *subentries on* **Women's Rights; Women's Labor.**

Bibliography

Buckley, Peter G. "The Culture of 'Leg-work': The Transformation of Burlesque after the Civil War." In *The Myth-making Frame of Mind: Social Imagination and American Culture.* Edited by James Gilbert et al. Belmont, Calif.: Wadsworth, 1993.

Chan, Sucheng. "The Exclusion of Chinese Women, 1870–1943." In *Entry Denied: Exclusion and the Chinese Community in America, 1882–1943.* Edited by Sucheng Chan. Philadelphia: Temple University Press, 1991.

Dudden, Faye E. *Women in the American Theatre: Actresses and Audiences, 1790–1870.* New Haven, Conn.: Yale University Press, 1994.

Green, Rayna. "The Pocahontas Perplex: The Image of the Indian Woman in American Culture." *Massachusetts Review* 16 (Autumn 1975): 698–714.

Jacobson, Matthew Frye. *Whiteness of a Different Color: European Immigrants and the Alchemy of Race.* Cambridge, Mass.: Harvard University Press, 1998.

Lecauday, Hélène. "Behind the Mask: Ex-Slave Women and Interracial Sexual Relations." In *Discovering the Women in Slavery: Emancipating Perspectives on the American Past.* Edited by Patricia Morton. Athens: University of Georgia Press, 1996.

Loeb, Lori Anne. *Consuming Angels: Advertising and Victorian Women.* New York: Oxford University Press, 1994.

Morton, Patricia. *Disfigured Images: The Historical Assault on Afro-American Women.* New York: Greenwood, 1991.

Perdue, Theda. *Cherokee Women: Gender and Cultural Change, 1700–1835.* Lincoln: University of Nebraska Press, 1998.

Russett, Cynthia Eagle. *Sexual Science: The Victorian Construction of Womanhood.* Cambridge, Mass.: Harvard University Press, 1989.

Showalter, Elaine. *Sexual Anarchy: Gender and Culture at the Fin de Siècle.* New York: Viking, 1990.

Smith-Rosenberg, Carroll. *Disorderly Conduct: Visions of Gender in Victorian America.* New York: Knopf, 1985.

Srebnick, Amy Gilman. *The Mysterious Death of Mary Rogers: Sex and Culture in Nineteenth-Century New York.* New York: Oxford University Press, 1995.

Stansell, Christine. *City of Women: Sex and Class in New York, 1789–1860.* New York: Knopf, 1986.

Welter, Barbara. "The Feminization of American Religion, 1800–1860." In *Clio's Consciousness Raised: New Perspectives on the History of Women.* Edited by Mary S. Hartman and Lois Banner. New York: Harper and Row, 1974.

AMANDA FRISKEN

WORK

[This entry includes seven subentries:
Agricultural Labor
Domestic Labor
Artisans and Craftsworkers
The Workshop
Factory Labor
Child Labor
Middle-Class Occupations
See also **Slavery** and **Women**, subentry on **Women's Labor**.]

AGRICULTURAL LABOR

The rhythm of the seasons determined the general patterns of agricultural labor, while a diversity of farm tasks characterized specific agricultural work during the nineteenth century. Spring brought plowing and seeding time, cultivating and harvesting came with summer for most crops, while tobacco and cotton matured in the autumn. Threshing, ginning, and pork packing occupied considerable time during the winter months.

The Role of Family

Throughout the nineteenth century, farming was a family and group activity that required at least two people—a man and a woman—to ensure success. All farmers performed many similar tasks, but often both region and gender determined who performed certain work. In general, the male head of a household usually conducted the fieldwork, such as plowing and planting and the harvesting of corn and small grain crops. The farmer's wife had responsibility for raising poultry, churning butter, and tending the vegetable garden, which provided both food and income for the family. In the northern United States the men milked the cows, while the women performed

this task in the South. In another regional variance, northern farmers picked the ears from the corn stalks while southerners commonly shocked their corn for removal of the ears later. In the South, white women worked in the fields, cultivating and harvesting cotton and tobacco. In the North, women seldom worked in the fields but instead conducted a host of jobs, primarily related to food production and preservation, as well as child rearing and homemaking. African American women also worked in the fields, first as slaves before the Civil War, and then as sharecroppers or tenant farmers during the remainder of the nineteenth century. Children also performed a host of chores, determined by age and gender. Couples who had a large number of children could cultivate more land and produce more commodities for sale, thereby increasing their income and often their wealth in terms of land ownership, than families with fewer children.

Although new implements and machines, such as reapers, threshing machines, and steam engines, replaced some human labor, farmwork did not lend itself to assembly-line processes. The seasonal cycles of farmwork mandated the completion of certain jobs sequentially. Many tasks could not be performed simultaneously, and most forms of labor depended on unpaid family labor, particularly from children. With the exception of plantation agriculture based on slave labor, successful farming depended on family labor, supplemented by hired labor or shared labor among neighbors, the latter particularly evident at threshing time and barn raisings.

The success of a family farm also depended more on labor than on capital. In the Midwest and Great Plains, for example, men and women with little money could rent a farm. In time, many of these tenants accumulated capital to buy their own farms. They emphasized cash crops while meeting most of their own food needs. Since they did not pay a wage to themselves or their children, their labor costs only involved expenses for part-time workers, especially at harvest and threshing time.

Hired Workers

Land clearing remained the most difficult and expensive agricultural labor during the nineteenth century. Farmers often hired male workers to help cut down trees and remove stumps. During the early nineteenth century, farmers could expect to pay from five to twenty dollars per acre for clear-cutting trees, the cost determined by the number of trees per acre. Then the stumps had to be removed, usually by using a team of horses or oxen along with ax and fire. Farmers conducted this work as well as the cutting of fire-

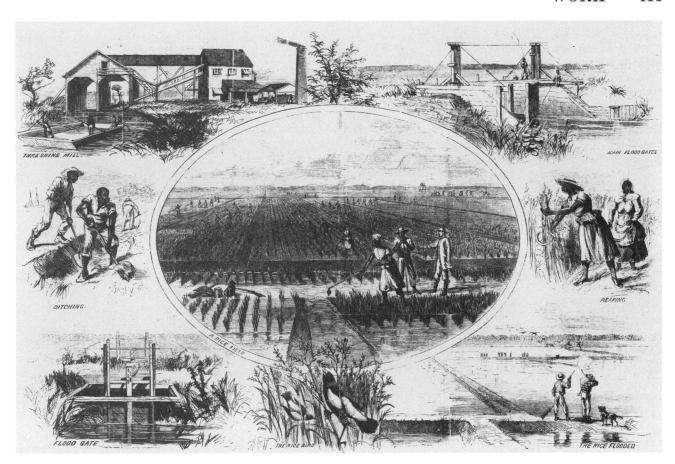

"Rice Culture on the Ogeechee, near Savannah, Georgia." Wood engraving by A. R. Ward. *Harper's Weekly*, 5 January 1867. LIBRARY OF CONGRESS

wood and the building of rail fences during the winter. In the region of the prairies and plains, farmers often hired workers with a special plow to break, or turn over, the heavy sod. These prairie-breaking teams plowed approximately three acres per day at a cost of approximately three dollars per acre.

Although the agricultural workday often stretched from sunup to sundown, in the North and Midwest the pace was often slow and irregular except during harvest, threshing, and haying time. Twelve-hour days were customary for agricultural workers in the North, but the ten-hour day had gained popularity by 1840, particularly for hired workers. Periodic rests, noontime meals, trips to town, visits from salesmen, and a host of tasks, however, provided relief and variety during the workday. Most agricultural workers were hired on a seasonal rather than annual basis to complete specific jobs, such as harvesting or threshing. Usually, their period of employment ran from six to eight months or from March through October. Men retained after the harvest season found that their wages usually decreased until

longer days and more pressing work began again in the spring. A six-day workweek was the norm, with Sunday a free day for hired laborers. Workers hired by the day were more expensive than those hired by the month, season, or year. Shortages of labor, often caused by westward migration, frequently drove wages above the average for specific areas. American-born farmhands, however, usually earned higher wages than immigrant workers. Many farmworkers labored with the intent of saving enough money to buy a farm. Few acquired sufficient capital to do so, and most became tenant farmers before they could save enough money to buy their own farms.

In California during the late nineteenth century, the large-scale farmers called growers, who raised fruits and vegetables, needed many workers to plant, cultivate, and harvest their crops. During the 1850s, these farmers began employing Chinese immigrant workers because they were hardworking, reliable, and docile as well as knowledgeable about agricultural tasks. With the boom in demand for produce that followed the completion of the first transcontinental

"The Last Load." Harvest photograph by Paul W. England of Massachusetts. LIBRARY OF CONGRESS

railroad in 1869, many Chinese workers sought employment in the rapidly expanding vegetable fields, orchards, and vineyards. During the 1870s, California growers also preferred to hire Chinese workers because they were readily available and their numbers helped keep wages low. By 1882, Chinese workers comprised approximately 50 percent of the farm labor force and as much as 75 percent of the workforce that handled specialty crops in California.

Western growers, who had a need for hired agricultural labor, did not employ Mexicans in great numbers until the twentieth century. In the absence of cheap, docile, Chinese labor, they preferred to recruit white, European immigrants and native-born whites from the eastern United States, whom they believed would not create social and racial problems. A cheap and reliable labor force drawn from the eastern white population never materialized, and after the turn of the twentieth century, western growers increasingly relied on Mexican workers to meet their agricultural labor needs.

Slave Labor

In contrast to independent farmers and hired workers, African American agricultural workers labored under sweatshop conditions in the South prior to the Civil War. African American slaves, who worked in the cotton fields, often labored in large groups called gangs. They had only marginal control over their labor, usually in the form of work slowdowns or illnesses that gave some relief from the fast pace set by their supervisors, called drivers. In the rice-producing areas along the coast of South Carolina and Georgia, as well as in the tobacco and hemp regions of the Upper South, slaves often conducted their work by task, that is, they were given a specific assignment to complete during the day, after which they were free to tend their own personal or family affairs on the farm or plantation.

The Beginning of Change

By the end of the nineteenth century, family workers provided most of the labor on farms. California proved the exception because highly perishable crops and the necessity to ship them to market quickly necessitated the employment of a large number of seasonal workers. Technological change, however, had increasingly reduced the hours needed to complete certain tasks, such as plowing, harvesting, and threshing. New forms of agricultural technology also diminished the need for hired workers and compensated for shortages in the workforce as better jobs lured farm laborers to the towns and cities. This trend rapidly accelerated change in agricultural labor during the twentieth century.

See also **Agriculture; California; Homesteading; Women,** *subentry on* **Women's Labor.**

Bibliography

Daniel, Cletus E. *Bitter Harvest: A History of California Farmworkers, 1870–1941.* Ithaca, N.Y.: Cornell University Press, 1981.

Hahamovitch, Cindy. *The Fruits of Their Labor: Atlantic Coast Farmworkers and the Making of Migrant Poverty, 1870–1945.* Chapel Hill: University of North Carolina Press, 1997.

Kolchin, Peter. *American Slavery, 1619–1877.* New York: Hill and Wang, 1993.

Nelson, Daniel. *Farm and Factory: Workers in the Midwest, 1880–1990.* Bloomington: Indiana University Press, 1995.

Schob, David E. *Hired Hands and Plowboys: Farm Labor in the Midwest, 1815–1860.* Urbana, Ill.: University of Illinois Press, 1975.

R. DOUGLAS HURT

DOMESTIC LABOR

Domestic work in nineteenth-century America generally was performed by women: wives and mothers of the household, paid employees, or black slaves. In the early part of the century, similar chores needed to be completed in households at all class levels. Only toward the end of the 1800s would piped water, gas, electricity, and labor-saving appliances become commonplace in upper- and middle-class households. Whether in the city or the country, domestic laborers had to draw water from the pump, make meals, clean the dishes and laundry, and preserve food. The difference between wealthy and more modest households was not the type of work performed, but the number of servants or slaves available to perform it. In households of limited means, one servant would complete all of the cooking and cleaning; in wealthier households, several workers would divide up these tasks.

The North

In the early nineteenth century, "hired help" was the most common form of domestic labor in the urban and rural areas of the North. Women hired "girls" for specific duties, such as the production of dairy items that could be sold at the market. Mistresses worked alongside their help in order to get household chores done.

Domestic labor patterns changed in the 1820s and 1830s, as the industrial revolution took hold in the United States. Women who traditionally would have entered domestic service now were being employed by textile mills. American-born, young, white women were the most likely to be hired by factories, such as those in Lowell, Massachusetts. Mill work paid better than domestic positions, and employees did not have to live with their employers. The teaching profession also began to attract women workers. Increasingly, domestic service became the domain of immigrants. In particular, the Irish became the most popular choice for domestic servants in urban areas, overshadowing the employment of free blacks and of immigrants whose first language was not English, such as Scandinavians and Germans. Immigrant groups such as the Germans found domestic work mainly in homes that spoke their native language. However, as new job opportunities opened up for women toward the end of the century, upper- and middle-class women had difficulty hiring help from any ethnic group, even with the continuing influx of new immigrants.

Domestic labor needs and trends continued to change in the 1840s and 1850s. In rural areas, the old patterns of domestic service prevailed, with employ-

"Before the Conquest." Black women increasingly entered domestic service in the late nineteenth century. Photograph by S. L. Stein, 1897. LIBRARY OF CONGRESS

Women Ironing. Lithograph advertisement, c. 1885. LIBRARY OF CONGRESS: PRINTS AND PHOTOGRAPHS DIVISION

ers and employees working together on market-oriented tasks, without the aid of modern utilities. But in the growing cities, bourgeois women became less and less involved in their household's domestic labor. The mass production of goods meant these women could buy many of the items previously produced in the home, such as dairy goods and textiles. Servants now could be employed to focus on daily chores, including nursing duties. In middle-class households, maids took over these tasks; in wealthy households, work continued to be divided among many servants. Middle-class households, in particular, desired maids who were self-sacrificing and eager to fulfill all of the mistress's expectations.

This period, and the decades following the Civil War, also saw the professionalization of domestic service. Women like Catharine Beecher (1800–1878) helped standardize household practices while reinforcing the family values of the "cult of domesticity." At the same time, reformers were supporting the "Americanization" of immigrants. These cultural trends met in the home, where mistresses tried to instill middle-class values, such as temperance, among their lower-class servants. Many maids complained that their mistresses were too involved in their private lives, restricting access to their beaux and scrutinizing how the servants spent their earnings. Certainly domestic help often spent money on "frivolous" items, like clothes and nights on the town,

rather than saving funds in a bank. But spending money as they wished helped servants assert their freedom as well as show they did not necessarily accept such middle-class values as thrift and deferred gratification.

The South

In the antebellum South, most domestic work for upper- and middle-class families was performed by slaves. On big plantations, house slaves were considered higher on the slave hierarchy than field slaves. They usually had better clothes and food, along with more chances to ingratiate themselves with the master or mistress. However, the master's proximity could be an enormous restriction on what little freedom slaves could find on a plantation. Large plantations had a wide variety of domestic slaves: cooks, maids, nurses, waiting maids, coachmen, and butlers. Both women and men were house slaves, though their jobs were segregated, with women doing more of the domestic work of cleaning, cooking, and sewing. There were exceptions, such as the highly trained male chefs owned by Thomas Jefferson (1743–1826); also, some male slaves ended up as tailors within the plantation economy. In general, though, the gender segregation of slave duties allowed female slaves to create a reputation as skilled laborers. Word of a fine slave cook or seamstress often spread beyond the plantation.

The average slave owner was not part of this southern aristocracy of elite planters. Slaves involved in domestic service outside a large plantation had to perform a greater number of household chores, and often there was only one slave in the household to do the cooking and cleaning. After the Civil War, African American women found that working in domestic service was one of their only options for earning wages, since most jobs were reserved for white employees. African American women preferred postwar situations where they did not have to live in the house, since that reminded them too much of slavery. From 1890 to 1920 the number of white women domestic workers declined by 33 percent, while black women's participation rose by 43 percent.

The West

Through the post–Civil War period, frontier households usually were much poorer than their eastern counterparts. There were fewer domestic servants in frontier homes, though hired girls still were found in these areas. Homesteading families often lived a subsistence existence. Wives or daughters did all the chores, and their work clearly was much harder than in the cities, especially after utilities were introduced in urban areas. Mining towns, with their relative wealth, were some of the only white settlements where women could earn wages as domestic servants.

In the Mexican territories that eventually would be ceded to the United States, such as California, a different domestic hierarchy prevailed. There, Mexicans of Spanish descent owned the large plantations. Domestic servants came from the Indian Mexican population. After the Mexican-American War (1846–1848), white squatters began seizing much of the Mexican-owned land. This illegal takeover changed the makeup of domestic labor in the area. Afterward, Mexicans of all races worked as domestics in white households, a trend that held steady through the turn of the century, especially as more Mexicans moved to the regions once owned by Mexico.

Domestic labor proved to be one of the few ways women could earn wages in the nineteenth century. Along with factory work, teaching, and taking in boarders, domestic work was supported by a gender-segregated workforce. The shifting patterns of domestic service reflected the larger U.S. cultural and political trends. By the beginning of the twentieth century, domestics mostly were women from racially or ethnically marginalized groups.

See also **Domestic Life; Food; Homesteading; Housing; Immigration and Immigrants,** *subentry on* **The Immigrant Experience; Plantation, The; Slavery,** *subentry on* **Slave Life; Women;** *subentry on* **Women's Labor.**

Bibliography

Aptheker, Bettina. *Woman's Legacy: Essays on Race, Sex, and Class in American History.* Amherst: University of Massachusetts Press, 1982.

Armitage, Susan, and Elizabeth Jameson, eds. *The Women's West.* Norman: University of Oklahoma Press, 1987.

Dudden, Faye E. *Serving Women: Household Service in Nineteenth-Century America.* Middletown, Conn.: Wesleyan University Press, 1983.

Fox-Genovese, Elizabeth. *Within the Plantation Household: Black and White Women of the Old South.* Chapel Hill: University of North Carolina Press, 1988.

Hine, Darlene Clark, ed. *Black Women in United States History: From Colonial Times through the Nineteenth Century.* 4 vols. Brooklyn, N.Y.: Carlson, 1990.

Katzman, David M. *Seven Days a Week: Women and Domestic Service in Industrializing America.* Urbana: University of Illinois Press, 1981.

Matthaei, Julie A. *An Economic History of Women in America: Women's Work, the Sexual Division of Labor, and the Development of Capitalism.* New York: Schocken Books, 1982.

Stansell, Christine. *City of Women: Sex and Class in New York, 1789–1860.* Urbana: University of Illinois Press, 1987.

JUSTINE S. MURISON

ARTISANS AND CRAFTSWORKERS

Artisans and craftsworkers were known for the thoughtful, artistic, and skilled work that they did by hand and with the use of tools. Although artisans have often been described as having one profession or trade, such as making sails or carts, many craftsworkers had multiple occupations, sometimes simultaneously, over the course of their lives. For example, an artisan might be a wage worker at a textile factory during good economic times and work at home as an independent weaver or furniture maker, as a seller of used clothing, or as a seller of backyard-raised poultry. In the first part of the nineteenth century craftsworkers were affected by the decline of small shops that specialized in custom-made goods for particular customers. Artisans increasingly found themselves working for large factories that made standardized, mass-produced goods for producers and consumers. Even as larger economies of scale and urban centralization became established, many workers with handicraft skills continued to juggle both formal and informal jobs.

Throughout the United States artisans and craftsworkers were associated with different types of profit-oriented production, including the small artisan shop. Owner-run crafts operations employed indentured servants, apprentices, and in the South slaves, who were paid with room, board, training, and sometimes wages. Even though many people primarily associate artisans with these small shops, craftsworkers also worked for other businesses and for themselves in their homes.

In both rural and urban areas, shop- and home-based craftswork continued to sustain the economy and to be an integral part of U.S. production. Rural landholders had craftswork done by wage laborers, enslaved laborers (before emancipation), and tenants and sharecroppers (especially in the southern states after the Civil War). This craftswork included blacksmithing, the making of some farm equipment and tools, maintaining wagons, and the preparation of agricultural products, such as wool, tobacco, sugar, meat, and animal hides, for the market. Craftswork took place in putting-out operations, where employers organized weaving production in laborers' homes. Owners of manufactories increased their profits and stimulated massive protests by workers when they placed large numbers of craftsworkers such as shoemakers in wage labor factories, where the work process was divided into small components. Craftsworkers from urban and rural areas often became displaced from their trades, working at steam-powered, mechanized industrial production sites.

Craftswork also took place in laborers' homes and in working-class streets and neighborhoods, outside of the domain of profit-related work. Households created goods, services, and consumable items to make ends meet, and this included making and sometimes selling craft items. Handcrafted items like vending apparatus and baskets were made to help households sell goods at urban neighborhood markets, at local and regional markets, and at fairs in rural areas. In the West workingpeople organized independent gold-mining operations that required craft skills. This type of self-organized work was an essential activity because most workers' wages and the combined wages of household members typically did not cover the full cost of household needs. Instead of completely undermining skilled work done by hand, industrial production was exploitative and sporadic and thereby encouraged low- to moderate-income families to keep doing craftswork and to maintain local markets to trade with others in similar circumstances.

Social definitions of ethnic and gender identity shaped the contexts in which craftswork was conducted. In large cities racism and residential segregation often meant that African Americans carried out many trades, including carpentry, herbal healing, and midwifery, within African American communities. Although women's craftswork and trades typically are described as housework, women often were skilled artisans in the trades of sewing, quilting, breadmaking, canning, cultivation, animal husbandry, and preparation of wild animal meat.

The process of separating laboring people from the tools, land, resources, skills, and knowledge needed to conduct artisan work proceeded slowly. Contrary to common perceptions that the appearance of large-scale industrial production, the so-called Industrial Revolution, brought the quick end of artisans, these workers continued to engage in their trades, especially in rural settings and at home. Artisan work was an integral but subordinate part of many formal industrial settings. Craftswork flourished in neighborhoods and communities where income and bartered goods enabled families to sustain themselves economically and culturally.

Low-income and rural households continued to do craftswork with noncommercial goods and resources until the end of the nineteenth century and even into the twentieth. The decline of home-based craftswork was associated with several processes, including the gradual disappearance of open land and forests in rural areas; urbanization and the development of vacant city lots; the enhancement of transportation systems and roads; the commercialization of various resources needed for living, such as water and fuel; the creation of new state health and work regulations; and the eventual commercialization of the clothing and food industries. All these changes meant that laboring families crafted fewer goods; engaged in more service provision, such as washing and ironing clothes; vended fewer homemade goods and more commercially made items; and depended more on store-bought and recycled items. Whereas early-nineteenth-century rural women frequently designed and sewed their own clothes, perhaps with hand-woven cloth, late-century urban women often secured recycled factory-made clothes and altered them.

Late in the century more consumer and producer goods came from factories, reducing the control that craftsworkers had over their work and the materials that went into them. By the end of the century basket makers rarely stripped willows when they made their wares, and turtle meat vendors rarely caught and processed their own turtles. Craftswork was shaped by the wage labor and consumer goods markets, and craftsworkers purchased factory-made handicraft materials with which to do artisan work. Money had become the center of home-based transactions, and artisan work was subjected to the rules of the global marketplace.

See also **Cities and Urbanization; Country Fairs; Industrialization and the Market; Labor Force; Women,** *subentry on* **Women's Labor; Work,** *subentries on* **Domestic Labor, Factory Labor.**

Bibliography

Dickinson, Torry D. *Common Wealth: Self-Sufficiency and Work in American Communities, 1830 to 1993.* Lanham, Md.: University Press of America, 1995.

Du Bois, W. E. B. *The Philadelphia Negro: A Social Study.* New York: Benjamin Bloom, 1967. First published in 1899.

Jones, Jacqueline. *The Dispossessed: America's Underclasses from the Civil War to the Present.* New York: Basic Books, 1992.

Laurie, Bruce. *Artisans into Workers: Labor in Nineteenth-Century America.* New York: Hill and Wang, 1989.

Tryon, Rolla Milton. *Household Manufactures in the United States, 1640–1860.* New York: A. M. Kelley, 1966.

Ward, David. *Cities and Immigrants: A Geography of Change in Nineteenth Century America.* New York: Oxford University Press, 1971.

Wilentz, Sean. *Chants Democratic: New York City and the Rise of the American Working Class, 1788–1850.* New York: Oxford University Press, 1984.

TORRY D. DICKINSON

THE WORKSHOP

While the scope and scale of production and the flow of the workday changed as the nineteenth century progressed, the production of consumer goods, from shoes and housewares to luxury coaches, remained located in artisan workshops. These workshops varied by size, region, and especially by type of craft, but overall they functioned as a small arena where workers produced entire commodities by hand. Rather than being quickly replaced by factories as the nation's economy developed, workshops consistently adapted to fill the areas of production that factories did not handle. Over the century, the integration of national markets and more cost-effective forms of transportation forced workshop owners to divide craft skills during production, add extra hands, and mechanize craft work. Often, however, these moves resulted in labor conflict. Workshops were predominantly the domain of white male workers, and attempts, whether by bosses, women, or minority male workers, to alter established work patterns were met with resistance. As the site where artisans spent much of their time and labor, the nineteenth-century workshop was not only a place of work, but also one of the central locations where unions formed and fought for the rights of workers.

In the early years of the century, in seaport cities like Boston, New York, Philadelphia, and Baltimore, artisans could account for over 50 percent of the adult male population, and most found employment in the cities' hundreds of workshops. These shops were usually located on the ground level of two- or three-floor buildings where master craftsmen's families lived. A master craftsman and his family presided over a handful of journeymen, and perhaps an apprentice or two, all working in close quarters with nothing but crude benches, hand tools, and their acquired skills. When journeymen acquired enough tools and a small amount of capital they often tried to set up their own workshop. The pace and quantity of production varied by craft, but generally shops had no great access to distant markets, so local and regional consumers set the agenda for work. Artisans in larger population centers like New York had more work, and subsequently more competition, whereas workers in smaller cities on the western frontier like Cincinnati were more in demand and could command higher wages. Operating within a premarket sensibility, many of these early nineteenth-century workshops barely functioned on Mondays, and they were often paced both by alcohol consumption and by preferences for quality over quantity. Although these small workshops dominated production in early nineteenth-century cities, they were often financially unstable and operated close to the margin with a minimum of capital investment. Many of them closed quickly after a fire, an illness, or a death, or the inability to repay a small debt.

Except for the interruptions of the panics of 1819, 1837, and 1857, the nation experienced great economic growth before the Civil War, largely spurred on by transportation advancements. The Erie Canal, completed in 1825, and early railroads connected western and southern markets to northern cities, thus making possible dramatic increases in workshop productivity and size. With the ability to sell to a larger number of consumers, market sensibilities took hold of workshop owners, who became more like businessmen and less like craftsmen. Increasing competition with factory production and an undercutting subcontracting market forced workshop owners to expand and adapt quickly, or risk losing their shops and becoming dependent workers themselves. Whereas one master had worked closely with a few journeymen in the early nineteenth-century workshop, by the middle of the century in larger seaport cities it was common to have twenty or thirty workers and even a foreman.

The rapid growth in the number of employees in a workshop often occurred within a decade or two, and quickly dashed the hopes of most journeymen of ever setting up their own workshop. One reason for this was that most of this growth was accomplished not by greatly increasing capital investment, but by cutting labor costs, subdividing skills, and decreasing workshop size. Unlike the workshops of earlier times, which were integrated into the master craftsmen's homes and neighborhoods, these shops were set up in lower-rent manufacturing districts or wherever inexpensive space could be found. Cellars and garrets were often utilized as workspaces. In these increasingly cramped spaces or "sweatshops," entire products might still be produced, but often by a number of people, each doing only one aspect of the job. In the push to increase production, keep costs low, and maintain workshop survival, craft skills that had been passed from master to journeyman and apprentice for centuries were divided and lost.

Faced with increased workers' hours, diminished skill levels, lower pay, and more dangerous and unhealthy conditions, labor unions battled with owners for reforms. Whereas earlier in the century journeymen viewed master craftsmen as fellow artisans whom they one day hoped to emulate, the changes in the economics of the workshop separated the two groups. At first journeymen tried numerous methods to protect their skills and economic independence, such as opening their own workshops or establishing local journeymen's mutual benefit societies. However, under the increasing economic weight of larger manufacturers, wholesalers, and workshop owner associations, workers were forced to form larger, even national, unions. During the nineteenth century many of the members of the largest and most powerful national unions—the National Trades Union, the National Labor Union, and the American Federation of Labor—were drawn from unified groups of workshop-based craftsmen.

The relationship between workers and workshop owners was often contentious, and the relationships among the workers themselves could be strained as well. The same dynamics that produced racism, nativism, and prejudice in the larger society could seep into the operation of a small workshop. In a city like Richmond, Virginia, before the Civil War, for example, white artisans were often in competition for workshop employment with free blacks or slaves who had been hired out as day labor. On a number of occasions, white workers protested these developments and threatened to boycott or strike against workshops that hired blacks. This scenario was repeated throughout the nineteenth century around the country, against a variety of ethnic groups: Chinese workers in San Francisco, Irish workers in Boston, Italian and Jewish workers in New York and Philadelphia. Throughout the nation, female workers were subject to harsh treatment when they sought jobs, and usually they were segregated into specific types of workshops, such as textiles sweatshops, that were deemed suitable for women. These divisions not only hurt the work prospects and economic success of female and ethnic minority workers, but also weakened the labor unions that attempted to reform workshop conditions for all workers.

By the end of the nineteenth century, factories run by large corporations with large capital investments had taken over much of the manufacturing that had once been accomplished in smaller workshops. The production of goods such as handmade cigars or luxury furniture that still survived within cramped garrets was limited, and even most textile sweatshops had become mechanized with sewing machines. In cities where the majority of the labor force at the dawn of the century was composed of artisans, the proportion of artisans in the labor force was greatly reduced by the end of the century, and most workshop laborers were unskilled immigrants. However, the triumph of the factory was never complete, and there were always workshops filling the gaps between larger centers of production.

See also **Industrialization and the Market; Industry (The Work Ethic); Labor Force; Labor Movement; Women,** subentry on **Women's Labor; Work,** subentry on **Factory Labor.**

Bibliography

Laurie, Bruce. *Artisans into Workers: Labor in Nineteenth Century America.* New York: Hill and Wang, 1989.
Gilje, Paul A., and Howard B. Rock, eds. *Keepers of the Revolution: New Yorkers at Work in the Early Republic.* Ithaca, N.Y.: Cornell University Press, 1992.
Rodgers, Daniel T. *The Work Ethic in Industrial America, 1850–1920.* Chicago: University of Chicago Press, 1978.
Ross, Steven. *Workers on the Edge: Work, Leisure, and Politics in Industrializing Cincinnati, 1788–1890.* New York: Columbia University Press, 1985.
Stott, Richard B. *Workers in the Metropolis: Class, Ethnicity, and Youth in Antebellum New York City.* Ithaca, N.Y.: Cornell University Press, 1990.
Wilentz, Sean. *Chants Democratic: New York City and the Rise of the American Working Class, 1788–1850.* New York: Oxford University Press, 1984.

JOSHUA R. GREENBERG

FACTORY LABOR

To "manufacture" literally means to make things by hand, a definition at odds with modern notions of factories and industrial production. Yet at the beginning of the nineteenth century, manufacturing did consist of handicrafts made primarily at home and occasionally in small "manufactories." Although early Americans worked mostly in agriculture, a significant number also produced nonagricultural goods. In fact, Alexander Hamilton championed manufacturing efforts as a complement to agriculture, particularly for women and children.

Scope of U.S. Manufacturing and Working Conditions for Laborers

Only 75,000 Americans worked in industry in 1810. Fledgling factory owners found competing for workers hard, particularly when day wages were high during harvest. The leading industries at that time produced textiles, hides and skins, liquor, iron, machines, wood products, cable, and cordage. Many of these early manufactories consisted of rented workshops where workers could come and go freely. Factory work, like agriculture, was often seasonal. For example, antebellum midwestern meat packers worked only in the fall and winter.

Firms grew larger and more complicated after 1820, with greater division of labor and an increased proportion of women and children on the payroll. Although President Martin Van Buren set a ten-hour workday for federal employees in 1840, the typical industrial worker at that time worked about 11.5 hours a day, often six days a week. By 1860 the workday had shortened to 10.5 or 11 hours. More than 1.3 million people worked in manufacturing on the eve of the Civil War, many of them employed around New York, Boston, and Philadelphia. Still, antebellum factories tended to be widely dispersed, simple, small, and rural. Some large plants did exist, particularly in flour milling and textiles. These began to incorporate as joint stock companies with publicly traded stock, although shares sold at a high unit price and attracted only a few shareholders.

The advent of larger firms and greater fixed investment meant the implementation of fixed hours of work, increased factory discipline, and work coordination efforts. Factory gates, mandatory attendance, and restrictions on worker interactions were commonplace among large firms. In some places, particularly in the garment districts of New York, Philadelphia, and Boston, sweatshops with horrible conditions emerged. For a time after the Civil War, small, relatively unstructured firms continued to operate as local monopolies. After transportation costs began to fall in the 1870s, however, consolidation became quite profitable and large firms were the order of the day.

Between 1860 and 1920 the proportion of the U.S. labor force working in industry went from 14 to 27 percent. In 1880 the Midwest had become a large manufacturing center, and Chicago surpassed Boston in importance. Agriculture was the chief source of national wealth through the 1880s, but in 1890 the value of U.S. manufactured goods was three times the value of U.S. agricultural products. By the century's end, mass production and distribution had created the modern business enterprise, complete with middle management. Many workers won a ten-hour workday in the 1880s through legislation passed ostensibly to protect women and children.

A prominent feature of nineteenth-century American industry was its labor-saving technology. Manufacturing tended to be resource-intensive, and multiple technical innovations improved U.S. industry. For example, Americans took an early lead in the ma-chine tool industry. Despite the mythology, truly interchangeable parts did not emerge in most industries until the 1870s with the exception of the weapons industry, which was bankrolled by the federal government.

Wages

Although industrial wages fluctuated through the 1800s, researchers generally agree that real earnings increased over the century. Wild price swings through the period apparently did little to aggravate employment or real activity. Cross-sectional firm data indicate large growth rates in compensation from 1820 until the late 1840s and early 1850s. Wages stagnated or even fell during the 1850s and early 1860s as immigration increased and mechanization spread throughout the nation. Wages then rose fairly continuously in postbellum years. Skilled workers virtually always earned more than the unskilled, and the gap widened as industrialization progressed. The skill premium ranged from 40 to 60 percent in 1830 to 60 to 80 percent in 1850. Price Fishback and Shawn Kantor have discovered that nineteenth-century workers also earned premiums for occupational hazards and unemployment risks. These premiums disappeared with the onset of workers' and unemployment compensation programs.

Through much of the century, manufacturing wages were quoted by the day although effectively they were paid by the piece. As a result, expected output dominated the size of the daily run. Because daylight hours varied across regions and months, work intensity also varied over place and time. In addition, workers typically were not day laborers but tended to stay with one employer for a relatively long time, encountering periods of unemployment along the way.

The Role of Women and Minorities

Industrialization gave rise to increased labor force participation by women, particularly in textiles. As late as 1890 about 70 percent of female laborers still worked in textiles or apparel. At the beginning of the 1800s New England textile mills quickly took advantage of a growing pool of underemployed farm women. Many enterprises adopted the Waltham system of hiring only young, unmarried women. (A separate system developed in Rhode Island, where factory owners hired entire families.) Under the Waltham system young women typically worked long hours, about 11.5 hours a day, six days a week in 1830, with mandatory Sunday school attendance. Many never saw a paycheck because mill owners often paid wages directly to the women's fathers. The

Leaving a Shoe Factory at Lynn, Massachusetts. Photograph by F. B. Johnson, 1895. LIBRARY OF CONGRESS

composition of the mill-weaving workforce changed over the century. Before 1845 about 95 percent of workers were native-born, but this figure dropped to 60 percent by the 1850s as Irish immigrants swarmed into the United States. About the same time, work intensity increased, and women became responsible for more looms.

One attraction of bringing women into the labor force was the relatively high pay offered in manufacturing. In Massachusetts, women working in agriculture received about 29 percent of the male wage in 1815, whereas women working in manufacturing earned about 30 to 37 percent of male wages. In 1832 and 1850 the wage gap narrowed to 40 to 45 percent and 50 percent respectively in manufacturing. The increase in female labor force participation through the century gave rise to disgruntled male workers, particularly in times of mass industrial unemployment. These sentiments arose during the financial panics of the 1870s and 1890s, although data show little evidence of displacement of male workers by females.

The welcoming of women into northern textile mills was not duplicated for African Americans in the South, where very few blacks worked in textile mills. However, about half the labor force in southern sawmills and planing mills and a majority in tobacco, iron, and steel plants did consist of African Americans. One explanation for this difference is that textile work required much learning by doing. Parents passed on these skills to their children, therefore African Americans had little chance to enter the industry. In addition, they had no incentive to work in textiles for lower wages than whites because they could earn wages in agriculture comparable to those of whites.

The Labor Movement

During the first part of the century, unions were considered criminal conspiracies. The Massachusetts chief justice Lemuel Shaw's watershed opinion in *Commonwealth v. Hunt* (1842) declared that unions were simply organizations. Shaw also opined that unions' requests for closed shops seemed reasonable.

Much of the early labor movement rose among skilled craftsmen, but employer hostility and business slumps in the late 1830s and early 1840s meant that few workers joined unions. At the time of the Civil War fewer than 2 percent of workers were union members. By 1864 about 200,000 workers carried union cards.

The Knights of Labor, the first national union that admitted any worker, formed in 1869. The depression of the 1870s was hard on labor generally and even harder on unions. Nevertheless the Knights of Labor rallied in the 1880s and conducted strikes against Jay Gould's railroads despite difficult economic conditions. Labor unions held a successful strike in 1885, but public sentiment turned against the unions after the May 1886 bombing and rioting in Chicago's Haymarket Square. Also in 1886 Samuel Gompers, a cigarmaker, organized a new national craft union, the American Federation of Labor. At this time over 700,000 workers were union members, representing about 10 percent of industrial wage earners. Despite rising enthusiasm among workers, a general strike called in May 1886 failed, and many skilled workers left the union ranks.

The financial panic of the 1890s brought significant labor troubles. In 1892 a strike by iron and steel workers in Homestead, Pennsylvania, turned bloody. In early 1894 the economic slump toppled nearly six hundred banks. Subsequently, Pullman workers walked out, reinforced by Eugene Debs's sympathetic railway workers. After the financial crisis subsided, strike activity abated, union membership rose, and labor shared in the prosperity that accompanied the turn of the century.

See also **Labor Force; Labor Movement,** *subentry on* **Unions and Strikes; Panics and Depressions; Textiles; Women,** *subentry on* **Women's Labor.**

Bibliography

Atack, Jeremy. "Economies of Scale and Efficiency Gains in the Rise of the Factory in America, 1820–1900." In *Quantity and Quiddity: Essays in U.S. Economic History.* Edited by Peter Kilby. Middletown, Conn.: Wesleyan University Press, 1987.

———. *A New Economic View of American History.* New York: Norton, 1994.

Bateman, Fred, and Thomas Weiss. "Comparative Regional Development in Antebellum Manufacturing." *Journal of Economic History* 35 (1975): 182–208.

Clark, Gregory. "Factory Discipline." *Journal of Economic History* 54 (1994): 128–163.

Fishback, Price V., and Shawn Everett Kantor. "'Square Deal' or Raw Deal? Market Compensation for Workplace Disamenities, 1884–1903." *Journal of Economic History* 52 (1992): 826–848.

Goldin, Claudia. *Understanding the Gender Gap: An Economic History of American Women.* New York: Oxford University Press, 1990.

Goldin, Claudia, and Robert Margo. "Wages, Prices, and Labor Markets before the Civil War." In *Strategic Factors in Nineteenth-Century American Economic Growth.* Edited by Claudia Goldin and Hugh Rockoff. Chicago: University of Chicago Press, 1992.

Goldin, Claudia, and Kenneth L. Sokoloff. "Women, Children, and Industrialization in the Early Republic: Evidence from the Manufacturing Censuses." *Journal of Economic History* 42 (1982): 741–774.

Lazonick, William, and Thomas Brush. "The 'Horndal Effect' in Early U.S. Manufacturing." *Explorations in Economic History* 22 (1985): 53–96.

Long, Clarence D. *Wages and Earnings in the United States, 1860–1890.* Princeton, N.J.: Princeton University Press, 1960.

Margo, Robert A., and Georgia C. Villaflor. "The Growth of Wages in Antebellum America: New Evidence." *Journal of Economic History* 47 (1987): 873–895.

Rosenburg, Nathan. *Technology and American Economic Growth.* New York: Harper and Row, 1972.

Sokoloff, Kenneth, and Georgia Villaflor. "The Market for Manufacturing Workers during Early Industrialization: The American Northeast, 1820 to 1860." In *Strategic Factors in Nineteenth-Century American Economic Growth.* Edited by Claudia Goldin and Hugh Rockoff. Chicago: University of Chicago Press, 1992.

JENNY BOURNE WAHL

CHILD LABOR

Although most labor historians focus on adult male employment, women and children constituted the majority of America's first factory workers. Observing the desperate economic circumstances of many widows and fatherless children after the American Revolution, Alexander Hamilton and other Federalists encouraged economic policy that included wage labor for women and children. John Slater's Rhode Island textile mill, often cited as the nation's first "factory," employed almost one hundred workers, all under twelve years of age. By the 1820s many middle-class farm families sent their adolescent daughters to mill towns like Lowell, Massachusetts, to seek employment in textile mills. But as the nineteenth century progressed a growing number of Americans began to believe that wage labor encouraged exploitation and threatened individual liberty. This shifting perception of wage work is perhaps clearest when examining the history of child labor.

The concept of childhood itself changed during the nineteenth century. In the early Republic most Americans viewed childhood as a short-lived period that, for everyone but the wealthy, ended at about age fourteen. Based on policies rooted in England's 1598 Elizabethan Poor Law, the apprenticeship and indenture of orphans and other poor children as young as eight years old seemed normal. Even after

Coal Breaker Boys, Kingston, Pennsylvania. Dry-plate negative from Detroit Publishing Company Collection. LIBRARY OF CONGRESS: PRINTS AND PHOTOGRAPHS DIVISION. (DETROIT PUBLISHING COMPANY PHOTOGRAPH COLLECTION)

the Civil War thousands of "orphans," not all of whom were actually without parents or relatives, passed through Charles Loring Brace's Children's Aid Society in New York. These youngsters boarded trains to midwestern "foster" families, who often viewed the children simply as farm laborers. Adolescents from middle-class families frequently obtained job skills by working as apprentices or farm laborers in exchange for room and board. Older girls sometimes served as live-in domestics or child care providers. Even those children living with their own parents constituted a significant labor force in rural America. Immigrant children often worked alongside their parents in the nation's expanding factories. In southern states African American children as young as six labored long hours as field hands and domestic "help" under slavery and emancipation. Children imitated and participated in the work world of adults.

After the Civil War some social reformers began to call attention to what they saw as the growing exploitation of children by greedy parents and industrialists. Ignoring the real-life circumstances of many antebellum children, postwar popular opinion held that earlier forms of child labor within the household

and on the farm had resulted in emotional attachments that protected child workers from abuse. Reformers lamented that, as a rising number of workers joined the industrial labor force, a growing army of children also toiled long hours for low wages as migrant agricultural workers, in mines and factories, as pieceworkers in unhealthy city tenements, and on crowded urban streets as vendors and messengers. Popular novels of the period, such as Horatio Alger's *Ragged Dick* (1867), told of the dangers that faced urban working youth. But as Alger's novels suggest, not everyone thought child labor was evil. Some believed that work could be good for children and resisted calls for reform.

The number of working children is difficult to assess. Census data conservatively suggest that in 1870 approximately 740,000 children ages ten through fifteen (13.2 percent of that age cohort) worked for wages in the United States. By 1900 more than 1.75 million (18.2 percent of children in that age range) worked, and in 1910 they numbered 1,990,225 (18.4 percent). This count does not include those under ten who performed piecework at home, were illegally employed, labored in agriculture, or worked as "inde-

but because adult salaries were so low, the meager wages of children helped improve a poor family's circumstances. Other parents willingly sent their children to work because they believed it developed strong character. Some also gave little value to schooling above the elementary grades.

Despite such beliefs, by the late nineteenth century muckraking journalists like John Spargo and other child welfare advocates persuasively argued that young persons who spent their hours working for wages were denied what the advocate Florence Kelley called "a right to childhood." Consequently, these children grew to be unproductive, unhealthy adults with criminal tendencies. States with the highest percentages of child workers were also those with some of the nation's worst infant mortality rates and highest poverty levels. In addition in 1900 these states had the nation's lowest literacy rates for persons aged ten to fourteen: Louisiana, 67.12 percent; South Carolina, 70.44 percent; Alabama, 71.11 percent; Georgia, 77.21 percent; Mississippi, 77.62 percent; and North Carolina, 78.25 percent. Boys were more likely to work for wages than girls, but girls' labor often consisted of overlooked, unpaid domestic and child care duties, which also kept girls from attending school.

Regional labor disputes highlighted the problems of child workers. The popular press generally depicted children who worked for wages as innocent waifs. The 1902 anthracite coal strike in Pennsylvania provided a national forum for examining the circumstances of the era's child workers. Pennsylvania's laws established fourteen as the minimum age of employment, but as in most states, officials and employers ignored such restrictions. Young boys, some as young as ten and eleven, laboring in the coal mines were generally illiterate, malnourished, anemic, and had permanent physical deformities. A few worked deep in the mines, but most toiled aboveground as breakers. They stooped for ten or eleven hours a day, six days a week, picking slate, stone, and other waste materials from mined coal passing on conveyor belts below their feet. Experienced workers nicknamed new recruits "red tops" because the skin on their inexperienced fingers bled until it hardened. Strikers argued that the presence of such young workers lowered the wages of adults, and unions became significant supporters of child labor reform.

Although some states passed child labor laws during the nineteenth century, the number of young workers continued to rise. Reformers failed in several attempts to gain federal legislation restricting child labor during the Progressive Era. Finally the adult employment crisis of the Great Depression in the 1930s prompted passage and enforcement of federal

"Shine, Sir?" An African American bootblack c. 1899, possibly in Savannah, Georgia. LIBRARY OF CONGRESS: PRINTS AND PHOTOGRAPHS DIVISION

pendent merchants." Furthermore some parents and employers lied about the ages of young workers to avoid compulsory school attendance laws passed in some states. Massachusetts and Connecticut passed the nation's first child labor regulations in 1842, limiting the workday to ten hours for children under twelve in Massachusetts and under fourteen in Connecticut. But generally such laws went unenforced. Some parents reluctantly sent their children to work,

child labor laws under the 1938 Fair Labor Standards Act.

See also **Industry (The Work Ethic); Labor Force; Life Cycle,** *subentry on* **Childhood and Adolescence; Muckrakers; Orphans and Orphanages; Reform, Social.**

Bibliography

Felt, Jeremy P. *Hostages of Fortune: Child Labor Reform in New York State.* Syracuse, N.Y.: Syracuse University Press, 1965.

Hiner, N. Ray, and Joseph M. Hawes, eds. *Growing Up in America: Children in Historical Perspective.* Urbana: University of Illinois Press, 1985.

King, Wilma. *Stolen Childhood: Slave Youth in Nineteenth-Century America.* Bloomington: Indiana University Press, 1995.

Lindenmeyer, Kriste. *A Right to Childhood: The U.S. Children's Bureau and Child Welfare, 1912–1946.* Urbana: University of Illinois Press, 1997.

Spargo, John. *The Bitter Cry of the Children.* 1906. Reprint, Chicago: Quadrangle, 1968.

Trattner, Walter I. *Crusade for the Children: A History of the National Child Labor Committee and Child Labor Reform in America.* Chicago: Quadrangle, 1970.

KRISTE LINDENMEYER

MIDDLE-CLASS OCCUPATIONS

In nineteenth-century America the middle class emerged as a distinct social group, particularly in the nation's cities. Middle-class, or nonmanual, workers experienced great changes in the work world. As industrialization expanded markets and spawned bureaucratization in the second half of the century, the three main sectors in the middle-class workforce, professionals, proprietors, and clerical and sales personnel, expanded vastly. New jobs were created and old ones redefined.

Defining Middle-Class Work

The term "middle class," as it pertains to employment, is vague. Middle-class workers generally benefited from more education than their working-class counterparts. They drew salaries rather than hourly wages, and their work emphasized mental skills over manual abilities or physical strength. Many middle-class workers experienced greater independence from supervision than the working class. This was especially true for the owners of small businesses and for professionals, who were often their own bosses. Middle-class work conferred higher social status than manual work, and it was often steadier and more lucrative.

Exceptions complicated the nature of the nineteenth-century middle class. In rural America small farms that produced crops for market were in many ways small businesses, yet farmwork comprised manual labor. For much of the nineteenth century, urban artisans, such as cobblers, coopers, and tailors, simultaneously produced and sold goods; to some degree, they were small-business owners. Thus thousands of artisans and small-scale, market-oriented farmers formed part of the nineteenth-century middle class.

American concepts of middle-class work were unclear at the beginning of the 1800s. Workers who toiled with their hands often worked alongside those who did not. Middle-class workplaces were not separate from areas of manual production. By mid-century industrialization highlighted the distinctions between working-class and middle-class work spaces. Inside fledgling factories, office work areas were separated from manual production. Geographically, middle-class work zones began to emerge in urban areas. Cities developed shopping areas anchored by department stores. Banking centers as well as centralized office-building districts also emerged. Some blurring occurred. Middle-class work often lent itself to intimate connection with residential zones. For example, individual neighborhoods had their own banks and retail stores. By the second half of the century, Americans, particularly in the nation's larger cities, began to develop clearer notions of middle-class work.

Professionals

For much of the first half of the nineteenth century, individuals became professionals, such as teachers, ministers, medical doctors, and lawyers, through self-education or apprenticeship. Someone interested in lawyering apprenticed with an experienced lawyer. As late as the mid–nineteenth century, entrance into the professions, especially the legal and medical realms, was not regulated. No established courses of education dominated medical training.

In the last quarter of the century, with the quest for hierarchical organization and bureaucracy that industrialization engendered, fields like teaching, medicine, law, and journalism developed associations that helped regulate professional standards and ethics. For example, the American Bar Association was founded in 1878. A new wave of college-trained professionals emerged in the second half of the nineteenth century, and apprenticeship waned. Throughout the 1800s the professions remained predominantly the domain of native-born white men. Only teaching offered women significant employment opportunities.

Small Business Owners

During much of the nineteenth century, small business owners such as wholesalers, retailers, artisans, small-scale manufacturers, peddlers, and farmers produced and sold most of the goods in the American market. Small businesses served significant social roles as well. For example, ethnic grocery stores were important places of socialization and interaction for immigrants. Rural peddlers often brought necessities, news, and newfangled goods to rural areas in the early nineteenth century.

Throughout the century, small business owners—proprietors who supervised fifty or fewer employees—experienced great occupational instability. Small business failure rates were high, and changes brought on by industrialization dramatically altered the sector. Early in the century, artisans made up a significant proportion of small business owners. By the 1880s artisans had been largely superseded by retailers who sold manufactured goods. Early in the century, retailers dealt in a large variety of products ranging from hardware to foodstuffs. Because of market expansion in the second half of the century, specialization in lines of goods, such as women's clothing, reigned in urban America.

While native-born whites dominated the proprietary sector in the nineteenth century, small business ownership was more attainable by immigrants than was professional or office work. Immigrants often ran neighborhood bakeries, saloons, butcher shops, and groceries. For immigrants, proprietorship was the only realistic middle-class occupational opportunity. From 1870 to 1900 in Philadelphia, immigrants accounted for one-third of all small business owners. For women, boardinghouse ownership was the most feasible small business option. Typical small business owners worked long hours, and unpaid family members were often the most important laborers in the enterprises. In fact, for many small business owners, home and business were intimately connected, as work areas and living areas often occupied the same structure. Even with unpaid family help, profit margins were slim, and regional or national economic downturns meant extremely difficult times that strained family resources and family stability.

Clerical and Sales Workers

Office and sales work were dominated by native-born white males throughout the 1800s. During the first half of the nineteenth century, male office employees viewed their jobs as apprenticeships—preparation for eventual business ownership. They toiled behind office desks to learn firsthand how to run a business. After the Civil War (1861–1865) industrialization transformed the status of clerical and sales work as well as its composition. Industrial-era businesses needed many new workers to process the mountains of information required for the companies to run profitably. From 1870 to 1900 the clerical and sales sectors expanded tremendously. The growing need for workers to organize information led to the rise of business colleges and commercial high schools, which prepared many thousands for the office world. Most office skills were no longer conferred on the job. Thus in the second half of the century, notions of office apprenticeship were on the wane. Industrialization also mechanized the office, with the introduction of office machines such as typewriters and Dictaphones.

In the last two decades of the nineteenth century, a sizable influx of young, single white women into offices and retail workplaces occurred. By the century's end department store sales staffs were mostly female. Managers saw women as less costly and more tractable than their male counterparts, and women in the paid labor force had been historically linked with machines in light manufacturing. So, as in working-class occupations, women were placed in the most mechanized, routinized, and managerially scrutinized jobs in the office world. For instance, in the late nineteenth century, office management quickly defined the newly created job of typewriting as women's work. Female typists transcribed reams of documents under strict managerial supervision. Male clerks, bookkeepers, secretaries, and sales personnel experienced higher levels of promotion and pay than did women. At the start of their careers male clerical and sales workers may not have earned as much as the best-paid skilled blue-collar workers, but they enjoyed greater possibilities for promotion and increased income.

The vast expansion of the clerical and sales sectors also encouraged an important shift in the overall makeup of the urban middle-class workforce between 1870 and 1900. In 1870 proprietors formed the largest single segment of the middle-class workforce. By the end of the century clerical and sales workers outnumbered proprietors. Overall, the complexion of middle-class employment shifted away from the autonomy and prestige of small business ownership and professional vocation toward the increasingly circumscribed work world of the office and sales floor. This trend continued into the twentieth century.

See also **Class, Social; Education,** *subentry on* **Graduate and Professional Education; Entrepreneurs; Entrepreneurs, Women; Industry (The Work Ethic); Labor Force; Professions; Small Businesses; Women,** *subentries on* **Women's Labor, Women in the Professions.**

Bibliography

Aron, Cindy. *Ladies and Gentlemen of the Civil Service: Middle-Class Workers in Victorian America.* New York: Oxford University Press, 1987.

Bledstein, Burton J. *The Culture of Professionalism: The Middle Class and the Development of Higher Education in America.* New York: Norton, 1976.

Blumin, Stuart M. *The Emergence of the Middle Class: Social Experience in the American City, 1760–1900.* Cambridge, U.K.: Cambridge University Press, 1989.

Bruchey, Stuart, ed. *Small Business in American Life.* New York: Columbia University Press, 1980.

Hatch, Nathan O., ed. *The Professions in American History.* Notre Dame, Ind.: University of Notre Dame Press, 1988.

JEROME P. BJELOPERA

WORKING-CLASS CULTURE As the nation's political economy shifted in the nineteenth century from a system of small independent producers to one made up of wage earners and employers—a process that began with the market revolution (1815) and accelerated in the post–Civil War years—the shared culture of the broadly defined producing classes ruptured. Employers and their allies in the pulpit, the classroom, and the community demanded new kinds of behavior from the growing number of employees. The new code of employers demanded what the English historian E. P. Thompson has called "time discipline" as well as a strict morality both in and out of the workplace. In stark contrast to the old world of work, employers of wage earners in factories and elsewhere—for this was true even of those who hired domestic labor in the home—often forbade singing, drinking, joking, smoking, or conversations on the job, and they denied the growing numbers of ethnic workers time to celebrate their holidays and holy days. This was no small matter: a Polish wedding in a Pennsylvania mining town might last three to five days; the Greek church had more than eighty festivals throughout the year; many Slavs observed Saint's days as holidays; Orthodox Jews would not work on Saturdays, their Sabbath day.

Resistance to Middle-class Morality

The attempt by the bourgeoisie, the employing class, to inculcate an "industrial morality," which as the historians Alan Dawley and Paul Faler noted "located the virtues of self-control, self-denial, and self-improvement at the center of the moral universe," met with mixed success (1979, p. 61). While some workers embraced self-improvement, evangelical religion, and temperance, all characteristics promoted by the bourgeoisie, many rejected the value system associated with industrial work. Workers esteemed hard work, but they looked with suspicion on the "work ethic" promulgated by their employers, which seemed to sanction long days and short wages for those who worked for a living and big profits for managers and shareholders, the "nonproducers" and "idlers" who did not. Called "traditionalists" by some historians, workers who took this point of view adhered to customs and values that went against the grain of industrial discipline: they continued to enjoy the fellowship and mutuality of the saloon (and even the odd "dram" on the job), to take the occasional "Blue Monday" off (a sociable day spent sharpening tools, carrying in stock, and discussing current events), and to reject the prerogatives of managers who aimed to control the work process. As late as 1877, a New York City manufacturer complained that too many cigar makers "come down to the shop in the morning; roll a few cigars and then go to a beer saloon and play pinnicio or some other game . . . working probably two or three hours a day" (Gutman, 1975, pp. 36–37).

Factory workers were not the only employees to desire autonomy at work and a realm of leisure untrammeled by middle-class expectations. African American domestic workers preferred not to "live in" with their white employers and engaged in preindustrial forms of resistance, such as "toting" food (taking it home without the authorization of their employer) and refusing to wear uniforms at work. Outside of the workplace, they treated community-sanctioned holidays as days off, strolled the streets in their own distinct (and distinctly unbourgeois) fashions, and frequented dance halls, as well as other sites of "cheap amusements." Like other industrial workers, African American workers participated in a world of leisure that they saw as a more important mark of their identity than their form of employment.

Working-class culture, then, developed both in the workplace and outside of it, particularly in the cities of industrializing America. One of the characteristics of urban life was a vibrant, heterosocial public sphere. Wage work loosened domestic obligations, especially for young working women, many of whom participated in the culture of the streets by dressing in flamboyant clothing; going to theaters, ice-cream parlors, amusement parks; or simply by promenading. In so doing, working women rejected bourgeois female decorum and the notion of separate spheres, which bound middle-class women to the private sphere. Although working-class men continued to value the homosocial leisure space of the saloon, their participation in the mixed-sex culture of the streets—

"The Wickedest Man in New York." New York City dance house scene. Wood engraving published in *Frank Leslie's Illustrated Newspaper*, 8 August 1868. LIBRARY OF CONGRESS

some of it rough rather than respectable—set them apart from middle-class ideals of manhood, which stressed sobriety, decorum, and individualism.

Even as the working class was being remade by immigration, the in-migration of rural folk, and new work processes, the first large cohort of wage earners shared similar experiences that brought them together in spite of their heterogeneity. Thus, although divisions of skill, gender, race, and ethnicity made impossible a monolithic laborers' culture, a distinctive working-class culture emerged, one that defined itself in opposition to middle-class values and norms.

Formation of Working-class Identity

Opposition to middle-class morality provided just one means by which workers formulated an identity. Workers who were intent on defining themselves as "white" during the nineteenth century condemned their fellow immigrant and African American workers as much as they did their bosses. Many of these people had an ambivalent relationship to those they

saw as nonwhite. They often covertly envied African Americans and recent immigrants who, they believed, had retained the spontaneous, lively, preindustrial cultures that they, as "respectable" white workers, had been forced to leave behind. Thus, the appeal of the most popular form of working-class entertainment, the minstrel show, was that it mocked industrial morality, while simultaneously allowing audience members to feel superior to the bumpkins and bumblers in blackface, whose inability to meet the challenges of the new economy was racialized in comforting ways. Similarly, the movement to exclude Chinese immigrants, a popular working-class cause that contributed to the passage of the Chinese Exclusion Act in 1882, depended on caricatures of the Chinese as miserly—an exaggerated version of the value of thrift that native-born Protestant workers had once celebrated but came to see as inimical to workers' well-being in an industrial economy driven by consumer demand. (In parallel fashion, male workers dismissed women's efforts to secure decent jobs as mere desire to earn "pin money," while prizing their own ability to enjoy the "comforts of life" as the essence of masculine republican citizenship.)

Working-class culture was "traditional" in that workers often sought to preserve old customs in the workplace and to defend holidays, rituals, and leisure prerogatives that characterized the world they had lost. Yet it would be inaccurate to interpret working-class culture as backward looking. Workers helped to shape the consumer culture that we closely associate with modernity through new modes of public behavior and through consuming goods like clothing, jewelry, and cosmetics in styles quite different from those of the middle class. The alternative culture they embraced often expressed itself in political opposition to middle-class values, which one labor pamphlet labeled "the rot of a false-named culture." Moreover workers theorized in original ways about how consumption patterns affected the political economy and democratic citizenship. To them, questions of leisure time and standards of living were as much about politics as about pleasure. One of the consistent demands of organized labor from the Jacksonian era through the end of the century was for a shorter workday. Advocates of an "American Standard of Living" deemed a minimal level of material well-being to be a prerequisite for citizenship. The trade unionist and writer George McNeill called for working people to be able to use "the morning hours in the duties and pleasures of the sunlit home; taking his morning bath before his morning work, reading his morning paper in the well-equipped reading room of the manufactory" (*The Labor Movement: The Problem of To-day* [Boston, 1887], p. 466). McNeill called the working-class claims of entitlement to their fair share of leisure and wealth the "new revolution." The cultural battle was clearly also a political one.

At the turn of the nineteenth century, the culture of workers would not have appeared altogether distinct from the culture of farmers and middle-class shopkeepers, all of whom were generally lumped under the category of "producers." By the end of the century, as wage-earners came to be seen as a permanent class in society, the culture that these workers created had become a distinct presence in American life. Although defined largely by opposition to the middle class, working-class culture ultimately contributed more to the making of modern America than it did to the persistence of tradition. For the culture most workers championed—the celebration of street life, the development of an urban style, the consumerist demands for the fruits of industrial production, and, sadly, the racism that so often accompanied these developments—became staples of American life in the twentieth century.

See also **Cities and Urbanization; Class, Social; Clothing; Consumerism and Consumption; Holidays; Minstrel Shows; Recreation; Work,** *subentries on* **Agricultural Labor, Factory Labor.**

Bibliography

Cantor, Milton, ed. *American Workingclass Culture: Explorations in American Labor and Social History.* Westport, Conn.: Greenwood Press, 1979.

Couvares, Francis G. *The Remaking of Pittsburgh: Class and Culture in an Industrializing City, 1877–1919.* Albany: State University of New York Press, 1984.

Dawley, Alan, and Paul Faler. "Workingclass Culture and Politics in the Industrial Revolution: Sources of Loyalty and Rebellion." In *American Workingclass Culture: Explorations in American Labor and Social History.* Edited by Milton Cantor. Westport, Conn.: Greenwood Press, 1979.

Gutman, Herbert G. *Work, Culture and Society in Industrializing America.* New York: Knopf, 1975.

Hunter, Tera. *To 'Joy My Freedom: Southern Black Women's Lives and Labors After the Civil War.* Cambridge, Mass.: Harvard University Press, 1997.

Roediger, David R. *The Wages of Whiteness: Race and the Making of the American Working Class.* New York: Verso, 1991.

Rosenzweig, Roy. *Eight Hours for What We Will: Workers and Leisure in an Industrial City, 1870–1920.* New York: Cambridge University Press, 1983.

Stansell, Christine. *City of Women: Sex and Class in New York, 1789–1860.* Urbana: University of Illinois Press, 1987.

Weir, Robert E. *Beyond Labor's Veil: The Culture of the Knights of Labor.* University Park: Penn State University Press, 1996.

LAWRENCE B. GLICKMAN

WORLD'S FAIRS By the 1800s, multinational trade fairs had been known to many parts of the world for centuries, and national exhibitions of arts and industrial products had become popular in western Europe beginning in the eighteenth century. Nevertheless the fair opened by Queen Victoria in London on 1 May 1851 created a new standard. Nearly fourteen thousand exhibitors, half of them from Britain and its colonies, sent their products to be displayed and judged competitively. Joseph Paxton's Crystal Palace exhibit hall, which enclosed nineteen of the twenty-six acres of the fairgrounds, dramatically demonstrated what modern architectural engineers could do with steel and glass. By the time the exhibition closed five months later, this first true world's fair had drawn more than six million visitors.

Following the success of the London World's Fair, from 1851 until World War I world's fairs were important institutions of Western culture. Reflecting the accelerating pace of technological innovation,

The World's Columbian Exposition in Chicago, 1893. The most extensive public exhibition of the century helped introduce the Beaux Arts style to America. LIBRARY OF CONGRESS

commercial expansion, and international competition, succeeding fairs also gave space to displays of natural history, agriculture, education, and the fine arts, all of which were arranged to demonstrate evolutionary, as opposed to revolutionary, progress and the superiority of Western civilization. Participation by non-Western, indigenous, or colonial peoples, when included, was often characterized by racial stereotyping and demeaning comparisons. Beginning in Paris in 1889, international meetings called "congresses" were held concurrently with the fairs to provide an opportunity to address the nonmaterial, intellectual, or spiritual aspects of human culture.

Although the essential form and character of the world's fair was developed by England and France, the United States produced the largest number of fairs. Between 1853 and 1916, Americans hosted nineteen exhibitions that included international representation, five of which (Philadelphia in 1876, Chicago in 1893, Buffalo in 1901, St. Louis in 1904, and San Francisco in 1915) rank as major world's fairs.

American interest and participation, like that of the French and British, reflected the expansion of nationalism, competitive enterprise, and international consciousness. World's fairs in the United States, however, as with American representation in foreign fairs, depended more heavily on private than on governmental management and financial support. Since the United States lacked a single dominant metropolis the equivalent of Paris or London, the process of selecting a suitable site in which to hold a world's fair often spurred urban and regional rivalries.

The first world's fair held in the United States was not a great success. Hastily conceived by New York businesspeople to capitalize upon the success of London's great fair, the New York World's Fair of 1853 opened two months behind schedule and, in spite of the newspaperman Horace Greeley's promotion and the showman P. T. Barnum's management, closed with little fanfare the next year.

Following the Civil War and Reconstruction, however, the one-hundredth anniversary of the Declara-

World's Fairs in the United States, 1853–1916

City	Dates	Size (acres)	Attendance (×1,000)
New York	Jul. 1853–Nov. 1854	4	1,150
Philadelphia	May 1876–Nov. 1876	285	9,789
Atlanta	Oct. 1881–Dec. 1881	19	290
Boston	Sep. 1883–Jan. 1884	3	300
Louisville	Aug. 1883–Nov. 1883	45	971
New Orleans	Dec. 1884–Jun. 1885	249	1,159
Chicago	May 1893–Oct. 1893	686	27,529
San Francisco	Jan. 1894–Jun. 1894	160	1,356
Atlanta	Sep. 1895–Dec. 1895	189	780
Nashville	May 1897–Oct. 1897	200	1,167
Omaha	Jun. 1898–Oct. 1898	200	2,614
Buffalo	May 1901–Nov. 1901	350	8,120
Charleston	Dec. 1901–Jun. 1902	160	—
St. Louis	Apr. 1904–Dec. 1904	1,272	19,695
Portland	Jun. 1905–Oct. 1905	400	2,554
Jamestown	Apr. 1907–Nov. 1907	400	2,851
Seattle	Jun. 1909–Oct. 1909	250	3,741
San Francisco	Feb. 1915–Dec. 1915	635	18,876
San Diego	Jan. 1915–Dec. 1916	400	3,748

Source: Findling, ed., *Historical Dictionary of World's Fairs and Expositions, 1851–1988*, pp. 376–379.

tion of Independence approached, and hosting an American world's fair appeared to be a good way both to help heal the nation's wounds and to demonstrate to the world the restoration and maturity of the American Union. Congress appropriately chose Philadelphia as the centennial city, and on 10 May 1876 President Ulysses S. Grant opened the first grand American world's fair in Fairmount Park. Occupying 285 acres, the fair presented over 150 temporary structures erected by states, territories, and foreign governments. By the time it closed on 10 November, over 9 million people had visited the 30,000 exhibits representing 32 countries. The focus of the Philadelphia Centennial was unquestionably the machine. American industrial devices and dynamos were greatly admired, and the seven-hundred-ton Corliss engine was the fair's most popular attraction. In the absence of adequate federal financial backing, the officials of the Centennial Exhibition, and indeed those of subsequent American fairs, were forced to depend upon gate receipts and revenues from concessions and popular amusements. In the United States, popular show business grew up with the world's fairs and was an important element in all of them.

After the Philadelphia Centennial, a series of fairs of primarily regional significance were held in the former Confederate States to demonstrate the vision of an industrial and commercial New South promoted by the Atlanta booster Henry W. Grady. The first of

these, Atlanta's International Cotton Exposition of 1881, was followed by expositions in Louisville (1883), New Orleans (1884), Atlanta (1887), Nashville (1897), Charleston (1901), and Norfolk, Virginia (1907). The Cotton States and International Exposition hosted by Atlanta in 1895 featured the first building dedicated to the exhibits of black Americans, and there Booker T. Washington delivered his famous "Atlanta Compromise" address.

In 1893 the United States and the city of Chicago hosted a world's fair to commemorate the four-hundredth anniversary of the European discovery of the New World. Challenged by the impressive Paris World's Fair of 1889, for which the Eiffel Tower was constructed, the World's Columbian Exposition was the most extensive public exhibition in America in the nineteenth century. It marked the emergence of Chicago, the American West, and the United States itself as major international forces. Chief among the expressions of an American imperial unity and dignity at Chicago was the beaux arts, uniformly white Court of Honor, with its great exhibit halls, statuary, and elaborate decoration designed by America's leading architects, sculptors, and painters. Constructed primarily in Jackson Park, eight miles south of Chicago's central business district, the artistically conceived White City contrasted dramatically with the chaotic and soot-blackened city to the north. It influenced American architecture, encouraging the use of classic Renaissance design in public buildings into the 1930s, and urban planning, encouraging the City Beautiful movement. As memorable and influential as the White City, the Midway Plaissance was the most extensive popular entertainment area of any world's fair up to that time. Its main attraction, a giant mechanical wheel created by George Ferris, carried riders high above the crowds on the Midway and in the Court of Honor. The Chicago World's Fair was notable for the attention given to women and for the extensiveness of the international conferences associated with it.

St. Louis had lobbied hard for the Columbian Exposition, and Governor David K. Francis of Missouri was particularly disappointed when Congress awarded the prize to Chicago. As the centennial of the Louisiana Purchase of 1803 approached he was determined to see St. Louis produce a bigger and better world's fair. The St. Louis World's Fair of 1904 was the site of the third modern Olympic Games, and it boasted the largest fairgrounds of any fair to that date. But in attempting to outdo Chicago, St. Louis failed to offer much that was original. The design of the major exhibit halls, for example, amounted to little more than an elaborate imitation of the classic renaissance style of Chicago.

Eleven years after the St. Louis Fair, the Panama Pacific International Exposition in San Francisco attracted nearly as many visitors, some eighteen million, to celebrate the opening of the Panama Canal and the resurgence of a city that had been devastated by earthquake and fire only nine years earlier. The San Francisco World's Fair of 1915 has been described as the last collective American expression of an unqualified faith in competitive nationalism and material progress as agents of universal peace and human happiness. Be that as it may, by the time of U.S. entry into World War I nearly every American town had its own microcosmic version of the world's fair in the form of a department store, a supermarket, an amusement park, and that ultimate fantasyland, the movie theater.

See also **Architecture; Boosterism; Chicago; Inventors and Inventions; Philadelphia; Recreation; St. Louis; San Francisco; Theater.**

Bibliography

Badger, Reid. *The Great American Fair: The World's Columbian Exposition and American Culture.* Chicago: N. Hall, 1979.

Curti, Merle. "America at the World Fairs, 1851–1893." *American Historical Review* 55 (1950): 833–856.

Findling, John E., ed. *Historical Dictionary of World's Fairs and Expositions, 1851–1988.* New York: Greenwood, 1990.

Rydell, Robert W. *All the World's a Fair: Visions of Empire at American International Expositions, 1876–1916.* Chicago: University of Chicago Press, 1984.

Smithsonian Institution. *The Books of the Fairs: Materials about World's Fairs, 1834–1916, in the Smithsonian Institution Libraries.* Chicago: American Library Association, 1992.

Trachtenberg, Alan. *The Incorporation of America: Culture and Society in the Gilded Age.* New York: Hill and Wang, 1982.

REID BADGER

WYOMING   The high, arid plains of Wyoming, located in the Rocky Mountains, were home to the Oglala and Brulé Sioux, Crows, Arapahos, and Shoshones until white fur trappers, soldiers, and migrants to the West Coast passed through, beginning in the 1830s. As the transcontinental railroad moved westward in the 1860s, the towns of Cheyenne, Laramie, and Evanston were established. On 25 July 1868 Congress granted the area territorial status. A year later the first territorial legislature gave women the right to vote and hold office, largely as a means of attracting settlers. Wyoming was the first state to grant women suffrage when it entered the Union in 1890.

Aside from employment by the Union Pacific Railroad and the federal government, the main occupation of residents of the new territory was cattle ranching. The range cattle boom of the 1890s spurred development and solidified the economic power of the Wyoming Stock Growers' Association. The end of the cattle expansion brought in smaller ranchers, farmers, and sheep raisers. Tension between large and small cattle ranchers led to the Johnson County War of 1892, in which federal troops had to save a vigilante expedition of large ranchers from death at the hands of their intended targets, the small ranchers. Thanks to their dominance of Wyoming courts, the "Invaders," as they were known, escaped legal punishment. The war remained a divisive issue in the state for decades.

Wyoming became the forty-fourth state on 10 July 1890. Because of its identification with woman suffrage, it gained the nickname "The Equality State." Aside from advancing suffrage, however, the state was politically conservative. Democrats and Republicans had battled on even terms in the 1880s until the restrictive land policies of President Grover Cleveland's first administration and the territorial governor Thomas Moonlight turned voters' sentiment toward the Republicans. In the aftermath of the drive for statehood, two Republican senators, Francis E. Warren and Joseph M. Carey, were sent to Washington. Warren drew the two-year term; Carey, the four-year term. Once political allies, the two men fell out and became bitter foes. Their rivalry shaped the history of the Wyoming Republican Party for a generation. Within two years the Johnson County War had aroused public unhappiness with the Republicans, giving the Democrats a chance at power.

The new Democratic governor, John E. Osborne, took office months before the depression of 1893 hit. The hard times hurt the Democrats, especially when Congress reduced the tariff on wool in the Wilson-Gorman Tariff of 1894. As a result the Republicans were victorious in the 1894 elections. Warren defeated Carey's reelection bid in 1895 and began a Senate career that lasted until his death in 1929. Clarence Don Clark held the other Senate seat.

Public life in Wyoming turned on issues of raising cattle and sheep. In national affairs the state's representatives favored the tariff on cattle hides and wool and eagerly pursued appropriations for military bases. Thinly populated, with only 92,531 inhabitants in 1900, and economically underdeveloped, Wyoming was on the margin of American life at the end of the nineteenth century.

See also **Ranching and Livestock Raising; Territorial Government; West, The; Women's Rights.**

Bibliography

Gould, Lewis L. *Wyoming: From Territory to Statehood.* Worland, Wyo.: High Plains, 1989.
Larson, Taff Alfred. *History of Wyoming.* 2d ed. Lincoln: University of Nebraska Press, 1978.

LEWIS L. GOULD

YOUNG AMERICA MOVEMENT In promoting the image of the United States as a vigorous individual approaching the full powers of adulthood, the Young America movement of the 1840s and 1850s captured the optimistic, democratic, and expansionist tendencies of the early Republic. Several manifestations linked primarily by one individual constituted the movement. In various incarnations Young America addressed creation of a unique, democratic, and American literature and culture; the advancement of young Democratic Party leaders clustered around U.S. Senator Stephen A. Douglas of Illinois; and finally, expansion of territorial boundaries to the Pacific and the annexation of Cuba. John L. O'Sullivan of New York City, an editor, filibusterer, and diplomat in the Franklin Pierce administration, provided the common link.

Descended from a colorful line of exiled Irish soldiers and adventurers, O'Sullivan founded the *United States Magazine and Democratic Review,* commonly known as the *Democratic Review,* in the fall of 1837. Among the goals outlined by the twenty-four-year-old editor were carrying the political cause of democracy and the Democratic Party into the cultural realm, thereby nurturing a literature that reflected the political and social systems of the United States. "The vital principle of an American national literature must be democracy," O'Sullivan wrote in the first issue, calling for the rewriting of history and political science "in light of the democratic principle" ("The Introductory Statement," *Democratic Review I*, October 1837, pp. 14–15). Although the magazine struggled during its first years of existence in Washington, O'Sullivan lured to its columns writers associated with the American Renaissance. Ralph Waldo Emerson, Henry David Thoreau, Walt Whitman, Edgar Allan Poe, and Nathaniel Hawthorne were *Democratic Review* contributors. Hawthorne, who developed a lifelong friendship with O'Sullivan, placed more articles and sketches in the magazine than in any other publication.

After moving the magazine to New York in 1841, O'Sullivan became associated with the Tetractys Club, the nucleus of the literary Young America movement. Evert A. Duyckinck, a critic who promoted a unique and democratic American literature, was the catalyst in forming the club, which eventually reached into suburban Boston and the Berkshires of Massachusetts. Conviction that the United States stood on the brink of a new era was also felt in the South. In 1845 Edwin De Leon, a South Carolinian, published *The Position and Duties of Young America,* a speech arguing that nations, like humans, went through growth stages from infancy to old age. De Leon envisioned the United States at the stage of "exulting manhood" and ready for the energetic leadership of a new generation. In April of the same year Duyckinck became literary editor of the *Democratic Review.* O'Sullivan needed assistance in producing the magazine because by 1845 he was deeply involved in politics and also edited a daily newspaper, the *New York Morning News.* In two essays, "The Great Nation of Futurity" (*Democratic Review IV,* November 1839, pp. 426–430) and "Democracy" (*Democratic Review VII,* March 1840, pp. 215–229), O'Sullivan laid the foundations for what became known as "Manifest Destiny." The notion that the United States was ordained by God to extend its boundaries and spread democracy gained its name when O'Sullivan welcomed the annexation of Texas in July 1845 with the essay "Annexation" (*Democratic Review XVII,* July–August 1845, pp. 5–10). On page five, he termed the action "the fulfillment of our manifest destiny to overspread the continent allotted by Providence for the free development of our yearly multiplying millions." Six months later he repeated the phrase in a *Morning News* editorial on the Oregon question (27 December 1845).

O'Sullivan sold the magazine in June 1846 and embarked on various speculative ventures, including two failed attempts to invade Cuba and overthrow the Spanish authorities. The Young America movement flickered as slavery increasingly roiled domestic politics and, especially, the Democratic Party. As the 1852 Democratic nominating convention approached, the name "Young America" was applied to backers of Douglas, then thirty-eight years old. George N. Sanders, who purchased the *Democratic Review* in December 1851, turned it into a Douglas organ. However, Sanders was so bitter in his attacks on older Democratic candidates and leaders, whom he termed "old fogeys," that he severely crippled Douglas's bid. The eventual nominee and winner of the presidential contest, Franklin Pierce, welcomed a number of Young Americans, who were also associated with aggressive territorial expansion. After serving as a go-between for Pierce and the Martin Van Buren faction of the New York Democratic Party, O'Sullivan was appointed as consul to Portugal. Other Young Americans sent abroad by Pierce included Sanders, Daniel Stickles, John Y. Mason, and Pierre Soulé. The latter two, along with James Buchanan, signed the Ostend Manifesto, an 1854 call for the immediate purchase of Cuba by the United States.

As the debate over slavery in the territories mounted, the territorial goals of Young America were frustrated, and by 1856 even the Democratic Party abandoned its formerly aggressive expansionist plank. O'Sullivan, who provided the primary link among the three phases of the movement, went into self-imposed exile in Europe during the Civil War, serving there as a Confederate agent. In the decades after the Civil War the onetime Young Americans were themselves well into "old fogeyism" and, like the ideals they once espoused, slowly died away.

Nurturing a unique American literature was Young America's greatest success. The efforts of O'Sullivan and Duyckinck provided support and context for the development of American writers like Hawthorne, Herman Melville, and Whitman. Politically, while failing to nominate and elect Douglas, the Young Americans did have influence within the Pierce administration. The treaty ending the Mexican War marked the high point of Young America's territorial achievements. Cuba and Central America, despite numerous filibustering attempts, never became part of the United States. O'Sullivan's phrase "Manifest Destiny" was Young America's most visible and controversial legacy.

See also **Cuba; Democratic Party; Elections,** *subentry* **on Presidential Elections; Expansion; Filibusters; Literature,** *subentry on* **The Essay; Manifest Destiny.**

Bibliography

Chaffin, Tom. *Fatal Glory: Narciso López and the First Clandestine U.S. War against Cuba.* Charlottesville: University of Virginia Press, 1996. Argues that López and O'Sullivan were motivated by democratic ideals in their failed Cuban annexation projects.

Harris, Sheldon Howard. "The Public Career of John Louis O'Sullivan." Ph.D. diss., Columbia University, 1958.

Johannsen, Robert W. *Stephen A. Douglas.* New York: Oxford University Press, 1973. Best account of the Young America movement to nominate Douglas in 1852.

Miller, Perry. *The Raven and the Whale: The War of Words and Wits in the Era of Poe and Melville.* New York: Harcourt, Brace, 1956. Classic work on literary Young America.

Riepma, Siert F. " 'Young America': A Study in American Nationalism before the Civil War." Ph.D. diss., Case Western Reserve University, 1939.

Sampson, Robert Dean. "'Under the Banner of the Democratic Principle': John Louis O'Sullivan, the Democracy, and the *Democratic Review.*" Ph.D. diss., University of Illinois at Urbana-Champaign, 1995.

Widmer, Edward L. *Young America: The Flowering of Democracy in New York City.* New York: Oxford University Press, 1999. Argues that two distinct Young America movements existed, one literary and cultural, the other territorial.

ROBERT D. SAMPSON

ZOOS   Exotic animals were first exhibited in the United States when a lion was taken to Boston in 1716. Traveling menageries began in the early 1800s and were soon joined by circus menageries. Urban menageries appeared in the mid-1800s, and the first zoo, the Philadelphia Zoological Garden, opened in 1874. Many of the early urban menageries did not survive, and little is known about them. Of those existing at the end of the nineteenth century, thirty-two developed into zoos and aquariums during the twentieth century.

Four major zoos opened during the nineteenth century in Philadelphia (1874), Cincinnati (1875), Washington, D.C. (1889), and New York (1899). All except the National Zoological Park, a federal institution operated by the Smithsonian Institution, were managed by private zoological societies. However, some early zoos and most later zoos were established or encouraged by urban civic leaders and were handled by municipal parks departments. Founders of municipal zoos, usually well traveled and familiar with the great European zoos, felt zoos should be included among the many cultural institutions, such as art museums and botanical gardens, that American cities were developing. Zoo creation accompanied the

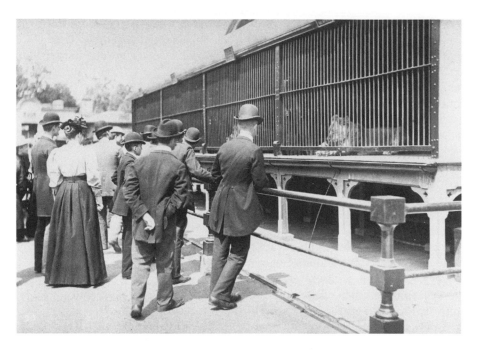

Central Park Zoo, New York City. Viewing the lion cages, 1895. BYRON/MUSEUM OF THE CITY OF NEW YORK/ARCHIVE PHOTOS

urban park movement, the professionalization of the natural sciences, exploration, the discovery of new species, and the first nationwide concern for wildlife conservation.

The first American zoos were concerned variously with recreation, education, scientific research, and conservation. These efforts were particularly well developed by the New York Zoological Park during the final years of the century, coinciding with the first national conservation movement. The New York Zoological Park, other zoos, and private ranches played significant roles in this movement, which saved the American bison from extinction.

Aquariums were first developed in Britain in the 1850s and quickly became popular in the United States. Unlike zoos, however, the first public aquariums in the United States were commercial endeavors. In 1856 Phineas T. Barnum established an aquarium at his American Museum in New York. Boston's Aquarial Gardens opened in 1859 and merged with the Barnum aquarium in 1862. Two public aquariums dating from this period survived through the twentieth century: the National Aquarium, which opened in Washington, D.C., in 1873 and should not be confused with the National Aquarium in Baltimore, and the New York Aquarium, which opened in 1896.

Exhibits were uniform in nineteenth-century zoos. Barred cages were designed to be sturdy and easily cleaned because animal husbandry and veterinary medicine were not well advanced. Animal collections were taxonomic, resembling living museums, and zoos displayed representative specimens of as many species as possible. While native animals were of interest, it was the exotic animals from distant lands that attracted the most attention, such as lions, tigers, elephants, rhinoceroses, giraffes, and other large mammals. Curators obtained animals from dealers, from expeditions operated by their zoos, or from other zoos. As knowledge and technology improved, animal husbandry, veterinary medicine, exhibition techniques, and other zoo programs advanced also. The most significant improvements occurred during the next century, particularly after World War II.

See also **Circuses; Conservation; Geography and Ecology; National Parks; Nature; Parks and Landscape Architecture; Recreation.**

Bibliography

Kisling, Vernon N., Jr. "The Origin and Development of American Zoological Parks to 1899." In *New Worlds, New Animals: From Menagerie to Zoological Park in the Nineteenth Century.* Edited by R. J. Hoage and William A. Deiss. Baltimore: Johns Hopkins University Press, 1996.

Stott, R. Jeffrey. "The Historical Origins of the Zoological Park in American Thought." *Environmental Review* 5, no. 2 (1981): 52–65.

Wirtz, Patrick. "Zoo City: Bourgeois Values and Scientific Culture in the Industrial Landscape." *Journal of Urban Design* 2, no. 1 (1997): 61–82.

VERNON N. KISLING JR.

Systematic Outline of Contents

The systematic outline provides a general overview of the conceptual scheme of the Encyclopedia, listing the titles of each entry and subentry.

The outline is divided into eight parts:

1 Defining the Nineteenth Century
2 Population
3 Contexts
4 Slavery and Sectionalism
5 Civil War and Reconstruction
6 Philosophy and the Arts
7 Popular Culture
8 Print, Books, Reading
9 Key Concepts
10 Foreign Relations and War
11 Places

Most parts are divided into several sections. Because the section headings are not mutually exclusive, certain entries in the Encyclopedia are listed in more than one section. The main entry on a topic may appear at the beginning of a section, out of alphabetical order.

1 DEFINING THE NINETEENTH CENTURY

Nineteenth Century
Jeffersonian Era
Era of Good Feeling
Jacksonian Era

Gilded Age
Foreign Observers
Interpretations of the Nineteenth Century

Popular Interpretations of the Frontier West
Twentieth-Century Film and Media

2 POPULATION

This part includes the entry on Population, as well as sections on American Indians, African Americans, women, other groups, immigration and emigration, and migration to the West and patterns of settlement.

Population

American Indians

American Indian Societies
    New England
    The Middle Atlantic Region
    The Southeast
    The Great Lakes
    The Plains
    California
    The Northwest Plateau
    The Southwest
    Alaska

American Indians
    Overview
    Law in Indian Communities
    Wars and Warfare
    Treaties and Treatymaking
    U.S. Government Policies
    Indian Removal
    The Image of the Indian

African Americans

African Americans
    Overview
    Free Blacks before the Civil War

    Blacks in the West
Segregation
    Segregation and Civil Rights
Education
    School Segregation

Women

Women
    Overview
    Women's Rights
    Women's Labor
    Women in the Professions
    Woman as Image and Icon

Gender
    Interpretations of Gender
    Gender and the Law
Education
    Education of Girls and
        Women
Voters and Voting
    The Women's Vote
Republican Motherhood
Clubs
    Women's Clubs and
        Associations
Magazines, Women's

Other Groups

Creoles
Mexican Americans

Immigration and Emigration

Immigration and Immigrants
    An Overview
    The Immigrant Experience

Immigration Policy and Law
Anti-immigrant Sentiment
Ireland
Great Britain
France and the Low Countries
Germany
Central and Eastern Europe
Jewish Immigrants
Scandinavia and Finland
Southern Europe
The Ottoman Empire and the
    Middle East
Canada
Mexico and Latin America
Asia
Barrios
Chinese Exclusion Act
Chinatowns

**Migration to the West and
    Patterns of Settlement**

Alaska Purchase
Boomtowns

Boosterism
Conservation
Cowboys and Cowgirls
Expansion
Exploration and Explorers
Federal Land Policy
Frontier
Fur Trade
Geography and Ecology
Gold Rushes and Silver Strikes
Gunfighters
Homesteading
Hunting and Trapping
Lewis and Clark Expedition
Manifest Destiny
Mexican Cession
National Parks
Natural Resources
Outlaws
Statehood and Admission
Territorial Government
Trails to the West
Travel, Technology of

3   CONTEXTS

This part includes sections on political contexts, legal contexts, economic contexts, social contexts, social problems and social reform, everyday life, cultural concepts, science and technology, religious groups, and religious contexts. Several of these sections are in turn divided into subsections.

Political Contexts

Politics
    Political Thought
    Political Culture
    The First Party System
    The Second Party System
    The Third Party System
    Corruption and Scandals
Federalist Party
Democratic Party
Whig Party
Republican Party
Third Parties
Nationalism
    1800–1865
    1861–1900
Progressivism
Internal Improvements
Populism
Radicalism
Race and Racial Thinking
Miscegenation
Cartoons, Political
Reform, Political

The Presidency

Presidency
    The Presidency as an
        Institution

1801–1829
1829–1849
1849–1861
1861–1877
1877–1901
Washington, George

Political Culture

Bosses, Political
First Ladies
Muckrakers
Patriotic and Genealogical
    Societies
Politics
    Party Organization and
        Operations
    Parties and the Press
    Machines and Bosses
Religion
    Religion as a Political Issue
Revolutionary War Remembered
Slogans, Songs, and Nicknames,
    Political
Young America Movement

Political Objectives

Assassinations
Banking and Finance

The Politics of Banking
Foreign Trade and Tariffs
    The Politics of Tariffs

Government and Policy

Cabinet
Civil Service Reform
Congress
Currency Policy
Elections
    Campaigns and Elections
    Presidential Elections
Federal-State Relations
    1800–1833
    1831–1865
    1861–1900
Government
Local Government
State Government
States' Rights
Taxation and Public Finance
Voters and Voting
    White Male Franchise
    Black Voters before the Civil
        War
    Black Voters after the Civil
        War
    The Women's Vote

9 KEY CONCEPTS

Character
Civilization
Home
Industry (The Work Ethic)

Liberty
Manliness
Nature
Progress, Idea of

Reform, Idea of
Republicanism
Women
    Woman as Image and Icon

10 FOREIGN RELATIONS AND WAR

This part includes sections on foreign countries and possessions, diplomacy, armed forces, and wars.

Foreign Countries and Possessions

Cuba
Filibusters
Foreign Parts
Gadsden Purchase
Haiti
Louisiana Purchase
Mexico
Overseas Possessions
Puerto Rico
Virgin Islands

Diplomacy

Diplomatic Corps
Foreign Parts

Foreign Relations
    Overview
    1789–1860
    The Civil War
    1865–1917
Monroe Doctrine
Canada
Great Britain, Foreign Relations with
Europe, Foreign Relations with
Central America and the Caribbean
South America, Foreign Relations with
Africa, Foreign Relations with
Asia, Foreign Relations with

Armed Forces

Militia, State
Army
Navy
Marines, U.S.
Military Service
African Americans
    Blacks in the Military
Military Technology
Naval Technology

Wars

Barbary War
War of 1812
Seminole Wars
Mexican War
Civil War
Spanish-American War

11 PLACES

This part includes sections on regions, states and territories, and cities.

Regions

New England
Mid-Atlantic States
South, The
    The South before the Civil War
    The New South after Reconstruction
Appalachia
Border States
Midwest, The
Great Plains
West, The

States and Territories

Alabama
Alaska
Arizona
Arkansas
California
Colorado
Connecticut
Delaware

District of Columbia
Florida
Georgia
Hawaii
Idaho
Illinois
Indian Territory
Indiana
Iowa
Kansas
Kentucky
Louisiana
Maine
Maryland
Massachusetts
Michigan
Minnesota
Mississippi
Missouri
Montana
Nebraska
Nevada
New Hampshire
New Jersey

New Mexico
New York State
North Carolina
North Dakota
Northwest Territory
Ohio
Oregon
Pennsylvania
Rhode Island
South Carolina
South Dakota
Tennessee
Texas
Utah
Vermont
Virginia
Washington State
West Virginia
Wisconsin
Wyoming

Cities

Baltimore
Boston

Brooklyn
Buffalo, N.Y.
Charleston
Chicago
Cincinnati
Denver

Detroit
Kansas City
Los Angeles
Miami
New Orleans
New York City

Philadelphia
Richmond
San Francisco
Seattle
St. Louis
Washington, D.C.

Directory of Contributors

W. A. ACHENBAUM
Institute of Gerontology, University of Michigan
   Life Cycle: Old Age

SEAN ADAMS
University of Central Florida
   Iron

THOMAS G. ALEXANDER
Brigham Young University
   Mormonism

DOUGLAS C. ALLEN
Georgia Institute of Technology
   Parks and Landscape Architecture

MARTIN R. ANSELL
Carrollton, Texas
   Petroleum
   Transportation: Railroads

CINDY S. ARON
University of Virginia
   Offices and Office Work

LARRY CATÁ BACKER
College of Law, University of Tulsa
   Politics: Political Culture

REID BADGER
University of Alabama
   World's Fairs

PAUL A. BAGLYOS
Zion Lutheran Church, Harrisburg, Pa.
   Protestantism: Lutherans

BARRY BAIN
The American Planning Association
   City and Regional Planning
   Local Government
   Police
   Suburbs

GORDON MORRIS BAKKEN
California State University, Fullerton
   African Americans: Blacks in the
     Military
   Law: Federal Law

LOIS W. BANNER
University of Southern California
   Beauty Contests
   Women: Women's Rights

ROBERT BANNISTER
Swarthmore College
   Evolution

DIANE BARNES
West Virginia University
   Boosterism

GEORGIA BRADY BARNHILL
Andrew W. Mellon Curator of Graphic Arts, American Antiquarian Society
   Lithography and Prints

MARK BARROW
Virginia Polytechnic Institute and State University
   Conservation

ABEL A. BARTLEY
University of Akron
   Florida
   Miami

FRANK L. BATTISTI
New England Conservatory
   Bands and Band Concerts

HUGO A. BEDAU
Tufts University
   Capital Punishment

JANET R. BEDNAREK
University of Dayton
   Bicycling

MICHAEL LES BENEDICT
Ohio State University
   Civil Rights
   Presidency: 1861–1877
   Reconstruction: The Politics of
     Reconstruction

DAVID H. BENNETT
Syracuse University
   Immigration and Immigrants:
     Anti-immigrant Sentiment

RICHARD BENSEL
Cornell University
   Civil War: Consequences of the
     Civil War

KEITH R. BENSON
University of Washington, Seattle
   Biology
   Medicine

EUGENE BERWANGER
Colorado State University
   Civil War: The West
   Reconstruction: The West

JEROME BJELOPERA
Temple University
   Work: Middle-Class Occupations

KAREN J. BLAIR
Central Washington University
   Clubs: Women's Clubs and
     Associations

BURTON J. BLEDSTEIN
University of Illinois, Chicago
   Professions

GEOFFREY BLODGETT
Oberlin College
   Reform, Political

LORI BOGLE
United States Naval Academy
   Marines, U.S.
   Navy

TRACEY J. BOISSEAU
University of Akron
   Grand Tour

JEROME D. BOWERS II
The Madeira School, McLean, Va.
   Mid-Atlantic States
   National Parks
   Revivalism

PAUL S. BOYER
Institute for Research in the Humanities, University of Wisconsin, Madison
   Character

PAUL F. BRAIM
Embry Riddle University
Army

ANN LEE BRESSLER
Davidson College
Unitarianism and Universalism

GREGORY M. BRITTON
Minnesota Historical Society Press
Printing Technology

W. FITZHUGH BRUNDAGE
University of Florida
Lynching

PAUL BUHLE
Brown University
Radicalism

PATRICIA BURGESS
Independent Scholar, Shaker Heights, Ohio
Chicago
Civil Engineering: Building
Technology
Reform, Social

SCOTT BURNET
Independent Scholar, Charlottesville, Va.
Maine
Pennsylvania

O. VERNON BURTON
University of Illinois, Urbana-Champaign
Civil War: The Home Front in the
South

GREGORY BUSH
University of Miami
Advertising

CHARLES W. CALHOUN
East Carolina University
Gilded Age

COLIN G. CALLOWAY
Dartmouth College
American Indian Societies: New
England

BALLARD CAMPBELL
Northeastern University
Government
State Government

CHARLES W. CAREY
Lynchburg College
Central Virginia Community College
Corporations and Big Business
Cotton
Entrepreneurs
Gold Rushes and Silver Strikes

Immigration and Immigrants:
Great Britain
Internal Improvements
Market Revolution
Presidency: 1829–1849
Presidency: 1849–1861
Regulation of Business
Third Parties
Trusts

RODNEY P. CARLISLE
History Associates
Maritime Technology

BETTY BOYD CAROLI
*Kingsborough Community College,
City University of New York*
First Ladies

STEPHANIE CARPENTER
Murray State University
Federal Land Policy

EDWARD J. CASHIN
*Center for the Study of Georgia
History, Augusta State University*
Georgia

SCOTT E. CASPER
University of Nevada, Reno
Book Publishing

EDWARD CASTILLO
Sonoma State University
American Indian Societies:
California

ANDREW R. L. CAYTON
Miami University, Oxford, Ohio
Midwest, The
Northwest Territory

MARY K. CAYTON
Miami University, Oxford, Ohio
Protestantism: Congregationalists

ROBERT J. CHANDLER
Historical Services, Wells Fargo Bank
Travel, Technology of
Wells Fargo

GABRIEL CHIN
*College of Law, University of
Cincinnati*
Immigration and Immigrants:
Immigration Policy and Law

LAWRENCE O. CHRISTENSEN
University of Missouri–Rolla
Missouri

GENE CLANTON
*Washington State University,
Emeritus*
Populism

JAMES W. CLARKE
University of Arizona
Assassinations

THOMAS CLARKIN
University of Texas at San Antonio
Seattle
Transportation: Roads and
Turnpikes

MATT CLAVIN
American University
Minstrel Shows
Slavery: Slave Life

STANLEY COBEN
University of California, Los Angeles
Victorianism

JEFFREY COHEN
Fordham University
Cabinet

LOUIS COHEN
Cambridge, Massachusetts
Astronomy

MARGARET CONNELL SZASZ
University of New Mexico
American Indian Societies: The
Southwest

JAMES CONNOLLY
Ball State University
Politics: Machines and Bosses

STEPHEN COOK
*Curator, Mashantucket Pequot
Museum and Research Center*
American Indians: American
Indian Art

CONSTANCE COOPER
Historical Society of Delaware
Delaware

ROBERT COTTROL
George Washington University
African Americans: Free Blacks
before the Civil War

EDWARD COUNTRYMAN
Southern Methodist University
Civilization
Jeffersonian Era

DAVID T. COURTWRIGHT
University of North Florida
Violence

ROBERT M. CRAIG
Georgia Institute of Technology
Parks and Landscape Architecture

SARAH GARDNER CUNNINGHAM
Marymount School of New York
Christian Science

HELEN DAMON-MOORE
Cornell College, Mt. Vernon, Iowa
Literacy and Reading Habits

REBECCA DAMRON
University of Tulsa
Language

DAVID B. DANBOM
North Dakota State University
North Dakota

ROGER DANIELS
University of Cincinnati
Chinese Exclusion Act
Immigration and Immigrants: An
Overview
Immigration and Immigrants: The
Immigrant Experience
Immigration and Immigrants:
Asia

JANET M. DAVIS
University of Texas at Austin
Circuses

LANCE E. DAVIS
California Institute of Technology
Whaling

MARY A. DE CREDICO
United States Naval Academy
Naval Academy, U.S.

RENÉ DE LA PEDRAJA
Canisius College, Buffalo, N.Y.
Steam Power

ARNOLDO DE LEÓN
Angelo State University
Barrios
Mexican Americans

TORRY D. DICKINSON
Kansas State University
Work: Artisans and Craftsworkers

LEONARD DINNERSTEIN
*Committee on Judaic Studies,
University of Arizona*
Anti-Semitism
Immigration and Immigrants:
Jewish Immigrants

BRIAN DIPPIE
University of British Columbia
American Indians: The Image of
the Indian

JOHN DIZIKES
University of California, Santa Cruz
Music: Opera

GORDON B. DODDS
Portland State University
Oregon
Washington State

JAY P. DOLAN
University of Notre Dame
Catholicism

JESSICA DORMAN
*Pennsylvania State University,
Harrisburg*
Muckrakers

RICHARD DOTY
*Smithsonian Institution, Curator of
Numismatics*
Money and Coins

PAUL DOWNES
University of Toronto
Literature: Fiction

RACHEL L. DRENOVSKY
Indiana University, Indianapolis
Immigration and Immigrants:
France and the Low Countries
Immigration and Immigrants:
Central and Eastern Europe
Immigration and Immigrants:
Southern Europe

ARIELA R. DUBLER
Yale University
Marriage

DANIEL MARTIN DUMYCH
*County of Niagara, New York (d.
2000)*
Inventors and Inventions
Waterpower

KEITH EDGERTON
Montana State University, Billings
Prisons and Punishment

MICHAEL EDMONDS
*Library Division, State Historical
Society of Wisconsin,*
Wisconsin

DOUGLAS R. EGERTON
LeMoyne College
Colonization, African American

MARK R. ELLIS
University of Nebraska, Lincoln
Great Plains
Trails to the West

RICHARD E. ELLIS
State University of New York, Buffalo
Federal-State Relations: 1800–
1833
States' Rights

WILLIAM E. ELLIS
Eastern Kentucky University
Kentucky

ROBERT S. ELLWOOD
*University of Southern California,
Emeritus*
Non-Western Religions

JAMES W. ELY
Vanderbilt School of Law
Constitutional Law: After the
Civil War
Economic Regulation
Property

LINDA EIKMEIER ENDERSBY
University of Missouri–Columbia
Museums: Science and Technology
Museums
Textiles

DANIEL R. ESS
Purdue University
Agricultural Technology

DAVID M. FAHEY
Miami University, Oxford, Ohio
Temperance Movement

JOHN D. FAIRFIELD
Xavier University, Cincinnati
Cincinnati

MARY FARMER
Bowling Green State University
Voters and Voting: The Women's
Vote

HAYWARD FARRAR
*Virginia Polytechnic Institute and
State University*
Newspapers, African American

JAMES E. FICKLE
University of Memphis
Lumber and Timber Industry

PAUL FINKELMAN
College of Law, University of Tulsa
Bill of Rights
Compromise of 1850
Constitutional Law: Before the
Civil War
Federal-State Relations: 1831–
1865
Fugitive Slave Laws
Kansas-Nebraska Act
Law: An Overview
Massachusetts
Missouri Compromise
Nineteenth Century
Race Laws
Sectionalism
Slavery: Runaway Slaves
Slavery: Law of Slavery
Slavery: Defense of Slavery
Supreme Court: Slavery

Voters and Voting: Black Voters
before the Civil War

GAYLE V. FISCHER
Salem State College, Massachusetts
Women: Overview

DONALD L. FIXICO
*Director of Indigenous Nations
Studies, University of Kansas*
American Indians: Wars and
Warfare

LAURA ANN FOSTER
University of Cincinnati
Women: Women's Labor
Women: Women in the Professions

LAWRENCE FOSTER
Georgia Institute of Technology
Communitarian Movements and
Groups
Polygamy, Mormon

WALTER J. FRASER
Georgia Southern University
Charleston

DONALD S. FRAZIER
McMurry University
Geography and Cartography

CHARLES S. FREEMAN
Tallahassee, Florida
Music: Orchestral Music

KRIS FRESONKE
Iowa State University
Interpretations of the Nineteenth
Century: Twentieth-Century
Film and Media

AMANDA FRISKEN
*State University of New York College
at Old Westbury*
Women: Woman as Image and
Icon

KATHRYN WAGNILD FULLER
University of Minnesota, Duluth
Academic and Professional
Societies

WAYNE FULLER
*University of Texas at El Paso,
Emeritus*
Pony Express
Post Office

PATRICK J. FURLONG
Indiana University, South Bend
Indiana

LISA GABBERT
Indiana University, Bloomington
Folktales and Tall Tales

J. MATTHEW GALLMAN
Loyola College in Maryland
Civil War: The Home Front in the
North
Philadelphia

L. DEE GARRISON
Rutgers University
Libraries

TIM ALAN GARRISON
Portland State University
American Indians: Treaties and
Treatymaking
American Indian Societies: The
Middle Atlantic Region
American Indian Societies: The
Southeast
American Indian Societies: The
Great Lakes
Civil War: Indian Territory
Race and Racial Thinking

EUGENE GARVER
St. John's University
Philosophy
Pragmatism

GEOFFREY GILBERT
Hobart and William Smith College
Economic Theory

LAWRENCE B. GLICKMAN
University of South Carolina
Working-class Culture

ANDREW GODLEY
*University of Reading, United
Kingdom*
Foreign Investment

DOUGLAS GOMERY
University of Maryland
Movies

LESLEY GORDON
University of Akron
Revolutionary War Remembered
Veterans Organizations

LEWIS L. GOULD
*University of Texas at Austin,
Emeritus*
Congress
Democratic Party
Elections: Presidential Elections
Europe, Foreign Relations with
Federal-State Relations: 1861–
1900
Foreign Relations: 1865–1917
Foreign Trade and Tariffs: Trade
and Tariffs
Foreign Trade and Tariffs: The
Politics of Tariffs
Overseas Possessions

Presidency: The Presidency as an
Institution
Presidency: 1877–1901
Puerto Rico
Republican Party
Virgin Islands
Wyoming

VIRGINIA MEACHAM GOULD
Our Lady of Holy Cross College
Creoles
Louisiana
New Orleans

ROGER GRANT
Clemson University
Railroads
Spiritualism
Transportation: Animal Power

WILLIAM D. GREEN
Augsburg College, Minneapolis
Minnesota

JOSHUA R. GREENBERG
*Ph.D. Candidate, American
University*
Work: The Workshop

CLYDE GRIFFEN
Vassar College
Manliness

DAVID A. GRIMSTED
University of Maryland, College Park
Theater

FRANK E. GRIZZARD
*Papers of George Washington,
University of Virginia*
Washington, George

STEPHEN B. GROVE
United States Military Academy
Military Academy, U.S.

CAROLE HABER
University of Delaware
Life Cycle: Childhood and
Adolescence
Life Cycle: Adulthood

GLADYS HADDAD
Case Western Reserve University
Education: Education of Girls and
Women

MICHAEL R. HAINES
Colgate University
Population

PETER HALL
Yale University
Philanthropy

THOMAS D. HAMM
Earlham College, Indiana
Quakers

DAVID HAUS
Bowling Green State University
 Glass

STEVE HAYCOX
University of Alaska, Anchorage
 Alaska
 American Indian Societies: Alaska

CHRISTINA DALLETT HEMPHILL
Ursinus College
 Manners

LINNEA HENDRICKSON
University of New Mexico
 Literature: Children's Literature

DAVID F. HERR
Independent Scholar, Urbana, Illinois
 Merchandising: The General Store

STEPHEN HESS
The Brookings Institution
 Cartoons, Political

WALTER L. HIXSON
University of Akron
 Asia, Foreign Relations with
 Crime: Overview
 Crime: Sensational Crimes
 War of 1812

GRAHAM RUSSELL HODGES
Colgate University
 Brooklyn
 New York City
 New York State

CLIFTON HOOD
Wichita State University
 Kansas City
 Transportation: Urban and
  Interurban Transportation

HERBERT T. HOOVER
University of South Dakota
 South Dakota

ANGELA HOWARD
University of Houston at Clear Lake
 Magazines, Women's

THOMAS HOWARD
*Virginia Polytechnic Institute and
State University*
 Africa, Foreign Relations with
 Liberia

BARBARA J. HOWE
*Center for Women's Studies, West
Virginia University*
 Housing

LISA NEUMAN HOWORTH
Independent Scholar, Oxford, Miss.
 Folk Arts

FREDERICK E. HOXIE
The Newberry Library
 American Indians: Overview

BARBARA HUGHETT
Independent Scholar, Chicago, Ill.
 Barbary War
 Connecticut
 Patriotic and Genealogical
  Societies

ELLEN HUPPERT
*Institute for Historical Study,
National Coalition of Independent
Scholars*
 Foreign Observers

R. DOUGLAS HURT
Iowa State University
 Agriculture
 Work: Agricultural Labor

WAYNE A. HUSS
Gwynedd-Mercy College
 Masons

JAMES L. HUSTON
Oklahoma State University
 Panics and Depressions

HAROLD HYMAN
Rice University
 Supreme Court: The Court during
  the Civil War and
  Reconstruction

PAUL ISRAEL
*Thomas A. Edison Papers, Rutgers
University*
 Telegraph

WILLIAM ISSEL
San Francisco State University
 San Francisco

DAVID JAMISON
University of Akron
 Constitutional Amendments:
  Twelfth Amendment
 Constitutional Amendments:
  Thirteenth, Fourteenth, and
  Fifteenth Amendments
 Magazines
 Newspapers and the Press

ROBERT L. JENKINS
Mississippi State University
 Mississippi

RICHARD JENSEN
University of Illinois, Chicago Circle
 Elections: Campaigns and
  Elections
 Federalist Party
 Politics: The Second Party System
 Politics: The Third Party System

THOMAS C. JEPSEN
*National Coalition of Independent
Scholars*
 Communications

DEIDRE JOHNSON
*West Chester University,
Pennsylvania*
 Dime Novels and Story Papers

HERBERT A. JOHNSON
*University of South Carolina School of
Law*
 Supreme Court: The Marshall
  Court

PAUL E. JOHNSON
University of South Carolina
 Religion: Religion as a Political
  Issue

BARBARA M. JONES
*Rare Book/Special Collections
Library, University Of Illinois at
Urbana-Champaign*
 Clothing
 Personal Appearance

KAREN JONES
*University of Bristol, United
Kingdom*
 Nature

ERVIN L. JORDAN
University of Virginia
 Civil War: Black Soldiers
 Slavery: Slave Insurrections

HANNAH JOYNER
Gallaudet University
 Education: Education of the Blind
  and Deaf

CARMELA A. KARNOUTSOS
Jersey City State University
 New Jersey

PETER KARSTEN
University of Pittsburgh
 Law: Common Law

ROBERT KASTENBAUM
Arizona State University
 Cemeteries and Burial
 Death and Dying

MORTON KELLER
Brandeis University
 Supreme Court: The Economy

VAGEL KELLER
Carnegie Mellon University
 Steel and the Steel Industry

WALTER KENDRICK
Fordham University
 Pornography

PAUL KENS
Southwest Texas State University
 Supreme Court: The Gilded Age

JOSEPH KEY
University of Arkansas, Fayetteville
Fisheries

CLARA SUE KIDWELL
University of Oklahoma
Missions: Indian Responses to
White Missionaries

FRANK KIRKPATRICK
Trinity College, Hartford, Conn.
Evangelicalism
Millennialism and Adventism
Protestantism: Overview
Social Gospel

VERNON N. KISLING
Marston Science Library, University of Florida
Zoos

JOHN M. KLEEBERG
American Numismatic Society
Currency Policy

NANCY KOEHN
Graduate School of Business Administration, Harvard University
Consumerism and Consumption

LAWRENCE F. KOHL
University of Alabama
Jacksonian Era

MICHAEL L. KRENN
University of Miami
Alaska Purchase
Central America and the
Caribbean
Cuba
Diplomatic Corps
Filibusters
Foreign Parts
Gadsden Purchase
Haiti
Mexican Cession
Mexico
Monroe Doctrine
South America, Foreign Relations
with
Spanish-American War

KENNETH KUSMER
Temple University
Hobos, Tramps, and the Homeless
Segregation: Urban Segregation

LAWRENCE H. LARSEN
University of Missouri–Kansas City
Nebraska
St. Louis

EUGENE E. LEACH
Trinity College, Hartford, Conn.
Liberalism
Liberty

Progress, Idea of
Reform, Idea of
Republicanism

BILL LEONARD
Dean, Wake Forest Divinity School
Protestantism: Baptists

STEPHEN J. LEONARD
Metropolitan State College of Denver
Colorado
Denver

ALAN H. LESSOFF
Texas A&M University, Corpus Christi
Washington, D.C.

DAVID R. LEWIS
Utah State University
American Indians: U.S.
Government Policies
Utah

RONALD L. LEWIS
West Virginia University
Coal

SUSAN INGALLS LEWIS
State University of New York, Binghamton
Entrepreneurs, Women

KRISTE A. LINDENMEYER
Tennessee Technological University
Work: Child Labor

DONALD W. LINEBAUGH
University of Kentucky
Archaeology

JUDY LITOFF
Bryant College
Midwives

MONROE LITTLE
Indiana University–Purdue University, Indianapolis
Education: School Segregation

JAMES W. LOEWEN
*Catholic University of America
National Museum of American History*
Monuments and Memorials

EDWARD LORENZ
Alma College
Civil Service Reform
Settlement Houses
Welfare and Charity

GLORIA RICCI LOTHROP
California State University, Northridge
California

ODD S. LOVOLL
*St. Olaf College
University of Oslo*
Immigration and Immigrants:
Scandinavia and Finland

STEPHEN E. LUCAS
University of Wisconsin, Madison
Orators and Oratory

JORDAN D. LUTTRELL
Meyer Boswell Books, Inc.
Law Books

BONNIE LYNN-SHEROW
Kansas State University
American Indians: Indian
Removal

JAMES D. MCBRIDE
Arizona State University
Arizona

WILLIAM M. MCBRIDE
United States Naval Academy
Naval Technology

MAUREEN A. MCCARTHY
Independent Scholar, Toronto, Ontario, Canada
Clubs: Religious Clubs and
Organizations

JOSEPH A. MCCARTIN
Georgetown University
Labor Movement: Unions and
Strikes

BERNADETTE MCCAULEY
Hunter College, City University of New York
Hospitals

ALLEN L. MCDERMID
New York City
Slavery: Domestic Slave Trade
and Migration

ROBERT MCGLONE
University of Hawaii at Manoa
Bleeding Kansas

JAMES B. MCKEE
Michigan State University, Emeritus
Sociology

ROBERT R. MACKEY
United States Military Academy
Military Service
Military Technology
Militia, State

THOMAS C. MACKEY
University of Louisville
Courts, State and Federal

JOHN R. MCKIVIGAN
West Virginia University
    Harpers Ferry and John Brown

THOMAS MCMULLIN
University of Massachusetts, Boston
    Boston

JOHN K. MAHON
University of Florida, Emeritus
    Seminole Wars

TIMOTHY R. MAHONEY
University of Nebraska, Lincoln
    Industrialization and the Market
    Interstate Commerce
    Social Life: Urban Social Life

RICHARD J. C. MAJOR
Ames, Iowa
    South Carolina

MATTHEW J. MANCINI
Southwest Missouri State University
    Convict Leasing

MINA MAREFAT
Principal, Design Research Inc.,
Washington, D.C.
    Architecture: Vernacular
    Architecture

ROBERT MARGO
Vanderbilt University
    Labor Force

ARNOLD MARKOE
Brooklyn College, City University of
New York
    Sports: Baseball

HARVEY MARKOWITZ
D'Arcy McNickle Center for
American Indian History, The
Newberry Library
    Missions: North American Indians

DONALD B. MARTI
Indiana University, South Bend
    Country Fairs

MARTIN E. MARTY
University of Chicago, Emeritus
    Protestantism: Episcopalians
    Religion: Religion in Nineteenth-
    Century America

JULIAN MATES
C. W. Post College, Long Island
University
    Vaudeville and Burlesque

GLENNA MATTHEWS
Institute of Urban and Regional
Development, University of California,
Berkeley
    Domestic Life

PAUL H. MATTINGLY
New York University
    Education: Public Policy toward
    Education

TIMOTHY J. MEAGHER
Center for Irish Studies, Catholic
University of America
    Immigration and Immigrants:
    Ireland

DEVON A. MIHESUAH
Northern Arizona State University
    Education: Indian Schools

CHRISTOPHER L. MILLER
University of Texas–Pan American
    American Indian Societies: The
    Northwest Plateau

DAVID REED MILLER
Saskatchewan Indian Federated
College, University of Regina
    American Indian Societies: The
    Plains

H. CRAIG MINER
Wichita State University
    Kansas

JAMES C. MOHR
University of Oregon
    Reconstruction: The North

CARL H. MONEYHON
University of Arkansas at Little Rock
    Arkansas
    Reconstruction: The South

ELIZABETH BRAND MONROE
Indiana University, Indianapolis
    Civil Engineering: Bridges and
    Tunnels

R. DAN MONROE
Illinois Historical Survey, University
of Illinois at Urbana-Champaign
    Illinois

JILL G. MORAWSKI
Wesleyan University
    Psychology

MICHAEL A. MORRISON
Purdue University
    Manifest Destiny

MARIAN MORTON
John Carroll University
    Orphans and Orphanages

RICHARD P. MULCAHY
University of Pittsburgh at Titusville
    Mining and Extraction

JUSTINE S. MURISON
University of Pennsylvania
    Industry (The Work Ethic)
    Work: Domestic Labor

IAN MYLCHREEST
Surrey Hills, Victoria, Australia
    Blue Laws
    Era of Good Feeling
    History
    Idaho

THOMAS H. NEALE
The Library of Congress
    Politics: Corruption and Scandals
    Slogans, Songs, and Nicknames,
    Political
    Voters and Voting: White Male
    Franchise

DANIEL NELSON
University of Akron
    Rubber

ROGER L. NICHOLS
University of Arizona
    American Indians: American
    Indian Religions

STEVEN NOLL
University of Florida
    Asylums
    Mental Illness

RICHARD T. OAKES
Hamline University School of Law
    Firearms

KATHRYN J. OBERDECK
University of Illinois, Urbana-
Champaign
    Class, Social

GAIL W. O'BRIEN
North Carolina State University
    North Carolina

CECILIA O'LEARY
California State University at
Monterey Bay
    Nationalism: 1861–1900

ROWENA OLEGARIO
University of Michigan Business
School
    Small Businesses

SANDRA L. OLIVER
Publisher and Editor,
Food History News
    Food

PATRICK M. O'NEIL
State University of New York, Broome
Community College
    Anti-Catholicism
    Foreign Relations: 1789–1860

Great Britain, Foreign Relations
    with
Judicial Review
Nullification
Slavery: African Slave Trade
Statehood and Admission
Territorial Government

GREGORY ORFALEA
*U.S. Department of Health and
Human Services*
    Immigration and Immigrants: The
        Ottoman Empire and the
        Middle East

GREY OSTERUD
Acton, Massachusetts
    Social Life: Rural Social Life

PHILIPPE OSZUSCIK
University of South Alabama, Mobile
    Painting
    Sculpture

TED OWNBY
University of Mississippi
    Poverty

DOROTHY R. PARKER
*Eastern New Mexico University,
Emerita*
    New Mexico

DONALD E. PEASE
Dartmouth College
    Realism and Naturalism
    Romanticism

THOMAS R. PEGRAM
Loyola College in Maryland
    Progressivism

CHRISTOPHER W. PHILLIPS
University of Cincinnati
    Baltimore

MADELINE PLASENCIA
College of Law, University of Tulsa
    Homosexuality

ELIZABETH PLECK
*University of Illinois, Urbana-
Champaign*
    Holidays

DANIEL POPE
University of Oregon
    Merchandising: Chain Stores
    Merchandising: Mail Order
    Merchandising: Department
        Stores

EDWARD RAFFERTY
*Mary Baker Eddy Collections and
Library*
    Education: Graduate and
        Professional Education
    Politics: Political Thought

DONALD RAKESTRAW
Georgia Southern University
    Foreign Relations: The Civil War

JOHN DAVID RAUSCH
West Texas A&M University
    Constitutional Amendments:
        Amending the Constitution

JAMES W. REED
Rutgers University
    Sexual Morality

WILLIAM J. REESE
University of Wisconsin, Madison
    Education: Elementary and
        Secondary Schools

DAVID REICHARD
*California State University at
Monterey Bay*
    Cities and Urbanization
    Los Angeles

LEX RENDA
University of Wisconsin, Milwaukee
    Whig Party

STEVEN A. RIESS
Northeastern Illinois University
    Recreation
    Sports: Sports and the Sporting
        Life

GLENDA RILEY
Ball State University
    Divorce and Desertion
    Gender: Interpretations of Gender

ERIC W. RISE
University of Delaware
    Law: State Law

DONALD A. RITCHIE
United States Senate Historical Office
    Politics: Parties and the Press

DANA L. ROBERT
*Truman Collins Professor of World
Mission, Boston University*
    Missions: Foreign Missions

JESSICA FORBES ROBERTS
University of Michigan
    Literature: Poetry

KEVIN D. ROBERTS
University of Texas at Austin
    African Americans: Blacks in the
        West
    Education: Education of African
        Americans
    Outlaws
    South, The: The South before the
        Civil War
    Wild West Shows

AUGUSTA ROHRBACH
*Bunting Fellow, The Radcliffe
Institute for Advanced Study, Harvard
University*
    Literature: Women's Literature

FRED S. ROLATER
Middle Tennessee State University
    Border States
    Tennessee

WILLIAM J. RORABAUGH
University of Washington, Seattle
    Alcoholic Beverages
    Brewing and Distilling
    Saloons and the Drinking Life

R. B. ROSENBURG
University of North Alabama
    Civil War: Remembering the Civil
        War

WILLIAM G. ROSS
*Cumberland School of Law, Samford
University*
    Legal Profession
    Supreme Court: Supreme Court
        Justices

JOHN DAVID ROTH
Goshen College
    Protestantism: Mennonites

WILLIAM D. ROWLEY
University of Nevada, Reno
    Nevada

JUDITH V. ROYSTER
University of Tulsa
    American Indians: Law in Indian
        Communities

ROBERT O. RUHLING
George Mason University
    Health Consciousness and Fitness

JOHN RURY
DePaul University
    Education: Colleges and
        Universities

PEGGY RUSSO
*Pennsylvania State University at
Mont Alto*
    Literature: The Influence of
        Foreign Literature

ROBERT A. RUTLAND
University of Tulsa
    Presidency: 1801–1829

CAMERON L. SAFFELL
*New Mexico Farm and Ranch
Heritage Museum*
    Cowboys and Cowgirls
    Meatpacking
    Peanuts
    Ranching and Livestock Raising

ROBERT D. SAMPSON
University of Illinois, Urbana-Champaign
  Young America Movement

GARY SCHARNHORST
University of New Mexico
  Alger, Horatio

MARC J. SCHNEIBERG
University of Arizona
  Insurance

JOHN C. SCHNEIDER
Tufts University
  Detroit

FRANK SCHUMACHER
University of Erfurt, Germany
  Immigration and Immigrants:
    Germany
  Slavery: Indian Slaveholding

LARRY E. SCHWEIKART
University of Dayton
  Banking and Finance: The
    Banking Industry
  Banking and Finance: The Politics
    of Banking
  Taxation and Public Finance

DOROTHY A. SCHWIEDER
Iowa State University
  Iowa

ANDREW R. SEAGER
Ball State University
  Architecture: Professional
    Architects and Their Work

SHARON SEAGER
Ball State University
  Civil War: Women on the Front

PAUL M. SEARLS
University of Vermont
  Vermont

MILTON SERNETT
Syracuse University
  African Americans: African
    American Religions
  Underground Railroad

WALTER G. SHARROW
Canisius College, Buffalo, N.Y.
  Buffalo, N.Y.

RONALD E. SHAW
Oxford, Ohio
  Transportation: Canals and
    Waterways

JIM SHEROW
Kansas State University
  Homesteading

DAVID W. SHIDELER
University of Hawaii at Manoa
  Hawaii

PHILLIP R. SHRIVER
Miami University, Oxford, Ohio
  Ohio

DAVID SICILIA
University of Maryland
  Chemicals

JOEL H. SILBEY
Cornell University
  Politics: Party Organization and
    Operations
  Politics: The First Party System

BROOKS D. SIMPSON
Arizona State University
  Civil War: Battles and
    Combatants
  Lincoln-Douglas Debates

MELVIN SMALL
Wayne State University
  Foreign Relations: Overview

CHARLES L. SMITH
Appalachian State University
  Natural Resources

DUANE A. SMITH
Fort Lewis College
  Boomtowns

NORMAN W. SMITH
Rhode Island College
  Rhode Island

FRED SOMKIN
Cornell University
  Nationalism: 1800–1865

J. RONALD SPENCER
Trinity College, Hartford, Conn.
  Civil War: Causes of the Civil
    War

SARAH STAGE
Arizona State University
  Patent Medicines

JOHN STAUFFER
Harvard University
  Popular Culture

SUSAN M. STEINER
*Freelance Writer and Translator,
Morristown, N.J.*
  Labor Movement: People of Color

LOUISE STEVENSON
Franklin and Marshall College
  Home

STEVEN STOWE
Indiana University, Bloomington
  Health and Disease

WILLIAM W. STOWE
Wesleyan University
  Vacations and Resorts

SHARON H. STROM
Narragansett, Rhode Island
  Labor Movement: Women

LANCE J. SUSSMAN
*State University of New York,
Binghamton*
  Judaism

W. R. SWAGERTY
University of Idaho
  Fur Trade
  Hunting and Trapping

JONATHAN SWAINGER
*University of Northern British
Columbia*
  Canada
  Immigration and Immigrants:
    Canada

RICHARD E. SYLLA
*Stern School of Business, New York
University*
  Investment and Capital
    Formation

MARCY TANTER
*Tarleton State University,
Stephenville, Tex.*
  Literature: The Essay

JOHN E. TAPIA
*Missouri Western State College, St.
Joseph*
  Lyceums

MARK TEBEAU
Cleveland State University
  Disasters
  Fires and Firefighting

GORDON C. THOMASSON
*State University of New York, Broome
Community College*
  Anti-Mormonism

DANIEL B. THORP
*Virginia Polytechnic Institute and
State University*
  Expansion
  Lewis and Clark Expedition

PETER J. THUESEN
Yale University
  Bible and Bible Reading, The

BRYANT F. TOLLES
University of Delaware
  Museums: Art Museums

BENSON TONG
Wichita State University
  Chinatowns

DAVID TREVIÑO
Texas A&M University, Kingsville
  Immigration and Immigrants:
    Mexico and Latin America
  Music: Folk Songs, Parlor Music,
    and Popular Music

ERIC TSCHESCHLOK
Auburn University
  Confederate States of America
  Supreme Court: The Antebellum
    Court

LIANN TSOUKAS
University of Pittsburgh
  Law: Women and the Law

DEBORAH BINGHAM VAN
BROEKHOVEN
Ohio Wesleyan University
  Abolition and Antislavery

SANDRA F. VANBURKLEO
Wayne State University
  Contraception and Abortion
  Gender: Gender and the Law
  Republican Motherhood

LAWRENCE F. VAN HORN
*Denver Service Center, National Park
Service, U.S. Department of the
Interior*
  Exploration and Explorers

NICHOLAS VARGA
Loyola College in Maryland
  Maryland

ARTHUR VERSLUIS
Michigan State University
  Transcendentalism

DEBRA VILES
Wayne State University
  Contraception and Abortion

JOELLEN MCNERGNEY VINYARD
Eastern Michigan University
  Michigan

RUDI VOLTI
Pitzer College
  Transportation: Automobiles

ANN WAGNER
St. Olaf College, Emerita
  Dance and Ballet

JENNY BOURNE WAHL
Carleton College
  Monetary Policy
  Stock Markets

  Wealth
  Work: Factory Labor

SHIRLEY WAJDA
Kent State University
  Photography

CHRIS WALDREP
Eastern Illinois University
  Montana
  Vigilantes

HENRY WALKER
Vanderbilt University
  Alabama

NANCY A. WALKER
Vanderbilt University
  Humor

PETER WALLENSTEIN
*Virginia Polytechnic Institute and
State University*
  Appalachia
  Chain Gangs
  Emancipation
  Education: Education of the Blind
    and Deaf
  Louisiana Purchase
  Miscegenation
  New England
  New Hampshire
  Richmond
  Segregation: Segregation and Civil
    Rights
  Slavery: Overview
  South, The: The New South after
    Reconstruction
  Virginia

JAMES D. WATKINSON
Randolph-Macon College
  Clubs: Fraternal Societies and
    Clubs

LOUIS WEEKS
*Union Theological Seminary and
Presbyterian School of Christian
Education, Richmond, Va.*
  Protestantism: Presbyterians

MARK K. WELLS
United States Air Force Academy
  Balloons

MICHAEL C. WENDL
*School of Medicine, Washington
University*
  Mathematics and Numeracy

DOROTHY C. WERTZ
*Shriver Center for Mental
Retardation, Inc.*
  Birth and Childbearing

ELLIOT WEST
University of Arkansas, Fayetteville
  Games and Toys, Children's
  Indian Territory

FRANK T. WHEELER
Tusculum College
  Dueling
  Gunfighters

JAMES C. WILLIAMS
De Anza College
  Civil Engineering: Sewage and
    Sanitation
  Electricity

JOHN ALEXANDER WILLIAMS
Appalachian State University
  West Virginia

LOU FAULKNER WILLIAMS
Kansas State University
  Ku Klux Klan

PETER W. WILLIAMS
Miami University, Oxford, Ohio
  Protestantism: Liberal
    Protestantism

VERNON J. WILLIAMS
Purdue University
  Anthropology

JOHN WILLS
*University of Bristol, United
Kingdom*
  Geography and Ecology

BRUCE WINDERS
Historian and Curator, The Alamo
  Mexican War

CARY WINTZ
Texas Southern University
  Literature: African American
    Literature
  Texas

GAIL WOLDU
Trinity College, Hartford, Conn.
  Music: Spirituals and African
    American Music

SHARON E. WOOD
University of Nebraska, Omaha
  Prostitution

DONALD R. WRIGHT
*State University of New York,
Cortland*
  African Americans: Overview

DAVID M. WROBEL
Widener University
  Frontier
  Interpretations of the Nineteenth
    Century: Popular
    Interpretations of the Frontier
    West

JOHN R. WUNDER
University of Nebraska, Lincoln
Great Plains

WANG XI
Indiana University of Pennsylvania
Voters and Voting: Black Voters
after the Civil War

JEFF YOUNG
Georgia Southern University
Plantation, The

CHARLES YRIGOYEN
*Theological and Graduate Schools,
Drew University*
Protestantism: Methodists

SUSAN ZAESKE
University of Wisconsin, Madison
Orators and Oratory

SCOTT ZEMAN
*New Mexico Institute of Mining and
Technology*
West, The

Index

Page numbers in boldface refer to the main entry on the subject.
Page numbers in italics refer to illustrations, figures, tables, and maps.

A

Abbey, Edward, 2:387
Abbot, Francis Ellingwood, 3:38, 322
Abbot, J. Stephen, 2:414; 3:311
Abbott, Charles, 2:179
Abbott, Edith, 3:147
Abbott, Emma, 2:376
Abbott, Grace, 3:146
Abbott, John, 1:408
Abbott, Lyman, 1:445
Abdülhamid II, 2:93
Abe Lincoln in Illinois (film), 2:124
Abenakis (Abenaquis), 1:85; 3:327
Abolition and antislavery, 1:1–7, 430–
  432; 3:89–90
  anti-Mormonism and, 1:99–100
  attacks on abolitionists, 1:4
  in border states, 1:157–158
  in Boston, 1:159–160
  in Cincinnati, 1:206
  Civil War and, 1:236, 255
  Compromise of 1850 and, 1:296–
    298
  constitutional amendments, 1:313–
    317
  essays on, 2:209
  evangelicalism and, 1:442
  foreign missions and, 2:347
  gag rule against, 1:143, *144*
  legal system and, 2:169
  Mexican War and, 2:301
  in the Mid-Atlantic states, 2:314
  millennialism in, 2:331
  in minstrel shows, 2:342
  Missouri Compromise and, 3:136–
    137
  in New England, 2:272; 3:134, 328
  and newspapers, 2:420, 423, 543
  in Ohio, 2:450
  in political culture, 2:507
  religion and, 1:281
  republicanism and, 3:104
  runaway slaves, 3:165
  Secret Six, 2:15
  in the South, 3:192–193
    southern laws against, 3:163

telegraph and, 1:289
temperance movement and, 3:266
women and, 1:532; 3:90, 349–350
women in, 3:400–401
Abortion, 1:327–328, 536
  Comstock and, 2:430
  criminalization of, 2:177; 3:149
  fertility rates and, 2:535
  prostitution and, 3:16
Abraham, 3:171
Abraham Lincoln (Barnard), 3:131
Abstinence, 3:266
Academic and professional societies,
  1:7–9
Academies, 1:391
  for women, 1:401, 408
Accounting
  railroad use of, 3:53
  rise of corporations and, 1:332, 333,
    334
Acheson, Edward G., 2:129
Across the Continent (Bowles), 3:378
Actuarial methods, 1:469–470
Adams, Abigail Smith, 1:472, 473
Adams, Alvin, 3:312
Adams, Andy, 2:117
Adams, Charles Francis, 1:508–509
Adams, Charles Kendall, 1:403
Adams, Henry, 1:25; 2:25–26, 556;
  3:48
  Democracy: An American Novel,
    1:545
  Education of Henry Adams, The,
    1:545–546
  on progress, 3:12
Adams, Herbert Baxter, 2:25–26;
  3:48
Adams, John
  as attorney, 2:168
  background of, 3:388
  on cider, 1:48
  corruption charges against, 2:521
  death of, 2:141
  Declaration of Independence and,
    2:270
  election of, 1:422

electoral college and, 1:313
as Federalist, 1:457
foreign relations under, 1:504
Library of Congress and, 2:192
on Madison, 2:556
at Massachusetts constitutional
  convention, 3:343
Mercy Otis Warren and, 3:106
navy created by, 2:2
on the novel, 2:529
partisanship and, 1:438; 2:551
Sedition Act of 1798 and, 1:143
transfer of power from, 2:435
U.S. Marine Band and, 1:131
Adams, John Quincy, 2:270, *557*
  abolitionist gag rule and, 1:4
  Adams-Onís Treaty and, 2:295
  Alaska and, 1:47
  cabinet of, 1:167
  Cuba and, 1:355
  in diplomatic corps, 1:374
  1828 election, 1:423
  electoral college and, 1:305
  as elitist, 3:389
  on gag rules, 1:320
  George Washington and, 3:361
  Jackson and, 1:363; 2:513
  Jefferson and, 2:140
  on Manifest Destiny, 2:248
  Mexican War and, 2:301
  Monroe Doctrine and, 1:*505*, 505–
    506; 2:358–359
  on observatories, 1:124
  opposition to abolitionist gag rule,
    1:*144*
  presidency of, 2:556–557
  Quadruple Alliance and, 2:6
  removal treaty and, 1:543–544
  as secretary of state, 1:502; 2:556
  on South America, 3:198, 199
  War of 1812 and, 1:504; 2:3;
    3:360
Adams, Louisa Catherine Johnson,
  1:*472*, 473
Adams, Robert, 1:*372*
Adams Female Academy, 1:409

prostitution and, 3:16
qualities attributed to, 2:252
racial thinking and, 3:45–50
racist depictions of, 3:413
radicalism and, 3:51
Reconstruction and, 3:63, 69–70, 193–194
in reform, 3:84
religion and, 3:98
  Baptist, 3:20, 33–34, 95
  Episcopalian, 3:20
  Methodist, 3:20, 27–29
  Presbyterian, 3:25, 26
  Quaker, 3:42
  religious organizations, 1:281
  revivalism, 3:113
rural social life of, 3:179–180
in San Francisco, 3:128
in San Juan, 3:*208*
small businesses and, 3:176
social life and, 3:186–187
spirituals, 2:374
sports and, 3:213
  in baseball, 3:*216*, 218
as strikebreakers, 2:52
"stylin' " among, 1:277
suffrage, 3:343, *348*
  voters after the Civil War, 3:345–349
  voters before the Civil War, 3:344–345
in Texas, 3:273, 275
and Underground Railroad, 3:319–320
and vacationing, 3:325
and Victorian character, 3:330
violence toward, 3:74–75
in Virginia, 3:336
Virginians, 3:336–337
in Washington, D.C., 3:364–365
in the West, 3:79–80, 383
women
  clubs, 1:280; 3:404
  organizations, 3:405
  roles, 1:531, 537
African Methodist Episcopal Church, 3:27
bishops of, 1:*30*
founded, 1:23
missionaries from, 1:12–13, 31
organization of, 1:30–31
African Methodist Episcopal Zion Church, 3:28
Africans in racial hierarchy, 1:498
Afro-American, 2:427
Afterglow (La Farge), 2:467
After the Hunt (Harnett), 2:467
Agassiz, Louis, 1:*19*, 146; 3:325
as anti-Darwinian, 1:444
ethnology and, 1:96

Museum of Comparative Zoology, 2:371
Age, median, 2:532, 534
Age of Anxiety, 2:303–307
Age of consent, 3:17
Age of Excess (Ginger), 1:546
Age of Innocence, The (film), 2:124
Age of Innocence, The (Wharton), 2:219
Age of Reform, 3:89
Agrarian parties, 1:547
Agrarian revolt, 1:42–43
  in Arkansas, 1:113
Agrarian revolution, 2:107
Agricultural censuses, 2:532
Agricultural implements manufacture, 1:201
  in Chicago, 1:199
Agricultural Museum (journal), 2:242
Agricultural technology, 1:32–36; 2:127–128
  haying machinery, 1:*39*
  markets and, 2:107
Agricultural Wheel, 1:113; 2:540
Agriculture, 1:36–44
  in Arizona, 1:112
  big companies in, 3:381–382
  in California, 2:230
  as chief source of wealth, 3:423
  city planning and, 1:217
  during Civil War, 1:257, 263
  crop-lien system, 2:287
  crop rotation, 1:540
  dairy products, 3:328
  defeat of agrarian reform, 3:85
  division of labor in, 3:179
  ecological effects of, 1:540
  fairs and, 1:341–342
  family in, 3:414
  in Florida, 1:477
  foreign relations and, 1:512
  the Gilded Age and, 1:547
  on the Great Plains, 1:459–460
  Hatch Act and, 1:406
  hired workers in, 3:414–416
  Hispanics in, 2:166
  immigrants in, 3:415–416
    Arab, 2:94
    British, 2:74, 75
    Eastern European, 2:83
    Mexican, 2:96–97
    Scandinavian, 2:88
  impact of on the Civil War, 1:241
  Jacksonian era, 2:137
  in Kentucky, 2:150–151
  labor in, 3:414–417
  market farming, 2:107
  market revolution and, 2:261–262
  in Michigan, 2:311–312
  in the Mid-Atlantic states, 2:313

in the Midwest, 2:319
migrant workers in, 2:26, 54
in Missouri, 2:351
Native Americans and, 1:72, 75
natural resource utilization in, 2:391
in Nebraska, 2:407–408
in New Hampshire, 2:415
newspapers on, 2:420
in New York, 2:432
in Ohio, 2:450
panic of 1873 and, 2:472–473
percent of labor force in, 1:36
Populism and, 2:538–541
ranching and livestock, 3:57–60
sectionalism and, 3:136
shift of labor from, 2:156
slaves in, 3:416
in St. Louis, 3:123
tariffs and, 1:517
transformation of, 2:434–435
in Virginia, 3:339
War of 1812 and, 3:357, 359
wealth and, 3:371
in the West, 3:135
in West Virginia, 3:384
women in, 3:407
Agriculture, Department of, 1:40–41, 555
cabinet status of, 1:167
Division of Forestry, 1:310–311
road management by, 3:297
Aguinaldo, Emilio, 1:121; 2:*13*, 459
Aid to Dependent Children, 2:11, 456
Aiken, George L., 2:222
Akimel O'odham, 1:93–94
Alabama, 1:44–45
Black Belt region of, 1:336–337
plantations in, 2:500
segregation in, 3:139
state banks in, 1:138
Alabama, 1:176, 512; 2:403, 414
claims, 1:177; 2:5
Alaska, 1:45–47
acquisition of, 1:450
boundary disputes, 1:178, 515
citizenship and, 2:64
ecological damage in, 1:552
fur trade, 1:526
gold in, 1:549–550; 2:473; 3:367
Manifest Destiny and, 2:250–251
Native Americans in, 1:94
Russian Orthodox church in, 2:84
seal hunting in, 2:46
Skagway, 1:552
Alaska Purchase, 1:47–48
Alaska Territory, 3:352
Albany Evening Journal, 2:517
Albany Lyceum of Natural History, 1:146

Bickley, George W. L., 1:*124*
Bicycling, 1:142; 3:120–121, 211, *211*
  road improvements and, 3:297
Biddle, Nicholas, 1:356; 2:337, 353
  Bank of the United States and, 1:134–135
  panic of 1819 and, 2:469
Bidwell-Bartleson party, 1:169
Bierce, Ambrose
  Tales of Soldiers and Civilians, 2:207
  Tales of Soldiers and Courage, 1:264
Bierstadt, Albert, 1:521; 2:393, 463
  Rocky Mountains, The, 2:464, *466*
Bigamy, 2:264
Bigelow, Jacob, 2:360
Big Foot, 1:58, 70; 3:383–384
Biglow Papers, The (Lowell), 2:44, 302
Billings, Josh Shaw, 2:191
Bill of Rights, 1:142–145, 232–233
  constitutional law and, 1:318
  limits on power in, 1:552
Billy the Kid, 1:522; 2:11
  as outlaw, 2:458
Bimetallic monetary standard, 1:357; 2:355, 541
Bingham, George Caleb, 1:*520*, 521; 2:138, 226
  Fur Traders Descending the Missouri River, 2:464
Bingham, Hiram, 2:16
Bingham, John Armour, 1:143, *305*
  Fourteenth Amendment and, 1:315–316
Bingham, Kingsley, 2:311
Biographical Memoir of Daniel Boone, The (Flint), 1:521
Biographies, 2:124, 215
  political, 3:172
Biological Survey of the United States, 2:48
Biology, 1:145–147
Bird, Isabella, 1:489, 491–492
Bird, Robert Montgomery, 3:284
Birmingham, Alabama, 1:*211*
  industry in, 3:195–196
  steel in, 1:540; 3:*194*, 230
Birney, James G., 1:5, 157, 206; 2:450; 3:285
  African colonization and, 1:287
  American Anti-Slavery Society and, 1:3
  American Churches, The: The Bulwarks of American Slavery, 1:4
Birth and childbearing, 1:147–150
Birth control, 1:148
  Comstock Act and, 1:145; 2:542
  fertility rates and, 2:535
  laws on, 2:177

prostitution and, 3:16
  and women's rights, 1:532, 536, 537
Birth of a Nation, The (film), 2:121, *122*, 153
Birthrates, 2:436
Bishallany, Antonios, 2:92
Bison
  annihilation of, 2:9
  conservation and, 1:310
  fur trade and, 1:525, 526
  railroad's impact on, 1:54
Bituminous coal, 1:282; 2:333–334
Bjørnson, Bjørnstjerne, 1:495
Black, Frank, 1:164
Black ball ships, 3:312
Black belt region, 1:336–337; 3:197
Black-billed Cuckoo (Audubon), 2:463
Black Brigade of Cincinnati, 1:250
"Black Cat, The" (Poe), 2:205
Black codes, 3:71, 346
  Fourteenth Amendment and, 1:315–316
  poverty and, 2:548
  Reconstruction and, 1:19; 3:64
  segregation and, 3:138
Black communities, 3:383
Black Crook, The, 1:360
Black Elk, 2:346
Blackfeet, 2:8
Black Friday, 3:234
Black Hawk, 1:79, 88; 2:104; 3:394
  Catlin's painting of, 2:464
  resistance of, 1:52, 65–66
Black Hawk War (1832), 1:79, 115; 2:50; 3:394
  militias in, 2:322, 329
Black Hills (South Dakota), 2:7
  gold in, 1:549, 552
  mining of, 1:542
Black Kettle, 1:69
Black Legend, 3:198–199
Black-lung disease, 2:335
Black powder, 1:198
Black rule, 3:73–75
Blacksmiths, 3:420
  slaves as, 3:160
Blackstone, William, 2:168, 176, 179, 180
Black towns, 1:25; 3:80
Blackwell, Alice, 2:244
Blackwell, Elizabeth, 1:149; 2:283; 3:401, 405, 409
Blackwell, Henry
  on marriage, 1:531
  marriage to Stone, 3:401–402
  woman suffrage and, 3:403
Bladensburg Races, 2:328
Blagden, George, 1:*106*
Blaine, James G., 1:306; 2:248; 3:108, 329

Cleveland and, 2:579
  as Democrat, 1:367
  Garfield and, 2:579
  nicknames of, 3:174
  Pan-American Congress, 1:512
  on South America, 3:200
  as speaker of the House, 1:553
Blair, Francis P., 2:517
Blair, Francis Preston, Jr., 1:365
Blair, Henry W., 1:465
Blair, Montgomery, 1:290
Blair, Walter, 2:42
Blair bill, 1:465
Blake; or, The Huts of America (Delany), 2:220
Blakelock, Ralph, 2:467
Blak Hills Pioneer (newspaper), 2:424
Blanchet, François, 2:454
Bland, James, 2:381
Bland-Allison Act (1878), 1:357; 2:579
  panic of 1893 and, 2:472
Blassingame, John W., 1:14–15
Blast furnaces, 3:228
Blatchford, Samuel, 1:345; 3:*255*
Bleaches, 1:198, 199
Bleeding Kansas, 1:150, 158; 2:9; 3:273
  abolitionism and, 1:5
  Missouri and, 2:350–351
  Missouri Compromise and, 2:353
  violence of, 1:350; 3:218–219
Blind education, 1:416–417; 2:411; 3:375
  asylums and, 1:127
  in Massachusetts, 2:271–272
  segregation in, 3:140
Bliss, Betty, 1:473
Bliss, William D. P., 3:21, 178
Blister steel, 3:229–230
Blithedale Romance, The (Hawthorne), 1:294; 2:204; 3:118
Blodget, Samuel, 2:534
Bloodletting, 2:278–279, 284
Blood transfusions, 1:149
Bloody shirt campaigns, 1:265
Bloomer, Amelia Jenks, 1:274, *274*, 277; 3:401
  Lily, 2:246
  temperance and, 2:31
Bloomers, 1:274, *274*; 3:*211*
  bicycling and, 1:142
Blue-Backed Speller (Webster), 1:393
Blue books, 3:184
Blue Hole, Flood Waters, Little Miami River, The (Duncanson), 2:467
Blue laws, 1:151; 3:93, 101
  sports and, 3:213
Blues music, 2:381
Blumenbach, Johann F., 1:95; 3:45–46

state law and, 2:172
  Supreme Court on, 2:170; 3:243,
    247, 251–252, 256
Duer, William, 3:232
Dugdale, Richard, 3:373
Dulles, John Foster, 2:117
Dumas, Francis E., 1:251
Dumbbell tenements, 1:218
Dunbar, Paul Laurence, 2:211, 213,
  214, 220
Dunbar-Nelson, Alice, 2:218
Duncan, John, 2:361
Duncanson, Robert Stuart, 2:467
Duniway, Abigail Scott, 2:454
Dunlap, William, 3:283
Dunmore, Lord, 1:1, 430
Du Pont company, 1:158
Du Pont family, 1:198; 2:77
Dupuy de Lôme, Enrique, 3:205
Durand, Asher Brown, 2:463; 3:117
  nationalism and, 2:384
Durrie, George Henry, 2:224
Duryea, Charles E., 2:129; 3:311
Duryea, J. Frank, 2:129; 3:311
Duse, Eleonora, 3:283
Duvall, Gabriel, 3:238
Duveneck, Frank, 2:466
Duyckinck, Evert A., 2:204
  Young America Movement and,
    3:436–437
Duyckinck, George, 2:204
Dvořák, Antonin, 2:374
Dwight, John Sullivan, 2:373, 374
Dwight, Theodore, 3:6
Dwight, Timothy, 2:529
  "America," 2:248
Dyestuffs, 1:198–199, 273
Dying Tecumseh, The (Pettrich),
  1:83
Dynamic psychiatry, 2:285
Dynamic Sociology (Ward), 1:446;
  3:187
Dyniewicz, Wladyslaw, 2:84

E

Eads, James, 1:226
Eakins, Thomas, 2:465, 466–467, 489
  Clinic of Dr. Gross, The, 2:467
Early, Jubal, 1:247
Earnings Acts (1860, 1868), 2:176
Earp, Wyatt, 2:458
  as gunfighter, 2:11–12
  O.K. Corral gunfight, 1:155
Earthquakes, 1:376, 379
Eastern Orthodox Christians, 3:98
Eastern Trunk Line Association,
  3:314
Eastman, George, 2:128, 498–499
  popular photography and, 2:530–
    531

East Side Railway, 3:309
Eastwood, Clint, 2:118, 122
Eaton, Dorman, 3:85, 88
Eaton, William, 2:401
  Tripolitan War and, 1:139
Eclectic physicians, 2:279
École des Beaux-Arts, 1:105, 108;
  2:466
  sculpture and, 3:131
Ecology, science of, 1:147
Economic development
  in Canada, 1:172
  Civil War and, 1:254–255, 263–
    264
  constitutional law and, 1:321–322
  consumerism and, 1:324–327
  general stores and, 2:286–287
  labor force, 2:155
  Midwest and, 2:315
  railroads and, 1:487–488
  Supreme Court on, 3:239–240, 249–
    254
  workshops and, 3:421–422
Economic mobility, 2:537
Economic regulation, 1:387–388
Economics
  among slaves, 3:156
  domestic life and, 1:382–383
  Gilded Age and, 1:547, 555–556
  government assistance in, 1:554
  households, 2:29–30, 38
  idea of progress and, 3:12–13
  immigration and, 2:54
  industrialization and markets in,
    2:106–110
  insurance and, 2:112–114
  investment and capital formation,
    2:129–131
  liberalism and, 2:184–186
  proslavery arguments and, 3:169–
    170
  of slavery, 3:150–151
  vernacular architecture and,
    1:110
Economic theory, 1:388–390
Economies of scale, 2:109
Ecumenical Missionary Conference,
  2:348
Eddy, Mary Baker, 1:205; 2:414;
  3:99
  health consciousness of, 2:23
  *Science and Health with Key to the
    Scriptures*, 1:205, *205*
*Edgar Huntly; or, Memoirs of a Sleep-
  Walker* (Brown), 2:202
Edgerton, Sidney, 2:360
Edison, Thomas A., 1:*428*; 2:128
  incandescent lighting and, 1:427–
    428
  kinetoscope, 3:211

laboratories of, 2:373, 415
  movies and, 2:365
  telephone and, 3:265
Edison Electric Company, 2:41
Edmonds, Sarah, 1:253
Edmunds, John, 3:208
Edmunds Act (1882), 1:100; 3:221,
  324
Edmunds-Tucker Act (1887), 1:100;
  3:221, 324
Education, 1:390–419
  anti-Catholic sentiment and, 2:66
  in architecture, 1:105
  assimilation role of, 2:91
  Baptist, 3:32
  in Boston, 1:159, 161
  childhood and, 2:194
  Cincinnati as center of, 1:206
  civil engineering, 1:222
  cult of true womanhood and, 3:396–
    397
  economic theory in, 1:388–389
  federalism and, 1:465
  federal land-grant system
    in Virginia, 3:338
  geography, 1:538–539
  German, 2:77
  German immigrant, 2:80
  government support of, 3:78, 390
  graduate, 1:158
  the grand tour and, 2:1, 2
  in Ireland, 2:70
  land grants for, 1:554
  legal, 1:8; 2:169, 181
  liberty and, 2:188
  library, 2:192
  local government in, 2:229
  lyceums and, 2:236–238
  Mann and, 1:159
  in mathematics, 2:273
  medical, 1:7; 2:20, 21–22
  in medicine, 2:278, 280, 281
  Methodism and, 3:29
  in the Midwest, 2:318
  in midwifery, 2:320
  military, 1:117, 118
  museums and, 2:368, 369–373
  music, 2:375
  nationalism and, 2:385
  Native American, 1:77; 2:346
  naval officer, 2:403–404
  in New England, 2:411
  in North Carolina, 2:439
  in nursing, 2:37
  oratory in, 2:452–453
  parochial, 1:184–185, 186
  preparatory schools, 3:79
  professional, 3:8
  professionalization and, 1:8
  progressivism and, 3:13

R

R. G. Dunn and Company, 1:435
Rabelais, François, 2:223
Raccoons, hunting and trapping, 2:46
Race
  AFL and, 2:162
  childhood and, 2:195
  cultural constructions of, 1:269–270
  hierarchies of, 1:497–498
  homosexuality and, 2:34
  labor force structure and, 2:157
  politics and, 2:505, 506–507
  proslavery arguments and, 3:168–169
  South America and, 3:198–199
  third party system and, 2:515–517
  urbanization and, 1:215
Race and Revolution (Nash), 1:1
Race relations
  in Charleston, 1:198
  in the Civil War, 1:259
  emancipation and, 1:429
  federalism and, 1:466
  in firefighting, 1:469
  foreign observers on, 1:493–494
  nationalism and, 2:386–387
  planters and poor whites and, 3:191–192
  in the South, 3:161
  Whigs on, 3:390–391
Racism, 2:436
  Addams and, 3:146
  anthropology and, 1:95–95
  asylums and, 1:127
  in capital punishment, 1:180
  in cemeteries, 1:188
  Democratic Party and, 1:365–366
  exceptionalism and, 1:231
  expansionism and, 1:237
  Haiti and, 2:13
  idea of progress and, 3:12
  immigrant policy and, 2:62–66
  Jewish immigrants and, 2:65
  lynching and, 2:238–239
  Manifest Destiny and, 1:502; 2:251–252
  Mexican Cession and, 2:294–295
  Mexico and, 2:305
  in the Mid-Atlantic states, 2:313–314
  militias and, 2:323
  in minstrel shows, 2:342, 531
  in the North, 3:76
  the Philippines and, 1:121
  race laws, 3:50–51
  racial thinking, 3:45–50
  scientific, 1:21
  social life and, 3:179–180

South America and, 3:198, 200
  in welfare/charity, 3:377
Radicalism, 3:51–53
  in New York, 2:432–433
  saloons and, 3:126
Radical Reconstruction, 1:316–317
Radical Republicans
  GAR and, 3:328
  Reconstruction and, 1:19
  support of black enfranchisement, 3:346
  in Washington, D.C., 3:365
Radio, 1:291
Ragged Dick (Alger), 1:51; 2:111, 215, 253; 3:426
Railroads, 3:53–57, 302–307, *303 map*
  African, 1:13
  in Alabama, 1:44
  animal power in, 3:294
  Appalachia and, 1:103
  boom after the Civil War, 3:76
  boomtowns and, 1:155
  in Buffalo, 1:164
  building technology and, 1:221
  in California, 1:170
  in Canada, 1:177
  cartography and, 1:539
  in Chicago, 1:*200*; 2:51
  Chinese labor on, 2:97–98
  circuses and, 1:209
  city planning and, 1:217
  Cleveland and, 2:581
  coal industry and, 1:282–283, 284; 2:334
  commuter, 2:434
  consumerism and, 1:324
  in Detroit, 1:371
  electric railways, 3:116, 309
  elevated railways, 3:226, *309*, 309–310
  entrepreneurs in, 1:433–434
  federal land policy and, 1:460
  foreign investment in, 1:487–488
  foreign observers and, 1:489
  gauge in, 3:305–306
  in Georgia, 1:544
  the Gilded Age and, 1:547
  government funding of, 2:114–116
  immigration and, 2:54–55
  impact on buffalo, 1:54
  in Indiana, 2:101, 102
  Indian lands and, 1:76, 261
  in Indian Territory, 2:105
  industrialization and markets and, 2:109
  in Iowa, 2:131
  iron industry and, 2:133–135
  Italian immigrants and, 2:*91*
  in Kansas, 2:148
  Kansas City as rail hub, 2:148

in Kentucky, 2:151
  land grants and, 3:93
  locomotives, 3:229
  logging and, 2:233, 235, 338
  lyceum lecturers and, 2:237
  mail and, 1:289; 2:544, *545*
  mail order and, 2:289
  market revolution and, 2:262, 263
  meatpacking and, 2:275–277
  Mexican immigrants in, 2:96
  in Mexico, 2:308–309
  Midwest and, 2:318
  military technology and, 2:327
  in Minnesota, 2:340
  national parks and, 2:388
  in Nebraska, 2:408
  in Nevada, 2:408
  in New Mexico, 2:416
  in New York, 2:431
  in North Carolina, 2:439
  in North Dakota, 2:441
  notes issued by, 1:134
  in Ohio, 2:450
  orphan trains and, 2:456
  panic of 1873 and, 2:472; 3:77
  paper currency and, 2:357
  passenger coaches, 3:306
  passenger service, 3:304
  peddler car service, 2:276
  in Pennsylvania, 2:480
  pools, 3:314
  public mistrust of, 3:306
  publishing and, 1:25, 152
  refrigerated cars, 2:275–276; 3:58
  regulation of, 1:387; 2:126, 171; 3:87, 94
  rise of corporations and, 1:331–333
  scheduling, 1:289
  sectionalism and, 3:302
  section workers, 2:26
  securities, 3:234
  settlement encouraged by, 1:542; 2:8
  in the South, 3:192, 194
  sports and, 3:210
  St. Louis and, 3:123
  Standard Oil and, 2:487
  state law and, 2:172
  steam-powered, 3:225, 312
  steel in, 3:227, 228–230
  strikes in, 3:12, 51, 54
  suburbs and, 3:*235*, 236
  Supreme Court on, 1:322; 3:252
  tort law and, 2:175
  track design, 3:304–305
  transcontinental, 3:305–306
    completion of, 3:*54*, 56–57
    federal land policy and, 1:460
    Washington state and, 3:367
  urbanization and, 1:211

Mexico under, 2:307
Texas Revolution and, 2:*304*
Santa Barbara, 1:140
Santa Fe, 2:298
Santa Fe Trail, 2:416; 3:288, 289,
297
in Missouri, 2:350
Santa Fe Trail (film), 2:120
Sante, Luc, 1:9
Santee and Cooper Canal, 3:299
Santees, 1:68
Santo Domingo, 1:192
occupied by Spanish, 2:14
Sapir, Edward, 1:97
Sara Crewe (Burnett), 2:215
Sargent, Charles Sprague, 2:476
Sargent, Dudley, 2:24; 3:213
Sargent, John Singer, 2:465, 489
Sarmiento, Domingo, 1:491, 495
Saroyan, William, 2:93
My Name Is Aram, 2:94
Sartain, John, 2:226
Saturday Evening Gazette (magazine),
2:241
Saturday Evening Post (magazine),
1:371; 2:242
Saturday Review of Literature
(periodical), 3:*332*
Sauks, 1:115
in Iowa, 2:131
removal of, 1:65
trade allies of, 1:52
war dance of, 1:*67*
in Wisconsin, 3:394
Savage, James D., 1:67
Savages, Indians as, 1:82–84
Savannah (ship), 1:169; 2:258
Saw-making industry, 2:74
Sawmills, 2:232–233
Say, J. B., 1:388
Sayer, Pierre-Guillaume, 1:175
Scalawags, 1:*262*; 3:72, 73
Scandinavian immigrants, 2:86–88
in Chicago, 1:200
in the Midwest, 1:540; 2:317
numbers of, 2:58
settlement patterns of, 2:56, 59
stereotypes of, 1:498
Scarlet Letter, The (Hawthorne),
1:234; 2:204
Schechter, Solomon, 2:143
Schley, Winfield S., 2:406
Schmucker, Samuel Simon, 3:34
Schoellkopf, Jacob, 1:164
Scholte, Hendrik, 2:76
Schools. *See* Education
*Schooners before Approaching Storm
off Owl's Head* (Lane), 2:464
Schroeder, John Frederick, 3:363
Schultz, Stanley, 1:216

Schurz, Carl, 2:80, 185–186; 3:85, 88
Ute War and, 1:70
Schuyler, David, 1:209
Schwartz, Anna, 2:472
Schweninger, Loren, 3:164
Science
education in, 1:403, 406
evangelicalism and, 1:443
exploration and, 1:451–456
food and, 1:485–486
foreign observers and, 1:490–491
history as, 2:26
medical, 2:281–282
in medicine, 2:21–22
museums, 2:369–373
of ranching, 3:58–59
response to evolution, 1:444–445
view of foreign parts in, 1:499
*Science and Health with Key to the
Scriptures* (Eddy), 1:205, *205*
Science (journal), 1:8
Science of Wealth, The (Walker),
1:389
Scientific American (magazine), 1:222;
2:*128*
Scoops, 1:353
Scopes, John Thomas, 1:445
Scorsese, Martin, 2:124
Scott, Dred, 3:247–249
Scott, Harvey, 2:454
Scott, Orange, 3:28
Scott, Tom, 2:480
Scott, Walter
influence of, 2:221–222
monument of, 2:360
Waverly, 2:203
Scott, Winfield, 1:*115*, 364; 2:*296*
Anaconda Plan, 1:241
in the Civil War, 1:116
Compromise of 1850 and, 1:297,
297
Mexican War and, 1:116; 2:298,
299–301, 302
navy and, 2:403
Pierce and, 2:567
second party system and, 2:514
Southern perceptions of, 3:391
Trist and, 2:301
in the War of 1812, 1:114
Scottish immigrants, 2:75
in coal industry, 1:284
language and, 2:167
numbers of, 2:73
Scouts of the Prairies (play), 1:521
Scribner's (magazine), 1:428; 2:210,
243, 244
Scribner's Monthly (magazine), 1:153
Scripps, E. W., 2:518
Scripture, E. W., 3:39
Scudder, John, 1:145–146; 2:370, 371

Scudder, Vida, 3:21
Sculpture, 3:129–131. *See also*
Monuments and memorials
Seabury, Samuel, 3:19–20
Sea Cotton, 1:336
Sea Gull, 2:396
Seals, 2:48
hunting, 1:526; 2:46
in Alaska, 1:46
Aleuts and, 1:94
trapping, 2:46
Sealsfield, Charles, 1:495
Seaman's Aid Society, 2:246
Seamen
controversy, 2:444
impressment of, 1:171, 504–505;
2:553
War of 1812 and, 3:356
Sea otters, hunting and trapping of,
2:46
Searchers, The (film), 2:122
Sears, Richard W., 2:52, 289
Sears, Roebuck and Company, 1:325,
334; 2:263, 289–290, *290*; 3:211
Seattle, 1:213; 3:131–132
Secchi de Casali, Giovanni Francesco,
2:90
Secession
Buchanan and, 2:570
Civil War and, 1:262, 464–465
the Hartford Convention and, 2:*28*,
29, 409
Lincoln and, 1:239–240, 464
in Mississippi, 2:349
Missouri Compromise and, 2:352
Reconstruction and, 3:62–63
in South Carolina, 3:202
states' rights and, 1:461–462; 3:222,
223
Second American Party System,
1:364
Second Bank of the United States,
1:134–135; 2:115
bond defaults and, 3:233
era of good feeling and, 1:438
Jackson and, 1:363–364
monopoly rights of, 1:138
National Republicans and, 3:389
panic of 1819 and, 2:469–470
recharter of, 1:134–135
uniform currency and, 2:263
Second Confiscation and Militia Act
(1862), 1:249–250
Second Cumberland Presbyterian
Church, 3:25
Second Great Awakening, 1:441–442;
3:18, 95, 112
asylums and, 1:126, 127
Baptists and, 3:31, 32
blue laws and, 1:151

548   Index

Washington Monument, 2:361, *362,* 363, 388; 3:364

Washington Monument Society, 3:362

Washington State
  communitarian groups in, 1:295
  woman suffrage in, 3:352

Water
  city planning and, 1:218
  conservation of, 1:311
  sewage and sanitation, 1:228–230
  tunnels, 1:227

Water cures, 2:23

Waterhouse, Benjamin, 2:279–280

Water law, 2:168
  state law and, 2:172

Waterpower, 3:367–370
  in cotton, 1:338
  in Minnesota, 2:340
  steam and, 3:224

Waterways, 3:297–301

Waterwheels, 3:367–368

Watie, Stand, 1:261

Watkins, Frances Ellen
  African colonization and, 1:287

Watson, Elkanah, 1:340

Watson, Thomas A., 1:427

Watson, Thomas E., 1:544; 2:540, 541

Watt, James, 3:224, 302

Waud, A. R., 3:*72*

Waverly (Scott), 2:203

Wayland, Francis
  Elements of Political Economy, 1:388
  reforms at Brown by, 1:401

Wayland, J. A., 1:295

Wayne, Anthony, 1:52

Wayne, James M., 3:255, 257

Wayne, John, 2:117, 121

Ways and Means Committee, 1:304, 305

Wayside Press, 1:154

"Way to Wealth, The" (Franklin), 2:110

Wealth, 3:370–372
  agricultural, 3:423
  distribution of, 2:537
  Episcopalian church and, 3:21
  foreign observers on, 1:492–493
  inequities of, 2:189
  philanthropy and, 2:489–494
  Protestant views of, 3:19
  reform and, 3:90
  rise of corporations and, 1:335
  Social Gospel and, 3:176–177
  women's, 1:536

"Wealth" (Carnegie), 2:492

Weatherby, Carrie, 2:*316*

Weatherford, William, 1:52

Weaver, James B., 1:43; 2:132

Webb, Alexander Russell, 2:439

Webb, Mary, 3:33

Webb, Walter Prescott, 2:7

Weber, Max, 2:110

Webster, Daniel, 2:270; 3:3:*389*
  Anti-Masons and, 3:390
  Canadian-U.S. dispute and, 2:4
  Compromise of 1850 and, 1:297, *297*
  Dartmouth College case, 1:400
  debate with Hayne, 1:320
  Fillmore and, 2:566
  Harrison's inaugural speech by, 2:561
  Hayne debate with, 1:306
  local control and, 1:396
  at Massachusetts constitutional convention, 3:343
  on natural resources, 2:389
  in New Hampshire, 2:413
  no-colonization policy and, 1:506
  nullification debate, 1:462
  as orator, 2:451
  Sandwich Islands and, 2:6
  Washington's influence on, 3:363
  Webster-Ashburton Treaty and, 1:173

Webster, Noah
  American Dictionary of the English Language, 1:194; 2:167
  Blue-Backed Speller, 1:393
  journalism of, 2:419

Webster, Thomas, 2:482

Webster-Ashburton Treaty (1842), 1:439, 501; 2:3, 5, 410
  Aroostock War and, 1:506
  Canada and, 1:173
  Maine borders in, 2:248
  slave trade and, 1:507; 3:155

Wedgwood, Josiah, 1:*2*

Weed, Thurlow, 2:517

Weeks, James, 1:163

Weems, Mason Locke
  Life and Memorable Actions of George Washington, The, 3:114, 363
  Life of Washington the Great, The, 2:215

Weidenmann, Jacob, 2:476

Weir, Julian, 2:464

Weismann, August, 1:446

Weiss, John, 3:292

Weld, Theodore, 1:442

Weld, Theodore Dwight, 1:3; 2:452

Welfare and charity, 2:170; 3:372–378
  Catholic agencies of, 1:185
  disaster recovery and, 1:377–378
  government support of, 3:78
  medical, 2:21
  philanthropy in, 2:489–494

Welles, Gideon, 1:308; 2:251, 397
  Navy under, 2:403

Wells, Fargo, and Company, 1:169; 3:312

Wells, Henry, 3:312, 378

Wells, Horace, 2:282

Wells-Barnett, Ida B., 3:334
  antilynching crusade of, 3:404
  Free Speech and Headlight, 2:244
  newspaper of, 2:427
  as orator, 2:452
  Red Record, The, 3:413
  reforms of, 3:84
  Southern Horrors: Lynch Law in All Its Phases, 2:218
  transportation segregation and, 3:141
  women's organizations and, 1:280

Wells Fargo, 3:378–379

Welsh immigrants, 2:75
  coal industry and, 1:284
  numbers of, 2:73

Wendell, Barrett, 3:48

Wernwag, Lewis, 1:224

Wesley, John, 3:26–27, 28
  Thoughts on Slavery, 1:2

Wesleyan Methodist Connection, 3:28–29

West, Benjamin, 1:499; 2:461

West, The, 3:379–384
  in advertising, 2:118–120
  African Americans in, 1:24–26
  agriculture in, 1:38
  bachelor subculture in, 3:80–81
  boomtowns in, 1:155
  canals in, 3:301
  Civil War in, 1:259–261
  clothing in, 1:276
  coal in, 1:283
  domestic labor in, 3:419
  exploration of, 1:538
  in films, 2:117–118
  gender roles in, 2:197
  gold rushes in, 1:549–550
  law in, 2:11
  in literature, 3:60
  lynchings in, 2:239
  marriage in, 3:398
  newspapers in, 2:424
  outlaws in, 2:457–458
  police in, 2:502–503
  popular interpretations of, 2:117–120
  population increases in, 1:213
  prisons in, 3:5–6
  prostitution in, 3:16
  Reconstruction in, 3:78–80
  sectionalism and, 3:135
  slavery in, 1:24–25
  tall tales and, 1:480–481

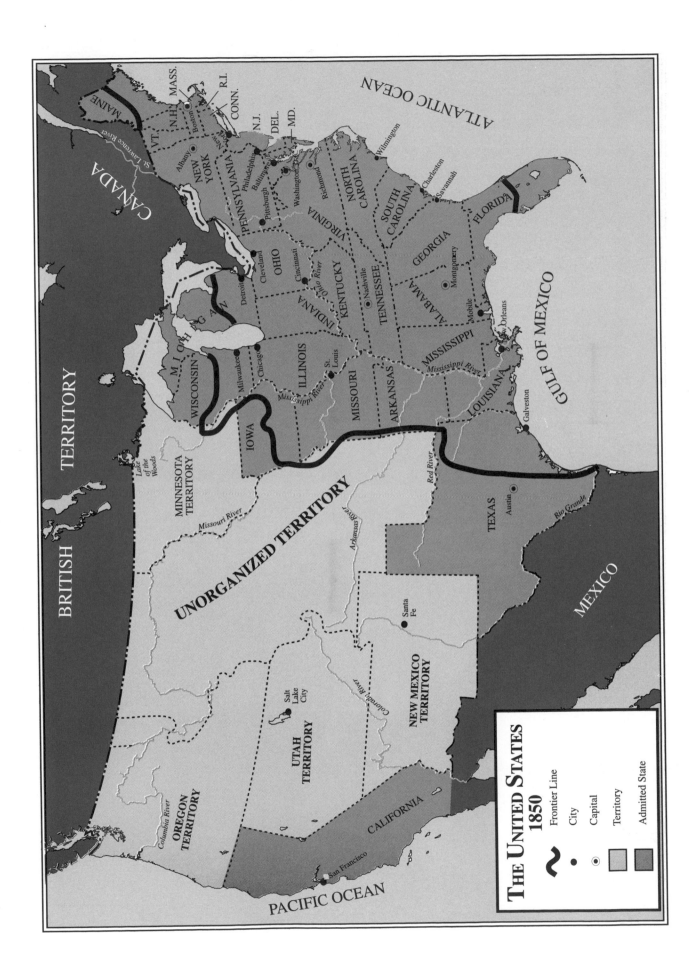

CANADA

ATLANTIC OCEAN

MAINE

N.H. MASS.
VT.
Boston R.I.
Albany CONN.
NEW YORK N.J.
Philadelphia DEL.
PENNSYLVANIA MD.
Pittsburgh Baltimore
Washington, D.C.
Cleveland OHIO Richmond
Cincinnati VIRGINIA Wilmington
Ohio River NORTH CAROLINA
Detroit INDIANA KENTUCKY Nashville SOUTH CAROLINA Charleston
Savannah
TENNESSEE
MICHIGAN GEORGIA
Milwaukee ILLINOIS Montgomery FLORIDA
Chicago St. Louis ALABAMA
WISCONSIN MISSISSIPPI Mobile
Mississippi River MISSOURI ARKANSAS New Orleans
IOWA Mississippi River LOUISIANA
Lake of the Woods Galveston GULF OF MEXICO
St. Lawrence River
Columbia River

BRITISH TERRITORY

MINNESOTA TERRITORY

Missouri River

UNORGANIZED TERRITORY

Red River

Arkansas River

TEXAS
Austin
Rio Grande

MEXICO

Santa Fe
NEW MEXICO TERRITORY

Salt Lake City
UTAH TERRITORY

Colorado River

OREGON TERRITORY

CALIFORNIA

San Francisco

PACIFIC OCEAN

THE UNITED STATES 1850

Frontier Line
City
Capital
Territory
Admitted State